INDIA

COOKBOOK

INDIA

COOKBOOK

QUALITY
ASSURANCE

Written by:

PUSHPESH PANT

THE ONLY BOOK ON INDIAN FOOD YOU'LL EVER NEED

PRODUCE OF INDIA   **1000 RECIPES**   REAP #: 1-0-06-205

WWW.PHAIDON.COM

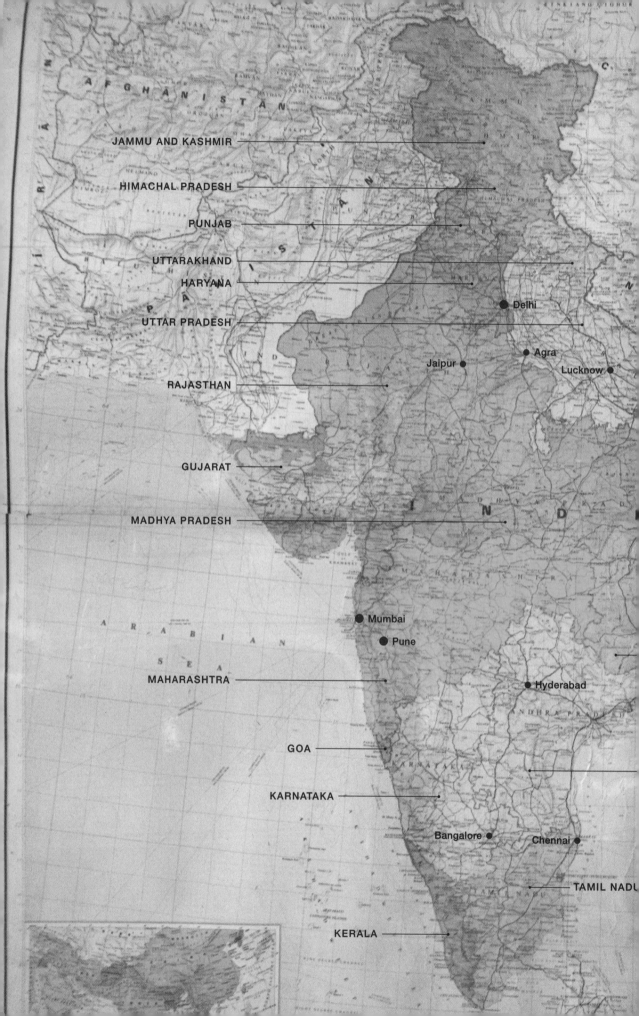

INTRODUCTION

SIKKIM

ARUNACHAL PRADESH

ASSAM

NAGALAND

MEGHALAYA

BIHAR

MANIPUR

JHARKHAND

TRIPURA

WEST BENGAL

MIZORAM

Kolkata

ORISSA
CHHATTISGARH

ANDHRA PRADESH

For many people Indian cuisine is synonymous with the food of the Mughal shahs, the illustrious rulers of most of India from the sixteenth to the nineteenth century. And, while it is true that a wonderful gastronomic revival took place during their reign – bringing us famous dishes such as korma and biryani – it must be remembered that there is far, far more to Indian food than curries alone.

—

Introduction

A Brief History of Indian Food

The foods of India are as significant to its civilization as its majestic monuments, art and literature. Indian food has taken on influences from as far afield as central Asia, southeast Asia and Turkey. The Europeans, too, have left an indelible imprint on Indian cuisine and introduced ingredients that are now widely used alongside native foods. These influxes of exotic produce, new crops and cooking techniques introduced by traders, pilgrims and soldiers have combined to create a unique and dazzlingly varied cuisine.

———— The story of the world's love affair with Indian food dates back to the first millennium when an ancient Greek envoy described sugar cane as 'Indian bamboo filled with honey'. Arab traders were later lured to India's Malabar coast in the southwest by a wealth of aromatic pepper, cloves, cardamom and cinnamon. It was also the lucrative spice trade that drew the Portuguese explorer Vasco da Gama to India in 1498. At that time spices were worth many times their weight in gold and the expenses incurred on Gama's expedition were recovered several times over by the quantities he took back with him. It is estimated that one of his shipments alone consisted of 1,500 tons of pepper, twenty-eight tons of ginger, eight tons of cinnamon and seven tons of cloves. And, while India's spices attracted Europeans to the area, the traders brought with them the culinary secrets of leavened bread, baking and noodles. In return the Indians introduced the Europeans to the joys of curry, mangoes and chutney.

———— During the nineteenth century the British came to India and were conquered by the myriad smells, sights and sounds of the subcontinent. Many of the British colonists acquired a taste for local delicacies and Indian flavours and native ingredients soon found their way back to Britain, as can be seen in the fish and rice breakfast dish kedgeree, and in the spicy meat soup mulligatawny. At the same time many British visitors chose to stay and make India their home, and across the country many spicy Anglo-Indian foods can still be found today.

———— In more recent years, India's changing demographic profile, along with its economic development, has broken many food taboos. The younger generation, better educated than its predecessors and more widely travelled, is far more adventurous. Access to pre-packaged processed foods, such as tamarind extract and coconut milk, has greatly reduced the drudgery of daily kitchen chores. More time and energy can now be devoted to innovation, and fusion cuisine is flourishing as a result. Traditional and experimental recipes now coexist happily, and Indian cuisine seems poised on a promising and exciting threshold. With its wide variety of flavours, styles, ingredients and techniques, it should come as no surprise that the popularity of Indian food is on the increase around the world.

Ayurveda and Indian Food

Ayurveda is a traditional system of Hindu medicine, which is based on the idea of balance in bodily systems. It is an ancient art of living a good life and forms the bedrock of Indian culinary philosophy. Many Indians place great emphasis on matching food with individual body types and temperaments, and the Ayurvedic system contains a vast repertoire of recommendations that enable individuals to prepare dishes tailored to their specific requirements and mood. According to Ayurveda, all foods have distinct properties that have an effect on our health tand mental balance.

———— Ayurvedic thinking states that each of us has a different combination of the three *doshas* or types — *kapha, vata* and *pitta* — that create our unique mental and physical characteristics, and which need to be balanced for optimum health and happiness. Most of us have one or two *doshas* that are most active, and Ayurveda seeks to redress this imbalance, primarily through diet. According to the Ayurvedic system, ailments are first treated with food and only later with medication if required.

———— Each *dosha* is related to the five great elements — earth, water, fire, air and ether — and one of these elements predominates in each season. So an individual's diet should vary according to their personal *doshas* and the climate. Good health can only be enjoyed when the three *doshas* are balanced, and can be impaired by eating against one's type, or being oblivious to the season. In the summer, light, cooling and re-hydrating foods are preferred; whilst in winter, richer ingredients strengthen the metabolism.

———— Ayurveda divides all foods into the *shadrasa*, or the six basic flavours: *madhur* (sweet), *amla* (sour), *katu* (pungent), *tikta* (bitter), *kashaya* (astringent) and *lavana* (salty). Each of these is essential for good health and dining pleasure. Ayurvedic lore makes a clear distinction between the 'taste' that our palate discerns and the 'taste' that our body experiences when it starts to metabolize what we have eaten.

———— It is not difficult to appreciate how food can affect our health and moods. Food may be solely nutritious, as a tonic or an intoxicant it can tranquillize or excite, and it can even be harmful at times. Ayurveda urges us to consider how the food we eat will influence our bodies and minds. To open the mind to Ayurvedic culinary wisdom is to try to ensure lasting good health while continuing to enjoy both life and food.

Food Regions of India

In order to describe the rich and varied history of Indian cuisine I have identified ten major culinary regions in India, which are explored in detail in the following pages. Each area has its own gastronomic traditions, but the regions have blurred boundaries and there are many shared techniques and tastes. Although Indian cuisine is constantly evolving and the emergence of a pan-Indian style is discernible, it can even be argued that regional foods play a more significant role in defining cultural identity than the officially recognized spoken languages that were the basis for the reorganization of states in post-Independence India.
————— Over the centuries India's cartographic borders have changed many times and it is impossible to describe India's rich and varied culinary heritage within modern day perimeters. For the purposes of discussing India's historic food culture as fully as possible, I have chosen the following regions to best describe the evolution of Indian cuisine. Some of them historically covered a greater area than they do in modern India, and include parts of modern Pakistan, Afghanistan and Bangladesh.

Kashmir

According to myth, the valley of Kashmir emerged out of a vast lake when the sage Kashyap vanquished a villainous demon who was tormenting local villagers. Kashyap drained the lake by creating a depression on its western side; this valley was christened Kashyap-mar, which eventually became Kashmir.
————— A historic region of the Indian subcontinent, Kashmir has breathtaking natural beauty. It is also renowned throughout the world for its wonderful range of exquisite architecture, fabulous houseboats, mosques and Mughal gardens. The land is associated with saffron, with its subtle and seductive aroma and alluring golden tint. The valleys of Kashmir are resplendent with purple carpets of saffron crocuses; in some places, the fields extend as far as the eye can see. Saffron is extravagantly expensive and, as well as being used in food, it also has a place in ritual worship, and is used to make *kumkum*, a colourful paste, which is painted on statues of the gods.
————— When the British discovered the coolness of the Kashmiri valleys, they made them their summer holiday destination. Because it was the domain of an Indian Prince, they were not allowed to buy land there, so luxurious houseboats began to appear. These mansion-like floating residences have become an integral part of the Kashmiri landscape and many of them, with their elegant furnishings and ornately carved ceilings, are a joy to behold. The wooden boats known as *shikara* were originally created for service rather than residences, acting as anything from taxis to floating department stores. They sold ingredients such as *nadru* (lotus stems) and a variety of spinach called *haak*,

which are mainstays of the Kashmiri vegetarian repertoire, as well as fish from the local waters.

———— Kashmiri cuisine is quite different from that of any other region in India, because for centuries it has been influenced not only by the mainland, but also by central Asia and Tibet. The preferred meat is lamb, while elsewhere in the country kid and goat are favoured. There are two main cooking styles, one Hindu and the other Muslim. The Hindu Pandit style almost completely does away with onions and garlic, replacing them with aniseed and ginger powders, and has a great number of strictly vegetarian dishes, which are used during religious ceremonies.

———— The traditional cooks in Kashmir — who claim descent from fifteenth-century immigrants from Samarkand in central Asia — are called *waaza* and their kitchens-cum-condiments shops are called *waan*. These two words combine in the term for a Kashmiri banquet: *wazwan*. At such a feast, people sit in groups of four — which is considered an auspicious number — to sample a little taste of many different dishes. The concept of *wazwan* is unique, reflecting a blend of Persian, central Asian, Afghan and Punjabi culinary influences. The traditional *wazwan* consists of thirty-six courses, though now twenty-course meals are more usual. Originally, the host had to lay out all the food before the most important guest, who, for his part, was expected to do full justice to the meal.

———— The feast is served on a *trami*, a large, ornate plate covered with a copper filigree dome to keep the food warm. The *trami* arrives piled high with rice and the first few courses. As each *trami* is eaten, the empty plate is removed and a new one brought in, until the meal is completed. Contemporary diners who are more health conscious and prefer lighter meals often treat the first *trami* as a mini *wazwan* in itself, but traditionally, each successive course followed separately, to allow diners to enjoy their distinctive flavours. Kashmiris favour lamb, especially the cuts with a lot of fat. Some of the specialities of the feast might be lamb ribs or a rich lamb curry such as *Rhogan Josh* (page 438) and — perhaps the most renowned recipe — a dish of meatballs in a cardamom sauce known as *Gushtaba* (page 436). The miniature balls are tightly packed but retain a silken, spongy texture. Making the *gushtaba* is a time-consuming process and they are usually bought from professional cooks. *Gushtaba* are the crowning glory of Kashmiri cuisine and are usually served last to announce the conclusion of a banquet.

———— The meal will always include *kahwa* (green tea), a favourite Kashmiri beverage which is traditionally brewed in ornate samovars and is served throughout the day as well as with meals. It is sweetened, and often laced with green cardamom and enriched with slivers of almond. And, as with most foods in Kashmir, saffron can make an appearance, although saffron *kahwa* does not use tea leaves, but is solely an infusion of fragrant saffron stamens.

————

Punjab
Punjab, the 'Land of the Five Rivers' — the Beas, Satluj, Ravi, Chenab and Jhelum rivers cross the region; in Persian *Punj* means five and *aab* means waters —

is India's granary, producing more than half the wheat, rice and millet grown in the country. The fertility of its fields and the richness of its dairy produce are the envy of the subcontinent. The earliest references to the region's food were made in the ancient Hindu *Veda* scriptures more than 3,000 years ago. The region has also given us tandoori food, tandoor ovens and, arguably, the Indian restaurant.

———— Situated at the crossroads of the Silk Route between south and central Asia, Punjab has experienced diverse culinary influences. Its proximity to Persia, Afghanistan and central Asia brought a taste for fresh and dried fruits and exotic nuts. The rich streams of Hindus, Sikhs and nomadic Pathan tribes have, over the millennia, enriched the cuisine, and Punjabi people have lovingly cherished and preserved their far-reaching tastes and eclectic cooking traditions.

———— The Partition of India in 1947 brought unprecedented numbers of Punjabi refugees to the rest of the country, who carried with them the rich diversity of their food. A string of Punjabi roadside restaurants called *dhabas* sprang up all over the larger cities and proliferated along every highway. They introduced the rest of India to the joys of tandoori cuisine and the pleasures of eating out. *Dhabas* started not as a business proposition, but as the refugees' strategy for survival. The food is mostly cooked in a tandoor oven, the menu is limited, ingredients are fresh and the food is simple yet delicious and excellent value for money.

———— The remains of an ancient tandoor oven have been discovered in an excavation at the Indus Valley. Today, the oven's widespread popularity should be credited to the intrepid and extremely mobile Punjabi people. In days gone by, the tandoor in a small village served as community kitchen, providing the focus for social life. The ovens could be easily set up and wholesome food could be cooked and served inexpensively, which popularized them with non-Punjabis. Such is their success that portable tandoor ovens, powered by gas or electricity, are now being manufactured. Punjabi Sikhs, in common with other Sikhs, still put great emphasis on *langar* (community kitchens) and sharing food, and they make up the majority of the Punjabi people.

———— *Dal Makhani* (Creamy Black Dal, page 582), is as much a signature dish in Punjab as tandoori chicken and is indispensable at any banquet. A pot of lentils is left in the tandoor to cook overnight with ginger, garlic and tomatoes, then mashed to a satin-smooth texture and served with butter on top. The dal is so tasty that it does not require the usual tempering of fried spices. It has become popular throughout India and often appears on the menu in fine restaurants.

———— *Butter Chicken* (page 501) started as a recipe for re-using leftover tandoori chicken, but it has now evolved into an international favourite. These days, it is a delicate dish made with aromatics such as fenugreek, cardamom and cinnamon. The reasons for its popularity are easy to understand. It is colourful and gentle on the palate, and it is possible to cut out the fat for a more health-conscious version. It can also be made in next to no time.

———— The cuisine in Punjab is exceptionally responsive to the changing seasons. Winter is welcomed with *Makke ki Roti* (Corn Bread, page 619) and *Sarson da Saag* (Classic Mustard Greens, page 262), a combination that is thought to be extremely nutritious. The greens are slow-cooked and mashed, sometimes with the addition of a few radishes or turnips. In common with many meals in this dairy-rich state, the dish is considered incomplete without the addition of some home-churned butter.

———

Rajasthan

Present-day Rajasthan was formed from a colourful mixture of dozens of large and small princely states that merged when an independent India was formed. The land is dotted with historical monuments, magnificent palaces and towering forts, such as Mehrangarh at Jodhpur and the grand citadel at Chittor. In addition the Golden Fort at Jaisalmer, the Lake Palace at Udaipur and the Ummaid Bhawan at Jodhpur are all landmark tourist destinations. An ancient trade route passed through this region, bearing the traffic from the central Asian silk route to the port cities in Gujarat. Flourishing commerce brought waves of immigrants from different directions and, along with them, myriad tastes and flavours to enrich the local cuisine. The main culinary imports have been from three communities: Rajput, Muslim and Marwari. These diverse influences have mingled in Rajasthan to evolve a robust and simple yet sublime range of dishes.

——— Although most of the population in Rajasthan is vegetarian, there is no shortage of meat dishes. This, after all, is the domain of chivalrous Rajput princes: heroic and bloodthirsty warriors who vied with each other to excel in battle and in the hunt. They had no food taboos prohibiting beef and the fiery *lal maas* (red meat dishes) and milder *safed maas* (white meat dishes) remain exceptional regional delicacies.

——— The rulers of Jaipur, the capital of present-day Rajasthan, were the first to make peace and establish alliances with the Mughals, creating a civic stability that allowed the Mughals to patronize both the performing and culinary arts. This special bond is reflected in the exceptionally high standards of Mughal cooking in Jaipur. The Muslim delicacies blend the powerful dishes of the Rajputs with the refinement of the Mughals.

——— The Jains are an illustrious and strict religious community in India who follow a very stringent vegetarian code, and they comprise an important segment of the Rajasthani community. Orthodox Jain food does not use roots or tubers such as potatoes, but rather than hinder them, this has inspired cooks to improvise and create unique versions of the common delicacies enjoyed by others. A festive Jain banquet can equal any other, both in taste and appearance, but great emphasis is placed on cleanliness, purity of ingredients and following Ayurvedic principles.

——— In Ajmer, the mausoleum of a Sufi saint is a major place of pilgrimage for both Hindus and Muslims. As a result, Ajmer has a long-standing tradition of cooking and sharing food with pilgrims and visitors. Large cooking vessels placed near the entrance to the shrine remind travellers of the role that consecrated food plays here. At the annual celebration of the Urs, biryani is cooked in these huge pots and distributed to the devotees.

————— Millet is the countryside staple in Rajasthan and the scarcity of fresh vegetables in this arid region is compensated for by an imaginative use of lentils. A typical Rajasthani spread might include a number of lentil-based dishes, such as *Khasta Kachori* (Savoury Deep-fried Snack, page 134) as well as lentil pancakes and steamed or boiled lentil dumplings. To avoid these recipes becoming too bland, and to spice up the flavour, Rajasthanis use plenty of chillies and asafoetida – a pungent flavouring, which, when cooked, has a taste reminiscent of onions and garlic. Generous quantities of ghee are also consumed.

————— Jodhpur, the second-largest city in Rajasthan, boasts more than a hundred varieties of the snack *Mirchi Vada* (Batter-fried Green Chillies, page 102). Made in the alleyways of the city, this street food is more than a mouthful. The large green chillies are stuffed with a tangy potato filling, coated with a thin batter and deep-fried.

———

Agra and Delhi: The Mughals' Imperial Cities

The grand Mughals are arguably the most illustrious dynasty to have ruled India, and can justifiably be compared to the Medici in Renaissance Italy; like them, the Mughals were patrons of the arts and great lovers of gastronomy. At the start of the eighteenth century, the height of the empire, the Mughals controlled most of India. Wherever the imperial Mughal army marched, it was accompanied by a large kitchen brigade to cater for the princely commanders and their courtiers. As such, culinary traditions and recipes spread outward from the imperial cities of Agra and Delhi to the frontier outposts and important garrison cities.

————— Agra is internationally known for the the Taj Mahal, the white marble mausoleum built by the Mughal emperor Shah Jahan in memory of his favourite wife and completed around 1653. However, years before the building was even commissioned, talented cooks flocked to Agra to serve the Mughal emperors, bringing the city an outstanding culinary reputation that survives to this day.

————— In the sixteenth century the Delhi Sultanate was absorbed by the Mughul empire and in the mid-seventeenth century Agra was upstaged when the Mughals moved their capital north to Delhi. As the imperial centre moved, it transformed both the landscape and the eating habits of Delhi. Legend has it that the waters of the Jamuna river were quite polluted even then, and were considered a health hazard. The royal doctor could not persuade the shah to move back to Agra, so he prescribed a strong dose of chillies in his master's daily diet. To balance the heat and pungency of this food, a much larger amount of cooking fat was used. This combination has lent both the meat and vegetarian dishes of Delhi their piquancy and richness. Few can visit Delhi and not succumb to the seductions of its famous *Murg Mumtaz* (Celebratory Chicken Korma, page 502).

————— Rajasthan and Punjab have also deeply influenced the food of Delhi. The imperial city's famous Red Fort was built with vividly coloured sandstone imported from Rajasthan and most Delhi sweet-sellers can trace their lineage there as well.

Today, Delhi is a fascinating mix of the legacy of the Sultanates, Mughals, British and Partition refugees, and the influx continues with people from all over India moving here.

————— Dishes served in a classic Mughal meal are very familiar to those in the West; in fact, Mughal food is often mistakenly regarded as the entirety of Indian cuisine — in part, perhaps, because it has been influenced so much by other cuisines of the country. For example, a Mughal meal usually begins with kebabs, both on skewers and cooked on a griddle, followed by a variety of kormas, Kashmiri-influenced *kaliyas* — lighter meat curry dishes — and *do pyaza* lamb curries from Rajasthan, accompanied by an assortment of breads, such as naan, *rumali* and roti. The rice course will be an aromatic biryani and pulao, served with raita. A typical dessert would be the ice cream-like *Kulfi* (page 691).

————— When a train station was built at Delhi, numerous *Poori* (page 592) stalls sprouted around it. *Poori*, a deep-fried bread, is a favourite of travellers because it keeps so well. Prepared in ghee or oil, the dough is ideally made with milk instead of water, which might contaminate the bread. Delhi *poori* is considered particularly special, since it is less oily and crisper than other regional varieties. Delhi has also made its mark on another India staple, *Paratha* (page 609), a layered, shallow-fried Indian bread that can be eaten plain or stuffed. Giant *paratha* are baked then fried on a huge heavy griddle. A single *paratha* with accompaniments can serve as a full meal for a family.

————— The kebab makers of Delhi have always considered themselves unrivalled. They make fun of the delicate Awadhi kebabs as food only fit for the aged or the infirm. The kebab in Delhi, whether cooked on the skewer, griddle, or in the oven, has a more robust flavour. The *Mutton Barra Kebab* (Roasted Lamb Kebab, page 182), made with the choicest cuts of the animal, may have originated in the north-western frontier, but it is in Delhi that it reached sublime heights.

————— The residents of Delhi are notorious for their love of street food, and are addicted to both vegetarian and meaty snacks. A plate of savoury snacks, or *chaat*, is a unique Indian speciality, a truly moveable feast consisting of a variety of dishes such as *Aloo Tikki* (Potato Patties, page 108) and *Pani Poori* (Puffed Biscuits [Cookies] with Tangy Water, page 155). However, it is the accompanying spicy sprinkles and sweet-and-sour chutneys that give *chaat* its special character.

—————

Awadh

Awadh, a region in modern-day Uttar Pradesh, was governed in the imperial period by loyal followers of the Mughal emperors who were addressed as *nawab*. The *nawabs* were great patrons of the arts, especially music and dance, and the capital Lucknow's reputation as a city of culture and fine cuisine stems from this time.

————— In culinary matters, no-one can match the splendour of an Awadhi spread. Lucknow is famous for *dum pukht* (meaning 'slow oven'), the art of steam cooking slowly in a sealed clay pot. According to legend, this exquisite cuisine was created in the eighteenth-century kitchens of Nawab Asaf-ud-Daula when he ordered a most ambitious food-for-work programme to fuel the construction of his Bara Imambara shrine in 1784. He directed his cooks to put rice, meat and spices into a gigantic cooking pot, seal it with dough and let it cook overnight while the huge famished labour force worked round the clock on the building. This biryani would be fed to the workers every morning. His generosity is recalled in the saying 'Asaf-ud-Daula provides for even those unfortunates whom the good Lord has overlooked'.

————— The British gained control over the province in the mid-nineteenth century, but the *nawabs'* art of elegant living was preserved and extended by the landed aristocracy. This was the golden era of north-Indian cuisine, when innovation was encouraged. Women from respectable families were discouraged from eating outside the home, so bamboo kiosks containing a small griddle upon which an assortment of savouries could be cooked were carried from door to door. This was fast food, Indian style. The standard fare has remained unchanged for generations. Today, if you take a walk through Lucknow's atmospheric old market, you will find a maze of lanes lined with shops selling authentic local cuisine.

————— Old-timers will tell you that one lifetime is not enough to savour the culinary joys of Lucknow. Lamb kebabs, such as *Galouti*, *Seekh Gilafi* (both page 186) and *Kakori* (page 180), are some of the signature dishes of Lucknow. *Galouti* means a delectable morsel that melts in the mouth. Residents of Lucknow – particularly members of the nobility – considered it uncouth to be seen biting into meat or chewing it, so the court cooks were asked to create delicacies which avoided this. Meats were tenderized with raw papaya paste and, for kebabs, meat was ground three times before use until it had a pâté-like consistency.

————— *Kakori*, perhaps the most delicate of all the kebabs, derives its name from a small town near the outskirts of Lucknow. There are interesting and varying accounts explaining its origin and smooth texture. According to folklore, the pleasure-loving *nawabs* aged before their time; their flesh became increasingly weak but their yearning for good food remained strong, so the lighter-than-air kebab was devised to tempt their toothless palates. Perhaps closer to the truth is another story which suggests that the kebab was prepared for the aged pilgrims who thronged to a local shrine.

————— Silver leaf is the favourite garnish in Awadh. It adorns delicacies both sweet and savoury, and no korma or pulao can be served without it. Making it is a very laborious process, in which small, thin coins of silver are placed between layers of leather and paper and beaten for hours until transformed into a foil. On rare and very special occasions gold is used instead. Silver was eaten enthusiastically in the days of *nawabs*, as it was thought to have aphrodisiac properties.

———

Bengal

Bengal was a historical region in northeast of the Indian subcontinent. Today it is mainly divided between the Indian state of West Bengal and Bangladesh. The red terracotta temples of Bishnupur lie to the west; to the south are the dense mangrove swamps where Royal Bengal tigers roam; and the quaint hill stations of Darjeeling and Kalimpong are in the north. Bengal is a fascinating tapestry of culture, colour, natural beauty and an extremely well-developed cuisine. Kolkata served for generations as the capital of British colonial administration and has continued as a bustling centre of commerce. Bengal also lead the way in adopting and adapting foreign mores in both its costume and cuisine.

———— Though Bengal boasts a wonderful repertoire of delicate sweetmeats and irresistible fish curries, these are just the beginning of the region's delicious temptations. They have their own garam masala with a definite identity: *Paanch Phoren* (Five Spice Mix, page 55), which means literally 'the spice that crackles five times'. Bengalis also like a bit of sugar in their dishes.

———— A traditional Bengali meal is a mix of seasonal vegetables, with an accent on bitter flavours. Bengal cuisine gives equal importance to the *shadrasa,* the six basic flavours in Ayurveda, particularly *tikta* (the bitter taste) which is believed to cleanse the palate and aid the digestive system. As such, Bengali cooking shows a marked preference for mustard, as a paste or as an oil, and mustard-flavoured fish is a quintessential dish. Bengalis love Dijon and English mustards and, more recently, have come to love Japanese wasabi, too. The local mustard, *kashundi,* is strong and very tasty. Grinding it is an art that is difficult but worth mastering. Folklore has it that Bengali mothers-in-law traditionally tested the cooking skills of their sons' new wives by putting them to this test.

———— Similarly, much of Bengali cuisine embraces other cultures: *Aloo Chop* (Potato with Minced [Ground] Lamb, page 214) and the *Kathi Kebab* (Boneless Lamb Kebab, page 183), for example, were both created in response to flavours introduced by immigrants. A small roadside eatery in Kolkata has even acquired legendary status by popularizing the wrap in India. This is no surprise, since, like the people of Delhi, the Bengalis enjoy their snacks. Favourites such as *Singhara* (Bengali Samosas, page 132) or *Pata Bhaja* (Batter-fried Spinach, page 103) are light meals that can serve as a bite to eat grabbed on the run; it is fast finger food, not junk food.

———— The nine-day-long festival of Durga Puja, dedicated to the worship of the mother goddess, is widely celebrated in West Bengal and the surrounding states. Food is a central part of the celebrations and numerous temporary stalls spring up around idols of the goddess. There is lively competition between the stallholders, with everyone from housewives to chefs showing off their cooking skills.

———— Hilsa, the Indian salmon, is particularly popular in the region. In West Bengal they serve a deliciously tropical dish of *Illich Maachh Annanas* (Hilsa with Pineapple, page 353). Hilsa have a life-cycle very similar to that of the western salmon: born in fresh water, the fish school together and swim out to the ocean before returning, years later, to spawn inland. Many that are caught during the monsoon period contain roe, a delicacy that local people consider akin to caviar.

———— The famous sweet *sandesh* is made with *Chhena* (page 59), the solid part of curdled milk. It is turned out of moulds to look like flowers and fruits, and can be flavoured with orange peel, jackfruit, saffron or essence of rose. The *chhena* encases a large globe of jaggery (palm sugar) molasses, and is a highly prized delicacy in winter.

Hyderabad

A historic region, Hyderabad was once the largest princely state of the Indian
subcontinent and was governed, from the eighteenth century to the mid-twentieth
century, by hereditary rulers called *nizams*. At its centre was the spellbinding
city of Hyderabad, now the capital of the modern southern region of Andhra
Pradesh. To the west of the city is the great Golconda Fort, a fortified citadel
of grand palaces, mosques and gardens. Golconda is also famous for the great
hoard of diamonds, mined nearby, which included the celebrated Koh-i-noor
diamond, which is now part of the British Crown Jewels.

——————— Hyderabad has a composite culture, a mixture of Hindu and Muslim
customs, mingled with Arab, Persian and Turkish influences, which is evident
in its language, food, manners and arts. Some of the most delicious food in town
can be found in the most unappetizing-looking hole-in-the-wall eateries, yet
Hyderabad also boasts spectacular delicacies. Legend has it that the seventeenth-
century *nizams* spent more time on culinary matters than on battle strategy.
As a result these days the city has, arguably, the most exotic cuisine in the land.

——————— Hyderabad's signature dish is biryani. In Persian, the word biryani means
fried or roasted rice. In the Indian culinary context it has come to mean rice
roasted with meat, spices and herbs. The art of cooking biryani is in its perfect
timing; the marinated meat must cook in the same time as the part-cooked
rice when the two are sealed together in a pot. The grains of rice should remain
unbroken and separate, and should have absorbed the flavourful stock.

——————— Kid is the most popular meat in Hyderabadi cuisine, with chicken coming
a poor second. Most of all, Hyderabadis prize the meat of the male goat. It will
always be found in *Lukhmi* (page 192), a favourite local appetizer of thin pastry
stuffed with a delicately spiced filling, resembling a mini samosa. *Halim* (page 421)
is an exceptionally nutritious and flavourful porridge commonly prepared during
Ramadan, the month of daylight fasting and prayer observed by Muslims. It is
made with meat, cereal, ghee and spices. Yet despite their love of meat dishes, of
all the Muslim Indian cuisines, Hyderabadi is the only one that can boast a major
vegetarian element. The wide variety of their tasty vegetarian recipes include
Aloogadda Vepudu (Spicy Potatoes, page 235), *Bhuni Besan Bhindi* (Fried Okra
Coated in Gram [Chickpea] Flour, page 244) and *Dum Kathhal* (Spicy Baked Jackfruit,
page 267), a local favourite.

——————— The key flavours in Hyderabadi cuisine are a blend of north and south
Indian ingredients: the chillies and cumin seeds of the north are mixed with
the mustard seeds and curry leaves of southern dishes. The people love coconut,
tamarind, peanuts and sesame seeds, and great emphasis is placed on sour
flavours. Dishes without a sour tang are rare, as it is believed that the city's dry
heat makes the appetite sluggish, and sour food revives the palate. Once, the
ingredient that created the sour flavour reflected social status: the poor used
tamarind leaves; the lower-middle class, tamarind fruit and lemon; the middle
classes, raw mango; the upper-middle class, under-ripe grapes; whilst the
affluent used pomegranate. These days, the class distinctions have vanished.

————— The desserts of Hyderabad are breathtaking. The sweet porridge-like *Gil e Behisht* (Milky Clay of Paradise, page 692) is a celebration of dairy produce with a hint of cardamom. *Khoobani ka Meetha* (Stewed Apricots with Clotted Cream, page 671) is one of the most sublime desserts of Hyderabad. It requires extraordinary culinary skills. The apricots within it should be completely free from fibre, and it should be topped with just the right amount of clotted cream to balance the sweetness.

—

Tamil Nadu

This is the homeland of the Tamils, a people who can lay claim to a civilization that is the oldest in India. There was a time when the domain of the Tamil rulers extended from the banks of the River Ganges to the Indian Ocean. Tamil Nadu is known the world over for its majestic temples with soaring *shikhars* (towers) and intricate stone carvings. The Brihadishvara Temple in Thanjavur, the temple city of Madurai, and the exquisite shore temple at Mamallapuram are all testimony to the people's architectural genius.

————— The food in the region has remained true to its roots. The staples are vegetarian and heavily reliant on rice. A common meal, eaten off plantain leaves, would contain rice, vegetables, curd and a slice of pickle, along with *Rasam* (page 561), a tamarind dal flavoured with seeds; *Sambhar* (page 543), a vegetable dal; and *Nariyal ki Chutney* (page 67), a coconut chutney. Tamarind and asafoetida are used as souring agents, while mustard seeds and curry leaves are common.

————— Many eateries in Tamil Nadu thrive on their tiffin food, such as *Idli* (page 149), which are steamed dumplings made from lentils or rice, *Dosa* (page 141) which are thin rice pancakes, and *Vada* (see chapter 3), which are deep-fried lentil-based patties that come in countless variations. The word 'tiffin' dates back to the Raj, but the tradition of taking tiffin — a light 'meal between meals' often eaten at midday — existed long before the arrival of the Europeans, as the midday heat turned a heavy lunch into an unappetizing proposition. *Dosa* and *idli*, served with chutneys, are not just tiffin, but are also eaten a main dish.

————— *Idli* are an ancient Indian food and were first recorded in a tenth-century story in which a lady offers an *idli* to a monk asking for alms. *Idli* made with lentil flour and spiced with pepper and asafoetida are also mentioned in the *Manasollasa*, an encyclopaedic work written in the twelfth century which discusses, among many topics, contemporary culinary habits. This prototype *idli* was made without rice and was fried, not steamed. The steaming method used today seems to have been introduced from Indonesia, where a similar dish exists. *Idli* are usually accompanied by a *sambhar* or chutney.

————— *Dosa* are thin pancakes made of rice and shallow-fried in a pan. When stuffed with spiced mashed potato, they are called *Masala Dosa* (page 143). The recipe for *dosa* has remained largely unchanged for centuries, but these days it has interesting variations. The paneer *dosa* was created, it seems, by popular demand, to please the dairy-loving Punjabi palate which is partial to cheese. There is an onion version, another that is butter roasted, as well as a spongy *dosa* served with chutney. Restaurants specializing in *dosa* take pride in making them paper-thin, and bringing them to the table shaped into a cone. Today, there are also non-vegetarian *dosa* made with chicken or lamb, or even seafood.

————— *Vada* are arguably the oldest snack in India, and are especially popular in south India. They are eaten with *sambhar* and chutney as a light meal or at breakfast. There are many variations (see chapter 3): some are highly spiced with green chillies, curry leaves and pepper, while others are soaked in yoghurt.

————— In January the Hindu festival of Makar Sankranti is celebrated all over India in a variety of ways. In Tamil Nadu this is the time for Pongal, the winter solstice celebrations. Cows are garlanded with mango leaves and a pot of rice is put on the fire and allowed to boil over, symbolizing plenty and prosperity in the household. The porridge-like breakfast dish *Venu Pongal* (Rice with Moong Dal, page 665) is spiced with cumin, pepper, ginger and asafoetida.

————— Most of the inhabitants of Tamil Nadu are vegetarian. Although the non-Brahmin communities, particularly those of Chettinadu in the south, are not averse to eating meat. Their repertoire makes uninhibited use of non-vegetarian ingredients and shows the influence of Andhra cuisine, from where they are thought to have emigrated.

————— No meal in Tamil Nadu is complete unless complemented by two or three flavoursome chutneys. These are not seen as mere accompaniments, but as important side dishes with a distinct personality. Coconut chutney is ubiquitous and invariably served with *idli*, *dosa* and *vada*. Tomato and garlic versions are also very popular.

————— Coffee is an integral part of dining in Tamil Nadu. In common with the rest of India and the world, purists take theirs unadulterated by sugar or milk and in thimble-sized espresso portions. A more traditional drink is made from freshly roasted and ground coffee beans mixed with chicory, diluted with a boiling mix of milk and water, and sweetened generously.

——

Kerala

Legend has it that the land of Kerala, in the southwest of the country, emerged out of the sea when the warrior-sage Parashuram flung in his battle-axe, displacing the water. Kerala is referred to as 'God's own country' because of its astounding natural beauty and exceptional fertility. The landscape is extremely verdant, the backwaters reach deep inland and a multitude of coconut trees sway gently in the breeze. Tea gardens and coffee plantations stretch out for miles in the highlands, as do the bountiful gardens of spices. Kerala has been famous for thousands of years for the quality of its spices. It was an important centre on the spice route that connected Arabia with southeast Asia. Sailors from China and the Persian Gulf also visited regularly and left their influences.

————— Kerala is where both Islam and Christianity came to India, and is also home to a type of Ayurveda which is quite distinct from the Ayurveda practised in the north of India. The food in Kerala shows the influence of this variety of cultures, fused into a unique identity by Ayurveda. Fish figures prominently in the daily diet, and the staples are rice and tapioca. Beef is commonly eaten by the non-Hindu community.

———— The Namboodiri community in Kerala is strictly vegetarian and avoids garlic. A traditional Nambodari *thoran*, a dry dish of finely chopped vegetables, is *Muttokos Thoran* (Kerala Stir-fried Cabbage with Coconut, page 261).

———— The Muslims of Kerala claim descent from Arab traders and have a different style of cuisine. The Arab influence is easily discernible in a number of their meat and wheat porridge dishes. The bread they eat is a flat, thin chapati made with a boiled mash of rice, baked on a griddle and dipped in coconut milk.

———— Keralan Christians are mostly non-vegetarian. A favourite dish is *Erachi Verthathu Rachathu* (Lamb Cooked with Ground Coconut, page 461), which contains onions, tomatoes and chillies with spicy ground coconut paste. Another popular dish is *Ga Archa Meen Kari* (Fish Curry with Coconut, page 365).

———— *Kadalaparippu Payasam* (Chana Dal Dessert, page 706) is a typical Keralan dessert, a creamy sweet porridge made from *chana dal*, coconut cream and ground cardamom, which is then garnished with browned grated coconut, raisins and cashew nuts.

———— The Keralan *Appam* (page 627) is perhaps the most beautiful of Indian breads. These delicate rice pancakes made with coconut milk are cooked over a hot griddle and form a delicate lace-like pattern at the edges while remaining soft and spongy in the centre. When well made, *appam* blossoms like a white lotus bud. Some types of batter incorporate *toddy*, an alcoholic coconut drink, and are fermented overnight. In other varieties, the batter is steamed in a banana leaf parcel with jackfruit, jaggery (palm sugar) and coconut.

———— Kerala has an abundance of fish, both from the sea and fresh waters. However, it is the *karimeen*, the pearl-spot fish, that is most prized. An inhabitant of shallow brackish waters, it can be cooked in a spicy marinade, wrapped in banana leaves, cooked on a griddle, or fried encrusted with coconut, garlic and chillies. It is difficult to decide which recipe is the most delicious, but a firm favourite is *Karimeen Polichattu* (Pearl Fish Pan Grilled in Banana Leaf, page 359), in which the pearl spot fish is marinated, wrapped in a banana leaf and cooked over a griddle.

———— *Puttu* (page 631) is a very unusual staple. Powdered rice mixed with grated coconut is steamed in bamboo or copper tubes to make a 'bread' that is usually eaten with a lentil curry. It has the texture of an *idli* but is less fluffy, and a single helping is as filling as a plateful of rice.

———— *Prathaman* is the name given to Keralan sweets based on milk or coconut milk. They can contain fruits such as bananas and jackfruits, fried in ghee, or even moong beans, coconut and jaggery (palm sugar). Cardamom and ginger powder are used to enhance flavour, while fried cashew nuts, raisins and coconut enrich the taste.

The Western Coast

————— The western coast of India stretches from the state of Gujarat, through Maharashtra and the glittering city of Mumbai, to the white sand beaches of Goa, the thriving port of Mangalore in Karnataka and the historic Malabar region. Within this stretch of land is a great variety of foods and flavours, but the coastal people are united by their penchant for seafood. While Goa, Konkan and North Karnataka display the most interesting recipes — and naturally fish and coconut are the dominant ingredients — each area and the different communities within it have made their own interpretations of these ingredients.

————— Goa remained under Portuguese rule for many centuries, and its food includes flavours which are alien to the rest of the country. The daily diet here is more similar to Western food than elsewhere in India. Traditional Goan food is cooked in earthenware on a wood fire, lending an unique flavour which cannot easily be duplicated in a modern kitchen. Apart from fish and seafood, Goan cuisine displays a great variety of meat and vegetable dishes, such as *Caril de Galinha* (Goan Chicken Curry, page 508), or *Tamba di Bhaji* (Red Amaranthus Leaves, page 264), a delicious dish of amaranthus leaves simmered with coconut.

————— The state of Maharashtra lies to the west of the country and is currently the richest state in the whole of India (thanks in part Mumbai's 'Bollywood', the largest film production centre in the world). Maharashtrian cuisine ranges from robust rural foods to the elaborate and elegant regal menus favoured by the food-lovers of Pune, the state's second largest city after Mumbai. The subtle sweet strained yoghurt dish *Shrikhand* (page 693) would rival the lightest soufflé, while their spicy lamb curry *Mutton Kolhapuri* (Maharashtrian Hot Lamb Curry, page 431) has enough fire to put even the hottest Mexican delicacies to shame.

————— The city of Mumbai was given in dowry by the Portuguese to a British Prince. A small fishing village at the time, it grew rapidly under British rule. It has acted as a crucible to blend diverse ingredients and techniques into a unique cuisine, and the food in the city is possibly the most impressive illustration of its eclectic cosmopolitanism.

————— Mumbai is a fast-paced city, and sustains its millions of inhabitants on fast food. *Pao Bhaji* (Mini Loaves with Tangy Vegetables, page 139) is to Mumbai what hamburgers and hot dogs are to New York. *Pao* is a squarish small loaf of bread served with *bhaji*, a mixed potato and vegetable mash drenched in puréed tomato and liberally spiced with onions, green chillies and ginger. The *bhaji* is cooked in front of the customer on a large griddle, which also toasts the bread. It is served with liberal amounts of butter to create the illusion of richness for the poor man who may be surviving on one meal a day.

————— Udupi is a tranquil town in south Karnataka that has become famous for its south Indian fast food outlets. The food — *idli*, *dosa* and *vada* — is inexpensive, extremely well prepared and consistent in flavour and quality. The menu may be small, but it ensures value for money.

————— The Gujarati favourite that has conquered the land are the steamed lentil cakes called *Dhokla* (page 150). Gujarati cuisine is predominantly vegetarian

and what distinguishes it is the use of sugar, even in savoury dishes. Millet
and lentils are widely used and much significance is attached to snacks, which
are central to Gujarati eating habits and usually bought from a shop.

—————— The Parsis, originally from Persia, are the smallest minority in the
western coast, but have contributed substantially to the cuisine. They have
adopted the cooking techniques of Gujarat and Maharashtra, where the majority
of them live, but their food retains a distinct identity. Parsis are enthusiastic
Westernizers and many of their dishes display European influences, while their
sweet and sour dishes use vinegar. Their *Dhansak* (page 462) is a unique dish that
combines pulao, kebab, lentils and vegetables in a rich one-dish meal. *Patrani
Machli* (Fish Cooked in Banana Leaf Wraps, page 365) is another favourite.

—

Tribal Food

The tribal population may only make up a small percentage of India, but their
significance should not be underestimated. From the tribes of the trans-Himalayan
region and those that dwell in the tropical rainforest, to the inhabitants of
Indian Ocean islands, the indigenous peoples present a bewildering diversity. The
tiny Onges and Jarwas tribes in the Andaman Islands, in the Bay of Bengal to the
West of India, lead an existence that has hardly changed in millennia, while the
Shaukas and Bhotias in Uttarakhand in the north, or the Meenas of Rajasthan, are
now almost indistinguishable from the non-tribal population.

—————— While some nomadic tribes have incorporated elements of cuisine from
the people they have come into contact with, other tribes have shunned contact
with outsiders and remain fiercely parochial and exclusive in matters of food.

—————— What is common to all tribal people is the belief that food must
be nutritious, easy to cook or to preserve, well-balanced and free from additives
that could adulterate or dilute its natural goodness. Organic food has gained
currency in recent years in the West, but the tribal diet has always been organic.
The dishes are always seasonal, natural textures and flavours are seldom
interfered with, and the best use is made of whatever is available locally.

—————— Tribal recipes are rarely written down and have been blended and
incorporated into the various local cuisines of India over many years. It is hard
to pinpoint their origins precisely, and the foods described in the following texts,
which have been favoured by tribespeople over the centuries, are intended
to provide an insight into the tribes' culinary culture, rather than specific dishes.

—

Trans-Himalayan Region

Ladakh, meaning 'the land of high passes', is in the far north of Kashmir and
Jammu, lying between the Kunlun mountains and the Himalayas. Given this
location it is no surprise that the tribal food in Ladakh shows a remarkable
influence from Tibet, seen in dishes such as *momo*, steamed dumplings that are

close cousins of the Chinese variety and *thupka*, pieces of dough cooked in a broth enriched with vegetables. *Gudgud*, a tea-like brew drunk by the tribes is very different from the beverage most people know as tea. Instead, it is an entire meal, made by stirring roasted barley flour with yak butter and salt in a green tea leaf brew. Most of the tribes consume alcohol in the form of a light invigorating beer-like drink called *chang* or *dzu*.

————— The Shaukas and Bhotias of neighbouring Uttarakhand were intrepid traders. They frequently travelled to Tibet and this is reflected in their food. Himalayan chives and aromatic grasses are used with lentils and vegetables. Roasted black soy beans and amaranth grain are greatly valued as nutrients. The practice of drying meats and vegetables for winter continues in the highest altitude villages, and *churbi* — a cheese made with yak's milk — is also greatly enjoyed.

The North and Northeast

The Bhils are legendary warriors who inhabit the hilly region near Udaipur that borders Gujarat. Some of Rajasthan's roasted meat delicacies, such as a whole rabbit cooked in a pit, appear to have been acquired from the Bhils. The tribal people in Bastar have a famous chicken delicacy, the *karak nag murga*, which uses generous quantities of alcohol and is served with local short-grained rice.

————— The Nagas descended from Mongols and, until very recently, remained outside Hindu-Buddhist civilization. They have a whole range of indigenous ingredients used for flavouring. Cooked dishes are seasoned mostly with shallots, garlic, ginger and turmeric. Common techniques are steaming and Chinese-style stir-frying. The emphasis is always on retaining maximum nutrition. Fermented fish and soy beans are extremely popular ingredients. Manipuris relish *eronba*, a vegetable chutney with a pinch of fermented fish, which provides its distinct identity.

How to Eat an Indian Meal

A traditional Indian meal — whether eaten in the north, south, east or west — follows a very different pattern from that of Europe, the Mediterranean or the Far East. There are no starters, the meal is not served in courses, and desserts are not necessarily served at the end. Often the meal will appear on the table 'pre-plated' in small bowls arranged on a *thali* (a large round plate or a clean plantain leaf), along with the staples bread and rice.

——————— Crunchy snacks, such as *Samosas* (page 131) or *Onion Bhajiya* (Onion Bhaji, page 98), are enjoyed alongside the main dishes, which, for non-vegetarians, would be chicken, fish or mutton kebabs, or curry. Vegetarians often eat a main dish of paneer, mushrooms or seasonal vegetables. It is common to serve at least one dry dish and one dish with sauce. In addition, a dal, *sambhar* or *karhi* (yoghurt dumplings) is almost compulsory. Bread and rice are taken according to personal preference. Dairy produce is included in the form of plain yoghurt or raita, and is indispensable in all but the most frugal fare. Chutneys, pickles and preserves accompany daily meals at home, ensuring that all the basic flavours are on offer as well as providing a variety of colours and textures. A sweet dish, such as rice pudding or a serving of *halwa* (see chapter 8), is also offered. Beverages (mostly sherbets (see chapter 9), made with fruit juice added to milk, cream or egg whites) are offered to guests before eating, although some drinks, such as buttermilk, are sipped during the meal.

——————— The guiding principle of Indian meals is that they should be appropriate to the season and occasion. More elaborate celebratory banquets have much greater variety, including different kinds of fish, quail and partridge, and use more complex and uncommon recipes.

——————— It is not unusual to mix and match dishes from different culinary zones: for example, Punjabi tandoori tikka, Awadhi korma and Hyderabadi biryani could easily share the centre spread with Gujarati snacks, Kerala breads and Bengali sweets. And in fact, except for ritual meals, most Indians mix and match at home. However, this should in no way inhibit an enthusiast from creating a regional menu that is deeply satisfying.

——————— Finally, an Indian gourmet does not use knives, forks and spoons: the fingers, assisted by a variety of breads, are best to fully enjoy the temperature and texture of the food.

Notes on the Recipes

The recipes in this book have been gathered from all over India during the last twenty years. They reflect both the similarities and the differences across all the regions, and represent the best of traditional Indian cooking. Armed with the recipes in this book you can look forward to cooking authentic Indian food and enjoying its kaleidoscope of flavours.

———— Authentic Indian recipes often use a generous amount of ghee or other cooking oil, but once you have followed the recipe the first time and cooked the traditional version of the dish, you may like to reduce the amount of ghee you use in the future.

———— Similarly, the amount of spice in Indian recipes can be changed to suit your palate. Each recipe in the book contains a rating to let you know how hot the dish is in its traditional form, but feel free to experiment – adding more or less chilli and other spices as you wish.

———— In India, the most commonly used meat is goat, known as 'mutton'. The 'mutton' recipes in this book have been adapted for lamb, which is much more readily available outside India, but goat can also be used. It will usually require a longer cooking time. The cheaper cuts of lamb, often sold in supermarkets as stewing or casserole lamb, such as shoulder, neck, breast or shank, need to be cooked for longer than more expensive cuts. Whichever cut you buy, simmer the meat until it is tender, checking it regularly making sure the sauce does not reduce too much. Marinating the lamb, in raw papaya for example, will tenderize the meat and is one way to reduce the cooking time. Meat in India is often cooked on the bone, and all the recipes in this book can be cooked with meat either on or off the bone, unless otherwise stated.

———— To save time, an electric spice grinder and blender are handy tools in the kitchen. Ready-made extracts, such as coconut milk and tamarind extract, can also reduce the burden in the kitchen.

———— Lastly, many of the exotic-sounding ingredients can be substituted for produce more commonly found outside India, or simply omitted if unavailable. A complete list of Indian ingredients can be found in the glossary at the back of the book.

SPICE MIXTURES
AND PASTES

Indian spices are treasured around the world and have drawn travellers to the country for centuries. Spices are undeniably at the heart of Indian cooking and give the cuisine its unique flavour and aroma. In India, almost all spices are believed to have therapeutic properties and they are used in recipes in harmony with the changing seasons.

1

Spice Mixtures and Pastes

Garam Masala (I)
Garam Masala (I)

Origin Delhi/Punjab/Awadh
Preparation time 15 minutes
Makes 500g / 1lb 2oz

200g / 7oz (2 cups) cumin seeds
75g / 2½oz (1 cup) coriander seeds
45g / 1½oz (½ cup) black cardamom pods
45g / 1½oz (⅓ cup) black peppercorns
40g / 1½oz (½ cup) green cardamom pods
40g / 1½oz (½ cup) ground ginger

Put all the ingredients in a mortar and pound with a pestle, or grind in a spice grinder, to make a fine powder. Sieve (strain) and store in a sterilized (see page 791), dry and airtight container.

Garam Masala (II)
Garam Masala (II)

Origin Delhi/Punjab/Awadh
Preparation time 15 minutes
Makes 500g / 1lb 2oz

100g / 3½oz (1 cup) cumin seeds
75g / 2½oz (⅔ cup) black cardamom seeds
75g / 2½oz (⅔ cup) black peppercorns
45g / 1½oz (½ cup) green cardamom pods
35g / 1¼oz (⅓ cup) coriander seeds
35g / 1¼oz (⅓ cup) fennel seeds
25g / 1oz (¼ cup) cloves
20 cinnamon sticks, about 2.5cm / 1 inch long
25g / 1oz (¼ cup) mace
25g / 1oz (¼ cup) black cumin seeds
20g / ¾oz (2⅔ cups) bay leaves
20g / ¾oz (1 cup) dried rose petals
3 tablespoons ground ginger
3 nutmegs, grated

Put all the ingredients, except the ground ginger and nutmeg, in a mortar and pound with a pestle, or grind in a spice grinder, to make a fine powder. Transfer to a clean, dry bowl, add the ground ginger and nutmeg and mix well. Sieve (strain) and store in a sterilized (see page 791), dry and airtight container.

Khas Garam Masala
Aromatic Garam Masala

Origin Punjab
Preparation time 15 minutes
Makes 500g / 1lb 2oz

175g / 6oz (2 cups) green cardamom pods
125g / 4¼oz (1 cup) cumin seeds
125g / 4¼oz (1 cup) black peppercorns
20 cinnamon sticks, about 2.5cm / 1 inch long
20g / ¾oz (¼ cup) cloves
2 nutmegs, grated

Put all the ingredients, except the nutmeg, in a mortar and pound with a pestle, or grind in a spice grinder, to make a fine powder. Transfer to a clean, dry bowl, add the nutmeg and mix well. Sieve (strain) and store in a sterilized (see page 791), dry and airtight container.

Chaat Masala
Chaat Masala

Origin Punjab/Delhi
Preparation time 15 minutes
Makes 500g / 1lb 2oz

75g / 2½oz (¾ cup) cumin seeds
70g / 2½oz (⅔ cup) black peppercorns
5 tablespoons black salt
35g / 1¼oz (2⅔ cups) dry mint leaves
3 teaspoons ajwain seeds
2 teaspoons asafoetida
1 teaspoon tartaric acid
150g / 5oz (1⅓ cups) amchoor
3½ tablespoons salt
4 tablespoons ground ginger
4 tablespoons yellow chilli powder

Put all the ingredients, except the amchoor, salt, ground ginger and yellow chilli powder, in a mortar and pound with a pestle, or grind in a spice grinder, to make a fine powder. Transfer to a clean, dry bowl, add the remaining ingredients and mix well. Sieve (strain) and store in a sterilized (see page 791), dry and airtight container.

Sambhar Masala (I)
Sambhar Masala (I)

Origin Tamil Nadu
Preparation time 30 minutes
Makes about 400g / 14oz

125g / 4¼oz (1½ cups) coriander seeds
4 tablespoons cumin seeds
1½ tablespoons fenugreek seeds
1½ tablespoons black peppercorns
1½ tablespoons mustard seeds
2 teaspoons poppy seeds, ground
2 cinnamon sticks
½ cup curry leaves
2 teaspoons chana dal, rinsed and drained
2 teaspoons arhar or toor (toover) dal, rinsed and drained
1 tablespoon vegetable oil
2 cups dried red chillies
2 teaspoons ground turmeric

Dry-roast each ingredient individually, except the oil, dried red chillies and turmeric, in a dry frying pan (skillet) over medium heat for a few moments, or until the spices and curry leaves are fragrant and the dals are golden.

Add the oil to the pan and heat through, then add the dried red chillies and stir-fry for about 1 minute, or until fragrant. Mix all the ingredients together in a mortar and pound with a pestle, or grind in a spice grinder, to make a fine powder. Store in an airtight container and use as required.

Sambhar Masala (II)
Sambhar Masala (II)

Origin Tamil Nadu
Preparation time 30 minutes, plus cooling time
Makes about 400g / 14oz

2 tablespoons groundnut (peanut) oil, for frying
60g / 2oz (⅓ cup) urad dal, rinsed and drained
60g / 2oz (⅓ cup) chana dal, rinsed and drained
1 tablespoon asafoetida chunks
120g / 4oz (1½ cups) coriander seeds
80g / 2¾oz (¾ cup) cumin seeds
4 tablespoons black peppercorns
3 tablespoons mustard seeds
3 tablespoons fenugreek seeds
20 dried red chillies
4 tablespoons ground turmeric
1 tablespoon ground garlic

Heat the oil in a kadhai, wok or deep, heavy-based pan over medium heat, add the dals and fry for 1–2 minutes until light golden. Remove and drain on kitchen paper (paper towels) and allow to cool.

Reheat the oil in which the lentils were fried over medium heat, add the asafoetida and fry for about 20 seconds until it swells up. Remove and drain on kitchen paper and allow to cool, then break it up into little pieces.

Put all the ingredients, except the turmeric and garlic, in a mortar and pound with a pestle, or grind in a spice grinder, to make a fine powder. Transfer to a clean, dry bowl, add the remaining ingredients and mix well. Sieve (strain) and store in a sterilized (see page 791), dry and airtight container.

Garam Masala (I)
p.31

Sambhar Masala (I)
p.32

Coconut Paste
p.57

Garlic Paste
p.57

Cashew Nut Paste
p.58

Ginger Paste
p.57

Assorted Spices

Egyptian Lentil
Chutney   p.63

Coconut Chutney
p.67

Ginger Pickle   p.84

Mildly Spiced
Chicken   p.499

Yoghurt Chutney
p.69

Prawn (Shrimp)
Balchao   p.408

Beetroot (Beet)
Chutney   p.69

Coconut Chutney
with Seasoning p.68

Curry Leaf Chutney
p.70

Spicy Potato
Stuffed Bread   p.611

Tomato Chutney
p.70

Raw Mango Pickle
from Telangana   p.76

Creamy Black Dal
p.582

Pineapple Raita
p.86

Chettinad Sambhar Podi
Chettinad Sambhar Powder

Origin Tamil Nadu
Preparation time 20–25 minutes, plus standing time
Makes about 600g / 1lb 5oz

250g / 9oz dried red chillies

3 tablespoons vegetable oil

280g / 10oz (3½ cups) coriander seeds

¾ teaspoon fennel seeds

¾ teaspoon cumin seeds

6–8 black peppercorns

2 tablespoons basmati rice, rinsed and drained

2 tablespoons chana dal, rinsed and drained

2 tablespoons arhar or toor (toover) dal, rinsed
   and drained

Remove the stalks from the dried red chillies and dry them in the sun for 1–2 days or stir-fry lightly in a dry frying pan (skillet) until fragrant and roasted. Set aside.

Heat a few drops of oil at a time in a frying pan and fry each ingredient individually for a few moments, or until the spices are fragrant and the rice and dals are golden. If drying the chillies in the sun, fry them as well, for 1 minute, or until they turn a shade darker.

Mix all the ingredients together in a mortar and pound with a pestle, or grind in a spice grinder, to make a fine powder. Store in an airtight container and use as required.

Kotu Podi
Kootu Powder

Origin Tamil Nadu
Preparation time 25 minutes
Makes about 500g / 1lb 2oz

75g / 2½oz (¾ cup) grated copra or
   desiccated (dried flaked) coconut

2 tablespoons vegetable oil

12–14 dried red chillies

1 tablespoon black peppercorns

1 tablespoon cumin seeds

4 teaspoons coriander seeds

1 teaspoon asafoetida

200g / 7oz (1 cup) chana dal, rinsed and drained

150g / 5oz (¾ cup) urad dal, rinsed and drained

Stir-fry the copra or desiccated coconut in a dry frying pan (skillet) over low heat for about 2–3 minutes, or until roasted. Remove from the pan and set aside.

Heat a few drops of oil at a time in the same pan and fry each ingredient individually for 30–45 seconds, or until the chillies and spices are fragrant and the dals are golden.

Mix all the ingredients in a mortar and pound with a pestle, or grind in a spice grinder, to make a coarse powder.

Store in an airtight container and use as required.

Poriyal Podi
Poriyal Powder

Origin Tamil Nadu
Preparation time 20 minutes
Makes about 400g / 14oz

75g / 2½oz (1 cup) coriander seeds
1 teaspoon asafoetida
100g / 3½oz (½ cup) urad dal, rinsed and drained
50g / 1¾oz (½ cup) grated copra or desiccated (dried flaked) coconut
3 tablespoons vegetable oil
15 dried red chillies
1 teaspoon salt

Stir-fry the coriander seeds, asafoetida and dal individually in a dry frying pan (skillet) over medium heat for 30–45 seconds, or until the spices are fragrant and the dal is golden. Remove from the pan and set aside.

Add the copra or desiccated coconut to the pan and roast, stirring constantly, until there is a red tinge. Remove from the pan. Pour the oil into the pan and heat through. Add the dried red chillies and fry for about 1–2 minutes, or until fragrant.

Mix all ingredients together in a mortar and pound with a pestle, or grind in a spice grinder, to make a coarse powder. Store in an airtight container and use as required.

Dosai Milagu Podi
Dosai Chilli Powder

Origin Tamil Nadu
Preparation time 20 minutes
Makes about 750g / 1lb 9oz

150g / 5oz (1 cup) white sesame seeds
2 tablespoons vegetable oil
1 cup dried red chillies
300g / 11oz (1½ cups) urad dal, rinsed and drained
150g / 5oz (¾ cup) chana dal, rinsed and drained
70g / 2½oz (½ cup) shelled peanuts
4–5 tablespoons jaggery or soft brown sugar
1 teaspoon salt

Stir-fry the sesame seeds in a dry frying pan (skillet) over medium heat for about 30 seconds, or until golden, then remove from the pan and set aside. Pour 1 tablespoon oil into the pan and heat through. Add the dried red chillies and stir-fry for 1–2 minutes or until fragrant, then remove from the pan and set aside.

Pour the remaining oil into the pan and heat through. Add the dals and fry for about 1 minute, or until golden. Mix all the ingredients together in a mortar and pound with a pestle, or grind in a spice grinder, to make a coarse powder.

Store in an airtight container and use as required.

Dum ka Masala
Spice Mixture for Dum Dishes

Origin Awadh
Preparation time 20 minutes
Makes about 125g / 4¼oz

45g / 1½oz (⅓ cup) fennel seeds
45g / 1½oz (⅓ cup) ground ginger
20g / ¾oz (¼ cup) green cardamom pods
20g / ¾oz (¼ cup) black cardamom pods

Put all the ingredients in a mortar and pound with a pestle, or grind in a spice grinder, to make a fine powder. Sieve (strain) and store in a sterilized (see page 791), dry and airtight container.

Tandoori Chaat Masala
Tandoori Chaat Masala

Origin Punjab
Preparation time 20 minutes
Makes about 450g / 1lb

50g / 1¾oz (½ cup) cumin seeds
50g / 1¾oz (scant ½ cup) black peppercorns
3½ tablespoons black salt
30g / 1¼oz (2⅓ cups) dried mint leaves
2 tablespoons fenugreek seeds
30 green cardamom pods
15 cloves
5 cinnamon sticks, about 2.5cm / 1 inch long
2 teaspoons ajwain seeds
1 teaspoon asafoetida
½ teaspoon ground mace
125g / 4¼oz (1 cup) amchoor
2½ tablespoons salt
3 tablespoons ground ginger
3 tablespoons yellow chilli powder

Put all the ingredients, except the amchoor, salt, ground ginger and yellow chilli powder, in a mortar and pound with a pestle, or grind in a spice grinder, to make a fine powder. Transfer to a clean, dry bowl, add the remaining ingredients and mix well. Sieve (strain) and store in a sterilized (see page 791), dry and airtight container.

Karpodi
Lentil Powder

Origin Andhra Pradesh
Preparation time 20 minutes
Makes about 125g / 4¼oz

2 teaspoons chana dal, rinsed and drained
½ teaspoon urad dal, rinsed and drained
2 teaspoons red chilli powder
pinch of ground mustard seeds
dash of asafoetida
2 teaspoons desiccated (dried flaked) coconut
salt

Heat a tawa or heavy-based frying pan (skillet), add the dals and dry-roast for about 1 minute, or until light brown. Roast each of the spices, except the salt, separately, including the coconut.

Put the dals into a mortar and pound with a pestle, or grind in a spice grinder, to make a powder. Add the coconut and process together. Transfer to a bowl, add the rest of the ingredients, season with salt, and mix together to make a dry reddish powder. This is sprinkled over Idlis (see pages 137–149) together with melted ghee and Sambhar (see page 32).

✺ ✵ ❈

Karepaku Karam
Spicy Ground Flavouring

Origin Tamil Nadu
Preparation time 20 minutes
Makes about 450g / 1lb

3 tablespoons vegetable oil
40 curry leaves
1 tablespoon coriander seeds
1 teaspoon cumin seeds
3 dried red chillies
1 teaspoon garlic powder
2 tablespoons urad dal, rinsed and drained
pinch of asafoetida
1 teaspoon ground black pepper
salt

Heat the oil in a frying pan (skillet) over medium heat, add the curry leaves and stir-fry for 30 seconds, or until crisp, then remove from the pan. Fry the rest of the ingredients, except the salt, individually, for about 45 seconds, or until light brown, then put into a a mortar and pound with a pestle, or grind in a spice grinder, add the curry leaves, season with salt and process to make a powder. Store in an airtight container and serve sprinkled on yoghurt or as flavouring to any lightly flavoured dish.

✺ ✵ ❈

Kandi Podi
Spicy Lentil Powder

Origin Andhra Pradesh
Preparation time 20 minutes
Makes about 750g / 1lb 10oz

180g / 6½oz (¾ cup) ghee
500g / 1lb 2oz (2⅔ cups) chana dal, rinsed and drained
30 dried red chillies
6 curry leaves
1 teaspoon cumin seeds
1 teaspoon coriander seeds
½ dried coconut, grated
1 clove garlic
salt

For the tempering

½ teaspoon ghee or vegetable oil
pinch of asafoetida
1 teaspoon mustard seeds
2 dried red chillies

Heat the ghee in a frying pan (skillet) over medium heat, add the chana dal and stir-fry for about 1 minute, or until golden. Remove from the pan and add the dried red chillies and stir-fry for about 1–2 minutes, or until they turn a shade darker. Remove from the pan and add the curry leaves. Stir-fry for about 30 seconds, or until fragrant. Put the dal, dried red chillies, cumin and coriander seeds and curry leaves in a mortar and pound with a pestle, or grind in a spice grinder, season with salt and process to make a fine powder. Add the grated coconut and garlic and process together.

Heat the ghee or oil for the tempering in a small frying pan over medium heat, add all the tempering ingredients and stir-fry for about 1–2 minutes, or until the seeds start to splutter and the chilies turn a shade darker. Pour over the ground mixture, mix well, then store in a sterilized, dry and airtight container.

✳ ✳ ✳
___

Moongphali Masala
Spicy Peanut Masala

Origin Andhra Pradesh/Hyderabad
Preparation time 20 minutes
Makes about 450g / 1lb

140g / 4¾oz (1 cup) shelled peanuts, with skin
1 teaspoon cumin seeds
1 teaspoon coriander seeds
½ teaspoon vegetable oil
20 dried red chillies
1 head garlic, peeled

Fry the peanuts lightly in a dry frying pan (skillet) over medium heat, then remove and peel off the skins by rubbing them between the palms of your hands. Stir-fry the cumin and coriander lighly on a hot tawa or in a dry frying pan until light brown, then remove from the pan. Heat the oil in a small frying pan over medium heat, add the dried red chillies and stir-fry for about 1–2 minutes, or until they turn a shade darker. Add the garlic and stir-fry briefly. Transfer all the ingredients to a mortar and pound with a pestle, or grind in a spice grinder, to make a powder. Store in a dry and airtight container. This can be sprinkled over Idlis (see pages 137–149).

✳ ✳ ✳
___

Rasam Podi
Spice Mixture for Pepper Water

Origin Tamil Nadu
Preparation time 20 minutes
Makes about 750g / 1lb 10oz

100g / 3½oz (½ cup) masoor dal, rinsed and drained
150g / 5oz (¾ cup) chana dal, rinsed and drained
50g / 1¾oz (¼ cup) urad dal, rinsed and drained
40g / 1½oz (½ cup) coriander seeds
250ml / 8fl oz (1 cup) vegetable oil
225g / 8oz dried red chillies
4 tablespoons black peppercorns
1 teaspoon asafoetida
2 tablespoons cumin seeds
2 teaspoons fenugreek seeds

Heat a tawa or heavy-based frying pan (skillet), add the dals and coriander seeds and dry-roast for about 1 minute, or until light brown.

Heat the oil in a frying pan over medium heat, add the dried red chillies, peppercorns and asafoetida and fry for about 1–2 minutes, or until the chillies turn a shade darker. Transfer all the ingredients to a mortar and pound with a pestle, or grind in a spice grinder, to make a powder. Store in an airtight container and use as required.

❋ ❋ ❋

Puliyadorai Masala
Spice Mixture for Tamarind Rice

Origin Tamil Nadu
Preparation time 20 minutes
Makes about 450g / 1lb

4 tablespoons vegetable oil
100g / 3½oz (½ cup) chana dal, rinsed and drained
100g / 3½oz (½ cup) arhar or toor (toover) dal, rinsed and drained
pinch of asafoetida
1 cup dried tamarind
1 tablespoon sesame seeds, roasted
salt

To be fried separately

50g / 1¾oz (⅓ cup) shelled peanuts
1 teaspoon chana dal, rinsed and drained
1 teaspoon urad dal, rinsed and drained
2 red chillies
2 green chillies
6 curry leaves
4 tablespoons vegetable oil

Heat the oil in a frying pan (skillet) over medium heat, add the dals and asafoetida and fry for about 1–2 minutes, or until the dals are golden. Add the tamarind, then transfer to a mortar and pound with a pestle, or grind in a spice grinder, add the sesame seeds and process until ground. Separately fry the items listed in the second section, then mix both together in a bowl, season with salt and store them in an airtight container. When the Tamarind Rice (see page 642) is to be made, take 4 cups cooked rice, heat a little oil in a pan, then add 2 tablespoons of the spice mixture and mix with the hot oil. Add to the rice and mix together.

❋ ❋

Bhruchi Masala
Bhruchi Curry Powder

Origin Coastal/Gujarat
Preparation time 20 minutes
Makes about 2kg / 4½lb

100g / 3½oz dried red Goa chillies
1kg / 2¼lb (5¼ cups) chana dal, roasted
100g / 3½oz (¾ cup) ground turmeric
250g / 9oz (2⅔ cups) cumin seeds
250g / 9oz (3 cups) small coriander seeds
250g / 9oz (1¾ cups) poppy seeds
10g / ¼oz (1½ tablespoons) ground cinnamon
2 tablespoons cloves
20g / ¾oz (¼ cup) white cardamom pods, seeds only
1 tablespoon black peppercorns
2 nutmegs, grated
2 tablespoons ground mace

Heat a tawa or heavy-based frying pan (skillet) and dry-roast all the ingredients separately, until light brown, then allow to cool. Put each into a mortar and pound with a pestle, or grind in a spice grinder, to make a powder. Mix them all together in a bowl, then sieve (strain) and store in an airtight glass jar.

Dhansak Masala
Dhansak Masala

Origin Gujarat
Preparation time 15 minutes
Makes about 125g / 4¼oz

45g (1½ oz) fenugreek seeds
45g (1½ oz) cloves
45g (1½ oz) black cardamom pods

Pound all the ingredients in a mortar with a pestle to make a fine powder. Sieve and store in a sterilized (see page 791), dry and airtight container.

Valsadi Masala
Traditional Valsad Masala (Dry)

Origin Gujarat
Preparation time 20 minutes
Makes about 450g / 1lb

1 × 10-cm / 4-inch piece fresh ginger, peeled
1 clove garlic
2 teaspoons ground turmeric
10–15 dried red chillies
2 teaspoons cumin seeds
1 tablespoon coriander seeds
1 cinnamon stick, about 5cm / 2 inches long
6–7 cloves
5–6 white cardamom pods, seeds only
8–10 black peppercorns
1 tablespoon poppy seeds
3 teaspoons salt

Put all the ingredients in a mortar and pound with a pestle, or grind in a spice grinder, to make a powder. Store in an airtight glass jar for up to 5–6 days, and longer in the refrigerator.

Valsadi Hara Masala
Traditional Valsad Masala (Green)

Origin Gujarat
Preparation time 20 minutes
Makes about 450g / 1lb

1 × 10-cm / 4-inch piece fresh ginger, peeled
1 clove garlic
2 teaspoons ground turmeric
10–15 green chillies, roughly chopped
2 teaspoons cumin seeds
1 tablespoon coriander seeds
1 cinnamon stick, about 5cm / 2 inches long
6–7 cloves
5–6 white cardamom pods, peeled
8–10 black peppercorns
1 tablespoon poppy seeds
3 teaspoons salt

Put all the ingredients in a mortar and pound with a pestle, or grind in a spice grinder, to make a powder. Store in an airtight glass jar for up to 2–3 days, and a little longer in the refrigerator.

Paanch Phoren
Five Spice Mix

Origin West Bengal
Preparation time 15 minutes, plus standing time
Makes about 150g / 5oz

60g / 2oz (⅔ cup) cumin seeds
60g / 2oz (½ cup) fennel seeds
2½ tablespoons fenugreek seeds
2½ tablespoons yellow mustard seeds
4 tablespoons kalonji (nigella) seeds

Dry the spices in the sun for 1–2 days or in a very low oven for several hours. Put them in a mortar and pound with a pestle, or grind in a spice grinder, to make fine powder. Sieve (strain) and store in an airtight container.

Parappu Podi
Lentil Spice Powder

Origin Andhra Pradesh
Preparation time 20 minutes
Makes about 200g / 7oz

100g / 3½oz (½ cup) moong dal, rinsed and drained
100g / 3½oz (½ cup) chana dal, rinsed and drained
4 dried red chillies
pinch of asafoetida
salt

Heat a tawa or heavy-based frying pan (skillet) and dry-roast all the ingredients, except the salt, until light brown. Transfer to a mortar and pound with a pestle, or grind in a spice grinder, season with salt and process to make a fine powder. Sieve (strain) and store in an airtight container.

Molaggai Podi
Pungent Chilli Powder

Origin Andhra Pradesh/Tamil Nadu
Preparation time 20 minutes
Makes about 250g / 9oz

2 teaspoons vegetable oil
10 teaspoons urad dal, rinsed and drained
10 teaspoons chana dal, rinsed and drained
10 dried red chillies
5 teaspoons sesame seeds
1 teaspoon asafoetida
salt

Heat the oil in a frying pan (skillet) over medium heat, add the dals and stir-fry for 2–3 minutes, or until fragrant. Add the dried red chillies and sesame seeds and stir-fry for about 1–2 minutes, or until they start to splutter and are fragrant. Add the asafoetida and stir-fry for 1 minute.

Season with salt. Transfer all the ingredients to a mortar and pound with a pestle, or grind in a spice grinder, to make a fine powder. Sieve (strain) and store in an airtight container.

✸ ✸ ✸

Kariveppilai Podi
Curry Leaf Powder

Origin Andhra Pradesh
Preparation time 20 minutes
Makes about 250g / 9oz

1 teaspoon vegetable oil
2 cups curry leaves
4 tablespoons urad dal, rinsed and drained
5 dried red chillies
1 marble-size ball of tamarind
salt

Heat the oil in a frying pan (skillet) and lightly fry all the ingredients, except the salt, individually. Transfer them to a mortar and pound with a pestle, or grind in a spice grinder, season with salt and process to make a coarse powder. Sieve (strain) and store in an airtight container.

✸ ✸ ✸

Kothimalli Podi
Coriander Leaf Powder

Origin Andhra Pradesh
Preparation time 20 minutes
Makes about 250g / 9oz

1 teaspoon vegetable oil
30g / 1¼oz (¾ cup) coriander (cilantro) leaves
4 tablespoons urad dal, rinsed and drained
5 dried red chillies
1 marble-size ball of tamarind
salt

Heat the oil in a frying pan (skillet) and lightly fry all the ingredients, except the salt, individually. Transfer them to a mortar and pound with a pestle, or grind in a spice grinder, season with salt and process to make a coarse powder. Sieve (strain) and store in an airtight container.

Garam Masala Kashmiri
Kashmiri Garam Masala

Origin Jammu and Kashmir
Preparation time 20 minutes
Makes about 500g / 1lb 2oz

120g / 4oz (1¼ cups) cumin seeds
3 tablespoons cloves
120g / 4oz (1⅛ cups) black cardamom pods
2 cinnamon sticks, 5cm / 2 inches long
120g / 4oz (⅔ cup) fenugreek seeds
3 tablespoons green cardamom pods
120g / 4oz aniseeds
10 bay leaves
2 teaspoons ground mace
2 nutmegs, grated

Heat a heavy-based pan, add the cumin seeds, cloves, black cardamom pods, cinnamon and fenugreek seeds and dry-roast over medium heat for about 1–2 minutes, or until they change colour to reddish brown. Transfer to a mortar and pound with a pestle, or grind in a spice grinder, add all the remaining ingredients and process to make a fine powder. Sieve (strain) and store in sterilized (see page 791), dry and airtight container and use as required.

p.35

Pisi Adrak
Ginger Paste

Origin Pan-India
Preparation time 20 minutes, plus chilling time
Makes about 250g / 9oz

1 × 14-cm / 5½-inch piece fresh ginger, peeled and
   roughly chopped

Put the ginger in a blender, add 3 tablespoons water
and process to make a smooth paste. Transfer to
a container and chill in the refrigerator. This paste
can be stored for up to 3 days in the refrigerator.

p.35

Pisi Lehsun
Garlic Paste

Origin Pan-India
Preparation time 15 minutes, plus chilling time
Makes about 200g / 7oz

200g / 7oz (about 5 heads) roughly chopped garlic

Put the garlic in a blender, add 3 tablespoons water
and process to make a fine paste. Transfer to
a container and chill and in the refrigerator. This paste
can be stored for up to 3 days in the refrigerator.

p.35

Pisa Nariyal
Coconut Paste

Origin Pan-India
Preparation time 25 minutes, plus chilling time
Makes about 150g / 5oz

1 coconut, peeled and grated, reserving any coconut
water

Put the coconut in a blender, add 5 tablespoons water,
preferably coconut water from the coconut, and
process to make a smooth paste. Transfer to
a container and chill in the refrigerator. This paste
can be stored for up to 12 hours in the refrigerator.

Ubala Pisa Pyaz
Boiled Onion Paste

Origin Awadh/Delhi/Hyderabad
Preparation time 25–30 minutes
Makes 1kg / 2¼lb

1kg / 2¼lb (7 medium) onions, roughly chopped
3 bay leaves
3 black cardamom pods

Put the onions in a handi or heavy-based pan, add
the bay leaves, cardamom pods and 250ml / 8fl oz
(1 cup) water. Bring to the boil, then reduce the
heat to medium and simmer for 20 minutes until
the onions are transparent and the liquid has
evaporated. Transfer to a blender and process to
make a smooth purée. This paste can be stored
for 24 hours in the refrigerator.

Tala Pisa Pyaz
Fried Onion Paste

Origin Awadh/Delhi/Hyderabad
Preparation time 15 minutes
Makes about 1kg / 2¼lb

3 tablespoons groundnut (peanut) oil, for frying
1kg / 2¼lb (7 medium) onions, sliced
100ml / 3½fl oz (½ cup) natural (plain) yoghurt

Heat the oil in a kadhai, wok or deep, heavy-based
pan over medium heat, add the onions and fry for
about 5–7 minutes, or until brown. Remove the
onions from the pan and spread them out on kitchen
paper (paper towels) to drain. Allow to cool.

When cool, transfer to a blender, add the yoghurt
and process to make a fine paste. This paste can be
stored for up to 3 days in the refrigerator.

Pisa Kaju
Cashew Nut Paste

Origin Pan-India
Preparation time 15 minutes, plus soaking time
Makes about 250g / 9oz

140g / 4¾oz (1 cup) cashew nuts

Soak the cashew nuts in a bowl of water for 30 minutes, then drain and break into pieces.

Put the cashew nuts in a blender, add 2 teaspoons water and process to make a smooth paste. Transfer to a container and chill in the refrigerator. This paste can be stored for up to 24 hours in the refrigerator.

Pisi Khas Khas
Poppy Seed Paste

Origin Pan-India
Preparation time 10 minutes, plus soaking time
Makes about 330g / 11oz

150g / 5oz (1 cup) poppy seeds

Soak the poppy seeds in bowl of warm water for 30 minutes, then drain.

Put the poppy seeds in a small blender, add 100ml / 3½fl oz (½ cup) water and process to make a smooth paste. Transfer to a container and chill in the refrigerator. This paste can be stored for up to 24 hours in the refrigerator.

Imli ka Sutt
Tamarind Extract

Origin Tamil Nadu
Preparation time 10 minutes, plus soaking time
Makes about 75ml / 3fl oz (4 tablespoons)

50g / 1¾oz tamarind

Put the tamarind in a bowl, add 4 tablespoons lukewarm water and soak for 30 minutes. Press through a sieve (strainer) into a bowl. Discard the residue. Tamarind extract should be made as needed, it does not store.

Khoya
Khoya

Origin North India
Preparation time 1½ hours, plus cooling time
Makes about 400g / 14oz

2 litres / 3½ pints (8½ cups) whole milk

Put the milk in a kadhai, wok or deep, heavy-based pan and bring to the boil. Reduce the heat to low and cook, stirring after every 5 minutes until the milk is reduced by half. Stirring constantly and continually scraping in the dried layer of milk that sticks to sides of the pan, continue to cook until reduced to a mashed potato consistency. Transfer to a bowl and allow to cool. When cool, this paste can be stored in the refrigerator for up to 2 days. It can also be dried and stored as a solid: spoon the paste into a clean piece of muslin (cheesecloth), then place in the sink, weigh down with something heavy and leave to drain for about 1 hour. The resulting solid should be stored in the refrigerator, and can be grated or crumbled as required.

Paneer
Paneer

Origin Punjab
Preparation time 30 minutes, plus standing time
Makes about 750g / 26oz

2 litres / 3½ pints (8½ cups) milk

2 tablespoons lemon juice

Heat the milk in a pan over a medium heat. When boiling, add the lemon juice. As the milk curdles the whey will separate. Strain the curdled milk through a piece of clean muslin, catching all the solids. Bring up and tie the edges of the muslin to form a pouch around the solids. Do not squeeze the muslin. Hang the pouch over a container and leave until all the water has been drained. Transfer the solids, still covered with muslin, to the sink and weigh down for 2–3 hours to produce a block of paneer that can be cut to the desired shape.

Chhena
Chhena

Origin West Bengal
Preparation time 1 hour, plus cooling time
Makes about 400g / 14oz

2 litres / 3½ pints (8½ cups) whole milk

160ml / 5½fl oz (⅔ cup) white vinegar

Put the milk in a handi or large, heavy-based pan and bring to the boil, then remove and allow to cool to 49°C/120°F. Add the vinegar in a steady stream over the entire surface and stir for about 3 minutes. Pour the curdled milk on to a piece of muslin (cheesecloth) in a sieve (strainer) placed over the sink to drain out the whey, then hold the four corners of the muslin and prod and gently squeeze the residue until a 'milky' whey starts to ooze out. Transfer the residue – chhena – while it is still warm on to a flat tray and knead firmly with the palm of your hand to mash the granules. Allow to cool, then wrap in foil and store in the refrigerator for up to 24 hours.

Chashni
Sugar Syrup

Origin Pan-India
Preparation time 20–25 minutes
Makes about 625ml / 21fl oz (2½ cups)

600g / 1lb 5oz (3 cups) sugar

1 teaspoon milk

1 teaspoon lime juice

Put the sugar and 250ml / 8fl oz (1 cup) water in a heavy-based pan over low heat and heat gently, stirring until the sugar dissolves completely.

Increase the heat and bring the syrup to the boil without stirring. When it comes to the boil, add the milk mixed with 1 teaspoon water. The scum will rise to the surface.

Boil for about 10 minutes, then strain the syrup through a piece of muslin (cheesecloth). Do not squeeze the muslin.

Meanwhile, rinse the pan. Return the syrup to the pan and bring to the boil once more. Add the lime juice. This prevents crystallization of the syrup. In case more scum rises to the surface, remove it with a slotted spoon.

To test, take some syrup between your thumb and forefinger (index finger). Be careful, as the syrup is very hot. Draw your fingers slightly apart. The syrup will form fine threads. The numbers of threads it forms, will give you the correct consistency.

SPECIAL P

Special Ma
CHILLI PICK
Lemon Pic
GARLIC PIC

MIXED PICKLE
Ginger Pic
RED CHILL
Kair Pickle

CKLES

go Pickle

LE IN OIL

lee in oil

LE IN OIL

N OIL

le in oil

IN OIL

in oil

In warm climates it is essential to find ways of preserving foodstuffs and prevent spoiling. As such, Indian pickles and chutneys are more than mere accompaniments – they are an intrinsic part of India's gastronomic heritage. Vital components of any meal, a fiery pickle made with chillies can increase the heat of a dish, while mild fruit chutneys or yoghurt-based raitas provide a cooling touch.

2
—

Pickles, Chutneys and Raitas

Masoor ki Chutney
Egyptian Lentil Chutney

Origin Hyderabad
Preparation time 20 minutes
Makes 250g / 9oz

1 tablespoon vegetable oil
4 tablespoons whole (sabut) masoor dal, rinsed and drained
6 dried red chillies
¼ teaspoon coriander seeds
¼ teaspoon cumin seeds
pinch of asafoetida
125ml / 4½fl oz (½ cup) Tamarind Extract (see page 58)
1 × 5-cm / 2-inch piece dried coconut
½ teaspoon Garlic Paste (see page 57)
salt

For the tempering

1 teaspoon vegetable oil
6 curry leaves
2 dried red chillies
½ teaspoon mustard seeds
1 onion, chopped

Heat the oil in a frying pan (skillet) over medium heat, add the dal and fry for about 1–2 minutes, or until they change colour, then remove from the pan and set aside. Add the red chillies, coriander and cumin seeds and the asafoetida and stir-fry for about 1 minute, or until the seeds start to splutter. Remove and transfer to a blender. Add the dal, tamarind extract, coconut, garlic paste and season with salt, then process until ground. Transfer to a serving bowl.

Heat the oil for the tempering in the frying pan over medium heat, add the curry leaves, dried red chillies and mustard seeds and stir-fry for about 1–2 minutes, or until they turn dark brown. Add the onion and fry for about 5 minutes, or until brown.

Add the tempering to the dal mixture and mix all the ingredients together. Transfer to an airtight container and store for up to 2 days in the refrigerator. This chutney can be served with Dosa (see page 141) or vadas (see pages 102–157).

Pyaz ki Chutney
Onion Chutney

Origin Hyderabad
Preparation time 35 minutes, plus cooling time
Makes 400g / 14oz

3 tablespoons tamarind pulp
6 tablespoons groundnut (peanut) oil
100g / 3½oz (½ cup) urad dal, rinsed, drained and dried
pinch of asafoetida
250g / 9oz (1½ cups) onions, chopped
2 dried red chillies
10g / ¼oz (5 slices) ginger, roughly chopped
2½ teaspoons roughly chopped garlic
salt

For the tempering

2 teaspoons groundnut (peanut) oil
2 dried red chillies
½ tablespoon mustard seeds

Put the tamarind pulp in a bowl, add 2 tablespoons water and mix together.

Heat the oil in a frying pan (skillet) over medium heat, add the dal and stir-fry for about 2 minutes, or until light golden. Add the asafoetida and onions and stir-fry for 1–2 minutes, or until pink in colour. Add the tamarind pulp mixture, dried red chillies, ginger and garlic, and stir-fry for 1–2 minutes. Remove from the heat and allow to cool.

When the mixture is cool, transfer to a blender or food processor, add 4 tablespoons water and process to make a rough paste. Put in a bowl.

Heat the oil for the tempering in a separate frying pan over medium heat, add the dried red chillies and stir-fry for a few seconds, then add the mustard seeds and stir-fry for about 1 minute, or until they start to splutter. Pour the mixture over the chutney and mix well. Season with salt. This chutney should be eaten immediately.

Illigada Chutney
Garlic Chutney

Origin Andhra Pradesh
Preparation time 35–40 minutes
Makes 250g / 9oz

125ml / 4½fl oz (½ cup) sesame oil
3 tablespoons red chilli powder
1 tablespoon ground fenugreek
juice of 20 limes
100g / 3½oz garlic, cut into vertical slices
salt

For the tempering
1 tablespoon vegetable oil
2 dried red chillies
4 curry leaves
1 tablespoon mustard seeds

Heat the oil in a frying pan (skillet) over low heat, add the chilli powder and fenugreek and fry for about 30 seconds. Season with salt, add the lime juice and cook for 5 minutes. Add the garlic and cook gently for 15 minutes.

Heat the oil for tempering in a separate frying pan, add the dried red chillies, curry leaves and mustard seeds and stir-fry for about 1–2 minutes, or until dark brown, then pour over the garlic mixture. This chutney is very good for digestion and can be stored for up to 1 week in the refrigerator.

Adrak ki Chutney
Ginger Chutney

Origin Awadh
Preparation time 20 minutes
Makes 250g / 9oz

1 tablespoon sesame oil
1 × 5-cm / 2-inch piece fresh ginger, peeled
    and chopped
125ml / 4½fl oz (½ cup) Tamarind Extract
    (see page 58)
1 teaspoon jaggery or soft brown sugar
1 teaspoon cumin seeds
½ teaspoon chopped garlic
1 teaspoon mustard seeds
4 curry leaves
3 dried red chillies
pinch of asafoetida
salt

Heat the oil in a heavy-based pan over low heat, add the ginger and stir-fry for 3 minutes, then remove from the pan with a slotted spoon. Set the pan and oil aside.

Put the tamarind extract in a blender, add the ginger and jaggery or sugar and process until ground. Transfer to a bowl.

Reheat the oil in the pan over medium heat, add the cumin seeds, garlic, mustard seeds, curry leaves and dried red chillies and stir-fry for about 1 minute, or until the mustard seeds start to splutter. Add the asafoetida and season with salt. Remove from the heat, place in a mortar and pound coarsely with a pestle, or process in a food processor or blender, then add to the ginger mixture and mix well. This chutney should be consumed on the day it is made.

Chintapandu Koythamira Chutney
Tamarind & Coriander (Cilantro) Chutney

Origin Coastal/Tamil Nadu
Preparation time 30 minutes, plus standing time
Makes 500g / 1lb 2oz

350g / 12oz coriander (cilantro) leaves

125ml / 4½fl oz (½ cup) vegetable oil

¼ teaspoon asafoetida

8 green chillies, de-seeded (optional)
    and roughly chopped

½ teaspoon coriander seeds

½ teaspoon cumin seeds

1 teaspoon jaggery or soft brown sugar

125ml / 4½fl oz (½ cup) Tamarind Extract
    (see page 58)

pinch of ground turmeric

2 dried red chillies

4 curry leaves

¼ teaspoon mustard seeds

salt

Wash the coriander leaves and drain, then pat dry
with kitchen paper (paper towel) and set aside for
10 minutes.

Heat 1 teaspoon oil in a frying pan (skillet) over
medium heat, add the asafoetida, green chillies,
coriander seeds and cumin seeds and stir-fry for
about 1 minute, or until the seeds start to splutter.
Set aside.

Put the jaggery, tamarind extract, turmeric and
coriander leaves in a blender, season with salt and
process until ground. Set aside.

Heat the remaining oil in a large frying pan over
medium heat, add the dried red chillies, curry leaves
and mustard seeds and stir-fry for about 1–2
minutes, or until they turn dark brown. Add all the
other ingredients to the pan, mix together and fry
together for a few minutes. This chutney should be
consumed on the day it is made.

Imli Aur Adrak ki Saunth
Tamarind & Ginger Chutney

Origin Delhi/Punjab
Preparation time 15–20 minutes, plus cooling time
Make 500g / 1lb 2oz

500ml / 18fl oz (2¼ cups) Tamarind Extract
    (see page 58)

2 teaspoons ground ginger

1 teaspoon cumin seeds, roasted

6 cloves garlic, crushed

3 tablespoons brown sugar

1 teaspoon chilli powder

1 teaspoon sliced ginger

1 tablespoon raisins

salt

Put the tamarind extract into a large bowl, add the
remaining ingredients, except the raisins. Season
with salt, then transfer the mixture to a large,
heavy-based pan and cook over medium heat for
about 5 minutes. Add the raisins and stir for about
5 minutes. Allow to cool and serve. This chutney
should be eaten immediately.

Chintapandu Thokku
Raw Tamarind Chutney

Origin Andhra Pradesh
Preparation time 50 minutes, plus cooling and
standing time
Makes 750g / 1lb 10oz

500g / 1lb 2oz tamarind
2 cloves garlic
4–5 bunches mint leaves
10–15 green chillies, de-seeded (optional) and roughly chopped
salt

For the tempering

180ml / 6fl oz (¾ cup) vegetable oil
1 teaspoon mustard seeds
1 teaspoon cumin seeds
¼ teaspoon fenugreek seeds
4 dried red chillies

Remove the seeds from the tamarind because they
spoil the taste of the chutney. Put all the ingredients,
except the tempering ingredients and salt, in a
blender and process, adding a little water if
necessary, to make a smooth paste. Season with salt.

Heat the oil for the tempering in a frying pan (skillet)
over medium heat, add all the tempering ingredients
and stir-fry for about 1–2 minutes, or until the seeds
start to splutter and the chillies turn a shade darker.
Pour the hot tempering over the chutney and mix
well. Allow to cool.

When cool, put into a sterilized bottle (see page 791)
with a well-fitting lid. Keep at room temperature and
use after one week. The chutney can be stored in the
refrigerator for up to a year.

Pudine ki Chutney
Mint Chutney

Origin Punjab/Delhi/Awadh
Preparation time 10 minutes
Makes 250g / 9oz

16 cloves garlic, crushed
10 green chillies, de-seeded (optional) and roughly chopped
1 large bunch coriander (cilantro) leaves
5 large bunches mint leaves
125ml / 4½fl oz (½ cup) Tamarind Extract (see page 58)
salt

Put the garlic, chillies, coriander and mint leaves in
a blender and process until ground, then transfer to
a bowl, add the tamarind extract and mix together.
Season with salt. The amount of chillies and salt can
be increased or decreased to taste. This chutney
should be consumed on the day it is made.

Nariyal Tamatar ki Chutney
Tomato Coconut Chutney

Origin Tamil Nadu/Karnataka
Preparation time 35 minutes
Makes 1kg / 2¼lb

500g / 1lb 2oz (3 medium) ripe tomatoes

½ coconut, roughly chopped

2 tablespoons fried chana dal

pinch of ground turmeric

1 tablespoon chilli powder

1 bunch coriander (cilantro) leaves, ground

225g / 8oz (3 small) onions

1 teaspoon sugar

juice of 1 lime

salt

For the tempering

1 tablespoon vegetable oil

3 dried red chillies

½ teaspoon mustard seeds

½ teaspoon urad dal, rinsed and drained

½ teaspoon cumin seeds

8 curry leaves

pinch of asafoetida

Put the tomatoes, coconut, dal, turmeric and chilli powder in a blender or food processor, season with salt and process to make a purée. Pass through a sieve (strainer) into a bowl.

Put the coriander leaves in the blender and process to make a purée. Set aside.

Cook the onions in a pan of salted boiling water for 2–3 minutes, or until soft, then drain.

Heat the oil for the tempering in a heavy-based pan over medium heat, add the dried red chillies, mustard seeds, urad dal, cumin, curry leaves and asafoetida and stir-fry for about 1–2 minutes, or until dark brown. Add the boiled onions and fry lightly, then stir in the tomato-coconut purée until it thickens. Add the sugar, coriander purée and lime juice to taste, then cook for 1–2 minutes, or until heated through. This chutney can be stored for up to 2 days in the refrigerator.

Nariyal ki Chutney
Coconut Chutney

Origin Tamil Nadu/Karnataka
Preparation time 20 minutes
Makes 500g / 1lb 2oz

½ coconut, peeled and finely grated

6 green chillies, roughly chopped

1 bunch coriander (cilantro) leaves

1 teaspoon cumin seeds

pinch of asafoetida (optional)

juice of 1 lime

salt

Keep a spoonful of the grated coconut aside for the garnish, then put the rest in a blender or food processor with the remaining ingredients, except the lime juice. Season with salt and process, adding a little water if necessary to make a paste. Transfer to a bowl and mix in the lime juice and garnish with reserved grated coconut. This chutney should be consumed on the day it is made.

Kobari Pachadi
Coconut Chutney with Seasoning

Origin Tamil Nadu
Preparation time 30 minutes
Makes 400g / 14oz

1 coconut, peeled and grated
250ml / 8fl oz (1 cup) natural (plain) yoghurt
salt

For the tempering

1 tablespoon vegetable oil
1 teaspoon urad dal, rinsed and drained
1 dried red chilli
1 teaspoon mustard seeds

Mix the coconut and yoghurt together in a bowl, then season with salt. Transfer to a blender and process until ground.

Heat the oil in a frying pan (skillet) over medium heat, add the urad dal and chilli and stir-fry for about 1–2 minutes, or until they start to brown. Add the mustard seeds and stir-fry for about 1 minute, or until they start to splutter. Pour over the coconut paste and mix together. This chutney can be stored in an airtight container for up to 2 days in the refrigerator.

Topa Kooler Achar
Preserved Indian Plums

Origin West Bengal
Preparation time 30 minutes, plus cooling and standing time
Makes 2kg / 4½lb

250ml / 8fl oz (1 cup) mustard oil
pinch of ground turmeric
50g / 1¾oz (½ cup) chilli powder
1kg / 2¼lb Indian plums or ordinary ripe plums
250g / 9oz (¾ cup) cane molasses
250g / 9oz (1¼ cups) sugar
50g / 1¾oz ground Paanch Phoren (see page 55), roasted

Heat the mustard oil in a large stainless-steel pan over medium heat, add the turmeric and chilli powder. Add the plums and bring to the boil, stirring gently. Add the cane molasses and sugar and cook over medium heat for 15 minutes. Before removing from the heat, add the paanch phoren. The consistency should be slightly sticky.

Allow to cool, then bottle into sterilized jars (see page 791). Keep at room temperature and use after 1 week. The preserved plum can be stored in the refrigerator.

☀ / 📷 p.41

Dahi ki Chutney
Yoghurt Chutney

Origin Awadh
Preparation time 35 minutes
Makes 250g / 9oz

2 teaspoons vegetable oil
1 tablespoon chana dal, rinsed and drained
1 tablespoon urad dal, rinsed and drained
1 piece fresh coconut, 7.5 × 5 × 2.5cm / 3 × 2 × ½ inches, roughly chopped
4 green chillies, de-seeded (optional) and roughly chopped
1 teaspoon chopped ginger
12 curry leaves
4 tablespoons natural (plain) yoghurt, whisked
juice of ½ lime
salt

For the tempering

1 teaspoon mustard seeds
1 tablespoon chana dal, rinsed and drained
1 tablespoon urad dal, rinsed and drained
2 dried red chillies

Heat 1 teaspoon oil in a frying pan (skillet) over medium heat, add the dals and stir-fry for about 1–2 minutes, or until they turn dark brown.

Put the coconut, green chillies, ginger, curry leaves, and the fried dals in a blender or food processor and process, adding a little water, if necessary, to make a paste. Transfer to a bowl.

Heat the remaining oil in a frying pan over medium heat, add the tempering ingredients and stir-fry for about 1–2 minutes, or until the seeds start to splutter and the chillies turn a shade darker. Add them to the ground paste and mix well, then add the yoghurt and lime juice. Season with salt, then add a little water if required and mix to a chutney consistency. This chutney can be stored for up to 2 days in the refrigerator.

☀ / 📷 p.42

Beetroot Thuviyal
Beetroot (Beet) Chutney

Origin Tamil Nadu
Preparation time 20–25 minutes
Makes 400g / 14oz

2–3 tablespoons vegetable oil
1½ teaspoons mustard seeds
1½ tablespoons urad dal, rinsed and drained
1 tablespoon chana dal, rinsed and drained
½ teaspoon asafoetida
2 dried red chillies
1 green chilli, de-seeded and chopped
2 medium-sized beetroots (beets), peeled and grated
4 tablespoons Tamarind Extract (see page 58)
2 tablespoons grated fresh coconut
2 tablespoons chopped coriander (cilantro) leaves
salt

Heat half the oil in a frying pan (skillet) over medium heat, add the mustard seeds, dals, asafoetida, dried red chillies and green chilli and stir-fry for about 2 minutes, or until the spices are fragrant and dals turn golden. Remove from the pan and set aside.

Add the remaining oil to the pan and heat through. Add the beetroot (beet) and fry for about 5 minutes, or until tender.

Combine all the ingredients in a blender or food processor, season with salt, add 2–3 tablespoons water process to a smooth consistency. This chutney should be eaten immediately.

Karipatta Chutney
Curry Leaf Chutney

Origin Hyderabad
Preparation time 25–35 minutes
Makes 250g / 9oz

2 tablespoons vegetable oil
1 teaspoon mustard seeds
1 cup curry leaves
6 green chillies, de-seeded (optional) and roughly chopped
1 onion
1 teaspoon ground fresh ginger
2 teaspoons ground garlic
½ fresh coconut, grated
juice of 2–3 limes
1 tablespoon sesame seeds, roasted
salt

Heat the oil in a frying pan (skillet) over medium heat, add the mustard seeds and stir-fry for about 1–2 minutes, or until dark brown. Add the curry leaves and stir-fry lightly for about 30 seconds. Remove from the heat and transfer to a blender or food processor, add all the remaining ingredients, season with salt and process until ground. You can add or decrease ingredients to taste. This chutney should be consumed on the day it is made.

Tonk
Tomato Chutney

Origin West Bengal
Preparation time 30 minutes, plus standing time
Makes 2½kg / 5½lb

2kg / 4½lb tomatoes, cut into quarters
400g / 14oz (2 cups) sugar
250ml / 8fl oz (1 cup) malt (white) vinegar
2 teaspoons chilli powder
4 teaspoons ground garlic
2 tablespoons raisins
2 teaspoons sliced ginger
4 dried red chillies, cut into pieces
4 green chillies, de-seeded and roughly chopped
salt

Cook all the ingredients together in a large, stainless steel pan over low heat for about 20 minutes, or until the tomatoes are pulpy and thick. Leave for 1–2 hours before eating, to allow the flavours to develop, or transfer to an airtight container. This chutney can be stored for up to 2 weeks in the refrigerator.

Til ki Chutney
Sesame Seed Chutney

Origin Awadh
Preparation time 20 minutes
Makes 500g / 1lb 2oz

4 tablespoons sesame seeds
3 tablespoons peanuts
1–2 tablespoons vegetable oil (optional)
6–8 green chillies, de-seeded (optional) and roughly chopped
1 tablespoon ground garlic
2 onions, sliced
20g / ¾oz (½ cup) coriander (cilantro) leaves
125ml / 4½fl oz (½ cup) Tamarind Extract (see page 58)
salt

The sesame seeds and peanuts can either be dry-roasted separately in a small frying pan (skillet) for about 2 minutes, or until they change colour, or they can be fried. If frying, heat the oil in a frying pan over medium heat, add the sesame seeds and stir-fry for about 1 minute, or until they change colour, then remove from the pan. Add the peanuts to the pan and stir-fry for about 1–2 minutes, or until they turn golden.

Transfer them to a blender, add the sesame seeds and the remaining ingredients, then season with salt and process until ground. Grind all the ingredients together. One can add or lessen any ingredients according to taste. This chutney should be consumed on the day it is made.

Simla Mirch ki Chutney
(Bell) Pepper Chutney

Origin Awadh
Preparation time 30 minutes, plus cooling time
Makes 1½kg / 3¼lb

125ml / 4½fl oz (½ cup) vegetable oil
6 cloves garlic, chopped
3 large dried red chillies, slit in half lengthways and de-seeded
1 teaspoon cumin seeds
1 teaspoon mustard seeds
4 tablespoons brown sugar
250ml / 8fl oz (1 cup) malt (white) vinegar
6 tablespoons vegetable oil
6 red or green (bell) peppers, de-seeded and cut into quarters
salt

Heat the 125ml / 4½fl oz (½ cup) oil in a pan until hot, then remove from the heat and allow to cool.

Put the garlic, dried red chillies, cumin seeds, mustard seeds, brown sugar and vinegar in a blender and process to make a smooth paste. Set aside.

Heat the 6 tablespoons oil in a large frying pan (skillet) over medium-low heat, add the pepper quarters and stir-fry for about 5 minutes. Add the ground spices and cook for a further 10 minutes. Add the cooled oil and remove from the heat. Allow to cool completely, before storing in sterilized jars (see page 791).

Sarson ki Chutney
Mustard Chutney

Origin New
Preparation time 20 minutes
Makes 125g / 4½oz

80g / 2¾oz (1 cup) mustard powder
1½ teaspoons mustard
2 tablespoons lemon juice
4 teaspoons malt (white) vinegar
1 teaspoon ground turmeric
2 teaspoons vegetable oil
salt

Mix all the ingredients, except the oil, together
in a large bowl, then season with salt. Gradually
add the oil to the mixture, whisking all the time
until combined. This chutney should be consumed
on the day it is made.

Moongphali ki Chutney
Peanut Chutney

Origin Hyderabad
Preparation time 25 minutes
Makes 750g / 1lb 10oz

125ml / 4½fl oz (½ cup) vegetable oil
185g / 6½oz (1¼ cups) shelled peanuts, fried
12 green chillies
10g / ¼oz tamarind
1 × 2.5-cm / 1-inch piece dried coconut
3–4 onions, finely chopped
salt

For the tempering

3 dried red chillies
pinch of asafoetida
6 curry leaves
½ teaspoon cumin seeds

Heat the oil in a frying pan (skillet) over medium
heat, add the peanuts and cook for 1 minute, then
remove with a slotted spoon and set aside.
Add the green chillies to the pan and fry for about
1–2 minutes, or until they change colour, then
remove from the pan and set aside. Reserve the oil
in the pan.

Put the fried peanuts in a blender, add the tamarind,
coconut and green chillies, then season with salt and
process until ground.

Heat the oil again over medium heat, add the dried
red chillies, asafoetida, curry leaves and cumin for
about 1 minute, or until the cumin seeds start to
splutter. Add the finely chopped onions and fry for
about 5–7 minutes, or until the onions are golden
brown. Add the peanut mixture and fry briefly, then
transfer to a serving dish. This chutney should be
consumed on the day it is made.

Moong Dal ki Chutney
Moong Dal Chutney

Origin Awadh
Preparation time 15 minutes, plus cooling time
Makes 400g / 14oz

2 teaspoons vegetable oil

¼ teaspoon fenugreek seeds

8 dried red chillies

½ teaspoon mustard seeds

100g / 3½oz (½ cup) moong dal, rinsed and drained

6 green chillies, de-seeded (optional)
    and roughly chopped

1 teaspoon ground fresh ginger

1 onion, cut into quarters

125ml / 4½fl oz (½ cup) Tamarind Extract
    (see page 58)

½ teaspoon icing (confectioners') sugar

salt

Heat the oil in a frying pan (skillet) over medium heat, add the fenugreek seeds, dried red chillies, mustard seeds and dal and stir-fry for about 1–2 minutes, or until dark brown. Remove from the heat and allow to cool, then mix with the green chillies, ginger, onion and tamarind extract in a bowl. Transfer to a blender and process, adding a little water if necessary to form a smooth paste.

Add the sugar and mix well. Transfer to a serving bowl to serve with Dosa (see page 141) as well as other dishes, or transfer to an airtight contained and store for up to 2 days in the refrigerator.

Chenigapappu Chutney
Chana Dal Chutney

Origin Tamil Nadu
Preparation time 20–25 minutes
Makes 500g / 1lb 2oz

250g / 9oz (1⅓ cups) chana dal, roasted

1 teaspoon chopped ginger

½ bunch coriander (cilantro) leaves

40g / 1½oz (½ cup) grated fresh coconut

6 green chillies, de-seeded (optional)
    and roughly chopped

juice of 2–3 limes

For the tempering

1 tablespoon vegetable oil

10 curry leaves

1 teaspoon mustard seeds

pinch of asafoetida

salt

Put the roasted chana dal, ginger, coriander leaves, coconut, chillies and lime juice in a blender and process until ground. Transfer to a bowl.

Heat the oil for the tempering in a frying pan (skillet) over medium heat, add the curry leaves and mustard seeds and stir-fry for about 1 minute, or until they splutter. Add the asafoetida and season with salt, then remove from the heat and mix with the ground chutney. This chutney should be consumed on the day it is made.

Molgai Podi
Dry Ground Chutney

Origin Andhra Pradesh
Preparation time 20 minutes
Makes 400g / 14oz

4 tablespoons vegetable oil
100g / 3½oz (½ cup) split and skinned urad dal rinsed and drained
100g / 3½oz (½ cup) chana dal, rinsed and drained
30g / 1¼oz (⅓ cup) desiccated (dried flaked) coconut
8–10 pieces of dried red chilli
½ teaspoon asafoetida
few curry leaves
salt

Heat a little oil in a frying pan (skillet) over medium heat, add the dals and stir-fry for about 1–2 minutes, or until golden, then remove from the pan and set aside. Add the coconut to the pan and stir-fry for about 30 seconds, or until golden brown. Remove from the pan and set aside with the dals, then add the chillies to the pan and stir-fry for about 1–2 minutes, or until they turn a shade darker. Add to the coconut and dals. Season the mixture with salt and add the asafoetida and curry leaves, then transfer to a blender and process until coarsely ground. Put in a jar and use as required.

Dakshini Hari Chutney
Southern Green Chutney

Origin New
Preparation time 25–30 minutes, plus cooling time
Makes 500g / 1lb 2oz

2 tablespoons groundnut (peanut) oil
200g / 7oz curry leaves
100g / 3½oz (1 cup) grated fresh coconut
50g / 1¾oz (1 cup) coriander (cilantro) leaves
50g / 1¾oz (⅓ cup) sesame seeds
10g / ¼oz (5 slices) ginger, roughly chopped
½ teaspoons roughly chopped garlic
1 tablespoon lemon juice
2 tablespoons chopped, stoned (pitted) raw mango
salt

For the tempering

4 teaspoons groundnut (peanut) oil
2 tablespoons chana dal, rinsed and drained
4 dried red chillies
10 curry leaves

Heat the oil in a large frying pan (skillet) over medium heat, add all the ingredients, except the lemon juice, mango and salt, and stir-fry for a few seconds. Remove from the heat and allow to cool.

When cool, transfer the mixture to a blender or food processor, add the mango and lemon juice and season with salt, then process, adding a little water if necessary to make a smooth paste. Transfer the paste to a bowl.

Heat the oil for the tempering in a frying pan over medium heat, add the chana dal and stir-fry for about 1–2 minutes, or until light golden. Add the dried red chillies and curry leaves and stir-fry for a few seconds. Mix well with the chutney. This chutney should be eaten immediately.

Kairi ki Mhithi Chutney
Sweet Green Mango Chutney

Origin Hyderabad/Awadh
Preparation time 45–50 minutes, plus standing time
Makes 1kg / 2¼lb

5 medium-sized raw green mangoes, stoned (pitted) and cut into 2.5-mm / ⅛-inch pieces
1 teaspoon sesame oil
6 tablespoons chilli powder
150g / 5oz (½ cup) salt
1½ tablespoons mustard powder
2 teaspoons turmeric powder
¼ teaspoon fenugreek seeds
¼ teaspoon ground cloves
1 teaspoon chopped ginger
125g / 4½oz (1 cup) icing (confectioners') sugar
250ml / 8fl oz (1 cup) sesame oil

For the tempering

1 dried red chillies
¼ teaspoon mustard seeds
2 curry leaves, fried

Put the mangos in a large bowl.

Put all the ingredients for the tempering in a blender and process until ground. Set aside.

Heat the 1 tablespoon oil in a heavy-based pan over medium heat, add the spices and sugar and stir-fry for about 1 minute. Add half to the chopped mangoes, then put them into sterilized jars (see page 791). Add the tempering to the jars and pour in the remaining spiced oil, then cover with the lids and keep for 3 days.

On the third day, put the jars in a sunny or warm place for 2 hours. With the lid tightly fitted, turn the jars upside down, then straighten and keep the lids well closed. This chutney can be stored for in a cool place for several months.

Kairi ki Chutney
Raw Green Mango Chutney

Origin Hyderabad/Awadh
Preparation time 50 minutes, plus cooling time
Makes 500g / 1lb 2oz

125ml / 4½fl oz (½ cup) sesame oil
1 tablespoons mustard powder
1 teaspoon fenugreek seeds
¼ teaspoon asafoetida
5 small green mangoes, stoned (pitted) and cut into bite-sized pieces
6 tablespoons chilli powder
½ teaspoons ground turmeric
salt

For the tempering

1 teaspoon vegetable oil
2 dried red chillies
¼ teaspoon chana dal, rinsed and drained
¼ teaspoon urad dal, rinsed and drained
¼ teaspoon mustard seeds

Heat 1 tablespoon of the oil in a frying pan (skillet) over low heat, add the mustard powder, fenugreek and asafoetida and stir-fry for about 30 seconds.

Heat 375ml / 13fl oz (1½ cups) oil in a large, heavy-based pan over low heat, add the mangoes and fry for 20 minutes, or until they soften. Remove from the heat and allow to cool. Transfer to a blender or a food processor and add the fried spices, chilli powder, turmeric and remaining oil and season with salt, then process until ground. Transfer to a bowl.

Heat the oil for the tempering in a frying pan over medium heat, add all the ingredients and stir-fry for about 1–2 minutes, or until brown. Remove from the heat and allow to cool, then mix with the mango and spice mixture. When cool, this chutney can be stored in airtight ceramic jars for several months.

Seb ki Chutney
Apple Chutney

Origin Uttarakhand
Preparation time 1 hour 15 minutes, plus cooling time
Cooking time 1 hour
Makes 1kg / 2¼lb

6 green apples, peeled and cut into cubes
2 teaspoons sliced ginger
2 tablespoons raisins
6 cloves
125ml / 4½fl oz (½ cup) malt (white) vinegar
250g / 9oz (1¼ cups) sugar
12 cloves garlic
salt

Put the apples together with all the other ingredients in a large, heavy-based pan and cook over medium heat for about 1 hour, or until the water is absorbed and the apple chutney thickens. Allow to cool completely and store in sterilized bottles or jars (see page 791).

Bhaang ki Chutney
Tangy Chutney of Hemp Seeds & Mint

Origin Uttarakhand
Preparation time 15 minutes
Makes 100g / 3½oz

3½ tablespoons hemp seeds
2 green chillies, de-seeded (optional) and roughly chopped
3 tablespoons lemon juice
2 tablespoons chopped mint leaves
salt

Stir-fry the hemp seeds on a tawa or in a dry frying pan (skillet) over low-medium heat for about 1 minute, or until roasted, then transfer them to a blender and process until ground. Add the chillies, lemon juice, mint leaves, 3 tablespoons water and season with salt, then process again, to make a smooth paste.

This chutney makes a versatile accompaniment to any dish, and can be stored in the refrigerator for up to 24 hours.

❋ ❋ ❋ / 📷 pp.47, 117, 595

Avakk
Raw Mango Pickle from Telangana

Origin Andhra Pradesh
Preparation time 20–25 minutes, plus standing time
Makes 500g / 1lb 2oz

250g / 9oz sour green mangoes, stoned (pitted) and chopped into 2.5-cm / 1-inch pieces
1kg / 2¼lb (5¾ cups) mustard seeds
1kg / 2¼lb red chillies, ground
sesame oil
4 tablespoons fenugreek seeds
coarse salt

Put the mangoes in a ceramic or stone jar or bowl and set aside.

Rub the mustard seeds between the palms of your hands to try to remove the dark husk as much as possible, then put them in a mortar or spice grinder and pound with a pestle or process until ground.

Spread the salt and ground chillies out on clean tea (dish) towels and let them dry so there is no moisture left.

Mix the mustard powder, ground chillies and salt together in a large bowl, adding a little oil to make a paste. Add the paste and the fenugreek seeds to the mangoes in the jar or bowl for 12 hours and leave them with a cloth covering the jar or bowl until the mangoes release water. Drain out the water gently. After draining out the water, pour in enough oil to stand about 8–10cm / 3–4 inches above the mangoes. Mix the spices and mangoes well with a dry wooden spoon and make sure there is still 10cm / 4 inches oil on top of the mangoes mixture.

Aam ka Achar
Mild Raw Mango Pickle

Origin Awadh
Preparation time 35–40 minutes, plus standing time
Makes 750g / 1lb 10oz

For stage a

450g / 1lb (2¾ cups) raw green mangoes, stoned (pitted) and cut into small squares
1 teaspoon ground turmeric
2 tablespoons lime juice
salt

For stage b

¾ level tablespoon kalonji (nigella) seeds
1 heaped (heaping) tablespoon fenugreek seeds
1 heaped (heaping) tablespoon mustard seeds
2 heaped (heaping) tablespoons cumin seeds
2 level tablespoons coriander seeds
4 heaped (heaping) tablespoons red chilli powder
¾ cup garlic, partially ground

For the tempering

500ml / 18fl oz (2¼ cups) sesame oil
¾ teaspoon fenugreek seeds
¾ teaspoon mustard seeds
½ teaspoon kalonji (nigella) seeds
10 dried red chillies
10 cloves garlic

For stage a, put the mangoes in a large bowl, add the turmeric, then sprinkle some salt over and mix well. Leave in a partially closed glass or ceramic dish for 3 days. Gently shake them around once or twice a day. Some water will be released by the mangoes, which should be retained. On the third day, add the lime juice, then mix together and leave for another day.

For stage b, on the fourth day, add all the spices to the mangoes and mix thoroughly, then add the garlic and mix well. Set aside.

Heat the oil for the tempering, in a deep frying pan (skillet) over medium heat. Add the fenugreek, mustard and kalonji seeds, then add the dried red chillies and garlic and fry for about 1–2 minutes, or until brown. Remove from the heat and allow to cool.

When the tempering is cool, slowly add it in 3–4 batches to the pickle mixture, stirring the mixture thoroughly while adding. Leave for 4–5 days in a partially closed dish or bowl, mixing daily. Make sure there is enough oil to cover the pickle. If not, heat a little more oil, then allow it to cool and add it to the pickle. Bottle into sterilized jars (see page 791).

Gurh Keri
Mango Pickle with Jaggery

Origin Gujarat
Preparation time 20 minutes, plus standing time
Makes 3½kg / 7lb 11oz

6 large raw mangoes, stoned (pitted) and cut into cubes
2 tablespoons ground turmeric
115g / 4oz (1 cup) chilli powder
275g / 10oz (1½ cups) split mustard seeds
2 tablespoons split fenugreek seeds
5 teaspoons asafoetida
1.4kg / 3lb jaggery, chopped, or soft brown sugar
salt

Put the mango pieces in a large bowl, season with salt, and add the turmeric and toss until the mango pieces are coated. Spread them out on a clean cloth or tea (dish) towel and dry overnight.

The next day, put the remaining spices, jaggery and mango pieces in a large bowl and toss gently to mix. Transfer the mixture to a wide-mouthed glass jar and cover with muslin. Leave in a cupboard in a cool place, stirring with a clean spoon once in 2 days. The pickle is ready when the jaggery has melted and the mango pieces are slightly softened. Remove 1–2 cups at a time and put into a small jar for everyday use.

Meetha Nimboo ka Achar
Sweet Lime Pickle

Origin Punjab/Delhi
Preparation time 20 minutes, plus standing time
Makes 750g / 1lb 10oz

12 limes
1 teaspoon chilli powder
1 teaspoon ground turmeric
1 teaspoon Garam Masala (see page 31)
6 tablespoons jaggery or soft brown sugar
salt

Cut the limes into 8 pieces each, and put them in a large glass sterilized jar (see page 791). Mix all the remaining ingredients together in a large bowl and season with salt. Pour over the limes, shake the jar and mix well. Tie a muslin cloth (cheesecloth) on top of the jar and keep the jar on the window in the kitchen. It will be ready to eat in 15 days time. Shake it daily.

Nimboo ka Achar
Lime Pickle

Origin Punjab
Preparation time 35 minutes, plus standing time
Makes 750g / 1lb 10oz

1kg / 2¼lb limes, cut into quarters and de-seeded
juice of ½ lime
125g / 4¼oz (⅓ cup) salt
30 cloves garlic
40g / 1½oz (⅓ cup) chilli powder

For the tempering

100ml / 3½fl oz (½ cup) vegetable oil
30g / 1¼oz (⅓ cup) cumin seeds
2 tablespoons mustard seeds
pinch of asafoetida

Prick each lime quarter with a fork.

Put the limes in a heatproof bowl, add the juice, salt, garlic and chilli powder and mix together, then put them in a steamer and steam for about 10 minutes, or until the slices soften. If you don't have a steamer, use a large pan with a lid and place a trivet or upside-down plate in the base (bottom). Pour in enough water so it stays below the top of the trivet and cover with the lid. Place the bowl carefully on top of the trivet or upside-down plate, cover and steam for 10 minutes, or until soft.

Transfer the limes to a bowl, cover with muslin (cheesecloth) and leave in the sun or in a warm place for 2 days. If leaving outside, bring indoors at night to avoid damp air.

Heat the oil for the tempering in a frying pan (skillet) over medium heat, add the cumin and mustard seeds and stir-fry for about 1 minute, or until they start to splutter. Add the asafoetida and mix well. Pour the mixture over the limes and mix well. Cover with muslin and leave in the sun or on a windowsill for 2 more days, then remove the cloth and bottle into sterilized jars (see 791).

Papite ka Achar
Papaya Pickle

Origin Punjab
Preparation time 35–40 minutes, plus cooling and standing time
Makes 500g / 1lb 2oz

1 large raw green papaya, peeled
500ml / 18fl oz (2¼ cups) vegetable oil
¼ teaspoon asafoetida
6 cloves garlic, crushed
1 teaspoon cumin seeds
1 teaspoon aniseeds
1 teaspoon ground turmeric
1 tablespoon sliced ginger
1 teaspoon chilli powder
salt

Bring 1 litre / 1¾ pints (4¼ cups) water to the boil in a large pan, add the papaya and cook for about 10 minutes, or until soft, then drain and spread the papaya out on a baking tray (sheet) and let it dry it completely.

Heat the oil in a large pan over medium heat, add the asafoetida, garlic, cumin, aniseeds, turmeric and ginger and stir-fry for about 2 minutes. Remove the pan from the heat and allow to cool.

When cool, add the chilli powder and papaya, then season with salt. Cover with muslin (cheesecloth) and leave overnight in the pan.

The next morning, put into sterilized glass jars (see page 791).

Kurmo Pachadi
Jackfruit Pickle

Origin Tamil Nadu
Preparation time 25–30 minutes, plus cooling time
Makes 1kg / 2¼lb

2 tablespoons ground turmeric
1kg / 2¼lb jackfruit, peeled and de-seeded wearing gloves (see page 793), and cut into 2.5-cm / 1-inch pieces, seeds reserved
375ml / 13fl oz (1½ cups) vegetable oil
2 tablespoons mustard seeds
3 tablespoons ground cumin
3 tablespoons kalonji (nigella) seeds
1 tablespoon amchoor
3 tablespoons chilli powder
salt

Bring 1 litre / 1¾ pints (4¼ cups) water to the boil in a large pan. Season with salt and add half the turmeric. Add the jackfruit pieces and seeds and boil for 2 minutes, then drain and wipe dry on a clean cloth or tea (dish) towel. Put the jackfruit pieces and seeds in a large bowl, sprinkle some salt over and rub it in.

Heat 1 tablespoon of the oil in a large frying pan (skillet) over medium heat, add the mustard seeds and stir-fry for about 1–2 minutes, or until they start to brown. Remove from the heat and allow to cool.

Mix all the ingredients except the remaining oil together in a large bowl. Heat the oil in a pan over medium heat, then allow to cool slightly.

Bottle the pickle into sterilized jars (see 791), then pour the oil over the top, cover with the lids and store for 2 weeks before serving. The oil should float on top of the bottled pickle. If there is not enough, heat the required amount, allow to cool and cover.

Kathhal ka Meetha Achar
Sweet Jackfruit Pickle

Origin Hyderabad
Preparation time 1 hour, plus standing time
Makes 1kg / 2¼lb

1kg / 2 ¼lb jackfruit, peeled wearing gloves (see page 793), and cut into 4-cm / 1½-inch pieces
250g / 9oz (1¼ cups) jaggery or soft brown sugar
250ml / 8fl oz (1 cup) malt (white) vinegar
50g / 1¾oz (½ cup) ground coriander
50g / 1¾oz (½ cup) aniseeds
50g / 1¾oz (½ cup) chilli powder
4 tablespoons ground ginger
salt

Cook the jackfruit in a large pan of boiling salted water for about 30 minutes, or until soft. Drain and spread out on a piece of muslin (cheesecloth) or tea (dish) towel and let it dry for about 5–6 hours.

Boil the jaggery or sugar and vinegar in a pan for about 5 minutes, or until the jaggery dissolves completely. Pass it through a sieve (strainer) into a bowl, then season with salt and add the ground coriander, aniseeds, chilli powder and ginger. Add the dried jackfruit, then mix together and store in sterilized jars (see page 791).

Kamrakh ka Achar
Star Gooseberry Pickle

Origin Awadh
Preparation time 25–30 minutes
Makes 500g / 1lb 2oz

125ml / 4¼oz (½ cup) vegetable oil
12 cloves garlic
20 curry leaves
4–6 dried red chillies
1 teaspoon mustard seeds
5 tablespoons Garlic Paste (see page 57)
2 tablespoons chilli powder
1 tablespoon malt (white) vinegar
250g / 9oz star gooseberries, cut in half and de-seeded
salt

Heat the oil in a large pan over medium heat, add the garlic, curry leaves and dried red chillies and stir-fry for about 2 minutes, or until they turn brown. Add the mustard seeds and stir-fry for about 1 minute, or until they start to splutter. Add the garlic paste and stir-fry for 2–3 minutes, then add the chilli powder, vinegar and fruit and season with salt. Reduce the heat to very low and simmer for 5 minutes. Remove from the heat and allow to cool. When cool, bottle into sterlized jars (see page 791). If you can't find star gooseberries for this recipe, you can use regular gooseberries.

Tamatar ka Achar
Tomato Pickle

Origin Awadh
Preparation time 45 minutes, plus cooling time
Makes 4kg / 9lb

500ml / 18fl oz (2¼ cups) sesame oil

3 tablespoons mustard powder

1 tablespoon ground fenugreek

¼ teaspoon asafoetida

225g / 8oz (2 cups) red chilli powder

3kg / 6lb 10oz ripe, firm tomatoes, cut into quarters

750ml / 1¼ pints (3¼ cups) Tamarind Extract
    (see page 58)

2 tablespoons ground turmeric

For the tempering

8 dried red chillies

3 tablespoons chana dal, rinsed and drained

3 tablespoons urad dal, rinsed and drained

3 tablespoons mustard seeds

500g / 1lb 2oz (1¾ cups) salt

Heat 2 tablespoons of the oil in a small frying pan (skillet) over medium heat, add the mustard powder, fenugreek, asafoetida and chilli powder and stir-fry for about 1 minute, or until fragrant. Set aside.

Heat almost all the remaining oil in a large, heavy-based pan over low heat, add the tomatoes and fry for 10 minutes, or until well cooked. Remove from the heat and allow to cool.

When cool, put the tomatoes in a blender or food processor, add the fried mustard powder mixture, the tamarind extract and turmeric and process until mixed together. Transfer to a bowl.

Heat the remaining oil in a large frying pan over medium heat, add the tempering ingredients, except the salt, and stir-fry for about 1–2 minutes, or until dark brown. Add the salt and allow to cool, then add it to the tomato mixture and mix well. Store in a sterilized (see page 791) airtight ceramic jar for up to 2 weeks in the refrigerator.

Pyaz ka Achar
Onion Pickle

Origin Punjab
Preparation time 55 minutes, plus standing and cooling time
Makes 1kg / 2¼lb

20 baby (pearl) onions

250ml / 8fl oz (1 cup) malt (white) vinegar

200g / 7oz (1 cup) jaggery or soft brown sugar

1 teaspoon chilli powder

1 teaspoon cumin seeds, crushed

1 teaspoon Garam Masala (see page 31)

6 cloves garlic, crushed

salt

Put the whole onions in a large bowl, then season with salt and mix together. Put them in sterilized jars (see page 791) and tie muslin (cheesecloth) over the top, then leave in a sunny or warm place for 2 days, shaking daily.

Open the jars and drain the onions and place them on kitchen paper (paper towels) for about 2 hours.

Put the vinegar in a deep pan, add the jaggery, all the spices, and garlic and season with salt, then bring to the boil and cook for about 10 minutes.

Add the onions and cook for a further 5–10 minutes. Remove from the heat and allow to cool overnight.

The next day, put the mixture into sterilized jars (see page 791), cover with muslin and leave on the windowsill for a week, shaking it daily. It will be ready to eat after 7–10 days.

Aloo Matar ka Achar
Potato & Pea Pickle

Origin Awadh
Preparation time 40–45 minutes, plus cooling and standing time
Makes 2kg / 4½lb

1kg / 2¼lb (10 small) potatoes, unpeeled

500g / 1lb 2oz (3½ cups) peas, shelled if fresh

50g / 1¾oz (½ cup) mustard powder

3 tablespoons ground turmeric

4 tablespoons chilli powder

2–3 teaspoons dried fenugreek leaves

375ml / 13fl oz (1½ cups) vinegar

250ml / 8fl oz (1 cup) mustard oil

2 tablespoons Garlic Paste (see page 57)

2 tablespoons Ginger Paste (see page 57)

salt

Cook the potatoes in a large pan of boiling water for about 20 minutes, or until soft. Drain and peel off the skins, then set aside. Cook the peas in a separate pan of boiling water for about 5–7 minutes, or until tender, then set aside.

Mix the mustard powder, turmeric, chilli powder, fenugreek leaves and vinegar together in a bowl, then season with salt.

Heat the oil in a large pan over medium heat, add the garlic paste and stir-fry for about 1–2 minutes, or until it turns light golden. Add the ginger paste and stir-fry for about 1–2 minutes, or until light brown. Add the vinegar with the spices, then add the peas and potatoes and cook for about 1 minute. Mix well, remove from the heat and allow to cool.

When cool, bottle into sterilized jars (see page 791) and leave for 1–2 days.

Sirkewala Achar
Mixed Vegetable Pickle

Origin Punjab
Preparation time 15 minutes, plus standing time
Makes 250g / 9oz

4 tablespoons malt (white) vinegar

½ teaspoon sugar

4 tablespoons sliced carrot

4 tablespoons thin strips cucumber

65g / 2½oz (½ cup) small cauliflower, cut into florets

3 large flakes garlic or ½ clove garlic, sliced

1 onion, cut into pieces

1 tablespoon olive oil

salt

Bring 250ml / 8fl oz (1 cup) water to the boil with vinegar, salt and sugar in a large pan, then remove from the heat. Add all the vegetables and olive oil, then mix and season to taste. Set aside for about 2 hours, then transfer to sterilized jars (see page 791).

Lal Imli ka Achar
Red Tamarind Pickle

Origin Hyderabad
Preparation time 30 minutes, plus cooling time
Makes 750g / 1lb 10oz

500g / 1lb 2oz fresh ripe tamarind
250ml / 8fl oz (1 cup) sesame oil, plus extra for filling up, if necessary
6 dried red chillies
2 teaspoons mustard seeds
6 sprigs curry leaves
6 cloves garlic, coarsely ground
½ cup Garlic Paste (see page 57)
2 tablespoons chilli powder
2 tablespoons vinegar
salt

Remove the seeds from the tamarind and cut into slices.

Heat the oil in a large frying pan (skillet) over medium heat, add the dried red chillies and stir-fry for about 1–2 minutes, or until they turn a shade darker. Add the mustard seeds and stir-fry for about 1 minute, or until they start to splutter. Add the curry leaves and coarsely ground garlic and cover the pan with a lid.

After 3–4 minutes, remove the lid and check that the garlic is light brown. Add the garlic paste and fry for a few minutes. Add the chilli powder, then season with salt and cook for 1 minute. Add the tamarind and cook for a few minutes, then add the vinegar and mix well. Remove from the heat and allow to cool.

When cool, bottle into sterilized jars (see page 791) with enough oil to cover the surface of the pickle. If the oil does not cover the pickle, mold will develop. This pickle can be stored for up to 3 weeks in the refrigerator.

Gongura Pachadi
Sorrel Leaf Pickle

Origin Andhra Pradesh
Preparation time 20 minutes
Makes 750g / 1lb 10oz

250ml / 8fl oz (1 cup) vegetable oil
400g / 14oz gongura or sorrel leaves
10–20 green chillies, de-seeded and roughly chopped
1 teaspoon coriander seeds
¼ teaspoon fenugreek seeds
½ teaspoon cumin seeds
75g / 2½oz (½ cup) sesame seeds
pinch of ground turmeric
salt

For the tempering

3 dried red chillies
6 curry leaves
½ teaspoon mustard seeds
½ teaspoon urad dal, rinsed and drained

Heat 125ml / 4½fl oz (½ cup) of the oil in a frying pan (skillet) over medium heat, add the leaves and green chillies and fry for 90 seconds. Set aside.

Heat 4 tablespoons of the oil in another frying pan over medium heat, add the coriander, fenugreek, cumin and sesame seeds for about 1 minute, or until they turn brown. Transfer them to a blender, add the leaves and chillies and turmeric and process to a paste.

Heat the remaining oil in a frying pan over medium heat, add the tempering ingredients and stir-fry for about 1–2 minutes, or until dark brown. Pour the tempering over the gongura mixture and mix well, then allow to cool. Season with salt. When cool, bottle in a ceramic jar or sterilized glass jars (see page 791).

Inji Thokku
Ginger Pickle

Origin Tamil Nadu
Preparation time 20 minutes, plus cooling time
Makes 250g / 9oz

6 teaspoons sesame oil
2 teaspoons mustard seeds
6 green chillies, de-seeded and roughly chopped
150g / 5oz (1 cup) grated ginger
125ml / 4½fl oz (½ cup) thick Tamarind Extract (see page 58)
salt

Heat the oil in a frying pan (skillet) over medium heat, add the mustard seeds and stir-fry for about 1 minute, or until they starts splutter. Add the chillies and a pinch of salt and stir-fry for 2 minutes. Add the tamarind extract and grated ginger and season with salt, if necessary.

Reduce the heat to low and cook for 5 minutes, or until the ginger is soft and the extract thickens. Remove from the heat and allow to cool. Store in an airtight container.

Ande ka Achar
Egg Pickle

Origin Hyderabad
Preparation time 50–55 minutes, plus cooling time
Makes 500g / 1lb 2oz

500ml / 18fl oz (2¼ cups) vegetable oil
½ teaspoon mustard seeds
¼ teaspoon fenugreek seeds
12 hard-boiled eggs, shelled
4 tablespoons Ginger Paste (see page 57)
4 tablespoons Garlic Paste (see page 57)
225g / 8oz (2 cups) chilli powder
10 cloves, ground
3 cinnamon sticks, about 2.5cm / 1 inch long, ground
10 green cardamom pods, ground
500ml / 18fl oz (2¼ cups) lime juice
salt

Heat about 1 tablespoon of the oil in a frying pan (skillet) over medium heat, add the mustard and fenugreek seeds and stir-fry for about 1 minute, or until they start to splutter. Set aside.

Heat the rest of the oil in a large, heavy-based pan over medium heat, add the eggs and fry for a few minutes, then remove from the pan with a slotted spoon and set aside. Reduce the heat to low, add the ginger and garlic pastes, chilli powder, cloves, cinnamon and cardamom and fry lightly for about 1–2 minutes. Add the eggs and cook for 3–4 minutes, then add the fried mustard and fenugreek seeds. Remove from the heat and allow to cool.

When cool, season with salt, add the lime juice and mix well. Bottle into airtight, sterilized jars (see page 791). This pickle can be stored for up to 3 weeks in the refrigerator.

Gosht ka Achar
Lamb Pickle

Origin Punjab
Preparation time 1 hour, plus cooling time
Makes 750g / 1lb 10oz

1kg / 2¼lb boneless lamb, cut into 2.5-cm / 1-inch cubes
500ml / 18fl oz (2¼ cups) vegetable oil
15 green chillies, de-seeded (optional)
½ clove garlic
1 × 5-cm / 2-inch piece fresh ginger, peeled and thinly sliced
100g / 3½oz (1 cup) chilli powder
1 teaspoon ground turmeric
1 teaspoon ground fresh ginger
1 teaspoon ground garlic
125ml / 4½fl oz (½ cup) malt (white) vinegar
1 tablespoon sugar
salt

Put the lamb in a large, heavy-based pan, season with salt and pour in enough water to cover, then bring to the boil and cook for about 10 minutes, or until tender. Allow the water to evaporate when the meat is cooked, so do not pour in too much water while cooking.

Heat the oil in another large pan over medium heat, add the lamb and fry for about 10 minutes, or until brown. Remove from the pan with a slotted spoon and set aside.

Add the chillies, garlic and ginger to the pan and lightly brown for about 1 minute. Add the ground spices, ground ginger and garlic, vinegar and sugar, then season with salt and brown together for a few minutes. Bring to the boil, add the meat, then reduce the heat and simmer for 3 minutes. Remove from the heat and allow to cool. When cool, put in an airtight ceramic container or glass jar, cover and set aside in the refrigerator. This pickle can be stored for up to 3 weeks in the refrigerator.

 p.195

Mooli ka Raita
Mooli Raita

Origin Jammu and Kashmir
Preparation time 15 minutes, plus chilling time
Makes 750ml / 1¼ pints (3¼ cups)

1 mooli (daikon), peeled and grated
500ml / 18fl oz (2¼ cups) natural (plain) yoghurt
1 green chilli, de-seeded and chopped
1 teaspoon cumin seeds, roasted and ground
few coriander (cilantro) leaves, chopped
salt

Put the mooli and the yoghurt in a large bowl. Add all the ingredients, season with salt and mix well. Chill for 30 minutes before serving.

Matar ka Raita
Green Pea Raita

Origin Awadh
Preparation time 15 minutes, plus chilling time
Makes 750ml / 1¼ pints (3¼ cups)

500ml / 18fl oz (2¼ cups) natural (plain) yoghurt
250g / 9oz (1½ cups) peas, lightly cooked
1 teaspoon cumin seeds, roasted
1 teaspoon sugar
1 teaspoon chilli powder
1 green spring onion (scallion), trimmed and chopped
salt

Put the yoghurt and peas in a large bowl. Add all the other ingredients, then season with salt and mix together. Chill for 30 minutes before serving.

Karam Kalle ka Raita
Spicy Cabbage & Peanut Raita

Origin New
Preparation time 15 minutes, plus soaking and chilling time
Makes 750ml / 1¼ pints (3¼ cups)

½ cabbage, thinly sliced
1 tablespoon cumin seeds, roasted and crushed
1 teaspoon peanuts, roasted and crushed
few coriander (cilantro) leaves, chopped
500ml / 18fl oz (2¼ cups) natural (plain) yoghurt, whisked
1 teaspoon chilli powder
1 teaspoon sugar
1 green chilli, de-seeded and chopped
salt

Soak the shredded cabbage in a bowl of warm salted water for about 30 minutes, then drain in a colander for about 30 minutes.

Put the cabbage in a bowl with the yoghurt and all the other ingredients then season with salt and mix well. Chill for 30 minutes before serving.

Ankur ka Raita
Mung Bean Sprout Raita

Origin Coastal
Preparation time 20 minutes, plus chilling time
Makes 750ml / 1¼ pints (3¼ cups)

500ml / 18fl oz (2¼ cups) natural (plain) yoghurt
115g / 4oz (1 cup) mung bean sprouts
1 green chilli, de-seeded and chopped
1 teaspoon sugar
1 onion, chopped
½ teaspoon chilli powder
1 teaspoon cumin seeds, roasted
salt
few coriander (cilantro) leaves, chopped, to garnish

Whisk the yoghurt in a large bowl. Add the sprouts and all the other ingredients, then season with salt and mix well. Garnish with coriander leaves. Chill for 30 minutes before serving.

Lauki ka Raita
Bottle Gourd (Calabash) Raita

Origin Awadh
Preparation time 30–35 minutes, plus chilling time
Makes 750ml / 1¼ pints (3¼ cups)

1 tablespoon raisins
60g / 2oz (½ cup) coarsley grated bottle gourd (calabash) or courgette (zucchini)
500ml / 18fl oz (2¼ cups) natural (plain) yoghurt
1 green chilli, de-seeded and chopped
1 teaspoon sugar
1 teaspoon cumin seed, roasted and ground
½ teaspoon dried mint
salt

Rinse the raisins in a bowl of water, then drain.

Cook the grated bottle gourd in a pan of boiling water for about 5 minutes, or until soft. Drain and pat dry with kitchen paper (paper towels), then grate again and squeeze it lightly to remove excess water.

Put the yoghurt in a large bowl, add the grated bottle gourd, raisins and the rest of the ingredients. Mix together and chill for 1 hour before serving.

📷 p.48

Annanas ka Raita
Pineapple Raita

Origin Punjab/Delhi
Preparation time 20 minutes, plus chilling time
Makes 625ml / 21fl oz (2½ cups)

500ml / 18fl oz (2¼ cups) natural (plain) yoghurt
3 slices canned pineapple, cut into small pieces
½ teaspoon black peppercorns, crushed
1 teaspoon roasted cumin seeds
1 teaspoon sugar
salt

Put the yoghurt in a bowl and mix with the pineapple pieces. Add all the spices and sugar, then season with salt and mix well. Chill for 30 minutes before serving.

Arabi ka Raita
Colocasia (Taro Root) Raita

Origin Awadh
Preparation time 25 minutes
Makes 1 litre / 1¾ pints (4 cups)

6 colocasias (taro roots), boiled and peeled

125ml / 4½fl oz (½ cup) vegetable oil

500ml / 18fl oz (2¼ cups) natural (plain) yoghurt

½ teaspoon chilli powder

1 teaspoon cumin seeds, roasted

salt

few coriander (cilantro) leaves, to garnish

Press the colocasia between the palms of your hands.

Heat the oil in a kadhai, wok or deep, heavy-based pan over medium heat, add each colocasia to the hot oil and fry for 2 minutes on both sides until it is crisp and golden. Remove from the pan with a slotted spoon and drain on kitchen paper (paper towels).

Put the yoghurt in a large bowl and add all the spices, then season with salt. Add the fried colocasia and mix together. Garnish with coriander leaves and serve.

Chane aur Aloo ka Raita
Potato, Yoghurt & Chickpea (Garbanzo Bean) Raita

Origin Awadh
Preparation time 2½–3 hours, plus soaking and chilling time
Cooking time 1½–2½ hours
Makes 1 litre / 1¾ pints (4 cups)

200g / 7oz (1 cup) dried chickpeas (garbanzo beans)

500ml / 18fl oz (2¼ cups) natural (plain) yoghurt, whisked

1 teaspoon cumin seeds, roasted and ground

1 teaspoon coriander seeds, roasted and crushed

2 dried red chillies, roasted and crushed

1 boiled potato, cut into cubes

1 tablespoon Tamarind Extract (see page 58)

1 teaspoon sugar

salt

Soak the chickpeas in a large bowl of water overnight.

The next day, drain the chickpeas and cook them in a pan of boiling water for about 1½–2 hours, or until soft. Drain.

Put the yoghurt in a large bowl, add the potatoes and chickpeas together with all the other ingredients and stir. Chill for 30 minutes before serving.

Snacks are wildly popular in India, where city streets are lined with kiosks selling kebabs, stuffed breads, crispy fritters, bhajis and samosas. These light meals range in flavour from delicately spiced to aromatic and full bodied, and can have a soft or crisp texture. Often eaten alone, they can also be an integral part of a larger meal and no Indian banquet is complete without a number of them to accompany the main dishes.

3
———

Snacks and Appetizers

Vegetables

Subz Seekh
Vegetarian Seekh Kebabs

Origin Awadh
Preparation time 1 hour 15 minutes, plus
cooling time
Cooking time 5–7 minutes
Serves 4

150g / 5oz (1 cup) peeled and grated yam

75g / 2½oz (⅓ cup) cauliflower

3 medium-sized potatoes, unpeeled

75g / 2½oz (½ cup) peas, shelled if fresh

3½ tablespoons vegetable oil

100g / 3½oz (½ cup) snake gourd or courgette
    (zucchini), grated

75g / 2½oz (⅔ cup) grated carrots

200g / 7oz Paneer (see page 59), grated

2 tablespoons chopped coriander (cilantro) leaves

1 × 2.5-cm / 1-inch piece fresh ginger, peeled
    and finely chopped

6 green chillies, de-seeded and chopped

1 teaspoon ground dried pomegranate seeds

24 almonds, flaked (slivered)

24 dried plums, chopped

salt

Mint Chutney, (see page 66), to serve

For the subz seekh masala

5 teaspoons amchoor

1 teaspoon ground black pepper

1 teaspoon ground coriander

½ teaspoon ground green cardamom

½ teaspoon ground mace

½ teaspoon black rock salt

salt

Cook the yam in a pan of boiling water for about
10 minutes, or until soft. Cook the cauliflower in
another pan of boiling water for 5 minutes, or until
just tender. Drain and grate.

Cook the potatoes in a third pan of boiling water
for about 20 minutes, or until soft, then drain and
allow to cool. When the potatoes are cool, peel off
their skins, return to the pan and mash.

Meanwhile, cook the peas in a separate pan of
boiling water for about 5–7 minutes, or until soft,
then drain, return to the pan and mash.

Prepare a tandoor for a moderate heat, or alternatively
preheat the grill (broiler) to medium, if using. Heat
the oil in a pan, add all the vegetables and stir-fry
over medium heat until the moisture has completely
evaporated. Remove and spread the vegetables on
a flat surface or board to cool immediately.

When the vegetables are cool, put them in a
large bowl with the paneer, coriander, ginger,
chillies, ground pomegranate seeds, almonds and
dried plums. Season with salt. Add all the masala
ingredients, mix well, then mash with a potato
masher. Divide the mixture into 12 equal portions
and roll into balls.

Using damp hands, spread the balls along the length
of metal skewers, flattening the mixture into
a sausage shape until the kebabs are 10cm / 4 inches
long and leaving 5cm / 2 inches between each one.
You can make 2 kebabs on one long skewer.

Roast the kebabs in a moderately hot tandoor or
under the hot grill for about 2–3 minutes, or until
golden brown. Turn the kebabs gently during
cooking so they colour evenly. Remove the kebabs
from the skewers and serve with Mint Chutney.

Subz ke Kakori
Vegetarian Skewers

Origin Awadh
Preparation time 1½ hours
Cooking time 3–4 minutes
Serves 4

500g / 1lb 2oz colocasia (taro root),
about 5cm / 2 inches long

200g / 7oz Paneer (see page 59), grated

120g / 4oz Khoya (see page 58), grated
or 120g / 4oz (¾ cup) milk powder (dry milk)

2 tablespoons mint leaves, chopped

1 × 2.5-cm / 1-inch piece fresh ginger, peeled
and grated

6 green chillies, de-seeded and chopped

1 teaspoon ground dried pomegranate seeds

20–22 almonds, flaked (slivered)

15 dried plums, chopped

generous pinch of ground dried fenugreek leaves

salt

For the aromatic potli

8 cloves

4 green cardamom pods

2 black cardamom pods

¼ nutmeg

For the masala for sprinkling

5 teaspoons amchoor

1 teaspoon ground black pepper

1 teaspoon ground cumin

½ teaspoon ground green cardamom

½ teaspoon ground mace

½ teaspoon ground black rock salt

Prepare a tandoor for moderate heat, or
alternatively preheat the grill (broiler) to medium.
Put all the ingredients for the aromatic potli in
a piece of muslin (cheesecloth) and tie together
with kitchen string (twine) to make a pouch. Bring
a pan of water to the boil, add the potli together
with the colocasia and boil until the colocasia is soft.
Drain, discarding the potli, then peel off the skin,
return to the pan and mash until smooth.

Put all the ingredients for the masala for sprinkling
in a bowl and mix together.

Put the mashed colocasia, paneer, khoya, mint,
ginger, chillies, ground pomegranate seeds, almonds,
plums, ground fenugreek and salt to taste, add three-
quarters of the masala, mix well, then mash with
a potato masher. Divide the mixture into 12 equal
portions and roll into balls. Using damp hands,
spread the balls along the length of 4 metal skewers,
flattening the mixture into a sausage shape until the
kebabs are 10cm / 4 inches long. You could make
2 kebabs along one skewer if the skewers are long.

Roast in a moderately hot tandoor or under the hot
grill for 3–4 minutes, or until golden. Remove gently
from the skewers, arrange on a platter and sprinkle
over the remaining masala.

Jaipuri Subz Seekh
Rajasthani Vegetarian Skewers

Origin Rajasthan
Preparation time 1½ hours, plus cooling time
Cooking time 3–4 minutes
Serves 4

500g / 1lb 2oz colocasia (taro root)

1 teaspoon ground dried pomegranate seeds

150g / 5oz Paneer (see page 59), grated

125g / 4¼oz Khoya (see page 58), grated
or 125g / 4¼oz (¾ cup) milk powder (dry milk)

generous pinch of ground dried fenugreek leaves,
crushed

1 × 2.5-cm / 1-inch piece fresh ginger, peeled
and chopped

2 tablespoons mint leaves

2 teaspoons chopped green chilli

salt

For the aromatic potli

8 cloves

2 black cardamom pods

4 green cardamom pods

¼ nutmeg

For the masala

5 teaspoons amchoor
½ teaspoon ground green cardamom
1 teaspoon ground black pepper
¼ teaspoon ground mace
1 teaspoon ground cumin
1 teaspoon black rock salt

Put all the ingredients for the aromatic potli in a piece of muslin (cheesecloth) and tie together with kitchen string (twine) to make a pouch. Bring a pan of water to the boil, then carefully add the colocasia pieces and the potli and boil until the colocasia is soft. Drain, discarding the potli, and allow to cool. Once the colocasia is cool, peel off the skin, return to the pan and mash until smooth.

Put the mashed colocasia, pomegranate seeds, paneer, khoya, fenugreek, ginger, mint and chillies in a large bowl. Season with salt and add all the ingredients for the masala, mix well and mash with a potato masher. Divide the mixture into 12 equal portions and roll into balls.

Heat a charcoal grill or preheat a grill (broiler) to medium. Using damp hands, spread the balls along the length of metal skewers, flattening the mixture into a sausage shape until the kebabs are 10cm / 4 inches long. You can make 2 kebabs along the length of a long skewer.

Roast the kebabs over the charcoal grill or under the grill for 3–4 minutes, or until golden.

Lauki ki Seekh
Skewered Pumpkin

Origin Awadh
Preparation time 30–40 minutes, plus cooling time
Cooking time 8–10 minutes
Serves 4

300g / 11 oz (2⅔ cups) peeled and grated pumpkin
300g / 11oz Paneer (see page 59), grated
3 tablespoons chopped onion
1 × 1-cm / ½-inch piece fresh ginger, peeled and chopped
4 tablespoons chopped carrot
1 tablespoon chopped green chilli
20g / ¾oz (½ cup) chopped coriander (cilantro) leaves
pinch of ground allspice
pinch of ground ground cardamom and mace
30g / 1¼oz green chilli paste
1–2 tablespoons fresh breadcrumbs, for binding
ground white pepper
salt

Parboil the grated pumpkin with a pinch of salt in a pan of boiling water for about 5 minutes, or until soft. Drain, then put the pumpkin into a bowl of cold water to cool.

Prepare a tandoor or charcoal grill for a moderate heat, or alternatively preheat the grill (broiler) to medium. When cold, put the pumpkin into a clean towel and squeeze to remove any excess water. Transfer to a clean bowl, and add the paneer, onion, ginger, carrot, chilli, and coriander and mix well. Season with salt and white pepper, then add the ground spices, green chilli paste and breadcrumbs and mix thoroughly until the mixture binds together. Divide the mixture into 16 equal portions.

Using damp hands, mould some of the mixture into a sausage shape along the length of metal skewers. Roast in a moderately hot tandoor, over a charcoal grill or under the hot grill for 8–10 minutes.

Hariali Paneer Tikka
Green Paneer Skewers

Origin Punjab
Preparation time 30–35 minutes, plus marinating time
Cooking time 10–15 minutes
Serves 4

1kg / 2¼lb Paneer (see page 59), cut into
    medium-sized pieces

For the marinade

375ml / 13fl oz (1½ cups) hung natural (plain) yoghurt
    (see page 793)

2 tablespoons double (heavy) cream

4 teaspoons Garlic Paste (see page 62)

1 tablespoon coriander (cilantro) leaves

2 tablespoons red chilli paste

1½ teaspoons green chilli paste

90g / 3¼oz (⅓ cup) Mint Chutney (see page 66)

2½ tablespoons gram (chickpea) flour, roasted

3 tablespoons mustard oil

black rock salt

To prepare the marinade, put the yoghurt, cream, garlic paste, coriander leaves, red and green chilli pastes, chutney, roasted gram flour and oil in a large bowl. Season with salt and mix together.

Coat the paneer with the marinade and set aside for about 2 hours.

Prepare a charcoal grill, or alternatively preheat the oven to 180°C/350°F/Gas Mark 4. Take a metal skewer and thread the marinated paneer cubes through it, leaving a 2.5-cm / 1-inch gap between each cube.

Roast over a charcoal grill or in the preheated oven for 10–15 minutes.

Paneer Tikka Kali Mirch
Peppery Paneer Skewers

Origin Punjab
Preparation time 30–35 minutes, plus marinating time
Cooking time 10–15 minutes
Serves 4

1kg / 2¼lb Paneer (see page 59), cut into
    medium-sized pieces

small onion wedges or cubes, or potato
    or pepper (bell pepper) slices (optional)

For the marinade

4 tablespoons double (heavy) cream

5 teaspoons Boiled Onion Paste (see page 57)

2 teaspoons Ginger Paste (see page 57)

2 teaspoons Garlic Paste (see page 57)

3 tablespoons black peppercorns, crushed

2 lemon rinds

50g / 1¾oz (⅓ cup) plain (all-purpose) flour, roasted

3 tablespoons vegetable oil

salt

Make a deep criss-cross in each paneer cube without going right through the cheese.

To prepare the marinade, put the cream, boiled onion paste, ginger and garlic pastes, crushed pepper, lemon rinds, flour and oil in a large bowl. Season with salt and mix together.

Coat the paneer pieces with this marinade, making sure that some of the marinade goes into the slits. Set aside for about 2 hours.

Prepare a charcoal grill, or alternatively preheat the oven to 180°C/350°F/Gas Mark 4. Take a metal skewer and thread the marinated paneer pieces through it, leaving a 2.5-cm / 1-inch gap between each portion. If you like, you may use a small onion, potato or a slice of pepper (bell pepper) in between the paneer cubes to prevent them from slipping off the skewer.

Roast over a charcoal grill or in the preheated oven for 10–15 minutes.

Achari Paneer Tikka
Grilled (Broiled) Paneer in Pickling Spices

Origin Punjab
Preparation time 30 minutes, plus cooling and marinating time
Cooking time 10–12 minutes
Serves 2

4 tablespoons mustard oil
few fenugreek seeds
½ teaspoon mustard seeds
¼ teaspoon kalonji (nigella) seeds
1 teaspoon fennel seeds
850g / 1¾lb Paneer (see page 59), cut into cubes
300ml / ½ pint (1⅓ cups) hung natural (plain) yoghurt (see page 793)
1½ teaspoons Ginger Paste (see page 57)
1½ teaspoons Garlic Paste (see page 57)
1 teaspoon yellow chilli powder
1 teaspoon ground turmeric
100g / 3½oz (½ cup) Mango Pickle with Jaggery (see page 77)
salt

Heat the mustard oil in a pan, add the fenugreek seeds and stir-fry for 1 minute, or until they start to crackle. Add the mustard seeds, kalonji and fennel seeds and stir-fry for a further 2 minutes. Remove from the heat and set aside to cool.

Whisk the hung yoghurt in a bowl, then add the ginger and garlic pastes, cooled mustard seed mixture, chilli powder, turmeric and mango pickle. Season with salt and mix well. Add the paneer cubes to the mixture and mix until the paneer is coated. Allow to marinate in the refrigerator for 2–3 hours.

Prepare a tandoor or charcoal grill for a moderate heat, or alternatively preheat the grill (broiler) to medium. Thread the marinated paneer on to several metal skewers leaving a 2.5-cm / 1-inch gap between each them. Roast in a moderately hot tandoor, over a charcoal grill or under the hot grill for 6–8 minutes, or until the paneer is cooked.

Bhutta Seekh Kebab
Corn Kebabs on Skewers

Origin Punjab
Preparation time 30 minutes, plus cooling time
Cooking time 10 minutes
Serves 4

700g / 1lb 8½oz (11 cups) fresh sweetcorn (corn) kernels or canned kernels
1 tablespoon ground turmeric, plus a pinch
250g / 9oz (1 cup) cottage cheese, drained
1 tablespoon green chilli, de-seeded and chopped
½ teaspoon Ginger Paste (see page 57)
½ teaspoon Garlic Paste (see page 57)
3 tablespoons finely chopped coriander (cilantro) leaves
1 teaspoon finely grated ginger
1 teaspoon Kashmiri red chilli powder
1 tablespoon Garam Masala (see page 31)
1 teaspoon Chaat Masala (see page 31)
1 teaspoon Tandoori Masala (see page 51)
1 tablespoon melted butter
about 1–2 tablespoons breadcrumbs, for binding
salt

Prepare a tandoor or charcoal grill for a moderate heat, or alternatively preheat the grill (broiler) to medium. If using fresh sweetcorn, cook the kernels with the pinch of turmeric in a pan of boiling water or about 5 minutes, or until tender. Drain and set aside to cool.

Put the cheese, 600g / 1lb 5oz (3¾ cups) cooked or canned sweetcorn, the chilli, ginger and garlic pastes, the spices, melted butter and enough breadcrumbs to bind the mixture together. Season with salt and mix well with your hands. Divide the mixture into 16 equal portions and roll into balls.

Using damp hands, spread the balls along the length of metal skewers, flattening the mixture into a sausage shape until the kebabs are 10cm / 4 inches long, and leaving 5cm / 2 inches between each one. You can make 2 kebabs on one long skewer. Put the remaining corn on top of the kebabs and roast in a moderately hot tandoor, over a charcoal grill or under the hot grill for 10 minutes.

Nargisi Seekh Kebab
Vegetable & Egg Skewers

Origin Awadh
Preparation time 30 minutes, plus cooling time
Cooking time 15 minutes
Serves 4

300g / 11oz (3 medium) potatoes, unpeeled
15g / ½oz mint leaves
15g / ½oz curry leaves
300 g (11 oz) Paneer (see page 59), grated
1 egg
2 tablespoons Garlic Paste (see page 57)
2 tablespoons chopped onion
2 tablespoons chopped tomato
2 tablespoons chopped red (bell) pepper
20g / ¾oz (½ cup) chopped coriander (cilantro) leaves
60g / 2oz (⅓ cup) chopped carrot
2½ tablespoons chopped garlic
2 tablespoons chopped green chilli
60g / 2oz (⅓ cup) sesame seeds
1 tablespoon ground white pepper
¼ teaspoon ground cardamom
¼ teaspoon mace powder
1 tablespoon Chaat Masala (see page 31)
about 1–2 tablespoons breadcrumbs, for binding
salt

Cook the potatoes in a pan of boiling water for about 15 minutes, or until cooked but still firm. Drain and allow to cool. When cool, peel off the skins and grate the flesh. Set aside.

Prepare a tandoor or charcoal grill for a moderate heat, or alternatively heat the grill (broiler). Put the mint and curry leaves in a small dry frying pan (skillet) and fry for about 1 minute, or until fragrant. Remove from the heat and set aside.

Mix the grated potatoes, paneer, egg, garlic paste, onion, tomatoes, red pepper, coriander, carrot, garlic, chilli, fried mint and curry leaves and sesame seeds together in a large bowl. Season with salt, then mix in the white pepper, cardamom, mace, chaat masala and enough breadcrumbs to bind the mixture together. Divide the mixture into 16 equal portions and roll into balls.

Using damp hands, spread the balls along the length of metal skewers, flattening the mixture into a sausage shape until the kebabs are 10cm / 4 inches long and leaving 5cm / 2 inches between each one. You can make 2 kebabs on one long skewer. Roast in a moderately hot tandoor, over a charcoal grill (broiler) or under the hot grill for 6–8 minutes.

Khumb Shabnam
Button (White) Mushrooms in Yoghurt Sauce

Origin Awadh
Preparation time 20 minutes, plus cooling time
Cooking time 10 minutes
Serves 4

250ml / 8fl oz (1 cup) natural (plain) yoghurt
1 teaspoon ground cumin
1 teaspoon Garam Masala (see page 31)
1 teaspoon Kashmiri chilli powder
pinch of ground turmeric
1 tablespoon vegetable oil
200g / 7oz (3 cups) button (white) mushrooms, sliced
2 green chillies, slit lengthways
salt

Beat the yoghurt with the ground spices in a bowl and set aside.

Heat the oil in a non-stick frying pan (skillet), add the mushrooms and stir-fry over a low heat for about 10 minutes, or until cooked. Remove from the heat and allow to cool.

When the mushrooms are cool, pour in the spiced beaten yoghurt and mix well. Season with salt and then garnish with the chillies.

Tandoori Achari Khumb
Grilled Mushrooms in Pickling Spices

Origin Punjab
Preparation time 1 hour, plus marinating time
Cooking time 10 minutes
Serves 4

32 large fresh mushrooms, stems removed
250ml / 8fl oz (1 cup) hung natural (plain) yoghurt (see page 793)
100g / 3½oz achari paste
5 teaspoons Ginger Paste (see page 57)
5 teaspoons Garlic Paste (see page 57)
½ teaspoon mustard powder
2 teaspoons kalonji (nigella) seeds
3 tablespoons gram (chickpea) flour, roasted
150ml / ¼ pint (⅔ cup) mustard oil
1 egg
1 teaspoon ground turmeric
2 teaspoons Garam Masala (see page 31)
2 teaspoons red chilli paste
salt

Parboil the mushrooms in a pan of boiling water for about 3–5 minutes, then drain and put into a bowl of cold water. Drain again and squeeze out any excess water from the mushrooms. Set aside.

Put the hung yoghurt, achari paste, ginger and garlic pastes, mustard powder, kalonji seeds, roasted gram flour, mustard oil, egg, turmeric, garam masala and red chilli paste into a large bowl, then season with salt and mix well. Add the mushrooms to the marinade and set aside for about 2 hours.

Prepare a tandoor or charcoal grill for a moderate heat, or alternatively preheat the grill (broiler) to medium. Thread the mushrooms one by one onto several metal skewers and drizzle over the remaining marinade. Roast in a tandoor at a moderate temperature, over a charcoal grill or under the hot grill for 4 minutes.

Pakoras
Deep-fried Vegetable Fritters

Origin Tamil Nadu
Preparation time 10 minutes
Cooking time 20 minutes
Serves 3–4

250g / 9oz (1⅔ cups) gram (chickpea) flour
½ teaspoon baking powder
½ teaspoon chilli powder
1 teaspoon chopped coriander (cilantro) leaves
1 green chilli, de-seeded and chopped
pinch of ground turmeric
1 onion, chopped or sliced
vegetable oil, for deep-frying
salt

Put the flour, baking powder, chilli powder, coriander, chilli, turmeric and onion in a large bowl.
Season with salt and mix together with enough water to make a thick batter.

Heat enough oil for deep-frying in a kadhai or deep, heavy-based pan to 180°C/350°F, or until a cube of bread browns in 30 seconds. Working in batches, drop spoonfuls of the batter into the hot oil and deep-fry for 3–4 minutes, or until golden brown. Remove from the heat with a slotted spoon and drain on crumpled up kitchen paper (paper towels). Serve plain.

Mangupullu
Crispy Deep-fried Savoury Rings

Origin Andhra Pradesh/Tamil Nadu
Preparation time 10 minutes
Cooking time 20 minutes
Serves 12

100g / 3½oz (½ cup) moong dal, rinsed and dried
200g / 7oz (1 cup) basmati rice, rinsed and drained
75g / 2½oz (½ cup) gram (chickpea) flour
1 teaspoon sesame seeds
1 teaspoon cumin seeds
1 tablespoon ghee
vegetable oil, for frying
salt

Put the moong dal and rice into a blender or food processor and process until finely ground. Transfer to a bowl and add the gram flour, sesame and cumin seeds and ghee. Season with salt and mix, gradually adding enough water to make a smooth, stiff paste. Put the paste into a murukulu shaper or piping (pastry) bag.

Heat enough oil for deep-frying in a kadhai or deep, heavy-based pan to 180°C/350°F, or until a cube of bread browns in 30 seconds, Working in batches, hold a murukulu shaper or pastry bag over the hot oil and carefully squeeze out the paste, making circles, each one in several rings around a central one and deep-fry for about 2–3 minutes, or until crisp. Remove with a slotted spoon and drain on kitchen paper (paper towels). Allow to cool. Store in an airtight jar or container.

Onion Bhajiya
Onion Bhaji

Origin Tamil Nadu
Preparation time 15 minutes
Cooking time 15 minutes
Serves 10

150g / 5oz (1 cup) gram (chickpea) flour
½ teaspoon bicarbonate of soda (baking soda)
2 teaspoons ajwain seeds
1kg / 2¼lb (6 large) onions, cut into thin rings
vegetable oil, for deep-frying
salt

Put the gram flour in a large bowl and stir in enough water to make a thick batter. Add the bicarbonate of soda and ajwain seeds and season with salt. Add the onion rings and mix well to coat the onions in the batter.

Heat enough oil for deep-frying in a kadhai or deep, heavy-based pan to 180°C/350°F, or until a cube of bread browns in 30 seconds. Using a ladle, very carefully drop spoonfuls of the coated onion into the hot oil and deep-fry for about 3–4 minutes, or until golden brown. Remove with a slotted spoon and drain on kitchen paper (paper towels). Keep the fritters warm, while making the others in the same way.

☀ / 📷 p.115

☀ ☀

Vengayya
Onion Fritters

Origin Tamil Nadu
Preparation time 15 minutes
Cooking time 10 minutes
Serves 4

150g / 5oz (1 cup) gram (chickpea) flour
1 teaspoon rice flour
1 teaspoon ajwain seeds
3 green chillies, de-seeded and chopped
few coriander (cilantro) leaves, chopped
vegetable oil, for deep-frying
3 onions, sliced
salt

Put the flours, ajwain, chillies and coriander
in a large bowl. Season with salt and mix, adding
enough water to make a thick batter.

Heat enough oil for deep-frying in kadhai or deep,
heavy-based pan to 180°C/350°F, or until a cube of
bread browns in 30 seconds. Working in batches,
dip each onion slice in the batter and then carefully
drop into the hot oil and deep-fry for about 2 minutes,
or until golden brown. Remove with a slotted spoon
and drain on kitchen paper (paper towels).

Vengayya Pakora
Onion Pakoras

Origin Tamil Nadu
Preparation time 10 minutes
Cooking time 15 minutes
Serves 4

150g / 5oz (1 cup) gram (chickpea) flour
2 tablespoons rice flour
175ml / 6fl oz (¾ cup) vegetable oil
3 medium-sized onions, finely chopped
1½ teaspoons chilli powder
2 tablespoons finely chopped coriander (cilantro) leaves
salt
vegetable oil, for deep-frying

Combine the flours, oil, onions, chilli powder and
coriander together in a bowl. Season with salt and
mix in 1 teaspoon water to make a stiff batter.

Heat enough oil for deep-frying in a kadhai or a deep
frying pan (skillet) to 180°C/350°F, or until a cube of
bread browns in 30 seconds, then reduce the
heat slightly. Working in batches, drop spoonfuls
of the batter into the hot oil and deep-fry, turning
frequently for about 2–3 minutes, or until golden
and crisp. Remove the pakoras with a slotted spoon
and drain on kitchen paper (paper towels).

Milgai Bhajiya
Andhra Chilli Fritters

Origin Tamil Nadu
Preparation time 30 minutes
Cooking time 30 minutes
Serves 6

12 medium-sized chillies

vegetable oil, for deep-frying

For the filling

4 medium-sized onions, chopped

2 green chillies, de-seeded and chopped

2 dried red chillies

½ teaspoon asafoetida

1 tablespoon Tamarind Extract (see page 58)

salt

For the batter

150g / 5oz (1 cup) gram (chickpea) flour

2 tablespoons rice flour

pinch of salt

Slit the chillies to be stuffed lengthways down one side only, making sure they are still joined at the stem.

Put all the ingredients for the filling into a blender or food processor, add 1 tablespoon water and process to make a thick smooth paste. Stuff the chillies with the filling and set aside.

To make the batter, whisk the flours with 250ml / 8fl oz (1 cup) water together in a bowl until thick.

Heat the oil for deep-frying in a kadhai or deep frying pan (skillet) to 180°C/350°F, or until a cube of bread browns in 30 seconds, then reduce the heat. Working in batches, dip the stuffed chillies in the batter and carefully lower into the hot oil and deep-fry, turning frequently, for about 4 minutes, or until golden brown and crisp. Remove with a slotted spoon and drain on kitchen paper (paper towels).

Kalmi Bare
Chana Dal Fritters

Origin Delhi
Preparation time 45 minutes, plus soaking time
Cooking time 30 minutes
Serves 6–8

200g / 7oz (1 cup) chana dal, rinsed and drained

200g / 7oz (1 cup) urad dal, rinsed and drained

2 teaspoons coriander seeds

1 teaspoon black peppercorns

1–2 green chillies, de-seeded and finely chopped

2 tablespoons chopped coriander (cilantro) leaves

vegetable oil or ghee, for deep-frying

green chutney, such as Mint Chutney (see page 66), to serve

For sprinkling

1 teaspoon Garam Masala (see page 31)

1 teaspoon Chaat Masala (see page 31)

salt

Soak the lentils in a large bowl of water overnight.

The next day, put the coriander seeds in a mortar and coarsely pound with a pestle. Set aside.

Drain the lentils, then transfer them to a blender or food processor and processor to make a fine paste. Put the paste in a large bowl and add the peppercorns, chillies, coriander seeds and chopped coriander and beat together thoroughly until light and fluffy.

Heat enough oil or ghee for deep-frying in a kadhai or deep, heavy-based pan to 180°C/350°F, or until a piece of bread browns in 30 seconds. Working in batches, drop large tablespoonfuls of the paste carefully into the hot oil and deep-fry, turning frequently, for about 5 minutes, or until light golden colour. Remove the fritters with a slotted spoon and drain on kitchen paper (paper towels). Allow to cool. Set the oil or ghee aside.

When ready to serve, cut each fritter into slices. Reheat the oil or ghee in the kadhai or pan to 180°C/350°F, or until a piece of bread browns in 30 seconds and re-fry the slices for about 2 minutes, or until crisp. Sprinkle the garam masala and chaat masala over, season with salt and serve with a green chutney.

Pesaru Punukulu
Green Lentil Fritters

Origin Andhra Pradesh
Preparation time 15–20 minutes, plus soaking time
Cooking time 20 minutes
Serves 4–6

200g / 7oz (1 cup) sabut moong, rinsed and drained
40g / 1½oz (¼ cup) basmati rice, rinsed and drained
4 green chillies, de-seeded and coarsely chopped
2 medium-sized onions, chopped
2 tablespoons coriander (cilantro) leaves, roughly chopped
1 sprig curry leaves, roughly chopped
vegetable oil, for deep-frying
salt

Soak the sabut moong and rice in a large bowl of water for 2–3 hours. Drain, rinse and drain again.

Transfer the lentils and rice to a blender or food processor, add the chillies and 2–3 tablespoons water and process to a thick coarse batter. Stir in the onions, coriander leaves and curry leaves and season with salt.

Heat enough oil for deep-frying in a kadhai or deep frying pan (skillet) to 180°C/350°F, or until a cube of bread browns in 30 seconds, then reduce the heat. Working in batches, carefully drop spoonfuls of the batter into the hot oil and deep-fry the fritters, turning frequently, for about 5 minutes, or until golden brown and crisp. Remove with a slotted spoon and drain on kitchen paper (paper towels).

Kathirakkai
Aubergine (Eggplant) Fritters

Origin Tamil Nadu
Preparation time 15–20 minutes
Cooking time 10 minutes
Serves 4

4 long aubergines (eggplants)
150g / 5oz (1 cup) gram (chickpea) flour
1 teaspoon rice flour
pinch of asafoetida
1 teaspoon ajwain seeds
1 teaspoon coarsely ground chilli powder
vegetable oil, for deep-frying
salt
Tamarind & Coriander Chutney (see page 65), to serve

Cut the aubergine into vertical thin slices.

Put the flours and spices in a bowl. Season with salt and mix in enough water to make a thick batter of pouring consistency.

Heat enough oil for deep-frying in a kadhai or deep, heavy-based pan to 180°C/350°F, or until a cube of bread browns in 30 seconds. Working in batches, dip each aubergine slice in the batter and then carefully drop into the hot oil and deep-fry for about 2 minutes, or until golden brown. Remove with a slotted spoon and drain on kitchen paper (paper towels). Serve hot with Tamarind & Coriander Chutney.

☀ ☀ / p.116

☀ ☀

Molagai
Chilli Fritters

Origin Tamil Nadu
Preparation time 10 minutes
Cooking time 10 minutes
Serves 4

150g / 5oz (1 cup) gram (chickpea) flour
1 teaspoon ajwain seeds
10 green chillies
4 teaspoons amchoor
vegetable oil, for deep-frying
salt

Put the flour and ajwain in a bowl. Season with salt and mix in enough water to make a thick batter.

Slit the chillies lengthways down one side and fill with a little amchoor and salt. Heat enough oil for deep-frying in a kadhai or deep, heavy-based pan to 180°C/350°F, or until a cube of bread browns in 30 seconds. Working in batches, dip each chilli into the batter and then carefully drop into the hot oil and deep-fry for about 2–3 minutes, or until golden brown. Remove with a slotted spoon and drain on kitchen paper (paper towels).

Mirchi Vada
Batter-fried Green Chillies

Origin Rajasthan
Preparation time 40 minutes, plus cooling time
Cooking time 20–25 minutes
Serves 4–5

500g / 1lb 2oz large, plump green chillies
250g / 9oz (4 small) potatoes, unpeeled
1 teaspoon amchoor
1 tablespoon chopped coriander (cilantro) leaves
pinch of icing (confectioners') sugar
1 teaspoon ground cumin
75g / 2½oz (½ cup) gram (chickpea) flour
vegetable oil, for deep-frying
salt

Make a deep slit in one side of the chillies and de-seed. Put the chillies in a large bowl and pour in 500ml / 18fl oz (2¼ cups) water and add a little salt. Set aside.

Cook the potatoes in a pan of boiling water for about 20 minutes, or until soft, then drain and allow to cool. When the potatoes are cool, peel off their skins, return to the pan and mash. Season with salt to taste, then add the amchoor, chopped coriander, sugar and ground cumin and mix to combine. Fill the chillies with the mixture.

Put the flour in a bowl and whisk in enough water to make a smooth batter.

Heat enough oil for deep-frying in a kadhai or deep, heavy-based pan to 180°C/350°F, or until a cube of bread browns in 30 seconds. Working in batches, dip the chillies in the batter and deep-fry until light brown and crisp. Remove with a slotted spoon and drain on kitchen paper (paper towels).

Beguni
Batter-fried Aubergine (Eggplant)

Origin West Bengal
Preparation time 10–15 minutes
Cooking time 15 minutes
Serves 4–6

300g / 10½oz (2 cups) gram (chickpea) flour
1 teaspoon chilli powder
1 teaspoon ground cumin
pinch of bicarbonate of soda (baking soda)
vegetable oil, for deep-frying
2 medium aubergines (eggplants), thinly sliced lengthways
salt

To serve
80g / 2¾oz (4½ cups) puffed rice
½ fresh coconut, sliced

To make the batter, put the flour in a bowl and add enough water to make a thick batter. Add the chilli powder, cumin, bicarbonate of soda and salt to taste and mix well.

Heat enough oil for deep-frying in a kadhai or deep, heavy-based pan to 180°C/350°F, or until a cube of bread browns in 30 seconds. Dip the aubergines in the batter and lower carefully into the hot oil. Deep-fry for about 2 minutes, or until golden and crisp. Remove with a slotted spoon and drain on kitchen paper (paper towels). Serve with puffed rice and sliced coconut.

Pata Bhaja
Batter-fried Spinach

Origin West Bengal
Preparation time 5 minutes
Cooking time 10 minutes
Serves 6

3 tablespoons plain (all-purpose) flour
salt
250ml / 8fl oz (1 cup) mustard oil
12 large single spinach leaves

Put the flour, salt and a few drops of mustard oil in a bowl and mix in just enough water to form a thin batter.

Heat the remaining mustard oil in a kadhai or wok until smoking, then reduce the heat. Dip each spinach leaf in the batter and fry individually until crisp and golden. Remove with a slotted spoon and drain on kitchen paper (paper towels).

Poongobi Pakora
Cauliflower Fritters

Origin Tamil Nadu
Preparation time 10 minutes
Cooking time 10 minutes
Serves 4

150g / 5oz (1 cup) gram (chickpea) flour
1 teaspoon rice flour
1 teaspoon ajwain seeds
1 teaspoon coarsely ground chilli powder
200g / 7oz (2 cups) cauliflower florets
vegetable oil, for deep-frying
salt

Put the flours, ajwain and chilli powder in a bowl. Season with salt and mix in enough water to make a thick batter or pouring consistency.

Heat enough oil for deep-frying in a kadhai or deep, heavy-based pan to 180°C/350°F, or until a cube of bread browns in 30 seconds. Working in batches, dip each cauliflower floret into the batter and then carefully drop into the hot oil and deep-fry for about 2 minutes, or until golden brown. Remove with a slotted spoon and drain on kitchen paper (paper towels).

☀

Methi Pakora
Fenugreek Fritters

Origin Awadh
Preparation time 30 minutes
Cooking time 20 minutes
Serves 3–4

150g / 5oz (1 cup) gram (chickpea) flour
1 teaspoon crushed peanuts
1 small onion, chopped
1 teaspoon Garam Masala (see page 31)
½ teaspoon chilli powder
1 green chilli, de-seeded and chopped
1 bunch fenugreek leaves, chopped
250ml / 8fl oz (1 cup) vegetable oil
salt

Put the gram flour, peanuts, chopped onion, garam masala, chilli powder and chopped chilli in a bowl and mix together. Add enough water to make a batter. Now, stir in the fenugreek leaves.

Heat the oil in a kadhai or deep frying pan (skillet) to 180°C/350°F, or until a cube of bread browns in 30 seconds. Working in batches, carefully drop spoonfuls of the batter into the hot oil and deep-fry for 3–4 minutes, or until golden brown all over. Remove from the pan and drain kitchen paper (paper towels). Make the others in the same way.

 ☀ ☀

Mundhiri Parappu Pakora
Cashew Nut Fritters

Origin Andhra Pradesh/Tamil Nadu
Preparation time 20–25 minutes
Cooking time 30 minutes
Serves 4–6

¼ teaspoon bicarbonate of soda (baking soda)
2 tablespoons ghee
75g / 2½oz (½ cup) gram (chickpea) flour
4 tablespoons rice flour
1 teaspoon chilli powder
1 green chilli, de-seeded and finely chopped
1 × 1-cm / ½-inch piece ginger, peeled and grated
1 sprig curry leaves
1–2 tablespoons chopped coriander (cilantro) leaves
150g / 5oz (1¼ cups) cashew nuts, chopped
vegetable oil, for deep-frying
salt

Put the bicarbonate of soda and ghee in a bowl and whisk together until frothy. Mix in the flours, chilli powder, chilli, ginger, curry leaves and coriander. Season with salt. Gradually stir in 4 tablespoons water to make a very thick batter. Stir in the cashew nuts.

Heat enough oil for deep-frying in a kadhai or deep frying pan (skillet) to 180°C/350°F, or until a cube of bread browns in 30 seconds, then reduce the heat slightly. Working in batches, carefully drop spoonfuls of the batter into the hot oil and deep-fry, turning frequently, for 2–3 minutes, or until the pakoras are golden brown and crisp. Remove with a slotted spoon and drain on kitchen paper (paper towels).

Cheese ke Bhajiya
Cheese Fritters

Origin Fusion
Preparation time 15 minutes, plus standing time
Cooking time 10 minutes
Serves 4

3½ tablespoons self-raising flour, sifted
85g / 3oz (¾ cup) Cheddar cheese, grated
1 teaspoon Garam Masala (see page 31)
2 eggs, beaten
6 tablespoons milk
1 teaspoon baking powder
vegetable oil, for frying
salt
ground black pepper
ketchup, to serve

Put the flour, grated cheese, garam masala, eggs and milk into a large bowl, season with salt and pepper and stir to make a smooth paste. Add the baking powder and stir well, then set aside for about half an hour.

Heat a little oil in a wok or deep, heavy-based frying pan (skillet) and carefully add spoonfuls of the batter, about 6 at a time, to the hot oil. Cook until golden brown, then turn the fritters over and cook the other side until golden. Remove them with a slotted spoon and drain on kitchen paper (paper towels). Serve hot with ketchup.

Vaarzhaikkai
Banana Fritters

Origin Kerala
Preparation time 15 minutes
Cooking time 10 minutes
Serves 4

3 raw bananas
150g / 5oz (1 cup) gram (chickpea) flour
1 teaspoon rice flour
pinch of asafoetida
1 teaspoon ajwain seeds
1 teaspoon coarsely ground chilli powder
few curry leaves, chopped
vegetable oil, for deep-frying
salt
Tamarind & Coriander Chutney (see page 65), to serve

Peel the bananas and cut into vertical thin slices.

Put the flours, spices and curry leaves in a bowl. Season with salt and mix in enough water to make a thick batter of pouring consistency.

Heat enough oil for deep-frying in a kadhai or deep, heavy-based pan to 180°C/350°F, or until a cube of bread browns in 30 seconds. Working in batches, dip each banana slice in the batter and then carefully drop into the hot oil and deep-fry for 3–4 minutes, or until golden brown. Remove with a slotted spoon and drain on kitchen paper (paper towels). Serve hot with Tamarind & Coriander Chutney.

Poha Pulao
Pressed Rice with Vegetables

Origin Maharashtra
Preparation time 25–35 minutes, plus soaking time
Cooking time 15–20 minutes
Serves 4

100g / 3½oz (½ cup) pressed rice
100g / 3½oz (⅔ cup) peas, shelled if fresh
1 tablespoon vegetable oil, plus extra for stir-frying
½ teaspoon mustard seeds
¼ teaspoon ground turmeric
½ teaspoon chilli powder
½ teaspoon Garam Masala (see page 31)
150g / 5oz (1½ cup) cauliflower, cut into florets
1 medium-sized potato, cut into small pieces
100g / 3½oz French (green) beans, sliced
2 carrots, diced
2 medium-sized tomatoes, cut into quarters
50g / 1¾oz Paneer (see page 59), cut into small pieces
1 teaspoon sugar
1 tablespoon lemon juice
2–3 green chillies, de-seeded
1 × 2.5-cm / 1-inch piece fresh ginger, peeled and grated
salt
1 large sprig coriander (cilantro) leaves, chopped, to garnish

Soak the pressed rice in a bowl of water for 10 minutes then spread out delicately to dry. Meanwhile, cook the peas in a pan of water for 5–7 minutes, or until soft. Set aside.

Heat the oil in a large flat pan or frying pan (skillet), add the mustard seeds and ground spices and stir-fry for 1 minute. Add the rice, turning lightly with a flat spatula. Cover, reduce the heat to very low and leave for 1 minute, then remove from the heat.

Heat a little more oil in another frying pan, add the cauliflower and stir-fry until browned, then add the potatoes, French beans, peas and carrots and stir-fry for about 5 minutes. Add the tomatoes and cook until the tomatoes are just scalded. Add the paneer at the end and cook for a few minutes until it is heated through. Stir in the sugar, lemon juice, chillies and ginger, then season with salt. Arrange the rice and vegetables in layers in a serving dish and garnish with coriander.

Kaikari Masala Vada
Mixed Vegetable Patties

Origin Tamil Nadu
Preparation time 15 minutes, plus soaking time
Cooking time 30 minutes
Makes 12–14

100g / 3½oz (½ cup) chana dal, rinsed and drained
4 tablespoons urad dal, rinsed and drained
2 tablespoons plain (all-purpose) flour
25g / 1oz (¼ cup) finely chopped cabbage
100g / 3½oz (¾ cup) chopped carrot
2 medium-sized onions, finely chopped
1 × 5-mm / ¼-inch piece fresh ginger
4 green chillies, de-seeded and finely chopped
2 tablespoons chopped coriander (cilantro) leaves
1 sprig curry leaves
1½ teaspoons dry-roasted chana dal
vegetable oil, for deep-frying
salt

Soak the lentils in a large bowl of water for 1 hour.

Drain the lentils well and transfer to a blender or food processor. Process, gradually adding about 2 tablespoons water, until thick. Transfer the batter to a clean bowl and mix in the flour, vegetables, ginger, chillies, coriander, curry leaves and roasted chana dal. Season with salt.

Heat enough vegetable oil for deep-frying in a kadhai or deep, heavy-based pan to 180°C/350°F, or until a cube of bread browns in 30 seconds, then reduce the heat slightly so that the vadai will not brown too quickly. Working in batches, take a ladleful of the mixture and, using damp hands, flatten it into a 5cm / 2 inch round patty. Gently lower the patty into the hot oil and deep-fry, turning carefully, for about 2–3 minutes, or until golden brown and crisp. Remove with a slotted spoon and drain and on kitchen paper (paper towels). Repeat until all the mixture is used up.

Subz ke Shami
Vegetarian Patties

Origin Awadh
Preparation time 3½ hours, plus cooling time
Cooking time 10–15 minutes
Makes 16

100g / 3½oz (2 small) potatoes, unpeeled	
100g / 3½oz French (green) beans	
150g / 5oz (2 medium) carrots	
50g / 1¾oz cauliflower, cut in pieces	
1–2 tablespoons vegetable oil	
3½ tablespoons ghee, plus extra for cooking	
1 teaspoon coriander seeds	
100g / 3½oz (⅔ cup) onions, sliced	
1 teaspoon ground cumin	
1 teaspoon Ginger Paste (see page 57)	
1 teaspoon Garlic Paste (see page 57)	
1 teaspoon amchoor	
2 tablespoons Cashew Nut Paste (see page 58)	
1 tablespoon chironji kernel paste	
1 teaspoon chilli powder	
1 teaspoon ground black pepper	
1 tablespoon ground coriander	
tiny pinch of ground green cardamom	

Cook the potatoes in a pan of boiling water for about 20 minutes, or until soft, then drain and allow to cool. When the potatoes are cool, peel off their skins, return to the pan and mash.

Meanwhile, cook the beans in another pan of boiling water for 5 minutes or until tender, then drain and set aside. Cook the carrots in a separate pan of boiling water for about 15 minutes, or until soft. Drain and cut into dice. Cook the cauliflower in another pan of boiling water for 5 minutes, or until just tender. Drain and grate.

Heat the oil in a frying pan (skillet) and lightly fry the potato, beans, carrots and cauliflower.

Melt the ghee in a separate pan, add the coriander seeds and half the onions and lightly fry until golden brown and crisp. Drain on kitchen paper (paper towels), then crumble with your hands and allow to cool.

Reheat the ghee, add the cumin and stir-fry over medium heat until it begins to splutter. Add the remaining onions and lightly fry for about 5 minutes until they are translucent. Add the ginger and garlic pastes and stir-fry for another 5 minutes, until the onions are light golden brown. Stir in the amchoor then add the cashew nut paste, chironji kernel paste and the remaining spices and mix well.

Add the mixture and the fried onions to the vegetables and mix well. Divide the mixture into 16 equal portions. With damp hands, roll into balls and then flatten to make 2.5-cm / 1-inch thick patties. Heat the ghee on a tawa or flat griddle or in a frying pan (skillet). Working in batches, shallow-fry the patties over medium heat, for about 3 minutes on each side, or until they are evenly brown, turning once. Remove with a slotted spoon and drain on kitchen paper (paper towels).

Aloo Tikki
Potato Patties

Origin Punjab/Delhi
Preparation time 1 hour, plus cooling time
Cooking time 5–10 minutes
Makes 12

For the potatoes

500g / 1lb 2oz (3 medium) potatoes, unpeeled
3 teaspoons ground cumin
3 teaspoons ground black pepper
3 teaspoons black rock salt
2 teaspoons ajwain seeds
3 teaspoons amchoor
1 tablespoon yellow chilli powder
2 tablespoons dried mint leaves, ground
4 green chillies, de-seeded and chopped
1 large sprig coriander (cilantro), chopped
ghee, for shallow-frying
salt

For the filling

large pinch of asafoetida or garlic or onion powder
250g / 9oz (1¾ cups) peas, shelled if fresh
4 tablespoons ghee
1 teaspoon cumin seeds
1 × 2.5-cm / 1-inch piece fresh ginger, peeled and finely chopped
4 green chillies, de-seeded and chopped
1½ teaspoons amchoor
1 teaspoon ground black pepper

For the filling, dissolve the asafoetida in 2 tablespoons water and set aside.

Cook the potatoes in a pan of boiling water for about 20 minutes, or until soft, then drain and allow to cool. When the potatoes are cool, peel off their skins, return to the pan and mash.

Cook the peas for the filling in a separate pan of boiling water for about 5–7 minutes, or until soft, then drain, return to the pan and mash. Set aside.

Put the mashed potatoes, spices, mint, chillies and coriander in a bowl and mix well. Divide into 12 equal portions and roll into balls.

To make the filling, heat the ghee in a pan, add the cumin seeds and stir-fry over medium heat until they begin to splutter.

Add the reserved asafoetida, the ginger and chillies and stir-fry for a few seconds, then add the mashed peas and stir-fry until the mixture becomes dry. Remove the pan from the heat and stir in the amchoor and black pepper. Adjust the seasoning and allow to cool. When the mixture is cool, mash with a potato masher and divide into 12 equal portions.

With damp hands, flatten each potato ball to make round patties. Place a portion of the filling in the middle, roll into balls again to enclose the filling and then flatten to make 1-cm / ½-inch thick round patties.

Heat the ghee for shallow-frying on a thick tawa or flat griddle or in a frying pan (skillet) over medium heat. Working in batches, add the patties and shallow-fry, turning once, for about 3–5 minutes on both sides, or until a thick crust is formed. Remove with a slotted spoon and drain on kitchen paper (paper towels). Cook the remaining patties in the same way.

✳ / 📷 p.119

Aloo Tikki Awadhi
Potato & Pea Patties

Origin Awadh
Preparation time 45 minutes, plus cooling time
Cooking time 15–20 minutes
Makes 12

1kg / 2¼lb (6–7 medium) potatoes, unpeeled
250g / 9oz (1¾ cups) peas, shelled if fresh
1 tablespoon vegetable oil or ghee, plus extra for shallow-frying
1 teaspoon cumin seeds
1 × 5-cm / 2-inch piece fresh ginger, peeled and finely chopped
6–8 green chillies, de-seeded and finely chopped
1 teaspoon chilli powder
1 teaspoon ground coriander
1 teaspoon Chaat Masala (see page 31)
1 teaspoon Garam Masala (see page 31)
1 tablespoon coriander (cilantro) leaves, finely chopped, plus extra to garnish
2 tablespoons gram (chickpea) flour
salt
a Green Mango Chutney (see page 75) or Tamarind & Coriander Chutney (see page 65), to serve

Cook the potatoes in a pan of boiling water for about 20 minutes, or until soft, then drain and allow to cool. When the potatoes are cool, peel off their skins, return to the pan and mash. Cook the peas in another pan of boiling water for 5–7 minutes, or until soft.

Heat the oil or ghee in a pan, add the cumin seeds and stir-fry for about 1 minute, or until they begin to splutter, then add the cooked peas, ginger, chillies, and spices, including the chaat masala, and season with salt. Continue to stir-fry for a further 1 minute. Add the potatoes, garam masala, chopped coriander and flour and fry for another 1 minute. Remove from the heat and divide the mixture into 12 equal portions. Roll into balls, then with damp hands, flatten them slightly and shape them into round patties.

Heat enough oil or ghee for shallow-frying on a thick tawa or flat griddle or in a frying pan over medium-high heat. Working in batches, add the patties and shallow-fry for 3–4 minutes, or until golden brown and crisp on both sides. Remove and set aside while the remaining patties are cooked. To serve, place the patties on serving plates, then spoon the chutneys over the top and garnish with coriander.

Aloo ke Kebab
Potato Kebabs

Origin Awadh
Preparation time 35–40 minutes, plus cooling time
Cooking time 20–30 minutes
Makes 20

500g / 1lb 2oz (3 medium) potatoes, unpeeled

1 teaspoon chilli powder

1 teaspoon cumin seeds, roasted

1 green chilli, chopped

1 tablespoon lemon juice

3 tablespoons grated cheese

2 tablespoons gram (chickpea) flour

1 teaspoon baking powder

few coriander (cilantro) leaves, chopped

85g / 3oz (½ cup) semolina (farina)

250ml / 8fl oz (1 cup) vegetable oil, for shallow-frying

salt

Cook the potatoes in a pan of boiling water for about 20 minutes, or until soft, then drain and allow to cool. When the potatoes are cool, peel off their skins, return to the pan and mash.

Blend the potatoes with all the other ingredients except the semolina. Divide the mixture into 20 equal portions and roll into balls. With damp hands, flatten the balls into small burger patty-like shapes.

Spread the semolina out on a flat plate and use to coat the kebabs evenly on both sides.

Heat the oil for shallow-frying in a suitable pan over medium-high heat. Add 4–6 kebabs and shallow-fry for about 2–3 minutes, then gently turn with the spatula to fry the other side for another 2–3 minutes. Remove with a slotted spoon and drain on kitchen paper (paper towel). Repeat with the rest of the kebabs.

Khumb ki Tikki
Mushroom Patties

Origin Awadh
Preparation time 40 minutes
Cooking time 20 minutes
Makes 8

100g / 3½oz (1⅓ cups) button (white) mushrooms,
   chopped

---

1 small onion, chopped

---

100 g / 3½oz (¾ cup) cauliflower florets, chopped

---

2 tablespoons shelled peanuts

---

1 teaspoon yeast extract

---

1 tablespoon chopped coriander (cilantro) leaves

150g / 5oz (1½ cups) dried breadcrumbs,
   plus 60g / 2oz (½ cup) for coating

---

5 tablespoons vegetable oil

---

salt

To serve

---

onion rings

---

cherry tomatoes

Cook the mushrooms in a non-stick frying pan
(skillet) without any oil. Keep stirring briskly
for about 10 minutes until all the moisture has
evaporated from the mushrooms.

Put the onion, vegetables and nuts in a food
processor or blender and process until they bind
together and form a thick mixture. Transfer to
a bowl, season with salt and stir in the yeast extract,
coriander and breadcrumbs. With damp hands,
roll the mixture into 8 balls and flatten to make
round patties.

Spread the breadcrumbs out on a plate and roll each
patty in the breadcrumbs until coated.

Heat the oil in a non-stick frying pan (skillet) and
working in batches, cook the patties for about
5 minutes, or until crisp and golden brown on both
sides. Remove from the pan and keep warm in a low
oven while you cook the rest. Serve with onion rings
and cherry tomatoes.

Saboodana Vada
Sago Patties

Origin Coastal
Preparation time 40 minutes, plus soaking time
Cooking time 20 minutes
Makes 12

---

3 tablespoons sago

---

2 potatoes, unpeeled

150g / 5oz (1 cup) shelled peanuts

4–5 green chillies, finely chopped

---

vegetable oil, for deep-frying

---

rock salt

Soak the sago in a large bowl of water for about
1 hour. Drain and set aside.

Meanwhile, cook the potatoes in a pan of boiling
water for about 20 minutes, or until soft, then drain
and allow to cool. When the potatoes are cool, peel
off their skins, return to the pan and mash.

Heat a kadhai or large wok, add the peanuts and
stir-fry for about 2 minutes, or until roasted.
Transfer the peanuts to a mortar and pestle and
pound until crushed.

Separate the sago so that it is free of any lumps then
sprinkle over 250ml (8fl oz/1 cup) water. Add the
potatoes, chillies, peanuts and salt, and mix well.

Divide the mixture equally into 12 small portions and
shape into flat patties. If the patties are sticking to
your hands, then you may need to oil your hands
with a little oil.

Heat enough oil for deep-frying in a kadhai or deep,
heavy-based pan to 180°C/350°F, or until a cube
of bread browns in 30 seconds. Carefully lower the
patties, in batches, into the hot oil and deep-fry
for about 2 minutes, or until golden brown. Remove
with a slotted spoon and drain on kitchen paper
(paper towels).

Dahi ke Kebab
Yoghurt Patties

Origin Awadh
Preparation time 45 minutes, plus cooling time
Cooking time 10–15 minutes
Makes 16

250ml / 8fl oz (1 cup) hung natural (plain) yoghurt (see page 793), whisked
250g / 9oz (2 cups) plain (all-purpose) flour
125g / 4¼oz (¾ cup) onion, chopped
1–2 green chillies, de-seeded and chopped
1 tablespoon chopped coriander (cilantro) leaves
1 × 5-cm / 2-inch piece fresh ginger, peeled and chopped
1 tablespoon Garam Masala (see page 31)
1 tablespoon ground dried fenugreek leaves
1 tablespoon ground turmeric
1½ tablespoons chilli powder
125ml / 4½fl oz (½ cup) vegetable oil or ghee, for shallow-frying
salt

Put the whisked yoghurt and flour in a bowl and mix together, then strain the mixture through a sieve (strainer) and set aside.

Put the onions, chillies, coriander, ginger, garam masala, fenugreek, turmeric and chilli powder in another bowl and season with salt. Mix together and set aside.

Pour both mixtures into a large pan, stir, and lightly fry over medium heat ensuring that it does not stick to the base (bottom) of the pan for 5–10 minutes, or until thick. Remove from the heat and allow to cool.

When the mixture is cool, divide into 16 equal portions. With damp hands, roll into balls and flatten into patties.

Heat the oil for shallow-frying in a deep, heavy-based pan over medium-high heat. Working in batches, shallow-fry the patties for about 3–4 minutes, or until they are golden brown and crispy. Remove with a slotted spoon and set aside while you cook the remaining patties.

Nadru ke Kebab
Lotus Root Kebabs

Origin Jammu and Kashmir
Preparation time 30–35 minutes, plus cooling time
Cooking time 20–30 minutes
Makes 25

1kg / 2¼lb lotus roots
1½ tablespoons chopped coriander (cilantro)
1½ tablespoons chopped green chillies
2 teaspoons black cumin seeds
1 teaspoon ground dried mint
¼ teaspoon ground cinnamon
1 teaspoon Kashmiri red chilli powder
¼ teaspoon ground black pepper
6 tablespoons breadcrumbs
vegetable oil, for shallow-frying
salt

Roast the lotus roots over a coal fire for about 5 minutes, or until large brown specks appear all over, then allow to cool slightly. Alternatively, preheat the grill (broiler) to medium and grill (broil) the lotus roots. When the lotus roots are cool enough to handle, peel the skin, then chop the roots into thin slices, transfer to a blender or food processor and process to make a coarse paste.

Put the paste in a bowl and add the chopped coriander, chillies and spices and mix well. Season with salt, add the breadcrumbs and mix well again. With damp hands, divide the mixture into 25 small balls, then flatten each ball into a round patty.

Heat enough oil for shallow-frying in a kadhai or deep frying pan (skillet) over medium-high heat. Working in batches, add the patties to the hot oil and shallow-fry for about 3–4 minutes, or until light brown. Remove with a slotted spoon and drain on kitchen paper (paper towels).

Avasara Vada
Coconut & Gram (Chickpea)
Flour Patties

Origin Tamil Nadu
Preparation time 15 minutes
Cooking time 30 minutes
Makes 20–25

150g / 5oz (1 cup) rice flour

60g / 2oz (½ cup) plain (all-purpose) flour

75g / 2½oz (½ cup) gram (chickpea) flour

1 teaspoon white sesame seeds

½ teaspoon cumin seeds

½ teaspoon asafoetida

6 tablespoons freshly grated coconut

3 green chillies, de-seeded and chopped

1 × 1-cm / ½-inch piece fresh ginger, peeled
and chopped

2 tablespoons chopped coriander (cilantro) leaves

1½ tablespoons ghee

vegetable oil, for deep-frying

salt

Combine all the ingredients, except the ghee and oil,
in a bowl and mix well. Season with salt, then
gradually mix in 125ml /4½fl oz (½ cup) water to make
a thick, stiff batter.

Heat the ghee in a small pan until melted and mix it
into the paste.

Heat enough vegetable oil for deep-frying in
a kadhai or deep, heavy-based pan to 180°C/350°F,
or until a cube of bread browns in 30 seconds, then
reduce the heat. Working in batches, take a ladleful
of the batter and, using damp hands, flatten it into
a 5cm / 2 inch round patty. Gently lower the patty
into the hot oil and deep-fry, turning carefully, for
about 2–3 minues, or until golden brown and crisp.
Remove with a slotted spoon and drain and on
kitchen paper (paper towels). Repeat until all the
batter is used up.

Arabi ke Kebab
Colacasia (Taro Root) Kebabs

Origin Awadh
Preparation time 40 minutes, plus cooling time
Cooking time 25 minutes
Makes 8

225g / 8oz colacasia (taro root), unpeeled

1 tablespoon vegetable oil

1 onion, chopped

1 teaspoon chilli powder

½ teaspoon ground ginger

1 teaspoon ground coriander

pinch of asafoetida

½ teaspoon Garam Masala (see page 31)

1 × 2.5-cm / 1-inch piece fresh ginger, chopped

50g / 1¾oz (½ cup) gram (chickpea) flour

1 bunch coriander (cilantro) leaves, chopped

60g / 2oz (½ cup) dried breadcrumbs

salt

Put the colacasia in a pan, cover with water and boil
until soft. Drain and allow to cool, then peel off
the skins, return to the pan and mash with a fork or
potato masher.

Heat the 1 tablespoon oil in a frying pan (skillet), add
the onion and fry until brown. Transfer to a bowl
and season with salt, then add the spices, fresh
ginger, flour, coriander and mashed yam and mix to
combine. Shape the mixture into 8 balls, then flatten
them into patties.

Spread the breadcrumbs out on a plate and roll the
kebabs in the breadcrumbs until coated.

Heat enough oil for deep-frying in a kadhai or deep
frying pan to 180°C/350°F, or until a cube of bread
browns in 30 seconds. Working in batches, deep-fry
the kebabs for about 3–4 minutes, or until crisp
and golden brown. Remove with a slotted spoon and
drain on kitchen paper (paper towels). Serve hot.

Grilled Mushrooms
in Pickling Spices p.97

Batter-fried Aubergine
(Eggplant)   p.103

Samosas p.131

Coconut Chutney p.67

Onion Fritters p.99

Chilli Fritters
p.102

Raw Mango Pickle
from Telangana   p.76

Fried Moong Dal
Dumplings   p.578

Batter-fried
Spinach   p.103

Pressed Rice with
Vegetables   p.106

Sesame Seed &
Coconut Balls p.155

Potato & Pea
Patties   p.108

Shredded Chicken with
(Bell) Peppers   p.221

Lukhmi
      p.192

Stuffed Potatoes
p.159

Tomato Chutney
p.70

Mini Loaves with
Tangy Vegetables p.139

Semolina Pancakes
p.142

Sambhar with Fresh
Ground Spices   p.565

Lentil-filled
Puffed Bread   p.157

Stuffed Lamb
Kebabs   p.188

Stuffed Grilled
Cauliflower   p.160

Baked Fish
p.174

Savoury Semolina
with Vegetables   p.164

Milk-based Sherbet
p.721

Baked Fish
p.174

Fish Patties

p.176

✵ ✵

Vazhaiappoo Vada
Plantain Flower Patties

Origin Kerala
Preparation time 35–40 minutes, plus soaking time
Cooking time 30 minutes
Makes 10

1 plantain flower
1 tablespoon natural (plain) yoghurt, whisked
3 teaspoons vegetable oil
¼ teaspoon mustard seeds
¼ teaspoon cumin seeds
¼ teaspoon fennel seeds
1 sprig curry leaves
1 medium-sized onion, finely chopped
vegetable oil, for deep-frying

For the batter

100g / 3½oz (½ cup) chana dal, rinsed and drained
100g / 3½oz (½ cup) toover dal, rinsed and drained
1 teaspoon cumin seeds
1 teaspoon fennel seeds
3 dried red chillies
salt

To make the batter, soak both dals in a large bowl of water for 2 hours.

Drain the dals and transfer to a food processor or blender with the cumin and fennel seeds and dried chillies. Season with salt, then process, gradually adding about 2–3 tablespoons water until it is a coarse, stiff batter.

Remove the outer layers of the plantain flower until you reach the finger-shaped white florets. Remove the stamens from the florets and chop the florets finely. Keep removing the inner layers and chopping the florets until you get 1 cup chopped flowers. Put the yoghurt and water in a large bowl, add the chopped flowers and allow to soak until needed.

Heat the 3 teaspoons oil in a frying pan (skillet) over medium heat, add the mustard, cumin and fennel seeds and curry leaves and stir-fry for about 1 minute, or until the mustard seeds start spluttering. Add the onion and stir-fry for about 1–2 minutes.

Drain the plantain flowers, squeeze out any excess water, add to the pan and fry for about 1–2 minutes. Pour the contents of the pan into the batter and mix well.

Heat enough oil for deep-frying in a kadhai or deep frying pan to 180°C/350°F, or until a cube of bread browns in 30 seconds, then reduce the heat slightly. With damp hands, take a ladleful of the batter and flatten it into a 5cm / 2 inch round patty. Working in batches, slip the patties gently into the hot oil and deep-fry, turning frequently, for 3–4 minutes, or until golden brown and crisp. Remove with a slotted spoon and drain on kitchen paper (paper towels).

✵ ✵

Maddur Vada
Semolina & Rice Patties

Origin Karnataka
Preparation time 10 minutes
Cooking time 30 minutes
Makes 18–20

150g / 5oz (1 cup) rice flour
4 tablespoons fine semolina (semolina flour)
2 tablespoons chana dal, roasted
3–4 green chillies, de-seeded and finely chopped
2 tablespoons ghee
¾ teaspoon asafoetida
2 tablespoons chopped coriander (cilantro) leaves
vegetable oil, for deep-frying
salt

Combine all the ingredients, except the oil, in a bowl. Season with salt and gradually stir in 4 tablespoons water to make a thick, stiff batter.

Heat enough oil for deep-frying in a kadhai or deep frying pan (skillet) to 180°C/350°F, or until a cube of bread browns in 30 seconds, then reduce the heat slightly. With damp hands, take a ladleful of the batter and flatten it into a 5cm / 2 inch round patty. Working in batches, slip the patties gently into the hot oil and deep-fry, turning frequently, for 2–3 minutes, or until the patties are golden brown and crisp. Remove with a slotted spoon and drain on kitchen paper (paper towels).

☀ / 📷 p.119

Lukhmi
Vegetable-filled Pastries

Origin Hyderabad
Preparation time 50 minutes, plus resting time
Cooking time 1 hour
Makes 8

---

3 tablespoons vegetable oil

2 teaspoons Ginger Paste (see page 57)

2 teaspoons Garlic Paste (see page 57)

½ teaspoon chilli powder

100g / 3½oz (1⅓ cups) button (white) mushrooms, stalks removed and finely chopped

50g / 1¾ oz (⅓ cup) carrot, finely chopped

6–8 green chillies, slit in half lengthways and de-seeded

100g / 3½oz Paneer (see page 59), crumbled

1 × 2.5-cm / 1-inch piece fresh ginger, peeled and finely chopped

100g / 3½oz (⅔ cup) peas, shelled if fresh

2 tablespoons lemon juice

½ red (bell) pepper, finely chopped

½ yellow (bell) pepper, finely chopped

3 tablespoons pomegranate seeds

1 teaspoon black cumin seeds

½ teaspoon ground cumin

30g / 1¼oz (1 cup) coriander (cilantro) leaves, chopped

vegetable oil, for deep-frying

salt

For the pastry

4 tablespoons ghee

2 tablespoons natural (plain) yoghurt, whisked

250g / 9oz (2 cups) plain (all-purpose) flour, plus extra for dusting

First, make the pastry. Put the ghee, yoghurt, a little salt and the flour in a large bowl and mix with enough water to make a soft dough. Cover the dough and set aside for 30 minutes in a cool place, preferably a refrigerator.

Heat the oil in a pan, add the ginger and garlic pastes, chilli powder, salt and the finely chopped mushrooms and lightly stir-fry for about 2 minutes, or until all the moisture has evaporated.

Add the carrots, chillies and paneer and continue frying for about 1 minute, then add the ginger and peas and sprinkle with lemon juice. Now add the peppers and pomegranate seeds and stir to mix well. Sprinkle over the black cumin seeds.

Divide the dough into equal portions, then roll each portion into a round ball. Dust with a little flour and shape each ball into ovals. Place a little vegetable mixture in the middle, fold over to cover the vegetables and seal the edges. Trim off the uneven sides with a sharp knife to make neat rectangular or triangular lukhmi.

Heat enough oil for deep-frying in a kadhai or deep, heavy-based pan to 180°C/350°F, or until a cube of bread browns in 30 seconds. Working in batches, carefully lower the lukhmis into the hot oil and deep-fry until golden brown. Remove with a slotted spoon and drain on kitchen paper (paper towels) before serving.

Samosa
Samosas

Origin Punjab/Awadh/Delhi
Preparation time 45 minutes, plus cooling time
Cooking time 15–20 minutes
Makes 10

500g / 1lb 2oz (4 cups) plain (all-purpose) flour, plus
    extra for dusting

vegetable oil, for deep-frying

For the filling

100g / 3½oz (2 small) potatoes, unpeeled

150g / 5oz (1 cup) peas, shelled if fresh

4 tablespoons ghee

1 teaspoon cumin seeds

1 × 5-cm / 2-inch piece fresh ginger, peeled
    and finely chopped

4–5 green chillies, de-seeded and chopped

1 teaspoon chilli powder

¼ teaspoon ground turmeric

1 teaspoon ground coriander

1 teaspoon pomegranate seeds

1 tablespoon chopped coriander (cilantro) leaves

salt

Put the flour in a large bowl and mix with enough water to form a stiff dough. Divide the dough into 10 equal portions and roll into balls. Cover with a damp cloth.

For the filling, cook the potatoes in a pan of boiling water for about 20 minutes, or until soft, then drain and allow to cool. When the potatoes are cool, peel off their skins, return to the pan and mash. Cook the peas in another pan of boiling water for 5–7 minutes, or until soft.

Heat the ghee in a deep, heavy-based pan, add the cumin seeds and fry over medium heat for about 15 seconds. Add the ginger, chillies, chilli powder, turmeric, coriander and season with salt. Stir-fry for about 1 minute, then add the mashed potatoes and peas and stir-fry for another minute. Add the pomegranate seeds and chopped coriander and stir. Taste and adjust the seasoning, if necessary, then remove from the heat and allow to cool. When the filling is cool, divide it into 10 equal portions.

Place the balls of dough on a lightly floured surface and roll into rounds of about 12cm / 5 inches diameter. Moisten the edges with water, then place a portion of filling in the centre, fold over and press all around to seal the edges.

Heat enough oil for deep-frying in a kadhai or deep, heavy-based pan to 180°C/350°F, or until a cube of bread browns in 30 seconds. Working in batches, add the samosas carefully to the hot oil and deep-fry for about 2–3 minutes, or until golden brown. Remove with a slotted spoon and drain on kitchen paper (paper towels).

Singhara
Bengali Samosas

Origin West Bengal
Preparation time 40 minutes, plus cooling time
Cooking time 20 minutes
Makes 12 samosas

625g / 1lb 7oz (5 cups) plain (all-purpose) flour

4 tablespoons vegetable oil

1 teaspoon salt

vegetable oil, for deep-frying

For the filling

1 teaspoon ground turmeric

1 teaspoon ground cumin

2 teaspoons ground coriander

1 teaspoon chilli powder

5 tablespoons vegetable oil

1 tablespoon chopped onion

2 teaspoons Ginger Paste (see page 57)

2 teaspoons Garlic Paste (see page 57)

150g / 5oz (1 cup) potatoes, diced

150g / 5oz (1½ cups) cauliflower, chopped or grated

50g / 1¾oz (⅓ cup) peas, shelled if fresh

50g / 1¾oz (⅓ cup) shelled peanuts

salt

Put the flour in a large bowl, add the oil and salt and rub until the mixture becomes crumbly. Add enough water to make a soft dough.

For the filling, put the ground spices and a little salt in a small bowl, add 2 tablespoons water and stir until dissolved.

Heat the oil in a kadhai or wok until smoking, then reduce the heat, add the onion and stir-fry for about 5 minutes, or until golden brown. Add the ginger and garlic pastes and stir-fry until the oil separates. Add the dissolved ground spices and stir-fry for about 5 minutes. Add the vegetables and cook until done. Add the peanuts and mix well. Remove from the heat and allow to cool.

Divide the dough into 12 equal portions, then roll out each portion into a 5-cm / 2-inch disc and cut it in half. Place 1 tablespoon of the filling in each of the crescents and fold over to enclose the filling, pressing the edges firmly to seal.

Heat enough oil for deep-frying in a kadhai or deep, heavy-based pan to 180°C/350°F, or until a cube of bread browns in 30 seconds. Lower the samosas carefully into the hot oil and deep-fry until golden brown. Remove with a slotted spoon and allow to drain on kitchen paper (paper towels) before serving.

Rava Bonda
Fried Semolina Dumplings

Origin Karnataka
Preparation time 20 minutes
Cooking time 20–25 minutes
Makes 25–30

200g / 7oz (1 cup) fine semolina (semolina flour)

4 tablespoons sour yoghurt (see page 793)

3–4 green chillies, de-seeded and finely chopped

½ teaspoon asafoetida

1 × 2.5-cm / 1-inch piece fresh ginger, peeled and grated

2 tablespoons cashew nuts, finely chopped

1–2 tablespoons chopped coriander (cilantro) leaves

vegetable oil, for deep-frying

salt

Combine all the ingredients, except the oil, in a bowl. Season with salt and gradually stir in 2 tablespoons water to make a stiff batter. Shape the batter into small lime-sized balls.

Heat enough oil for deep-frying in a kadhai or deep frying pan (skillet) to 180°C/350°F, or until a cube of bread browns in 30 seconds, then reduce the heat slightly. Slip 6–8 bonda at a time into the hot oil and deep-fry, turning frequently, for 3–4 minutes, or until golden brown and crisp. Remove with a slotted spoon and drain on kitchen paper (paper towels).

Khuzhi Paniyaram
Fried Rice Dumplings from Chettinad

Origin Tamil Nadu
Preparation time 45 minutes, plus soaking and fermenting time
Cooking time 1½ hours
Makes 28–30

200g / 7oz (1 cup) basmati rice, rinsed and drained
180g / 6¼oz (1 cup) parboiled rice, rinsed and drained
70g / 2½oz (⅓ cup) urad dal, rinsed and drained
1 teaspoon fenugreek seeds, rinsed and drained
2 tablespoons chopped coriander (cilantro) leaves
vegetable oil, for cooking
salt
Coconut Chutney (see page 67), to serve

For the tempering

2 tablespoons vegetable oil
1 teaspoon mustard seeds
2 medium-sized onions, chopped
4 tablespoons grated fresh coconut

Soak the basmati rice and parboiled rice in a large bowl of water for 6 hours. At the same time, soak the lentils and fenugreek seeds in another large bowl of water for 6 hours.

Drain the rice, transfer to a blender or food processor and process, gradually adding about 500ml / 18fl oz (2¼ cups) water to make smooth batter. Transfer to a bowl.

Drain the lentils, transfer to a blender or food processor and process, gradually adding 2–3 tablespoons water to make a smooth batter. Combine both batters, season with salt and set aside to ferment for 6–8 hours. The batter should be of a thick pouring consistency, so add a little more water, if necessary.

Heat the 2 tablespoons oil for the tempering in a frying pan (skillet), add the mustard seeds and stir-fry for 1 minute, or until they start spluttering, then add the onions and fry for a further 1–2 minutes. Mix in the coconut and fry for 1 minute. Stir the contents of the pan into the batter and mix in the coriander leaves.

Heat a dumpling pan and fill each depression with a little oil. When heated, add enough batter to come halfway up the depressions and fry over low heat for about 3 minutes.

Turn the dumpling over gently with a skewer and fry the other side for about 3 minutes, or until golden. Remove and drain on kitchen paper (paper towels). Serve with Coconut Chutney.

You will need a special paniyaram pan for this dish, but a Danish aebleskiver pan, used for making Danish-style pancakes, is a perfect substitute. You could also use an egg poacher.

Kele ke Dahi Bare
Green Banana Dumplings in Yoghurt

Origin Delhi
Preparation time 20 minutes
Cooking time 30 minutes
Makes 20

6 green unripe bananas, unpeeled
1 litre / 1¾ pints (4 cups) natural (plain) yoghurt
1 teaspoon sugar
½ teaspoon ground cumin
1–2 green chillies, de-seeded and chopped
2 teaspoons chopped coriander (cilantro) leaves
310g / 11oz (1¼ cups) ghee, for frying
salt

Pour 2 litres / 8 cups water into a large pan and bring to the boil. Add the bananas and cook for about 20 minutes. Drain and allow to cool slightly. Meanwhile, put the yoghurt and sugar in a bowl, season with salt and whisk to combine. Set aside.

Peel the bananas, transfer to a food processor and roughly blend. Transfer to a large bowl and finish mashing with a potato masher or fork. Add the cumin, chillies and chopped coriander and mix together. Divide the mixture into equal portions and roll into balls, then flatten between the palms of your hands.

Heat the ghee in a kadhai or deep, heavy-based pan until a cube of bread browns in 40 seconds. Working in batches, add the dumplings and fry for about 3 minutes, or until golden, turning once. Remove with a slotted spoon, drain on kitchen paper (paper towel), sprinkle with a little salt and set aside.

When ready to serve, place the banana dumplings in the seasoned yoghurt, making sure they are covered in the yoghurt.

Masala Siyam
Fried Rice & Black Lentil Dumplings

Origin Tamil Nadu
Preparation time 30–40 minutes, plus soaking time
Cooking time 30 minutes
Makes 30–35

200g / 7oz (1 cup) good-quality basmati rice, rinsed and drained

150g / 5oz (¾ cup) urad dal, rinsed and drained

vegetable oil, for deep-frying

For the tempering

1 tablespoon vegetable oil

1 teaspoon mustard seeds

1 sprig curry leaves

2 medium-sized onions, chopped

40g / 1½oz (½ cup) grated fresh coconut

3 tablespoons chopped coriander (cilantro) leaves

salt

Combine the rice and lentils in a large bowl, pour in enough water to cover and allow to soak in water for 3–4 hours.

Drain the rice and lentils, transfer to a blender or food processor and process, gradually adding 500ml / 18fl oz (2¼ cups) water to make to a smooth, stiff batter.

Heat the 1 tablespoon oil for the tempering in a small, heavy-based frying pan (skillet), add the mustard seeds and stir-fry for about 1 minute, or until they start spluttering, then add the curry leaves and onions and stir-fry for about 2 minutes. Stir in the coconut and fry for a further 2 minutes, then put the contents of the pan into the batter. Season with salt and stir in the coriander leaves.

Heat enough oil for deep-frying in a kadhai or deep frying pan (skillet) to 180°C/350°F, or until a cube of bread browns in 30 seconds, then reduce the heat slightly. Working in batches, shape the batter into small lime-sized balls, then slip them gently into the hot oil and deep-fry, turning frequently for about 1–2 minutes, or until golden brown and crisp. Remove with a slotted spoon and drain on kitchen paper (paper towels).

Khasta Kachori
Savoury Deep-fried Snack

Origin Rajasthan/Dellhi/Awadh
Preparation time 25–35 minutes, plus soaking and cooling time
Cooking time 18–20 minutes
Makes 12

500g / 1lb 2oz (4 cups) plain (all-purpose) flour

1 teaspoon bicarbonate of soda (baking soda)

4 tablespoons ghee

70g / 2½oz (⅓ cup) urad dal, rinsed and drained

1 tablespoon vegetable oil, plus extra for deep-frying

2 tablespoons fresh ginger, peeled and chopped

1 tablespoon green chilli, de-seeded and chopped

2 teaspoons chilli powder

1½ teaspoons ground fennel

1½ teaspoons ground cumin

pinch of asafoetida

1 teaspoon ground coriander

½ teaspoon sugar

salt

Sift the flour with a little salt and the bicarbonate of soda into a large bowl. Add the ghee and rub the mixture between your fingers until breadcrumbs form. Mix in enough water to form a soft dough. Cover with a damp cloth and set aside.

Soak the urad dal in a bowl of water for 45 minutes. Drain and transfer the urad dal to a blender or food processor, add a little water and process until coarsely ground. You do not want a paste.

Heat the oil in a pan, add the chopped ginger, green chilli, chilli powder, ground fennel, cumin, asafoetida and coriander and stir well. Add the ground dal and cook until all the moisture has evaporated. Add the sugar, then season with salt to taste and mix well. Remove the pan from the heat and allow to cool.

Divide the dough into 12 equal portions and roll into balls, then flatten slightly. Place a little of the urad dal stuffing in the centre and bring the edges together to form a ball; flatten slightly.

Heat enough oil for deep-frying in a deep, heavy-based pan to 170°C/325°F, or until a cube of bread browns in 30 seconds. Carefully slide the balls into the oil and deep-fry until golden brown and crisp. Remove with a slotted spoon and drain on kitchen paper (paper towel) before serving.

Batata Vada
Deep-fried Potato Dumplings

Origin Maharashtra
Preparation time 30–35 minutes, plus cooling time
Cooking time 10 minutes
Makes 12

500g / 1lb 2oz (3 medium) potatoes, unpeeled
6 tablespoons vegetable oil
2½ teaspoons Garlic Paste (see page 57)
2½ teaspoons Ginger Paste (see page 57)
1½ teaspoons green chilli paste
pinch of asafoetida
¾ teaspoon ground turmeric
2½ teaspoons lemon juice
2 tablespoons chopped coriander (cilantro) leaves
vegetable oil, for deep-frying
salt

For the batter
150g / 5oz (1 cup) gram (chickpea) flour
1½ teaspoons ground cumin

Cook the potatoes in a pan of boiling water for about 20 minutes, or until soft, then drain and allow to cool. When the potatoes are cool, peel off their skins, return to the pan and mash.

Heat the oil in a pan, add the garlic paste and fry for about 2 minutes. Add the remaining ingredients except the oil for deep-frying and cook for another 2 minutes. Remove from the heat, mix in the mashed potatoes, then divide the mixture into 12 walnut-sized balls.

Put the gram flour and cumin in a bowl and mix together, adding enough water to make a thin batter.

Heat enough oil for deep-frying in a kadhai or deep, heavy-based pan to 180°C/350°F, or until a cube of bread browns in 30 seconds. Dip the potato balls in the batter and carefully drop them into the hot oil. Deep-fry until golden brown, then remove with a slotted spoon and drain on kitchen paper (paper towels). You may need to cook the potato balls in batches.

Masala Vada
Fried Lentil Dumplings

Origin Tamil Nadu
Preparation time 20 minutes, plus soaking time
Cooking time 30 minutes
Makes 16

250g / 9oz (1⅓ cups) chana dal, rinsed and drained
1 teaspoon fennel seeds
4 dried red chillies
250g / 9oz (1½ cups) onions, chopped
1 × 1-cm / ½-inch piece fresh ginger, peeled and finely chopped
20–25 curry leaves, finely chopped
vegetable oil, for deep-frying
salt

To serve
chutney of your choice, such as Tamarind & Coriander Chutney (see page 65)

Put the chana dal in a pan, add the fennel seeds and chillies and pour in enough water to cover. Set aside for about 2 hours.

Drain the chana dal, reserving the fennel seeds and chillies, and set aside 50g / 1¾ oz (¼ cup) of the dal. Put the remaining dal, the fennel seeds and red chillies in a blender or food processor and process to make a coarse paste.

Transfer the paste to a bowl and add the onions, ginger, curry leaves and the reserved dal. Season with salt and mix well. Divide the mixture into 16 equal portions. With damp hands, roll into balls and flatten to make 5cm / 2 inch diameter patties.

Heat enough oil for deep-frying in a kadhai or deep, heavy-based pan to 180°C/350°F, or until a cube of bread browns in 30 seconds. Working in batches, add the patties to the hot oil and deep-fry for about 5 minutes, or until golden brown. Remove with a slotted spoon and drain on kitchen paper (paper towels). Serve with chutney.

※ ※

Raj Kachori
Deep-fried Lentil Snacks

Origin Rajasthan
Preparation time 50 minutes, plus rising
and cooling time
Cooking time 30 minutes
Makes 15–20

500g / 1lb 2oz (4 cups) plain (all-purpose) flour

150g / 5oz (¾ cup plus 2 tablespoons) semolina
(farina)

1 teaspoon bicarbonate of soda (baking soda)

3 tablespoons vegetable oil, warmed

100ml / 3½fl oz (½ cup) vegetable oil, for deep-frying

salt

For the filling

125g / 4¼oz (2 small) potatoes, unpeeled

1½ tablespoons chilli powder

5 green chillies, de-seeded and chopped

150g / 5oz (⅔ cup canned/1 cup cooked and drained)
chickpeas (garbanzo beans) (see page 37)

150g / 5oz (¾ cup) whole moong beans, cooked
and drained (see page 326)

1 large sprig coriander (cilantro), leaves only, chopped

For the masala for sprinkling

1 teaspoon dried pomegranate seeds

1 teaspoon icing (confectioners') sugar

1 teaspoon ground cumin

¼ teaspoon rock salt

½ teaspoon amchoor

½ teaspoon ground cloves

To finish

100g / 3½oz (⅓ cup) Raw Tamarind Chutney
(see page 66)

100g / 3½oz (⅓ cup) Mint Chutney (see page 66)

100ml / 3½fl oz (¾ cup) natural (plain) yoghurt,
whisked

Sift the plain flour, semolina, bicarbonate of soda
and a little salt together into a large bowl. Add the
warm oil and enough water to make a stiff dough.
Set aside for about 30 minutes, or until risen.

For the filling, cook the potatoes in a pan of boiling
water for about 20 minutes, or until soft, then drain
and allow to cool. When the potatoes are cool, peel
off their skins, return to the pan and cut into dice.

Put the diced potatoes, chilli powder, chillies,
chickpeas, moong beans and chopped coriander into
a large bowl and mix together.

Put all the ingredients for the masala for sprinkling
in a bowl and mix together, then set aside.

Divide the dough into equal portions and roll into
15–20 balls. Flatten each ball between the palms of
your hands and place a portion of the filling in the
middle. Shape again into balls then, using a rolling
pin, roll into discs of about 10cm / 4 inches diameter.

Heat the oil for deep-frying in a kadhai or deep,
heavy-based pan to 180°C/350°F, or until a cube of
bread browns in 30 seconds. Working in batches,
carefully lower the kachoris into the hot oil and
deep-fry, turning frequently, for about 2–3 minutes,
or until coloured evenly all over. Remove with
a slotted spoon and drain on kitchen paper (paper
towels). Allow to cool.

Pinch a hole in the top of each kachori and stuff it
with the rest of the filling.

To finish, spoon the chutneys and whisked
yoghurt over the top, sprinkle with the masala and
serve immediately.

Rava Sevai Idli
Savoury Steamed Vermicelli Dumplings

Origin Tamil Nadu
Preparation time 45 minutes, plus standing time
Cooking time 30 minutes
Serves 4

3 tablespoons ghee
½ teaspoon chana dal, rinsed and drained
½ teaspoon urad dal, rinsed and drained
½ teaspoon mustard seeds
1 tablespoon vegetable oil, plus extra for oiling
2 onions, chopped
5 cashew nuts, chopped
4 green chillies, de-seeded and chopped
½ teaspoon Ginger Paste (see page 57)
60g / 2oz (½ cup) vermicelli (thick sevai), broken into 1-cm / ½-inch pieces
200g / 7oz (1 cup) fine semolina (semolina flour)
175ml / 6fl oz (¾ cup) natural (plain) yoghurt
½ teaspoon bicarbonate of soda (baking soda)
½ bunch coriander (cilantro) leaves, chopped
juice of ½ lime
salt

Heat the ghee in a frying pan (skillet), add the dals and mustard seeds and fry for about 1 minute, or until they turn dark brown. Transfer to a large bowl and set aside

Heat the oil in a large pan, add the onions, cashew nuts and chillies, and stir-fry for about 2 minutes. Add the ginger paste, vermicelli and semolina and stir-fry for a further 2 minutes. Remove from the heat and slowly add the yoghurt, bicarbonate of soda, coriander, lime juice and season with salt. Mix well, then add this mixture to the dals and set aside for about 30 minutes.

Oil idli moulds with a little oil and pour a ladleful of the mixture into them. Steam in a steamer or pressure cooker for about 8–10 minutes, or until cooked. To check if the idlis are done, insert a cocktail stick (toothpick) into the middle and if it comes out clean, they are cooked. If using a pressure cooker, don't apply the weight or whistle. Carefully remove from the steamer and cool for 1–2 minutes.

If you don't have idli moulds then use small heatproof bowls, such as ramekins. Oil them lightly before filling them with the batter and steaming them in either a double boiler or an egg poacher.

Paitham Parappu Idli
Steamed Green Lentil Dumplings

Origin Andhra Pradesh/Tamil Nadu
Preparation time 25 minutes, plus soaking and fermenting time
Cooking time 20 minutes
Serves 4

200g / 7oz (1 cup) basmati rice, rinsed and drained
100g / 3½oz (½ cup) moong dal, rinsed and drained
100g / 3½ oz (½ cup) urad dal, rinsed and drained
4 tablespoons pressed rice, rinsed and drained
85g / 3oz (1 cup) grated fresh coconut
2–3 green chillies, de-seeded and finely chopped
1 × 2.5-cm / 1-inch piece fresh ginger
2 tablespoons chopped coriander (cilantro) leaves
vegetable oil, for oiling
salt

Soak the rice and lentils in 2 separate large bowls of water for 1 hour.

Drain the rice, transfer to a blender or food processor and process, gradually adding about 125ml / 4½fl oz (½ cup) water to make a coarse batter. Transfer to a bowl.

Drain the lentils, transfer to a blender or food processor and process until almost smooth but still a little grainy. Add the pressed rice, coconut, chillies, ginger and coriander leaves and process, gradually adding 4 tablespoons water to make a smooth batter. Combine both batters, season with salt and set aside to ferment for about 4 hours. The batter should be of a thick pouring consistency, so add a little more water, if necessary.

Oil idli moulds with a little oil and pour 4 tablespoons of the batter into them. Steam in a steamer or pressure cooker for about 20 minutes, or until cooked. To check if the idlis are done, insert a cocktail stick (toothpick) into the middle and it comes out clean, they are cooked. If using a pressure cooker, don't apply the weight or whistle. Carefully remove from the steamer and allow to cool for 1–2 minutes.

If you don't have idli moulds then use small heatproof bowls, such as ramekins. Oil them lightly before filling them with the batter and steaming them in either a double boiler or an egg poacher.

✳ ✳
___

Masala Idli
Spicy Steamed Rice Dumplings

Origin Tamil Nadu
Preparation time 20–30 minutes, plus soaking
and fermenting time
Cooking time 40 minutes
Serves 4–6

360g / 12½oz (2 cups) parboiled rice, rinsed and
   drained

200g / 7oz (1 cup) urad dal, rinsed and drained

4 tablespoons chana dal, rinsed and drained

128g / 4½oz (1½ cups) grated fresh coconut

1 × 2.5-cm / 1-inch piece fresh ginger, peeled
   and grated

4 green chillies, de-seeded and chopped

3 tablespoons chopped coriander (cilantro) leaves

vegetable oil, for oiling

salt

For the tempering

2 teaspoons vegetable oil

1 teaspoon mustard seeds

1 teaspoon cumin seeds

½ teaspoon asafoetida

1 sprig curry leaves

Soak the rice and urad dal in 2 separate bowls of
water for 6 hours.

Drain the rice, transfer to a blender or food
processor and process, gradually adding 375ml /
13fl oz (1½ cups) water to make a coarse batter.
Transfer to a bowl.

Drain the urad dal, transfer to a blender or food
processor and process, gradually adding 250ml / 8fl oz
(1 cup) water to make a smooth batter. Combine both
batters, season with salt and set aside to ferment for
10 hours. The batter should be thicker than dosai
batter, but of a pouring consistency, so add a little
more water if necessary.

An hour before cooking, soak the chana dal in
a bowl of water. Drain well and add to the
batter, then stir in the coconut, ginger, chillies
and coriander leaves.

Heat the 2 teaspoons oil for tempering in a small,
heavy-based frying pan (skillet), add the mustard
and cumin seeds, asafoetida and curry leaves and
stir-fry for 1 minute, or until the mustard seeds
start spluttering. Stir the contents of the pan into
the batter.

Oil idli moulds with a little oil and pour 4 tablespoons
of the batter into them. Steam in a steamer or
pressure cooker for about 15–20 minutes, or until
cooked. To check if the idlis are done, insert
a cocktail stick (toothpick) into the middle and it it
comes out clean, they are cooked. If using a pressure
cooker, don't apply the weight or whistle. Carefully
remove from the steamer and allow to cool for
1–2 minutes.

If you don't have idli moulds then use small heatproof
bowls, such as ramekins. Oil them lightly before
filling them with the batter and steaming them in
either a double boiler or an egg poacher.

※ ※ / 📷 p.121

Pao Bhaji
Mini Loaves with Tangy Vegetables

Origin Maharashtra
Preparation time 25 minutes, plus cooling time
Cooking time 20 minutes
Makes 6

1kg / 2¼lb (7 medium) potatoes, unpeeled
2 teaspoons Garlic Paste (see page 57)
180g / 6oz (¾ cup) ghee or vegetable oil
360g / 12½oz (2 cups) tomatoes, chopped
160g / 5½oz (1 cup) onions, chopped
6 green chillies, de-seeded and chopped
1 × 4-cm / 1½-inch piece fresh ginger, peeled and finely chopped
1½ teaspoons ground turmeric
1 teaspoon chilli powder
180g / 6oz (¾ cup / 1½ sticks) butter
2 teaspoons Garam Masala (see page 31)
2 tablespoons chopped coriander (cilantro) leaves
3 tablespoons lemon juice
12 Pav (mini bread loaves)
salt

Cook the potatoes in a pan of boiling water for about 20 minutes, or until soft, then drain and allow to cool. When the potatoes are cool, peel off their skins, return to the pan and mash.

Put the garlic and ginger pastes in separate bowls and stir in 125ml / 4½fl oz (½ cup) water. Set aside.

Heat the ghee or oil in a heavy-based frying pan (skillet), add the tomatoes, onions, chillies, ginger and turmeric and stir-fry over medium heat for about 4–5 minutes. Reduce the heat, add the mashed potatoes, chilli powder and salt, mix thoroughly and continue to cook, mashing and stirring for about 5 minutes. Add the garlic and ginger paste mixtures, then increase the heat, add 4 tablespoons butter and mix well. Sprinkle the garam masala, chopped coriander and lemon juice over and stir well.

Slice the pav in half. Heat the remaining butter in a pan and, when melted, add the pav halves and fry until light brown. Remove from the pan and serve with the mashed vegetables.

Undrally
Steamed Rice Balls

Origin Tamil Nadu
Preparation time 20 minutes, plus cooling time
Cooking time 10 minutes
Serves 8

225g / 8oz (1 cup) rice, rinsed and dried
120g / 4oz (⅔ cup) chana dal, rinsed and drained
salt

To serve

Raw Tamarind Chutney (see page 66)

Put the rice in a blender or food processor and process until finely ground and the rice resembles semolina. Transfer to a large pan, pour in about 475ml / 16fl oz (2 cups) water (twice the amount of water to rice) and bring to the boil. Season with salt, then reduce the heat and cook over low heat, stirring constantly, for about 5 minutes, or until the rice is cooked. Remove from the heat and put the rice on a wide plate.

Cook the chana dal in another pan of boiling water for about 10 minutes, or until slightly soft, then drain and allow to cool.

Add the chana dal to the cooked rice and mix well. Using your hands, shape the mixture into lemon-sized balls. Transfer the balls to a steamer and cook for 5 minutes. If you don't have a steamer, use a large pan with a lid and place a trivet or upside-down plate in the base. Pour in enough water so it stays below the top of the trivet and cover with the lid. Place the balls on a plate and carefully put on top of the trivet or upside-down plate. Serve with Raw Tamarind Chutney and a raita.

Cheela
Vegetarian Pancakes

Origin Delhi/Punjab/Awadh
Preparation time 20 minutes
Cooking time 15 minutes
Serves 4

250g / 9oz (2¾ cups) gram (chickpea) flour
1 medium-sized tomato, finely chopped
4–6 green chillies, de-seeded and finely chopped
1 teaspoon cumin seeds
½ bunch coriander (cilantro) leaves, chopped
125ml / 4½fl oz (½ cup) vegetable oil, for frying
salt

Put the flour in a large bowl and stir in enough water to make a smooth batter. It should have a thin pouring consistency. Add the tomato, chillies, cumin seeds and chopped coriander. Season with salt and beat lightly with a fork for 1 minute.

Heat 1 tablespoon oil in a non-stick frying pan (skillet). When hot, pour in a ladleful of the batter and tilt the pan slightly to spread it over the base into a circular pancake. Fry for about 2 minutes, or until brown on one side, then turn the pancake over, adding more oil if required and fry for a further 2 minutes, or until brown. Remove from the pan and keep warm in a low oven. Make the others in the same way, adding more oil as needed.

Dibba Roti
Thick Pancakes

Origin Hyderabad
Preparation time 15 minutes, plus soaking time
Cooking time 40 minutes
Serves 4

200g / 7oz (1 cup) urad dal, rinsed and drained
400g / 14oz (2 cups) rice, rinsed and drained
1 tablespoon ground cumin, roasted
vegetable oil, for oiling
salt
spicy chutney, such as Ginger Chutney (see page 64)

Soak the urad dal in a large bowl of water for 2 hours, then drain the dal and transfer to a blender or food processor. Process until coarsely ground, then set aside.

Put the rice in a blender or food processor and process until ground, then transfer to a large bowl and add the dal and cumin. Mix, and add enough hot water to make a batter. Season with salt.

Oil a curved, deep tawa or a heavy-based frying pan (skillet) and heat it. When hot, pour in a ladleful of the batter and spread it over the base. Cook over a low heat for about 2 minutes, or until golden brown, then flip the pancake over and cook the other side for a further 2 minutes, or until done. The pancake will be thicker in the middle. Transfer to a serving plate and serve hot with a spicy chutney. Make the others in the same way.

Dosa
Savoury Rice Pancakes

Origin Tamil Nadu/Karnataka/Kerala
Preparation time 30 minutes, plus soaking
and standing time
Cooking time 20 minutes
Serves 4

350g / 12oz (2 cups) parboiled rice
700g / 1lb 8½oz (3¾ cups) basmati rice, rinsed
¼ teaspoon fenugreek seeds
1 tablespoon pressed rice (optional)
250g / 9oz (1⅓ cups) urad dal, rinsed and drained
¼ teaspoon baking powder
250g / 9oz (1 cup) ghee
salt

To serve

savoury potatoes
chutney, such as Coconut Chutney (see page 67)
Sambhar (see page 543)

Soak the parboiled rice and basmati rice in a large
bowl of water for 10 hours. Drain the rice, then rinse
in cold water and transfer to a blender or food
processor with the fenugreek seeds and process to
make a very fine paste. If you prefer a softer dosa,
then add the pressed rice with the fenugreek seeds
in the blender.

Meanwhile, soak the urad dal in a separate bowl of
water to cover for about 4–5 hours. Drain, place in
a blender or food processor and process to make
a very fine paste. Transfer to a large bowl and add
the ground rice. Mix together and season with salt.
Cover and allow to stand overnight. The mixture is
left to ferment, so leave it in a warm place.

The next day, mix in the baking powder and beat the
mixture until it is a very smooth, fluffy batter.

Heat a very smooth flat tawa or a non-stick frying
pan (skillet) and sprinkle a few drops of water on it.
When the tawa dries, add a little ghee or oil, then
pour over a ladleful of the batter and spread it out
to make a round thin pancake. Fry on one side for
about 2–3 minutes, or until golden brown, very lacy
around the edges and thicker in the centre. A dosa
can be soft like a pancake or crisp. Transfer to
a serving plate. Dosas are usually served hot with
savoury potatoes, chutney and Sambhar. Make the
others in the same way.

Pesarattu
Spicy Lentil Pancakes

Origin Andhra Pradesh
Preparation time 20 minutes, plus soaking time
Cooking time 15 minutes
Serves 4

250g / 9oz (1⅓ cups) moong dal, rinsed and drained
1 teaspoon chopped fresh ginger
4 green chillies, de-seeded
2 onions, sliced
½ teaspoon ground cumin
½ bunch coriander (cilantro) leaves, chopped
250ml / 8fl oz (1 cup) vegetable oil
salt

To serve

Sambhar (see page 543)
pickle, such as Tomato Pickle (see page 31) or Mint
    or Raw Tamarind Chutney (page 66)

Soak the moong dal in a bowl of water for 2–3 hours.

Drain the dal, reserving 250ml (8fl oz/1 cup) of the
water, and transfer the dal to a blender or food
processor. Add the ginger and chillies and season
with salt, then process to make a paste. Put the
paste in a bowl and mix in enough of the reserved
water to make a thick batter.

Put the sliced onion in a separate bowl, add the
ground cumin and chopped coriander and set aside.

Heat a frying pan (skillet) and, when hot, pour in
1 teaspoon of the oil. Pour 1 ladleful of the batter
into the frying pan and spread it out like a thin
pancake, then pour ½ teaspoon of the oil around the
edges and cook over medium heat for about
2 minutes, or until golden brown. Sprinkle some of
the chopped onion mixture in the middle of the
pancake and spread it around. When the pancake is
well cooked, add a little more oil and fry for
a further 1 minute, or until the edges are crispy. Fold
the pancake in half, remove from the pan and keep
warm in a covered dish. Make the others in the same
way. Serve hot with Sambhar and any pickle, or Mint
or Raw Tamarind Chutney.

Rava Dosa
Semolina Pancakes

Origin Tamil Nadu/Karnataka
Preparation time 20–25 minutes, plus standing time
Cooking time 15 minutes
Serves 4

125g / 4½oz (1 cup) plain (all-purpose) flour
35g / 1¼oz (¼ cup) rice flour
100g / 3½oz (½ cup) fine semolina (semolina flour)
125ml / 4½fl oz (½ cup) buttermilk
½ teaspoon melted butter
½ onion, chopped
2 green chillies, de-seeded and chopped
¼ teaspoon cumin seeds
salt
vegetable oil, for frying

To serve

Coconut Chutney (see page 67)
Sambhar (see page 543)

Put the flours and semolina in a large bowl and mix together. Add the buttermilk, melted butter, onion, chillies and cumin seeds and stir to combine. Season with salt then set aside for 20 minutes.

Put the mixture in a blender or food processor and process, until very fine, smooth and fluffy, adding water as required to make a batter. Transfer the puréed mixture to a clean bowl and allow to stand for 12 hours. If the mixture thickens a little on standing, stir through a little water to thin it out.

Oil a tawa or heavy-based frying pan (skillet) and heat it. When hot, add 1 teaspoon oil and pour in a ladleful of the dosa batter, spreading it all around like a thin pancake. Reduce the heat slightly and fry for 2 minutes on both sides, or until the dosa becomes crisp around the edges and golden brown. If the dosa is sticking to the pan, pour a little amount of oil around the edges. Fold 2 sides inwards and transfer to a serving plate. The dosas must be served hot with Coconut Chutney and piping hot Sambhar. Make the others in the same way.

Tapala Chakku Athi
Rice & Lentil Pancakes

Origin Andhra Pradesh
Preparation time 45 minutes, plus soaking time
Cooking time 30 minutes
Serves 4

250g / 9oz (1⅓ cups) basmati rice, rinsed and drained
125g / 4¼oz (⅔ cup) chana dal, rinsed and drained
250g / 9oz (2⅔ cups) desiccated (dried flaked) coconut
250ml / 8fl oz (1 cup) vegetable oil
salt

For the tempering

1 teaspoon vegetable oil, for frying
1 teaspoon cumin seeds
1 teaspoon mustard seeds
4 curry leaves
3 dried red chillies
½ teaspoon urad dal, rinsed and drained
pinch of asafoetida

Put the rice and chana dal in a large bowl, pour in 250ml / 8fl oz (1 cup) water and soak for 1 hour. Drain, then transfer to a blender or food processor, add the coconut and about 250ml / 8fl oz (1 cup) water. Process to make a smooth paste, then transfer to a bowl and set aside.

Heat 1 teaspoon oil in a small, heavy-based frying pan (skillet), add all the ingredients for the tempering and stir-fry for 1 minute, or until they are dark brown. Blend with the ground rice and lentil mixture.

Heat 1 teaspoon oil in a non-stick frying pan over low heat. Pour a ladleful of the mixture into the frying pan. Spread it over the base like a pancake and fry for about 2 minutes, or until golden brown. Flip it over with a spatula and fry the other side for a further 1 minute, or until golden brown. Transfer to a serving plate and repeat with rest of the mixture.

Masala Dosa
Spicy Stuffed Pancakes

Origin Tamil Nadu
Preparation time 30 minutes, plus soaking and fermenting time
Cooking time 30 minutes
Serves 6–8

For the dosai

600g / 1lb 5oz (3¼ cups) basmati rice, rinsed
    and drained

200g / 7oz (1 cup) urad dal, rinsed and drained

250g / 9oz (4 small) potatoes, unpeeled

2 tablespoons vegetable oil

1 teaspoon mustard seeds

1 teaspoon chana dal

10–12 curry leaves

1 onion, sliced

1 teaspoon chilli powder

1 teaspoon ground turmeric

1 tablespoon lemon juice

250g / 9oz (1 cup) ghee or vegetable oil, for frying

salt

To serve

Coconut Chutney (see page 67)

Sambhar (see page 543)

Soak the rice and urad dal in 2 large bowls of water overnight. Drain the rice and lentils separately, then transfer the rice to a blender or food processor and process until ground. Transfer to a clean bowl. Do the same with the lentils, then add the ground rice and mix together. Season with salt, cover with a damp cloth and allow to ferment overnight.

The next day, cook the potatoes in a pan of boiling water for about 15 minutes, or until soft, then drain and allow to cool. When the potatoes are cool, peel off their skins, return to the pan and mash.

To prepare the filling, heat the oil in a pan add the mustard seeds, chana dal and curry leaves and stir-fry for about 3 minutes. Add the onion and fry for about 2 minutes, then add the chilli powder and turmeric and cook for a further 2–3 minutes. Finally, add the mashed potatoes and stir to combine.

When you are ready to cook the dosas, add enough water to the rice and lentil paste to make a batter of thick pouring consistency.

Heat a large, non-stick flat tawa, pan or a cast-iron griddle and brush it lightly it with a little ghee or oil. Pour in 2 tablespoons of the dosa batter and quickly spread it evenly into a circle of about 15cm / 6 inches diameter. Flatten the surface with the back of a ladle then pour a little oil around the edges of the dosa so it does not stick to the pan. Cover the pan for 1 minute, or until crisp and golden, then flip it over to cook the other side. Transfer to a serving plate, place some of the filling in the centre and fold the dosa in half. The dosas must be served hot with Coconut Chutney and piping hot Sambhar. Make the others in the same way.

Utthapam
Vegetable Pancakes

Origin Tamil Nadu/Karnataka
Preparation time 30 minutes, plus standing time
Cooking time 15 minutes
Serves 4

4 green chillies, de-seeded and chopped

3 medium-sized tomatoes, chopped

1 teaspoon chopped coriander (cilantro) leaves

1 medium-sized onion, chopped

100g / 3½oz (½ cup) semolina (farina)

125ml / 4½fl oz (½ cup) natural (plain) yoghurt

vegetable oil, for frying

salt

Put the chillies, tomatoes, coriander and onions into a bowl and mix together.

Put the semolina and yoghurt in another bowl and mix together. Season with salt and stir in enough water to make a smooth mixture. Let the mixture stand for about 30 minutes.

Heat a frying pan (skillet) and add a very small amount of oil. Pour 2 tablespoons of the semolina mixture into the pan and spread it over the base into a thick pancake. Sprinkle a spoonful of the chopped onion mixture lightly over the pancake and cover the pan. Cook for about 2 minutes, then remove the cover and turn the pancake over, adding a little more oil and cook for a further 2 minutes, or until browned. Transfer to a serving plate and make more pancakes in the same way.

Paper Dosa
Crisp Wafer-thin Pancakes

Origin Tamil Nadu
Preparation time 20 minutes, plus soaking and standing time
Cooking time 10 minutes
Serves 4

150g / 5oz (¾ cup) basmati rice, rinsed and drained
150g / 5oz (¾ cup) urad dal, rinsed and drained
1 teaspoon fenugreek seeds
ghee or vegetable oil, for frying
salt

To serve

Coconut Chutney (see page 67)
Sambhar (see page 543)

Put the rice in a blender or food processor and process to make a thick, grainy paste. Transfer the paste to a bowl, add enough water to cover and soak overnight. Put the urad dal in a separate bowl, pour in enough water to cover and soak overnight.

The next day, drain the urad dal and transfer to a blender or food processor. Add the fenugreek seeds and process to make a fine paste. Mix the 2 pastes together and allow the mixture to stand overnight. Season with salt.

Heat a large, non-stick frying pan (skillet) or a large, flat tawa or griddle over medium heat. Pour 1 ladleful of the batter into the centre of the pan and spread it out in a circular motion with the back of the ladle to a thin layer. Cook for about 2 minutes, or until dry, then spread some ghee or oil in the centre and along the sides and cook for a further 2 minutes, or until the dosa is golden brown and crisp. Roll it up and transfer to a serving plate. The dosas must be served hot with Coconut Chutney and piping hot Sambhar. Make the others in the same way.

Saboodana Utthapam
Sago Pancakes with Chopped Greens

Origin Tamil Nadu
Preparation time 30 minutes, plus soaking time
Cooking time 15 minutes
Serves 6

75g / 2½oz (½ cup) sago
250ml / 8fl oz (1 cup) natural (plain) yoghurt
300g / 10½oz (2 cups) rice flour
1 onion, sliced
4 curry leaves, chopped
6 green chillies, de-seeded and chopped
1 bunch coriander (cilantro) leaves, chopped
125ml / 4½fl oz (½ cup) vegetable oil
salt

Soak the sago and yoghurt in a bowl of water for about 2 hours.

Add the rice flour, onion, curry leaves, chillies and coriander to the sago and yoghurt mixture, then season with salt and add enough water to make a batter of pouring consistency.

Heat a little oil in a frying pan (skillet) over medium-low heat and pour a ladleful of the batter into the frying pan. Spread it over the base like a pancake and fry for about 2 minutes, or until golden brown. Flip it over with a spatula and fry the other side for a further 2 minutes, or until golden brown. Transfer to a serving plate and repeat with rest of the mixture.

Mysore Masala Dosa
Rice Pancakes from Mysore

Origin Karnataka
Preparation time 1 hour, plus soaking, fermenting and cooling time
Cooking time 15 minutes
Serves 4

200g / 7oz (1 cup) basmati rice, rinsed and drained

135g / 4½oz (¾ cup) parboiled rice, rinsed

4 tablespoons urad dal, rinsed and drained

4 tablespoons chana dal, rinsed and drained

2 teaspoons fenugreek seeds

70g / 2½oz (⅓ cup) pressed rice

vegetable oil, for shallow-frying

salt

For the tempering

1 tablespoon vegetable oil

1 teaspoon mustard seeds

½ teaspoon cumin seeds

½ teaspoon asafoetida

1 dried red chilli, halved

½ teaspoon urad dal

1 sprig curry leaves

For the filling

3 medium-sized potatoes, unpeeled

120g / 4oz (¾ cup) peas, shelled if fresh

2 medium onions, finely chopped

1 × 2.5-cm / 1-inch piece fresh ginger, peeled and grated

3 green chillies, de-seeded and finely chopped

2 tablespoons chopped mint leaves

½ teaspoon ground turmeric

1 teaspoon salt, or to taste

1 tomato, chopped

To serve

4–6 tablespoons Coconut Chutney (see page 67)

120g / 4oz (½ cup / 1 stick) butter

Soak the basmati rice and parboiled rice in a large bowl of water for 6 hours. At the same time, soak both lentils and the fenugreek seeds in another large bowl of water for 6 hours.

Drain the rice and transfer to a blender or food processor and process, gradually adding 250ml / 8fl oz (1 cup) water, to make a smooth batter.

Drain the lentils, put into a clean bowl and mix in the pressed rice, transfer to a blender or food processor and process, gradually adding 250ml / 8fl oz (1 cup) water, until light and fluffy.

Combine both batters in a large, clean bowl, season with salt and set aside to ferment for 8–10 hours. When ready to cook the dosas, add a little water, if necessary, to make a thick batter of pouring consistency.

For the filling, cook the potatoes in a pan of boiling water for about 20 minutes, or until soft. Drain and allow to cool. When cool, peel off the skins, return to the pan and mash. Cook the peas in a separate pan of boiling water, for 5–7 minutes, or until soft. Drain and set aside.

Heat the oil for tempering in a heavy-based pan, add the remaining ingredients for the tempering and stir-fry for 1 minute, or until the mustard seeds start spluttering. Add the onions, ginger and chillies for the filling and stir-fry for a further 2 minutes. Stir in the mint, turmeric, salt, tomato and 250ml / 8fl oz (1 cup) water, then cover the pan and simmer for about 5 minutes, or until the onions and tomato are soft. Mix in the potatoes and peas. The filling should be dry, so if there is too much water, cook, uncovered, over low heat until all the moisture has evaporated. Remove from the heat and stir in the lime juice.

Heat a tawa, flat griddle or frying pan (skillet) over high heat until it sizzles when a few drops of water are sprinkled on it. Reduce the heat and smear a very thin film of oil evenly over the the tawa. Pour a ladleful of batter into the centre of tawa and spread it out quickly using a circular motion with the back of the ladle to form a 15cm / 6 inch round dosa. Drizzle 1 teaspoon oil around the edges, then increase the heat and cook for about 2 minutes, or until the base is golden brown. Turn the dosa carefully and fry for a further 2 minutes, or until golden brown. Transfer to a serving plate, place a little of the filling in the middle and fold over. Serve hot with a little Coconut Chutney smeared over the top and some butter. Make the others in the same way.

Vendaya Keerai Adai
Rice & Fenugreek Leaf Pancakes

Origin Tamil Nadu
Preparation time 20–30 minutes, plus soaking time
Cooking time 35–45 minutes
Serves 4

100g / 3½oz (½ cup) basmati rice, rinsed and drained

90g / 3¼oz (½ cup) parboiled rice, rinsed and drained

4 tablespoons chana dal, rinsed and drained

2 tablespoons urad dal, rinsed and drained

6 dried red chillies

½ teaspoon asafoetida

85g / 3oz (1 cup) grated fresh coconut

90g / 3¼oz (1½ cups) finely chopped fenugreek
    leaves

vegetable oil, for shallow-frying

salt

Soak the basmati rice and parboiled rice in a large bowl of water for 1 hour. At the same time, soak the lentils in another large bowl of water for 1 hour.

Drain the rice, transfer to a blender or food processor and add the red chillies and asafoetida. Process, gradually adding 3 tablespoons water to make a coarse batter. Transfer to a clean bowl.

Drain the lentils, transfer to a blender or food processor and process, gradually adding 2 tablespoons water to make a coarse batter. Combine the rice and lentil batters and mix in the coconut, fenugreek leaves and season with salt. Stir in a little water, if necessary, to make a thick batter of pouring consistency.

Heat a tawa, flat griddle or frying pan (skillet) over high heat until it sizzles when a few drops of water are sprinkled on to it. Reduce the heat and smear a very thin film of oil evenly over the tawa. Pour a ladleful of the batter into the centre of the tawa and spread it out quickly using a circular motion with the back of the ladle to form a 15cm / 6 inch round adai. Make a hole in the centre and drizzle 1 teaspoon oil around the edges and centre. Cook for about 2 minutes, or until the base is golden. Turn carefully with a spatula and fry the other side for a further 2 minutes, or until crisp and golden. Transfer to a serving plate and serve hot. Make the others in the same way.

Payatham Parappu Dosa
Green Lentil Pancakes

Origin Andhra
Preparation time 30 minutes, plus soaking
and fermenting time
Cooking time 40–45 minutes
Serves 4–6

180g / 6½oz (1 cup) parboiled rice, rinsed and drained

4 tablespoons moong dal, rinsed and drained

2 teaspoons fenugreek seeds, rinsed and drained

1 × 1-cm / ½-inch piece fresh ginger, peeled
    and grated

3–4 green chillies, de-seeded and finely chopped

1 sprig curry leaves

1–2 tablespoons finely chopped coriander
    (cilantro) leaves

1 teaspoon cumin seeds

vegetable oil, for shallow-frying

salt

Soak the rice in a bowl of water for 6 hours. At the same time, soak the lentils and fenugreek seeds in another bowl of water for 6 hours.

Drain the rice, then transfer to a blender or food processor and process, gradually adding 125ml / 4½fl oz (½ cup) water to make a fine batter. Transfer to a clean bowl.

Drain the lentils and fenugreek seeds, transfer to a blender or food processor and process, gradually adding 3 tablespoons water to make a fine batter. Combine the rice and lentil batters and season with salt. Set aside to ferment for 8 hours.

Mix the ginger, chillies, curry leaves, coriander leaves and cumin seeds into the batter, then stir in a little water, if necessary, to make a thick batter of pouring consistency.

Heat a tawa, flat griddle or frying pan (skillet) over high heat until it sizzles when a few drops of water are sprinkled on to it. Reduce the heat and smear a very thin film of oil evenly over the tawa. Pour a ladleful of batter into the centre of tawa and spread it out quickly using a circular motion with the back of the ladle to form a 15cm / 6 inch round dosa. Drizzle 1 teaspoon oil around the edges, then increase the heat and cook for about 2 minutes, or until the base is golden brown. Turn the dosa carefully and fry for a further 2 minutes, or until golden brown. Remove from the pan and serve hot. Make the others the same way.

Malabar Adai
Rice & Lentil Pancakes from Malabar

Origin Kerala
Preparation time 15 minutes, plus soaking time
Cooking time 45–55 minutes
Serves 6–8

180g / 6¼oz (1 cup) parboiled rice, rinsed and drained

70g / 2½oz (⅓ cup) sabut urad, rinsed and drained

70g / 2½oz (⅓ cup) chana dal, rinsed and drained

70g / 2½oz (⅓ cup) toovar dal, rinsed and drained

1 × 2.5-cm / 1-inch piece fresh ginger, peeled and grated

4–6 green chillies, de-seeded and chopped

1 sprig curry leaves

¼ cup fresh coconut, cut into 1-cm / ½-inch cubes

vegetable oil, for shallow-frying

salt

Soak the rice and lentils in 2 separate large bowls of water for 1 hour.

Drain the rice, transfer to a blender or food processor and process, gradually adding about 125ml / 4½fl oz (½ cup) water to make a coarse batter. Transfer to a bowl.

Drain the lentils, transfer to a blender or food processor, add the ginger and chillies and process, gradually adding 250ml / 8fl oz (1 cup) water to make a coarse batter. Combine both batters, then season with salt and add the curry leaves, coconut and a little more water, if necessary, to make a thick batter of pouring consistency.

Heat a tawa, flat griddle or frying pan (skillet) over high heat until it sizzles when a few drops of water are sprinkled on to it. Reduce the heat and smear a very thin film of oil evenly over the tawa. Pour a ladleful of the batter into the centre of the tawa and spread it out quickly using a circular motion with the back of the ladle to form a 15cm / 6 inch round pancake. Make a hole in the centre and drizzle 1 teaspoon oil around the edges and centre. Cook for about 2 minutes, or until the base is golden, then turn carefully with a spatula and fry the other side for a further 2 minutes, or until crisp and golden. Transfer to a serving plate and serve hot. Make the others in the same way.

Verum Arisi Adai
Lacy Rice Pancakes from Palakkad

Origin Tamil Nadu
Preparation time 10–20 minutes, plus soaking and fermenting time
Cooking time 40–45 minutes
Serves 6–8

270g / 10oz (1½ cups) parboiled rice, rinsed and drained

40g / 1½oz (½ cup) grated fresh coconut

vegetable oil, for shallow-frying

salt

Soak the rice in a bowl of water for 6–8 hours.

Drain the rice, transfer to a blender or food processor and process, gradually adding about 250ml / 8fl oz (1 cup) water to make a smooth batter. Transfer to a bowl and season with salt. Set aside to ferment for 6–8 hours.

Stir in the grated coconut. The batter should be of a thin pouring consistency, so add a little more water, if necessary.

Heat a tawa, flat griddle or frying pan (skillet) over high heat until it sizzles when a few drops of water are sprinkled on to it. Reduce the heat and smear a very thin film of oil evenly over the tawa. Trickle a ladleful of the batter along the outer edges of the tawa and continue trickling it inwards to form a wafer-thin, 15cm / 6 inch round adai. Fill any gaps with more batter. Drizzle 1 teaspoon oil around the edges and fry for about 2 minutes, or until the base is golden, then lift the edges carefully and turn the adai over. Cook the other side for 2 minutes, or until crisp and golden. Transfer to a plate and serve hot. Make the others in the same way.

Avasara Adai
Quick Semolina (Farina) & Gram
(Chickpea) Pancakes

Origin Tamil Nadu
Preparation time 20–25 minutes
Cooking time 45–55 minutes
Serves 4–6

400g / 14oz (2¼ cups) semolina (farina)

150g / 5oz (1 cup) gram (chickpea) flour

6–8 tablespoons grated fresh coconut

1 medium-sized onion, finely chopped

2–3 green chillies, finely chopped

1 × 1-cm / ½-inch piece fresh ginger, peeled
and grated

1–2 tablespoons finely chopped coriander
(cilantro) leaves

salt

vegetable oil, for shallow-frying

For the tempering

2 teaspoons vegetable oil

1 teaspoon mustard seeds

1 teaspoon cumin seeds

½ teaspoon asafoetida

5–6 dried red chillies, halved

1 sprig curry leaves

Roast the semolina in a dry frying pan (skillet) over
low heat for about 4 minutes. Transfer to a bowl and
add the flour, coconut, onion, chillies, ginger and
coriander. Season with salt and mix to combine.

Heat the 2 teaspoons oil for the tempering in a small,
heavy-based pan, add the mustard and cumin seeds,
asafoetida, red chillies and curry leaves and
stir-fry for 1 minute, or until the mustard seeds start
spluttering. Stir the contents of the pan into
the semolina mixture, then continue to stir, gradually
adding about 250ml / 8fl oz (1 cup) water to make
a thick batter of pouring consistency.

Heat a tawa, flat griddle or frying pan (skillet) over
high heat until it sizzles when a few drops of water
are sprinkled on to it. Reduce the heat and smear
a very thin film of oil evenly on the tawa. Pour a
ladleful of the batter into the centre of the tawa and
spread it out quickly using a circular motion with the
back of the ladle to form a 15cm / 6 inch round
pancake. Make a hole in the centre and drizzle
1 teaspoon oil around the edges and centre.

Cook for about 2 minutes, or until the base is golden
brown, then turn it over carefully and fry the other
side for a further 2 minutes, or until crisp and
golden. Transfer to a plate and serve hot. Make the
others in the same way.

Plain Utthapam
Savoury Eggless Pancakes

Origin Tamil Nadu
Preparation time 15 minutes, plus fermenting time
Cooking time 10 minutes
Serves 4

500ml / 18fl oz (2¼ cups) Dosai batter (see page 141),
fermented overnight

vegetable oil, for frying

To serve

Coconut Chutney (see page 67)

Sambhar (see page 543)

Make the batter according to the recipe on page 141
and allow to stand overnight.

The next day, heat the oil in a non-stick frying pan
(skillet) over medium-low heat and pour a ladleful of
the batter into the frying pan. Spread it over the base
like a pancake and fry for 2 minutes, or until golden
brown. Flip it over with a spatula and fry the other
side for 2–3 minutes, or until golden brown. Transfer
to a serving plate and repeat with rest of the mixture.
Serve hot with Coconut Chutney and Sambhar.

Idli
Steamed Spongy Cakes

Origin Tamil Nadu
Preparation time 30 minutes, plus soaking time
Cooking time 15 minutes
Serves 6

120g / 4oz (½ cup) urad dal, rinsed and drained

125g / 4¼oz (¾ cup) fine semolina (semolina flour)

135g / 4½oz (¾ cup) parboiled rice

1 teaspoon baking powder

salt

To serve

Sambhar (see page 543)

Karpodi (see page 51)

Soak the urad dal in a bowl of water overnight.

The next day, drain the dal, transfer to a blender or food processor and process to make a smooth paste. Put the ground dal in a clean bowl, add the semolina and set aside overnight.

Meanwhile, soak the rice in another bowl of water for 15 minutes. Drain the rice, transfer to a blender or food processor and process to make a smooth paste. Put the ground rice in a clean bowl and set aside overnight.

The next day, line idli moulds with a damp cloth. Mix the ground dal mixture and rice together. Add the baking powder and season with salt, then whisk for about 2 minutes. Put spoonfuls of the mixture in the prepared idli moulds and steam in a steamer or pressure cooker for 8–10 minutes, or until cooked. To check if the idlis are done, insert a cocktail stick (toothpick) into the middle and if it comes out clean, they are cooked. If you use a pressure cooker, don't apply the weight or whistle.

If you don't have idli moulds then use small heatproof bowls, such as ramekins. Oil them lightly before filling them with the rice and dal mixture and steaming them in either a double boiler or an egg poacher.

Allow to cool for 1–2 minutes, then remove the idlis and serve with Sambhar and karpodi.

Rava Idli
Steamed Semolina Cakes

Origin Tamil Nadu/Karnataka
Preparation time 45 minutes, plus standing time
Cooking time 25 minutes
Serves 4

125ml / 4½fl oz (½ cup) vegetable oil, plus extra
    for oiling

1 tablespoon urad dal, rinsed and drained

1 tablespoon chana dal, rinsed and drained

400g / 14oz (2¼ cups) fine semolina (semolina flour)

250ml / 8fl oz (1 cup) natural (plain) yoghurt

½ teaspoon baking powder

½ teaspoon Ginger Paste (see page 57)

12 curry leaves, chopped

½ teaspoon asafoetida

6 green chillies, de-seeded and chopped

1 teaspoon mustard seeds

salt

Heat the oil in a large pan, add the lentils and semolina and fry for about 2 minutes, or until lightly roasted.

Put the yoghurt, baking powder, ginger paste, curry leaves, asafoetida, chillies, mustard seeds and 250ml / 8fl oz (1 cup) water in a large bowl, season with salt and mix together. Set aside for 30 minutes, then whisk the mixture to make a batter. Set aside for 4–6 hours.

Oil idli moulds with a little oil and pour a ladleful of the batter into them. Steam in a steamer or pressure cooker for about 10–12 minutes, or until cooked. To check if the idlis are done, insert a cocktail stick (toothpick) into the middle and if it comes out clean, they are cooked. If using a pressure cooker, don't apply the weight or whistle. Carefully remove from the steamer and allow to cool for 1–2 minutes.

If you don't have idli moulds then use small heatproof bowls, such as ramekins. Oil them lightly before filling them with the batter and steaming them in either a double boiler or an egg poacher.

Dhokla
Steamed Lentil Sponge Cake

Origin Gujarat
Preparation time 30 minutes, plus soaking
and standing time
Cooking time 50–60 minutes
Serves 4

500g / 1lb 2oz (2⅔ cups) chana dal, rinsed
    and drained

1 × 2.5-cm / 1-inch piece fresh ginger, peeled
    and finely chopped

2 teaspoons lemon juice

2–3 green chillies, coarsely ground

1 teaspoon sugar

1 teaspoon bicarbonate of soda (baking soda)

5 tablespoons vegetable oil, plus extra for oiling

salt

Raw Tamarind Chutney or Mint Chutney
    (see page 66), to serve

For the tempering

10–15 fresh curry leaves

6–7 green chillies, deseeded and finely chopped

2 teaspoons black mustard seeds

Soak the chana dal in a bowl of water overnight.

Drain the dal, then place in a blender or food
processor and process until ground and a soft
dropping consistency.

Oil a 1.5-litre / 2½-pint (6¼-cup) round container, such
as a cake tin (pan), that fits inside a steamer,
then place the tin inside the steamer and heat. If you
don't have a steamer, use a large saucepan or Dutch
oven with a lid and place a trivet or upside-down
plate in the base. Pour in enough hot water to come
half way up the side of the cake tin. Place over
medium heat.

Put the ground dal, ginger, lemon juice, chillies, sugar,
bicarbonate of soda (baking soda), 3 tablespoons oil
and salt to taste in a large bowl, add 250ml / 18fl oz
(1 cup) lukewarm water and mix quickly.

Pour the batter into the heated tin. It should be just
over half full, then carefully cover with a clean cloth
or a round of baking paper (parchment) and put on
the lid. The steamer should remain sealed. Steam for
about 50–60 minutes, or until done. It will be risen
and firm to the touch. Carefully remove the tin from
the steamer and let stand for 15 minutes.

Leave the dhokla (cake) in the container. Cut into
wedges while still warm.

For the tempering, heat the remaining oil in
a heavy-based pan, then when the oil is hot, reduce
the heat, add the curry leaves and stir-fry for
1 minute. Add the green chillies and black mustard
seeds and stir-fry for about 2 minutes, or until the
spices start to crackle. Add 125ml / 4½fl oz (½ cup)
water and pour the mixture on top of the dhokla.
Serve with chutney.

Upama
Semolina (Farina) Snack

Origin Tamil Nadu/Karnataka
Preparation time 20 minutes
Cooking time 15 minutes
Serves 4

½ teaspoon ghee

1 teaspoon ground ginger

4 green chillies, de-seeded and chopped

2 onions, finely sliced

200g / 7oz (1 cup) coarse semolina (farina)

1 bunch coriander (cilantro) leaves, chopped

juice of 1 lime

salt

For the tempering

1 tablespoon chana dal, rinsed and drained

1 teaspoon urad dal, rinsed and drained

½ teaspoon mustard seeds

½ teaspoon cumin seeds

6 cashew nuts

Heat half the ghee in a medium-sized, heavy-based
frying pan (skillet), add the ginger and stir-fry for
1 minute. Add all the ingredients for the tempering
and stir-fry for about 2 minutes, or until they turn
dark brown. Add the chillies and onions and cook
over low heat for about 4 minutes.

Bring 500ml / 18fl oz (2¼ cups) salted water to the
boil in a pan. Add the semolina to the ingredients in
the frying pan, then, stirring constantly, pour in the
hot salted water. Continue to stir until all the water
is absorbed. Add the rest of the ghee and the
chopped coriander and cook until the ghee has
melted. Remove from the heat, add the lime juice
and serve hot.

Rava Pongal
Semolina & Green Lentil Savoury

Origin Tamil Nadu
Preparation time 20 minutes–1 hour
Cooking time 30 minutes
Serves 4

8 tablespoons ghee
100g / 3½oz (½ cup) moong dal, rinsed and drained
1 teaspoon cumin seeds
1 teaspoon black peppercorns
200g / 7oz (1 cup) fine semolina (semolina flour)
10 cashew nuts, to garnish
salt
1 × 2.5-cm / 1-inch piece fresh ginger, peeled and grated
1 sprig curry leaves
½ teaspoon ground turmeric

Heat a kadhai or heavy-based, deep frying pan (skillet) over medium heat. When hot, add 4 tablespoons ghee, then add the lentils and roast for about 4 minutes. Set the ghee aside in the pan.

Put the cumin seeds and peppercorns into a spice grinder and process until coarsely ground. Alternatively, use a mortar and pestle. Set aside.

Transfer the lentils to a pressure cooker, add 375ml / 13fl oz (1½ cups) water and cook under pressure for 5 minutes. Set aside. Alternatively, put the lentils and water in a pan, bring to the boil, then reduce the heat and cook for about 40 minutes, or until soft.

Heat the reserved ghee in the pan, then add the semolina (farina) and fry for about 1 minute, or until golden. Remove from the pan and set aside. Add a further 2 tablespoons ghee to the pan and heat through. Add the cashew nuts for the garnish and fry for 1–2 minutes, or until golden. Remove from the pan and set aside.

Pour 1 litre / 1¾ pints (4¼ cups) water into the pan. Add 1 teaspoon salt, the grated ginger and bring to the boil, then reduce the heat and gradually add the fried semolina, about 2 tablespoons at a time, stirring vigorously after each addition to blend well and prevent any lumps. Continue to cook, stirring constantly, for 8–10 minutes, or until the water is almost absorbed and the semolina is cooked.

Fold in the cooked lentils, then stir in the curry leaves, turmeric, the coarsely ground cumin seeds and peppercorns and a further 2 tablespoons ghee and remove from the heat. Garnish with the reserved cashew nuts and serve.

Pongal
Pepper-flavoured Porridge

Origin Tamil Nadu
Preparation time 15 minutes
Cooking time 20 minutes
Serves 6

400g / 14oz (2 cups) basmati rice, rinsed and drained
200g / 7oz (1 cup) moong dal, dry-roasted
4 tablespoons ghee
pinch of asafoetida
1 teaspoon mustard seeds
3 dried red chillies
8–10 curry leaves
10–15 cashew nuts
1 teaspoon black peppercorns
juice of 1 lime
salt

Put the rice in a blender or food processor and process until it is coarsely ground and looks like semolina (farina). Transfer the rice to a dry frying pan (skillet) and fry for 2–3 minutes, or until golden. Remove from the heat and set aside.

Put the lentils in a large pan, add enough water to cover, then bring to the boil and cook for about 10–12 minutes, or until soft. Drain, return to the pan and mash with a potato masher or fork. Add the dry-roasted ground rice, season with salt and pour in 1 litre / 1¾ pints (4¼ cups) water. Cook over medium heat for about 15 minutes, or until all the water is fully absorbed.

Heat the ghee in a frying pan, add the asafoetida and other spices and fry for 1 minute, or until fragrant. Add the cashew nuts and peppercorns and fry for a further 2 minutes, or until the nuts are golden. Remove from the heat and pour over the porridge. Add the lime juice before serving hot.

Matthi
Flaky Savoury Biscuits (Crackers)

Origin Punjab
Preparation time 30–35 minutes
Cooking time 40 minutes
Makes 30–35

1kg / 2¼lb (8 cups) plain (all-purpose) flour, plus
    extra for dusting

1 teaspoon salt

250ml / 8fl oz (1 cup) vegetable oil or ghee, plus
    extra for frying

2 tablespoons black peppercorns, coarsely ground

Sift the flour and salt into a bowl, then mix in the
oil or ghee, add the pepper and mix well. Slowly
add enough water to make a stiff dough. Divide the
dough into 16–18 equal portions and roll out each
portion on a lightly floured surface into a thick disc,
about 8cm / 3 inches in diameter. Prick each disc on
one side with a fork.

Heat enough oil or ghee for deep-frying in a kadhai
or deep, heavy-based pan to 180°C/350°F. or until
a cube of bread browns in 30 seconds. Working in
batches, drop 4 discs at a time carefully into the
hot oil and deep-fry, turning frequently, for about
5 minutes, or until golden brown. Remove with
a slotted spoon and drain on kitchen paper (paper
towels). Allow to cool completely, then serve or
store them in an airtight container.

Papri
Gram (Chickpea) Flour Biscuits (Crackers)

Origin Delhi
Preparation time 20 minutes
Cooking time 10 minutes
Makes 20–25

250g / 9oz (1⅔ cups) gram (chickpea) flour, plus
    extra for dusting

pinch of cream of tartar

½ teaspoon chilli powder

pinch of asafoetida

6 fenugreek leaves, finely chopped

2 tablespoons mustard oil, plus extra for oiling

500ml / 18fl oz (2¼ cups) mustard oil,
    for shallow-frying

salt

Mix the flour, cream of tartar, spices and chopped
fenugreek together in a large bowl. Gradually add
enough water to make very stiff dough, then knead
2 tablespoons mustard oil, a little at a time, into the
dough. With oiled hands, roll the dough into a long
rope about 2.5cm / 1 inch in diameter, then cut off
2.5-cm / 1-inch pieces of dough and flatten each into
a circle. Dust the work surface with flour and roll
out the papris as thinly as possible. They should be
15cm / 6 inches in diameter.

Heat the oil for shallow-frying in a large kadhai or
deep, heavy-based pan over high heat. Reduce the
heat and fry the papris, in batches, for about
1–2 minutes, or until cooked through, crisp and pale
golden. Do not allow the biscuits to become too
dark. Remove with a slotted spoon, drain on kitchen
paper (paper towels) and allow to cool. Serve or
store carefully in an airtight container.

Dahi ki Gujiya
Savoury Pastry Crescents

Origin Delhi
Preparation time 30 minutes, plus soaking time
Cooking time 45 minutes
Makes 10–12

For the gujia

200g / 7oz (1 cup) urad dal, rinsed and drained
½ teaspoon bicarbonate of soda (baking soda)
pinch of asafoetida
1 × 5-cm / 2-inch piece fresh ginger, peeled and finely chopped
2–3 green chillies, de-seeded and finely chopped
2 teaspoons finely chopped mint leaves
2 tablespoons raisins or sultanas (golden raisins)
vegetable oil or ghee, for deep-frying
choice of chutney, such as Green Mango Chutney (see page 75) or Mint Chutney (see page 66), to serve

For the spicy yoghurt

2 teaspoons cumin seeds
500ml / 18fl oz (2¼ cups) natural (plain) yoghurt
¼ teaspoon chilli powder
salt

Soak the lentils in a bowl of water overnight.

The next day, drain the lentils, transfer them to a blender or food processor and process them to make a fine paste. Put the paste in a clean bowl and mix in the bicarbonate of soda and asafetida, then whisk the mixture until fluffy.

Mix the ginger, chillies, mint and raisins together in a bowl, then set aside.

Stretch a damp piece of muslin (cheesecloth) over the rim of a glass. Dampen the palms of your hands, shape the mixture into small balls, then flatten lightly on the muslin.

Heat enough oil or ghee for deep-frying in a kadhai or deep, heavy-based pan to 180°C/350°F, or until a cube of bread browns in 30 seconds. Place a small amount of the ginger mixture in the centre and fold over to make a semicircle, using the muslin to help you, then gently press the edges to enclose the filling.

Using a metal spatula or slotted spoon, very carefully and gently slide each gujiya into the hot oil and deep-fry for about 3–4 minutes, or until pale golden. Remove with a slotted spoon and drain on kitchen paper (paper towels). Make the others in the same way.

Put the deep-fried gujiyas in a bowl of warm, salted water and allow to stand for 10 minutes.

Meanwhile, to make the spicy yoghurt, put the cumin seeds in a dry frying pan (skillet) and roast for about 1 minute, or until fragrant, then transfer them to a mortar and pestle or spice grinder and pound or process until ground. Whisk the yoghurt in a bowl, then stir in the roasted ground cumin and chilli powder. Season with salt.

Remove the gujias from the bowl and gently squeeze them with the palms of your hands to extract any excess water. Arrange them in a serving bow and pour the spicy yoghurt over the top. Serve with your choice of chutney.

Dahi Papri ki Chaat
Biscuits (Crackers) in Spicy Yoghurt

Origin Delhi
Preparation time 45 minutes–1 hour
Cooking time 10–15 minutes
Serves 6–8

3–4 teaspoons cumin seeds
250g / 9oz (2 cups) plain (all-purpose) flour, plus extra for dusting
1 teaspoon chilli powder
2 tablespoons ghee, melted
vegetable oil or ghee, for frying
500ml / 18fl oz (2¼ cups) natural (plain) yoghurt
2–3 teaspoons cumin seeds
salt

To serve

Tamarind Chutney (see page 64), Ginger Chutney (see page 64) or Mango Chutney (see page 75)
chopped red chillies
Chaat Masala (see page 31)

Put 1 teaspoon cumin seeds in a dry frying pan (skillet) and roast for about 1 minute, or until fragrant. Transfer to a mortar and, using a pestle, grind to a powder. Set aside.

To make the papri, sift the flour and 1 teaspoon salt together. Add the chilli powder and enough cold water to make stiff dough. Knead thoroughly for about 5 minutes, incorporating the melted ghee into the dough. Roll the dough out thinly on a lightly floured surface and cut out circles 2.5cm / 1 inch in diameter. Prick the papris with a fork.

Heat some oil or ghee in a pan and fry the papris, a few at a time, for about 5 minutes, or until golden brown. Remove and drain on kitchen paper (paper towels) and set aside.

Put the yoghurt in a large bowl and whisk, then add the remaining cumin seeds and season with salt. Set aside.

Just before serving, arrange the papris on a platter, pour the seasoned yoghurt and chutney on top and sprinkle over the ground roasted cumin seeds, red chillies and chaat masala. Serve immediately.

Palakkayalu
Coconut Biscuits (Crackers)

Origin Tamil Nadu/Andhra Pradesh
Preparation time 30 minutes
Cooking time 20 minutes
Makes 20–24

500g / 1lb 2oz (3 cups) rice flour
1 teaspoon sesame seeds
2 tablespoons butter
1 teaspoon chilli powder, or to taste
½ fresh coconut, grated
250g / 9oz (1 cup) ghee
salt

Put the rice flour, sesame seeds, butter and chilli powder into a large bowl. Season with salt and add and 1 tablespoon water. Add the coconut and mix well to make a dough. If it is too dry, add a little more water.

Using your hands, roll the mixture into 20–24 small balls, then flatten them in the palms of your hands to make small rounds.

Heat the ghee in a kadhai or deep, heavy-based pan to 180°C/350°F, or until a cube of bread browns in 30 seconds, then reduce the heat slightly. Working in batches, gently lower the biscuits (crackers) into the hot oil and deep-fry for about 1–2 minutes, or until golden brown. Remove with a slotted spoon and drain on kitchen paper (paper towels).

Allow to cool. These can be stored in an airtight container for 10 days.

☀ ☀

Pani Poori
Puffed Biscuits (Cookies) with Tangy Water

Origin Delhi
Preparation time 50 minutes, plus cooling and standing time
Cooking time 15 minutes
Makes 50

65g / 2½oz (½ cup) wholemeal (whole-wheat) flour, plus extra for dusting	
70g / 2½oz (½ cup) semolina (farina)	
2 tablespoons ghee	
500g / 1lb 2oz (2 cups) ghee or vegetable oil, for deep-frying	
Chaat Masala (see page 31), for sprinkling	
100g / 3½oz (½ cup) Tamarind & Ginger Chutney (see page 65)	
1 quantity Jal Jeera (see page 727)	

For the filling

2 medium-sized potatoes, unpeeled	
120g / 4oz (½ cup) canned chickpeas (garbanzo beans), drained	

To make the filling, cook the potatoes in a pan of boiling water for 15 minutes, or until cooked but still firm. Drain and allow to cool, then peel off the skins and cut into small dice. Set aside.

Sift the flour and semolina together into a large bowl. Add the 2 tablespoons ghee and rub it in with your fingertips, then mix in enough water to make a stiff dough. Cover with a damp cloth and set aside for about 30 minutes.

Pinch off marble-sized pieces of dough and roll out thinly on a lightly floured surface or board into 4-cm / 1½-inch discs.

Heat the ghee or oil in a kadhai or deep, heavy-based pan to 180°C/350°F, or until a small cube of bread browns in 30 seconds, then reduce the heat. Working in batches, deep-fry the discs for about 1–2 minutes, or until they puff up and are golden in colour. Remove as soon as they begin to brown with a slotted spoon, drain on kitchen paper (paper towels) and set aside.

Punch a hole in the top of the discs with your thumb and fill with about ½ teaspoon of the potatoes and ½ teaspoon of the chickpeas. Sprinkle over some chaat masala and pour ½ teaspoon of the chutney over the top. Alternatively, dip the pooris in a pan of cold jal jeera to fill with tangy cumin-mint flavoured water and serve.

☀ / 📷 p.118

Uppu Vada
Sesame Seed & Coconut Balls

Origin Tamil Nadu
Preparation time 30–45 minutes, plus drying time
Cooking time 10 minutes
Serves 10

1kg / 2¼lb (6 cups) rice flour	
100g / 3½oz (½ cup) urad dal, rinsed and drained	
120g / 4oz sesame seeds	
½ fresh coconut, grated	
pinch of asafoetida	
1 tablespoon butter	
vegetable oil, for deep-frying	
salt	

Put the rice flour in a dry frying pan (skillet) and cook for about 30 seconds, or until roasted. Transfer to a bowl and set aside. Put the urad dal in the frying pan and cook for about 1 minute, or until roasted, then transfer to a blender and process until finely ground. Transfer to the rice flour.

Put the sesame seeds in the frying pan and cook for about 30 seconds, or until roasted. Add to the rice flour and urad dal and add the grated coconut, asafoetida and butter. Season with salt and mix, adding enough water to make a soft, pliable dough. Divide the dough into small marble-sized balls and place them on a piece of cloth to dry for about 1 hour.

Heat the oil for deep-frying in a kadhai or deep, heavy-based pan to 180°C/350°F, or until a cube of bread browns in 30 seconds. Working in batches, deep-fry the balls for about 2 minutes, or until they are a medium brown colour. Remove with a slotted spoon and drain on kitchen paper (paper towels). These balls can be kept in an airtight container for a month.

Pappuchakkalu
Savoury Fried Rice Flour Biscuits
(Crackers)

Origin Andhra Pradesh
Preparation time 20–25 minutes, plus soaking time
Cooking time 10 minutes
Makes 12–15

1 teaspoon cumin seeds
1–2 green chillies, de-seeded and chopped
2–4 curry leaves
1 teaspoon moong dal, rinsed and drained
1 teaspoon chana dal, rinsed and drained
150g / 5oz (1 cup) rice flour
4 tablespoons gram (chickpea) flour
1 tablespoon desiccated (dried flaked) coconut
1 teaspoon melted butter
vegetable oil, for deep-frying
salt

Put the cumin seeds, chillies and curry leaves in
a spice grinder, season with salt and process
until coarsely ground. Alternatively, use a mortar
and pestle.

Soak the lentils in a bowl of water for about
10 minutes. Drain and put into a clean bowl, then
add the flours, coconut and melted butter. Mix
well, adding enough water to make a dough. Divide
the dough into 12–15 equal portions and roll into
balls, then shape the balls into triangles or rounds
about 6cm / 2½ inches in diameter and about 5mm /
¼ inch thick.

Heat the oil for deep-frying in a kadhai or deep,
heavy-based pan to 180°C/350°F, or until a cube of
bread browns in 30 seconds. Working in batches,
deep-fry the triangles for 3–4 minutes, or until
golden brown on all sides. Remove with a slotted
spoon and drain on kitchen paper (paper towels).
Allow to cool. These can be stored in an airtight
container for 10 days.

Thatte Vada
Rice Flour & Cashew Nut Biscuits
(Crackers)

Origin Tamil Nadu
Preparation time 30–35 minutes
Cooking time 20 minutes
Serves 8

75g / 2½oz (½ cup) urad dal, rinsed and drained
1kg / 2¼lb (6 cups) rice flour, plus extra for dusting
50g / 1¾oz (about ⅓ cup) cashew nuts
75g / 2½oz (¼ cup) ghee
pinch of asafoetida
½ teaspoon ground cumin
pinch of ground black pepper
½ teaspoon chilli powder
vegetable oil, for frying
salt

Put the urad dal on a tawa or flat griddle or in
a dry frying pan (skillet) and fry for about 1 minute,
or until roasted. Transfer to a spice grinder and
process until finely ground.

Put the rice flour on a tawa or flat griddle or in a dry
frying pan and cook for about 1 minute, or until
roasted. Remove from the heat.

Put the cashew nuts into the spice grinder and
process to a coarse powder. Mix the ground
ingredients together in a large dish. Season with salt.

Put the asafoetida in a small bowl, add 1 tablespoon
water and stir until dissolved.

Heat the ghee in a pan, add the ground mixture and
asafoetida mixture and heat through.

Remove from the heat and put the mixture into
a clean bowl. Knead into a dough, adding a little
water, if necessary, then roll out on a lightly floured
surface or board and cut into flat thin 3-cm /
1¼-inch rounds.

Heat the oil for deep-frying in a kadhai or deep,
heavy-based pan to 180°C/350°F, or until a cube of
bread browns in 30 seconds. Working in batches,
deep-fry the rounds for about 2–3 minutes, or until
golden brown. Remove with a slotted spoon and
drain on kitchen paper (paper towels). These biscuits
(crackers) can be stored in an airtight container for
2–3 weeks.

❋ / 📷 p.123

❋❋

Dal ki Kachori
Lentil-filled Puffed Bread

Origin Delhi
Preparation time 30 minutes, plus soaking
and standing time
Cooking time 30 minutes
Serves 4

120g / 4 oz (⅔ cup) urad dal, rinsed and drained

1 teaspoon red chilli powder

1 teaspoon peppercorns, coarsely crushed

1 teaspoon coriander seeds

1 tablespoon self-raising flour

4 tablespoons vegetable oil

500ml / 18fl oz (2¼ cups) vegetable oil for shallow-frying

salt

Soak the urad dal in a bowl of water overnight.

Drain the urad dal, transfer to a blender or food
processor and process to make a coarse paste.
Mix in the chilli powder, peppercorns and coriander
seeds, and season with salt. Set aside.

Using your hands, mix the flour and oil together in
a large bowl. Slowly add enough water to make
a stiff dough. Knead thoroughly and then set aside
for 1 hour.

Knead the dough again, then divide it into 12–14
equal-sized portions, roll into balls, then make
a slight depression in the centre and fill with a little
of the dal paste. Cover the dal paste completely
with the dough and flatten the dough between the
palms of your hands. Roll the bread lightly on
a board until it is about 8cm / 3 inches in diameter.
Repeat until all the dough and dal paste are used up.

Heat the oil for shallow-frying in a kadhai or deep,
heavy-based pan over high heat, then reduce the
heat to low. Working in batches, shallow-fry the
breads for about 2 minutes, or until golden brown,
then turn them over and fry the other side until
golden brown. Remove with a slotted spoon and
drain on kitchen paper (paper towels). Repeat until
all the breads are cooked.

These breads can be eaten either hot or cold and are
good for school lunches, picnics or long journeys.

Chatpate Kulche
Baked Bread with Savoury Topping

Origin Punjab
Preparation time 20 minutes
Cooking time 10 minutes
Serves 2

1 tablespoon vegetable oil

1 large-sized tomato, chopped

1 medium-sized onion, chopped

½ teaspoon ground coriander

½ teaspoon Kashmiri chilli powder

½ teaspoon ground cumin

½ teaspoon Chaat Masala (see page 31)

50g / 1¾oz (¾ cup) button (white) mushrooms,
cut into dice

1 red or green (bell) pepper, chopped

2 kulcha from the baker

salt

chutney, such as Sweet Green Mango Chutney
(see page 75) or pickle, such as Mango Pickle
with Jaggery (see page 77)

Heat the oil in a non-stick frying pan (skillet), add
the tomato and fry for about 5 minutes, or until
most of the moisture has evaporated. Add the onion
together with the ground spices, then season
with salt and stir-fry for a further 1 minute. Add the
mushrooms and continue to cook over high
heat, stirring briskly, for 1–2 minutes. Sprinkle the
chopped (bell) pepper over the top, then remove
from the heat and spread the mixture evenly on
the kulcha. Slice like regular pizza and serve with
a choice of chutney or pickle.

❋ ❋

Bervin Poori
Poori Filled with Black Lentils

Origin Awadh
Preparation time 45 minutes, plus soaking time
Cooking time 10–15 minutes
Serves 4–6

125g / 4¼oz (½ cup) urad dal
1½ teaspoons aniseed
½ teaspoon chilli powder
3 teaspoons coriander seeds, crushed
2 teaspoons finely chopped fresh ginger
2 teaspoons finely chopped coriander (cilantro)
1 quantity Poori Dough (see page 55)
plain (all-purpose) flour, for dusting
vegetable oil, for deep-frying

Soak the urad dal in a bowl of water overnight.

The next day, drain the lentils, place in a food processor and process to make a smooth, stiff paste. Mix in the spices, ginger and chopped coriander. Set aside.

Divide the poori dough into 10 equal portions and shape into small balls. Flatten the dough slightly, then put 1 level teaspoon of the paste into the centre and fold the dough over to enclose the filling completely. Dust each ball with a little flour and, using a rolling pin, roll the balls out carefully into rounds.

Heat enough oil for deep-frying in a kadhai or deep, heavy-based pan to 180°C/350°F, or until a cube of bread browns in 30 seconds. Working in batches, carefully lower the pooris into the hot oil and deep-fry for 1–2 minutes, or until puffed up and golden brown. Remove with a slotted spoon and drain on kitchen paper (paper towels).

❋ / 📷 p.196

Aloo Chholey
Potato & Chickpea (Garbanzo Bean) Snack

Origin Punjab
Preparation time 10 minutes, plus soaking and cooling time
Cooking time 20 minutes–2 hours
Serves 4

200g / 7oz (1 cup) dried chickpeas (garbanzo beans), soaked overnight
500g / 1lb 2oz (3 medium) potatoes, unpeeled
1 teaspoon amchoor
1 teaspoon ground cumin
2 teaspoons ground coriander
1 teaspoon rock salt
½ teaspoon chilli powder
½ teaspoon lemon juice
salt

Drain the chickpeas and cook them in a pressure cooker with 500ml / 18fl oz (2¼ cups) water for about 10 minutes. Alternatively, put the chickpeas in a pan with the water and cook for about 2 hours, or until soft. Drain and set aside.

Cook the potatoes in a pan of boiling water for about 20 minutes, or until soft, then drain and allow to cool. When the potatoes are cool, peel off their skins, return to the pan and cut into dice.

Put the chickpeas, potatoes and all the remaining ingredients in a bowl, the season with salt and mix together.

Aloo Chaat
Piquant Potatoes in Spicy Yoghurt

Origin Delhi
Preparation time 45 minutes, plus cooling time
Cooking time 5 minutes
Serves 4

500g / 1lb 2oz (3 medium) potatoes, unpeeled
2 tablespoons vegetable oil
2 teaspoons ground ginger
1½ teaspoons chilli powder
1½ teaspoons coriander seeds
1 × 2.5-cm / 1-inch piece fresh ginger, peeled and chopped
6 green chillies, de-seeded and chopped
2 teaspoons Chaat Masala (see page 31)
1½ tablespoons lemon juice
1½ tablespoons chopped coriander (cilantro) leaves
salt
1 lemon, cut into wedges, to garnish

Cook the potatoes in a pan of boiling water for about 10 minutes, or until cooked but still firm, then drain and allow to cool. When the potatoes are cool, peel off their skins and cut the potatoes into 2.5-cm / 1-inch cubes.

Heat the oil in a pan, add the potato cubes and stir-fry for about 1 minute over medium heat. Remove from the heat and allow to cool.

When the potatoes are cool, add the remaining ingredients and toss gently, making sure the potatoes are not mashed. Arrange equal portions of the chaat in 4 serving dishes and garnish with lemon wedges.

Aloo ke Khulle
Stuffed Potatoes

Origin Punjab
Preparation time 30 minutes, plus soaking time
Cooking time 15 minutes
Serves 6

12 medium-sized potatoes, unpeeled
vegetable oil, for shallow-frying
100g / 3½oz (½ cup) cottage cheese, drained
100ml / 3½fl oz (½ cup) hung natural (plain) yoghurt (see page 793)
50g / 1¾oz (⅓ cup) carrots, finely chopped
1 teaspoon Chaat Masala (see page 31), plus more for sprinkling
1–2 green chillies, de-seeded and chopped
2 teaspoons chopped coriander (cilantro) leaves
juice of 2 limes
salt

Cook the potatoes in a pan of boiling, salted water for about 20 minutes, or until soft. Drain and allow to cool. When cool enough to handle, peel off the skins.

Heat enough oil for shallow-frying in a kadhai or wok over medium-high heat. Add the potatoes and shallow-fry for about 10 minutes, or until golden brown. Remove and drain on kitchen paper (paper towels).

Put the cottage cheese in a bowl, add the yoghurt and stir to combine.

Cut a thin slice off the top of each potato and set aside. Using a sharp knife, make a hollow in the potatoes, making sure the skin is not punctured, and scoop out the potato flesh into a bowl with a teaspoon. Set the hollows aside.

Season the scooped out potatoes with salt, then add the carrots, chaat masala, chopped chillies, coriander and lime juice. Mix well, then add the yoghurt and cottage cheese mixture and stir until combined. Stuff the potato hollows with the filling, put the reserved potato slice on top and sprinkle over some chaat masala before serving.

☀ / 📷 p.124

Bharwan Phoolgobi
Stuffed Grilled (Broiled) Cauliflower

Origin Punjab
Preparation time 1 hour, plus cooling and
marinating time
Cooking time 8–10 minutes
Serves 4

1 medium-sized head cauliflower
5 peppercorns
3 large cardamom pods
5 small cardamom pods
2 cinnamon sticks, about 2.5cm / 1 inch long
5 cloves
60ml / 2½fl oz (⅓ cup) vegetable oil
2 teaspoons urad dal, ground
1 tablespoon cashew nuts, chopped
1 tablespoon almonds, sliced
4 teaspoons green chillies, de-seeded and chopped
3 tablespoons coriander (cilantro) leaves, chopped
2 tablespoons grated Khoya (see page 58)
1 tablespoon Ginger Paste (see page 57)
1 tablespoon Garlic Paste (see page 57)
1 teaspoon mustard paste
1 teaspoon ground turmeric
1 tablespoon lemon juice
3 tablespoons grated Paneer (see page 59)
100ml / 3½fl oz (½ cup) double (heavy) cream
4 tablespoons natural (plain) yoghurt
1 tablespoon ground white pepper
salt

First, divide the cauliflower into large florets and
cut away as much of the stem as possible without
cutting it all the way through. Put the cauliflowers
into a large pan half filled with water. Add the
peppercorns, cardamom pods, cinnamon sticks and
cloves and bring to the boil. Reduce the heat and
simmer for 7–8 minutes, or until just tender.
Drain and allow to cool, then place, stem-side up,
in a single layer in an ovenproof dish.

Heat the oil in a pan. When hot, add the ground
urad dal and fry for about 1–2 minutes. Transfer it
to a bowl and add the cashew nuts, almonds, half
the chopped chillies, 1½ tablespoons coriander and
the khoya. Season with salt and mix well. Stuff
the mixture inside and all around the cauliflower
and set aside.

Put the ginger and garlic pastes, mustard paste,
turmeric and remaining oil in another bowl. Season
with salt and mix well. Spread the marinade all
around the cauliflower and set aside for 1 hour.

Put the lemon juice, grated paneer, cream, yoghurt,
the remaining chopped chillies, remaining chopped
coriander and the white pepper in another bowl.
Season with salt and mix well. Spread this marinade
over the cauliflower and set aside for a further
1 hour.

Prepare a tandoor for a moderate heat or preheat
the grill (broiler) to medium. Take a metal skewer
and thread the cauliflower pieces on to it, leaving
a 2.5-cm / 1-inch gap in between each piece. Roast
in a moderately hot tandoor or under the grill for
about 8–10 minutes.

Tandoori Bharwan Tamatar
Grilled Stuffed Tomatoes

Origin Punjab
Preparation time 30 minutes, plus cooling time
Cooking time 10 minutes
Serves 4

8 large tomatoes

For the stuffing

2 teaspoons vegetable oil

1 teaspoon cumin seeds

300g / 11oz Paneer (see page 59), cut into cubes

300g / 11oz (2 cups) small boiled potatoes, cut
   into dice

150g / 5oz (1 cup) peas, cooked

3 tablespoons raisins

½ ground turmeric

1 teaspoon chilli powder

salt

For the marinade

2 eggs

100g / 3½oz (⅔ cup) gram (chickpea) flour

pinch of salt

pinch of ajwain seeds

100g / 3½oz (½ cup) hung natural (plain) yoghurt
   (see page 793)

To serve

salad

chutney, such as Tamarind & Ginger Chutney
   (see page 65)

Cut the tops off the tomatoes, scoop out the seeds using a teaspoon, then rinse under cold running water and pat dry with kitchen paper (paper towels).

To make the stuffing, heat the oil in a non-stick pan, add the cumin seeds and fry for about 1 minute, or until they start to crackle, then add the paneer cubes, diced potato, peas, raisins, turmeric, and chilli powder, and season with salt. Stir-fry for 1–2 minutes, then transfer the mixture to a bowl and allow to cool.

Prepare a tandoor or charcoal grill for moderate heat, or alternatively preheat the grill (broiler) to medium. When the stuffing is cool, fill each tomato with the mixture. Replace the tops and individually tie each tomato with a piece of kitchen string (twine).

To make the marinade, mix the eggs, flour, salt, ajwain and hung yoghurt together thoroughly in a large bowl. Coat the tomatoes with the marinade, then thread the tomatoes onto 2 metal skewers, leaving at least a 2.5-cm / 1-inch gap in between. You can also put a cut onion or potato half or at the end to prevent the tomatoes slipping off the skewers. Roast in a tandoor, over a charcoal grill or under a grill for 3–5 minutes, or until the tomatoes are cooked and the filling is piping hot. Serve hot with choice of salad and chutney.

Mysore Bonda
Fried Spicy Onion Snacks

Origin Karnataka
Preparation time 15–20 minutes, plus soaking time
Cooking time 20 minutes
Serves 4

200g / 7oz (1 cup) urad dal, rinsed and drained

1 teaspoon basmati rice, rinsed and drained

2 teaspoons peppercorns

1 onion, chopped

2 green chillies, de-seeded and chopped

1 × 2.5-cm / 1-inch piece fresh coconut, grated

chopped coriander (cilantro) leaves

vegetable oil, for deep-frying

salt

Soak the urad dal and rice in a bowl of water for 3 hours.

Transfer the dal and rice to a blender or food processor, season with salt and process to make a stiff, smooth batter. Add the remaining ingredients, except the oil, and mix well, then shape the batter into lemon-sized balls.

Heat enough oil for deep-frying in a kadhai or deep, heavy-based pan to 180°C/350°F, or until a cube of bread browns in 30 seconds, then reduce the heat to low. Working in batches, deep-fry the bonda for 3–4 minutes, or until golden brown and crisp. Remove with a slotted spoon and drain on kitchen paper (paper towels). Serve hot.

Paneer Jhaal Frazie
Stir-fried Paneer

Origin Awadh
Preparation time 20–30 minutes
Cooking time 10 minutes
Serves 2

100g / 3½oz tofu, cut into medium-sized cubes
100g / 3½oz Paneer (see page 59), cut into medium-sized cubes
1–2 tablespoons vegetable oil
2 dried red chillies
2 green chillies, slit lengthways and de-seeded
2 small carrots, cut into small pieces
1 small head broccoli or cauliflower, cut into florets
½ teaspoon ground coriander
½ teaspoon ground cumin
½ teaspoon Kashmiri red chilli powder
¼ teaspoon ground turmeric
1 large tomato or red (bell) pepper, de-seeded and cut into slices
½ teaspoon lemon juice
salt

Heat a tawa, flat griddle or frying pan (skillet) until hot. Add the tofu and paneer cubes and cook for about 7 minutes, or until golden brown on all sides. Make sure they do not burn.

Heat the oil in a broad, shallow pan, add the red chillies, green chillies, carrots, broccoli or cauliflower, ground spices, the tofu, paneer and the tomato or red pepper and stir-fry over high heat for 3–4 minutes. Toss the vegetables to combine. Season with salt, then sprinkle lemon juice over the top and serve hot.

Lehsuni Paneer Tikka
Garlic-flavoured Paneer

Origin Punjab
Preparation time 20–30 minutes, plus marinating time
Cooking time 6–8 minutes
Serves 4

750g / 1¾lb Paneer (see page 59)
5g / ¼oz (¼ pepper) green chilli, de-seeded
250g / 9oz (1¾ cups) natural (plain) yoghurt, whisked
4 tablespoons double (heavy) cream
5 teaspoons Garlic Paste (see page 57)
6 tablespoons ground coriander
1 tablespoon chilli powder
½ tablespoon ground turmeric
1 tablespoon Garam Masala (see page 31)
1 tablespoon ajwain seeds
1 tablespoon Chaat Masala (see page 31)
4 tablespoons gram (chickpea) flour
1 teaspoon vinegar
2 tablespoons vegetable oil or ghee
salt

For the stuffing

2 tablespoons Tandoori Chaat Masala (see page 51)
2 tablespoons Garlic Paste (see page 57)

Prepare a charcoal grill or preheat the oven to 180°C/350°F/Gas Mark 4, if using. Cut the paneer into cubes and make a deep slit in the centre but do not cut all the way through. Put the chilli in a mortar or small blender and coarsely pound with a pestle or process to make a paste.

To make the stuffing, mix the tandoori masala and garlic paste together in a bowl, then put some of the mixture inside the slit in the paneer and rub some of the mixture on the outside of the paneer; set aside.

Put the whisked yoghurt, cream, chilli, garlic paste, spices, gram flour, vinegar and oil in a large bowl, season with salt to taste and mix thoroughly. Add the paneer to the marinade and set aside for about 2 hours.

Thread the paneer pieces on to 2–4 metal skewers making sure the pieces are about 2.5cm / 1 inch apart. Grill over a charcoal grill or in the preheated oven for about 6–8 minutes.

Tandoori Bharwan Paneer
Grilled Stuffed Paneer

Origin Punjab
Preparation time 35 minutes, plus marinating time
Cooking time 5–7 minutes
Serves 4

500g / 1lb 2oz Paneer (see page 59)
vegetable oil, for shallow-frying
1 tablespoon cumin seeds
1 teaspoon ground turmeric
200g / 7oz (2¼ cups) cabbage, chopped
50g / 1¾oz (⅓ cup) carrots, chopped
1 teaspoon Chaat Masala (see page 31)
1 large sprig coriander (cilantro), chopped
melted butter, for basting
salt

For the marinade

400ml / 14fl oz (3 cups) hung natural (plain) yoghurt (see page 793)
½ tablespoon Ginger Paste (see page 57)
½ tablespoon Garlic Paste (see page 57)
1 tablespoon chilli powder
1 teaspoon Garam Masala (see page 31)
1 teaspoon ground dried fenugreek leaves
1 teaspoon lemon juice
1 tablespoon vegetable oil

To serve

salad
chutney, such as Tomato Chutney (see page 70) or Sweet Green Mango Chutney (see page 75)

Cut the paneer into 5 x 5-cm /2-inch pieces, then cut each piece into 1-cm / ½-inch slices and pat dry with kitchen paper (paper towels). Heat the oil for shallow-frying in a deep, heavy-based pan over medium heat. Add the paneer and shallow-fry for about 10 minutes, or until golden brown. Remove the paneer with a slotted spoon and set aside.

Reheat the oil in the same pan, add the cumin seeds and stir-fry until they begin to splutter. Add the turmeric, cabbage and carrots and fry for about 2–3 minutes.

Season with salt, then add the chaat masala, chopped coriander and cook for another 5 minutes, or until the vegetables are crisp. Remove them from the pan and set aside.

Place the paneer slices on a flat surface or tray and spread the vegetables evenly over each slice, then roll each slice into a cylindrical shape. Secure with cocktail sticks (toothpicks) at both ends to hold the filling in place. Set aside.

To make the marinade, put the hung yoghurt, ginger and garlic pastes, chilli powder, salt to taste, the garam masala, ground fenugreek, lemon juice and the oil in a large shallow dish and mix well. Put the paneer rolls into the marinade and set aside for about 1 hour.

Preheat a tandoor or charcoal grill to a moderate heat, or alternatively preheat the grill (broiler) to medium. Thread the marinated paneer rolls on to metal skewers, leaving a 2.5-cm / 1-inch gap in between each roll. Roast in a moderately hot tandoor, over a charcoal grill or under the grill for 5–7 minutes, basting with melted butter during cooking. Cut each roll in 2–3 slices. Serve hot with a choice of salad and chutney.

✵ / 📷 p.126

Kurugayulu Upama
Savoury Semolina with Vegetables

Origin Tamil Nadu
Preparation time 15–20 minutes
Cooking time 15 minutes
Serves 4

125ml / 4½fl oz (½ cup) vegetable oil
2 medium-sized onions, sliced
1 small sprig curry leaves
6 green chillies, de-seeded and chopped
1 teaspoon Ginger Paste (see page 57)
1 teaspoon Garlic Paste (see page 57)
3–4 cloves
pinch of ground turmeric
75g / 2½oz (½ cup) mixed seasonal vegetables
1 medium-sized tomato, chopped
200g / 7oz (1 cup) fine semolina (semolina flour)
125ml / 4½fl oz (½ cup) natural (plain) yoghurt
1 bunch coriander (cilantro) leaves, chopped
juice of 1 lime
salt

For the tempering

½ teaspoon urad dal, rinsed and drained
¼ teaspoon mustard seeds
¼ teaspoon cumin seeds

Heat the oil in a heavy-based kadhai or wok. Add all the ingredients for the tempering and stir-fry for about 1 minute, or until they start to splutter. Add the onions, curry leaves, chopped chillies, ginger and garlic pastes, cloves and turmeric, season with salt and stir-fry for a further 5 minutes.

Add the mixed vegetables and tomato, then cover with a lid and cook over medium heat for about 5 minutes. Uncover, add the semolina, 375ml /13fl oz (1½ cups) hot water and the yoghurt and stir constantly over the heat for about 3–5 minutes, or until all the moisture is absorbed. Sprinkle over the chopped coriander, then season with salt and add the lime juice. Remove from the heat.

✵

Arisi Upama
Savoury Rice Snack

Origin Tamil Nadu
Preparation time 20–30 minutes, plus soaking time
Cooking time 30 minutes
Serves 6

½ teaspoon asafoetida
400g / 14oz (2¼ cups) coarsely broken rice, rinsed and drained
85g / 3oz (1 cup) grated fresh coconut
1 teaspoon ground black pepper
salt

For the tempering

125ml / 4½fl oz (½ cup) vegetable oil
1 teaspoon mustard seeds
1 teaspoon cumin seeds
1 dried red chilli, halved
2 teaspoons urad dal, rinsed and drained
1 sprig curry leaves

For the dal paste

4 tablespoons toovar dal, rinsed and drained
4 green chillies

Soak the toover dal for the paste in a bowl of water for 15 minutes. Drain the dal, transfer to a blender or food processor, add the chillies and 1 tablespoon water and process to make a paste.

Heat the oil for the tempering in a kadhai or heavy-based, deep frying pan (skillet), add the mustard and cumin seeds, red chilli, urad dal and curry leaves and stir-fry for 1 minute, or until the mustard seeds start spluttering. Add the asafoetida, dal paste and 1 litre / 1¾ pints (4¼ cups) water. Season with salt and bring to the boil.

Stir in the broken rice, reduce the heat, cover and simmer for 15–20 minutes, or until the water is absorbed and the rice is cooked. Stir gently every 5 minutes. Mix in the coconut and pepper and remove from the heat.

Pao Bhaji
Spicy Vegetables with Buttered Bread

Origin New
Preparation time 30–35 minutes
Cooking time 10–15 minutes
Serves 4

6–8 Pav (mini bread loaves)
250g / 9oz (4 small) potatoes, unpeeled
500g / 1lb 2oz (3 medium) tomatoes
100g / 3½oz (⅔ cup) peas, shelled if fresh
100g / 3½oz (7 tablespoons) butter, plus extra to serve (optional)
200g / 7oz (2 cups) cauliflower florets
1 teaspoon chilli powder
1 teaspoon Garam Masala (see page 31)
¼ teaspoon rock salt
½ teaspoon ground coriander
½ teaspoon ground cumin

To garnish

6 green chillies, de-seeded and chopped
1 × 5-cm / 2-inch piece fresh ginger, peeled and sliced
few coriander (cilantro) leaves, chopped
salt

Cut the pav in half.

Cook the potatoes in a pan of boiling water for 20 minutes, or until soft. Drain and allow to cool, then peel off the skins, return to the pan and mash.

Make a small cross in the top of the tomatoes with a knife, then put them in a bowl of hot water and allow to stand for about 5 minutes. Drain and allow to cool slightly, then peel off the skins. Set the tomato pulp aside.

Cook the peas in another pan of boiling water for 5–7 minutes, or until soft.

Heat a large tawa or flat griddle and coat it with a thin film of butter by rotating the slab of butter all over the pan. Once tawa is coated, remove the butter and set aside. Place the sliced pav on it and cook for about 3–4 minutes, or until slightly browned, then remove to a corner of the pan and flatten a little with a spatula.

Return the butter to the tawa or griddle, concentrating half in the centre, where it is hottest, and when very hot, add the tomato pulp, mashed potatoes and other vegetables. Add the ground spices and ontinue to mash with a spatula until extremely well blended. You may decide upon the consistency of the bhaji according to individual taste.

Serve hot, garnished with chillies, ginger and coriander, accompanied with the pav and a small knob (pat) of butter, if desired.

Carrot Bonda
Fried Spicy Carrot Snacks

Origin New
Preparation time 20 minutes, plus soaking time
Cooking time 20 minutes
Serves 4

200g / 7oz (1 cup) urad dal, rinsed and drained
1 teaspoon basmati rice, rinsed and drained
2 teaspoon peppercorns
2 medium-sized carrots, grated
2 green chillies, de-seeded and finely chopped
1 × 2.5-cm / 1-inch piece fresh ginger, peeled and chopped
few coriander (cilantro) leaves, chopped
vegetable oil, for deep-frying
salt

Soak the urad dal and rice in a bowl of water for 3 hours.

Transfer the dal and rice to a blender or food processor, season with salt and process to make a stiff, smooth batter. Add the remaining ingredients, except the oil, and mix well, then shape the batter into lemon-sized balls.

Heat enough oil for deep-frying in a kadhai or deep, heavy-based pan to 180°C/350°F, or until a cube of bread browns in 30 seconds, then reduce the heat to low. Working in batches, deep-fry the bonda for 3–4 minutes, or until golden brown and crisp. Remove with a slotted spoon and drain on kitchen paper (paper towels). Serve hot.

Gobi Tandoori
Grilled (Broiled) Cauliflower

Origin Punjab
Preparation time 20 minutes, plus cooling
and marinating time
Cooking time 10 minutes
Serves 4

1 large cauliflower head, cut into medium-sized florets
6 black peppercorns
2 cinnamon sticks
4 large cardamom pods
4 cloves
375ml / 13fl oz (1½ cups) hung natural (plain) yoghurt (see page 793)
½ tablespoon Ginger Paste (see page 57)
½ tablespoon Garlic Paste (see page 57)
1½ tablespoons yellow chilli powder
vegetable oil, for frying the tumeric
3 tablespoons Garam Masala (see page 31)
1 tablespoon ground turmeric
salt

To serve

green salad
choice of chutney, such as Ginger Chutney (see page 64)

Put the cauliflower florets in a large pan, pour in enough water to just cover, then add the peppercorns, cinnamon sticks, cardamom pods and cloves. Season with salt and blanch the cauliflower for about 5 minutes, or until it is two-thirds cooked. Drain and allow to cool.

Put the hung yoghurt in a large bowl and add the ginger and garlic pastes, chilli powder and garam masala. Season with salt and mix well.

Heat the oil in a pan, add the turmeric and stir-fry for 30 seconds, or until it starts to smell fragrant. Pour into the yoghurt mixture and mix well. Add the cooled cauliflower florets to the marinade and set aside for 1 hour.

Prepare a tandoor or charcoal grill for moderate heat, or alternatively preheat the grill (broiler) to medium. Thread the marinated cauliflower florets through several metal skewers, drizzle the remaining marinade over the top and roast in a tandoor, over a charcoal grill or under the hot grill for 6–8 minutes. Serve hot with choice of salad and chutney.

☀ / 📷 p.193

Khandavi
Gram (Chickpea) Flour Rolls

Origin Gujarat
Preparation time 10–15 minutes, plus setting time
Cooking time 15 minutes
Serves 4

vegetable oil, for greasing
100g / 3½oz (⅔ cup) gram (chickpea) flour
250g / 9oz (1 cup) natural (plain) yoghurt
1 teaspoon Ginger Paste (see page 57)
¼ teaspoon ground turmeric
1 teaspoon green chilli paste
chilli powder, to taste
salt

For the tempering

1 tablespoon vegetable oil
1 teaspoon fenugreek seeds
1 teaspoon cumin seeds
¼ teaspoon asafoetida
2 dried red chillies
1 teaspoon sesame seeds
1 tablespoon curry leaves

Oil a flat tray (baking pan) and set aside.

Put the gram flour, yoghurt, ginger paste, turmeric, green chilli paste, chilli powder and 250ml / 8fl oz (1 cup) water in a bowl. Season with salt and stir until it is a smooth paste. Pour the mixture into a kadhai or wok and cook for about 10 minutes, or until it is thick in consistency, then spread the mixture evenly over the prepared tray (pan) and allow to set.

When the mixture has set, use a rolling pin to roll from one end to other, then cut it into 3-cm / 1¼-inch pieces and set aside.

Heat the oil for the tempering in a small, heavy-based frying pan (skillet), add all the tempering ingredients and stir-fry for 1–2 minutes, or until the spices smell fragrant. Pour the spice mixture over the gram flour pieces and serve.

Puli Bongaralu
Rice Flour & Lentil Snacks

Origin Andhra Pradesh
Preparation time 30–40 minutes, plus standing and soaking time
Cooking time 20 minutes
Makes 30–35

300g / 10½oz (2 cups) rice flour
1 tablespoon chana dal, rinsed and drained
200g / 7oz (1 cup) urad dal, rinsed and drained
2 curry leaves
2 onions, finely sliced
2 green chillies, de-seeded and chopped
1 teaspoon chopped fresh ginger
vegetable oil, for deep-frying
salt

For the tempering

1 tablespoon vegetable oil
½ teaspoon mustard seeds
2 dried red chillies
½ teaspoon urad dal, rinsed and drained
pinch of asafoetida

Put half of the rice flour into a pan and add 1 tablespoon water. Bring to the boil, then remove from the heat and mix with the remaining half of the rice flour. Set aside for 24 hours.

Soak the urad dal in water for 4 hours. Soak the chana dal in another bowl of water for 1 hour. Drain. Drain most of the water from the urad dal, transfer to a blender or food processor and process to make a fine paste. Transfer to a bowl, add the rice flour, curry leaves, onions, chillies, ginger and season with salt. Mix together, then add the chana dal and mix well.

Heat the 1 tablespoon oil for tempering in a small, heavy-based frying pan (skillet), add the mustard seeds, chillies, ½ teaspoon urad dal and asafoetida and stir-fry for about 1 minute, or until dark brown. Remove from the heat and add to the rice flour mixture. Mix well, then shape the mixture into 5-cm / 2-inch rounds about 2cm / ¾ inch thick.

Heat the oil for deep-frying in a kadhai or deep, heavy-based pan to 180°C/350°F, or until a cube of bread browns in 30 seconds. Working in batches, deep-fry the rounds for about 2–3 minutes, or until golden brown. Remove with a slotted spoon and drain on kitchen paper. Allow to cool. This snack will keep for several days in an airtight container.

Moru Kalli
Yoghurt & Rice Flour Savoury

Origin Tamil Nadu
Preparation time 10–15 minutes
Cooking time 15 minutes
Serves 6

5 tablespoons sesame oil
125ml / 4½fl oz (½ cup) sour yoghurt (see page 793), whisked
150g / 5oz (1 cup) rice flour
2 tablespoons chopped coriander (cilantro) leaves
salt

For the tempering

2 tablespoons sesame seed oil
1 teaspoon mustard seeds
1 teaspoon asafoetida
2 dried red chillies, halved
6 green chillies, de-seeded and finely chopped
1 teaspoon urad dal, rinsed and drained
1 sprig curry leaves

Oil a plate, that has a 2.5-cm /1-inch rim with 1 teaspoon oil and set aside.

Whisk the yoghurt with 250ml / 8fl oz (1 cup) water in a bowl. Add the rice flour, a spoonful at a time, beating well between each addition to make a smooth batter without any lumps. Season with salt and stir in the coriander leaves.

Heat the 2 tablespoons oil for the tempering in a kadhai or deep, heavy-based frying pan (skillet), add the mustard seeds, asafoetida, chillies, urad dal, and curry leaves and stir-fry for 1 minute, or until the mustard seeds start spluttering. Pour in 250ml / 8fl oz (1 cup) water and bring to the boil over high heat. Reduce the heat, then pour in the batter and cook over low heat for 5–7 minutes, or until the water is almost absorbed, stirring constantly to prevent lumps. Add 4 tablespoons oil and keep stirring until the mixture leaves the sides of the pan. Pour onto the oiled plate, flatten with a spatula and allow to cool.

Cut into diamond-shaped pieces before serving.

Arisi Pulao
Steamed Rice & Coconut Snacks

Origin New
Preparation time 20–30 minutes
Cooking time 15 minutes
Serves 4

125g / 4oz (¾ cup) rice flour

pinch of salt

125ml / 4½fl oz (½ cup) fresh coconut water
   (see page 781)

40g / 1½oz (½ cup) grated fresh coconut

fresh ripe bananas as required

sugar as required

Mix the rice flour, salt and coconut water together
in a bowl to make a moist but powdery dough.

Fill a tube with 3 spoonfuls of grated coconut, then
dough, then continue to fill alternately until the
dough and coconut are finished. The fillings should
be tight at each step.

Put the lid on and steam in the puttu maker for
7 minutes. Remove from the heat and tilt the
cylindrical-shaped puttu on to a serving plate. Break
the puttu at the coconut joints and eat with bananas
and sprinkle with sugar.

A special pan called a puttu maker is needed to
make these Keralan snacks. The puttu maker comes
in two parts: the lower part is a steamer and the
upper part is a cylindrical tube where the rice and
coconut are placed. The upper portion has
a perforated lid at the bottom where steam rises
up from the steamer and a tight-fitting lid at the top
with small holes to allow the steam to escape.

Saboodana Khichari
Sago Flavoured with Coconut
& Coriander (Cilantro)

Origin Maharashtra
Preparation time 30 minutes, plus soaking time
Cooking time 15 minutes
Serves 6

500g / 1lb 2oz sago

300g / 11oz (2 cups) shelled peanuts

2 tablespoons grated coconut

1 teaspoon cumin seeds

½ teaspoon sugar

2 teaspoons lemon juice

1½ tablespoons ghee or vegetable oil

2 potatoes, finely chopped

4–5 green chillies, finely chopped

3 tablespoons chopped coriander (cilantro) leaves

rock salt

Soak the sago in a large bowl of water for about
2 hours. Drain and set aside.

Heat a kadhai or large wok, add the peanuts and
stir-fry for about 2 minutes, or until roasted.
Transfer the peanuts to a plate to cool, then crush
with a mortar and pestle.

Separate the sago so that it is free of any lumps by
sprinkling over a little water and crumbling the sago
between your fingers. Put the sago in a bowl with
the crushed peanuts, grated coconut, cumin seeds,
sugar and lemon juice and mix well. Season with
rock salt, then set aside.

Heat the ghee or oil in a pan, add the potatoes and
stir-fry over medium heat for about 8 minutes, or
until they become soft. Add the chillies and continue
to stir-fry for about 1 minute. Reduce the heat to low,
add the sago mixture and stir to blend. Sago is
sensitive to heat so make sure the heat is reduced to
very low before adding the sago mixture, then cook
for about 5 minutes, stirring once or twice. Remove
from the heat as soon as the sago softens. Season
with salt, add the chopped coriander and mix well.

Beej
Sugared Marsh Melon Seeds

Origin Awadh
Preparation time 10 minutes
Cooking time 10 minutes
Makes 20–25

100g / 3½oz marsh melon seeds
3–4 heaped (heaping) tablespoons boora
or caster (superfine) sugar

Dry-roast the melon seeds in a kadhai or wok for about 2 minutes. Add the boora or sugar, then sprinkle in 125ml / 4½fl oz (½ cup) of water with your fingers and stir until the seeds are coated with the sugar. Transfer to a plate and allow to cool.

Store the sugared seeds in an airtight container.

Vazhaippazham Chips
Banana Chips

Origin Tamil Nadu/Kerala
Preparation time 20 minutes
Cooking time 15 minutes
Serves 4–5

750ml–1 litre / 1¼–1¾ pints (3¼–4 cups) vegetable oil
1kg / 2¼lb large, green bananas or plantains, peeled
and cut in half
salt

Heat the oil in a kadhai or deep, heavy-based pan to 180°C/350°F, or until a cube of bread browns in 30 seconds, then working in batches, carefully slice the plantains halves directly into the oil. Alternatively, slice the plantain halves first and add them to the hot oil in batches. Season with salt and deep-fry for 3–4 minutes, or until golden brown, then turn over and continue deep-frying for a further 3–4 minutes, or until crisp. Remove with a slotted spoon and drain on kitchen paper (paper towels).

Allow to cool, then store in airtight containers.

Phalon ki Chaat
Tangy Fresh Fruit

Origin Delhi
Preparation time 30 minutes
Serves 4

2 teaspoons cumin seeds
2 apples, peeled, cored and cut into cubes
2 guavas, peeled and cut into cubes
3 oranges, peeled and cut into segments
3 bananas, peeled and sliced
150g / 5oz (1 cup) seedless green grapes
1½ teaspoons amchoor
½ teaspoon black rock salt
2 teaspoons sugar
1 teaspoon ground black pepper
1 teaspoon ground dried mint
1 teaspoon lemon juice

Put the cumin seeds into a dry frying pan (skillet) and fry over high heat for 30 seconds, or until browned and fragrant. Be careful not to burn them. Remove from the heat, transfer to a spice grinder or mortar and process or pound with a pestle until ground.

Put all the fruits together in a glass bowl and mix with a salad fork and spoon. Add all the remaining ingredients including the roasted ground cumin and mix well. Chill a little before serving.

Fish and Seafood

✳
—

Mahi Tikka Ajwaini
Thyme-flavoured Fish

Origin Punjab
Preparation time 30 minutes, plus marinating time
Cooking time 15 minutes
Serves 6

1kg / 2¼lb skinless firm white fish fillets, such
    as monkfish or halibut, trimmed and cut
    into bite-sized cubes
300ml / ½ pint (1¼ cups) hung natural (plain) yoghurt
    (see page 793)
melted butter, for basting
salt

For the first marinade
4 teaspoons lemon juice
1 tablespoon Ginger Paste (see page 57)
1 tablespoon Garlic Paste (see page 57)
1 tablespoon yellow chilli powder
2 tablespoons ajwain seeds
1 tablespoon ground turmeric

For the second marinade
½ tablespoon Garam Masala (see page 31)
1 tablespoon chana dal, roasted and ground
3 tablespoons mustard oil

To serve
salad
chutney, such as Sweet Mango Chutney (see page 75)

To make the first marinade, mix the lemon juice, half
of the ginger and garlic pastes, half of the yellow
chilli powder, half of the ajwain seeds and half of
the turmeric together in a large shallow dish. Season
with salt, add the fish cubes and rub well to coat
in the marinade. Cover and allow to marinate in the
refrigerator for 30 minutes.

Whisk the hung yoghurt in a large bowl, then add
the remaining ginger and garlic pastes, the garam
masala, the remaining yellow chilli powder and the
ground roasted chana dal. Season with salt and mix
well. Heat the mustard oil in a pan and when hot,
remove from the heat. Add the remaining ajwain
seeds and turmeric to the oil and immediately add
this to the yoghurt mixture and mix well.

Remove the marinated fish cubes from the first
marinade and remove any excess moisture by lightly
squeezing them with the palm of your hand, then put
the fish into the yoghurt mixture and turn until all
the fish is coated in the second marinade. Cover and
allow to marinate in the refrigerator for 2 hours.

Prepare a tandoor or charcoal grill for a moderate
heat, or alternatively preheat the grill (broiler)
to medium. Thread the fish cubes onto several metal
skewers, 2.5cm / 1 inch apart, and coat with the
remaining marinade.

Roast in a moderately hot tandoor, over a charcoal
grill or under the grill for about 6–8 minutes, or
until the fish is cooked.

Remove the skewers from the heat and hang them up
over a tray for about 5 minutes to allow any excess
moisture to drain out completely. Put the skewers
in a dish, baste with melted butter and roast again in
the tandoor or under the grill for about 3 minutes.
Serve hot with a choice of salad and chutney.

✳ ✳ / p.472

Hara Mahi Tikka
Roast Fish with Mint

Origin Punjab
Preparation time 30 minutes, plus marinating time
Cooking time 15 minutes
Serves 6

3 tablespoons chopped green chilli

100g / 3½oz (2⅔ cups) coriander (cilantro) leaves

18 mint leaves

2 curry leaves

2 tablespoons pomegranate seeds

1 onion, coarsely chopped

300ml / ½ pint (1¼ cups) hung natural (plain) yoghurt
    (see page 793)

1kg / 2¼lb fish fillets, trimmed and cut
    into large cubes

melted butter, for basting

For the marinade

½ tablespoon finely chopped ginger

½ tablespoon Garlic Paste (see page 57)

60g / 2oz (2 tablespoons) peanut paste

1 teaspoon ground cinnamon

pinch of ground allspice

1 teaspoon crushed black peppercorns

1 tablespoon crushed pomegranate seeds

1 teaspoon ajwain seeds

1½ tablespoons cornflour (cornstarch)

1 tablespoon gram (chickpea) flour, roasted

4 teaspoons lemon juice

3 tablespoons vegetable oil

salt

Put the chilli, coriander leaves, mint leaves, curry leaves, pomegranate seeds and onion in a blender or food processor and process to make a smooth paste. Transfer to a bowl and set aside.

Whisk the hung yoghurt in a bowl, then add all the ingredients for the marinade and the spice paste, season with salt and mix well. Add the fish cubes and turn until the fish is coated. Cover and allow to marinate in the refrigerator for about 2 hours.

Prepare a tandoor or charcoal grill for a moderate heat, or alternatively preheat the grill (broiler) to medium. Thread the fish cubes on to several metal skewers, 2.5cm / 1 inch apart, and coat with the remaining marinade.

Roast in a moderately hot tandoor, over a charcoal grill or under the grill for 6–8 minutes, or until cooked.

Remove the skewers from the heat and hang them up over a tray for about 2–3 minutes to allow any excess moisture to drain out completely. Put the skewers in a dish and baste with melted butter then roast again for a further 2–4 minutes.

✳ ✳

Talela Bangda
Fried Fresh Mackerel

Origin Coastal
Preparation time 20 minutes, plus marinating time
Cooking time 20 minutes
Serves 4

2 teaspoons cumin seeds

2 teaspoons coriander seeds

8 large dried red chillies

1 teaspoon ground turmeric

2 tablespoons tamarind pulp

12 medium-sized whole mackerels, gutted, rinsed
    and patted dry with kitchen paper (paper towels)

vegetable oil, for shallow-frying

salt

lime wedges, to serve

To make the marinade, put the cumin and coriander seeds, dried red chillies, turmeric and tamarind pulp into a mortar or blender, season with salt and pound with a pestle or process to make a smooth paste. Arrange the fish in a single layer in a large shallow dish and spread the paste evenly over. Cover and allow to marinate in the refrigerator for 20 minutes.

Heat enough oil for shallow-frying in a pan over high heat, then reduce the heat to medium. Working in batches, add the fish together with the marinade and fry for 2–3 minutes on one side until golden brown and crisp. Turn the fish over and fry the other side for 2 minutes, or until golden brown. Remove with a slotted spoon and serve hot with lime wedges.

Khatti Meethi Machhali
Sweet & Sour Fish

Origin Awadh
Preparation time 30 minutes, plus cooling and marinating time
Cooking time 15 minutes
Serves 6

1kg / 2¼lb sole, cleaned and cut into large cubes

½ tablespoon ground white pepper

1 tablespoon lemon juice

250ml / 8fl oz (1 cup) hung natural (plain) yoghurt (see page 793)

1 tablespoon red chilli paste

melted butter, for basting

salt

For the tamarind sauce

100g / 3½oz (¾ cup) tamarind pulp

4 tablespoons jaggery or soft brown sugar

1 teaspoon chilli powder

1 teaspoon ground cumin

½ teaspoon Garam Masala (see page 31)

To prepare the tamarind sauce, heat the tamarind pulp in a pan with a little water. Add the jaggery, chilli powder, cumin and garam masala, then season with salt and simmer until the sauce is reduced. Remove from the heat and allow to cool.

Put the fish cubes in a bowl, season with salt, then add the white pepper and lemon juice. Cover and allow to marinate in the refrigerator for about 30 minutes.

Whisk the hung yoghurt in a large bowl, then add the red chilli paste and cooled tamarind sauce and mix well. Remove the fish cubes from the first marinade and remove any excess moisture by lightly squeezing them with the palm of your hand, then put the fish into the yoghurt mixture and turn until all the fish is coated in the second marinade. Cover and allow to marinate in the refrigerator for 1 hour.

Prepare a tandoor or charcoal grill for a moderate heat, or alternatively preheat the grill (broiler) to medium. Thread the fish cubes on to several metal skewers, 2.5cm / 1 inch apart, and coat with the remaining marinade.

Roast in a moderately hot tandoor, over a charcoal grill or under the grill for 6–8 minutes, or until cooked.

Remove the skewers from the heat and hang them up over a tray for about 2–3 minutes to allow any excess moisture to drain out completely. Put the skewers in a dish and baste with melted butter then roast again for a further 4 minutes.

Samudri Seekh
Seafood Skewers

Origin Punjab
Preparation time 20–30 minutes
Cooking time 5–7 minutes
Serves 6

500g / 1lb 2oz skinless firm white fish fillets, finely chopped

500g / 1lb 2oz large prawns (shrimp), peeled, deveined, rinsed and patted dry with kitchen paper (paper towels), then chopped

½ tablespoon Ginger Paste (see page 57)

½ tablespoon Garlic Paste (see page 57)

½ tablespoon ground white pepper

3½ tablespooons chopped coriander (cilantro) leaves

3 green chillies, de-seeded and chopped

4 teaspoons cream

melted butter, for basting

Salt

Prepare a tandoor or charcoal grill for a moderate heat, or alternatively preheat the grill (broiler) to medium. Mix the fish and prawns together in a bowl, then add the ginger and garlic pastes, white pepper, coriander and chillies. Season with salt and mix until the fish and prawns are coated in the mixture. Add the cream and mix again.

Divide the mixture into 16 equal portions, then spread each portion evenly along the length of metal skewers, flattening the mixture into a sausage shape until the kebabs are 10cm / 4 inches long and leaving 2.5cm / 1 inch between each one. You can make 2 kebabs on one long skewer.

Roast in a moderately hot tandoor, over a charcoal grill or under the grill for 4–5 minutes, or until cooked.

Remove the skewers from the heat and hang them up over a tray for about 5 minutes to allow any excess moisture to drain out completely. Put the skewers in a dish and baste with melted butter then roast again for a further 1–2 minutes.

Ambat Dahyatil Machhi
Fried Soured Cream Fish

Origin Coastal
Preparation time 15 minutes, plus marinating time
Cooking time 20 minutes
Serves 4

500ml / 18fl oz (2¼ cups) soured cream
4 teaspoons ground black pepper
1 tablespoon Ginger Paste (see page 57)
1 tablespoon Garlic Paste (see page 57)
800g / 1¾lb firm white fish fillets, such as surmai or haddock, trimmed, rinsed and patted dry with kitchen paper (paper towels)
300g / 10½oz (2 cups) rice flour
vegetable oil, for deep-frying
salt

Put the soured cream, pepper, and ginger and garlic pastes in a shallow dish that is large enough to hold the fish in a single layer. Season with salt and mix well. Put the fish fillets into the dish and rub each well with the mixture. Cover and allow to marinate in the refrigerator for 15 minutes.

Spread the rice flour out on to a flat tray and coat each fish fillet evenly on both sides by pressing firmly into the flour.

Heat enough oil for deep-frying in a kadhai or deep frying pan (skillet) to 180°C/350°F, or until a cube of bread browns in 30 seconds, then reduce the heat. Working in batches, carefully lower the fish into the hot oil and deep-fry for about 5 minutes, or until golden brown on all sides. Remove with a slotted spoon and drain on kitchen paper (paper towels).

Taleli Gaboli
Spicy Fried Fish Roe

Origin Coastal
Preparation time 30 minutes, plus standing time
Cooking time 20 minutes
Serves 4

1kg / 2¼lb fish roe, cleaned
vegetable oil, for shallow-frying

For the dry masala

1 teaspoon ground turmeric
2 teaspoons chilli powder
2 teaspoons ground cumin
2 teaspoons ground coriander
1 teaspoon Garam Masala (see page 31)
salt

For the green masala paste

4 green chillies, de-seeded and chopped
1 × 2.5-cm / 1-inch piece fresh ginger, peeled and chopped
6 cloves garlic, chopped
3 bunches coriander (cilantro) sprigs, leaves only, chopped
1 teaspoon sugar
1 teaspoon salt
2 tablespoons lime juice

Cook the roe in a steamer for about 10–15 minutes, then remove the membrane and cut into slices.

Mix all the ground spices together in a bowl, season with salt and rub the dry masala mix gently on each slice of roe. Cover and allow to stand for 5 minutes.

To make the green masala paste, put the chillies, ginger, garlic, coriander, sugar, salt and lime juice in a mortar or blender and pound with a pestle or process to make a smooth paste. Rub this paste on the fish roe slices in the bowl, then cover again and allow to stand for a further 5 minutes.

Heat enough oil for shallow-frying in a large shallow pan over high heat, then reduce the heat to medium. Working in batches, put the roe slices into the hot oil, making sure there is enough space between them so they do not break when turned over. Shallow-fry for about 5 minutes, or until golden brown on both sides. Remove with a slotted spoon.

Mith Miryatii Machhi
Salt & Pepper Fish

Origin Coastal
Preparation time 15 minutes, plus marinating time
Cooking time 20 minutes
Serves 4

1 large banana leaf (optional)
1kg / 2¼lb white fish fillets, such as haddock, tilapia or halibut, trimmed, rinsed and patted dry with kitchen paper (paper towels)
2 tablespoons black peppercorns, crushed
1 teaspoon ground black pepper
few sprigs coriander (cilantro) leaves
2 tablespoons lime juice
2 tablespoons butter or ghee
salt

To soften the banana leaf, hold it over the low flame of a gas cooker (stove top burner) for a few seconds, or until soft. Alternatively, use a cook's blowtorch or submerge each leaf into a pan of boiling water, remove immediately with tongs, rinse under cold water and dry well. Cut the banana leaf into 4 x 25-cm / 10-inch squares.

Put the fish fillets in a shallow dish and rub each fillet with a little salt, the pepper, coriander leaves and lime juice. Cover and allow to marinate in the refrigerator for 15 minutes.

Heat the butter or ghee in a large frying pan (skillet) over medium heat, add the fish and fry for 5–10 minutes on each side.

Place a piece of fish in the centre of a prepared banana leaf, fold over the sides to form a neat parcel and secure with kitchen string (twine). If using foil, bring the edges up and seal at the top to make an airtight but loose package.

Heat a tawa, griddle or non-stick frying pan over medium heat. When hot, add the parcels and fry for 5 minutes on each side. Serve hot in the banana parcels.

※ ※ / 📷 pp.125, 127

Bhajela Saranga
Baked Fish

Origin Coastal
Preparation time 30–40 minutes, plus marinating time
Cooking time 40 minutes
Serves 8

1kg / 2¼lb whole rawas or salmon, gutted, rinsed and patted dry with kitchen paper (paper towel)
1 teaspoon ground turmeric
1 tablespoon lime juice
banana leaves (optional)
vegetable oil, for frying
salt

For the spice paste

1 onion, chopped
2 red chillies, de-seeded and chopped
2 cloves garlic, crushed
1 × 2.5-cm / 1-inch piece fresh ginger, peeled and chopped
30g / 1¾oz (⅓ cup) desiccated (dried flaked) coconut

Cut the head and fins off the fish, then using a sharp knife, score slashes on both sides. Mix the turmeric and lime juice together in a bowl and season with salt. Arrange the fish in a large dish and rub the turmeric and lime mixture evenly all over the fish. Cover and allow to marinate in the refrigerator for 15 minutes.

Soften the banana leaves (see left), then cut them into 8 x 25-cm / 10-inch squares. Alternatively, use foil squares.

To make the spice paste, put the onion, chillies, garlic, ginger and desiccated coconut into a blender or food processor and process, adding a little water to make a smooth paste. Cut the fish into 4 individual portions and coat thickly on both sides with the spice paste.

Spread out the banana leaf or foil squares on a clean flat surface, place a fish portion in the centre, then fold over to make a neat parcel and secure with kitchen string (twine).

Heat a thin film of oil on a tawa, griddle or a frying pan (skillet) over low-medium heat. Pan-fry the parcels for 10 minutes on each side. Remove and unwrap carefully so as not to break the fish fillets.

❋❋

Kala Saranga
Black Pomfret

Origin Coastal
Preparation time 20 minutes
Cooking time 30 minutes
Serves 4

1kg / 2¼lb whole pomfret (butterfish), gutted, rinsed
    and patted dry with kitchen paper (paper towels)

1 teaspoon ground turmeric

2 tablespoons lime juice

½ teaspoon salt

12 cloves

12 cardamom pods

20 black peppercorns

5 cinnamon sticks, about 2.5cm / 1 inch long

1 tablespoon aniseed

1 tablespoon cumin seeds

4 tablespoons tamarind pulp

1 teaspoon sugar

1 large banana leaf (optional)

salt

Cut the head and fins off the fish. Using a knife,
score deep slashes on both sides of the fish. Mix
the turmeric, lime juice and salt together in a bowl.
Arrange the fish in a large dish and rub the turmeric
and lime mixture evenly all over the fish.

Roast the whole spices gently together with the aniseed
and cumin seeds on a tawa, griddle or in a dry frying
pan (skillet) for about 30 seconds, or until they
darken. Transfer to a mortar and, using a pestle, pound
until coarsely ground or grind in a spice grinder.
Transfer to a bowl, add the tamarind pulp and sugar,
then season with salt and mix together, adding
a little water if necessary to make a paste. Rub the
paste all over the fish including in the slashes.

Soften the banana leaf (see page 174), or use a large
piece of foil.

Wrap the fish tightly in the banana leaf or foil and
secure with cocktail sticks (toothpicks). Heat a tawa,
griddle or non-stick frying pan. When hot, add
the fish parcel and cook for 5 minutes on each side,
or until the fish is cooked. Serve hot.

❋❋❋

Tikaht Modaka
Spicy Whitebait

Origin Coastal
Preparation time 15–30 minutes
Cooking time 15 minutes
Serves 4–6

---

2 tablespoons vegetable oil

1 teaspoon cumin seeds

1 large sprig coriander (cilantro), leaves only, chopped

1 tablespoon Garlic Paste (see page 57)

4 green chillies, de-seeded and chopped

1 teaspoon sugar

1kg / 2¼lb whitebait or herring, gutted, rinsed
    and patted dry with kitchen paper (paper towels)

2 tablespoons lime juice

1 teaspoon Garam Masala (see page 31)

salt

Heat the oil in a pan over medium heat, add the
cumin seeds and stir-fry for about 1 minute, or until
they change colour. Add the chopped coriander,
garlic paste, chillies, sugar and season with salt. Fry
for 1 minute. Add the whitebait or herring, stir to
mix and add the lime juice. Reduce the heat, cover
and simmer for 10 minutes, or until the fish is
cooked. Sprinkle the garam masala over the top
just before serving.

Machhi Kebab
Fish Patties

Origin Hyderabad
Preparation time 50 minutes, plus cooling time
Cooking time 25 minutes
Serves 4

2 medium-sized potatoes, peeled and cut into cubes

500g / 1lb 2oz skinless firm white fish fillets, such as whiting or haddock, trimmed

3 tablespoons vegetable oil, plus extra for oiling

4 spring onions (scallions), trimmed and chopped

1 × 5-cm / 2-inch piece fresh ginger, peeled and chopped

4 green chillies, de-seeded and finely chopped

2 eggs

about 60g / 2oz (½ cup) dried breadcrumbs, for coating

ground black pepper

salt

lemon wedges, to serve

Cook the potatoes in a pan of boiling water for 20 minutes, or until soft. Drain, return to the pan and mash with a potato masher. Allow to cool.

Meanwhile, put the fish into a steamer, cover with the lid and steam over low heat for about 10 minutes, or until cooked. If you don't have a steamer, put a trivet or upturned plate into the base (bottom) of a large pan and pour in enough boiling water to come up to the trivet. Place the fish on a lightly oiled plate, cover with another plate or a piece of lightly oiled foil and carefully put into the pan. Cover and cook.

Remove from the heat, uncover and allow to cool. Flake the fish into a bowl, add the mashed potatoes, spring onions, ginger, chillies and 1 egg. Season with and mix well to combine. Divide into 20 small balls, then flatten them into small burger patty-like shapes.

Put the remaining egg in a shallow dish and beat lightly, then spread the breadcrumbs out on a plate. Dip the patties first in the beaten egg, then in the breadcrumbs to coat.

Heat the oil in a non-stick frying pan (skillet) over low heat. Working in batches, fry the patties for about 8–10 minutes, or until golden brown on both sides and hot all the way through. Remove with a slotted spoon and drain on kitchen paper (paper towels). Serve with lemon wedges.

Karhai Jhinga
Stir-fried Prawns (Shrimp)

Origin Punjab
Preparation time 40–45 minutes
Cooking time 20 minutes
Serves 4

8 dried red chillies

2 teaspoons coriander seeds

100g / 3½oz (scant ½ cup) ghee or vegetable oil

160g / 5½oz (1 medium) onion, chopped

3½ teaspoons Garlic Paste (see page 57)

2 teaspoons ajwain seeds

750g / 1lb 10oz (4 cups) chopped tomatoes

40g / 1½oz (⅓ cup) chopped ginger

6 green chillies, de-seeded and chopped

750g / 1lb 10oz prawns (shrimp), peeled, deveined, rinsed and patted dry with kitchen paper (paper towels), then and heads and tails removed

2 teaspoons Garam Masala (see page 31)

1½ teaspoons ground fenugreek

4 tablespoons lemon juice

6 tablespoons chopped coriander (cilantro) leaves

salt

Put the red chillies and coriander seeds in a mortar and pound with a pestle or grind in a spice grinder. Set aside.

Heat the ghee or oil in a kadhai or wok, add the onions and sauté over medium heat for about 5 minutes, or until golden brown. Add the garlic paste and stir-fry for 15 seconds, then add the ounded spices, ajwain seeds and stir-fry for a further 30 seconds. Add the tomatoes, then increase the heat to high and add three-quarters of the ginger and chillies. Reduce the heat to medium and cook for about 5 minutes, or until the oil separates from the sauce.

Add the prawns and continue to cook for a further 5 minutes, or until the prawns are cooked. If there is some liquid left, then increase the heat to high and cook for a further 1–2 minutes until the liquid has evaporated. Season with salt, then sprinkle over the garam masala, fenugreek, lemon juice and coriander. Stir to combine and serve hot.

Shevandi Kada
King Prawns (Jumbo Shrimp) with Baby (Pearl) Onions

Origin Coastal
Preparation time 15 minutes
Cooking time 20 minutes
Serves 4

2 tablespoons vegetable oil

8 curry leaves

1 large onion, chopped

1 teaspoon sugar

2 tablespoons coconut vinegar

1½ tablespoons ground black pepper

36 baby (pearl) onions, peeled

8 king prawns (jumbo shrimp), peeled, deveined, rinsed and patted dry with kitchen paper (paper towels), heads removed but tails left intact

375ml / 13fl oz (1½ cups) coconut feni or coconut vinegar or white-wine vinegar

salt

Heat the oil in a pan over medium heat, add the curry leaves and stir-fry for about 1 minute, or until they begin to change colour. Add the chopped onion and fry for about 5 minutes, or until translucent. Add the sugar, vinegar, pepper and season with salt. Fry for a further 1 minute. Prick the baby onions with a fork and add to pan. Fry for 3 minutes.

Prick the king prawns with a fork and add to the pan. Reduce the heat, then cover with a lid and simmer for 5 minutes. Uncover the pan, pour in the feni, cover again and cook for a further 5 minutes, or until the prawns are done.

Jhinga Adraki
Grilled (Broiled) Ginger Prawns (Shrimp)

Origin Punjab
Preparation time 30 minutes, plus marinating time
Cooking time 20 minutes
Serves 4

250ml / 8fl oz (1 cup) hung natural (plain) yoghurt (see page 793)

½ tablespoon yellow chilli powder

1 tablespoon ground ginger

1 tablespoon Ginger Paste (see page 57)

1 tablespoon lemon juice

3 tablespoons mustard oil

½ tablespoon ground turmeric

20 large prawns (shrimp), peeled, deveined, rinsed and patted dry with kitchen paper (paper towels), heads removed but tails left intact

melted butter, for basting

salt

Put the hung yoghurt in a large bowl and beat with a fork, then add the chilli powder, ginger, ginger paste and lemon juice. Season with salt and mix well.

Heat the oil in a pan to 180°C/350°F, or until a cube of bread browns in 30 seconds. Add the turmeric and pour this over the yoghurt mixture. Cover the bowl with a tight lid for 2 minutes, then mix well.

Add the prawns to the yoghurt mixture and turn until they are evenly coated. Cover and allow to stand for 30 minutes.

Prepare a tandoor or charcoal grill for a moderate heat, or alternatively preheat the grill (broiler) to medium. Thread the prawns through several metal skewers and cover with the remaining marinade.

Cook in a moderately hot tandoor, over a charcoal grill or under the hot grill for 8–10 minutes, or until the prawns are cooked.

Remove the skewers from the heat and hang them up over a tray for about 5 minutes to allow any excess moisture to drain out completely. Put the skewers in a dish, baste with melted butter and roast again in the tandoor or under the grill for about 2 minutes.

✳ ✳
___

Hare Jhinga
Prawns (Shrimp) in Green Chutney

Origin Punjab
Preparation time 40 minutes, plus marinating time
Cooking time 15 minutes
Serves 4–6

15–20 curry leaves
20g / ¾oz (½ cup) coriander (cilantro) leaves
3 tablespoons mint leaves
6–8 green chillies
1 tablespoon Ginger Paste (see page 57)
1 tablespoon Garlic Paste (see page 57)
2 tablespoons ground dried fenugreek leaves
2 tablespoons lime juice
20 large prawns (shrimp), peeled, deveined, rinsed and patted dry with kitchen paper (paper towels), heads removed but tails left intact
200ml / 7fl oz (scant 1 cup) hung natural (plain) yoghurt (see page 793)
4 tablespoons cream
1 egg, beaten
1 teaspoon yellow chilli powder
½ teaspoon ajwain seeds
½ teaspoon Garam Masala (see page 31)
125ml / 4½fl oz (½ cup) vegetable oil
melted unsalted butter, for basting
salt

To make the green spice paste, put the curry, coriander and mint leaves and chillies in a mortar or blender. Season with salt and pound with a pestle or process, adding a little water, if necessary, to make a smooth paste. Set aside.

Put half of the ginger and garlic pastes, the ground, dried fenugreek and lime juice in a large bowl and mix together. Add the prawns and turn until they are evenly coated in the mixture. Cover and allow to marinate for 20 minutes.

Put the yoghurt and cream in a bowl and beat with a fork, then add the green spice paste, beaten egg, ground spices, the remaining ginger and garlic pastes and the oil, and mix well.

Remove the prawns from the marinade and allow them to drain to remove any excess liquid, then add the prawns to the yoghurt mixture and turn until they are evenly coated. Cover and allow to marinate in the refrigerator for 1 hour.

Prepare a tandoor or charcoal grill for a moderate heat, or alternatively preheat the grill (broiler) to medium. Thread the prawns on to several metal skewers, then cover with the remaining mixture.

Cook the skewers in a moderately hot tandoor, over a charcoal grill or under the hot grill for 8–10 minutes, or until the prawns are cooked. Make sure the prawns are not overcooked, otherwise they will be tough and rubbery.

Remove the skewers from the heat and hang them up over a tray for about 5 minutes to allow any excess moisture to drain out completely. Put the skewers in a dish, baste with melted butter and roast again in the tandoor or under the grill for about 2 minutes.

☀ ☀
___

Shahalyat Kalve
Oysters in Green Masala

Origin Coastal
Preparation time 30 minutes, plus marinating time
Cooking time 7–8 minutes
Serves 4–6

½ teaspoon ground turmeric
1 teaspoon chilli powder
1 teaspoon ground cumin
½ teaspoon ground coriander
1 tablespoon coconut vinegar
1kg / 2¼lb large oysters, shucked and rinsed
2 tablespoons vegetable oil
salt

For the spice paste

60g / 2oz (⅔ cup) desiccated (dried flaked) coconut
1 × 2.5-cm / 1-inch piece fresh ginger, peeled
3 green chillies, de-seeded
1 small bunch coriander (cilantro)
1 small bunch mint
flesh of 6 tender coconuts

To make the the marinade, put the ground spices and vinegar in a shallow dish and season with salt. Add the oysters and rub them all over with the mixture, then cover and allow to marinate in the refrigerator for 15 minutes.

To make the spice paste, put the desiccated coconut, ginger, chillies, coriander and mint leaves into a mortar or blender and pound with a pestle or process, adding a little water, if necessary, to make a smooth paste.

Heat the oil in a pan over medium heat, add the spice paste and the coconut flesh and stir-fry for 2 minutes. Add the oysters together with the marinade and stir-fry for 2–3 minutes. Cover with a lid and cook for a further 2 minutes, or until the oysters are cooked.

Meat

✻ ✻ ✻ / 📷 p.193

Kakori Kebab
Minced (Ground) Lamb Skewers

Origin Awadh
Preparation time 30 minutes
Cooking time 10 minutes
Serves 4

750g / 1lb 10oz minced (ground) lamb

1 teaspoon Ginger Paste (see page 57)

1 teaspoon Garlic Paste (see page 57)

3 tablespoons Cashew Nut Paste (see page 58)

1 tablespoon Poppy Seed Paste (see page 58)

1 tablespoon Garam Masala (see page 31)

1 tablespoon yellow chilli powder

2 tablespoons ghee

melted butter, for basting

salt

To serve

---

onion rings

chutney, such as Mint Chutney (see page 66)

Prepare a tandoor or charcoal grill for a moderate heat, or alternatively preheat the grill (broiler) to medium. Put the meat, pastes, ground spices and ghee into a large bowl. Season with salt and mix well. Divide the mixture into 16 equal portions and roll into balls. Thread the balls on to several metal skewers and, with damp hands, flatten them into a long sausage shape.

Cook over a moderately hot charcoal grill or under the hot grill for about 5–8 minutes, turning frequently to ensure even roasting. Baste with melted butter and cook for a further 1–2 minutes, or until cooked. Serve hot with onion rings and chutney.

✻

Kursi Miyani
Sedan-Chair Kebab

Origin Hyderabad
Preparation time 45 minutes
Cooking time 5 minutes
Serves 4–6

---

6 eggs

1 green chilli, de-seeded (optional)

3 tablespoons cooked minced (ground) lamb

1 tablespoon gram (chickpea) flour

½ teaspoon ground dried pomegranate seeds

4 tablespoons chopped coriander (cilantro) leaves

100g / 3½oz (¾ cup) plain (all-purpose) flour

1 teaspoon red chilli powder

vegetable oil, for frying

salt

Cook the eggs in a pan of boiling water for 8–10 minutes, or until hard-boiled. Drain and allow to cool. Put the chilli in a small blender and process until ground to a paste. Set aside.

Cut the eggs into halves, then scoop out the yolks and put into a bowl. Add the mince, gram flour, green chilli, ground pomegranate seeds and chopped coriander and mix well. Divide the mixture into 12 equal portions and fill the egg white hollows with it. 'Join' 2 halves and secure with a long wooden skewer.

Sift the plain flour and red chilli powder into a large bowl. Season with salt and whisk, gradually adding enough water (about 150 ml / ¼ pint (½ cup)) to make medium batter – not too thick or thin.

Half-fill a deep, heavy-based pan with oil, and heat over medium heat until a cube of bread browns in 30 seconds. Dry the eggs well, then dip them in the batter and fry for 3–4 minutes, or until golden brown and slightly crusted. Drain on kitchen paper (paper towel), and sprinkle with a little salt.

✳ ✳
___

Maans ke Soole
Skewered Spicy Lamb Fillet

Origin Rajasthan
Preparation time 45 minutes–1 hour, plus
marinating time
Cooking time 20 minutes
Serves 4

1kg / 2¼lb lamb fillet (sirloin)
6 cloves (optional)
4 teaspoons hot ghee (optional)
about 2 tablespoons melted butter, for basting

For the first marinade

1 tablespoon raw papaya paste
½ tablespoon Ginger Paste (see page 57)
½ tablespoon Garlic Paste (see page 57)
2 tablespoons red chilli paste
4 teaspoons malt (white) vinegar
4 teaspoons vegetable oil or ghee
salt

For the second marinade

250ml / 8fl oz (1 cup) hung natural (plain) yoghurt (see page 793), whisked
300g / 11oz Onion Paste (see page 57)
2 tablespoons red chilli paste
2 tablespoons Garam Masala (see page 31)
1 tablespoon ground white pepper
4 tablespoons lemon juice
4 tablespoons vegetable oil
pinch of salt

Put the meat on to a board and, using a meat mallet, beat to flatten slightly, then score the meat gently with a knife.

To make the first marinade, put the pastes, vinegar and oil into a large shallow dish, season with salt and mix well. Add the meat and spread the mixture evenly over to coat. Cover and allow to marinate in the refrigerator for at least 2 hours.

Mix the yoghurt with all the other ingredients for the second marinade in a large shallow dish. Remove the meat from the first marinade, wiping off any excess moisture from the first marinade and add it to the second marinade. Cover and allow to marinate in the refrigerator for a further 3 hours.

Prepare a moderately hot charcoal grill or preheat the oven to 190°C/375°F/Gas Mark 5. If you would like to smoke the meat, place the marinated meat pieces in a large, heavy-based pan leaving a hole in the centre. Set the remaining marinade aside.

Put 3–4 pieces of burning charcoal into a small heatproof bowl and place it in the middle of the pan. Add the cloves and pour over hot ghee, then immediately cover the pan with a lid and leave for 3–5 minutes so that the smoke imparts its unique flavour to the meat.

Thread the meat on to several metal skewers, making sure there is a 2.5-cm / 1-inch gap between each piece of meat. Coat with the remaining marinade. Roast over a moderately hot charcoal grill or in the oven for about 15 minutes, or until the meat is cooked.

Remove the skewers from the heat and hang up to drain out any excess moisture. Put the skewers into a dish and baste with the melted butter, then roast for a further 3–4 minutes. Serve hot.

☸☸☸☸ / 📷 p.194

Rajasthani Boti Kebab
Spicy Lamb Tikka on Skewers

Origin Rajasthan
Preparation time 30 minutes, plus marinating time
Cooking time 25 minutes
Serves 4

1kg / 2¼lb boneless lamb, cut into chunks
2 tablespoons melted butter, for basting

For the first marinade
2 tablespoons raw papaya paste
½ tablespoon Ginger Paste (see page 57)
½ tablespoon Garlic Paste (see page 57)
1 tablespoon red chilli paste
4 teaspoons vinegar
4 teaspoons vegetable oil
salt

For the second marinade
250ml / 8fl oz (1 cup) hung natural (plain) yoghurt (see page 793), whisked
½ tablespoon Ginger Paste (see page 57)
½ tablespoon Garlic Paste (see page 57)
3 tablespoons red chilli paste
1 tablespoon Garam Masala (see page 31)
1 tablespoon ground dried fenugreek leaves
2 tablespoons lemon juice
3 tablespoons mustard oil
pinch of salt

To make the first marinade, put all the ingredients into a large bowl, season with salt and mix well. Add the meat, coat evenly, then cover and allow to marinate in the refrigerator for about 2 hours.

Mix the yoghurt with all the ingredients for the second marinade in a large bowl or shallow dish. Remove the meat from the first marinade. Using a knife scrape off any excess moisture from the first marinade and add the meat to the second marinade. Cover and allow to marinate in the refrigerator for a further 3 hours.

Prepare a moderately hot charcoal grill or preheat the oven to 190°C/375°F/Gas Mark 5. Thread the meat on to several metal skewers and roast over the grill or in the oven for about 15 minutes, or until the meat is cooked. Remove the skewers from the heat and hang up to drain any excess moisture. Put the skewers into a dish and baste with the melted butter, then roast for a further 3–4 minutes. Serve hot.

☸

Mutton Barra Kebab
Roasted Lamb Kebabs

Origin Punjab
Preparation time 30 minutes, plus marinating time
Cooking time 15–20 minutes
Serves 4

3 tablespoons raw papaya paste
1 tablespoon Garlic Paste (see page 57)
1 tablespoon Ginger Paste (see page 57)
1 teaspoon ground black pepper
1 teaspoon black cumin seeds
125ml / 4½fl oz (½ cup) natural (plain) yoghurt, whisked
3 tablespoons malt (white) vinegar
1kg / 2¼lb lamb chops and shanks
melted butter, for basting
salt

For sprinkling
½ teaspoon ground black cardamom
½ teaspoon ground green cardamom
¼ teaspoon ground cinnamon
¼ teaspoon ground cloves
pinch of ground black rock salt

Put all the pastes, black pepper, cumin, yoghurt and vinegar in a large shallow dish. Season with salt and mix well. Add the meat and rub evenly all over to coat. Cover and allow to marinate in the refrigerator overnight.

Prepare a tandoor or charcoal grill for a moderate heat, or alternatively preheat the grill (broiler) to medium. Put all the spices for sprinkling in a small bowl and mix together, then set aside.

Thread the meat on to several metal skewers and place a tray under them to collect any juices. Roast in a moderately hot tandoor, over a charcoal grill or under the hot grill for about 10 minutes.

Remove the skewers from the heat and hang up to drain out any excess moisture. Put the skewers into a dish and baste with the melted butter, then roast for a further 5 minutes, or until cooked. Sprinkle with the spice mixture just before serving.

Kathi Kebab
Boneless Lamb Kebabs

Origin Bengal
Preparation time 30 minutes, plus soaking
and marinating time
Cooking time 30 minutes
Serves 6–8

1kg / 2¼lb boneless lamb, cut into 2.5-cm / 1-inch
cubes

4 tablespoons melted ghee or butter

vegetable oil, for oiling

For the marinade

8 dried kachri (optional)

4 dried figs

4 onions, cut into rings

8–10 cloves garlic, crushed

1 × 2.5-cm / 1-inch piece fresh ginger, peeled

1 × 5-cm / 2-inch piece raw papaya

10–12 black peppercorns, dry-roasted

1½ tablespoons yellow mustard seeds, dry-roasted

1 teaspoon cumin seeds, dry-roasted

4 tablespoons natural (plain) yoghurt, whisked

salt

To serve

onion rings

lime wedges

Soak the dried kachri, if using, and figs in a bowl of
water for 4 hours.

To make the marinade, drain the kachri and figs,
then transfer to a blender or food processor and
add the onions, garlic, ginger and papaya. Process to
make a smooth paste, then transfer to a large bowl
or shallow dish.

Put the roasted spices into a mortar and pound
with a pestle until ground. Alternatively, use a spice
grinder. Add to the onion paste with the yoghurt and
season with salt. Mix thoroughly. Add the meat and
turn until the meat is coated in the mixture. Cover
and allow to marinate in the refrigerator overnight.

Prepare a charcoal grill for a moderate heat, or
alternatively, preheat the grill (broiler) to medium.
Thread the meat on to several metal skewers and
cook over the charcoal grill or under the grill,
turning frequently, for about 10 minutes, or until
evenly browned. Baste with the melted ghee or
butter and cook, turning occasionally, for a further
10 minutes, or until the meat is cooked.

Remove the meat from the skewers (be careful, as
the metals skewers will be hot) and transfer to an
oiled frying pan (skillet) until ready to serve.

When ready to serve, heat the meat for a few minutes
or until piping hot, and serve with onion rings and
lime wedges.

Kashmiri Seekh Kebab
Minced (Ground) Lamb Kebabs
on Skewers

Origin Jammu and Kashmir
Preparation time 30 minutes, plus marinating time
Cooking time 7–9 minutes
Serves 4

750g / 1lb 10oz minced (ground) lamb

1 × 2.5-cm / 1-inch piece fresh ginger, peeled
and chopped

50g / 1¾oz (⅓ cup) onions, chopped

3½ tablespoons chopped mint leaves

1 large sprig coriander (cilantro), chopped

½ tablespoon Ginger Paste (see page 57)

½ tablespoon Garlic Paste (see page 57)

2 tablespoons red chilli paste

1 teaspoon Garam Masala (see page 31)

1 teaspoon ground dried fenugreek leaves

1 tablespoon vegetable oil

melted butter, for basting

salt

Put the meat in a large bowl and add the ginger, onions, herbs, pastes, garam masala, fenugreek and oil. Season with salt and mix well. Cover and allow to marinate in the refrigerator for about 30 minutes.

Prepare a tandoor or charcoal grill for a moderate heat, or alternatively preheat the grill (broiler) to medium. Divide the mince mixture into 16 equal portions and roll into balls. With damp hands, spread the balls along the length of metal skewers, flattening the mixture into a sausage shape until the kebabs are 10cm / 4 inches long and leaving 5cm / 2 inches between each one. You can make 2 kebabs on one long skewer.

Roast in a moderately hot tandoor, over a charcoal grill or under the hot grill for 5–6 minutes. Remove from the heat and baste with melted butter then cook for a further 2–3 minutes.

Pasande ki Seekh
Lamb Fillets on Skewers

Origin Delhi
Preparation time 45–50 minutes, plus soaking time
Cooking time 45 minutes
Serves 4

6 dried kachri (optional)

2 dried figs

5 teaspoons poppy seeds

250g / 9oz (1 large) onion

20 cloves garlic, crushed

250 ml / 8fl oz (1 cup) natural (plain) yoghurt

1 kg (2¼ lb) Pasandas (see page 187)

2 teaspoons ghee

1 teaspoon Garam Masala (see page 31)

½ teaspoon chilli powder

salt

To garnish

onion rings

lime wedges

Soak the dried kachri, if using, and figs in a bowl of water for 4 hours. Drain and transfer to a blender or food processor, add the poppy seeds, onion and garlic and process to make a paste. Transfer to a large shallow dish, season with salt and add half the yoghurt. Add the meat and mix well.

If you would like to smoke the meat, put the meat mixture into a large, heavy-based pan and make a depression in the centre. Put the ghee into a piece of foil and place it in this depression. Hold a small piece of coal with a pair of tongs over a flame until red hot, then place it into the ghee. Immediately cover as tightly as possible and allow the meat to smoke for 4 hours.

Prepare a charcoal grill for a moderate heat, or alternatively preheat the grill (broiler) to medium. Remove the coal, pour the ghee on to the meat, add the garam masala and chilli powder and mix well. Wrap pieces of the meat around several metal skewers and tie in place with wet kitchen string (twine). Cook over a charcoal grill or under the hot grill, turning frequently, for about 45 minutes, or until golden brown and tender.

Serve garnished with onion rings and lime wedges.

Kachhe Keeme ki Tikya
'Uncooked' Meat Patties

Origin Hyderabad
Preparation time 45 minutes, plus marinating time
Cooking time 50 minutes
Makes 30–35

---

1 × 2.5-cm / 1-inch piece raw papaya

1 × 2.5-cm / 1-inch piece fresh ginger, peeled

1kg / 2¼lb finely minced (ground) lamb

2 tablespoons ghee

2 onions, sliced

100ml / 3½fl oz (½ cup) hung natural (plain) yoghurt (see page 793), whisked

100g / 3½oz (½ cup) chana dal, rinsed and drained, then roasted

3 level tablespoons poppy seeds, dry-roasted

2 teaspoons chironji seeds, dry-roasted

1½ teaspoons Garam Masala (see page 31)

1 cinnamon stick, about 2.5cm / 1 inch long

250g / 9oz (1 cup) ghee, for greasing and frying

salt

For the filling

1 × 3-cm / 1-inch piece fresh ginger, peeled and chopped

2–3 green chillies, de-seeded and chopped

4 tablespoons chopped coriander (cilantro) leaves

Put the papaya in a small blender or food processor and process until ground to a paste, then transfer to a bowl. Put the ginger in the blender and process until ground, then add to the papaya. Season with salt and add the meat and mix well. Cover and allow to marinate in the refrigerator for 1 hour.

Heat the 2 tablespoons ghee in a frying pan (skillet) over medium heat, add the onions and fry for about 5–7 minutes, or until golden brown. Transfer to a blender or food processor and process until ground. Transfer to the bowl of meat and add the yoghurt, chana dal, poppy and chironji seeds, garam masla and cinnamon stick. Mix together to combine.

Mix together all the ingredients for the filling in another bowl. Using greased hands, take small amounts of the meat mixture and roll into balls. Make depressions in the centre of each ball and put in a little filling. Pinch together to enclose the filling and flatten into patties.

Heat a little ghee on an iron griddle or in a heavy-based frying pan (skillet) over low heat. Working in batches, add a few patties to the griddle or pan, then cover with a domed lid and cook for 5 minutes on each side until golden brown. Drizzle a little ghee on the griddle or in the pan during cooking.

Chapali Kebab
Sandal Kebab

Origin Hyderabad
Preparation time 25–35 minutes
Cooking time 15 minutes
Serves 6

100g / 3½oz (1 medium) onion, cut into large chunks

1 × 8-cm / 3-inch piece fresh ginger, peeled and roughly chopped

4–6 dried red chillies

4 green chillies, de-seeded (optional)

750g / 1lb 10oz minced (ground) lamb with fat

30g / 1¼oz (¾ cup) chopped coriander (cilantro) leaves

1 tablespoon ground dried pomegranate seeds

1 tablespoon ground coriander

3 tablespoons gram (chickpea) flour

2 eggs, beaten

ghee, for frying

salt

Put the onion, ginger, and red and green chillies in a spice grinder or food processor and process until ground. Transfer to a bowl. Add the remaining ingredients, except the ghee and season with salt. Mix well to combine, then divide into 24 equal portions and, using damp hands, roll into balls. Flatten slightly, then shape each flattened ball into 5cm / 2 inch long and 2-cm / ¾-inch thick oval patties, like the sole of a chappal (sandal).

Heat the ghee in a heavy-based frying pan (skillet) over medium heat, then reduce the heat to low. Working in batches, add the kebabs in a single layer in the pan and fry for about 6–8 minutes, or until cooked and brown on both sides.

Seekh Gilafi
Vegetable-coated Skewers

Origin Awadh
Preparation time 45 minutes
Cooking time 7–10 minutes
Serves 4

600g / 1lb 5oz minced (ground) lamb

1 tablespoon Ginger Paste (see page 57)

1 tablespoon Garlic Paste (see page 57)

4 tablespoons chopped onion

6 tablespoons chopped spring onion (scallion)

4 tablespoons chopped tomato

4 tablespoons chopped (bell) pepper

2 tablespoons chopped green chilli

3 tablespoons chopped coriander (cilantro) leaves

2 tablespoons Kashmiri red chilli powder

pinch of ground allspice

2 tablespoons Garam Masala (see page 31)

2 tablespoons lemon juice

2 tablespoons melted butter, for basting

salt

Prepare a tandoor or charcoal grill for a moderate heat, or alternatively preheat the grill (broiler) to medium. Put the meat, ginger and garlic pastes, 2 tablespoons each of the chopped onion, spring onion, tomato and pepper into a bowl. Add all the remaining ingredients, except the butter, and season with salt. With damp hands, mix well, then divide the mixture into 16 equal portions and roll into balls. Spread the balls evenly along the length of metal skewers, flattening the mixture into sausage shapes until the kebabs are 10-cm / 4-inches long and leaving 2.5cm / 1 inch between each one. You can make 2 kebabs on one long skewer. Spread the remaining chopped vegetables evenly over each skewer.

Roast in a moderately hot tandoor, over a charcoal grill or under the hot grill for 5–6 minutes. Remove the skewers from the heat and hang them up over a tray for about 2–3 minutes to allow any excess moisture to drain out completely. Put the skewers in a dish, baste with melted butter and roast again in the tandoor, on the charcoal grill or under the grill for a further 2–3 minutes.

Galouti
'Melt in the Mouth' Smoked Kebabs

Origin Awadh
Preparation time 1 hour, plus standing and smoking time
Cooking time 15 minutes
Serves 4

750g / 1lb 10oz very finely minced (ground) lamb

100g / 3½oz (½ cup) raw papaya paste

4 tablespoons gram (chickpea) flour, roasted

1 teaspoon Garam Masala (see page 31)

4 tablespoons ghee, plus an extra 1 tablespoon

4 green cardamom pods, lightly crushed

salt

Mix the lamb and raw papaya paste together in a bowl. Cover and set aside in the refrigerator for about 30 minutes.

Add the roasted gram flour to the lamb mixture, mix well, cover again and set aside for a further 10 minutes.

Add the masala to the lamb, season with salt and mix to combine.

Heat a little ghee in a frying pan (skillet) over low heat, add the crushed cardamom pods and stir-fry for about 1–2 minutes, or until red. Remove from the pan and set aside.

If you would like to smoke the lamb, place the meat in a large pan, make a hollow in the middle and place a heatproof bowl into the hole. Put a few pieces of live charcoal into the bowl, sprinkle the seeds of the cardamom pods together with 1 tablespoon of ghee on the charcoal, cover immediately with a lid and smoke for about 30 minutes. Uncover, remove the bowl and discard its contents.

Divide the smoked lamb into 12 equal portions, roll into balls and then flatten them between your hands into 2-cm / ¾-inch thick patties.

Heat the remaining ghee on a large flat tawa, griddle or frying pan (skillet), gently arrange the patties on it and fry over very low heat for 3–4 minutes, carefully turning once. Remove and drain on kitchen paper (paper towels).

You can omit the smoking of the meat if you prefer, but make sure the patties are fully cooked before serving them.

Shami Kebab
Classic Kebabs

Origin Delhi
Preparation time 1 hour 10 minutes, plus cooling time
Cooking time 5–7 minutes
Serves 5–6

1kg / 2¼lb finely minced (ground) lamb

75g / 2½oz (⅓ cup) chana dal, rinsed and drained

2 tablespoons masoor dal, rinsed and drained

3–4 black cardamom pods

5–6 green cardamom pods

4–6 dried red chillies

6–8 black peppercorns

1 cinnamon stick, about 2.5cm / 1 inch long

4–5 cloves

1 × 2.5-cm / 1-inch piece fresh ginger

1 large sprig coriander (cilantro), chopped

1½ tablespoons chopped green chilli

vegetable oil, for deep-frying

salt

Mint Chutney (see page 66) or Raw Green Mango
   Chutney (see page 75), to serve

Place the meat, dals, cardamoms pods, red chillies, peppercorns, cinnamon stick, cloves and ginger in a pan. Season with salt and then pour in 175ml / 6fl oz (¾ cup) water and bring to the boil. Reduce the heat to medium and cook until the meat is completely dry, about 45 minutes. Remove and allow to cool.

Discard the whole spices and transfer the meat to a blender or food processor and process to make a fine paste. Transfer the paste to a bowl, add the chopped coriander and green chilli and mix well.

Divide the mixture into 20 equal portions and roll into balls. With damp hands, flatten them into small patty-like shapes.

Heat enough oil for deep-frying in a kadhai or deep pan to 180°C/350°F, or until a cube of bread browns in 30 seconds. Working in batches, carefully lower the patties into the hot oil and deep-fry until golden brown and crisp. Remove with a slotted spoon and drain on kitchen paper (paper towels). Serve with chutney.

Pasanda Kebab
Lamb Kebabs

Origin Hyderabad
Preparation time 30 minutes, plus standing time
Cooking time 20 minutes
Serves 8

1kg / 2¼lb lamb fillet, trimmed

1 × 5-cm / 2-inch piece papaya

1 × 5-cm / 2-inch piece fresh ginger

6 cloves garlic, crushed

2 onions, sliced

6 black peppercorns

2 green chillies, de-seeded and finely chopped

1 teaspoon red chilli powder, or to taste

pinch of ground asafoetida

1 teaspoon Garam Masala (see page 31)

100g / 3½oz (½ cup) ghee

salt

Cut the meat into 8-cm / 3-inch pieces that are 1cm / ½ inch thick. Place on a board and, using a meat mallet, beat lightly on one side to flatten and make pasandas (thin slices).

Put the papaya, ginger, garlic, onions, peppercorns and chillies in a blender or food processor and process to make a smooth paste. Transfer to a bowl, season with salt and add the chilli powder, asafoetida and garam masala and mix to combine. Smear this mixture on both sides of the pasandas, cover and set aside in the refrigerator for about 1 hour.

Preheat the grill (broiler) to medium, if using. Now roll each pasanda up and secure with a piece of kitchen string (twine). Heat the ghee in a large frying pan (skillet) and fry the pasandas over low heat for about 10 minutes. Cover with a lid, place some live charcoals on top and cook for about 5–7 minutes, or until reddish brown. Alternatively, transfer the pasandas to the hot grill and cook for about 5 minutes, or until reddish brown.

☀ / 📷 p.124

Sikampoor Kebab (I)
Stuffed Lamb Kebabs

Origin Awadh
Preparation time 1 hour, plus cooling time
Cooking time 20–25 minutes
Serves 6–8

1kg / 2¼lb minced (ground) lamb

100g / 3½oz (½ cup) chana dal, rinsed and drained

3 black cardamom pods

5 green cardamom pods

5 dried red chillies

5 black peppercorns

½ teaspoon ground turmeric

30g / 1¼oz (¾ cup) chopped coriander (cilantro) leaves

1½ tablespoons green chillies, de-seeded
    and chopped

vegetable oil, for deep-frying

salt

For the stuffing

1 onion, finely chopped

2 boiled egg whites, chopped

5 black peppercorns, crushed

To serve

salad

chutney, such as Mint Chutney (see page 66)

Put the minced meat, chana dal, cardamom pods, red chillies, black peppercorns and turmeric in a large pan. Season with salt and add enough water to cover. Cook over low heat for about 30 minutes, or until the meat is cooked and all the water has evaporated. Remove the spices and discard and allow the meat to cool.

Transfer the cooled meat to a food processor and process to a fine paste. Put the paste into a bowl, add the chopped coriander and chillies and mix to combine.

To make the stuffing, put the chopped onion, chopped egg whites and crushed black peppercorns in a bowl. Season with salt and mix together.

Divide the meat mixture into 20 equal portions, and, with damp hands, shape the mixture into balls. Make a hollow in the center of each ball with your thumb and place a teaspoon of stuffing mixture in each hole.

Close by pinching the meat mixture over the top, roll into balls again and then flatten to make round patties.

Heat the oil for deep-frying in a kadhai or deep, heavy-based pan to 180°C/350°F, or until a cube of bread browns in 30 seconds. Working in batches, carefully lower the patties into the hot oil and deep-fry for about 5 minutes until golden brown and crisp on both sides. Remove with a slotted spoon and drain on kitchen paper (paper towels). Serve hot with choice of salad and chutney.

Moti Kebab
Succulent Spicy Lamb

Origin Awadh
Preparation time 30 minutes, plus marinating time
Cooking time 15–20 minutes
Serves 4–6

---

1 tablespoon raw papaya paste

4 tablespoons malt (white) vinegar

1kg / 2¼lb boneless lamb, cut into small cubes

4 tablespoons vegetable oil or ghee

2 tablespoons butter

salt

For the marinade

250ml / 8fl oz (1 cup) natural (plain) yoghurt, whisked

2 tablespoons Ginger Paste (see page 57)

2 tablespoons Garlic Paste (see page 57)

2 tablespoons red chilli paste

2 teaspoons Garam Masala (see page 31)

Put the papaya paste and vinegar in a large bowl, season with salt and mix well. Add the meat and mix until it is evenly coated in the mixture. Cover and allow to stand in the refrigerator for at least 30 minutes.

Put all the ingredients for the marinade in a large bowl or shallow dish, season with salt and mix well. Add the meat and mix until it is evenly coasted. Cover and allow to marinate in the refrigerator overnight.

Heat the oil or ghee in a very shallow or wide flat pan. Add the meat, together with the marinade, and cook over low-medium heat, turning frequently with a spatula, for about 15 minutes, or until cooked and very little moisture remains.

Sikampoor Kebab (II)
Lamb Patties

Origin Awadh
Preparation time 1 hour, plus cooling time
Cooking time 10–20 minutes
Serves 4

500g / 1lb 2oz minced (ground) lamb

4 tablespoons chana dal, rinsed and drained

10 cloves garlic

1 teaspoon black cumin seeds

5 green cardamom pods

2 cinnamon sticks, about 2.5cm / 1 inch long

5 cloves

2 tablespoons vegetable oil, plus more for deep frying

2 tablespoons lemon juice

1 teaspoon chilli powder

salt

For the filling

2 tablespoons finely chopped onions

1 large sprig mint, chopped

4 green chillies, de-seeded and chopped

pinch of salt

Put the lamb, chana dal, garlic, cumin, cardamom pods, cinnamon sticks and cloves in a large pan. Pour in 175ml / 6fl oz (¾ cup) water and bring to the boil, then reduce the heat to medium and cook until the meat is completely dry, about 45 minutes. Add the oil and fry over medium heat for about 2–3 minutes. Remove from the heat and let cool.

Transfer the lamb to a blender or food processor and process to a fine paste. Transfer the paste to the pan, add the lemon juice and chilli powder and season with salt. Mix well, then divide the mixture into 8 equal portions and roll into balls.

Put all the ingredients for the filling in a bowl and mix to combine, then divide into 8 equal portions.

With wet hands, flatten each lamb ball, then place a portion of the filling in the middle, seal and flatten again into round patties. Heat enough oil for deep-frying in deep, heavy-based pan to 180°C/350°F, or until a cube of bread browns in 30 seconds. Working in batches, deep-fry the patties for about 5 minutes on each side until dark brown. Remove and drain on kitchen paper (paper towels). You may shallow-fry the patties if you prefer.

Patthar Kebab
Kebab Cooked on a Stone

Origin Hyderabad
Preparation time 20 minutes, plus marinating time
Cooking time 15–20 minutes
Serves 6–8

6–8 green chillies, de-seeded

1kg / 2¼lb boneless lamb, cut into flat steaks, about 2cm / ¾ inch thick

1 teaspoon ground allspice

1 teaspoon ground black pepper

1½ teaspoons Ginger Paste (see page 57)

1½ teaspoons Garlic Paste (see page 57)

1 teaspoon green papaya paste

vegetable oil, for brushing

salt

To serve

2–3 onions, finely sliced

2–3 lemons

few mint leaves

Mint Chutney (see page 66)

Put the chillies in a small blender or food processor and process to a paste. Set aside.

Put the meat on a board and gently pound with a meat mallet to flatten.

Put the chilli paste, allspice, pepper and pastes into a large shallow dish. Season with salt and mix well. Add the meat and rub the marinade all over until coated. Cover and allow to marinate in the refrigerator for 4–5 hours.

Take a flat piece of rough granite, wash it and place it on 2 bricks making sure it is stable. Heat the granite well by placing live charcoals under it. Sprinkle a little oil on the granite and, working in batches, add the marinated meat pieces. Cook, turning a couple of times and brushing them lightly with oil, for about 4–5 minutes on each side. Remove with tongs and keep warm. Alternatively, cook the meat over a charcoal grill or on a griddle (ridged grill pan). Serve with sliced onions, lemon wedges, mint leaves and fresh mint chutney.

Dum ke Kebab
Kebabs Baked in a Slow Oven

Origin Hyderabad
Preparation time 30 minutes, plus marinating time
Cooking time 45 minutes
Serves 4

1 tablespoon raw papaya
1kg / 2¼ lb boneless lamb, cut into flat pieces
2 tablespoons vegetable oil or ghee
4 onions, sliced
250ml / 8fl oz (1 cup) natural (plain) yoghurt, whisked
1 cinnamon stick, about 5cm / 2 inches long
8 cardamom pods
6 cloves
6 green chillies, de-seeded (optional)
1½ bunches coriander (cilantro), leaves only, chopped
1 teaspoon black caraway seeds
1 teaspoon chironji seeds
2 teaspoons poppy seeds
1 × 2.5-cm / 1-inch piece dry coconut
1½ teaspoons Garlic Paste (see page 57)
1 teaspoon Ginger Paste (see page 57)
6 dried red chillies
salt

For the seasoning

250g / 9oz (1 cup) ghee
1 teaspoon ground allspice
125ml / 4½fl oz (½ cup) single (light) cream
3 teaspoons gram (chickpea) flour, roasted
juice of 2 limes

To garnish

few sprigs mint
2 limes, cut into slices

Put the papaya in a small blender and process until ground to a paste.

Put the lamb on a board and, using a meat mallet, pound to flatten.

Heat half the oil or ghee in a large, heavy-based pan over medium heat, add the onions and fry for 5–7 minutes, or until golden brown. Drain and set aside.

Put the ground papaya and yoghurt in a large shallow dish, add the lamb and the rest of the ingredients, then season with salt. Mix well, making sure the meat is evenly coated with the mixture. Cover and allow to marinate in the refrigerator for 1 hour.

Preheat the oven 180°C/350°F/Gas Mark 4. Crush most of the fried onions, setting aside a handful for the garnish.

To make the seasoning, put the crushed onions, ghee, allspice, cream and roasted gram flour in a bowl and mix together. Add the marinated lamb and mix well. Arrange the lamb in a baking dish and spread the seasoning over it, then cover with foil and place in the middle of the oven (not near the source of the heat) and cook for 35–40 minutes, or until cooked and browned on top. After 20 minutes of cooking, uncover and turn the meat over in the baking pan. Add the lime juice, then return to the oven and leave uncovered for the remaining cooking time.

Serve garnished with the reserved fried onions, mint sprigs and lime slices.

Tatti Gosht
'Bamboo Curtain' Kebab

Origin Hyderabad
Preparation time 15 minutes, plus marinating time
Cooking time 30 minutes
Serves 4–6

8–10 green chillies, de-seeded (optional)
½ teaspoon ground black pepper
1 large sprig coriander (cilantro), chopped
1½ teaspoons Ginger Paste (see page 57)
1½ teaspoons Garlic Paste (see page 57)
1 teaspoon raw papaya paste
1kg / 2¼lb boneless lamb, cut into fillets about 1cm / ½ inch thick
125ml / 4½fl oz (½ cup) vegetable oil, for brushing
1 onion, sliced, to serve
2 tablespoons lemon juice, to serve
salt

Put the chillies in a small blender or food processor and process until ground.

Put the pepper and coriander, pastes and ground chillies into a large bowl, season with salt and mix well. Spread the paste evenly over the meat, put into a large, shallow dish, cover and allow to marinate in the refrigerator for 1–1 ½ hours.

Prepare a tandoor or charcoal grill for a moderate heat, or alternatively preheat the grill (broiler) to medium. Lightly brush a wire mesh or grill rack with oil. Place the marinated meat on the mesh or rack and cook over a moderately hot charcoal grill or under the hot grill for about 30 minutes, basting the meat with oil, until the meat is cooked. Serve with sliced onions and a little lemon juice sprinkled over the top.

Khusk Pasande
Dry Meat Kebabs

Origin Hyderabad
Preparation time 20–30 minutes, plus marinating time
Cooking time 2½ hours
Serves 4

200g / 7oz garlic, crushed
1 × 5-cm / 2-inch piece fresh ginger
4 tablespoons lime juice
pinch of chilli powder
1½ teaspoons salt
2kg / 4½lb Pasanda (see page 187)
150g / 5oz chironji seeds
3 tablespoons poppy seeds
500ml / 18fl oz (2¼ cups) natural (plain) yoghurt
2 tablespoons ghee
lime wedges and onion rings to garnish

Put the garlic and ginger in a mortar or small blender and pound with a pestle or process until ground. Transfer to a bowl and add the lime juice and chilli powder. Season with salt and mix together. Add the meat and rub the mixture evenly over to coat. Cover and allow to marinate in the refrigerator for at least 4 hours.

Preheat the oven to 200°C/400°F/Gas Mark 6. Roast the chironji seeds and poppy seeds gently in a dry frying pan (skillet). Transfer to a spice grinder and process until ground. Add to the ground meat, then add the yoghurt and ghee to the meat and mix well.

Transfer the meat to a shallow baking dish and cook in the oven for 1½ hours. Reduce the oven temperature to 180°C/350°F/Gas Mark 4 and cook for a further 1 hour, or until the meat is very tender, turning the meat once or twice during cooking.

☀ / 📷 p.119

___

Lukhmi
Lukhmi

Origin Hyderabad
Preparation time 1 hour, plus cooling and standing time
Cooking time 20 minutes
Makes 35

___

500g / 1lb 2oz minced (ground) lamb

½ teaspoon chilli powder

½ teaspoon ground cumin

1 × 2.5-cm / 1-inch piece fresh ginger, peeled and finely chopped

2 teaspoons Ginger Paste (see page 57)

2 teaspoons Garlic Paste (see page 57)

3 tablespoons vegetable oil, plus extra for deep-frying

20g / ¾oz (½ cup) chopped coriander (cilantro) leaves

6–8 green chillies, de-seeded and chopped

2 tablespoons lemon juice

salt

For the pastry

250g / 9oz (2 cups) plain (all-purpose) flour, plus extra for dusting

4 tablespoons ghee

2 tablespoons natural (plain) yoghurt, whisked

Place the meat, chilli powder, cumin, chopped ginger and ginger and garlic pastes in a pan. Season with salt and then pour in 175ml / 6fl oz (¾ cup) water and bring to the boil. Reduce the heat to medium and cook for about 45 minutes, or until the mince is cooked.

Heat the 3 tablespoons oil in a frying pan (skillet), add the coriander and chillies and fry for 1 minute. Add the boiled meat and fry until there is no water left. Allow to cool, then add the lemon juice.

To make the pastry, put all the pastry ingredients in a large bowl, season with salt and mix, gradually adding enough water to make a soft dough. Cover the dough and set aside in a cool place, preferably the refrigerator for 30 minutes.

Divide the dough into 35–40 equal portions and roll into round balls. Dust each ball with a little flour and shape each into an oblong. Place a little of the meat mixture in the centre, fold over to cover the mixture and seal the edges.

Trim off the uneven sides with a sharp knife to make neat rectangles, called lukhmi. Heat enough oil for deep-frying in a kadhai or deep, heavy-based pan to 180°C/350°F, or until a cube of bread browns in 30 seconds. Working in batches, carefully lower the lukhmis into the hot oil and deep-fry for about 5 minutes, or until golden brown all over. Remove with a slotted spoon and drain on kitchen paper (paper towels). Serve hot.

☀ / 📷 p.206

___

Tabak Maaz
Deep-fried Spare Ribs

Origin Jammu and Kashmir
Preparation time 1½ hours
Cooking time 45 minutes
Serves 4

___

1kg / 2¼lb ribs of lamb

2 tablespoons Garlic Paste (see page 57)

2 teaspoons ground ginger

8–10 cloves

8–10 black cardamom pods

2 tablespoons ground turmeric

500ml / 18fl oz (2¼ cups) vegetable oil or ghee

salt

Boil the ribs in a large pan of water, removing the scum with a slotted spoon, for about 30 minutes, or until the water is clear and until the ribs are half done. Stir in the garlic paste and boil for 15 minutes. Season with salt, cover with a lid and boil for a further 15 minutes, or until the membrane between the ribs can be pierced with your fingers. Remove the pan from the heat and drain off the water. Allow the ribs to cool, then wash thoroughly, reserving the washing water, and set aside.

Using a sharp heavy knife, separate the ribs into 8 rectangular pieces.

Put the reserved washing water into a large pan and bring to the boil. Add the chopped ribs, ginger, cloves, cardamom pods and turmeric. Season with saltand mix well. Allow to boil until the bones can beextracted from the membrane easily. Remove the pan from the heat and remove the ribs with a slotted spoon.

Arrange the ribs in a large frying pan (skillet) (ensuring that they do not overlap), add the oil or ghee and fry, turning gently for 45 minutes, or until they are evenly browned. Drain out the excess fat before serving.

Kashmiri Red
Kidney Beans   p.586

Gram (Chickpea)
Flour Rolls   p.166

Minced (Ground)
Lamb Skewers   p.180

Boneless Lamb
Kebab   p.183

Kashmiri Red
Kidney Beans   p.586

Gram (Chickpea)
Flour Rolls   p.166

Minced (Ground)
Lamb Skewers   p.180

Spicy Lamb Tikka on Skewers   p.182

Mooli Raita
p.85

Spinach Paratha
p.613

Potato & Chickpea
(Garbanzo Bean) Snack
p.158

Masala chai
p.726

Spicy Grilled
Chicken Pieces p.217

Paneer in Pickling
Spices   p.313

Ginger-flavoured
Chops   p.212

Making
Paneer   p.59

Assorted
Spices

Preparing Fresh
Coconut   p.781

Deep-fried
Spare Ribs   p.192

Ribbed Gourd with
Chana Dal   p.296

Raw Tamarind
Chutney   p.66

Boneless Lamb
Kebab   p.183

✷ ✷
___

Keeme ke Samose
Lamb Samosas

Origin Awadh
Preparation time 1 hour, plus cooling time
Cooking time 20 minutes
Makes 40

For the pastry

250g / 9oz (2 cups) plain (all-purpose) flour, plus extra
    for dusting

pinch of salt

5 level tablespoons ghee or butter

For the filling

8 cloves garlic, chopped

3 tablespoons ghee

2 onions, chopped

1 × 1-cm / ½-inch piece fresh ginger, peeled
    and chopped

½ teaspoon ground turmeric

1 teaspoon coriander seeds, ground

4 tablespoons natural (plain) yoghurt

500g / 1lb 2oz finely minced (ground) lamb

2 tablespoons chopped coriander (cilantro) leaves

500g / 1lb 2oz (2¼ cups) ghee or vegetable oil,
    for deep-frying

salt

To make the pastry, sift the flour and salt together into a large bowl, add the ghee or butter and rub it in with your fingertips until it resembles breadcrumbs. Add enough water to make a stiff dough and knead until smooth. Cover with a damp cloth and set aside while you make the filling.

Put the garlic in a small blender and process until ground to a paste.

Heat the 3 tablespoons ghee over medium heat, add the onions and stir-fry for about 5–7 minutes, or until golden. Add the garlic, ginger, turmeric and coriander, stir and cook, adding the yoghurt, a little at a time. Season with salt, add the meat and cook for 5 minutes, or until the meat is evenly browned. Pour in 250ml / 8fl oz (1 cup) water, cover with a lid and cook for 30–45 minutes, or until the mince is tender and completely dry. Stir in the chopped coriander, then remove from the heat and allow to cool completely before using.

To assemble the samosas, pinch off small pieces of dough and roll out thinly on a lightly dusted board or work surface into rounds. Cut each round in half. Dampen half the cut edge with water and fold over the other half to make a cone shape and press firmly to seal. Hold the cone open in one hand and fill with 2–3 teaspoons meat. Dampen the top edge and seal to enclose the filling. Crimp the edges.

Heat enough ghee or oil for deep-frying in a kadhai or deep, heavy-based pan to 180°C/350°F, or until a cube of bread browns in 30 seconds, then reduce the heat. Working in batches, carefully lower the samosas into the hot oil and deep-fry for about 5 minutes, or until golden on all sides. Remove with a slotted spoon and drain on kitchen paper (paper towels).

※ ※
___

Tawe de Tikke
Boneless Pan-fried Lamb

Origin Punjab
Preparation time 35–40 minutes, plus marinating time
Cooking time 20 minutes
Serves 4

1kg / 2¼lb lamb shoulder, cut into cubes

125g / 4¼oz (½ cup) ghee or vegetable oil

8 flakes garlic or 1 small clove garlic, chopped

200g / 7oz (1¼ cups) chopped onions

3 teaspoons chopped ginger

4–5 green chillies, de-seeded

3 large tomatoes, chopped

1½ teaspoons ground cumin

1½ teaspoons ground black pepper, dry-roasted

½ teaspoon ground black cardamom

¼ teaspoon ground cloves

¼ teaspoon ground cinnamon

2 tablespoons dark rum

3 tablespoons chopped coriander (cilantro) leaves

1 tablespoon lemon juice

1 teaspoon fenugreek leaves

salt

For the marinade

6 green cardamom pods

6 cloves

3 black cardamom pods

3 cinnamon sticks, about 2.5cm / 1 inch long

2 teaspoons chilli powder

5 teaspoons Garlic Paste (see page 57)

3½ teaspoons Ginger Paste (see page 57)

250ml / 8fl oz (1 cup) natural (plain) yoghurt, whisked

100g / 3½oz (1 medium) onion, fried

To make the marinade, put the spices, pastes, yoghurt and fried onion in a large shallow dish and mix well. Add the meat cubes and rub evenly all over to coat. Cover and allow to marinate in the refrigerator for about 2 hours.

Transfer the marinated meat to a large pan and stir-fry over medium heat until the juices begin to boil. Reduce the heat and stir-fry for about 5 minutes, or until the juices have completely evaporated and the meat is cooked. Set aside.

Heat a little ghee or oil on an iron griddle or in a frying pan (skillet), add the garlic and stir-fry over medium heat for about 30 seconds, or until it turns light golden. Add the chopped onions and stir-fry for 2 minutes, or until they become translucent. Now, add the ginger and chillies and stir-fry for a few seconds. Add the tomatoes and stir-fry for about 5 minutes, or until they become soft. Next, add the cooked meat pieces and stir-fry for a further 2–3 minutes. Add the ground cumin, pepper, cardamom, cloves and cinnamon, then season with salt and stir. Now, add the rum and mix to combine. Finally, add the coriander and lemon juice, then sprinkle over the fenugreek leaves and give everything a final stir. Remove from the heat and adjust the seasoning, if necessary.

✳ ✳

Raan Patialashai
Royal Patiala Leg of Lamb

Origin Punjab
Preparation time 30 minutes, plus marinating time
Cooking time 1 hour 10 minutes
Serves 4

1kg / 2¼ lb leg of lamb
melted butter, for basting

For the marinade

1 tablespoon raw papaya paste
2 cinnamon sticks, crushed
1 teaspoon ground cardamom
1 teaspoon ground cloves
1 teaspoon ground aniseed
1½ teaspoons ground cumin
1½ tablespoons ground coriander
½ teaspoons ground nutmeg
1 tablespoon ground ginger

For the whisked yoghurt paste

300ml / ½ pint (1¼ cups) hung natural (plain) yoghurt (see page 793)
4 tablespoons Garlic Paste (see page 57)
2 tablespoons green chilli paste
2 tablespoons red chilli paste
2 tablespoons chopped garlic
½ tablespoon ground turmeric
½ tablespoon ground cinnamon
3½ tablespoons lemon juice
2 teaspoons vegetable oil
2 tablespoons melted butter
salt

Remove the blade bone of the lamb leg and, using a sharp knife, make incisions all over the meat.

To make the marinade, put the papaya paste, crushed cinnamon and ground spices in a large shallow dish and mix well. Add the meat and rub the mixture evenly all over to coat. Cover and allow to marinate in the refrigerator for about 2 hours.

To make the whisked yoghurt paste, put the yoghurt, pastes, the chopped garlic, turmeric, cinnamon, lemon juice, oil and butter in another large dish. Season with salt and mix well. Remove the meat from the first marinade, wiping off any excess moisture from the first marinade and add the meat to the second marinade.

Rub the paste evenly all over the meat, then cover and allow to marinate in the refrigerator for a further 2 hours.

Preheat the oven to 190°C/375°F/Gas Mark 5. Place the lamb leg with any remaining marinade into a large roasting dish or tin (pan) and roast the leg in the oven for about 1 hour, or until it is nearly cooked. Remove and cut the leg into 3–4 pieces along the bone.

Prepare a tandoor or charcoal grill for a moderate heat, or alternatively preheat the grill (broiler) to medium. Thread the lamb pieces on to several metal skewers and roast in a moderately hot tandoor or under the hot grill for 7–8 minutes. Remove from the heat and baste with melted butter, then roast for a further 3–4 minutes. Slice the meat and serve hot.

Tash Kebab
Steamed Slices of Lamb

Origin Awadh
Preparation time 15 minutes, plus marinating time
Cooking time 45 minutes
Serves 4

1 tablespoon Garam Masala (see page 31)
½ teaspoon Ginger Paste (see page 57)
½ teaspoon Garlic Paste (see page 57)
1 teaspoon chilli powder
350g / 12oz (1½ cups) ghee
pinch of saffron threads
375ml / 13fl oz (1½ cups) natural (plain) yoghurt
juice of 2 limes
500g / 1lb 2oz boneless lamb, cut into slices
1kg / 2¼lb (6–7 medium) onions, finely sliced
salt

Put the garam masala, ginger and garlic pastes, chilli powder, ghee, saffron, yoghurt and lime juice in a large shallow dish. Season with salt and mix well. Add the lamb slices and turn until the meat is evenly coated. Cover and allow to marinate in the refrigerator for 3 hours.

Preheat the oven to 140°C/275°F/Gas Mark 1, if using. Put half the onions in a large casserole dish. Put the lamb slices on top, then cover with the rest of the onions. Cover with a tight-fitting lid, put a few burning charcoals on the lid and cook over low heat. Alternatively, cook in the oven for 45 minutes, or until the meat and onions are cooked in their own steam.

Adraki Chaamp
Ginger-flavoured Chops

Origin Punjab
Preparation time 30 minutes, plus marinating time
Cooking time 15–20 minutes
Serves 4

1kg / 2¼lb lamb chops, rinsed and patted dry
    with kitchen paper (paper towels)
melted butter, for basting

For the first marinade
4 tablespoons unripe papaya paste
1 tablespoon red chilli paste
2 tablespoons Ginger Paste (see page 57)
1 tablespoon Garlic Paste (see page 57)
1 tablespoon chopped ginger
1 tablespoon malt (white) vinegar
1 tablespoon vegetable oil
salt

For the second marinade
250ml / 8fl oz (1 cup) natural (plain) yoghurt, whisked
1 tablespoon chopped ginger
1 tablespoon Garlic Paste (see page 57)
4 tablespoons Ginger Paste (see page 57)
1 × 6-cm / 2½-inch piece ginger, peeled and chopped
3 tablespoons vegetable oil

To make the first marinade, put the pastes, chopped ginger, vinegar and oil in a large shallow dish. Season with salt and mix well. Add the chops and spread the marinade evenly over to coat. Cover and allow to marinate in the refrigerator for about 6 hours.

Mix the yoghurt with all the other ingredients for the second marinade in a large shallow dish. Remove the meat from the first marinade, wiping off any excess moisture from the first marinade and add the meat to the second marinade. Cover and allow to marinate in the refrigerator for a further 3 hours.

Prepare a tandoor or charcoal grill for a moderate heat, or alternatively preheat the grill (broiler) to medium. Thread the chops on to metal skewers, leaving 2.5cm / 1 inch between them. Make sure they do not fall off the skewers. Roast in a moderately hot tandoor, over a charcoal grill or under the hot grill for about 10 minutes. Remove the skewers from the heat and hang up to drain. Put the skewers into a dish and baste with the melted butter, then roast for a further 5 minutes, or until cooked. Serve hot.

Khageena
Savoury Scrambled Eggs

Origin Hyderabad
Preparation time 15 minutes
Cooking time 15 minutes
Serves 4

2 tablespoons vegetable oil
2 onions, sliced
2 tomatoes, finely chopped
3 green chillies, de-seeded and chopped
½ teaspoon ground turmeric
½ teaspoon chilli powder
¼ teaspoon Ginger Paste (see page 57)
¼ teaspoon Garlic Paste (see page 57)
6 eggs, beaten
1 tablespoon butter or ghee
½ bunch coriander (cilantro), leaves only, chopped
salt
Handkerchief Roti (see page 616), to serve

Heat the oil in a frying pan (skillet) over medium heat, add the onions and fry for about 5–7 minutes, or until golden brown. Reduce the heat, add the tomatoes, chillies, ground spices and the ginger and garlic pastes and stir together over low heat. Continue to cook for about 5 minutes, or until the tomatoes are softened and the liquid has evaporated.

Beat the eggs in a bowl.

Melt the butter or ghee in another pan over low heat. Add the beaten eggs and coriander leaves, season with salt and reduce the heat to low. Cook, stirring briskly, for 3–4 minutes, or until the eggs are scrambled, but still remain moist. Add the onion and tomato mixture and stir for 1 minute until warmed through. Serve with Roti.

Bhune Kebab
Savoury Baked Minced (Ground) Lamb

Origin Hyderabad
Preparation time 30–35 minutes, plus cooling time
Cooking time 40–50 minutes
Serves 4

225g / 8oz minced (ground) lamb

4 brown cardamom pods

2 cloves

1 teaspoon ground ginger

4 small dried kachri optional

4 onions, sliced

100g / 3½oz (½ cup) ghee

1 tablespoon gram (chickpea) flour, roasted

1 × 8-cm / 3-inch square piece papaya with skin,
    ground

1 teaspoon chilli powder

To garnish

5 green chillies, de-seeded and chopped

few sprigs mint leaves

1 bunch coriander (cilantro), leaves only, chopped

To serve

few limes, cut into slices

chutney, such as Mint Chutney (see page 66)
    or Raw Green Mango Chutney (see page 75)

Preheat the oven to 180°C/350°F/Gas Mark 4. Put the mince into a food processor and process until finely ground. Transfer to a bowl.

Remove the seeds from the cardamom pods and put into a blender or food processor with the cloves, ginger and kachri, if using. Add 2 of the onions and a teaspoon of water and process until ground. Add to the mince and mix well.

Heat half the ghee in a frying pan (skillet) over medium heat, add the remaining 2 onions and fry for 5–7 minutes, or until golden brown. Using a spoon, transfer to a blender or food processor and process until ground. Add to the mince mixture with the gram flour, papaya and chilli powder and mix well.

Heat the remaining ghee in the pan until melted, then remove from the heat and allow to cool for 20 minutes.

Preheat the grill (broiler) to medium. Put a little ghee in your hands and roll the mince mixture into balls. Arrange them neatly next to each other in a large baking dish. Cover with a lid or foil and bake in the oven for 30–40 minutes, or until the mince is cooked and browned. Do not allow the mince to burn. When the mince is cooked, place under the hot grill for a few minutes to brown the top a little more. Garnish with chopped chillies, mint and coriander leaves and serve with slices of lime and chutney.

Aloo Chop
Potato with Minced (Ground) Lamb

Origin West Bengal
Preparation time 30 minutes, plus cooling
and chilling time
Cooking time 20 minutes
Serves 4

500g / 1lb 2oz (3 medium) potatoes
½ teaspoon ground white pepper
pinch of ground nutmeg
1 tablespoon chopped coriander (cilantro) leaves
2 eggs
120g / 4oz (¾ cup) dried breadcrumbs
vegetable oil, for shallow-frying
salt

For the filling

2 tablespoons vegetable oil
2 tablespoons butter
60g / 2oz (⅓ cup) onions, chopped
8 cloves garlic, chopped
1 × 2.5-cm / 1-inch piece fresh ginger, peeled and chopped
4 green chillies, de-seeded and chopped
450g / 1lb minced (ground) lamb
2 teaspoons lemon juice
generous pinch of basil leaves, chopped
pinch of ground green cardamom
small pinch of ground cloves
small pinch of ground cinnamon
60g / 2oz (½ cup) cheese, grated
1 teaspoon Tabasco sauce

Cook the potatoes in a large pan of boiling water for 20 minutes, or until soft. Drain and allow to cool. When cool, peel off the skins and return the potato to the pan. Mash with a potato masher.

Put the mashed potatoes, white pepper, nutmeg and coriander in a large bowl, season with salt and mix well. Divide into 16 equal portions and roll into balls. Put the balls on a large plate, cover and allow to chill in the refrigerator for 15 minutes.

To make the filling, heat the oil and butter in a frying pan (skillet) over medium heat, add the onions and garlic and stir-fry for about 2 minutes, or until the onions are translucent. Add the ginger and chillies and stir-fry for a further 3–4 minutes, or until the onions are golden. Add the lamb, season with salt and stir-fry for about 7–8 minutes, or until the lamb is cooked, sprinkling over a little water, if necessary, to prevent the lamb sticking to the pan. Stir in the lemon juice, basil and ground spices, then season with salt. Remove from the heat and allow to cool slightly.

When the filling has cooled slightly, add the cheese and Tabasco and adjust the seasoning, if necessary. Mix well and divide into 16 equal portions.

With damp hands, flatten each potato ball to make round patties, then place a portion of the filling in the middle, roll into balls again to enclose the filling and then flatten into 2-cm / ¾-inch thick oval patties, making sure that the filling does not ooze out. Put on a large plate, cover and allow to chill for 15 minutes.

Put the eggs in a shallow dish and beat lightly. Spread the breadcrumbs out on a large plate. Remove the patties from the refrigerator and dip them first into the beaten eggs and then roll in the breadcrumbs until evenly coated.

Heat enough oil for shallow-frying in a frying pan over medium heat. Working in batches, add the patties and shallow-fry, turning once, for about 3 minutes on each side, or until golden brown. Remove with a slotted spoon and drain on kitchen paper (paper towels).

※ ※
___

Keema Upama
Vermicelli with Minced (Ground) Lamb

Origin New
Preparation time 15 minutes
Cooking time 50–60 minutes
Serves 4

125ml / 4½fl oz (½ cup) vegetable oil
2 onions, sliced
1 teaspoon Ginger Paste (see page 57)
1 teaspoon Garlic Paste (see page 57)
1 teaspoon ground coriander, dry-roasted
8 curry leaves
3 green chillies, de-seeded and chopped
½ teaspoon chilli powder
1 cinnamon stick, about 2.5cm (1 inch) long
3 cardamom pods
3 cloves
250g / 9oz minced (ground) lamb
240g / 8½oz vermicelli (thick variety)
½ bunch coriander (cilantro), leaves only, chopped
juice of 1 lime

To garnish

fried whole red chillies
cumin seeds, dry-roasted

Heat the oil in a large, heavy-based pan over medium heat, add the onions and fry for 5–7 minutes, or until golden brown. Add the ginger and garlic pastes, coriander, curry leaves, chillies, chilli powder, cinnamon stick, cardamom pods and cloves and fry for 2 minutes. Add the lamb and fry for a further 5 minutes, or until browned. Add 500ml / 18fl oz (2¼ cups) water and cook for about 30–40 minutes, or until the lamb is tender and the water has evaporated. Continue to fry for a further 1–2 minutes until brown.

Add the vermicelli to the pan and fry for 1 minute. Add another 250ml / 8fl oz (1 cup) water, cover with a lid and cook over low heat for about 8 minutes. Sprinkle over the coriander leaves and lime juice and garnish with fried red chillies and cumin.

※ ※
___

Kaleji Kebab
Deep-fried Liver Koftas

Origin Punjab
Preparation time 30 minutes
Cooking time 30 minutes
Serves 6–8

500g / 1lb 2oz liver, trimmed
50g / 1¾oz (⅓ cup) natural (plain) yoghurt, whisked
1 teaspoon chilli powder, or to taste
2 onions, chopped
1 × 5-cm / 2-inch piece fresh ginger, peeled and ground
pinch of ground asafoetida
2 green chillies, de-seeded and chopped
1 teaspoon ground ginger
1 teaspoon Garam Masala (see page 31)
1 teaspoon ground coriander
50g / 1¾oz (1 cup) chopped coriander (cilantro) leaves
2 tablespoons rice flour
150g / 5oz (⅔ cup) ghee or vegetable oil, for deep-frying
salt

Cut the liver into 2.5-cm / 1-inch pieces.

Cook the liver in a pan of 250ml / 8 fl oz (1 cup) boiling water for about 6 minutes. Add the whisked yoghurt, chilli powder, onions, fresh ginger, asafoetida, chillies and ground ginger and cook for a few more minutes until the liver is tender and dry.

Remove the liver from the pan, place on a grinding stone and grind it to a fine paste. Alternatively, use a food processor or mincer. Transfer the ground liver to a bowl and add the garam masala, both corianders and the rice flour. Season with salt and mix to combine. Divide the mixture into 15–20 equal portions and roll into koftas.

Heat the ghee or oil for deep-frying in a kadhai or deep pan to 180°C/350°F, or until a cube of bread browns in 30 seconds. Working in batches, carefully lower the koftas into the hot oil and deep-fry for 5 minutes, or until golden brown. Remove with a slotted spoon and drain on kitchen paper (paper towels).

Murg Dalcha Kebab
Chicken & Lentil Kebabs

Origin Hyderabad
Preparation time 30 minutes, plus soaking
and marinating time
Cooking time 10 minutes
Serves 4

250g / 9oz (1⅓ cups) chana dal

750g / 1lb 10oz skinless, boneless chicken breasts

2 teaspoons Ginger Paste (see page 57)

2 teaspoons Garlic Paste (see page 57)

2 tablespoons lemon juice

3 teaspoons yellow chilli powder

1 teaspoon Garam Masala (see page 31)

300ml / ½ pint (1¼ cups) hung natural (plain) yoghurt
   (see page 793), whisked

150ml / ¼ pint (⅔ cup) single (light) cream

pinch ground nutmeg

5½ tablespoons vegetable oil

melted butter, for basting

salt

Soak the chana dal in a bowl of water overnight.

The next day, drain the chana dal, then transfer
to a blender or food processor and process to
make a smooth paste. Put the paste into a bowl
and set aside.

Cut each chicken breast in half and pat dry with
kitchen paper (paper towels).

Put the ginger and garlic pastes, lemon juice, chili
powder and garam masala in a large shallow dish.
Season with salt and mix. Add the chicken and rub
the mixture evenly over to coat. Cover and allow
to marinate in the refrigerator for 1 hour.

Put the hung yoghurt in another large shallow dish,
add the chana dal paste, cream, nutmeg and oil
and mix well. Remove the chicken from the first
marinade and squeeze out the excess moisture, put
the chicken in the second marinade and rub the
mixture evenly over to coat. Cover and allow to
marinate in the refrigerator for a further 2–3 hours.

Prepare a tandoor or charcoal grill for a moderate
heat, or alternatively preheat the grill (broiler) to
medium. Thread the chicken on to several metal
skewers and place a dish underneath to collect any
juices. Roast in the hot tandoor, charcoal grill or
under the grill for 6–7 minutes, or until half done.

Remove the skewers from the heat and hang them
up over a tray for about 2–3 minutes to allow any
excess moisture to drain out completely. Put the
skewers in a dish, baste with melted butter and roast
again in the tandoor or on the charcoal grill or under
the grill for a further 3–4 minutes, or until cooked.
Transfer the chicken to a plate and serve hot.

Murg Kali Mirch
Pepper Chicken

Origin Punjab
Preparation time 5 minutes, plus marinating time
Cooking time 15–25 minutes
Serves 4

4 tablespoons natural (plain) yoghurt, whisked

1 teaspoon Ginger Paste (see page 57)

1 teaspoon Garlic Paste (see page 57)

1½ tablespoons freshly ground black pepper

1 large onion, sliced

500g / 1lb 2oz skinless, boneless chicken pieces

4 tablespoons vegetable oil

salt

Put the yoghurt in a large shallow dish and add
the ginger and garlic pastes, black pepper and
onions. Season with salt and mix well. Add the
chicken and turn until the chicken is evenly coated
in the marinade. Cover and allow to marinate in
the refrigerator for at least 2 hours.

Remove the onions from the marinade. Heat the oil
in a large, heavy-based pan over medium heat, add
the marinated onions and fry for about 5–7 minutes,
or until golden brown. Add the chicken with any
remaining marinade and fry for 5–6 minutes, or
until all the moisture has evaporated. Pour in 125ml
/ 4½fl oz (½ cup) water and cook for a further 5–10
minutes, or until the chicken is cooked.

Kashmiri Murg Kebab
Chicken Kebabs

Origin Jammu and Kashmir
Preparation time 30 minutes, plus marinating time
Cooking time 10 minutes
Serves 4

750g / 1lb 10oz skinless, boneless chicken legs

melted butter, for basting

For the marinade

1 teaspoon Cashew Nut Paste (see page 58)

1 tablespoon green chilli paste

375ml / 13fl oz (1½ cups) hung natural (plain) yoghurt
 (see page 793)

200ml / 7fl oz (1 cup) single (light) cream

2 eggs

2 teaspoons plain (all-purpose) flour

2 tablespoons malt (white) vinegar

3 tablespoons ground white pepper

2 teaspoons ground green cardamom

5½ tablespoons vegetable oil

2 tablespoons Ginger Paste (see page 57)

2 tablespoons Garlic Paste (see page 57)

2 tablespoons rose petals, ground

salt

Cut each chicken leg into 4 pieces.

Mix all the ingredients for the marinade together
in a large shallow dish. Season with salt, add the
chicken pieces and rub the marinade evenly over to
coat. Cover and allow to marinate in the refrigerator
for 2 hours.

Prepare a tandoor or charcoal grill for a moderate
heat, or alternatively preheat the grill (broiler) to
medium. Thread the chicken pieces on to several
metal skewers and place a tray underneath to collect
any juices. Roast the chicken pieces in a moderately
hot tandoor, over a charcoal grill or under the grill
for 6–7 minutes, or until half done.

Remove the skewers from the heat and hang them
up over a tray for about 2–3 minutes to allow any
excess moisture to drain out completely. Put the
skewers in a dish, baste with melted butter and roast
again in the tandoor or under the grill for a further
3–4 minutes, or until cooked. Transfer the chicken
to a plate and serve.

❋ ❋ ❋ / 📷 p.197

Teekha Murg Tikka
Spicy Grilled (Broiled) Chicken Pieces

Origin Punjab
Preparation time 15–20 minutes, plus marinating time
Cooking time 10 minutes
Serves 4

750g / 1lb 10oz skinless, boneless chicken legs

melted butter, for basting

For the marinade

3 tablespoons Ginger Paste (see page 57)

3 tablespoons Garlic Paste (see page 57)

2 tablespoons Boiled Onion Paste (see page 57)

1 tablespoon gram (chickpea) flour, roasted

2 tablespoons chopped coriander (cilantro) leaves

2 tablespoons chopped onion

1 tablespoon chopped green chilli

2 tablespoons Garam Masala (see page 31)

2 tablespoons amchoor

1 tablespoon ground dried fenugreek leaves

1 tablespoon Chaat Masala (see page 31)

1 tablespoon Kashmiri red chilli powder

½ tablespoon ajwain seeds

5 tablespoons malt (white) vinegar

125ml / 4½fl oz (½ cup) vegetable oil

salt

Cut each chicken leg into 4 pieces.

Put all the ingredients for the marinade in a large
shallow dish, season with salt and mix well. Add the
chicken pieces to the marinade and rub the mixture
evenly over to coat. Cover and allow to marinate in
the refrigerator for 2 hours.

Prepare a tandoor or charcoal grill for a moderate
heat, or alternatively preheat the grill (broiler) to
medium. Thread the chicken on to several metal
skewers and place a dish underneath to collect any
juices. Roast in a moderately hot tandoor, over
a charcoal grill or under the grill for 6–7 minutes,
or until half done.

Remove the skewers from the heat and hang them
up over a tray for about 2–3 minutes to allow any
excess moisture to drain out completely. Put the
skewers in a dish, baste with melted butter and roast
again in the tandoor, on the charcoal grill or under
the grill for a further 3–4 minutes, or until cooked.
Transfer the chicken to a plate and serve hot.

Tandoori Murg
Grilled (Broiled) Chicken

Origin Punjab
Preparation time 15 minutes, plus marinating time
Cooking time 20 minutes–1½ hours
Serves 4

1 × 800g / 1¾lb chicken, cleaned

melted butter, for basting

2 tablespoons Chaat Masala (see page 31)

4 tablespoons lemon juice

For the first marinade

½ tablespoon Ginger Paste (see page 57)

½ tablespoon Garlic Paste (see page 57)

1 tablespoon red chilli paste

2 tablespoons lemon juice

salt

For the second marinade

400ml / 14fl oz (1⅔ cups) hung natural (plain) yoghurt
    (see page 793), whisked

½ tablespoon Ginger Paste (see page 57)

½ tablespoon Garlic Paste (see page 57)

2 tablespoons Garam Masala (see page 31)

1 tablespoon ground dried fenugreek leaves

5½ tablespoons vegetable oil

Using a sharp knife, make 3 incisions on the breast and leg of the chicken.

For the first marinade, put the pastes and lemon juice in a large shallow dish. Season with salt and mix well. Add the chicken and rub the mixture evenly over to coat. Cover and allow to marinate in the refrigerator for 1 hour.

Put the yoghurt in another large shallow dish, add the ginger and garlic pastes, garam masala, ground dried fenugreek and oil and mix well. Add the marinated chicken to this mixture, and rub the marinade evenly over to coat. Cover and allow to marinate in the refrigerator for a further 2–3 hours.

Prepare a tandoor or charcoal grill for a moderate heat, or alternatively preheat the oven to 200°C/400°F/ Gas Mark 6. Thread the marinated chicken from the tail to the head on to a metal skewer. Roast in a moderately hot tandoor or over a charcoal grill for 12–15 minutes, or until half done.

If roasting the chicken in the oven, place the chicken in a roasting tin (pan), cover with foil and roast for about 1–1½ hours, or until the juices run clear when a skewer is inserted into the thickest part of the meat. Halfway through cooking, baste the chicken with any remaining marinade.

Remove the skewer from the heat and hang it up for about 2–3 minutes to allow any excess moisture to drain out completely. Put the skewer in a dish, baste with melted butter and roast again in the tandoor, over the charcoal grill or in the oven for a further 5–7 minutes, or until cooked. Transfer the chicken to a board and cut into 4 pieces. Sprinkle over the chaat masala and lemon juice, and serve hot.

Lehsuni Murg Tikka
Garlic-flavoured Chicken

Origin Punjab
Preparation time 30 minutes, plus marinating time
Cooking time 10–15 minutes
Serves 4

4 tablespoons Garlic Paste (see page 57)
1½ tablespoons yellow chilli powder
3 teaspoons lemon juice
750g / 1lb 10oz boneless chicken breasts
100g / 3½oz (⅔ cup) gram (chickpea) flour, roasted
200ml / 7fl oz (1 cup) vegetable oil
melted butter, for basting
salt

Put the garlic paste, chilli powder and lemon juice in a large shallow dish, season with salt and mix well. Add the chicken breasts and rub evenly all over to coat. Cover and allow to marinate in the refrigerator for 1 hour.

Now, place the chicken in a tray, add the flour and mix well. Add the oil and mix again.

Prepare a tandoor or charcoal grill for a moderate heat, or alternatively preheat the grill (broiler) to medium. Thread the chicken on to several metal skewers and place a tray underneath to collect any juices. Roast in a moderately hot tandoor, over a charcoal grill or under the hot grill for 6 minutes, or until half done.

Remove the skewer from the heat and hang it up for about 2–3 minutes to allow any excess moisture to drain out completely. Put the skewer in a dish, baste with melted butter and roast again in the tandoor or under the grill for a further 4 minutes, or until cooked. Transfer the chicken to a plate and serve hot.

Kandahari Murg Tikka
Pomegranate-flavoured Chicken

Origin Punjab
Preparation time 20 minutes, plus marinating time
Cooking time 8–10 minutes
Serves 4

750g / 1lb 10oz skinless, boneless chicken breasts
1 tablespoon pomegranate seeds
1 teaspoon dried mint leaves
10–12 curry leaves
1 tablespoon chopped coriander (cilantro) leaves
6–8 green chillies, de-seeded (optional) and chopped
½ tablespoon Ginger Paste (see page 57)
½ tablespoon Garlic Paste (see page 57)
200ml / 7fl oz (1 cup) hung natural (plain) yoghurt (see page 793)
1 tablespoon chopped onion
1 tablespoon finely chopped ginger
1 teaspoon Kashmiri red chilli powder
1 teaspoon ground dried fenugreek leaves
1 tablespoon lemon juice
4 tablespoons vegetable oil
melted butter, for basting
salt

Put the chicken on a board and, using a meat mallet, pound gently to flatten.

To make a paste, put the pomegranate seeds, mint, curry and coriander leaves and the chillies in a small blender and process to a smooth paste.

Put the ginger and garlic pastes, pomegranate paste, yoghurt, onion, ginger, chilli powder, ground dried fenugreek, lemon juice and oil in a large shallow dish and mix together. Add the chicken pieces and rub the mixture evenly over to coat. Cover and allow to marinate in the refrigerator for about 4 hours.

Prepare a charcoal grill for a moderate heat, or preheat the oven to 190°C/375°F/Gas Mark 5. Thread the chicken pieces on to several metal skewers. Roast over a moderately hot charcoal grill or in the oven, for 6–7 minutes, or until half done.

Remove the skewers from the heat and hang them up for about 2–3 minutes to allow any excess moisture to drain out completely. Put the skewers in a dish, baste with melted butter and roast again on the grill or in the oven for a further 2–3 minutes, or until cooked. Transfer the chicken to a plate and serve hot.

☀

Murg Methi Tikka
Fenugreek-flavoured Chicken

Origin Punjab
Preparation time 30 minutes, plus cooling
and marinating time
Cooking time 10 minutes
Serves 4

250g / 9oz fenugreek leaves

4 tablespoons mustard oil

½ teaspoon fenugreek seeds

½ tablespoon Ginger Paste (see page 57)

1 tablespoon Garlic Paste (see page 57)

2 tablespoons lemon juice

750g / 1lb 10oz boneless chicken pieces

300ml / ½ pint (1¼ cups) hung natural (plain) yoghurt
    (see page 793), whisked

3 tablespoons ground dried fenugreek leaves

2–3 green chillies, de-seeded and chopped

1 teaspoon chilli powder, or to taste

1 tablespoon gram (chickpea) flour

1 tablespoon vegetable oil

melted butter, for basting

salt

Bring a small pan of water to the boil, add the
fenugreek leaves and blanch for a few minutes, or
until soft then drain. Transfer the fenugreek leaves
to a mortar or blender and pound with a pestle or
process to make a smooth purée.

Heat the mustard oil in a frying pan (skillet) over
low-medium heat, add the fenugreek seeds and
stir-fry for 30 seconds, or until they start to splutter,
then add the fenugreek purée and cook for about
10 minutes. Remove from the heat and allow to cool.

Put the ginger and half the garlic paste with 1
tablespoon lemon juice into a large shallow dish.
Season with salt and mix well. Add the chicken
breasts and rub the mixture evenly over to coat.
Cover and allow to marinate in the refrigerator
for about 1 hour.

Put the yoghurt in another large shallow dish,
add the remaining garlic paste, ground dried
fenugreek, chillies, ginger, chilli powder, cooked
fenugreek purée, remaining lemon juice, gram
flour and oil and mix well. Adjust the seasoning,
if necessary. Add the chicken breasts and rub the
mixture evenly over to coat. Cover and allow to
marinate for a further 2 hours.

Prepare a tandoor or charcoal grill for a moderate
heat, or alternatively preheat the grill (broiler) to
medium. Thread the chicken breasts on to several
metal skewers and place a tray underneath to collect
any juices. Roast in a moderately hot tandoor, over
a charcoal grill or under the grill for 5 minutes, or
until half done.

Remove the skewers from the heat and hang them
up for about 2–3 minutes to allow any excess
moisture to drain out completely. Put the skewers
in a dish, baste with melted butter and roast again
in the tandoor, on the charcoal grill or under
the grill for a further 3–4 minutes, or until cooked.
Transfer the chicken to a plate and serve hot.

☀ ☀ / 📷 p.119

Murg ke Parche
Chicken Fillet Kebabs

Origin Awadh
Preparation time 30 minutes, plus marinating time
Cooking time 10–15 minutes
Serves 4

1 tablespoon Ginger Paste (see page 57)
1 tablespoon Garlic Paste (see page 57)
1 tablespoon freshly ground white pepper
1 tablespoon black cumin seeds
1 tablespoon vegetable oil
750g / 1lb 10oz boneless chicken breasts
100ml / 3½fl oz (½ cup) hung natural (plain) yoghurt (see page 793)
1 egg white
200ml / 7fl oz (1 cup) cream
½ tablespoon ground green cardamom
¼ tablespoon ground mace
6–8 green chillies, de-seeded and chopped
1 large sprig coriander (cilantro), chopped
melted butter, for basting
salt

Put the ginger and garlic pastes, half the white pepper, the black cumin seeds and oil in a large shallow dish. Season with salt and mix well. Add the chicken breasts and rub evenly over to coat. Cover and allow to marinate in the refrigerator for 1 hour.

Put the yoghurt, egg white and cream in another large shallow dish and mix together to make a smooth paste. Season with salt and add the remaining white pepper, the ground cardamom and mace, chopped chillies and coriander and mix well. Put the chicken breasts into this second marinade and turn until they are evenly coated. Cover and allow to marinate in the refrigerator for a further 2 hours.

Prepare a tandoor or charcoal grill for a moderate heat, or alternatively preheat the grill (broiler) to medium. Thread the chicken on to several metal skewers. Roast over a charcoal grill or under the hot grill for 6–7 minutes, or until half done.

Remove the skewers from the heat and hang them up for about 2–3 minutes to allow any excess moisture to drain out completely. Put the skewers in a dish, baste with melted butter and roast again in the tandoor, on the charcoal grill or under the grill for a further 3–4 minutes, or until cooked. Transfer the chicken to a plate and serve hot.

Chooza Chaat
Shredded Chicken with (Bell) Peppers

Origin Delhi
Preparation time 15 minutes, plus cooling time
Cooking time 5 minutes
Serves 4

1 red (bell) pepper
1 yellow (bell) pepper
1 green (bell) pepper
200g / 7oz skinless, boneless chicken breasts, grilled (broiled) and cut into thin strips
3–4 cloves garlic, chopped
1 teaspoon lemon juice
½ teaspoon olive oil
½ teaspoon black peppercorns, coarsely ground
1 teaspoon mustard paste
salt
4 tablespoons walnuts, to garnish

Scald the peppers on an open flame on the gas stove, ensuring that these are charred evenly on all sides but not burnt to taste bitter. Alternatively, preheat the grill (broiler), cut the peppers in half, de-seed and cook them under the hot grill, turning frequently, for about 8–10 minutes, or until the skin is blistered and blackened.

Place the charred peppers in a plastic bag, seal tight and allow to cool for about 10 minutes. Remove from the bag, peel, cut in half and de-seed, if you haven't done so already. Cut the flesh into strips or squares.

Place the chicken and peppers in a bowl, sprinkle over all the other ingredients, adjust the seasoning, if necessary and toss well. Garnish with walnuts.

Murg Manpasand
Steamed Chicken Patties

Origin Awadh
Preparation time 15 minutes, plus chilling time
Cooking time 20–30 minutes
Serves 2

250g / 9oz lean minced (ground) chicken
1 onion, chopped
2 green chillies, de-seeded and chopped
1 red (bell) pepper or tomato, diced
½ teaspoon Garlic Paste (see page 57)
½ teaspoon Ginger Paste (see page 57)
½ teaspoon black peppercorns, ground
½ teaspoon Garam Masala (see page 31)
1 tablespoon chopped coriander (cilantro) leaves
1 teaspoon vegetable oil, plus extra for frying (optional)
salt

Put all the ingredients into a blender or food processor, season with salt and process to make a paste. Transfer to a large bowl, cover and allow to chill in the refrigerator for about 1 hour.

Shape the mixture into plump patties, place in idli moulds and steam in a steamer or pressure cooker for about 10 minutes, or until cooked. If using a pressure cooker, don't apply the weight or whistle. If you don't have idli moulds, steam the patties in a steamer. Remove the patties and lightly pat on kitchen paper (paper towels) to remove any extra moisture.

Heat a little oil in a non-stick pan over medium heat, add the patties and cook, pressing with a wooden spatula, for about 10 minutes, or until lightly browned on both sides.

Murg Parche
Spicy Chicken Supremes

Origin Parsi
Preparation time 20–30 minutes, plus marinating time
Cooking time 15 minutes
Serves 2

2–3 green chillies, de-seeded
2 tablespoons natural (plain) yoghurt, whisked
1 teaspoon Garlic Paste (see page 57)
1 teaspoon Ginger Paste (see page 57)
1 tablespoon dried mint, crumbled, plus extra to garnish
250g / 9oz boneless chicken breasts
1–2 tablespoons vegetable oil
1 banana leaf (optional)
green chillies in vinegar, to garnish
salt

To serve

lemon slices
onion rings

Put the chillies in a mortar and, using a pestle, pound until ground.

Put the ground chillies, whisked yoghurt, garlic and ginger pastes and dried mint into a blender or food processor, then season with salt and process to make a smooth paste. Transfer to a large shallow dish, add the chicken and rub the paste evenly all over to coat. Cover and allow to marinate in the refrigerator for 1 hour.

Heat a little oil in a non-stick pan over medium heat, add the chicken and cook for about 5 minutes on each side, or until cooked. If you prefer to steam the chicken, place the chicken in a clean banana leaf square, fold over to make a parcel and secure with cocktail sticks (toothpicks). Use a large pan with a lid and place a trivet or upside-down plate or small bowl in the base. Pour in enough water so it stays below the top of the trivet or plate and cover with the lid. Place the banana leaf on a plate and carefully put on top of the trivet, plate or bowl, cover with a lid and steam for about 10 minutes, or until the chicken is cooked.

Sprinkle some green chillies in vinegar and a little dried mint on top of the chicken and serve with a slice of lemon and onion rings.

Chicken Pakora
Chicken Pakora

Origin Punjab
Preparation time 30 minutes, plus chilling time
Cooking time 15–20 minutes
Serves 4

---

1 whole chicken, cleaned

vegetable oil, for deep-frying

Chaat Masala (see page 31), for sprinkling

1 lemon, cut into wedges, for serving

For the batter

125g / 4¼oz (¾ cup) gram (chickpea) flour

1½ tablespoons Ginger Paste (see page 57)

8–10 green chillies, de-seeded and chopped

2½ teaspoons chilli powder

2½ teaspoons Garam Masala (see page 31)

1½ tablespoons Garlic Paste (see page 57)

1 × 2.5-cm / 1-inch piece fresh ginger, peeled
  and ground to a paste

3 tablespoons lemon juice

2 eggs

2½ teaspoons coriander seeds, coarsely ground

salt

Cut the chicken into 12 pieces, remove and discard
the skin, and set the pieces aside.

To make the batter, put all the ingredients for the
batter into a large bowl, add 150ml / ¼ pint (2/3 cup)
water and mix well. The batter should be of coating
consistency. Add the chicken to the batter and turn
until the pieces are evenly coated. Cover and allow
to chill in the refrigerator for 2½ hours.

Heat enough oil for deep-frying in a kadhai or
deep, heavy-based pan to 180°C/350°F, or until
a cube of bread browns in 30 seconds, then reduce
the heat. Working in small batches, add the battered
chicken and deep-fry for 2–3 minutes, or until
golden brown and cooked. Remove with a slotted
spoon and drain on kitchen paper (paper towels).
Sprinkle over the chaat masala and serve with
lemon wedges.

MAIN DISHES

Throughout India it is customary to offer guests two main dishes, one dry and one with a sauce. Fortunately there is a dizzying array of recipes to suit all palates and diets – some are vegetarian and others contain meat; some are lighter and lend themselves to the summer months, while others are more hearty and robust. These plates form the core of an Indian meal and it is not uncommon for an entire menu to be carefully composed to compliment them.

4
—
Main Dishes

Vegetables

Heeng Jeere ke Aloo
Asafoetida & Cumin-flavoured Potatoes

Origin Rajasthan
Preparation time 20 minutes
Cooking time 5–6 minutes
Serves 4

500g /1lb 2oz (10 small) new (baby) potatoes
6 tablespoons ghee
generous pinch of asafoetida
2 teaspoons cumin seeds
2 teaspoons chopped ginger
2 green chillies, de-seeded and chopped
1 tablespoon ground dried pomegranate seeds
1 teaspoon chilli powder
1 teaspoon ground turmeric
salt

Cook the potatoes in a large, heavy-based pan of salted boiling water for about 12 minutes, or until cooked but not mushy. Drain and set aside.

Heat the ghee in a large, heavy-based pan over medium heat, add the asafoetida and stir-fry for about 30 seconds, or until it puffs up. Add the cumin seeds and stir-fry for 1 minute, or until they start to splutter. Add the ginger and chillies and stir-fry for about 30 seconds, then add the potatoes and stir-fry for 1 minute. Add the ground pomegranate seeds, chilli powder and turmeric and stir-fry for a further 1–2 minutes, or until the masala turns dark brown and evenly coats the potatoes. Remove from the heat and adjust the seasoning, if necessary.

Aloo Posto
Potatoes with Poppy Seed Paste

Origin West Bengal
Preparation time 10 minutes
Cooking time 25–30 minutes
Serves 6

100g / 3½oz (¾ cup) poppy seeds
8–10 dried red chillies
175ml / 6fl oz (¾ cup) vegetable oil
1kg / 2¼lb (9 medium) potatoes, cut into quarters
juice of 2 lemons
salt

Put the poppy seeds and dried red chillies in a mortar and pound with a pestle or in a spice grinder and process, adding a little water if necessary, to make a paste.

Heat the oil in a kadhai, wok or large, heavy-based pan over medium heat, add the potatoes and fry for 15–20 minutes, or until golden brown and soft. Remove with a slotted spoon and drain on kitchen paper (paper towels).

Add the poppy seed paste to the same oil and fry for about 2–3 minutes, then add the fried potatoes and season with salt. Pour in 125 ml / 4½fl oz (½ cup) boiling water, stirring constantly, then cover and cook for about 5 minutes, or until all the water has evaporated. Remove from the heat and add the lemon juice.

☀ / 📷 p.393

Aloo Dum
Potato Curry

Origin Jammu and Kashmir
Preparation time 15 minutes, plus soaking time
Cooking time 35 minutes
Serves 6

1kg / 2¼lb (9 medium) potatoes, halved

4–6 dried red chillies

pinch of asafoetida

1 tablespoon milk

250g / 9oz (1 cup) ghee, plus more to garnish

2 green cardamom pods

3 cloves

2 cinnamon sticks, about 2.5cm / 1 inch long

1 teaspoon Ginger Paste (see page 57)

250ml / 8fl oz (1 cup) natural (plain) yoghurt, whisked

2 tablespoons sugar

2 bay leaves

1 teaspoon ground turmeric

50g / 1¾oz grated Khoya (see page 58) or
    5½ tablespoons milk powder (dry milk)

1 tablespoon hot ghee or butter

salt

Soak the potatoes in a large bowl of water for about
1 hour. Prick them over once or twice during soaking
so that they are quite soft. Drain and pat dry with
kitchen paper (paper towels).

Meanwhile soak the chillies in a bowl of water for
1 hour, then drain and transfer to a small blender.
Process, adding a little water if necessary, to make
a paste.

Put the asafoetida in a small bowl, add the milk and
allow to soak until required.

Heat the ghee in a kadhai or heavy-based pan over
high heat, then reduce the heat to low. Add the
potatoes and fry for about 15 minutes, or until half
cooked. Remove with a slotted spoon and drain
on kitchen paper (paper towels). Pour out all
but 2 tablespoons of ghee, then return the pan
to the heat, add the cardamom pods, cloves,
cinnamon, chilli and ginger pastes and fry gently
for 2–3 minutes.

Remove the pan from the heat and add the yoghurt.
Stir well, then return to low heat and simmer for
5 minutes. Add the potatoes, sugar, bay leaves and
turmeric, and season with salt.

Stir, then cover and simmer for about 5–10 minutes,
or until the potatoes are cooked.

Add the asafoetida and grated khoya and stir well
until the potatoes are evenly coated with the sauce.
Remove from the heat and stir in a tablespoon of
hot ghee or butter before serving.

☀

Dahi ke Aloo
Potatoes with Yoghurt

Origin Awadh
Preparation time 15 minutes
Cooking time 20 minutes
Serves 4

---

4 tablespoons vegetable oil or ghee

¼ teaspoon asafoetida

1 teaspoon mustard seeds

3 Kashmiri red chillies or other mild chillies

10–15 curry leaves

500g / 1lb 2oz (4 medium) potatoes, cut into cubes

1 teaspoon ground coriander

1 teaspoon ground cumin

1 teaspoon chilli powder

½ tablespoon ground turmeric

1 teaspoon Garam Masala (see page 31)

1 tablespoon gram (chickpea) flour

500ml / 18fl oz (2¼ cups) natural (plain) yoghurt,
    whisked

salt

Heat the oil in a large, heavy-based pan over medium
heat, add the asafoetida, mustard seeds, chillies
and curry leaves and fry for about 1 minute. Add
the potatoes together with all the ground spices,
season with salt, then reduce the heat, cover and cook
over low heat for about 8–10 minutes, or until the
potatoes are soft. Pour a little hot water into the pan
to prevent the potatoes from sticking to the base
(bottom) of the pan.

Put the gram flour and yoghurt into a bowl and mix
together, then add this mixture to the potatoes.
Bring almost to the boil, then reduce the heat and
simmer for about 7 minutes, or until the sauce
becomes thick.

Dum Aloo
Rich & Spicy Potatoes

Origin Jammu and Kashmir
Preparation time 15 minutes, plus cooling time
Cooking time 1 hour
Serves 4–6

750g / 1lb 10oz (6 medium) potatoes, unpeeled

½ tablespoon Kashmiri red chilli powder

125ml / 4½fl oz (½ cup) vegetable oil

6 green cardamom pods

3 cinnamon sticks, about 2.5cm / 1 inch long

4 cloves

2 black cardamom pods

2 teaspoons ground fennel

1 teaspoon finely chopped ginger

½ teaspoon ground turmeric

2 teaspoons ground coriander

125ml / 4½fl oz (½ cup) natural (plain) yoghurt,
    whisked

½ tablespoon Kashmiri chilli water

salt

Parboil the potatoes in a large pan of lightly salted
boiling water for 5–7 minutes. Drain and allow
to cool, then peel off the skins and pierce all over
with a fork.

Put the chilli powder in a bowl, pour in 750ml /
1¼ pints (3¼ cups) water and mix together. Set aside.

Heat the oil in a large, heavy-based frying pan
(skillet) over very low heat, add the potatoes and
fry for at least 45 minutes, or until crisp and golden
brown on the outside but soft inside. Remove from
the pan with a slotted spoon and drain on kitchen
paper (paper towels).

In the same pan, heat about 6 tablespoons oil over
medium heat, add the whole spices and stir-fry
for 1–2 minutes, or until they start to splutter,
then add the ground spices and stir-fry briskly for
1 minute. Add the yoghurt and cook for a further
2 minutes. Add the chilli water and potatoes and
season with salt. Simmer over very low heat for
about 10 minutes, or until the potatoes are done.

Aloo Baigan Sookha
Potatoes with Aubergine (Eggplant)

Origin Awadh
Preparation time 10 minutes
Cooking time 12–15 minutes
Serves 4–6

---

3 tablespoons vegetable oil

2 teaspoons cumin seeds

3 dried red chillies, broken into 2–3 pieces each

2 large potatoes, peeled and cut into 8 pieces each

1kg / 2¼lb (2 medium long) aubergines (eggplants),
    rinsed and cut lengthways into quarters

salt

Heat the oil in a large, heavy-based pan over medium
heat, add the cumin seeds and dried red chillies
and fry for 1–2 minutes, then add the potatoes and
aubergines and season with salt. Sauté for 2 minutes,
then reduce the heat, cover and cook over low
heat for about 10 minutes, or until the vegetables are
done. Add 1–2 tablespoons water, if the vegetables
are sticking to the base (bottom) of the pan.

Aloo Vadiyan
Spicy Lentil Dumplings with Potatoes

Origin Punjab
Preparation time 30 minutes
Cooking time 35–40 minutes
Serves 4

---

5 tablespoons ghee

2 teaspoons cumin seeds

150g / 5oz (1 medium) onion, chopped

3½ teaspoons Ginger Paste (see page 57)

1¾ teaspoons Garlic Paste (see page 57)

150g / 5oz (1 medium) tomato, puréed

4 potatoes, cut into thin chips (French fries)

250g / 9oz (1⅓ cups) urad dal vadi

generous pinch of ground fenugreek

salt

1 tablespoon chopped coriander (cilantro) leaves,
    to garnish

For the marinade

150ml / ¼ pint (⅔ cup) natural (plain) yoghurt

1 tablespoon ground coriander

1 teaspoon chilli powder

1 teaspoon ground turmeric

To make the marinade, put the yoghurt in a large
bowl, add the spices and whisk well.

Heat the ghee in a large, heavy-based pan, add the
cumin seeds and stir-fry for about 1 minute, or until
they start to splutter. Add the onion and stir-fry
for about 5 minutes, or until it turns light golden.
Add the ginger and garlic pastes and stir-fry for
about 2–3 minutes, or until the onion is golden brown.
Remove from the heat, stir in the yoghurt mixture,
then return to the heat and stir-fry for about 2–3
minutes, or until the oil starts to separate out and
rise to the surface. Add the puréed tomato and
the potatoes and stir-fry for a further 2–3 minutes,
or until the oil separates out.

Pour in 1 litre / 1¾ pints (4¼ cups) water and season
with salt. Bring to the boil, then reduce the heat to
low and simmer, stirring frequently, for 10 minutes,
or until the potatoes are three-quarters cooked.

Add the urad dal vadi and bring to the boil. Reduce
the heat to low and simmer, stirring frequently,
for 10 minutes, or until the potatoes are cooked
and the sauce is a thin consistency. Sprinkle over
the ground fenugreek, stir and remove from the
heat. Adjust the seasoning, if necessary. Garnish
with chopped coriander.

Uralikizhan Moru Kozhambu
Potato & Yoghurt Curry

Origin Tamil Nadu
Preparation time 15 minutes, plus soaking time
Cooking time 15–20 minutes
Serves 4–6

2–3 potatoes, cut into 1-cm / ½-inch cubes

½ teaspoon ground turmeric

600ml / 1 pint (2½ cups) natural (plain) yoghurt,
    whisked

salt

For the spice paste

1 tablespoon chana dal, rinsed and drained

½ teaspoon fenugreek seeds

½ teaspoon mustard seeds

4–5 green chillies, de-seeded and chopped

2 tablespoons chopped coriander (cilantro) leaves

1 × 1-cm / ½-inch piece fresh ginger, peeled
    and chopped

100g / 3½oz (1¼ cups) grated fresh coconut

Soak the dal for the spice paste in a bowl of water
for 20 minutes. Drain well and set aside.

To make the spice paste, put the fenugreek seeds in
a kadhai or small, heavy-based dry frying pan (skillet)
over medium heat and stir-fry for 1–2 minutes, or
until roasted. Remove from the pan and transfer to
a small blender. Add all the remaining ingredients,
including the soaked dal and 4 tablespoons water and
process to make a smooth paste.

Bring 375ml / 13 fl oz (1½ cups) water to the boil in
a large, heavy-based pan. Add the potatoes and
turmeric and season with salt. Cover, reduce the heat
to medium and simmer for about 10–12 minutes, or
until the potatoes are tender. Stir in the spice paste
and simmer for 1–2 minutes. Stir in the yoghurt and
heat through, stirring constantly to prevent curdling
for a further 1–2 minutes, or until hot.

❀❀

Chharra Aloo
'Marbled' Potatoes in Sauce

Origin Awadh
Preparation time 15–20 minutes
Cooking time 15 minutes
Serves 4–6

500g / 1lb 2oz marble-sized potatoes

1 teaspoon ground cumin

½ teaspoon chilli powder

½ teaspoon ground turmeric

½ teaspoon ground black pepper

2 teaspoons amchoor

½ teaspoon Garam Masala (see page 31)

1 teaspoon ground aniseed

2 tablespoons ghee

1 bay leaf

2 green chillies, de-seeded and chopped

2 cloves

2 black cardamom pods

1 teaspoon ground coriander

salt

Remove the skin from the potatoes by rubbing vigorously, then crush lightly with the side of a heavy knife or a grinding stone.

Put the ground spices in a small bowl, add 4 tablespoons water and mix together.

Heat the ghee in a kadhai or large, heavy-based pan over medium heat, add the bay leaf, chillies and whole spices and stir-fry for about 1–2 minutes, or until they turn darker. Add the ground spice mixture and stir-fry for 30 seconds, then add the potatoes. Stir to mix well and pour in 750ml / 1¼ pints (3¼ cups) water. Bring to the boil, then reduce the heat, season with salt, cover and simmer for about 10 minutes. Uncover, mash the potatoes a little with the back of a ladle or wooden spatula and simmer for a further 2 minutes.

❀❀

Aloo Tamatar ka Chokha
Mashed Potato & Tomato

Origin Bihar
Preparation time 20 minutes, plus cooling time
Cooking time 10 minutes
Serves 4

250g / 9oz (2 medium) potatoes

4 green chillies, de-seeded and finely chopped

1 × 2.5-cm / 1-inch piece fresh ginger, peeled and finely chopped

¼ teaspoon chilli powder

1 tablespoon mustard oil

4–6 tomatoes

salt

1 large sprig coriander (cilantro), to garnish

For the tempering (optional)

2 teaspoons vegetable oil

½ teaspoon cumin seeds

Cook the potatoes in a large pan of boiling water for about 20 minutes, or until soft. Drain and allow to cool, then peel off the skins and transfer the potatoes to a large bowl. Add the chillies, ginger, chilli powder, mustard oil and season with salt. Use your hands to mix everything together and mash well.

Chargrill the tomatoes over the open flame of a gas cooker (gas stove top) for a few minutes, or until the skins are blackened, then peel off the skins, transfer the flesh to a bowl and mash with a spoon. Alternatively, put the tomatoes in a large heatproof bowl of boiling water for 30 seconds, then plunge them in cold water, drain, allow to cool slightly and remove the skins.

Heap the mashed potato mixture on a serving plate, arrange the mashed tomato decoratively around and garnish with coriander.

If using, heat the oil for the tempering in a small frying pan (skillet) over medium heat, add the cumin seeds and stir-fry for about 1 minute, or until they start to splutter. Pour over the mashed potato and tomato.

Aloo Matar Rasedar
Potatoes & Peas in Sauce

Origin Awadh
Preparation time 30 minutes
Cooking time 10 minutes
Serves 6–8

---

6 tablespoons vegetable oil or ghee, plus extra
    for frying

500g / 1lb 2oz (4 medium) potatoes, cut into
    medium-sized pieces

pinch of asafoetida

1 teaspoon cumin seeds

500g / 1lb 2oz (4 cups) peas, shelled if fresh

2 cloves

¼ teaspoon chilli powder

1 teaspoon Kashmiri Garam Masala (see page 56)
    (optional)

1 teaspoon ground coriander

2 tomatoes (optional)

finely chopped fenugreek leaves or 2 tablespoons
    dried fenugreek leaves (optional)

salt

Heat enough oil for frying in a large, heavy-based frying pan (skillet) over medium heat, add the potatoes and fry for about 15–20 minutes, or until cooked and light golden. Remove from the pan and set aside.

Heat the oil or ghee in a heavy-based pan over medium heat, add the asafoetida and cumin seeds and stir-fry for 1 minute, or until the seeds start to splutter. Add the peas and 125ml / 4½fl oz (½ cup) water, then cover and cook for about 5 minutes, shaking the pan lightly every few minutes or stirring carefully with a ladle so that the peas are well mixed without breaking, or until nearly done. Add the cloves and chilli powder and Kashmiri garam masala. When nearly done, add the fried potatoes and sprinkle over the ground coriander.

If you would like to add tomatoes to this dish, first put them in a bowl of boiling water for about 30 seconds, then drain, allow to cool slightly and remove the skins. Put the flesh into a bowl and mash to a pulp. Add the pulp to the pan containing the potatoes and cook for a few minutes, or until done.

If you are using dried fenugreek add it with the fried potatoes, sprinkle over a little water, mix well and simmer for a few more minutes until done.

☀ / 📷 p.475

Aloo Simla Mirch
Savoury Potatoes & (Bell) Peppers

Origin Delhi
Preparation time 10 minutes
Cooking time 17–20 minutes
Serves 4–6

---

3 tablespoons ghee or 100g / 3½oz (7 tablespoons)
    butter with 2 teaspoons vegetable oil

8 potatoes, cut into quarters

4 green (bell) peppers, de-seeded and cut into quarters

salt

Heat the ghee or butter and oil in a medium-sized, heavy-based pan over low heat, add the potatoes and season with salt. Cover and cook for about 15 minutes, or until the potatoes are cooked. Sprinkle over 1 tablespoon water if the potatoes are browning too much. Uncover, add the peppers and simmer for a further 2–3 minutes. Mix gently before serving.

※

Aloo Kele ki Bhujiya
Spiced Potatoes & Bananas in Yoghurt

Origin Awadh
Preparation time 30–40 minutes
Cooking time 25–30 minutes
Serves 4–6

4 tablespoons ghee or vegetable oil

6 potatoes, cut into 3-cm / 1-inch cubes

6 unripe green bananas, peeled and cut into rounds,
    about 1cm / ½ inch thick

pinch of asafoetida

½ teaspoon cumin seeds

¼ teaspoon fenugreek seeds

¼ teaspoon kalonji (nigella) seeds

½ teaspoon red chilli powder

½ teaspoon ground ginger

½ teaspoon ground coriander

4 tablespoons natural (plain) yoghurt, whisked

salt

Heat 3 tablespoons ghee or oil in a heavy-based
frying pan (skillet) over medium heat, and working
in batches fry the potatoes for 10–15 minutes, or
until golden brown. Remove from the heat. Place
on kitchen paper (paper towel) to drain.

Add the bananas to the pan and fry for 2 minutes
making sure not to scorch the bananas, then set aside.

Heat the remaining ghee or oil in a second large,
heavy-based pan over medium heat. Add the
asafoetida, cumin seeds, fenugreek and kalonji
seeds and stir-fry for 1 minute, or until the
seeds start to splutter. Add the fried bananas,
potatoes and the remaining spices, then
season with salt. Shake the pan a couple of
times and pour in 250ml / 8fl oz (1 cup) water.

Reduce the heat, cover and simmer for 10–15
minutes, or until the potatoes are soft. Add the
yoghurt, cover and simmer over very low heat
for a further 10 minutes.

※ / 🖻 p.279

Khatte Aloo
Sour Potatoes

Origin Awadh
Preparation time 15 minutes
Cooking time 20 minutes
Serves 4–6

150ml / ¼ pint (⅔ cup) mustard oil

pinch of asafoetida

1 teaspoon cumin seeds

500g / 1lb 2oz (4 medium) potatoes, cut into
    bite-sized pieces

½ teaspoon chilli powder

1 teaspoon ground turmeric

1 teaspoon ground coriander

2 cloves

¼ teaspoon fenugreek seeds

1 teaspoon ground ginger

2 green chillies

1 × 2.5-cm / 1-inch piece fresh ginger, peeled
    and finely chopped

2 teaspoons amchoor

salt

Heat the oil in a large, heavy-based pan over
medium heat, add the asafoetida and cumin seeds
and stir-fry for 1 minute, or until the seeds start to
splutter. Add the potatoes and chilli powder and
stir-fry for 1 minute, before adding the remaining
ingredients, except the amchoor, and seasoning
with salt. Stir-fry for a further 1 minute, then pour
in 500ml / 18fl oz (2¼ cups) water. Bring to the boil,
reduce the heat to medium, cover and simmer for
10–15 minutes.

Add the amchoor and simmer for another few minutes.

Dahiwale Aloo
Potatoes in Yoghurt Sauce

Origin Awadh
Preparation time 15 minutes
Cooking time 20–25 minutes
Serves 4

4 tablespoons vegetable oil or ghee
¼ teaspoon asafoetida
1 teaspoon mustard seeds
3–4 dried red chillies
10–15 curry leaves
500g / 1lb 2oz (4 medium) potatoes, cut into cubes
1 teaspoon ground coriander
1 teaspoon ground cumin
1 teaspoon chilli powder
½ tablespoon ground turmeric
1 teaspoon Garam Masala (see page 31)
500ml / 18fl oz (2¼ cups) natural (plain) yoghurt, whisked
salt

Heat the oil or ghee in a large, heavy-based pan over medium heat, add the asafoetida, mustard seeds, dried red chillies and curry leaves and stir-fry for about 1 minute. Add the potatoes together with all the ground spices, season with salt, then cover, reduce the heat to low and cook for about 10–15 minutes, or until the potatoes are soft. Pour a little water on the lid and tilt into the pan when hot to prevent the potatoes from sticking to the base (bottom) of the pan.

Remove the pan from the heat, add the yoghurt slowly, stirring constantly, then return to the heat and simmer for about 5 minutes, or until the sauce is thick, but do not allow to boil.

Aloo Methi
Potatoes with Fenugreek

Origin Punjab/Awadh
Preparation time 15 minutes, plus soaking time
Cooking time 20 minutes
Serves 2

15g / ½oz (¾ cup) fresh fenugreek leaves
3 tablespoons vegetable oil
2 cloves garlic, crushed
1 green chilli, de-seeded and chopped
250g / 9oz (2 medium) potatoes, cut into cubes
⅛ teaspoon ground turmeric
4 sprigs dill, chopped
1 tablespoon chopped coriander (cilantro) leaves
salt

Soak the fenugreek leaves in a bowl of lightly salted water for about 30 minutes. Drain, pat dry and chop.

Heat the oil in a large, heavy-based frying pan (skillet) over medium heat, add the garlic and chilli and mix, then add the fenugreek leaves and fry for about 1 minute. Add the potatoes and turmeric, season with salt and stir-fry for about 2 minutes. Now add the dill and coriander leaves.

Reduce the heat to low, cover and cook for about 10 minutes, or until the potatoes are soft. If the mixture is too dry and the potatoes are browning too much, sprinkle over a little water.

Aloogadda Vepudu
Spicy Potatoes

Origin Hyderabad/Andhra Pradesh
Preparation time 1 hour
Cooking time 15–20 minutes
Serves 4

350g / 12oz (3 medium) potatoes, cut into
   2.5-cm /1-inch pieces

2 tablespoons ghee

½ teaspoon mustard seeds

½ teaspoon cumin seeds

salt

For the masala

1 tablespoon coriander seeds

1 teaspoon cumin seeds

10–12 whole black peppercorns

4 dried red chillies

4 green cardamom pods

3 cloves

1 cinnamon stick, about 2.5cm / 1 inch long

1 teaspoon ground turmeric

2 teaspoons lemon juice

For the tempering

2 teaspoons vegetable oil

1 onion, sliced

15–20 curry leaves

Put the potatoes into a heavy-based pan, add half the turmeric and season with salt. Pour in enough water to cover, then bring to the boil and cook for about 12–15 minutes, or until soft. Drain and set aside.

To make the masala, heat a tawa, griddle or small, heavy-based frying pan (skillet) over very low heat, add the coriander seeds and stir-fry for about 3 minutes, or until fragrant and roasted. Remove from the pan and roast the cumin seeds, black peppercorns, dried red chillies, green cardamom pods, cloves and cinnamon separately in the same way. Transfer all the roasted spices, turmeric and lemon juice to a blender and process until ground. Pass through a sieve (strainer) and set aside.

Heat the ghee in a large, heavy-based pan over medium heat, add the mustard and cumin seeds and stir-fry for about 1 minute, or until they start to splutter.

Add the potatoes and season with salt, then stir-fry for 2 minutes. Add the masala and stir-fry for a further 2 minutes, before removing from the heat and adjusting the seasoning, if necessary.

Heat the oil for the tempering in a small frying pan over medium heat, add the sliced onion and fry for about 5–7 minutes, or until golden, then add the curry leaves. Stir and spread over the potatoes.

✵ / 📷 p.273

Aloo ke Gutake
Potatoes Tempered with Cumin

Origin Uttarakhand
Preparation time 10 minutes
Cooking time 20 minutes
Serves 4

---

3 tablespoons mustard oil

1½ teaspoons cumin seeds

pinch of ground turmeric

500g / 1lb 2oz (4 medium) potatoes, cut into
   slices lengthways

salt

To garnish

2–3 dried red chillies

1 sprig coriander (cilantro), chopped

Heat the oil in a kadhai or heavy-based pan over high heat, then reduce the heat. Add the cumin seeds and stir-fry for about 30 seconds, or until they start to splutter. Add the turmeric and immediately afterwards the sliced potatoes. Stir well and sprinkle over a very little amount of water just to make them damp.

Season with salt, then reduce the heat to very low, cover and cook for about 15–20 minutes, or until the potatoes are tender, stirring once or twice and sprinkling very small amounts of water whenever required during cooking, so the potatoes do not burn or catch on the base (bottom) of the pan. Garnish with dried red chillies and chopped coriander.

Cheera Thoran
South Indian Spinach & Potatoes

Origin Tamil Nadu
Preparation time 15 minutes
Cooking time 20 minutes
Serves 6

2–3 tablespoon coconut oil
1 teaspoon mustard seeds
1 teaspoon urad dal, rinsed and drained
1 large onion, chopped
1 × 2.5-cm / 1-inch piece fresh ginger, peeled and grated
4–8 green chillies, de-seeded and chopped
10–12 curry leaves
250g / 9oz (2 medium) potatoes, cut into small cubes
750g / 1lb 10oz red spinach, shredded
100g / 3½oz (1 cup) grated fresh coconut
salt

Heat the oil in a large, deep heavy-based pan over medium heat, add the mustard seeds and stir-fry for 1 minute, or until they start to splutter. Add the urad dal and stir-fry for about 1 minute, or until light golden, then add the onion and stir-fry for about 2 minutes, or until translucent and glossy. Add the ginger and chillies and stir-fry for a few seconds, before adding the curry leaves. Stir, then add the potatoes and stir-fry for about 5 minutes, or until the potatoes are half cooked.

Now add the spinach and coconut and season with salt. Cover with a lid and cook for 3 minutes or until the spinach has wilted. Remove the cover and stir-fry for 3–5 minutes, or until all the moisture has evaporated and the potatoes are soft. Remove from the heat and adjust the seasoning, if necessary.

Aloo Matar Sookhe
Potatoes with Peas

Origin Awadh/Punjab
Preparation time 25 minutes, plus cooling time
Cooking time 15–20 minutes
Serves 4–6

8 potatoes, in their jackets (skins)
350g / 12oz (2½ cups) peas, shelled if fresh
2–3 tablespoons ghee or vegetable oil
1 tablespoon mustard seeds
1 tablespoon cumin seeds
1 tablespoon ground turmeric
2 tomatoes, chopped (optional)
2–3 green chillies, chopped
1 tablespoon chopped coriander (cilantro) leaves
salt

Cook the potatoes in a large pan of boiling water for about 10 minutes, or until half done. Drain, allow to cool, then peel off their skins. Cut the potatoes into cubes.

Cook the peas in another pan of boiling water for 5–7 minutes, or until soft, then drain and refresh immediately in cold water so they do not lose their colour. Set aside.

Heat the ghee or oil in a heavy-based pan over medium heat, add the mustard seeds and cumin seeds and stir-fry for 1 minute, or until they start to splutter. Add the turmeric, then add the potatoes and tomatoes, if using. Season with salt and fry for about 5–10 minutes, or until done.

Add the peas, chillies and coriander leaves to the pan, mix well and serve hot.

Aloo Masala
Curried Spice Potatoes

Origin Awadh
Preparation time 20 minutes, plus cooling time
Cooking time 10–15 minutes
Serves 4

250g / 9oz (2 medium) potatoes, unpeeled
8–10 teaspoons vegetable oil
1 teaspoon ground aniseed
2 teaspoons chilli powder
2 pinches of ground turmeric
1 cinnamon stick, about 2.5cm / 1 inch long
6 cloves
6 green cardamom pods
1 teaspoon poppy seeds
4 tablespoons gram (chickpea) flour
1 teaspoon mustard seeds
1 teaspoon urad dal, rinsed and drained
2–4 green chillies, de-seeded and chopped
150g / 5oz (1 medium) onion, sliced
2 teaspoons hot ghee
15–20 curry leaves
salt

Cook the potatoes in a large pan of boiling water for 20 minutes, or until soft. Drain, allow to cool and peel off the skins. Cut the potatoes into large pieces.

Heat 1 teaspoon oil in a small frying pan (skillet) over medium heat, add half the aniseed and the rest of the spices and stir-fry for about 30 seconds. Transfer to a mortar and pound with a pestle or process in a spice grinder to a powder. Set aside.

Put the gram (chickpea) flour in a small bowl, pour in 250ml / 8fl oz (1 cup) water and stir together until blended. Set aside.

Heat the remaining oil in a large frying pan over medium heat, add the mustard seeds and urad dal and stir-fry for about 1 minute, or until they start to splutter. Add the remaining aniseed and stir-fry for a few seconds. Add the chillies and onion and fry for about 2 minutes, or until the onion is translucent. Now add the potatoes and season with salt. Fry for about 1 minute.

Pour the flour paste into the curry and keep stirring until the sauce thickens considerably. Sprinkle over the ground spices, then pour over the ghee and add a few curry leaves. Mix well and cook for about 5 minutes, before removing from the heat.

Bharwan Aloo
Stuffed Potatoes

Origin Rajasthan
Preparation time 20 minutes
Cooking time 15 minutes
Serves 6

6 potatoes
1 tablespoon vegetable oil, plus extra for deep frying
½ teaspoon black cumin seeds
200g / 7oz Paneer (see page 59), cut into cubes
¼ teaspoon Kashmiri chilli powder
large pinch of dried mint
¼ teaspoon Garam Masala (see page 31) (optional)
1 teaspoon raisins
1 teaspoon pine nuts
¼ red (bell) pepper, cut into small diamonds
salt

Scoop out the centres of the potatoes ensuring that about a 1-cm / ½-inch shell remains intact.

Heat enough oil for deep-frying in a kadhai or deep, heavy-based pan to 180°C/350°F, or until a cube of bread browns in 30 seconds. Carefully add the potato shells to the hot oil and deep-fry for about 2–3 minutes, or until they acquire a golden hue and appear crisp. Remove with a slotted spoon and drain on kitchen paper (paper towels).

Heat the 1 tablespoon oil in a non-stick pan over medium heat, add the black cumin seeds and stir-fry for 1 minute, or until they start to splutter. Add the paneer and quickly stir-fry for about 2 minutes. Season with salt, then add the chilli powder, dried mint and garam masala, if using. Add the raisins, pine nuts and red pepper and stir well to blend. Remove from the heat and fill the hollowed potatoes with this mixture.

Uralaikizhan Sagu
Potato Curry with Coconut

Origin Tamil Nadu
Preparation time 40 minutes, plus cooling time
Cooking time 20–25 minutes
Serves 6

7–8 potatoes, unpeeled

3 onions, chopped

2–3 green chillies, de-seeded and chopped

1 × 1-cm / ½-inch piece fresh ginger, peeled
　and grated

4 tomatoes, chopped

½ teaspoon ground turmeric

375ml / 13fl oz (1½ cups) coconut milk, fresh
　(see page 781) or canned

salt

For the spice paste

1 teaspoon poppy seeds, ground

3–4 dried red chillies

1 tablespoon chana dal, roasted

1 tablespoon coriander seeds

½ teaspoon fennel seeds

1 cinnamon stick, about 1cm / ½ inch long

For the tempering

6 tablespoons vegetable oil

1 teaspoon mustard seeds

1 teaspoon cumin seeds

1 teaspoon urad dal, rinsed and drained

1 teaspoon chana dal, rinsed and drained

1 sprig curry leaves

Cook the potatoes in a pan of boiling water for
about 20 minutes, or until soft. Drain and allow to
cool, then peel off the skins. Cut the potatoes into
1-cm / ½-inch cubes.

Put all the ingredients for the spice paste in
a blender with a little water, if necessary, and
process to make a smooth paste. Set aside.

Heat the oil for the tempering in a kadhai or deep,
heavy-based frying pan (skillet) over medium heat,
add all the ingredients for the tempering and stir-fry
for 1 minute, or until the mustard seeds start to
splutter. Add the onions and stir-fry for 5 minutes,
or until golden.

Mix in the chillies, ginger, tomatoes and turmeric,
and season with salt. Fry for about 1–2 minutes.

Pour 250ml / 8fl oz (1 cup) water into the pan, stir,
then reduce the heat, cover and simmer for about
5 minutes.

Mix in the spice paste and potatoes and simmer,
uncovered, for a further 5 minutes, or until well
blended. Pour in the coconut milk and simmer
for about 1–2 minutes.

Chakra Vazhikilangu Poriyal
Spicy Sweet Potatoes

Origin Tamil Nadu
Preparation time 10 minutes
Cooking time 10–15 minutes
Serves 4–6

350g / 12oz (2 medium) sweet potatoes, peeled
　and cut into cubes

2 green chillies, de-seeded and chopped

½ teaspoon ground turmeric

1 tablespoon Poriyal Powder (see page 50)

salt

For the tempering

2 teaspoons vegetable oil

1 teaspoon mustard seeds

1 teaspoon cumin seeds

1 dried red chilli, halved

1 teaspoon urad dal, rinsed and drained

1 sprig curry leaves

Heat the oil for the tempering in a large, heavy-
based frying pan over medium heat, add all the
ingredients for the tempering and stir-fry for
1 minute, or until the mustard seeds start to splutter.
Add the sweet potatoes, chillies, turmeric and
season with salt.

Pour 125ml / 4½fl oz (½ cup) water into the pan, then
reduce the heat, cover and simmer for about 10–15
minutes, or until the sweet potatoes are cooked and
all the water is completely absorbed. Sprinkle in the
poriyal powder, mix well and remove from the heat.

Aloo ka Qorma
Braised Potatoes

Origin Awadh
Preparation time 30 minutes
Cooking time 10 minutes
Serves 6

500g / 1lb 2oz (2 large) potatoes, cut into
    quarters lengthways
¼ teaspoon ground turmeric
1 teaspoon poppy seeds
1 × 2.5-cm / 1-inch piece fresh ginger, peeled
1 teaspoon ground garlic
6 cashew nuts
½ tablespoon desiccated (dried flaked) coconut
125ml / 4½fl oz (½ cup) vegetable oil or ghee
2 green cardamom pods
2 cinnamon sticks, about 2.5cm / 1 inch long
2 cloves
6 green chillies, de-seeded and chopped
1½ teaspoon ground coriander
4 tomatoes, chopped
½ teaspoon chilli powder
250ml / 8fl oz (1 cup) natural (plain) yoghurt
1 bunch coriander (cilantro) leaves, chopped
juice of 1 lime
salt

Cook the potatoes together with the turmeric in
a large pan of boiling water for about 15 minutes,
or until tender. Drain and set aside.

Put the poppy seeds, ginger, garlic, cashew nuts
and coconut in a mortar and pound with a pestle
or a spice grinder and process until ground.

Heat the oil or ghee in a heavy-based pan over
medium heat, add the whole spices and chillies
and lightly fry for about 1–2 minutes. Add the ground
spices and ground coriander and fry for about
1 minute, or until fragrant.

Add the tomatoes together with the boiled potatoes
to the pan and cook for a few minutes. Season with
salt, then add the chilli powder and yoghurt. Reduce
the heat to low and simmer for a few minutes. Add
the chopped coriander and remove the pan from the
heat. Stir in the lime juice and serve.

Aloo ki Tarkari
Potatoes in Sauce

Origin Awadh
Preparation time 35 minutes
Cooking time 10–15 minutes
Serves 6

500g / 1lb 2oz (4 medium) potatoes, unpeeled
3 tablespoons dried fenugreek leaves
1 teaspoon ground turmeric
1 teaspoon ground cumin powder
1 teaspoon Kashmiri red chilli powder
½ teaspoon amchoor
125ml / 4½fl oz (½ cup) vegetable oil
small pinch of asafoetida
6 cloves
1 bay leaf
1 × 5-cm / 2-inch piece fresh ginger, peeled
    and crushed
salt

Cook the potatoes in a large pan of boiling water
for about 20 minutes, or until soft. Drain, allow to
cool, then peel off the skins. Return the potatoes
to the pan and mash with a potato masher. Set aside.

Soak the dried fenugreek leaves in a bowl of water
for a few minutes, then drain and crumble. Set aside.

Put the ground spices in a small bowl, add
1 tablespoon water and stir together.

Heat the oil in a kadhai, wok or deep, heavy-based
frying pan (skillet) over medium heat, add the
asafoetida and stir-fry for about 30 seconds. Add
the cloves and bay leaf and stir-fry for a further
30 seconds. Add the ground spice mixture and the
ginger and fry for another 30 seconds.

Pour in about 1 litre / 1¾ pints (4¼ cups) water and
bring to the boil. Add the mashed potatoes and
season with salt. Reduce the heat and cook for
about 8 minutes, or until it has reached the desired
consistency. Add the crumbled fenugreek leaves
and mix well.

※ ※
—

Aloo Chutneywale
Chutney-coated Potatoes

Origin Hyderabad
Preparation time 45 minutes
Cooking time 20–25 minutes
Serves 4

---

groundnut (peanut) oil, for deep frying

750g / 1lb 10oz (6 medium) potatoes, cut into
    barrel shapes

salt

For the filling

125g / 4¼oz Paneer (see page 59), grated

4 green chillies, de-seeded and finely chopped

1 teaspoon finely chopped fresh ginger

10 cashew nuts, crushed

For the chutney

150g / 5oz (3½ cups) coriander (cilantro) leaves

3 tablespoons unripe mangoes, peeled and
    roughly chopped

75g / 2½oz (1½ cups) mint leaves

For the sauce

100g / 3½oz (scant ½ cup) ghee

1¾ teaspoons cumin seeds

150g / 5oz Boiled Onion Paste (see page 57)

4 teaspoons Ginger Paste (see page 57)

4 teaspoons Garlic Paste (see page 57)

50g / 1¾oz Cashew Nut Paste (see page 58)

1 teaspoon chilli powder

10g / ¼oz Garam Masala (see page 31)

100g / 3½oz (1 small) tomato, chopped

300ml / ½ pint (1¼ cups) natural (plain) yoghurt,
    whisked

pinch of salt

Heat enough oil for deep-frying in a kadhai or deep,
heavy-based pan to 180°C/350°F, or until a cube
of bread browns in 30 seconds. Working in batches,
add the potatoes to the hot oil and deep-fry for
1–2 minutes, or until three-quarters cooked and
light brown in colour. Remove with a slotted spoon
and drain on kitchen paper (paper towels). When
cool, scoop out the centres leaving a 5-mm / ¼-inch
gap from the sides.

For the filling, mix all the ingredients together
in a bowl. Season with salt and stuff the scooped
potatoes with the filling.

To make the chutney, put the coriander and
mangoes in a blender or food processor and process
to make a paste. Add the mint and process again
to make a smooth paste.

To make the sauce, heat the ghee in a large,
heavy-based pan over medium heat, add the cumin
seeds and stir-fry for about 1 minute, or until they
start to splutter. Add the pastes and stir-fry for
1–2 minutes, or until the moisture has evaporated.
Now add the ground spices and a pinch of salt,
then add the tomatoes and stir-fry for about
2–3 minutes, or until the moisture has evaporated.

Remove the pan from the heat, stir in the yoghurt,
then return to a low heat, add the potatoes
and simmer gently for a few minutes until hot.

Aloo Tamatar
Curried Potatoes with Tomato

Origin Punjab/Awadh
Preparation time 10 minutes
Cooking time 15–20 minutes
Serves 4

250ml / 8fl oz (1 cup) mustard oil
2–3 dried red chillies
1½ tablespoons coriander seeds
pinch of asafoetida
4 tomatoes, chopped
½ teaspoon ground turmeric
1 teaspoon chilli powder
150g / 5oz (1 medium) potato, cut into chunks
4–5 green chillies, slit in half lengthways and de-seeded
salt
4 tablespoons chopped coriander (cilantro) leaves, to garnish

Heat the oil in a heavy-based pan over high heat, then reduce the heat, add the dried red chillies and coriander seeds and stir-fry for 1 minute, or until the seeds start to splutter and the chillies turn a shade darker. Add the asafoetida, stir, then add the tomatoes and cook for about 1 minute. Add the turmeric and chilli powder, then season with salt. Cook for about 2–3 minutes, or until the tomatoes become soft and well blended.

Pour in 250ml / 8fl oz (1 cup) water and bring to the boil. Add the potato and green chillies and cook for about 8–10 minutes, or until the potatoes are soft and the sauce is thick. Garnish with chopped coriander.

Aloo Methi ki Sabzi
Potatoes with Fenugreek Leaves

Origin Punjab/Awadh
Preparation time 15 minutes
Cooking time 20 minutes
Serves 4

2 tablespoons vegetable oil or ghee
1 teaspoon cumin seeds
150g / 5oz (1 medium) potato, cut into dice
¼ teaspoon chopped green chilli
500g / 1lb 2oz fenugreek leaves, finely chopped
¼ teaspoon ground turmeric
salt

Heat the oil or ghee in a heavy-based pan over medium heat, add the cumin seeds and stir-fry for 1 minute, or until they start to splutter. Add the potatoes and chilli and season with salt. Cover and cook for about 8–10 minutes, or until the potatoes are soft, stirring once or twice to make sure the potatoes do not brown and sprinkling over a little water if necessary to prevent the potatoes burning and catching on the base (bottom) of the pan.

Add the fenugreek leaves and turmeric and cook for a further 10 minutes.

Dum ki Arabi
Slow-cooked Colocasia (Taro Root)

Origin Awadh
Preparation time 25–30 minutes, plus cooling time
Cooking time 20 minutes
Serves 4–6

500g / 1lb 2oz (1 root) colocasia (taro root)

2 bay leaves

½ teaspoon black cumin seeds

½ teaspoon grated nutmeg

4 black cardamom pods

6–8 cloves

2 cinnamon sticks, about 2.5cm / 1 inch long

125ml / 4½fl oz (½ cup) vegetable oil, plus extra
     for frying

2 onions, sliced

125ml / 4½fl oz (½ cup) natural (plain) yoghurt,
     whisked

1 teaspoon chilli powder

1 teaspoon ground coriander

1 teaspoon cumin seeds

½ teaspoon ground turmeric

2 tablespoons Boiled Onion Paste (see page 57)

2 teaspoons Ginger Paste (see page 57)

2 teaspoons Garlic Paste (see page 57)

salt

Cook the colocasia in a large, heavy-based pan of
boiling water for about 10–15 minutes. Drain, allow
to cool slightly, then peel off the skin and prick
all over with a fork.

Put the bay leaves and whole spices in a mortar and
pound with a pestle or process in a spice grinder until
coarsely ground, then set aside.

Heat enough oil for deep-frying in a kadhai or
deep, heavy-based pan to 180°C/350°F, or until
a cube of bread browns in 30 seconds, then reduce
the heat. Carefully lower the colocasia into the
hot oil and deep-fry for about 2–3 minutes, or
until it firms up slightly and acquires a rich golden
brown hue. Remove from the pan with a slotted
spoon and drain on kitchen paper (paper towels).

Heat the measured oil in another heavy-based pan
over medium heat, add the onions and fry for about
5 minutes, or until lightly browned.

Remove from the heat and slowly stir in the yoghurt,
all the ground spices and the onion, ginger and
garlic pastes. Season with salt and return the pan
to the heat. Stir-fry for a few minutes until the oil
separates out and the spice mixture is well browned.
Pour in 500ml / 18fl oz (2 cups) water and add the
colocasia. Cover and simmer over very low heat for
about 10 minutes.

Masala Arabi
Spicy Colocasia (Taro Root)

Origin Awadh
Preparation time 20 minutes, plus cooling time
Cooking time 15–20 minutes
Serves 5–6

500g / 1lb 2oz (1 root) colocasia (taro root), peeled
     and sliced into chunks

2 tablespoons ghee

1 × 5-cm / 2-inch piece fresh ginger, peeled
     and chopped

2–3 green chillies, de-seeded and chopped

pinch of asafoetida

¼ teaspoon ajwain seeds

½ teaspoon salt

½ teaspoon ground turmeric

1 teaspoon ground coriander

2 tablespoons natural (plain) yoghurt, whisked

2 tablespoons chopped coriander (cilantro) leaves

Cook the colocasia in a large, heavy-based pan of
boiling water for 8–10 minutes. Drain, allow to cool
slightly, then peel off the skin and slice into chunks.

Heat the ghee in a large, heavy-based pan over
medium heat, add the ginger and stir-fry for about
2–3 minutes. Add the chillies, asafoetida and ajwain
seeds and stir-fry for 1 minute. Add the colocasia
together with the salt, turmeric and ground coriander
seeds. Pour in 250ml / 8fl oz (1 cup) water and cook
for 10 minutes until the water is absorbed and the
colocasia is tender. Remove from the heat and add
the yoghurt and chopped coriander.

Ajwaini Arabi
Ajwain-flavoured Colocasia (Taro Root)

Origin Banaras/Awadh
Preparation time 20 minutes, plus cooling time
Cooking time 10 minutes
Serves 4–5

250g / 9oz (½ root) colocasia (taro root)
200g / 7oz (¾ cup) ghee
pinch of asafoetida
½ teaspoon ajwain seeds
½ teaspoon chilli powder
salt

Cook the colocasia in a large, heavy-based pan of boiling water for about 10–15 minutes. Drain and allow to cool, then peel off the skins, cut in half lengthways and flatten with your hands.

Reserve 1 tablespoon of ghee and heat the remaining ghee in a frying pan (skillet) over medium heat. Add the colocasia and fry for a few minutes until crisp and golden. Remove with a slotted spoon and drain on kitchen paper (paper towels). Return to the frying pan.

Heat the remaining ghee in a small frying pan over medium heat, add the asafoetida and ajwain seeds and stir-fry for 1 minute. Remove from the heat, stir in the chilli powder and season with salt. Pour over the colocasia, then cover and cook over very low heat for a further 5 minutes.

Rajasthani Arabi
Colocasia (Taro Root) in Yoghurt Sauce

Origin Rajasthan
Preparation time 30 minutes, plus cooling time
Cooking time 20 minutes
Serves 4–6

300g / 11oz (⅔ root) colocasia (taro root)
250ml / 8fl oz (1 cup) natural (plain) yoghurt
2 teaspoons gram (chickpea) flour
½ tablespoon Ginger Paste (see page 57)
½ tablespoon Garlic Paste (see page 57)
1 teaspoon chilli powder
1 teaspoon ground turmeric
4 tablespoons vegetable oil
3–4 cloves
2 black cardamom pods
1 teaspoon ajwain seeds
1 teaspoon Garam Masala (see page 31)
salt

Bring 750ml / 1¼ pints (3¼ cups) water to the boil in a large, heavy-based pan, add the colocasia, cover, reduce the heat to medium and cook for 20 minutes. Drain, allow to cool, then peel off the skins and cut into 1-cm ½-inch thick slices.

Put the yoghurt, gram flour, ginger and garlic pastes, chilli powder, turmeric and 250ml / 8fl oz (1 cup) water in a large bowl. Season with salt and mix together. Set aside.

Heat the oil in another large, heavy-based pan over medium heat, add the cloves, cardamom pods and ajwain seeds and stir-fry for about 1 minute, or until they start to splutter. Season with salt and add the garam masala, and stir-fry briskly for 15 seconds. Add the colocasia and fry for about 10 minutes, or until there is no more stickiness and the colocasia turns light brown.

Reduce the heat and add the yoghurt mixture. Stir and cook for about 5 minutes.

Dum ki Bhindi
Slow-cooked Okra in Yoghurt Sauce

Origin Awadh
Preparation time 15–20 minutes, plus soaking time
Cooking time 25 minutes
Serves 4

500g / 1lb 2oz okra

3 teaspoons chilli powder, or to taste

150ml / ¼ pint (⅔ cup) natural (plain) yoghurt, whisked

1½ teaspoons Garam Masala, plus extra for sprinkling (see page 31)

4 teaspoons chopped green chillies

3 tablespoons vegetable oil

2 teaspoons Ginger Paste (see page 57)

2 teaspoons Garlic Paste (see page 57)

1½ teaspoons ground turmeric

3 teaspoons ghee

salt

Slit the okra lengthways but keep them joined at the stem.

Put the yoghurt in a bowl, add the chilli powder, garam masala and 1 teaspoon chopped green chillies. Season with salt and mix together. Add the okra to the yoghurt mixture and set aside for about 20 minutes to soak.

Heat the oil in a heavy-based pan over medium heat, add the ginger and garlic pastes, turmeric and the remaining green chillies and stir-fry for 1–2 minutes. Now add the okra and yoghurt mixture and cook for a further 5 minutes. Add the ghee and sprinkle over a little garam masala, then reduce the heat to low, cover and cook for about 10 minutes.

Remove the lid and continue cooking for about 5 minutes, or until the yoghurt mixture coats the okra.

Bhuni Besan Bhindi
Fried Okra Coated in Gram (Chickpea) Flour

Origin Hyderabad
Preparation time 20–25 minutes
Cooking time 15 minutes
Serves 4

---

vegetable oil, for deep frying

750g / 1lb 10oz okra, topped and tailed (trimmed)

5 teaspoons ground coriander

1 tablespoon amchoor

1 teaspoon chilli powder

1 teaspoon ground turmeric

5 tablespoons ghee

50g / 1¾oz (½ cup) gram (chickpea) flour

1 teaspoon ground black pepper

½ teaspoon ground black cardamom

½ teaspoon ground nutmeg

salt

Heat enough oil for deep-frying in a kadhai or deep-heavy-based pan to 180°C/350°F, or until a cube of bread browns in 30 seconds. Working in batches, add the okra to the hot oil and deep-fry for 2–3 minutes, or until crisp. Remove with a slotted spoon and drain on kitchen paper (paper towels).

Put the coriander, amchoor, chilli powder and turmeric in a small bowl, add 3 tablespoons water and mix together.

Heat the ghee in a heavy-based pan over medium-low heat, add the gram flour and stir-fry for about 1 minute, or until it is fragrant. Add the deep-fried okra and the ground spices mixture and stir-fry for a few seconds. Season with salt and stir-fry for about 5 minutes, or until the gram flour coats the okra. Sprinkle over the ground pepper, cardamom and nutmeg, then remove from the heat and adjust the seasoning, if necessary.

Bharwan Bhindi
Stuffed Okra

Origin Punjab
Preparation time 30 minutes
Cooking time 20–25 minutes
Serves 4

500g / 1lb 2oz okra, topped and tailed (trimmed), cut in half lengthways then de-seeded
salt

For the filling

1 teaspoon ground turmeric
1 teaspoon ground black cardamom
1 teaspoon ground fennel
1½ teaspoons ground cumin
1 teaspoon ground black pepper
2½ tablespoons vegetable oil or ghee
1 tablespoon amchoor
1 teaspoon ground coriander
2 teaspoons chilli powder
¼ teaspoon ground nutmeg
pinch of salt

For the sauce

1½ teaspoons chilli powder
½ teaspoon ground turmeric
4 tablespoons vegetable oil or ghee
125g / 4¼oz (1 small) onion, sliced
750ml / 1¼ pints (3¼ cups) natural (plain) yoghurt, whisked

To make the filling, mix all the ingredients together in a bowl. Fill the okra with equal quantities of the mixture and set aside.

To make the sauce, mix the chilli powder and turmeric in a small bowl with 2 tablespoons water.

Heat the oil or ghee in a deep, heavy-based pan over low heat, add the onion and fry for 3–4 minutes, or until translucent and glossy. Add the chilli powder mixture and stir-fry for about 3–4 minutes, or until all the moisture has evaporated, then add the stuffed okra, increase the heat to medium, cover and cook, stirring occasionally, for 7–8 minutes.

Remove from the heat, stir in the yoghurt and season with salt. Return to the heat and cook, stirring occasionally, but carefully, for about 5 minutes, or until the sauce is quite thick. Remove from the heat and adjust the seasoning, if necessary.

Sabut Bhindi
Whole Spicy Okra

Origin Awadh
Preparation time 20 minutes
Cooking time 35–40 minutes
Serves 4

500g / 1lb 2oz okra, topped and tailed (trimmed)
3 teaspoons vegetable oil
1 teaspoon cumin seeds
2 onions, chopped
1 teaspoon ground ginger
10 cloves garlic, crushed
1 teaspoon ground turmeric
2 teaspoons ground coriander
1 teaspoon amchoor
1 teaspoon Garam Masala (see page 31)
1 teaspoon chilli powder
1 teaspoon ground cumin
pinch of asafoetida
2 tomatoes, chopped
salt

Slit the okra lengthways down one side without slicing them in two.

Heat the oil in a large, heavy-based pan over medium heat, add the cumin seeds and stir-fry for about 1 minute, or until they start to splutter. Add the onions, ginger and garlic and stir-fry for about 5 minutes.

Add the okra and fry for a further 15 minutes. Now add all the spices and the tomatoes, then season with salt and mix well. Reduce the heat, cover and simmer for about 15 minutes, stirring occasionally to stop the okra from sticking to the pan. Remove from the heat and keep covered until ready to serve.

Vendakkai Masala Pachadi
Spicy Southern Okra

Origin Tamil Nadu
Preparation time 25 minutes
Cooking time 20–25 minutes
Serves 4

groundnut (peanut) oil, for deep frying
750g / 1lb 10oz okra, topped and tailed (trimmed), then cut into 2.5-cm / 1-inch pieces
2 tablespoons cashew nuts
75g / 2½oz (1 cup) grated fresh coconut
1 teaspoon cumin seeds
1 teaspoon mustard seeds
2 tablespoons urad dal, rinsed and drained
3 dried red chillies
8–10 curry leaves
125g / 4¼oz (1 small) onion, chopped
250g / 9oz (1 large) tomato, chopped
1 teaspoon chilli powder
½ teaspoon ground turmeric
1 tablespoon ground coriander
100ml / 3½fl oz (½ cup) natural (plain) yoghurt, whisked
salt

Heat the oil for deep-frying in a kadhai or deep, heavy-based pan to 180°C/350°F, or until a cube of bread browns in 30 seconds. Working in batches, add the okra pieces to the hot oil and deep-fry for about 2–3 minutes, or until crisp. Remove with a slotted spoon and drain on kitchen paper (paper towels). Reserve the oil.

Put the cashews and coconut into a small blender or food processor and process, adding a little water if necessary, to make a paste.

Heat the reserved oil in a large, heavy-based pan over medium heat, add the cumin seeds, mustard seeds, urad dal, dried red chillies and curry leaves and stir-fry for about 1 minute, or until the seeds start to splutter. Add the onion and stir-fry for about 5–7 minutes, or until golden brown. Now add the tomato, stir and add the chilli powder, turmeric and coriander and season with salt. Stir-fry for about 2–3 minutes, or until the oil separates out. Reduce the heat to low, add the cashew and coconut paste and fry for a further 2 minutes.

Remove the pan from the heat, stir in the yoghurt, then pour in 400ml / 14fl oz (1⅔ cups) water, return to the heat and bring to the boil.

Now add the deep-fried okra, reduce the heat and simmer for about 3–4 minutes, or until coated in the sauce. Adjust the seasoning, if necessary, before serving.

Bhindi Pyaz
Crispy Okra with Onions

Origin Punjab
Preparation time 10 minutes, plus soaking time
Cooking time 15 minutes
Serves 4

500g / 1lb 2oz okra
2 tablespoons vegetable oil
4 onions, chopped
4–6 green chillies, de-seeded and chopped
1 teaspoon cumin seeds, crushed
salt

Soak the okra in a large bowl of lightly salted water for about 5 minutes.

Now trim away the stem just above the ridge, then slice the okra into miniature wheels.

Heat the oil in a non-stick frying pan (skillet) over medium heat, add the onions and fry for about 5 minutes, or until the onions are browned. Add the chillies and fry for about 2 minutes, or until they are pale green. Add the cumin seeds and fry for about 30 seconds, then add the okra and season with salt. Stir well and cook, stirring frequently to prevent the okra from sticking to the pan, for about 8 minutes, or until done.

Vendakkai Pulussu
Okra in Tamarind Sauce

Origin Tamil Nadu
Preparation time 20 minutes
Cooking time 25 minutes
Serves 4

4 tablespoons vegetable oil

500g / 1lb 2oz okra, topped and tailed (trimmed)

For the sauce

2 teaspoons ground coriander

1 teaspoon chilli powder

¼ teaspoon ground turmeric

160g / 5½oz (1 medium) onion, chopped

1 teaspoon Garlic Paste (see page 57)

2 green chillies, de-seeded and chopped

200g / 7oz (2 small) tomatoes, puréed

½ tablespoon Tamarind Extract (see page 58)

1 teaspoon sugar

salt

For the tempering

1 tablespoon vegetable oil

½ teaspoon mustard seeds

½ teaspoon fenugreek seeds

10–15 curry leaves

Heat half the oil in a large, heavy-based pan. Add the okra and stir-fry for 1 minute.

Put the ground coriander, chilli powder and turmeric in a small bowl, add 2 tablespoons water and stir together.

Heat the remaining oil in a heavy-based pan over medium heat, add the onion and a pinch of salt and stir-fry for about 2 minutes, or until the onion is translucent. Add the garlic paste, and continue frying for a further 2 minutes, or until the onion is light golden. Add the green chillies and stir-fry for about 30 seconds, then add the coriander mixture and stir-fry for about 2–3 minutes, or until all the moisture has evaporated. Add the puréed tomatoes and stir-fry for about 2–3 minutes, or until the oil has separated out and rises to the surface.

Add the tamarind extract and stir-fry for 1 minute, then pour in 250ml / 8fl oz (1 cup) water, add the sugar and season with salt. Bring to the boil, then reduce the heat to low and simmer for about 2–3 minutes. Now add the okra and simmer for about 5 minutes, while you make the tempering.

Heat the oil for the tempering in a small frying pan (skillet) over medium heat. Add the mustard seeds and stir-fry for about 1 minute, or until they start to splutter. Add the fenugreek seeds and curry leaves and stir-fry for 1–2 minutes, or until the leaves stop spluttering. Pour over the simmering okra, then remove from the heat and adjust the seasoning, if necessary.

Khara Bheeda
Savoury Okra

Origin Parsi
Preparation time 15 minutes
Cooking time 10–15 minutes
Serves 8

1kg / 2¼lb young, small, tender okra, topped and tailed (trimmed)

2 large onions, sliced

1 teaspoon ground turmeric

2 tablespoons vegetable oil

2 medium-sized tomatoes

4 green chillies, de-seeded and chopped

salt

2 tablespoons chopped coriander (cilantro) leaves with tender stems, to garnish

Cut the okra into 5mm slices, place in a shallow dish and sprinkle with salt.

Heat the oil in a heavy-based frying pan (skillet) over medium heat, add the onions and fry for about 5 minutes. Add the remaining ingredients, including the okra and cook for about 6–7 minutes, or until the okra are tender. Garnish with chopped coriander.

Vendakkai Nouvala Pod
Stir-fried Okra with Sesame Seeds from Andhra

Origin Tamil Nadu
Preparation time 25 minutes
Cooking time 10 minutes
Serves 6

walnut-sized lump of tamarind

500g / 1lb 2oz okra, topped and tailed (trimmed), then cut into 1-cm / ½-inch pieces

¼ teaspoon ground turmeric

3 tablespoons sesame seeds, ground

1 teaspoon salt, or to taste

For the tempering

2 tablespoons vegetable oil

1 teaspoon mustard seeds, roasted and ground

1 teaspoon cumin seeds

½ teaspoon asafoetida

1 dried red chilli, halved

1 teaspoon urad dal, rinsed and drained

1 sprig curry leaves

Put the tamarind in a bowl, add 2 tablespoons water and soak for 10 minutes. Using your hands, mix well then squeeze out the pulp through a sieve (strainer). Set the extract aside and discard the pulp.

Heat the oil for the tempering in a large, heavy-based frying pan (skillet) over medium heat, add all the ingredients for the tempering and stir-fry for about 1 minute, or until the mustard seeds start to splutter. Add the okra, turmeric and tamarind extract, then cover and cook for about 5 minutes, or until the okra are tender and all the moisture has evaporated. Add the ground sesame seeds and season with salt, then stir-fry over high heat for a further 2 minutes, or until everything is well mixed and dry.

Vendakkai Igguru
Spicy Fried Okra

Origin Tamil Nadu
Preparation time 10 minutes
Cooking time 20–25 minutes
Serves 4

2 teaspoons cumin seeds

3 teaspoons coriander seeds

175ml / 6fl oz (¾ cup) vegetable oil

2 onions, chopped

½ teaspoon ground turmeric

2 teaspoons ground fresh ginger

2 teaspoons ground garlic

2 tomatoes, chopped

500g / 1lb 2oz tender okra, topped and tailed

1 tablespoon ground coconut

1 bunch mint leaves, chopped

1 bunch coriander (cilantro) leaves, chopped

4 green chillies, de-seeded and chopped

1 teaspoon chilli powder

250ml / 8fl oz (1 cup) coconut milk, fresh (see page 781) or canned

salt

For the seasoning

4 dried red chillies

1 teaspoon mustard seeds

6 garlic cloves

8–10 curry leaves

Put the cumin and coriander seeds in a small dry frying pan (skillet) over medium heat and stir-fry for a few minutes until roasted. Set aside.

Heat the oil in a large, heavy-based pan over medium heat, add all the ingredients for the seasoning and fry for 1–2 minutes, or until the mustard seeds start to splutter. Add the onions and fry for 5–7 minutes, or until golden brown. Add the turmeric, ginger and garlic and sauté for 2 minutes, then add the roasted cumin and coriander seeds and stir well.

Add the tomatoes and cook for 2–3 minutes, or until the tomatoes are well cooked and the oil has separated out and risen to the surface. Add the okra, stir, then add the coconut and mix well. Add the chopped mint and coriander leaves, green chillies, chilli powder and season with salt. Stir well, then pour in 500ml / 18fl oz (2¼ cups) water and the coconut milk, reduce the heat and simmer for a few minutes until hot.

Dahi ma Bheeda
Okra in Yoghurt Sauce

Origin Parsi
Preparation time 15 minutes
Cooking time 15 minutes
Serves 4–6

1kg / 2¼lb small, tender okra, topped and tailed (trimmed)
4–6 tablespoons vegetable oil
2 tablespoons Ginger Paste (see page 57)
2 tablespoons Garlic Paste (see page 57)
1 teaspoon ground turmeric
2 teaspoons chilli powder
3 teaspoons ground cumin
450ml / 16fl oz (2 cups) natural (plain) yoghurt, whisked
salt

Cut the okra into 1-cm / ½-inch thick pieces, place in a bowl and sprinkle with salt.

Heat the oil in a deep, heavy-based frying pan (skillet) over high heat, then reduce the heat to medium. Add the okra and fry for 2–3 minutes, or until it is crisp but remains green. Remove with a slotted spoon and drain on kitchen paper (paper towels).

Put the ginger and garlic pastes and ground spices into the same pan and stir-fry for about 2 minutes. Sprinkle over a little water if the spices seem to be sticking to the base (bottom) of the pan and burning. Remove from the heat and slowly stir in the yoghurt. Return to very low heat and simmer for 2–3 minutes. Season with salt and add the fried okra. Simmer for a further 2 minutes, or until the okra are hot.

Bhareli Vangi
Stuffed Spicy Aubergines (Eggplant) from Maharashtra

Origin Coastal
Preparation time 20–25 minutes
Cooking time 10 minutes
Serves 6–8

500g / 1lb 2oz (2 small) small round aubergines (eggplants), trimmed
85g / 3oz (1 cup) grated fresh coconut
4 tablespoons sesame seeds
2 teaspoons coriander seeds
2½ teaspoons cumin seeds
½ teaspoon tamarind powder
120g / 4oz (1¼ cups) peanuts, ground
1½ tablespoons jaggery or soft brown sugar
2 teaspoons Ginger Paste (see page 57)
1½ teaspoons Garlic Paste (see page 57)
1 teaspoon chilli powder
2 tablespoons Garam Masala (see page 31)
2 tablespoons vegetable oil
1 teaspoon cumin seeds
pinch of asafoetida
1 teaspoon ground turmeric
salt

Slit the aubergines horizontally and vertically with the stem intact, then rinse the aubergines in salt water and set aside.

Put the coconut, sesame seeds, coriander and cumin seeds in a dry frying pan (skillet) over medium heat and stir-fry for about 1 minute, or until light brown. Transfer to a blender or mortar and add the tamarind, ground peanuts, jaggery or sugar, ginger and garlic pastes, chilli powder and garam masala. Season with salt and process or pound with a pestle to make a paste. Stuff the aubergines with this paste.

Heat the oil in a large, heavy-based pan over high heat, then reduce the heat, add the cumin seeds and stir-fry for about 1 minute, or until the seeds start to splutter. Add the asafoetida, turmeric and stuffed aubergines, increase the heat and stir-fry over high heat for about 2 minutes.

✳ / 📷 p.395

Baghare Baigan
Spicy Sweet & Sour Aubergines (Eggplant)

Origin Hyderabad
Preparation time 45 minutes, plus cooling time
Cooking time 25 minutes
Serves 6–8

1kg / 2¼lb (2 medium) aubergines (eggplants), trimmed
2 tablespoons grated fresh coconut
1 teaspoon sesame seeds
1 teaspoon cumin seeds
2 tablespoons shelled peanuts
1 teaspoon coriander seeds
1 tablespoon molasses
1 tablespoon chopped coriander (cilantro) leaves
1 tablespoon chilli powder
1 teaspoon ground turmeric
1 tablespoon Ginger Paste (see page 57)
1 teaspoon Garlic Paste (see page 57)
1 teaspoon parched gram (chickpea) powder or lightly roasted (chickpea) gram flour
1 teaspoon Garam Masala (see page 31)
125ml / 4½fl oz (½ cup) sesame oil
50g / 1¾oz (½ small) onion, chopped
1 tablespoon Tamarind Extract (see page 58)
salt

Slice the aubergines lengthways into quarters, keeping them joined at the stem. Put them in a large, shallow dish.

Put the coconut in a small, dry frying pan (skillet) over medium heat and stir-fry for about 1 minute, or until roasted. Remove from the pan and set aside. Put the sesame seeds, cumin seeds and peanuts into the pan and stir-fry for about 1 minute, or until roasted. Remove from the pan and set aside. Put the coriander seeds in the pan and stir-fry for 1 minute, or until roasted, then transfer to a mortar and pound with a pestle or grind in a spice grinder until ground.

Put the roasted coconut, sesame seeds, cumin seeds, peanuts, molasses and coriander leaves in a blender or mortar with a little water and process or pound with a pestle to make a paste.

Season with salt, then add the chilli powder, ground coriander seeds, turmeric, ginger and garlic pastes, parched gram and garam masala and mix well.

Stuff the aubergines with the spice paste and spread the remainder of the spice paste over the aubergines.

Heat the oil to 180°C/350°F, or until a cube of bread browns in 30 seconds, then remove from the heat and allow to cool. Return to the heat and, working in batches, fry the aubergines lightly over medium heat for 2 minutes. Remove from the pan with a slotted spoon and set aside. Add the onion to the pan and fry for about 5 minutes, or until light golden. Add the aubergines and tamarind extract, then cover, reduce the heat to low and simmer for about 10 minutes, stirring occasionally and taking care not to break the aubergines, until all the moisture has evaporated and only a little sauce remains.

❋ / 📷 p.398

Baigan ka Bharta
Roasted Mashed Aubergine (Eggplant)

Origin Pan-India
Preparation time 30 minutes, plus cooling time
Cooking time 20 minutes
Serves 4

4 large aubergines (eggplants), trimmed

8 flakes garlic or 2 cloves garlic, chopped

8 cloves

½ teaspoon groundnut (peanut) oil, for brushing

½ teaspoon ground turmeric

125g / 4½oz (½ cup) ghee

1 teaspoon cumin seeds

250g / 9oz (1 large) onion, chopped

1 × 2.5-cm / 1-inch piece fresh ginger, peeled
    and chopped

4 green chillies, de-seeded and chopped

1 teaspoon chilli powder

pinch of ground turmeric

350g / 12oz (2 medium) tomatoes, chopped

2½ tablespoons chopped coriander (cilantro) leaves,
    to garnish

salt

Preheat the tandoor or charcoal grill to moderately hot, or alternatively preheat the grill (broiler) to medium-low. Using a sharp knife, make 4 small holes in each aubergine, then press 2 flakes garlic and 2 cloves into each aubergine and brush with some oil and the turmeric. Roast the aubergines for 12–15 minutes, turning frequently, until the skin is blackened. Remove and allow to cool, then peel off the skin and put the flesh in a bowl and mash with a spoon.

Heat the ghee in a kadhai, wok or large, heavy-based frying pan (skillet) over medium heat, add the cumin seeds and stir-fry for 1 minute, or until the seeds start to splutter. Add the onions and stir-fry for about 2 minutes, or until they turn translucent. Add the ginger and chillies and stir-fry for a few seconds. Add the mashed aubergine flesh, chilli powder and turmeric and stir-fry for a few minutes, or until the oil separates out.

Now add the tomatoes to the pan and season with salt. Stir-fry for about 5 minutes, or until the oil separates out, then remove from the heat and adjust the seasoning, if necessary. Garnish with chopped coriander.

Dahi ke Baigan
Aubergine (Eggplant) in Mild Yoghurt Sauce

Origin Coastal
Preparation time 15 minutes
Cooking time 15–20 minutes
Serves 2

250g / 9oz (1 small) aubergine (eggplant), trimmed

½ teaspoon ground cumin

pinch of chilli powder

pinch of ground turmeric

1 tablespoon vegetable oil, plus extra for frying

1½ teaspoons Ginger Paste (see page 57)

1½ teaspoons Garlic Paste (see page 57)

2–3 green chillies, de-seeded and chopped

200ml / 7fl oz (1 cup) natural (plain) yoghurt

salt

For the tempering

pinch of asafoetida

½ teaspoon mustard seeds

1–2 dried red chillies (optional)

sprig of curry leaves

Cut the aubergine into round slices. For smaller ones, you can choose not to separate them at the stem. Put the ground spices in a small bowl, season with salt and add 1 tablespoon of water. Mix together.

Coat a non-stick pan with a thin film of oil over medium heat, add the ginger paste, garlic paste and green chillies and stir-fry for about 1 minute. Add the aubergine and cook for 3–5 minutes, stirring once or twice with a wooden spatula, then remove from the pan and set aside. Put the yoghurt in another pan and mix with a little water, then bring almost to the boil, stirring constantly to ensure that it does not curdle.

Heat the remaining oil in a heavy-based frying pan (skillet) over medium heat, add the asafoetida and mustard seeds and stir-fry for 1 minute, or until the seeds start to splutter. Add the dried red chillies, if using, and stir-fry for about 2 minutes, or until they turn a shade darker, then add the curry leaves. Pour the tempering over the yoghurt mixture, add the aubergines and simmer for a further 2 minutes, or until the yoghurt and aubergine are hot.

Tsuk Wangun
Sour Kashmiri Aubergines (Eggplant)

Origin Jammu and Kashmir
Preparation time 20 minutes, plus marinating time
Cooking time 30 minutes
Serves 4

8 round aubergines (eggplants), trimmed

vegetable oil, for deep frying

For the marinade

½ teaspoon ground turmeric

2 tablespoons lemon juice

salt

For the spice paste

2 teaspoons Ginger Paste (see page 57)

2 teaspoons Garlic Paste (see page 57)

1 tablespoon ground coriander

1 teaspoon red chilli paste

1 teaspoon ground turmeric

For the sauce

30g / 1¾oz (¼ cup) tamarind pulp

2 tablespoons vegetable oil

6 cloves

2 cinnamon sticks

90g / 3¼oz (1 small) tomato, puréed

4 teaspoons Fried Onion Paste (see page 57)

Slice the aubergines lengthways, keeping them joined at the stem.

To make the marinade, mix the turmeric and lemon juice together in a bowl. Season with salt and rub the aubergines all over with the marinade. Place the aubergines in a large shallow dish, then cover and set aside for 30 minutes.

Heat enough oil for deep-frying in a kadhai or deep, heavy-based pan to 180°C/350°F, or until a cube of bread browns in 30 seconds. Carefully lower the aubergines into the hot oil and deep-fry for about 2–3 minutes, or until cooked, working in batches if necessary. Remove with a slotted spoon and drain on kitchen paper (paper towels).

Put all the ingredients for the spice paste in a bowl, add 4 tablespoons water and mix well.

To make the sauce, put the tamarind pulp in a pan, add 125ml / 4½fl oz (½ cup) water, bring to the boil, then reduce the heat to low and simmer for 5–7 minutes until reduced by half. Strain through a sieve (strainer), discarding the fibres in the sieve and set the extract aside.

Heat the oil in a heavy-based pan over medium heat, add the cloves and cinnamon and stir-fry for a few seconds, then add the spice paste and stir-fry for about 2 minutes, or until the oil separates out. Add the puréed tomato and continue frying for 2–3 minutes, then add the tamarind extract and fry for about 1 minute, before adding the fried onion paste. Continue to cook until the oil separates out and rises to the top.

Pour in 250ml / 8fl oz (1 cup) water, then bring to the boil, reduce the heat and simmer, stirring occasionally, until the sauce is a thin consistency. Lower the aubergines carefully into the sauce and simmer for a further 5 minutes. Remove from the heat and adjust the seasoning, if necessary.

Sabut Achari Baigan
Whole Aubergines (Eggplant)
in Pickling Spices

Origin Awadh
Preparation time 15 minutes
Cooking time 10–15 minutes
Serves 4–6

750g / 1lb 10oz (3 small) aubergines
   (eggplants), trimmed

4 tablespoons mustard oil

½ teaspoon fenugreek seeds

½ teaspoon mustard seeds

1 teaspoon kalonji (nigella) seeds

1 teaspoon ground aniseed

1 teaspoon ground coriander

1 teaspoon amchoor

½ teaspoon ground turmeric

salt

Cut a criss-cross in the aubergines, keeping the aubergines whole at the stem.

Put a large pinch of salt in a small bowl, add 2 tablespoons water and stir until dissolved.

Heat the oil in a kadhai or deep, heavy-based pan over high heat. Reduce the heat, add the fenugreek seeds, mustard seeds and kalonji seeds and stir-fry for 1 minute, or until all the seeds start to splutter. Add the ground spices together with the salt mixture and stir-fry for 30 seconds. Remove the pan from the heat. Fill the aubergines with equal quantities of the mixture, then place the aubergines back in the pan, cover and cook over very low heat for 5–7 minutes, turning gently once or twice, until hot.

Bharwan Baigan
Aubergines (Eggplant) with Spicy Filling

Origin Awadh
Preparation time 15 minutes, plus cooling time
Cooking time 10–15 minutes
Serves 6

500g / 1lb 2oz (2 small) aubergines
   (eggplants), trimmed

4 tablespoons mustard oil

2 onions, chopped

1 teaspoon Ginger Paste (see page 57)

1 teaspoon Garlic Paste (see page 57)

¼ teaspoon ground cloves

2 teaspoons ground coriander

1 teaspoon ground turmeric

½ teaspoon Garam Masala (see page 31)

½ teaspoon chilli powder

250g / 9oz (1 large) tomato, diced

salt

Slice the aubergines lengthways, keeping them joined at the stem. Place in a large shallow dish, sprinkle with salt and set aside.

Heat the oil in a kadhai or heavy-based pan over high heat. Reduce the heat, add the onions and fry for 2 minutes, or until translucent. Add the ginger and garlic pastes and stir-fry for 1 minute, then sprinkle over 1 teaspoon water. Add the ground spices together with the tomato and season with salt. Stir-fry over medium heat for 2 minutes, then remove from the heat and allow to cool.

When cool, fill the aubergines evenly with this mixture, then place them back in the same pan, cover and simmer for 5–7 minutes, turning once or twice, until hot.

Gutti Vengkayya
Stuffed Aubergines (Eggplant)
from Andhra

Origin Hyderabad
Preparation time 40 minutes
Cooking time 30 minutes
Serves 4–6

2 teaspoons vegetable oil
½ teaspoon ground turmeric
3 tablespoons coriander seeds
1 teaspoon cumin seeds
¼ teaspoon asafoetida
6 dried red chillies
1 teaspoon chana dal, rinsed and drained
1 teaspoon urad dal, rinsed and drained
1 teaspoon Tamarind Extract (see page 58)
500g / 1lb 2oz (2 small) aubergines (eggplants), trimmed
½ teaspoon ground turmeric
salt

For the tempering

6 tablespoons vegetable oil
1 teaspoon mustard seeds
½ teaspoon cumin seeds
1 dried red chilli, halved
10–12 curry leaves
1 teaspoon urad dal, rinsed and drained
2 onions, chopped

Heat the oil in a deep, heavy-based pan over medium heat, add the turmeric, coriander seeds, cumin seeds, asafoetida, dried red chillies and the dals and stir-fry for about 2 minutes, or until all the spices and chillies are fragrant and the dals turn golden. Put the tamarind extract in a bowl, add the spice and dal mixture and season with salt. Transfer the mixture to a mortar or small blender and pound with a pestle or process until ground.

Slice the aubergines into quarters, keeping them joined at the stem. Fill the aubergines with the spice mixture and set aside.

Heat the oil for the tempering in a large, heavy-based pan over medium heat, add the mustard seeds, cumin seeds, dried red chilli, curry leaves and dal and stir-fry for 1 minute, or until the mustard seeds start to splutter. Add the onions and stir-fry for about 1–2 minutes. Add the aubergines and turmeric, then season with salt and fry for about 2 minutes, turning the aubergines around gently. Sprinkle over 1–2 tablespoons water, then reduce the heat, cover and simmer, turning them occasionally and taking care not to break them, for about 15–20 minutes, or until the aubergines are cooked. Serve hot.

Namak ke Baigan
Fried Aubergines (Eggplant)

Origin Awadh
Prepration time 10 minutes, plus standing time
Cooking time 15 minutes
Serves 8

500g / 1lb 2oz long aubergines (eggplants), trimmed
3 tablespoons mustard oil
salt

Slice the aubergines lengthways. Place in a large shallow dish, sprinkle with salt and set aside for 30 minutes.

Heat the oil in a kadhai or deep heavy-based pan over high heat. Reduce the heat, add the aubergines together with a little salt to the pan, cover and simmer for about 15 minutes, turning gently twice or three times until hot.

Venkayya Thuvaiyal
Tangy Mashed 'Southern' Aubergines (Eggplant)

Origin Tamil Nadu
Preparation time 5 minutes, plus cooling time
Cooking time 12–15 minutes
Serves 4

1 aubergine (eggplant), trimmed
1 tablespoon urad dal, rinsed and drained
2 tablespoons chana dal, rinsed and drained
2 dried red chillies
pinch of asafoetida
1 tablespoon vegetable oil
1 teaspoon tamarind extract
1 green chilli, de-seeded (optional)
salt

Roast the aubergine over an open flame of a gas cooker (gas stove top), rotating frequently until the skin is blistered and charred evenly all over. Alternatively, preheat the grill (broiler) to medium and cook the aubergine under the grill for about 12–15 minutes, turning frequently until blackened all over. Allow to cool, then peel off the skin, put the flesh in a bowl and mash well with a spoon.

Put the remaining ingredients in a blender or food processor, season with salt and process to make a smooth paste. Add the mashed aubergine and mix well before serving.

Khatte Meethe Baigan
Sweet & Sour Minty Aubergine (Eggplant)

Origin Awadh
Preparation time 20 minutes
Cooking time 30–35 minutes
Serves 2–4

250g / 9oz (1 small) aubergine (eggplant), trimmed
1 quantity Mint Chutney (page 66)
2 teaspoons ground dried mint
5 tablespoons vegetable oil
1½ teaspoons cumin seeds
100g / 3½oz (1 small) onion, thinly sliced
1 tablespoon Ginger Paste (see page 57)
2 tablespoons Garlic Paste (see page 57)
½ teaspoon ground turmeric
1 tablespoon ground coriander
2 teaspoons ground cumin
1 tablespoon Tamarind Extract (see page 58)
1 teaspoon chilli powder
1 teaspoon Garam Masala (see page 31)
2 tablespoons jaggery, crumbled, or soft brown sugar
salt
few mint leaves, to garnish

Slice the aubergine lengthways into quarters, keeping it joined at the stem. Fill the aubergine generously with the mint chutney and also spread some chutney on the outer skin. Spread the dried mint out on a plate and roll the aubergine in it to coat. Set aside.

Heat the oil in a large, heavy-based pan over medium heat, add the cumin seeds and stir-fry for about 1 minute, or until they start to splutter. Add the onion and stir-fry for about 5–7 minutes, or until the onions are golden brown. Now add the ginger and garlic pastes and stir-fry for about 2 minutes. Gently place the stuffed aubergine into the pan and carefully fry for about 2 minutes.

Pour 250ml / 8fl oz (1 cup) hot water into the pan, add the tamarind extract and the remaining spices and season with salt. Reduce the heat slightly, cover and simmer for about 10 minutes. Carefully turn the aubergine over once and sprinkle over the jaggery or sugar and 125ml / 4½fl oz (½ cup) hot water, if necessary, and stir. Cover and simmer for a further 10 minutes.

Remove the pan from the heat, adjust the seasoning, if necessary and garnish with mint leaves.

Kathirakkai Poriyal
Curried Aubergines (Eggplant)

Origin Tamil Nadu
Preparation time 30 minutes
Cooking time 10–15 minutes
Serves 4–6

500g / 1lb 2oz (2 small) aubergines
    (eggplants), trimmed
½ teaspoon ground turmeric
2 onions, thinly sliced
salt

For the spice powder
4 teaspoons vegetable oil
1 tablespoon coriander seeds
½ teaspoon asafoetida
2–3 dried red chillies
2 teaspoons urad dal, rinsed and drained
2 tablespoons grated fresh coconut
1 teaspoon Tamarind Extract (see page 58)

For the tempering
2 tablespoons vegetable oil
1 teaspoon mustard seeds
1 dried red chilli, halved
1 sprig curry leaves

Cut the aubergines into quarters and set aside.

To make the spice powder, heat 2 teaspoons oil in
a deep, heavy-based frying pan (skillet) over medium
heat. Add the coriander seeds, asafoetida, dried red
chillies and dal and stir-fry for about 2 minutes, or
until the spices are fragrant. Remove from the pan
and set aside.

Heat 2 more teaspoons oil in the pan over medium
heat. Add the coconut and stir-fry for about
1–2 minutes, or until golden brown. Make sure
the coconut doesn't burn.

Combine the coconut with the fried spices and dal
in a bowl. Add the tamarind extract and season
with salt. Transfer the mixture to a blender and
process until ground.

Heat the oil for the tempering in the same pan over
medium heat, add the mustard seeds, dried red chilli
and curry leaves and stir-fry for 1 minute, or until
the mustard seeds start to splutter Add the onions
and fry for about 2 minutes.

Add the aubergines, turmeric, 4 tablespoons
water and season with salt. Reduce the heat, cover
and simmer for about 10 minutes, or until the
aubergines are tender and all the moisture has
evaporated. Sprinkle in the spice powder and
stir gently before serving.

Rasedar Baigan
Curried Aubergine (Eggplant)
in Coconut Sauce

Origin Coastal
Preparation time 15–20 minutes
Cooking time 15–18 minutes
Serves 4

250g / 9oz (1 small) aubergine (eggplant), trimmed
pinch of asafoetida
4–5 teaspoons vegetable oil
½ teaspoon ground turmeric
1 teaspoon chilli powder
250ml / 8fl oz (1 cup) coconut milk, fresh
    (see page 781) or canned
salt

Cut the aubergine into slices.

Put the asafoetida in a small bowl, add 1 tablespoon
water and stir until dissolved.

Heat the oil in a heavy-based pan over medium heat,
add the aubergine, season with salt, then add the
turmeric, chilli powder and asafoetida mixture and
stir-fry for about 2 minutes. Reduce the heat to low
and simmer for about 10 minutes.

Remove the pan from the heat, stir in the coconut
milk, then return to a low heat and simmer for about
3–4 minutes. Adjust the seasoning, if necessary.

Kamala Phoolkopi
Cauliflower with Oranges

Origin West Bengal
Preparation time 15–20 minutes
Cooking time 20 minutes
Serves 4

500g / 1lb 2oz (1 small head) cauliflower, cut into
    2.5-cm / 1-inch florets

4 potatoes, cut into 2.5-cm / 1-inch pieces

1 teaspoon ground turmeric

4 tablespoons vegetable oil

2 bay leaves

1 tablespoon ground fresh ginger

2 onions, ground

1 teaspoon chilli powder

2 teaspoons ground cumin

1 teaspoon sugar

3 oranges, peeled and de-seeded, pith removed,
    reserving flesh

3–4 green chillies, de-seeded and chopped

salt

For the garam masala

4 cloves

2 green cardamoms

1 cinnamon stick, about 5cm / 2 inches long

Put the vegetables in a large bowl, add the turmeric
and toss until they are lightly coated.

Mix all the ingredients for the garam masala together
in a bowl.

Heat the oil in a large, heavy-based pan over high
heat, then reduce the heat. Add the vegetables
and stir-fry for 2–3 minutes, or until they are light
brown. Remove from the pan with a slotted spoon
and set aside.

Add the bay leaves and garam masala to the pan and
stir-fry for about 1 minute, or until fragrant. Add the
ground ginger, onions, chilli powder, cumin and sugar
and stir-fry for a further 1 minute, or until the spices
change colour. Sprinkle over a few drops of water
to prevent burning, if necessary. Add the vegetables,
season with salt and stir thoroughly.

Add the flesh of 2 oranges, reserving the rest for
the garnish. Mix well, then pour in 125ml / 4½fl oz
(½ cup) water, cover and cook over low heat for
about 15 minutes.

About 5 minutes before the end of the cooking time,
add the chillies. There should be very little sauce left
in the pan. Garnish with the reserved orange.

☼ ☼

Gobi Kali Mirch
Peppery Cauliflower Curry

Origin Awadh
Preparation time 10 minutes
Cooking time 12–15 minutes
Serves 4

---

2 teaspoons vegetable oil

1½ teaspoons mustard seeds

1½ teaspoons cumin seeds

1½ teaspoons urad dal, rinsed and drained

500g / 1lb 2oz (1 small head) cauliflower, cut into
    small florets

1½ teaspoons ground black pepper

salt

Heat the oil in a large, heavy-based pan over medium
heat, add the mustard seeds and cumin seeds and
stir-fry for 1 minute, or until they start to splutter.
Add the dal and stir-fry for a further 1 minute, or until
they change colour, then add the cauliflower and just
enough water to cook the vegetables.

Reduce the heat and simmer for about 5 minutes,
or until the cauliflower is almost done. Season with
salt, add the pepper and stir. Remove from the heat
and keep covered for a further 5 minutes.

※ ※ / p.467

Chatpati Gobi
Piquant Cauliflower

Origin Delhi
Preparation time 45 minutes, plus soaking and standing time
Cooking time 20 minutes
Serves 4

500g / 1lb 2oz (1 small head) cauliflower, cut into florets
250g / 9oz (1 large) tomato, puréed
2 teaspoons ground coriander
½ teaspoon chilli powder
1 teaspoon amchoor
3 teaspoons gram (chickpea) flour
4 potatoes, cut into quarters
5½ tablespoons vegetable oil
1 teaspoon cumin seeds
1 × 5-cm / 2-inch piece fresh ginger, peeled and finely chopped
10 green chillies, de-seeded and chopped
½ teaspoon ground black pepper
generous pinch of fenugreek seeds
salt
pomegranate seeds, to garnish

Put the cauliflower florets in a large bowl of salted iced water. Drain just before cooking.

Put the puréed tomato in a bowl, add the coriander, ¼ teaspoon chilli powder and the amchoor and mix well. Now cut the potatoes into quarters and then halve each quarter lengthways. Put them in a large shallow dish and sprinkle the remaining ¼ teaspoon chilli powder over them. Season with salt and set aside for about 15 minutes. Sprinkle over the gram flour and mix well.

Heat 4½ tablespoons oil in a large, heavy-based pan over medium heat, add the potatoes and fry for about 15–20 minutes, or until soft, golden brown and crisp.

Heat the remaining oil in another pan over medium heat, add the cumin seeds and stir-fry for 1 minute, or until they start to splutter. Add the ginger and chillies and stir-fry for about 10 seconds before adding the tomato mixture and stir-frying for a further 10 seconds. Add the cauliflower florets and reduce the heat to low. Cover and cook for about 8–10 minutes, or until the cauliflower is almost cooked.

Now add the potatoes and stir until all the moisture has completely evaporated. Sprinkle over the pepper and stir carefully. Crush the fenugreek seeds between your hands and sprinkle them into the pan and stir. Remove from the heat and adjust the seasoning, if necessary. Garnish with pomegranate seeds.

※

Phool Gobi
Cauliflower Masala

Origin Punjab
Preparation time 15 minutes
Cooking time 10 minutes
Serves 4–6

125ml / 4¼oz (½ cup) vegetable oil
pinch of asafoetida
1 teaspoon cumin seeds
½ teaspoon fenugreek seeds
1 × 2.5-cm / 1-inch piece fresh ginger, peeled and crushed
1 teaspoon ground ginger
1 large or 2 small heads cauliflowers, cut into 5-cm / 2-inch florets
½ teaspoon chilli powder
1 teaspoon ground succh bari or Kashmiri Garam Masala (see page 56)
1 teaspoon sugar
1 teaspoon ground turmeric
bunch of coriander (cilantro) leaves, chopped
salt

Heat the oil in a kadhai or deep, heavy-based pan over medium heat, sprinkle over a little water, then add the asafoetida, cumin seeds, fenugreek seeds, and crushed and ground ginger and fry for a few seconds. Add the cauliflower, season with salt, then add the chilli powder, succh bari or garam masala, sugar and turmeric and shake the pan, so that the masala is well mixed. Add 2 tablespoons water, reduce the heat to low and cook for about 8–10 minutes, or until the cauliflower is cooked. Add the coriander and toss again.

※ ※

Gobi Rajwadi
Spicy Cauliflower & Yam

Origin Rajasthan
Preparation time 35–45 minutes
Cooking time 8–10 minutes
Serves 4

750g / 1lb 10oz (1 medium head) cauliflower, cut into florets
250g / 9oz yam, peeled and cut into cubes
5 tablespoons ghee
1 teaspoon cumin seeds
100g / 3½oz (1 small) onion, chopped
6 flakes garlic or 2 cloves garlic, chopped
3 teaspoons chopped ginger
2 teaspoons Kachri Powder (see page 774)
2 teaspoons ground coriander
1 teaspoon chilli powder
1 teaspoon ground turmeric
1 teaspoon amchoor
salt

For the smoking (optional)

2 green cardamom pods
1 teaspoon ghee

Blanch the cauliflower florets in a large pan of boiling salted water, then drain and refresh in iced water.

Cook the yam in another large pan of boiling water for about 20 minutes, or until soft.

If you would like to smoke the yam, put a few small pieces of hot charcoal in a small heatproof bowl and place the bowl in a large, heavy-based pan. Arrange the boiled yam cubes around the bowl, then place the cardamom pods on the charcoal, pour on the ghee and, as the smoke bellows, cover with a lid and set aside for about 15 minutes.

Heat the ghee in a deep, heavy-based pan over medium heat, add the cumin seeds and stir-fry for about 1 minute, or until they start to splutter. Add the onion, garlic and ginger and stir-fry for about 2 minutes, or until the onion is translucent and glossy. Add the cauliflower and smoked yam and stir-fry for 1 minute, before adding the kachri powder, coriander, chilli powder, turmeric and amchoor. Season with salt and stir-fry, adding 2 tablespoons water at frequent intervals, for about 5 minutes. Remove from the heat and adjust the seasoning, if necessary.

 ※ ※

Achari Gobi
Cauliflower in Pickling Spices

Origin Awadh
Preparation time 20 minutes, plus soaking time
Cooking time 15–20 minutes
Serves 4

1 large head cauliflower, cut into florets
3 teaspoons vegetable oil
½ teaspoon mustard seeds
½ teaspoon kalonji (nigella) seeds
1 teaspoon coriander seeds, crushed
½ teaspoon cumin seeds
1 teaspoon crushed dried red chillies
5 cloves garlic, coarsely chopped
1 teaspoon amchoor
1 teaspoon oil from any pickle
salt

Soak the cauliflower in a heatproof bowl of hot salted water for about 10 minutes.

Heat the oil in a kadhai or large, heavy-based pan over medium heat, add all the seeds and stir-fry for 1 minute, or until they start to splutter.

Drain the cauliflower and add to the pan and stir-fry for about 10 minutes. Add the chillies and garlic and sprinkle over 1 teaspoon of hot water. Season with salt, then cover and cook for about 5 minutes. Stir and add the amchoor and the oil from any pickle.

Ganth Gobi
Kohlrabi

Origin Jammu and Kashmir
Preparation time 10 minutes
Cooking time 25–30 minutes
Serves 4–6

125g / 4¼oz (½ cup) ghee or vegetable oil
pinch of asafoetida
2 cloves
750g / 1lb 10oz kolhrabi with leaves, peeled
4 green chillies
1 teaspoon ground coriander
1 teaspoon ground succh bari or Kashmiri Garam Masala (see page 56)
1 teaspoon ground ginger
salt

Heat the ghee or oil in a large, heavy-based pan over medium heat, add the asafoetida and cloves and stir-fry for about 1 minute, or until the cloves change colour. Add the kohlrabi, shake the pan, then reduce the heat, cover and simmer for 10 minutes.

Add the remaining ingredients to the pan, season with salt and fry for 2–3 minutes. Pour in 250ml / 8fl oz (1 cup) water and simmer over low heat for about 15 minutes.

Muttakose Kilangu
Stir-fried Cabbage & Carrots

Origin Tamil Nadu
Preparation time 20 minutes
Cooking time 10–15 minutes
Serves 4

3 tablespoons vegetable oil
1 teaspoon mustard seeds
1 teaspoon chana dal, rinsed and drained
1 teaspoon urad dal, rinsed and drained
10–15 curry leaves
2–4 green chillies, de-seeded and cut into long strips
250g / 9oz (½ small head) green cabbage, finely shredded
3 tablespoons grated fresh coconut
salt

Heat the oil in a large, heavy-based frying pan (skillet) over medium heat, add the mustard seeds and stir-fry for 1 minute, or until they start to splutter. Add the dals and stir-fry for 1 minute, or until the dals change colour. Add the curry leaves and stir-fry for a further 1 minute. Add the chillies and stir, then add the cabbage and stir once to mix. Season with salt and mix again.

Reduce the heat to low, cover and cook for about 6 minutes, or until the cabbage is nicely glazed but still retains its crunch.

Add the coconut to the pan and mix it in with the cabbage, stirring vigorously for 1 minute.

Muttokos Thoran
Kerala Stir-fried Cabbage
with Coconut

Origin Kerala
Preparation time 10 minutes
Cooking time 15 minutes
Serves 4–6

3 tablespoons grated fresh coconut

2–3 shallots

2 green chillies, de-seeded (optional)

500g / 1lb 2oz (1 small head) cabbage, chopped

salt

For the tempering

2 teaspoons coconut oil

1 teaspoon mustard seeds

1 teaspoon cumin seeds

1 dried red chilli, halved

1 teaspoon urad dal, rinsed and drained

1 sprig curry leaves

Put the grated coconut, shallots, chillies and
1–1½ tablespoons water in a food processor or
blender and process to make a paste.

Heat the oil for the tempering in a large, heavy-
based frying pan (skillet) over medium heat. Add
all the ingredients for the tempering and stir-fry
for 1 minute, or until the mustard seeds start
to splutter. Add the cabbage and season with salt.
Reduce the heat, cover and simmer for about
10 minutes, or until the cabbage is cooked and
all the moisture is absorbed.

Add the coconut-shallot paste and stir-fry for a few
minutes until well mixed.

Kosu Podi
Fried Savoury Cabbage

Origin Coastal
Preparation time 20 minutes
Cooking time 10–15 minutes
Serves 2

225g / 8oz (½ small head) cabbage, cut into
1-cm / ½-inch pieces

2 tablespoons vegetable oil

1 tablespoon chana dal, rinsed and drained

½ teaspoon urad dal, rinsed and drained

½ teaspoon cumin seeds

1 onion, sliced

1 teaspoon ground garlic

1 bunch coriander (cilantro) leaves, chopped

6–8 green chillies, de-seeded and chopped

3 tablespoons grated fresh coconut

salt

Pour in 125ml / 4½fl oz (½ cup) water into a kadhai
or large, heavy-based pan, add a little salt and the
cabbage, then cover and simmer over very low heat
for 10 minutes, or until tender. Remove from the
heat and set aside.

Heat the oil in a large, heavy-based frying pan (skillet)
over medium heat, add the dals and cumin seeds
and stir-fry for about 1 minute, or until they are dark
brown. Add the onion and garlic and stir-fry for about
5 minutes, or until the onion is golden brown, then
add the cabbage and cook for a few minutes to reduce
any extra water. Add the coriander and chillies and
season with salt. Mix well, then remove from the heat.
Sprinkle over the grated coconut and mix.

Karamkalla
Dry Cabbage in Masala

Origin Awadh
Preparation time 15 minutes
Cooking time 15 minutes
Serves 4–6

125ml / 4½fl oz (½ cup) vegetable oil

pinch of asafoetida

1 teaspoon cumin seeds

½ teaspoon fenugreek seeds

1 × 2.5-cm / 1-inch piece fresh ginger, peeled
   and crushed

2 green chillies, de-seeded and chopped

1 teaspoon ground ginger

1 large cabbage, cut into large pieces

1 teaspoon chilli powder, or to taste

1 teaspoon sugar

1 teaspoon ground turmeric

1 teaspoon ground coriander

salt

1 sprig coriander (cilantro), leaves only, chopped,
   to garnish

Heat the oil in a large, heavy-based pan over high
heat, then reduce the heat, add the asafoetida and
cumin and fenugreek seeds and stir-fry for 1 minute,
or until the seeds start to splutter. Add the ginger,
chillies and ground ginger and stir-fry briskly for
15 seconds, then add the cabbage and season with
salt. Add the chilli powder, sugar and other ground
spices and stir-fry for about 10 minutes, or until all
the moisture has evaporated. Garnish with coriander.

Sarson da Saag
Classic Mustard Greens

Origin Punjab
Preparation time 30 minutes
Cooking time 3 hours
Serves 4

750g / 1lb 10oz mustard greens, chopped

250g / 9oz spinach, chopped

100g / 3½oz mooli (daikon) leaves, chopped

30g / 1¼oz amaranthus, washed well and
   chopped

8 green chillies, slit in half lengthways and de-seeded

1 × 2.5-cm / 1-inch piece ginger, diced

4 tablespoons mustard oil

4 tablespoons basmati rice

2 tablespoons cornflour (cornstarch)

225g / 8oz (1 cup / 2 sticks) butter, softened,
   to garnish

salt

Put all the ingredients except the flour and butter
in a large, heavy-based pan. Season with salt and
pour in 2 litres / 3½ pints (8½ cups) water. Bring to
the boil, then reduce the heat to low and simmer
for about 1¾ hours.

Remove the pan from the heat and churn with a
wooden churner or transfer to a blender or food
processor and process until blended. Put the mixture
back in the pan and return to the heat.

Add the cornflour, then cover and simmer over very
low heat, stirring frequently, for about 1 hour. Remove
and adjust the seasoning, then transfer to a serving
bowl and garnish with large dollops of butter.

※

Pata Bhaja
Batter-fried Spinach Leaves

Origin West Bengal
Preparation time 15 minutes
Cooking time 10 minutes
Serves 6

3 tablespoons gram (chickpea) flour
250ml / 8fl oz (1 cup) mustard oil, plus a few drops
12 large single leaves of spinach
salt

Put the gram flour, a pinch of salt and a few drops of mustard oil in a bowl and mix together, adding enough water to make a fairly thin batter.

Heat the mustard oil in a kadhai, wok or deep heavy-based pan over high heat, then reduce the heat. Working in batches, if necessary, dip each spinach leaf into the batter and carefully drop them into the hot oil. Fry for about 1 minute, or until crisp and golden. Remove with a slotted spoon and drain on kitchen paper (paper towels).

Palak
Spiced Spinach

Origin Awadh
Preparation time 15 minutes
Cooking time 15 minutes
Serves 4–6

100ml / 3½fl oz (½ cup) mustard oil
1 teaspoon coriander seeds
2–3 dried red chillies
500g / 1lb 2oz spinach, stems removed and chopped
salt

Heat the oil in a kadhai or deep, heavy-based pan over high heat, then reduce the heat. Add the coriander seeds and stir-fry for about 1 minute, or until they start to splutter. Add the dried red chillies and stir-fry for about 1 minute, or until the chillies turn a shade darker. Add the spinach, mix well, season with salt, stir once again, then reduce the heat to very low, cover and simmer for about 10 minutes.

Uncover and simmer for about 1–2 minutes, or until all the moisture has evaporated.

※ / 📷 p.276

Haak
Kashmiri Leafy Greens

Origin Jammu and Kashmir
Preparation time 15 minutes
Cooking time 20 minutes
Serves 4

1 tablespoon vegetable oil
pinch of asafoetida
½ teaspoon chilli powder
1 teaspoon ground ginger
2 dried red chillies
1kg / 2¼lb collard greens
1 teaspoon ground succh bari or Kashmiri Garam Masala (see page 56)
salt

Heat the oil in a large, heavy-based pan over medium heat. Add the asafoetida and stir-fry for about 30 seconds, or until it dissolves. Add the chilli powder, ground ginger and dried red chillies and stir-fry for 10 seconds, then add the leafy greens. Crumble over the succh bari or Kashmiri Garam Masala and stir.

Reduce the heat to low, cover and cook for about 15 minutes. Don't let all the moisture evaporate, as the dish should have a little sauce. Adjust the seasoning.

In Kashmir, collard greens are called haak. Collard greens are similar to kale and spring greens so use them instead if you cannot find collard greens.

✸

Arbai ke Patte
Yam Leaf Wraps
with Spicy Lentil Paste Filling

Origin Awadh
Preparation time 25 minutes, plus soaking time
Cooking time 20–25 minutes
Serves 4–6

250g / 9oz (1⅓ cups) urad dal, rinsed and drained
12 yam leaves
pinch of asafoetida
2 teaspoons ground cumin
1 teaspoon chilli powder
1 teaspoon ground ginger
1 teaspoon ground coriander
1 × 2.5-cm / 1-inch piece fresh ginger, peeled and grated
6–8 green chillies, de-seeded and very finely chopped
250ml / 8fl oz (1 cup) vegetable oil
1 teaspoon ground turmeric
2 teaspoons amchoor
salt
1 sprig coriander (cilantro) leaves, to garnish

Soak the urad dal in a bowl of water for 2 hours. Drain, transfer to a blender or food processor and process, adding a little water if necessary, to make a smooth thin paste. Transfer to a bowl.

Remove the central stem from the yam leaves. Mix all the spices, except the amchoor and turmeric together in a bowl. Season with salt, then mix into the lentil paste.

Smear the mixture lightly over each yam leaf. Roll the leaves into 2.5-cm /1-inch thick flat rolls and place them on a board. Cut each leaf into 5-cm / 2-inch pieces and seal the ends with the reserved lentil paste. Continue this process until everything is used up.

Heat half the oil in a kadhai or deep, heavy-based pan over high heat. Add 3 or 4 yam leaves at a time to the hot oil and fry for about 2 minutes, or until golden brown. Remove with a slotted spoon and drain on kitchen paper (paper towels).

Add the remaining oil to a separate large, heavy-based pan, pour in 500ml / 18fl oz (2¼ cups) water and bring to the boil. As it boils, add the turmeric and the fried yam leaves, then reduce the heat and simmer for about 10 minutes until they are tender, but not too soft as they may break.

When there is a little sauce left in the pan, sprinkle over the amchoor and shake the pan lightly. Remove from the heat and garnish with coriander leaves.

If you can't find yam leaves, you could use large spinach leaves, but the flavour of the dish will be quite different. If you use spinach leaves make sure you reduce the simmering time by half, to 5 minutes.

Tamba di Bhaji
Red Amaranthus Leaves

Origin Coastal
Preparation time 30 minutes
Cooking time 20 minutes
Serves 6–8

1 tablespoon vegetable oil
1 onion, sliced
4 cloves garlic, chopped
2 green chillies, de-seeded (optional) and chopped
1 large bunch red amaranthus leaves
1 tablespoon grated fresh coconut
salt

Make sure the amaranthus leaves are well washed before using. You may need to wash them about three times to get rid of all the dirt. If you cannot buy amaranthus then use spinach instead. Roughly chop.

Heat the oil in a large, heavy-based pan over medium heat, add the onion and fry for about 5 minutes, or until they are light golden brown. Add the garlic and chillies and stir-fry for about 30 seconds. Add the amaranthus leaves, then cover, reduce the heat and cook for about 15 minutes, stirring occasionally.

Finally, add the grated coconut and season with salt.

Palang ka Kapha
Puréed Spinach

Origin Uttarakhand
Preparation time 20 minutes
Cooking time 30 minutes
Serves 4

1kg / 2¼lb spinach, chopped
1 tablespoon vegetable oil
pinch of asafoetida
2 onions, sliced
1 tablespoon Ginger Paste (see page 57)
3–4 green chillies, slit in half lengthways and de-seeded
2 tablespoons rice flour
1 tablespoon ghee
2–3 dried red chillies
6 garlic cloves, chopped (optional)
salt
1 × 5-cm / 2-inch piece fresh ginger, peeled and cut into strips, to garnish freshly cooked Rice (see page 631) or Roti (see page 616), to serve

Bring 250ml / 8fl oz (1 cup) water to the boil in a heavy-based pan, add the spinach and cook for a few minutes until the spinach is cooked. Remove from the heat and mash it well with a wooden churner or in a blender or food processor. Set aside.

Heat the oil in a kadhai or deep, heavy-based pan over medium heat, add the asafoetida and stir-fry for about 30 seconds, or until it dissolves. Add the onions and stir-fry for about 2 minutes, or until they are translucent. Add the ginger paste and continue stir-frying for about 1 minute.

Add the spinach purée and green chillies to the pan, then pour in 500ml / 18fl oz (2¼ cups) hot water and mix well. Slowly add the rice flour, stirring constantly to make sure that no lumps form, then bring to the boil. Season with salt and reduce the heat to medium-low and cook for about 20 minutes.

Heat the ghee in a small frying pan (skillet) over medium heat, add the dried red chillies and garlic cloves, if using, and stir-fry for about 1 minute, or until they change colour. Pour over the spinach mixture and serve hot garnished with ginger strips and accompanied with Rice or Roti.

Kurma Pulussu
Raw Jackfruit Curry

Origin Tamil Nadu
Preparation time 30 minutes
Cooking time 45 minutes
Serves 6

1 teaspoon fresh ginger
1 teaspoon garlic
1 teaspoon poppy seeds
1 teaspoon grated coconut
1 teaspoon chilli powder
1 tablespoon chopped coriander (cilantro) leaves
175ml / 6fl oz (¾ cup) vegetable oil
3 green cardamom pods
3 cloves
1 cinnamon stick, about 2.5cm / 1 inch long
1kg / 2¼lb raw jackfruit, peeled, de-seeded and cut into 4-cm / 1½-inch pieces wearing gloves (see page 793)
4 onions, thinly sliced
1 bay leaf
250ml / 8fl oz (1 cup) natural (plain) yoghurt, whisked
salt

Put the ginger, garlic, poppy seeds, coconut, chilli powder and chopped coriander in a spice grinder or mortar and process or pound with a pestle until ground. Set aside.

Heat the oil in a large, heavy-based pan over medium heat, add the cardamom pods, cloves and cinnamon and stir-fry for about 1 minute, or until they start to splutter. Add the jackfruit and stir-fry for 10–15 minutes, or until brown, then remove from the pan.

Add the onions to the oil in the pan and fry for about 3 minutes, then add the ground ingredients and bay leaf and season with salt. Stir-fry for a few minutes until fragrant. Add the jackfruit and fry briefly, then pour in 500ml / 18fl oz (2¼ cups) water. Reduce the heat, add the yoghurt and simmer for about 15 minutes, or until the jackfruit is cooked, adding a little water if it gets too dry.

Kathhal Dopyaza
Jackfruit with Onions

Origin Awadh
Preparation time 1 hour
Cooking time 10 minutes
Serves 4–5

1kg / 2¼lb jackfruit, peeled, de-seeded and cut into small pieces wearing gloves (see page 793)
1½ teaspoons ground turmeric
1 tablespoon vegetable oil, plus extra for deep frying
4 onions, sliced
16 baby (pearl) onions
1½ tablespoons ground coriander
1 teaspoon chilli powder
2 tablespoons ghee
5 dried red chillies
4 green chillies, slit in half lengthways and de-seeded (optional)
2 bay leaves
5 cloves
2 black cardamom pods
¼ teaspoon ground green cardamom
¼ teaspoon ground cinnamon
very small pinch of ground cloves
very small pinch of ground nutmeg
salt
1 tablespoon chopped coriander (cilantro) leaves, to garnish

Bring a large pan of water to the boil, add the jackfruit, ½ teaspoon of the ground turmeric and 1 teaspoon salt and boil for about 15 minutes, or until soft. Drain and pat the jackfruit dry with kitchen paper (paper towels).

Heat the oil in a large frying pan (skillet) over medium heat, add the sliced onions and fry for about 5–7 minutes, or until golden brown. Remove from the heat and set aside.

Heat enough oil for deep-frying in a deep, heavy-based pan to 180°C/350°F, or until a cube of bread browns in 30 seconds. Working in batches, carefully lower the jackfruit into the hot oil and deep-fry for 1–2 minutes, or until golden brown. Remove from the pan with a slotted spoon and drain on kitchen paper (paper towels).

Reduce the heat slightly, add the baby onions and stir-fry for about 2–3 minutes, or until golden brown. Remove from the pan with a slotted spoon and drain on kitchen paper (paper towels).

Put the ground coriander, the remaining turmeric and the chilli powder in a small bowl, add 3 tablespoons water and mix together.

Heat the ghee in a separate deep, heavy-based pan over medium heat, add the red and green chillies and stir-fry for about 1–2 minutes, or until the chillies change colour.

Add the bay leaves together with the whole spices and stir-fry for about 10 seconds. Add half the ground spice mixture and stir, then add the fried jackfruit, sliced onions and the baby onions, and season with salt.

Fry for a further 2 minutes, before adding the remaining ground spices. Stir and remove from the heat. Garnish with chopped coriander.

Dum Kathhal
Spicy Baked Jackfruit

Origin Hyderabad
Preparation time 30 minutes
Cooking time 30–45 minutes
Serves 4

750g / 1lb 10oz jackfruit
250ml / 8fl oz (1 cup) mustard oil
300g / 11oz (6 small) potatoes, cut in half
100g / 3½oz (scant ½ cup) ghee or vegetable oil
pinch of asafoetida
½ teaspoon cumin seeds
½ teaspoon fenugreek seeds
1 teaspoon ground ginger
1 teaspoon chilli powder
1 × 2.5-cm / 1-inch piece fresh ginger, peeled and chopped
1 teaspoon Garam Masala (see page 31)
1 tablespoon chopped coriander (cilantro) leaves
salt

Wearing gloves (see page 793), slice the jackfruit into 8cm / 3 inches long by 4cm / 1½ inches wide pieces and peel off the outer comb. Remove the seeds.

Heat the mustard oil in a large, heavy-based pan over medium heat, add the jackfruit and potatoes and fry for 15 minutes, or until they turn golden brown. Remove from the pan and set aside. You may need to do this in batches.

Heat the ghee or oil in another large, heavy-based pan over medium heat, add the asafoetida, cumin seeds and fenugreek seeds and stir-fry for about 1 minute, or until the seeds start to splutter.

Next, add the fried jackfruit and potatoes and all the remaining ingredients, except the chopped coriander. Pour in 500ml / 18fl oz (2¼ cups) water, reduce the heat slightly and simmer for 15 minutes, shaking the pan frequently. When the jackfruit and potatoes are soft to the touch, add the chopped coriander.

Kathhal ki Subzi
Braised Jackfruit with Yoghurt Sauce

Origin Awadh
Preparation time 30 minutes
Cooking time 45 minutes
Serves 4

500g / 1lb 2oz jackfruit
2 teaspoons ground coriander
½ teaspoon ground turmeric
1 teaspoon chilli powder
250g / 9oz (1 cup) vegetable oil or ghee
pinch of asafoetida
1½ teaspoons cumin seeds
250ml / 8fl oz (1 cup) natural (plain) yoghurt, whisked
1 teaspoon Garam Masala (see page 31)
1 teaspoon amchoor
salt

Wearing gloves (see page 793), peel the jackfruit and cut into 5-cm / 2-inch pieces, peel the seeds as well.

Put the ground coriander, turmeric and chilli powder in a small bowl, add 2 tablespoons water and stir together.

Heat the oil or ghee in a large, heavy-based pan over medium heat, add the jackfruit, not the seeds, and fry for about 10 minutes, or until golden brown. Remove from the pan and set aside.

Add the asafoetida to the pan and stir-fry for about 30 seconds, or until dissolved, then add the cumin seeds and stir-fry for about 1 minute, or until they start to splutter. Add the ground spice mixture, then season with salt and stir-fry for about 2–3 minutes.

Add the fried jackfruit, the seeds and 250ml /8fl oz (1 cup) water to the pan. Reduce the heat to low, cover and cook for about 30 minutes, or until the jackfruit is tender. Add the yoghurt, garam masala and amchoor and cook for a further 15 minutes.

Dhingri Dulma
Mushroom, (Bell) Pepper
& Paneer Curry

Origin Awadh
Preparation time 20 minutes
Cooking time 10–15 minutes
Serves 4

4 tablespoons vegetable oil or ghee
1 teaspoon black cumin seeds
4 spring onions (scallions), trimmed and chopped
4 teaspoons Ginger Paste (see page 57)
4 teaspoons Garlic Paste (see 57)
1 teaspoon chilli powder
500g / 1 lb 2oz (2 cups) chopped tomatoes
200g / 7oz (3 cups) button (white) mushrooms, sliced
1 green (bell) pepper, de-seeded and thinly sliced
1 red (bell) pepper, de-seeded and thinly sliced
1 yellow (bell) pepper, de-seeded and thinly sliced
450g / 1lb Paneer (see page 59), cut into 1-cm / ½-inch cubes
1 teaspoon ground black pepper, roasted
generous pinch of ground green cardamom
generous pinch of ground cloves
generous pinch of ground fenugreek
generous pinch of ground black rock salt
1 × 2.5-cm / 1-inch piece fresh ginger, peeled and cut into juliennes
salt
chopped coriander (cilantro) leaves, to garnish

Heat the oil or ghee in a large, heavy-based pan over medium heat, add the cumin seeds and stir-fry for about 30 seconds, or until they start to splutter. Add the chopped spring onions and fry for about 1–2 minutes, or until light golden. Add the ginger and garlic pastes and stir-fry for about 10 seconds, then add the chilli powder. Stir, add the tomatoes and stir-fry for 2–3 minutes, or until all the moisture has evaporated.

Add the mushrooms to the pan and stir-fry for about 3–4 minutes, or until the mushroom liquor has evaporated. Now add the peppers and stir-fry for about 1 minute. Add the paneer and season lightly with salt. Stir-fry for 1 minute, then add the roasted black pepper and the remaining ground spices and ginger juliennes. Stir well, then remove from the heat and adjust the seasoning, if necessary. Garnish with chopped coriander.

Khumb Hara Pyaz
Mushrooms with Spring Onions
(Scallions)

Origin Punjab
Preparation time 20 minutes
Cooking time 20 minutes
Serves 4

600g / 1lb 5oz button (white) mushrooms, stalks removed
150g / 5oz (⅔ cup) ghee
5 green cardamom pods
1 black cardamom pod
5 cloves
1 cinnamon stick, about 2.5cm / 1 inch long
1 bay leaf
150g / 5oz Boiled Onion Paste (see page 57)
25g / 1oz Ginger Paste (see page 57)
25g / 1oz Garlic Paste (see page 57)
1 × 2.5-cm / 1-inch piece fresh ginger, peeled and finely chopped
4 green chillies, de-seeded and chopped
1 teaspoon chilli powder
pinch of ground mace
½ teaspoon ground coriander
200ml / 7fl oz (1 cup) natural (plain) yoghurt, whisked
300g / 11oz spring onions (scallions), trimmed
salt

Cut the mushrooms in half and set aside.

Heat the ghee in a large, heavy-based pan over medium heat, add the whole spices and stir-fry for 1–2 minutes, or until they start to change colour. Add the boiled onion paste and stir-fry for 2 minutes, then add the ginger and garlic pastes and stir-fry for 30 seconds. Add the ginger and green chillies and stir-fry for a further 30 seconds, then add the chilli powder, ground mace and coriander and stir-fry for 30 seconds.

Remove the pan from the heat and stir in the yoghurt. Season with salt, then return to the heat, pour in 125ml / 4½fl oz (½ cup) water and bring to the boil. Reduce the heat and simmer for about 2–3 minutes, or until the oil has separated out. Add the mushrooms and simmer for a further 2 minutes, before adding the spring onions and simmering for 1 minute. Remove the pan from the heat and adjust the seasoning, if necessary.

Bharwan Guchhi
Stuffed Morels

Origin Punjab
Preparation time 30 minutes
Cooking time 20–25 minutes
Serves 4–6

8–10 dried morels
125ml / 4½fl oz (½ cup) vegetable oil or ghee
2 cloves
2 green cardamom pods
salt

For the filling
1–2 teaspoons vegetable oil
50g / 1¾oz (1cup) chopped spring onions (scallions)
2 tablespoons Khoya (see page 58)
3 tablespoons chopped mint leaves
4 tablespoons chopped coriander (cilantro) leaves
2 tablespoons lemon juice

For the sauce
pinch of saffron threads
3 tablespoons milk
25g / 1oz (½ cup) finely chopped spring onions
    (scallions)
2 teaspoons Ginger Paste (see page 57)
2 teaspoons Garlic Paste (see page 57)
2 teaspoons green chilli paste
2 tablespoons Cashew Nut Paste (see page 58)
250ml / 8fl oz (1 cup) hung natural (plain) yoghurt
    (see page 793), whisked
1 teaspoon Garam Masala (see page 31)

Soak the morels in a bowl of warm water for
10 minutes. Drain, then cook in a pan of boiling
water for about 15 minutes. Drain and set aside.

For the sauce, put the saffron in a small bowl, add
the milk and soak until required.

To make the filling, heat a little oil in a small frying
pan (skillet), add the chopped spring onions and fry
for about 3–4 minutes, or until golden brown. Put all
the ingredients for the filling, including the spring
onions in a bowl and mix together. Stuff the morels
with the mixture.

Heat the oil or ghee in a large, heavy-based pan,
add the cloves and cardamom pods and stir-fry for
1–2 minutes, or until they change colour. Remove
and discard.

To make the sauce, reheat the oil or ghee in the
same pan over medium heat, add the finely chopped
spring onions and lightly fry for about 1–2 minutes,
or until translucent. Add the ginger and garlic pastes
and stir-fry for 2 minutes, or until the water has
evaporated and they change colour. Add the green
chilli and cashew nut pastes and stir-fry for another
1–2 minutes, or until well blended and their colour
changes. Reduce the heat, add the yoghurt and
season with salt. Stir and simmer for a few minutes
until it is a sauce-like consistency.

Add the garam masala and saffron milk to the pan
and stir to mix well. Add the stuffed morels and
125ml / 4½fl oz (½ cup) water and simmer for about
10 minutes, coating the morels with the sauce.

Khumb Dopyaza
Mushrooms Cooked with Onions

Origin Awadh
Preparation time 15 minutes
Cooking time 10 minutes
Serves 6

1 tablespoon butter
2–3 dried red chillies, wiped with a damp cloth
400g / 14oz (2½ cups) sliced onions
400g large button (white) mushrooms, stalks trimmed
2 green chillies, slit in half lengthways and de-seeded
1 × 5-cm / 2-inch piece fresh ginger, peeled
    and cut into strips
salt

Melt the butter in a large, heavy-based pan over
medium heat, add the dried red chillies and fry for
about 2–3 minutes, or until glazed. Remove from the
pan and set aside.

Reheat the butter over medium heat, add the onions
and stir-fry for about 2 minutes, or until the onions
are translucent. Add the mushrooms and season with
salt, then stir-fry over high heat for about 3 minutes,
or until all the moisture has evaporated. Add the
green chillies, glazed dried red chillies and ginger
strips and stir-fry for about 2 minutes.

Bharwan Khumb
Stuffed Mushrooms

Origin Awadh
Preparation time 30–40 minutes
Cooking time 30 minutes
Serves 6–8

200g / 7oz mushrooms

4–5 green cardamom pods

juice of ½ lemon

salt

For the filling

1 tablespoon vegetable oil

2 onions, chopped

50g / 1¾oz Khoya (see page 58) or 5½ tablespoons
    milk powder (dry milk)

1 × 1-cm / ½-inch piece fresh ginger, peeled
    and grated

1 tablespoon cashew nuts, crushed

3 tablespoons pomegranate seeds

4 tablespoons chopped coriander (cilantro) leaves

½ teaspoon ground black pepper

½ teaspoon ground cumin, roasted

½ teaspoon Garam Masala (see page 31)

For the paste

90g / 3¼oz (⅓) red pomegranate

2 onions, sliced

1 × 1-cm / ½-inch piece fresh ginger, peeled
    and grated

4 dried red chillies

For the sauce

4 tablespoons vegetable oil

½ teaspoon Garam Masala (see page 31)

½ teaspoon chilli powder

½ teaspoon ground turmeric

1 teaspoon ground coriander

Preheat the oven to 200°C/400°F/Gas Mark 6.

Remove and reserve the stalks from the mushrooms.
Put the cardamom pods in a mortar and pound with
a pestle, then set aside.

Pour about 1 litre / 1¾ pints (4¼ cups) water into
a large, heavy-based pan. Add 2 teaspoons salt
and the lemon juice and bring to the boil. Add the
mushrooms and cook for about 2 minutes. Drain and
refresh under cold running water. Drain again, then
wipe and dry well on kitchen paper (paper towels).

To make the filling, heat the oil in a kadhai, wok or
heavy-based frying pan (skillet) over medium heat,
add the onions and fry for about 4–5 minutes, or
until soft. Add the khoya and mix well, then add the
grated ginger, crushed cashew nuts, pomegranate
seeds, chopped coriander, the ground spices and
the ½ teaspoon garam masala. Season with salt
and mix well. Remove from the heat and stuff each
mushroom with the mixture.

Place the mushrooms on several large baking sheets
and put into the hot oven for about 5 minutes, then
remove from the oven and set aside.

To make the paste, put the pomegranates into
a blender, pour in 375ml / 13fl oz (1½ cups) water
and process briefly. Trim the leftover mushroom
stalks and transfer to a blender or food processor.
Add the onions, ginger and dried red chillies
and process, adding a little water, if necessary,
to make a smooth paste.

For the sauce, heat the 4 tablespoons oil in a heavy-
based wok or frying pan (skillet) over low heat,
add the reserved cardamom pods and stir-fry for
about 1 minute, then add the onion-mushroom paste
and cook for about 10 minutes, or until the paste
turns light brown. Add the remaining ground spices
and season with salt. Add the pomegranate juice,
then bring to the boil, reduce the heat and simmer
for about 5 minutes. Add the stuffed mushrooms to
the sauce and simmer gently until hot.

Kan Guchhi
Spiced Morels

Origin Jammu and Kashmir
Preparation time 20 minutes, plus soaking time
Cooking time 20 minutes
Serves 8

100g / 3½oz dried morels
2 teaspoons Kashmiri red chilli powder
6 tablespoons vegetable oil
4 cinnamon sticks, about 5cm / 2 inches long
8 cloves
8 green cardamom pods
9 black cardamom pods
1 teaspoon Garlic Paste (see page 57)
1 teaspoon ground turmeric
1 teaspoon ground ginger
100ml / 3½fl oz (½ cup) hung natural (plain) yoghurt (see page 793), whisked
1 tablespoon Fried Onion Paste (see page 57)
¼ teaspoon saffron threads
1 teaspoon black cumin seeds
¼ teaspoon dried mint
salt

Soak the dried morels in a bowl of warm water for 20 minutes. Drain and rinse well in cold water to remove any grit. Cut in half.

Put the chilli powder in a small bowl, add 1 tablespoon water and stir well. Set aside.

Heat the oil in a large frying pan (skillet) over medium heat, add the morels, cinnamon sticks, cloves and cardamom pods, then mix well and fry for a few minutes until all the water has evaporated. Add the garlic paste, turmeric, chilli mixture and ginger and season with salt. Fry for a further 2 minutes, or until all the water has completely evaporated.

Add the yoghurt to the pan and stir until completely absorbed. Pour in about 200ml / 7fl oz (¾ cup) water, then add the onion paste and saffron, mix well and reduce the heat to low. Simmer for 5 minutes, then sprinkle over the black cumin seeds and dried mint.

Batani Kadala Kari
Pea & Mushroom Curry

Origin Kerala
Preparation time 20 minutes
Cooking time 20–25 minutes
Serves 4

750g / 1lb 10oz (5 cups) peas, shelled if fresh
150ml / ¼ pint (⅔ cup) groundnut (peanut) oil
750g / 1lb 10oz mushrooms, stalks removed
2 teaspoons cumin seeds
1 teaspoon mustard seeds
1 teaspoon fenugreek seeds
2 tablespoons urad dal, rinsed and drained
125g / 4¼oz (1 medium) onion, sliced
4 teaspoons Ginger Paste (see page 57)
4 teaspoons Garlic Paste (see page 57)
1 teaspoon chilli powder
2 teaspoons ground coriander
1 teaspoon ground turmeric
250g / 9oz (1 large) tomato, chopped
60g / 2oz (¾ cup) grated fresh coconut
30g / 1¼oz (¼ cup) cashew nuts
20 curry leaves
salt
1 sprig coriander (cilantro) leaves, chopped, to garnish

Cook the peas in a small pan of lightly salted water for 5–7 minutes, or until soft. Drain and set aside.

Heat 3 tablespoons of oil in a large, heavy-based pan over medium heat, add the mushrooms and stir-fry for about 4–5 minutes.

Heat the remaining oil in a large, heavy-based frying pan (skillet) over medium heat, add the cumin, mustard and fenugreek seeds and urad dal and stir-fry for about 1 minute, or until the seeds start to splutter. Add the onions and stir-fry for about 5 minutes, or until light brown, then add the ginger and garlic pastes and stir-fry for about 1–2 minutes, or until the moisture has evaporated. Add the ground spices and season with salt. Stir, add the tomato and stir-fry for about 5 minutes, or until the oil separates out.

Reduce the heat to low, add the coconut, cashew nuts and curry leaves, stir for 1 minute, then pour in about 500ml / 18fl oz (2¼ cups) water and bring to the boil. Add the boiled peas and stir-fried mushrooms, reduce the heat and simmer for about 5 minutes. Remove from the heat and adjust the seasoning, if necessary, and garnish with coriander.

Khumb Shabnam
Mushrooms in Yoghurt Sauce

Origin Awadh
Preparation time 10 minutes, plus cooling time
Cooking time 10 minutes
Serves 4

200ml / 7fl oz (1 cup) natural (plain) yoghurt
1 teaspoon Kashmiri red chilli powder
1 teaspoon ground cumin
1 teaspoon Kashmiri Garam Masala (see page 56)
pinch of ground turmeric
1 tablespoon vegetable oil
200g / 7oz (3 cups) button (white) mushrooms, sliced
salt
2 green chillies, slit in half lengthways and de-seeded, to garnish

Put the yoghurt in a bowl, add the ground spices, season with salt and whisk to combine, then set aside.

Heat the oil in a non-stick frying pan (skillet) over high heat, add the mushrooms and stir-fry for about 5 minutes, or until there is a small amount of moisture left. Take care that the mushrooms do not scorch or dry up. Remove from the heat and allow the mushrooms to cool.

When the mushrooms are cool, pour in the spiced beaten yoghurt and mix. Return to the heat and simmer for a few minutes until hot. Garnish with slit green chillies.

Kaju Khumb Makhane
Mushrooms with Cashew Nuts

Origin Rajasthan
Preparation time 20 minutes
Cooking time 30 minutes
Serves 4

1½ teaspoons chilli powder
1 teaspoon ground turmeric
1 teaspoon ground coriander
125g / 4¼oz (½ cup) ghee
150g / 5oz (1 medium) onion, grated
1 teaspoon kalonji (nigella) seeds
1 teaspoon cumin seeds
2½ tablespoons Ginger Paste (see page 57)
1½ tablespoons Garlic Paste (see page 57)
250g / 9oz (1 large) tomato, chopped
175ml / 6fl oz (¾ cup) natural (plain) yoghurt, whisked
500g / 1lb 2oz (7 cups) mushrooms, chopped
75g / 2½oz (½ cup) cashew nuts, roasted
75g / 2½oz lotus puffs
salt
1 large sprig coriander (cilantro), chopped, to garnish

Put the ground spices in a small bowl, add 4 tablespoons water and mix together.

Heat the ghee in a large, heavy-based pan over medium heat, add the onions and fry for about 5–7 minutes, or until golden brown. Add the kalonji and cumin seeds and stir-fry for about 1 minute, or until they start to splutter. Add the ginger and garlic pastes and stir-fry for about 1–2 minutes, then add the ground spice mixture and stir-fry for 2 minutes. Add the tomatoes and fry for about 5 minutes, or until the oil separates out.

Remove the pan from the heat and slowly stir in the yoghurt. Season with salt, then return to the heat and pour in about 250ml / 8fl oz (1 cup) water. Bring almost to the boil, then reduce the heat and simmer for a few minutes until the sauce thickens. Add the mushrooms and simmer for a further 5 minutes. Add the cashew nuts and lotus puffs and stir to mix well. Remove from the heat, adjust the seasoning, if necessary, and garnish with chopped coriander.

Fried Green
Peas   p.304

Dry Khichari
p.638

Lamb Stew (I)
p.431

Tomato Curry with
Coconut & Spinach p.316

Tangy Curried Tomatoes   p.317

Stuffed Green
Chillies   p.320

Kumhare ki Subzi
Dry Spicy Pumpkin

Origin Awadh
Preparation time 15–30 minutes
Cooking time 30 minutes
Serves 4

---

3 tablespoons vegetable oil or ghee

1 teaspoon fenugreek seeds

1 teaspoon cumin seeds

1½ teaspoons chilli powder

1 teaspoon ground turmeric

2 teaspoons ground coriander

2 teaspoons amchoor

2–3 green chillies, de-seeded and chopped

500g / 1lb 2oz (4 cups) pumpkin, peeled, de-seeded
and cut into cubes

2 teaspoons sugar

salt

To garnish

whole green chillies

few coriander (cilantro) leaves

Heat the oil or ghee in a large, heavy-based pan over
low heat, add the fenugreek and cumin seeds and
stir-fry for about 3–4 minutes, or until they start to
splutter. Add the remaining spices and stir-fry for
about 7 minutes.

Add the green chillies and the remaining
ingredients and mix well. Cover and cook for
about 15–20 minutes, or until the pumpkin
is tender. Remove from the heat and mash well
with a wooden spatula or potato masher. Garnish
with green chillies and coriander leaves.

Sitaphal ki Subzi
Pumpkin Curry

Origin Awadh
Preparation time 20 minutes
Cooking time 10–15 minutes
Serves 4

500g / 1lb 2oz (4 cups) pumpkin, peeled and cut into
5-cm / 2-inch pieces

pinch of ground turmeric

4 teaspoons vegetable oil

1 teaspoon mustard seeds

1 teaspoon urad dal, rinsed and drained

2 dried red chillies

100g / 3½oz (½ cup) jaggery, crumbled, or soft
brown sugar

4 tablespoons grated fresh coconut

4 tablespoons rice flour

salt

Put the pumpkin in a large pan of boiling salted
water, add the turmeric and cook, stirring
frequently, for about 10–15 minutes, or until soft
but not overcooked and mushy.

Heat the oil in a large frying pan over medium
heat, add the mustard seeds, urad dal and dried
red chillies and stir-fry for about 1 minute, or until
the mustard seeds start to splutter. Add the boiled
pumpkin and jaggery or sugar. When the jaggery
begins to dissolve, add the grated coconut and
rice flour. Cook for about 5 minutes, turning the
vegetables over a few times, until the pumpkin
is tender. Remove from the heat and serve.

Khatta Meetha Kaddu
Sweet & Sour Pumpkin

Origin Uttarakhand
Preparation time 35 minutes
Cooking time 10 minutes
Serves 4–6

1kg / 2¼lb pumpkin, peeled and cut into chunks

2 tablespoons mustard oil

pinch of asafoetida

1 teaspoon kalonji (nigella) seeds

1 teaspoon cumin seeds

½ teaspoon mustard seeds

1 teaspoon fennel seeds

½ teaspoon fenugreek seeds

1 tablespoon lemon juice

4 tablespoons jaggery, grated, or soft brown sugar

½ tablespoon ghee or mustard oil

4–6 dried red chillies

To garnish

whole green chillies

few coriander (cilantro) leaves

Cook the pumpkin in a large pan of boiling water for 20–25 minutes, or until soft. Drain, return to the pan and mash with a potato masher.

Heat the oil in a large, heavy-based pan over medium heat, add the asafoetida and stir-fry for 30 seconds, then add the remaining spices and stir-fry for about 1 minute. Stir in the mashed pumpkin, pour in the lemon juice, add the jaggery or sugar and season with salt. Cook for a further 2–3 minutes.

Heat the ghee in a small frying pan (skillet) over medium heat, add the dried red chillies and stir-fry for about 1 minute, or until they turn a shade darker. Pour over the mashed pumpkin mixture and garnish with coriander leaves and green chillies.

Kumbalanga Olan
Ash Gourd Curry with Coconut Milk

Origin Tamil Nadu
Preparation time 15 minutes–1½ hours, plus soaking time
Cooking time 35 minutes
Serves 6

100g / 3½oz (½ cup) red cowpeas
    (black eyed peas), rinsed

200g / 7oz (1¾ cups) ash gourd,
    peeled and cut into 2.5-cm / 1-inch pieces

6 green chillies, slit in half lengthways and de-seeded

15 curry leaves

250ml / 8fl oz (1 cup) coconut milk, fresh
    (see page 781) or canned

2 tablespoons vegetable oil

salt

Soak the cowpeas in a bowl of water overnight.

The next day, drain, rinse and put the cowpeas in the pressure cooker. Cook under pressure for 10 minutes. Alternatively, cook in a large pan of water for 1–1½ hours, or until soft.

Bring a large pan of water to the boil and add the ash gourd, chillies and 10 curry leaves. Season with salt and cook for about 30 minutes. Drain and allow to cool in a bowl, then mash with a wooden spatula or potato masher. Mix in the cowpeas and add the coconut milk. Transfer to a clean pan and simmer for 2 minutes.

Heat the oil in a small frying pan (skillet) over high heat. Reduce the heat, add the remaining curry leaves and stir-fry for about 30 seconds, or until they change colour. Pour over the ash gourd mixture.

Rasakalan
Yoghurt Curry with Ash Gourd
from Palakkad

Origin Kerala
Preparation time 15 minutes
Cooking time 15 minutes
Serves 4–6

500ml / 18fl oz (2¼ cups) natural (plain) yoghurt, whisked	
2 tablespoons jaggery, ground, or soft brown sugar	
115g / 4oz (1 cup) ash gourd, cut into 1-cm / ½-inch cubes	
½ teaspoon ground turmeric	
salt	

For the spice paste

2 teaspoons coconut oil
1 teaspoon fenugreek seeds
2–3 dried red chillies
2–3 green chillies, de-seeded (optional)
80g / 2¾oz (1 cup) grated fresh coconut
1 teaspoon basmati rice, rinsed and drained

For the tempering

2 teaspoons coconut oil
1 teaspoon mustard seeds
1 dried red chilli, halved
1 sprig curry leaves

Heat the oil for the spice paste in a kadhai or deep, heavy-based frying pan (skillet) over medium heat, add the fenugreek seeds and dried red chillies and stir-fry for about 1 minute, or until fragrant. Remove from the heat and mix in the coconut, rice and 2–3 tablespoons water. Transfer to a blender and process to make a smooth paste. Transfer to a large bowl, add the yoghurt and jaggery or sugar, then season with salt and whisk together. Set aside.

Bring 250ml / 8fl oz (1 cup) water to the boil in the pan used for frying the spices. Add the ash gourd and turmeric, then reduce the heat and simmer for 5–7 minutes. Remove from the heat, drain the ash gourd and set aside.

Heat the oil for the tempering in the same pan over medium heat. Add all the ingredients for the tempering and stir-fry for 1 minute, or until the seeds start to splutter. Stir in the yoghurt mixture and ash gourd, then reduce the heat to low and cook for 3 minutes, stirring constantly to prevent curdling.

Mai Kan
Fried Ash Gourd

Origin Tribal North East India
Preparation time 15 minutes
Cooking time 20 minutes
Serves 4

1 tablespoon vegetable oil	
2 large onions, chopped	
500g / 1lb 2oz ash gourd, peeled and de-seeded and cut into 5-cm / 2-inch cubes	
4 dried red chillies	
1 teaspoon ground turmeric	
salt	

Heat the oil in a kadhai or deep, heavy-based pan over medium heat, add the onions and fry for about 5 minutes, or until light brown. Add the remaining ingredients, season with salt and fry, stirring gently, for a further 10–12 minutes, or until the ash gourd is tender.

✳ ✳
___

Bharwan Karele
Slow-cooked Stuffed Bitter Gourds

Origin Awadh
Preparation time 30 minutes, plus standing time
Cooking time 30 minutes
Serves 4

250g / 9oz (2 small) bitter gourds

2 teaspoons Ginger Paste (see page 57)

2 teaspoons Garlic Paste (see page 57)

1 teaspoon ground turmeric

vegetable oil or ghee, for oiling and basting

salt

For the filling

1 × 5-cm / 2-inch piece fresh ginger, peeled

50g / 1¾oz (⅓ cup) peanuts

1 tablespoon sesame seeds

2 teaspoons cumin seeds

1 onion, chopped

100g / 3½oz Paneer (see page 59), cut into
   small cubes

2 green chillies, de-seeded (optional) and chopped

1 tablespoon chopped coriander (cilantro) leaves

1 tablespoon jaggery, crumbled, or soft brown sugar

2 tablespoons Tamarind Extract (see page 58)

1 tablespoon Garam Masala (see page 31)

For the tempering

3 tablespoons vegetable oil

½ teaspoon cumin seeds

½ teaspoon mustard seeds

½ teaspoon fenugreek seeds

Slit the bitter gourds lengthways and de-seed, then rub all over with salt. Place on a large tilting tray (roasting pan) and set aside for 1 hour.

For the filling, put the ginger in a mortar and pound with a pestle or process in a blender to make a paste. Set aside.

To blanch the bitter gourds, heat enough water to cover the gourds in a large pan, season with salt and add the ginger and garlic pastes and turmeric. Bring to the boil, then add the bitter gourds and blanch for 3–4 minutes, or until soft. Drain and set aside.

To make the filling, put the peanuts, sesame seeds, cumin seeds and onion in a blender or food processor, pour in 4 tablespoons water and process to make a paste. Transfer to a large bowl and add the paneer, ginger, green chillies, coriander, jaggery or sugar, tamarind extract and garam masala. Season with salt and mix well.

Preheat the oven to 140°C/275°F/Gas Mark 1 and oil a large roasting tray (pan).

To make the tempering, heat the oil in a frying pan (skillet) over medium heat, add the cumin, mustard and fenugreek seeds and stir-fry for about 1 minute, or until they start to splutter. Remove and pour over the filling, then mix well and divide the mixture into equal portions, one for each gourd.

Stuff the bitter gourds with the filling and arrange in the prepared roasting tray with the open side on top. Cover with foil, punch a couple of holes in the foil and cook in the hot oven for 30 minutes, basting with oil or ghee at regular intervals. Serve hot.

Pavakka Theeyal
Bitter Gourd Curry with Fried Coconut

Origin Tamil Nadu
Preparation time 30–40 minutes, plus standing time
Cooking time 30 minutes
Serves 2–4

100g / 3½oz (1) bitter gourd
1 tablespoon vegetable oil
8 shallots, chopped
3 green chillies, de-seeded
1 tablespoon Tamarind Extract (see page 58)
salt

For the spice paste

1 tablespoon vegetable oil
1 coconut, peeled and grated
4 shallots
10 dried red chillies
6 whole black peppercorns
10–15 curry leaves
1 teaspoon ground coriander
1 teaspoon ground turmeric

For the tempering

1 tablespoon vegetable oil
1 teaspoon mustard seeds
2 dried red chillies
3–4 shallots, coarsely chopped
1 sprig curry leaves

Slit the bitter gourd in half lengthways and de-seed, then cut into 2.5-cm / 1-inch pieces. Place on a tilting tray (roasting pan), sprinkle with salt and set aside for 30 minutes.

To make the spice paste, heat the oil in a frying pan (skillet) over medium heat, add all the ingredients except the ground spices and fry, stirring constantly, for about 2 minutes, or until the coconut turns brown. Remove from the heat, stir in the ground spices and transfer to a small blender or food processor. Add 250ml / 8fl oz (1 cup) water and process to make a smooth paste.

Heat 1 tablespoon oil in a large, heavy-based pan over medium heat, add the bitter gourd, shallots and green chillies, and fry for a few minutes, or until the bitter gourd is well browned. Add the tamarind extract and stir in the spice paste. Season with salt and pour in 250ml / 8fl oz (1 cup) water. Bring to the boil and cook for 10 minutes, then remove the pan from the heat.

To make the tempering, heat the oil in a small frying pan (skillet) over medium heat, add the mustard seeds and stir-fry for about 1 minute, or until they start to splutter. Add the dried red chillies and stir-fry for a few moments. Add the remaining ingredients and fry for about 3–4 minutes, or until the shallots are browned. Pour the tempering into the curry, stir well and serve.

Kurkure Karele
Fried Bitter Gourd

Origin Punjab
Preparation time 15 minutes
Cooking time 10 minutes
Serves 4

250g / 9oz (2) small bitter gourds
pinch of ground turmeric
1 teaspoon Tamarind Extract (see page 58)
1 teaspoon vegetable oil
1 teaspoon urad dal, rinsed and drained
½ teaspoon mustard seeds
2 dried red chillies
pinch of asafoetida
10–15 curry leaves
2 teaspoons jaggery, crumbled, or soft brown sugar
1 teaspoon rice flour
salt

Bring 375ml / 13fl oz (1½ cups) water to the boil in a large, heavy-based pan. Add the bitter gourds, turmeric and tamarind extract and cook for 5–7 minutes. Season with salt and cook for a further 5–7 minutes. Drain.

Heat the oil in a large frying pan (skillet) over medium heat, add the urad dal, mustard seeds, chillies and asafoetida and stir-fry for about 1 minute. Add the bitter gourds, curry leaves and the jaggery or sugar and cook for about 5 minutes. Stir in the rice flour and cook for a further 1 minute, then remove from the heat.

✳ ✳

Koorina Kakarkaya
Stuffed Bitter Gourds in Mustard Sauce

Origin Tamil Nadu
Preparation time 40 minutes, plus standing time
Cooking time 35–40 minutes
Serves 4–8

1kg / 2¼lb (8) bitter gourds

1 tablespoon Tamarind Extract (see page 58)

2 tablespoons sugar

¼ teaspoon chilli powder

¼ teaspoon ground turmeric

vegetable oil, for shallow frying

salt

For the filling

2 tablespoons vegetable oil

1 teaspoon cumin seeds

1 × 5-cm / 2-inch piece fresh ginger, peeled and
  finely chopped

8–10 cloves garlic, chopped

4 green chillies, de-seeded and chopped

125g / 4¼oz (1 small) onion, chopped

125g / 4¼oz (1 medium) potato, cut into dice

125g / 4¼oz (2 medium) carrots, cut into dice

2 tablespoons chopped coriander (cilantro) leaves

2 teaspoons lemon juice

pinch of salt

For the sauce

2 tablespoons vegetable oil

1 teaspoon fennel seeds

½ teaspoon mustard seeds

¼ teaspoon fenugreek seeds

10–15 curry leaves

150g / 5oz (1 medium) onion, chopped

1 tablespoon Ginger Paste (see page 57)

1 tablespoon Garlic Paste (see page 57)

1 teaspoon ground coriander

1 teaspoon red chilli powder

½ teaspoon ground turmeric

400g / 14oz (2–3 medium) tomatoes, puréed

2 tablespoons sugar

Slit the bitter gourds in half lengthways, de-seed
and rub with salt. Place on a tilting tray (roasting
pan) and set aside for 30 minutes.

Bring 500ml / 18fl oz (2¼ cups) water to the boil in
a large, heavy-based pan, add the tamarind extract,
sugar, chilli powder and turmeric. Season with salt,
then reduce the heat to medium, add the bitter gourds
and cook for about 5 minutes, or until the liquid has
almost evaporated and the gourds are tender when
pierced with a knife. Drain and set aside.

To make the filling, heat the oil in a large, heavy-
based frying pan (skillet) over medium heat, add the
cumin seeds and stir-fry for about 1 minute, or until
they start to splutter. Add the ginger, garlic and
green chillies and fry for about 1–2 minutes, or until
the garlic is lightly coloured. Add the onion and fry
for about 2 minutes, or until translucent. Add the
potato, and carrots and season with salt. Stir-fry
for 5 minutes, then remove from the heat and allow
to cool.

When cool, add the chopped coriander and lemon
juice and mix well. Divide the mixture into equal
portions and stuff a portion in each of the boiled
bitter gourds and secure with kitchen string (twine).

Heat enough oil for shallow-frying in a large, non-
stick frying pan over medium heat, add the stuffed
bitter gourds and shallow-fry for 3 minutes, or until
lightly coloured and crisp. Remove with a slotted
spoon and drain on kitchen paper (paper towels).

To make the sauce, heat the oil in a large, heavy-
based pan over medium heat, add the fennel,
mustard and fenugreek seeds and stir-fry for about
1 minute, or until they start to splutter. Add the curry
leaves and stir-fry for another minute, or until they
stop spluttering. Add the onion and fry for about
5 minutes, or until light golden, then add the ginger
and garlic pastes and stir-fry for a further 1 minute,
or until the moisture has evaporated.

Put the coriander, chilli powder and turmeric in
a small bowl, add 2 tablespoons water and mix
together. Add this mixture to the pan and stir-fry for
1 minute, or until the liquid has evaporated. Add
the puréed tomatoes and season with salt, then stir-
fry for about 5 minutes, or until specks of oil start
to appear on the surface.

Pour 500ml / 18fl oz (2¼ cups) water into the pan,
then bring to the boil. Reduce the heat to medium-
high and simmer for 8–10 minutes, or until reduced
by half. Add the fried bitter gourds and sugar, and
bring to the boil. Reduce the heat to low and simmer
for 2–3 minutes, then remove from the heat and
adjust the seasoning, if necessary.

Chooran ke Karele
Tangy Deep-fried Bitter Gourds

Origin Hyderabad
Preparation time 30 minutes, plus standing and cooling time
Cooking time 20 minutes
Serves 4–6

500g / 1lb 2oz (4) bitter gourds

vegetable oil, for deep-frying

1 teaspoon kalonji (nigella) seeds

3 tablespoons fennel seeds

3 tablespoons coriander seeds

3 tablespoons amchoor

1 teaspoon chilli powder

¼ teaspoon ground turmeric

salt

Place the bitter gourds on a large tilting tray (roasting pan) and sprinkle with salt. Set aside for 30 minutes.

Bring a pan of water to the boil and place a steamer basket or colander over the water. Steam the bitter gourds for about 10 minutes. Allow to cool and cut into small pieces. Remove and discard the seeds.

Heat enough oil for deep-frying in a deep, heavy-based pan to 180°C/350°F, or until a cube of bread browns in 30 seconds. Working in batches, carefully slide the bitter gourds into the hot oil and deep-fry for 1–2 minutes, or until crisp. Remove with a slotted spoon and drain on kitchen paper (paper towels).

Transfer about 3 tablespoons of the deep-frying oil to a fresh pan and heat over a medium heat. Add the kalonji, fennel and coriander seeds and stir-fry for about 1 minute, or until they start to splutter. Add the ground spices and season with salt, then stir-fry for about 1 minute, or until all the moisture has evaporated. Add the bitter gourd and stir well. Serve hot.

Bhuni Mungphali
Dry-fried Bitter Gourds

Origin Hyderabad/Andhra Pradesh
Preparation time 20 minutes, plus soaking time
Cooking time 15 minutes
Serves 6

500g / 1lb 2oz (4) bitter gourds, peeled and chopped into small pieces

¼ teaspoon ground turmeric

1 tablespoon Tamarind Extract (see page 58)

1 tablespoon gram (chickpea) flour

2 teaspoons chilli powder

1 teaspoon Garlic Paste (see page 57)

1 × 2.5-cm / 1-inch piece dried coconut, grated or 4 tablespoons desiccated (dried flaked) coconut

3 tablespoons vegetable oil

5 onions, chopped

2 teaspoons jaggery, crumbled, or soft brown sugar

salt

Put the bitter gourds in a large bowl, season with salt and add the turmeric and tamarind extract. Mix together and soak for 5 minutes. Squeeze the bitter gourds well and drain out any excess liquid, then soak in a large bowl of fresh water for 10 minutes. Squeeze out the water again and place the bitter gourds on a plate.

Put the gram flour, chilli powder, garlic paste and coconut in a bowl. Season with salt and mix together.

Heat the oil in a large, heavy-based frying pan (skillet) over medium heat and lightly fry the bitter gourds for about 2 minutes. Remove from the pan with a slotted spoon and set aside.

Add the onions to the pan and fry for about 5 minutes, or until light brown. Add the fried bitter gourds and fry for 2 minutes. Add the coconut and garlic spice mixture and stir-fry for a further 2 minutes, then add the jaggery or sugar and cook for 3–4 minutes.

Veerakkaikura
Ribbed Gourd with Chana Dal

Origin Tamil Nadu
Preparation time 40 minutes, plus cooling time
Cooking time 10–15 minutes
Serves 4

2 tablespoons chana dal, rinsed and drained

2 ribbed gourds, peeled and cut into
    4-cm / 1½-inch pieces

2 tomatoes, chopped

6 green chillies, de-seeded and chopped

1 tablespoon vegetable oil

1 teaspoon chopped garlic

¼ teaspoon chilli powder

½ teaspoon ground coriander, roasted

¼ teaspoon ground turmeric

¼ teaspoon ground cumin

salt

1 bunch coriander (cilantro) leaves, to garnish

For the seasoning

1 tablespoon vegetable oil

2 dried red chillies

½ teaspoon mustard seeds

4–6 curry leaves

Bring 375ml / 13fl oz (1½ cups) water to the boil in a large, heavy-based pan, add the dal and cook for about 10 minutes. Add the gourd, tomatoes and chillies and cook for about 20 minutes, or until the gourd is soft and tender but not mushy.

Heat the oil in another pan over medium heat, add the garlic, ground spices and season with salt, then stir-fry for about 1 minute. Add the vegetables and simmer for 5 minutes. Remove from the heat and allow to cool.

Heat the oil for the seasoning in a small frying pan (skillet) over medium heat. Add all the ingredients and fry for about 2 minutes, or until brown. Pour over the vegetables and cover immediately. Garnish with coriander leaves and serve.

Pappu Dosakai
Bottle Gourd (Calabash) with Chana Dal

Origin Hyderabad/Andhra Pradesh
Preparation time 30 minutes
Cooking time 25–30 minutes
Serves 6

100g / 3½oz (½ cup) chana dal, rinsed and drained

4 green chillies, slit in half lengthways and de-seeded

500g / 1lb 2oz bottle gourd (calabash), peeled
    and cut into 2.5-cm / 1-inch pieces

2 onions, sliced

2 tomatoes, chopped

1 teaspoon chilli powder

½ teaspoon ground coriander, roasted

pinch of ground turmeric

½ teaspoon Garlic Paste (see page 57)

¼ dried coconut, ground

salt

coriander (cilantro) leaves, to garnish

Bring 500ml / 18fl oz (2¼ cups) water to the boil in a large, heavy-based pan. Add the dal and cook for about 20 minutes, or until almost cooked but not completely soft. Drain, reserving about 250ml / 8fl oz (1 cup) of the cooking water.

Add the green chillies, bottle gourd, onions and tomatoes to the pan and simmer over low heat for about 15 minutes, or until the gourd is half cooked. Add the ground spices and garlic paste, then season with salt and cook for a further 5 minutes. Add the coconut, chana dal and continue to cook for 2 minutes, adding a little water if necessary. Add the coriander leaves and remove from the heat.

Lauki Musallam
Whole Stuffed Bottle Gourd (Calabash)

Origin Awadh
Preparation time 40 minutes, plus standing time
Cooking time 30 minutes
Serves 4

1 x 500g / 1lb 2oz bottle gourd (calabash)
pinch of saffron threads
1 teaspoon kewra water
100ml / 3½fl oz (½ cup) vegetable oil
2 onions, chopped
8–10 cashew nuts
1 tablespoon chironji kernel paste
200g / 7oz Khoya (see page 58)
or 200g / 7oz (1⅓ cups) milk powder (dry milk)
2 tablespoons poppy seeds
6 cloves
6 green cardamom pods
1 blade mace
250ml / 8fl oz (1 cup) natural (plain) yoghurt, whisked
1 teaspoon chilli powder
salt
chopped coriander (cilantro) leaves, to garnish

Peel and remove the pith from the bottle gourd and prick the outside uniformly with a fork. Hollow out the inside of the gourd, then rub some salt all over the outside. Place on a tray and set aside for about 30 minutes.

Put the saffron in a small bowl, add the kewra water and soak until required.

Heat the oil in a large, heavy-based pan over medium heat, add the onions and fry for about 5–7 minutes, or until golden brown. Using a slotted spoon, transfer the onions to a small blender or food processor and process to make a paste. Set aside.

Add the cashew nuts and chironji kernel paste to the pan and fry for about 1 minute, or until they turn pink. Remove from the pan and chop the nuts with a sharp knife, then set aside.

Return the pan to the heat and add the khoya. Fry for a few minutes until it changes colour, then mix in the fried nuts and remove from the heat. Reserve the oil left in the pan.

Put the poppy seeds in a small, dry frying pan (skillet) over medium heat and stir-fry for about 30 seconds until roasted.

Transfer to a mortar or small blender, add the cloves, cardamom pods and mace and pound or process, adding a little water if necessary, to make a paste.

Pat dry the bottle gourd with kitchen paper (paper towels) and fry in the reserved oil for a few minutes until evenly browned. Remove from the pan.

Mix the khoya and nut mixture with a little salt and 2 tablespoons yoghurt, then use to fill the inside of the gourd. Mix the onion paste, chilli powder-poppy seed paste and the saffron mixture together in a bowl and season with salt.

Place the bottle gourd in a large flat pan and pour the yoghurt mixture on and around it. Use a spatula to push some of the mixture underneath it. Pour the remainder of the yoghurt on top and cover with a tight-fitting lid. Place over low-medium heat and cook for about 30 minutes. Garnish with chopped coriander.

☀ / 📷 p.397

Dum ki Lauki
Spicy Baked Bottle Gourd (Calabash)

Origin Jammu and Kashmir
Preparation time 20 minutes
Cooking time 30–35 minutes
Serves 4–6

100g / 3½oz (scant ½ cup) ghee or vegetable oil
pinch of asafoetida
½ teaspoon cumin seeds
¼ teaspoon fenugreek seeds
1kg / 2¼lb bottle gourd (calabash), peeled and cut into 4-cm / 1½-inch pieces
½ teaspoon chilli powder, or to taste
2 green chillies, de-seeded and finely chopped
1 teaspoon ground succh bari or Kashmiri Garam Masala (see page 56)
1 teaspoon ground ginger
1 x 2.5-cm / 1-inch piece fresh ginger, peeled and ground
1 teaspoon ground coriander
1 bunch coriander (cilantro) leaves, finely chopped,
salt

Heat the ghee in a large, heavy-based pan over medium heat, add the asafoetida, and seeds and stir-fry for about 1 minute, or until they start to splutter. Add the bottle gourd and remaining ingredients, but no water, then cover, and cook for about 30 minutes, or until soft. Remove from the heat and add the finely chopped coriander.

Alubokhara Kofta
Kofta Stuffed with Dried Plums

Origin Punjab
Preparation time 50–55 minutes
Cooking time 20–25 minutes
Serves 8

500g / 1lb 2oz bottle gourd (calabash), peeled,
    de-seeded and grated

16 dried plums

16 almonds

100g / 3½oz (1 cup) gram (chickpea) flour

2 green chillies, de-seeded and chopped

2½ teaspoons Ginger Paste (see page 57)

½ teaspoon coarsely ground black pepper, roasted

5–6 tablespoons groundnut (peanut) oil

1 tablespoon ground coriander

1 teaspoon chilli powder

½ teaspoon ground turmeric

3½ tablespoons ghee

3 green cardamom pods

2 cloves

1 cinnamon stick

1 bay leaf

100g / 3½oz (1 small) onion, grated

1 teaspoon Ginger Paste (see page 57)

1 teaspoon Garlic Paste (see page 57)

675g / 1lb 7oz (6 large) tomatoes, puréed

½ teaspoon ground black cardamom

generous pinch of ground fenugreek

salt

chopped coriander (cilantro) leaves, to garnish

Put the bottle gourd in a large pan, add a little salt
and water and boil for 3 minutes, or until soft. Drain
and squeeze in a clean tea (dish) towel to remove
all the excess moisture. Remove the stones (pits) from
the dried plums and replace them with almonds.

Put the gram flour, chillies, ginger paste, roasted
black pepper and bottle gourd in a large bowl,
season with salt and mix well with your hands.
Divide the mixture into 16 equal portions and roll
into balls. With damp hands, flatten the balls
and place a stuffed dried plum in the middle, then
shape into balls again.

Heat the oil in a kadhai or deep, heavy-based pan
over high heat, then reduce the heat to medium.
Working in batches, carefully lower the balls into the
hot oil and fry for about 2 minutes turning constantly,
or until golden brown. Remove with a slotted spoon
and drain on kitchen paper (paper towels).

Put the ground coriander, chilli powder and
turmeric in a small bowl, add 3 tablespoons water
and stir together.

Heat the ghee in a large, heavy-based pan over
medium heat, add the cardamom pods, cloves,
cinnamon and bay leaf and stir-fry for about
1 minute, or until the cardamom pods start to change
colour. Add the onion and stir-fry for about
2 minutes, or until translucent. Add the ginger and
garlic pastes and stir-fry for about 1–2 minutes,
then add the ground spice mixture and season with
salt. Stir-fry for 1–2 minutes, or until the moisture
has evaporated.

Add the puréed tomatoes to the pan and stir-fry
for about 5 minutes, or until specks of oil begin to
appear on the surface. Pour in 250ml / 8fl oz (1 cup)
water and bring to the boil. Reduce the heat to
low and simmer, stirring frequently, for 2 minutes,
Add the fried kofta and simmer for a further
2 minutes. Sprinkle over the remaining ground spices,
stir and remove from the heat. Adjust the seasoning,
if necessary and garnish with chopped coriander.

☀ / 📷 pp.281, 394

Bharwan Parwal
Stuffed Wax Gourd

Origin Awadh
Preparation time 1 hour 15 minutes
Cooking time 15 minutes
Serves 5–6

16 small wax gourds

vegetable oil, for deep frying

For the filling

2 tablespoons vegetable oil or ghee

1 onion, chopped

¼ teaspoon ground turmeric

100g / 3½oz (½ cup) chana dal, rinsed and drained

½ teaspoon cumin seeds

4 green chillies, de-seeded and chopped

1 teaspoon chopped coriander (cilantro) leaves

2 teaspoons amchoor

1 teaspoon ground black pepper

For the sauce

250ml / 8fl oz (1 cup) natural (plain) yoghurt, whisked

3 teaspoons ground coriander

2 teaspoons chilli powder

½ teaspoon ground turmeric

2 tablespoons ghee

2 tablespoons Boiled Onion Paste (see page 57)

1 tablespoon Ginger Paste (see page 57)

2 teaspoons Garlic Paste (see page 57)

5 tomatoes, puréed

3 teaspoons Garam Masala (see page 31)

salt

Slit the wax gourds lengthways on 1 side and de-seed.

To make the filling, heat the oil or ghee in a large, heavy-based pan over medium heat, add the onion and fry for 5–7 minutes, or until golden brown. Add the turmeric and chana dal, then reduce the heat and cook for about 30 minutes, or until the dal is soft. You may need to add a little water. Transfer to a blender or food processor and process until ground, then transfer to a bowl and add the cumin seeds, chillies, chopped coriander, amchoor and black pepper. Mix well and divide the mixture into 16 equal portions. Stuff the wax gourds with the filling and set aside.

To make the sauce, put the yoghurt in a bowl, add the ground coriander, chilli powder and turmeric and stir to blend well.

Heat the ghee in a large, heavy-based pan over medium heat, add the boiled onion paste and fry for about 2–3 minutes, or until golden brown. Add the ginger and garlic pastes and fry for 1 minute. Reduce the heat and add the yoghurt mixture, stirring constantly until the oil separates out and rises to the surface, about 2–3 minutes. Add the puréed tomatoes, season with salt, then increase the heat to medium and cook for a few minutes until the mixture is a thick paste. Pour in 500ml / 18fl oz (2¼ cups) water and bring to the boil.

Add the stuffed wax gourds to the sauce, then reduce the heat and simmer for about 5 minutes. Add the garam masala and stir carefully until the sauce is thick. Remove from the heat.

Torai Jeerewali
Cumin-tempered Gourd

Origin Awadh
Preparation time 10 minutes
Cooking time 20 minutes
Serves 4

1 tablespoon ghee

1 teaspoon cumin seeds

500g / 1lb 2oz wax gourd, peeled and cut into rounds

2–3 green chillies, slit in half lengthways and de-seeded

salt

Heat the ghee in a large, heavy-based pan over medium heat, add the cumin seeds and stir-fry for about 1 minute, or until they start to splutter. Add the wax gourd and green chillies, then season with salt, reduce the heat to low, cover and cook for about 20 minutes, or until all the moisture has evaporated. Do not add any water.

Potoler Dolma
Wax Gourd Curry

Origin West Bengal
Preparation time 25–30 minutes
Cooking time 30 minutes
Serves 4

300g / 11oz wax gourds, peeled

150ml / ¼ pint (⅔ cup) mustard oil, for deep-frying

1 teaspoon cumin seeds

2 teaspoons chopped onions

2 teaspoons Ginger Paste (see page 57)

2 teaspoons Garlic Paste (see page 57)

1 teaspoon chilli powder

2 teaspoons chopped tomatoes

1 teaspoon Garam Masala (see page 31)

1 teaspoon chopped coriander (cilantro) leaves

For the filling

200g / 7oz Paneer (see page 59)

2 teaspoons coriander (cilantro) leaves

1 teaspoon chopped green chillies

2 teaspoons raisins

salt

Slit the wax gourds lengthways on 1 side and de-seed. To make the filling, put all the ingredients in a bowl and mix together. Set aside.

Heat the oil in a kadhai, wok or deep, heavy-based frying pan (skillet) to 180°C/350°F, or until a cube of bread browns in 30 seconds. Carefully add the wax gourds to the hot oil and deep-fry for about 2–3 minutes, or until half done. Remove with a slotted spoon and drain on kitchen paper (paper towels). Reserve the oil. Stuff the wax gourds with the filling.

Heat 6 tablespoons of the reserved oil in a large, heavy-based pan over medium heat, add the cumin seeds and stir-fry for 1 minute, or until they start to splutter. Add the onion and stir-fry for about 5–7 minutes, or until golden brown. Add the ginger and garlic pastes and stir-fry for a further 2–3 minutes. Add the chilli powder and tomatoes and stir-fry for another 1–2 minutes, or until the oil separates out and rises to the surface.

Pour 125ml / 4½fl oz (½ cup) water into the pan and bring to the boil. Add the stuffed wax gourds, then cover and simmer over low heat for 10–15 minutes, or until tender. Sprinkle over the garam masala and the chopped coriander and stir, then remove from the heat.

Dahiwali Lauki
Spicy Wax Gourd in Yoghurt Sauce

Origin Uttarakhand
Preparation time 15 minutes
Cooking time 20–25 minutes
Serves 4–6

---

1 tablespoon Kashmiri red chilli powder

4 tablespoons mustard oil

small pinch of asafoetida

1kg / 2¼lb wax gourd, peeled and cut
   into rounds

1 teaspoon ground ginger

250ml / 8fl oz (1 cup) hung natural (plain) yogurt (see
   page 793), whisked

1 teaspoon ground fennel

1 teaspoon Garam Masala (see page 31)

salt

Put the chilli powder in a small bowl, add 1 teaspoon water and mix together. Set aside.

Heat the oil in a kadhai or heavy-based pan over high heat. Reduce the heat, add the asafoetida and stir-fry for 30 seconds, or until it dissolves. Add the chilli powder mixture and stir briskly for 15 seconds. Add the wax gourd and fry very lightly for about 1½ minutes. Add the ground ginger and yoghurt and stir well. Add the ground fennel, garam masala and season with salt, then cover and cook, stirring occasionally, for about 15–20 minutes, or until the gourd is tender but still has a little bite. Serve hot. This dish can be served covered in its sauce or the spicy slices can be enjoyed separately.

❃

Bharwan Ghiy
Stuffed Marrow

Origin Awadh
Preparation time 40 minutes, plus cooling time
Cooking time 45–55 minutes
Serves 6–8

750g / 1lb 10oz marrow or bottle gourd (calabash)

chopped coriander (cilantro) leaves, to garnish

For the stuffing

250g / 9oz (2 medium) potatoes, unpeeled

2 tablespoons ghee

200g / 7oz (2 small) onions, chopped

1 × 5-cm / 2-inch piece fresh ginger, peeled and
    finely chopped

2–3 green chillies, de-seeded and chopped

2 tablespoons coriander (cilantro) leaves

salt

For the masala

4 tablespoons ghee

250g / 9oz (1 large) onion, grated

10 garlic cloves, ground

1 × 2.5-cm / 1-inch piece ginger, ground

1 teaspoon cumin seeds, roasted and ground

3 teaspoons coriander seeds, ground

½ teaspoon ground turmeric

1 teaspoon salt

500g / 1lb 2oz (3 medium) tomatoes, chopped

Preheat the oven to 180°C/350°F/Gas Mark 4, if using.

Cook the potatoes for the stuffing in a large pan of
boiling water for about 20 minutes, or until soft. Drain
and allow to cool, then peel off the skins, return the
flesh to the pan and mash. Set aside.

Cut off a thin slice along the length of the marrow
and, using a spoon, carefully scoop out the insides,
leaving a 1-cm / ½-inch rim all around. Chop the
marrow flesh and set aside.

To make the stuffing, heat 2 tablespoons ghee in
a large, heavy-based pan over medium heat, add the
onions and fry for about 2–3 minutes, or until lightly
coloured. Add the chopped marrow flesh and cook
for 3–5 minutes. Remove from the heat and mix in
the mashed potatoes, ginger, chillies and coriander
and season with salt. Stuff the marrow with the
mixture and set aside.

To make the masala, heat 4 tablespoons ghee in
a large, heavy-based pan over medium heat, add the
grated onions and fry for about 4–5 minutes, or until
golden. Stir in the garlic, ginger, cumin, coriander,
turmeric and salt and cook, stirring, for 5 minutes,
adding 1–2 teaspoons water occasionally to prevent
it burning and catching on the base (bottom) of the
pan. Add the tomatoes and cook for 5–7 minutes, or
until the mixture is paste-like. Pour in 125ml / 4½fl oz
(½ cup) water and cook for a further 5–7 minutes.

Put the stuffed marrow in the masala, cover and
cook over medium heat for 20–30 minutes. You can
also put the marrow into a greased baking dish, pour
the masala around it and bake in the hot oven for
30 minutes. Sprinkle with chopped coriander and serve.

Lauki ke Kofte
Bottle Gourd (Calabash) Kofta

Origin Awadh
Preparation time 30 minutes
Cooking time 40 minutes
Makes 6–8

1kg / 2¼lb marrow or bottle gourd (calabash),
    peeled and grated
2 tablespoons gram (chickpea) flour
1 × 2.5-cm / 1-inch piece fresh ginger, peeled
    and chopped
2 tablespoons chopped coriander (cilantro) leaves
2–3 green chillies, de-seeded and chopped
250g / 9oz (1 cup) ghee, for frying

For the sauce

1 × 2.5-cm / 1-inch piece fresh ginger, peeled
10 garlic cloves
1 tablespoon coriander seeds
½ tablespoon cumin seeds
4 tablespoons ghee
3 onions, grated
4 tomatoes, chopped
100ml / 3½fl oz (½ cup) natural (plain) yoghurt
salt

Grate the marrow and squeeze out all the moisture by
pressing it between your hands. Put into a large bowl,
add the gram flour, ginger, coriander and chillies and
mix together. Roll the mixture into walnut-sized balls.

Heat the ghee in a kadhai or deep, heavy-based
pan over medium heat. Working in batches, gently
lower the koftas into the hot ghee and fry for about
2–3 minutes, or until golden. Remove with a slotted
spoon and set aside.

To make the sauce, put the ginger, garlic, coriander
and cumin seeds in a small blender or food
processor and process until ground. Set aside.

Heat 4 tablespoons ghee in a large, heavy-based
pan over medium heat, add the grated onions and
fry for about 3 minutes, or until golden brown. Stir
in the ground paste and stir-fry for 5 minutes, adding
1–2 teaspoons water occasionally to prevent the
mixture burning and catching on the base (bottom)
of the pan.

Add the tomatoes and cook for a further 5–7
minutes, or until the ghee separates from the paste.
Season with salt and add the yoghurt.

Pour in 375ml / 13fl oz (1½ cups) water and simmer for
15 minutes.

Just before serving, add the koftas to the sauce and
simmer over low heat for about 5 minutes, or until
the koftas are hot.

☀ / 📷 pp.282, 594

Bharwan Tinde
Stuffed Round Gourd

Origin Punjab
Preparation time 20 minutes
Cooking time 20–30 minutes
Serves 4–6

500g / 1lb 2oz tinda (round gourd), peeled
1 teaspoon salt
½ teaspoon ground turmeric
½ teaspoon chilli powder
1 teaspoon ground fennel
1 teaspoon coriander seeds, ground
½ teaspoon amchoor
10–15 sultanas (golden raisins)
100g / 3½oz (scant ½ cup) ghee
pinch of asafoetida
½ teaspoon cumin seeds

Cut a slice off the stalk end of the tinda, then
carefully scoop out the insides with a spoon, keeping
the tinda whole. Chop the tinda flesh, discarding any
hard seeds, and put into a large bowl. Add the salt,
ground spices and sultanas (golden raisins) and mix
together. Stuff the tindas with this mixture.

Heat the ghee in a large, heavy-based pan over
medium heat, add the asafoetida and cumin seeds
and stir-fry for about 1 minute, then remove
from the heat and place the tindas in the pan in a
single layer. Pour in 500ml / 18fl oz (2¼ cups) water,
cover and cook over low heat for 20–30 minutes,
or until the tindas are tender.

Torai
Snake Gourd Curry

Origin Uttarakhand
Preparation time 15 minutes
Cooking time 20–25 minutes
Serves 6–8

100g / 3½oz (scant ½ cup) ghee or vegetable oil

½ teaspoon cumin seeds

¼ teaspoon fenugreek seeds

pinch of asafoetida

2 cloves

1kg / 2¼lb snake gourd, peeled and cut into
   1-cm / ½-inch thick rounds

½ teaspoon chilli powder

1 teaspoon ground coriander

1 teaspoon ground turmeric

½ teaspoon ground ginger

1 × 2.5-cm / 1-inch piece ginger, peeled and crushed

salt

chopped coriander (cilantro) leaves, to garnish

Heat the ghee or oil in a large, heavy-based pan over medium heat, add the cumin and fenugreek seeds, asafoetida and cloves and stir-fry for a few seconds. Add the snake gourd, cover and simmer for 15–20 minutes. You don't need to add any water as the snake gourd releases its own water during cooking. Stir the snake gourd once or twice, then season with salt and add the rest of the spices. Cook for about 5 minutes, or until the oil separates out and rises to the surface, and all the water has evaporated. Garnish with chopped coriander.

Zimikand-Matar
Elephant's Foot Yam with Green Peas

Origin Punjab
Preparation time 20 minutes
Cooking time 35 minutes
Serves 4–6

500g / 1lb 2oz Indian yam, peeled and cut into
   large pieces

180g / 7oz (¾ cup) ghee

pinch of asafoetida

½ teaspoon cumin seeds

½ teaspoon ground turmeric

½ teaspoon chilli powder

1 teaspoon coriander seeds, ground

1 teaspoon salt

2 tomatoes, chopped

1kg / 2¼lb (7 cups) peas, shelled if fresh

125ml / 4½fl oz (½ cup) natural (plain) yoghurt,
   whisked

1 teaspoon Garam Masala (see page 31)

½ teaspoon amchoor

Cook the yam in a large pan of boiling water for about 10 minutes, or until tender. Drain and cut into 4-cm / 1½-inch cubes.

Heat the ghee in a large, heavy-based pan over medium heat, add the yam and fry for about 5 minutes, or until golden. Remove with a slotted spoon and set aside.

Add the asafoetida and cumin seeds to the pan and stir-fry for 1–2 minutes. Stir in the turmeric, chilli powder, coriander, salt and tomatoes and cook for a further 2–3 minutes. Add the fried yam and peas, then pour in 250ml / 8fl oz (1 cup) water, reduce the heat to low, cover and cook, stirring occasionally, for 15–20 minutes, or until the vegetables are tender.

Add the yoghurt, garam masala and amchoor and cook for a further 10 minutes.

☼ / 📷 p.283

Chunke Matar
Fried Green Peas

Origin Awadh
Preparation time 20 minutes, plus soaking time
Coking time 20 minutes
Serves 5

1kg / 2¼lb fresh peas, shelled if fresh

2 tablespoons ghee

2 teaspoons cumin seeds

2 onions, sliced

pinch of asafoetida

5 green chillies, de-seeded and chopped

½ teaspoon ground coriander

1½ teaspoons black pepper

½ teaspoon ground black cardamom

1 teaspoon amchoor

2 pieces fresh ginger, peeled

2 tablespoons lemon juice

salt

Remove the stems from the peas and soak in a large bowl of water for a few minutes. Drain and set aside.

Heat the ghee in a large, heavy-based pan over medium heat, add the cumin seeds and stir-fry for about 1 minute, or until they start to splutter. Add the onions and asafoetida and fry for about 5–7 minutes, or until the onions are golden brown. Add the chillies, ground spices and ginger, season with salt, and fry for about 1 minute, then add the peas and cook for 7–8 minutes, stirring occasionally. Sprinkle over the lemon juice and serve.

☼ / 📷 p.284

Matar ki Phali
Peas in the Pod

Origin Awadh
Preparation time 15 minutes
Cooking time 15–20 minutes
Serves 4

2 tablespoons vegetable oil

pinch of asafoetida

½ teaspoon cumin seeds

500g / 1lb 2oz peas in the pod

3 teaspoons amchoor

¼ teaspoon Garam Masala (see page 31)

salt

Heat the oil in a large frying pan (skillet) over medium heat, add the asafoetida and cumin seeds and fry for about 1 minute, then add the peas, amchoor and garam masala and season with salt. Mix well, then reduce the heat, cover and cook, stirring occasionally, for about 15 minutes, or until the peas are tender. Adjust the seasoning, if necessary, and serve.

Matar ki Tarkari
Green Pea Curry

Origin Awadh
Preparation time 15 minutes
Cooking time 20–25 minutes
Serves 4

400g / 14oz (2¾ cups) peas, shelled if fresh
2 dried red chillies
1 teaspoon ground turmeric
1 teaspoon salt
1 tablespoon vegetable oil
1 teaspoon chopped ginger
5 chives
2 tomatoes
1 teaspoon ground coriander
½ teaspoon ground fenugreek
½ teaspoon ground cumin

Place the peas in a pressure cooker with 500ml /
18fl oz (2¼ cups) water and cook under pressure for
5 minutes. Open the cooker and mix in the dried red
chillies, turmeric and salt. Cover lightly and simmer
without pressure over low heat for 10–15 minutes.
Alternatively, cook the peas with the water, spices
and salt in a large, heavy-based pan for about 5–10
minutes, or until soft.

Heat the oil in another large, heavy-based pan over
medium heat, add the ginger, chives, tomatoes and
ground spices and stir-fry for about 2–3 minutes, or
until the tomatoes have disintegrated. Add the peas
with any liquid remaining in the cooker and simmer
for 2–3 minutes.

Khoya Matar
Peas with Thickened Milk

Origin Rajasthan
Preparation time 10–15 minutes
Cooking time 10–12 minutes
Serves 4

125g / 4¼oz (½ cup) ghee or vegetable oil
pinch of asafoetida
4 cloves
1 teaspoon cumin seeds
500g / 1lb 2oz Khoya (see page 58)
or 500g / 1lb 2oz (3½ cups) milk powder (dry milk)
250g / 9oz (1⅔ cups) peas, shelled if fresh
½ teaspoon chilli powder
2 green chillies, de-seeded and chopped
1 teaspoon ground ginger
1 teaspoon ground cumin
1 teaspoon ground coriander
1 teaspoon Garam Masala (see page 31)
1 × 2.5-cm / 1-inch piece fresh ginger, peeled
and finely chopped
salt

Heat the ghee or oil in a heavy-based pan over
medium heat, add the asafoetida, cloves and cumin
seeds and stir-fry for about 1 minute, or until the
cumin seeds start to splutter. Add the khoya and
stir-fry for about 2–3 minutes, or until it turns
reddish brown. Add the peas, remaining spices and
500ml / 18fl oz (2¼ cups) water, then season with
salt. Bring to the boil, reduce the heat and simmer
for 5–7 minutes, or until the peas are cooked.

Dum ki Bharwan Mirch
Stuffed (Bell) Peppers

Origin Hyderabad
Preparation time 50 minutes, plus cooling time
Cooking time 20–25 minutes
Serves 4

8 large (bell) peppers

For the filling

400g / 14oz (3 medium) potatoes, unpeeled

1 teaspoon cumin seeds

1 tablespoon sesame seeds

50g / 1¾oz (⅓ cup) roasted peanuts

1 teaspoon coarsely ground black pepper, roasted

2 tablespoons jaggery, crumbled, or soft brown sugar

10–12 mint leaves

vegetable oil, for frying and greasing

salt

For the sauce

1 teaspoon chilli powder

1 teaspoon ground turmeric

4 teaspoons Ginger Paste (see page 57)

2½ teaspoons Garlic Paste (see page 57)

4 tablespoons Tamarind Extract (see page 58)

1 teaspoon ground cumin

5 tablespoons groundnut (peanut) oil

pinch of salt

For the spice paste for the sauce

4 tablespoons peanuts, roasted

2 tablespoons desiccated (dried flaked) coconut

4½ tablespoons sesame seeds

250g / 9oz (2 small) onions

For the tempering

1 tablespoon groundnut (peanut) oil

½ teaspoon cumin seeds

½ teaspoon mustard seeds

pinch of fenugreek seeds

10 curry leaves

Preheat the oven to 180°C/350°F/Gas Mark 4 and grease a large roasting tray (pan).

Cook the potatoes for the filling in a large pan of boiling water for about 20 minutes, or until soft. Drain and allow to cool, then peel off the skins, return the flesh to the pan and mash. Set aside.

Cut the tops off the peppers and reserve. Remove the core and discard, keeping the peppers whole.

To make the filling, mix the cumin and sesame seeds with the peanuts and about 4 tablespoons water together in a bowl, then transfer to a small blender or food processor and process to make a paste. Transfer to a clean bowl, add the roasted black pepper, jaggery or sugar, mint and mashed potato and mix well. Fill the peppers with the mixture, then arrange the stuffed peppers on the prepared roasting tray and cook in the oven for about 10 minutes.

To make the spice paste for the sauce, put all the ingredients in a small blender or food processor and process to make a smooth paste, adding a little water if necessary. Set aside.

To make the sauce, put the chilli powder and turmeric in a small bowl, add 2 tablespoons water and stir together.

Heat the remaining oil in a large, heavy-based pan over medium heat, add the ginger and garlic pastes and stir-fry for a few seconds, then add the chilli powder mixture and stir-fry for about 2–3 minutes. Add the spice paste and stir-fry for about 1–2 minutes, or until the oil separates out, adding a little water towards the end, if necessary, to ensure that the spice paste does not stick to the pan or burn. Add the tamarind extract and season with salt, then cook for about 4–5 minutes, stirring constantly.

Now add 375ml / 13fl oz (1½ cups) water, bring to the boil, then reduce the heat to low and simmer for 10 minutes, or until the mixture is a sauce consistency. Sprinkle over the ground cumin, stir and remove from the heat.

Heat the oil for the tempering in a small frying pan (skillet) over medium heat, add the cumin, mustard and fenugreek seeds and stir-fry for about 1 minute, or until they start to splutter. Add the curry leaf and stir-fry for 1 minute, or until they are glazed, then pour the tempering over the sauce.

Kairas
(Bell) Pepper & Peanut Curry

Origin Coastal
Preparation time 40 minutes
Cooking time 30 minutes
Serves 4

150g / 5oz (1 cup) unsalted peanuts

5–6 (bell) peppers, cored, de-seeded and cut
    into squares

1 tablespoon jaggery, crumbled, or soft brown sugar

salt

For the spice paste

2 teaspoons vegetable oil

2 teaspoons asafoetida

2 teaspoons coriander seeds

2 teaspoons sesame seeds

4 dried red chillies

1 teaspoon chana dal, rinsed and drained

3 tablespoons grated fresh coconut

1 teaspoon Tamarind Extract (see page 58)

For the tempering

2 teaspoons vegetable oil

1 teaspoon mustard seeds

1 teaspoon cumin seeds

1 dried red chilli, halved

10–12 curry leaves

Cook the peanuts in a pan of boiling water for about
30 minutes. Drain and set aside.

To make the spice paste, heat the oil in a large, heavy-
based pan over medium heat, add the asafoetida,
coriander and sesame seeds, dried red chillies and
dal and stir-fry for about 1 minute, or until the spices
and chillies are fragrant and the dal changes colour.
Remove from the heat and mix in the coconut
and tamarind extract. Transfer to a blender or food
processor, add ½ cup water and process to make
a smooth paste.

Heat the oil for the tempering in a large frying pan
(skillet) over medium heat, add all the ingredients
for the tempering and stir-fry for about 1 minute,
or until the mustard seeds start to splutter. Add
the pepper squares, then sprinkle over a little water,
cover and simmer for about 10 minutes. Remove
from the heat and set aside.

Heat about 250ml / 8fl oz (1 cup) water in a large
pan and add the spice paste and jaggery or sugar,
then season with salt. Stir and bring to the boil, then
reduce the heat and simmer for about 10 minutes.
Add the peanuts and (bell) peppers and simmer for
a further 5 minutes until well blended.

Bhopali Mirchi Peeth
Green (Bell) Pepper Curry

Origin Coastal
Preparation time 10 minutes
Cooking time 15 minutes
Serves 6

225g / 8oz (1½ cups) gram (chickpea) flour

3 teaspoons chilli powder

1½ teaspoons ground turmeric

1 teaspoon sugar

2 tablespoons vegetable oil

3 teaspoons mustard seeds

½ teaspoon asafoetida

6 green (bell) peppers, cored, de-seeded and cut
    into pieces

salt

2 teaspoons coriander (cilantro) leaves, to garnish

Put the gram flour, the chilli powder, ½ teaspoon
turmeric and the sugar in a large bowl. Season with
salt and mix together.

Heat the oil in a deep, heavy-based pan over medium
heat, add the mustard seeds, asafoetida and the
remaining turmeric and stir-fry for about 1 minute.
Add the green peppers and cook over high heat for
a few minutes until they are half tender.

Reduce the heat to medium and add the gram flour
mixture. Mix well until the peppers are well coated
with the flour. Cook for a further 5 minutes until the
peppers are crisp and golden. Serve hot, garnished
with coriander leaves.

Paneer Pasanda
Stuffed Paneer in a Spicy Tomato Sauce

Origin Awadh
Preparation time 30 minutes
Cooking time 25–30 minutes
Serves 4

500g / 1lb 2oz Paneer (see page 59)

vegetable oil, for frying

1 small sprig mint, to garnish

For the stuffing

100g / 3½oz vegetables of choice

1 tablespoon chopped raisins

2 tablespoons broken cashew nuts

50g / 1¾oz (½ cup) Mixed Pickle (see page 787),
    chopped

For the batter

150g / 5oz (1⅔ cups) gram (chickpea) flour

50g / 1¾oz (⅓ cup) rice flour

1 teaspoon chilli powder

pinch of salt

For the sauce

100g / 3½oz (scant ½ cup) ghee

1 tablespoon Ginger Paste (see page 57)

1 tablespoon Garlic Paste (see page 57)

1 teaspoon chilli powder

4 green chillies, de-seeded and chopped

250g / 9oz (2 small) tomatoes, puréed

3 tablespoons Fried Onion Paste (see page 57)

2 tablespoons Cashew Nut Paste (see page 58)

1 teaspoon Garam Masala (see page 31)

salt

Cut the paneer into 1-cm / ½-inch pieces, about 4cm /
1½ inches thick.

To make the stuffing, cook the vegetables in a pan
of boiling water for about 10 minutes, or until soft.
Drain and finely chop, then transfer to a bowl, add
the raisins, cashew nuts and mixed pickle and mix
together. Divide into 8 equal portions and place
each portion between 2 slices of paneer. Set aside.

Put the flours, chilli powder and salt in a bowl and
mix in enough water to make a thick batter.

Heat enough oil for deep-frying in a kadhai or
deep, heavy-based pan to 180°C/350°F, or until
a cube of bread browns in 30 seconds, then reduce
the heat. Working in batches, if necessary, dip the
stuffed paneer 'sandwiches' into the batter, then
carefully lower them into the hot oil and deep-fry
for about 2 minutes, or until light brown. Remove
with a slotted spoon and drain on kitchen paper
(paper towels).

To make the sauce, heat the ghee in a heavy-based
pan over medium heat, add the ginger and garlic
pastes and stir-fry for 1 minute. Add the chilli powder
and green chillies and stir-fry for 30 seconds. Add
the puréed tomatoes and fry for about 2–3 minutes,
or until the oil separates out, then add the fried
onion paste, 250ml / 8fl oz (1 cup) water and season
with salt. Bring to the boil, then lower the heat and
simmer for about 10 minutes, or until the sauce has
reduced by two-thirds. Now add the cashew nut paste
and cook for about 2 minutes, or until the oil has
separated out. Adjust the seasoning, if necessary,
sprinkle over the garam masala and stir. Add the
cooked paneer 'sandwiches' and cook for a further
1 minute. Garnish with mint and serve.

Paneer Jaipuri
Rajasthani Curried Paneer

Origin Rajasthan
Preparation time 30 minutes
Cooking time 45 minutes
Serves 4

100g / 3½oz (1 small) onion, coarsely chopped
250ml / 8fl oz (1 cup) natural (plain) yoghurt, whisked
¼ teaspoon Fried Onion Paste (see page 57)
2 tablespoons Cashew Nut Paste (see page 58)
2 teaspoons ground coriander
1 teaspoon ground turmeric
1 teaspoon yellow chilli powder
1 teaspoon saffron threads
2 tablespoons lukewarm milk
1 teaspoon ghee or vegetable oil
3 green cardamom pods
2 cloves
1 cinnamon stick, about 2.5cm / 1 inch long
750ml / 1¼ pints (3¼ cups) vegetable stock
1 teaspoon Ginger Paste (see page 57)
3 teaspoons Garlic Paste (see page 57)
750g / 1lb 10oz Paneer, (see page 59), cut into 5-cm / 2-inch squares
½ teaspoon ground green cardamom
½ teaspoon ground mace
¼ teaspoon ground cinnamon
2 tablespoons single (light) cream
salt

Put the onion in a blender or food processor, add 2 tablespoons water and process to make a paste. Set aside.

Put the yoghurt in a bowl, add the fried onion paste, cashew nut paste, ground coriander, turmeric and yellow chilli powder, then season with salt, whisk to combine and set aside.

Put the saffron threads in a mortar or spice grinder and crush with a pestle or process until crushed. Put the milk in a small bowl, add the crushed saffron and stir to make a paste. Set aside.

Heat the ghee or oil in a heavy-based pan over medium heat, add the whole spices and stir-fry for about 1 minute, or until the cardamom changes colour. Add the puréed onions and fry for about 1–2 minutes, or until translucent. Add the ginger and garlic pastes and stir-fry for about 2–3 minutes, or until the moisture has evaporated. Remove from the heat, stir in the yoghurt mixture, then return to the heat and stir-fry for about 3–4 minutes, or until the oil separates out.

Add the vegetable stock and bring to the boil. Remove from the heat and pass the sauce through fine muslin (cheesecloth) or a fine sieve (strainer) into a separate pan. Return the sauce to the heat, bring to the boil, add the paneer, reduce the heat and simmer, stirring occasionally, for 10 minutes, or until the sauce is a thin consistency. Sprinkle over the ground spices and stir gently, then add the cream and the reserved saffron paste and serve immediately.

Malai Kofta
Stuffed Paneer Dumplings

Origin Rajasthan
Preparation time 45 minutes
Cooking time 35 minutes
Serves 8

750g / 1lb 10oz Paneer (see page 59)

50g / 1½oz (⅓ cup) gram (chickpea) flour

vegetable oil, for deep-frying

For the filling

few saffron threads

1 tablespoon milk

150g / 5oz (⅔ cup) clotted cream

10–15 cashew nut halves

150g / 5oz Paneer (see page 59), mashed

16 raisins

30g / 1¾oz Khoya (see page 58)
    or 3 tablespoons milk powder (dry milk)

1 tablespoon chopped coriander (cilantro) leaves

1 teaspoon finely chopped ginger

1 teaspoon black cumin seeds

pinch of salt

For the sauce

1 tablespoon ground coriander

1 teaspoon Kashmiri red chilli powder

3 tablespoons ghee or vegetable oil

3 green cardamom pods

2 cloves

1 black cardamom pod

2 bay leaves

1 cinnamon stick, about 2.5cm / 1 inch long

2 teaspoons Ginger Paste (see page 57)

1 tablespoon Cashew Nut Paste (see page 58)

750g / 1lb 10oz (5 medium) tomatoes, chopped

1 litre / 1¾ pints (4¼ cups) vegetable stock

1 teaspoon ground green cardamom

1 teaspoon ground mace

¼ teaspoon ground cloves

¼ teaspoon ground cinnamon

salt

Put the paneer in a bowl and mash with a potato masher or a fork, then add the flour and mix together. Divide into 8 equal portions and shape into balls or ovals.

For the filling, put the saffron in a small bowl with the milk and soak until required.

Put all the ingredients for the filling, including the saffron and milk, in a large bowl and mix together. Divide into 8 equal portions.

Flatten the paneer balls or ovals between your hands, place a portion of the filling in the middle and reshape into balls or ovals.

Heat enough oil for deep-frying in a kadhai or deep, heavy-based pan to 180°C/350°F, or until a cube of bread browns in 30 seconds, then reduce the heat. Working in batches, if necessary, carefully lower the stuffed kofta into the hot oil and deep-fry for 2–3 minutes, or until golden brown. Remove with a slotted spoon and drain on kitchen paper (paper towels).

To make the sauce, mix the ground coriander, chilli powder and 3 tablespoons water together in a small bowl.

Heat the ghee in a heavy-based pan over medium heat, add the whole spices and bay leaves and stir-fry for about 1 minute, or until the cardamom pods begin to change colour. Add the ginger paste and stir-fry for 1 minute, then add the ground coriander and chilli powder mixture and stir-fry for about 2–3 minutes, or until all the water has evaporated.

Add the cashew nut paste and stir-fry for a further 2 minutes, or until the oil separates out. Add the tomatoes, bring to the boil, then reduce the heat to low and simmer for 5–7 minutes.

Add the stock, bring to the boil, then reduce the heat to low and simmer for a further 10 minutes. Place the fried kofta in the sauce and simmer for 3–4 minutes. Mix all the ground spices together, then sprinkle them over.

Paneer Makhani
Paneer in Creamy Tomato Sauce

Origin Punjab
Preparation time 30 minutes
Cooking time 20 minutes
Serves 4

500g / 1lb 2oz (3 medium) tomatoes, chopped

3½ tablespoons butter

500g / 1lb 10oz Paneer (see page 59), cut into cubes

4 tablespoons vegetable oil

1 teaspoon chilli powder

2–3 teaspoons ground green cardamom

1 teaspoon Garam Masala (see page 31)

2 tablespoons Ginger Paste (see page 57)

2 tablespoons Garlic Paste (see page 57)

1 tablespoon poppy seeds

2 tablespoons crushed ginger

1 bay leaf

3–4 cloves

2 cinnamon sticks, about 2.5cm / 1 inch long

1 teaspoon dried fenugreek leaves, crushed

1 teaspoon sugar

125ml / 4½fl oz (½ cup) single (light) cream

salt

4 tablespoons coriander (cilantro) leaves, to garnish

Blanch the tomatoes by putting them in a large heatproof bowl of boiling water for 30 seconds, then plunging them in cold water. Remove the skin and chop the flesh.

Heat the butter in a heavy-based frying pan (skillet) over medium heat, add the paneer and fry for about 8–10 minutes, or until evenly golden brown all over. Remove with a slotted spoon and soak in a bowl of water to keep succulent.

Heat the oil in a heavy-based pan, add the tomatoes and stir-fry for 2 minutes. Add all the ground spices, the ginger and garlic pastes and poppy seeds and continue frying for 2–3 minutes, or until the oil separates out. Add the crushed ginger, bay leaf, cloves and cinnamon and pour in 250ml / 8fl oz (1 cup) hot water. Bring to the boil and cook over high heat for about 5–7 minutes. Reduce the heat and simmer for a further 3–4 minutes, or until the sauce is thick. Add the dried fenugreek, sugar and cream, then stir, remove from the heat and set aside.

Add the paneer to the sauce, season with salt and heat before serving. Garnish with coriander leaves.

Thanda Achari Paneer
Cold Paneer in Pickling Spices

Origin Punjab
Preparation time 15 minutes
Cooking time 15 minutes
Serves 4

500ml / 18fl oz (2¼ cups) natural (plain) yoghurt, whisked

1 teaspoon ground coriander

pinch of ground turmeric

1 teaspoon yellow or Kashmiri red chilli powder

3 tablespoons mustard oil

½ teaspoon mustard seeds

½ teaspoon kalonji (nigella) seeds

1 teaspoon fennel seeds

2 dried red chillies

500g / 1lb 2oz Paneer (see page 59), cut into 5-cm / 2-inch cubes

½ teaspoon amchoor

salt

3–4 green chillies, slit in half lengthways and de-seeded, to garnish

---

Put the yoghurt in a large bowl, add the coriander, turmeric and chilli powder and season with salt. Stir well and set aside.

Heat 2 tablespoons of the oil in a heavy-based pan over medium heat, add the mustard seeds, kalonji seeds and fennel seeds and stir-fry for about 1 minute, or until the seeds start to splutter. Add the dried red chillies and stir-fry for a further 2 minutes, or until the chillies turn a shade darker.

Add the paneer together with the amchoor and stir-fry for about 5 minutes, or until all the moisture has evaporated. Season with salt, then remove from the heat and stir in the yoghurt mixture. Pour the remaining mustard oil on top and garnish with green chillies.

Palak Paneer
Paneer with Spinach

Origin Punjab
Preparation time 20 minutes, plus cooling time
Cooking time 20–25 minutes
Serves 2

100g / 3½oz Paneer (see page 59)
250g / 9oz fresh spinach, chopped
2 green chillies, de-seeded and chopped
½ teaspoon chopped ginger
pinch of salt
2 tablespoons vegetable oil
pinch of fenugreek seeds
1 onion, chopped
1 clove garlic, chopped
¼ teaspoon cumin seeds
250g / 9oz (1 cup) puréed tomatoes

Cut the paneer into 5-cm / 2-inch square pieces, about 2.5cm / 1 inch thick and set aside.

Put the spinach, chillies, ginger, salt and a sprinkling of water in a large, heavy-based pan and cook over medium heat for about 3–4 minutes, or until cooked. Allow to cool, squeeze dry, then transfer to a blender or food processor and process to make a purée. Set aside.

Heat the oil in a heavy-based pan over medium heat, add the fenugreek seeds and stir-fry for about 30 seconds. Add the onion and stir-fry for about 5 minutes, or until it is lightly coloured. Add the garlic and cumin seeds and fry for 30 seconds, then add the puréed tomatoes and fry for a further 5 minutes, or until the liquid from the tomatoes has evaporated. Add the paneer and stir gently, then add the puréed spinach and cook for 2 minutes before serving.

Paneer di Bhurji
Paneer Scramble

Origin Punjab
Preparation time 20 minutes
Cooking time 20–25 minutes
Serves 4–6

½ teaspoon ground turmeric
1 teaspoon chilli powder
4 tablespoons ghee
1 teaspoon cumin seeds
90g / 3¼oz (1 small) onion, chopped
2½ teaspoons Ginger Paste (see page 57)
2½ teaspoons Garlic Paste (see page 57)
175g / 6oz (1 medium) tomato, chopped
300g / 11oz (1½ cups) cooked chana dal
450g / 1lb Paneer (see page 59), mashed
4 green chillies, de-seeded and cut into long strips
1 teaspoon coarsely ground black pepper
1 teaspoon ground green cardamom
1 teaspoon ground cloves
1 teaspoon ground nutmeg
1 teaspoon ground fenugreek
salt

To garnish

1 × 4-cm / 1½-inch piece fresh ginger, peeled and cut into juliennes
4 tablespoons chopped coriander (cilantro) leaves

Put the turmeric and chilli powder in a small bowl, add 2 tablespoons water and mix together.

Heat the ghee in a heavy-based pan over medium heat, add the cumin and stir-fry for about 1 minute, or until the seeds begin to splutter. Add the onion and fry for 5 minutes, or until it turns light golden. Add the ginger and garlic pastes and stir-fry for 1 minute, or until all the moisture has evaporated. Add the turmeric mixture and fry for a further 30 seconds, or until all the liquid has evaporated.

Add the tomato and fry for about 5 minutes, or until all the moisture has evaporated. Now add the chana dal and stir-fry for about 2 minutes, or until the oil separates out. Add the mashed paneer and stir, then add the chillies and season with salt. Stir-fry for about 1 minute, before adding the ground spices. Stir, then remove from the heat and adjust the seasoning, if necessary. Transfer to a serving dish and garnish with ginger juliennes and chopped coriander.

Karhai Paneer
Paneer & (Bell) Peppers in Tomato Sauce

Origin Punjab
Preparation time 20 minutes
Cooking time 15 minutes
Serves 4

½ teaspoon ground turmeric
1 teaspoon chilli powder
3 tablespoons ghee
90g / 3¼oz (1 small) onion, chopped
1½ teaspoons Ginger Paste (see page 57)
3½ teaspoons Garlic Paste (see page 57)
1 teaspoon coriander seeds, dry roasted
350g / 12oz (1½ cups) puréed tomatoes
750g / 1lb 10oz Paneer (see page 59), cut into bite-sized chunks
3 green (bell) peppers, cut into quarters
¾ teaspoon ground cumin
½ teaspoon ground mace
1 cinnamon stick
4 black cardamom pods
4 cloves
generous pinch of fenugreek seeds
salt
1 tablespoon chopped coriander (cilantro) leaves, to garnish

Put the turmeric and chilli powder in a small bowl, add 2 tablespoons water and mix together.

Heat the ghee in a heavy-based pan over medium heat, add the onion and fry for about 2 minutes, or until the onion is translucent. Add the ginger and garlic pastes and stir-fry for about 1–2 minutes, or until all the moisture has evaporated. Add the coriander seeds and stir-fry for 30 seconds, then add the turmeric mixture and stir-fry for a further 1–2 minutes, or until all the liquid has evaporated.

Add the puréed tomatoes and season with salt. Stir-fry for about 5 minutes, or until the oil begins to appear on the surface. Add the paneer and peppers and stir-fry for 1 minute, before adding the ground spices, cinnamon, cardamoms, cloves, and fenugreek seeds and stirring carefully. Remove from the heat and adjust the seasoning, if necessary. Garnish with chopped coriander.

Achari Paneer
Paneer in Pickling Spices

Origin Punjab
Preparation time 20 minutes, plus marinating time
Cooking time 15 minutes
Serves 6

1 teaspoon ground turmeric
1 teaspoon chilli powder
500g / 1lb 2oz Paneer (see page 59)
4 tablespoons vegetable oil
2½ teaspoons aniseeds
1 teaspoon fenugreek seeds
1 teaspoon mustard seeds
½ teaspoon kalonji (nigella) seeds
1 teaspoon cumin seeds
3 onions, chopped
6–8 green chillies, de-seeded and chopped
½ teaspoon Garlic Paste (see page 57)
1 teaspoon Ginger Paste (see page 57)
250ml / 8fl oz (1 cup) natural (plain) yoghurt, whisked
1½ teaspoons amchoor
¾ teaspoon Garam Masala (see page 31)
3 green (bell) peppers, cut into bite-sized pieces
salt
2–3 green chillies, slit in half lengthways and de-seeded, to garnish

Put half the turmeric and chilli powder in a small bowl, add 2 tablespoons water and mix together. Cut the paneer into 5-cm / 2-inch cubes and with a sharp knife, score them all over lightly. Put them in a large, shallow dish and pour over the turmeric mixture. Season and set aside for about 10 minutes.

Heat 1 tablespoon of oil in a heavy-based pan over medium heat, add all the spice seeds at once and stir-fry for 1 minute, or until they start to splutter.

Add the onions and chillies and cook for about 5 minutes, or until the onions turn light brown. Add the ginger and garlic pastes and the remaining turmeric and stir-fry for about 1 minute. Stir in the yoghurt, then while stirring, sprinkle over the amchoor and garam masala and season with salt. Reduce the heat to low and cook for about 2 minutes, or until the moisture has reduced a little, but make sure that the liquid does not dry up completely. Add the marinated paneer and peppers and cook for a further 3 minutes, then remove from the heat and allow to cool. Heat just before serving and garnish with slit green chillies.

Chaaman
Kashmiri Paneer

Origin Jammu and Kashmir
Preparation time 15 minutes
Cooking time 20 minutes
Serves 4–6

125g / 4¼oz (½ cup) ghee or vegetable oil
500g / 1lb 2oz Paneer (see page 59), cut into 2.5-cm / 1-inch cubes
1 teaspoon chilli powder
1 teaspoon ground ginger
2 teaspoons Garam Masala (see page 31)
1 teaspoon ground cumin
pinch of asafoetida
1 teaspoon ground coriander
1 teaspoon ground turmeric
salt
1 sprig coriander (cilantro) leaves, to garnish

Heat half the ghee or oil in a large, heavy-based frying pan (skillet) over medium heat, add the paneer and fry for about 5 minutes, or until golden brown all over. Remove with a slotted spoon and drain on kitchen paper (paper towels).

Heat the remaining ghee or oil in another heavy-based pan over low heat, add the paneer and all the remaining ingredients, except the garnish, season with salt and pour in 375ml / 13fl oz (1½ cups) water. (When frying the paneer, make sure the oil is hot enough, otherwise it may stick to the base (bottom) of the frying pan.) Simmer over low heat for about 10 minutes, then garnish with coriander leaves.

Tamatar Chaaman
Paneer in Thick Tomato Sauce

Origin Jammu and Kashmir
Preparation time 15 minutes
Cooking time 25 minutes
Serves 6

250ml / 8fl oz (1 cup) vegetable oil
500g / 1lb 2oz Paneer (see page 59), cut into 2.5-cm / 1-inch cubes
pinch of asafoetida
5 cloves
5 green cardamom pods
2 cinnamon sticks
750g / 1lb 10oz (3 cups) puréed tomatoes
2 teaspoons ground fennel
1 teaspoon ground ginger
1½ teaspoons ground coriander
1 teaspoon ground cumin
1½ teaspoons Kashmiri red chilli powder
1 teaspoon Kashmiri Garam Masala (see page 56)
salt
1 small sprig coriander (cilantro) leaves, to garnish

Heat the oil in a large, heavy-based frying pan (skillet) over medium heat, add the paneer and fry for about 5 minutes, or until golden brown all over. Remove with a slotted spoon and drain on kitchen paper (paper towels). Add the asafoetida and whole spices to the pan and stir-fry for about 1 minute, or until they change colour.

Add the puréed tomatoes to the pan and cook for about 5 minutes, or until all the liquid has evaporated. Pour in 250ml / 8fl oz (1 cup) hot water together with all the ground spices, except the garam masala, and season with salt. Bring to the boil and add the paneer. Reduce the heat to low and cook for 5 minutes. Sprinkle over the garam masala and stir gently, then simmer for a further 2–3 minutes. Garnish with coriander leaves.

Dakhani Paneer
Paneer in Tamarind Coconut Curry

Origin Hyderabad
Preparation time 50 minutes
Cooking time 20–25 minutes
Serves 5

5 tablespoons vegetable oil, plus extra for deep-frying

1 onion, chopped

2 tomatoes, chopped

500ml / 18fl oz (2¼ cups) coconut milk, fresh
    (see page 781) or canned

300g / 11oz Paneer (see page 59), cut
    into 2.5-cm / 1-inch cubes

salt

For the spice paste
120g / 4oz (1½ cups) grated fresh coconut

8–10 dried red chillies, shredded

1 teaspoon cumin seeds

1 tablespoon coriander seeds

pinch of ground turmeric

2 tablespoons Tamarind Extract (see page 58)

1 × 2.5-cm / 1-inch piece fresh ginger

5–6 cloves garlic

For the batter
75g / 2½oz (½ cup) gram (chickpea) flour

3 tablespoons chopped coriander (cilantro) leaves

1 teaspoon Garam Masala (see page 31)

1 teaspoon ground black pepper

To make the spice paste, put all the ingredients in a blender or food processor and process, adding enough water to make a paste. Set aside.

Heat 4–5 tablespoons oil in a large, heavy-based pan over medium heat, add the onion and fry for about 5–7 minutes, or until golden brown. Add the tomatoes and cook for 5–6 minutes, or until the oil separates out. Reduce the heat to low, add the spice paste and continue cooking for about 10 minutes. Stir in the coconut milk and season with salt. Stir, remove from the heat and set aside.

Mix all the ingredients for the batter together in a large bowl and stir in 125ml / 4½fl oz (½ cup) water until thick.

Heat enough oil for deep-frying in a kadhai or deep, heavy-based pan to 180°C/350°F, or until a cube of bread browns in 30 seconds, then reduce the heat.

Working in batches, dip the paneer pieces into the batter, then carefully lower them into the hot oil and deep-fry for 2–3 minutes, or until golden brown. Remove with a slotted spoon and drain on kitchen paper (paper towels).

Place the fried paneer on a serving dish and pour the sauce over the top.

Matar Paneer
Paneer & Pea Curry

Origin Awadh
Preparation time 20 minutes
Cooking time 20 minutes
Serves 4–6

150g / 5oz (⅔ cup) ghee or vegetable oil

500g / 1lb 2oz Paneer (see page 59), cut into
    5-cm / 2-inch cubes

1 bay leaf

4 cloves

2 black cardamom pods

1 cinnamon stick, about 2.5cm / 1 inch long

1 teaspoon ground cumin

1 teaspoon chilli powder

½ teaspoon ground turmeric

2 teaspoons ground coriander

1 teaspoon Garam Masala (see page 31)

1 × 2.5-cm / 1-inch piece fresh ginger, peeled
    and chopped

250g / 9oz (1⅔ cups) peas, shelled if fresh

salt

Heat the ghee or oil in a kadhai or deep, heavy-based pan over medium heat, add the paneer and fry for about 5 minutes, or until golden brown all over. Remove with a slotted spoon and drain on kitchen paper (paper towels).

Reheat the ghee or oil in the same pan, add the bay leaf and whole spices and fry for about 1 minute, or until they change colour. Add the ground spices, season with salt and pour in 4 tablespoons water. Stir-fry over medium heat for 2 minutes. Add the ginger, paneer, peas and 500ml / 18fl oz (2¼ cups) water. Bring to the boil, reduce the heat, cover and simmer for 5–7 minutes, or until the peas are cooked. Adjust the seasoning, if necessary.

Working in batches, dip the paneer pieces into the batter, then carefully lower them into the hot oil and deep-fry for 2–3 minutes, or until golden brown. Remove with a slotted spoon and drain on kitchen paper (paper towels).

Place the fried paneer on a serving dish and pour the sauce over the top.

___

Matar Paneer
Paneer & Pea Curry

Origin Awadh
Preparation time 20 minutes
Cooking time 20 minutes
Serves 4–6

150g / 5oz (⅔ cup) ghee or vegetable oil
500g / 1lb 2oz Paneer (see page 59), cut into 5-cm / 2-inch cubes
1 bay leaf
4 cloves
2 black cardamom pods
1 cinnamon stick, about 2.5cm / 1 inch long
1 teaspoon ground cumin
1 teaspoon chilli powder
½ teaspoon ground turmeric
2 teaspoons ground coriander
1 teaspoon Garam Masala (see page 31)
1 × 2.5-cm / 1-inch piece fresh ginger, peeled and chopped
250g / 9oz (1⅔ cups) peas, shelled if fresh
salt

Heat the ghee or oil in a kadhai or deep, heavy-based pan over medium heat, add the paneer and fry for about 5 minutes, or until golden brown all over. Remove with a slotted spoon and drain on kitchen paper (paper towels).

Reheat the ghee or oil in the same pan, add the bay leaf and whole spices and fry for about 1 minute, or until they change colour. Add the ground spices, season with salt and pour in 4 tablespoons water. Stir-fry over medium heat for 2 minutes. Add the ginger, paneer, peas and 500ml / 18fl oz (2¼ cups) water. Bring to the boil, reduce the heat, cover and simmer for 5–7 minutes, or until the peas are cooked. Adjust the seasoning, if necessary.

✳ ✳ / ▣ pp.286, 468

Tamatar Bhatkalikura
Tomato Curry with Coconut & Spinach

Origin Tamil Nadu
Preparation time 20 minutes
Cooking time 20–30 minutes
Serves 4

500g / 1lb 2oz (2¾ cups) tomatoes, chopped
2 green chillies, de-seeded and chopped
6 curry leaves
2 onions, sliced
½ teaspoon Garlic Paste (see page 57)
1 teaspoon ground cumin
½ dried coconut, ground
pinch of ground turmeric
45g / 1½oz (1½ cups) chopped spinach
salt

For the tempering

2 teaspoons vegetable oil
3 dried red chillies
1 teaspoon mustard seeds

Bring 750ml / 1¼ pints (3¼ cups) water to the boil in a large, heavy-based pan. Add the tomatoes, chillies, curry leaves and half of the onions, season with salt and reduce the heat slightly. Continue to boil for about 5 minutes. Add the garlic paste, ground cumin, coconut, turmeric and spinach, then reduce the heat and simmer for a few minutes until the moisture has evaporated.

Heat the oil for the tempering in a large frying pan (skillet) over medium heat, add the remaining onions, the dried red chillies and mustard seeds and stir-fry for about 5–7 minutes, or until the onions are golden brown. Pour over the tomatoes and cover immediately to retain the aroma.

Tamatar Mooli
Spicy Tomatoes & Radishes

Origin Jammu and Kashmir
Preparation time 15 minutes
Cooking time 25 minutes
Serves 4–6

50ml / 2fl oz (¼ cup) vegetable oil

½ teaspoon cumin seeds

pinch of asafoetida

¼ teaspoon fenugreek seeds

750g / 1lb 10oz (6 large) tomatoes, finely chopped

500g / 1lb 2oz (2) radishes, cut into 1cm / ½ inch
    wide rounds

1 teaspoon sugar

1 teaspoon chilli powder

1 teaspoon ground ginger

1 teaspoon ground coriander

1 × 2.5-cm / 1-inch piece fresh ginger, peeled and
    grated

salt

4 sprigs coriander (cilantro) leaves, chopped,
    to garnish

Heat the oil in a large, heavy-based pan over medium
heat, add the cumin, asafoetida and fenugreek seeds
and stir-fry for about 1 minute, or until the seeds
start to splutter. Now add the tomatoes and fry for
about 2–3 minutes. When they are half done, add
the radishes, sugar and the rest of the spices and the
fresh ginger, then season with salt. Cover and cook
for about 15 minutes, or until the radishes become
soft, adding a little water if necessary. Garnish with
chopped coriander.

Tamatar ka Kut
Tangy Curried Tomatoes

Origin Hyderabad
Preparation time 30 minutes
Cooking time 30 minutes
Serves 6

1kg / 2¼lb tomatoes

1 teaspoon Ginger Paste (see page 57)

1 teaspoon Garlic Paste (see page 57)

15–20 curry leaves

½ teaspoon fenugreek seeds

1 teaspoon cumin seeds

5 tablespoons vegetable oil

2–3 onions, sliced

1 teaspoon ground turmeric

1 teaspoon chilli powder

1 tablespoon sesame seeds

2 tablespoons gram (chickpea) flour, roasted

salt

For the tempering

1 tablespoon vegetable oil

½ tablespoon cumin seeds

¼ teaspoon mustard seeds

¼ tablespoon fenugreek seeds

¼ tablespoon kalonji (nigella) seeds

7–8 dried red chillies

8–10 curry leaves

Bring 250ml / 8fl oz (1 cup) water to the boil in
a large, heavy-based pan, add the tomatoes,
½ teaspoon each of the ginger and garlic pastes,
the curry leaves, fenugreek seeds and cumin
seeds and cook for 10 minutes. Pass through
a sieve (strainer) to make a smooth purée.

Heat the oil in a large, heavy-based pan over
medium heat, add the onions and fry for about 5–7
minutes, or until golden brown. Add the remaining
ginger and garlic pastes and fry for about 2 minutes.
Add the puréed tomatoes, turmeric, chilli powder
and sesame seeds, then season with salt.

Put the roasted gram flour in a small bowl, add a little
water and stir together, then add to the pan. Add
a little more water, if required. The dish should have
a thick soup-like consistency. Simmer over medium
heat for about 10 minutes.

※ ※
—

Bhare Baghare Tamate
Stuffed Tomatoes

Origin Hyderabad
Preparation time 1¼ hours
Cooking time 30 minutes
Serves 4

12 tomatoes

salt

For the filling

unsalted butter, for frying

150g / 5oz (2 cups) chopped mushrooms

250g / 9oz Paneer (see page 59), grated or crumbled

1 tablespoon chopped coriander (cilantro) leaves

4 green chillies, slit in half lengthways and de-seeded

24 cashew nut halves

1 teaspoon black cumin seeds

For the paste

4 tablespoons peanuts, roasted

2 tablespoons desiccated (dried flaked) coconut

4½ tablespoons sesame seeds

250g / 9oz (2 small) onions

4 teaspoons ground coriander

1 teaspoon ground cumin

For the sauce

1 teaspoon ground turmeric

1½ teaspoons chilli powder

125ml / 4½fl oz (½ cup) vegetable oil

½ teaspoon mustard seeds

1 teaspoon cumin seeds

16 curry leaves

150g / 5oz (1 medium) onion, sliced

3 tablespoons Ginger Paste (see page 57)

1 teaspoon Garlic Paste (see page 57)

100g / 3½oz Fried Onion Paste (see page 57)

¼ teaspoon Tamarind Extract (see page 58)

Blanch the tomatoes by putting them in a large heatproof bowl of boiling water for 30 seconds, then plunging them in cold water. Remove the skin and slice off the top neatly with a sharp knife, then remove the core, taking care not to pierce the flesh.

To make the filling, melt the butter in a large, heavy-based pan over medium heat, add the mushrooms and lightly fry for about 2–3 minutes, or until the moisture has evaporated. Transfer to a bowl, then add all the other ingredients for the filling, season with salt and mix together. Put a portion of the filling in each of the blanched tomatoes and set aside.

To make the paste, put all the ingredients in a blender or food processor, with a little water if necessary, and process to make a paste. Set aside.

To make the sauce, put the turmeric and chilli powder in a small bowl, add 2 tablespoons water and stir together.

Heat the oil in another large, heavy-based pan over medium heat, add the mustard and cumin seeds and stir-fry for about 1 minute, or until they start to splutter. Add the curry leaves, stir, then add the onions and lightly fry for about 2 minutes, or until they are translucent. Add the ginger and garlic pastes and stir-fry for about 2–3 minutes, or until the onions are golden.

Add the ground spice mixture to the pan and stir-fry for 2–3 minutes, or until the moisture has evaporated, then add the pastes and stir-fry for about 2–3 minutes, or until the oil has separated out. Pour in 750ml / 1¼ pints (3¼ cups) water and season with salt. Bring to the boil, then stir in the tamarind extract. Reduce the heat and simmer for about 5 minutes, stirring occasionally, until it is a thin sauce consistency.

Place the stuffed tomatoes in the sauce, cover and simmer for 2–3 minutes. Uncover and simmer for about 5 minutes, or until the sauce is thick. Remove from the heat and adjust the seasoning, if necessary.

Tamatar Pachadi
Tangy Tomatoes in Yoghurt

Origin Tamil Nadu
Preparation time 10 minutes, plus cooling time
Cooking time 10 minutes
Serves 4

1 teaspoon vegetable oil
½ teaspoon mustard seeds
1 teaspoon urad dal, rinsed and drained
3–4 dried red chillies
pinch of asafoetida
1 large tomato, chopped
250ml / 8fl oz (1 cup) natural (plain) yoghurt, whisked
salt

Heat the oil in a large frying pan (skillet) over high heat, then reduce the heat. Add the mustard seeds, urad dal, dried red chillies and asafoetida and stir-fry for 1 minute. Add the tomato, reduce the heat to low and cook for about 5 minutes. Remove from the heat and allow to cool.

When cool, add the yoghurt and season with salt, then mix well.

☀ / 📷 p.290

Mirchi ka Salan
Stuffed Green Chillies

Origin Hyderabad
Preparation time 30–35 minutes
Cooking time 20 minutes
Serves 8

1 tablespoon coriander seeds
1 teaspoon cumin seeds
3 tablespoons sesame seeds
4 tablespoons peanuts
1 teaspoon poppy seeds
1 tablespoon grated coconut
100g / 3½oz (1 small) onion
1 × 2.5-cm / 1-inch piece fresh ginger, peeled
1 tablespoon Garlic Paste (see page 57)
½ teaspoon ground turmeric
1 teaspoon chilli powder
1 teaspoon jaggery, crumbled, or soft brown sugar
4 tablespoons Tamarind Extract (see page 58)
250ml / 8fl oz (1 cup) vegetable oil
5–6 green chillies
10–15 curry leaves
1 teaspoon fenugreek seeds
salt

Put the coriander seeds, cumin seeds, sesame seeds, peanuts, poppy seeds and grated coconut in a dry frying pan (skillet) and cook for about 2–3 minutes, or until roasted. Remove from the heat.

Put the onions, roasted spices, ginger, garlic paste, turmeric, chilli powder, jaggery or sugar and tamarind extract in a blender or food processor. Season with salt and process to make a paste.

Heat the oil in a heavy-based pan over medium heat, add the chillies and stir-fry very lightly for about 15 seconds. Add the curry leaves and fenugreek seeds and stir-fry for a further 30 seconds, then add the spice paste and cook, stirring once or twice, for about 10 minutes, or until the oil separates and rises to the surface.

❋ / 📷 p.288

Mirchi ka Salan
Stuffed Green Chillies

Origin Hyderabad
Preparation time 30–35 minutes
Cooking time 20 minutes
Serves 8

1 tablespoon coriander seeds
1 teaspoon cumin seeds
3 tablespoons sesame seeds
4 tablespoons peanuts
1 teaspoon poppy seeds
1 tablespoon grated coconut
100g / 3½oz (1 small) onion
1 × 2.5-cm / 1-inch piece fresh ginger, peeled
1 tablespoon Garlic Paste (see page 57)
½ teaspoon ground turmeric
1 teaspoon chilli powder
1 teaspoon jaggery, crumbled, or soft brown sugar
4 tablespoons Tamarind Extract (see page 58)
250ml / 8fl oz (1 cup) vegetable oil
5–6 green chillies
10–15 curry leaves
1 teaspoon fenugreek seeds
salt

Put the coriander seeds, cumin seeds, sesame seeds, peanuts, poppy seeds and grated coconut in a dry frying pan (skillet) and cook for about 2–3 minutes, or until roasted. Remove from the heat.

Put the onions, roasted spices, ginger, garlic paste, turmeric, chilli powder, jaggery or sugar and tamarind extract in a blender or food processor. Season with salt and process to make a paste.

Heat the oil in a heavy-based pan over medium heat, add the chillies and stir-fry very lightly for about 15 seconds. Add the curry leaves and fenugreek seeds and stir-fry for a further 30 seconds, then add the spice paste and cook, stirring once or twice, for about 10 minutes, or until the oil separates and rises to the surface.

❋ / 📷 p.385

Baghare Gajar
Savoury Fried Carrots

Origin Hyderabad
Preparation time 20 minutes
Cooking time 20 minutes
Serves 4–6

500g / 1lb 2oz (9 medium) carrots, cut into 1-cm / ½-inch pieces
1 teaspoon chilli powder
2 tablespoons ghee
2 dried red chillies
½ teaspoon cumin seeds
6 curry leaves
1 tablespoon grated fresh coconut
salt

Cook the carrots with the chilli powder in 250ml / 8fl oz (1 cup) of lightly salted boiling water for about 10–12 minutes, or until tender. The water should be absorbed by the time they are cooked.

Put the ghee in a heavy-based frying pan (skillet) over medium heat, add the dried red chillies, cumin seeds and curry leaves and stir-fry for about 1 minute, or until the chillies have turned a shade darker. Immediately pour over the boiled carrots and sprinkle over the grated coconut and serve hot.

Shalgam ki Subzi
Curried Turnips

Origin Punjab
Preparation time 25 minutes, plus standing time
Cooking time 30–35 minutes
Serves 2–4

250g / 9oz (4 small) turnips, peeled
2 tablespoons vegetable oil
1 teaspoon ground turmeric
1 cinnamon stick
4 green cardamom pods
4 black cardamom pods
1 tablespoon Fried Onion Paste (see page 57)
2 tablespoons Kashmiri red chilli powder
1 tablespoon Garlic Paste (see page 57)
120ml / 4oz (1 small) tomato, puréed
salt

Put the turnips in a bowl, add 1 teaspoon salt and
mix well. Set aside for 15 minutes, then rinse well
and pat dry on kitchen paper (paper towels). Heat
the oil in a non-stick pan over medium heat, add the
turnips and fry for about 5 minutes, or until light
brown. Remove from the pan and set aside.

Pour 250ml / 8fl oz (1 cup) water into a deep, heavy-
based pan, add the turmeric, cinnamon, cardamom
pods, fried onion paste, chilli powder and garlic
paste, then season with salt. Bring the mixture to the
boil, stirring constantly, and boil for 7–8 minutes.
Add the fried turnip and cook for about 20 minutes,
or until the turnip is tender. Remove from the heat,
stir in the puréed tomato and stir for 2–3 minutes.

Sol Karhi
Kokum Curry

Origin Coastal
Preparation time 15–20 minutes, plus soaking time
Cooking time 10 minutes
Serves 4–6

10–12 kokum, rinsed well
1 tablespoon gram (chickpea) flour
about 1.25 litres / 2 pints (5 cups) coconut milk, fresh (see page 781) or canned
3–4 green chillies, de-seeded
1 × 5-cm / 2-inch piece fresh ginger, peeled
2 teaspoons cumin seeds
pinch of asafoetida
2 tablespoons coriander (cilantro) leaves, chopped
sugar, to taste

For the seasoning

1 tablespoon ghee
1–2 dried red chillies, broken into 2–3 pieces
2–3 strips curry leaves

Make sure the kokum is cleaned of all grit, then
soak in a bowl of warm water for 30 minutes. Purée
on a curry stone or in a blender then transfer to a
non-metallic bowl if not using immediately.

Put the gram flour in a small bowl, add 2 tablespoons
coconut milk and soak until required.

Put the green chillies, ginger, cumin seeds and
asafoetida in a small blender or food processor and
process until ground.

Mix all the ingredients, except the seasoning,
together in a large, heavy-based pan and bring to the
boil just once.

Heat the ghee for the seasoning in a small frying pan
(skillet) over medium heat, add all the ingredients
and stir-fry for 1 minute. Pour over the curry, then
stir well and remove from the heat.

Injipuli
Ginger Curry

Origin Kerala
Preparation time 15–20 minutes
Cooking time 25 minutes
Serves 4

4 tablespoons vegetable oil
40g / 1½oz (½ cup) grated fresh coconut
2–3 dried red chillies
small pinch of ground turmeric
¼ teaspoon mustard seeds
3 green chillies, de-seeded and chopped
20–30 curry leaves
1 x 2.5-cm / 1-inch piece ginger, peeled and cut into very small pieces
30g / 1¼oz coconut pieces
1 tablespoon Tamarind Extract (see page 58)
salt

Heat about 1 tablespoon oil in a small frying pan (skillet) over medium heat, add the grated coconut and dried red chillies and stir-fry for about 1 minute, or until the coconut changes colour. Add the turmeric, mix well and remove from the heat. Transfer the mixture to a blender or food processor and process, without adding any more water, until ground.

Heat the remaining oil in a large frying pan, add the mustard seeds and stir-fry for about 1 minute, or until they start to splutter. Add the green chillies, curry leaves, ginger pieces and coconut pieces and fry for 3–4 minutes.

Add the ground coconut mix to the pan together with the tamarind and season with salt. Pour in 500ml / 18fl oz (2¼ cups) water and bring to the boil. Cook for about 15 minutes, or until the sauce thickens.

Mor Kozhambu
Buttermilk Curry

Origin Tamil Nadu
Preparation time 15–20 minutes
Cooking time 10–15 minutes
Serves 4

250ml / 8fl oz (1 cup) buttermilk (slightly sour)
½ tablespoon rice flour
pinch of ground turmeric
10–15 curry leaves
2 tablespoons vegetable oil
1 tablespoon coriander seeds
1 teaspoon urad dal, rinsed and drained
pinch of asafoetida
2 dried red chillies
3 tablespoons grated fresh coconut
2 green chillies, de-seeded (optional)
1 teaspoon mustard seeds
salt

Put the buttermilk into a large pan, add the rice flour, turmeric and some curry leaves, then season with salt. Set aside.

Heat 1 tablespoon oil in a frying pan (skillet) over medium heat, add the coriander seeds, dal, asafoetida and dried red chillies and stir-fry for about 1 minute, or until the seeds start to splutter and the chillies turn a shade darker. Transfer to a small blender or food processor, add the coconut and green chillies and process, adding a little water if necessary, to make a smooth paste.

Blend this paste into the buttermilk mixture and bring to the boil. Cook for 10 minutes over medium heat.

To make the tempering, heat the remaining oil in a small frying pan over medium heat, add the mustard seeds and stir-fry for about 1 minute, or until they start to splutter, then pour over the curry.

Gwar Phali
Cluster Bean Curry

Origin Punjab/Awadh
Preparation time 15 minutes, plus cooling time
Cooking time 20 minutes
Serves 4

250g / 9oz cluster beans, cut into pieces

200ml / 7fl oz (¾ cup) mustard oil

pinch of asafoetida

½ teaspoon ajwain seeds

1 teaspoon chopped ginger

1 teaspoon amchoor

pinch of chilli powder

salt

Bring 1 litre / 1¾ pints (4¼ cups) water to the boil in a large, heavy-based pan, add the beans and cook for 10 minutes over medium heat. Drain, allow to cool and remove the string.

Heat the oil in a frying pan (skillet) over medium heat, add the asafoetida and stir-fry for 30 seconds, or until dissolved. Add the ajwain seeds and ginger and stir-fry for about 2 minutes. Add the beans, reduce the heat to low, cover and cook for 15 minutes. Remove from the heat and stir in the amchoor and chilli powder, then season with salt.

Chukandar ki Subzi
Beetroot (Beet) Curry

Origin Punjab
Preparation time 15 minutes
Cooking time 20–25 minutes
Serves 4

---

1 tablespoon vegetable oil

2 cloves

pinch of asafoetida

½ teaspoon ground cumin

¼ teaspoon fenugreek seeds

500g / 1lb 2oz (6) beetroot (beet), peeled
    and cut into 5-mm / ¼-inch thick pieces

½ teaspoon ground ginger

1 teaspoon ground coriander

½ teaspoon chilli powder

250g / 9oz (2 small) tomatoes, chopped

salt

Heat the oil in a large, heavy-based pan over medium heat, add the cloves, asafoetida, cumin and fenugreek seeds and stir-fry for about 1 minute, or until the seeds start to splutter. Add the beetroot, increase the heat to high and stir-fry for 1 minute, then pour in 250ml / 8fl oz (1 cup) water and bring to the boil. Reduce the heat to medium, cover and cook for about 10 minutes.

Add the remaining spices and tomatoes and season with salt, then cook for a further 10 minutes.

Andhra Pulussu
Andhra Tamarind Curry

Origin Hyderabad/Andhra Pradesh
Preparation time 30 minutes
Cooking time 25–30 minutes
Serves 4–6

1 teaspoon Tamarind Extract (see page 58)
1 (vegetable) drumstick, cut into 8-cm / 3-inch pieces
2 aubergines (eggplant), trimmed and cut into quarters
1 sweet potato, peeled
and cut into 2.5-cm / 1-inch cubes
60g / 2oz (½ cup) ash gourd, peeled
and cut into 2.5-cm / 1-inch cubes
2 green chillies, slit in half lengthways and de-seeded
1 × 1-cm / ½-inch piece fresh ginger, peeled
and chopped
½ teaspoon ground turmeric
1 tablespoon jaggery, crumbled, or soft brown sugar
1 tablespoon gram (chickpea) flour
salt

For the tempering

2 tablespoons sesame seed oil
1 teaspoon mustard seeds
½ teaspoon fenugreek seeds
½ teaspoon asafoetida
2 dried red chillies, halved
1 teaspoon urad dal, rinsed and drained
1 sprig curry leaves

Heat the oil for the tempering in a frying pan (skillet) over medium heat, add all the ingredients for the tempering and stir-fry for about 1 minute, or until the mustard seeds start to splutter. Add the tamarind extract, vegetables, chillies, ginger, turmeric and jaggery or sugar and season with salt. Mix well, reduce the heat slightly, cover and simmer for 20–25 minutes, or until the vegetables are tender and the sauce has reduced to half.

Put the gram flour in a bowl, pour in 125ml / 4½fl oz (½ cup) water and whisk well, then pour into the curry. Simmer, uncovered, for about 5 minutes, stirring frequently, until well blended.

Kachnar ki Kali
Flowers of the Bauhinia Tree

Origin Awadh
Preparation time 15 minutes
Cooking time 30 minutes
Serves 4–6

500g / 1lb 2oz kachnar flowers
100ml / 3½fl oz (½ cup) vegetable oil
½ teaspoon cumin seeds
2 cloves
pinch of asafoetida
1 teaspoon chilli powder
1 teaspoon ground coriander
1 teaspoon Garam Masala (see page 31)
½ teaspoon ground ginger
1 × 2.5-cm / 1-inch piece fresh ginger, peeled
and crushed
250ml / 8fl oz (1 cup) natural (plain) yoghurt, whisked
coriander (cilantro) leaves, to garnish

Boil the kachnar flowers in a large pan of water until soft. Drain and remove the green outer stalks.

Heat the oil in a heavy-based pan over medium heat, add the cumin seeds, cloves and asafoetida and stir-fry for about 1 minute, or until the seeds start to splutter. Add the kachnar flowers and remaining spices and ginger and fry for another 1 minute until they turn reddish brown. Pour in 125ml / 4½fl oz (½ cup) water and simmer for 10 minutes.

Add the yoghurt to the kachnar flowers and garnish with coriander leaves.

※
___

Charchari
Stir-fried Peelings and Scraps

Origin West Bengal
Preparation time 50 minutes
Cooking time 30 minutes
Serves 6

150g / 5oz (1 medium) potato, cut into cubes
    and peel reserved

150g / 5oz (3) new potatoes, cut into cubes
    or kept whole if small and peel reserved

150g / 5oz (⅓ small head) cauliflower, cut into florets,
    including stalks and tender leaves

150g / 5oz (1¼ cups) pumpkin, cut into cubes
    and peel reserved

150g / 5oz (1¼ cups) bottle gourd (calabash), cut into
    cubes and peel reserved

2 aubergines (eggplant), trimmed and cut into quarters,
    trimmings reserved

few spinach leaves, roughly chopped

150g / 5oz (2⅓ cups) pea pods

1½ teaspoons sugar

salt

For the masala

1½ teaspoons cumin seeds

1 teaspoon poppy seeds

1 teaspoon ground turmeric

5–6 dried red chillies

1 teaspoon mustard seeds

2 onions, chopped

4 cloves garlic

1 small piece fresh ginger, peeled and chopped

For the tempering

2½ tablespoons mustard oil

1½ teaspoons Paanch Phoren (see page 55)

2 bay leaves

3 dried red chillies

Put all the ingredients for the masala in a blender or food processor and process until ground. Set aside.

Heat the mustard oil for the tempering in a kadhai, wok or large, heavy-based pan over medium heat, add the paanch phoren, bay leaves and dried red chillies and stir-fry for 1 minute, or until the chillies turn a shade darker. Add the ground masala and fry for a further 2 minutes.

Rinse all the vegetable peelings (trimmings) well to remove any dirt and set them aside as they will be cooked with the rest of the vegetables.

Add the potatoes and cauliflower to the pan and stir-fry for a few minutes until lightly brown. Add the remaining vegetables and peelings. Stir constantly to ensure even cooking, then add the sugar and season with salt.

Reduce the heat, cover and cook for about 15–20 minutes, or until the vegetables are tender and the oil has separated out. Add a little water if the vegetables appear too dry.

Tali Sem ki Phali
Broad (Fava) Beans with Coriander
(Cilantro)

Origin Awadh
Preparation time 15 minutes
Cooking time 15–20 minutes
Serves 6

400g / 14oz coriander (cilantro) leaves
4–6 green chillies, de-seeded and chopped
3 teaspoons sugar
2 tablespoons vegetable oil
½ teaspoon kalonji (nigella) seeds
1 tablespoon Ginger Paste (see page 57)
400g / 14oz (3 cups) broad (fava) beans
salt

Put the coriander leaves, chillies, 1 teaspoon sugar
and a little salt in a small blender or food processor
and process, adding a little water if necessary, to a
paste. Set aside.

Heat the oil in a kadhai, wok or large, heavy-based
pan over low heat. Add the kalonji seeds and stir-fry
for about 30 seconds, then add the ginger paste and
stir-fry for about 3–4 minutes.

Add the broad beans to the pan and mix well, then
add the coriander paste and stir thoroughly. Add the
remaining sugar and season with salt. Simmer over
medium heat for about 10–15 minutes, or until all the
moisture has evaporated and the beans are tender.
Remove from the heat.

Gota Siddho
Whole Moong Beans
& Vegetable Casserole

Origin West Bengal
Preparation time 40 minutes, plus soaking time
Cooking time 30 minutes
Serves 8

500g / 1lb 2oz (2⅔ cups) whole moong beans, rinsed and drained
8 small new potatoes, cut into cubes
8 peas in their pods
8 broad (fava) beans, podded
2 sweet potatoes, peeled and cut into cubes
1 mooli (daikon), peeled and cut into cubes
10–15 whole black peppercorns
4–6 cloves
1 cinnamon stick, about 5cm / 2 inches long
4–5 green cardamom pods
1 × 2.5-cm / 1-inch piece fresh ginger, peeled and sliced
1 bunch spinach leaves with shoots and roots, if possible
1 tablespoon ghee
4 tablespoons milk
salt

Soak the whole moong beans in a large bowl of
water for about 40 minutes, or overnight.

Drain the beans and cook them on a hot tawa,
griddle or in a frying pan (skillet) for a few minutes
until roasted. Transfer them to a pressure cooker,
add 600ml / 1 pint (2½ cups) water and cook under
pressure for about 15 minutes. Alternatively, cook
the beans with the water in a large, heavy-based
pan for about 30 minutes, or until soft. Drain and
transfer to a clean plan.

Add the potatoes, peas in the pod, broad beans,
sweet potatoes, mooli, peppercorns, cloves,
cinnamon, cardamom pods and ginger. Pour in 125ml /
4½fl oz (½ cup) water and season with salt. Cover and
cook for about 15–20 minutes, or until the vegetables
are done and the dal is thick. Add the spinach and
cook for a further 5 minutes. Add the ghee and milk,
then immediately remove the pan from the heat.

Kath Kaha
Mixed Vegetable Curry

Origin Kerala
Preparation time 50 minutes
Cooking time 1 hour
Serves 6–8

---

2 tablespoons vegetable oil

pinch of asafoetida

½ teaspoon mustard seeds

½ teaspoon cumin seeds

¼ teaspoon ground turmeric

2 bay leaves

1 onion, chopped

1 blade mace

125g / 4¼oz yam, peeled and cut into
     medium-sized pieces

100g / 3½oz (2 medium) carrots, cut into
     medium-sized pieces

125g / 4¼oz (1 medium) potato, cut into
     medium-sized pieces

75g / 2½oz French (green) beans

75g / 2½oz (½ cup) peas, shelled if fresh

1 teaspoon lemon juice

salt

For the roasted coconut paste

1 tablespoon vegetable oil

80g / 2¾oz (1 cup) grated fresh coconut

6 dried red chillies

2 teaspoon coriander seeds

4 cloves

8–10 whole black peppercorns

2 cinnamon sticks, about 5cm / 2 inches long

1 onion, sliced

To make the paste, heat the oil in a large frying pan
(skillet) over low heat, add the coconut and stir-fry
for about 5 minutes, or until roasted. Remove from
the pan and put in a large bowl. In the same pan,
add the dried red chillies and coriander seeds and
stir-fry for about 3 minutes. Add the cloves, black
peppercorns and cinnamon sticks and stir-fry for
a further 2–3 minutes. Remove and mix with the
coconut. Transfer the mixture to a blender or food
processor, add the sliced onion, then pour in
125ml / 4½fl oz (½ cup) water and process to make
a paste. Set aside.

Heat the 2 tablespoons oil in another pan over
medium heat, add the asafoetida, mustard seeds,
cumin seeds and turmeric and stir-fry for about
1 minute, or until the seeds start to splutter. Add the
bay leaves and chopped onion and stir-fry for about
5–7 minutes, or until the onion is golden brown.

Pour in the spice paste and add the mace to
the pan, then cook for about 5 minutes. Pour in
about 1 litre / 1¾ pints (4¼ cups) water and season
with salt. Mix well, then add the yam first and cook
for 8–10 minutes. Add the carrots, followed by the
potatoes. After about 5 minutes, add the beans,
and finally the peas. Cook over low heat until the
vegetables are tender and the sauce is slightly thick.
Remove from the heat and stir in the lemon juice.

Ondhiya
Gujarati Vegetables

Origin Gujarat
Preparation time 1½ hours
Cooking time 30 minutes
Serves 4

1 teaspoon ajwain seeds

generous pinch of bicarbonate of soda (baking soda)

200g / 7oz (1¾ cups) small French (green) beans, cut
   into diamonds

salt

For the vegetables

200g / 7oz (1½ cups) sweet potatoes, peeled
   and cut into cubes

4 potatoes

3 unripe green bananas, peeled and cut into cubes

16 baby aubergines (eggplant), trimmed and sliced

For the dumplings

75g / 2½oz (½ cup) gram (chickpea) flour

50g / 1¾oz (1 cup) fenugreek leaves, chopped

1 teaspoon sugar

2 green chillies, de-seeded and finely chopped

2 teaspoons sesame seeds

1 teaspoon vegetable oil, plus extra for deep frying

For the masala

45g / 1½oz (½ cup) grated coconut

15g / ½oz (⅓ cup) coriander (cilantro) leaves, chopped

4 green chillies, de-seeded and finely chopped

5 teaspoons Tamarind Extract (see page 58)

1 teaspoon ground turmeric

1 teaspoon sugar

To make the dumplings, put the gram flour,
fenugreek leaves, sugar, a pinch of salt, chillies,
sesame seeds and 1 teaspoon oil in a large bowl and
mix together until a stiff dough is formed. Divide
the dough into 20 equal portions and press with
a fist to form dumplings.

Heat enough oil for deep-frying in a kadhai or deep,
heavy-based pan to 180°C/350°F, or until a cube of
bread browns in 30 seconds. Working in batches,
carefully lower the dumplings into the hot oil and
deep-fry for about 2 minutes, or until golden brown.
Remove with a slotted spoon and drain on kitchen
paper (paper towels).

Mix all the masala ingredients together in a bowl.
Set aside.

Reheat the same oil to 180°C/350°F, or until a cube
of bread browns in 30 seconds, then reduce the
heat. Working in batches, deep-fry the vegetables
separately over medium heat for 7–8 minutes,
or until half cooked. Remove with a slotted spoon
and drain on kitchen paper (paper towels).

Bring about 500ml / 18fl oz (2¼ cups) water to the
boil in a large, heavy-based pan. Add the ajwain
seeds and bicarbonate of soda, then add the small
beans and continue to boil for a few minutes until
half cooked.

Add the deep-fried vegetables in the same order in
which they were deep-fried, and boil until all the
ingredients are cooked to taste. Add the masala, stir
and reduce the heat to low, then cover and simmer,
stirring occasionally, for 4–5 minutes. Remove from
the heat and adjust the seasoning, if necessary.

Flower Batata Bhaji
Cauliflower with Potatoes

Origin Parsi
Preparation time 15 minutes
Cooking time 30 minutes
Serves 6

1½ tablespoons vegetable oil
1 teaspoon cumin seeds
small pinch of asafoetida
1½ teaspoons ground turmeric
1 teaspoon Ginger Paste (see page 57)
1½ teaspoons Garlic Paste (see page 57)
6 green chillies, de-seeded and chopped
1 onion, sliced
4 potatoes, cut into cubes
2 cauliflowers, cut into florets
1 teaspoon Garam Masala (see page 31)
salt

Heat the oil in a large, heavy-based pan over high heat, then reduce the heat. Add the cumin seeds and stir-fry for about 1 minute, or until they start to splutter. Add the asafoetida and turmeric and stir-fry for 30 seconds, then add the ginger and garlic pastes and stir-fry for 1 minute. Add the chillies and onion and fry for 5 minutes, or until the onion turns golden.

Add the potatoes and cauliflower florets to the pan, increase the heat to high and cook for about 2 minutes. Pour in 750ml / 1¼ pints (3¼ cups) water, mix well, cover and cook for about 8–10 minutes, stirring occasionally. Add the garam masala and season with salt. Reduce the heat and simmer uncovered for about 5 minutes to thicken the sauce.

Majjige Huli
Mixed Vegetable Curry from Karnataka

Origin Coastal
Preparation time 30 minutes, plus soaking time
Cooking time 40 minutes
Serves 4

200g / 7oz (1 cup) chana dal, rinsed and drained
500g / 1lb 2oz ash gourd, cut into cubes
120g / 4oz chayote squash sliced
150g / 5oz (1 medium) potato, cut into cubes
110g / 3½oz (1 cup) French (green) beans, topped and tailed (trimmed), then cut into 2.5-cm / 1-inch pieces
1 tablespoon grated ginger
1 tablespoon mustard powder
½ coconut, grated
1 sprig coriander (cilantro), chopped
10–15 curry leaves
4–6 green chillies, de-seeded and chopped
1 litre / 1¾ pints (4¼ cups) buttermilk
salt

For the tempering

2 tablespoons ghee
1 teaspoon mustard seeds
10–15 curry leaves, chopped
1 tablespoon chilli powder

Soak the chana dal in a large bowl of water overnight. The next day, bring 250ml / 8fl oz (1 cup) salted water to the boil in a large, heavy-based pan and add all the vegetables.

Meanwhile, drain the chana dal, transfer to a blender or food processor and add the ginger, mustard powder, coconut, chopped coriander, curry leaves and chillies. Process, adding a little water if necessary, to make a paste.

Pour the buttermilk into a large bowl, add the spice paste and mix together, then pour the mixture into the pan in which the vegetables are being cooked. Bring to the boil, then reduce the heat, cover and cook until the vegetables are cooked.

To make the tempering, heat the ghee in a frying pan (skillet) over medium heat, add the mustard seeds and stir-fry for about 1 minute, or until they start to splutter. Add the curry leaves and chilli powder and stir-fry for a few seconds before pouring over the vegetables.

Avial
Mixed Vegetables (I)

Origin Kerala
Preparation time 30 minutes
Cooking time 30 minutes
Serves 4

125g / 4½oz (½ cup) ghee or vegetable oil
1 teaspoon mustard seeds
1½ teaspoons chopped ginger
4 cloves garlic, chopped
125g / 4¼oz (1 medium) onion, chopped
3 green chillies, de-seeded and chopped
1 teaspoon ground turmeric
1 tablespoon ground coriander
1kg / 2¼lb choice of mixed vegetables, chopped or sliced
80g / 2¾oz (1 cup) grated fresh coconut
125ml / 4½fl oz (½ cup) coconut milk, fresh (see page 781) or canned
2 tablespoons chopped coriander (cilantro) leaves
salt

Heat the ghee or oil in a deep, heavy-based pan over medium heat, add the mustard seeds and stir-fry for about 1 minute, or until they start to splutter. Add the ginger and garlic and stir-fry for 1 minute, then add the onions and chillies and stir-fry for about 5–7 minutes, or until the onions are golden brown. Add the turmeric and ground coriander and mix well.

Add the vegetables to the pan and mix well. Add the grated coconut and season with salt, then pour in the coconut milk. Mix well and bring to a rapid boil. Reduce the heat and cook for about 8 minutes, or until the vegetables are cooked but still have a bite.

Bhutta Methi Palak
Corn with Mixed Greens

Origin New
Preparation time 35 minutes
Cooking time 12 minutes
Serves 4

1½ teaspoons ground coriander
3 tablespoons vegetable oil
1 garlic clove, chopped
1 × 2.5-cm / 1-inch piece fresh ginger, peeled and chopped
4 green chillies, de-seeded and chopped
1 teaspoon cumin seeds
1 teaspoon fennel seeds
100g / 3½oz (1 small) onion, sliced
32 baby corn, cut into 2.5-cm / 1-inch pieces
450g / 1lb fenugreek leaves, chopped
450g / 1lb spinach, chopped
1 tablespoon lemon juice
½ teaspoon coarsely ground black pepper, roasted
¼ teaspoon ground nutmeg
¼ teaspoon ground cloves
salt

Put the ground coriander in a small bowl, add 1 tablespoon water and mix together.

Heat the oil in a deep, heavy-based pan over medium heat, add the garlic and stir-fry for about 1 minute, or until it begins to change colour. Add the ginger and chillies and stir-fry for a few seconds. Add the cumin and fennel seeds and stir-fry for a few more seconds, before adding the onion and frying for about 2 minutes, or until translucent.

Add the baby corn to the pan and stir-fry for 2 minutes, then add the coriander mixture and stir-fry for another 1–2 minutes, or until the moisture has almost evaporated. Add the fenugreek and spinach, and stir-fry for a further 2–3 minutes, or until the moisture has almost evaporated. Add the lemon juice, stir, add the ground spices, stir again, then remove from the heat and adjust the seasoning, if necessary.

Puragayalu Pulussu
Mixed Vegetable Curry

Origin Tamil Nadu
Preparation time 40 minutes
Cooking time 30 minutes
Serves 4–6

1 teaspoon chilli powder

1 teaspoon ground turmeric

100g / 3½oz (1 cup) pumpkin, peeled
    and cut into cubes

100g / 3½oz (1 cup) bottle gourd (calabash), peeled
    and cut into cubes

100g / 3½oz (1¼ cups) aubergines (eggplant),
    trimmed and cut into cubes

100g / 3½oz (¾ cup) sweet potatoes, peeled
    and cut into cubes

2 (vegetable) drumsticks, cut into
    4-cm / 1½-inch pieces

3 dried red chillies

2 tablespoons chana dal, rinsed and drained

1 teaspoon coriander seeds

1 teaspoon basmati rice, rinsed and drained

½ teaspoon fenugreek seeds

¼ teaspoon mustard seeds

pinch of asafoetida

1 teaspoon Tamarind Extract (see page 58)

salt

For the tempering:

1 tablespoon vegetable oil

1 teaspoon urad dal, rinsed and drained

½ teaspoon cumin seeds

1 teaspoon mustard seeds

6 curry leaves

pinch of asafoetida

Put 750ml / 1¼ pints (3¼ cups) water in a large, heavy-based pan, season with salt, add the chilli powder and turmeric and bring to the boil. Add the vegetables, except the drumsticks, and cook over medium heat for about 10 minutes.

Cook the drumsticks separately in a pan of boiling salted water for about 10 minutes, or until soft. Drain, then squeeze and scrape out the pulp. When all the vegetables are cooked, put them in a large bowl and mash together.

Roast the dried red chillies, chana dal, coriander seeds, rice, fenugreek and mustard seeds and asafoetida separately in a dry frying pan (skillet) over medium heat for about 1–2 minutes each, then add them to the mashed vegetables. Put the mixture in a large pan, add the tamarind extract and simmer over low heat for about 5 minutes.

Heat the oil for the tempering in a frying pan over medium heat, add the urad dal, cumin and mustard seeds, curry leaves and asafoetida and stir-fry for about 1 minute, or until the dal turns golden and the seeds start to splutter. Pour over the vegetables and immediately cover to retain the aroma. Mix together before serving.

Muthapappu
Moong Dal, Coconut & Vegetable Curry

Origin Hyderabad/Andhra Pradesh
Preparation time 30–40 minutes
Cooking time 15 minutes
Serves 4

100g / 3½oz (½ cup) moong dal, rinsed and drained

275g / 10oz (2½ cups) French (green) beans,
    topped and tailed (trimmed), then cut into
    2.5-cm / 1-inch pieces

250g / 9oz (2 small) courgettes (zucchini), cut into
    2.5-cm / 1-inch pieces

½ tablespoon ground coriander

½ teaspoon rice powder

1 teaspoon chilli powder

¼ teaspoon mustard powder

¼ teaspoon ground turmeric

pinch of asafoetida

¼ dried coconut, ground

salt

Cook the moong dal in a medium-sized pan of water for about 20–30 minutes, or until soft. Drain and set aside.

Put the vegetables in a pan, cover with water, then season with salt and cook for 8 minutes, or until tender but not too soft. Add all the spices, moong dal and coconut and cook for a few more minutes until the curry has a thick sauce-like consistency.

✳

Tengaipal Pitha Kotu
Mixed Vegetable Stew with Coconut Milk

Origin Kerala
Preparation time 20–50 minutes
Cooking time 15 minutes
Serves 4–6

100g / 3½oz (½ cup) moong dal, rinsed and drained

120g / 4oz (1 cup) snake gourd, cut into cubes

120g / 4oz (1 cup) ribbed gourd, cut into cubes

½ teaspoon ground turmeric

1 teaspoon Sambhar Masala (see page 32)

125ml / 4½fl oz (½ cup) coconut milk, fresh
    (see page 781) or canned

salt

For the spice paste

2 teaspoons ghee

1 teaspoon whole black peppercorns

1 tablespoon urad dal, rinsed and drained

½ teaspoon asafoetida

2 teaspoons basmati rice, rinsed and drained

1 teaspoon cumin seeds

For the tempering

2 teaspoons ghee

1 teaspoon mustard seeds

1 dried red chilli, halved

1 sprig curry leaves

Place the moong dal in a kadhai or deep frying pan
(skillet) and roast over medium heat for 1–2 minutes.
Rinse well and drain, then place in a pressure
cooker with 250ml / 8fl oz (1 cup) water and cook
under pressure for 5 minutes. Alternatively, put
the dal in a pan with the water and cook for about
20–30 minutes, or until soft.

To make the spice paste, heat the ghee in the pan
used to roast the dal. Add the remaining ingredients
for the spice paste, except the cumin seeds, and fry
over medium heat for 1–2 minutes, or until the urad
dal turns golden.

Remove from the heat, transfer to a blender and
add the cumin seeds. Add 2 tablespoons water and
process to make a paste.

Place the vegetables, turmeric, sambhar masala and
1 litre / 1¾ pints (4¼ cups) water in the same pan.

Season with salt, then cover and simmer over
medium heat for about 10 minutes, or until the
vegetables are tender.

Blend in the spice paste and simmer for another
minute. Add the cooked moong dal and simmer
for a further 5 minutes, stirring occasionally, until
well blended.

Heat the ghee for the tempering in a small frying pan
over medium heat, add all the ingredients for the
tempering and stir-fry for about 1 minute, or until
the mustard seeds start to splutter. Pour over the
vegetables and stir well, then remove from the heat
and stir in the coconut milk.

Subzi Panchmel
Mixed Vegetables (II)

Origin New
Preparation time 25 minutes
Cooking time 10–12 minutes
Serves 4

100g / 3½oz (3 small) new (baby) potatoes
3 tablespoons mustard oil
2 onions, chopped
8 cloves garlic, chopped
10 baby corn
400g / 14oz mushrooms, stalks removed
1 red (bell) pepper, cut into juliennes
1 yellow (bell) pepper, cut into juliennes
120g / 4oz (1 small) tomato, puréed
1½ teaspoons coriander seeds, roasted, then pounded in a mortar and pestle
1 teaspoon coarsely ground black pepper, roasted
1 × 2.5-cm / 1-inch piece fresh ginger, peeled and sliced
2 tablespoons chopped coriander (cilantro) leaves
salt

Cook the potatoes in a medium-sized pan of water for about 10 minutes, or until soft. Drain and set aside.

Heat the oil in a large, heavy-based pan over high heat, then reduce the heat to medium. Add the onions and fry for about 2 minutes, or until translucent. Add the garlic and fry for about 2–3 minutes, or until the onions turn light golden. Add the baby corn, potatoes, mushrooms and peppers, then increase the heat to high and stir fry for about 2 minutes, or until the baby corns are cooked. Add the puréed tomato and stir-fry for a further 1 minute to ensure that the purée coats the vegetables evenly. Sprinkle over the coriander seeds, pepper, ginger and season with salt, then stir. Add the chopped coriander leaves and stir again. Remove from the heat and adjust the seasoning, if necessary.

Kaliya Baans Singhara
Bamboo Shoot & Water Chestnut Sauce

Origin Awadh
Preparation time 35 minutes
Cooking time 25 minutes
Serves 4

125ml / 4½fl oz (½ cup) natural (plain) yoghurt
2 teaspoons ground coriander
1 teaspoon Kashmiri red chilli powder or paprika
¼ teaspoon ground turmeric
200g / 7oz (1 large) onion, roughly chopped
½ teaspoon saffron threads
3½ tablespoons ghee
3½ teaspoons Ginger Paste (see page 57)
1 teaspoon Garlic Paste (see page 57)
500ml / 18fl oz (2¼ cups) clear vegetable stock
2 × 225g / 8oz cans water chestnuts, drained
500g / 1lb 2oz bamboo shoots
1½ teaspoons shahi masala or other garam masala
salt

Put the yoghurt in a bowl, add the coriander, chilli powder and turmeric and whisk using a fork.

Put the onions in a small blender and process, adding water if necessary, to make a paste. Set aside.

Crush the saffron, then put in a small bowl, add 1 tablespoon of lukewarm water and soak for about 5 minutes. Transfer to a mortar and pound with a pestle or process in a small blender to make a paste.

Heat the ghee in a large, heavy-based pan over medium heat, add the ginger and garlic pastes and stir-fry for about 1–2 minutes, or until the moisture has evaporated. Add the onion paste and stir-fry for 5 minutes, or until specks of oil begin to appear on the surface. Remove from the heat, stir in the yoghurt mixture, then return to the heat and stir-fry for about 2–3 minutes, or until the oil separates out.

Pour in the stock and season with salt. Bring to the boil, then reduce the heat to medium, add the water chestnuts, return to the boil, reduce the heat to low and simmer, stirring occasionally, until the chestnuts are cooked.

Add the bamboo shoots, bring to the boil, then reduce the heat and simmer, stirring occasionally, until the sauce is of a desired consistency. Stir in the shahi masala together with the saffron paste, then remove from the heat and adjust the seasoning.

Methi Makhani Palak
Corn with Mixed Greens

Origin Punjab
Preparation time 25 minutes
Cooking time 10–12 minutes
Serves 4

1½ teaspoons ground coriander

4 tablespoons vegetable oil

6 cloves garlic, chopped

1 × 2.5-cm / 1-inch piece fresh ginger, peeled
    and chopped

4 green chillies, de-seeded and chopped

1 teaspoon cumin seeds

1 teaspoon fennel seeds

100g / 3½oz (1 small) onion, chopped

32 baby corn, cut into 2.5-cm / 1-inch pieces

450g / 1lb fenugreek leaves, chopped

450g / 1lb spinach leaves, chopped

1 tablespoon lemon juice

½ teaspoon whole black peppercorns, coarsely
    ground and roasted

¼ teaspoon ground nutmeg

½ teaspoon ground cloves

salt

Put the ground coriander in a small bowl, add
1 tablespoon water and mix together.

Heat the oil in a deep, heavy-based pan over medium
heat, add the garlic and stir-fry for about 1 minute,
or until it changes colour. Add the ginger and chillies
and stir-fry for 20 seconds. Add the cumin and
fennel seeds and stir-fry for 30 seconds, then add
the onions and stir-fry for about 2 minutes, or until
the onions are translucent.

Add the baby corn to the pan and stir-fry for about
2 minutes. Add the ground coriander mixture and
stir-fry for about 1 minute, or until the moisture has
almost evaporated. Add the fenugreek and spinach
and stir-fry for 1–2 minutes, or until the moisture
has almost evaporated. Now add the lemon juice and
ground spices and stir well. Remove from the heat
and adjust the seasoning.

Erisseri
Elephant's Foot Yam & Plantain Curry
with Fried Coconut

Origin Kerala
Preparation time 45 minutes
Cooking time 45 minutes
Serves 4–5

---

1 coconut, peeled and grated

1 teaspoon cumin seeds

500g / 1lb 2oz yam, cut into 2.5-cm / 1-inch pieces

20 unripe plantains, peeled and slit in half lengthways,
    then cut into 1-cm / ½-inch pieces

1 teaspoon chilli powder

1 teaspoon ground turmeric

salt

For the tempering

2 tablespoons coconut oil

2 teaspoons mustard seeds

3 dried red chillies, torn into pieces

1 coconut, grated

20 curry leaves

Put the coconut and cumin seeds in a blender or
food processor and process, adding a little water if
necessary, to make a paste.

Bring 500ml / 18fl oz (2¼ cups) water to the boil in a
large pan, add the yam, plantains, ground spices and
then season with salt. Cook for about 20 minutes.
Add the coconut-cumin paste and boil for a further
2 minutes. Reduce the heat and simmer for about
10 minutes, or until the sauce thickens. Remove the
pan from the heat.

Heat the oil for the tempering in a frying pan
(skillet), add the mustard seeds and stir-fry for about
1 minute, or until they start to splutter. Add the dried
red chillies and stir-fry for 10 seconds shaking the
pan constantly. Add the remaining ingredients and
stir-fry, stirring constantly, until the coconut
is browned. Pour into the curry, mix well and serve.

Kande ki Subzi
Spicy Onions in Sauce

Origin Rajasthan
Preparation time 25 minutes, plus standing time
Cooking time 30 minutes
Serves 4

500g / 1lb 2oz (4 medium) onions
1 tablespoon ground coriander
1 teaspoon chilli powder
1 teaspoon ground turmeric
3 tablespoons vegetable oil or ghee
1 teaspoon cumin seeds
5 teaspoons Garlic Paste (see page 57)
1 teaspoon Ginger Paste (see page 57)
2–4 green chillies, de-seeded and chopped
200g / 7oz tomatoes, coarsely chopped
salt
pinch of dried fenugreek leaves, to garnish

For the filling

1 teaspoon amchoor
½ teaspoon ground turmeric
1 teaspoon ground coriander
1 teaspoon ground cumin
pinch of rock salt
½ teaspoon chilli powder

Using a sharp knife, make deep incisions in the shape of a cross on top of the onions, cutting half-way through the onions.

To make the filling, mix all the ingredients together in a large bowl and season with salt.

Stuff equal quantities of the filling between the incisions in the onions and set aside for about 30 minutes.

Put the ground coriander, chilli powder and turmeric in a small bowl, add 4 tablespoons water and stir together.

Heat the oil or ghee in a large, heavy-based pan over medium heat, add the cumin seeds and stir-fry for about 1 minute, or until they start to splutter. Add the garlic and ginger pastes and stir-fry for about 1–2 minutes, or until the moisture has evaporated, then add the chillies and stir-fry for a further 1 minute. Add the ground spice mixture and stir-fry for 1 minute, then add the tomatoes and 250ml / 8fl oz (1 cup) water and stir-fry for about 5 minutes, or until the tomatoes are reduced to a pulp.

Place the onions in the sauce and season with salt. Stir, then reduce the heat to low, cover and cook, stirring occasionally, for about 20 minutes, or until the onions are cooked, but not soft. Remove from the heat and adjust the seasoning, if necessary. Sprinkle over the dried fenugreek leaves before serving.

✳ ✳

Amrud ki Subzi
Guava Curry

Origin Rajasthan
Preparation time 20 minutes
Cooking time 10–15 minutes
Serves 2

1 teaspoon ground coriander
1 teaspoon chilli powder
¼ teaspoon ground turmeric
2 tablespoons vegetable oil
1 teaspoon cumin seeds
1 teaspoon Garlic Paste (see page 57)
sugar to taste
2 tablespoons lime juice
500g / 1lb 2oz (1) guava, de-seeded and cut into bite-sized pieces
salt

Put the ground coriander, chilli powder and turmeric in a small bowl, add 4 tablespoons water and mix together.

Heat the oil in a medium-sized pan over medium heat, add the cumin seeds and stir-fry for about 1 minute, or until they start to splutter. Reduce the heat to low, add the garlic paste and ground spice mixture and stir-fry for about 5 minutes. If using sugar, add it now, then pour in the lime juice and cook for a further 1 minute.

Add the guava and continue cooking for about 5 minutes, ensuring that all the fruit is evenly coated with the spices. Adjust the seasoning.

Rasgulle ki Subzi
Rosogolla Curry

Origin Rajasthan
Preparation time 20 minutes
Cooking time 30 minutes
Serves 4

12 Rosogolla (see page 701)
125ml / 4½fl oz (½ cup) natural (plain) yoghurt
7 teaspoons ground coriander
2 teaspoons chilli powder
1 teaspoon ground turmeric
100g / 3½oz (scant ½ cup) ghee
5 teaspoons Ginger Paste (see page 57)
2 tablespoons Chaar Magaz paste
225g / 8oz (2 small) tomatoes, puréed
1 teaspoon ground cumin
¾ teaspoon ground green cardamom
¼ teaspoon ground mace
½ teaspoon ground rose petals
salt

Squeeze out the sweet syrup from the rosogolla, put them in a bowl of water and set aside.

Whisk the yoghurt in a bowl, add the ground coriander, chilli powder and turmeric, then season with salt and whisk to combine.

Heat the ghee in a large, heavy-based pan over medium heat, add the ginger paste together with 125ml / 4½fl oz (½ cup) water and stir until all the moisture has evaporated. Remove from the heat, add the yoghurt mixture, return to the heat and stir-fry for a few minutes until the oil separates out. Add the chaar magaz paste and stir-fry for about 2 minutes, or until the oil separates out, then add the puréed tomatoes and stir-fry for about 2–3 minutes, or until the oil separates out.

Pour in 250ml / 8fl oz (1 cup) water, bring to the boil, then reduce the heat and add the rosogolla. Return to the boil, then reduce the heat to low and simmer, stirring occasionally, for about 2 minutes. Sprinkle over the remaining ground spices, then remove from the heat and adjust the seasoning, if necessary.

Dhaniya Aloo Mangodi
Lentil Dumpling with Coriander & Potatoes

Origin Rajasthan
Preparation time 45 minutes
Cooking time 10–15 minutes
Serves 4

4 potatoes, cut into cubes
vegetable oil, for deep-frying
150g / 5oz mongodi
1 tablespoon ground coriander
1 teaspoon chilli powder
1 teaspoon ground turmeric
3½ tablespoons ghee
2 teaspoons cumin seeds
1 × 5-cm / 2-inch piece fresh ginger, peeled and ground to a paste
250g / 9oz coriander (cilantro) leaves, roughly chopped
225g / 8oz (2 small) tomatoes, puréed
1 teaspoon coarsely ground black pepper
salt

Cook the potatoes in a pan of salted boiling water for about 8–10 minutes, or until cooked but not soft. Drain and set aside.

Heat enough oil for deep-frying in a deep, heavy-based pan to 180°C/350°F, or until a cube of bread browns in 30 seconds. Carefully lower the mongodi into the oil and fry for 2–3 minutes, until golden. Remove with a slotted spoon and drain on kitchen paper (paper towels), then put in a pan of water to soften.

Put the ground coriander, chilli powder and turmeric in a small bowl, add 4 tablespoons water and mix.

Heat the ghee in a large, heavy-based pan over medium heat, add the cumin seeds and stir-fry for about 1 minute, or until they start to splutter. Add the ginger paste and stir-fry for about 1 minute, or until the moisture has evaporated. Add the chopped coriander, along with the ground spice mixture and stir-fry for about 1–2 minutes, or until the moisture has evaporated. Add the puréed tomatoes and stir-fry for 5 minutes, or until the sauce splits.

Add the potatoes and mongodi to the pan, then season with salt. Stir-fry for about 2–3 minutes, or until the coriander coats the potatoes and the mongodi. Sprinkle over the remaining ground spices and stir, then remove from the heat and adjust the seasoning, if necessary.

Methi Kishmish
Fenugreek Seeds with Raisins

Origin Rajasthan
Preparation time 45 minutes, plus soaking time
Cooking time 10 minutes
Serves 8

200g / 7oz (1 cup plus 2 tablespoons) fenugreek seeds
500ml / 18fl oz (2¼ cups) milk
45g / 1½oz unripe mango
5 teaspoons ground coriander
2 teaspoons chilli powder
2 teaspoons ground turmeric
125ml / 4½fl oz (½ cup) vegetable oil
generous pinch of asafoetida
100g / 3½oz (⅔ cup) raisins
4 tablespoons amchoor
salt

Put the fenugreek seeds in a bowl, add the milk and soak overnight.

Put the unripe mango in a bowl of water and set aside for 30 minutes or until soft, then drain.

Put the fenugreek seeds and the milk into a pan with 200ml / 7fl oz (¾ cup) boiling water, then reduce the heat to low and simmer for about 30 minutes, stirring occasionally, until the liquid is fully absorbed. Drain and rinse the boiled fenugreek under cold running water, then drain and set aside.

Put the ground coriander, chilli powder and turmeric in a small bowl, add 5 tablespoons water and stir together.

Heat the oil in a deep, heavy-based pan over medium heat, add the asafoetida and stir-fry for about 30 seconds. Add the ground spice mixture and stir-fry for about 1–2 minutes, or until the moisture has evaporated. Add the fenugreek seeds and soaked mango and stir-fry for about 4–5 minutes. Add the raisins and amchoor and season with salt, then stir-fry for about 1–2 minutes, before removing from the heat and adjusting the seasoning, if necessary.

Kochu Sagar Ghonto
Arum Stalk Curry

Origin West Bengal
Preparation time 30–40 minutes, plus soaking time
Cooking time 10 minutes
Serves 4

4 arum stalks, cut into 8-cm / 3-inch pieces
lime juice, for soaking
1 teaspoon ground turmeric
4 tablespoons roasted whole moong dal
1 teaspoon ground coriander
1 teaspoon ground black pepper
2 green cardamoms seeds
2 teaspoons sugar
1 tablespoon ghee
1 teaspoon ground aniseed
2 bay leaves
2 dried red chillies
1 tablespoon ground coconut
2 tablespoons milk
salt

Soak the arum stalks in a bowl of lime-flavoured water for about 30 minutes. Drain.

Cook the arum stalks with the turmeric and roasted whole moong dal in a pan of boiling water for about 20–30 minutes, or until the dal is soft and the stalks almost mushy. Drain, put into a bowl and mash with a wooden spatula. Add the ground coriander, black pepper, cardamom seeds and sugar and season with salt.

Heat the ghee in a kadhai or large pan over medium heat, add the aniseed, bay leaves and dried red chillies and stir-fry for about 1 minute, or until the chillies turn a shade darker. Add the mashed arum stalks and mix well. Cover and cook for about 5 minutes, or until the oil separates out and rises to the surface. Add the ground coconut and milk and mix well.

※

—

Mochar Paturi
Banana Flowers Wrapped
in Banana Leaves

Origin West Bengal
Preparation time 20–30 minutes, plus soaking time
Cooking time 20 minutes
Serves 5

1 large banana leaf (optional)
250g / 9oz banana flowers
1¼ teaspoons ground turmeric
200g / 7oz wax gourd, de-seeded and cut into dice
125g / 4¼oz (1 medium) onion, chopped
½ teaspoon chilli powder
6 green chillies, de-seeded and chopped
salt

For the mustard paste

125g / 4¼oz (¾ cup) yellow and black mustard seeds
2 green chillies, de-seeded and chopped
1 teaspoon sugar
125ml / 4½fl oz (½ cup) mustard oil, plus extra for oiling

If using the banana leaf, soften the leaf (see page 174) and cut into 10 pieces the size of your tawa or griddle. Alternatively, use foil.

Peel the red covering sheaths off the banana flowers and pick out the yellow flowers. Remove the stamens from the centre and the tough calyx at the bottom. Chop the tender flower petals and soak them in water with 1 teaspoon of turmeric for at least 1 hour, and preferably overnight. Drain and squeeze out the water.

For the mustard paste, put the mustard seeds, 2 chillies, the sugar, 2 tablespoons water and the mustard oil in a blender or mortar and season with salt. Process or pound with a pestle to make a paste.

Put the prepared banana flowers, wax gourd, onions, chilli powder, the rest of the turmeric, 6 green chilies and the mustard paste in a large bowl and mix together.

Place 5 pieces of banana leaf on an oiled tawa or griddle and spoon the vegetable mixture on top. Cover with the remaining 5 pieces of leaf. Tuck the edges of the top pieces under the vegetable mixture, then bring the ends of the lower 5 pieces up and tie over the top to make a parcel.

Place the tawa or griddle over high heat and chargrill until the leaves burn off one by one, to leave the last leaf. Flip the parcel over carefully and repeat the process. When ready to serve, open the parcel.

※ / 📷 p.391

—

Nadru Yakhani
Lotus Root Curry

Origin Jammu and Kashmir
Preparation time 15 minutes
Cooking time 35 minutes
Serves 4

500g / 1lb 2oz lotus roots
3½ tablespoons ghee
2 black cardamom pods
4 green cardamom pods
5 cloves
2 cinnamon sticks, about 2.5cm / 1 inch long
1 teaspoon ground aniseed
1 teaspoon ground ginger
250ml / 8fl oz (1 cup) natural (plain) yoghurt
salt

Cook the lotus roots in a pan of boiling water for 10 minutes, or until half done.

Heat the ghee in another pan over low heat, add the whole spices together with the aniseed and ground ginger, then season with salt and cook for about 10 minutes stirring constantly. Add the lotus roots, reduce the heat and simmer for a further 10 minutes, or until tender. Stir in the yoghurt and simmer over low heat for 2 minutes.

Dum Nadru
Spicy Baked Lotus Roots

Origin Jammu and Kashmir
Preparation time 20 minutes
Cooking time 20 minutes
Serves 4

150g / 5oz (⅔ cup) ghee or vegetable oil
500g / 1lb 2oz lotus roots, cut diagonally
500g / 1lb 2oz (4 medium) potatoes, cut in half
pinch of asafoetida
4 cloves
1 teaspoon cumin seeds
500g / 1lb 2oz (3½ cups) peas, shelled if fresh
2 green chillies de-seeded (optional) and chopped
1 teaspoon chilli powder
2 teaspoons ground coriander
1 × 2.5-cm / 1-inch piece fresh ginger, peeled and chopped
1 teaspoon ground ginger
2 teaspoons sugar
1 teaspoon Kashmiri Garam Masala (see page 56)
salt

Heat 125g / 4½ oz (about ½ cup) ghee or oil in a large, heavy-based frying pan (skillet) over medium heat, add the lotus roots and potatoes and fry for about 5 minutes, or until light brown. Remove from the heat and set aside.

Heat the remaining ghee or oil in another large pan over medium heat, add the asafoetida, cloves and cumin seeds and stir-fry for about 1 minute, or until the seeds start to splutter. Add the lotus roots, potatoes, peas, 250ml / 8fl oz (1 cup) water, the rest of the spices and the sugar. Season with salt and simmer for 15 minutes, tossing the vegetables occasionally, or until soft.

Gajar Matar
Peas & Carrots

Origin Punjab
Preparation time 25 minutes
Cooking time 20–25 minutes
Serves 4

2½ tablespoons vegetable oil or ghee
1 teaspoon cumin seeds
2 onions, chopped
2 green chillies, de-seeded and chopped
1 clove garlic, chopped
1 × 1-cm / ½-inch piece fresh ginger, peeled and chopped
1 teaspoon ground coriander
1 teaspoon ground cumin
½ teaspoon chilli powder
1 tomato, chopped
250g / 9oz (1¾ cups) peas, shelled if fresh
125g / 4¼oz (2 medium) carrots, cut into dice
salt

Heat the oil or ghee in a large, heavy-based pan over high heat, then reduce the heat, add the cumin seeds and stir-fry for 30 seconds, or until they start to splutter. Add the onions and fry over medium heat for about 5–7 minutes, or until golden brown.

Add the chillies, garlic and ginger and stir-fry for 2 minutes. Add the ground spices, then season with salt and stir-fry for a further 2 minutes. Sprinkle in 3 tablespoons water and stir. Continue cooking the spices for a further 2 minutes, then add the chopped tomato and cook for 2–3 minutes. Add the peas and carrots, reduce the heat to low, cover and cook for about 5–8 minutes, or until the vegetables are done.

Gogji
Black Cumin-flavoured Turnips

Origin Jammu and Kashmir
Preparation time 20 minutes, plus soaking time
Cooking time 30–40 minutes
Serves 4–6

500 g / 1lb 2oz (4 medium) turnips, peeled
    and cut into quarters

2 tablespoons Kashmiri red chilli powder

vegetable oil, for shallow-frying

3 teaspoons ground turmeric

5 cinnamon sticks, about 2.5cm / 1 inch long

8 green cardamom pods

5 black cardamom pods

1 tablespoon Fried Onion Paste (see page 57)

1 tablespoon garlic water

125g / 4½oz (½ cup) ghee

1½ tablespoons sugar

½ teaspoon black cumin seeds

salt

Put the turnips in a bowl or shallow dish, add
1 teaspoon salt and mix together. Set aside for about
15 minutes, then rinse and pat dry on kitchen paper
(paper towels).

Put the chilli powder in a small bowl, add
4 tablespoons water and mix together.

Heat enough oil for shallow-frying in a kadhai or
deep, heavy-based pan over medium heat, add the
turnips and shallow-fry for 5–7 minutes, or until
reddish brown. Remove with a slotted spoon and
drain on kitchen paper (paper towels).

Bring 500ml / 18fl oz (2¼ cups) water to the boil in
a deep, heavy-based pan. Add the turmeric, cinnamon
sticks, cardamom pods, fried onion paste, Kashmiri
chilli powder mixture, garlic water and ghee and
season with salt. Continue to boil for about 8 minutes.

Add the fried turnips and sugar to the pan and cook
for about 15–20 minutes, or until the turnips are
tender. Sprinkle over the black cumin seeds and
simmer for about 3 minutes.

Mujh
Radishes in Thick Yoghurt Sauce

Origin Jammu and Kashmir
Preparation time 15 minutes, plus cooling time
Cooking time 15–20 minutes
Serves 4

1 tablespoon mustard oil

400g / 14oz (3½ cups) mooli (daikon), sliced into
    discs, about 1cm / ½ inch thick

pinch of asafoetida

1 teaspoon Kashmiri red chilli powder

250ml / 8fl oz (1 cup) natural (plain) yoghurt, whisked

1 teaspoon sugar

1 teaspoon ground ginger

1½ teaspoons ground aniseed

1 teaspoon Kashmiri Garam Masala (see page 56)

salt

Heat the oil in a heavy-based pan over high heat.
When hot, remove from the heat and allow to cool
for a short while. Reheat the oil over medium heat,
add the mooli and stir-fry for 1–2 minutes, or until
light brown. Remove from the pan with a slotted
spoon and set aside.

In the same oil, add the asafoetida and chilli
powder and stir-fry for a few seconds, then reduce
the heat to low, add the yoghurt, sugar and season
with salt. Continue cooking for 5–7 minutes,
stirring constantly to make sure it does not curdle.
When the oil separates out, add the fried radish
pieces and 250ml / 8fl oz (1 cup) water. Add the
ground ginger and aniseed and bring to the boil.
Cook over medium heat for about 5 minutes, then
sprinkle over the garam masala and stir.

Munakkaigguru
Drumstick Curry

Origin Tamil Nadu
Preparation time 30 minutes, plus cooling time
Cooking time 30 minutes
Serves 6

250g / 9oz (4 small) potatoes

6 (vegetable) drumsticks, cut into 6-cm / 2½-inch
    pieces and tied in bundles

3 tablespoons vegetable oil

3 onions, sliced

2 tomatoes, chopped

1 teaspoon Ginger Paste (see page 57)

1 teaspoon Garlic Paste (see page 57)

¼ teaspoon ground turmeric

1 teaspoon chilli powder

1 teaspoon ground coriander

1 teaspoon ground cumin

3 green chillies, slit in half lengthways and de-seeded

1 bunch coriander (cilantro) leaves, chopped

250ml / 8fl oz (1 cup) coconut milk, fresh
    (see page 781) or canned

1 tablespoon lime juice

Cook the potatoes in a pan of boiling water for
about 10 minutes, or until soft. Drain, allow to cool,
then peel off the skins.

Bring 500ml / 18fl oz (2¼ cups) water to the boil in
a large, heavy-based pan, add the drumsticks and
cook for 10 minutes, or until soft. Drain, reserving
250ml / 8fl oz (1 cup) water.

Heat the oil in a large, heavy-based pan over
medium heat, add the onions and fry for about
5–7 minutes, or until golden. Add the potatoes,
tomatoes, ginger and garlic pastes and the ground
spices and fry well. Add the drumsticks and the
reserved water and bring to the boil. Cook for
5–10 minutes, then reduce the heat, add the chillies,
coriander leaves and the coconut milk and simmer
for a few minutes. Stir in the lime juice and remove
from the heat.

Vazhai Thandu Kari
Banana Stem Curry

Origin Tamil Nadu
Preparation time 20 minutes, plus standing time
Cooking time 10–15 minutes
Serves 4

1 x 30-cm / 12-inch long banana stem

2 teaspoons moong dal, rinsed and drained

250ml / 8fl oz (1 cup) sour buttermilk

1 teaspoon vegetable oil

½ teaspoon mustard seeds

1 teaspoon urad dal, rinsed and drained

1 dried red chilli

2 teaspoons grated fresh coconut

salt

Remove the outer skin from the banana stem and
slice it, then cut the slices into pieces. Add the
moong dal and buttermilk to the chopped stems,
then season with salt and mix well. Set aside for
about 15 minutes.

Heat the oil in a large, heavy-based pan over
medium heat, add the mustard seeds and stir-fry for
about 1 minute, or until they start to splutter. Add
the urad dal and dried red chilli and stir-fry for
1 minute. Reduce the heat to low.

Add the buttermilk and vegetable mixture to the pan,
and keep stirring over low heat for about 10 minutes,
or until the banana stem is cooked. Add the grated
coconut and mix well, then simmer for a further
2 minutes before serving.

Kachche Kele ke Kofte
Spicy Green Banana Balls in Sauce

Origin Hyderabad
Preparation time 40 minutes
Cooking time 15–18 minutes
Serves 4

400g / 14oz (2¾ cups) peas, shelled if fresh
500g / 1lb 2oz unripe green bananas
1½ teaspoons ground turmeric
3 tablespoons green chilli paste
1½ tablespoons Kashmiri Garam Masala (see page 56)
2 tablespoons gram (chickpea) flour
125ml / 4½fl oz (½ cup) vegetable oil, for deep-frying
1 tablespoon vegetable oil or ghee
1 teaspoon ground cumin
1 teaspoon cumin seeds
250ml / 8fl oz (1 cup) hung natural (plain) yoghurt (see page 793), whisked
1 large sprig coriander (cilantro) leaves, chopped
salt

For the spice paste

1 teaspoon cumin seeds
1 tablespoon ground coriander
80g / 2 ¾oz (1 cup) grated coconut
4–6 green chillies
2 tablespoons sugar

Cook the peas in a pan of boiling water for 5–7 minutes, or until soft. Drain, return to the pan and mash with a wooden spatula or potato masher. Set aside.

Boil the bananas in a pan of boiling water for about 5–7 minutes, then drain, allow to cool slightly and peel off the skins. Put the bananas in a large bowl and mash with a potato masher or fork, then mix in the turmeric, green chilli paste, garam masala and gram flour, and season with salt. Divide the mixture into equal portions and roll into balls or shape like small sausages.

Heat the oil for deep-frying in a kadhai or deep, heavy-based pan to 180°C/350°F, or until a cube of bread browns in 30 seconds, then reduce the heat. Working in batches, carefully lower the koftas into the hot oil and deep-fry for about 1–2 minutes, or until golden brown. Remove with a slotted spoon and drain on kitchen paper (paper towels).

To make the spice paste, put all the ingredients in a blender or food processor and process to make a paste.

Put the ground cumin in a small bowl, add 2 tablespoons water and stir together.

Heat the ghee in a frying pan (skillet) over medium heat, add the cumin seeds and stir-fry for 1 minute, or until they start to splutter. Add the cumin mixture and stir fry for about 2 minutes. Remove from the heat and slowly stir in the yoghurt.

Return the pan to the heat, add the mashed peas with the spice paste, and cook for 2 minutes. Pour in 250ml / 8fl oz (1 cup) water and bring to the boil, then reduce the heat and simmer for about 2 minutes. Gently lower the koftas into the sauce and simmer for 2 minutes. Add the coriander, remove from the heat and adjust the seasoning.

Rotuai
Bamboo Shoots with Green Chillies

Origin Tribal North East India
Preparation time 10 minutes
Cooking time 30 minutes
Serves 4

500g / 1lb 2oz tender bamboo shoots
20–25 green chillies
salt

Bring 1.5 litres / 2½ pints (6¼ cups) water to the boil in a large, heavy-based pan. Add the bamboo shoots and green chillies, then reduce the heat and simmer for about 20 minutes until tender.

Drain and reserve the chillies. Put the chillies with a little salt in a small blender or food processor and process to make a smooth paste. Cut the bamboo shoots into 5-cm / 2-inch pieces and mix with the chilli paste before serving.

Gaderi ki Dahidali Subzi
Yam in Yoghurt Sauce

Origin Uttarakhand
Preparation time 30 minutes
Cooking time 35 minutes
Serves 4–6

125ml / 4½fl oz (½ cup) mustard oil

1kg / 2 ¼lb yam, peeled and cut into small pieces

500ml / 18fl oz (2¼ cups) natural (plain) yoghurt,
   whisked

salt

For the spice paste
4–5 dried red chillies

2 teaspoons coriander seeds

1 teaspoon ground turmeric

For the tempering
1 tablespoon ghee

3–4 dried red chillies

To garnish
8 tablespoons coriander (cilantro) leaves

2–3 green chillies

To make the spice paste, put all the ingredients in
a small blender or food processor and process to
make a rough paste.

Heat the oil in a kadhai or deep, heavy-based pan
over high heat, then reduce the heat. Add the yam
pieces and stir-fry for about 1 minute, then add the
spice paste and season with salt. Gently stir in the
yoghurt, then pour in about 500ml / 18fl oz (2¼ cups)
water, reduce the heat to low and simmer for about
30 minutes.

Heat the ghee for the tempering in a small pan over
low heat, add the dried red chillies and fry for
2 minutes, or until the chillies turn a shade darker.
Pour over the yam and cover for about 30 seconds.
Stir and garnish with coriander leaves and whole
green chillies.

Kappa Puzhukku
Cassava Porridge

Origin Kerala
Preparation time 20 minutes
Cooking time 35–40 minutes
Serves 6

500g / 1lb 2oz (2½ cups) cassava, thickly peeled
   and cut into 1-cm / ½-inch pieces wearing gloves
   (see below)

salt

For the coconut paste
1 coconut, grated

6 shallots, chopped

10–12 dried red chillies

¼ teaspoon cumin seeds

1 teaspoon ground turmeric

For the tempering
½ tablespoon vegetable oil

1 teaspoon mustard seeds

1 small sprig curry leaves

Cassava contains a toxin under the skin, which
cooking destroys, but when peeling the root it
is advisable to remove a thick scraping of the
skin and to wash your hands thoroughly after
preparation.

To make the coconut paste, put all the ingredients
in a food processor or blender and process to make
a coarse paste.

Cook the cassava in a large, heavy-based pan of
boiling water over high heat for 30 minutes, or until
cooked. Drain, return to the pan, then season with
salt and mash with a potato masher.

Return the pan to low heat, add the coconut paste
and blend well, then cook for 5 minutes, stirring
2 or 3 times.

Heat the oil for the tempering in a small frying pan
(skillet) over medium heat, add the mustard seeds
and stir-fry for about 1 minute, or until they start
to splutter. Add the remaining ingredients and stir-
fry for a further 1 minute. Pour over the cassava,
mix well and serve.

Thor Muri Ghonto
Banana Stem Cooked with Rice

Origin West Bengal
Preparation time 45 minutes, plus soaking and
standing time
Cooking time 35–40 minutes
Serves 4

25-cm / 10-inch long banana stem, cut into
    6-cm / 2½-inch pieces

pinch of ground turmeric

200g / 7oz (1 cup) basmati rice, rinsed and drained

½ tablespoon raisins

1–2 tablespoons vegetable oil

2 potatoes, cut into 1-cm / ½-inch dice

1½ tablespoons poppy seeds

½ tablespoon ground cumin

½ tablespoon ground coriander

1 teaspoon chilli powder

100g / 3½oz (scant ½ cup) ghee, plus 2 extra
    tablespoons (optional)

4 bay leaves

4–5 green cardamom pods

6–8 cloves

1 cinnamon stick, about 5cm / 2 inches long

salt

Put the banana stem into a large bowl and mix in the
turmeric, then season with salt. Set aside for about
1 hour.

Soak the basmati rice in a large bowl of water for
about 10–15 minutes. Drain and dry the rice out as
much as possible by spreading it out on a large plate.

Put the raisins in a bowl, pour in 125ml / 4½fl oz
(½ cup) water and soak until required.

Heat the oil in a large, heavy-based pan over
medium heat, add the potatoes and fry for about
7–8 minutes, or until golden brown. Remove
from the pan and set aside. Drain the raisins and
add them to the pan. Stir-fry for about 2 minutes.

Put the poppy seeds in a spice grinder or mortar and
process or pound with a pestle until ground. Transfer
to a bowl and mix in the ground cumin powder,
coriander, chilli powder and 2 tablespoons water.

Heat the ghee in a kadhai, wok or large, heavy-
based pan over medium heat, add the bay leaves,
cardamom pods, cloves and cinnamon and stir
fry for 2–3 minutes, then add the poppy seed mixture
and fry for about 1–2 minutes, or until the spices
change colour and smell fragrant. Add the rice and
stir-fry for 10 minutes.

Squeeze out all the water from the banana stems and
knead it with your hands to a pulp. Add to the pan,
mix well with the rice, then pour in about 500ml /
18fl oz (2¼ cups) water and season with salt. Cover
and simmer over medium heat for about 15 minutes,
or until the rice is nearly done.

Add the fried potatoes and raisins, stir, then reduce
the heat, cover and cook for a further 3–5 minutes,
or until the rice is done. If the dish appears too dry,
add 2 tablespoons ghee. Remove from the heat and
serve hot.

Hingwali Chukandar
Beetroot (Beet) with Asafoetida

Origin Jammu and Kashmir
Preparation time 20 minutes
Cooking time 35 minutes
Serves 4

¼ teaspoon asafoetida
1 tablespoon ground coriander
½ teaspoon ground turmeric
1 teaspoon chilli powder
2 large beetroot (beet), peeled and cut into dice
2 large potatoes, cut into small cubes
2½ tablespoons natural (plain) yoghurt
2 tablespoons vegetable oil
1 teaspoon fenugreek seeds
1 teaspoon aniseed seeds
1 teaspoon ajwain seeds
2 green chillies, de-seeded and chopped
1 teaspoon ajwain seeds, ground
1 tablespoon lime juice (optional)
salt

Put the asafoetida in a small bowl, add 2 tablespoons water and mix together. Set aside.

Put the ground coriander, turmeric and chilli powder in a medium-sized bowl, pour in 750ml / 1¼ pints (3¼ cups) water and stir together, then strain through a sieve (strainer) into a large, heavy-based pan and bring to the boil. Add the vegetables, reduce the heat and simmer for 15–20 minutes, or until they are soft. Remove from the heat, add the yoghurt and season with salt. Return to a low heat and simmer gently for a further 5 minutes.

Heat the oil in a large, heavy-based pan over high heat, then reduce the heat. Add the fenugreek, aniseed and ajwain seeds and stir-fry for 1 minute, or until they start to splutter. Pour over the vegetables, then cover and simmer for a few minutes, before removing from the heat.

Add the asafoetida mixture to the pan, stir, cover, return to the heat and cook for a further 2 minutes. Add the chillies and ground ajwain and stir in the lime juice if the beetroot is too sweet.

Artikai Kura
Curried Bananas with Coconut

Origin Tamil Nadu
Preparation time 20 minutes, plus cooling time
Cooking time 15–20 minutes
Serves 4

4 unripe green bananas
½ cup desiccated (dried flaked) coconut
pinch of ground turmeric
1 tablespoon gram (chickpea) flour
6 tablespoons vegetable oil or ghee
4 cloves
1 teaspoon Garlic Paste (see page 57)
2 onions, chopped
4 green chillies, de-seeded and chopped
salt

Cook the bananas with the skin on in a large, heavy-based pan of boiling water for about 7 minutes, or until soft. Remove from the pan and allow to cool, then peel. Cut each banana into 2.5-cm / 1-inch pieces.

Mix the grated coconut and turmeric together in a bowl and season with salt. Add the gram flour to the coconut mixture. Set aside.

Heat the oil or ghee in a large frying pan (skillet) over medium heat, add the cloves and garlic paste and stir-fry for about 1 minute. Add the onions and chillies and stir-fry for about 10 minutes until lightly browned, then add the bananas and coconut mixture and fry for 2 minutes.

Artikai Podi
Savoury Green Bananas

Origin Tamil Nadu
Preparation time 20 minutes, plus soaking time
Cooking time 20–25 minutes
Serves 4–6

---

walnut-sized lump of tamarind

1 tablespoon urad dal, rinsed and drained

1 tablespoon chana dal, rinsed and drained

10–12 curry leaves

4 dried red chillies, broken into pieces

½ teaspoon mustard seeds, ground

4 unripe green bananas

1 × 2.5-cm / 1-inch piece fresh ginger, peeled
  and ground

salt

For the tempering

2 tablespoons sesame oil

1 teaspoon cumin seeds

few green chillies

Put the tamarind in a bowl, add 2 tablespoons water
and soak for 10 minutes. Using your hands, mix well
then squeeze out the pulp through a sieve (strainer).
Set the extract aside and discard the pulp.

Heat a tawa, griddle or dry frying pan (skillet) over
medium heat, add the dals, curry leaves, broken red
chillies and mustard seeds and stir-fry briefly until
roasted and fragrant. Transfer to a spice grinder and
process to make a coarse powder.

Peel and cut the bananas into 2.5-cm / 1-inch long
pieces. Place the pieces in a large, heavy-based pan,
pour in 125ml / 4½fl oz (½ cup) water and cook over
low heat for 5 minutes. Add the ground spices and
ginger, and season with salt, then cook, adding a
little water if it sticks to the base (bottom) of the
pan, for about 15 minutes. Add the tamarind extract
and simmer for a few minutes.

Heat the oil for the tempering in a small frying pan
over medium heat, add the cumin seeds and chillies
and stir-fry for about 1–2 minutes, or until the seeds
start to splutter and the chillies change colour. Add
to the cooked mixture and mix well, then simmer
together for 1 minute. Serve hot.

Artikai Vepudu
Savoury Bananas

Origin Hyderabad/Andhra Pradesh
Preparation time 15 minutes
Cooking time 15–20 minutes
Serves 4

---

4 unripe green bananas

125ml / 4½fl oz (½ cup) vegetable oil

pinch of ground turmeric

1 tablespoon ground coriander

½ teaspoon chilli powder

¼ dried coconut, ground

1 teaspoon gram (chickpea) flour

salt

Peel and cut the bananas into slices 1cm / ½ inch
thick. Set aside.

Heat the oil in a large frying pan (skillet) over
medium heat, add the bananas and turmeric and fry
for about 12–15 minutes. Add a little water, cover and
let the bananas simmer gently for about 2 minutes.

Add the ground spices, ground coconut and gram
flour to the bananas, then season with salt and fry
for a further 2 minutes.

Chikkudu Vepudu
Stir-fried Broad (Fava) Beans

Origin Hyderabad/Andhra Pradesh
Preparation time 15 minutes
Cooking time 10 minutes
Serves 4

250g / 9oz (1⅔ cups) tender broad (fava) beans, cut into 2.5-cm / 1-inch pieces
pinch of ground turmeric
1 × 2.5-cm / 1-inch piece dried coconut, grated
1 teaspoon ground coriander
1 tablespoon fried chana dal
1 teaspoon chilli powder
1 onion, chopped
½ teaspoon ground garlic
½ teaspoon jaggery or soft brown sugar
salt

For the tempering

1½ tablespoons vegetable oil
5–6 curry leaves
¼ teaspoon mustard seeds
½ teaspoon cumin seeds
½ teaspoon urad dal, rinsed and drained
2 dried red chillies

Put the broad beans and turmeric in just enough water to cover and cook for about 8 minutes, or until tender. All the water should be absorbed while cooking.

Mix the grated coconut, ground coriander powder, fried chana dal and chilli powder together in a bowl.

Heat the oil for the tempering in a large frying pan (skillet) over high heat, add all the ingredients and stir-fry for about 30 seconds, or until the seeds start to splutter and the chillies turn a shade darker. Add the onion and stir-fry for about 2–3 minutes, then add the garlic and broad beans and fry for 2 minutes until coated with spices. Reduce the heat to low, then stir in the spice mixture and jaggery or sugar and cook for about 4 minutes.

Artikai Pachadi
Bananas in Spicy Yoghurt Sauce

Origin Tamil Nadu
Preparation time 25 minutes plus cooling time
Cooking time 10 minutes
Serves 4

2 unripe green bananas
½ teaspoon chopped ginger
pinch of ground turmeric
6 green chillies, de-seeded and ground
250ml / 8fl oz (1 cup) natural (plain) yoghurt
1 tablespoon vegetable oil
1 teaspoon urad dal, rinsed and drained
½ teaspoon chana dal, rinsed and drained
few dried red chillies
¼ teaspoon mustard seeds
salt

To garnish

1 bunch coriander (cilantro) leaves, chopped
juice of ½ lime

Cook the bananas with the skin on in a large, heavy-based pan of boiling water for about 7 minutes, or until soft. Remove from the pan and allow to cool, then peel. Cut each banana into 2.5-cm / 1-inch pieces.

Mix the chopped ginger, turmeric, green chillies and yoghurt together in a large heatproof bowl. Season with salt and add the bananas.

Heat the oil in a large, heavy-based pan over medium heat, add the dals, dried red chillies and mustard seeds and stir-fry for about 1 minute, or until the seeds start to splutter and the dals turn golden. Pour over the yoghurt mixture and cover immediately to retain the aroma. After about 5 minutes, uncover and garnish with chopped coriander leaves and lime juice and serve immediately.

Chowgara
Mixed Vegetables from Deccan

Origin Hyderabad
Preparation time 1½–2 hours
Cooking time 20–30 minutes
Serves 6

about 4–6 tablespoons vegetable oil, for frying
100g / 3½oz (2 small) potatoes, cut into pieces
250g / 9oz (1¾ cups) peas, shelled if fresh
150g / 5oz (2 medium) carrots, cut into pieces
150g / 5oz (1⅓ cups) French (green) beans, topped and tailed (trimmed), then cut into small pieces
200g / 7oz (1½ cups) cauliflower, cut into florets
150g / 5oz (1¾ cups) aubergines (eggplant), trimmed and cut into medium-sized pieces
½ teaspoon ground turmeric
1 teaspoon chilli powder
2 green cardamom pods
4 cloves
1 bay leaf
1 cinnamon stick, about 2.5cm / 1 inch long
½ teaspoon caraway seeds
100g / 3½oz (1 small) onion, sliced
1 teaspoon Ginger Paste (see page 57)
1 teaspoon Garlic Paste (see page 57)
125ml / 4½fl oz (½ cup) natural (plain) yoghurt, whisked
1 tablespoon lemon juice
salt

Heat half the oil in a large, heavy-based pan over medium heat and fry the potatoes, peas, carrots, beans, cauliflower and aubergines (eggplant) separately for about 5–10 minutes, or until more than half done. Set aside.

Put the turmeric and chilli powder in a small bowl, add 2 tablespoons water and mix together. Set aside.

Put the cardamom pods, cloves, bay leaf, cinnamon and caraway seeds in a mortar and pound with a pestle, or grind in a spice grinder. Set aside.

Heat the remaining oil over medium heat, add the onion and fry for 3 minutes, or until light brown. Now add the ginger and garlic pastes and fry for about 1 minute. Season with salt and add the turmeric mixture. Add the fried vegetables, then stir in the yoghurt, cover and cook over medium heat for about 5 minutes, or until the vegetables are done. Sprinkle over the ground spices and lemon juice, and season.

Aloo Gobi Methi ka Tuk
Cauliflower with Fenugreek & Potatoes

Origin New
Preparation time 25 minutes
Cooking time 15–20 minutes
Serves 4

150g / 5oz (1 medium) potato, cut into quarters
750g / 1lb 10oz (1 medium head) cauliflower, cut into medium-sized florets
6 tablespoons vegetable oil
1 teaspoon mustard seeds
20–25 curry leaves
3½ teaspoons Ginger Paste (see page 57)
1½ teaspoons Garlic Paste (see page 57)
200g / 7oz (3⅓ cups) fenugreek leaves, chopped
1 teaspoon yellow chilli powder
1 teaspoon amchoor
½ teaspoon ground cumin powder
½ teaspoon coarsely ground black pepper
generous pinch of dried fenugreek leaves, crumbled
salt

Cook the potato quarters in a large pan of boiling water for about 10 minutes, or until still quite firm. Drain and set aside.

Meanwhile, blanch the cauliflower in another pan of boiling water for a few minutes. Drain and set aside.

Heat the oil in a pan over medium heat, add the mustard seeds and stir-fry for about 1 minute, or until they start to splutter. Add the curry leaves and stir-fry for a few seconds, then add the ginger and garlic pastes and stir-fry for about 1–2 minutes, or until the moisture has evaporated.

Add the fenugreek leaves and stir-fry for about 15 seconds, then add the cauliflower and yellow chilli powder and season with salt. Stir, then reduce the heat to low, cover and cook for about 5 minutes.

Uncover, increase the heat, add the potatoes and stir-fry for 2–3 minutes. Sprinkle over the remaining ground spices and the dried fenugreek, then stir, remove from the heat and adjust the seasoning, if necessary.

Subz Khara Masala
Mixed Vegetables with Whole Spices

Origin Awadh
Preparation time 30 minutes
Cooking time 25 minutes
Serves 4–6

150ml / ¼ pint (⅔ cup) groundnut (peanut) oil

7 teaspoons Ginger Paste (see page 57)

3 teaspoons Garlic Paste (see page 57)

100g / 3½oz (½ cup) spring onions (scallions),
    trimmed and chopped

100g / 3½oz (½ cup) French (green) beans, topped
    and tailed (trimmed), then cut diagonally
    into small pieces

100g / 3½oz (⅔ cup) peas, shelled, if fresh

100g / 3½oz (⅔ cup) carrots, cut into dice

150g / 3½oz potatoes, cut into cubes

250g / 3½oz cauliflower, cut into florets

½ teaspoon ground turmeric

1 teaspoon chilli powder

100g / 3½oz (1 small) tomato

4 green chillies, de-seeded and chopped

4 dried red chillies

20g / ¾oz (½ cup) chopped coriander (cilantro) leaves

250ml / 8fl oz (1 cup) natural (plain) yoghurt, whisked

4 tablespoons chopped fenugreek leaves

salt

Heat the oil in a large, heavy-based pan over
medium heat, add the ginger and garlic pastes and
stir-fry for about 30 seconds. Add the spring onions
and fry for 1 minute. Add the beans, peas, carrots,
potatoes and cauliflower and stir-fry for about
1 minute, then add the turmeric and chilli powder
and stir to mix.

Add the tomatoes to the pan with both chillies and
the coriander and stir-fry for about 1 minute. Slowly
stir in the yoghurt, then add the fenugreek and
stir again. Add 375ml / 13fl oz (1½ cups) water, bring
almost to the boil, then reduce the heat and simmer
for about 15 minutes, or until all the vegetables are
cooked and the moisture has evaporated. Adjust the
seasoning, if necessary.

Istoo
Vegetable Stew

Origin Kerala
Preparation time 15 minutes
Cooking time 20 minutes
Serves 6

250g / 9oz mixed vegetables of your choice, chopped

1 onion, chopped

250ml / 8fl oz (1 cup) coconut milk, fresh
    (see page 781) or canned

10–15 curry leaves

2 tablespoons vegetable oil

1 × 2.5-cm / 1-inch piece fresh ginger, peeled
    and chopped

1 teaspoon ground black pepper

salt

Cook the vegetables in a large pan of lightly salted
boiling water for about 10 minutes, or until soft. Stir
in the coconut milk, add the curry leaves and simmer
for 1 minute.

Heat the oil in a small pan over medium heat, add
the ginger and stir-fry for about 1 minute. Pour into
the vegetables, mix well, then add the black pepper
and serve.

Pulinkari
Sour Vegetable Curry

Origin Kerala
Preparation time 20–30 minutes
Cooking time 20–30 minutes
Serves 6

200g / 7oz (2 cups) pumpkin, peeled, de-seeded and
   cut into 2.5-cm / 1-inch cubes

100g / 3½oz (¾ cup) cucumber, peeled and cut into
   2.5-cm / 1-inch cubes

1 tablespoon Tamarind Extract (see page 58)

1 tablespoon vegetable oil

1 teaspoon mustard seeds

2 green chillies, de-seeded and chopped

salt

For the coconut-spice paste

1 coconut, grated

10 dried red chillies

1 teaspoon fenugreek seeds

Cook the pumpkin and cucumber in a large pan
of lightly salted water for about 10 minutes, or
until tender.

To make the coconut spice paste, put the coconut in
a dry frying pan (skillet) and stir-fry over medium
heat for about 1 minute. Add the red chillies and
fenugreek seeds and stir-fry for another minute, or
until roasted. Transfer to a small blender or food
processor and process until ground.

Stir the tamarind extract into the pan with the
vegetables, add the coconut-spice paste, then bring
to the boil and remove from the heat immediately.

Heat the oil in a small frying pan over medium heat,
add the mustard seeds and chillies and stir-fry for
about 1 minute, or until the seeds start to splutter,
then pour over the cooked vegetables.

Papad Methi ki Subzi
Rajasthani Fenugreek

Origin Rajasthan
Preparation time 20 minutes
Cooking time 15 minutes
Serves 4

---

8 papad

1 teaspoon ground coriander

1 teaspoon ground turmeric

1 teaspoon chilli powder

3 tablespoons vegetable oil

1 teaspoon cumin seeds

1 tablespoon Ginger Paste (see page 57)

2 green chillies, de-seeded and chopped

100g / 3 ½oz (1 small) tomato, chopped

500g / 1lb 2oz fenugreek leaves, chopped

1 tablespoon lemon juice

salt

Roast the papad in a dry frying pan (skillet) until
crisp, then set aside.

Put the ground coriander, chilli powder and
turmeric in a small bowl, add 2 tablespoons water
and stir together.

Heat the oil in a large, heavy-based pan over
medium heat, add the cumin seeds and stir-fry for
about 1 minute, or until they start to splutter. Add
the ginger paste, chillies and ground spice mixture
and stir-fry for about 1 minute.

Add the tomato and stir-fry for about 5 minutes, or
until the tomato is completely mashed, then add the
fenugreek and season with salt. Stir-fry for a few
minutes until the fenugreek is cooked.

Crush 6 of the papads and add to the pan with the
lemon juice. Stir gently for about 1 minute, then
remove from the heat and adjust the seasoning, if
necessary. Break the remaining papads into pieces
and use as a garnish.

Shukto
Mixed Vegetables with Bitter Gourd

Origin West Bengal
Preparation time 1 hour
Cooking time 20 minutes
Serves 6

1 teaspoon black mustard seeds
2 tablespoons mustard oil
12 small matar dal bori or 2 tablespoons masala
100g / 3½oz (¾ cup) sweet potatoes, peeled and cut into 4-cm / 1½-inch pieces
100g / 3½oz (1 medium) potato, peeled and cut into 4-cm / 1½-inch pieces
100g / 3½oz (vegetable) drumstick, cleaned and cut into 4-cm / 1½-inch lengthways pieces
100g / 3½oz (1 small) bitter gourd, peeled and cut into 4-cm / 1½-inch pieces
100g / 3½oz (1 cup) mooli (daikon), peeled and cut into 4-cm / 1½-inch pieces
100g / 3½oz plantains, peeled and cut into 4-cm / 1½-inch pieces
100g / 3½oz (⅔ cup) broad (fava) beans, podded (shelled)
100g / 3½oz (½ small) aubergine (eggplant), trimmed and cut into pieces
2 teaspoons Ginger Paste (see page 57)
½ teaspoon ajwain seed paste
2 bay leaves
1 teaspoon ghee
2 tablespoons milk
Paanch Phoren (see page 55), for sprinkling
salt

Put the black mustard seeds and 1 teaspoon water in a small blender and process to make a paste. Set aside. Heat the mustard oil in a kadhai, wok or deep, heavy-based pan over high heat, then reduce the heat. Add the matar dal bor and fry for a few minutes, then remove from the pan and set aside.

Add the sweet potatoes, potatoes, drumsticks and bitter gourd to the pan and stir-fry for about 2 minutes. Add the rest of the vegetables and stir-fry for a further 2 minutes. Put the ginger paste, black mustard paste and ajwain seed paste in a bowl and mix in a little water, then add to the vegetables. Season with salt, cover and cook for about 10 minutes, or until the vegetables are done. Add the bori, bay leaves and ghee and cook for a further 2 minutes. Add the milk, cover and remove the pan from the heat. Sprinkle with paanch phoren.

Deewani Handi
Mixed Vegetables (III)

Origin Awadh
Preparation time 30 minutes
Cooking time 45 minutes
Serves 4–6

100ml / 3½fl oz (½ cup) vegetable oil
pinch of asafoetida
½ teaspoon cumin seeds
¼ teaspoon fenugreek seeds
500g / 1lb 2oz (2 small) aubergines (eggplant), trimmed and finely chopped
125g / 4¼oz (4 cups) spinach, finely chopped
30g / 1¼oz (½ cup) fenugreek leaves, finely chopped
1 mooli (daikon), peeled and finely chopped
1 onion, finely chopped
1 tablespoon soy beans, fresh or frozen
125ml / 4½fl oz (½ cup) milk
½ teaspoon chilli powder
1 teaspoon ground turmeric
1 teaspoon ground coriander
1 teaspoon ground ginger
1 × 2.5-cm / 1-inch piece fresh ginger, peeled and crushed
salt
coriander (cilantro) leaves, to garnish

Heat the oil in a large, heavy-based pan over medium heat, add the asafoetida, cumin and fenugreek seeds and stir-fry for about 1 minute, or until the seeds start to splutter. Immediately add the vegetables, then cover and cook for about 20 minutes, or until the liquid from the vegetables has evaporated. With a ladle or wooden spoon, keep stirring the vegetables so they fry well.

Add the milk and the remaining spices to the pan, then season with salt and stir-fry for a few more minutes until the milk is absorbed by the vegetables and oil appears on the surface. Remove from the heat and garnish with coriander leaves.

Fish and Seafood

Maachher Jhol
Spicy Fish with Vegetables

Origin West Bengal
Preparation 30 minutes
Cooking time 30 minutes
Serves 4

500g / 1lb 2oz rui or any other firm white fish, such
    as red snapper or halibut, cleaned and rinsed
1½ teaspoons ground turmeric
1 teaspoon chilli powder
1½ teaspoons ground cumin
1½ teaspoons ground coriander
250ml / 8fl oz (1 cup) mustard oil
4 potatoes, cut into quarters
pinch of asafoetida
6 boris
150g / 5oz wax gourd, peeled, de-seeded
    and sliced lengthways
100g / 3½oz (vegetable) drumsticks, cut into
    5-cm / 2-inch pieces
1 teaspoon sugar
salt

For the tempering
2 teaspoons mustard oil
1 teaspoon Paanch Phoren (see page 55)
2 dried red chillies
1 bay leaf

Cut the fish into 2.5-cm / 1-inch thick steaks with the
bone, then place in a large shallow dish and rub with
the turmeric and a little salt. Cover and set aside.

Put all the ground spices in a small bowl, pour in
750ml / 1¼ pints (3¼ cups) water and mix together.

Heat the oil in a large, heavy-based pan over
high heat, then reduce the heat. Add the asafoetida
and stir-fry for about 30 seconds, or until it
has dissolved.

Add the boris and stir-fry for 2 minutes, or until they
darken in colour. Remove with a slotted spoon and
drain on kitchen paper (paper towels).

Reduce the heat to low, then working in batches if
necessary, add the fish to the pan and fry for about
1 minute on both sides. Remove with a slotted spoon
and set aside.

Pour out all but 2 tablespoons of the oil, add the
vegetables and stir-fry for about 5 minutes. Pour
the ground spice mixture over the vegetables, add
the sugar and season with salt. Cover and continue
cooking until all the vegetables are done to your
taste. Add the fish and boris and cook for a further
5 minutes, or until cooked.

Heat the mustard oil for the tempering in a small
frying pan (skillet) over medium heat, add the
paanch phoren, dried red chillies and bay leaf and
stir-fry for about 1 minute, or until the paanch
phoren begins to splutter and smell fragrant and
the chillies turn a shade darker. Pour over the
fish and simmer for 1 minute.

Illich Maachh Annanas
Hilsa with Pineapple

Origin West Bengal
Preparation 20 minutes, plus standing time
Cooking time 25 minutes
Serves 4

600g / 1lb 5oz hilsa (shad) or other large firm fish
    fillets, such as haddock or mackerel, trimmed

1½ teaspoons ground turmeric

1 × 2.5-cm / 1-inch piece fresh ginger, peeled
    and grated

1 tablespoon aniseeds

125ml / 4½fl oz (½ cup) mustard oil

2 bay leaves

4 cloves

4 green cardamom pods

1 cinnamon stick, about 2.5cm /1 inch long

1 teaspoon chilli powder

6 slices fresh or canned pineapple, chopped

salt

Cut the fish into equal-sized pieces, then place in
a large shallow dish and rub the fish with the turmeric
and a little salt. Cover and set aside in the refrigerator
for about 30 minutes.

Put the ginger in a mortar with a little water and
pound with a pestle or process in a small blender
to make a smooth paste, then set aside. Add the
aniseeds to the mortar or blender with a little water
and pound to make a smooth paste. Set aside.

Heat 2 tablespoons mustard oil in a kadhai or large,
heavy-based frying pan (skillet) over low heat, then,
working in batches if necessary, add the fish and
lightly fry for about 1 minute on both sides. Remove
from the pan with a slotted spoon and set aside.

Heat the remaining oil in the pan over medium heat,
add the bay leaves and whole spices and stir-fry for
about 2 minutes, or until they change colour. Add the
ground spices together with the ginger and aniseed
pastes and stir-fry for about 2–3 minutes, or until
the oil separates out. Add the pineapple pieces and
season with salt.

Pour in 125ml / 4½fl oz (½ cup) water, bring to
the boil, then reduce the heat to low and simmer
for 5 minutes. Add the fish, cover and cook for
about 15 minutes, turning the fish once, taking care
it does not break, or until it is cooked.

Poshto Maachh
Fish with Poppy Seeds

Origin West Bengal
Preparation time 25 minutes plus cooling time
Cooking time 15 minutes
Serves 4

500g / 1lb 2oz pomfret (butterfish) fillets or other flat
    fish, trimmed

1 teaspoon ground turmeric

5 tablespoons mustard oil

4 dried red chillies

10 curry leaves

1 teaspoon coriander seeds

1½ tablespoons poppy seeds

1 teaspoon cumin seeds

2–3 green chillies, de-seeded and chopped

1 teaspoon sugar

salt

Cut the fish into equal-sized pieces, place in a large
shallow dish and rub with the turmeric and a little
salt. Cover and set aside.

To make the spice paste, heat the oil in a large,
heavy-based pan over high heat, then reduce the
heat. Add the dried red chillies and curry leaves and
stir-fry for about 2 minutes. Remove from the heat
and allow to cool.

When the chillies and curry leaves are cool, transfer
them to a blender, add the coriander, poppy seeds,
cumin seeds and green chillies and process, adding
a little water if necessary, to make a smooth paste.

Reheat the oil in the pan over high heat, add the
spice paste and stir-fry over high heat for 1 minute,
sprinkling with a little water to avoid burning. Pour
in 125ml / 4½fl oz (½ cup) water, bring to the boil,
add the sugar and season with salt. Stir, then add
the fish pieces, reduce the heat and simmer for
7–8 minutes, or until the fish is cooked.

Paturi Maachh
Fish in Banana Leaves

Origin West Bengal
Preparation time 25 minutes
Cooking time 25 minutes
Serves 4

banana leaves (optional)
400g /14oz any firm white fish of choice, cut into 8 fillets, trimmed
1 teaspoon yellow mustard seeds
1 teaspoon black mustard seeds
2 green chillies, de-seeded (optional) and chopped
1 teaspoon ground turmeric
125ml / 4½fl oz (½ cup) mustard oil, plus extra for cooking
1 teaspoon sugar
salt

If using banana leaves, soften the leaves (see page 174) and cut into 20-cm / 8-inch squares. Alternatively, use squares of foil.

Put the fish fillets in a large shallow dish and rub gently and evenly with salt. Cover and set aside.

Put the yellow and black mustard seeds, green chillies, turmeric, mustard oil and sugar in a blender or food processor, season with salt and process to make a smooth paste. Spread the paste evenly over the the fish.

Arrange the banana leaf or foil squares on a clean flat surface, placing one strip over the other to form a cross. Place one fillet each in the centre of the crosses and fold the strips over to form neat parcels resembling envelopes. Secure with kitchen string (twine).

Coat a tawa, griddle or non-stick frying pan (skillet) with a thin film of oil and heat over low heat. Working in batches, place the parcels in the pan and cook for 5–6 minutes gently turning once, or until the fish is cooked.

Maachher Roast
Roast Fish

Origin West Bengal
Preparation time 20 minutes, plus standing time
Cooking time 20 minutes
Serves 4

500g /1lb 2oz skinless parshey, red mullet or red snapper fillets, trimmed
½ teaspoon ground turmeric
1 onion, roughly chopped
1 × 2.5-cm / 1-inch piece fresh ginger, peeled
3 tablespoons ghee
½ teaspoon chilli powder
½ teaspoon Kashmiri red chilli powder
1 tablespoon vinegar
1 teaspoon sugar
3–4 green chillies, slit lengthways and de-seeded
salt

Using a sharp knife, score the fish on the side that had the skin, then place in a large shallow dish and rub with the turmeric and a little salt. Cover and set aside in the refrigerator for 30 minutes.

Meanwhile, put the onion and ginger in a blender or food processor and process, adding a little water if necessary, to make a paste.

Heat 2 tablespoons of the ghee in a large, heavy-based pan over medium heat, add the fish and fry for 1–2 minutes on both sides until light golden in colour. Remove from the pan with a slotted spoon and drain on kitchen paper (paper towels).

Add another tablespoon of ghee to the pan and heat over high heat, then reduce the heat. Add the chilli powders and stir-fry for about 2 minutes, or until the spices change colour. Add the vinegar and sugar and season with salt. Add the green chillies and stir-fry for 2 minutes. Pour in 125ml / 4½fl oz (½ cup) water, then place the fish gently into the pan, spooning the sauce over the fish, reduce the heat, cover and simmer for a further 5 minutes, until the fish is cooked.

Musallam Bharwan Machhali
Whole Stuffed Fish

Origin Awadh
Preparation time 30–40 minutes, plus marinating time
Cooking time 40 minutes
Serves 4

---

1 × 1-kg / 2¼-lb whole bhetki fish, or any other firm white fish, such as red snapper, cleaned

---

1 lime

---

vegetable oil, for oiling

For the filling

2 tablespoons ghee

---

3 large onions, thinly sliced

---

1 tablespoon Ginger Paste (see page 57)

---

2 teaspoons Garlic Paste (see page 57)

---

1 teaspoon chilli powder

50g / 1¾oz (1 cup) chopped mint leaves

50g / 1¾oz (1 cup) chopped coriander (cilantro) leaves

---

salt

Using a sharp knife, score the fish on both sides, place in a large shallow dish and rub salt all over, then squeeze over the lime. Cover and marinate in the refrigerator for 2 hours.

Heat the ghee in a large frying pan (skillet) over medium heat, add the onions and stir-fry for about 5–7 minutes, or until golden brown. Add the ginger and garlic pastes, chilli powder, and chopped herbs, season with salt and stir-fry for 2–3 minutes, then remove from the heat.

Stuff the fish with the mixture and secure with kitchen string (twine), then place it in a large oiled shallow kadhai or frying pan and cook over low heat for about 30 minutes.

Dum ki Machhali
Slow-cooked Aromatic Fish

Origin Awadh
Preparation time 30 minutes, plus marinating time
Cooking time 15 minutes
Serves 4

1kg / 2¼lb skinless, firm white fish fillets, trimmed

100g / 3½oz (scant ½ cup) ghee

¼ teaspoon ground cinnamon

¼ teaspoon ground nutmeg

¼ teaspoon black cumin seeds, ground

¼ teaspoon ground green cardamom

¼ teaspoon ground cloves

For the marinade

2 tablespoons desiccated (dried flaked) coconut

---

2 tablespoons poppy seeds

---

1 teaspoon mustard seeds

---

5 teaspoons Ginger Paste (see page 57)

---

3 teaspoons Garlic Paste (see page 57)

125ml / 4½fl oz (½ cup) natural (plain) yoghurt, whisked

---

1 teaspoon chilli powder

---

1 teaspoon ground cumin

---

2 tablespoons lemon juice

---

salt

To make the marinade, heat a tawa, griddle or dry frying pan (skillet), add the desiccated coconut and poppy and mustard seeds and stir-fry for about 1 minute, or until roasted and fragrant. Transfer to a blender, add a little water and process to make a moist but coarse paste. Transfer to a bowl, add the ginger and garlic pastes, yoghurt, chilli powder, ground cumin and lemon juice, then season with salt and mix well.

Put the fish fillets in a large shallow dish and rub the marinade evenly over them. Cover and marinate in the refrigerator for 1 hour.

Melt the ghee in a large frying pan over very low heat, add the marinated fish with the marinade, then add the ground spices, cover and cook for 15 minutes, or until the fish is cooked.

✳ / ⬚ p.400

Machhali Musallam
Stuffed Fish

Origin Awadh
Preparation time 1 hour
Cooking time 20 minutes
Serves 4–6

1 × 1-kg / 2-¼lb whole fish, cleaned

150ml / ¼ pint (⅔ cup) vegetable oil, plus extra
  for deep-frying and oiling

1 tablespoon gram (chickpea) flour, roasted

1 teaspoon Garam Masala (see page 31)

½ teaspoon coarsely ground black pepper, roasted

pinch of ground nutmeg

melted butter, for basting

salt

For the marinade

3 teaspoons Ginger Paste (see page 57)

1½ teaspoons Garlic Paste (see page 57)

1 teaspoon chilli powder

1 teaspoon ground cinnamon

4 tablespoons lemon juice

For the spice paste

100g / 3½oz Fried Onion Paste (see page 57)

3 tablespoons Garlic Paste (see page 57)

2 teaspoons Ginger Paste (see page 57)

250ml / 8fl oz (1 cup) natural (plain) yoghurt

1 teaspoon chilli powder

Preheat the oven to 150°C/300°G/Gas Mark 2.

Using a sharp knife, score the fish with 3 deep slashes
on each side. Place the fish in a large shallow dish.

To make the marinade, mix all the ingredients
together in a bowl and season with salt. Rub
the marinade evenly over the fish. Cover and set
aside for about 5 minutes.

Heat enough oil for deep-frying in a deep, heavy-
based pan to 180°C/350°F, or until a cube of bread
browns in 30 seconds, then reduce the heat slightly.
Carefully add the fish to the hot oil and deep-fry
for about 4 minutes, or until crisp and golden brown
on both sides. Remove with a slotted spoon and
drain on kitchen paper (paper towels).

To make the spice paste, mix the fried onion,
garlic and ginger pastes, yoghurt and chilli powder
together in a bowl, then season with salt.

Heat the oil in a large frying pan (skillet), add the
spice paste and stir-fry for about 2–3 minutes, or until
specks of oil appear on the surface. Add the roasted
gram flour and stir-fry for a further 2–3 minutes.
Remove the pan from the heat, add the remaining
ingredients, stir and season with salt.

Arrange the fried fish in a large oiled roasting tray
(pan). Thickly spread half the paste on top, then turn
the fish over and spread the remaining paste on the
other side. Cover and bake in the oven for about
20 minutes, basting with butter frequently.

Machhali ka Salan
Curried Fish from Hyderabad

Origin Awadh
Preparation time 30 minutes
Cooking time 30 minutes
Serves 4

800g / 1¾lb firm white fish fillets, cleaned
1½ teaspoons ground turmeric
5 tablespoons vegetable oil
3 onions, sliced
2 teaspoons Ginger Paste (see page 57)
1 teaspoon Garlic Paste (see page 57)
1½ teaspoons chilli powder
3 teaspoons ground coriander
4 tomatoes, chopped
4–6 dried red chillies
1 tablespoon Tamarind Extract (see page 58)
125ml / 4½fl oz (½ cup) coconut milk, fresh
    (see page 781) or canned
salt

Put the fish fillets in a large shallow dish and
rub with the turmeric and a little salt. Cover and
set aside.

Heat the oil in a large frying pan (skillet) over medium
heat, add the onions and stir-fry for about 5 minutes,
or until light brown. Add the ginger and garlic pastes
and season with salt, then add the chilli powder and
ground coriander and continue to stir-fry for a further
2 minutes. Add the chopped tomatoes, chillies and
tamarind extract and cook for about 5 minutes,
or until the moisture has evaporated and the spices
are blended.

Pour in about 250ml / 8fl oz (1 cup) water and bring
to the boil. Carefully lower the fish fillets into the
pan, reduce the heat, cover and simmer for 8–10
minutes, or until the fish is cooked. Uncover, add the
coconut milk and stir gently. Simmer for 2 minutes
before serving.

Masala Pomfret
Spicy Stuffed Pomfret (Butterfish)

Origin Coastal
Preparation time 30 minutes, plus soaking and
marinating time
Cooking time 10–12 minutes
Serves 6–8

1 × 500-g /1lb 2-oz whole pomfret (butterfish), plaice
    (flounder) or grey (striped) mullet, cleaned, head,
    tail and fins removed
125ml / 4½fl oz (½ cup) vegetable oil, for
    shallow-frying

For the marinade
4 dried red chillies, de-seeded
1 tablespoon vinegar
1½ teaspoons cumin seeds
10–12 cloves garlic
1 × 2.5-cm / 1-inch piece fresh ginger, peeled
1 teaspoon sugar
salt

To make the marinade, put the dried red chillies
in a bowl, add the vinegar and soak for about
15 minutes.

Transfer the dried red chillies to a blender or food
processor, add the cumin seeds, garlic, ginger and
sugar, season with salt and process to make a paste.

Put the fish in a large shallow dish and rub the
fish well inside and out with the paste. Cover and
marinate in the refrigerator for at least 3–4 hours.

Heat the oil in a large frying pan (skillet) over low
heat, add the fish and shallow-fry for about 5–6
minutes on each side. Remove from the pan and
drain on kitchen paper (paper towels).

Bhunee Machhali
Grilled (Broiled) Trout

Origin Jammu and Kashmir
Preparation time 35 minutes, plus marinating time
Cooking time 10–12 minutes
Serves 4

---

4 trouts, cleaned and rinsed

3 tablespoons mustard oil

1½ teaspoons ground turmeric

melted butter, for basting

salt

For the first marinade

1½ teaspoons yellow chilli powder

1 teaspoon Ginger Paste (see page 57)

1 teaspoon Garlic Paste (see apge 57)

2 teaspoons lemon juice

For the second marinade

375ml /13fl oz (1½ cups) natural (plain) yoghurt

1 teaspoon Ginger Paste (see page 57)

1 teaspoon Garlic Paste (see page 57)

1½ teaspoons yellow chilli powder

1 teaspoon Garam Masala (see page 31)

Using a sharp knife, make 4 deep incisions on each side of the fish and pat dry with kitchen paper (paper towels). Set aside.

To make the first marinade, mix all the ingredients, including a pinch of salt, together in a bowl.

Put the fish in a single layer in a large shallow dish and spread the marinade evenly over. Cover and marinate in the refrigerator for 30 minutes.

To make the second marinade, mix all the ingredients together in a bowl. Season with salt and set aside.

Heat the oil in a large frying pan (skillet) over medium-high heat, add the turmeric and stir-fry for about 10 seconds, then remove the pan from the heat and slowly pour in the yoghurt mixture and stir to combine. Rub this mixture over the fish, then cover and marinate for a further 1 hour.

Prepare a charcoal grill for a moderate heat or preheat the oven to 180°C/350°F/Gas Mark 4.

Thread the fish on to several metal skewers and roast over the charcoal grill or in the oven for 7–8 minutes. Remove the skewers from the heat and hang them up over a tray for about 5 minutes to allow any excess moisture to drain out completely. Put the skewers in a dish, baste with melted butter and roast again for about 3–4 minutes.

Ranith Gaad
Kashmiri Fish Curry

Origin Jammu and Kashmir
Preparation time 15 minutes
Cooking time 1 hour
Serves 6

250ml / 8fl oz (1 cup) mustard oil

1kg / 2¼lb skinless, firm white fish fillets, trimmed

1½ teaspoons chilli powder

1 teaspoon ground turmeric

1 teaspoon ground ginger

1 teaspoon ground aniseed

2 cloves

small pinch of asafoetida

1 teaspoon cumin seeds

1 teaspoon caraway seeds

1 teaspoon Kashmiri Garam Masala (see page 56)

salt

Heat the oil in a deep, heavy-based pan to 180°C/350°F, or until a cube of bread browns in 30 seconds. Working in batches, carefully add the fish to the hot oil and deep-fry for about 1 minute, or until golden brown. Remove with a slotted spoon and drain on kitchen paper (paper towels).

Pour about 500ml / 18fl oz (2¼ cups) water into a large, heavy-based pan and add all the spices, except the Kashmiri garam masala, then season with salt. Stir the mixture and bring to the boil. Once the water starts boiling gently add the fried fish pieces, reduce the heat to medium and cook for about 30 minutes, or until the sauce thickens and the oil separates out and rises to the surface. Sprinkle over the Kashmiri garam masala and simmer for a further 2 minutes.

❀ ❀ / 📷 p.396

Karimeen Polichattu
Pearl Fish Pan Grilled in Banana Leaf

Origin Kerala
Preparation time 15 minutes, plus marinating time
Cooking time 20–30 minutes
Serves 4

4 × 200g / 7oz pearl spot fish or pomfret (butterfish) fillets, trimmed

4 banana leaves, softened (see page 174) (optional)

vegetable oil, for frying

For the marinade

75g / 2½oz baby (pearl) onions, crushed

4 tablespoons lemon juice

2 tablespoons Garlic Paste (see page 57)

2½ teaspoons Ginger Paste (see page 57)

1½ teaspoons chilli powder

20 curry leaves

4 tablespoons coconut oil

salt

To make the marinade, put the onions in a large bowl, add the remaining ingredients, season with salt and mix well. Place the fish in a single layer in a large shallow dish and rub the marinade evenly over. Cover and set aside in the refrigerator for 15 minutes.

Wrap 1 fish fillet in each banana leaf, if using, then, fold over the sides and set aside. Alternatively, use squares of foil.

Heat a tawa, griddle or large non-stick frying pan (skillet) over medium heat. Sprinkle with a little water and clean thoroughly, then spread a little oil on the pan and, working in batches, arrange the wrapped fish fillets on top. Cook for 5–7 minutes, turning 2 to 3 times, adding a little oil each time you turn the parcels.

❀ ❀ / 📷 p.397

Tikha Maslyatil Tali Macchi
Piquant Fish Fry

Origin Coastal
Preparation time 30 minutes, plus marinating time
Cooking time 20 minutes
Serves 4

1kg / 2¼lb surmai or mackerel fillets, trimmed

vegetable oil, for frying

salt

For the marinade

1 teaspoon ground turmeric

1 teaspoon chilli powder

1 tablespoon Ginger Paste (see page 57)

1 teaspoon Garlic Paste (see page 57)

2 tablespoons lime juice

For the spice paste

6 green chillies, slit in half lengthways and de-seeded

2 teaspoons ground cumin

2 teaspoons ground coriander

Put the fish in a large shallow dish. Mix the turmeric, chilli powder, the ginger and garlic pastes, a little salt and the lime juice together in a bowl. Rub the mixture evenly over the fish, then cover and set aside in the refrigerator for 15 minutes.

To make the spice paste, put the chillies, ground spices and a little salt in a food processor or small blender and process, adding a little water if necessary, to make a paste. Coat the fish with the paste.

Heat enough oil for frying in a large frying pan (skillet) over medium heat. Working in batches, add the fish and fry for 5 minutes on each side. Remove and drain on kitchen paper (paper towels).

Dhan-Dal Patio
Fish with Lentils

Origin Parsi
Preparation time 45 minutes–1 hour
Cooking time 40–45 minutes
Serves 4

450g / 1lb firm white fish, such as pomfret
    (butterfish), cleaned

100g / 3½oz (scant ½ cup) ghee

250g / 9oz (2 small) onions, sliced

½ teaspoon ground turmeric

6 tablespoons chopped coriander (cilantro) leaves

1 teaspoon Dhansak Masala (see page 54)

90g / 3¼oz (1 small) tomato, chopped

3 tablespoons Tamarind Extract (see page 58)

1 tablespoon jaggery or soft brown sugar

100g / 3½oz (1¼ cups) aubergines (eggplant),
    trimmed and cut into small pieces

salt

For the spice paste

1 tablespoon chopped garlic

10 dried red chillies

2¾ teaspoons cumin seeds

For the mori dal

150g / 5oz (¾ cup) toor (toover) dal, rinsed
    and drained

½ teaspoon ground turmeric

125g / 4½oz (½ cup) ghee

1 teaspoon chopped garlic

Cut the fish into 2.5-cm / 1-inch thick steaks with
the bone.

To make the spice paste, put all the ingredients in
a blender and season with salt. Process, adding
a little water if necessary, to make a smooth paste.
Set aside.

Put the dal in a medium-sized, heavy-based pan, add
the turmeric and 1 litre / 1¾ pints (4¼ cups) water,
then season with salt and bring to the boil. Cook
for about 25 minutes, or until the dal is soft. Remove
from the heat and press the dal through a sieve
(strainer) into a bowl.

Heat 100g / 3½oz (scant ½ cup) ghee in a large, heavy-
based pan over medium heat, add half the sliced
onions and fry for about 5–7 minutes, or until
brown. Add the spice paste and turmeric and stir-fry
for 1 minute, then add the coriander and dhansak
masala and stir-fry for about 30 seconds. Add the
tomatoes and stir-fry for about 5 minutes, or until
the masala becomes smooth.

Pour 400ml / 14fl oz (1⅔ cups) water into the pan
and bring to the boil. Reduce the heat, cover and
simmer for about 5 minutes. Season with salt,
then add the tamarind extract and jaggery or sugar
and simmer for a further 2–3 minutes. Add the
aubergines and adjust the seasoning, if necessary.
Add the fish to the pan and simmer gently for about
5 minutes, or until the fish is cooked.

Heat the remaining ghee in a separate medium-
sized, heavy-based pan over medium heat, add the
remaining onions and fry for about 5–7 minutes, or
until brown. Reserve half the onions for the garnish,
add the garlic to the pan and stir-fry for about 1–2
minutes, or until brown. Add the puréed dal and stir-
fry for 2 minutes. Adjust the seasoning, if necessary.

Serve the fish with the mori dal and garnished with
the fried onions.

Dahi ki Machhali
Fish Cooked in Yoghurt Sauce

Origin Awadh
Preparation time 30 minutes, plus standing time
Cooking time 15–20 minutes
Serves 4

1kg / 2¼lb skinless, firm white fish fillets, cut into pieces
1 teaspoon ground turmeric
3–4 onions, sliced
2 teaspoons Ginger Paste (see page 57)
2 teaspoons Garlic Paste (see page 57)
3 cinnamon sticks
6–7 cloves
8 green cardamom pods
2 black cardamom pods
1 teaspoon black peppercorns
500ml / 18fl oz (2¼ cups) natural (plain) yoghurt
200ml / 7fl oz (¾ cup) vegetable oil
2 teaspoons ground coriander
1 teaspoon chilli powder
salt
chopped coriander (cilantro) leaves, to garnish

Put the fish in a large shallow dish, and rub with the turmeric and a little salt. Cover and set aside in the refrigerator for 30 minutes.

Put the onions, ginger and garlic pastes in a blender or food processor and process, adding a little water if necessary, to make a paste. Transfer to a bowl.

Put the cinnamon, 2–3 cloves, 5 green cardamom pods, the black cardamom pods and the peppercorns in a spice grinder and process to make your own masala.

Put the yoghurt in a large bowl and beat with a fork, then add the masala, stir to combine and set aside.

Heat the oil in a deep, heavy-based pan over medium heat, add the remaining whole spices and stir-fry for about 1 minute, or until they start to splutter. Add the onion paste and stir-fry for 2–3 minutes, or until the paste is golden brown. Add the ground coriander and chilli powder and season with salt, then add the fish and fry for about 5 minutes.

Reduce the heat and slowly stir in the yoghurt mixture, then cover and cook for about 3 minutes, or until the fish is cooked and oil floats on the top. Garnish with coriander leaves.

Muj Gaad
Fish with Radishes

Origin Jammu and Kashmir
Preparation time 30 minutes, plus standing time
Cooking time 25–30 minutes
Serves 4–6

750g / 1lb 10oz radishes
2 teaspoons Kashmiri red chilli powder dissolved in 1 teaspoon Kashmiri bari paste or Kashmiri Garam Masala (see page 56) mixed with a little water
3–4 tablespoons vegetable oil
800g / 1¾lb firm white river fish fillets, such as salmon, cleaned and cut into 8-cm / 3-inch long pieces
1 tablespoon Garlic Paste (see page 57)
4 cinnamon sticks, about 2.5cm / 1 inch long
4 black cardamom pods
4 green cardamom pods
5–8 cloves
2 teaspoons ground ginger
3 teaspoons ground turmeric
1½ tablespoons Fried Onion Paste (see page 57)
½ teaspoon black cumin seeds
½ teaspoon ground black pepper
1 teaspoon black cardamom seeds
salt

Slice the radishes into rounds, then halve them into crescents and put them in a large bowl. Sprinkle with salt and set aside for 30 minutes.

Put the chilli powder in a small bowl, add about ½ cup water and mix together.

Heat the oil in a large frying pan (skillet) over low heat, add the fish and fry for about 2–3 minutes, or until reddish brown. Remove with a slotted spoon and drain on kitchen paper (paper towels). Set aside.

Reheat the remaining oil in a kadhai, wok or deep, heavy-based pan over medium heat, add the garlic paste and radishes and stir-fry for about 2 minutes, or until the radishes turn light brown around the edges. Stir in the red chilli powder mixture and bring to the boil. Add the whole spices, ground ginger, turmeric and onion paste and season with salt. Mix well and cook for 10–12 minutes.

Add the fried fish and bring to the boil again, then boil rapidly for 2 minutes. Sprinkle over the black cumin seeds, black pepper and black cardamom seeds and serve.

❋ ❋ / 📷 p.399

Amritsari Machhali
Fried Fish from Amritsar

Origin Punjab
Preparation time 30 minutes, plus marinating time
Cooking time 15–25 minutes
Serves 4

800g / 1¾lb fish fillets, preferably sole
4 tablespoons cumin seeds
4 tablespoons black peppercorns
4 tablespoons black rock salt
5 teaspoons dried mint leaves
2 teaspoons ajwain seeds
1 teaspoon asafoetida
150g / 5oz (1⅓ cups) amchoor
4 teaspoons ground ginger
1 tablespoon yellow chilli powder
vegetable oil, for deep-frying
salt
lemon wedges, to serve

For the marinade

3 tablespoons gram (chickpea) flour
5 teaspoons Garlic Paste (see page 57)
3 teaspoons Ginger Paste (see page 57)
1 teaspoon chilli powder
1 teaspoon ajwain seeds
½ teaspoon asafoetida

Put the fish in a large shallow dish.

To make the marinade, mix all the ingredients with 4 tablespoons water together in a large bowl. Spread the batter evenly over the fish, then cover and set aside in the refrigerator for about 30 minutes.

To make the fish masala, mix the cumin seeds, peppercorns, black rock salt, dried mint leaves, ajwain seeds, asafoetida, amchoor, ginger and chilli powder together. Transfer the mixture to a mortar and pound with a pestle or grind in a spice grinder to make a powder. Transfer to a clean bowl, season with salt and mix well.

Heat enough oil for deep-frying in a deep, heavy-based pan to 180°C/350°F, or until a cube of bread browns in 30 seconds. Working in batches, carefully lower the fish into the hot oil and deep-fry for about 2–3 minutes, or until light golden. Remove with a slotted spoon and drain on kitchen paper (paper towels). Allow the fish to cool and reserve the oil.

When the fish are cool, make one slit down the middle along the length and 4 slits across the breadth. Now, reheat the oil in a deep, heavy-based pan to 180°C/350°F, or until a cube of bread browns in 30 seconds. Working in batches, deep-fry the fish pieces again for 3–5 minutes, or until golden and crusty. Remove with a slotted spoon and drain on kitchen paper (paper towels) before serving sprinkled with the fish masala and with lemon wedges alongside.

Machhali Tamatarwali
Fish in Tomato Sauce

Origin Punjab
Preparation time 30 minutes
Cooking time 25 minutes
Serves 4–6

800g / 1¾lb firm white fish fillets, cleaned
500g / 1lb 2oz (3 medium) ripe tomatoes
100g / 3½oz (scant ½ cup) ghee or vegetable oil
pinch of asafoetida
½ teaspoon ground cumin
2 onions, chopped
1 teaspoon chilli powder
1 teaspoon ground ginger
1 teaspoon ground coriander
½ teaspoon semolina (farina)
2 green chillies, de-seeded and chopped
salt
1 sprig coriander (cilantro) leaves, chopped, to garnish

Cut the fish into 8-cm / 3-inch pieces.

Cook the fish in a pan of boiling water for 2 minutes, or until tender. Drain and allow to cool.

Blanch the tomatoes by putting them in a large heatproof bowl of boiling water for 30 seconds, then plunging them in cold water. Remove the skin, put the flesh in a bowl and mash to pulp with a potato masher.

Heat the ghee or oil in a large, heavy-based pan over medium-low heat, add the asafoetida, ground cumin and onions and stir-fry for about 5–7 minutes, or until the onions are golden brown. Add the tomato pulp, chilli powder and the remaining ingredients, then season with salt. Cook for 3–4 minutes, or until the sauce thickens, then reduce the heat to very low and add the fish. Cook for about 8 minutes, or until the fish is cooked. Garnish with chopped coriander.

Machhali ke Kofte
Fish Kofte

Origin Awadh
Preparation time 1 hour, plus cooling time
Cooking time 20 minutes
Serves 4–6

800g / 1¾lb firm white fish fillets, cleaned

6 potatoes

2 teaspoons ground coriander

½ teaspoon chilli powder

3 tablespoons ghee or vegetable oil

2 onions, chopped

2 eggs

1 teaspoon lemon juice

1 bunch coriander (cilantro) leaves, chopped

2 tablespoons rice flour or breadcrumbs

vegetable oil, for deep-frying

Cut the fish into 8-cm / 3-inch pieces. Put into a bowl and, using a potato masher or wooden spoon, mash well.

Meanwhile, cook the potatoes in a large pan of boiling water for 20 minutes, or until soft. Drain and allow to cool, then peel off the skins, return the flesh to the pan and mash.

Add the mashed potatoes to the fish, then add the ground coriander and chilli powder and season with salt. Mix well.

Heat 1 tablespoon of ghee or oil in a large frying pan (skillet) over medium-low heat, add the fish and potato mixture and stir-fry for a few minutes until the moisture is absorbed, taking care not to burn it. Remove from the pan and set aside.

Heat the remaining ghee or oil in a separate pan over medium heat, add the onions and stir-fry for 5–7 minutes, or until golden brown. Transfer the onions with a slotted spoon to the fish mixture, then break an egg over the mixture and mix well. Add the lemon juice and mix lightly until combined. Sprinkle over the chopped coriander and with damp hands, shape into sausage-like koftas, about 8cm / 3 inches long and 2cm / ¾ inches thick.

Put the remaining egg in a shallow bowl and beat lightly, then spread the rice flour or breadcrumbs out on a plate. Dip the koftas first in the beaten egg, then roll in the flour until coated.

Heat enough oil for deep-frying in a kadhai or deep, heavy-based pan to 180°C/350°F, or until a cube of bread browns in 30 seconds. Working in batches, carefully lower the koftas into the hot oil and deep-fry for about 2–3 minutes, or until light brown all over. Remove with a slotted spoon and drain on kitchen paper (paper towels).

Fish Fry
Fried Fish Fillets

Origin Anglo-Indian
Preparation time 30 minutes, plus marinating time
Cooking time 30 minutes
Serves 4

750g /1lb 10oz skinless, firm white fish fillets, trimmed

2 eggs, beaten

120g / 4oz (1 cup) breadcrumbs

250ml / 8fl oz (1 cup) vegetable oil

For the marinade

1 × 2.5-cm / 1-inch piece ginger, peeled and chopped

1 onion, sliced

4–5 cloves garlic, crushed

3–4 green chillies, de-seeded and roughly chopped

2 tablespoons malt (white) vinegar or lime juice

1 teaspoon ground black pepper

salt

To make the marinade, put the ginger, onion, garlic and chillies in a blender or food processor and process, adding a little water to make a paste. Transfer to a bowl, add the vinegar or lime juice and black pepper. Mix well.

Put the fish in a large shallow dish and rub the marinade all over the fish. Cover and set aside in the refrigerator for at least about 2 hours.

Put the beaten eggs in a shallow dish and spread the breadcrumbs out on a piece of brown paper or on a large flat plate. Dip the fish first in the beaten eggs, then in the breadcrumbs to coat.

Heat the oil in a large frying pan (skillet) over medium heat. Add the fillets 2 at a time to the hot oil and fry for 3–4 minutes on one side, then turn gently and fry for a further 1 minute, or until golden brown. Remove with a slotted spoon and drain on kitchen paper (paper towels).

✵ ✵

___

Madras Fish Curry
Fish Curry from Madras

Origin Tamil Nadu
Preparation time 2 minutes, plus marinating time
Cooking time 30 minutes
Serves 4

1kg / 2¼lb skinless, firm white fish fillets, trimmed
juice of 1 lime
2 teaspoons vinegar
½ teaspoon ground fenugreek
1 teaspoon ground cumin
125ml / 4½fl oz (½ cup) vegetable oil
1 teaspoon mustard seeds
350g / 12oz (3 medium) onions, chopped
20–30 curry leaves
1 teaspoon ground coriander
1 teaspoon ground turmeric
2 teaspoons chilli powder
1 teaspoon Tamarind Extract (see page 58)
salt

For the spice paste

250g / 9 oz (3 cups) grated fresh coconut
50g / 1¾oz chopped ginger
½ clove garlic
500g /1lb 2oz (3 medium) tomatoes, chopped
2 tablespoons Poppy Seed Paste (see page 58)

Put the fish in a large shallow dish, add the lime juice, vinegar and a little salt, then turn to coat, cover and set aside in the refrigerator for 30 minutes.

To make the spice paste, put the grated coconut, ginger, garlic, tomatoes and poppy seed paste into a food processor or blender and process to make a paste. Do not add any water. Set aside.

Mix the ground fenugreek and cumin together in a small bowl and set aside.

Heat the oil in a large, heavy-based pan over medium heat, add the mustard seeds and stir-fry for about 1 minute, or until they start to splutter. Add the onions and stir-fry for about 2 minutes, or until translucent, then add the curry leaves and stir-fry for a further 2–3 minutes, or until the onions are light brown. Add the ground spices and stir-fry for 1 minute, then add the spice paste and stir-fry for about 5 minutes.

Add the tamarind extract and 500ml / 18fl oz (2¼ cups) water to the pan. Season with salt, then bring to the boil, reduce the heat and simmer for 3 minutes. Now gently slip in the fish pieces and turn the heat down to low. Sprinkle over the fenugreek mixture and cook for about 8–10 minutes, or until the fish is cooked.

✵ ✵

___

Meen Thala Kari
Fish Head Curry

Origin Tamil Nadu
Preparation time 30 minutes, plus standing time
Cooking time 40–45 minutes
Serves 2

1 medium-sized fish head, cleaned and rinsed
1 teaspoon ground turmeric
2 tablespoons vegetable oil
1 teaspoon ground cumin
1 teaspoon ground coriander
1 teaspoon chilli powder
2 tomatoes, chopped
5–6 green chilies, de-seeded and chopped
1 tablespoon grated ginger
1 tablespoon Tamarind Extract (see page 58)
1.25 litres / 2 pints (5 cups) coconut milk, fresh (see page 781) or canned
10–12 okra, topped and tailed (trimmed), then cut in half
6 small aubergines (eggplant), trimmed and cut in half
salt

Rub the fish head with turmeric and a little salt, then place in a dish, cover and set aside in the refrigerator for about 30 minutes.

Heat the oil in a large, heavy-based pan over low heat, add the ground spices, then season with salt and stir-fry for about 2 minutes. Add the tomatoes, chillies, ginger and tamarind extract and fry for a further 2 minutes. Cover the pan and cook for about 5 minutes.

Pour half the coconut milk into the pan and bring to the boil over medium heat. Add the fish head, okra and aubergines, then cover and cook over medium heat for 20 minutes. Pour in the rest of the coconut milk and simmer for a further 2 minutes.

Ga Archa Meen Kari
Fish Curry with Coconut

Origin Kerala
Preparation time 30 minutes
Cooking time 20 minutes
Serves 6

500g / 1lb 2oz skinless, firm white fish fillets, trimmed

1 tablespoon vegetable oil

2 sprigs curry leaves

1 onion, chopped

1 × 3-cm / 1¼-inch piece fresh ginger, peeled

2 green chillies, slit in half lengthways and de-seeded

3–4 petals cambodge

4 teaspoons chilli powder

1 teaspoon ground coriander

1 teaspoon ground turmeric

1 teaspoon ground black pepper

salt

For the spice paste

½ dried coconut, grated

2 shallots, chopped

2 cloves garlic, crushed

1 teaspoon cumin seeds

½ teaspoon ground turmeric

For the tempering

1 teaspoon mustard seeds

1 teaspoon fenugreek seeds

2 shallots

Cut the fish into about 4-cm / 1½-inch pieces.

To make the spice paste, put all the ingredients, except the the cumin and tumeric into a blender or food processor and process, adding a little water if necessary, to make a paste.

Put the cumin seeds and turmeric, powder in a small blender or spice grinder and process, adding a little water if necessary to make a paste.

Heat the oil in a large heavy-based pan over low heat, add the fish pieces, curry leaves, onions, ginger, chillies, cambodge petals, ground spices and 1 litre / 1¾ pints (4¼ cups) water and season with salt. Cook for 10 minutes, then stir in the spice paste, bring to the boil and remove from the heat.

Patrani Machli
Fish Cooked in Banana Leaf Wraps

Origin Parsi
Preparation time 30 minutes
Cooking time 10 minutes
Serves 6–8

800g / 1¾lb any firm white fish fillets, such as pomfret (butterfish), cut into 8 pieces

4 banana leaves (optional)

salt

For the spice paste

1 coconut, peeled and grated

6 green chillies, de-seeded and chopped

4 tablespoons coriander

2 teaspoons cumin seeds

2 teaspoons sugar

6 cloves garlic, chopped

2 tablespoons lemons juice

If using the banana leaves, soften the leaves (see page 174) and cut into 16 strips. Alternatively, use foil.

To make the spice paste, put all the ingredients except the lemon juice into a blender or food processor and process, adding a little water if necessary, to make a smooth paste. Add the lemon juice to the paste.

Place the fish in a large shallow dish and rub the fish with the paste.

Arrange the banana leaf strips into crosses, making 8 crosses, 1 for each fillet of fish. Place a fillet in the centre of each cross and fold the banana leaf strips over to make envelopes. Tie the envelopes with kitchen string (twine).

Place the fillets in a small wire or bamboo steamer basket. Cover the basket with a cloth and lower it over a large pan of boiling water. Steam for about 10 minutes, or until the fish is cooked. Alternatively, a large steamer may be used.

Vatticha Mathi Kari
Spicy Sardines

Origin Tamil Nadu
Preparation time 30 minutes
Cooking time 30 minutes
Serves 6

2–3 petals cambodge

750g /1lb 10oz sardines, cleaned

3 tablespoons vegetable oil

2 onions, chopped

6 cloves garlic, chopped

1 × 4-cm / 1½-inch piece fresh ginger, peeled
   and grated

15–20 curry leaves

1½ teaspoons ground turmeric

salt

For the spice paste
10–20 dried red chillies

10 black peppercorns

2 teaspoons coriander seeds

1 teaspoon fenugreek seeds

Soak the cambodge petals in a bowl of water
until required.

If the sardines are large remove the heads, then cut
the fish into pieces.

To make the spice paste, put all the ingredients and a
little water in a blender and process to make a paste.

Heat 1 tablespoon oil in a small frying pan (skillet)
over medium heat, add the onions, garlic, ginger,
curry leaves and turmeric and stir-fry for 2 minutes,
or until the onions are translucent. Add the spice
paste and stir-fry for a further 2 minutes, then
remove the pan from the heat.

Heat the remaining oil in a large frying pan over
medium-low heat, add the sardines and spread the
onion mixture on top. Add the cambodge petals
with their soaking water and pour in enough water
to just cover the fish, then bring to the boil. Season
with salt, reduce the heat to low and simmer for 10
minutes, or until the fish are cooked.

Aa
Fish Stew

Origin Tribal North East India
Preparation time 15 minutes
Cooking time 25 minutes
Serves 4

800g / 1¾lb fish fillets, such as rohu, hilsa (shad)
   or red snapper, cleaned

3–4 green chillies, chopped

4 onions, chopped

4 cloves garlic, chopped

2 small fermented fish

salt

Cut the fish into 5-cm / 2-inch long pieces.

Bring 750ml / 1¼ pints (3¼ cups) water to the boil
in a large pan over high heat, add the fish pieces
and boil for about 2 minutes. Add the remaining
ingredients, reduce the heat and simmer for
about 20 minutes, or until the fish is tender and
the sauce thickens.

Bombil Machli, Baingan aur Chigur
Dried Bombay Duck Cooked with
Aubergines (Eggplant) & Tamarind
Leaves

Origin Hyderabad
Preparation time 20 minutes
Cooking time 20 minutes
Serves 4–6

8 sun-dried Bombay duck or fresh firm white fish fillets
180ml / 6fl oz (²⁄₃ cup) vegetable oil
2 onions, sliced
1 teaspoon Ginger Paste (see page 57)
1 teaspoon Garlic Paste (see page 57)
½ teaspoon ground turmeric
1 teaspoon chilli powder
250g / 9oz (1 small) aubergine (eggplant), trimmed
   and cut into 4-cm / 1½-inch pieces
4–6 green chillies, de-seeded and chopped
120g / 4oz (1 cup) chigur, young tamarind leaves
salt

Cut the fish into 4-cm / 1½-inch pieces, then rinse
under cold running water and pat dry.

Heat the oil in a large, heavy-based pan over medium
heat, add the fish and fry until crisp. Remove from
the pan with a slotted spoon and set aside.

Reheat the oil in the same pan over medium heat,
add the onions and stir-fry for about 5–7 minutes, or
until golden brown. Add the ginger and garlic pastes,
turmeric and chilli powder and stir-fry for 1 minute.
Add the aubergine and continue stir-frying for a
further 3 minutes. Add the chillies and chigur leaves,
then season with salt and pour in 250ml / 8fl oz (1 cup)
water and simmer together until the chigur is soft.

Chapa Pulussu
South Indian Fish Curry

Origin Tamil Nadu
Preparation time 20 minutes, plus marinating time
Cooking time 20–25 minutes
Serves 4

400g /14oz firm white fish fillets, such as pomfret
   (butterfish) or cod, cleaned
1 teaspoon ground turmeric
1 teaspoon Garlic Paste (see page 57)
3 tablespoons vegetable oil
3 onions, sliced
1 teaspoon mustard seeds
4 dried red chillies
2 tablespoons ground coriander
2 tablespoons sesame seeds
10 curry leaves
500ml /18fl oz (2¼ cups) coconut milk, fresh
   (see page 781) or canned
2 tomatoes, chopped
20g / ¾oz (½ cup) chopped coriander (cilantro) leaves
salt

Cut the fish into 5-cm / 2-inch pieces and place in
a large shallow dish.

To make the marinade, mix the turmeric and the
garlic paste together in a bowl, then season with
salt. Rub the marinade over the fish, cover and set
aside in the refrigerator for 30 minutes.

Heat the oil in a large frying pan (skillet) over
medium heat, add the onions, mustard seeds and
dried red chillies and stir-fry for about 5–7 minutes,
or until the onions are golden brown. Add the rest
of the spices and sesame seeds and stir-fry for
1 minute, then pour in half of the coconut milk and
cook for a few minutes. Add the fish, the rest of the
coconut milk, the tomatoes and 250ml / 8fl oz (1 cup)
water and simmer for about 10 minutes, or until the
fish is cooked. Add the chopped coriander leaves,
then bring to the boil and remove from the heat.
Adjust the seasoning, if necessary.

Meen Dakhani
Fish Curry from Deccan

Origin New
Preparation time 25–30 minutes, plus marinating time
Cooking time 15–20 minutes
Serves 6

800g / 1¾lb skinless, firm white fish fillets, trimmed

1 teaspoon Ginger Paste (see page 57)

2 teaspoons Garlic Paste (see page 57)

1 teaspoon chilli powder

¼ teaspoon ground turmeric

3 tablespoons vegetable oil

1 teaspoon cumin seeds

½ teaspoon mustard seeds

3 onions, sliced

4 green chillies, de-seeded and chopped

1½ tablespoons Tamarind Extract (see page 58)

20 curry leaves

1 bunch coriander (cilantro) leaves, chopped

salt

Cut the fish into bite-sized chunks and place in a large bowl.

To make the marinade, mix the ginger and garlic pastes, chilli powder and turmeric together in a bowl. Season with salt and rub the fish evenly with the marinade. Cover and set aside in the refrigerator for 30 minutes.

Heat the oil in a large, heavy-based pan over high heat, then reduce the heat. Add the cumin and mustard seeds and stir-fry for about 1 minute, or until they start to splutter. Add the onions and stir-fry for about 5–7 minutes, or until golden brown.

Add the fish to the pan together with the chillies and lightly fry for 2 minutes. Add the tamarind extract and 250ml / 8fl oz (1 cup) water, then increase the heat to high and boil for 2 minutes. Reduce the heat to low and simmer for about 3 minutes, or until the fish is cooked.

Add the curry leaves and chopped coriander, then cook for a further 1 minute before removing the pan from the heat.

☀ / 📷 p.274

Mahi Kaliya
Spicy Fish Curry with Tamarind

Origin Awadh
Preparation time 25 minutes
Cooking time 25 minutes
Serves 4–6

---

2 tablespoons ground coriander

2 tablespoons ground cumin

1 tablespoon chironji kernels

1 tablespoon poppy seeds

2 tablespoons sesame seeds

¼ dried coconut, grated

125ml / 4½fl oz (½ cup) vegetable oil

8 curry leaves

½ teaspoon mustard seeds

1 teaspoon kalonji (nigella) seeds

1 tablespoon Tamarind Extract, (see page 58), plus 1 teaspoon

½ teaspoon ground turmeric

3 onions, chopped

1½ teaspoons chopped ginger

1½ teaspoons chopped garlic

1 teaspoon chilli powder

2 bay leaves

1kg / 2¼lb skinless, firm white fish fillets, rinsed

1 bunch coriander (cilantro) leaves, chopped

salt

Dry roast separately the ground coriander and cumin, chironji kernels, poppy seeds, sesame seeds and coconut in a dry frying pan (skillet) for about 1 minute each. Allow to cool, then transfer them to a spice grinder and grind. Set aside.

Heat the oil in a large frying pan over medium heat, add the curry leaves, mustard seeds and kalonji seeds and stir-fry for about 1 minute, or until the seeds start to splutter. Add the 1 teaspoon taramind extract, the turmeric and onions and stir-fry for about 5–7 minutes, or until the onions are lightly browned. Add the ginger and ground garlic and stir-fry for 1 minute. Reduce the heat to low, mix in the ground spices and chilli powder and continue to cook for a few minutes. Season with salt, then add the bay leaves and remaining tamarind extract and mix well.

Add the fish to the pan. Pour in 250ml / 8fl oz (1 cup) water and cover. Cook for 7–8 minutes, or until the fish is cooked through. Remove the fish and keep warm. Boil the sauce for 5 minutes, or until it thickens. Remove the bay leaves. Add the chopped coriander and stir. Pour over the fish.

✺ ✺
___

Meen Godavari
Andhra Fish Curry

Origin Hyderabad/Andhra Pradesh
Preparation time 20 minutes
Cooking time 15 minutes
Serves 4

1 tablespoon ground coriander
80g / 2¾oz (1 cup) grated fresh coconut
½ teaspoon fenugreek seeds
1 tablespoon Tamarind Extract (see page 58)
1 tablespoon chilli powder
¼ teaspoon ground turmeric
250ml / 8fl oz (1 cup) vegetable oil
400g / 14oz skinless, firm white fish fillets, trimmed and cut into 6-cm / 2½-inch pieces
3 green chillies, de-seeded and chopped
¼ teaspoon ground black pepper
salt

Roast the coriander, grated coconut and fenugreek seeds on a tawa, griddle or in a dry frying pan (skillet) over low heat for a few minutes until evenly brown. Transfer to a small blender or food processor, add the tamarind extract, chilli powder and turmeric. Season with salt and process until ground.

Heat the oil in a large frying pan over low heat, add the mixture and fry for about 5 minutes. Add the fish and stir-fry for 2 minutes. Pour in 250ml / 8fl oz (1 cup) water and simmer for about 5 minutes, or until the fish is cooked. Add enough water as necessary to make a little sauce and sprinkle the chillies and pepper over the top, then cook for 1 minute, stirring gently so that the fish does not break. Remove from the heat.

✺ ✺
___

Podi Chapa
Andhra Fried Fish

Origin Hyderabad/Andhra Pradesh
Preparation time 15–20 minutes
Cooking time 15 minutes
Serves 4–6

1kg / 2¼lb skinless, firm white fish fillets, trimmed
1 teaspoon ground turmeric, plus extra for rinsing
1 teaspoon chilli powder
2 teaspoon Garlic Paste (see page 57)
1 × 5-cm / 2-inch piece fresh ginger, peeled and grated
1 teaspoon ground coriander
juice of 2 limes
500ml / 18fl oz (2¼ cups) vegetable oil for deep-frying
1 teaspoon pepper
salt

Cut the fish into pieces and rinse in water with a little salt and turmeric has been added. Place the fish in a large shallow dish.

Mix the turmeric, chilli powder, garlic paste, ginger, coriander and lime juice together in a bowl. Season with salt and the pepper. Rub the mixture evenly over the fish.

Heat the oil for deep-frying in a kadhai or deep heavy-based pan to 180°C/350°F, or until a cube of bread browns in 30 seconds. Working in batches, if necessary, carefully lower the fish into the hot oil and deep-fry for 2–3 minutes, or until golden brown. Remove with a slotted spoon and drain on kitchen paper (paper towels).

Shai Dum ki Machhali
Baked Masala Fish

Origin Hyderabad
Preparation time 20–25 minutes, plus marinating time
Cooking time 40 minutes
Serves 4

1 × 1-kg / 2¼-lb fish, such as rohu, hilsa (shad) or red snapper, cleaned
250ml / 8fl oz (1 cup) sesame oil
4 onions, sliced
1 teaspoon ground turmeric
juice of 3 limes
salt

For the marinade

15g / ½ oz (⅓ cup) coriander (cilantro) leaves
8 tablespoons mint leaves
10 green chillies, slit in half lengthways and de-seeded
2 tablespoons Garlic Paste (see page 57)
1 tablespoon Ginger Paste (see page 57)
1 teaspoon ground turmeric

For the spice paste

2 tablespoons ground cumin, roasted
½ dried coconut, grated
1 tablespoon sesame seeds
1 tablespoon poppy seeds

To garnish

1 tablespoon sesame oil
3 onions, sliced

To make the marinade, put the coriander and mint leaves, chillies, garlic and ginger pastes and turmeric in a blender and season with salt. Process until ground. Place the fish in a large shallow dish and rub the marinade all over the fish. Cover and marinate in the refrigerator for 1 hour.

Preheat the oven to 220°C/425°F/Gas Mark 7. Put the cumin, coconut and sesame and poppy seeds in a blender and process, adding a little water if necessary, to make a smooth paste.

Heat 2 tablespoons of the oil in a pan over medium heat, add the onions and stir-fry for 5 minutes, or until light brown. Add the turmeric and continue stir-frying for about 30 seconds. Add the spice paste and fry for about 1–2 minutes.

Drain off any excess oil, then add the lime juice and 500ml / 18fl oz (2¼ cups) water. Stir, reduce the heat and simmer for 5 minutes.

Heat the remaining oil in a large frying pan (skillet), add the fish and lightly fry for a few minutes. Place the fish carefully into a large flat dish and add the hot spices and sauce. Cover with a tight-fitting lid or foil and bake in the oven for about 15–20 minutes, or until the fish is cooked.

Meanwhile, heat the oil for the garnish in a small frying pan over low heat, add the onions and fry for about 10 minutes, or until golden brown.

Remove the fish from the oven, spread the fried onions on top and serve.

Year Chapa
Fried Fish in Tomato Sauce

Origin Tribal North East India
Preparation time 20 minutes, plus standing time
Cooking time 15 minutes
Serves 4

500g / 1 lb 2oz skinless, firm white fish fillets, trimmed

½ teaspoon ground turmeric

4 large tomatoes, roughly chopped

4 onions, sliced

1 teaspoon Ginger Paste (see page 57)

2 teaspoons Garlic Paste (see page 57)

1 teaspoon ground coriander

1 teaspoon ground cumin

4 tablespoons vegetable oil, plus enough for
    deep-frying

3 potatoes, sliced

1 teaspoon chilli powder

salt

Cut the fish into 8-cm / 3-inch long pieces, then
place in a large shallow dish and rub, with the
turmeric. Cover and set aside in the refrigerator
for 20 minutes.

Put the tomatoes, onions, ginger and garlic pastes,
the ground coriander and cumin in a blender or food
processor and process to make a smooth paste.

Heat the oil for deep-frying in a deep, heavy-based
pan to 180°C/350°F, or until a cube of bread browns in
30 seconds. Working in batches, if necessary, carefully
lower the fish into the hot oil and deep-fry for
2–3 minutes, or until brown. Remove with a slotted
spon and drain on kitchen paper (paper towels).
Sprinkle with a little salt.

In the same oil, fry the potatoes lightly, in batches,
for 5 minutes or until golden. In a large pan, heat the
remaining oil over medium heat. Add the spice paste
and stir-fry for 2 minutes. Add the chilli powder then
pour in 250ml / 8fl oz (1 cup) water and bring to the
boil. Reduce the heat, add the fish and potatoes and
simmer for 5 minutes, or until the fish is cooked.

Taleli Masala Boomla
Fried Spiced Bombay Duck

Origin Coastal
Preparation time 40 minutes, plus marinating time
Cooking time 15–20 minutes
Serves 4

8 fresh Bombay duck fish (see page 367)

½ teaspoon ground fenugreek

1 teaspoon ground cumin

juice of 2 limes

rice flour as required

sesame seed oil, for shallow-frying

salt

For the spice paste

4 green chillies, chopped

1 × 5-cm / 2-inch piece fresh ginger, peeled

6 cloves garlic

1 teaspoon ground turmeric

5 dried red chillies

1 teaspoon ground cumin

2 teaspoons ground coriander

1 teaspoon fenugreek seeds

1 cinnamon stick, about 5cm / 2 inches long

2–3 cloves

2 green cardamom pods

½ teaspoon whole black peppercorns

Clean the fish, cut off the heads and fins and the bone
that juts along the tail. Slit the belly carefully ensuring
that the skin is not pierced, then remove all the
entrails and rinse well under cold running water.

To make the spice paste, put all the ingredients in a food
processor or blender and process to a smooth paste.

Put the ground fenugreek and cumin in a small
bowl and mix together, then rub the mixture inside
the fish. Put the fish in 2–3 large shallow dishes.

To make the marinade, mix the lime juice and spice
paste in a bowl and season. Spread the marinade
evenly over the fish, then cover and set aside in the
refrigerator for 30 minutes. Spread the rice flour out
on a large plate and coat the fish in it.

Heat enough oil for shallow-frying in a large frying
pan (skillet) over medium heat, then reduce the heat.
Working in batches, fry the fish for 2–3 minutes on
each side, or until crisp.

Meen Moily
Fish Curry Cooked with Coconut

Origin Kerala
Preparation time 30–40 minutes, plus standing time
Cooking time 15–20 minutes
Serves 4

800g / 1¾lb pomfret (butterfish) or haddock
  fillets, cleaned

juice of 2 limes

2 tablespoons sesame seed oil

500ml / 18fl oz (2¼ cups) coconut milk, fresh
  (see page 781) or canned

1 × 5-cm / 2-inch piece fresh ginger, peeled and sliced

4–6 green chillies, slit in half lengthways and de-seeded

20 curry leaves

salt

For the spice paste

1 teaspoon cumin seeds

1 tablespoon coriander seeds

1 tablespoon poppy seeds

2 tablespoons desiccated (dried flaked) coconut

2 tablespoons peanuts

2 tablespoons cashew nuts

2 tablespoons roasted gram (chickpea) flour

1 tablespoon basmati rice, rinsed and drained

2 onions, sliced

1 small sprig fresh coriander (cilantro) leaves, chopped

4–8 dried red chillies

6 cloves garlic, crushed

Cut the fish into 1-cm / ½-inch thick slices and place
in a large shallow dish. Rub a little of the lime juice
and salt over the fish, then cover and set aside in
the refrigerator for 30 minutes.

To make the spice paste, put all the ingredients
in a blender or food processor and process to make
a smooth paste.

Heat the oil in a large, heavy-based pan over
low-medium heat, add the spice paste and stir-fry
for about 3–4 minutes, or until the oil separates out.
Remove from the heat, slowly stir in the coconut
milk, then add the ginger, green chillies and curry
leaves, and season with salt. Stir, then return to
the heat and simmer for 3–4 minutes. Add the fish
and simmer for about 7 minutes. Remove from the
heat and sprinkle over the lime juice.

Machhali ka Qorma
Curried Braised Fish

Origin Awadh
Preparation time 30 minutes
Cooking time 15–20 minutes
Serves 5–6

---

1 teaspoon cumin seeds

2 tablespoons coriander seeds

2 tablespoons poppy seeds

2 tablespoons sesame seeds

2 tablespoons chironji kernels

100g / 3½oz (scant ½ cup) ghee

2 small onions, sliced

1 teaspoon Garlic Paste (see page 57)

1 teaspoon Ginger Paste (see page 57)

½ teaspoon ground turmeric

200ml / 7fl oz (¾ cup) natural (plain) yoghurt, whisked

800g / 1¾lb skinless, firm white fish fillets, trimmed
  and cut into 5-cm / 2-inch long pieces

salt

Stir-fry the cumin, coriander, poppy and sesame
seeds and the chironji kernels separately in a dry
frying pan (skillet) for about 1 minute, or until
roasted. Do not let them burn. Transfer the seeds
to a spice grinder or mortar and process or pound
with a pestle until ground. Set aside in a bowl.

Heat the ghee in a large, heavy-based pan over
medium heat, add the onions and stir-fry for
5–7 minutes, or until golden-brown. Remove with
a slotted spoon and set aside.

Add the garlic and ginger pastes, turmeric and
yoghurt to the ground spices. Season with salt and
mix together, then add to the pan in which the
onions were fried and cook over medium heat for
1 minute. Remove from the heat and crumble in the
fried onions and mix thoroughly. Add the fish pieces,
then return to low heat and simmer for 10 minutes,
or until the fish is cooked.

※ ❋

Sookhe Masala ki Machhali
Spicy Fried Fish

Origin Bihar/ West Bengal
Preparation time 20–30 minutes, plus standing time
Cooking time 15 minutes
Serves 4

1kg / 2¼lb skinless, firm white fish fillets, trimmed
    and cut into 5-cm / 2-inch long pieces

1 teaspoon Garlic Paste (see page 57)

1 teaspoon Ginger Paste (see page 57)

2 teaspoons ground coriander

½ teaspoon chilli powder

juice of ½ lime

120g / 4oz (1 cup) breadcrumbs

250g / 9oz (1 cup) ghee

salt

Put the fish in a large shallow dish, and rub the
fish with the garlic and ginger pastes and coriander
and a little salt. Mix the chilli powder and lime
juice together in a bowl. Pour the mixture evenly
over the fish, then cover and set aside in the
refrigerator for 1 hour.

Spread the breadcrumbs out on a large plate and roll
the fish pieces in it to coat.

Heat the ghee in a large frying pan (skillet) over
medium heat. Working in batches, add the fish
and fry for 2–3 minutes, or until golden brown
on each side.

※ ❋

Chincheche Talwan
Fish & Tamarind Curry

Origin Coastal
Preparation time 30 minutes, plus standing time
Cooking time 20 minutes
Serves 4

750g / 1lb 10oz skinless, firm white fish fillets, trimmed

1 teaspoon ground turmeric

1 tablespoon lime juice

½ teaspoon chilli powder

1 tablespoon vegetable oil

500g / 1lb 2oz mixed seasonal vegetables, cut into
    bite-sized pieces

1 tablespoon Tamarind Extract (see page 58)

1 tomato, skinned (see page 232)

½ teaspoon sugar

¼ teaspoon Garam Masala (see page 31)

salt

For the spice paste

1 large sprig coriander (cilantro) leaves

4 green chillies, chopped

1 × 2.5-cm / 1-inch piece fresh ginger, peeled

6 cloves garlic

Place the fish in a large shallow dish. Mix the
turmeric and lime juice together in a bowl, then rub
the fish with the turmeric mixture and sprinkle over
some salt. Cover and set aside in the refrigerator
for 15 minutes.

To make the spice paste, put all the ingredients in
a food processor or blender, season with salt and
process, adding a little water to make a paste.

Heat the oil in a large, heavy-based pan over
medium-low heat, add the spice paste and stir-fry
lightly, ensuring that it doesn't brown. Add the
mixed vegetables, then pour in 250ml / 8fl oz (1 cup)
water, bring to the boil, reduce the heat, cover
and simmer for 7–8 minutes.

Uncover, add the tamarind extract, tomatoes and
marinated fish together with the marinade. Pour in
250ml / 8fl oz (1 cup) water, add the sugar and season
with salt. Cover and cook for 5 minutes, or until the
fish is done. Remove from the heat and sprinkle over
the garam masala before serving.

Goan Fish Curry (I)
Goan Fish Curry (I)

Origin Coastal
Preparation time 30 minutes, plus soaking
and marinating time
Cooking time 30 minutes
Serves 4

600g /1lb 5oz skinless, firm white fish fillets, trimmed
 and cut into large cubes

2 tablespoons vegetable oil

1 onion, sliced

1 tomato, puréed

3 green chillies, slit in half lengthways and de-seeded

few okra, topped and tailed (optional)

salt

chopped coriander (cilantro) leaves, to garnish

For the marinade

1 teaspoon lemon juice

pinch of ground turmeric

pinch of salt

For the spice paste

8 dried red chillies

80g / 2¾oz (1 cup) grated fresh coconut

3 teaspoons coriander seeds

1 onion, chopped

1 teaspoon cumin seeds

1 teaspoon ground turmeric

1½ teaspoons chopped garlic

1 teaspoon Tamarind Extract (see page 58)

For the spice paste, put the dried red chillies in
a bowl, pour in 250ml / 8fl oz (1 cup) water and
soak for about 15 minutes. Drain, reserving 1–2
tablespoons of the soaking water.

To make the marinade, mix the lemon juice with
a pinch each of turmeric and salt together in a bowl.
Put the fish in a large shallow dish and rub with
the marinade. Cover and marinate in the refrigerator
for 30 minutes.

To make the spice paste, put the soaked dried red
chillies, coconut, coriander seeds, chopped onion,
cumin seeds, turmeric powder, garlic, tamarind
extract and the reserved soaking water in a blender
or food processor and process to make smooth paste.

Heat the oil in a wide, shallow pan over medium heat,
add the sliced onion and stir-fry for about 7–8
minutes. Add the spice paste and cook for 6–7
minutes, or until golden brown, adding a little water
if necessary to prevent the spice paste burning on
the base (bottom) of the pan. Pour in 1 litre / 1¾ pints
(4¼ cups) water and cook for a few minutes until the
oil starts to separate from the spices. Add the puréed
tomato, green chillies and okra, if using, and season
with salt. Continue to cook for about 6 minutes, then
add the fish and cook for about 4–5 minutes, or until
the fish is cooked. Garnish with coriander.

☀ ☀

Goan Fish Curry (II)
Goan Fish Curry (II)

Origin Coastal
Preparation time 30 minutes, plus standing and
soaking time
Cooking time 20 minutes
Serves 4

600g / 1lb 5oz skinless, firm white fish fillets, trimmed

½ teaspoon ground turmeric

6 large dried red chillies

2 teaspoons coriander seeds

pinch of ground mace or nutmeg

2 tablespoons grated fresh coconut

1 tablespoon vegetable oil

6 cloves garlic, crushed

1 large onion, chopped

1 teaspoon Tamarind Extract (see page 58)

salt

Put the fish in a large shallow dish and rub the fish
with the turmeric and a little salt. Cover and set
aside in the refrigerator for 30 minutes.

Soak the dried red chillies in a bowl of lukewarm
water for 15 minutes. Drain, reserving the water,
then cut in half and de-seed.

Put the chillies, coriander seeds, ground spices and
coconut in a small blender and process, adding
a little reserved water to make a smooth paste.

Heat the oil in a large, heavy-based pan over
medium-low heat, add the garlic and onion and
the spice paste and stir-fry lightly, ensuring that it
doesn't turn brown. Pour in 500ml / 18fl oz (2¼ cups)
water, bring to the boil and reduce the heat. Add the
fish together with the marinade and the tamarind
extract. Season with salt. Simmer for 10 minutes, or
until the fish is cooked.

Laal Kalwan
Coconut Red Chilli Curry

Origin Coastal
Preparation time 30 minutes, plus soaking and standing time
Cooking time 25 minutes
Serves 4

750g / 1lb 10oz skinless, firm white fish fillets, trimmed

1 level teaspoon ground turmeric

½ teaspoon sugar

1 tablespoon lime juice

1 tablespoon oil

1 potato, cut into cubes

salt

For the red spice paste

8 dried red chillies

30g / 1¼oz (⅓ cup) desiccated (dried flaked) coconut

6 cloves garlic, crushed

1 tablespoon malt (white) vinegar

Place the fish in a large shallow dish. Mix the turmeric, sugar and lime juice together in a bowl, then rub the fish with the turmeric mixture and sprinkle over some salt. Cover and set aside in the refrigerator for 15 minutes.

To make the red spice paste, soak the dried red chillies in a bowl of lukewarm water for 15 minutes, then drain, reserving the water, cut in half and de-seed.

Put the chillies, coconut, garlic and the reserved water in a food processor or blender and process to make a paste.

Heat the oil in a large, heavy-based pan over medium-low heat, add the red spice paste and fry lightly, ensuring the bright red colour is not lost due to browning.

Put the potatoes in a large pan, pour in 250ml / 8fl oz (1 cup) water and bring to the boil. Reduce the heat, cover and simmer for 10 minutes. Add the marinated fish together with the marinade and red spice paste, then pour in 250ml / 8fl oz (1 cup) water and season with salt. Cover and cook for 10 minutes, or until the fish is cooked.

Kane Kari
Curried Ladyfish

Origin Coastal
Preparation time 20 minutes, plus standing time
Cooking time 20 minutes
Serves 4

12 whole ladyfish or other small whole fish, cleaned

1 teaspoon ground turmeric

1 tablespoon vegetable oil

8–10 curry leaves

salt

For the spice paste

1 teaspoon cumin seeds

1 teaspoon coriander seeds

1 large onion

6 cloves garlic, chopped

6 large dried red chillies

4 tablespoons grated fresh or desiccated
   (dried flaked) coconut

Put the fish in a large shallow dish, score the sides of the fish with a knife, then rub the fish with the turmeric and a little salt. Cover and set aside in the refrigerator for 30 minutes.

To make the spice paste, put all the ingredients in a food processor or blender, season with salt and process, adding a little water to make a smooth paste.

Heat the oil in a large, heavy-based pan over medium heat, add the spice paste and stir-fry for 2 minutes. Pour in 500ml / 18fl oz (2¼ cups) water, bring to the boil, then reduce the heat. Add the fish together with the marinade and curry leaves. Cover and simmer for 7–8 minutes, or until the fish is cooked.

Lal Machhali
Fish in Red Chilli Chutney

Origin Coastal
Preparation time 25–30 minutes, plus standing time
Cooking time 15–20 minutes
Serves 4

750g / 1lb 10oz skinless, firm white fish fillets, trimmed

1 tablespoon vegetable oil

salt

For the marinade
1 level teaspoon ground turmeric

4 cloves garlic, crushed

1 tablespoon lime juice

½ teaspoon sugar

For the red spice paste
6 dried red chillies

40g / 1½oz (⅓ cup) desiccated (dried flaked) coconut

1 teaspoon malt (white) vinegar

Mix the turmeric, garlic, lime juice, sugar and a little salt together in a bowl. Put the fish in a large shallow dish and rub the fish with the turmeric mixture, then cover and set aside in the refrigerator for 30 minutes.

To make the red spice paste, put the dried red chillies, desiccated coconut and vinegar in a food procesor or small blender and process to make a paste, adding a little water only if necessary.

Heat the oil in a pan over high heat, add the red spice paste and stir-fry lightly for about 1 minute, ensuring the bright red colour is not lost due to browning. Reduce the heat, add the fish with 125ml / 4½fl oz (½ cup) water, stir and simmer for 7–8 minutes, or until the fish is cooked.

Doi Maachh
Fish in Yoghurt Sauce

Origin West Bengal
Preparation time 30 minutes, plus standing time
Cooking time 25 minutes
Serves 4

750g / 1lb 10oz skinless, firm white fish fillets, trimmed

1 teaspoon turmeric

125ml / 4½fl oz (½ cup) mustard oil, plus 1 tablespoon

4 green chillies, slit in half lengthways and de-seeded

1 teaspoon yellow mustard seeds

500ml / 18fl oz (2¼ cups) natural (plain) yoghurt, whisked

salt

Put the fish in a large shallow dish and rub with the turmeric and a little salt. Cover and set aside in the refrigerator for 30 minutes.

Heat the oil in kadhai, wok or large frying pan (skillet) over high heat. Working in batches, if necessary, add the fish and fry for 2–3 minutes or until golden brown. Remove with a slotted spoon and drain on kitchen paper (paper towels).

Put the chillies and mustard seeds in a spice grinder and process until ground. Add to the yoghurt and beat well, then add 1 tablespoon oil and mix well to combine.

Return the pan to low heat and add the fish and yoghurt mixture. Cover and simmer for 20 minutes.

Dhyatle Sukha
Dried Fish with Yoghurt

Origin Coastal
Preparation time 20–25 minutes, plus soaking and
marinating time
Cooking time 25 minutes
Serves 4

12 dried Bombay duck (see page 367)
4 tablespoons white sesame seeds
2 tablespoons vegetable oil
1 tablespoon Ginger Paste (see page 57)
1 tablespoon Garlic Paste (see page 57)
4 green chillies, slit lengthways and de-seeded
500ml / 18fl oz (2¼ cups) natural (plain) yoghurt, whisked
4 potatoes, boiled and sliced
salt

For the marinade

¾ teaspoon ground turmeric
1 teaspoon ground cumin
3 tablespoons lime juice

Soak the fish in a bowl of lukewarm water for
15 minutes. Drain and pat dry. Using a sharp knife,
carefully slit open to remove the backbone. Place
the fish in a large shallow dish.

To make the marinade, mix the ground spices and
lime juice together in a bowl. Spread the mixture
evenly over the fish, then cover and set aside in the
refrigerator for 15 minutes.

Put the sesame seeds in a mortar or in a food
processor or small blender, add 2 tablespoons water
and pound with a pestle or process to make a paste.

Heat the oil in a frying pan (skillet) over medium
heat, add the ginger, garlic and sesame seed paste
together with the chillies and stir-fry for 2 minutes.
Pour in 500ml / 18fl oz (2¼ cups) water, then bring to
the boil. Add the fish and cook for 2 minutes, then
reduce the heat, cover and simmer for 10 minutes.

Slowly stir in the yoghurt and cook for 3–4 minutes.
Add the potatoes, stir once and cook, uncovered, for
2 minutes.

Chutney ani Kelwatla Saranga
Pomfret (Butterfish) with Green Masala
Chutney & Bananas

Origin Coastal
Preparation time 30 minutes, plus marinating time
Cooking time 20–25 minutes
Serves 4

4 large whole pomfrets (butterfish), plaice (flounder) or grey (striped) mullet
2 teaspoons ground turmeric
2 tablespoons lime juice
1 large ripe banana
1 tablespoon vegetable oil
salt

For the green spice paste

8 tablespoons chopped coriander (cilantro) leaves
4 sprigs mint, chopped
4–6 green chillies, slit in half lengthways and de-seeded

Clean the fish, cut off the heads and fins, then rinse
under cold running water and pat dry with kitchen
paper (paper towels). Using a sharp knife, score on
both sides. Place the fish in 1–2 large shallow dishes.
Mix the turmeric, lime juice and a little salt together
in a bowl, then rub the mixture evenly over the fish.
Cover and set aside in the refrigerator for 20 minutes.

To make the green spice paste, put the coriander,
mint and green chillies in a small blender and
process, adding a little water if necessary, to make
a paste.

Peel the banana, then halve lengthways. Halve again
lengthways, making four pieces in all.

Heat the oil in a pan over medium heat, add the
banana and fry lightly for about 2 minutes, or
until golden brown. Add the green spice paste and
stir-fry for 2 minutes. Add the fish together with
500ml / 18fl oz (2¼ cups) water, then reduce the
heat, cover and simmer for 15–20 minutes, or until
the fish is cooked.

Mugatli Machhi
Fish & Moong Dal Sprout Stew

Origin Coastal
Preparation time 30 minutes, plus marinating time
Cooking time 25 minutes
Serves 4

---

4 large pomfrets (butterfish) or grey (striped)
    mullets, cleaned

2 tablespoons vegetable oil

6 curry leaves

½ teaspoon chilli powder

1 teaspoon ground cumin

1 teaspoon ground coriander

500g / 1lb 2oz green whole moong dal sprouts

salt

For the marinade

1 teaspoon ground turmeric

2 tablespoons lime juice

For the green spice paste

8 green chillies, slit in half lengthways and de-seeded

1 large sprig coriander (cilantro), chopped

1 sprig mint, chopped

Clean the fish, cut off the heads and fins, then rinse under cold running water and pat dry with kitchen paper (paper towels). Using a sharp knife, score the fish on both sides and make a slit in the belly. Place the fish in 1–2 large shallow dishes. Mix the turmeric, lime juice and a little salt together in a bowl, then rub the mixture evenly over the fish. Cover and set aside in the refrigerator for 15 minutes.

To make the green spice paste, put the chillies coriander and mint leaves in a food processor or small blender and process, adding a little water to make a paste.

Heat the oil in a large, heavy-based pan over medium heat, add the curry leaves and stir-fry for about 1 minute, or until they start to change colour and turn crisp. Add the green spice paste, ground spices and sprouts, then season with salt. Pour in 250ml / 8fl oz (1 cup) water, bring to the boil, then reduce the heat and simmer for 10 minutes.

Add the fish to the pan, cover and simmer for 10 minutes, or until the fish is cooked.

Kothmiratil Machhi
Coriander (Cilantro)-flavoured Fried Fish

Origin Coastal
Preparation time 30–35 minutes, plus marinating time
Cooking time 20 minutes
Serves 4

1kg / 2¼lb whitebait or herring, cleaned, rinsed
    and patted dry with kitchen paper (paper towels)

150g / 5oz (1 cup) rice flour

vegetable oil, for shallow-frying

salt

For the marinade

1 teaspoon ground turmeric

1 teaspoon lime juice

1 teaspoon sugar

For the spice paste

200g / 7oz (4¾ cups) coriander (cilantro) leaves, chopped

4 green chillies, slit in half lengthways and de-seeded

1 × 2.5-cm / 1-inch piece fresh ginger, peeled
    and chopped

8 cloves garlic, crushed

Using a sharp knife, score the fish on both sides and place in a large shallow dish.

Mix the turmeric, lime juice, sugar and a little salt together in a bowl. Rub the mixture evenly over the fish, then cover and set aside in the refrigerator for 15 minutes.

To make the spice paste, put all the ingredients in a food processor or blender and process, adding a little water to make a smooth paste. Spread the paste evenly over the fish and set aside for a further 15 minutes.

Spread the rice flour out on large plate and coat the fish evenly with it.

Heat enough oil for shallow-frying in a large frying pan (skillet) over medium heat. Working in batches, add the fish and shallow-fry for 5 minutes on each side. Remove and drain on kitchen paper (paper towels).

Maspatotia
Fish Roasted in Banana Leaves

Origin Coastal
Preparation time 20–25 minutes, plus standing time
Cooking time 15 minutes
Serves 4

800g / 1¾lb firm white fish fillets, cleaned

4 green chillies, slit in half lengthways and de-seeded

1 teaspoon mustard seeds

1 teaspoon mustard oil

3 banana leaves (optional)

Put the fish in a large shallow dish.

Put the chillies, mustard seeds and mustard oil in a food processor or small blender and process to make a paste, then spread the paste evenly over the fish. Cover and set aside in the refrigerator for 15 minutes.

If using the banana leaves, soften the leaves (see page 174) and cut into squares or rectangles. Alternatively, use foil.

Place one fish fillet on a piece of banana leaf and fold over the sides to form a neat parcel. Secure with kitchen string (twine). Repeat with the remaining fillets.

Heat a tawa or griddle pan over medium heat, then working in batches, place the parcels on the pan and grill for 3 minutes on both sides until the leaf is burnt.

Masor Tenga
Sour Fish

Origin West Bengal
Preparation time 25 minutes, plus standing time
Cooking time 20–25 minutes
Serves 4

500g / 1lb 2oz river fish, such as salmon or trout, cleaned

½ teaspoon ground turmeric

4 tablespoons mustard oil

2 teaspoons fenugreek seeds

500g / 1lb 2oz bottle gourd (calabash), peeled and grated

4 tomatoes, chopped

1 teaspoon lime juice

salt

Put the fish in a large shallow dish. Rub with the turmeric and a little salt, then cover and set aside in the refrigerator for 15 minutes.

Heat the oil in a kadhai, wok or deep, heavy-based pan over high heat, add the fish and fry for about 1–2 minutes, or until light brown on both sides. Remove with a slotted spoon and drain on kitchen paper (paper towels).

Reduce the heat to low, add the fenugreek seeds and stir-fry for about 2 minutes, or until light brown. Add the grated bottle gourd and fry for 5 minutes. Add the tomatoes and fry for 3–4 minutes. Pour in 500ml / 18fl oz (2¼ cups) water, bring to the boil, add the fish and simmer for 10 minutes. Stir in the lime juice and remove from the heat.

Mathok Brenga
Fish in Hollow Bamboo

Origin Tribal North East India
Preparation time 25 minutes
Cooking time 20 minutes
Serves 4

1kg / 2¼lb small rui, hilsa (shad) or any small firm
    white fish, cleaned

1 small onion, chopped

4 green chillies, de-seeded and chopped

pinch of bicarbonate of soda (baking soda)

1 short length of hollow bamboo, about 8cm /
    3 inches in diameter and 13cm / 5 inches long

salt

Remove all the bones from the fish and chop
into pieces.

Mix the fish, onion, chillies, a little salt and the
bicarbonate of soda together in a large bowl, and fill
the bamboo hollow with it. Seal the bamboo with
a banana leaf and secure with kitchen string (twine).

Cook over a preheated charcoal fire or barbecue,
rotating the bamboo hollow frequently, for about
20 minutes, or until the bamboo is almost charred.
Remove from the fire and allow to cool. Remove
the leaf 'cap' and empty the contents into a bowl.

Fish Stew
Fish Stew

Origin Anglo-Indian
Preparation time 15–20 minutes
Cooking time 20 minutes
Serves 2

---

2 spring onions (scallions), trimmed and roughly chopped

150g / 5oz (1 medium) potato, quartered

250ml / 8fl oz (1 cup) coconut milk, fresh (see page
    781) or canned

250ml / 8fl oz (1 cup) fish stock

1 bay leaf

150g / 5oz (1 cup) broccoli or cauliflower florets

400g / 14oz skinless, firm white fish fillets, trimmed

150g / 5oz (1 cup) sweetcorn kernels

pinch of ground black pepper

salt

Place the spring onions and potato in a large, heavy-
based pan, add the coconut milk, stock and bay leaf
and bring to the boil. Reduce the heat, cover and
simmer for about 10 minutes.

Uncover, add the broccoli or cauliflower, fish and
sweetcorn. Season with salt and pepper, then cover
and simmer for a further 5 minutes. Discard the
bay leaf before serving.

Karhai Machhali
Stir-fried Spicy Fish

Origin Punjab
Preparation time 30 minutes
Cooking time 30 minutes
Serve 4

10g / ¼oz dried red chillies
2 teaspoons coriander seeds
100ml / 3½fl oz (scant ½ cup) mustard oil or ghee
1½ teaspoons ajwain seeds
1 teaspoon fenugreek seeds
2 tablespoons Garlic Paste (see page 57)
750g / 1lb 10oz (6 medium) tomatoes, chopped
1 × 5-cm / 2-inch piece fresh ginger, peeled and chopped
5–10 green chillies, de-seeded and chopped
600g / 1lb 5oz skinless, firm white fish fillets, such as pomfret (butterfish), cut into medium-sized pieces
2 teaspoons Garam Masala (see page 31)
4 tablespoons lemon juice
1 large sprig coriander (cilantro), chopped
salt

Put the dried red chillies and coriander seeds in a mortar and pound with a pestle, then transfer to a spice grinder and process until ground.

Heat the oil or ghee in a large, heavy-based pan over medium heat, add the ajwain and fenugreek seeds and stir-fry for about 1 minute, or until they start to splutter. Add the garlic paste and stir-fry for about 30 seconds. Add the pounded spices and stir-fry for a further 30 seconds. Now add the tomatoes, bring to the boil and add half of the ginger and green chillies, then season with salt. Stir, reduce the heat to low and fry for about 3–4 minutes, or until the oil separates out and rises to surface.

Add the fish and simmer for about 5 minutes, or until the fish is cooked, stirring constantly to prevent sticking. Adjust the seasoning, if necessary. Sprinkle the garam masala, lemon juice, coriander and the remaining ginger and green chillies over the fish, stir and serve hot.

Jhingri Maach Malai
Prawn (Shrimp) Malai Curry

Origin West Bengal
Preparation time 15–20 minutes
Cooking time 20 minutes
Serves 4

500g / 1lb 2oz prawns (shrimp), peeled and deveined
½ teaspoon ground turmeric
2 tablespoons ghee
4 green cardamom pods
6 cloves
1 cinnamon stick, about 2.5cm / 1 inch long
1 bay leaf
250ml / 8fl oz (1 cup) coconut milk, fresh (see page 781) or canned
2 green chillies, slit in half lengthways and de-seeded
pinch of ground mace
125ml / 4½fl oz (½ cup) coconut cream, fresh (see page 781) or canned
salt

Put the prawns in a large shallow dish and rub them with the turmeric and a little salt.

Heat the ghee in a large frying pan (skillet) over high heat, add the prawns and stir-fry for 2 minutes. Remove from the pan and set aside.

Reduce the heat to low, then add the whole spices and bay leaves to the pan and stir-fry for about 1–2 minutes, or until they change colour. Pour in the coconut milk and simmer for 2 minutes. Add the prawns, and chillies and season with salt, then simmer for a further 5 minutes. Sprinkle over the ground mace and simmer for about 2 minutes, then stir in the coconut cream. Heat through, adding a couple of tablespoons of water, if necessary.

Doi Jhingri
Prawns (Shrimp) Cooked in Yoghurt

Origin West Bengal
Preparation 20 minutes
Cooking time 20 minutes
Serves 4

300g / 11oz small prawns (shrimp), peeled and deveined
100ml / 3½fl oz (½ cup) natural (plain) yoghurt
1 tablespoon Ginger Paste (see page 57)
1 teaspoon chilli powder
4 tablespoons ghee
1 bay leaf
2 green cardamom pods
4 cloves
1 cinnamon stick, about 2.5cm / 1 inch long
2 onions, thinly sliced
½ clove garlic, crushed
2 potatoes, cut into bite-sized pieces
1 teaspoon sugar
salt

Put the prawns in a shallow dish and sprinkle over some salt. Cover and set aside.

Put the yoghurt in a bowl and whisk briefly, then add the ginger paste and chilli powder and mix together.

Heat the ghee in a large, heavy-based pan over high heat. Reduce the heat, add the bay leaf and whole spices and stir-fry for about 2 minutes, or until they change colour. Add the onions and garlic and stir-fry for 2 minutes, or until the onions are translucent. Add the potatoes and stir-fry for 5 minutes, sprinkling over a little water if required.

Remove the pan from the heat and slowly stir in the yoghurt mixture, then return to medium heat, add the sugar and cook for 5 minutes. Reduce the heat to low, add the prawns and cook for about 5 minutes, or until they turn pink and are cooked through.

Sembharachi Kodi
Goan Prawn (Shrimp) Curry

Origin Coastal
Preparation time 20–25 minutes, plus standing time
Cooking time 25 minutes
Serves 4

250g / 9oz dried prawns (shrimp)
250g / 9oz prawns (shrimp), peeled and deveined
3 tablespoons Sambhar Masala (see page 32)
250ml / 8fl oz (1 cup) coconut milk, fresh (see page 781) or canned
4 tablespoons vegetable oil
150g / 5oz (1 medium) onion, sliced
1 × 2.5-cm / 1-inch piece fresh ginger, peeled and grated
10 cloves garlic, crushed
10 green chillies, de-seeded and finely chopped
3 tablespoons Tamarind Extract (see page 58)
salt

Put the dried and fresh prawns in a large bowl, season with salt and mix together. Cover and set aside in the refrigerator for 30 minutes.

Blend the sambhar masala with the coconut milk in a bowl.

Heat the oil in a large, heavy-based pan over low heat, add the onion, ginger and garlic and stir-fry for about 8–10 minutes, or until golden brown, stirring constantly to ensure the onion doesn't stick to the pan. Add the prawns and chillies and stir-fry for 3 minutes.

Pour the sambhar masala mixture into the pan, increase the heat and bring to the boil. Stir in the tamarind extract and mix well, then reduce the heat to medium and cook for about 2–4 minutes.

Kurumulagail Verthatu Chemeen
Pepper Prawns (Shrimp)

Origin Kerala
Preparation time 15–20 minutes, plus marinating time
Cooking time 15–20 minutes
Serves 4

24 prawns (shrimp), peeled and deveined, heads
    removed but tails intact

1 tablespoon cornflour (cornstarch)

3 tablespoons vegetable oil

250g / 9oz (2 medium) onions, chopped

1 teaspoon Ginger Paste (see page 57)

2 teaspoons Garlic Paste (see page 57)

1 teaspoon chilli powder

60g / 2oz (1 cup) spring onion (scallion) greens,
    trimmed and cut into long thin strips

2 tablespons chopped spring onions (scallions)

1 tablespoon lemon juice

1 tablespoon chopped coriander (cilantro)

generous pinch of coarsely ground black pepper

salt

For the marinade

3 tablespoons lemon juice

2 tablespoons Ginger Paste (see page 57)

5 teaspoons Garlic Paste (see page 57)

2 teaspoons black peppercorns, crushed

To make the marinade, mix all the ingredients
together in a large bowl, then add the prawns and
rub evenly with the marinade. Cover and set aside
for 15 minutes.

Put the cornflour in a small bowl, add 3 tablespoons
water and mix together. Set aside.

Heat the oil in a deep, heavy-based pan over medium
heat, add the onions and stir-fry for about 2 minutes,
or until translucent and glossy. Add the ginger and
garlic pastes and stir-fry for 2–3 minutes, or until the
onions are light golden. Add the chilli powder and
stir-fry for about 1–2 minutes, or until the moisture
has evaporated.

Add the marinated prawns, increase the heat to high
and stir-fry for 2 minutes. Add the spring onions
and stir-fry for 1 minute, then pour in 125ml / 4½fl
oz (½ cup) water. Stir, then add the lemon juice
and coriander and season with salt. Stir, add the
cornflour mixture and continue to stir for about
2–3 minutes, or until the moisture has almost
evaporated. Sprinkle over the ground black pepper,
stir, remove from the heat and adjust the seasoning,
if necessary.

❋ / 📷 pp.554, 555

Chemeen Ada
Prawn (Shrimp) Cutlets

Origin Kerala
Preparation time 15–20 minutes, plus cooling time
Cooking time 20–30 minutes
Serves 5–6

500g / 1lb 2oz prawns (shrimp), peeled and deveined

150g / 5oz (1 cup) rice flour

6 green chillies, chopped

10 shallots, chopped

1 × 2.5-cm / 1-inch piece fresh ginger

2 sprigs curry leaves

250ml / 8fl oz (1 cup) vegetable oil

salt

Bring a large pan of water to the boil, add the
prawns and cook for 5 minutes. Remove from the
heat, drain and allow to cool.

When the prawns are cool, mash well with a
potato masher, then blend with all the remaining
ingredients except the oil. Roll the mixture into
small balls then with damp hands, flatten and shape
into cutlets, or balls if you prefer.

Heat the oil in a large frying pan (skillet) over
medium heat. Working in batches, fry the cutlets
for about 3–4 minutes on each side until golden.
Remove with a slotted spoon and drain on kitchen
paper (paper towels).

Erha Meen Mulkitathu
Prawns (Shrimp) & Sole in Fennel Sauce

Origin Kerala
Preparation time 40 minutes, plus soaking
and marinating time
Cooking time 45 minutes
Serves 4

---

8 large prawns (shrimp), peeled and deveined, heads
    removed but tails intact

8 sole or pomfret (butterfish) fillets, trimmed

vegetable oil, for shallow-frying

salt

For the marinade

3 teaspoons Ginger Paste (see page 57)

7 teaspoons Garlic Paste (see page 57)

3 tablespoons lemon juice

½ teaspoon ground turmeric

1 tablespoon chopped coriander (cilantro) leaves

4 teaspoons grated fresh coconut

For the sauce

2 teaspoons ground coriander

1 teaspoon chilli powder

½ teaspoon ground turmeric

2 tablespoons vegetable oil

1 teaspoon fennel seeds

½ teaspoon mustard seeds

½ teaspoon fenugreek seeds

125g / 4¼oz (1 small) onion, chopped

7 teaspoons Garlic Paste (see page 57)

4 green chillies, de-seeded and chopped

20–25 curry leaves

400g / 14oz (3 small) tomatoes, puréed

3 tablespoons Tamarind Extract (see page 58)

Soak several wooden skewers in a large bowl of
water for 30 minutes before using.

Thread the prawns on to the soaked wooden skewers
from the tail to the head. Set aside in a large shallow
dish. Put the fish in another shallow dish.

To make the marinade, mix all the ingredients
together in a large bowl and rub the fish and
prawns evenly with the marinade. Cover and set
aside in the refrigerator for 30 minutes.

To make the sauce, put the ground coriander,
chilli powder and turmeric in a small bowl, add
2 tablespoons water and mix together.

Heat the oil in a large, heavy-based pan over medium
heat, add the fennel, mustard and fenugreek seeds
and stir-fry for about 1 minute, or until they start to
splutter. Add the onions and stir-fry for 5 minutes,
or until light golden, then add the garlic paste and
stir-fry for a further 2–3 minutes, or until the onions
are golden brown. Add the chillies and curry leaves
and stir-fry for 30 seconds, then add the ground spice
mixture and stir-fry for about 2–3 minutes, or until
the moisture has evaporated.

Add the puréed tomatoes to the pan and stir-fry
for about 5 minutes, or until specks of oil begin to
appear on the surface, then add the tamarind extract
and stir-fry for 1 minute. Pour in about 500ml /
18fl oz (2¼ cups) water, bring to the boil, then reduce
the heat to low and simmer.

Heat enough oil for shallow-frying in a large frying
pan (skillet) over medium heat. Working in batches,
add the fish and shallow-fry for about 1 minute
on each side until evenly coloured, then transfer
to the sauce.

Heat a little more oil in the same pan over medium
heat. Slide the prawns off the skewers and into
the pan and shallow-fry for about 1 minute on each
side, turning once, until evenly coloured, then transfer
to the sauce and bring to the boil. Check to make
sure the fish and prawns are cooked, then remove
from the heat and adjust the seasoning, if necessary.

Savoury Fried
Carrots   p.320

Paneer in Thick
Tomato Sauce   p.314

Broad Beans with
Coriander (Cilantro) p.326

Spicy Onions
in Sauce   p.335

Pounded Meatballs in
Light Cardomom Sauce p.436

Lotus Root Curry
p.338

Peas & Carrots p.339

Spicy Chicken in Thick Sauce p.510

Potato Curry

p.228

Fish Cooked in Banana
Leaf Wraps   p.365

Spicy Sweet & Sour Aubergines
(Eggplants)   p.250

Kokum Curry
          p.321

Goan Fish
Curry (I)   p.374

Pearl Fish Pan Grilled
in Banana Leaf   p.359

Spicy Baked Bottle
Gourd (Calabash)   p.297

Piquant
Fish Fry   p.359

Roasted Mashed Aubergine
(Eggplant)
                    p.251

Fried Fish from Amritsar   p.362

Dry Black Lentils   p.583

Stuffed Fish   p.356

Konju Masala
Spicy Prawn (Shrimp) Curry

Origin Kerala
Preparation time 15–20 minutes
Cooking time 25 minutes
Serves 4

5 teaspoons ground coriander
4 teaspoons chilli powder
1 teaspoon ground turmeric
3 tablespoons coconut oil
300g / 11oz (2 cups) chopped onions
1 × 2.5-cm / 1-inch piece fresh ginger, peeled and chopped
4 green chillies, de-seeded and chopped
2½ teaspoons Ginger Paste (see page 57)
2½ teaspoons Garlic Paste (see page 57)
400g / 14oz (2¼ cups) chopped tomatoes
45g / 1½oz kokum
16 prawns (shrimp), peeled and deveined, heads removed but tails intact
20–25 curry leaves
125ml / 4½fl oz (½ cup) coconut milk, fresh (see page 781) or canned
salt

Put the ground coriander, chilli powder and turmeric in a small bowl, add 4 tablespoons water and mix together.

Heat the oil in a large, heavy-based pan over medium heat, add the onions and stir-fry for about 2 minutes, or until translucent. Add the ginger and chillies and stir-fry for 2–3 minutes, or until the onions are light golden. Add the ginger and garlic pastes and stir-fry for 1–2 minutes, or until the moisture has evaporated. Add the ground spice mixture and stir-fry for a further 2–3 minutes, or until the moisture has evaporated.

Add the tomatoes and kokum to the pan, stir, then pour in 500ml / 18fl oz (2¼ cups) water and season with salt. Bring to the boil, reduce the heat to low and simmer for about 5 minutes, or until reduced to half its original volume.

Add the prawns, return to the boil, then reduce the heat to low, add the curry leaves and simmer for 3–4 minutes. Remove from the heat, stir in the coconut milk, then return to low heat and simmer for a further 2–3 minutes. Remove from the heat and adjust the seasoning, if necessary.

Jhinga Dopyaza
Curried Prawns (Shrimp) with Onions

Origin Awadh
Preparation time 20–25 minutes
Cooking time 15–20 minutes
Serves 6

250ml / 8fl oz (1 cup) vegetable oil
750g / 1lb 10oz (6 medium) onions, sliced
½ teaspoon ground turmeric
1 tablespoon Ginger Paste (see page 57)
1 tablespoon Garlic Paste (see page 57)
2 teaspoons chilli powder
3 teaspoons ground coriander
12 curry leaves
6 green chillies, de-seeded and chopped
1kg / 2¼lb prawns (shrimp), peeled and deveined
2 tablespoons chopped coriander (cilantro) leaves
salt

Heat the oil in a shallow kadhai, wok or frying pan (skillet) over medium heat, add the onions and turmeric and stir-fry for about 5 minutes, or until light brown.

Reduce the heat to low, add the ginger and garlic pastes, chilli powder, ground coriander, curry leaves and green chillies, then season with salt and stir-fry for 5 minutes. Add the prawns and keep stir-frying for about 5 minutes, or until they change colour and are well cooked. Add the chopped coriander and remove from the heat.

Tamatarwale Jhinge
Prawns (Shrimp) with Tomato

Origin Punjab
Preparation time 20–25 minutes, plus marinating time
Cooking time 15–20 minutes
Serves 4

500g / 1lb 2oz prawns (shrimp), peeled and deveined
1 teaspoon sugar
125ml / 4½fl oz (½ cup) vegetable oil
4 dried red chillies
¼ teaspoon fenugreek seeds
¼ teaspoon mustard seeds
6 cloves garlic, chopped
2 onions, sliced
½ teaspoon ground cumin
6 green chillies, de-seeded and chopped
500g / 1lb 2oz (3 medium) tomatoes, puréed
salt

For the marinade

½ teaspoon ground turmeric
1 teaspoon Ginger Paste (see page 57)
1 teaspoon Garlic Paste (see page 57)
juice of 1 lime

For the tempering

1 tablespoon vegetable oil
½ teaspoon cumin seeds

To make the marinade, mix the turmeric, ginger and garlic pastes and the lime juice together in a bowl, then season with salt. Place the prawns in a large shallow dish and rub the marinade all over, then cover and set aside in the refrigerator for 1 hour.

Put the sugar in a small bowl, add 1 tablespoon water and stir until dissolved. Set aside.

Heat the oil in a large, heavy-based pan over medium heat, add the red chillies, fenugreek seeds, mustard seeds and garlic and stir-fry for about 1 minute, or until they change colour. Add the onions and stir-fry for 5–7 minutes, or until golden brown. You may need to reduce the heat slightly to prevent the seeds burning.

Add the ground cumin to the pan and stir, then add the marinated prawns and stir-fry for about 2 minutes. Add the green chillies and mix well.

Reduce the heat to low, add the puréed tomatoes and cook for about 5 minutes, or until the tomatoes are cooked and the oil rises to surface. Add the dissolved sugar mixture, then season with salt and mix.

Heat the oil for the tempering in a small frying pan (skillet) over high heat, add the cumin seeds and stir-fry for about 30 seconds, or until they start to splutter, then pour over the prawns.

Chemeen Kari
Home-style Prawn (Shrimp) Curry

Origin Kerala
Preparation time 30 minutes
Cooking time 8–10 minutes
Serves 4

4 teaspoons chilli powder
1 teaspoon ground coriander
1 teaspoon ground turmeric
3 green chillies, de-seeded and chopped
8 shallots, chopped
3 petals cambodge, shredded
1 × 3-cm / 1¼-inch piece fresh ginger, peeled
1 coconut, shrimp
500g / 1lb 2oz prawns (shrimp), peeled and deveined, heads removed but tails intact
15–20 curry leaves
1 tablespoon vegetable oil
salt

Bring 500ml / 18fl oz (2¼ cups) water to the boil in a large, heavy-based pan, add all the ground spices together with the chillies, shallots, cambodge petals, ginger, and coconut, then season with salt. Add the prawns, reduce the heat to low and cook for about 6 minutes, or until the prawns are cooked and the sauce thickens.

Mix in the curry leaves and oil, then remove the pan from the heat.

Royya Alu Pulussu
Prawn (Shrimp) Curry

Origin Hyderabad/Andhra Pradesh
Preparation time 20 minutes, plus marinating time
Cooking time 20 minutes
Serves 4

¼ teaspoon ground turmeric

1 teaspoon chilli powder

500g / 1lb 2oz prawns (shrimp), peeled and deveined

1 teaspoon ground coriander

1 teaspoon ground cumin

125ml / 4½fl oz (½ cup) vegetable oil

4 onions, sliced

1 teaspoon Ginger Paste (see page 57)

1 teaspoon Garlic Paste (see page 57)

250ml / 8fl oz (1 cup) coconut milk, fresh
(see page 781) or canned

40g / ½oz (½ cup) desiccated (dried flaked) coconut

4 green chillies, de-seeded and chopped

4 cloves

6 black peppercorns

10 mint leaves, chopped

6 curry leaves, chopped

juice of 1 lime

1 teaspoon Tamarind Extract (see page 58)

salt

To make the marinade, mix the turmeric and chilli powder together in a large bowl and season with salt. Add the prawns and turn until coated, then cover and set aside in the refrigerator for 15 minutes.

Put the ground coriander and cumin in a small bowl, add 4 tablespoons water and mix together.

Heat the oil in a large frying pan (skillet) over medium heat, add the onions and stir-fry for 2 minutes, or until translucent.

Reduce the heat to low, add the prawns to the pan and fry for 3 minutes. Add the ginger and garlic pastes together with the ground coriander mixture and fry for 2 minutes. Pour in the coconut milk and add the desiccated coconut, chillies, cloves, peppercorns, chopped mint and curry leaves and simmer for about 5 minutes. Add the lime juice and tamarind extract and simmer for a further 5 minutes, then remove from the heat.

Thotikura Tetakaya
Spinach with Dried Prawns (Shrimp)

Origin Tamil Nadu
Preparation time 20 minutes, plus soaking time
Cooking time 10–12 minutes
Serves 4

60g / 2oz dried prawns (shrimp), rinsed

125ml / 4½fl oz (½ cup) vegetable oil

½ teaspoon mustard seeds

1 onion, sliced

1 teaspoon Ginger Paste (see page 57)

1 teaspoon Garlic Paste (see page 57)

¼ teaspoon ground turmeric

3–6 green chillies, de-seeded and chopped

500g / 1lb 2oz spinach or similar greens

salt

Soak the dried prawns in a bowl of lukewarm water for 20 minutes.

Put the onion in a blender or food processor and process until ground.

Heat the oil in a large, heavy-based pan over high heat, then reduce the heat. Add the mustard seeds and stir-fry for about 1 minute, or until they start to splutter. Add the onion, ginger and garlic pastes, turmeric, green chillies and prawns and stir-fry for 3–4 minutes.

Add the spinach or greens and continue to fry for about 2 minutes, then season with salt. Stir, reduce the heat to low and cook for a further 2–3 minutes, or until the water released by the greens is absorbed.

Veinchana Royyaalu
Curried Prawns (Shrimp)

Origin Hyderabad/Andhra Pradesh
Preparation time 30 minutes, plus marinating time
Cooking time 15 minutes
Serves 4

2 teaspoons Ginger Paste (see page 57)
2 teaspoons Garlic Paste (see page 57)
1 teaspoon ground turmeric
juice of 2 limes
500g / 1lb 2oz prawns (shrimp), peeled and deveined, heads removed but tails intact
1 teaspoon ground coriander
2 teaspoons chilli powder
100ml / 3½fl oz (½ cup) vegetable oil
4 cardamom pods
4 cloves
¼ teaspoon aniseeds
2 onions, thinly sliced
2 tomatoes, chopped
4 green chillies, slit in half lengthways and de-seeded
salt

To make the marinade, put half the ginger and garlic pastes in a bowl, season with salt and add the turmeric and lime juice. Add the prawns and rub them with the marinade. Cover and marinate in the refrigerator for 30 minutes.

Put the ground coriander and chilli powder in a small bowl, add 2 tablespoons water and mix together.

Heat the oil in a large, heavy-based pan over medium heat, add the cardamom pods, cloves and aniseeds and stir-fry for about 1 minute, or until the cardamom pods darken and swell. Add the onions and stir-fry for about 4–5 minutes, or until light brown. Add the remaining ginger and garlic pastes and stir-fry for 30 seconds. Add the ground coriander mixture and stir-fry for another minute. Add the tomatoes and fry for a further 2 minutes. Add the prawns, then season with salt and add the chillies. Stir, add 250ml / 8fl oz (1 cup) water, bring to the boil, then reduce the heat and cook for about 5 minutes, or until the prawns are cooked.

Nariyalna Doodh ma Bheeda ne Colmi
Prawns (Shrimp) with Okra
in Coconut Milk

Origin Parsi
Preparation time 20 minutes
Coking time 15–20 minutes
Serves 4

500g / 1lb 2oz prawns (shrimp), peeled and deveined
4 tablespoons rice flour
1 teaspoon ground turmeric
juice of 1 lime
3 tablespoons vegetable oil or ghee
4 onions, chopped
250g / 9oz okra, topped and tailed (trimmed)
500ml / 18fl oz (2¼ cups) coconut milk, fresh (see page 781) or canned
½ teaspoon Tamarind Extract (see page 58)
sugar to taste
salt

For the spice paste

6–8 green chillies, roughly chopped
1 clove garlic, crushed
4 teaspoons ground cumin
1 tablespoon malt (white) vinegar

Put the prawns in a dish and rub them with the rice flour, turmeric, lime juice and some salt. Cover and set aside.

To make the spice paste, put all the ingredients in a food processor or blender and process to make a smooth paste.

Heat the oil or ghee in a large, heavy-based pan over medium heat, add the onions and stir-fry for about 4–5 minutes, or until light brown. Add the prawns and stir-fry for 2–3 minutes, then add the spice paste and fry for 1 minute. Add the okra and cook for a further 2–3 minutes. Reduce the heat, pour in the coconut milk and simmer for 3–4 minutes, then add the tamarind extract and sugar and season with salt.

Jhingri Machher Malikari
Prawns (Shrimp) in Coconut Sauce

Origin West Bengal
Preparation time 25–30 minutes
Cooking time 20 minutes
Serves 4–6

4 tablespoons mustard oil
3 onions, sliced
2kg / 4½lb prawns (shrimp), peeled and deveined
1 teaspoon ground turmeric
½ teaspoon ground coriander
½ teaspoon ground cumin
½ teaspoon chilli powder
1 teaspoon sugar
125ml / 4½fl oz (½ cup) coconut milk, fresh (see page 781) or canned
salt
steamed Rice (see page 631), to serve

Place a kadhai, wok or large frying pan (skillet) over medium heat and add the oil. When hot, add the onion slices and fry for about 2–3 minutes, or until golden brown. Remove with a slotted spoon and drain on kitchen paper (paper towels).

Add the prawns and fry for 1 minute, then add the ground spices and sugar and stir-fry for 1 minute. Pour in the coconut milk, reduce the heat, cover and cook for 10 minutes.

Garnish with the crispy fried onions and serve with freshly steamed Rice.

Chinchi Gulatala Jawla
Sweet & Sour Prawns (Shrimp)

Origin Coastal
Preparation time 25 minutes, plus standing time
Cooking time 20 minutes
Serves 4–6

1kg / 2¼lb prawns (shrimp), peeled and deveined
½ teaspoon ground turmeric
1 tablespoon vegetable oil
2 onions, chopped
1 tablespoon grated ginger
1 tablespoon finely chopped garlic
1 teaspoon ground coriander
1 teaspoon ground cumin
1 teaspoon chilli powder
4 tablespoons jaggery, crumbled, or soft brown sugar
1 tablespoon Tamarind Extract (see page 58)
salt

Put the prawns in a large bowl or dish and rub them with the turmeric and a little salt. Cover and set aside in the refrigerator for 20 minutes.

Heat the oil in a large, heavy-based pan over medium heat, add the onions, ginger, garlic and ground spices and stir-fry for about 5 minutes, or until the onions are brown. Add the jaggery or sugar, tamarind extract, 250ml / 8fl oz (1 cup) water and season with salt. Mix well and cook for 5 minutes. Add the prawns with 125ml / 4½fl oz (½ cup) water. Reduce the heat slightly, cover and simmer for 7–8 minutes, or until the moisture has evaporated and the prawns are cooked.

✳ ✳
___

Kolambini Bharaleli Bhaji
Prawns (Shrimp) with Stuffed Steamed (Bell) Peppers

Origin Coastal
Preparation time 1 hour, plus soaking, standing and cooling time
Cooking time 15 minutes
Serves 4

250g / 9oz fresh or dried small prawns (shrimp)
4 potatoes, (unpeeled)
4 red or green (bell) peppers
2 tablespoons vegetable oil
1 large onion, chopped
1 teaspoon ground coriander
1 teaspoon ground cumin
1 teaspoon chilli powder
1 teaspoon Ginger Paste (see page 57)
1 teaspoon Garlic Paste (see page 57)
2 tomatoes, chopped
1 teaspoon sugar
1 teaspoon Garam Masala (see page 31)
salt

For the marinade
1 teaspoon ground turmeric
1 teaspoon salt
1 teaspoon lime juice

If using fresh prawns, peel, devein, rinse under cold running water and pat dry with kitchen paper (paper towels). If using dried prawns, soak in a bowl of cold water for about 10 minutes.

To make the marinade, mix the turmeric, salt and the lime juice together in a bowl, then rub the mixture over the prawns. Cover and set aside in the refrigerator for 15 minutes.

Cook the potatoes in a large pan of boiling water for about 20 minutes, or until soft. Drain, allow to cool then peel off the skins. Return the flesh to the pan and mash with a potato masher.

Slice the tops off the peppers and reserve. Remove the core and seeds and discard.

Heat the oil in a large, heavy-based pan over medium heat, add the onion and stir-fry for 2 minutes, or until they are translucent. Add the ground spices, season with salt and fry for a further 2 minutes. Add the ginger and garlic pastes, tomatoes, mashed potatoes and sugar, then mix well. Reduce the heat, cover and simmer for 10 minutes.

Add the prawns together with the marinade and cook for 2–3 minutes, or until the prawns are cooked. Remove from the heat, sprinkle over the garam masala and stir. Allow the stuffing to cool to room temperature.

Rub the remaining oil over the outer skin of the peppers and stuff them loosely with the filling. Replace the tops and cook in a steamer for 15 minutes

You can use aubergines or tomatoes instead of peppers, if you prefer.

Bhaji ani Kolambicha Stew
Prawns (Shrimp) with Stewed Vegetables

Origin Coastal
Preparation time 30–35 minutes, plus soaking and standing time
Cooking time 20–25 minutes
Serves 4

450g / 1lb small or medium-sized fresh or dried
    prawns (shrimp)
2 tablespoons vegetable oil
2 onions, chopped
4 tablespoons desiccated (dried flaked) coconut
2 green chillies, de-seeded and chopped
1 teaspoon grated ginger
1 teaspoon finely chopped garlic
½ teaspoon ground green cardamom
1 teaspoon ground coriander
1 teaspoon ground cumin
1 teaspoon chilli powder
2 teaspoons sugar
1 teaspoon salt
1 small cabbage, shredded
100g / 3½oz (⅔ small) unripe papaya, peeled and cut
    into cubes
4–6 small new (baby) potatoes
100g / 3½oz (1 cup) French (green) beans,
    topped and tailed (trimmed)
½ teaspoon Garam Masala (see page 31)
2 tablespoons chopped coriander (cilantro),
    to garnish

For the marinade
½ teaspoon ground turmeric
1 teaspoon lime juice
½ teaspoon salt

If using fresh prawns, peel, devein, remove the heads but keep the tails intact, then rinse under cold running water and pat dry with kitchen paper (paper towels). If using dried prawns, soak in cold water for 10 minutes.

To make the marinade, mix all the ingredients together, then pour the mixture over the prawns. Cover and set aside in the refrigerator for 15 minutes.

Heat the oil in a large, heavy-based pan over medium heat, add the onions and stir-fry for 2 minutes or until translucent. Add the coconut and stir-fry for 1 minute, making sure that it does not turn brown. Add the chillies, ginger, garlic, ground spices, sugar, salt and the vegetables and mix thoroughly. Pour in 500ml / 18fl oz (2¼ cups) water, then reduce the heat, cover and cook for about 10 minutes, or until the vegetables are almost done.

Add the prawns together with the marinade, then cover and cook for 5 minutes, or until the vegetables are almost dry and the prawns are cooked. Remove from the heat, sprinkle over the garam masala and cover for 2 minutes. Garnish with chopped coriander and serve immediately.

Hirvya Kelyatil Jawla
Prawns (Shrimp) with Raw Green Bananas

Origin Coastal
Preparation time 20 minutes, plus marinating time
Cooking time 15–20 minutes
Serves 4

1kg / 2¼lb prawns (shrimp), peeled and deveined
2 tablespoons lime juice
1 tablespoon ghee
1½ tablespoons coarsely ground black pepper
170g / 6oz (1¾ cups) desiccated
    (dried flaked) coconut
1kg / 2¼lb raw green bananas, peeled and cut
    into slices
salt

Put the prawns in a large bowl, add the lime juice and turn until the prawns are coated. Cover and set aside in the refrigerator for 15 minutes.

Heat the ghee in a large heavy-based pan over medium heat, add the black pepper and coconut and stir-fry for about 1 minute, or until the coconut turns light brown. Be careful not to burn it.

Add the banana slices and 250ml / 8fl oz (1 cup) water, then reduce the heat, cover and cook for 5 minutes. Add the prawns together with the marinade, cover and simmer for about 7 minutes, or until the prawns are cooked.

Balchao
Prawn (Shrimp) Balchao

Origin Coastal
Preparation time 40 minutes
Cooking time 15 minutes
Serves 4

150ml / ¼ pint (⅔ cup) groundnut (peanut) oil, plus extra for deep-frying

160g / 5½oz (1 medium) onion, chopped

120g / 4oz (1 small) tomato, chopped

1kg / 2 ¼lb small prawns (shrimp), peeled and deveined

10 curry leaves

2½ teaspoons sugar

salt

For the paste

20 dried red chillies

4 cinnamon sticks, about 2.5cm / 1 inch long

15 green cardamom pods

15 cloves

1 teaspoon whole black peppercorns

1 teaspoon cumin seeds

1 tablespoon chopped garlic

3 tablespoons chopped ginger

150ml / ¼ pint (⅔ cup) malt (white) vinegar

Heat enough oil for deep-frying in a kadhai or deep, heavy-based pan to 180°C/350°F, or until a cube of bread browns in 30 seconds. Working in batches, carefully lower the prawns into the hot oil and deep-fry for 2 minutes. Remove with a slotted spoon and drain on kitchen paper (paper towels).

To make the paste, put all the ingredients in a food processor or blender and process to make a smooth paste.

Heat the oil in a handi or large frying pan (skillet) over medium heat, add the onion and fry for about 5–7 minutes, or until golden brown. Add the tomato, stir for 1 minute, then add the paste and stir-fry for a further 2 minutes. Add the prawns and stir-fry for about 5 minutes, or until the prawns are cooked. Now add the curry leaves and sugar and stir. Adjust the seasoning, if necessary.

This dish is known for its piquant character. It is more like a pickle relish and is consumed in moderation.

Rechiado Prawns
Portuguese-style Spicy Fried Prawns (Shrimp)

Origin Goa
Preparation time 15–20 minutes
Cooking time 10 minutes
Serves 6

1kg / 2¼lb large prawns (shrimp), peeled and deveined, heads removed but tails intact

1 tablespoon whole black peppercorns

2 teaspoons cloves

½ tablespoon ground cinnamon

1 x 1-cm / ½-inch piece fresh ginger, peeled and chopped

20 cloves garlic, crushed

10–20 dried red chillies, de-seeded

1 tablespoon cumin seeds

1½ teaspoons ground turmeric

125ml / 4½fl oz (½ cup) malt (white) vinegar

vegetable oil, for frying

plain (all-purpose) flour, for dusting

salt

Put the prawns in a large bowl or dish.

Put the whole spices, ginger, garlic, dried red chillies, cumin seeds and turmeric in a blender or food processor, season with salt and process, adding as much vinegar as required to make a smooth paste, then coat the prawns liberally with the spice paste.

Heat the oil in a frying pan (skillet) over medium heat. Dust each prawn lightly with flour and fry for 3–4 minutes, or until golden brown and cooked.

Roya Vepaddu
Golden Fried Prawns (Shrimp)

Origin Hyderabad/Andhra Pradesh
Preparation time 15 minutes
Cooking time 15 minutes
Serves 4

8–10 prawns (shrimp), peeled and deveined, heads
    removed but tails intact

---

vegetable oil, for deep-frying

---

salt

For the batter

100g / 3½oz (⅔ cup) rice flour

---

3 tablespoons desiccated (dried flaked) coconut

---

1 egg yolk

150ml / ¼ pint (⅔ cup) coconut milk

---

1 teaspoon ground black pepper

Put the prawns in a shallow dish and sprinkle over
some salt.

To make the batter, mix the flour and desiccated
coconut together in a large bowl, then gradually stir
in the egg yolk, coconut milk and black pepper, and
season with salt.

Heat enough oil for deep-frying in a kadhai or deep
heavy-based pan to 180°C/350°F, or until a cube of
bread browns in 30 seconds. Dip the prawns into the
batter one by one, then carefully lower them into
the hot oil and deep-fry for about 2 minutes, turning
with a slotted spoon a few times. Remove from the
pan with a slotted spoon and drain on kitchen paper
(paper towels). Serve hot.

Nejandu Thoran
Crab Curry with Coconut

Origin Kerala
Preparation time 45 minutes–1 hour
Cooking time 30 minutes
Serves 4

500g / 1lb 2oz crabmeat

---

2 green chillies, slit in half lengthways and de-seeded

---

1 × 3-cm / 1¼-inch piece fresh ginger,
    peeled and chopped

---

1 tablespoon coconut oil

15–20 curry leaves

---

salt

For the paste

3 teaspoons chilli powder

---

1 teaspoon ground coriander

---

1 teaspoon ground turmeric

---

2 coconuts, grated

---

2 cloves garlic, crushed

---

4 shallots, chopped

---

1 teaspoon cumin seeds

Pick over the crabmeat and remove and discard any
pieces of shell.

To make the paste, put the ground spices in a small
bowl, add 3 tablespoons water and mix together.
Put the grated coconut, garlic, shallots, cumin seeds
and the ground spice mixture in a blender or food
processor and process to make a paste.

Put the crabmeat in a large pan, add the chillies,
ginger, the paste and 250ml / 8fl oz (1 cup) water, then
season with salt and cook over low heat for about
30 minutes, or until all the water has evaporated.

Heat the oil in a small frying pan (skillet) over
medium heat, add the curry leaves and stir-fry for
about 1 minute, or until they change colour. Pour
over the crab mixture, stir well and serve.

☀ ☀

Kande Batatyatli Machhi
Shellfish in Onion Masala

Origin Coastal
Preparation time 25 minutes, plus marinating time
Cooking time 25 minutes
Serves 4

750g / 1lb 10oz live mussels or clams
¼ teaspoon ground green cardamom
¼ teaspoon ground coriander
¼ teaspoon ground cumin
1 tablespoon vegetable oil
1 teaspoon grated ginger
1 teaspoon finely chopped garlic
2 cloves
1 cinnamon stick, about 2.5cm / 1 inch long
2 green chillies, de-seeded and chopped
2 onions, sliced
1 large potato, cut into cubes
1 teaspoon jaggery, crumbled, or soft brown sugar
1 large tomato, skinned
pinch of ground mace or nutmeg
1 tablespoon coconut feni
salt

For the marinade

1 teaspoon ground turmeric
½ teaspoon chilli powder
1 teaspoon lime juice

Rinse the mussels or clams very well to remove all grit and dirt, then remove or retain shell as preferred.

Mix the turmeric, chilli powder, lime juice and a little salt together. Coat the mussels or clams all over with the turmeric mixture, then cover and set aside in the refrigerator for 20 minutes.

Put the ground spices, except the mace, in a small bowl, add 2 tablespoons water and mix together.

Heat the oil in a large, heavy-based pan over high heat, add the ginger, garlic and whole spices and stir-fry for about 1 minute, or until the spices start to splutter. Add the green chillies, ground spice mixture and stir-fry for 30 seconds. Add the onions and stir-fry for 2 minutes, or until they are translucent.

Add the potatoes and jaggery or sugar, then season with salt and pour in 250ml / 8fl oz (1 cup) water. Reduce the heat, cover and simmer for 10 minutes.

Add the shellfish together with the marinade, the tomatoes and 125ml / 4½fl oz (½ cup) water. Cover and simmer for a further 10 minutes, or until the sauce is thick.

Sprinkle over the ground mace powder and remove the from heat. Stir in the coconut feni.

☀ ☀

Nejandu Kari
Crab Curry

Origin Kerala
Preparation time 30 minutes
Cooking time 30 minutes
Serves 4

1kg / 2¼lb crabmeat
3 tablespoons chilli powder
1 tablespoon ground coriander
1 teaspoon ground turmeric
3 tablespoons vegetable oil
1 teaspoon mustard seeds
1 teaspoon fenugreek seeds
1–15 curry leaves
2 tomatoes, chopped
4–6 green chillies, de-seeded and chopped
6–8 cloves garlic, chopped
1 × 2.5-cm / 1-inch piece fresh ginger, peeled and chopped
2 tablespoons Tamarind Extract (see page 58)
salt

Pick over the crabmeat and remove and discard any pieces of shell.

Put the ground spices in a small bowl, add 4 tablespoons water and mix together.

Heat the oil in a large, heavy-based pan over medium heat, add the mustard seeds and stir-fry for about 1 minute, or until they start to splutter. Add the fenugreek seeds and curry leaves and stir-fry for about 1 minute, or until they turn black. Immediately add the ground spice mixture, then increase the heat to high and stir-fry for a minute or so.

Reduce the heat, add the tomatoes, chillies, garlic and ginger and simmer for about 5 minutes. Add the tamarind extract, bring to the boil and gently stir in the crabmeat. Season with salt, then cover the pan and cook over low heat for about 20 minutes.

Chimbori Shengdanya Kalwan
Crab Curry with Peanuts

Origin Coastal
Preparation time 20 minutes, plus marinating time
Cooking time 40 minutes
Serves 4

4 medium-sized crabs, rinsed well
4 tablespoons vegetable oil
1 large onion, chopped
300g / 11oz (2 cups) peanuts, roughly pounded and roasted
1 large tomato, skinned and chopped
1 teaspoon Ginger Paste (see page 57)
½ tablespoon Garlic Paste (see page 57)
2 teaspoons chilli powder
1 teaspoon ground turmeric
1 teaspoon ground green cardamom
1 teaspoon ground coriander
1 teaspoon ground cumin
1 teaspoon ground aniseed
2 tablespoons lime juice
1 teaspoon Garam Masala (see page 31)
2 teaspoons sugar
125ml / 4½fl oz (½ cup) coconut feni
salt

For the marinade
1 teaspoon ground turmeric
1 tablespoon lime juice

To make the marinade, mix all the ingredients together in a bowl and rub into the crabs. Place the crabs in a large dish, cover and marinate in the refrigerator for 15 minutes.

Heat the oil in a pan over medium heat, add the onion and stir-fry for 5–7 minutes, or until golden brown. Add the peanuts and fry for 2 minutes. Add the rest of the ingredients, except the coconut feni and crabs, then season with salt and fry for 3 minutes. Pour in 1 litre / 1¾ pints (4¼ cups) water, cover and cook for a further 5 minutes.

Add the marinated crabs together with the marinade and a little water if necessary. Cover and cook for 20 minutes, or until the flesh of the crabs is opaque. Add the coconut feni, stir, cover again and cook for a few more minutes until heated through.

Bhuna Kekra
Grilled Lobster

Origin Punjab
Preparation time 30 minutes, plus marinating time
Cooking time 10–12 minutes
Serves 8

8 lobsters, peeled and deveined with tail intact
melted butter, for basting
salt

For the first marinade
½ tablespoon Ginger Paste (see page 57)
½ tablespoon Garlic Paste (see page 57)
1½ tablespoons red chilli paste
pinch of salt
½ teaspoon vinegar
1 teaspoon vegetable oil

For the second marinade
250ml / 8fl oz (1 cup) natural (plain) yoghurt, whisked
½ tablespoon Ginger Paste (see page 57)
½ tablespoon Garlic Paste (see page 57)
1½ tablespoons red chilli paste
½ teaspoon vinegar
1 tablespoon Garam Masala (see page 31)
½ tablespoon ground dried fenugreek leaves

To make the first marinade, mix all the ingredients together in a bowl.

Place the lobsters in a large shallow dish and rub the marinade evenly over. Cover and marinate in the refrigerator for 1 hour.

To make the second marinade, mix all the ingredients together in a separate bowl and season with salt. Rub this paste all over the lobsters, cover again and marinate in the refrigerator for a further 1–2 hours.

Prepare a charcoal grill for a moderate heat or preheat the oven to 180°C/350°F/Gas Mark 4.

Thread the marinated lobsters on to metal skewers and spread any of the remaining marinade over them. Roast the lobsters over the charcoal grill or in the oven, over a baking tray, for about 8–10 minutes, or until the excess moisture drains out completely. Remove from the charcoal grill or oven and baste with melted butter, then roast for a further 2–4 minutes, or until the lobster is cooked. Serve hot.

Meat

Aloo Gosht
Lamb with Potatoes

Origin Delhi
Preparation time 40 minutes
Cooking time 1½–2 hours
Serves 4–6

1½ teaspoons ground coriander
1½ teaspoons ground cumin
1½ teaspoons chilli powder
1 teaspoon Garam Masala (see page 31)
125ml / 4½fl oz (½ cup) vegetable oil or ghee
2 bay leaves
1 teaspoon cumin seeds
5 large potatoes, cut into quarters
225g / 8oz (2 medium) onions, finely sliced
1 cinnamon stick, about 5cm / 2 inches long
4–6 cloves
seeds from 2–3 large black cardamom pods
4–6 green cardamom pods, crushed
pinch of ground mace
1 × 2.5-cm / 1-inch piece fresh ginger, peeled and chopped
2 tablespoons chopped garlic
750g / 1lb 10oz lamb, cut into medium-sized pieces
250g / 9oz (2 small) tomatoes, finely chopped
salt

Put the ground spices in a small bowl, add
1 tablespoon water and mix together to make a
paste. Set aside.

Heat the oil or ghee in a large, heavy-based pan over
medium heat, add the bay leaves and cumin seeds
and stir-fry for about 1 minute, or until the seeds
start to splutter. Add the potatoes and fry for about
10–15 minutes, or until golden. Remove from the pan
with a slotted spoon and drain on kitchen paper
(paper towels).

Add the onions to the oil in the pan and fry, stirring
occasionally, for about 5 minutes, or until medium
brown. Add the cinnamon, cloves, black cardamom
seeds, green cardamoms and the mace and stir-fry
for about 2 minutes, or until the onions are well
browned. Add the ground spice mixture and stir-fry
for a further 1–2 minutes. Add 2 tablespoons water,
then add the ginger and garlic and fry for about
30 seconds.

Now add the meat and stir-fry for about 5 minutes.
Add the tomatoes and let the meat fry in this
mixture for about 5 minutes, or until the moisture
has evaporated.

Pour in 750ml / 1¼ pints (3¼ cups) water, season
with salt, cover and cook over a low heat for about
1–1½ hours, or until the meat is tender. Add the
fried potatoes and heat through.

Lehm e Murgan
Invigorating Lamb Curry

Origin Awadh
Preparation time 45 minutes, plus marinating time
Cooking time 2½ hours
Serves 4

1kg / 2¼lb lamb shanks

salt

For the marinade

2 tablespoons lemon juice

For the majoon paste

1 tablespoon ghee

15 cashew nuts

2½ teaspoons chironji kernels

1 teaspoon poppy seeds

1½ teaspoons desiccated (dried flaked) coconut

For the aromatic potli

8 cloves

4 green cardamom pods

2 black cardamom pods

1 flower mace

1 stick cinnamon, about 2.5cm /1 inch long

For the sauce

4 tablespoons natural (plain) yoghurt, whisked

1½ teaspoons ground coriander

½ teaspoon chilli powder

100g / 3½oz (scant ½ cup) ghee or vegetable oil

1 large onion, sliced

1 tablespoon Onion Paste (see page 57)

1 teaspoon Garlic Paste (see page 57)

½ teaspoon Ginger Paste (see page 57)

625ml / 1 pint (2½ cups) stock

1 teaspoon coarsely ground black pepper, roasted

very small pinch of ground green cardamom

small pinch of ground black cardamom

small pinch of ground mace

small pinch of ground cloves

very small pinch of ground nutmeg

1 drop kewra water or rosewater

Put the meat in a large shallow dish and rub the meat well with the lemon juice and a little salt, then cover and set aside for about 15 minutes.

To make the majoon paste, heat the ghee in a small frying pan (skillet) over medium heat, add the cashew nuts and fry for about 1 minute, or until golden. Remove from the pan and set aside. In the same ghee, add the chironji kernels, poppy seeds and desiccated coconut and stir-fry for about 1 minute, then remove from the pan and put into a blender or food processor with the cashew nuts. Process, adding a little water if necessary, to make a smooth paste. Set aside.

Put all the ingredients for the aromatic potli in a mortar and pound with a pestle to break the spices, then place in a piece of muslin (cheesecloth), fold over to make a 'pouch' and secure with kitchen string (twine) to hang over the rim of the pan.

Mix the yoghurt, ground coriander and chilli powder together in a bowl and set aside.

Heat the ghee or oil in a large, heavy-based pan over medium heat, add the sliced onions and lightly fry for 5–7 minutes, or until golden brown. Add the meat, then season with salt and stir-fry for about 2 minutes. Add the onion, garlic and ginger pastes and stir-fry for 1 minute.

Remove the pan from the heat, stir in the yoghurt mixture, then return the pan to the heat, add the aromatic potli and stir-fry for about 2–3 minutes, or until the oil separates out. Add the stock, bring to the boil, then reduce the heat to medium, cover and simmer for 2 hours, stirring occasionally, until the meat is tender.

Reduce the heat, stir in the majoon paste and then cover and simmer, stirring occasionally, for about 5 minutes. Now reduce the heat to very low, add the ground spices, stir, cover and simmer for about 10 minutes. Remove from the heat, then remove and discard the potli, add the kewra water, then stir, and adjust the seasoning, if necessary.

Qorma dum Pukht
Braised Lamb in Aromatic Sauce

Origin Awadh
Preparation time 30 minutes, plus cooling time
Cooking time 2¼ hours
Serves 3–4

few saffron threads

1 teaspoon kewra water or rosewater

250ml / 8fl oz (1 cup) vegetable oil

6–7 onions, sliced

50g / 1¾oz (⅓ cup) almonds

4 green chillies, de-seeded and chopped

2 bay leaves

1 tablespoon chopped ginger

1 tablespoon chopped garlic

2 teaspoons ground coriander

1 teaspoon Garam Masala (see page 31)

1kg / 2¼lb lamb shanks and chops

2 teaspoons chilli powder

3 tablespoons natural (plain) yoghurt, whisked

¼ teaspoon ground mace

¼ teaspoon ground green cardamom

1 teaspoon lime juice (optional)

salt

Put the saffron in a small bowl, add the kewra water and soak until required.

Heat half the oil in a large, heavy-based pan over medium heat, add the onions and fry for about 4 minutes, or until light brown. Add the almonds and continue to fry until the onions are deep brown. Remove from the pan and allow to cool.

When cool, transfer to a blender or food processor, reserving the oil, and process, adding a little water if necessary, to make a smooth paste.

Reheat the oil in the pan over medium heat, add the chillies, bay leaf, ginger, garlic, ground coriander, half the garam masala and the meat, then season with salt and fry for about 10 minutes, stirring constantly. Reduce the heat to low, add the chilli powder and yoghurt, mix well and continue to cook for 3–4 minutes. Simmer until there is hardly any moisture left. Add the fried onion-almond paste and mix well, then sprinkle over the remaining garam masala, add the ground mace and cardamom and fry for 2 minutes. Pour in about 1 litre / 1¾ pints (4¼ cups) water and cook for 2 hours, or until the meat is tender. Stir in the lime juice, if using. Sprinkle over the soaked saffron just before serving.

Taar Qorma
Lamb with Rich Sauce

Origin Hyderabad
Preparation time 30 minutes
Cooking time 1¾ hours
Serves 5–6

250g / 9oz (1 cup) ghee

7–8 green cardamom pods

5–6 cloves

2 cinnamon sticks, about 2.5cm / 1 inch long

1kg / 2¼lb lamb shoulder, cut into pieces

4 teaspoons Garlic Paste (see page 57)

3 teaspoons Ginger Paste (see page 57)

1½ teaspoons ground coriander

1 teaspoon Kashmiri red chilli powder

250ml / 8fl oz (1 cup) natural (plain) yoghurt

4 tablespoons Fried Onion Paste (see page 57)

2 tablespoons Cashew Nut Paste (see page 58)

1.5 litres / 2½ pints (6¼ cups) lamb stock
    (see page 636)

½ teaspoon coarsely ground black pepper, roasted

¼ teaspoon ground green cardamom

¼ teaspoon ground nutmeg

¼ teaspoon ground clove

¼ teaspoon ground mace

½ teaspoon kewra water or rosewater

salt

Heat the ghee in a large, heavy-based pan over medium heat, add the cardamom pods, cloves and cinnamon and stir-fry for about 30 seconds. Add the meat and season with salt. Increase the heat to high and sear for 1–2 minutes, then reduce the heat to low, add the garlic and ginger pastes and stir-fry for 1 minute. Add the ground coriander and chilli powder and stir-fry for 1–2 minutes, or until the moisture has evaporated. Remove the pan from the heat, stir in the yoghurt, then return the pan to the heat and stir-fry for 2 minutes, or until the oil has separated out.

Now add the fried onion paste and stir-fry for another 1–2 minutes, or until the oil has separated out. Add the cashew nut paste and stir-fry for about 1 minute, then pour in the stock. Bring almost to the boil, reduce the heat to low and simmer, stirring occasionally, for about 1½ hours, or until tender.

Sprinkle over the aromatic spices and stir, then sprinkle over the kewra water and stir again. Remove from the heat and adjust the seasoning.

Kundan Kaliya
Golden Lamb Curry

Origin Awadh
Preparation time 1 hour
Cooking time 1½ hours
Serves 4–6

---

pinch of saffron threads

1 teaspoon milk

1kg / 2¼lb lamb shoulder or leg, cut into cubes

400g / 14oz (1⅔ cups) ghee or vegetable oil

500g / 1lb 2oz (3 medium) onions, sliced

250ml / 8fl oz (1 cup) hung natural (plain) yoghurt
(see page 793), whisked

3 tablespoons Ginger Paste (see page 57)

2 tablespoons Garlic Paste (see page 57)

2 teaspoons ground coriander

2 teaspoons chilli powder

2 teaspoons ground turmeric

4–6 cloves

4–6 green cardamom pods

large pinch of ground mace

½ teaspoon whole black peppercorns

4 cinnamon sticks, about 2.5cm / 1 inch long

200ml / 7fl oz (¾ cup) single (light) cream

10 edible gold leaves

salt

Put the saffron threads in a small bowl, add the milk and soak until required.

Blanch the meat in a large pan of boiling water for about 10 minutes, then drain and set aside.

Heat the ghee or oil in a large, heavy-based pan over medium heat, add the onions and fry for about 5–7 minutes, or until golden brown. Remove from the pan with a slotted spoon and drain on kitchen paper (paper towels). Reserve the ghee or oil in the pan.

Crush the onions into small pieces with your fingers and mix with 2 tablespoons yoghurt. Add the ginger and garlic pastes and mix together, then put in the pan with the lamb and stir-fry over medium-low heat for about 10 minutes.

Add the ground coriander, chilli powder and turmeric to the pan and stir-fry for a further 5 minutes. Slowly stir in the remaining yoghurt and stir-fry for about 2 minutes, or until the ghee or oil separates out.

Pour in 250ml / 8fl oz (1 cup) water and add all the aromatic spices. Cover and cook for 1 hour, or until the lamb is tender. When done, remove the lamb from the sauce and set aside.

Strain the sauce through a muslin cloth (cheesecloth) or a fine sieve (strainer) into the pan. Add the cream, then return the lamb pieces to it, stir in the soaked saffron and cook over low heat for about 5 minutes.

Set aside a little gold leaf for the garnish and mix the rest into the sauce with a fork. Garnish with the reserved gold leaf.

Chippa Gosht
Lamb Cooked in a Clay Pot

Origin Hyderabad
Preparation time 10 minutes, plus marinating time
Cooking time 1¼–1¾ hours
Serves 6–8

½ teaspoon ground turmeric

2 teaspoons chilli powder

2 teaspoons Ginger Paste (see page 57)

1½ teaspoons Garlic Paste (see page 57)

½ teaspoon raw papaya paste

1kg / 2¼lb lamb, cut into 5-cm / 2-inch pieces

125ml / 4½fl oz (½ cup) vegetable oil

1 tablespoon lemon juice

salt

few sprigs coriander (cilantro) leaves, chopped,
to garnish

To make the marinade, mix the turmeric, chilli powder, ginger, garlic and the papaya pastes together in a large shallow dish, then season with salt. Place the meat in the marinade and mix well until coated evenly all over. Cover and set aside in the refrigerator for 1½ hours.

Heat the oil in a chippe or earthenware pot or in a heavy-based casserole dish over low-medium heat, add the marinated meat and fry for about 15 minutes, or until the moisture has evaporated. Pour in about 125ml / 4½fl oz (½ cup) water, then cover and cook for 1–1½ hours, or until the meat is tender. Add a little more water if it is too dry.

Sprinkle over the lemon juice and garnish with chopped coriander before serving.

Musallam Raan
Slow-cooked Aromatic Leg of Lamb

Origin Awadh
Preparation time 40 minutes, plus marinating time
Cooking time 30 minutes
Serves 4–6

1 × 1-kg / 2¼-lb leg of lamb, trimmed and rinsed
100g / 3½oz raw papaya paste
1 teaspoon chilli powder
2 tablespoons ghee or vegetable oil, plus 250ml / 8fl oz (1 cup) for cooking
4 onions, sliced
200g / 7oz (1½ cups) cashew nuts
50g / 1¾oz Poppy Seed Paste (see page 58)
25g / 1oz chironji kernels
1 tablespoon desiccated (dried flaked) coconut
2 tablespoons Ginger Paste (see page 57)
2 tablespoons Garlic Paste (see page 57)
250ml / 8fl oz (1 cup) natural (plain) yoghurt, whisked
pinch of saffron threads
1 tablespoon gram (chickpea) flour, roasted
8–10 green cardamom pods
4 black cardamom pods
1 teaspoon whole black peppercorns
6–8 cloves
¼ nutmeg, grated
1 blade mace
salt

To garnish

3 edible silver leaves
1 tablespoon almonds, finely chopped

Place the meat in a large shallow dish and prick well with a fork. Rub the raw papaya paste, chilli powder and a little salt all over, then cover and set aside in the refrigerator for 3–4 hours, preferably overnight.

Heat the ghee or oil in a large, heavy-based pan over medium heat, add the onions and fry for about 5–7 minutes, or until golden brown. Remove from the pan, put into a blender and process, adding a little water if necessary, to make a paste.

Roast the cashew nuts and poppy seed paste lightly on a tawa or in a dry frying pan (skillet) for about 1 minute.

Add the chironji kernels and fry briefly, then transfer to a small blender or food processor, add the desiccated coconut and process, adding a little water if necessary, to make a paste.

Mix the poppy seed paste with the ginger and garlic pastes, yoghurt, saffron and roasted gram flour together in a bowl, then season with salt. Massage the lamb leg with the marinade, making sure the leg is evenly coated all over, then cover and set aside for a further 2 hours. Sprinkle over the aromatic spices and rub again.

Heat the ghee or oil in a flat-based pan over medium heat, place the leg of lamb with the marinade in it, then cover and cook for about 30 minutes, or until the meat is done. Remove from the heat and serve garnished with silver leaf and finely chopped almonds.

Sasranga
Baked Spicy Minced (Ground) Meat

Origin Awadh
Preparation time 45 minutes
Cooking time 1¼ hours
Serves 6–8

3½ tablespoons ghee or vegetable oil, plus extra for brushing
2 tablespoons blanched almonds, slivered
50g / 1¾oz (⅓ cup) raisins, chopped
60g / 2oz (½ cup) sliced onions
1kg / 2¼lb minced (ground) lamb, preferably from leg or shoulder
1 × 2.5-cm / 1-inch piece fresh ginger, peeled and chopped
10–15 green chillies, de-seeded and chopped
1 large sprig coriander (cilantro) leaves, chopped
4 eggs
1 tablespoon lime juice
125ml / 4½fl oz (½ cup) single (light) cream
salt

Preheat the oven to 190°C/375°F/Gas Mark 5.

Heat the ghee or oil in a large, heavy-based pan over medium-low heat, add the almonds and stir-fry for about 30 seconds, then remove from the pan with a slotted spoon. Add the raisins and stir-fry for another 30 seconds, then remove from the pan and set aside.

Add the onions to the pan and stir-fry for 5–7 minutes, or until golden brown. Remove from the pan with a slotted spoon, drain on kitchen paper (paper towels) and crush coarsely. Set aside.

Put the minced lamb in the same pan, season with salt and cook over medium heat for 10 minutes, or until the moisture has evaporated, then stir-fry for about 1 minute. Pour in about 1 litre / 1¾ pints (4¼ cups) water, then bring to the boil. Reduce the heat and simmer for about 30 minutes, or until the mince is tender and the liquid dries completely.

Mix the almonds, raisins, fried onions, ginger, green chillies and coriander leaves together in a bowl. Put the eggs in another bowl and beat lightly, then stir in the lime juice.

Brush a 20cm / 8 inch round baking dish with oil and line it with baking (parchment) paper. Spread half of the meat on the paper and pour half of the cream over the top. Sprinkle over half of the almond and raisin mixture, then pour over half of the egg and lime juice mixture. Pat gently with your fingers to level the mixture, then repeat the process until everything is used up.

Bake in the oven for about 30 minutes, or until the mince becomes firm. Allow to cool, then cut into wedges.

Shahi Qorma
Prince-like Curry

Origin Awadh
Preparation time 30 minutes
Cooking time 1½–2 hours
Serves 4

pinch of saffron threads

1 teaspoon warm milk

150g / 5oz (⅔ cup) ghee or vegetable oil

10 green cardamom pods

5–6 cloves

2 cinnamon sticks, about 2.5cm / 1 inch long

2 bay leaves

150g / 5oz (1 medium) onion, sliced

3 tablespoons Ginger Paste (see page 57)

3 tablespoons Garlic Paste (see page 57)

2 teaspoons ground coriander

1 teaspoon chilli powder

1kg / 2¼lb lamb, cut into pieces

250ml / 8fl oz (1 cup) natural (plain) yoghurt, whisked

1 teaspoon Garam Masala (see page 31)

1 teaspoon ground mace

1 teaspoon ground green cardamom

1 teaspoon ground white pepper

2 drops kewra water or rosewater

salt

To garnish

20 blanched almonds, cut into slivers

2 edible silver leaves

Put the saffron threads in a small bowl, add the warm milk and soak until required.

Heat the ghee or oil in a large, heavy-based frying pan (skillet) over medium heat, add the cardamom pods, cloves, cinnamon and bay leaves and stir-fry for about 1 minute, or until they start to splutter. Add the onions and stir-fry for about 5–7 minutes, or until golden brown. Add the ginger and garlic pastes and fry for a further 2–3 minutes. Add the ground coriander and chilli powder, then season with salt and stir for a few minutes.

Add the meat to the pan and stir-fry for about 10 minutes. Reduce the heat and slowly stir in the yoghurt, then bring almost to the boil and pour in enough water to make a gravy.

Reduce the heat to medium, cover and cook, stirring occasionally, for about 1–1½ hours, or until the meat is tender. You may have to add some more water to the pan if it dries out.

Add the remaining ground spices to the pan and simmer for a further 8–10 minutes. Just before serving, add the kewra water together with the soaked saffron and stir, then garnish with almonds and silver leaves.

Tala Gosht
Fried Lamb

Origin Hyderabad
Preparation time 15 minutes, plus marinating time
Cooking time 30 minutes
Serves 4

1 tablespoon Ginger Paste (see page 57)

1 teaspoon Garlic Paste (see page 57)

1 teaspoon raw papaya paste

1½ teaspoons chilli powder

1 teaspoon ground allspice

½ teaspoon ground turmeric

1 teaspoon whole black peppercorns, coarsely pounded

1kg / 2¼lb boneless lamb, cut into bite-sized pieces

250ml / 8fl oz (1 cup) vegetable oil

salt

To make the marinade, mix the ginger, garlic and raw papaya pastes, chilli powder, ground allspice and turmeric together in a large bowl. Season with salt and add the pounded peppercorns. Place the meat in the marinade, then cover and set aside in the refrigerator for at least 1½ hours.

Heat the oil in a large, heavy-based pan over high heat, add the meat and sear briefly to seal in all the juices. Reduce the heat, cover and cook for about 30 minutes, or until the meat is tender. Sprinkle over a little water while frying to prevent the meat sticking to the base (bottom) of the pan or burning.

Dalcha Gosht
Lamb with Lentils

Origin Hyderabad
Preparation time 45 minutes
Cooking time 1½–2 hours
Serves 4–6

200g / 7oz (1 cup) chana dal, rinsed and drained

1 tablespoon coriander seeds

10–15 curry leaves

100g / 3½oz (scant ½ cup) ghee

1 bay leaf

5–6 green cardamom pods

1 black cardamom pod

5–6 cloves

1 cinnamon stick, about 2.5cm / 1 inch long

100g / 3½oz (1 small) onion, sliced

2 tablespoons Ginger Paste (see page 57)

2 tablespoons Garlic Paste (see page 57)

2 teaspoons de-seeded and chopped green chillies

500g / 1lb 2oz lamb, cut into pieces

small pinch of ground mace

2 teaspoons chilli powder

½ teaspoon ground turmeric

1 teaspoon ground coriander

500ml / 18fl oz (2¼ cups) natural (plain) yoghurt

4 tablespoons lemon juice

salt

steamed rice, to serve

For the tempering

2 tablespoons ghee

5 cloves garlic

4 dried red chillies

Cook the dal in a pan of water for about 30 minutes, or until soft. Drain, then process in a blender or food processor to a purée. Set aside.

Put the coriander seeds and curry leaves in a small piece of muslin (cheesecloth) and secure the top with kitchen string (twine) to make a pouch.

Heat the ghee in a large, heavy-based pan over medium heat, add the bay leaf, cardamom pods, cloves and cinnamon and stir-fry for about 1 minute, or until they start to splutter. Add the onion and stir-fry for about 5–7 minutes, or until golden brown.

Add the ginger and garlic pastes and green chillies and stir-fry for 15 seconds, then add the lamb and fry for 3–4 minutes. Add the mace, chilli powder, turmeric and ground coriander and stir. Pour in about 1.5 litres / 2½ pints (6¼ cups) water and bring to the boil.

Remove the pan from the heat, stir in the yoghurt, then return to the heat and bring to just below boiling point. Suspend the aromatic pouch in the pot, then cover and simmer for 1–1½ hours, or until the lamb is tender.

Add the dal purée, bring back almost to the boil, then reduce the heat and simmer for about 15 minutes. Remove and discard the aromatic pouch, sprinkle with lemon juice and stir. Adjust the seasoning, if necessary.

Heat the ghee for the tempering in a small frying pan (skillet) over medium heat, add the garlic and lightly fry for about 1 minute, or until golden brown. Add the dried red chillies and stir. Pour the tempering over the lamb stew and stir. Serve with steamed rice.

Bund Gosht
Fennel-flavoured Lamb Cooked in a Sealed Pot

Origin Awadh
Preparation time 30 minutes
Cooking time 1¼–1¾ hours
Serves 4

125ml / 4½fl oz (½ cup) vegetable oil
3–4 green cardamom pods, cracked
2–3 cinnamon sticks, about 2.5cm / 1 inch long
4–6 cloves
3 tablespoons Fried Onion Paste (see page 57)
1 tablespoon Ginger Paste (see page 57)
3 tablespoons Garlic Paste (see page 57)
1 teaspoon turmeric paste
1kg / 2¼lb lamb chops
250ml / 8fl oz (1 cup) natural (plain) yoghurt, whisked
1 teaspoon chilli powder
1 tablespoon ground fennel
about 150g / 5oz dough (optional), for sealing the lid (see page 783)
salt

Heat the oil in a large, heavy-based pan over medium heat, add the cardamom pods, cinnamon and cloves and stir-fry for about 1 minute, or until they start to splutter. Add the onion paste and stir-fry for about 1 minute, then add the ginger and garlic pastes and stir-fry for another 1 minute, or until the onion paste is lightly browned. Add the turmeric paste and continue frying for about 1–2 minutes, or until the moisture has evaporated.

Add the chops to the pan, season with salt, then remove the pan from the heat. Slowly stir in the yoghurt and 1 tablespoon of water, then return to the heat, add the chilli powder and slowly increase the heat. Mix well and cook for 2–3 minutes. Add the ground fennel, reduce the heat to low, cover and seal the lid with dough, if using, or with foil and cook for about 1–1½ hours, or until the meat is tender.

Baadam Pasanda
Lamb Fillets with Cashews & Almonds

Origin Delhi
Preparation time 20 minutes
Cooking time 40–50 minutes
Serves 4

750g / 1lb 10oz boneless lamb fillets
250g / 9oz (1 cup) ghee
5–6 cloves
3–4 green cardamom pods
200g / 7oz Boiled Onion Paste (see page 57)
1 tablespoon Ginger Paste (see page 57)
1 tablespoon Garlic Paste (see page 57)
1 tablespoon chilli powder
1 tablespoon ground coriander
250ml / 8fl oz (1 cup) natural (plain) yoghurt
3 tablespoons Cashew Nut Paste (see page 58)
2 teaspoons Garam Masala (see page 31)
¼ teaspoon ground green cardamom
¼ teaspoon ground nutmeg
¼ teaspoon ground mace
salt

To garnish

1 sprig coriander (cilantro) leaves, chopped
50g / 1¾oz (⅓ cup) blanched almonds

Place the meat on a board and, using a meat mallet, beat lightly on one side to flatten, then lightly score the meat with a sharp knife.

Heat the ghee in a large, heavy-based pan over medium heat, add the cloves and cardamom pods and stir-fry for about 15 seconds. Add the boiled onion paste and stir-fry for about 1–2 minutes, or until the oil separates out. Add the ginger and garlic pastes and stir-fry for about 1 minute, then add the chilli powder, ground coriander, and yoghurt and season with salt, then stir-fry for about 1–2 minutes, or until the oil separates out. Pour in about 300ml / ½ pint (1¼ cups) water and bring almost to the boil. Add the meat fillets and simmer for about 25–30 minutes, or until tender.

Add the cashew nut paste, bring to the boil, then reduce the heat to medium and cook for about 1–2 minutes, or until the oil separates out. Sprinkle over the remaining ground spices and stir. Adjust the seasoning and garnish with chopped coriander and almonds.

※

Qorma Asafjahi
The Sovereign's Favourite

Origin Hyderabad
Preparation time 30 minutes
Cooking time 1½ hours
Serves 4–6

pinch of saffron threads
1 teaspoon warm milk
125g / 4¼oz (½ cup) ghee
1 tablespoon Garlic Paste (see page 57)
1 tablespoon Ginger Paste (see page 57)
1kg / 2¼lb lamb shoulder, cut into 5-cm / 2-inch pieces
1 tablespoon blanched almonds, cut into slivers
1 tablespoon raisins
2 onions, finely chopped
2 teaspoons chilli powder
½ teaspoon Garam Masala (see page 31)
½ teaspoon peppercorns, pounded
1 teaspoon sugar
10 green chilies, de-seeded and finely chopped
250ml / 8fl oz (1 cup) natural (plain) yoghurt, whisked
1 tablespoon chopped coriander (cilantro) leaves
salt

Put the saffron threads in a small bowl, add the warm milk and soak until required.

Heat half the ghee in a large, heavy-based pan over medium heat, add the garlic and ginger pastes and stir-fry for 1–2 minutes, until golden brown. Add the meat, season with salt and keep stir-frying, sprinkling over a little water whenever the moisture dries up, for 30 minutes. Add very little water at a time, as the meat should be fried not boiled.

Heat the remaining ghee in a separate pan over medium-low heat, add the almonds and stir-fry for 30 seconds, or until golden, then remove from the pan. Add the raisins to the pan and stir-fry for 30 seconds, or until golden, then remove from the pan.

Add the onions to the pan and fry for about 5–7 minutes, or until golden brown. Add the chilli powder, garam masala, peppercorns, sugar, chillies and 2 tablespoons water and cook, stirring well, until the water has evaporated. Add the mixture to the meat and stir, then add the almonds, raisins, yoghurt, soaked saffron and coriander leaves and mix well. Reduce the heat to low and simmer for 45 minutes, then serve immediately.

※ ※

Halim
Ceremonial Meat Porridge

Origin Hyderabad
Preparation time 30 minutes
Cooking time 1½–2 hours
Serves 6–8

250g / 9oz (1 cup) ghee or vegetable oil
6 large onions, sliced
4 large onions, ground
10 cloves garlic, ground
2 tablespoons Ginger Paste (see page 57)
2 tablespoons Garlic Paste (see page 57)
2 teaspoons turmeric
2 tablespoons chilli powder
1kg / 2¼lb lamb shoulder, cut into 5-cm / 2-inch pieces
200g / 7oz (1½ cups) bulgar wheat
4 tablespoons Garam Masala (see page 31)
2 tablespoons chopped coriander (cilantro) leaves
salt
lime wedges, to serve

Heat the ghee or oil in a large, heavy-based pan over medium heat, add the sliced onions and stir-fry for about 5 minutes, or until brown. Add the ground onion and garlic, ginger and garlic pastes, turmeric and chilli powder and stir-fry for about 1 minute, or until the spices change colour. Add the meat and stir-fry for 15 minutes.

Add the bulgar wheat to the pan and mix thoroughly, then stir-fry for about 15 minutes. Season with salt. Pour in 2 litres / 3½ pints (8 cups) water, reduce the heat to low and cook for 1½ hours. As the bulgar tends to stick to the base (bottom) of the pan it is best to uncover the pan at least twice and stir the mixture. Continue cooking until nearly all the water is absorbed and the oil rises to the surface.

Sprinkle over the garam masala and chopped coriander and serve with lime wedges.

Achari Gosht
Lamb in Pickling Spices

Origin Punjab
Preparation time 30 minutes
Cooking time 1¼–1¾ hours
Serves 4–6

1kg / 2¼lb lamb, cut into pieces
1 teaspoon ground turmeric
250ml / 8fl oz (1 cup) mustard oil
15 dried red chillies
pinch of asafoetida
1 teaspoon black mustard seeds
1 teaspoon fenugreek seeds
1 teaspoon fennel seeds
15–20 curry leaves
5–6 cloves
2 teaspoons Ginger Paste (see page 57)
2 teaspoons Garlic Paste (see page 57)
½ tablespoon chilli powder
2 teaspoons cumin seeds
2 teaspoons kalonji (nigella) seeds
1 tablespoon brown sugar
3 tablespoons lemon juice
250ml / 8fl oz (1 cup) natural (plain) yoghurt, whisked
salt

For the fried onion paste

1 tablespoon vegetable oil
100g / 3½oz (1 small) onion, sliced

To make the fried onion paste, heat 1 tablespoon oil in a frying pan (skillet) over medium heat, add the onions and fry for about 5–7 minutes, or until golden brown. Transfer to a blender or food processor and process to make a paste. Set aside.

Bring 1 litre / 1¾ pints (4¼ cups) water to the boil in a large, heavy-based pan, add the meat and turmeric and cook for 5 minutes. Reduce the heat, cover and simmer for 1–1½ hours, or until the meat is done to your taste. Drain the meat, reserving the stock.

Heat the mustard oil in a large, heavy-based pan over high heat, then reduce the heat. Add the dried red chillies and stir-fry for 30 seconds, then remove and discard the chillies. Add the asafoetida, mustard seeds, fenugreek seeds, fennel seeds, curry leaves and cloves and stir-fry for about 1 minute, or until they start to splutter.

Add the boiled meat, ginger and garlic pastes, chilli powder, cumin seeds, kalonji seeds and the sugar, then stir and add the fried onion paste. Increase the heat, add the reserved stock and fry until the meat is browned. Sprinkle with lemon juice, reduce the heat and simmer for about 2 minutes. Remove from the heat, stir in the yoghurt, then return to the heat and cook until the oil separates and rises to the surface.

Bhuna Gosht (I)
Spicy Roast Lamb

Origin Punjab
Preparation time 15 minutes
Cooking time 2 hours
Serves 4

3 tablespoons vegetable oil
2 onions, sliced
1 tablespoon Ginger Paste (see page 57)
1 teaspoon Garlic Paste (see page 57)
1 teaspoon ground turmeric
1 teaspoon chilli powder
1kg / 2¼lb lamb on the bone, cut into medium-sized pieces
salt

Heat the oil in a large, heavy-based pan over medium heat, add the onions and fry for 8–10 minutes, or until golden brown. Add the ginger and garlic pastes and fry for about 2 minutes, then add the turmeric and chilli powder and season with salt. Add the meat and fry, stirring constantly, until the moisture has evaporated. Pour in about 125ml / 4½fl oz (½ cup) water, then cover and cook over low heat for about 1½ hours, until tender.

Uncover, bring to the boil and cook until all the water has evaporated and the oil rises to surface.

✵✵

Bhuna Gosht (II)
Roasted Lamb

Origin Awadh
Preparation time 30 minutes
Cooking time 1 hour
Serves 4

2 teaspoons ground coriander
1 teaspoon ground cumin
1 teaspoon ground turmeric
2 teaspoons chilli powder
125ml / 4½fl oz (½ cup) vegetable oil
1 bay leaf
3–4 cloves
1 teaspoon whole black peppercorns
2 black cardamom pods
1 cinnamon stick, about 2.5cm / 1 inch long
2 onions, sliced
1 tablespoon Ginger Paste (see page 57)
1 tablespoon Garlic Paste (see page 57)
1kg / 2¼lb lamb on the bone, cut into medium-sized pieces
salt

Put the ground coriander, cumin, turmeric and chilli powder in a small bowl, add 2 tablespoons water and mix together.

Heat the oil in a large, heavy-based pan over medium heat, add the bay leaf, cloves, peppercorns, cardamom pods and cinnamon and stir-fry for about 1 minute, or until they start to splutter and begin to change colour. Add the onions and fry for about 5–7 minutes, or until they are golden brown. Add the ginger and garlic pastes and the ground spice mixture and season with salt, then stir-fry for a further 1–2 minutes.

Now add the meat to the pan and fry for about 30 minutes, sprinkling with a little water if necessary to prevent the meat sticking to the pan. Pour in 250ml / 8fl oz (1 cup) hot water, bring to the boil, then reduce the heat and simmer for a further 15 minutes, or until the sauce thickens. Increase the heat and fry, stirring constantly, until the oil rises to the surface, then remove from the heat.

✵✵

Gol Maas Kaachar
Lamb with Kachri

Origin Rajasthan
Preparation time 45 minutes
Cooking time 1½–2 hours
Serves 4

100g / 3½oz (1 small) onion, roughly chopped
125ml / 4½fl oz (½ cup) natural (plain) yoghurt, whisked
150g / 5oz (1 medium) tomato, puréed
1 teaspoon chilli powder
6 tablespoons mustard oil
150g / 5oz (1 medium) onion, sliced
5 teaspoons Garlic Paste (see page 57)
½ teaspoon Ginger Paste (see page 57)
5 green cardamom pods
2 cloves
1 cinnamon stick, about 2.5cm / 1 inch long
1 bay leaf
1kg / 2¼lb lamb leg, cut into 2.5-cm / 1-inch cubes
250g / 9oz fresh kachri, cut into rounds, or 3 tablespoons lemon juice
salt

Put the roughly chopped onion in a blender and process to make a paste. Set aside.

Mix the yoghurt, puréed tomato and chilli powder together in a large bowl and season with salt. Set aside.

Heat the oil in a large, heavy-based pan over high heat. When the oil is hot, remove and sprinkle over a little water. Reheat over medium heat, add the sliced onions and stir-fry for about 4 minutes, or until light brown. Add the garlic and ginger pastes and stir-fry for about 1–2 minutes, or until the moisture has evaporated. Add the green cardamom pods, cloves, cinnamon and bay leaf and stir, then add the onion paste. Stir, add the meat and stir-fry for a few minutes until the oil separates out.

Remove the pan from the heat and stir in the yoghurt mixture, then return to the heat and bring almost to the boil. Reduce the heat to low, cover and simmer, stirring occasionally, for 1–1½ hours, or until the meat is tender.

Now add the kachri rounds or lemon juice, stir, increase the heat to medium and cook for about 10 minutes, or until the kaachri is cooked.

Safed Maas
Rajasthani Lamb in Rich White Sauce

Origin Rajasthan
Preparation time 1 hour, plus marinating time
Cooking time 1½–2 hours
Serves 4

10 blanched almonds
6 teaspoons poppy seeds
6 teaspoons grated fresh coconut
1kg / 2¼lb lamb, cut into cubes
5 tablespoons natural (plain) yoghurt, whisked
2 teaspoons chilli powder
1 teaspoon Ginger Paste (see page 57)
250g / 9oz (1 cup) ghee or vegetable oil
2 tablespoons Khoya (see page 58) or milk powder (dry milk)
125ml / 4½fl oz (½ cup) milk
3 tablespoons lemon juice
2 teaspoons ground aniseed
2 tablespoons khus essence (optional)
salt

Put the almonds in a small food processor or blender and process, adding a little water to make a paste. Set aside. Put the poppy seeds in a small blender or mortar and process or pound with a pestle, adding a little water to make a paste. Put the coconut in a small blender and process until ground.

Bring 1 litre / 1¾ pints (4¼ cups) water to the boil in a large, heavy-based pan, add the lamb and boil for about 5 minutes. It will remove the colour from the meat. Drain, place in a large bowl or dish and set aside.

To make a marinade, mix the yoghurt, chilli powder and ginger paste together in a bowl, then season with salt. Rub the marinade all over the meat, then cover and set aside in the refrigerator for about 2–3 hours.

Heat the ghee or oil in a large, heavy-based pan over medium heat, add the meat and stir-fry for about 5 minutes. Pour in a little water, then add the almond and poppy seed pastes, ground coconut, khoya and milk. Mix well and simmer for 1–1½ hours, or until the meat is tender and the oil rises to the surface. Stir in the lemon juice and ground aniseed and sprinkle over the khus essence, if using.

Amras ki Boti
Mango-flavoured Lamb

Origin Hyderabad
Preparation time 20 minutes
Cooking time 1 hour
Serves 6–8

½ teaspoon ground turmeric
½ teaspoon ground black pepper
1 teaspoon chilli powder
125ml / 4½fl oz (½ cup) vegetable oil
1 onion, sliced
2 teaspoons Ginger Paste (see page 57)
½ teaspoon Garlic Paste (see page 57)
1kg / 2¼lb lamb, cut into pieces
125ml / 4½fl oz (½ cup) milk
500ml / 18fl oz (2¼ cups) natural (plain) yoghurt, whisked
4 tablespoons chopped coriander (cilantro) leaves
6–8 green chillies, de-seeded and ground to a paste
4 teaspoons ground almonds
3 tablespoons melon seeds, ground
250g / 9oz canned mango pulp
few raisins
¼ teaspoon Garam Masala (see page 31)
large pinch of saffron threads
salt

Put the turmeric, black pepper and chilli powder in a small bowl, add 2 tablespoons water and mix together.

Heat half the oil in a large, heavy-based pan over medium heat, add half of the onion and stir-fry for 7 minutes, or until well browned. Add the ginger and garlic pastes and stir-fry for about 2–3 minutes, then add the ground turmeric mixture and milk and season with salt. Simmer for about 1 minute, then add the meat and fry for 10 minutes, or until the water has evaporated. Pour in 500ml / 18fl oz (2¼ cups) hot water and simmer for about 45 minutes.

Heat the remaining oil in another large, heavy-based pan over medium heat, add the remaining onion and fry for about 4 minutes, or until light brown. Add the yoghurt, stir to blend, then add the coriander, chilli paste, ground almonds and melon seeds together with the mango pulp, raisins and garam masala. Mix well, then add the cooked meat and sauce. Sprinkle over the saffron and simmer for a further 2–3 minutes. Serve hot.

Khare Masale ka Gosht
Lamb Cooked with Aromatic Whole Spices

Origin Awadh
Preparation time 30 minutes
Cooking time 1½–2 hours
Serves 4

250ml / 8fl oz (1 cup) natural (plain) yoghurt, whisked

1 tablespoon chopped coriander (cilantro) leaves

4 dried red chillies

½ teaspoon ground turmeric

5 tablespoons ghee

6 green cardamom pods

3 black cardamom pods

4 cloves

2 cinnamon sticks, about 2.5cm / 1 inch long

2 bay leaves

12 whole black peppercorns

1 teaspoon coriander seeds

500g / 1lb 2oz lamb, cut into pieces

5 teaspoons chopped garlic

1 × 5-cm / 2-inch piece fresh ginger, peeled and cut into strips

25g / 1oz (¼ cup) sliced onion

salt

Mix the yoghurt, chopped coriander, dried red chillies and turmeric together in a bowl, then set aside.

Heat the ghee in a large, heavy-based pan over medium heat, add the cardamom pods, cloves, cinnamon, bay leaves, peppercorns and coriander seeds and stir-fry for about 30 seconds, or until the cardamom pods start to change colour. Now add the meat and stir-fry for a few minutes, then add the garlic and ginger. Season with salt and stir-fry for about 1–2 minutes, or until the moisture has evaporated.

Remove from the heat and stir in the yoghurt mixture, then return to the heat and stir-fry for about 2 minutes, or until the oil separates out. Add the onion and stir-fry for about 2 minutes, or until the oil separates out. Pour in about 125ml / 4½fl oz (½ cup) water, bring almost to the boil, then reduce the heat to low and simmer, stirring occasionally, for about 1–1½ hours, or until the sauce is a thin sauce consistency and the meat is tender.

✳ ✳ / 📷 p.469

Jangli Maas
Rustic Hunter's Lamb

Origin Rajasthan
Preparation time 15 minutes
Cooking time 1 hour
Serves 4

200g / 7oz (¾ cup) ghee or vegetable oil

1kg / 2¼lb lamb, cut into pieces

5–6 dried red chillies

salt

Heat the ghee or oil in a large, heavy-based pan over low heat, add the meat and cook, stirring occasionally for about 10 minutes. Season with salt and add the dried red chillies. Sprinkle over a very small amount of water to ensure the meat does not stick to the base (bottom) of the pan, and cook for a further 10 minutes. Remember the meat should neither fry nor boil. Continue this process until the meat is tender. When tender, increase the heat slightly and cook for a few minutes until the moisture has evaporated.

Khatta Meetha Do Pyaza
Rajasthani Sweet & Sour Lamb

Origin Rajasthan
Preparation time 30 minutes, plus marinating time
Cooking time 1½ hours
Serves 4

1kg / 2¼lb lamb, cut into pieces

500ml / 18fl oz (2¼ cups) lamb stock (see page 636)

½ teaspoon dried basil

salt

For the marinade

150ml / ¼ pint (⅔ cup) natural (plain) yoghurt, whisked

2 tablespoons Garlic Paste (see page 57)

1 tablespoon Ginger Paste (see page 57)

½ teaspoon ground coriander powder

½ teaspoon Kashmiri red chilli powder

For the sauce

½ teaspoon Kashmiri red chilli powder

7 tablespoons ghee

6 green cardamom pods

2 black cardamom pods

6 cloves

2 cinnamon sticks, about 2.5cm / 1 inch long

2 bay leaves

150g / 5oz (1 medium) onion

5 teaspoons Ginger Paste (see page 57)

4 teaspoons Garlic Paste (see page 57)

5 teaspoons ground coriander

100g / 3½oz Fried Onion Paste (see page 57)

½ teaspoon ground black pepper

½ teaspoon ground green cardamom

¼ teaspoon ground nutmeg powder

¼ teaspoon ground cloves

generous pinch of dried fenugreek leaves

Mix all the ingredients for the marinade in a bowl, then season with salt. Place the meat in a large shallow dish and rub the marinade evenly over the meat, then cover and set aside in the refrigerator for about 3 hours.

Bring the stock to the boil in a large pan, add the basil, then reduce the heat to low and simmer for about 4–5 minutes. Remove from the heat and pass the stock through a fine sieve (strainer) into a separate pan. Set aside.

To make the sauce, put the chilli powder in a small bowl, add 2 tablespoons water and mix together.

When ready to cook, remove the meat from the marinade and reserve the marinade.

Heat the ghee in a large, heavy-based pan over high heat, then reduce the heat. Add the cardamom pods, cloves, cinnamon and bay leaf and stir-fry for about 30 seconds, or until the green cardamom pods start to change colour. Add the onion and stir-fry for about 4 minutes, or until light brown. Add the ginger and garlic pastes and stir-fry for about 1–2 minutes, or until the moisture has evaporated and the onion is golden brown.

Add the marinated meat to the pan, increase the heat to high and stir-fry for 3–4 minutes, or until seared. Reduce the heat to low, cover and cook, stirring occasionally, for about 20 minutes, adding small quantities of stock to prevent the meat sticking, if necessary.

Uncover and stir-fry for about 2 minutes, or until the liquid has evaporated, then add the ground coriander and a quarter of the marinade, and stir-fry for about 2 minutes, or until the liquid has evaporated. Add another quarter of the marinade and keep repeating the process until the marinade is used up.

Now add the chilli powder mixture and stir for a minute. Add the fried onion paste and stir, then reduce the heat to low and stir-fry for about 1–2 minutes, or until the oil separates out. Pour in 125ml / 4½fl oz (½ cup) stock, then bring to the boil, reduce the heat to low, cover and simmer, stirring occasionally, for 3–4 minutes.

Uncover, increase the heat to medium and stir-fry for about 2–3 minutes, or until the liquid has evaporated. Thereafter, add 2 tablespoons stock at a time and continue to stir-fry until the meat is cooked.

Add the caramelized onion, stir-fry for 1 minute, then add the ground spices and stir. Adjust the seasoning, if necessary, then crush the dried fenugreek leaves between your palms and sprinkle on top.

Chaamp Baadami
Almond Chops

Origin Awadh
Preparation time 45 minutes, plus marinating time
Cooking time 1¼ hours
Serves 4

12 lamb chops, trimmed
5 tablespoons unsalted butter, cut in knobs (pats)
2 eggs, beaten (optional)
salt

For the marinade

4 tablespoons malt (white) vinegar
125ml / 4½fl oz (½ cup) natural (plain) yoghurt, whisked
5 teaspoons Garlic Paste (see page 57)
3 teaspoons Ginger Paste (see page 57)
1 tablespoon Fried Onion Paste (see page 57)
2 teaspoons raw papaya paste
½ teaspoon chilli powder
½ teaspoon ground green cardamom
½ teaspoon ground cloves
pinch of ground nutmeg

For the sauce

6 tablespoons ghee or oil, plus extra for deep-frying
50g / 1¾oz (½ cup) blanched almonds
5 green cardamom pods
3 cloves
2 cinnamon sticks, about 2.5cm / 1 inch long
2 bay leaves
5 teaspoons Garlic Paste (see page 57)
3 teaspoons Ginger Paste (see page 57)
3 tablespoons Fried Onion Paste (see page 57)
1 tablespoon fried Garlic Paste (see page 57)
1 teaspoon chilli powder
½ teaspoon ground green cardamom
½ teaspoon ground cloves
½ teaspoon ground cinnamon
¼ teaspoon ground mace
¼ teaspoon ground nutmeg
1 drop ittar (optional)

Remove the 2 side ribs from the chops and then carefully scrape off the meat from the lower part of the bones. Place the meat in a large shallow dish or bowl.

Mix all the ingredients for the marinade together in a large bowl, then season with salt. Rub the chops with the marinade, then cover and set aside in the refrigerator for at least 3 hours.

To make the sauce, heat enough ghee or oil or deep-frying in a deep, heavy-based pan to 180˚C/350˚F, or until a cube of bread browns in 30 seconds. Add the almonds and deep-fry for about 1–2 minutes, or until light golden. Remove with a slotted spoon and drain on kitchen paper (paper towels) until cool.

When the almonds are cool, put them in a food processor or blender, add 250ml / 8fl oz (1 cup) water and process to make a smooth paste. Set aside.

Preheat the oven to 140˚C/ 275˚F/Gas Mark 1.

Arrange the chops in a greased roasting tray (pan) and spread the marinade evenly over the chops. Put the knobs (pats) of butter on top and spread a thin layer of beaten egg on top if using. Bake in the oven for about 25 minutes, or until cooked, basting at regular intervals with the marinade. Remove the chops and reserve the liquor.

Heat the ghee or oil in a large, heavy-based pan over medium heat, add the cardamom pods, cloves, cinnamon and bay leaves and stir-fry for about 30 seconds, or until the cardamom pods start to change colour. Add the garlic and ginger pastes and stir-fry for about 1–2 minutes, or until the moisture has evaporated. Reduce the heat to low, add the almond paste and stir-fry for about 1–2 minutes, or until brown, adding small quantities of water frequently to ensure that the paste does not burn and acquire a bitter taste.

Increase the heat to medium, add the fried onion and garlic pastes and stir-fry for about 1–2 minutes, or until the oil separates out. Add the chilli powder and stir-fry for 30 seconds, then add the reserved liquor and stir-fry for a further 2 minutes, or until the oil separates out.

Pour in about 500ml / 18fl oz (2¼ cups) water, bring to the boil, then reduce the heat to low and simmer for 4–5 minutes. Remove from the heat and pass the sauce through a fine-mesh sieve (strainer) into a separate pan and return to the heat. Season with salt, then add the ground spices, stir and bring to the boil. Reduce the heat to low, add the chops and simmer for 30 minutes, stirring occasionally, until tender. Remove, add the ittar (if using), stir and adjust the seasoning, if necessary.

Makki ka Soweta
Lamb with Sweetcorn (Corn) Kernels

Origin Rajasthan
Preparation time 50 minutes
Cooking time 2 hours
Serves 6–8

3 tablespoons ghee

6 cloves

4 black cardamom pods

2 cinnamon sticks, about 5cm / 2 inches long

2 bay leaves

1kg / 2¼lb lamb, cut into pieces

125ml / 4¼oz (½ cup) natural (plain) yoghurt, whisked

2 teaspoons chilli powder

3 teaspoons ground coriander

1 teaspoon ground turmeric

1 teaspoon cumin seeds

150g / 5oz (¼ cup) Fried Onion Paste (see page 57)

2 tablespoons Garlic Paste (see page 57)

1kg / 2¼lb ears fresh sweetcorn (corn), kernels removed and roughly puréed

1 tablespoon green chillies, de-seeded and chopped

1 tablespoon sugar

250ml / 8fl oz (1 cup) milk

60g / 2oz (⅓ cup) gram (chickpea) flour, mixed with a little water

1 tablespoon lime juice

1 tablespoon chopped coriander (cilantro) leaves

salt

Heat the ghee in a large, heavy-based pan over medium heat, add the cloves, cardamom pods, cinnamon and bay leaves and stir-fry for 1–2 minutes. Add the meat, yoghurt, chilli powder, ground coriander, turmeric, cumin seeds and onion and garlic pastes, then season with salt and fry the meat for about 10 minutes.

Pour in 600ml / 1 pints (2½ cups) water and stir, then simmer for 1½ hours, until the meat is nearly tender. Add the sweetcorn, chillies, sugar, milk and gram flour and stir well. Cook over medium heat for about 20 minutes, stirring all the time to avoid the sweetcorn sticking to the base (bottom) of the pan. The sweetcorn is cooked when it does not stick to the base (bottom) of the pan. Add the lime juice and chopped coriander and stir well.

Maas ki Karhi
Lamb in Gram (Chickpea) Flour & Yoghurt Curry

Origin Rajasthan
Preparation time 45 minutes
Cooking time 1½ hours
Serves 4–6

1½ teaspoons cumin seeds

375ml / 13fl oz (1½ cups) natural (plain) yoghurt, whisked

50g / 1¾oz (½ cup) gram (chickpea) flour

1 teaspoon chilli powder

½ teaspoon ground turmeric

125g / 4½oz (½ cup) ghee

generous pinch of asafoetida

1kg / 2¼lb boneless lamb, cut into chunks

120g / 4oz (½ cup) Boiled Onion Paste (see page 57)

3 tablespoons Garlic Paste (see page 57)

2 green chillies, slit in half lengthways and de-seeded

salt

6 tablespoons chopped coriander (cilantro) leaves

Plain Boiled Rice (see page 631), to serve

Lightly stir-fry half the cumin seeds on a tawa or in a dry frying pan (skillet) for about 1 minute, or until roasted, but not turned, then allow to cool. When cool, put them in a spice grinder and process to make a powder.

Whisk the yoghurt, gram flour, chilli powder and turmeric together in a bowl, then season and pour in 750ml / 1¼ pints (3¼ cups) water and whisk again.

Heat the ghee in a large, heavy-based pan over medium heat, add the remaining cumin seeds and asafoetida and stir-fry for about 1 minute, or until the seeds start to splutter. Add the meat and season, then stir-fry for about 4–5 minutes, or until the meat is light brown all over. Add the boiled onion and garlic pastes and stir-fry for about 5 minutes.

Now pour in 500ml / 18fl oz (2¼ cups) water and bring to the boil. Reduce the heat, cover and simmer for about 50 minutes, stirring occasionally, until the meat is almost tender. Add the yoghurt mixture, bring almost to the boil, then reduce the heat to medium and cook for 30 minutes, stirring constantly, until the sauce starts to thicken. Add the roasted ground cumin and green chillies, then stir and cook for 2–3 minutes. Adjust the seasoning, if necessary, and garnish with coriander. Serve with Boiled Rice.

✿✿

Rezhala
Lamb & Yoghurt Curry

Origin Bengal
Preparation time 45 minutes, plus marinating time
Cooking time 1¼ hours
Serves 8

1kg / 2 ¼lb lamb, cut into medium-sized pieces

200g / 7oz (¾ cup) ghee

10 small onions, chopped

6 dried sour plums

1 teaspoon pistachios, chopped

1 teaspoon almonds, chopped

1 teaspoon cashew nuts, chopped

10–15 green chillies, slit in half lenthways and de-seeded

¼ teaspoon ground turmeric

2 bay leaves

2 green cardamom pods

2 black cardamom pods

10 peppercorns

250ml / 8fl oz (1 cup) milk

salt

For the marinade

2 onions

1 × 5-cm / 2-inch piece fresh ginger, peeled

8 cloves garlic

1 tablespoon ground coriander

400ml / 14fl oz (1⅔ cups) natural (plain) yoghurt

To make the marinade, put all the ingredients separately into a blender and process, adding a little water if necessary, to make a paste. Put all the pastes in a bowl, add the ground coriander and yoghurt and mix together.

Put the meat in a large shallow dish or bowl and rub the marinade over the meat, then cover and set aside in the refrigerator for 1 hour.

Heat the ghee in a large, heavy-based pan over high heat, then reduce the heat slightly. Add the lamb and the marinade and fry over medium-high heat for 5 minutes. Reduce the heat and fry gently for 10 minutes until the meat is half done.

Add all the remaining ingredients to the pan and season with salt. Cover and simmer for about 1 hour, or until the meat is tender.

✿✿

Kossha Mangsho
Lamb Curry (I)

Origin Bengal
Preparation time 30 minutes, plus marinating time
Cooking time 1½–2 hours
Serves 4

1kg / 2¼lb boneless lamb, cut into 2.5-cm / 1-inch cubes

125ml / 4½fl oz (½ cup) mustard oil

300g / 11oz (3 medium) onions, sliced

2 tablespoons Ginger Paste (see page 57)

1 tablespoon Garlic Paste (see page 57)

2 teaspoons chopped green chillies

500ml / 18fl oz (2¼ cups) natural (plain) yoghurt, whisked

2 teaspoons chilli powder

1 teaspoon ground turmeric

3 teaspoons sugar

2 teaspoons ground black cardamom

salt

3 teaspoons chopped coriander (cilantro) leaves, to garnish

For the marinade

250ml / 8fl oz (1 cup) natural (plain) yoghurt, whisked

2 tablespoons mustard oil

1 teaspoon chilli powder

½ teaspoon ground turmeric

1 teaspoon sugar

To make the marinade, mix all the ingredients together in a large bowl, add the meat and turn until well coated. Cover and set aside in the refrigerator for 1 hour.

Heat the oil in a kadhai, wok or large frying pan (skillet) over medium heat, add the onions and stir-fry for about 5–7 minutes, or until golden brown. Add the ginger and garlic pastes and green chillies and stir-fry for 2–3 minutes. Increase the heat to high, add the yoghurt, chilli powder, turmeric and sugar, and the lamb and the marinade, then season with salt and stir-fry for 5–10 minutes.

Pour in about 1 litre / 1¾ pints (4¼ cups) water, then reduce the heat, cover and simmer for about 1–1½ hours, or until the meat is tender and the sauce is thick. Add the ground cardamom and adjust the seasoning, if necessary. Serve garnished with chopped coriander.

Panther Jhol
Lamb Stew (III)

Origin Bengal
Preparation time 30 minutes, plus marinating time
Cooking time 1¼ hours
Serves 4

500g / 1lb 2oz lamb, cut into 2.5-cm / 1-inch cubes
1 teaspoon ground turmeric
1 teaspoon chilli powder
1 teaspoon ground coriander
2 teaspoons ground cumin
1 tablespoon Ginger Paste (see page 57)
1 tablespoon mustard oil, plus extra for frying
6 green chillies, de-seeded and chopped
250g / 9oz (2 medium) potatoes, cut into quarters
1 teaspoon sugar
2 tablespoons ghee
¼ fresh coconut, peeled and diced
1 teaspoon cumin seeds
salt

For the marinade
pinch of ground turmeric
½ tablespoon mustard oil

Place the lamb in a large bowl or dish, add the marinade ingredients and turn until the meat is coated. Cover and set aside in the refrigerator for 30 minutes.

Put the turmeric, chilli powder, ground coriander, cumin and ginger paste in a large bowl, add 1.5 litres / 2½ pints (6¼ cups) water and mix together.

Heat the 1 tablespoon of mustard oil in a large, heavy-based pan over high heat, add the spice mixture and stir-fry for about 30 seconds, or until the oil separates out. Add the chillies, then reduce the heat, cover and simmer for 10–12 minutes. Add the marinated meat, cover and simmer for about 30 minutes, or until it is three-quarters done.

Heat about 2 tablespoons oil in a large frying pan (skillet) over medium heat, add the potatoes and fry for about 15–20 minutes, or until cooked and golden brown. Add the potatoes to the meat with the sugar and season with salt. Cover and cook for about 30–45 minutes, or until the meat is done.

Heat 1 tablespoon ghee in a small frying pan over medium-low heat, add the diced coconut and stir-fry for about 1–2 minutes, or until golden brown. Add the cumin seeds and fry for about 1 minute, or until they start to splutter, then pour the mixture over the meat and cover to retain the aroma. Remove from the heat.

Dhaniwal Qorma
Coriander (Cilantro)-flavoured Lamb

Origin Jammu and Kashmir
Preparation time 30 minutes
Cooking time 1–1½ hours
Serves 4–6

250g / 9oz (1 cup) ghee
125ml / 4½ fl oz (½ cup) natural (plain) yoghurt
5 onions, chopped
1kg / 2¼lb lamb, cut into pieces
2 teaspoons ground ginger
2 teaspoons ground fennel
3 teaspoons ground coriander
1 teaspoon whole black peppercorns
salt
1 bunch coriander (cilantro) leaves, to garnish

Heat the ghee in a large, heavy-based pan over low heat, add the yoghurt and onions and blend well. Now add the meat and the remaining ingredients and season with salt. Pour in 750ml / 1¼ pints (3¼ cups) water and bring to the boil, then reduce the heat and simmer for about 1–1½ hours, or until the meat is tender. Remove from the heat and garnish with coriander leaves.

✻ ✻ ✻

Mutton Kolhapuri
Maharashtrian Hot Lamb Curry

Origin Maharashtra
Preparation time 40 minutes, plus marinating time
Cooking time 1–1½ hours
Serves 5–6

1kg / 2¼lb lamb, cut into medium-sized pieces
250ml / 8fl oz (1 cup) vegetable oil
8 cloves
2 teaspoons whole black peppercorns
1 teaspoon poppy seeds
1 teaspoon coriander seeds
1 teaspoon aniseeds
7–8 dried red chillies
2 large onions, chopped
1 coconut, peeled and grated
4 large tomatoes, chopped
2 large potatoes, cut into cubes
15g / ½oz (⅓ cup) coriander (cilantro) leaves, chopped
salt

For the marinade

1 teaspoon ground turmeric
½ tablespoon Ginger Paste (see page 57)
½ tablespoon Garlic Paste (see page 57)

To make the marinade, mix the turmeric, ginger and garlic pastes and a pinch of salt together in a large bowl. Place the lamb pieces in a large dish or bowl and rub the marinade all over the meat, then cover and set aside in the refrigerator for about 3–4 hours.

Heat 2 tablespoons oil in a large, heavy-based pan over medium heat, add the cloves, peppercorns, poppy seeds, coriander seeds, aniseeds and dried red chillies and stir-fry for about 2 minutes. Add the onions and stir-fry for about 4 minutes, or until they are light brown. Add the coconut and tomatoes and season with salt, then cook for about 5 minutes, or until the moisture has evaporated. Remove the pan from the heat and allow to cool.

When the mixture is cool, put it into a blender or food processor and process to make a paste, then set aside.

Heat the remaining oil in a deep, heavy-based pan over medium heat, add the potatoes and fry for about 10 minutes, or until golden brown. Remove from the pan and set aside. Add the lamb and stir-fry for about 5 minutes, or until brown, then add the masala paste and season with salt. Pour in 500ml / 18fl oz (2¼ cups) hot water, bring to the boil, then reduce the heat, cover and simmer, stirring occasionally, for about 1–1½ hours, or until the meat is tender. You may need to add more water. Add the potatoes and cook for a further 5 minutes, then garnish with chopped coriander and serve hot.

✻ / 📷 p.285

Ishtoo (I)
Lamb Stew (I)

Origin Delhi/Bhopal
Preparation time 30 minutes
Cooking time 2 hours
Serves 4

250ml / 8fl oz (1 cup) vegetable oil or ghee
1kg / 2¼lb lamb chops and hind leg pieces, cut into pieces
1kg / 2¼lb (7 medium) onions, thinly sliced
250ml / 8fl oz (1 cup) natural (plain) yoghurt, whisked
10–12 dried red chillies
5–6 cloves
1 clove garlic
salt

Heat the oil or ghee in a large, heavy-based pan over very low heat. Mix all the ingredients together in a large bowl, then season with salt and add to the pan. Cover and cook for about 2 hours, or until the meat is tender.

Ishtoo (II)
Lamb Stew (II)

Origin Delhi/Bhopal
Preparation time 40 minutes
Cooking time 1¼–1¾ hours
Serves 4

200g / 7oz (2 medium) potatoes, cut into cubes

2 tablespoons coconut oil

8 green cardamom pods

4 cloves

4 bay leaf

2 cinnamon sticks, about 2.5cm / 1 inch long

300g / 11oz (2 medium) onions, sliced

1 × 2.5-cm / 1-inch piece fresh ginger, peeled and cut into juliennes

8 green chillies, de-seeded and cut into juliennes

24 curry leaves

2½ teaspoons Ginger Paste (see page 57)

2½ teaspoons Garlic Paste (see page 57)

250ml / 8fl oz (1 cup) coconut cream, fresh (see page 781) or canned

1kg / 2¼lb lamb chops and hind leg pieces, cut into pieces

125ml / 4½fl oz (½ cup) coconut milk, fresh (see page 781) or canned

½ teaspoon ground green cardamom

salt

desiccated (dried flaked) coconut, to garnish

Cook the potatoes in a large pan of salted boiling water for about 5 minutes, or until al dente, then drain and set aside.

Heat the oil in a large, heavy-based pan over medium heat, add the cardamom pods, cloves, bay leaf and cinnamon and stir-fry for about 30 seconds, or until the cardamom starts to change colour. Add the onions and stir-fry for about 2 minutes, or until translucent and glossy. Add the ginger, chillies and half the curry leaves and stir-fry for 1 minute, then add the ginger and garlic pastes and stir-fry for about 1–2 minutes, or until the moisture has evaporated.

Add the coconut cream and 375ml / 13fl oz (1½ cups) water and bring to the boil. Add the meat and season with salt, then stir and return to the boil. Reduce the heat to low, cover and simmer, stirring occasionally, for about 1–1½ hours, or until the meat is tender.

Uncover, add the remaining curry leaves and stir. Remove the pan from the heat and stir in the coconut milk. Return the pan to the heat, sprinkle over the ground cardamom, cover and simmer for about 5 minutes, or until beginning to boil. Remove from the heat, adjust the seasoning, if necessary, and garnish with desiccated coconut.

Do Pyaza
Spiced Lamb

Origin Awadh
Preparation time 40 minutes, plus cooling time
Cooking time 1 hour 10 minutes
Serves 4

250g / 9oz (2 small) onions, roughly chopped

1 × 5-cm / 2-inch piece fresh ginger, peeled

300g / 11oz (1¼ cups) ghee or vegetable oil

250g / 9oz (2 medium) onions, sliced

1kg / 2¼lb lamb, cut into pieces

4–6 cloves

250ml / 8fl oz (1 cup) natural (plain) yoghurt, whisked

6–8 green cardamom pods, crushed

2 teaspoons cumin seeds

1 teaspoon chilli powder

2 teaspoons garam masala (see page 31)

2 tablespoons chopped coriander (cilantro) leaves

salt

Put the chopped onions in a blender or food processor and process to make a paste. Set aside. Put the ginger in a small blender or food processor and process to make a paste. Set aside.

Heat the ghee or oil in a large, heavy-based pan over medium heat, add the sliced onions and fry for about 5–7 minutes, or until well browned. Remove from the pan with a slotted spoon and allow to cool. When cool, crush and set aside.

Add the meat, cloves, onion and ginger pastes, yoghurt, cardamom pods, cumin seeds and chilli powder to the pan and fry for about 30 minutes over medium heat, stirring frequently and sprinkling with a little water if required, to ensure that it does not burn. When the meat is cooked and very little sauce is left, add the crushed fried onions, garam masala, coriander leaves and 250ml / 8fl oz (1 cup) water. Bring to the boil, reduce the heat and simmer for about 30 minutes, then remove from the heat and serve.

Jardalu Boti
Lamb Cooked with Apricots

Origin Parsi
Preparation time 20 minutes, plus soaking time
Cooking time 1½–2 hours
Serves 6–8

250g / 9oz (1½ cups) dried apricots
1½ teaspoons chilli powder
1 tablespoon ground cumin
250ml / 8fl oz (1 cup) vegetable oil
150g / 5oz (1 medium) onion, finely chopped
1 × 2.5-cm / 1-inch piece fresh ginger, peeled and chopped
½ clove garlic, finely chopped
3–4 cinnamon sticks, about 5cm / 2 inches long
6–8 green cardamom pods
4 tomatoes, chopped
1kg / 2¼lb lamb, cut into bite-sized chunks
½ teaspoon Garam Masala (see page 31)
1½ teaspoons ground black pepper
1 teaspoon malt (white) vinegar
2 teaspoons sugar
salt

Soak the dried apricots in a bowl of water overnight.

The next day, put the chilli powder and ground cumin in a small bowl, add 2 tablespoons water and mix together. Drain the apricots and set aside.

Heat the oil in a large, heavy-based pan over low heat, add the onions and fry for 8–10 minutes, or until light brown. Now add the ginger and garlic and stir-fry for 3–4 minutes, then add the cinnamon and cardamom pods and cook for a further 1 minute.

Add the chilli powder mixture to the pan and stir well. Add the tomatoes and cook for about 5 minutes, then add the meat, garam masala and black pepper and season with salt. Stir-fry for about 5 minutes, then reduce the heat to very low and cook for about 1–1½ hours, or until the meat is tender. Pour in about of 125ml / 4½fl oz (½ cup) hot water, if it is drying out, and simmer for 1 minute. Sprinkle over the vinegar, then add the sugar and the drained apricots and cook for a further 2 minutes, then mix well to blend.

Nahari
Morning Delight

Origin Delhi
Preparation time 40 minutes
Cooking time 1¼–1¾ hours
Serves 4

125ml / 4½fl oz (½ cup) mustard oil
250g / 9oz (2 small) onions, sliced
8–10 black cardamom pods
4–5 cloves
2 cinnamon sticks, about 2.5cm / 1 inch long
3 tablespoons Ginger Paste (see page 57)
3 tablespoons Garlic Paste (see page 57)
3 teaspoons ground coriander
1 teaspoon chilli powder
1 teaspoon ground turmeric
150ml / ¼ pint (⅔ cup) natural (plain) yoghurt, whisked
500g / 1lb 2oz lamb, cut into pieces
1.5 litres / 2½ pints (6¼ cups) lamb stock (see page 636)
4 tablespoons gram (chickpea) flour, roasted
½ teaspoon ground black pepper
salt

Heat the oil in a large, heavy-based pan over medium heat, add half the onions and fry for about 5–7 minutes, or until golden and crisp. Remove from the pan with a slotted spoon and drain on kitchen paper (paper towels).

Reheat the oil over medium heat, add the whole spices and stir-fry for about 30 seconds, or until the cardamom pods start to change colour. Add the remaining onions, the ginger and garlic pastes, ground coriander, chilli powder, turmeric and yoghurt, then season with salt and stir-fry for about 2 minutes, or until the oil separates out.

Crush the reserved fried onions, then add them to the pan and stir-fry for 1 minute. Add the meat and stock and bring almost to the boil. Reduce the heat to low and simmer for about 1–1½ hours, or until the meat is tender.

Put the roasted gram flour in a small bowl, add 4 tablespoons water and mix together, then stir the mixture into the pan. Add the black pepper, mix well, cover and simmer for about 5 minutes. Uncover and adjust the seasoning, if necessary.

Elayachi Gosht
Cardamom-flavoured Lamb

Origin Hyderabad
Preparation time 30 minutes
Cooking time 1½–2 hours
Serves 4

125g / 4oz (½ cup) ghee

10 green cardamom pods, cracked

6 black cardamom pods, cracked

1kg / 2¼lb lamb, cut into pieces

1 × 2.5-cm / 1-inch piece fresh ginger, peeled and finely chopped

500g / 1lb 2oz (3 medium) onions, sliced

8–10 green chillies, de-seeded and chopped

400ml / 14fl oz (1⅔ cups) natural (plain) yoghurt, whisked

1 teaspoon chilli powder

1 teaspoon ground green cardamom

1 teaspoon ground coriander

salt

1 large sprig coriander (cilantro) leaves, to garnish

Heat the ghee in a large, heavy-based pan over medium heat, add the cardamom pods and stir-fry for about 1 minute, or until they start to splutter. Add the meat, increase the heat to high and stir-fry for about 5 minutes, or until it changes colour. Reduce the heat, add the ginger, onions and chillies and stir-fry for about 4 minutes, or until the onions are light brown. Remove the pan from the heat.

Mix the yoghurt and chilli powder together in a bowl, then season with salt. Stir into the pan, then return to the heat and bring almost to the boil. Pour in about 1 litre / 1¾ pints (4¼ cups) water and return almost to the boil. Reduce the heat, cover and simmer for about 1–1½ hours, or until the meat is cooked and tender. Sprinkle over the ground green cardamom and coriander and mix well. Adjust the seasoning, if necessary, and garnish with coriander leaves.

Meat Beliram
Punjabi Lamb Curry

Origin Punjab
Preparation time 30 minutes, plus marinating time
Cooking time 1 hour 10 minutes
Serves 6

1kg / 2¼lb lamb, cut into chunks

180g / 6oz (¾ cup) ghee

2 tablespoons coriander seeds, crushed

salt

For the marinade

750ml / 1¼ pints (3¼ cups) natural (plain) yoghurt, whisked

5 onions, sliced

4 tablespoons finely chopped ginger

4 tablespoons finely chopped garlic

2 teaspoons Kashmiri red chilli powder

10 green cardamom pods

2 cinnamon sticks, about 2.5cm / 1 inch long

5 cloves

To make the marinade, mix all the ingredients together in a large bowl and season with salt. Place the meat in a shallow dish and rub the marinade evenly over the meat, then cover and set aside in the refrigerator for about 2 hours.

Heat the ghee in a large, heavy-based pan over medium heat, add the coriander seeds and stir-fry for about 1 minute, or until they start to splutter. Now, add the chunks of meat together with the marinade and bring almost to the boil. Reduce the heat to medium, cover and cook for 30 minutes.

Now reduce the heat to low and simmer for about 30 minutes, then increase the heat to medium, uncover and cook for about 2–3 minutes, or until the oil separates out and the meat looks well fried. Adjust the seasoning, if necesary.

Rarha Meat
Pot-roasted Lamb

Origin Punjab
Preparation time 40 minutes, plus marinating time
Cooking time 1½–2 hours
Serves 2–3

250ml / 8fl oz (1 cup) natural (plain) yoghurt, whisked
1kg / 2¼lb lamb, cut into pieces
150g / 5oz (⅔ cup) ghee or vegetable oil
2 cinnamon sticks, about 2.5cm / 1 inch long
2½ black cardamom pods
1 bay leaf
100g / 3½oz (1 small) onion, finely chopped
4 teaspoons Ginger Paste (see page 57)
4 teaspoons Garlic Paste (see page 57)
½ teaspoon ground turmeric
2 teaspoons chilli powder
¾ teaspoon Garam Masala (see page 31)
100g / 3½oz (1 medium) tomato, chopped
salt
5–6 coriander (cilantro) leaves, chopped, to garnish

Put the yoghurt in a large dish or bowl, season with salt and add the meat. Turn until well coated, then cover and set aside in the refrigerator for about 1½ hours.

Heat the ghee or oil in a large, heavy-based pan over medium heat, add the cinnamon, cardamom pods and bay leaf and stir-fry for a few seconds. Now add the chopped onion and fry for about 5–7 minutes, or until the onion is golden brown. Add the ginger and garlic pastes, turmeric, chilli powder, garam masala and tomato, then season with salt. Cook for about 5 minutes, or until the tomato is mushy and the moisture has evaporated.

Now add the lamb together with the marinade and cook for about 2–3 minutes, or until the oil separates out. Pour in 750ml / 1¼ pints (3¼ cups) water and stir well. Bring almost to the boil, then reduce the heat to medium-low, cover and simmer for about 1–1½ hours, or until the meat is tender. Uncover, increase the heat and boil away any excess moisture. When very little sauce remains garnish with chopped coriander and serve.

Dahiwala Meat
Lamb in Yoghurt Sauce (I)

Origin Punjab
Preparation time 30 minutes, plus marinating time
Cooking time 2 hours
Serves 4

1kg / 2¼lb boneless lamb, cut into chunks
5 tablespoons ghee
3 onions, chopped
2 teaspoons Ginger Paste (see page 57)
2 teaspoons Garlic Paste (see page 57)
10 cloves
6 small cardamom pods
4 black cardamom pods
4 green chillies
2 cinnamon sticks, about 2.5cm / 1 inch long
1 teaspoon Garam Masala (see page 31)
salt
coriander (cilantro) leaves, to garnish

For the marinade

500ml / 18fl oz (2¼ cups) natural (plain) yoghurt, whisked
pinch of salt
1 teaspoon ground coriander
1 teaspoon chilli powder

To make the marinade, mix all the ingredients together in a large bowl. Add the meat and turn until well coated, then cover and set aside in the refrigerator for about 2 hours.

Heat the ghee in a large, heavy-based pan over low heat, add the onions and ginger and garlic pastes and stir-fry for 8–10 minutes, or until the onions are golden brown. Add the meat without any extra marinade and fry for about 5 minutes. Now, add all the remaining ingredients, except the garam masala and coriander, and the marinade and mix well. Pour in 400ml / 14fl oz (1¾ cups) water, then cover and cook over low heat for about 1½ hours, or until the meat is tender.

Add the garam masala and mix well. Cook for about 3 minutes, stirring frequently so that the sauce coats the lamb. Garnish with coriander leaves.

Masaledar Mutton
Lamb Masala

Origin Punjab
Preparation time 10 minutes
Cooking time 1½–2 hours
Serves 2–3

3 tablespoons ghee
1 bay leaf
3 onions, cut into rings
1½ tablespoons Garlic Paste (see page 57)
1 tablespoon Ginger Paste (see page 57)
500g / 1lb 2oz lamb, cut into pieces
2 tablespoons vegetable oil
½ teaspoon chilli powder
½ teaspoon Garam Masala (see page 31)
½ teaspoon ground turmeric
¾ teaspoon ground coriander
¾ teaspoon ground cumin
2 large tomatoes, puréed
salt

To garnish

2 green chillies, de-seeded and chopped
strips of fresh ginger

Heat the ghee in a large, heavy-based pan over medium heat, add the bay leaf and onion rings and stir-fry for about 4 minutes, or until the onions are light brown. Now add the ginger and garlic pastes and stir-fry for 1 minute. Add the lamb and all the remaining ingredients except the tomatoes and fry for about 10 minutes, or until the oil separates out and the meat looks well fried.

Add the puréed tomatoes to the pan and mix well. Pour in 180ml / 6½fl oz (¾ cup) water, mix well, then reduce the heat to low, cover and cook for about 1–1½ hours, or until the meat is tender. Alternatively, cook in a pressure cooker; close the lid, and after 6 minutes reduce the heat to low and cook for 25 minutes. The time will depend on the quality of the lamb.

Garnish with green chillies and ginger strips.

Gushtaba
Pounded Meatballs in Light Cardamom Sauce

Origin Jammu and Kashmir
Preparation time 1 hour
Cooking time 40 minutes
Serves 4

1kg / 2¼lb boneless lamb, cut into 5-cm / 2-inch pieces
125g / 4oz (½ cup) ghee, plus extra for meatballs
pinch of ground ginger
pinch of salt
3 black cardamom pods, ground
1.2 litres / 2 pints (5 cups) natural (plain) yoghurt
1 litre / 1¾ pints (4¼ cups) lamb stock (see page 636)
4 black cardamom pods
8 green cardamom pods
6 cloves
3 teaspoons ground fennel
3 teaspoons ground ginger
3 tablespoons garlic water
1 tablespoon Fried Onion Paste (see page 57)
½ teaspoon dried mint leaves
salt

Put the meat on a board and pound with a wooden mallet, adding small amounts of ghee, a pinch of ground ginger, salt and ground black cardamom, until the meat is pulped to a silken texture. Alternatively, put everything in a food processor and process until pulped and mixed together. With damp hands, shape the meat into balls about 4cm / 1½ inches in diameter.

Bring a large, heavy-based pan of water to the boil and place the meatballs in the pan with a slotted spoon. Cook for about 5 minutes, turning frequently, then remove from the heat and drain.

Add the meatballs, yoghurt, ghee and stock to a large, heavy-based pan and bring to a rapid boil. Add the cardamom pods, cloves and ground fennel and ginger, then cover and continue to boil for 10–12 minutes.

Add the garlic water, then season with salt and boil for a further 10 minutes. Add more hot water, if required, to maintain a soup-like consistency. Add the onion paste and cook for about 10–15 minutes, or until the meatballs are tender (spongy) to the touch and the sauce has thickened. Sprinkle over the dried mint leaves before serving.

※ ※
—

Rista
Pounded Meatballs in Piquant Sauce

Origin Jammu and Kashmir
Preparation time 1 hour
Cooking time 40 minutes
Serves 4

1kg / 2¼lb boneless lamb, cut into pieces

100g / 3½oz (scant ½ cup) ghee, plus more
  for the meatballs

4 teaspoons ground ginger

pinch of salt

3 black cardamom pods, ground

2 teaspoons ground fennel

1 teaspoon ground cinnamon

2 teaspoons chilli powder

6 black cardamom pods, ground

4 tablespoons Boiled Onion Paste (see page 57)

250ml / 8fl oz (1 cup) mawal extract

salt

Put the meat on a board and pound with a wooden mallet, adding small amounts of ghee, a pinch of ground ginger, salt and ground black cardamom, until the meat is pulped to a silken texture. Alternatively, put everything in a food processor and process until pulped and mixed together. With damp hands, shape the meat into balls about 4cm / 1½ inches in diameter.

Bring a large, heavy-based pan of water to the boil and place the meatballs in the pan with a slotted spoon. Cook for about 5 minutes, turning frequently, then remove from the heat and drain.

Heat the ghee in another large, heavy-based pan over high heat, add all the ingredients, except the onion paste and mawal extract, and pour in 500ml / 18fl oz (2¼ cups) water. Add the meatballs, then add the onion paste. Reduce the heat and simmer for about 20 minutes. Add the mawal extract and simmer for about 10–15 minutes, or until the oil separates out.

※ ※
—

Malgoba
Thick & Spicy Lamb Curry

Origin Rajasthan
Preparation time 30 minutes
Cooking time 2¼ hours
Serves 4–6

3 tablespoons ghee

5 black cardamom pods

20 cloves

20 whole black peppercorns

60g / 2oz onions, thinly sliced

1kg / 2¼lb lamb leg or shoulder, cut into pieces

2 teaspoons ground coriander

½ teaspoon ground turmeric

2 teaspoons chilli powder

2 teaspoons Ginger Paste (see page 57)

1 teaspoon plain (all-purpose) flour

1 litre / 1¾ pints (4¼ cups) natural (plain) yoghurt,
  whisked

1 tablespoon chopped coriander (cilantro) leaves

salt

Heat the ghee in a large, heavy-based pan over medium heat, add the cardamom pods, cloves and peppercorns and stir-fry for about 1 minute, or until they start to splutter. Add the onions and stir-fry for about 5–7 minutes, or until they are golden brown. Add the meat, season with salt, then add the ground coriander and turmeric and stir-fry for about 5 minutes, sprinkling with water if necessary.

Add the chilli powder and ginger paste and cook for a further 2–3 minutes. Pour in about 500ml / 2 pints (2½ cups) water and cook for about 1–1½ hours, or until the meat is tender.

Mix the flour and yoghurt together in a bowl. Add the yoghurt and coriander leaves to the meat and stir, then simmer for 30 minutes, or until the oil separates out and rises to the surface of the sauce.

Roghanjosh
Scarlet Rich Lamb Curry

Origin Jammu and Kashmir
Preparation time 30 minutes
Cooking time 1¼ hours
Serves 4–6

1 × 5-cm / 2-inch piece fresh ginger, peeled
few saffron threads
1 teaspoon hot water or milk
250g / 9oz (1 cup) ghee or vegetable oil
4 cloves
1 cinnamon stick, about 2.5cm / 1 inch long
pinch of asafoetida
1kg / 2¼lb lamb, cut into pieces
250ml / 8fl oz (1 cup) natural (plain) yoghurt, whisked
1 teaspoon ground ginger
1 teaspoon chilli powder
1 teaspoon sugar
2 teaspoons Garam Masala (see page 31)
salt

Put the ginger in a small blender and process to make a paste, then set aside. Put the saffron threads in a small bowl, add the hot water or milk and soak until required.

Heat the ghee or oil in a large, heavy-based pan over low heat, add the whole spices, asafoetida, meat, yoghurt, ground ginger, chilli powder, garam masala and ginger paste, then season with salt and cover. Simmer for 10 minutes, stirring frequently to prevent burning, until all the water has evaporated and a reddish sediment starts to appear. Sprinkle over about 2 tablespoons water, cover and continue to simmer, scraping the sediment frequently and turning the meat constantly.

Repeat this process for about 30 minutes, or until the meat turns reddish brown, then add the sugar and 250ml / 8fl oz (1 cup) water and cook for an additional 30–45 minutes or until the meat is tender. When the meat becomes tender, add the garam masala and soaked saffron, then cover and cook for a further 10 minutes. When the meat is nearly done, increase the heat to medium and cook until there is very little sauce left.

Martswangan Qorma
Chilli-flavoured Hot Lamb in Sauce

Origin Jammu and Kashmir
Preparation time 30 minutes
Cooking time 1¾ hours
Serves 4–6

20 dried red chillies
3 tablespoons vegetable oil or ghee
125ml / 4½fl oz (½ cup) natural (plain) yoghurt, whisked
1kg / 2¼lb shoulder of lamb, cut into pieces
4 teaspoons ground fennel
3 teaspoons ground cinnamon
4 green cardamoms
4 cloves
1 teaspoon cumin seeds
2 teaspoons ground ginger
4 tablespoons mawal extract
black rock salt

Soak the dried red chillies in a bowl of hot water for 2 minutes, then drain, reserving a little water. De-seed the chillies, then transfer to a small blender and process, adding a little soaking water to make a paste. Set aside.

Heat the ghee or oil in a large, heavy-based pan over low heat, add the yoghurt and cook for about 5 minutes, or until it turns brown. Add the meat and stir-fry for about 5 minutes, then add all the remaining ingredients, except the mawal extract, and season with salt.

Pass the chilli paste through a piece of fine muslin (cheesecloth) and add the extract to the meat and stir. Finally, add the mawal extract and simmer for about 1½ hours, or until the meat is tender and the oil rises to the surface.

Shabdeg
Overnight Meat Pot

Origin Jammu and Kashmir
Preparation time 3 hours, plus standing time
Cooking time 30 minutes, plus overnight
Serves 4–6

large pinch of saffron
2 tablespoons milk
250g / 9oz (2 medium) turnips, unpeeled
vegetable oil, for drizzling
½ teaspoon Garlic Paste (see page 57)
1 teaspoon ground turmeric
¼ teaspoon ground black pepper
125g / 4½oz (½ cup) ghee, plus more for deep-frying
500g / 1lb 2oz (6 medium) onions, thinly sliced
¼ teaspoon ground cloves
¼ teaspoon ground cinnamon
salt

For the yakhni

2½ tablespoons Garlic Paste (see page 57)
2½ tablespoons Ginger Paste (see page 57)
1kg / 2 ¼lb lamb, cut into pieces
500g / 1lb 2oz minced (ground) lamb
1 tablespoon raw papaya paste
2–4 green cardamom pods, ground to a paste
½ teaspoon Garam Masala (see page 31)

To finish

2 teaspoons Ginger Paste (see page 57)
2 teaspoons Garlic Paste (see page 57)
1 teaspoon ground cumin
1 teaspoon ground black cumin
3 teaspoons chilli powder
½ teaspoon Garam Masala (see page 31)
500ml / 18fl oz (2¼ cups) natural (plain) yoghurt, whisked
250g / 9oz (1 cup) clotted cream or crème fraiche
3 tablespoons almond paste
2 tablespoons lime juice
1 Kashmiri vadi or 1 tablespoon Kashmiri Garam Masala (see page 56)
1 teaspoon kewra water or rosewater

Preheat the oven to 200°C/400°F/Gas Mark 6. Put the saffron threads in a small bowl, add the milk and soak until required.

Put the turnips in a small roasting tin (pan), drizzle with oil and roast in the oven for about 30 minutes, or until cooked. Allow to cool, then remove the skin and prick all over with a fork. Put the turnips in a large shallow dish, add the garlic paste, turmeric, pepper and half of the saffron dissolved in milk, then season with salt and turn until well coated. Set aside for about 15 minutes.

Heat ½ cup of the ghee in a large, heavy-based pan over medium heat, add the turnips and fry for about 5–8 minutes, or until golden brown. Remove and set aside. Add the finely sliced onions and fry for about 5–7 minutes, or until browned and crisp. Drain off any excess oil.

Put the ground cloves and cinnamon in a small bowl, add a little water and mix to make a paste.

To make the yakhni, put half the fried onions, half the garlic paste, half the ginger paste, half the ground cloves mixture, half the lamb and enough water to cook the meat in a large, heavy-based pan. Cook for 2½ hours until the meat is tender and soft enough to be strained to make a thick soup. When the meat is done, mash to a pulp, extract any bones and strain through a sieve (strainer) or a piece of fine muslin (cheesecloth).

Mix the strained liquid with the minced lamb, papaya paste, remaining ginger, garlic and ground cloves mixture, the green cardamom paste and the garam masala in a large bowl. Allow to cool.

When the mixture is cool, shape it into balls or koftas about the size of the turnips. Heat the ghee for deep-frying in a kadhai or deep, heavy-based pan to 180°C/350°F, or until a cube of bread browns in 30 seconds. Working in batches, carefully lower the balls or koftas into the hot oil and deep-fry for about 2–3 minutes, or until golden brown, Remove with a slotted spoon and drain on kitchen paper (paper towels). Sprinkle with a little salt.

To finish the dish, put the remaining pieces of lamb in the hot ghee with the fried onions, ginger and garlic pastes, and the remaining ground spices and fry for about 5–7 minutes, or until the meat is well browned. Add the yoghurt, yakhni, cream, almond paste, fried turnips, lamb koftas and lime juice and stir gently. Add enough water for a thick sauce and to cook the meat. Crumble the Kashmiri vadi and stir it or the Kashmiri garam masala into the pan, then seal the lid with dough or foil. Add some live coals to the lid and below the pan and let it cook through the night, or cook it in a very low oven overnight.

The next day, add the remaining soaked saffron and the kewra water, stir and serve hot.

Aab Gosht
Lamb in Milk Sauce (I)

Origin Jammu and Kashmir
Preparation time 30 minutes
Cooking time 2 hours
Serves 4–6

1kg / 2¼lb lamb, cut into pieces
4–6 cloves garlic, crushed
2 teaspoons ground ginger
1 litre / 1¾ pints (4¼ cups) milk
6–8 green cardamom pods
250g / 9oz (1 cup) ghee
1 tablespoon Boiled Onion Paste (see page 57)
4 teaspoons ground fennel
5 cinnamon sticks, about 2.5cm / 1 inch long
4 cloves
1 tablespoon whole black peppercorns
salt

Place the meat with the garlic, ground ginger and a little salt in a large, heavy-based pan. Cover with cold water and bring to the boil. Simmer for about 5 minutes, or until the meat is firm. Drain, reserving the stock and set aside.

Boil the milk in another pan with the cardamom pods for about 1 hour, or until it thickens and is reduced to three-quarters of its original volume. Add the remaining ingredients and continue boiling. Now add the meat. Strain the remaining meat stock through a piece of fine muslin (cheesecloth) or sieve (strainer) and add it to the pan. Continue boiling for about 5 minutes, then reduce the heat and simmer for 1–1½ hours, or until the meat is tender.

Kabargah
Batter-fried Lamb Ribs

Origin Jammu and Kashmir
Preparation time 1 hour
Cooking time 30 minutes
Serves 4–6

4 green cardamom pods
2 teaspoons ground ginger
4 cloves
4 cinnamon sticks, about 2.5cm / 1 inch long
1 teaspoon fennel seeds
10 lamb breast pieces with 2 ribs each
250ml / 8fl oz (1 cup) milk
125g / 4¼oz (¾ cup) gram (chickpea) flour
5 tablespoons rice flour
1 teaspoon chilli powder
pinch of asafoetida
125g / 4oz (½ cup) ghee
salt

Put the cardamom pods, ground ginger, cloves, cinnamon and fennel in a piece of fine muslin (cheesecloth) and bring up the sides to form a bag. Tie the top with kitchen string (twine). Place this pouch with the meat, milk and 250ml / 8fl oz (1 cup) water in a deep, heavy-based pan and bring to the boil. Cook for about 30 minutes, or until the meat becomes tender and the liquid dries up.

Meanwhile, put the gram and rice flours in a large bowl and mix, adding enough water to make a light batter. To test the batter, drop a teaspoon of it into a cup of water. If the batter floats, the consistency is correct, if not beat again. Season with salt, then add the chilli powder and asafoetida and mix well.

Heat the ghee in a large frying pan (skillet) over medium heat. Dip the pieces of boiled meat into the batter and fry for 3–4 minutes, or until golden brown. Remove and drain on kitchen paper (paper towels).

Kaliya
Lamb in Yoghurt Sauce (II)

Origin Jammu and Kashmir
Preparation time 30 minutes
Cooking time 2 hours
Serves 4–6

50g / 2oz (¼ cup) ghee

pinch of asafoetida

4 cloves

250ml / 8fl oz (1 cup) natural (plain) yoghurt, whisked

1kg / 2¼lb lamb chops and breast piece with
  2 ribs each

1 teaspoon chilli powder

1 × 5-cm / 2-inch piece fresh ginger, peeled and
  ground

1 teaspoon ground ginger

1 teaspoon ground turmeric

1 teaspoon fennel seeds

250g / 9oz (2 medium) turnips or potatoes, cut into
  small pieces

2 teaspoons Kashmiri Garam Masala (see page 56)

1 teaspoon sugar

1 bunch of coriander (cilantro) leaves, chopped

salt

Heat the ghee in a large, heavy-based pan over low heat, add the asafoetida, cloves, yoghurt, meat, chilli powder and both gingers. Season with salt, then cover and simmer, stirring frequently to prevent burning, until all the water dries up and a reddish sediment starts to appear. Sprinkle over about 2 tablespoons water and cover, scraping the base (bottom) of the pan and turning the meat all the time to prevent the sediment from sticking and burning. Repeat the process for about 20 minutes until the meat turns a rich brown colour. Now add 500ml / 18½fl oz (2 cups) water and cook for at least 1½ hours. When the meat is tender, stir in the turmeric.

Put the fennel in a small muslin (cheesecloth) bag and place this bag in the pan with the meat. Add the turnips or potatoes and pour in more water to cover the meat and vegetables, if necessary. Cook until the vegetables are tender. Remove the muslin bag, skim off any excess fat, then add the garam masala, sugar and chopped coriander.

Darashahi Kaliya
Lamb Ribs in Sauce

Origin Jammu and Kashmir
Preparation time 15 minutes, plus cooling time
Cooking time 1¼ hours
Serves 5

250ml / 8fl oz (1 cup) milk

250ml / 8fl oz (1 cup) natural (plain) yoghurt, whisked

250ml / 8fl oz (1 cup) mustard oil

1kg / 2¼lb lamb ribs with fat

1 teaspoon ground ginger

2 teaspoons ground aniseed

small pinch of asafoetida

4 cloves

2 cinnamon sticks

1 teaspoon ground turmeric

1 teaspoon chilli powder

8 green cardamom pods

1 teaspoon Kashmiri Garam Masala (see page 56)

2½ tablespoons raisins

50g / 1¾oz (⅓ cup) cashew nuts, halved

salt

Mix the milk and yoghurt together in a bowl and set aside.

Heat the oil in a large, heavy-based pan over high heat. When hot, remove from the heat and allow to cool, then add the lamb pieces and return to the heat. Fry the meat over high heat for about 5 minutes, or until light golden. Pour in about 1 litre / 1¾ pints (4¼ cups) water, then add the ground ginger, aniseed, asafoetida, cloves, cinnamon, turmeric, chilli powder and cardamom pods and season with salt. Cover and cook for about 45 minutes. Remove from the heat and bring the pan to room temperature.

Uncover and add the mixture of milk and yoghurt to the pan and cook over medium-low heat for a further 15 minutes. Once the sauce thickens and the oil separates out, add the garam masala, raisins and halved cashews and simmer over low heat for another 10 minutes until the meat is tender and cooked.

Mutton Coconut Fry
Fried Lamb with Coconut

Origin Kerala
Preparation time 45 minutes, plus marinating time
Cooking time 2½ hours
Serves 4

750g / 1lb 10oz lamb chops

coconut oil, for brushing and basting

salt

For the marinade

2 teaspoons chilli powder

3 teaspoons Garlic Paste (see page 57)

7 teaspoons Ginger Paste (see page 57)

125ml / 4½fl oz (½ cup) toddy vinegar

For the braising

2 tablespoons coconut oil

6–8 green cardamom pods

5–6 cloves

2 cinnamon sticks, about 2.5cm / 1 inch long

2 bay leaves

pinch of salt

For the masala

1 coconut

6 dried red chillies

1 teaspoon black peppercorns

5 teaspoons coriander seeds

1 teaspoon cumin seeds

250ml / 8fl oz (1 cup) coconut milk, fresh
    (see page 781) or canned

For the sauce

1 tablespoon ground coriander

½ teaspoon ground turmeric

3 tablespoons coconut oil

10–15 curry leaves

250g / 9oz (2 medium) onions, thinly sliced

1 × 2.5-cm / 1-inch piece fresh ginger, peeled
    and grated

12 cloves garlic, crushed

250g / 9oz (2 small) tomatoes, chopped

3 tablespoons Tamarind Extract (see page 58)

Remove the side bones and the excess fat from the chops, then prick the chops all over with a fork, wash and pat dry with kitchen paper (paper towels). Place the chops in a large shallow dish and rub with the chilli powder and salt, then with the garlic and ginger pastes and vinegar. Cover and set aside for about 30 minutes.

Preheat the oven to 200°C/400°F/Gas Mark 6. Rub the chops with coconut oil and arrange in a large roasting tray (pan). Add all the braising ingredients and enough water to cover the chops and braise in the oven until the liquor begins to boil. Reduce the oven temperature to 150°C/300°F/Gas Mark 2 and braise for 1½ hours.

Remove the chops, brush with the coconut oil and set aside. Pass the liquor through a fine sieve (strainer) into a bowl and set aside for the sauce.

To prepare the masala, peel and grate the coconut. Roast all the ingredients, except the coconut milk, separately in a dry frying pan (skillet) over low heat for about 1 minute, or until fragrant. Transfer all the ingredients to a blender or food processor, add the coconut milk and process to make a coarse paste. Transfer to a bowl and set aside.

For the sauce, put the ground coriander and turmeric in a small bowl, add 2 tablespoons water and mix together.

Heat the oil in a kadhai, wok or deep, heavy-based pan over medium heat, add half the curry leaves and stir-fry for a few seconds. Add the onions and stir-fry for 2 minutes, or until they are translucent and glossy. Add the ginger and garlic and fry for about 3 minutes, or until the onions are golden brown, then add the masala and stir-fry for about 1–2 minutes, or until the masala is golden and the oil separates out. Add the ground coriander mixture and stir-fry for about 1–2 minutes, or until the moisture has evaporated. Add the tomatoes and tamarind and stir-fry for about 5 minutes, or until the oil separates out. Add the chops and the remaining curry leaves and season with salt. Pour in 375ml / 13fl oz (1½ cups) of the reserved liquor (add a little water if you don't have enough) and bring to the boil. Reduce the heat to low and simmer, stirring occasionally but very carefully, until the chops are cooked and tender. Remove from the heat and adjust the seasoning, if necessary.

※ ※

Attirachi Peralan
Lamb Curry (II)

Origin Tamil Nadu
Preparation time 45 minutes
Cooking time 1–1½ hours
Serves 8

1kg / 2¼lb boneless lamb
2 teaspoons malt (white) vinegar
4 tablespoons vegetable oil
1 teaspoon mustard seeds
1 onion, chopped
10 cloves garlic, chopped
1 × 5-cm / 2-inch piece fresh ginger, peeled and chopped
salt

For the spice paste

1 teaspoon ground black pepper
seeds from 2 green cardamom pods
4–5 cloves
1 cinnamon stick, about 2.5cm / 1 inch long, broken into pieces
1 teaspoon ground turmeric
1 teaspoon chilli powder
2 teaspoons ground coriander

Cut the meat into 5-cm / 2-inch long and 4-cm / 1½-inch wide strips, then place in a pan with the vinegar and 1 litre / 1¾ pints (4¼ cups) water. Season with salt and cook for 1–1½ hours.

Meanwhile, to make the spice paste, put all the ingredients in a blender and process, adding a little water if necessary, to make a paste.

Heat the oil in a large, heavy-based pan over low heat, add the mustard seeds and stir-fry for about 2–3 minutes, or until they start to splutter. Add the onion and stir-fry for about 4 minutes, or until translucent. Add the garlic and ginger and stir-fry for a further 2 minutes. Stir in the spice paste and fry for another 2 minutes. Continue cooking over low heat, stirring occasionally, until the sauce the thickens. Add the meat to the pan and heat through.

※ ※

Roast Mutton
Roast Lamb

Origin Kerala
Preparation time 15 minutes, plus marinating time
Cooking time 2½ hours
Serves 4

1 tablespoon Boiled Onion Paste (see page 57)
1 teaspoon Ginger Paste (see page 57)
1 tablespoon Garlic Paste (see page 57)
3 tablespoons Worcestershire sauce
250ml / 8fl oz (1 cup) vegetable oil
1 teaspoon black pepper
1 × 1-kg / 2¼-lb leg of lamb
6 large potatoes, cut into chunks
1 tablespoon plain (all-purpose) flour
salt

Mix the pastes, Worcestershire sauce, a little oil and the black pepper together in a large bowl, then season with salt.

Pierce the leg of lamb all over with a skewer and place in a large shallow dish. Massage the marinade all over the meat, then cover and set aside in the refrigerator overnight.

The next day, heat the remaining oil in a large, heavy-based pan over high heat, then reduce the heat to medium. Place the lamb in the pan and fry for about 10 minutes until browned all over, turning frequently. Pour in 500ml / 18fl oz (2¼ cups) water and bring to the boil. Reduce the heat, cover and simmer for about 2 hours, basting with the cooking juices occasionally, and turning once.

Uncover to check if the meat is cooked; when pierced with a sharp knife or skewer, the liquid that comes out should be a pale colour, not red. During the last 20 minutes of cooking, arrange the potatoes around the meat. When the meat and potatoes are cooked, lift out the meat and the potatoes, reserving the juices.

Put the pan containing the meat juices back on the heat and wait for the fat to bubble. Add the flour and brown well before adding 125ml / 4½fl oz (½ cup) warm water. Cook until the sauce thickens, then pour over the roast or serve separately after carving the meat into slices.

Maas Banjara
Gypsy Meat

Origin Rajasthan
Preparation time 20 minutes, plus marinating time
Cooking time 1¼–1¾ hours
Serves 4

1kg / 2¼lb lamb, cut into pieces
2 tablespoons Ginger Paste (see page 57)
2 tablespoons Garlic Paste (see page 57)
100g / 3½oz (scant ½ cup) ghee
150g / 5oz (1 medium) onion, sliced
1 teaspoon chilli powder
1–2 black cardamom pods
salt

For the marinade

400ml / 14fl oz (1⅔ cups) natural (plain) yoghurt, whisked
10g / ¼oz dried red chillies, shredded
1 × 5-cm / 2-inch piece fresh ginger, peeled and cut into thin strips
6–8 cloves garlic, crushed

To make the marinade, mix the yoghurt, dried red chillies, ginger and garlic together in a large bowl. Season with salt, then add the meat and turn until well coated. Cover and set aside in the refrigerator for at least 1 hour.

Put the ginger and garlic pastes in a small bowl, add 4 tablespoons water and mix together.

Heat the ghee in a large, heavy-based pan over medium heat, add the onions and stir-fry for about 5–7 minutes, or until golden brown. Add the ginger and garlic paste mixture and stir-fry for 15–20 seconds. Add the chilli powder and cardamom pods and stir-fry for 15 seconds. Now add the lamb together with the marinade and fry for 5 minutes. Pour in about 800ml / 1¼ pints (3¼ cups) water and bring almost to the boil. Reduce the heat and simmer for about 1–1½ hours, or until tender.

※ ※ ※ / ☐ p.471

Laal Maas
Red-Hot Lamb

Origin Rajasthan
Preparation time 40 minutes, plus standing time
Cooking time 1½–2 hours
Serves 4

45–50 milld dried red chillies
250ml / 8fl oz (1 cup) natural (plain) yoghurt, whisked
1 teaspoon cumin seeds
5 teaspoons ground coriander
1 teaspoon ground turmeric
100g / 3½oz (scant ½ cup) ghee
3 tablespoons sliced garlic
240g / 8½oz (2 medium) onions, thinly sliced
5 green cardamom pods
3 black cardamom pods
1kg / 2¼lb lamb shoulder, cut into cubes
salt
2 tablespoons chopped coriander (cilantro) leaves

Discard the stems of the dried red chillies and soak the chillies in a bowl of water for about 15 minutes. Drain and, wearing gloves, de-seed before using.

Mix the yoghurt, dried red chillies, cumin seeds and ground spices together in a bowl, then season with salt. Set aside for about 10 minutes.

Heat the ghee in a large, heavy-based pan over medium heat, add the garlic and stir-fry for 1–2 minutes, or until light golden. Add the onions and cardamom pods and stir-fry for 5–7 minutes, or until the onions are golden brown. Add the meat, increase the heat to high and stir-fry for 4–5 minutes, or until the meat changes colour. Reduce the heat to medium and stir-fry for a further 4–5 minutes.

Remove the pan from the heat and stir in the yoghurt mixture, then return to the heat and stir-fry for about 2–3 minutes, or until the liquid has evaporated. Now add about 1.5 litres /2½ pints (6¼ cups) water, then bring almost to the boil. Reduce the heat to low, cover and simmer, stirring occasionally, for about 1–1½ hours, or until the meat is tender and the sauce is a thin consistency. Remove from the heat and adjust the seasoning, if necessary. Garnish with chopped coriander.

This traditional dish from Rajasthan is famous for its fiery taste and striking crimson colour. If you can find them, use Kashmiri dried red chillies, as they are milder than the ordinary ones.

Baant
Lamb in a Spicy Sauce

Origin Uttarakhand
Preparation time 15 minutes
Cooking time 1¼–1¾ hours
Serves 4

1kg / 2¼lb mixed pieces of lamb
250ml / 8fl oz (1 cup) mustard oil
250g / 9oz (2 small) onions, thinly sliced
salt

For the spice paste

1 clove garlic
1 × 5-cm / 2-inch piece fresh ginger, peeled
1 teaspoon ground turmeric
1 teaspoon dried red chillies
2 teaspoons coriander seeds

To make the spice paste, put all the ingredients in a blender or food processor and process, adding a little water to make a smooth paste.

Heat the oil in a large, heavy-based pan over high heat, then reduce the heat. Add the onions and fry for about 4 minutes, or until light brown. Now add the spice paste, season with salt and stir-fry for about 1 minute. Add the lamb and keep stir-frying until the meat is nicely browned. Pour in about 2 litres / 3½ pints (8½ cups) warm water, then bring to the boil. Reduce the heat to medium and simmer for about 1–1½ hours, or until the meat is tender. Add a little more warm water if required during cooking.

Safed Saalan
Lamb in Milk Sauce (II)

Origin Awadh
Preparation time 20 minutes
Cooking time 1–1½ hours
Serves 6

1kg / 2¼lb lamb shoulder and breast pieces with 2 ribs attached
200g / 7oz (¾ cup) ghee
6 cloves
1 cinnamon stick, about 2.5cm / 1 inch long
20 whole black peppercorns
1 teaspoon chilli powder
1 teaspoon sugar
½ tablespoon Garam Masala (see page 31)
250ml / 8fl oz (1 cup) milk
salt

Cut the lamb shoulder into 8-cm / 3-inch pieces.

Heat the ghee in a large, heavy-based pan over medium heat, add the whole spices, chilli powder and meat, then season with salt. Fry and keep turning until the meat is light brown. Add the sugar and about 250ml / 8fl oz (1 cup) water and cook over medium heat for 1–1½ hours. When the meat is tender, add the garam masala and slowly pour in the milk, then reduce the heat to low and cook for another few minutes. The sauce will turn reddish white.

Chaamp
Chops

Origin Anglo-Indian
Preparation time 1 hour, plus marinating time
Cooking time 30 minutes
Serves 6

1kg / 2¼lb lamb chops with 2 ribs each
2 onions
6 cloves garlic, crushed
1 × 5-cm / 2-inch piece fresh ginger, peeled
1 × 5-cm / 2-inch piece raw papaya
1 cinnamon stick, about 1cm / ½ inch long
6 whole black peppercorns
2 teaspoons Garam Masala (see page 31)
chilli powder, to taste
1 tablespoon vinegar
4 tablespoons natural (plain) yoghurt
1 egg white
about 120g / 4oz (1 cup) dried breadcrumbs
125g / 4oz (½ cup) ghee
salt
1 large onion, shredded, to garnish

Remove a rib from each chop and trim. Flatten the chops using the blunt edge of a knife. Place the chops in a large shallow dish.

Put the onions, garlic, ginger, papaya, cinnamon and peppercorns in a blender or food processor and process, adding a little water if necessary, to make a paste. Transfer to a bowl, add the garam masala, chilli powder, vinegar and yoghurt, then season with salt and mix together. Smear the chops on both sides with the paste, then cover and set aside in the refrigerator for 1 hour.

Put the egg white in a shallow dish and beat briefly, then spread out the breadcrumbs on a plate. Drain the marinade from the chops and dip each chop into the egg white, then roll in the breadcrumbs to coat.

Heat 2 tablespoons ghee in a large frying pan (skillet) over medium heat. Working in batches, add the chops and fry for about 10 minutes on both sides until golden brown and cooked to your taste. Remove from the pan and set aside. Garnish with shredded onions.

Dum Raan
Spiced Lamb Baked with Yoghurt and Papaya

Origin Hyderabad
Preparation time 30 minutes, plus marinating time
Cooking time 1½–2 hours
Serves 6

1 × 1-kg / 2¼-lb lamb, such as hind leg
6 cloves garlic, crushed
1 × 5-cm / 2-inch piece fresh ginger, peeled
pinch of asafoetida
8 peppercorns
2 onions
1 × 5-cm / 2-inch piece raw papaya
½ tablespoon Garam Masala (see page 31)
250g / 9oz (1 cup) ghee
1 teaspoon chilli powder
1 teaspoon ground fennel
100g / 3½oz Khoya (see page 58) or 100g / 3½oz (⅔ cup) milk powder (dry milk)
1 teaspoon sugar
salt

For the marinade
250ml / 8fl oz (1 cup) natural (plain) yoghurt
juice of 1 lemon

To make the marinade, mix the yoghurt and lemon juice together in a bowl, then season with salt. Put the meat in a large shallow dish and rub the marinade evenly over, then cover and set aside in the refrigerator for 15 minutes.

Put the garlic, ginger, asafoetida, peppercorns, onions and papaya in a blender or food processor and process, adding a little water if necessary, to make a smooth paste. Rub this over the meat and prick it deeply all over with a fork. Rub the garam masala over the meat, then cover and set aside in the refrigerator for 2 hours.

Heat the ghee in a heavy-based degchi or casserole over low heat. Take a piece of muslin (cheesecloth) and place the meat, chilli powder, ground fennel, khoya and sugar in it. Tie the muslin and put it in the casserole with 250ml / 8fl oz (1 cup) water. Keep turning the meat over, so that it is cooked on both sides. Cook for 1½–2 hours, or until the meat is quite tender and the sauce has almost dried up. Take the meat out carefully, place it on a serving dish and squeeze the masala from the muslin over it.

Reshmai Gosht
Fried Slivers of Meat

Origin Hyderabad
Preparation time 15 minutes, plus cooling time
Cooking time 1½ hours
Serves 6

500g / 1lb 2oz boneless lamb shoulder
½ tablespoon Ginger Paste (see page 57)
½ tablespoon Garlic Paste (see page 57)
chilli powder, to taste
125g / 4oz (½ cup) ghee
salt

To garnish

1 onion, sliced into rings
8 cashew nuts, broken

Heat 250ml / 8fl oz (1 cup) water in a large pan, add the lamb and simmer over low heat for about 1 hour to soften. When the water dries out, put the meat on a grinding stone and pound to separate the meat into fine string-like shreds like vermicelli. Alternatively, put on a board and pound with a meat mallet until shredded. Discard any fat and sinew. Put the meat into a large bowl, season with salt, add the ginger and garlic pastes and chilli powder and mix well.

Heat the ghee in a large frying pan (skillet) or heavy-based pan, add the onions for the garnish to the pan and stir-fry for about 5–7 minutes, or until golden brown. Remove with a slotted spoon and allow to cool. Add the meat mixture to the pan and fry well for about 10 minutes, or until crisp on the edges. Remove with a slotted spoon and set aside. Crumble over the fried onions and garnish with the broken cashew nuts.

Podi Mamsam
Spicy Fried Lamb from Telangana

Origin Hyderabad/Andhra Pradesh
Preparation time 30 minutes, plus marinating time
Cooking time 1 hour
Serves 6

250ml / 8fl oz (1 cup) natural (plain) yoghurt, whisked
1 tablespoon chilli powder
¼ teaspoon ground turmeric
1 teaspoon ground ginger
500g / 1lb 2oz lamb on the bone, cut into small pieces
seeds from 4 green cardamom pods
3 cinnamon sticks, about 2.5cm / 1 inch long
3 cloves
125g / 4oz (½ cup) ghee or vegetable oil
2 onions, thinly sliced
1 tablespoon ground garlic
2 teaspoons ground coriander, roasted
1 teaspoon ground black pepper
2 teaspoons poppy seeds, ground
salt

Put the yoghurt, chilli powder, turmeric and ginger in a large bowl, then season with salt and add the lamb. Turn until coated, then cover and set aside in the refrigerator for 1 hour.

Put the cardamom seeds, cinnamon and cloves in a spice grinder and process until ground. Set aside.

Heat the ghee or oil in a large, heavy-based pan over medium heat, add the onions and fry for 5–7 minutes, or until golden brown. Add the garlic, ground spices, black pepper and poppy seeds and stir-fry for 2 minutes. Add the lamb and yoghurt mixture, reduce the heat to low and simmer for about 45 minutes–1 hour, or until the meat is tender, adding a little water if it starts sticking to the pan. Increase the heat and cook for a few minutes until the meat is well browned. Serve hot.

✳ ✳
___

Masala Chaamp
Battered Chops

Origin Punjab
Preparation time 30 minutes, plus cooling and rising time
Cooking time 15 minutes–1 hour
Serves 6

pinch of saffron threads
1 teaspoon milk
12 lamb chops
375ml / 13fl oz (1½ cups) milk
1 tablespoon dried mint leaves, ground
6 green chillies, de-seeded and chopped
2 teaspoons Garam Masala (see page 31)
1 cinnamon stick, about 2.5cm / 1 inch long
2 green cardamom pods
1 teaspoon red chilli powder
1 teaspoon ground fresh ginger
1 teaspoon ground garlic
2 onions, thinly sliced
150g / 5oz (1 cup) gram (chickpea) flour
½ teaspoon baking powder
180g / 6oz (¾ cup) vegetable oil or ghee
salt
2 limes, cut into slices, to garnish

Stir-fry the saffron lightly on a tawa or in a dry frying pan (skillet) for about 15 seconds, or until roasted, then transfer to a small bowl. Add the milk and soak until required.

Mix all the ingredients together with the chops, except the baking powder, saffron, gram flour and ghee. Put into a pressure cooker with 500ml / 18fl oz (2¼ cups) water and cook for 15 minutes. Allow to cool, then uncover and cook over low heat until the milk and spices reduce to a thick sauce. Alternatively, cook in a large, heavy-based pan for 1 hour until the chops are tender. Coat the chops with the sauce.

Meanwhile, put the gram flour in a large bowl and whisk in enough water to make a batter. Continue to whisk by hand for 15 minutes or 2 minutes with an electric mixer until the batter is light and fluffy. Add a little of the sauce to the batter together with the soaked saffron and baking powder and leave to rise for 30 minutes.

Heat the ghee in a kadhai or deep, heavy-based pan to 180°C/350°F, or until a cube of bread browns in 30 seconds. Dip each chop into the batter and carefully lower into the hot oil and deep-fry for about 3–4 minutes, or until golden brown. Remove with a slotted spoon and drain on kitchen paper (paper towels). When all the chops are done, lightly fry them in the hot oil again to make them crisper, then remove and drain on kitchen paper (paper towels). Serve garnished with lime slices.

✳
___

Paye ki Yakhni
Goats' Leg Soup

Origin Hyderabad
Preparation time 30 minutes
Cooking time 1 hour
Serves 6

3 teaspoons ghee
2 onions, chopped
2 tablespoons semolina (farina)
500g / 1lb 2oz goats' or lambs' legs, cut into 5-cm / 2-inch pieces with marrow intact
6 green cardamom pods
2 cloves
1 cinnamon stick, about 1cm / ½ inch long
1 teaspoon fennel seeds
salt

Heat the ghee in a kadhai or large, heavy-based pan over medium heat, add the onions and fry for 5–7 minutes, or until golden brown. Remove from the pan with a slotted spoon and set aside. Add the semolina and fry for a few minutes until light brown.

Put the bones and remaining ingredients in a pressure cooker and pour in 1.5 litres /2½ pints (6¼ cups) water. Cover and cook under pressure for about 30 minutes, or until the legs are done. Add the fried onions and semolina and cook for a further 30 minutes. Alternatively, cook everything in a large, heavy-based pan until the legs are cooked. Strain and serve.

Khawamdum
Lamb & Vegetable Korma

Origin Hyderabad
Preparation time 40 minutes, plus marinating time
Cooking time 1 hour
Serves 6

1½ teaspoons chironji kernels

1 × 5-cm / 2-inch piece dried coconut

1 teaspoon caraway seeds, plus a pinch

¼ teaspoon saffron threads

1 teaspoon milk

500g / 1lb 2oz lamb, cut into 4-cm / 1½-inch pieces

½ tablespoon Ginger Paste (see page 57)

½ tablespoon Garlic Paste (see page 57)

125g / 4oz (½ cup) ghee

4 onions, thinly sliced

350g / 12oz (3 medium) potatoes, cut into quarters

1½ teaspoons ground coriander, roasted

6 ground cloves

6 ground green cardamom pods, plus a little extra

1 cinnamon stick, about 2.5cm / 1 inch long, ground

125ml / 4½fl oz (½ cup) natural (plain) yoghurt, whisked

300g / 11oz (3 cups) pumpkin or ash gourd, peeled and cut into small pieces

salt

Plain Boiled Rice (see page 631) or roti (see pages 616–20), to serve

Put the chironji kernels, coconut and caraway seeds in a small blender or food processor and process until ground. Put the saffron in a small bowl, add the milk and soak until required.

Put the lamb in a large shallow dish, add the ginger and garlic pastes and mix together, then cover and set aside for for 15 minutes.

Heat about 5 tablespoons ghee in a heavy-based pan over medium heat, add the onions and fry for about 5–7 minutes, or until golden brown. Remove from the heat.

Heat about 3 tablespoons ghee in a separate frying pan (skillet) over medium heat, add the potatoes and fry for about 15–20 minutes, or until golden brown. Remove from the pan and set aside.

Mix the ground chironji kernels and coconut mixture, coriander, cloves, cardamom and cinnamon with the lamb. Add the yoghurt and mix to combine. Add the mixture to the onions and ghee and fry over medium heat for a few minutes until the liquid from the yoghurt and meat has evaporated, then continue frying for about 8 minutes, or until brown. Sprinkle with a little water if it is sticking to the pan, then stir well and continue to brown well. Add the fried potatoes and cook together for a few minutes, sprinkling with a little water if necessary.

Pour in 1 litre / 1¾ pints (4¼ cups) water and cook for 20 minutes, or until the meat is half done. You may need to add about 500ml / 18fl oz (2¼ cups) water for the sauce, if required. Add the pumpkin, pinch of caraway and extra green cardamom, then season with salt. Cook over low heat for 30 minutes until the oil separates out and rises to the surface. Serve hot with Rice or roti.

Aso Adin
Lamb Stew with Ginger

Origin Tribal North East India
Preparation time 20 minutes
Cooking time 1–1½ hours
Serves 5

1kg / 2¼lb lamb, cut into pieces

2 teaspoons Ginger Paste (see page 57)

6 green chillies, de-seeded and roughly chopped

salt

Bring 750ml / 1¼ pints (3¼ cups) water to the boil in a large, heavy-based pan, then add the meat and continue boiling for about 5 minutes. Stir in the remaining ingredients, season with salt, then reduce the heat, cover and simmer for about 1–1½ hours, or until the meat is tender and the sauce thickens.

Mutton Qorma
Lamb Korma (l)

Origin Delhi
Preparation time 20 minutes, plus marinating time
Cooking time 1 hour 30 minutes
Serves 6

50g / 1¾oz (about 1⅓ heads) garlic
1 × 5-cm / 2-inch piece fresh ginger, peeled
1kg / 2¼lb lamb, cut into pieces
50g / 1¾oz (⅓ cup) roughly chopped onions
1½ tablespoons poppy seeds
50g / 1¾oz (⅓ cup) almonds
6 tablespoons coriander seeds
10 cloves
8–10 seeds of green cardamom pods
1 cinnamon stick, about 2.5cm / 1 inch long
250g / 9oz (1 cup) ghee
150g / 5oz (1 medium) onion, sliced
250ml / 8fl oz (1 cup) natural (plain) yoghurt
2–3 drops kewra water or rosewater
salt
coriander (cilantro) leaves, to garnish

Put the garlic and ginger and a little salt in a small blender or mortar and pound or process until ground. Put the lamb in a large shallow dish, add the ground garlic mixture and rub over, then cover and set aside in the refrigerator for about 2 hours.

Put the roughly chopped onions into a blender or food processor, add the poppy seeds, almonds, coriander seeds, cloves, cardamom seeds and cinnamon and process until ground.

Heat the ghee in a large, heavy-based pan over medium heat, add the sliced onion and stir-fry for about 5–7 minutes, or until golden brown. Remove with slotted spoon and set aside, then put the ground onion and spice mixture into the pan and fry for 3 minutes. Add the marinated lamb and cook for about 5 minutes, or until the moisture has evaporated.

Pour about 250ml / 8fl oz (1 cup) warm water into the pan, then reduce the heat, cover and simmer for about 1 hour, stirring occasionally, until the meat is almost done.

Put the fried onion into a blender or food processor and process until ground, then add to the meat together with the yoghurt. Cover and cook for a further 15–20 minutes. Stir in the kewra water and garnish with coriander leaves.

Chintakkai Chaamp
Lamb Chops with Tamarind

Origin Tamil Nadu
Preparation time 20 minutes
Cooking time 45 minutes
Serves 6

125ml / 4½fl oz (½ cup) vegetable oil
500g / 1lb 2oz lamb chops
6 onions, thinly sliced
½ teaspoon mustard powder
1 teaspoon Ginger Paste (see page 57)
3 potatoes, sliced
4 green chillies, slit in half lengthways and de-seeded
2 tablespoons Tamarind Extract (see page 58)
1 teaspoon chilli powder
salt

To garnish

1 onion, sliced
1 bunch mint leaves

Heat the oil in a large frying pan (skillet) over low heat. Add the chops, onions, mustard powder and ginger paste. Season with salt, cover and cook over low heat for about 25 minutes, adding water a little at a time, until the chops are tender.

Add the potatoes and chillies and fry for about 10–15 minutes to brown the chops and fry the potatoes. Add the tamarind extract and chilli powder and simmer over low heat for about 5 minutes. There should be a little sauce, so add 125ml / 4½fl oz (½ cup) water and cook for a further 3 minutes. Garnish with sliced onions and mint leaves.

Qorma Dilpasand
Lamb Korma (II)

Origin Delhi
Preparation time 1¼ hours
Cooking time 1 hour
Serves 6

1kg / 2¼lb lamb, cut into pieces
3–4 cinnamon sticks, about 2.5cm / 1 inch long
2 bay leaves
8 green cardamom pods
10–12 cloves
½ teaspoon whole black peppercorns
large pinch of mace flakes
250g / 9oz (2 small) onions
1 × 5-cm / 2-inch piece fresh ginger, peeled
10 cloves garlic, crushed
2 tablespoons coriander seeds
2 dried red chillies
250g / 9oz (1 cup) ghee
500ml / 18fl oz (2¼ cups) natural (plain) yoghurt
1 teaspoon Garam Masala (see page 31)
salt

Put the lamb into a large, heavy-based pan with the cinnamon, bay leaves, cardamom pods, cloves, black peppercorns and mace. Cover with water, bring to the boil, then reduce the heat and simmer for about 30 minutes.

Put one-third of the onions with the ginger, garlic, coriander seeds and dried red chillies in a blender or food processor and process until ground. Thinly slice the remaining onions.

Heat the ghee in another large, heavy-based pan over medium heat, add the sliced onions and stir-fry for about 5–7 minutes, or until golden brown. Remove with a slotted spoon and set aside. Add the ground masala mixture into the pan and fry for a further 2 minutes.

Drain the meat, reserving the cooking water and discarding the whole spices, then add the meat to the masala mixture together with the cooking water and yoghurt. Season with salt.

Crush the fried onions and stir into the meat with the garam masala, then cover and cook over low heat, stirring occasionally for 30 minutes, or until the meat is tender.

Khare Masale ka Gosht
Lamb Cooked with Whole Spices

Origin Awadh
Preparation time 30 minutes
Cooking time 1½–2 hours
Serves 6

250g / 9oz (1 cup) ghee
250g / 9oz (2 small) onions, sliced
15–25 cloves garlic, cut into slices lengthways
1 × 8-cm / 3-inch piece fresh ginger, peeled and cut into strips
2 bay leaves
4 black cardamom pods
½ teaspoon whole black peppercorns
½ tablespoon coriander seeds
8 cloves
6 green cardamom pods
2 cinnamon sticks, about 2.5cm / 1 inch long
300g / 11oz (3 small) tomatoes, chopped
1kg / 2¼lb lamb, cut into pieces
500ml / 18fl oz (2¼ cups) natural (plain) yoghurt, whisked
salt

Heat the ghee in a large, heavy-based pan over medium heat, add the onions and stir-fry for about 5–7 minutes, or until golden brown. Add the garlic and ginger and stir-fry for 2 minutes. Add all the spices and stir-fry for 1 minute, then pour in 250ml / 8fl oz (1 cup) water and season with salt. Cover and cook for 5 minutes.

Stir in the tomatoes and cook for a further 5–10 minutes, or until the mixture is paste-like. Add the meat and yoghurt, then reduce the heat, cover and cook, stirring occasionally, for 1½ hours, or until the meat is tender. Add more water during cooking if necessary.

Dahi ka Dungara Gosht
Smoked Lamb Cooked with Yoghurt

Origin Rajasthan
Preparation time 1¾ hours
Cooking time 25 minutes
Serves 6

500g / 1lb 2oz lamb, cut into pieces

250g / 9oz (2 small) onions, sliced

8–10 cloves garlic, ground

1 × 5-cm / 2-inch piece fresh ginger, peeled and
   thinly sliced

pinch of chilli powder

2 tablespoons ground coriander

250g / 9oz (1 cup) ghee

2 tablespoons chopped mint leaves

3–4 green chillies, de-seeded and chopped

1 litre / 1¾ pints (4¼ cups) natural (plain) yoghurt,
   whisked

salt

Put the meat into a large, heavy-based pan with a
quarter of the sliced onions, the garlic, ginger, chilli
powder, coriander and 1½ teaspoons salt. Pour in
250ml / 8fl oz (1 cup) water, then cover and cook over
low heat for 1½ hours, or until the meat is tender.

Add the ghee to the pan, stir and cook until the
meat is well browned. Remove from the heat and
set aside.

Mix the remaining onions with the mint and green
chillies together in a bowl, then season with salt.

Add one-third of the yoghurt to the pan and cover
the meat, then top with one-third of the onions, then
another third yoghurt and so on.

Heat 2–3 small pieces of charcoal until red hot, then
place on a piece of foil and sprinkle with a few
drops of water. Place in the pan and immediately
cover as tightly as possible, then leave for 15–20
minutes on very low heat. Alternatively, just cover
the pan and leave over low heat until everything is
heated through. When serving, try to keep the layers
of meat, yoghurt and onions intact.

Aloo ka Salan
Lamb with Potatoes in Yoghurt Sauce

Origin Awadh
Preparation time 20 minutes
Cooking time 1½ hours
Serves 6

125g / 4oz (½ cup) ghee

100g / 3½oz (1 small) onion, sliced

100g / 3½oz (1 small) onion, finely chopped

10–12 cloves garlic, ground

1 × 2.5-cm / 1-inch piece fresh ginger, peeled
   and ground

2 teaspoons ground coriander

½ teaspoon ground turmeric

375ml / 13fl oz (1½ cups) natural (plain) yoghurt,
   whisked

500g / 1lb 2oz lamb, cut into pieces

1 teaspoon Garam Masala (see page 31)

1kg / 2¼lb (9 medium) potatoes, cut into quarters

salt

Heat the ghee in a large, heavy-based pan over
medium heat, add the sliced onions and fry for
about 5–7 minutes, or until golden brown. Remove
with a slotted spoon and set aside. Add the sliced
and chopped onions to the pan and fry for about
3–4 minutes, or until pale gold. Now add the garlic,
ginger, coriander and turmeric to the pan, then stir
and add 2 tablespoons yoghurt. Cook for about
5 minutes, or until the masala is brown and the
oil separates out.

Add the meat to the pan and season with salt, then
cook for about 5 minutes, stirring occasionally, until
the moisture has evaporated and the meat is browned.
Add the remaining yoghurt, the garam masala and
500ml / 18fl oz (2¼ cups) water and cook for about
30 minutes, or until the meat is almost done.

Add the potatoes to the meat, adding more water
if necessary, then cover and cook for a further 30
minutes, or until the meat and potatoes are tender.

Baadam Pasanda
Pasanda with Almonds

Origin Delhi
Preparation time 1 hour, plus soaking and marinating time
Cooking time 1¾ hours
Serves 6

1.5kg / 3¼lb Pasanda (see page 187)

For the marinade

3 dried figs

3 dried kachri or 1 × 2.5-cm / 1-inch piece raw
    papaya

3 onions, sliced

20 cloves garlic, crushed

1 × 5-cm / 2-inch piece fresh ginger, peeled

3 teaspoons poppy seeds

25 blanched almonds

Plain Boiled Rice (see page 631) or roti (see pages
    616–20), to serve

For the sauce

300g / 11oz (1⅓ cups) ghee

750g / 1lb 10oz (5 medium) onions, finely sliced

1 × 5-cm / 2-inch piece fresh ginger, peeled
    and chopped

10 cloves garlic, ground

2 bay leaves

1 cinnamon stick, about 5cm / 2 inches long

8 green cardamom pods

4 black cardamom pods, ground

3 teaspoons ground coriander

1 teaspoon Garam Masala (see page 31)

1 teaspoon chilli powder

500ml / 18fl oz (2¼ cups) natural (plain) yoghurt,
    whisked

250g / 9oz (2 small) tomatoes, skinned
    and chopped

pinch of saffron threads

salt

To garnish

20 blanched and split almonds

chopped coriander (cilantro) leaves

For the marinade, soak the figs and kachri, if using, in a bowl of water for 1–2 hours.

To make the marinade, put all the ingredients, including the soaked figs and kachri, in a blender or food processor and process until ground. Put the meat into a large shallow dish and rub the marinade mixture all over, then cover and set aside in the refrigerator for 4 hours.

To make the sauce, heat the ghee in a large frying pan (skillet) over medium heat, add the onions and stir-fry for about 5–7 minutes, or until golden brown. Stir in 2 teaspoons water, then add the ginger, garlic, bay leaves, cinnamon and cardamom and stir-fry for 1–2 minutes. Season with salt, then add the ground coriander, garam masala and chilli powder. Stir and cook, adding a little water for about 1–2 minutes, or until the oil separates out.

Add the meat together with the marinade to the pan, then reduce the heat to low, cover and cook for 1 hour, shaking the pan from time to time. Strain the yoghurt into the meat together with the tomatoes and cook for a further 30 minutes or until the meat is tender.

Put the saffron in a small bowl, add 1 teaspoon hot water and mix together, then add to the pan. Garnish with split almonds and chopped coriander. Serve with Rice or roti.

✿ ✿

Mansho Jhol
Lamb Curry (III)

Origin Bengal
Preparation time 45 minutes, plus marinating and soaking time
Cooking time 1–1½ hours
Serves 6

500g / 1lb 2oz lamb, cut into 2.5-cm / 1-inch pieces

2 tablespoons mustard oil

2 potatoes, cut into halves

500g / 1lb 2oz (2 medium) unripe papayas, peeled, de-seeded and cut into slices

salt

steamed rice (see page 631), to serve

For the marinade

2 large onions, chopped

1 tablespoon Garlic Paste (see page 57)

1 tablespoon Ginger Paste (see page 57)

1 tablespoon ground black pepper

1 teaspoon ground cumin

1 teaspoon ground coriander

¼ teaspoon ground turmeric

For the spice paste

3 black cardamom pods

1 cinnamon stick, about 8cm / 3 inches long

To make the marinade, mix all the ingredients together in a bowl, then season with salt. Put the meat into a large shallow dish and rub the mixture over the meat, then cover and set aside for 30 minutes. At the same time, put the cardamom pods and cinnamon for the spice paste in a bowl, add just enough water to cover and soak for 30 minutes.

Drain the spices, transfer to a small blender and process, adding a little water if necessary to make a paste. Set aside.

Heat the oil in a pressure cooker, add the lamb and fry, stirring occasionally until the oil separates out. Mix in the spice paste, potatoes, papaya and 500ml / 18fl oz (2¼ cups) water. Close the cooker and cook under pressure for 20 minutes. Alternatively, cook in a large, heavy-based pan for about 1–1½ hours, or until the meat is tender. Serve hot with steamed rice.

✿ ✿ ✿

Mutton Kolhapuri
Hot Lamb Curry with Local Spices

Origin Maharashtra
Preparation time 30 minutes
Cooking time 1¼–1¾ hours
Serves 6

3 teaspoons coriander seeds

3 teaspoons cumin seeds

1 tablespoon poppy seeds

1 teaspoon cloves

1 teaspoon whole black peppercorns

1 teaspoon ground star anise

1 cinnamon stick

4 teaspoons desiccated (dried flaked) coconut

200ml / 7fl oz (1 cup) vegetable oil

225g / 8oz (1⅓ cups) chopped onions

1 tablespoon Ginger Paste (see page 57)

1 tablespoon Garlic Paste (see page 57)

1kg / 2¼lb lamb, cut into 2.5-cm / 1-inch cubes

3 teaspoons chilli powder

1 teaspoon ground turmeric

tomatoes, chopped

salt

chopped coriander (cilantro), to garnish

Stir-fry all the whole spices, ground star anise and coconut lightly on a tawa or in a dry frying pan (skillet) for about 1 minute, or until roasted, then transfer to a spice grinder and process until ground.

Heat the oil in a large, heavy-based pan over medium heat, add the onions and stir-fry for about 4 minutes, or until light brown. Add the ginger and garlic pastes and fry well for about 2 minutes.

Add the lamb to the pan and fry for about 5 minutes, then add the chilli powder, turmeric and tomatoes and season with salt. Fry for about 5 minutes, then add all the ground spices and about 250ml / 8fl oz (1 cup) water. Reduce the heat, cover and cook for about 1–1½ hours, or until the meat is tender. Serve hot garnished with chopped coriander.

Bharwan Pasande
Stuffed Pasanda

Origin Awadh
Preparation time 1 hour, plus soaking time
Cooking time 1 hour 10 minutes
Serves 6

1kg / 2¼lb Pasanda (see page 187)

salt

For the filling

1 × 6-cm / 2½-inch piece fresh ginger, peeled and
    finely chopped

50g / 1¾oz (⅓ cup) blanched almonds,
    finely chopped

1 handful of coriander (cilantro), finely chopped

4–5 sprigs mint, finely chopped

4 hard-boiled eggs, finely chopped

juice of 1 lime

pinch of salt

For the sauce

2 dried figs

4–5 dried kachri

3 tablespoons poppy seeds

1 × 2.5-cm / 1-inch piece fresh ginger, peeled

3 tablespoons chopped garlic

250g / 9oz (1 cup) ghee

500g / 1lb 2oz (4 medium) onions, thinly sliced

1 teaspoon chilli powder

1½ teaspoons ground turmeric

3 teaspoons ground coriander

500ml / 18fl oz (2¼ cups) natural (plain) yoghurt,
    whisked

3 large tomatoes, finely chopped

6 green cardamom pods

To garnish

1 teaspoon Garam Masala (see page 31)

chopped coriander (cilantro) leaves

For the sauce, soak the figs and kachri in a bowl of water for 1–2 hours, then drain.

To make the filling, mix all the ingredients together in a bowl. Put a little filling in the centre of each pasanda and roll to enclose the filling, then tie with kitchen string (twine). Set aside.

To make the sauce, put the soaked figs and kachri into a blender or food processor with the poppy seeds, ginger and garlic and process until ground.

Heat the ghee in large, heavy-based pan over medium heat, add the sliced onions and stir-fry for about 5–7 minutes, or until golden brown. Remove with slotted spoon, put into a blender or food processor and process until ground, then set aside.

Stir the chilli powder, turmeric and ground coriander into the ghee. Season with salt and add the ground masala paste, then stir and cook adding 1–2 teaspoons yoghurt. Add the tomatoes and continue to cook for 5 minutes, or until the masala is a rich brown colour and the oil separates out. Add the remaining yoghurt and cardamom pods, then add the stuffed pasandas and cook, turning carefully, for about 5 minutes until all the liquid has evaporated. Add the fried onions and 500ml / 18fl oz (2¼ cups) water, then cover and cook over low heat for 1 hour, or until done, shaking the pan occasionally. Carefully remove the string from the pasandas and garnish with garam masala and chopped coriander.

Alubhokhara Qorma
Lamb in Plum Sauce

Origin Jammu and Kashmir
Preparation time 30 minutes, plus soaking time
Cooking time 1½–2 hours
Serves 6

100g / 3½oz (about 16) dried plums
1 tablespoon ghee or vegetable oil
125ml / 4½fl oz (½ cup) natural (plain) yoghurt
1kg / 2¼lb lamb shoulder or leg, cut into pieces
4 teaspoons ground fennel
2 teaspoons fennel seeds
½ teaspoon ground cinnamon
½ teaspoon cumin seeds
4 green cardamom pods
1 teaspoon chilli powder
250ml / 8fl oz (1 cup) mawal extract
salt
4 tablespoons blanched almonds, skinned and chopped in long pieces, to garnish

Soak the dried plums in a bowl of hot water for about 20 minutes, or until tender, then remove the stones (pits) and set aside.

Heat the ghee or oil in a large, heavy-based pan over low heat, add the yoghurt and cook for about 5 minutes, or until the yoghurt turns brown. Add the plums and stir until they dissolve. Now add the meat and stir for 5 minutes, then add the rest of the ingredients, except the mawal extract. Pour in 500ml / 18fl oz (2¼ cups) water, add the mawal extract and bring almost to the boil. Cook over medium heat for about 1–1½ hours, or until the meat is tender. To serve, garnish the dish with the almonds.

Daniwal Qorma
Lamb in Coriander (Cilantro) Sauce

Origin Jammu and Kashmir
Preparation time 20 minutes
Cooking time 1–1½ hours
Serves 6

1 tablespoon ghee
500ml / 18fl oz (2¼ cups) natural (plain) yoghurt
5 onions, chopped
1kg / 2¼lb lamb pieces, preferably from pelvic region and tail
2 teaspoons fennel seeds
2 teaspoons ground fennel
3 teaspoons ground coriander
1 teaspoon whole black peppercorns
1 bunch coriander (cilantro) leaves, finely chopped
salt

Heat the ghee in a large, heavy-based pan over low heat, add the yoghurt and chopped onions and stir them together until blended. Add the meat and the remaining ingredients, then pour in 750ml / 1¼ pints (3¼ cups) water and bring almost to the boil. Cook over medium heat for about 1–1½ hours, or until the meat is tender. Remove from the heat and garnish with chopped coriander.

Shorba Marag
Spicy Kid Soup

Origin Jammu and Kashmir
Preparation time 20 minutes
Cooking time 1¾–2¼ hours
Serves 6

500g / 1lb 2oz lamb, cut into 1-cm / ½-inch cubes
½ teaspoon ground black pepper
2 green chillies, de-seeded and chopped
½ bunch coriander (cilantro) leaves, chopped
½ bunch mint leaves, chopped
1 teaspoon ghee
1 onion, thinly sliced
salt
lime juice to taste (optional), to serve

Cook the lamb in a pressure cooker with a little salt and 2 litres / 3½ pints (8½ cups) water for 40 minutes. Alternatively, cook the lamb in a large, heavy-based pan with 4 litres / 5 pints (17 cups) water for 1–1½ hours, or until the meat is tender.

When the lamb is cooked, add the black pepper, green chillies, chopped coriander leaves and mint. There should be about 1.5 litres / 2½ pints (6¼ cups) soup.

Heat the ghee in a large frying pan (skillet) over medium heat, add the onion and stir-fry for about 4 minutes, or until light brown. Mix into the soup, then cook over low heat for 5 minutes. Serve hot in soup bowls, adding a few drops of lime juice if desired.

Mirchiwala Gosht
Peppery Lamb Curry

Origin New
Preparation time 20 minutes, plus marinating time
Cooking time 1¼–1¾ hours
Serves 6

250ml / 8fl oz (1 cup) natural (plain) yoghurt
½ teaspoon ground corinader
½ teaspoon ground cumin
½ teaspoon chilli powder
½ teaspoon Kashmiri red chilli powder
½ teaspoon yellow chilli powder
½ teaspoon ground ginger
pinch of ground turmeric
6 green chillies, de-seeded and chopped
1 teaspoon Garlic Paste (see page 57)
1kg / 2¼lb lamb shoulder, hind leg and chops, cut into pieces
250g / 9oz (1 cup) ghee or vegetable oil
1 cinnamon stick, about 2.5cm / 1 inch long
2 black cardamom pods
2 cloves
10 peppercorns
4 dried red chillies
400g / 14oz (2 large) onions, sliced
2 pieces of pipli or red (bell) pepper, about 5cm / 2 inches long
salt

To make a marinade, mix the yoghurt, ground spices, green chillies and garlic paste together in a large shallow dish. Add the meat and turn until well coated, then cover and set aside in the refrigerator for 2–3 hours.

Heat the ghee or oil in large, heavy-based pan over medium heat, add the whole spices and stir-fry for about 1 minute, or until they start to change colour, then add the dried red chillies. Add the onions and stir-fry for about 4 minutes, or until light golden. Now add the meat together with the marinade and pepper strips and stir-fry for about 3–4 minutes, or until the masala is well blended, the moisture has evaporated and the oil separates out. Pour in 125ml / 4½fl oz (½ cup) hot water, then reduce the heat to low and continue cooking for about 1–1½ hours, or until the meat is tender.

Gosht ki Khurchan
Mashed Pasanda

Origin Awadh
Preparation time 40 minutes, plus marinating time
Cooking time 15 minutes
Serves 4

2 tablespoons natural (plain) yoghurt, whisked
½ tablespoon Ginger Paste (see page 57)
½ tablespoon Garlic Paste (see page 57)
1 teaspoon cumin powder
1 teaspoon Kashmiri red chilli powder
1 teaspoon Garam Masala (see page 31)
500g / 1lb 2oz Pasanda (see page 187), cut into
    thin strips
3 tablespoons vegetable oil
1 onion, sliced
2 green chillies, de-seeded and chopped
1 × 2.5-cm / 1-inch piece fresh ginger, peeled
    and finely chopped
1 dried red chilli, chopped
salt

Mix the yoghurt, ginger and garlic pastes and ground
spices in a large bowl. Add the pasanda strips
and turn to coat, then cover and set aside in the
refrigerator for 30 minutes.

Heat the oil in a large, heavy-based frying pan (skillet)
over high heat, then reduce the heat. Add the onions
and stir-fry for about 5 minutes, or until brown. Add
the meat and the marinade, then increase the heat
and stir-fry briskly for about 5 minutes. Use a large
ladle or a wooden spatula to mash the meat at regular
intervals as it cooks. Sprinkle over the green chillies,
ginger and dried red chillies, then reduce the heat,
cover and cook for a further 5 minutes. Sprinkle
with a little water, if required. Remove from the heat
when the meat is cooked and adjust the seasoning,
if necessary.

Kashmiri Qorma
Saffron-flavoured Lamb

Origin Jammu and Kashmir
Preparation time 30 minutes
Cooking time 1–1½ hours
Serves 4–6

750g / 1lb 10oz lamb, cut into small chunks
pinch of saffron threads
1 tablespoon warm milk
125g / 4oz (½ cup) ghee
10 green cardamom pods
6 cinnamon sticks, about 2.5cm / 1 inch long
3 cloves
3 tablespoons garlic water
1 tablespoon sugar
2 teaspoons Tamarind Extract (see page 58)
145g / 4½oz (1 cup) raisins, fried
salt

Put the meat into a pan of water, bring to the boil
and boil for about 1 minute, then drain and set aside.

Put the saffron in a small bowl, add the warm milk
and soak until required.

Put the blanched meat in a shallow pan with the
ghee, cardamom pods, cinnamon sticks, and cloves
and fry for 2–3 minutes. Add about 250ml / 8fl oz
(1 cup) water and season with salt, then bring to
the boil. Add the garlic water, sugar and tamarind
extract and cook for about 1–1½ hours, or until the
meat is tender and the moisture has evaporated. Add
the saffron and raisins, mix well and heat through.

※

Shalgam Gosht
Lamb with Turnips

Origin Awadh
Preparation time 1 hour, plus draining time
Cooking time 1½ hours
Serves 4–6

250g / 9oz (4 small) turnips, peeled and cut into quarters

250g / 9oz lamb bones for stock

3 cloves garlic

1 teaspoon ground turmeric

1 bay leaf

5 tablespoons vegetable oil

400g / 14oz (2 large) onions, chopped

1 × 2.5-cm / 1-inch piece fresh ginger, peeled
    and chopped

1 clove garlic, chopped

2 tablespoons Kashmiri red chilli powder

1 teaspoon paprika

1 teaspoon ground turmeric

1½ teaspoons ground fennel

1 teaspoon ground coriander

2 black cardamom pods

4 green cardamom pods

1 cinnamon stick, about 2.5cm / 1 inch long

750g / 1lb 10oz lamb, cut into pieces

250g / 9oz (2 small) tomatoes, puréed

salt

Prick each turnip quarter several times with a fork or skewer, then place in a colander, sprinkle with a little salt and drain for about 10 minutes. Rinse off the salt and set the turnips aside.

To make a stock, put the lamb bones in a large, heavy-based pan, pour in 500ml / 18fl oz (2¼ cups) water, add the garlic, turmeric and bay leaf and bring to the boil, then boil for 45 minutes. Strain the stock into a clean pan and set aside.

Heat 3 tablespoons of the oil in a large frying pan (skillet) over medium heat, add the turnips and fry for about 20 minutes, or until they are pale gold and acquire a crisp skin. Keep turning during cooking so they are evenly coloured. Remove with a slotted spoon and drain on kitchen paper (paper towels).

Put the oil from the frying pan into a large casserole. Add 1 tablespoon of the remaining oil, then add the chopped onions and stir-fry over low heat for about 10–15 minutes, or until golden brown.

Add the chopped ginger and garlic and continue to stir for a further 5 minutes. Add the chilli powder, paprika, turmeric, fennel, coriander, cardamom pods, cinnamon, 2 tablespoons water, the remaining 1 tablespoon of oil and the lamb, and mix well. Fry the meat for 2 minutes so that it is evenly coated with spices, then cover and simmer for about 10 minutes, or until the meat releases moisture, which mixes with the spices and is then re-absorbed.

Uncover when the meat is almost dry, then, with a wooden spoon, stir and turn the meat over several times over 5 minutes. Season with 1 teaspoon salt, add the puréed tomatoes and stir and turn the meat. Pour in the reserved stock, cover and simmer for about 45 minutes. About 5 minutes before the meat is tender, add the turnips. Turn off the heat when the meat and turnips are tender.

Yakhni
Aromatic Lamb in a Tasty Sauce

Origin Jammu and Kashmir
Preparation time 30 minutes
Cooking time 1¼–1¾ hours
Serves 4–6

2 teaspoons Kashmiri red chilli powder
100g / 3½oz dried mawal flowers
½ teaspoon black cumin seeds
750g / 1lb 10oz lamb shoulder, shank and chops, cut into large pieces
1 teaspoon Garlic Paste (see page 57)
8 green cardamom pods
4 black cardamom pods
6 cloves
2 teaspoons ground turmeric
½ teaspoon ground ginger
1 tablespoon Boiled Onion Paste (see page 57)
250ml / 8fl oz (1 cup) natural (plain) yoghurt
100g / 3½oz (½ cup) ghee
½ teaspoon dried mint leaves
salt

Put the Kashmiri red chilli powder in a small bowl, add 4 tablespoons water and mix together.

Extract the mawal after soaking in ½ teaspoon black cumin seeds.

Bring a deep, heavy-based pan of water to the boil, add the lamb and cook for about 20 minutes, removing the scum that rises to the surface. When the water is clear, add the garlic paste and continue to boil for 4–5 minutes. Season with salt and cook for 10 minutes until the lamb is half done.

Add the cardamom pods, cloves, turmeric, ground ginger, onion paste, yoghurt, Kashmiri red chilli mixture and ghee. Season with salt, mix well, then reduce the heat, cover and cook for 45 minutes–1 hour until the lamb is tender.

Add the mawal flower extract and black cumin seeds and mix well, then sprinkle over the dried mint leaves.

Singhare ka Salan
Lamb Curry with Water Chestnuts

Origin Awadh
Preparation time 45 minutes
Cooking time 1½–2 hours
Serves 4–6

1 teaspoon dried red chillies
500g / 1lb 2oz lamb, cut into 4-cm / 1½-inch cubes
1½ teaspoons Ginger Paste (see page 57)
1½ teaspoons Garlic Paste (see page 57)
125g / 4oz (½ cup) ghee or vegetable oil
2 onions, thinly sliced
¼ teaspoon ground turmeric
4–6 green chillies, slit in half lengthways and de-seeded
8 curry leaves
120g / 4oz green water chestnuts, peeled and cut in half
3 tomatoes, chopped
2 bunches coriander (cilantro) leaves, chopped
salt

Put the dried red chillies in a small blender and process, adding a little water if necessary, to make a paste. Transfer to a bowl, add the lamb, ginger and garlic pastes, then season with salt and mix well.

Heat the ghee or oil in a large, heavy-based pan over medium heat, add the onions and stir-fry for about 5–7 minutes, or until golden brown. Add the turmeric and stir, then add the lamb mixture and stir-fry for about 5 minutes, or until well browned. Pour in 750ml / 1¼ pints (3¼ cups) water, add the green chillies and curry leaves, then reduce the heat and cook for about 1–1½ hours, or until the lamb is tender, adding water if required.

Add the water chestnuts and tomatoes and fry for 1–2 minutes, then add the chopped coriander, 180ml / 6½fl oz (¾ cup) water and cook over medium-high heat for about 5 minutes to slightly soften the water chestnuts.

Erachi Verthathu Rachathu
Lamb Cooked with Ground Coconut

Origin Kerala
Preparation time 45 minutes, plus cooling time
Cooking time 1–1½ hours
Serves 4

500g / 1lb 2oz lamb, cut into pieces

2 onions, sliced

3 tomatoes, sliced

3 green chillies, slit in half lengthways and de-seeded

1 × 5-cm / 2-inch piece fresh ginger, peeled
   and chopped

salt

For the spice paste

1 tablespoon coconut oil

1 coconut, grated

6–8 shallots, chopped

12 dried red chillies, broken into pieces

1 sprig curry leaves

2 teaspoons ground coriander seeds

1 teaspoon ground turmeric

2 cloves garlic, crushed

1 teaspoon ground black pepper

2 cinnamon sticks, about 2.5cm / 1 inch long, broken
   into pieces

4–6 cloves

1 teaspoon fennel seeds

For the tempering

1 tablespoon vegetable oil

1 teaspoon mustard seeds

4 shallots, chopped

1 sprig curry leaves

To make the spice paste, heat the oil in a frying pan (skillet) over medium-low heat, add the coconut, shallots, dried red chillies and curry leaves and stir-fry for about 1 minute, or until the coconut is brown. Sprinkle over the ground coriander, turmeric, garlic, black pepper, cinnamon, cloves and fennel, then mix and remove from the heat. Allow to cool, then transfer to a food processor or blender and process, adding 180ml / 6½fl oz (¾ cup) water to make a smooth paste. Set aside.

Bring 250ml / 8fl oz (1 cup) water to the boil in a large, heavy-based pan, add the meat, onions, tomatoes, green chillies and ginger and season with salt. Cook over medium heat for about 1–1½ hours, then stir in the spice paste and cook for 7–8 minutes, or until the sauce thickens.

Heat the oil for the tempering in a frying pan over medium heat, add the mustard seeds and stir-fry for about 1 minute, or until they start to splutter. Add the remaining ingredients and fry for about 3–4 minutes, or until the shallots turn brown. Pour this over the meat in the pan.

Kobarimasam Pulussu
Lamb in Coconut Sauce

Origin Tamil Nadu
Preparation time 30 minutes
Cooking time 2 hours
Serves 3–4

125ml / 4½fl oz (½ cup) vegetable oil

3 onions, thinly sliced

1 teaspoon grated fresh ginger

2 green chillies, de-seeded and chopped

1 teaspoon Garam Masala (see page 31)

500g / 1lb 2oz leg of lamb, cut into pieces with bones

2 potatoes, cut into quarters

6 curry leaves

250ml / 8fl oz (1 cup) coconut cream, fresh
   (see page 781) or canned

ground black pepper

salt

Heat the oil in a large, heavy-based pan over medium heat, add the onions, ginger, chillies, half the garam masala and the lamb and fry for about 15 minutes, or until the lamb is brown. Pour in about 500ml / 18fl oz (2¼ cups) water and cook for 1–1½ hours, or until the lamb is almost cooked and tender, adding more water if required.

Add the potatoes, curry leaves, coconut cream, salt and pepper and simmer until the lamb and potatoes are cooked. Increase the heat and boil the sauce until slightly thickened. You should finish with about 375ml / 13fl oz (1½ cups) sauce in the pan.

Dhansak
All-In-One Lamb, Dal, Vegetable & Rice Curry

Origin Parsi
Preparation time 1¾ hours, plus soaking time
Cooking time 1½–2 hours
Serves 4

200g / 7oz (¾ cup) ghee

200g / 7oz (2 small) onions, sliced

1 tablespoon chopped fresh ginger

1 tablespoon Garlic Paste (see page 57)

750g / 1lb 10oz leg of spring lamb, cut into pieces

100g / 3½oz (½ cup) toor (toover) dal, rinsed
and drained

100g / 3½oz (½ cup) masoor dal, rinsed and drained

50g / 1¾oz (⅓ cup) potato, cut into cubes

100g / 3½oz (¾ cup) aubergines (eggplant), trimmed
and cut into slices

100g / 3½oz (1 cup) pumpkin, peeled, de-seeded
and cut into small pieces

300g / 3½oz (1 small) tomato, chopped

1 teaspoon chilli powder

½ teaspoon ground turmeric

2 green chillies, de-seeded and chopped

10 whole black peppercorns

1 tablespoon Tamarind Extract (see page 58)

3½ tablespoons butter

1 teaspoon cumin seeds

2 dried red chillies

4 teaspoons Dhansak Masala (see page 54)

salt

20g / ¾oz (½ cup) chopped coriander (cilantro) leaves,
to garnish

For the kavab

3 slices bread

300g / 11oz minced (ground) lamb

100g / 3½oz (1 small) onion, chopped

1½ teaspoons Ginger Paste (see page 57)

1½ teaspoons Garlic Paste (see page 57)

½ teaspoon ground turmeric

1 large sprig coriander (cilantro) leaves, chopped

2 tablespoons chopped mint

4 green chillies, de-seeded and chopped

2 tablespoons Worcestershire sauce

1 egg, beaten

ghee, for deep-frying

150g / 5oz (1⅓ cups) dried breadcrumbs

For the rice

400g / 14oz (2 cups) basmati rice, rinsed and drained

5 teaspoons sugar

125g / 4oz (½ cup) ghee

125g / 4oz (1 small) onion, chopped

2 cinnamon sticks, about 2.5cm / 1 inch long

10 cloves

Soak the rice in a bowl of water for about
30 minutes, then drain.

To make the kavab, soak the bread in another
bowl of water for about 30 seconds and squeeze.
Place the bread in a large bowl with all the
remaining ingredients, except the breadcrumbs,
and mix together. Divide the mixture into equal
sized portions, then with damp hands roll each
portion into a ball and flatten them into small
patties. Spread the breadcrumbs out on a large
plate and roll the patties in the breadcrumbs to
coat, then set aside.

Heat the ghee in a kadhai or deep, heavy-based pan
to 180°C/350°F, or until a cube of bread browns in
30 seconds, then reduce the heat to low. Working in
batches, carefully lower the kavab into the hot oil
and deep-fry for about 3–4 minutes, or until cooked
and brown. Remove with a slotted spoon and drain
on kitchen paper (paper towels).

Preheat the oven to 180°C/350°F/Gas Mark 4. For
the rice, put the sugar in a small, heavy-based pan
and cook, stirring, over medium heat for a few
minutes until brown, don't let it burn. Add 180ml /
6½fl oz (¾ cup) water and simmer for a few minutes
until smooth.

Heat the ghee in a large, heavy-based ovenproof pan
over medium heat, add the onion and stir-fry for
about 5–7 minutes, or until golden brown. Remove
half the onions for the garnish. Add the cinnamon,
cloves and rice to the remaining half, then season
with salt and stir for 1 minute. Add the sugar mixture
and pour in 625ml / 1 pint (2½ cups) water. Bring to
the boil, then reduce the heat and simmer for about
4–5 minutes, or until the liquid has evaporated. Place
a wet cloth on top, cover and place a couple of hot
charcoals on top, if desired, then cook in the oven for
about 15 minutes. Alternatively, omit the charcoals.

For the meat and vegetables, heat the ghee in
another heavy-based pan or handi over medium
heat, add the onions, ginger and garlic pastes
and stir-fry for about 2 minutes.

Add the lamb and stir-fry for about 10 minutes, then add the dals, potatoes, aubergines, pumpkin, tomatoes, chilli powder, turmeric, green chillies and black peppercorns, then season with salt and stir fry for 2–3 minutes. Pour in 1.5 litres / 2½ pints (6¼ cups) water and bring to the boil, then reduce the heat, cover and simmer for about 1–1½ hours, or until the meat is tender and the lentils and vegetables are mashed. Remove the lamb from the pan and force the lentils and vegetables through a sieve (strainer) into a separate pan. Add the tamarind extract and stir, then adjust the seasoning.

Heat the butter in a separate large pan over medium heat, add the cumin, dried red chillies and dhansak masala and stir-fry for about 30 seconds. Add the cooked lamb and the strained mash and bring to the boil, then reduce the heat to low and cook for about 5 minutes. Garnish with the reserved fried onions and chopped coriander.

Achras
Minced (Ground) Lamb with Raw Mango

Origin Awadh
Preparation time 30 minutes, plus standing time
Cooking time 40 minutes
Serves 4

1 × 8-cm / 3-inch piece fresh ginger, peeled
1 tablespoon ground coriander
1½ teaspoons chilli powder
½ teaspoon ground turmeric
100g / 3½oz (scant ½ cup) ghee or vegetable oil
250g / 9oz (2 small) onions, chopped
1 teaspoon Garlic Paste (see page 57)
2 teaspoons Ginger Paste (see page 57)
750g / 1lb 10oz coarsely minced (ground) lamb
2 raw mangoes, stoned (pitted) and cut into dice
6–7 green chillies, de-seeded and chopped
1½ teaspoons chopped mint leaves
½ teaspoon coarsely ground black pepper, roasted
pinch of ground cloves
pinch of ground black cardamom
salt
chopped hard-boiled eggs, to garnish

Chop half of the ginger and cut the remaining half into juliennes and set aside.

Put the ground coriander, chilli powder and turmeric in a small bowl, add 4 tablespoons water and mix together.

Heat the ghee or oil in a large, heavy-based pan over medium heat, add the onions and stir-fry for about 2 minutes, or until translucent and glossy. Add the garlic and ginger pastes and stir-fry for about 5 minutes, or until the onions are golden. Add the ground spice mixture and continue to stir-fry for about 1–2 minutes, or until the oil separates out. Now add the minced lamb and stir-fry for about 8–10 minutes, or until light brown. Season with salt and pour in about 375ml / 13fl oz (1½ cups) water and cook for about 5–8 minutes, or until the oil separates out. Now add the diced mangoes, chopped ginger, green chillies and mint, then mix well, cover and remove from the heat (the heat of the cooked mince will soften the raw mangoes) for 10 minutes.

Uncover and adjust the seasoning. Sprinkle over the remaining ground spices and cover again until ready to serve. Garnish with chopped eggs.

Akha Peenda
Whole Roasted Leg of Lamb

Origin Rajasthan
Preparation time 1 hour, plus standing time
Cooking time 3 hours
Serves 8

1 × 2-kg / 4½-lb leg of lamb, trimmed

vegetable oil, for oiling and basting

For the studding

12 cloves

12 flakes garlic or 3 cloves garlic, thinly sliced

4 cinnamon sticks, about 2.5cm / 1 inch long

24 whole black peppercorns

For the marinade

1 tablespoon chilli powder

6 tablespoons rum

4 tablespoons malt (white) vinegar

3 tablespoons Ginger Paste (see page 57)

3½ teaspoons Garlic Paste (see page 57)

salt

For the roasting

5 green cardamom pods

2 black cardamom pods

2 cinnamon sticks, about 2.5cm / 1 inch long

2 bay leaves

12 black peppercorns

1 teaspoon black cumin seeds

2 tablespoons mustard oil, plus extra for rubbing

For the masala mix

5 teaspoons amchoor

1½ teaspoons kasoori methi powder

1 teaspoon ground black pepper

½ teaspoon ground black cardamom

½ teaspoon black rock salt

Prick the leg of lamb all over with a fork, then rinse and pat dry. Using a skewer or cooking needle, stud the leg with the cloves, garlic, cinnamon and peppercorns, then put in a large shallow dish, cover and set aside in the refrigerator for 30 minutes.

To make the marinade, mix the chilli powder and a little salt together in a bowl, then rub into the leg. Mix the remaining marinade ingredients together in a bowl and evenly rub over the leg, then cover and set aside in the refrigerator for 1 hour.

Preheat the oven to 150°C/300°F/Gas Mark 2. Put the leg in a large, deep roasting tray (pan), spread the roasting spices and mustard oil on and around the leg, then add enough water to cover the leg. Cover the pan with foil, puncture 2 holes in the foil and roast in the oven for 2½ hours.

Remove from the oven and evenly rub the leg with mustard oil.

To make the masala mix, combine the spices in a small bowl.

Prepare a charcoal grill or barbecue to a moderate heat, or alternatively preheat the oven again to 200°C/400°F/Gas Mark 6. Thread a skewer right down the middle horizontally and as close to the bone as possible, then arrange the leg on the rack of the charcoal grill or barbecue. Cover the grill and roast over medium heat for 10 minutes. Uncover, turn over and baste with vegetable oil, then roast again for 10 minutes. Alternatively, arrange the leg on an oiled roasting tray and roast in the oven for 30 minutes, basting occasionally with oil. Allow the roast to rest briefly, then carve into pieces and serve sprinkled with the masala mix.

Piquant Cauliflower
p.258

Tomato Curry with
Coconut & Spinach p.316

Slow-cooked Aromatic
Leg of Lamb   p.416

Chickpeas (Garbanzo Beans)
from Rowalpindi   p.568

Rustic Hunter's
Lamb   p.425

Stuffed (Bell)
Peppers   p.306

Red-Hot Lamb
p.444

Roast Fish with
Mint   p.171

Barbecued
Pork   p.533

Chops
          p.446

Saffron-flavoured
Lamb   p.458

Minced (Ground) Lamb
with Peas   p.483

Savoury Potatoes &
(Bell) Peppers   p.232

Chicken with Aromatic
Whole Spices
                    p.496

Pepper Chicken
from Chettinad p.513

Chicken with
Fenugreek Leaves p.520

Handkerchief
Bread   p.616

Quails Stuffed
with Chicken   p.527

Goan Pork
Curry   p.530

Nargisi Kofte
'Iris' Kofta

Origin Awadh
Preparation time 45 minutes
Cooking time 30 minutes
Serves 8

250g / 9oz (2 small) onions

250g / 9oz (1 cup) ghee or vegetable oil, plus extra
  for deep-frying

2 teaspoons Poppy Seed Paste (see page 58)

2 tablespoons Ginger Paste (see page 57)

2 tablespoons Garlic Paste (see page 57)

1 tablespoon cumin seeds, roasted

5–6 dried red chillies

400ml / 14fl oz (1⅔ cups) natural (plain) yoghurt,
  whisked

500g / 1lb 2oz minced (ground) lamb

8 hard-boiled eggs, peeled

2 tablespoons kewra water

salt

For the sauce

125g / 4¼oz (¾ cup) gram (chickpea) flour, roasted

8–10 black cardamom pods

6–8 cloves

10 whole black peppercorns

Slice half the onions and set aside, then roughly
chop the remaining onions, transfer to a blender
or food processor and process to make a paste.
Set aside.

Heat a little ghee or oil in a heavy-based pan over
medium heat, add the sliced onions and stir-fry for
about 5–7 minutes, or until golden brown. Remove
from the heat and put into a bowl with the poppy
seed paste, half the garlic and ginger pastes, the
roasted cumin and dried red chillies and mix together.
Transfer to a blender or food processor, add the
yoghurt and process until ground. Transfer to a bowl
and mix in the remaining ginger and garlic pastes and
the onion paste, then add the minced lamb and mix to
combine. Divide the mixture into 8 equal portions and
place 1 hard-boiled egg in the centre of each portion,
smoothing the mixture over the egg evenly.

Heat enough ghee or oil for deep-frying in a kadhai
or deep, heavy-based pan to 180°C/350°F, or until
a cube of bread browns in 30 seconds. Working in
2 batches, carefully lower the koftas into the hot oil
and deep-fry for about 2–3 minutes, or until cooked
and golden brown all over. Remove with a slotted
spoon and drain on kitchen paper (paper towels),
then cut them in half.

Heat the remaining ghee or oil in another pan over
medium heat, add the onion, ginger, garlic and red
chilli pastes and season with salt, then fry for a
few minutes until the oil separates out. Place the
koftas in the sauce and simmer for about 5 minutes.
Sprinkle with the kewra water just before serving.

※

Kairi ka do Pyaza
Savoury Green Mango, Lamb & Onions

Origin Hyderabad
Preparation time 30 minutes
Cooking time 1¼–1¾ hours
Serves 4–6

125ml / 4½fl oz (½ cup) vegetable oil
5 onions, thinly sliced
2 teaspoons ground fresh ginger
2 teaspoons ground garlic
½ teaspoon ground turmeric
1 teaspoon ground cumin
1 teaspoon Garam Masala (see page 31)
1 teaspoon chilli powder
500g / 1lb 2oz lamb breast, cut into 4-cm / 1½-inch pieces with bones
2 onions, ground
3 raw unripe mangoes, stoned (pitted) and cut into slices
1 teaspoon sugar
4 green chillies, de-seeded and chopped
1 bunch coriander (cilantro) leaves, ground
6 curry leaves, chopped
salt
Plain Boiled Rice (see page 631) or chapatti, to serve

For the tempering

1 tablespoon vegetable oil
3 dried red chillies
½ teaspoon mustard seeds
6 cloves garlic, chopped

Heat the oil in a large, heavy-based pan over medium heat, add the sliced onions and stir-fry for about 4 minutes, or until light brown. Add the ginger, garlic, turmeric and ground cumin, then stir in the garam masala, chilli powder and season with salt. Cook for 1 minute, then add the meat and stir-fry for about 5 minutes, or until browned. Add the ground onions and cook for a further 2 minutes. Pour in 750ml / 1¼ pints (3¼ cups) water and cook for about 30 minutes, or until the meat is nearly done.

Add the sliced mangoes, sugar and chillies and cook for about 30–45 minutes, or until the meat is tender, adding water as required. Mix in the ground coriander leaves and chopped curry leaves and cook for 5 minutes. The oil should rise to the surface and the water should reduce to 125ml / 4½fl oz (½ cup).

Heat the oil for the tempering in a frying pan (skillet) over medium heat, add the chillies, mustard seeds and garlic and stir-fry for about 1 minute, or until dark brown. Pour over the lamb and cover immediately to retain the aroma. Serve with Plain Boiled Rice or chapatti.

※ ※

Mamsummunakkai Pulussu
Lamb & Drumstick Curry

Origin Tamil Nadu
Preparation time 45 minutes
Cooking time 1¼–1¾ hours
Serves 4–6

1 tablespoon basmati rice, rinsed, drained and dried
1 tablespoon ghee
2 onions, thinly sliced
¼ tablespoon ground turmeric
1 teaspoon chilli powder
1 teaspoon ground coriander, roasted
½ teaspoon ground cumin
1½ teaspoons Ginger Paste (see page 57)
1½ teaspoons Garlic Paste (see page 57)
250g / 9oz lamb, cut into 4-cm / 1½-inch cubes
250g / 9oz (vegetable) drumsticks, peeled and cut into 5.5-cm / 2-inch lengths
1 teaspoon Tamarind Extract (see page 58) or lime juice
8 curry leaves
1 bunch coriander (cilantro) leaves, chopped
salt

Put the rice into a small blender and process, adding a little water if necessary, to make a paste. Put the paste into a bowl, add 250ml / 8fl oz (1 cup) water and mix until smooth. Set aside.

Heat the ghee in a large, heavy-based pan over medium heat, add the onions and stir-fry for about 4 minutes, or until light brown. Add the turmeric, chilli powder, coriander, cumin, ginger and garlic pastes and the lamb, then season and fry for about 5 minutes, or until the moisture has evaporated. Add the drumsticks and continue stirring for 1 minute.

Pour in 1 litre / 1¾ pints (4¼ cups) water and the tamarind extract or lime juice, then reduce the heat and simmer for about 1–1½ hours, or until the lamb is tender. Add the curry leaves, chopped coriander and rice paste mixture and cook for 5–10 minutes to thicken slightly.

MAIN DISHES

482

Bhuna Keema
Roasted Minced (Ground) Lamb

Origin Hyderabad
Preparation time 30 minutes
Cooking time 50 minutes
Serves 6–8

125ml / 4½fl oz (½ cup) vegetable oil
6 onions, sliced
2 teaspoons Ginger Paste (see page 57)
2 teaspoons Garlic Paste (see page 57)
½ teaspoon ground turmeric
1½ teaspoons chilli powder
1 large sprig coriander (cilantro) leaves, chopped
few small mint leaves, chopped
8–10 green chillies, de-seeded and chopped
1kg / 2¼lb minced (ground) lamb
2 tablespoons lemon juice
salt

Heat the oil in a large, heavy-based pan over medium heat, add the onions and stir-fry for about 5–7 minutes, or until golden brown. Add the ginger and garlic pastes and continue stir-frying for about 1–2 minutes, or until the paste changes colour. Season with salt, then add the turmeric and chilli powder and three-quarters of the chopped coriander, mint and chillies and fry over low-medium heat for 3–5 minutes. Add the minced lamb and fry for about 8–10 minutes, or until the moisture has evaporated and the mince is dry.

Add 250ml / 8fl oz (1 cup) water, cover and cook for about 20 minutes. Increase the heat and boil away any excess water. Sprinkle the lemon juice over the meat and garnish with the remaining coriander, mint and green chillies.

Keema Matar
Minced (Ground) Lamb with Peas

Origin Punjab
Preparation time 30 minutes, plus marinating time
Cooking time 45 minutes
Serves 3–4

500g / 1lb 2oz minced (ground) lamb

For the marinade

½ tablespoon chilli powder
½ tablespoon coriander seeds
1 teaspoon ground turmeric powder
1 teaspoon cumin seeds
115g / 4oz (1 small) onion, ground
2 tablespoons ground fresh ginger
250ml / 8fl oz (1 cup) natural (plain) yoghurt, whisked
125g / 4oz (½ cup) ghee
250g / 9oz (2 cups) shelled peas
1 tablespoon chopped and de-seeded green chillies
1 teaspoon Garam Masala (see page 31)
2 tablespoons lime juice
1 tablespoon chopped coriander (cilantro) leaves
salt

Put the minced lamb in a large bowl. To make the marinade, mix the chilli powder, coriander seeds, turmeric, cumin seeds, onions, ginger and yoghurt together in a bowl, then season with salt. Mix the paste into the mince, then cover and set aside in the refrigerator for about 30 minutes.

Heat the ghee in a large, heavy-based pan over medium heat, add the meat and cook for about 5–8 minutes, or until the meat is cooked. Add about 500ml / 18fl oz (2¼ cups) water and cook the meat for about 30 minutes, or until it is tender and a little water remains.

Add the peas and chopped chillies and reduce the heat, then cook for about 5–7 minutes, or until the peas are tender and the water has evaporated. Add the garam masala, lime juice and coriander leaves and stir.

Shyaem
Minced (Ground) Lamb Cutlets in
Yoghurt Sauce

Origin Jammu and Kashmir
Preparation time 1 hour
Cooking time 50 minutes
Serves 6

500ml / 18fl oz (2¼ cups) natural (plain) yoghurt
250ml / 8fl oz (1 cup) milk
1 teaspoon ground ginger
2 teaspoons ground aniseed
1 teaspoon sugar
125ml / 4½fl oz (½ cup) mustard oil
5 cloves
1 teaspoon cumin seeds
small pinch asafoetida
1 teaspoon Kashmiri Garam Masala (see page 56)
½ teaspoon caraway seeds
6 green cardamom pods
1 teaspoon ground black pepper
1 teaspoon ground black cardamom
1 teaspoon ground cinnamon
salt

For the koftas

1kg / 2¼lb minced (ground) lamb with extra fat
1 litre / 1¾ pints (4¼ cups) vegetable oil or ghee
1 teaspoon ground ginger
1 teaspoon ground aniseed
pinch of salt
1 teaspoon Kashmiri Garam Masala (see page 56)
1 teaspoon natural (plain) yoghurt
1 teaspoon asafoetida diluted in a little water

To make the koftas, mix the minced lamb, vegetable
oil or ghee, ginger, aniseed, salt, Kashmiri garam
masala, yoghurt and asafoetida together in a large
bowl, then use a wooden pestle and a large stone
mortar to pound it. Once pounded, divide the meat
into equal medium-sized portions and roll into
balls. Oil your hands and shape each ball into 8-cm
/ 3-inch long tubes and set aside on a plate.

Now mix the yoghurt, milk, ginger, aniseed and sugar
together in a medium-sized bowl, then season with
salt and set aside.

Bring 500ml / 18fl oz (2¼ cups) water to the boil in a
shallow pan.

Carefully add the cylindrical pieces of the beaten
minced meat to the water and boil for about
20 minutes. Remove the pan from the heat and
remove the pieces of minced meat with a slotted
spoon and reserve the soup. Add the soup to the
mixture of yoghurt and other masalas.

Heat the mustard oil in a separate pan over medium
heat, add the cloves, cumin seeds and the pinch
of asafoetida and fry for 30 seconds. Reduce the
heat and add the yoghurt masala and soup mixture,
stirring constantly until it thickens to a sauce. Now
add the minced meat slices to the boiling sauce
and cook for a further 15 minutes, shaking the pan
occasionally. Simmer for about 30 minutes, then add
the remaining spices and mix well.

Kashmiri Kofte
Lamb Koftas in Sauce

Origin Jammu and Kashmir
Preparation time 30 minutes
Cooking time 45 minutes
Serves 6–8

2 tablespoons vegetable oil
1 teaspoon Kashmiri Garam Masala (see page 56)
5 cloves
1 teaspoon cumin seeds
1 teaspoon asafoetida
1 teaspoon Kashmiri red chilli powder
1 teaspoon ground turmeric
235ml / 7¾fl oz (1 cup) natural (plain) yoghurt, whisked
1 teaspoon ground ginger
2 teaspoons ground aniseed
1 teaspoon sugar
salt

For the koftas

1kg / 2¼lb minced (ground) lamb with extra fat
2 tablespoons mustard oil, plus extra for oiling
1 teaspoon ground ginger
2 teaspoons ground aniseed
1 teaspoon Kashmiri red chilli powder
1 teaspoon asafoetida diluted in a little water
1 tablespoon natural (plain) yoghurt
1 teaspoon Kashmiri Garam Masala (see page 56)

To make the koftas, mix the minced lamb with the mustard oil, ginger, aniseed, chilli powder, asafoetida mixture, yoghurt, and the Kashmiri garam masala together in a large bowl, then season with salt. Divide the mixture into equal-sized portions and roll into balls. Oil your hands and shape each ball into 8-cm / 3-inch long sausages and set aside.

Heat the oil in a large, heavy-based pan over high heat, then allow to cool. Once cool, reheat the oil over medium heat and add the cloves, cumin seeds and asafoetida. Stir for about 3–4 minutes, then add the chilli powder, turmeric and 4 tablespoons water. Stir constantly for another 2 minutes until the oil becomes reddish brown and starts to separate.

Remove from the heat and slowly stir in the whisked yoghurt, then return to a low heat, stirring constantly, until the sauce blends into a thick reddish brown sauce.

Pour in 500ml / 18fl oz (2¼ cups) water, then add the ginger, aniseed and sugar and season with salt. Continue to stir otherwise the yoghurt may curdle. Gently lower all the koftas into the pan and boil for 30 minutes, or until the water has evaporated and the sauce thickens. Add the garam masala and mix gently.

Narangi Keema
Minced (Ground) Lamb with Orange Peel & Juice

Origin Hyderabad
Preparation time 15 minutes
Cooking time 15 minutes
Serves 5–6

peel and juice of 4 oranges
500g / 1lb 2oz (4½ cups) cooked minced (ground) lamb
juice of 1 lime
6 mint leaves, chopped
salt
chapati, Paratha (see page 609) or Naan (see page 591), to serve

Cut the orange peel into long narrow strips between 5mm / ¼ inch to 1cm / ½ inch wide and 2.5cm / 1 inch long, then cook the strips in a pan of boiling water for 2–3 minutes until soft. Drain and discard the water. Put the minced lamb into a large frying pan (skillet), add the orange strips and fry together for 7–8 minutes. Add the orange juice and lime juice, season with salt and fry for about 5 minutes, then sprinkle over the mint leaves. Serve hot with chapati, Paratha or Naan.

Kofta Curry
Meatball Curry

Origin Delhi
Preparation time 50 minutes
Cooking time 30 minutes
Serves 4

250ml / 8fl oz (1 cup) vegetable oil or ghee

3 onions, thinly sliced

½ teaspoon ground turmeric

1 teaspoon ground fresh ginger

1 teaspoon ground garlic

1 teaspoon ground aniseed

1 teaspoon poppy seeds

1 × 2.5-cm / 1-inch piece dried coconut

1 teaspoon chilli powder

pinch of saffron threads

4 cloves

5 cardamom pods

1 cinnamon stick, about 2.5cm / 1 inch long

180ml / 6½fl oz (¾ cup) natural (plain) yoghurt,
   whisked

350g / 12oz (3 cups) cooked minced (ground) lamb

1 egg

salt

Plain Boiled Rice (see page 631), chapatti or Paratha
   (see page 609), to serve

Heat 4 tablespoons oil or ghee in a large, heavy-based
pan over medium heat, add the onions and stir-fry
for about 5–7 minutes, or until golden brown. Add
the turmeric, ginger and garlic and fry for about
30 seconds. Add the aniseed, poppy seeds and coconut
and fry for about 1–2 minutes, or until fragrant.

Add the chilli powder, saffron, cloves, cardamom
pods, cinnamon and yoghurt, then season with salt.
Pour in 500ml / 18fl oz (2¼ cups) water and cook
over low heat for 5 minutes to make a sauce. If a
smooth sauce is preferred, allow to cool and process
in a blender for 30 seconds until smooth. If the
sauce is too thick, add 125ml / 4½fl oz (½ cup) water.

Put the minced lamb in a blender or food processor
and process until ground. Transfer the mince to a
frying pan (skillet) and cook over low heat to dry out
the water, otherwise the koftas will break when they
are fried. Beat the egg thoroughly in a bowl and mix
into the mince, then shape into walnut-sized balls.

Heat 175ml / 6fl oz (¾ cup) oil or ghee in a large
frying pan over medium heat. Working in batches,
fry the koftas for about 5–8 minutes, or until they
are golden brown all over. Remove from the pan
with a slotted spoon and drain on kitchen paper
(paper towels).

Put the koftas in a serving dish with the hot sauce.
The sauce should cover at least half the koftas. Serve
hot with cooked Rice, Chapatti or Paratha.

Lagan ka Keema
Baked Masala Minced (Ground) Lamb

Origin Awadh
Preparation time 45 minutes, plus soaking time
Cooking time 45 minutes
Serves 4

2 tablespoons vegetable oil or ghee
2 onions, thinly sliced
large pinch of saffron threads, roasted
1 teaspoon warm milk
500g / 1lb 2oz (4½ cups) minced (ground) lamb
1 bunch mint leaves, chopped
1 bunch coriander (cilantro) leaves, chopped
1 tablespoon ground coriander, roasted
125ml / 4½fl oz (½ cup) natural (plain) yoghurt, whisked
1 tablespoon ground fresh ginger
1 tablespoon ground garlic
1½ tablespoons chilli powder
1 teaspoon caraway seeds
1 teaspoon ground cumin
1 tablespoon poppy seeds, ground
1 tablespoon chironji kernels
½ teaspoon ground allspice
4 cloves, ground
1 cinnamon stick, about 2.5cm / 1 inch long, ground
4 small and 2 large green cardamom pods, ground
juice of 1 lime
salt
mint sprigs, to garnish

Preheat the oven to 180°C/350°F/Gas Mark 4.

Heat the oil or ghee in a large, heavy-based pan over medium heat, add the onions and stir-fry for about 5–7 minutes, or until crisp and golden brown. Remove from the heat and put half in a blender or food processor and process until ground. Keep the other half for garnishing.

Put the roasted saffron in a small bowl, add the warm milk and soak for 20 minutes, then place in a mortar and pound with a pestle.

Mix the minced lamb and all the ingredients together, including the oil or ghee in which the onions were fried and the saffron, in a large pan and fry over low heat for about 10 minutes, or until the mince is brown.

Spread the mince in a large baking dish and bake in the oven for about 40 minutes, or until the mince is cooked. Place under a hot grill (broiler) for a few minutes to brown the top.

If you like, remove from the grill and make a hollow in the mince. Place a hot piece of charcoal on an onion skin in the hollow and sprinkle a little oil or ghee over it, then cover the dish immediately. Leave it covered with the lid on for 10 minutes so that the aroma of charcoal permeates it. Garnish with the fried onions and mint sprigs.

Shufta
Minced (Ground) Lamb & Peas

Origin Jammu and Kashmir
Preparation time 25 minutes
Cooking time 40 minutes
Serves 6

300g / 11oz (1⅓ cups) ghee
pinch of asafoetida
4 cloves
1kg / 2¼lb coarsely minced (ground) lamb
250ml / 8fl oz (1 cup) natural (plain) yoghurt, whisked
1 teaspoon ground fennel
1 teaspoon chilli powder
1 × 5-cm / 2-inch piece fresh ginger, peeled and ground
1 teaspoon sugar
500g / 1lb 2oz (3½ cups) peas, shelled if fresh
250g / 9oz coriander (cilantro) leaves, chopped
1 teaspoon kewra water or rosewater
pinch of saffron threads, ground to a paste
2 teaspoons Garam Masala (see page 31)
1 teaspoon ground coriander
100g / 3½oz Khoya (see page 58) or 100g / 3½oz (⅔ cup) milk powder (dry milk)
salt

Heat the ghee in a degchi or large casserole over medium heat, add the asafoetida, cloves, meat, three-quarters of the yoghurt, the fennel, chilli powder and ginger then season with salt. Stir and cook for about 8–10 minutes, adding a little water occasionally to prevent burning, until the meat turns reddish brown. Add the sugar and peas and stir a few times. Pour in about 300ml / ½ pint (1¼ cups) water and allow the meat to simmer for about 20 minutes. When a little sauce is left, add the chopped coriander, kewra water, saffron, garam masala and ground coriander.

Next, dilute the khoya with the remaining yoghurt and add it to the pan, then cook for about 5 minutes, or until it turns light brown. If you like, place the pan over low heat, cover and put a few hot charcoals on the lid for a few minutes until the sauce thickens, then remove. Alternatively, cook for about 5 minutes, or until the sauce thickens, then remove from the heat.

Bhindi ka Patala Salan
Lamb, Potato & Okra Curry

Origin Awadh
Preparation time 30 minutes, plus marinating time
Cooking time 1¼ hours
Serves 4

500g / 1lb 2oz lamb, cut into 4-cm / 1½-inch cubes
1 teaspoon Ginger Paste (see page 57)
1 teaspoon Garlic Paste (see page 57)
4 tablespoons vegetable oil
2 tablespons ghee
2 potatoes, cut into slices
4 onions, sliced
¼ teaspoon ground turmeric
2 teaspoons chilli powder
1 teaspoon ground coriander, roasted
1 cinnamon stick, about 2.5cm / 1 inch long (optional)
3 green cardamom pods (optional)
4 cloves (optional)
10 okra, topped and tailed
2 tomatoes, chopped
1 bunch coriander (cilantro) leaves, chopped
few sprigs of mint
salt

Put the meat into a large shallow dish and rub the ginger and garlic pastes and the oil all over, then cover and set aside in the refrigerator for 1 hour.

Heat the ghee in a large frying pan (skillet) over low heat, add the potatoes and fry for about 10 minutes, or until lightly browned, then remove from the pan and set aside.

Add the onions to the pan and add the turmeric, chilli powder and coriander. Fry for about 8 minutes, or until the onions are light brown. Add the cinnamon, cardamom pods and cloves if desired, then add the lamb and fry for about 5 minutes, or until the liquid from the lamb has evaporated. Pour in 500ml / 18fl oz (2¼ cups) water and cook for about 30 minutes, or until the lamb is half cooked. Season with salt, then add the potatoes, whole okra, chopped tomatoes and a little more water and cook for a further 30 minutes, or until the lamb is tender. There should be about 500–750ml / 18–24fl oz (2–3¼ cups) liquid in the pan. Add the chopped coriander and mint leaves a few minutes before removing from the heat.

Chingur ka Salan
Lamb with Tender Tamarind Leaves
& Flowers

Origin Hyderabad
Preparation time 30 minutes
Cooking time 1¼–1¾ hours
Serves 4

1 tablespoon vegetable oil

5 onions, thinly sliced

8 green chillies, slit in half lengthways and de-seeded

¼ teaspoon ground turmeric

1 teaspoon Ginger Paste (see page 57)

1½ teaspoons Garlic Paste (see page 57)

500g / 1lb 2oz breast of lamb, cut into 4-cm
    1½-inch pieces

2 teaspoons ground cumin, roasted

2 full cups of tender chigur, rinsed well

6 curry leaves

chilli powder, to taste (optional)

salt

Plain Boiled Rice (see page 631), to serve

For the tempering
1 tablespoon vegetable oil

3 dried red chillies

6 cloves garlic

½ teaspoon mustard seeds

Heat the oil in a large, heavy-based pan over medium heat, add the onions and stir-fry for about 5–7 minutes, or until golden brown. Add the green chillies, turmeric, ginger and garlic pastes and fry for about 1–2 minutes. Add the lamb and fry for about 5 minutes. Pour in 750ml / 1¼ pints (3¼ cups) water and cook over medium heat for about 30–45 minutes, or until the meat has softened, and there is about 250ml / 8fl oz (1 cup) water left. Add the ground cumin and chigur and cook together for about 10 minutes, stirring occasionally until the chigur leaves soften. Add the curry leaves, then pour in 250–500ml / 8–18fl oz (1–2¼ cups) water and simmer for a further 10 minutes, seasoning with salt. Add the chilli powder if desired.

Heat the oil for the tempering in a frying pan (skillet) over medium heat, add the tempering ingredients, then reduce the heat and stir-fry for about 2 minutes, or until the chillies turn a shade darker. Pour over the chigur curry and cover immediately to retain the aroma. Serve with Plain Boiled Rice.

Dhoop Chhaun Keema
Minced (Ground) Lamb Cake Topped
with Eggs

Origin New
Preparation time 20 minutes
Cooking time 10–15 minutes
Serves 4

6 eggs

1kg / 2¼lb (9 cups) cooked minced (ground) lamb

vegetable oil, for oiling

2 bunches coriander (cilantro) leaves, chopped

2 bunches mint leaves, chopped

10–12 green chillies, de-seeded and chopped

salt

Paratha (see page 609), to serve

To garnish
2 teaspoons vegetable oil or ghee

few almonds, chopped

few cashew nuts, chopped

few pistachios, chopped

Preheat the grill (broiler) to medium. Beat the eggs in a bowl with a little salt.

Put the cooked minced lamb in a lightly oiled baking dish, about 4cm / 1½ inches high. Cover with the salted beaten eggs, then sprinkle over the chopped coriander, mint leaves and chopped chillies.

Heat the oil or ghee for the garnish in a frying pan (skillet) over medium heat, add all the nuts and stir-fry for about 1 minute, or until lightly toasted. Don't let them burn. Set aside.

In earlier days, the mince was covered with a metal cover or thali and lit charcoal was put on top. Today, put the baking dish under the hot grill and cook the eggs for 5–7 minutes, or until golden brown. When they are done, sprinkle the nuts over the top and serve with any Indian bread.

Dahi ka Keema
Lamb Cooked in Yoghurt

Origin Hyderabad
Preparation time 15 minutes
Cooking time 35 minutes
Serves 4

300ml / ½ pint (1¼ cups) natural (plain) yoghurt
1 cinnamon stick, about 2.5cm / 1 inch long
½ teaspoon ground cloves
groundnut (peanut) oil, for deep-frying
15 green chillies, slit in half lengthways and de-seeded
4 teaspoons Ginger Paste (see page 57)
4 teaspoons Garlic Paste (see page 57)
150g / 5oz (⅔ cup) ghee
5 green cardamom pods
1 black cardamom pod
5 cloves
1 bay leaf
pinch of ground mace
200g / 7oz (2 small) onions, finely chopped
2 teaspoons Garam Masala (see page 31)
2 teaspoons chilli powder
1kg / 2¼lb minced (ground) lamb
20g / ¾oz (½ cup) coriander (cilantro) leaves, chopped
salt

Put the yoghurt in a bowl and whisk with the cinnamon and ground cloves.

Heat enough oil for deep-frying in a kadhai or deep, heavy-based pan to 180°C/350°F, or until a cube of bread browns in 30 seconds. Carefully lower the chillies into the hot oil and deep-fry for 15–20 seconds. Remove with a slotted spoon and drain on kitchen paper (paper towels).

Put the ginger and garlic pastes in a small bowl, add 4 tablespoons water and mix together.

Heat the ghee in a kadhai, wok or large, heavy-based pan over medium heat, add the cardamom pods, cloves, bay leaf and mace and stir-fry for about 1 minute, or until they start to splutter. Add the onions and stir-fry for about 5–7 minutes, or until golden brown. Add the ginger and garlic pastes mixture and stir-fry for 30 seconds, then add the garam masala and chilli powder and stir-fry for 1½ minutes. Add the minced lamb and stir-fry for about 5 minutes, or until the liquid has evaporated. Now add the spiced yoghurt and bring almost to the boil.

Reduce the heat, cover and simmer for about 20 minutes, or until the lamb is cooked. Adjust the seasoning and sprinkle over the coriander and deep-fried green chillies and stir.

Gurde ka Keema
Lamb Kidney Curry

Origin Punjab
Preparation time 20 minutes
Cooking time 40 minutes
Serves 6

1 × 4-cm / 1½-inch piece fresh ginger, peeled
125g / 4oz (½ cup) ghee
½ teaspoon ground fennel
½ teaspoon chilli powder
pinch of asafoetida
2 cloves
100ml / 3½fl oz (½ cup) natural (plain) yoghurt
6 lambs' kidneys, cleaned, trimmed and cut in half lengthways
6 lambs' testes, cleaned, trimmed and cut in half lengthways
1 teaspoon ground coriander
1 teaspoon Garam Masala (see page 31)
¼ teaspoon kewra water or rosewater
1 bunch coriander (cilantro) leaves, chopped
salt

Put the ginger in a small food processor or blender and process, adding a little water if necessary, to make a paste. Set aside.

Heat the ghee in a large, heavy-based pan over low heat, add the ground fennel, chilli powder, asafoetida, cloves and yoghurt, then season with salt and fry for about 3–4 minutes, or until the masala turns red and the moisture has evaporated. Add the kidneys and fry for about 5 minutes, or until they are light brown, then add the testes and fry carefully (they break easily) for about 5 minutes, or until brown.

Pour in 250ml / 8fl oz (1 cup) water and simmer for 15 minutes. Test by hand to see if the kidneys have softened, then add the ground coriander, garam masala, ginger paste, kewra water and chopped coriander. If the kidneys are not done, add another 125ml / 4½fl oz (½ cup) water and simmer, making sure that the sauce is fairly thick.

Garhua
Lambs' Feet

Origin Uttarakhand
Preparation time 30 minutes
Cooking time 12 hours
Serves 4

12 lambs' feet
125ml / 4½fl oz (½ cup) mustard oil
200g / 7oz (1¼ cups) onion, chopped
1 bay leaf
1–2 black cardamom pods
1 × 2.5-cm / 1-inch piece fresh ginger, peeled and chopped
1 teaspoon black pepper
4–6 cloves garlic, crushed
salt

For the spice paste
2 teaspoons ground turmeric
1 × 2.5-cm / 1-inch piece fresh ginger, peeled and chopped
1 tablespoon coriander seeds

To garnish
10–12 dried red chillies, chopped
chopped coriander (cilantro) leaves

Clean and wash the feet, then split along the middle. Crack the attached shine bones to let the marrow escape during cooking.

To make the spice paste, put the turmeric, ginger and coriander seeds in a small blender and process, adding a little water to make a smooth paste. Set aside.

Heat the oil in a large, heavy-based pan over high heat, then reduce the heat. Add the onion and stir-fry for about 4 minutes, or until light brown. Now add the bay leaf, cardamom pods, ginger, black pepper and crushed garlic and fry for about 30 seconds. Add the spice paste, then season with salt and stir-fry for about 1 minute. Add the feet and stir-fry for about 1 minute to coat well with the masala. Pour in about 3 litres / 5¼ pints (12¾ cups) water, bring to the boil, then reduce the heat, cover and simmer over very low heat overnight. Garnish with chopped dried red chillies and chopped coriander.

Nalli aur Paye
Curry of Feet & Marrow Bones

Origin Awadh
Preparation time 30 minutes
Cooking time 2¼ hours
Serves 6

6 lambs' feet
180ml / 6fl oz (¾ cup) vegetable oil
3 onions, sliced
¼ teaspoon ground turmeric
1 tablespoon ground coriander, roasted
1 teaspoon chilli powder
1 tablespoon ground fresh ginger
1 tablespoon ground garlic
2 cinnamon sticks, about 2.5cm / 1 inch long
6 cloves
6 black cardamom pods
8 marrow bones
juice of 2 limes
1 bunch coriander (cilantro) leaves, chopped
few sprigs of mint
salt
Naan (see page 591), to serve

Get the butcher to clean the feet well and singe to remove all hair.

Heat the oil in a large, heavy-based pan over medium heat, add the onions and fry for about 5–7 minutes, or until golden brown. Add the turmeric, coriander, chilli powder, ginger and garlic and stir-fry for about 1–2 minutes, or until browned and fragrant. Add the cinnamon, cloves and cardamom pods, then season with salt and stir-fry together for about 1 minute. Add the feet, marrow bones and 1 litre / 1¾ pints (4¼ cups) water, then reduce the heat to low, cover and cook for about 30 minutes, or until the feet and marrow bones are softened, then continue cooking for another 1¾ hours or until done. Remove from the heat and allow to rest for a while. Spoon off the excess fat that rises to the surface, then return to the heat, add the lime juice, chopped coriander leaves and mint and simmer for 5 minutes. Remove from the heat and serve hot.

This dish should be served in large soup bowls with pieces of Naan dunked in it.

✳︎✳︎

___

Kaleji ka Salan
Liver Curry

Origin Awadh
Preparation time 15 minutes, plus marinating time
Cooking time 30 minutes
Serves 4

| 500g / 1lb 2oz liver, rinsed |
| 1 teaspoon ground fresh ginger |
| 1 teaspoon ground garlic |
| 1 teaspoon chilli powder |
| ½ teaspoon ground turmeric |
| 175ml / 6fl oz (¾ cup) natural (plain) yoghurt, whisked |
| 125ml / 4½fl oz (½ cup) vegetable oil |
| 2 onions, thinly sliced |
| 1½ teaspoons ground coriander, roasted |
| salt |
| few sprigs of mint |

Remove the membranes from the liver and rinse well, then cut the liver into 2.5-cm / 1-inch by 4-cm / 1½-inch pieces.

Mix the ginger, garlic, chilli powder, turmeric and yoghurt together in a large bowl and season with salt. Add the liver and turn to coat, then cover and set aside in the refrigerator for 15 minutes.

Heat the oil in a large, heavy-based pan over medium heat, add the onions and stir-fry for about 5–7 minutes, or until golden brown. Add the liver and fry for about 5 minutes, or until the liquid has evaporated. Add the roasted coriander and continue to fry for a few minutes. Pour in 500ml / 18fl oz (2¼ cups) water, then reduce the heat to low and simmer for about 15 minutes, or until the liver is cooked, adding more water if necessary. There should be about 250ml / 8fl oz (1 cup) sauce. Remove from the heat and garnish with mint sprigs.

✳︎✳︎

___

Kaleji Masala
Spicy Liver

Origin Punjab
Preparation time 45 minutes, plus marinating time
Cooking time 20 minutes
Serves 4

| 500g / 1lb 2oz liver, rinsed and cut into slices |
| 2 teaspoons Garlic Paste (see page 57) |
| 2 teaspoons Ginger Paste (see page 57) |
| 1 cinnamon stick, about 5cm / 2 inches long |
| 100g / 3½oz (scant ½ cup) ghee |
| 175g / 6oz (1 large) onion, thinly sliced |
| 2 tomatoes, finely chopped |
| salt |

For the marinade

| 4–5 green chillies, de-seeded and chopped |
| 8–10 whole black peppercorns |
| 1 teaspoon cumin seeds |
| 125ml / 4½fl oz (½ cup) malt (white) vinegar |
| ½ teaspoon sugar |

Put the liver slices in a large pan of water, add the garlic and ginger pastes and cinnamon and bring to the boil, then boil for about 10 minutes. Remove the slices from the pan, rinse, place in a large shallow dish and set aside. Reserve the residual stock for later use.

To make the marinade, mix all the ingredients together in a bowl and season with salt. Spread this paste on the liver slices, then cover and set aside in the refrigerator for about 30 minutes.

Heat the ghee in a large, heavy-based pan over medium heat, add the onion and stir-fry for about 5–7 minutes, or until golden brown. Season with salt, then add the liver slices together with the marinade and the reserved stock. Bring to the boil, add the chopped tomatoes and cook for about 10 minutes, or until all the liquid has evaporated.

Bhutua
Spicy Fried Offal (Variety Meats)

Origin Uttarakhand
Preparation time 45 minutes, plus cooling time
Cooking time 1 hour
Serves 4

1kg / 2¼lb mixed offal (variety meats), such as liver, lungs, stomach and intestines with a little roasted outer skin, rinsed very well

500ml / 18fl oz (2¼ cups) mustard oil

salt

For the spice paste

1 teaspoon ground turmeric

10–12 dried red chillies

1 tablespoon coriander seeds

Bring about 1 litre / 1¾ pints (4¼ cups) water with 1 teaspoon of salt to the boil in a large, heavy-based pan. Add the offal and the skin and boil for about 15 minutes. Remove from the water and rinse in cold water once again. Allow to cool, then cut into small bite-sized pieces.

Put the turmeric, chillies and coriander seeds in a small blender and process, adding a little water to make a smooth paste.

Heat the oil in a large, heavy-based pan over high heat, then reduce the heat slightly. Add the spice paste and season with salt, then stir-fry for about 30 seconds. Add the offal pieces and continue to stir-fry for a further 2 minutes over high heat. Reduce the heat to low and continue to simmer for about 1 hour.

Bheja
Sheep's Brains with Coconut Milk

Origin Hyderabad
Preparation time 25 minutes
Cooking time 20 minutes
Serves 4

½ coconut

125g / 4oz (½ cup) ghee

2 green cardamom pods

3 cloves

1 cinnamon stick, about 2.5cm / 1 inch long

1 onion, thinly sliced

1 teaspoon Ginger Paste (see page 57)

1 teaspoon Garlic Paste (see page 57)

½ teaspoon ground turmeric

6 green chillies, de-seeded and chopped

125ml / 4½fl oz (½ cup) milk

4 sheep's brains, rinsed and cut into 2.5-cm / 1-inch pieces

1 bunch coriander (cilantro) leaves, chopped

salt

Put the coconut in a blender or food processor and process, adding a little water if necessary, to make a paste. Set aside.

Heat the ghee in a large, heavy-based pan over medium heat, add the cardamom pods, cloves and cinnamon and stir-fry for about 1 minute, or until they start to splutter. Add the onion and stir-fry for 5–7 minutes, or until golden brown. Add the ginger and garlic pastes, turmeric and chillies and fry for 2 minutes.

Add the milk and a little water, if necessary, to the coconut and squeeze out the liquid. Add half the coconut milk and the brains to the fried ingredients and cook over low heat for about 10 minutes, or until the liquid has evaporated and the oil rises to the surface. Add the coconut paste and milk and season with salt, then cook for 1–2 minutes. Add the chopped coriander and stir, then remove from the heat.

Magaj Masala
Lambs' Brains

Origin Punjab
Preparation time 15 minutes, plus soaking time
Cooking time 30 minutes
Serves 4–6

8 lamb's brains, rinsed and patted dry

6 tablespoons ghee

1¾ teaspoons Garlic Paste (see page 57)

250g / 9oz (2 small) onions, chopped

3½ teaspoons Ginger Paste (see page 57)

2–3 green chillies, de-seeded and chopped

2 tablespoons Cashew Nut Paste (see page 58)

½ teaspoon ground green cardamom

½ teaspoon ground black cumin

¼ teaspoon ground cinnamon

¼ teaspoon ground cloves

2 teaspoons ground fennel

salt

For the yoghurt paste

125ml / 4½fl oz (½ cup) natural (plain) yoghurt, whisked

225g / 8oz (2¼ cups) ground coriander

2 teaspoons chilli powder

1½ teaspoons ground turmeric

For cooking the brains

500ml / 18fl oz (2¼ cups) milk

3 tablespoons brandy or rum

4 black cardamom pods

4 cloves

2 cinnamon sticks, about 2.5cm / 1 inch long

3 bay leaves

1 teaspoon cumin seeds

1 teaspoon fenugreek seeds

2 teaspoons lemon juice

few ginger juliennes

For cooking the brains, put the brains and milk into a large pan, add the brandy or rum and set aside overnight in the refrigerator.

The next day, put the remaining cooking ingredients in a large pan of water and bring to the boil. Drain the brains and add to the pan and boil for 2 minutes. Remove from the pan and set aside.

To make the yoghurt paste, whisk the yoghurt, coriander, chilli powder and turmeric together in a large bowl.

Next, heat the ghee in a large, heavy-based pan over medium heat, add the garlic paste and stir-fry for about 1–2 minutes, or until it turns light golden. Add the onions and stir-fry for about 2 minutes, or until the onions turn translucent and glossy. Add the ginger paste and chillies and stir for a few seconds. Add the yoghurt paste and stir-fry for about 2–3 minutes, or until the oil separates out.

Add the cashew nut paste and stir-fry for about 2–3 minutes, or until the oil separates out. Pour in 500ml / 18fl oz (2¼ cups) water and bring to the boil. Reduce the heat to low and sprinkle over the ground spices and stir again. Season with salt and stir. Cover and cook for about 20 minutes. Now, add the drained, cooked brains and stir-fry, using the side of the spatula to chop the brain into pieces until the sauce covers everything.

Khad Murg
Baked Chicken

Origin Rajasthan
Preparation time 30 minutes, plus marinating time
Cooking time 1 hour
Serves 4–6

1kg / 2¼lb skinless boneless chicken pieces
large pinch of saffron threads
1 tablespoon milk
500ml / 18fl oz (2¼ cups) clear chicken stock
3 green cardamom pods
2 cinnamon sticks, about 2.5cm / 1 inch long
2 cloves
2 bay leaves
2 black cardamom pods
8 Handkerchief Bread (page 616)
150ml / ¼ pint (⅔ cup) natural (plain) yoghurt, whisked
vegetable oil, for oiling

For the marinade

5 tablespoons ghee
3 tablespoons almond paste
3 tablespoons Garlic Paste (see page 57)
5 teaspoons Ginger Paste (see page 57)
½–1 tablespoon chilli powder
4 tablespoons lemon juice
1 teaspoon ground green cardamom
salt

Put the chicken in a large shallow dish and prick thoroughly with a fork.

To make the marinade, mix all the ingredients together in a large bowl, then season with salt. Rub the mixture all over the chicken, then cover and set aside in the refrigerator for 3–4 hours.

Put the saffron threads in a small bowl, add the milk and soak until required.

Preheat the oven to 200°C/400°F/Gas Mark 6.

Pour the stock into a heavy-based pan and add the cardamom pods, cinnamon, cloves and bay leaves. Bring to the boil, then reduce the heat, cover and simmer for about 15 minutes.

Arrange the chicken in a large roasting tray (pan), without overlapping the pieces, then pour over the sauce. Bake in the oven, basting frequently with the sauce, for about 30 minutes, or until cooked and the stock is completely absorbed. Remove from the oven and set aside. Reserve the fat. Keep the oven on.

Spread out 4 roti, overlapping each other by 3cm / 1 inch on an oiled baking tray. (These should form a surface large enough to wrap around the chicken.) Spread a little of the reserved fat on the roti. Sprinkle the soaked saffron over the chicken, then place half the chicken down the centre of the roti. Spoon over half the yoghurt. Fold the roti over the chicken, to make a parcel, and repeat with the remaining roti, chicken and yoghurt. Return both parcels to the oven for 15 minutes.

Chicken Masala
Chicken Masala

Origin Punjab
Preparation time 30 minutes, plus marinating time
Cooking time 35 minutes
Serves 4

1 chicken, cut into 10–12 pieces and skinned
250g / 9oz (1 cup) ghee
salt

For the marinade

2 green chillies, de-seeded and chopped
6–8 cloves garlic, crushed
8–10 black peppercorns
2 teaspoons ground coriander
1 teaspoon chilli powder
1 teaspoon ground turmeric
1 teaspoon ground aniseed

To make the marinade, put all the ingredients in a spice grinder or small blender and process until ground and mixed together. Place the chicken in a large shallow dish and rub the mixture all over, then cover and set aside in the refrigerator for about 2 hours.

Bring 125ml / 4½fl oz (½ cup) water with ½ teaspoon salt to the boil in a large, heavy-based pan, add the marinated chicken and return to the boil. Reduce the heat to low and simmer for about 25 minutes, or until dry and the chicken is cooked through.

Heat the ghee in a large frying pan (skillet) over low heat, add the chicken and fry for about 10 minutes, or until golden.

Khare Masale ka Murg
Chicken with Aromatic Whole Spices

Origin Rajasthan
Preparation time 30 minutes
Cooking time 30 minutes
Serves 4

125g / 4oz (½ cup) ghee
12 green cardamom pods
2 bay leaves
2 teaspoons cumin seeds
1 × 1-kg / 2¼-lb chicken, cut into large pieces and skinned
2 dried red chillies
1 teaspoon ground turmeric
2 tablespoons chopped garlic
1 × 2-cm / ¾-inch piece fresh ginger, peeled and chopped
300g / 11oz (2 medium) onions, sliced
125ml / 4½fl oz (½ cup) natural (plain) yoghurt, whisked
6 green chillies, slit in half lengthways and de-seeded
salt

Heat the ghee in a large, heavy-based pan over medium heat, add the cardamom pods, cloves, bay leaves and cumin seeds and stir-fry for about 1 minute, or until the seeds start to splutter. Add the chicken, increase the heat to high and cook for 2 minutes. Reduce the heat to medium, add the dried red chillies, turmeric, garlic and ginger, then season with salt and stir-fry for about 2–3 minutes, or until specks of oil start to appear on the surface.

Pour in 1 litre / 1¾ pints (4¼ cups) water and add the onions. Bring to the boil, then reduce the heat to low, cover and simmer for about 15 minutes. Uncover, stir in the yoghurt in a steady trickle and stir-fry for about 2–3 minutes, or until specks of oil start to appear on the surface. Now add the green chillies and stir-fry for about 5 minutes, or until the onions are mashed and the chicken is cooked through. Remove from the heat and adjust the seasoning, if necessary.

Murg Sheora-Natwara
Chieftain's Chicken

Origin Rajasthan
Preparation time 45 minutes
Cooking time 30 minutes
Serves 4

250ml / 8fl oz (1 cup) natural (plain) yoghurt, whisked
1 teaspoon ground coriander
125g / 4oz (½ cup) ghee
5 green cardamom pods
4 bay leaves
12 black peppercorns
150g / 5oz (1 medium) onion, chopped
1 clove garlic, chopped
1 × 2.5-cm / 1-inch piece fresh ginger, peeled and grated
1kg / 2¼lb chicken tikka breast, cut into 2.5-cm / 1-inch pieces
20g / ¾oz (½ cup) chopped coriander (cilantro) leaves
4 tablespoons chopped mint leaves
12 green chillies, de-seeded and chopped
½ teaspoon ground nutmeg
4 red chillies, de-seeded and cut into strips
about 150g / 5oz dough (optional), for sealing the lid (see page 783)
salt

Mix the yoghurt and ground coriander together in a large bowl and season with salt.

Heat the ghee in a large, heavy-based pan over medium heat, add the cardamom pods, bay leaves and peppercorns and stir-fry for about 1 minute, or until the cardamom pods start to change colour. Add the onions, garlic and ginger and stir-fry for about 2 minutes, or until the onion is translucent and glossy. Add the chicken, increase the heat to high and stir-fry for about 4 minutes.

Remove the pan from the heat, stir in the yoghurt mixture, then return to the heat, add the remaining ingredients except the dough, and pour in 250ml / 8fl oz (1 cup) water. Cover and seal the lid with dough, if using, or foil or a tight-fitting lid, then reduce the heat to low and cook, shaking the pan frequently, for a further 20 minutes. Remove from the heat, uncover, stir well and simmer for about 5 minutes, or until the sauce is thick and the chicken is cooked through. Remove from the heat and adjust the seasoning, if necessary.

✹ ✹

Handiwala Murg
Chicken Kebabs from the Pot

Origin Rajasthan
Preparation time 45 minutes, plus marinating time
Cooking time 30 minutes
Serves 4

12 skinless chicken thighs
6 tablespoons ghee, plus extra for shallow-frying
1 tablespoon ground coriander
1 teaspoon chilli powder
1 teaspoon ground turmeric
4 flakes garlic or ½ clove garlic, chopped
100g / 3½oz (1 small) onion, chopped
1 × 2.5-cm / 1-inch piece fresh ginger, peeled and chopped
4 green chillies, de-seeded and chopped
4 large tomatoes, chopped
400g / 14oz minced (ground) chicken
½ teaspoon ground green cardamom
½ teaspoon ground cloves
½ teaspoon ground cinnamon
1 tablespoon lemon juice
salt

For the marinade

2 tablespoons fresh coriander paste
3 teaspoons Ginger Paste (see page 57)
2 teaspoons Garlic Paste (see page 57)
1 teaspoon green chilli paste
2 tablespoons hung natural (plain) yoghurt (see page 793)
3 tablespoons lemon juice
1 teaspoon ground black pepper, roasted
½ teaspoon ground green cardamom
½ teaspoon ground cloves
½ teaspoon ground cinnamon

To garnish

2 hard-boiled eggs, quartered
4 tablespoons chopped coriander (cilantro) leaves

Carefully prise (pry) open the meat along the bone, pull the meat to the opposite end, ensuring that the bone does not get detached, then flatten with a meat mallet to make a 'lollypop'. Repeat with the remaining chicken thighs and place in a large shallow dish.

To make the marinade, mix all the ingredients together in a bowl and season with salt. Rub the marinade evenly over the lollypops, then cover and set aside in the refrigerator for 1 hour.

Heat enough ghee to cover a flat pan over very low heat. Add the marinated chicken, and shallow-fry for about 10–12 minutes, turning carefully once, until crisp and evenly golden. Remove from the pan and drain on kitchen paper (paper towels). Reserve the ghee.

Put the ground coriander, chilli powder and turmeric in a small bowl, add 3 tablespoons water and mix together.

Heat 6 tablespoons of the reserved ghee in a large heavy-based pan over medium heat, add the garlic and stir-fry for about 30 seconds, or until light golden. Add the onions and stir-fry for about 2 minutes, or until the onions are translucent and glossy. Add the ginger and green chillies and stir-fry for a few seconds, then add the ground spices mixture and stir-fry for about 1–2 minutes, or until the moisture has evaporated. Add the tomatoes and stir-fry for about 5 minutes, or until they become soft and release their juices. Now add the minced chicken and season with salt, then stir-fry for about 2 minutes. Add the chicken lollypops, stir carefully, then add the remaining ground spices and stir carefully. Cover and put a few hot charcoals on the lid for for 10 minutes. Alternatively, omit the charcoals and just cook for about 2 minutes, or until the chicken is cooked through.

Remove from the heat and keep the pan covered for a few minutes. Uncover, add the lemon juice, turn carefully with a spatula to incorporate, and adjust the seasoning, if necessary. Garnish with the quartered eggs and chopped coriander.

Murg ke Soole
Boneless Chicken on Skewers

Origin Rajasthan
Preparation time 30 minutes, plus marinating time
Cooking time 15–20 minutes
Serves 4

750g / 1lb 10oz boneless chicken thighs
250ml / 8fl oz (1 cup) hung natural (plain) yoghurt (see page 793), whisked
4 tablespoons Cashew Nut Paste (see page 58)
150ml / ¼ pint (⅔ cup) single (light) cream
2 tablespoons Fried Onion Paste (see page 57)
2 egg yolks
¼ teaspoon ground cinnamon
¼ teaspoon ground green cardamom
2 tablespoons chopped coriander (cilantro)
1 teaspoon chopped fresh ginger
1 teaspoon chopped green chilli
½ teaspoon black cumin seeds
1 tablespoon ginger
1 tablespoon Garlic Paste (see page 57)
2 teaspoons ground white pepper
1 teaspoon lemon juice
1 teaspoon malt (white) vinegar
1 tablespoon gram (chickpea) flour, roasted
2 teaspoons ghee (optional)
butter, for basting
salt

Put the chicken legs on a board and flatten with a meat mallet, then pat dry with a cloth and set aside.

To make the marinade, put the yoghurt in a large bowl and mix in all the ingredients, except the butter and ghee. Add the chicken pieces and turn to coat, then cover and set aside in the refrigerator for at least 3 hours.

Prepare a smoker or charcoal grill or alternatively preheat the oven to 200°C/400°F/Gas Mark 6.

If you would like to smoke the chicken, put the chicken and marinade in a heatproof pan, then place a small metal bowl with hot charcoals in the pan and pour some hot ghee over the charcoals. Cover immediately to allow the chicken to imbibe the smoky flavour. Alternatively, use a smoker or cook the chicken over a charcoal grill.

Thread the marinated chicken pieces through metal skewers. Keep a tray underneath to collect all the juices and roast over a charcoal grill or in the oven for about 10 minutes.

Remove the skewers from the heat and hang them up over a tray for about 5 minutes to allow any excess moisture to drain out completely. Put the skewers in a dish, baste with melted butter and roast again for about 5–10 minutes, or until the chicken is cooked through.

Trami Kokur
Saffron Chicken

Origin Jammu and Kashmir
Preparation time 20 minutes
Cooking time 45 minutes
Serves 4

3 tablespoons ghee
1 × 1-kg / 2¼-lb chicken, cut into 10–12 pieces
1 litre / 1¾ pints (4¼ cups) chicken stock
4 tablespoons Boiled Onion Paste (see page 57)
2 teaspoons ground fennel
10 cloves
2 teaspoons chilli powder
4 cinnamon sticks
5 teaspoons ground aniseed
large pinch of saffron threads
salt

Heat the ghee in a deep frying pan (skillet) over medium heat, add the chicken pieces and fry for about 5 minutes, or until light brown. Remove from the pan and set aside.

Put 2 tablespoons of the remaining ghee in a large, heavy-based pan, pour in the stock, add the chicken pieces, onion paste and the remaining ingredients, except the saffron, and bring to the boil, then reduce the heat to a simmer, put the saffron in a small bowl, add about 1 teaspoon water and soak until the water is a saffron colour, then stir to make a paste. Add the saffron to the pan and simmer for about 35 minutes, or until it is dry and the chicken is cooked through.

Murg ke Mokul
Mildly Spiced Chicken

Origin Rajasthan
Preparation time 30–45 minutes
Cooking time 50 minutes
Serves 4

2 teaspoons ground coriander
1 teaspoon chilli powder
1 teaspoon ground turmeric
5 tablespoons ghee
5 cloves
4 green cardamom pods
10 black peppercorns
2 bay leaves
2 blades mace
150g / 5oz (1 medium) onion, chopped
2½ tablespoons Garlic Paste (see page 57)
5 teaspoons Ginger Paste (see page 57)
150g / 5oz Boiled Onion Paste (see page 57)
2 tablespoons Cashew Nut Paste (see page 58)
750g / 1lb 10oz skinless, boneless chicken breasts, cut into 1-cm / ½-inch thick strips
2 tablespoons clotted cream or thick cream
250ml / 8fl oz (1 cup) natural (plain) yoghurt, whisked
salt

Put the ground coriander, chilli powder and turmeric in a small bowl, add 4 tablespoons water and mix together.

Heat the ghee in a large, heavy-based pan over medium heat, add the cloves, cardamom pods, peppercorns, bay leaves and mace and stir-fry for about 1 minute, or until the cardamom changes colour. Remove the whole spices, add the onions and sir-fry for about 2 minutes, or until translucent and glossy, then add the garlic and ginger pastes and stir-fry for about 2 minutes, or until the onions are light golden. Add the ground spice mixture and stir-fry for about 1–2 minutes, or until specks of oil start to appear on the surface. Add the boiled onion paste and stir-fry for about 1–2 minutes, or until the specks of oil start to reappear on the surface. Add the cashew nut paste and stir-fry for about 1–2 minutes, or until the specks of oil reappear, then add the chicken and cream and stir-fry for about 5 minutes. Pour in 500ml / 18fl oz (2¼ cups) water and bring to the boil.

Remove the pan from the heat and stir in the yoghurt, then return to the heat and bring almost to the boil.

Reduce the heat to low, cover and simmer, stirring occasionally, for about 30 minutes, or until the chicken is cooked through and the sauce is a thin sauce consistency. Remove from the heat and adjust the seasoning, if necessary.

Trami Kokur Safed
Chicken in White Sauce

Origin Jammu and Kashmir
Preparation time 20 minutes
Cooking time 35 minutes
Serves 4

3 tablespoons ghee or vegetable oil, plus extra for deep-frying
1 × 1-kg / 2¼-lb chicken, cut into 10–12 pieces
1 litre / 1¾ pints (4¼ cups) milk
5 teaspoons ground fennel
2 teaspoons ground ginger
10 cloves
5 cinnamon sticks
salt

Heat enough ghee or oil for deep-frying in a kadhai or deep, heavy-based pan to 180°C/350°F, or until a cube of bread browns in 30 seconds. Add the chicken pieces to the hot oil and deep-fry for about 3–4 minutes, or until light brown. Remove with a slotted spoon and drain on kitchen paper (paper towels).

Put the milk in a large, heavy-based pan and dilute it with 250ml / 8fl oz (1 cup) water, then add the fennel and ginger. Add all the remaining ingredients, season with salt and bring to the boil. Boil for 3–4 minutes, then add the chicken and simmer for about 30–35 minutes, or until dry and the chicken is cooked through.

Chandi Qorma
Sterling Chicken

Origin Awadh
Preparation time 1 hour, plus cooling time
Cooking time 45 minutes
Serves 4

125g / 4oz (½ cup) ghee
2 bay leaves
6–8 green cardamom pods
50g / 1¾oz (⅓ cup) blanched almonds
50g / 1¾oz (⅓ cup) cashew nuts, ground to a paste
250g / 9oz (2 medium) onions, chopped
2½ teaspoons Garlic Paste (see page 57)
2½ teaspoons Ginger Paste (see page 57)
1½ tablespoons Char Magaz (see page 780)
1 teaspoon poppy seeds, ground to a paste
4 green chillies, de-seeded and chopped
½ teaspoon rose petals, ground
1 tablespoon ghee
2–3 cloves
2 green chillies, slit in half lengthways and de-seeded
1kg / 2¼lb skinless, boneless chicken pieces, cut into cubes
250ml / 8fl oz (1 cup) hung natural (plain) yoghurt (see page 793), whisked
1¼ teaspoons ground nutmeg
4 tablespoons single (light) cream
salt

Heat the ghee in a large, heavy-based pan over medium heat, add the cardamom and bay leaves and stir-fry for about 1 minute, or until they change colour. Add the almonds and cashew nut paste and stir-fry for about 5 minutes, but do not let them brown. Add the onions and stir-fry for about 2 minutes, or until translucent. Add the garlic and ginger pastes and stir fry for about 1 minute, then add the char magaz paste, poppy seed paste, chopped green chillies and stir-fry for a further 3–4 minutes.

Pour in 250ml / 8fl oz (1 cup) hot water and the ground rose petals and continue to cook for about 10 minutes. Remove from the heat, discard the bay leaf and allow to cool.

Heat the 1 tablespoon ghee in another large, heavy-based pan, add the cloves, remaining garlic and ginger pastes and the slit green chillies and stir-fry for about 2 minutes, then add the chicken and let the chicken cook in its juices until almost dry. Remove from the heat and stir in the whisked yoghurt slowly to ensure that it does not curdle. Add the cooled spice paste mixture with the ground nutmeg and season with salt. Stir well and add 250ml / 8fl oz (1 cup) hot water. Cook over low heat for about 30 minutes, or until the chicken is cooked through. Gently stir in the cream gently and remove from heat after 1 minute.

Thokan
Chicken Curry (I)

Origin Tribal North East India
Preparation time 30 minutes
Cooking time 45 minutes
Serves 4

1 × 900-g / 2-lb chicken, cut into bite-sized pieces
2 tablespoons mustard oil
3 green chillies, de-seeded and chopped
3 onions, chopped
3 tomatoes, chopped
1 teaspoon dried mint, ground
1 tablespoon chopped garlic
salt
1 tablespoon chopped coriander (cilantro) leaves, to garnish

Put the chicken in a large, heavy-based pan over low heat, sprinkle over the oil and mix well. Increase the heat to medium and continue cooking, stirring frequently until the moisture has evaporated. Now add the remaining ingredients, except the garlic and coriander, and stir-fry for a further 5 minutes. Add the garlic and pour in 750ml / 1¼ pints (3¼ cups) water and bring to the boil. Reduce the heat and simmer for about 30 minutes, or until the chicken is cooked through and the sauce is thick. Garnish with chopped coriander.

Butter Chicken
Butter Chicken

Origin Punjab
Preparation time 30 minutes, plus marinating time
Cooking time 30 minutes
Serves 4

1 × 1-kg / 2¼-lb chicken, cut into pieces
6 tablespoons vegetable oil
salt

For the marinade

1 tablespoon Garlic Paste (see page 57)
1 tablespoon Ginger Paste (see page 57)
2 tablespoons Kashmiri red chilli powder
2 teaspoons ground coriander
1½ teaspoons ground cumin
½ teaspoon ground turmeric
1½ teaspoons Garam Masala (see page 31)
2 tablespoons lime juice
500ml / 18fl oz (2¼ cups) natural (plain) yoghurt, whisked

For the sauce

125g / 4¼oz (8 tablespoons/1 stick) chilled butter
750g / 1lb 10oz (6 medium) tomatoes, pureed
1 teaspoon chilli powder
2 teaspoons dried fenugreek leaves, crushed
½ teaspoon Garam Masala (see page 31)
3 tablespoons single (light) cream

To make the marinade, mix the garlic and ginger pastes, ground spices and lime juice together in a bowl and season with salt, then add the yoghurt and mix together. Put the chicken in a large shallow dish, pour over the marinade, then cover and put in the refrigerator for 2–3 hours, preferably overnight.

Heat the oil in a large, heavy-based pan over low heat, add the chicken and marinade, cover and cook, stirring occasionally, for 25 minutes, or until cooked.

For the sauce, melt 1 tablespoon butter in a frying pan (skillet), add the tomato and cook for 5 minutes until the moisture has evaporated. Add the rest of the butter, allow it to melt, then add the chilli powder and cook for 1 minute. Sprinkle over the crushed fenugreek leaves and garam masala, then season with salt. Stir in the cream just before serving.

Chicken Ishtoo
Indian-Style Chicken Stew

Origin Delhi
Preparation time 20–30 minutes
Cooking time 45 minutes
Serves 4

2 tablespoons vegetable oil
4 bay leaves
2 cinnamon sticks, about 2.5cm / 1 inch long
8 green cardamom pods
4 cloves
300g / 11oz (2 medium) onions, sliced
1 × 2.5-cm / 1-inch piece fresh ginger, peeled and chopped
8 green chillies, de-seeded and chopped
2½ teaspoons Ginger Paste (see page 57)
2½ teaspoons Garlic Paste (see page 57)
1 × 1-kg / 2¼-lb chicken, cut into pieces
½ teaspoon ground green cardamom
salt

Heat the oil in a large, heavy-based pan over medium heat, add the bay leaves, cinnamon, cardamom pods and cloves and stir-fry for about 1 minute, or until the cardamom starts to change colour.

Add the onions and stir-fry for about 2 minutes, or until translucent and glossy. Season with salt, then add the ginger and green chillies and stir-fry for a further 2 minutes. Add the ginger and garlic pastes, stirring constantly, otherwise the mixture may stick to the pan. Add the chicken and a little water and bring to the boil. Reduce the heat to low, cover and simmer, stirring occasionally, for about 30 minutes, or until the chicken is cooked through. Add the ground cardamom, then cover and simmer for about 3 minutes.

Murg Mumtaz
Celebratory Chicken Korma

Origin Delhi
Preparation time 1¼ hour, plus marinating and soaking time
Cooking time 45 minutes
Serves 4

375ml / 13fl oz (1½ cups) natural (plain) yoghurt, whisked

1 × 1-kg / 2¼-lb chicken, cut into pieces

⅓ teaspoon ground turmeric

2 teaspoons chilli powder

180g / 6oz (¾ cup) ghee

200g / 7oz (2 small) onions, sliced

1 tablespoon chopped ginger

4 green chillies, de-seeded and chopped

125ml / 4½fl oz (½ cup) single (light) cream

½ teaspoon ground mace

½ teaspoon ground green cardamom

salt

For the whole garam masala

5 green cardamom pods

1 black cardamom pod

5 cloves

1 cinnamon stick, about 2.5cm / 1 inch long

1 bay leaf

pinch of ground mace

For the spice paste

2 tablespoons poppy seeds

4 tablespoons blanched almonds

1–1.2kg / 2¼–2 ½lb cashew nuts

2 tablespoons melon seeds

To garnish

15 pistachio nuts, blanched

10 blanched almonds

10 cashew nuts

10 walnut halves

10 pine nuts

1 tablespoon raisins

1 tablespoon melon seeds

1 tablespoon sunflower seeds

To make a marinade, mix the yoghurt and a little salt together in a large bowl or shallow dish. Add the chicken and turn to coat, then cover and set aside in the refrigerator for at least 30 minutes.

To make the spice paste, soak the poppy seeds in a small bowl of water for 30 minutes, then drain.

Put the almonds, poppy seeds, cashew nuts, melon seeds and 125ml / 4½fl oz (½ cup) water in a blender or food processor and process to make a smooth paste. Set aside.

For the garnish, soak all the ingredients in a bowl of lukewarm water for 15 minutes, then drain.

Put the turmeric and chilli powder in a small bowl, add 2 tablespoons water and mix together.

Heat the ghee in a large, heavy-based pan over medium heat, add the ingredients for the whole garam masala and stir-fry for about 1 minute, or until it starts to splutter. Add the onions and stir-fry for about 5–7 minutes, or until golden brown. Add the ginger and chillies and stir-fry for 1 minute, then add the turmeric mixture and stir-fry for 2 minutes. Add the marinated chicken together with the marinade, then add 6 tablespoons water and bring to the boil. Reduce the heat, cover and simmer for about 25 minutes, or until the chicken is cooked through.

Now add the spice paste and bring to the boil. Reduce the heat and simmer for about 1–2 minutes, or until the oil rises to the surface. Add the cream and stir, then sprinkle over the ground mace and cardamom and half the garnish and stir again. Adjust the seasoning, if necessary, and add the remaining garnish.

Murg Shahjehani
Imperial Chicken

Origin Delhi
Preparation time 1 hour, plus marinating and cooling time
Cooking time 40 minutes
Serves 5

---

2 tablespoons vegetable oil

4 onions, sliced

5 cloves garlic, crushed

1 × 5-cm / 2-inch piece fresh ginger, coarsely chopped

8 cloves

1 teaspoon black peppercorns

2 cinnamon sticks

7 green cardamom pods

1 teaspoon poppy seeds

2 teaspoons cumin seeds

2 teaspoons coriander seeds

1 teaspoon chilli powder

250ml / 8fl oz (1 cup) natural (plain) yoghurt

1 × 1-kg / 2¼-lb chicken, cut into pieces

1 tablespoon rosewater

salt

Heat the oil in a large, heavy-based pan over medium heat, add the onions and stir-fry for about 5–7 minutes, or until golden brown. Remove from the heat, allow to cool slightly, then place in a blender or food processor and process, adding a little water if necessary, to make a paste. Set aside.

Put the garlic and ginger into a small blender and process, adding a little water if necessary, to make a paste. Set aside.

Lightly stir-fry the cloves, black peppercorns, cinnamon, cardamom pods, poppy seeds, cumin seeds, coriander seeds and chilli powder on a tawa or in a dry frying pan (skillet) for about 1 minute, or until roasted, then transfer to a blender. Add the yoghurt, season with salt and process to make a paste. Transfer to a large bowl or shallow dish and add the chicken pieces. Mix together until the chicken is coated, then cover and set aside in the refrigerator for about 45 minutes.

Put the onion paste in a large, heavy-based pan, add the chicken pieces and cook over low heat for about 40 minutes, or until the chicken is cooked through. Just before the end of cooking, add the rosewater.

Murg Qorma (I)
Mughlia Chicken in Rich Sauce

Origin Awadh
Preparation time 20 minutes
Cooking time 45 minutes
Serves 4

---

pinch of saffron threads

1 teaspoon milk

3 tablespoons vegetable oil

4 onions, chopped

750g / 1lb 10oz skinless, boneless chicken pieces

salt

For the spice paste

1 × 2.5-cm / 1-inch piece ginger, peeled and grated

2 cloves

1 cinnamon stick

4–5 dried red chillies

2 cardamom pods

1 teaspoon cumin seeds

Put the saffron in a small bowl, add the milk and soak until required.

To make the spice paste, put the ginger, cloves, cinnamon, dried red chillies, cardamom pods and cumin seeds in a blender and process, adding a little water if necessary, to a paste. Set aside.

Heat the oil in a large, heavy-based pan over medium heat, add the onions and fry for about 8–10 minutes, or until light brown. Reduce the heat to low and add the spice paste. Fry for about 2–3 minutes. Add the chicken pieces and fry for about 5 minutes, or until the chicken is well coated with the spices.

Pour in about 750ml / 1¼ pints (3¼ cups) hot water and bring to the boil, then reduce the heat and simmer for about 30 minutes, or until the chicken is cooked through. Sprinkle over the soaked saffron, adjust the seasoning, if necessary, then cover and cook over very low heat for about 2–3 minutes.

Murg Musallam
Whole Stuffed & Baked Chicken

Origin Awadh
Preparation time 50 minutes, plus soaking and marinating time
Cooking time 1½ hours
Serves 4

50g / 1¾oz (¼ cup) basmati rice, rinsed and drained

250ml / 8fl oz (1 cup) natural (plain) yoghurt, whisked

1 × 1-kg / 2¼-lb chicken, dressed (see page 780)

250g / 9oz (1 cup) ghee or vegetable oil

chilli powder to taste

pinch of asafoetida

2 tablespoons almonds

3 tablespoons raisins

15g / ½oz chironji kernels

100g / 3½oz Khoya (see page 58) or 100g / 3½oz (⅔ cup) milk powder (dry milk)

salt

For the masala

1 teaspoon ground fennel

1 × 5-cm / 2-inch piece fresh ginger, peeled

8 peppercorns

6 cloves garlic

3 onions, sliced

2 teaspoons Garam Masala (see page 31)

1 teaspoon sugar

1 teaspoon poppy seeds

Soak the rice in a bowl of water for 1 hour, then drain.

To make the masala, put all the ingredients in a spice grinder and process until ground. Transfer to a large bowl and add a little yoghurt. Put the chicken in a large shallow dish and prick it all over with a fork. Spread the remaining yoghurt and the ground masala over the chicken, then cover and set aside in the refrigerator for about 2 hours.

Prepare a charcoal grill or preheat the oven to 200°C/400°F/Gas Mark 6.

Heat 4 tablespoons ghee or oil in a large, heavy-based pan over medium heat, add the drained rice and stir-fry for about 4 minutes. Season with salt, then add the chilli powder, almonds, asafoetida, raisins, chironji kernels and khoya. Pour in 250ml / 8fl oz (1 cup) water and cook for about 12 minutes.

Stuff the chicken with this mixture and tie securely with kitchen string (twine) to prevent the ingredients from spilling out. Place the chicken in a degchi or large casserole with the remaining ghee and 125ml / 4½fl oz (½ cup) water and cook over a charcoal fire, covering the lid with hot charcoals, until the water is absorbed and the meat is cooked through. Alternatively, cook the chicken in a 180°C/350°F/Gas Mark 4 oven for about 1½ hours, or until the chicken is cooked through and the water is absorbed.

Cha Sha
Chicken

Origin Tribal North East India
Preparation time 20 minutes
Cooking time 45 minutes–1 hour
Serves 6

2 tablespoons vegetable oil

1 × 1-kg / 2¼-lb chicken, cut into pieces

2 onions, chopped

3 teaspoons chopped ginger

3 teaspoons chopped garlic

½ teaspoon ground turmeric

salt

1 teaspoon chilli powder, to garnish

Heat the oil in a large, heavy-based pan over low heat, add the chicken and cook for about 15 minutes. Add the onions, ginger, garlic and turmeric and season with salt. Stir-fry for about 2 minutes, then add water to cover and simmer for about 30–45 minutes, or until the meat is soft. Add the chilli powder.

Murg Qorma (II)
Spicy Chicken Drumsticks

Origin Jammu and Kashmir
Preparation time 1 hour, plus marinating time
Cooking time 30 minutes
Serves 4

12 chicken drumsticks
250ml / 8fl oz (1 cup) hung natural (plain) yoghurt (see page 793)
4 tablespoons Fried Onion Paste (see page 57)
2 tablespoons fried Garlic Paste (see page 57)
½ teaspoon chilli powder
6 tablespoons single (light) cream
about 150g / 5oz dough (optional), for sealing the lid (see page 783)

For the marinade

3 teaspoons Garlic Paste (see page 57)
3 teaspoons Ginger Paste (see page 57)
2 tablespoons white vinegar
salt

For the paste

3½ tablespoons almonds
3½ tablespoons poppy seeds

For the masala

2 teaspoons coriander seeds
3 green cardamom pods
2 cloves
1 cinnamon stick, about 2.5cm / 1 inch long
18 black peppercorns
4 blades mace
⅛ nutmeg
12 dried rose petals

To make the marinade, mix all the ingredients together in a large bowl. Put the chicken drumsticks in a large shallow dish and rub the marinade evenly over, then cover and set aside in the refrigerator for about 30 minutes.

To make the paste, put the almonds and poppy seeds in a blender and process, adding a little water to make a paste.

To make the masala, mix all the ingredients together and process in a spice grinder until ground.

Mix the yoghurt, the fried onion and garlic pastes, the almond and poppy seed paste, four-fifths of the masala and the chilli powder together in a bowl, and season with salt. Hold the chicken drumsticks up to drain the excess marinade, then rub them with this paste and arrange in a large pan with a gap between each drumstick. Pour on the excess paste, then evenly spread the cream on top.

Cook over medium heat for 5 minutes, then stir for a minute, cover and seal the lid with dough, if using, or foil, then put in the oven, place a couple of hot charcoals on top of the lid and cook for 15 minutes. Alternatively, just cover the pan with a tight-fitting lid and cook in a moderate oven for about 30 minutes, or until the drumsticks are cooked.

Remove from the oven, break the seal, then remove the drumsticks and set aside. Return the sauce to the heat and bring to the boil, then reduce the heat to low and simmer, stirring occasionally, until it thickens. Sprinkle over the remaining masala and stir. Remove from the heat and adjust the seasoning, if necessary.

Shahi Qorma
Prince-like Chicken Curry

Origin Awadh
Preparation time 30 minutes
Cooking time 1 hour
Serves 4

pinch of saffron threads
1 tablespoon warm milk
150g / 5oz (⅔ cup) ghee
10 green cardamom pods
5 cloves
2 cinnamon sticks, about 2.5cm / 1 inch long
2 bay leaves
150g / 5oz (1 medium) onion, chopped
3 tablespoons Ginger Paste (see page 57)
3 tablespoons Garlic Paste (see page 57)
2 teaspoons ground coriander
1 teaspoon chilli powder
1 × 1-kg / 2¼-lb chicken, in 2.5-cm / 1-inch pieces
salt
250ml / 8fl oz (1 cup) hung natural (plain) yoghurt (see page 793)
1 teaspoon Garam Masala (see page 31)
1 teaspoon ground mace
1 teaspoon ground cardamom
1 teaspoon ground white pepper
2 drops kewra water or rosewater

To garnish

20 blanched almonds, cut into slivers
edible silver leaf

Put the saffron in a small bowl, add the warm milk and soak until required.

Heat the ghee in a large, heavy-based pan over medium heat, add the cardamom pods, cloves, cinnamon and bay leaves and stir-fry for about 1 minute, or until they start to splutter. Add the onions and stir-fry for about 5–7 minutes, or until golden brown. Add the ginger and garlic pastes and stir-fry for a further 3 minutes. Add the coriander and chilli powder, then season, stir and add the chicken pieces. Stir-fry for about 5 minutes, then add the yoghurt and bring almost to the boil. Pour in 750ml / 1¼ pints (3¼ cups) water, cover and simmer for 30 minutes, or until cooked. Add the spices and simmer for 10 minutes. Adjust the seasoning, then add the kewra water and soaked saffron and stir. Garnish with almonds and silver leaf.

Chilli Chicken
Chilli Chicken

Origin New
Preparation time 30 minutes, plus marinating time
Cooking time 20 minutes
Serves 4

750g / 1lb 10oz skinless, boneless chicken pieces, cut into cubes
3 tablespoons vegetable oil
200g / 7oz (3⅔ cups) chopped spring onion (scallion)
75g / 2½oz (½ cup) green chillies, de-seeded and chopped
1 tablespoon crushed garlic
1 teaspoon mushroom soy sauce
1 tablespoon bottled chilli pepper paste
5 tablespoons coriander (cilantro) leaves, chopped

For the marinade

1 tablespoon crushed garlic
2 tablespoons mushroom soy sauce
2 teaspoons Chinese rice wine
2 tablespoons black bean and garlic paste

To make the marinade, mix all the ingredients together in a large shallow dish or bowl, add the chicken and turn to coat well. Cover and set aside in the refrigerator overnight. Before cooking, drain and roll the chicken in cornstarch.

Heat 2 tablespoons oil in a heavy-based non-stick wok over medium heat. Add the chicken and shallow-fry for about 10 minutes, or until golden brown and chicken. Remove from the wok and set aside.

Heat the remaining oil in a heavy-based pan over medium heat, add the spring onions, chillies and garlic and stir-fry for 2 minutes. Add the chicken, soy sauce and chilli pepper paste and stir well to coat. Cover and cook for 5 minutes.

Add the chopped coriander, stir thoroughly and remove from the heat.

Khatta Murg
Sour Chicken

Origin Hyderabad
Preparation time 1 hour, plus marinating time
Cooking time 30 minutes
Serves 4

8 large skinless boneless chicken breasts
180ml / 6½fl oz (⅔ cup) hung natural (plain) yoghurt (see page 793)
6 tablespoons single (light) cream
2 tablespoons almond paste
2½ teaspoons green chilli paste
1 teaspoon ground white pepper
1 teaspoon ground green cardamom
1½ tablespoons unsalted butter
1 tablespoon lemon juice
salt

For the marinade
5 teaspoons Garlic Paste (see page 57)
3 teaspoons Ginger Paste (see page 57)
1 tablespoon lemon juice
salt

For the filling
150g / 5oz (2¾ cups) spring onions (scallions), cut into rounds
1 × 2.5-cm / 1-inch piece fresh ginger, peeled and grated
4 green chillies, de-seeded and finely chopped
16–18 mint leaves
1 teaspoon black cumin seeds

Make a deep slit with a sharp knife along the thick edge of each chicken breast to make a pocket, taking care not to penetrate the flesh on the other side. Put the chicken in a large shallow dish.

To make the marinade, mix all the ingredients together in a bowl. Rub the chicken evenly with this mixture, then cover and set aside in the refrigerator for 20 minutes.

To make the filling, mix all the ingredients together in a bowl and divide into 8 equal portions. Stuff a portion into each 'pocket' of the marinated chicken and then seal each with the tip of a knife, ensuring that the flesh is not pierced.

Put the yoghurt in a large bowl, add half the cream and the remaining ingredients, except the lemon juice and butter, and whisk to mix well. Coat the stuffed chicken with this mixture and reserve the excess mixture.

Arrange the breasts, together with the marinade in a large, non-stick frying pan (skillet), pour on the reserved yoghurt mixture and then place little knobs (pats) of butter on top. Cover with foil and cook over medium heat for about 20–25 minutes. Remove the chicken breasts and set aside. Pass the sauce through a fine sieve (strainer) into a separate pan. Return the sauce to the heat, add the remaining cream and bring to just under the boil over medium heat, stirring constantly, until it is a sauce consistency. Stir in the lemon juice and adjust the seasoning, if necessary.

Kali Mirch ka Murg
Pepper Chicken in Thick Sauce

Origin Punjab
Preparation time 30 minutes, plus marinating time
Cooking time 45 minutes
Serves 4

1 teaspoon Garlic Paste (see page 57)
2 teaspoons Ginger Paste (see page 57)
1 tablespoon lemon juice
1 × 1-kg / 2¼-lb chicken, cut into pieces and skinned
125ml / 4½fl oz (½ cup) vegetable oil
100g / 3½oz (1 small) onion, sliced
100g / 3½oz (1 small) onion, ground to a paste
2 tablespoons black peppercorns
salt

To make the marinade, mix the garlic and ginger pastes and lemon juice together in a bowl and season with salt. Put the chicken pieces in a large shallow dish and rub the mixture all over, then cover and set aside in the refrigerator for about 2 hours.

Heat the oil in a large, heavy-based pan over medium heat, add the sliced onion and stir-fry for 2 minutes, or until translucent. Add the onion paste and peppercorns and stir-fry for about 1–2 minutes, or until light brown. Add the marinated chicken and fry for about 10 minutes, or until the moisture has evaporated. Pour in 125ml / 4½fl oz (½ cup) water and bring to the boil, then reduce the heat to low and simmer for about 10 minutes. Uncover, increase the heat and cook for about 20 minutes, or until the oil rises to the surface and the chicken is cooked.

Kairi Murg
Mango Chicken

Origin Hyderabad
Preparation time 30 minutes
Cooking time 50 minutes
Serves 4

4 tablespoons vegetable oil
1 × 750-g / 1lb 10-oz chicken, cut into 8–10 pieces
2 green chillies, de-seeded and chopped
⅓ teaspoon ground turmeric
1 teaspoon chilli powder
3 onions, sliced
1 teaspoon Ginger Paste (see page 57)
½ teaspoon Garlic Paste (see page 57)
2 raw mangoes, stoned (pitted) and cut into small pieces
few sprigs coriander (cilantro), chopped
salt

Heat about 2 tablespoons of oil in a large, heavy-based pan over medium heat, add the chicken pieces and stir-fry for about 8–10 minutes, or until they are evenly browned all over. Now add the chillies and turmeric with 250ml / 8fl oz (1 cup) water and bring to the boil. Reduce the heat and simmer for about 20 minutes, stirring occasionally.

Put the chilli powder in a small bowl, add 1 tablespoon water and mix together.

Heat the remaining oil in another pan over medium heat, add the onions and stir-fry for about 4 minutes, or until light brown. Add the ginger and garlic pastes and chilli powder mixture and season with salt, then fry for a further 2 minutes. Reduce the heat to low, cover and cook for 3 minutes to let the spices blend well.

Add the chicken and the raw mango and cook over low heat for about 10 minutes, then remove from the heat and adjust the seasoning, if necessary.

Caril de Galinha
Goan Chicken Curry

Origin Coastal
Preparation time 45 minutes
Cooking time 30 minutes
Serves 6–8

1 × 1-kg / 2¼-lb chicken, cut into pieces
2 tablespoons vegetable oil
100g / 3½oz (1 small) onion, sliced
250ml / 8fl oz (1 cup) coconut milk, fresh (see page 781) or canned
1 tablespoon Tamarind Extract (see page 58)
125ml / 4½fl oz (½ cup) coconut cream, fresh (see page 781) or canned
salt

For the spice paste
1 coconut, grated
1 tablespoon uncooked rice, rinsed and drained
8 cloves garlic, crushed
1 × 2.5-cm / 1-inch piece fresh ginger, peeled
10 dried Kashmiri red chillies
4 green chillies, slit in half lengthways and de-seeded
½ tablespoon cumin seeds
1 teaspoons coriander seeds
1 tablespoon poppy seeds
1 tablespoon ground turmeric

Put the chicken pieces in a large shallow dish and sprinkle over a little salt.

To make the spice paste, put half the grated coconut and the rice in a food processor or blender and process, adding a little water, to make a coarse paste. Set aside. Put the remaining grated coconut in the food processor or blender with the garlic, ginger, dried red chillies, green chillies and the spices and process until ground, then mix into the coarse paste.

Heat the oil in a large, heavy-based pan over medium heat, add the onion and cook for 4 minutes, or until light brown. Add the spice paste and stir-fry, stirring constantly, for 1–2 minutes, or until the oil separates out. Add the chicken and stir to coat. Add the coconut milk and season. Reduce the heat and simmer for 20 minutes, or until almost done.

Add the tamarind extract and stir in the coconut cream, then cook for 5–10 minutes until the chicken is cooked through.

✺ ✺ ✺
___

Kondapur Koli Thalna
Chicken Legs in Chilli Sauce

Origin Coastal
Preparation time 1 hour, plus marinating time
Cooking time 35 minutes
Serves 4

4 chicken legs
2 tablespoons lemon juice
ghee, for shallow-frying
salt

For the coondapur masala

125g / 4¼oz dried red chillies
60g / 2oz (¾ cup) coriander seeds
2½ teaspoons black peppercorns
1½ teaspoons fenugreek seeds
12 flakes garlic or 2 cloves garlic, chopped
1 teaspoon ground turmeric

For the sauce

3½ tablespoons ghee
6 flakes garlic or 1 clove garlic, chopped (unpeeled)
160g / 5½oz (1 medium) onion, chopped
½ coconut, grated and ground to a paste (see page 781)
375ml / 13fl oz (1½ cups) coconut milk, fresh (see page 781) or canned
4 tablespoons coconut cream, fresh (see page 781) or canned
salt

Halve the chickens legs lengthways and bone carefully, leaving the ankle knob intact, then place the halves between dry towels and flatten with a heavy steak hammer or rolling pin.

To make the masala, roast the red chillies and coriander seeds on a griddle or in a dry frying pan (skillet) over very low heat for 3–4 minutes. Remove and set aside. Roast the peppercorns for about 1 minute, or until they begin to puff up. Roast the fenugreek seeds for about 30 seconds, or until they begin to change colour. Put these in a spice grinder with the garlic and process until ground to a coarse powder. Transfer to a bowl and add the turmeric, then mix well and set aside.

To make a marinade, put 1 tablespoon of the masala in a bowl, add the lemon juice and a pinch of salt, then rub the mixture evenly over the chicken legs. Cover and set aside in the refrigerator for about 30 minutes.

To make the sauce, heat the ghee in a large, heavy-based pan over medium heat, add the garlic and stir-fry for about 30 seconds, or until it starts to change colour. Add the onion and stir-fry for 2 minutes, or until translucent and glossy. Add 2 tablespoons of the masala, stir, then add the coconut paste and the coconut milk. Bring to the boil, then reduce the heat to low, cover and simmer, stirring occasionally, until reduced by half.

Remove the pan from the heat, stir in the coconut cream and season with salt, then bring to just under the boil, ensuring that it does not boil or the coconut milk will curdle. Reduce the heat to low and simmer until the sauce is medium thick. Remove from the heat and adjust the seasoning, if necessary.

Heat half the ghee for shallow-frying in a frying pan over very low heat. Arrange the marinated chicken legs in it, 2 at a time, cover and cook, turning frequently, for 10–15 minutes, or until cooked. Remove with a slotted spoon and drain on kitchen paper (paper towels). Serve the chicken on a bed of sauce.

❋ ❋ / 📷 p.392

Chicken Xacuti
Spicy Chicken in Thick Sauce

Origin Goa
Preparation time 40 minutes, plus soaking time
Cooking time 30–40 minutes
Serves 6

125ml / 4½fl oz (½ cup) vegetable oil or ghee
120g / 4oz (1 small) onion, sliced
2½ teaspoons Garlic Paste (see page 57)
2 ½ teaspoons Ginger Paste (see page 57)
1 × 1-kg / 2¼-lb chicken, cut into 8–10 pieces
125ml / 4½fl oz (½ cup) lemon juice
salt

For the spice paste

10 dried red chillies
1 tablespoon ground coriander
1½ teaspoons cumin seeds
1½ teaspoons fenugreek seeds
10 black peppercorns
3 teaspoons poppy seeds
40g /1½oz (½ cup) grated fresh coconut
1 teaspoon ground turmeric
½ teaspoon ground green cardamom
½ teaspoon ground cloves
½ teaspoon ground cinnamon

To make the spice paste, soak the dried red chillies in a bowl of hot water for about 10 minutes, then drain.

Stir-fry all the ingredients separately, including the dried chillies, on a tawa or in a dry frying pan (skillet) for about 1 minute, or until roasted, then transfer to a blender and process, adding a little water if necessary, to make a paste. Set aside.

Heat the oil or ghee in a large, heavy-based pan over medium heat, add the onion and stir-fry for 5–7 minutes, or until golden brown. Add the spice paste with the garlic and ginger pastes and stir-fry for about 1–2 minutes, or until the oil separates out and rises to the surface.

Add the chicken pieces to the pan and season with salt. Stir to mix well and cook until the moisture has evaporated. Pour in 250ml / 8fl oz (1 cup) water, bring to the boil then reduce the heat to low, cover and simmer for about 25 minutes, or until the chicken is cooked through. Sprinkle over the lemon juice and stir well.

❋ ❋ ❋

Mangalorean Chicken Curry
Chicken Curry from Mangalore

Origin Coastal
Preparation time 30 minutes
Cooking time 40–45 minutes
Serves 4–5

125ml / 4½fl oz (½ cup) vegetable oil
1 onion, chopped
1 × 1-kg / 2¼-lb chicken, cut into pieces
250ml / 8fl oz (1 cup) coconut milk, fresh (see page 781) or canned
salt

For the spice paste

1 fresh coconut, grated and roasted
4 teaspoons coriander seeds, roasted
1 teaspoon fenugreek seeds, roasted
18–20 dried Kashmiri red chillies, roasted
1 teaspoon ground turmeric
6 cloves garlic, roasted

To make the spice paste, put all the ingredients in a food processor or blender and process, adding a little water to make a paste. Set aside.

Heat the oil in a large, heavy-based pan over medium heat, add the onions and stir-fry for 3–4 minutes, or until light brown. Add the chicken, reduce the heat and continue to cook for about 15 minutes. Add the spice paste, half of the coconut milk and season with salt, then stir and cook for about 15–20 minutes, or until the chicken is cooked through.

Now slowly stir in the remaining coconut milk and cook for a further 2 minutes.

✿ ✿

Chicken Chettinad
Chicken Chettinad (Dry)

Origin Tamil Nadu
Preparation time 45 minutes, plus marinating time
Cooking time 15–30 minutes
Serves 4

750g / 1lb 10oz boneless chicken legs, each cut
    into 4 pieces

butter, for basting

salt

For the coconut spice paste

1 tablespoon coconut oil

1 teaspoon mustard seeds

1 teaspoon chopped garlic

1 teaspoon chopped ginger

1 teaspoon coriander seeds

3–4 black cardamom pods

1 teaspoon cumin

2 green cardamom pods

10 cloves

10–12 curry leaves

2–3 whole red chillies

1 teaspoon ground coconut

For the marinade

pinch of ground turmeric

2 tablespoon Tamarind Extract (see page 58)

4 tablespoons coconut oil

2 tablespoons coconut milk, fresh (see page 781)
    or canned

½ tablespoon Ginger Paste (see page 57)

½ tablespoon Garlic Paste (see page 57)

1 teaspoon lemon juice

To make the coconut spice paste, heat the coconut oil in a large, heavy-based pan, add all the ingredients and fry for a few minutes until cooked. Allow to cool, then transfer to a blender and process, adding a little water if necessary, to make a smooth paste.

To make the marinade, blend the coconut spice paste with the turmeric, tamarind extract, coconut oil and milk in a bowl. Add the ginger and garlic pastes and lemon juice and season with salt. Put the chicken pieces in a large shallow dish and rub the mixture evenly over the chicken, then cover and set aside in the refrigerator for 1 hour.

Prepare a charcoal grill for moderate heat or preheat the oven 190°C/375°F/Gas Mark 5. Roast the chicken over a charcoal grill for about 15 minutes, or until cooked. Alternatively, roast the chicken in the oven for about 30 minutes, or until cooked through. Baste with butter several times during cooking.

✿ ✿

Gongura Chicken
Sorrel-flavoured Chicken

Origin Hyderabad
Preparation time 30 minutes, plus cooling time
Cooking time 1 hour
Serves 4

125ml / 4½fl oz (½ cup) vegetable oil

4 onions, chopped

1 teaspoon Ginger Paste (see page 57)

1 teaspoon Garlic Paste (see page 57)

1 × 750-g / 1lb 10-oz chicken, cut into pieces

pinch of salt

225–250g / 8–9oz (8–9 cups) gongura (sorrel)
    leaves, chopped

4–8 green chillies, de-seeded and chopped

1 teaspoon ground coriander

1 teaspoon ground cumin

1 teaspoon Garam Masala (see page 31)

1 teaspoon red chilli powder

1 teaspoon poppy seeds, roasted and ground to
    a paste

Heat the oil in a large, heavy-based pan over medium heat, add the onions and stir-fry for about 6–8 minutes, or until golden brown. Add the ginger and garlic pastes and continue frying for about 1–2 minutes, or until golden brown. Add the chicken pieces and the salt. Reduce the heat, cover and cook for about 40 minutes, or until the chicken is cooked through.

Meanwhile, bring two pans of water to the boil, add the gongura leaves to one and add the chillies to the other and cook for about 2 minutes. Drain both and allow to cool, then transfer to a food processor or blender and process, adding a little water if necessary, to make a paste.

Add the ground spices and poppy seed paste to the chicken and cook for 4 minutes. Now, add the gongura paste and cook for a further 2 minutes.

Bohri Chicken
Mild-tasting Chicken

Origin Gujarat
Preparation time 30 minutes, plus marinating time
Cooking time 40 minutes
Serves 6

1 × 750-g / 1lb 10-oz chicken, cut into 10–12 pieces

1 tablespoon lime juice

1 teaspoon ground black pepper

250ml / 8fl oz (1 cup) double (heavy) cream,
  lightly whipped

3½ tablespoons ghee, melted

salt

about 150g / 5oz dough (optional), for sealing the lid
  (see page 783)

For the spice paste

3 onions, chopped

1 × 2.5-cm / 1-inch piece fresh ginger, peeled
  and chopped

6 flakes garlic or 1 clove garlic, chopped

1 sprig coriander (cilantro) leaves, chopped

15–20 mint leaves

To make the spice paste, put all the ingredients
in a blender and process, adding a little water if
necessary, to make a paste. Set aside. Put the chicken
pieces in a large shallow dish and prick all over with
a fork. Rub the lime juice together with half the
ground paste over the chicken, then cover and set
aside in the refrigerator for about 2 hours.

Carefully place the marinated chicken pieces into
a large, heavy-based pan, spread the remaining
ground paste on top of the chicken and sprinkle
over the black pepper and some salt. Pour the
whipped cream over the top and add the melted
ghee around the sides of the chicken. Cover and seal
the lid with dough, if using, or foil. Alternatively,
use a tight-fitting lid. Cook over low heat for about
40 minutes or until the chicken is cooked through.

Chettinad Chicken Curry
Chicken Curry from Chettinad

Origin Tamil Nadu
Preparation time 1 hour
Cooking time 45 minutes
Serves 4

1 fresh coconut, peeled and cut into small pieces

2 teaspoons poppy seeds

1 teaspoon fennel seeds

1 cinnamon stick, about 2.5cm / 1 inch long

3–4 green cardamom pods

2–3 cloves

1 teaspoon ground turmeric

125ml / 4½fl oz (½ cup) vegetable oil

1 large onion, chopped

1 × 2.5-cm / 1-inch piece fresh ginger, peeled
  and chopped

4–6 cloves garlic, chopped

1 tablespoon chilli powder

1 × 1-kg / 2¼-lb chicken, cut into pieces

2 tomatoes, chopped

juice of 1 lime

1 small sprig fresh curry leaves

salt

4 tablespoons chopped coriander (cilantro) leaves,
  to garnish

Put the coconut, poppy and fennel seeds, cinnamon,
cardamom, cloves and turmeric into a food
processor or blender and process, adding a little
water if necessary, to make a smooth paste.

Heat half the oil in a large, heavy-based pan, add
the onion and fry for about 6–7 minutes, or until
light brown. Add the ginger, garlic and chilli powder
with the spice paste and continue frying for 1–2
minutes, then add the chicken and fry for a further
6–7 minutes. Add the tomatoes and fry for about
5 minutes, or until the moisture has evaporated.
Pour in 500ml / 18fl oz (2¼ cups) water and season
with salt, then stir well. Cook for about 30 minutes,
or until the chicken is cooked through. Sprinkle over
the lime juice and curry leaves and garnish with
the coriander leaves.

※ ※ / 📷 p.476

Koli Milagu Masala
Pepper Chicken from Chettinad

Origin Tamil Nadu
Preparation time 30 minutes
Cooking time 45 minutes
Serves 4

5 tablespoons vegetable oil
3 bay leaves
4–5 green cardamom pods
1 cinnamon stick, about 2.5cm / 1 inch long
1 teaspoon fennel seeds
3–4 cloves
1 teaspoon urad dal, rinsed and drained
15–20 curry leaves
2 onions, chopped
1 tomato, chopped
1 × 1-kg / 2¼-lb chicken, cut into pieces and skinned
salt

For the spice paste

1 tablespoon cumin seeds
8–10 dried red chillies
3 tablespoons coriander seeds
1 teaspoon fennel seeds
1 teaspoon white poppy seeds
1 teaspoon black peppercorns
5 cloves garlic
1 × 2.5-cm / 1-inch piece fresh ginger, peeled and roughly chopped
1 teaspoon ground turmeric

To make the spice paste, heat 1 tablespoon of the oil in a heavy-based pan over medium heat, add the cumin seeds, chillies, coriander seeds, fennel seeds, poppy seeds and black peppercorns and stir-fry for about 1 minute until lightly roasted. Remove, allow to cool, then transfer to a blender. Add the remaining ingredients, season with salt and process, adding a little water if necessary, to make a paste.

Heat the remaining oil in a pan over medium heat, add the bay leaves, cardamom pods, cinnamon, fennel seeds, cloves and urad dal and stir-fry for about 1–2 minutes, or until the urad dal changes colour. Add the curry leaves, then stir. Add the onions and stir-fry for about 3 minutes, or until soft and starting to change colour.

Add the spice paste and continue to stir-fry for about 5 minutes, sprinkling with a little water to prevent it sticking to the base (bottom) of the pan. Add the tomato and stir-fry for a further 3–4 minutes.

Add the chicken to the onion and spice mixture, then mix well and pour in 500ml / 18fl oz (2¼ cups) water. Bring to the boil, then reduce the heat to low, cover and simmer for 20–25 minutes until the chicken is almost cooked.

Remove the chicken from the sauce, increase the heat to thicken the sauce, then put the chicken back and reduce the heat to low. Cook for about 5 minutes, or until the chicken is cooked through.

Aksa Pok
Chicken with Ginger

Origin Tribal North East India
Preparation time 15 minutes
Cooking time 30 minutes
Serves 4

1 × 1-kg / 2¼-lb chicken, cut into small pieces
2½ tablespoons rice, rinsed and drained
2 tablespoons Ginger Paste (see page 57)
2 red chillies, de-seeded and chopped
salt

Heat a heavy-based pan over medium heat, add the chicken without any water or oil and cook, stirring to prevent it from burning, until the moisture has evaporated and the chicken is cooked through. Remove from the pan.

Bring 750ml / 1¼ pints (3¼ cups) water to the boil in the pan. Add the rice, then reduce the heat, cover and simmer until the rice is fluffy and soft. Uncover and keep stirring until the sauce thickens with the rice. Stir in the ginger paste, chillies and chicken and season with salt. Cook until the aroma of ginger is released.

✳ ✳

Kozhi Appakari
Ginger Chicken with Mustard

Origin Kerala
Preparation time 30 minutes, plus marinating time
Cooking time 30 minutes
Serves 4

1 × 750-g / 1lb 10-oz chicken, cut into pieces
5 tablespoons vegetable oil
5 dried red chillies, shredded
1 teaspoon brown mustard seeds
1 teaspoon urad dal, rinsed and drained
1 teaspoon fennel seeds
2 cinnamon sticks, about 2.5cm / 1 inch long
5–6 cloves garlic, chopped
1 onion, chopped
2 tomatoes, chopped
3–4 fresh red chillies
1 teaspoon black pepper
salt

For the marinade
1 × 8-cm / 3-inch piece fresh ginger, peeled
1 teaspoon ground turmeric
pinch of salt

For the marinade, put the ginger in a small food processor or blender and process to make a paste. Transfer to a bowl, add the turmeric and salt and mix together. Put the chicken in a large shallow bowl and rub the marinade all over the chicken, then cover and set aside in the refrigerator for about 4 hours.

Heat the oil in a large, heavy-based pan over medium heat, add the dried red chillies, mustard seeds, urad dal, fennel seeds and cinnamon and stir-fry for about 1 minute, or until the chillies turn a shade darker and the mustard seeds start to splutter.

Now add the garlic, stir and add the onion and stir-fry for about 4 minutes, or until the onion is soft and lightly browned. Add the tomatoes and stir-fry for 2–3 minutes, or until the tomatoes are soft. Add the chicken together with the marinade and the whole red chillies and season with salt. Increase the heat to high and stir-fry for about 8–10 minutes, or until the chicken is browned. Cover, reduce the heat to low and cook for about 10–15 minutes, stirring occasionally until the chicken is cooked through. Uncover and sprinkle over the black pepper.

✳ ✳

Murg Banjara
Spicy Chicken Legs

Origin Rajasthan
Preparation time 30 minutes, plus marinating time
Cooking time 10–12 minutes
Serves 4

850g / 1lb 14oz chicken legs, each cut into 4 pieces
melted butter, for basting
salt

For the first marinade
½ teaspoons Garlic Paste (see page 57)
½ teaspoons Ginger Paste (see page 57)
2 tablespoons lemon juice
pinch of salt

For the second marinade
250ml / 8fl oz (1 cup) hung natural (plain) yoghurt
  (see page 793), whisked
125g / 4¼oz roasted peanut paste
1 teaspoon amchoor
2 tablespoons chilli powder
2 tablespoons coriander paste
6 tablespoons mustard oil
1 tablespoon vinegar

Put the chicken in a large shallow dish. To make the first marinade, mix all the ingredients together in a bowl, then rub the mixture evenly over the chicken. Cover and set aside in the refrigerator for 1 hour.

To make the second marinade, mix all the ingredients together in another large shallow dish or bowl and season with salt. Remove the chicken legs from the first marinade and drain off the excess moisture, then place them in the second marinade. Rub the chicken pieces well with the mixture, then cover and set aside in the refrigerator for 2–3 hours.

Prepare a charcoal grill or preheat the grill (broiler) to medium. Thread the chicken legs through metal skewers and keep a tray underneath to collect all the juices, then roast over a charcoal grill or under the grill for 10–15 minutes, or until the chicken is almost cooked.

Remove the skewers from the heat and hang them up over a tray for about 2–3 minutes to allow any excess moisture to drain out completely. Put the skewers in a dish, baste with melted butter and roast again for another 3–4 minutes.

Acha Kozhi
Stuffed Chicken

Origin Kerala
Preparation time 1 hour, plus marinating time
Cooking time 30 minutes
Serves 6

1 × 1-kg / 2¼-lb chicken, with skin
750ml / 1¼ pints (3¼ cups) vegetable oil

For the stuffing

1 teaspoon chilli powder
4 hard-boiled eggs
3 tablespoons vegetable oil
3 onions, chopped
6 green chillies, de-seeded and chopped
1 × 2.5-cm / 1-inch piece fresh ginger, peeled and chopped
4 cloves garlic, chopped
salt

For the spice paste

1 × 2.5-cm / 1-inch piece fresh ginger, peeled and chopped
6 green chillies, de-seeded and chopped
4 cloves garlic, chopped
10–15 curry leaves
1 teaspoon chilli powder
1 teaspoon ground black pepper
1 teaspoon ground turmeric

To make the stuffing, mix the chilli powder and some salt together on a plate, prick the eggs with a fork and roll them in the mixture to coat.

Heat the oil in a large frying pan (skillet) over medium heat, add the eggs and lightly fry for a few minutes, then remove and drain on kitchen paper (paper towels). Add the onions to the same pan and fry for about 2 minutes, or until translucent. Add the chillies, ginger and garlic and stir-fry for about 5 minutes. Season with salt.

Stuff the chicken with the whole eggs and onion mixture and close the belly by sewing it with a trussing needle and kitchen string (twine). Put the chicken in a large shallow dish.

To make the spice paste, put all the ingredients in a food processor or blender and process, adding a little water if necessary, to make a paste. Rub the paste all over the chicken, then cover and set aside in the refrigerator for about 2 hours.

Heat enough oil for deep-frying in a deep, heavy-based pan to 180°C/350°F, or until a cube of bread browns in 30 seconds. Carefully lower the chicken into the hot oil and deep-fry for 20 minutes, turning frequently, so that it is evenly cooked and brown. Remove from the pan and drain on kitchen paper (paper towels).

Methi Murg
Fenugreek-flavoured Chicken

Origin Punjab
Preparation time 30 minutes
Cooking time 50 minutes
Serves 4–6

100ml / 3½fl oz (½ cup) vegetable oil
4 onions, sliced
5–6 green chillies, de-seeded
2 teaspoons Ginger Paste (see page 57)
2 teaspoons Garlic Paste (see page 57)
½ teaspoon ground turmeric
1 × 800-g / 1¾-lb chicken, cut into medium-sized pieces
100g / 3½oz (2 cups) tender fenugreek shoots
275g / 9½oz (2 medium) tomatoes, chopped
1½ teaspoons chilli powder
salt

Heat the oil in a large, heavy-based pan over medium heat, add the onions and fry for about 5–7 minutes, or until golden brown. Add the chillies, ginger and garlic pastes and turmeric and stir-fry for about 2 minutes. Add the chicken pieces and fenugreek shoots and fry for 10 minutes until the moisture has almost evaporated. Add the tomatoes and chilli powder, then season with salt and fry for a few more minutes, until the oil separates out and rises to the surface. Pour in some water and cook over medium heat for about 30 minutes, or until the chicken is cooked through and there is a little sauce to coat the chicken.

Murg Ishtoo
Chicken Stew

Origin Anglo-Indian
Preparation time 45 minutes
Cooking time 40 minutes
Serves 4

1 × 2.5-cm / 1-inch piece fresh ginger, peeled and
    cut into pieces

1 teaspoon black peppercorns

¼ teaspoon ground turmeric

2 onions, sliced

2–3 green chillies

160g / 5½oz (2 cups) grated fresh coconut

10–12 small new (baby) potatoes

pinch of ground turmeric

2 tablespoons vegetable oil

1 tablespoon ghee

½ teaspoon mustard seeds

1 bay leaf

2 cloves garlic, crushed

2 cinnamon sticks, about 2.5cm / 1 inch long

4 green cardamom pods

1 teaspoon Ginger Paste (see page 57)

3–4 cloves

20 curry leaves

750g / 1lb 10oz boneless chicken, cut into pieces

1 carrot, sliced

125ml / 4½fl oz (½ cup) coconut milk, fresh
    (see page 781) or canned

70g / 2½oz peas, shelled if fresh

1 × 2.5-cm / 1-inch piece fresh ginger, peeled and
    cut into juliennes

1 teaspoon Garam Masala (see page 31)

salt

Using a pestle, pound the ginger pieces, peppercorns
and the turmeric into a thick uneven paste in a
mortar. Mix the onions and chillies together in a
bowl. Mix the grated coconut and 500ml / 18fl oz
(2¼ cups) water together and pass through a sieve
(strainer) into a clean bowl. Set aside.

Parboil the potatoes in their skins with a pinch of
salt and the turmeric in a pan of boiling water for
about 5–8 minutes.

Heat the oil and ghee in a large, heavy-based pan
over medium heat, add the mustard seeds and stir-
fry for about 1 minute, or until they start to splutter.

Add the bay leaf and stir-fry for about 1 minute or
until it changes colour, then add the crushed garlic,
cinnamon and cardamom pods and stir-fry for
30 seconds. Add the ginger paste, cloves, curry
leaves and the chicken and fry in the spiced oil for
2–3 minutes. Season with salt, then add the potatoes
and carrot. Cover and cook for about 2 minutes.
Finally, stir in the coconut milk, 125ml / 4½fl oz
(½ cup) water, the peas and ginger juliennes.
Sprinkle with garam masala, then cover and
cook for about 30 minutes, or until the chicken
is cooked through.

Thanda Qorma
Cold Chicken Korma

Origin Hyderabad
Preparation time 15 minutes, plus cooling and chilling
time
Cooking time 35 minutes
Serves 4

2 tablespoons ghee

1 onion, sliced

1 teaspoon ground fresh ginger

1 teaspoon ground garlic

4 cloves

4 green cardamom pods

1 cinnamon stick, about 2.5cm / 1 inch long

1 × 1-kg / 2¼-lb chicken, cut into bite-sized pieces

4–5 black peppercorns

3 green chillies, slit in half lengthways and de-seeded

salt

Heat the ghee in a large, heavy-based pan over low
heat, add the onion, ginger and garlic and stir-fry
lightly without browning. Add the cloves, cardamom
pods and cinnamon and fry for about 1–2 minutes.
Add the chicken, stir well and cover immediately.
After about 1 minute, uncover and stir well again,
then lightly fry the chicken without browning it. Add
the peppercorns and chillies, then season with salt
and pour in about 625ml / 1 pint (2½ cups) water.
Cook for 25–30 minutes, or until the chicken is
cooked through and the sauce is almost dry. Remove
from the heat and allow to cool, then transfer to the
refrigerator. The little amount of sauce will set along
with the ghee. Serve cold.

Thengakkai Kori
Chicken Curry (II)

Origin Tamil Nadu
Preparation time 20 minutes, plus marinating time
Cooking time 45 minutes
Serves 6

150ml / ¼ pint (⅔ cup) natural (plain) yoghurt
2 teaspoons chilli powder
½ teaspoon ground turmeric, plus 1 teaspoon for rubbing
8 chicken breasts, with winglet bones
5 tablespoons vegetable oil
5–6 green cardamom pods
5–6 cloves
2 cinnamon sticks, about 2.5cm / 1 inch long
2 onions, chopped
7 teaspoons Garlic Paste (see page 57)
3 teaspoons Ginger Paste (see page 57)
750ml / 1¼ pints (3¼ cups) clear chicken stock
250ml / 8fl oz (1 cup) coconut milk, fresh (see page 781) or canned
½ teaspoon ground green cardamom
salt
4 teaspoons grated coconut, to garnish

Put the yoghurt in a bowl, add the chilli powder and turmeric and whisk until well mixed. Set aside.

Place the chicken in a large shallow dish. Mix a pinch of salt and the 1 teaspoon turmeric together in a bowl and rub evenly over the chicken, then cover and set aside in the refrigerator for 15 minutes.

Heat the oil in a large, heavy-based pan over medium heat, add the cardamom pods, cloves and cinnamon and stir-fry for about 1 minute, or until the cardamom starts to change colour. Add the onions and stir-fry for about 4 minutes, or until light golden. Then add the garlic and ginger pastes and stir-fry for about 1–2 minutes, or until the onions are golden. Remove from the heat, stir in the yoghurt mixture, then return to the heat and stir-fry for about 3–4 minutes, or until oil starts to appear on the surface.

Add the chicken stock and bring to the boil. Reduce the heat to low, add the chicken and season with salt, then simmer for about 30 minutes, or until the chicken is cooked. Remove the breasts and set aside. Pass the sauce through a fine sieve (strainer) into a separate pan, and return to the heat.

Add the cooked chicken and coconut milk, and bring to just under the boil, ensuring that it does not come to a bubble. Sprinkle over the ground cardamom and stir. Remove from the heat and adjust the seasoning, if necessary. Garnish with grated coconut just before serving.

Kori Gassi
Chicken with Curry Leaves

Origin Coastal
Preparation time 30 minutes
Cooking time 1 hour
Serves 4–6

125ml / 4½fl oz (½ cup) vegetable oil
10–15 fresh curry leaves
3 onions, sliced
1 × 1-kg / 2¼-lb chicken, cut into pieces
salt

For the spice paste

250ml / 8fl oz (1 cup) coconut milk, fresh (see page 781) or canned
4–6 dried red chillies
1 tablespoon coriander seeds
1 teaspoon fenugreek seeds
1 teaspoon cumin seeds
4 black peppercorns
1 teaspoon Garlic Paste (see page 57)
1 teaspoon ground turmeric

Heat 2 tablespoons of the oil in a large, heavy-based pan over medium heat. Add half the curry leaves and half the sliced onions and stir-fry for about 8–10 minutes, or until the onions are brown, then remove and set aside for the garnish.

Put all the ingredients for the spice paste, except the coconut milk, in a spice grinder and process, adding a little water if necessary, to make a paste. Stir into the coconut milk.

Heat the remaining oil in the pan. Add the spice mixture and fry for about 1–2 minutes, or until golden brown. Add the remaining sliced onions and curry leaves and fry for about 2 minutes. Now add the chicken and season with salt, then fry for about 8–10 minutes. Pour in 500ml / 1 pints (2¼ cups) water and cook over medium heat for about 45 minutes, or until the chicken is cooked through.

Murg Roganjosh
Chicken in a Rich Scarlet Sauce

Origin Jammu and Kashmir
Preparation time 20 minutes, plus marinating time
Cooking time 30 minutes
Serves 4

250ml / 8fl oz (1 cup) natural (plain) yoghurt, whisked

4 green cardamom pods

2 black cardamom pods

1 × 800-g / 1¾-lb chicken, cut into pieces

250ml / 8fl oz (1 cup) mustard oil

2 bay leaves

2 cinnamon sticks, about 2.5cm / 1 inch long

4 cloves

small pinch of asafoetida

1 teaspoon Kashmiri red chilli powder

1 teaspoon ground ginger

2½ teaspoons ground aniseed

1 teaspoon Kashmiri Garam Masala (see page 56)

salt

To make a marinade, mix the yoghurt and cardamom pods together in a bowl, then season with salt. Put the chicken in a large shallow dish and rub the marinade evenly over the chicken, then cover and set aside in the refrigerator for 3 hours.

Heat the oil in a large, heavy-based pan over medium heat, add the chicken, bay leaves, cinnamon, cloves and asafoetida and stir gently but constantly for about 10 minutes until the yoghurt dries and the oil separates out. Now reduce the heat and cook for a further 10 minutes, or until the chicken turns brown. Add 2 tablespoons water to the pan and mix in the chilli powder. Increase the heat and stir quickly, then add the ginger, aniseed powder and garam masala together with 250ml / 8fl oz (1 cup) water. Reduce the heat to low and cook for about 10 minutes, or until the sauce thickens. The dish is cooked once the oil separates out.

Chooza Makhani
Tandoori Chicken in Spicy Tomato Sauce

Origin Punjab
Preparation time 30 minutes
Cooking time 15 minutes
Serves 4

250g / 9oz (1 cup / 2 sticks) butter

3 teaspoons Ginger Paste (see page 57)

3 teaspoons Garlic Paste (see page 57)

1kg / 2¼lb (6 medium) tomatoes, chopped

1 teaspoon chopped ginger

8–10 green chillies, de-seeded and chopped

3 teaspoons Cashew Nut Paste (see page 58)

1 teaspoon chilli powder

2 Tandoori Chickens (see page 218)

125ml / 4½fl oz (½ cup) cream

salt

Heat half of the butter in a medium-sized, heavy-based pan over medium heat, add the ginger and garlic pastes and stir-fry for about 1–2 minutes, or until the liquid has evaporated. Add the tomatoes, season with salt and pour in 500ml / 18fl oz (2¼ cups) water, then cover and simmer until soft. Mash with the back of a spoon, then pass the sauce through a fine sieve (strainer) into a separate pan and set aside.

Melt the remaining butter in a large, heavy-based pan over medium heat, add the chopped ginger and chillies and stir-fry for about 2 minutes. Add the cashew nut paste and stir-fry for about 1–2 minutes, or until light brown, then add the chilli powder and stir in the sauce. Bring to a boil, add the tandoori chickens and simmer for about 10 minutes. Stir in the cream and adjust the seasoning, if necessary.

Korioora Munakkai
Chicken with Drumsticks in a Spicy Tamarind-flavoured Sauce

Origin Tamil Nadu
Preparation time 30 minutes, plus soaking time
Cooking time 1 hour
Serves 4

180g / 6oz (¾ cup) ghee
2 bay leaves
3 cinnamon sticks, about 2.5cm / 1 inch long
4 cloves
½ teaspoon fenugreek seeds
1 teaspoon kalonji (nigella) seeds
3 onions, sliced
½ teaspoon ground turmeric
½ teaspoons Ginger Paste (see page 57)
½ teaspoons Garlic Paste (see page 57)
1 tablespoon ground coriander, roasted
1 teaspoon sesame seeds
2 medium-sized chickens, each cut into 10 pieces
120g / 4oz (1 small) tomato, chopped
1 tablespoon grated fresh coconut
2 teaspoons chopped red chilli
15 curry leaves
4 tablespoons fresh toddy (see page 792) or beer
6 (vegetable) drumsticks, peeled and cut into 6-cm / 2½-inch pieces
12–15 black peppercorns
250ml / 8fl oz (1 cup) Tamarind Extract (see page 58)
1 tablespoon gram (chickpea) flour
salt

To garnish

6 green chillies, slit in half lengthways and de-seeded
1 bunch coriander (cilantro) leaves
6 sprigs mint

Heat the ghee in a large, heavy-based pan over medium heat, add the bay leaves, cinnamon, cloves and fenugreek and kalonji seeds and stir-fry for about 1 minute. Add the onions and stir-fry for about 5–7 minutes, or until golden brown. Add the turmeric and ginger and garlic pastes and stir-fry for about 1–2 minutes, then add the ground coriander and sesame seeds and stir well. When the oil rises to the surface, add the chicken and continue to stir-fry until it releases its juices, then continue to fry for about 8–10 minutes, or until the liquids have evaporated and the chicken is brown. Add the tomatoes, coconut, red chilli and curry leaves and cook for about 3 minutes. Add the toddy or beer and cook for a few minutes until the liquid is absorbed, then add the drumsticks, black peppercorns, 750ml / 1¼ pints (3¼ cups) water and the tamarind extract. Reduce the heat to low and simmer for about 30 minutes, or until the chicken and drumsticks are cooked.

Dry-roast the gram flour on a tawa, or griddle or in a small frying pan (skillet) for about 1 minute to remove the raw smell, then transfer to a bowl. Add 250ml / 8fl oz (1 cup) water and mix well. Add to the curry to thicken the sauce, then mix well and simmer for 5 minutes, or until the sauce thickens. Add more water if it is too thick. Garnish with green chillies, coriander and mint leaves.

Sika Murg
Charcoal-grilled Chicken

Origin Awadh
Preparation time 20 minutes, plus marinating time
Cooking time 45 minutes
Serves 4

125g / 4oz (½ cup) ghee, plus extra melted for brushing
2 × 1kg / 2¼lb chickens, each cut into 6 pieces
1 onion, sliced
1 teaspoon ground fresh ginger
1 teaspoon ground garlic
6 green chillies, de-seeded and ground
500ml / 18fl oz (2¼ cups) natural (plain) yoghurt, whisked
salt

To garnish

2 limes, cut into slices
1 onion, cut into rings

Rub the ghee and some salt over the chickens and set aside. Now mix the onion, ginger, garlic, chillies and yoghurt together in a large bowl or dish, add the chicken and turn until coated, then cover and set aside in the refrigerator for 12 hours.

Brush the chicken with some melted ghee and cook over a charcoal fire for about 45 minutes, or until cooked through. Garnish with lime slices and onion rings.

☀ ☀ / 📷 p.477

Methi Murg
Chicken with Fenugreek Leaves

Origin Punjab
Preparation time 30 minutes, plus marinating time
Cooking time 40–45 minutes
Serves 4

1 teaspoon Ginger Paste (see page 57)
1 teaspoon Garlic Paste (see page 57)
2 onions, sliced
2 tablespoons natural (plain) yoghurt, whisked
1 teaspoon chilli powder
½ teaspoon ground turmeric
1 medium-sized chicken, cut into pieces
180ml / 6½fl oz (¾ cup) vegetable oil
2 large cardamom pods
1 cinnamon stick, about 2.5cm / 1 inch long
3 green chillies, de-seeded and chopped
½ teaspoon ground caraway seeds
125g / 8oz (2 cups) fenugreek leaves, chopped
juice of 1 lime
salt

To make a marinade, mix the ginger and garlic pastes, 1 onion, the yoghurt, chilli powder and turmeric together in a large shallow dish or bowl and season with salt. Add the chicken and turn to coat well, then cover and set aside in the refrigerator for 20 minutes.

Heat half of the oil in a large, heavy-based pan over low heat, add the marinated chicken and cook for about 8–10 minutes, or until the chicken is browned. Pour in 750ml / 1¼ pints (3¼ cups) water and cook for about 30 minutes, or until two-thirds of the water has evaporated and the chicken is cooked.

Heat the rest of the oil in a frying pan (skillet) over medium heat, add the cardamom pods, cinnamon, chillies, ground caraway seeds and the remaining onion and fry for about 1–2 minutes, or until the cardamoms swell. Add the chopped fenugreek leaves and fry for 3–4 minutes. Add the cooked chicken and simmer together until the leaves are fragrant, then squeeze over the lime juice. There should be some thick green sauce with the chicken.

☀ ☀

Kori Tamatar
Savoury Chicken with Tomatoes

Origin Coastal
Preparation time 30 minutes
Cooking time 45 minutes
Serves 4

125g / 4oz (½ cup) ghee
6 black cardamom pods
1 cinnamon stick, about 2.5cm / 1 inch long
4 cloves
4 onions, sliced
1 teaspoon Ginger Paste (see page 57)
1 teaspoon Garlic Paste (see page 57)
1 tablespoon chilli powder
¼ teaspoon ground turmeric
1 teaspoon ground coriander, roasted
½ teaspoon ground cumin, roasted
1 × 1-kg / 2¼-lb chicken, cut into pieces
225g / 8oz (2 small) tomatoes, sliced
1 teaspoon tamarind pulp
6 curry leaves
4 green chillies, de-seeded and chopped
salt

Heat the ghee in a large, heavy-based pan over medium heat, add the cardamom pods, cinnamon and cloves and stir-fry for about 1 minute, or until the cardamoms swell. Add the onions and stir-fry for about 5–7 minutes, or until golden brown. Stir in the ginger and garlic pastes, chilli powder, turmeric, coriander, cumin and stir-fry for about 1 minute.

Add the chicken and fry for about 8–10 minutes, or until brown. Add the tomatoes and tamarind pulp and simmer for about 30 minutes until the chicken is cooked, adding 250ml / 8fl oz (1 cup) water or more as required. The tomatoes should be puréed and the oil should rise to the surface. Add the curry leaves and green chillies and season with salt, then cover and simmer for 2–3 minutes. Remove from the heat and serve.

Kobari Kori Pulussu
Chicken in Coconut Sauce

Origin Tamil Nadu
Preparation time 30 minutes
Cooking time 1 hour
Serves 4

10 dried red chillies
4 cloves
5 cardamoms
4 cinnamon sticks, about 2.5cm / 1 inch long
3 teaspoons ground coriander, roasted
1 teaspoon poppy seeds
¼ dried coconut
2 teaspoons Garlic Paste (see page 57)
1 teaspoon Ginger Paste (see page 57)
3 onions, thinly sliced
125g / 4oz (½ cup) ghee
1 × 1-kg / 2¼-lb chicken
500ml / 18fl oz (2¼ cups) coconut milk, fresh (see page 781) or canned
salt
Plain Boiled Rice (see page 631), to serve

To garnish

6 cashew nuts, fried
few sprigs mint

Put all the spices and pastes and the onions in a food processor or blender and process until ground. Stuff the chicken with the mixture and sew up with a trussing needle and kitchen string (twine), so that the stuffing does not come out.

Heat the ghee in a large, heavy-based pan over low heat, add the chicken and fry for 8–10 minutes turning so that each side browns. Pour 250ml / 8fl oz (1 cup) coconut milk over the chicken, then reduce the heat to medium-low and simmer for 10 minutes. Add the remaining coconut milk and season with salt. Continue cooking over low heat for 45 minutes, or until the chicken is cooked and the stuffing thickens into a sauce.

Cut the chicken into 8 pieces and arrange in a serving dish. Pour the sauce over the chicken. Garnish with cashew nuts and mint sprigs. Serve hot with Rice.

Hare Masale ka Murg
Chicken with Green Herbs

Origin Awadh
Preparation time 30 minutes
Cooking time 35 minutes
Serves 4

1 teaspoon ground fresh ginger
1 teaspoon ground garlic
1 × 800-g / 1¾-lb chicken, cut into pieces
125ml / 4½fl oz (½ cup) vegetable oil
10 blanched almonds
375ml / 13fl oz (1½ cups) natural (plain) yoghurt, whisked
250ml / 8fl oz (1 cup) single (light) cream
½ teaspoon ground cumin
½ teaspoon ground turmeric
6 green chillies, de-seeded and ground
15g / ½oz coriander (cilantro) leaves, ground
1 bunch mint leaves
½ fresh coconut, ground
salt

Rub the chicken all over with a little salt and the ginger and garlic.

Heat the oil in a large, heavy-based pan over low heat, add the chicken and fry for about 8–10 minutes, or until brown all over. Add the almonds and cook for 1 minute. Mix the yoghurt, cream, cumin and turmeric together in a bowl, then add to the chicken and cook for 5 minutes until most of the liquid has evaporated. Add the ground chillies, coriander, mint leaves and coconut, then increase the heat and and cook for 1 minute. Pour in 250ml / 8fl oz (1 cup) water, then reduce the heat to low and simmer for about 20–30 minutes, adding more water when required, until the chicken is cooked through and the oil rises to the surface.

Dum ka Murg
Baked Masala Chicken with Hard-boiled
Eggs & Potatoes

Origin Awadh
Preparation time 1 hour, plus marinating time
Cooking time 1 hour
Serves 4

½ teaspoon saffron threads

1 tablespoon milk

6 drops raw papaya milk

1 teaspoon chilli powder

1 medium-sized chicken, without skin

250g / 9oz (1 cup) ghee, melted

3 onions, sliced

1 tablespoon chopped ginger

1 tablespoon chopped garlic

1 teaspoon Garam Masala (see page 31)

1 tablespoon coriander seeds

1 tablespoon poppy seeds

1 teaspoon caraway seeds

2 cinnamon sticks, about 2.5cm / 1 inch long

5 green cardamom pods

4 cloves

1 litre / 1¾ pints (4¼ cups) hung natural (plain)
    yoghurt (see page 793)

juice of 2 limes

salt

Put the saffron in a small bowl, add the milk and
soak until required.

To make a marinade, mix a few drops of the raw
papaya milk with the chilli powder in a bowl and
then season with salt. Put the chicken in a large
shallow dish and rub the marinade evenly over,
then cover and set aside in the refrigerator, piercing
the chicken with a fork and rubbing it again every
15 minutes, for 1 hour.

Heat half the ghee in a large, heavy-based pan
over medium heat, add the onions and fry for 5–7
minutes, or until golden brown. Transfer the onions
to a blender and process until ground.

Add the ginger and garlic to the pan and stir-fry for
about 1 minute, then add the garam masala and the
whole spices and stir-fry for about 1 minute, or until
the cooked spices are fragrant and the ghee rises to
the top.

Mix the onions, fried masalas and yoghurt together
in a large bowl, then season with salt. Rub the
chicken with this masala all over and inside, then
cover and set aside in the refrigerator for 4 hours.

Preheat the oven to 180°C/350°F/Gas Mark 4. Put the
chicken in a deep baking dish and pour over the
saffron milk together with the rest of the melted ghee,
putting some also in the cavity. Pour over the lime
juice, then cover with a tight-fitting lid and roast in
the oven for about 1 hour, basting occasionally with
the pan juices and turning the chicken to check if it
is cooked. To test, pierce the chicken with a skewer
or the tip of a sharp knife in the thickest part of the
meat. If the juices run clear it is cooked, if not return
to the oven for a little longer then test again. When
done, transfer to a dish and serve whole.

Kundan Murg
White Chicken

Origin Awadh
Preparation time 20 minutes
Cooking time 45 minutes
Serves 4

500ml / 18fl oz (2¼ cups) natural (plain) yoghurt,
    whisked

5 green chillies

2 tablespoons ghee

5 whole green cardamom pods

2 bay leaves

1 × 800-g / 1¾-lb chicken, cut into pieces

250ml / 8fl oz (1 cup) milk

3 tablespoons desiccated (dried flaked) coconut

salt

Put the yoghurt into a large, heavy-based pan with the
chillies and stir over medium heat until it just comes
to the boil. Remove from the heat and set aside.

Heat the ghee in another heavy-based pan over
medium heat, add the cardamom pods and bay leaves
and stir-fry for 1 minute. Add the chicken and cook for
2–3 minutes. Do not allow the chicken to brown. Add
the milk and coconut and cook for 30 minutes.

Strain the yoghurt through a sieve (strainer) into
the pan with the chicken, discarding the chillies.
Season with salt and cook for 10 minutes, or until
the chicken is cooked thorough.

Sandali Murg
White Chicken Curry

Origin Awadh
Preparation time 20 minutes, plus soaking time
Cooking time 45 minutes
Serves 4

3 tablespoons chaar magaz (see page 780)
4 heaped (heaping) teaspoons poppy seeds
125g / 4oz (½ cup) ghee
1 × 800-g / 1¾-lb chicken, cut into pieces
750ml / 1¼ pints (3¼ cups) milk
2 tablespoons blanched almonds
2–3 blades mace
½ nutmeg, grated
seeds of 6 green cardamoms
salt

Soak the char magaz and poppy seeds separately in 2 bowls of water for 2–3 hours.

Heat the ghee in a large, heavy-based pan over medium heat, add the chicken and lightly fry for about 8 minutes. Remove from the heat and put into another pan with the milk and cook for 20–30 minutes, or until cooked through.

Drain the char magaz and poppy seeds and transfer to a blender, add the almonds, mace, nutmeg and cardamom seeds and process, adding a little water if necessary, to make paste. Put the paste in the ghee that has fried the chicken and fry for 2–3 minutes, then add to the cooked chicken and season with salt. Cover and simmer over very low heat for 10–15 minutes.

Arsa Llodos
Stir-fried Chicken

Origin Tribal North East India
Preparation time 40 minutes, plus marinating time
Cooking time 30 minutes
Serves 4

3½ tablespoons vegetable oil
2 onions, chopped
2 teaspoons chopped ginger
1 teaspoon chopped garlic
200g / 7oz skinless, boneless chicken, cut into 5-cm / 2-inch strips
2 green (bell) peppers, chopped
75g / 2½oz bamboo mushrooms, chopped
1 tomato, chopped
3 parkia seeds
1 teaspoon ground black pepper
180ml / 6½fl oz (¾ cup) chicken stock
2 teaspoons cornflour (cornstarch)
salt

For the marinade

1 teaspoon soy sauce
1 teaspoon thick red chilli sauce
2 tablespoons vegetable oil

Mix all the ingredients for the marinade together in a large bowl. Rub the marinade over the chicken, then cover and set aside in the refrigerator for 30 minutes.

Heat the oil in a kadhai, wok or deep, heavy-based pan over medium heat, add the onions, ginger and garlic and fry for about 5–7 minutes, or until the onions turn golden brown.

Add the chicken and the remaining ingredients, except the cornflour, then increase the heat to high and cook for 3 minutes. Combine the cornflour with 250ml / 8fl oz (1 cup) water and add to the pan. Cook, stirring constantly, for 20–30 minutes, or until the chicken is cooked through and the sauce thickens.

Chaar Magaz ka Murg
Chicken with Melon Seeds

Origin Hyderabad
Preparation time 1 hour, plus soaking time
Cooking time 1½ hours
Serves 4

1 × 1-kg / 2¼-lb chicken

For the stuffing
4 slices white bread, without crusts

125ml / 4½fl oz (½ cup) milk

2 tablespoons ghee

1 onion, chopped

2 hard-boiled eggs, chopped

salt

For the masala
6 tablespoons poppy seeds

150g / 5oz chaar magaz (see page 780)

pinch of saffron threads

5 tablespoons blanched almonds

seeds of 8–10 green cardamom pods

1 nutmeg, grated

9 cloves

50g / 2oz (¼ cup) ghee

125ml / 4½fl oz (½ cup) natural (plain) yoghurt,
   whisked

2–3 drops kewra water or rosewater

salt

For the masala, soak the poppy seeds and dried melon seeds separately in 2 bowls of water for 2–3 hours. Put the saffron threads in a small bowl, add 1 tablespoon hot water and soak until required.

Put the bread in a bowl, pour over the milk and soak for about 5 minutes. Heat 2 tablespoons ghee in a large, heavy-based pan over medium heat, add the onion and fry for about 5 minutes, or until just beginning to colour, then transfer to a bowl. Allow to cool. Squeeze out the bread and add to the onion, then add the eggs and season with salt. Mix well, then stuff the chicken with the mixture.

Drain the poppy seeds and melon seeds and transfer to a food processor or blender. Add the almonds, cardamom seeds, nutmeg and cloves and process, adding a little water if necessary, to make a paste.

Put the chicken in a large, heavy-based pan, add the paste and yoghurt and season with salt.

Pour in about 500ml / 18fl oz (2¼ cups) water, then cover and cook over low heat for 1½ hours, or until the chicken is cooked through. Add the soaked saffron and kewra water.

Joint the chicken before serving, if desired.

❅ ❅ / 📷 p.556

Sookhe Masale ka Murg
Dry Masala Chicken

Origin Awadh
Preparation time 25 minutes, plus marinating time
Cooking time 30 minutes
Serves 4

1 × 800-g / 1¾-lb chicken, cut into pieces

2 green chillies, de-seeded (optional) and
   roughly chopped

1 teaspoon chilli powder

2 teaspoons ground coriander

½ teaspoon turmeric powder

½ teaspoon ground aniseed

6–8 cloves garlic, crushed

5–6 black peppercorns

200g / 7oz (¾ cup) ghee

salt

Put all the ingredients except the chicken, ghee and salt into a food processor or blender and process until ground. Put the chicken in a large shallow dish and rub the mixture over, then cover and set aside in the refrigerator for 2 hours.

Pour 250ml / 8fl oz (1 cup) water into a large, heavy-based pan and add 1 teaspoon salt. Add the marinated chicken and bring to the boil, then reduce the heat and simmer for 15–20 minutes, or until the water has evaporated and the chicken is cooked through, but not overcooked.

Heat the ghee in another pan over low heat, add the chicken and fry for 10 minutes, or until golden. Serve immediately.

To Khan
Chicken Curry (III)

Origin Tribal North East India
Preparation time 20 minutes
Cooking time 30 minutes
Serves 4

1 × 1-kg / 2¼-lb chicken, cut into 5-cm / 2-inch pieces
1 tablespoon mustard oil
3 green chillies, de-seeded and chopped
3 onions, chopped
3 tomatoes, chopped
1 tablespoon chopped garlic
1 teaspoon dried mint
salt
1 tablespoon chopped ginger, to garnish

Place the chicken in a kadhai, wok or deep, heavy-based pan over low heat, sprinkle in the oil and mix by hand. Cook, stirring constantly, for about 5 minutes, or until the water from the chicken has evaporated. Add the remaining ingredients, except the ginger, and cook, stirring constantly for 5 minutes.

Pour in 625ml / 1 pint (2½ cups) water and simmer for about 20 minutes, or until the chicken is cooked through and the sauce thickens. Garnish with ginger.

Murg Rezhala
Chicken in Rezala Sauce

Origin Bengal
Preparation time 30 minutes
Cooking time 20 minutes
Serves 4

large pinch of saffron threads
125ml / 4½fl oz (½ cup) lukewarm milk
200g / 7oz chicken, minced (ground)
1 tablespoon Ginger Paste (see page 57)
2 teaspoon Garlic Paste (see page 57)
4–5 green cardamom pods
1 cinnamon stick, about 5cm / 2 inches long
250ml / 8fl oz (1 cup) natural (plain) yoghurt
100ml / 3½fl oz (½ cup) vegetable oil
5–6 green chillies, slit in half lengthways and de-seeded
1 teaspoon sugar
salt

Put the saffron in a small bowl, add the milk and soak until required.

Place a large, heavy-based pan over medium heat and add all the ingredients in, except the saffron soaked in milk and the green chillies. Mix well, then reduce the heat, cover and simmer for about 15 minutes.

Uncover and stir well until all the moisture has evaporated and the oil rises to the surface. Pour in the saffron and milk and add the green chillies, then cover again and simmer for 2 minutes before serving hot.

Murg Lazawab
Cold Curried Chicken

Origin New
Preparation time 1 hour, plus marinating, cooling and soaking time
Cooking time 40 minutes
Serves 4

4 tablespoons natural (plain) yoghurt, whisked

½ teaspoon Garam Masala (see page 31)

½ teaspoon yellow chilli powder

½ teaspoon ground turmeric

4 chicken breasts, with skin and bone

2 litres / 3½ pints (9 cups) clear chicken stock

10 green cardamom pods

5 cloves

1 bay leaf

salt

For the sauce

7 teaspoons butter

3 tablespoons gram (chickpea) flour

2½ tablespoons plain (all-purpose) flour

½ teaspoon Garam Masala (see page 31)

½ teaspoon yellow chilli powder

½ teaspoon ground turmeric

400ml / 14fl oz (1⅔ cups) clear chicken stock

pinch of salt

½ teaspoon ground mace

½ teaspoon ground green cardamom

2 teaspoons gelatine powder

7 tablespoons single (light) cream

Mix the yoghurt, garam masala, yellow chilli powder and turmeric in a bowl and season with salt. Put the chicken breasts in 1–2 large shallow dishes and rub the mixture over the chicken, then cover and set aside in the refrigerator for 45 minutes.

Put the stock in a large, flat-based handi or heavy-based pan, add the cardamom pods, cloves and bay leaf and bring to the boil. Reduce the heat and simmer until there is just enough sauce to cover the chicken. Arrange the chicken breasts, side by side, in the stock and simmer for 20–30 minutes, or until cooked. Remove from the stock and allow to cool.

When the chicken is cool, remove the skin and the bones carefully, ensuring that the surface remains smooth. Trim the edges, then transfer the chicken to a wire rack and put in the refrigerator.

To make the sauce, melt the butter in a kadhai or deep, heavy-based pan over low heat. Add the gram flour and plain flour and stir-fry for about 30 seconds–1 minute. Add the garam masala, yellow chilli powder, turmeric and salt, and stir. Whisk in the stock, then reduce the heat and simmer for 15 minutes. Adjust the seasoning, if necessary. Add the ground mace and cardamom, stir and remove from the heat. Strain into a large pan and allow to cool.

Put the gelatine in a heatproof bowl, add 3 tablespoons water and soak for about 10 minutes, then stir over a double boiler until dissolved. Stir into the sauce. Put some ice cubes in a large pan and cool the sauce until it starts to thicken.

Whip the cream in a bowl and fold into the sauce.

Remove the chicken from the refrigerator and carefully transfer the breasts to a silver platter. Serve cold with the sauce and a garnish of your choice.

Awushi Kulho
Chicken with Potatoes

Origin Tribal North East India
Preparation time 20 minutes
Cooking time 25 minutes
Serves 4

1 × 1-kg / 2¼-lb chicken, cut into
    medium-sized pieces

7 green chillies, de-seeded and cut into
    lengthways slices

1 tablespoon Ginger Paste (see page 57)

4 potatoes, cut into slices

salt

Place 1 litre / 1¾ pints (4¼ cups) water in a large, heavy-based pan and bring to the boil. Add the chicken, cover and cook for 10 minutes, or until the chicken is half done.

Mix in the remaining ingredients, cover again and cook for a further 10 minutes, or until the potatoes and chicken are tender.

Uncover, lightly crush the potatoes with a ladle or wooden spatula and continue cooking for a few more minutes until the sauce thickens.

Shola e Dil
Quails Stuffed with Savoury Minced (Ground) Chicken

Origin Awadh
Preparation time 2¼ hours, plus marinating time
Cooking time 1 hour
Serves 4

8 quails

2 medium-sized onions, sliced

3 green cardamom pods

3 cinnamon sticks, about 2.5cm / 1 inch long

2 black cardamom pods

2 cloves

2 bay leaves

1 litre / 1¾ pints (4¼ cups) clear chicken stock

butter, for basting

salt

For the marinade

125ml / 4½fl oz (½ cup) hung natural (plain) yoghurt
   (see page 793), whisked

3 tablespoons Ginger Paste (see page 57)

1 tablespoon Garlic Paste (see page 57)

1 teaspoon chilli powder

For the filling

250g / 9oz minced (ground) chicken

1 × 2.5-cm / 1-inch piece fresh ginger, peeled
   and chopped

1 green chilli, deseeded and chopped

8 roasted pistachios, halved

1 tablespoon toasted flaked almonds

¼ teaspoon ground green cardamom

½ teaspoon black cumin seeds

1 teaspoon coarsely ground black peppercorns,
   roasted

½ teaspoon saffron threads

½ teaspoon ground rose petals

For the sauce

large pinch of saffron threads

2 teaspoons rosewater

250ml / 8fl oz (1 cup) natural (plain) yoghurt, whisked

1 teaspoon ground coriander

1 teaspoon Kashmiri chilli powder

6 tablespoons ghee

1 teaspoon Garlic Paste (see page 57)

5 teaspoons Ginger Paste (see page 57)

3 tablespoons almond paste

2 tablespoons grated coconut, ground to a paste

1 tablespoon chironji kernel paste

3 tablespoons Fried Onion Paste (see page 57)

1 teaspoon ground green cardamom

¼ teaspoon ground mace

To make the marinade, mix all the ingredients together in a bowl. Put the quails in a large shallow dish and rub the marinade all over, then cover and set aside in the refrigerator for at least 1 hour.

To make the filling, mix all the ingredients together in a bowl and divide into 8 equal portions. Stuff the abdominal cavity of the quails with a portion of the filling; from the tail end, then double up the legs, ensuring that the drumsticks cover the opening through which the filling was stuffed, and tie firmly with kitchen string (twine).

Spread the onions in a large pan, sprinkle over the whole spices, then arrange the stuffed quails on top, leaving space between each bird. Pour on the chicken stock and bring to the boil, then reduce the heat to low, cover and simmer for 20–25 minutes, or until cooked. Remove the quails and set aside. Reserve the juice.

To make the sauce, soak the saffron in the rosewater, then crush lightly with a pestle or the back of a spoon and set aside. Put the yoghurt in a bowl, add the coriander and chilli powder and season with salt, then mix well.

Heat the ghee in a large, heavy-based pan over medium heat, add the garlic and ginger pastes and stir-fry for about 1–2 minutes, or until the moisture has evaporated. Remove the pan from the heat, stir in the yoghurt mixture, then return the pan to the heat and stir-fry over medium heat for about 2–3 minutes, or until specks of oil separates out. Add the almond, coconut and chironji pastes and stir-fry for about 1–2 minutes, or until the oil separates out. Add the fried onion paste and stir-fry for about 1–2 minutes, or until the oil separate out, then add the reserved juice and bring to the boil. Reduce the heat to low and simmer, stirring occasionally, for 4–5 minutes. Add the quails, baste with the butter, bring to the boil, then reduce the heat to low and simmer until it is a sauce consistency. Sprinkle over the ground cardamom and mace and stir, then add the saffron, stir, remove from the heat and adjust the seasoning, if necessary.

✳ ✳
___

Bataer Masaledar
Stuffed Quails in Spicy Sauce

Origin Punjab
Preparation time 1 hour, plus marinating time
Cooking time 1 hour
Serves 4

8 quails

250g / 9oz minced / (ground) chicken

1 teaspoon saffron threads

1 tablespoon warm milk

2 teaspoons ground coriander

1½ teaspoons chilli powder

6 tablespoons ghee

4 black cardamom pods

4 cloves

2 cinnamon sticks, about 2.5cm / 1 inch long

2 bay leaves

16 flakes garlic or 2 cloves garlic, chopped

250g / 9oz (2 medium) onions, grated

2 teaspoons chopped ginger

200g / 7oz (1 large) tomato, chopped

6 tablespoons natural (plain) yoghurt, whisked

2 tablespoons almond paste

1 teaspoon ground green cardamom

¼ teaspoon ground cinnamon

¼ teaspoon ground cloves

½ teaspoon ground mace

salt

For the quail marinade

6 tablespoons red wine

2 tablespoons malt (white) vinegar

1½ teaspoons Ginger Paste (see page 57)

1½ tablespoons Garlic Paste (see page 57)

1½ teaspoons chilli powder

For the minced (ground) chicken marinade

1½ tablespoons Garlic Paste (see page 57)

1½ teaspoons Ginger Paste (see page 57)

2 green chillies

16 roasted pistachios

16 raisins

½ teaspoon black cumin seeds

¾ teaspoon ground black pepper, roasted

1 teaspoon ground green cardamom

¼ teaspoon ground mace

pinch of salt

To garnish

1 tablespoon flaked (slivered) almonds

4–6 edible silver leaf

Put the quails in 2 large shallow dishes and prick with a fork. To make the marinade, mix all the ingredients together in a bowl and evenly rub the quails with the mixture. Cover and set aside in the refrigerator for at least 1 hour.

To make the marinade for the minced chicken, mix the mince with all the ingredients for the marinade in a large bowl and divide into 8 equal portions.

Stuff the abdominal cavity of the quails with a portion of the mixture. Cover the opening through which filling was stuffed and secure firmly with kitchen string (twine).

Put the saffron threads in a mortar and crush with a pestle, then put in a bowl, add the warm milk and soak until the milk is a saffron colour. Add the flaked almonds for the garnish and set aside.

Put the ground coriander and chilli powder in a small bowl, add 2 tablespoons water and mix together.

Heat the ghee in a large, heavy-based pan over medium heat, add the black cardamom pods, cloves, cinnamon and bay leaf and stir-fry for a few seconds, then add the garlic and stir-fry for about 1 minute, or until it changes colour.

Add the onions and stir-fry for about 4 minutes, or until light golden, then add the ginger and stir-fry briefly. Add the ground spice mixture and stir-fry for about 1–2 minutes, or until the moisture has evaporated.

Add the tomatoes, then season with salt and stir-fry for about 5 minutes, or until the oil separates out. Remove the pan from the heat and stir in the yoghurt, then return to the heat and stir-fry over medium heat until specks of oil start to appear on the surface. Add the almond paste and stir-fry for about 1–2 minutes, or until the oil separates out. Pour in about 1 litre / 1¾ pints (4¼ cups) water and bring to the boil. Reduce the heat to medium, add the quails and bring to the boil. Reduce the heat to low, cover and cook, stirring frequently, for 5–7 minutes, or until the quails are almost cooked.

Meanwhile, drain the almonds from the saffron, reserving the saffron milk. Uncover the pan, increase the heat slightly and cook until the sauce is a medium-thick consistency.

Sprinkle over the remaining ground spices and stir, then add the saffron mixture and stir again. Finally, remove from the heat and adjust the seasoning, if necessary. Garnish with the flaked almonds and silver leaf.

Doodhiya Bataer
Crispy Quail

Origin Awadh
Preparation time 25 minutes
Cooking time 1½ hours
Serves 4

2 teaspoons saffron powder
1.2 litres / 2 pints (5 cups) milk
½ teaspoon ground fennel
½ teaspoon chilli powder
100g / 3½oz (⅔ cup) gram (chickpea) flour
2 tablespoons lemon juice
1½ black peppercorns, pounded
12 quails, with skin
4 teaspoons fennel seeds
10 green cardamom pods
6–8 cloves
2 cinnamon stick, about 2.5cm / 1 inch long
2 bay leaves
vegetable oil, for deep-frying
salt

Mix half the saffron, 250ml / 8fl oz (1 cup) milk, the ground fennel, chilli powder, gram flour, a little salt and lemon juice together in a bowl to make a batter.

Boil the remaining milk in a large, heavy-based pan, add the pounded pepper and boil for a further 1 minute. Now add the quail and the remaining ingredients, except the oil, and boil over medium heat until tender. Remove the quails, reserving the masala.

Heat enough oil for deep-frying in a deep, heavy-based pan to 180°C/350°F, or until a cube of bread browns in 30 seconds. Dip the boiled quail in the batter, then carefully lower into the hot oil and deep-fry until a crisp cream-coloured layer is formed. Remove and drain on kitchen paper (paper towels), then serve.

Bhuja Haaz
Stir-fried Duck

Origin Tribal North East India
Preparation time 1 hour, plus soaking time
Cooking time 10 minutes
Serves 4

2 tablespoons sabut urad (whole black beans), rinsed and drained
1 × 1.5-kg / 3lb 5-oz duck
1 tablespoon mustard oil
8 dried red chillies, de-seeded and broken into small pieces
1 onion, sliced
1 green (bell) pepper, de-seeded and sliced
1 small head celery, shredded
2 cloves garlic, crushed
2 teaspoons sugar
1 tablespoon soy sauce
1 tablespoon vinegar

Soak the beans in a bowl of water for 30 minutes, then drain. Transfer to a blender and process, adding a little water if necessary to make a paste.

Debone and clean the duck, then slice into matchstick-sized strips.

Heat the oil in a large frying pan (skillet) over medium heat, add the dried red chillies and stir-fry for 1 minute. Remove the chillies and discard. Add the onion, green pepper, celery, garlic and bean paste to the pan and stir-fry for 5 minutes. Mix in the sugar, soy sauce and duck, and continue stir-frying for a further 2–3 minutes. Stir in the vinegar, fry for 10 seconds and serve.

Vindaloo
Goan Pork Curry

Origin Goa
Preparation time 1 hour, plus soaking and marinating time
Cooking time 1 hour
Serves 4

750g / 1lb 10oz pork, cut into cubes
100ml / 3½fl oz (½ cup) vegetable oil
3 onions, chopped
15–20 curry leaves
½ teaspoon jaggery or soft brown sugar, or to taste
salt

For the marinade
10–20 dried red chillies
1 teaspoon cumin seeds
6–8 cloves
2 cinnamon sticks, about 2.5cm / 1 inch long
10–12 black peppercorns
¼ star anise
1 teaspoon poppy seeds
1 × 5-cm / 2-inch piece fresh ginger, peeled
6 cloves garlic
1 tablespoon Tamarind Extract (see page 58)
4 teaspoons malt (white) vinegar

Soak the dried red chillies in a bowl of water for 10 minutes, then drain.

To make the marinade, put the chillies and all the spices in a blender, add the vinegar and process to make a smooth paste. Put the pork in a large shallow dish and rub half the paste all over, then cover and set aside in the refrigerator for 1 hour.

Heat the oil in a large, heavy-based pan over low heat, add the onions and stir-fry for about 15 minutes. Add the remaining spice paste and stir-fry for a further 5 minutes, stirring constantly, and add 1½ tablespoons water to prevent burning. Add the pork and continue cooking for about 5 minutes. Pour in 1 litre / 1¾ pints (4¼ cups) water and season with salt, then cook over low heat for about 30 minutes, or until the pork is cooked. Stir in the curry leaves and jaggery or sugar and simmer for 3–4 minutes. Serve hot.

Sorpatel
Spicy Pork & Liver Curry

Origin Goa
Preparation time 1 hour, plus cooling time
Cooking time 2 hours
Serves 6–8

1kg / 2¼lb pork, cut into pieces
300g / 11oz liver, cut into pieces
2 tablespoons olive oil
50g / 1¾oz (½ small) onion, sliced
1 clove garlic, crushed
6 teaspoons ground turmeric
2 cinnamon sticks, about 10cm / 4 inches long
1 teaspoon cumin seeds
12 black peppercorns
12 cloves
6 green cardamoms, seeds only
10–15 dried Kashmiri red chillies
1 teaspoon chilli powder
vinegar to taste
salt (optional)

Put the pork in a pan, add enough water to just cover and cook for about 30 minutes. Do the same with the liver in a separate pan. Drain both, reserving the cooking waters and allow to cool. Cut the pork and liver into smaller pieces when cool.

Heat the oil in a large, heavy-based pan over medium heat, add the onion and stir-fry for about 4 minutes, or until light brown. Add the garlic and spices and stir-fry for about 1 minute.

Starting with the fatty pieces of meat first, then using the lean pieces of meat and then the liver, add a few pieces to the pan at a time along with a little of the reserved cooking water. Fry over low heat, and when the liquid has been absorbed, add a few more pieces of meat and a little more liquid. Continue until all the meat and liver has been fried, then add the remaining cooking water, reduce the heat to very low and simmer for at least 2 hours. Add the vinegar and season with salt, if using. Remove and allow to cool, then set aside in the refrigerator for about 24 hours.

The next day, heat through over low heat. Adjust the seasoning and repeat this process for further 2 days.

Saanth-Bajrae ka Soweta
Pork Skin with Millet

Origin Rajasthan
Preparation time 1 hour, plus soaking time
Cooking time 2 hours
Serves 8–10

175g / 6oz (¾ cup plus 2 tablespoons) millet

4 teaspoons chilli powder

4 teaspoons ground coriander

2 tablespoons ground onions

4 teaspoons ground garlic

2 teaspoons ground fresh ginger

250ml / 8fl oz (1 cup) milk

6 tablespoons ghee

5 tablespoons split moong dal, rinsed and drained

2 tablespoons onions, thinly sliced

1kg / 2¼lb fresh pig skin with fat, cut into 4-cm /
   1½-inch pieces and boiled

4 tablespoons natural (plain) yoghurt, whisked

salt

Put the millet in a bowl, add a little water and soak for 30 minutes, then pound it lightly with a pestle in a mortar. Put the pounded millet through a sieve (strainer) and stir, remove and discard any over-pounded grains that have turned into powder. Soak the pounded millet in a bowl of water for about 30 minutes, then stir and drain.

To make the broth, put half the chilli powder, the coriander, ground onions, garlic and ginger and 1 litre / 1¾ pints (4¼ cups) water in a large, heavy-based pan and bring to the boil, then boil for about 15 minutes. Stir in the milk, remove from the heat and set aside.

Heat 1 tablespoon ghee in a large pan over medium-high heat. Slowly add enough water to cook the millet, and when it starts boiling add the millet and dal. Season with salt, then cover and cook for about 15 minutes. When half-cooked, add the broth and keep stirring until the millet is well cooked and thick.

Heat the remaining ghee in a separate large pan over medium heat, add the sliced onions and fry for about 5–7 minutes, or until golden brown. Remove and set aside. Add the boiled pig skin, remaining chilli powder and the yoghurt to the pan, then reduce the heat to very low, cover and cook for about 1 hour, or until the liquid has completely evaporated.

Add the pig skin and fried onions to the millet and mix well. Cook over low heat for about 30 minutes, until the oil rises to the surface.

Doi Nei
Pork in Dark Sauce

Origin Tribal North East India
Preparation time 25 minutes, plus soaking time
Cooking time 1 hour 20 minutes
Serves 4

150g / 5oz (¾ cup) dried black soya beans (soybeans)

1kg / 2¼lb pork, cut into medium-sized pieces

2 teaspoons vegetable oil

2 tablespoons Ginger Paste (see page 57)

3 green chillies, de-seeded and chopped

2 onions, chopped

salt

Soak the soya beans in a bowl of water overnight.

The next day, drain the beans, transfer to a blender and process, adding a little water if necessary, to make a paste.

Heat the oil in a large, heavy-based pan over medium heat, add the ginger paste, chillies and onions and stir-fry for about 5 minutes, or until brown. Now add the pork and stir-fry for about 30 minutes, or until the water from the pork has evaporated. Now add the black bean paste and season with salt. Pour in 500ml / 18fl oz (2¼ cups) water, then reduce the heat, cover and simmer for about 45 minutes, or until the pork is cooked.

Oma Eoni
Fried Pork

Origin Tribal North East India
Preparation time 20 minutes
Cooking time 45 minutes
Serves 5

---

2 tablespoons vegetable oil

1 tablespoon Ginger Paste (see page 57)

1 tablespoon Garlic Paste (see page 57)

1 tablespoon Boiled Onion Paste (see page 57)

1kg / 2¼lb pork, cut into 2.5-cm / 1-inch pieces

salt

Heat the oil in a kadhai or deep, heavy-based pan over medium heat, add the ginger, garlic and onion pastes, and stir-fry for about 1–2 minutes, or until golden brown. Add the pork, season with salt and mix, then fry for 7–8 minutes, or until brown, stirring frequently.

Sprinkle in 125ml / 4½fl oz (½ cup) water, reduce the heat, cover and simmer for 30 minutes, or until the pork is cooked.

Tabathyu
Naga-style Pork Stew

Origin Tribal North East India
Preparation time 20 minutes
Cooking time 40 minutes
Serves 4

1kg / 2¼lb pork

5 dried red chillies, broken into small pieces

2 teaspoons Ginger Paste (see page 57)

2 teaspoons Garlic Paste (see page 57)

salt

Cut the pork into pieces.

Bring 500ml / 18fl oz (2¼ cups) water to the boil in a large, heavy-based pan. Add the pork and boil for about 30 minutes.

Mix in the remaining ingredients and cook for a further 5 minutes.

Ili
Pork Stew with Ginger

Origin Tribal North East India
Preparation time 15 minutes
Cooking time 35 minutes
Serves 4

1kg / 2¼lb pork, cut into 5-cm / 2-inch pieces

200g / 7oz (1 cup) broken rice, rinsed
  and drained

1 × 8-cm / 3-inch piece fresh ginger, peeled and
  chopped

1 teaspoon red chilli powder

salt

Bring 1 litre / 1¾ pints (4¼ cups) water to the boil in a large, heavy-based pan, add the pork and rice and return to the boil, stirring constantly. Reduce the heat and simmer for 2 minutes, then add the remaining ingredients. Cover and cook for 30 minutes, or until the pork is tender and the sauce thickens.

Arek
Pork Stew with Bamboo Shoots

Origin Tribal North East India
Preparation time 20 minutes
Cooking time 30 minutes
Serves 4

1kg / 2¼lb pork, cut into 2.5-cm / 1-inch pieces

3 teaspoons bamboo shoots, chopped

1 teaspoon chopped ginger

1 teaspoon chopped garlic

1 tomato, cut into quarters

3–4 green chillies, de-seeded and chopped

salt

Place the pork in a large, heavy-based pan over high heat with enough water to cover, then just before it starts to boil, remove from the heat and drain. Return the pork to the pan, add fresh water to cover and bring to the boil.

Mix in the remaining ingredients, then reduce the heat, cover and simmer for 30 minutes, or until the pork is tender.

Oma Bedoi Saonai
Barbecued Pork

Origin Tribal North East India
Preparation time 15 minutes, plus soaking time
Cooking time 30 minutes
Serves 4

1kg / 2¼lb pork, cut into 2.5-cm / 1-inch pieces

salt

If using bamboo skewers, soak them in cold water for about 30 minutes before using to prevent them burning during barbecuing. Prepare a charcoal grill or preheat a grill (broiler) to medium. Put the pork in a large shallow dish and sprinkle over some salt and mix. Thread the pork on to soaked bamboo or metal skewers and roast over a charcoal grill or under the grill for 30 minutes, turning frequently until golden brown and tender.

Boksa Pok
Pork with Mustard Leaves

Origin Tibal North East India
Preparation time 15 minutes
Cooking time 45 minutes
Serves 4

2½ tablespoons short-grain rice, rinsed and drained

1kg / 2¼lb pork with fat, cut into 4-cm / 1½-inch pieces

500g / 1lb 2oz fresh mustard leaves

1 × 5-cm / 2-inch piece fresh ginger, peeled chopped

½ teaspoon bicarbonate of soda (baking soda)

1 teaspoon chilli powder

salt

Bring 625ml / 1 pint (2½ cups) water to the boil in a large, heavy-based pan, add the rice and return to the boil and continue boiling until the rice is fluffy and tender.

Add the pork, bring to the boil, then uncover and cook, stirring constantly, for about 15 minutes, or until the sauce thickens with the rice. Tear the mustard leaves into small pieces and add to the pan with the ginger and continue cooking and stirring for a further 10 minutes. Mix in the bicarbonate of soda and season with salt, then simmer for a further 5 minutes. Sprinkle in the chilli powder.

Wak Pura
Pork with Mustard Leaves and Rice

Origin Tribal North East India
Preparation time 15 minutes, plus soaking and drying time
Cooking time 1 hour
Serves 4

200g / 7oz (1 cup) short-grain rice, rinsed and drained

1kg / 2 ¼lb pork, cut into 5-cm / 2-inch pieces

500g / 1lb 2oz mustard leaves, shredded

2–3 green chillies, de-seeded and cut in half

pinch of bicarbonate of soda (baking soda)

salt

Soak the rice in a bowl of water for 15 minutes, then drain. Spread out to dry on a clean tea (dish) towel until dry again, then transfer to a spice grinder and process to make a powder.

Place the pork in a large, heavy-based pan over low heat without any oil or water, and cook for about 30 minutes, or until the water from the pork evaporates and a reddish sediment starts to appear, stirring occasionally to prevent burning. As the fat starts melting, mix in the mustard leaves and chillies, then season with salt and continue cooking and stirring until the mustard leaves disintegrate and are will mixed. Cover and cook over low heat for 5–10 minutes. Stir in 500ml / 18fl oz (2¼ cups) water, and cook for a further 10 minutes.

Blend in the rice powder and bicarbonate of soda, and simmer for another 15 minutes, or until the pork is cooked and the sauce thickens.

※ ※
—

Wak Al Galda
Pork with Sorrel Leaves

Origin Tribal North East India
Preparation time 20 minutes
Cooking time 25–45 minutes
Serves 4

1kg / 2¼lb pork, cut into 5-cm / 2-inch pieces

5 sorrel leaves, roughly torn

2 teaspoons Boiled Onion Paste (see page 57)

2 teaspoons chopped ginger

2 teaspoons chopped garlic

2 teaspoons green chilli paste

salt

Place the pork in a large, heavy-based pan over low heat without any oil or water, and cook for 20–35 minutes, stirring occasionally, until the water from the pork has evaporated.

Add the remaining ingredients and keep stirring and cooking until the sorrel leaves disintegrate and are well mixed. Stir in 125ml / 4½fl oz (½ cup) water, then increase the heat, bring to the boil and boil for about 15 minutes, or until the pork is cooked and the sauce thickens.

※ ※
—

Wak Me-A-Mesang Pura
Pork with Fermented Bamboo Shoots

Origin Tribal North East India
Preparation time 25 minutes
Cooking time 1½ hours
Serves 4

1kg / 2¼lb pork with fat and bones, cut into
   medium-sized pieces

500g / 1lb 2oz fermented bamboo shoots

2 teaspoons finely chopped green chillies

2 teaspoons finely chopped ginger

pinch of ground turmeric

½ cup rice powder

salt

Place the pork in a large heavy-based pan over low heat without any oil or water and cook for about 30 minutes, stirring occasionally, until the water from the pork has evaporated and it turns light brown. Add the bamboo shoots and 250ml / 8fl oz (1 cup) water and cook for a few minutes, stirring occasionally.

Mix in the chillies, ginger and turmeric, then season with salt and simmer until dry. Stir in 500ml / 18fl oz (2¼ cups) water and cook for about 15 minutes, or until the pork is cooked.

Blend in the rice powder to thicken the sauce and cook for a further 15 minutes.

Tungrumdai
Pork with Fermented Soya Beans (Soybeans)

Origin Tribal North East India
Preparation time 20 minutes
Cooking time 45 minutes
Serves 6

---

2 teaspoons vegetable oil

2 tablespoons onion, chopped

2 tablespoons Garlic Paste (see page 57)

200g / 7oz fermented soya beans (soybeans)

1kg / 2¼lb pork, cut into 5-cm / 2-inch pieces

1 teaspoon ground black sesame seeds

salt

Heat the oil in a large frying pan (skillet) over medium heat, add the onion and garlic paste and fry for about 5–7 minutes, or until golden brown. Stir in the soya beans and pork and fry for 7–8 minutes, or until the pork is golden brown.

Pour in 250ml / 8fl oz (1 cup) water and cook for 30 minutes, or until the pork is cooked, adding more water if required. Stir in the ground sesame seeds, then season with salt and cook for a further 15 minutes. Remove from the heat and serve.

Dohneiiong
Pork with Black Sesame Seeds

Origin Tribal North East India
Preparation time 20 minutes
Cooking time 30–40 minutes
Serves 6

1kg / 2¼lb pork, cut into 8-cm / 3-inch pieces

4 onions, sliced

2 tablespoons black sesame seeds

pinch of ground turmeric

salt

Place the pork in a pressure cooker over low heat and cook for about 15 minutes, stirring constantly, until the fat is released. Remove the meat from the cooker and set aside. Add the remaining ingredients to the cooker and cook, stirring frequently, for about 5 minutes, or until the fat separates out. Add the reserved pork and cook for about 5 minutes, stirring constantly.

Stir in 500ml / 18fl oz (2¼ cups) water, close the cooker and cook under pressure for 15 minutes. Alternatively, cook in a large, heavy-based pan for about 30 minutes, or until the pork is cooked.

Voksa
Pork Ribs

Origin Tribal North East India
Preparation time 1 hour, plus cooling time
Cooking time 30 minutes
Serves 6

1kg / 2¼lb pork ribs
300g / 11oz mustard leaves, torn
1 teaspoon ground black pepper
salt

Place the ribs over a smoking fire and smoke for about 1 hour. Allow to cool, then cut into 5-cm / 2-inch pieces. Place the ribs with 625ml / 1 pint (2½ cups) water in a large, heavy-based pan and boil for 20 minutes, or until half cooked.

Add the mustard leaves and continue boiling for 10 minutes, or until the ribs and leaves are cooked. Season and sprinkle over the pepper, and serve hot.

Aoshi
Pork with Fermented Soya Beans (Soybeans) & Tomatoes

Origin Tribal North East India
Preparation time 15 minutes
Cooking time 40 minutes
Serves 6

200g / 7oz fermented soya bean (soybean) paste
1kg / 2¼lb pork, cut into large pieces
10–15 ground black peppercorns
10 dried red chillies
2 teaspoons Ginger Paste (see page 57)
2 teaspoons Garlic Paste (see page 57)
2–3 tomatoes, chopped
salt

Pour 2 litres / 3½ pints (8½ cups) water into a large heavy-based pan, add the soya bean paste and bring to the boil. Add the pork and continue boiling for 30 minutes, or until tender.

Mix in the remaining ingredients, except the salt, and continue cooking, stirring occasionally, for about 5 minutes, or until the sauce thickens. Season.

Thevo Chu
Pork with Bamboo Shoots

Origin Tribal North East India
Preparation time 15 minutes
Cooking time 1¼ hours
Serves 6

1kg / 2¼lb pork, cut into 5-cm / 2-inch pieces
225g / 8oz canned bamboo shoots, rinsed and sliced
1 teaspoon Ginger Paste (see page 57)
1 teaspoon Garlic Paste (see page 57)
2 teaspoons chilli powder
salt

Place the pork in a pan over low heat without any water or oil and keep stirring for 5 minutes. As the pork starts releasing its water, add the bamboo shoots. Cover and cook over very low heat for 1 hour. Sprinkle in some water if it gets too dry.

Uncover, mix in the remaining ingredients, increase the heat to high and cook, stirring constantly, for 5–10 minutes.

Akshi
Pork with Dried Bamboo Shoots

Origin Tribal North East India
Preparation time 15 minutes
Cooking time 35 minutes
Serves 6

100g / 3½oz dried bamboo shoots
1kg / 2¼lb pork, cut into 8-cm / 3-inch pieces
1 teaspoon Ginger Paste (see page 57)
5 green chillies, de-seeded and finely chopped
salt

Bring 625ml / 1 pint (2½ cups) water to the boil in a large, heavy-based pan, add the bamboo shoots and cook for about 5 minutes. Reduce the heat and add the pork, then cover and simmer for 30 minutes, or until tender.

Add the ginger paste and chillies and cook for a few minutes longer. Season with salt.

Wookhan
Pork Stew

Origin Tribal North East India
Preparation time 15 minutes
Cooking time 45 minutes
Serves 6

1kg / 2¼lb pork, cut into medium-sized pieces
5 green chillies, de-seeded and chopped
3 large onions, chopped
1 teaspoon Ginger Paste (see page 57)
salt

Place the pork in a large, heavy-based pan with 625ml / 1 pint (2½ cups) water and bring to the boil. Reduce the heat, cover and simmer for about 30 minutes. Add the remaining ingredients and cook, stirring frequently, for a further 15 minutes.

Wak Serjak
Pork Curry

Origin Tribal North East India
Preparation time 20 minutes
Cooking time 40 minutes
Serves 6

2 teaspoons vegetable oil
2 tablespoons Ginger Paste (see page 57)
3 green chillies, de-seeded and chopped
2 onions, chopped
3 tomatoes, chopped
1kg / 2¼lb pork, cut into medium-sized pieces
salt

Heat the oil in a kadhai, wok or deep, heavy-based pan over medium heat, add the ginger paste, chillies, onions and tomatoes and fry for about 5 minutes, or until golden brown. Add the pork and stir-fry until the water from the pork has evaporated.

Season with salt and stir in 625ml / 1 pint (2½ cups) water, then cover and simmer for 30 minutes, or until the pork is cooked.

Machu Rasin Chisik
Beef with Sorrel Leaves

Origin Tribal North East India
Preparation time 15 minutes
Cooking time 1 hour
Serves 6

1kg / 2¼lb beef, cut into 2.5-cm /1-inch pieces
3 spring onions (scallions), trimmed and finely chopped
3 green chillies, de-seeded and finely chopped
5 sorrel leaves, torn
1 teaspoon alkaline water
pinch of bicarbonate of soda (baking soda)
salt

Place the beef in a large, heavy-based pan over low heat without any water or oil, and cook, stirring constantly, for 15 minutes, or until the water from the beef has evaporated.

Stir in 250ml / 8fl oz (1 cup) water and continue cooking and stirring until dry. Repeat until the beef is tender. It should take about 40 minutes.

Add the spring onions, green chillies and sorrel leaves and fry for about 2 minutes. Stir in 500ml / 18fl oz (2¼ cups) water, then bring to the boil and add the alkaline water. Reduce the heat and simmer for about 15 minutes.

Season with salt and sprinkle in the bicarbonate of soda, mix well and cook for a few minutes until the sauce thickens.

PULSES

Pulses (legumes) are eaten throughout India, and are an essential source of protein for the many vegetarians in the country. Sometimes served with breads or rice, and often cooked with vegetables or meat, pulses are surprisingly versatile and contribute to a great many favourite Indian dishes. Used whole, split, or ground they can add texture to stews and sambhars and bring richness to soups.

5

Pulses

✳

Kholamba
Spicy Pigeon Pea Curry from Mangalore

Origin Coastal
Preparation time 25–40 minutes
Cooking time 25 minutes
Serves 4

100g / 3½oz (½ cup) arhar dal or toor (toover) dal,
    rinsed and drained

250ml / 8fl oz (1 cup) Tamarind Extract (see page 58)

100g / 3½oz (1 cup) cauliflower florets

1 small carrot, cut into slices

1 small potato, cut into cubes

40g / 1½oz (¼ cup) peas, shelled if fresh

2–3 tomatoes, cut into quarters

2 green chillies, slit in half lengthways and
    de-seeded (optional)

½ teaspoon ground turmeric

2–3 curry leaves

salt

4 tablespoons coriander (cilantro) leaves, to garnish

For the spice paste

2 teaspoons vegetable oil

2 tablespoons coriander seeds

½ teaspoon cumin seeds

¼ teaspoon fenugreek seeds

¼ teaspoon black peppercorns

½ teaspoon asafoetida

2–3 dried red chillies

1 teaspoon chana dal, rinsed and drained

1 teaspoon urad dal, rinsed and drained

2–3 curry leaves

For the tempering

2 teaspoons vegetable oil

1 teaspoon mustard seeds

½ teaspoon fenugreek seeds

1 sprig curry leaves

Place the dal in a pressure cooker with 250ml /
8fl oz (1 cup) water and cook under pressure for
about 5 minutes. Using a whisk, whisk the dal
well and set aside. Alternatively, cook the dal
with the water in a large, heavy-based pan for
about 20 minutes, or until soft.

Heat the oil for the spice paste in a kadhai or deep,
heavy-based frying pan (skillet) over low heat, add
all the ingredients for the paste and stir-fry gently
for about 2–3 minutes, or until the spices and chillies
are fragrant and the dals are golden.

Mix in 4 tablespoons water, then transfer to a mortar
or spice grinder and pound with a pestle or process
to make a smooth paste.

Place the tamarind extract, vegetables, chillies,
turmeric and curry leaves in the pan used for frying
the spices, then season with salt and bring to the
boil. Reduce the heat, cover and simmer for about
15 minutes, or until the vegetables are tender. Stir
in the spice paste and simmer, uncovered, for a
further 5 minutes, or until well blended. Pour in the
cooked dal and simmer for another 1–2 minutes,
stirring gently until well blended.

Heat the oil for the tempering in a small frying pan
over medium heat, add all the ingredients for the
tempering and stir-fry for about 1 minute, or until the
mustard seeds start to splutter, then stir into the dal
and garnish with coriander leaves.

Arhar ki Dal
Pigeon Pea Dal

Origin Awadh/Delhi
Preparation time 10 minutes, plus soaking time
Cooking time 40 minutes
Serves 4

250g / 9oz (1⅓ cups) arhar dal or toor (toover) dal,
    rinsed and drained

pinch of asafoetida

1 teaspoon ground turmeric

1 teaspoon jaggery, crumbled, or soft brown sugar

3½ tablespoons ghee or vegetable oil

2 cloves

salt

Soak the dal in a large bowl of water for 1 hour,
then drain.

Bring 1 litre / 1¾ pints (4¼ cups) water to the boil
in a large, heavy-based pan. Add the dal with half
of the asafoetida and the turmeric, then season
with salt. Cover and continue to boil for about
15 minutes, or until the water has almost evaporated
and the dal shows signs of softening. Add 125ml /
4½fl oz (½ cup) water, cover again, reduce the heat
to low and simmer for about 10 minutes, or until the
dal is soft. Mash the cooked dal well with a wooden
spatula. Add 125ml / 4½fl oz (½ cup) hot water and
mix thoroughly to dilute the dal. Sprinkle over the
jaggery or sugar and cook over low heat for
a further 5 minutes.

Heat the ghee or oil in a frying pan (skillet) over
medium heat, add the cloves and the rest of the
asafoetida and stir-fry for 1 minute, or until the
cloves start to splutter, then immediately pour over
the dal and stir. Cover and simmer for 2 minutes,
or until hot.

Mandhiya
Pigeon Peas in Rice Konji

Origin Coastal
Preparation time 30 minutes
Cooking time 15–20 minutes
Serves 4

½ teaspoon fresh ginger

½ teaspoon ground kachri (optional)

½ teaspoon dried green mango

150g / 5oz (¾ cup) cooked arhar dal
    or toor (toover) dal, cooking water reserved

300ml / ½ pint (1¼ cups) natural (plain) yoghurt,
    whisked

½ teaspoon ground turmeric

½ teaspoon amchoor

pinch of chilli powder

2 green chillies, de-seeded and cut into 4 pieces

1 teaspoon ghee

2 cloves

½ teaspoon cumin seeds

pinch of asafoetida

salt

Put the ginger, kachri, if using, and dried green mango
in a mortar or small blender and pound with a pestle
or process in a food processor until ground.

Put the cooked dal, yoghurt, ground spices and
chillies in a large pan and season with salt. Pour
in 500ml / 18fl oz (2¼ cups) cooking water and
mix to combine.

Heat the ghee in a frying pan (skillet) over medium
heat, add the cloves, cumin seeds and asafoetida and
stir-fry for about 1 minute. Stir the spices into the dal
mixture and cook for about 5–10 minutes, or until
hot but not boiling. The consistency should remain
quite thin.

Sambhar
Tamil Nadu Dal with Drumsticks

Origin Tamil Nadu
Preparation time 30 minutes, plus soaking time
Cooking time 1 hour
Serves 4

200g / 7oz (1 cup) arhar or toor (toover) dal, rinsed

200g / 7oz (vegetable) drumsticks, cut into
    6-cm / 2½-inch pieces

1 teaspoon ground turmeric

1 teaspoon chilli powder

4 green chillies, slit in half lengthways

120g / 4oz (4–6 medium) shallots

300g / 11oz (2 medium) tomatoes, chopped

2 teaspoons Sambhar Masala (see page 32)

2 tablespoons Tamarind Extract (see page 58)

3 tablespoons chopped coriander (cilantro) leaves

salt

For the tempering

2 tablespoons vegetable oil

1 teaspoon cumin seeds

1 teaspoon coriander seeds

1 teaspoon black sesame seeds

1 teaspoon black mustard seeds

1 teaspoon urad dal, rinsed and drained

15–20 curry leaves

generous pinch of asafoetida

Soak the dal in a large bowl of water for 30 minutes.
Put the drained dal in a large, heavy-based pan,
add 1 litre / 1¾ pints (4¼ cups) water, the turmeric,
chilli powder, drumsticks, green chillies, shallots
and tomatoes, and season with salt. Bring to the
boil and cook for about 20 minutes, or until the dal
and drumsticks are cooked. Add the sambhar masala,
stir, then reduce the heat to very low and simmer,
stirring occasionally, for 5 minutes.

Heat the oil for the tempering in a frying pan
(skillet) over medium heat, add all the seeds together
with the urad dal and stir-fry briefly until the seeds
start to pop. Add the curry leaves and asafoetida
and stir-fry until the leaves stop spluttering. Pour
the tempering over the simmering sambhar, then add
the tamarind extract and stir. Reduce the heat to low
and simmer, stirring occasionally, for 10–12 minutes.
Add the chopped coriander, stir, remove from the
heat and adjust the seasoning, if necessary.

Tadka Dal
Tempered Yellow Dal

Origin Punjab
Preparation time 30 minutes
Cooking time 30–40 minutes
Serves 4–6

200g / 7oz (1 cup) arhar dal or toor (toover) dal, rinsed
    and drained

2 onions, 1 chopped and 1 sliced

1 teaspoon cumin seeds

3–4 cloves garlic

1 teaspoon chopped fresh ginger

2 tablespoons chopped coriander (cilantro) leaves

2 tomatoes

2 teaspoons coriander seeds

2 dried red chillies

2 tablespoons butter

1 black cardamom pod

1 cinnamon stick, about 2.5cm / 1 inch long

2 cloves

3 teaspoons chilli powder

salt

Bring 600ml / 1 pint (2½ cups) water to the boil in
a large, heavy-based pan, add the dal, reduce the
heat and cook for about 30 minutes, or until soft.
Drain, then return to the pan and set aside.

Put the chopped onion, the cumin seeds, garlic,
ginger, chopped coriander, tomatoes, coriander
seeds, and dried red chillies in a blender or food
processor and process until ground to a paste.

Melt the butter in another large, heavy-based pan
over medium heat, add the sliced onion, cardamom
pod, cinnamon and cloves and fry for about
7–8 minutes, or until the onions are golden brown.
Add the masala paste and fry for 10–15 minutes.
Now add the cooked dal, a little water if it is
too thick and season with salt. Boil for a further
15 minutes, or until cooked to your liking.

Chettinad Murungaikkai Sambhar
Drumstick Sambhar from Chettinad

Origin Tamil Nadu
Preparation time 15–30 minutes
Cooking time 35 minutes
Serves 6

150g / 5oz (¾ cup) arhar dal or toor (toover) dal,
    rinsed and drained

½ teaspoon ground turmeric

1½ teaspoons Chettinad Sambhar Powder
    (see page 49)

2 (vegetable) drumsticks, cut into 8-cm / 3-inch pieces

40g / 1½oz (¼ cup) chopped shallots

1 tomato, finely chopped

250ml / 8fl oz (1 cup) Tamarind Extract (see page 58)

salt

2 tablespoons finely chopped coriander (cilantro)
    leaves, to garnish

For the tempering

2 teaspoons vegetable oil

½ teaspoon mustard seeds

½ teaspoon fenugreek seeds

¼ teaspoon fennel seeds

½ teaspoon asafoetida

1 teaspoon urad dal, rinsed and drained

1 sprig curry leaves

Place the dal in a pressure cooker with 375ml / 13fl oz (1½ cups) water and cook under pressure for 5 minutes. Drain the dal, reserving the cooking water. Alternatively, cook the dal with the water in a large, heavy-based pan for about 20 minutes, or until soft.

Transfer the reserved dal water to a large, heavy-based pan. Add the turmeric, sambhar masala and vegetables and season with salt. Mix well and simmer for 10–12 minutes, or until the vegetables are tender. Stir in the tamarind extract and simmer for a further 10–15 minutes, or until the raw aroma of tamarind disappears. Add the drained dal and simmer for another 5 minutes, stirring occasionally, until blended.

Heat the oil for the tempering in a small frying pan (skillet) over medium heat, add the seeds, asafoetida, urad dal and curry leaves and stir-fry for about 1 minute, or until the mustard seeds start to splutter. Pour the mixture into the sambhar and garnish with chopped coriander.

Thenga Chertha Ulli Sambhar
Dal with Vegetables

Origin Tamil Nadu
Preparation time 30 minutes, plus cooling time
Cooking time 35 minutes
Serves 6

250g / 9oz (1⅓ cups) arhar dal or toor (toover) dal,
    rinsed and drained

500g / 1lb 2oz shallots

6 green chillies, slit in half lengthways
    and de-seeded (optional)

1 tablespoon Tamarind Extract (see page 58)

1 sprig coriander (cilantro), leaves only, chopped

For the spice paste

1 coconut, grated

4 tablespoons Sambhar Masala (see page 32)

1 teaspoon ground turmeric

1 teaspoon chilli powder

large pinch of asafoetida

salt

For the tempering

2 tablespoons coconut oil

1 teaspoon mustard seeds

1 teaspoon urad dal, rinsed and drained

2 dried red chillies, torn into pieces

2 sprigs curry leaves

Place the coconut for the spice paste in a frying pan (skillet) and dry-roast over low heat, stirring constantly, for about 2 minutes, or until it turns brown. Allow to cool, then transfer to a blender or food processor, add 250ml / 8fl oz (1 cup) water and process to make a fine paste. Mix in the ground spice powders and season with salt.

Put the dal in a large, heavy-based pan with the shallots, chillies and 125ml / 4½fl oz (½ cup) water and cook over high heat for about 25 minutes, or until soft. Using a wooden spatula, mash the mixture when cooked, then add the spice paste and stir well.

Meanwhile, heat the oil for the tempering in a small frying pan over medium heat, add the tempering ingredients and stir-fry for 1–2 minutes, or until the mustard seeds start to splutter and the dried red chillies turn a shade darker. Pour the mixture into the sambhar and garnish with coriander.

Split Red Dal
p.573

Sweet Yoghurt
Shake
p.719

Layered Paratha
p.609

Dal with Spinach
p.562

Beetroot (Beet)
Curry   p.323

Rice with Lentils
                  p.666

548

Sweet & Tangy
Yellow Dal   p.562

Mint Rasam
p.566

Fried Savoury
Cabbage   p.261

Dry Black
Lentils p.583

Mushrooms with
Cashew Nuts   p.272

Savoury Split Black
Lentil Dal   p.583

Prawn (Shrimp)
Cutlets   p.383

Vegetable
Stew   p.349

Ginger-flavoured
Moong Beans   p.576

Tomato Pepper
Water   p.585

Dry Masala Chicken
                p.524

Caulifower with
Oranges   p.257

Mixed Dal
p.562

Paneer with
Spinach p.312

Chana Dal with
Bottle Gourd   p.567

Jeera Rasam
Cumin Seed Rasam

Origin Tamil Nadu
Preparation time 10 minutes, plus soaking time
Cooking time 15 minutes
Serves 6

375ml / 13fl oz (1½ cups) Tamarind Extract
    (see page 58)

¾ teaspoon Spice Mixture for Pepper Water
    (see page 53)

salt

For the spice paste

1 teaspoon arhar dal or toor (toover) dal, rinsed
    and drained

1½ teaspoon cumin seeds

For the tempering

2 teaspoons ghee

1 teaspoon mustard seeds

2–3 dried red chillies, halved

1 sprig curry leaves

For the spice paste, put the dal and cumin seeds in a bowl, pour in 250ml / 8fl oz (1 cup) warm water and soak for 30 minutes.

Drain the dal and cumin, transfer to a small blender or food processor and process to a smooth paste. Transfer to a bowl, pour in 250ml / 8fl oz (1 cup) water and mix together. Set aside.

Combine the tamarind extract and spice mixture for pepper water in a heavy-based pan, season with salt and bring to the boil. Reduce the heat and simmer for about 10 minutes, or until the raw aroma of tamarind disappears. Mix in the spice paste with a little water, if necessary, and return to the boil. Reduce the heat and simmer for 5 minutes, or until the rasam froths up.

Heat the ghee for the tempering in a small frying pan (skillet) over medium heat, add all the ingredients for the tempering and stir-fry for about 1 minute, or until the mustard seeds start to splutter, then stir into the rasam.

Vendaya Rasam
Fenugreek Seed Rasam

Origin Tamil Nadu
Preparation time 30 minutes, plus soaking time
Cooking time 15 minutes
Serves 4–6

250ml / 8fl oz (1 cup) Tamarind Extract (see page 58)

1 teaspoon Spice Mixture for Pepper Water
    (see page 53)

½ teaspoon asafoetida

salt

1 tomato, cut into quarters

2 tablespoons chopped coriander (cilantro) leaves,
    to garnish

Plain Boiled Rice, to serve (see page 631)

For the spice paste

2 teaspoons ghee

½ teaspoon fenugreek seeds

2 teaspoons arhar dal or toor (toover) dal, rinsed
    and drained

For the tempering

2 teaspoons ghee

1 teaspoon mustard seeds

2–3 dried red chillies

1 sprig curry leaves

Heat the ghee for the spice paste in a deep, heavy-based frying pan (skillet) over medium heat, add the fenugreek seeds and dal and fry for about 1 minute, or until the dal turns golden. Put the fried seeds and dal in a bowl, pour in 125ml / 4½fl oz (½ cup) water and soak for about 30 minutes. Drain, transfer to a small blender and process to make a smooth paste.

Combine the tamarind extract, spice mixture for pepper water and asafoetida in the pan used for frying the spices. Season with salt, then place over medium heat and bring to the boil. Reduce the heat and simmer for about 10 minutes, or until the raw aroma of tamarind disappears. Add the tomato, spice paste and 250ml / 8fl oz (1 cup) water and simmer for about 5 minutes, or until the rasam froths up. Remove from the heat.

Heat the ghee for the tempering in a small frying pan over medium heat, add all the ingredients for the tempering and stir-fry for about 1 minute, or until the mustard seeds start to splutter. Stir into the rasam and garnish with chopped coriander.

☀ / 📷 pp.279, 559

Keoti Dal
Mixed Dal

Origin Hyderabad
Preparation time 45 minutes, plus soaking time
Cooking time 30 minutes
Serves 6

200g / 7oz (1 cup) toor (toover) dal, rinsed and drained
4 tablespoons masoor dal, rinsed and drained
½ teaspoon ground turmeric
4 tablespoons vegetable oil
100g / 3½oz (1 small) onion, sliced
1 teaspoon Ginger Paste (see page 57)
1 teaspoon Garlic Paste (see page 57)
2 green chillies, de-seeded and chopped
1 sprig coriander (cilantro), leaves only, chopped
1 teaspoon lemon juice
salt

For the tempering

1 tablespoon ghee or vegetable oil
½ teaspoon mustard seeds
½ teaspoon cumin seeds
4 whole dried red chillies
5–6 cloves garlic
few curry leaves

Soak both dals in a bowl of water for 2 hours. Drain.

Bring 1 litre / 1¾ pints (4¼ cups) water to the boil in a large, heavy-based pan. Add the dals, reserving half the toor dal, then add the turmeric and season with salt. Reduce the heat and simmer for about 20 minutes, or until soft. Drain, then return to the pan and mash lightly with a wooden spatula.

Put the reserved dal in another pan, pour in enough water to cover, then bring to the boil and cook for about 15 minutes, or until it is soft but still retains a bite. Drain and set aside.

Heat the oil in another large, heavy-based pan over medium heat, add the onions and fry for about 5 minutes, or until light brown. Add the ginger and garlic pastes and stir-fry for a further 1 minute. Now add the mashed dal and 250ml / 8fl oz (1 cup) water, bring to the boil, add the reserved dal, chopped chillies, coriander and the lemon juice, and stir. Reduce the heat and simmer for 5–10 minutes.

Heat the ghee or oil in a frying pan (skillet) over medium heat, add the mustard and cumin seeds, dried red chillies, garlic and curry leaves and stir-fry for about 1–2 minutes, or until the seeds start to splutter and the chillies turn a shade darker. Pour over the dal, stir, then cover and simmer for 2 minutes.

☀ / 📷 p.549

Aamati
Sweet & Tangy Yellow Dal

Origin Maharashtra
Preparation time 35 minutes, plus soaking time
Cooking time 15 minutes
Serves 7–8

100g / 3½oz (½ cup) toor (toover) dal, rinsed and drained
1 tablespoon vegetable oil
1 teaspoon mustard seeds
small pinch of asafoetida
1 teaspoon ground turmeric
1 onion, chopped
4 green chillies, de-seeded and chopped
2 tomatoes, chopped
1 teaspoon sugar
2 teaspoons Garam Masala (see page 31)
chopped coriander (cilantro) leaves, to garnish
salt

Soak the dal in a bowl of water for 1 hour.

Drain the dal, transfer to a medium-sized, heavy-based pan, pour in enough water to cover and bring to the boil. Reduce the heat and simmer for about 25 minutes, or until soft. Drain, return to the pan and mash with a wooden spatula.

Heat the oil in a medium-sized, heavy-based pan over medium heat, add the mustard seeds and stir-fry for 1 minute, or until they start to splutter, then add the asafoetida, turmeric, onion, and chillies and stir-fry for 5 minutes, or until the onion is light brown. Add the tomatoes and fry for 3–4 minutes, or until soft.

Add the mashed dal to the pan together with 250ml / 8fl oz (1 cup) water. Stir vigorously, then cook over high heat until bubbles start rising to the top. Reduce the heat to medium, season with salt, then add the sugar and garam masala. Mix well and simmer for a further 5 minutes. Remove from the heat and serve garnished with chopped coriander.

Moog aur Palak ki Dal
Dal with Spinach

Origin Awadh
Preparation time 20 minutes
Cooking time 30 minutes
Serves 6

250g / 9oz (1⅓ cups) toor (toover) dal, rinsed and drained
¼ teaspoon ground turmeric
4 tablespoons vegetable oil or ghee
1 teaspoon Ginger Paste (see page 57)
1 teaspoon Garlic Paste (see page 57)
250g / 9oz spinach, chopped
4 green chillies, de-seeded and cut in half
1 small sprig coriander (cilantro), leaves only, chopped
juice of 1 lemon
salt

For the tempering
1 tablespoon vegetable oil
4 dried red chillies
½ teaspoon mustard seeds
½ teaspoon cumin seeds
5–6 cloves garlic
few curry leaves

Bring 500ml / 18fl oz (2¼ cups) water to the boil in a large, heavy-based pan. Add the dal and turmeric and season with salt, then reduce the heat and cook for about 20 minutes, or until soft. Drain, then return to the pan and mash lightly with a wooden spoon or spatula, then set aside.

Heat the 4 tablespoons oil or ghee in a frying pan (skillet) over medium-low heat, add the ginger and garlic pastes and stir-fry for 1 minute, then add the spinach and cook for a few minutes until almost tender. Add the cooked spinach mixture to the dal, add a little water, then return to the heat and cook for 5–10 minutes. Stir in the chillies, coriander and lemon juice.

Heat the oil for the tempering in a small frying pan over medium heat, add all the ingredients for the tempering and stir-fry for 1–2 minutes, or until the mustard seeds start to splutter and the chillies turn a shade darker. Pour over the dal, cover and simmer for 2 minutes, or until hot.

The Rasam
Tamil Nadu Piquant Soup

Origin Tamil Nadu
Preparation time 15 minutes
Cooking time 25 minutes
Serves 4

2 tablespoons toor (toover) dal, rinsed and drained
2 teaspoons coriander seeds
1 tablespoon cumin seeds
2 teaspoons black peppercorns, roasted and coarsely ground
1 tablespoon Tamarind Extract (see page 58)
100g / 3½oz (1 small) tomato, chopped
1 teaspoon ground turmeric
4 cloves garlic, crushed
salt

For the tempering
1 tablespoon vegetable oil
2 dried red chillies, stems removed and wiped with a damp cloth
1 teaspoon mustard seeds
1 teaspoon cumin seeds
pinch of asafoetida
20 curry leaves

Heat a heavy-based frying pan (skillet) over low-medium heat, add the dal, coriander seeds, cumin seeds and roasted ground pepper and fry briefly until they smell fragrant. Transfer to a spice grinder or mortar and process or pound with a pestle to make a coarse powder. Set aside.

Put 500ml / 18fl oz (2¼ cups) water in a large, heavy-based pan, add the tamarind extract, tomato and turmeric and season with salt. Stir well, bring to the boil, then reduce the heat to low and simmer, stirring occasionally, for 8–10 minutes. Add the crushed garlic and the dal-pepper powder, stir, cover, increase the heat to medium and cook until the mixture begins to boil. Reduce the heat to low and simmer while you make the tempering.

Heat the oil for the tempering in a frying pan over medium heat, add the dried red chillies, mustard seeds and cumin seeds and stir-fry for about 1 minute, or until the seeds start to splutter. Add the asafoetida and curry leaves and stir-fry until the leaves stop spluttering. Pour over the rasam and mix well.

✻ ✻
___

Kathirikkai Rasam
Aubergine (Eggplant) Rasam

Origin Tamil Nadu
Preparation time 1 hour, plus soaking time
Cooking time 20 minutes
Serves 6

___

10–12 small aubergines (eggplant)

4 tablespoons toor (toover) dal, rinsed and drained

1 tomato, chopped

500ml / 18fl oz (2¼ cups) Tamarind Extract
   (see page 58)

½ teaspoon ground turmeric

salt

2–3 tablespoons chopped coriander (cilantro) leaves,
   to garnish

___

For the spice powder

3 teaspoons vegetable oil

2 teaspoons coriander seeds

½ teaspoon fenugreek seeds

½ teaspoon black peppercorns

½ teaspoon asafoetida

3–4 dried red chillies

1 teaspoon chana dal, rinsed and drained

2 teaspoons grated fresh coconut

___

For the tempering

2 teaspoons ghee or vegetable oil

1 teaspoon mustard seeds

1 teaspoon cumin seeds

1 dried red chilli, halved

1 sprig curry leaves

___

Cut the aubergines into quarters and soak in a bowl
of salted water.

Meanwhile, place the dal in a pressure cooker
with 375ml / 13fl oz (1½ cups) water and cook under
pressure for 5 minutes. Alternatively, cook the
dal with the water in a large, heavy-based pan for
about 20 minutes, or until soft.

Heat the oil for the spice powder in a deep, heavy-
based frying pan (skillet) over medium heat. Add all the
ingredients for the spice powder, except the coconut,
and stir-fry for 1–2 minutes, or until the spices are
fragrant and the dal is golden. Mix in the coconut, then
transfer to a mortar or spice grinder and pound with a
pestle or process to make a fine powder.

Heat the ghee or oil for the tempering in the pan used
for frying the spices, add all the ingredients for the
tempering and stir-fry over medium heat for about
1 minute, or until the mustard seeds start to splutter.
Drain the aubergines, add to the pan with the tomato
and stir over the heat for about 2 minutes.

Stir in the tamarind extract, turmeric and spice
powder, then season with salt and simmer for about
10–12 minutes, or until the raw aroma of tamarind
disappears and the aubergines are tender.

Add the cooked dal and if the rasam is too thick
add more water. Simmer for a further 5 minutes,
or until the rasam froths up. Remove from the heat
and garnish with chopped coriander.

✻ ✻
___

Masiyal
Spinach Mash

Origin Coastal
Preparation time 25 minutes
Cooking time 50 minutes
Serves 4

___

200g / 7oz (1 cup) toor (toover) dal, rinsed
   and drained

250ml / 8fl oz (1 cup) Tamarind Extract
   (see page 58)

1 teaspoon Sambhar Masala (see page 32)

15–20 curry leaves, shredded

2 tablespoons vegetable oil

1 teaspoon mustard seeds

3 dried red chillies

3 green chillies, de-seeded and chopped

500g / 1lb 2 oz spinach leaves

salt

___

Put the dal in a large, heavy-based pan, pour in
750ml / 1¼ pints (3¼ cups) water and bring to the boil.
Cook for about 40 minutes, or until the dal is soft.
Drain off any excess cooking water, then add the
tamarind extract, sambhar masala and curry leaves
and season with salt. Set aside.

Heat the oil in a frying pan (skillet) over medium heat,
add the mustard seeds and chillies and stir-fry for
about 1–2 minutes. Pour over the dal and return the dal
to the boil. Mash the dal well with a wooden spatula.

Boil the spinach in a separate pan for a few minutes, or
until wilted. Drain and squeeze, to remove any excess
cooking water, then chop roughly. Add to the dal and
mash together with a wooden spatula or potato masher.

___

Podi Sambhar
Sambhar with Fresh Ground Spices

Origin Tamil Nadu
Preparation time 25–50 minutes
Cooking time 30 minutes
Serves 6

___

150 g / 5oz (¾ cup) toor (toover) dal, rinsed
    and drained

1 green or red (bell) pepper, de-seeded and cut into
    small squares

1 mooli (daikon), cut into slices

1 (vegetable) drumstick, cut into 8-cm / 3-inch
    pieces

1 potato, cut into cubes

½ teaspoon ground turmeric

375ml / 13fl oz (1½ cups) Tamarind Extract
    (see page 58)

salt

2 tablespoons finely chopped coriander (cilantro)
    leaves, to garnish

For the spice paste

2 teaspoons vegetable oil

6 dried red chillies

1 tablespoon coriander seeds

½ teaspoon cumin seeds

¼ teaspoon fenugreek seeds

½ teaspoon asafoetida

2 teaspoons chana dal, rinsed and drained

2 tablespoons grated fresh coconut

For the tempering

2 teaspoons sesame oil

1 teaspoon mustard seeds

1 dried red chilli

1 sprig curry leaves

Heat 2 teaspoons oil for the spice paste in a deep, heavy-based frying pan (skillet) over medium heat, add the dried red chillies, spices and dal and stir-fry for about 2 minutes, or until the chillies and spices are fragrant and the dal is golden. Transfer to a bowl and set aside.

Place the dal in a pressure cooker with 375ml / 13fl oz (1½ cups) water and cook under pressure for about 5 minutes. Alternatively, put the dal and water in a large, heavy-based pan and cook for about 25 minutes, or until soft.

Add 1 teaspoon oil to the pan used to cook the spices and heat through. Add the grated coconut and fry for 1 minute. Add to the spices, then transfer to a mortar or small blender and pound with a pestle or process to make a smooth paste.

Combine the vegetables, turmeric and tamarind extract in the pan used for frying spices. Season with salt, then bring to the boil. Reduce the heat and simmer for about 10 minutes, or until the aroma of raw tamarind disappears and the vegetables are tender. Mix in the spice paste and simmer for about 5 minutes. Pour in the cooked dal and simmer for about 5 minutes, stirring occasionally, until well blended.

Heat the oil for the tempering in a small frying pan over medium heat, add all the ingredients for the tempering and stir-fry for about 1 minute, or until the mustard seeds start to splutter. Stir into the sambhar and garnish with chopped coriander.

___

Lachko Dal
Thick Yellow Toor (Toover) Dal

Origin North East India
Preparation time 20–35 minutes, plus cooling time
Cooking time 10 minutes
Serves 4

___

200g / 7oz (1 cup) toor (toover) dal or arhar dal,
    rinsed and drained

1 × 2.5-cm / 1-inch piece fresh ginger

¼ teaspoon ground turmeric

1 tablespoon ghee

¼ teaspoon asafoetida

salt

Cook the dal with 1 litre / 1¾ pints (4¼ cups) water, and the ginger and turmeric in a pressure cooker for about 15 minutes. Remove from the heat and allow to cool. Alternatively, cook the dal with the water and spices in a large, heavy-based pan for about 25 minutes, then allow to cool. Drain and put the dal into a clean pan.

Heat the ghee in a small frying pan (skillet) over medium heat, add the asafoetida and stir-fry for about 30 seconds, then pour over the cooked dal and mash with a wooden spatula or potato masher until smooth. Return to the heat, season with salt and simmer for about 10 minutes, or until thick, then serve.

※ / 📷 p.550

Pudina Rasam
Mint Rasam

Preparation time 40 minutes
Cooking time 15 minutes
Serves 6

100 g / 3½ oz (½ cup) arhar dal or toor (toover) dal,
   rinsed and drained
½ teaspoon ground turmeric
1 bunch mint leaves
2 green chillies, de-seeded (optional)
1½ teaspoons coriander seeds
¾ teaspoon cumin seeds
4 tablespoons black peppercorns
1½ tablespoons lime juice
salt
2 tablespoons coriander (cilantro) leaves, to garnish

For the tempering
2 teaspoons ghee
14 tablespoons mustard seeds
1 teaspoon cumin seeds
½ teaspoon asafoetida
1 dried red chilli
1 sprig curry leaves

Place the dal in a pressure cooker with the turmeric
and 250ml / 8fl oz (1 cup) water and cook under
pressure for about 5 minutes. Alternatively, put the
dal, turmeric and water in a heavy-based pan and
cook for about 25 minutes, or until the dal is soft.

Put the mint leaves, chillies, coriander seeds, cumin
seeds and peppercorns in a small blender, add
2 tablespoons water and process to a paste.

Transfer the dal to a heavy-based pan, add 500ml
/ 18fl oz (2¼ cups) water and whisk well. Add the
mint and spice paste, season with salt and mix well.
Place the pan over high heat and bring to the boil.
Add more water if the rasam is too thick. Reduce
the heat and simmer for about 5 minutes, or until
the rasam froths up. Remove from the heat and stir
in the lime juice.

Heat the ghee for the tempering in a small frying pan
(skillet) over medium heat, add all the ingredients
for the tempering and stir-fry for about 1 minute, or
until the mustard seeds start to splutter. Stir into
the rasam and garnish with coriander leaves. Serve
hot as an appetizer or with plain rice.

Chholar Dal
Chana Dal with Coconut

Origin West Bengal
Preparation time 30 minutes
Cooking time 45 minutes
Serves 4

2 bay leaves
1 cinnamon stick, about 5cm / 2 inches long
3–4 green cardamom pods, seeds removed
4–6 cloves
2 dried red chillies
1 teaspoon cumin seeds
250g / 9oz (1⅓ cups) chana dal, rinsed and drained
5–6 green chillies, split in half lengthways
   and de-seeded
1 teaspoon ground turmeric
3 teaspoons sugar
1 tablespoon ghee
1 small coconut, peeled and flesh cut into dice
50g / 1¾oz (⅓ cup) raisins
1 teaspoon chilli powder
1 teaspoon ground cumin
salt

Heat a tawa or frying pan (skillet) over medium-low
heat, add the bay leaves, cinnamon stick, cardamom,
cloves, dried red chillies and cumin seeds and roast
for about 2 minutes, or until they start to darken
and smell fragrant. Transfer to a mortar and pound
with a pestle or process in a spice grinder to make
a fine powder. Set aside.

Bring 1 litre / 1¾ pints (4¼ cups) water to the boil
in a pan, then add the dal, reduce the heat and cook,
stirring occasionally and removing the scum that
rises to the surface with a slotted spoon, for
30 minutes, or until the dal is soft. Add the split
chillies, turmeric and sugar and season with salt.

Heat the ghee in a small frying pan over high heat.
Reduce the heat to medium, add the coconut and
stir-fry for a few minutes, or until the coconut
is brown, then pour over the dal. Add the raisins,
cover and simmer for about 5 minutes. Sprinkle the
ground spices, chilli powder and ground cumin over
the dal and cover. Do not stir until ready to serve.

Chana Dal Lauki Waali
Chana Dal with Bottle Gourd

Origin Awadh
Preparation time 30 minutes, plus soaking time
Cooking time 35–40 minutes
Serves 7–8

400g / 14oz (2 cups) chana dal, rinsed and drained

200g / 7oz bottle gourd (calabash), rinsed, peeled
    and cut into medium-sized pieces

2 teaspoons chilli powder

2 tablespoons sliced fresh ginger

1½ teaspoons ground turmeric

3 teaspoons ground coriander

8 cloves garlic

1 tablespoon Garam Masala (see page 31)

salt

small bunch of mint leaves, chopped, to garnish

For the tempering

2 tablespoons ghee or vegetable oil

1 tablespoon cumin seeds, roasted

1 onion, sliced

Soak the dal in a large bowl of water for about
1 hour. Drain.

Put the dal in a deep, heavy-based pan together with
the bottle gourd and the spices and garlic. Bring to
the boil, then reduce the heat and cook for about
30 minutes, or until the dal is cooked. Remove from
the heat, season with salt and set aside.

Heat the ghee or oil for the tempering in a frying
pan (skillet) over medium heat, add the roasted
cumin seeds and onion and stir-fry for about
5–7 minutes, or until the onion is golden brown.
Make sure the cumin seeds do not burn. Pour
over the dal, then stir in the garam masala. Serve,
garnished with chopped mint.

Mangalore Saar
Rasam from Mangalore

Origin Coastal
Preparation time 25 minutes
Cooking time 20 minutes
Serves 6

3 teaspoons vegetable oil

1 teaspoon cumin seeds

¼ teaspoon fenugreek seeds

¾ teaspoon black peppercorns

2 teaspoons chana dal, rinsed and drained

1½ teaspoons urad dal, rinsed and drained

1 sprig curry leaves

2 teaspoons grated fresh coconut

500ml / 18fl oz (2¼ cups) Tamarind Extract
    (see page 58)

salt

2 tablespoons coriander (cilantro) leaves, to garnish

Plain Rice, to serve (see page 631)

For the tempering

2 teaspoons vegetable oil

1 teaspoon mustard seeds

½ teaspoon asafoetida

Heat 2 teaspoons oil in a kadhai or deep, heavy-
based frying pan (skillet) over medium heat. Add
the spices, dals and curry leaves and fry, stirring
constantly, for 1–2 minutes, or until the spices are
fragrant and the dals are golden. Transfer to a bowl.

Add 1 teaspoon oil to the pan and heat through.
Add the coconut and stir-fry for 2 minutes, or until
golden. Transfer the coconut to the bowl, add the
tamarind extract and season with salt. Transfer
to a small blender or food processor and process
to make a smooth paste. Return the spice paste
to the pan, pour in 600ml / 1 pint (2½ cups) water
and whisk well, then bring to the boil. Reduce
the heat and simmer for about 10 minutes, or until
the aroma of raw tamarind disappears.

Heat the oil for the tempering in a small frying pan
over medium heat, add all the ingredients for the
tempering and stir-fry for about 1 minute, or until
the mustard seeds start to splutter. Stir into the
rasam and garnish with coriander leaves. Serve hot
with Plain Rice.

✳ / 📷 p.469

Pindi Chana
Chickpeas (Garbanzo Beans) from Rawalpindi

Origin Punjab
Preparation time 1 hour, plus soaking and standing time
Cooking time 45 minutes
Serves 4

400g / 14oz (2¼ cups) dried chickpeas (garbanzo beans), rinsed and drained

4 tablespoons vegetable oil

1 teaspoon cumin seeds

1 tablespoon gram (chickpea) flour

1 teaspoon ajwain seeds

5 teaspoons ground pomegranate seeds

2 teaspoons amchoor

1 teaspoon chilli powder

1 teaspoon ground black rock salt

2 teaspoons ground fenugreek

generous pinch of bicarbonate of soda (baking soda)

salt

For the aromatic potli

6 black cardamom pods

4 cinnamon sticks, about 2.5cm / 1 inch long

4 cloves

1× 5-cm / 2-inch piece fresh ginger, peeled and crushed

2 teaspoons tea leaves

4 teaspoons vegetable oil

To garnish

1 × 5-mm / ¼-inch piece fresh ginger, cut into juliennes

2 tablespoons lemon juice

2 tomatoes, cut into wedges

1 onion, cut into rings

2 green chillies, de-seeded

3 lemons, cut into wedges

Soak the chickpeas in a large bowl of water for 2 hours.

Put the ginger juliennes for the garnish in a small bowl, add the lemon juice and set aside.

Drain the chickpeas, put into a large, heavy-based pan and pour in enough water to cover. Bring to the boil, then reduce the heat and simmer for 30 minutes. Remove from the heat, set aside for 1 hour and drain just before cooking.

To make the aromatic potli, put the cardamom pods, cinnamon sticks, cloves, crushed ginger and tea leaves in a small piece of muslin (cheesecloth) and secure the top with kitchen string (twine) to make a pouch.

Put the drained chickpeas in a large, heavy-based pan and add 1 litre / 1¾ pints (4¼ cups) fresh water. Bring to the boil, then reduce the heat to low and remove any scum from the surface with a slotted spoon. Add the 4 teaspoons oil and the potli, cover and simmer for about 25 minutes, or until cooked but still firm. Make sure the chickpeas are not too soft and their skins are not peeling off. Remove from the heat and set aside.

Heat the remaining oil in a kadhai or wok over medium heat, add the cumin seeds and stir-fry for about 1 minute, or until they start to splutter. Add the gram flour and stir-fry for about 30 seconds, or until fragrant, then add the remaining ingredients and stir-fry for about 1 minute. Season with salt. Add the cooked chickpeas and stir until well mixed. Remove from the heat and adjust the seasoning, if necessary. Transfer to a serving dish and garnish with tomatoes, onion rings, chillies, lemon wedges and the soaked ginger juliennes.

Add 125ml / 4½fl oz (½ cup) water if necessary and simmer for about 7 minutes, or until well blended. Stir in the spice paste and continue simmering for 7 minutes. Heat the oil for the tempering in a small frying pan over medium heat, add all the ingredients for the tempering and stir-fry for about 1 minute, or until the mustard seeds start to splutter, then stir into the chickpeas and mix well.

Ghashhi
Chickpea (Garbanzo Bean) Curry from Mangalore

Origin Coastal
Preparation time 1½–2½ hours, plus soaking time
Cooking time 25 minutes
Serves 6

200g / 7oz (1 cup) dried chickpeas (garbanzo beans), rinsed and drained

2 potatoes, cut into cubes

½ teaspoon ground turmeric

1 sprig curry leaves

salt

For the spice paste

1 teaspoon vegetable oil

4 dried red chillies

1 teaspoon coriander seeds

250ml / 8fl oz (1 cup) Tamarind Extract (see page 58)

80g / 2¾oz (1 cup) grated fresh coconut

For the tempering

2 teaspoons vegetable oil

½ teaspoon mustard seeds

½ teaspoon asafoetida

1 dried red chilli

2–3 curry leaves

Soak the chickpeas in a bowl of water for 8 hours or overnight.

Drain the chickpeas and rinse well. Place them in a pressure cooker with 500ml / 18fl oz (2¼ cups) water and season with salt. Cook under pressure for about 10 minutes. Alternatively, cook the chickpeas with the water in a large, heavy-based pan for about 1½–2½ hours, or until soft.

Heat the oil for the spice paste in a kadhai or deep frying pan (skillet) over medium heat, add the dried red chillies and coriander seeds and stir-fry for about 1–2 minutes, or until fragrant. Mix all the ingredients for the spice paste, including the tamarind extract, in a mortar or spice grinder and pound with a pestle or process to a smooth paste.

Transfer the chickpeas with the cooking liquid to the pan used for frying the spices and mix in the potatoes, turmeric and curry leaves and season with salt, if needed.

Khatte Chole
Sour Chickpeas (Garbanzo Beans)

Origin Punjab
Preparation time 1½–2 hours, plus soaking time
Cooking time 30 minutes
Serves 4

400g / 14oz (2 cups) dried chickpeas (garbanzo beans), rinsed and drained

2 tea bags

3 teaspoons vegetable oil or ghee

1 teaspoon cumin seeds

80g / 2¾oz (½ cup) grated onions

1 tablespoon finely grated fresh ginger

2 teaspoons Garam Masala (see page 31)

2 tomatoes, puréed

1 teaspoon amchoor

salt

To garnish

sliced onion

green chillies

chopped coriander (cilantro) leaves

Soak the chickpeas in a bowl of water overnight.

The next day, put the drained chickpeas in a large, heavy-based pan. Add the tea bags and water to cover and bring to the boil. Cover, reduce the heat and cook for 1½–2 hours, or until cooked. Drain.

Heat the oil or ghee in another large, heavy-based pan over medium heat, add the cumin seeds and stir-fry for about 1 minute, or until they start to splutter. Add the onions and ginger and stir-fry for about 3–4 minutes. Now add the garam masala and stir-fry for a further 1 minute. Pour in 750ml / 1¼ pints (3¼ cups) water, add the tomato purée and season. Add the chickpeas, stir well, sprinkle over the amchoor and cook for 10 minutes, or until dry. Serve hot, garnished with onions, chillies and coriander.

※ ※

Pesarcharu
Pepper Water with Green Chickpeas

Origin Andhra Pradesh
Preparation time 30 minutes
Cooking time 40 minutes
Serves 4

1kg / 2¼lb (5½ cups) hara chana, rinsed and drained

2 tablespoons vegetable oil

½ teaspoon ground cumin

¼ teaspoon ground fenugreek

2 cloves

1 cinnamon stick, about 2.5cm / 1 inch long

1 teaspoon chopped garlic

1 tablespoon chilli powder

250ml / 8fl oz (1 cup) Tamarind Extract (see page 58)

1 teaspoon sugar

1 teaspoon ground black pepper

pinch of ground turmeric

salt

For the tempering

4 dried red chillies

1 teaspoon mustard seeds

8 curry leaves

Put the hara chana in a pan, pour in about 600ml / 1 pint (2½ cups) water, bring to the boil and boil for about 20 minutes, or until soft. Drain, reserving the cooking water in another pan.

Heat 1 tablespoon of the oil in a frying pan (skillet) over medium heat, add the ground cumin, fenugreek, cloves, cinnamon and garlic and stir-fry for about 1–2 minutes, or until browned. Transfer to a mortar or spice grinder, add 1 tablespoon of the cooked hara chana and the chilli powder and pound with a pestle or process until ground.

Add the tamarind extract, sugar, ground fried spice mixture, pepper and turmeric to the reserved water. Season with salt, mix well and cook for 5–8 minutes.

Heat the remaining oil in a small frying pan over medium heat, add the ingredients for the tempering and stir-fry for about 2 minutes, or until the chillies turn a shade darker. Pour over the dal mixture, cover and cook for about 2 minutes.

※ ※

Rajasthani Karhi
Gram (Chickpea) Flour & Yoghurt Curry

Origin Rajasthan
Preparation time 10 minutes
Cooking time 20 minutes
Serves 4

200ml / 7fl oz (1 cup) natural (plain) yoghurt

50g / 1¾oz (⅓ cup) gram (chickpea) flour

1 teaspoon chilli powder

1 teaspoon ground turmeric

4 teaspoons groundnut (peanut) oil

1 teaspoon cumin seeds

pinch of asafoetida

2 teaspoons Garlic Paste (see page 57)

1 teaspoon chopped green chilli

salt

For the tempering

1 tablespoon ghee or vegetable oil

1 teaspoon cumin seeds

4 whole dried red chillies

Put the yoghurt in a large bowl, pour in 1 litre / 1¾ pints (4¼ cups) water and stir together. Now add the gram flour, chilli powde and turmeric and season with salt, then mix well.

Heat the oil in a heavy-based pan over low heat, add the cumin seeds, asafoetida, garlic paste and chilli and stir-fry for about 30 seconds. Add the yoghurt mixture and simmer for about 10 minutes, or until the karhi is cooked and of pouring consistency.

Heat the ghee or oil for the tempering in a frying pan (skillet) over medium heat, add the cumin seeds and stir-fry for about 1 minute, or until they start to splutter, then add the dried red chillies and fry for a further 2 minutes, or until they turn a shade darker. Pour over the karhi and adjust the seasoning, if necessary.

Dahi ki Karhi
Yoghurt & Gram (Chickpea) Flour Curry

Origin Awadh
Preparation time 1¼ hours, plus soaking
and standing time
Cooking time 15 minutes
Serves 6

For the karhi

500ml / 18fl oz (2¼ cups) soured natural (plain)
   yoghurt

2 tablespoons gram (chickpea) flour

½ teaspoon Ginger Paste (see page 57)

½ teaspoon Garlic Paste (see page 57)

2 teaspoons ground cumin

2 onions, thinly sliced

12 curry leaves

6 green chillies

½ teaspoon ground turmeric

6 cloves garlic

salt

Plain Boiled Rice, to serve (see page 631)

For the bhajias

3 tablespoons gram (chickpea) flour

pinch of salt

½ teaspoon chilli powder

pinch of baking powder

vegetable oil, for deep-frying

For the tempering

2 teaspoons vegetable oil

4 dried red chillies

½ teaspoon cumin seeds, ground

1 clove garlic, crushed

Process all the ingredients for the karhi in a food processor or blender. Transfer to a deep, heavy-based pan and cook, stirring occasionally so it doesn't stick to the base (bottom) of the pan, for about 45 minutes, or until the mixture is very smooth.

While the karhi is cooking, put the gram flour, a pinch of salt, the chilli powder and a pinch of baking powder in a bowl and mix in enough water to make a stiff paste. Set aside for about 20 minutes.

Divide the paste into small balls. Heat enough oil for deep-frying in a kadhai or deep, heavy-based pan to 180°C/350°F, or until a cube of bread browns in 30 seconds.

Working in batches, carefully drop the balls into the hot oil and deep-fry for a few minutes until golden brown. Remove with a slotted spoon, transfer to a bowl of tepid water, and leave for 5 minutes. Squeeze out the water, then drop the balls into the karhi.

Heat the oil for the tempering in a small frying pan (skillet) over medium heat, add the dried red chillies, cumin and garlic and stir-fry briefly until the chillies turn a shade darker. Pour over the cooked karhi and cover immediately to retain the aroma. Serve hot.

Karadla Igguru
Vegetable Curry with Crisp Gram (Chickpea) Flour Balls

Origin Andhra Pradesh
Preparation time 15–20 minutes
Cooking time 25 minutes
Serves 4

180g / 6oz (¾ cup) ghee

1 teaspoon mustard seeds

½ teaspoon fenugreek seeds

½ teaspoon cumin seeds

8 curry leaves

2 tablespoons gram (chickpea) flour

2 potatoes, cut into 1-cm / 1-inch cubes

12 green beans, cut into 1-cm / ½-inch pieces

1kg / 2¼lb (about 7 medium) tomatoes, puréed

8 green chillies

2 tablespoons sugar

2 bunches coriander (cilantro) leaves, chopped

1 cup small fried gram (chickpea) flour balls (see
   bhajias, left)

salt

Heat the ghee in a frying pan (skillet) over medium heat, add the mustard seeds, fenugreek seeds, cumin seeds and curry leaves and fry for about 1 minute, or until the mustard seeds start to splutter. Add the gram flour and fry for 1–2 minutes, or until fragrant. Add the potatoes and beans together with the puréed tomatoes, chillies, sugar and coriander leaves and season with salt. Reduce the heat slightly and simmer for about 15 minutes, or until cooked.

Remove from the heat and scatter the fried gram flour balls over the top just before serving so that they stay crisp.

Sindhi Karhi
Gram (Chickpea) Flour in Tamarind Curry

Origin Sindh
Preparation time 30 minutes
Cooking time 40 minutes
Serves 8

---

2 (vegetable) drumsticks, cut into pieces

3 tablespoons vegetable oil

1 teaspoon cumin seeds

pinch of asafoetida

½ teaspoon fenugreek seeds

3 teaspoons chopped ginger

8–10 curry leaves

4–6 green chillies, de-seeded and chopped

3–4 dried red chillies, broken in half

30g / 1oz (¼ cup) gram (chickpea) flour

100ml / 3½fl oz (½ cup) Tamarind Extract
  (see page 58)

2 carrots, sliced

20–30 French (green) beans, cut into short lengths

2 tomatoes, chopped

2 potatoes, peeled and cut into cubes

1 aubergine (eggplant), cut into cubes

1 tablespoon jaggery, crumbled, or soft brown sugar

1 teaspoon chopped coriander (cilantro) leaves,
  to garnish

salt

steamed rice, to serve

Boil the drumsticks in a pan of water for 15 minutes, then drain and set aside.

Heat the oil in a medium-sized, heavy-based pan over medium heat, add the cumin seeds, asafoetida, fenugreek seeds, ginger, curry leaves and chillies and stir-fry for about 1 minute. Now add the gram flour and stir-fry for about 3 minutes, or until lightly browned, then remove from the heat.

Add the tamarind extract, 750ml / 1¼ pints (3¼ cups) water and all the vegetables including the drumsticks. Reheat the pan over low heat and cook, stirring frequently, for about 25 minutes, or until all the vegetables are tender. Season with salt.

Add the jaggery and bring the mixture to the boil. Immediately remove from the heat and garnish with chopped coriander. Serve with steamed rice.

Kokam ni Karhi
Sweet & Sour Yoghurt Soup

Origin Gujarat
Preparation time 20 minutes
Cooking time 25 minutes
Serves 4

375ml / 13fl oz (1½ cups) natural (plain) yoghurt

4 tablespoons gram (chickpea) flour

1 litre / 1¾ pints (4½ cups) masoor dal
  cooking water (see page 573)

3–4 tablespoons jaggery or soft brown sugar

3–4 black kokum

1 tablespoon Ginger Paste (see page 57)

1 tablespoon chilli paste

2 tablespoons ghee or vegetable oil

½ teaspoon mustard seeds

½ teaspoon fenugreek seeds

½ teaspoon cumin seeds

½ teaspoon asafoetida

3–4 dried red chillies

few curry leaves

2 small aubergines (eggplant), trimmed
  and cut into cubes

1 white radish, cut into long thin slices

salt

Put the yoghurt, gram flour and cooking water in a large bowl and mix together until smooth. Add the jaggery or sugar, kokum and ginger and chilli pastes and season with salt. Transfer the mixture to a large, heavy-based pan and bring almost to the boil. Cook over medium heat, stirring occasionally.

Heat the ghee or oil in a small pan over medium heat, add the mustard seeds, fenugreek seeds and cumin seeds and stir-fry for about 1 minute, or until they start to splutter. Add the asafoetida, dried red chillies and curry leaves, then add the vegetables and cook for about 5 minutes, or until the vegetables are soft. Now add to the yoghurt mixture and bring almost to the boil. Reduce the heat and simmer for about 15 minutes before serving hot.

Masoor ki Dal
Red or Black Dal

Origin Pan-Indian
Preparation time 1 hour, plus soaking time
Cooking time 30 minutes
Serves 4

250g / 9oz (1⅓ cups) masoor dal
   (split red or whole black), rinsed and drained
pinch of asafoetida
1 teaspoon ground turmeric
chilli powder, to taste
1 teaspoon ground coriander
1× 2.5-cm / 1-inch piece fresh ginger, peeled
   and crushed
250ml / 8fl oz (1 cup) rice cooking water
   (see page 631)
3½ tablespoons ghee or vegetable oil
½ teaspoon cumin seeds
2 cloves
25g / 1oz dried mint
salt

Soak the dal in a bowl of water for 1 hour.

Drain the dal, then transfer it to a round, heavy-based pan, pour in enough water to cover, then add half the asafoetida and the turmeric and season with salt. Cover and bring to the boil. Cook for about 10 minutes, or until most of the water has evaporated and the dal shows signs of softening. Add about 125ml / 4½fl oz (½ cup) water, cover again, reduce the heat to low and cook for a further 10–15 minutes, or until the dal is soft. Let all the water evaporate and when the dal is almost dry, turn it with a ladle in a circular motion for about 5 minutes. Add the chilli powder, coriander, ginger and rice cooking water, and pour in 250ml / 8fl oz (1 cup) hot water. Make sure the water is hot or lumps will form in the dal. Continue to cook, stirring slowly, for about 5 minutes, or until the dal is fairly thick.

Heat the ghee or oil over medium heat, add the asafoetida, cumin seeds and cloves and stir-fry for about 1 minute, or until hot. Pour over the dal and sprinkle with dried mint.

✳ / 📷 p.545

Masoor Dal
Split Red Dal

Origin Awadh
Preparation time 25 minutes
Cooking time 10 minutes
Serves 4

250g / 9oz (1⅓ cups) masoor dal, rinsed and drained
1 teaspoon ground turmeric
1 teaspoon ghee or vegetable oil
4 dried red chillies
½ teaspoon ajwain seeds, ground
20g / ¾oz (½ cup) chopped coriander (cilantro) leaves
4 green chillies, split in half lengthways and de-seeded
salt

Put 1.2 litres / 2 pints (5 cups) water in a large, heavy-based pan and add the masoor dal and turmeric. Bring to the boil and remove the scum from the surface with a slotted spoon, then reduce the heat. Season with salt and simmer for about 20 minutes, or until the dal is soft. Stir to break up the dal.

Heat the ghee or oil in a frying pan (skillet) over medium heat, add the dried red chillies and ground ajwain seeds and stir-fry for about 2 minutes, or until the chillies turn a shade darker. Pour over the dal, then cover and simmer for about 2 minutes. Add the chopped coriander and green chillies before serving.

Aratidhoota Pappu
Dal with Banana Stems

Origin Andhra Pradesh
Preparation time 20 minutes
Cooking time 15 minutes
Serves 4

200g / 7oz (1 cup) masoor dal, rinsed and drained

1 cup banana stems

buttermilk, for soaking (optional)

2 tablespoons vegetable oil

1 teaspoon urad dal, rinsed and drained

1 teaspoon mustard seeds

1 teaspoon fenugreek seeds

1–2 dried red chillies

7–8 curry leaves

1 teaspoon asafoetida

½ teaspoon ground turmeric

4 tablespoons Tamarind Extract (see page 58)

2–3 teaspoons jaggery, crumbled, or soft brown sugar

salt

Put the dal in a large, heavy-based pan, pour in 375ml / 1¼ pints (1½ cups) water and cook for about 25 minutes, or until very soft. Drain well and set aside.

Discard the outer layer of the banana stems and chop them into thick, round slices. As you chop, discard the fibrous strands and soak the pieces in buttermilk or water to avoid any discoloration. Wash well and cut into small dice.

Heat the oil in a medium-sized pan over medium heat, add the urad dal and stir-fry for about 1–2 minutes, or until it turns golden. Add the mustard seeds and fenugreek seeds and stir-fry for about 1 minute, or until they turn brown. Reduce the heat and add the dried red chillies. Stir-fry for a further 2 minutes, or until they turn a shade darker, then stir in the curry leaves and asafoetida. Add the diced banana stems and stir for another minute. Add the turmeric, tamarind extract and jaggery or sugar and season with salt. Cook for about 5 minutes, or until the banana is well done. Finally, add the cooked masoor dal and simmer for few minutes until heated through.

Masoor Pappu Charu
Spicy Pepper Water

Origin Andhra Pradesh
Preparation time 25 minutes
Cooking time 30 minutes
Serves 4

4 tablespoons masoor dal, rinsed and drained

2 tablespoons ghee or vegetable oil

6 dried red chillies

1 tablespoon black peppercorns

1 tablespoon coriander seeds

1 teaspoon cumin seeds

pinch of asafoetida

4 onions, sliced

250ml / 8fl oz (1 cup) Tamarind Extract (see page 58)

½ teaspoon ground turmeric

½ teaspoon jaggery, crumbled, or soft brown sugar

1 bunch coriander (cilantro) leaves, finely chopped

salt

For the tempering

1 tablespoon vegetable oil

4 dried red chillies

1 teaspoon mustard seeds

10 curry leaves

Bring 500ml / 18fl oz (2¼ cups) water to the boil in a large pan, add the dal, reduce the heat and simmer for about 20 minutes, or until the dal is soft. Drain, then return to the pan and mash with a wooden spatula.

Heat the ghee or oil in a frying pan (skillet) over medium heat, add the dried red chillies, peppercorns, coriander seeds, cumin seeds and asafoetida and stir-fry for about 2 minutes, or until the chillies turn a shade darker. Remove from the heat and allow to cool.

Transfer the cooled spices to a small blender, add the onions and process until ground. Add the tamarind extract and turmeric, then season and mix into the dal. Add 750ml / 1¼ pints (3¼ cups) water and the jaggery and cook for 5 minutes.

Meanwhile, to prepare the tempering, heat the oil in a small frying pan over medium heat, add the dried red chillies, mustard seeds and curry leaves and stir-fry for 2 minutes, or until they turn dark brown. Pour over the dal and cover immediately to retain the aroma. Simmer for 2 minutes, then garnish with coriander.

Nimakai Rasam
Lime-flavoured Pepper Water

Origin Tamil Nadu
Preparation time 30 minutes, plus soaking time
Cooking time 30 minutes
Serves 4

200g / 7oz (1 cup) masoor dal, rinsed and drained
1 teaspoon ground coriander
½ teaspoon ground black pepper
¼ teaspoon ground cumin
juice of 2 limes
½ teaspoon ground garlic
4 dried red chillies, ground
pinch of asafoetida
1 bunch coriander (cilantro) leaves, chopped
salt

For the tempering
1 tablespoon vegetable oil
2 dried red chillies
½ teaspoon mustard seeds
5 curry leaves

Put the dal in a large bowl, pour in 500ml / 18fl oz (2¼ cups) water and soak for about 1 hour.

Drain the dal and transfer to a large pan. Pour in 750ml / 1¼ pints (3¼ cups) water, bring to the boil and cook for about 20 minutes. Drain, return to the pan and mash well with a wooden spatula.

Heat a tawa or frying pan (skillet) until hot. Add the ground coriander, pepper and cumin and stir-fry for about 30 seconds, or until roasted. Add the lime juice, then add the garlic, chillies, asafoetida, mashed dal and chopped coriander and season with salt. Pour in 1 litre / 1¾ pints (4¼ cups) water and mix to combine.

To prepare the tempering, heat the oil in a small frying pan over medium heat, add all the ingredients for the tempering and stir-fry for about 2 minutes, or until the chillies turn a shade darker. Pour the seasoning over the dal and immediately cover to retain the aroma. Bring to the boil and cook for a further 3 minutes.

Moong Dal
Yellow Dal with Vegetables

Origin Awadh
Preparation time 25–30 minutes
Cooking time 30 minutes
Serves 6

400g / 14oz (2 cups) moong dal, rinsed and drained
125ml / 4½fl oz (½ cup) vegetable oil, plus extra for frying
2 potatoes, cut into small pieces
200g / 7oz (2 cups) cauliflower florets
3 bay leaves
1 teaspoon cumin seeds
3–4 green chillies, de-seeded and finely chopped
2 teaspoons Ginger Paste (see page 57)
2 bunches spinach, finely chopped
1½ teaspoons sugar
1½ teaspoons Garam Masala (see page 31)
375g / 13oz (1½ cups) ghee
salt

Put the moong dal in a pan and fry, stirring constantly, for 2 minutes, or until golden. Moong dal tends to burn quickly after a certain temperature, so keep a careful eye on it. Remove from the heat and rinse the dal under cold running water, then transfer it to a large, heavy-based pan. Pour in enough water to cover and bring to the boil. Reduce the heat and simmer for 20 minutes, or until soft but not overcooked.

Heat the oil for deep-frying in a kadhai or deep, heavy-based pan to 180°C/350°F, or until a cube of bread browns in 30 seconds. Working in batches if necessary, deep-fry the potatoes and cauliflower for 2–3 minutes, or until well cooked but not too soft. Remove with a slotted spoon and drain on kitchen paper (paper towels). Remove all the debris, if any, from the oil.

Add the bay leaves and cumin seeds to the same oil and stir-fry over medium heat for 30 seconds, then add the chillies and ginger paste and stir-fry for a further 1 minute. Add the fried vegetables, the spinach, cooked dal and sugar and season with salt. Bring to the boil, add the garam masala and ghee and cook until heated through.

Moong Dal Khilwan
Ginger-flavoured Moong Beans

Origin Awadh
Preparation time 45 minutes, plus soaking time
Cooking time 20 minutes
Serves 4

300g / 11oz (1½ cups) whole moong beans, rinsed
  and drained

4 green chillies, split in half lengthways and de-seeded

3 tablespoons vegetable oil or ghee

1 teaspoon cumin seeds

generous pinch of asafoetida

4 dried red chillies

½ teaspoon ground turmeric

1 tomato, de-seeded and diced

generous pinch of ground black pepper

generous pinch of ground black cardamom

generous pinch of ground green cardamom

pinch of ground cloves

2 tablespoons lemon juice

salt

For the aromatic potli

1 × 2.5-cm / 1-inch piece fresh ginger

1 teaspoon cloves

2 black cardamom pods

6 black peppercorns, roasted and coarsely ground

1 teaspoon coriander seeds

1 teaspoon chilli powder

Soak the whole moong beans in a bowl of water overnight.

The next day, drain the whole moong dal. Put all the ingredients for the aromatic potli, except the ginger, in a mortar and pound with a pestle until crushed or process in a food processor, then wrap in a piece of muslin (cheesecloth) together with the ginger and secure with kitchen string (twine).

Put 750ml / 1¼ pints (3¼ cups) water in a large, heavy-based pan, add the moong beans, chillies and the aromatic potli. Bring to the boil, then reduce the heat to low, cover and simmer for about 30 minutes, or until the dal is soft and almost cooked. Uncover and remove and discard the aromatic potli.

Heat the oil or ghee in a large frying pan (skillet) over medium heat, add the cumin seeds and stir-fry for about 1 minute, or until they start to splutter. Add the asafoetida and stir-fry for 30 seconds, or until it puffs up. Add the dried red chillies, turmeric, 3 tablespoons water and season with salt. Stir-fry for about 3–4 minutes, or until all the liquid has evaporated.

Add the cooked dal and stir-fry gently for a further 4 minutes, making sure the dal does not get mashed. Add the tomatoes and stir-fry for 1 minute, then add the ground pepper, black cardamom, green cardamom and cloves, stir and add the lemon juice. Stir again to combine, then remove from the heat and adjust the seasoning, if necessary.

Payatham Pezhukku
Moong Bean Dal

Origin Kerala
Preparation time 10 minutes, plus soaking time
Cooking time 30 minutes
Serves 4

200g / 7oz (1 cup) whole moong dal, rinsed
  and drained

4 dried red chillies

2 teaspoons coconut oil

10–15 curry leaves

salt

Soak the whole moong beans in a bowl of water overnight.

The next day, drain the moong beans and cook them with the dried red chillies in a large, heavy-based pan of boiling water for about 30 minutes, or until soft. Drain and transfer to a serving dish.

Season the dal with salt, add the coconut oil and curry leaves and mix well.

Dal ka Kima
Moong Dal with Peas

Origin Awadh
Preparation time 40 minutes, plus soaking time
Cooking time 30 minutes
Serves 4

125g / 4¼oz (⅔ cup) moong dal, rinsed and drained

20 cloves garlic

1 × 2.5-cm / 1-inch piece fresh ginger, peeled

350g / 12oz (1½ cups) ghee

4 onions, ground to a paste

3 teaspoons coriander seeds, ground

½ teaspoon ground turmeric

3 tomatoes, skinned and chopped

250g / 9oz (1¾ cups) peas, shelled if fresh

½ teaspoon Garam Masala (see page 31)

6 tablespoons natural (plain) yoghurt, whisked

2 tablespoons chopped coriander (cilantro) leaves

salt

Soak the dal in a large bowl of water for 8–10 hours.

Drain the dal, transfer to a blender or food processor and process until coarsely ground. Transfer to a bowl.

Put the garlic and ginger in a small blender or food processor and process until ground. Set aside.

Heat 250g / 9 oz (1 cup) ghee in a frying pan (skillet) over medium heat, add the dal and fry, scraping the sides of the pan with a wooden spoon to prevent the dal sticking to the pan, for a few minutes until golden. Do not allow the dal to brown. Remove from the pan, drain and set aside.

Heat the remaining ghee in the frying pan over low-medium heat, add the ground onions and stir-fry for about 2 minutes, or until golden. Add the ground garlic and ginger and a little water and cook for about 1 minute. Stir in the ground coriander, turmeric and tomatoes and season with salt, then cook for about 7 minutes, or until the mixture is paste-like. Add the fried dal, pour in 500ml / 18fl oz (2¼ cups) water, cover, reduce the heat to low and cook for about 15 minutes. Add the peas and cook for a further 5–10 minutes, or until the peas are tender, adding more water, if necessary. Stir in the garam masala and yoghurt and cook, stirring, for a few more minutes until the mixture is dry. Sprinkle with chopped coriander and serve.

Aam Ada Diya Bhaaja Moong Dal
Roasted Split Moong Dal with Galangal

Origin West Bengal
Preparation time 35 minutes
Cooking time 30 minutes
Serves 4

250g / 9oz (1⅓ cups) split moong dal, rinsed and drained

1 teaspoon ground turmeric

1 teaspoon chilli powder

4 green chillies, de-seeded and chopped

1 teaspoon ghee or vegetable oil

1 teaspoon cumin seeds

2 dried red chillies

1 bay leaf

2 tablespoons galangal paste

1 teaspoon sugar

2 tablespoons milk

salt

Heat a tawa or frying pan (skillet) until hot, add the split moong dal and roast for a few minutes until golden brown. Remove from the heat and allow to cool, then rinse under cold running water.

Bring 1.2 litres / 2 pints (5 cups) water to the boil in a large pan, add the dal, turmeric and chilli powder, reduce the heat, cover and simmer for 10 minutes, removing the scum from the surface with a slotted spoon. Season with salt, then add the chillies and simmer for a further 20 minutes, or until the dal is soft.

Heat the ghee or oil in a frying pan over medium heat, add the cumin seeds, dried red chillies and bay leaf and stir-fry for about 2 minutes, or until the chillies turn a shade darker. Add to the dal, cover again and simmer for a further 3 minutes. Add the galangal paste, sugar and milk, and cook over low heat for about 2 minutes to allow the dal to absorb the flavours. Heat through without boiling before serving.

Karhi Pakori
Dumpling & Yoghurt Curry

Origin Punjab
Preparation time 20 minutes, plus soaking time
Cooking time 30 minutes
Serves 4

For the karhi

500ml / 18fl oz (2¼ cups) natural (plain) yoghurt

1 teaspoon ground turmeric

4 tablespoons gram (chickpea) flour

1 teaspoon chilli powder

salt

For the pakori

100g / 3½oz (½ cup) moong dal, rinsed and drained

pinch of salt

vegetable oil or ghee, for deep-frying

For the tempering

125g / 4oz (½ cup) ghee or vegetable oil

2 teaspoons cumin seeds

1 teaspoon mustard seeds

pinch of asafoetida

6–8 dried red chillies

To make the karhi, put the yoghurt in a bowl, add the remaining ingredients, season with salt and whisk to mix well. Pour in 1 litre / 1¾ pints (4¼ cups) water and whisk again. Set aside.

For the pakori, soak the dal in a bowl of water for about 2 hours. Drain, transfer to a blender or food processor, add the salt and about 500ml / 18fl oz (2¼ cups) water and process to make a fluffy batter. Transfer to a bowl.

Heat enough oil for deep-frying in a deep, heavy-based pan to 180°C/350°F, or until a cube of bread browns in 30 seconds. Working in batches, drop small ladlefuls of the batter into the hot oil and deep-fry for about 2–3 minutes, or until golden brown. Remove with a slotted spoon and drain on kitchen paper (paper towels).

Put the yoghurt mixture in a heavy-based pan, bring almost to the boil, then reduce the heat to low, cover and simmer, stirring occasionally, for 5–10 minutes, or until the yoghurt is a thin sauce consistency. Add the deep-fried pakori, return to the boil, reduce the heat to low and simmer, stirring occasionally, for 4–5 minutes.

Meanwhile, heat the ghee or oil for the tempering in a frying pan (skillet) over medium heat, add the cumin seeds and mustard seeds and stir-fry for about 1 minute, or until the seeds start to splutter. Add the asafoetida and stir-fry for about 30 seconds, or until the asafoetida puffs up, then add the dried red chillies and stir-fry for a further 2 minutes, or until they turn a shade darker. Pour over the simmering karhi, then remove from the heat and adjust the seasoning, if necessary.

✻ ✻ / 📷 p.117

Tali Mangori
Fried Moong Dal Dumplings

Origin Awadh
Preparation time 20 minutes, plus soaking time
Cooking time 25 minutes
Serves 4

200g / 7oz (1 cup) moong dal, rinsed and drained

250ml / 8fl oz (1 cup) ginger tomato sauce

250ml / 8fl oz (1 cup) mustard oil

2 tablespoons chopped coriander (cilantro) leaves, to garnish

salt

Soak the dal in a large bowl of water for 8–10 hours.

Drain the dal, then transfer to a blender or food processor and process to make to a very smooth paste. Transfer the paste to a bowl and, with your hand, beat well. Season with salt.

Put the ginger tomato sauce in a pan.

Heat the oil in a flat kadhai or large, heavy-based frying pan (skillet) over high heat. Take a handful of paste and, using your thumb and index finger, carefully squeeze pieces of the paste into the hot oil. Reduce the heat and fry without turning for a few minutes until bubbles appear on the surface. This allows the steam to escape and ensures that the mangories do not become hard. Turn the mangories over and fry for a few more minutes until golden brown. Remove with a slotted spoon and transfer to the ginger tomato sauce. Cook for a further 10–15 minutes, adding a little water, if necessary, until hot. Sprinkle with chopped coriander and serve.

Sookhi Mangori
Dried Moong Dal Dumplings

Origin Rajasthan
Preparation time 40 minutes, plus soaking
and drying time
Cooking time 40 minutes
Serves 4

For the mangori

250g / 9oz (1⅓ cups) moong dal, rinsed and drained

1× 1-cm / ½-inch piece fresh ginger, peeled

pinch of asafoetida

4 tablespoons ghee

For the sauce

2 tablespoons ghee

2 onions, grated

6 cloves garlic, ground

1 × 2.5-cm / 1-inch piece fresh ginger, peeled
   and ground

2 teaspoons ground coriander seeds

1 teaspoon ground turmeric

pinch of chilli powder

2 tomatoes, chopped

½ teaspoon Garam Masala (see page 31)

salt

Soak the dal in a large bowl of water for 8–10 hours.

Drain the dal and transfer to a blender or food
processor. Add the piece of ginger and the asafoetida
and process to make a smooth paste. Transfer to
a bowl and, using your hand, beat well.

Using your thumb and index fingers, carefully
squeeze a piece of the paste on to a straw mat and
repeat until all the paste is used up, then leave to
dry in the sun for 2–3 days.

Heat 4 tablespoons ghee in a pan over medium
heat, add the dried balls or mangories in batches,
if necessary, and fry lightly. Remove from the
heat and set aside.

To make the sauce, heat the 2 tablespoons ghee
in a frying pan (skillet) over medium heat, add
the onions and fry for about 5–7 minutes, or until
golden brown. Stir in 3–4 teaspoons water, add
the garlic and ginger and cook for 1 minute. Stir in
the coriander seeds, turmeric, chilli powder and
tomatoes and season with salt. Cook for about
5–7 minutes, or until the mixture is paste-like.

Add the mangories and cook for a further 1–2
minutes. Pour in 1 litre / 1¾ pints (4¼ cups) water,
cover and cook over low heat for 15–20 minutes,
or until the mangories are tender. Stir in the
garam masala before serving.

Molagootal
Moong Dal with Vegetables

Origin Tamil Nadu
Preparation time 35 minutes
Cooking time 15 minutes
Serves 4

100g / 3½oz (½ cup) moong dal, rinsed and drained

180g / 6¼oz (1 cup) chopped mixed vegetables

1 teaspoon vegetable oil

3–4 dried red chillies

1 teaspoon cumin seeds

30g / 1¼oz (½ cup) grated fresh coconut

1 teaspoon mustard seeds

1 teaspoon urad dal, rinsed and drained

10–15 curry leaves, to garnish

salt

Put the moong dal in a dry frying pan (skillet)
and stir-fry over medium heat for 2–3 minutes,
or until roasted.

Cook the chopped vegetables in a pan of boiling
salted water for about 3–5 minutes, or until soft.
Drain and set aside.

Heat ½ teaspoon oil in a small frying pan over low-
medium heat, add the dried red chillies and cumin
seeds and stir-fry for 1–2 minutes, or until the chillies
turn a shade darker. Transfer the fried spices to a
mortar or small blender, add the coconut and pound
with a pestle or process to make a smooth paste.

Combine the moong dal, cooked vegetables and
ground paste in a clean pan and mix well. Pour in
enough water to bring to the desired consistency,
and bring to the boil.

Meanwhile, heat the remaining oil in a small frying
pan over medium heat, add the mustard seeds and
urad dal and fry for about 1 minute, or until the
mustard seeds start to splutter. Remove the moong
dal and vegetable mixture from the heat and pour
over the mustard seeds and urad dal. Garnish with
curry leaves.

Dal ki Kaleji
Fried Moong Dal Cubes In Sauce

Origin Awadh
Preparation time 1¼ hours, plus soaking time
Cooking time 35 minutes
Serves 6

200g / 7oz (1 cup) moong dal, rinsed and drained

2 onions, cut into quarters

2 green chillies, de-seeded and chopped

1× 1-cm / ½-inch piece fresh ginger, peeled
    and finely chopped

2 teaspoons chopped coriander (cilantro) leaves

¼ teaspoon bicarbonate of soda (baking soda)

250g / 9oz (1 cup) ghee, for frying

salt

For the sauce

10 cloves garlic

1× 2.5-cm / 1-inch piece fresh ginger, peeled

100g / 3½oz (½ cup) ghee

4 onions, ground to a paste

3 teaspoons coriander seeds, ground

½ teaspoon ground turmeric

2–3 tomatoes, skinned

4 tablespoons natural (plain) yoghurt, whisked

pinch of salt

½ teaspoon Garam Masala (see page 31)

1 tablespoon fresh coriander (cilantro) leaves

For the sauce, put the garlic and ginger in a small blender or food processor and process until ground to a paste. Set aside.

Soak the dal in a large bowl of water for 8–10 hours.

Drain the dal, then transfer to a blender or food processor, add the onions and process to make a smooth paste. Transfer to a bowl, add the chillies, ginger, coriander and bicarbonate of soda and beat thoroughly. Put the mixture into a clean piece of muslin (cheesecloth), bring up the sides and secure the top with kitchen string (twine) to make a bag.

Put the muslin bag into a large pan of boiling water and boil for about 2 minutes, then reduce the heat and simmer for about 45 minutes. Lift out and allow to cool slightly. Unwrap the cooked dal and cut it into 1-cm / ½-inch cubes.

Heat the ghee for frying in a kadhai or deep, heavy-based pan over high heat. Working in batches, add the dal cubes and fry for 2–3 minutes, or until golden brown all over. Remove with a slotted spoon and drain on kitchen paper (paper towels).

To make the sauce, heat the ghee in a large frying pan (skillet), add the ground onions and fry for about 1–2 minutes, or until golden brown. Add the garlic and ginger and fry for about 2 minutes, adding 2 teaspoons water. Stir in the ground coriander, turmeric and tomatoes and cook for about 7 minutes until the mixture is paste-like. Remove from the heat, slowly stir in the whisked yoghurt, garam masala and coriander leaves, then season with salt, and pour in 500ml / 18fl oz (2¼ cups) water. Return to the heat and simmer for a further 5 minutes. Add the pieces of fried dal, cover and cook over low heat for 10 minutes until hot.

Moong Dal aur Palak
Moong Dal with Spinach

Origin Awadh
Preparation time 15 minutes
Cooking time 30 minutes
Serves 4

---

4 tablespoons vegetable oil

1 teaspoon chopped ginger

2 green chillies, de-seeded and chopped

pinch of asafoetida

½ teaspoon cumin seeds

200g / 7oz (1 cup) moong dal, rinsed and drained

250g / 9oz spinach, finely chopped

½ teaspoon ground turmeric

juice of ½ lime

salt

Heat the oil in a large, heavy-based pan over medium heat, add the ginger, chillies, asafoetida and cumin seeds and fry for about 1 minute. Add the dal and spinach and cook for a further 2 minutes. Season with salt, then add the turmeric and 1.5 litres / 2¼ pints (6¼ cups) water. Reduce the heat to low and cook, stirring from time to time, for about 25 minutes, or until the dal is soft. Stir in the lime juice and serve.

Hari Matar ke Kofte
Green Gram Balls in Yoghurt Sauce

Origin New
Preparation time 10 minutes
Cooking time 25–30 minutes
Serves 4

200ml / 7fl oz (1 cup) natural (plain) yoghurt
150g / 5oz (1 cup) moong dal flour
1 teaspoon chilli powder
1 teaspoon ground turmeric
4 teaspoons vegetable oil
1 teaspoon cumin seeds
pinch of asafoetida
2 teaspoons Garlic Paste (see page 57)
1 teaspoon chopped green chillies
vegetable oil, for deep-frying
salt

For the tempering

1 tablespoon ghee or vegetable oil
1 teaspoon cumin seeds
4 dried red chillies

Put the yoghurt in a large bowl, pour in 500ml / 18fl oz (2½ cups) water and stir well. Add 50g / 1¾oz (⅓ cup) moong dal flour, the chilli powder and turmeric, then season and mix well.

Heat the 4 teaspoons oil in a pan over low heat, add the cumin seeds, asafoetida, garlic paste and chillies and stir-fry for 25 seconds. Add the yoghurt mixture and simmer for 10 minutes, or until the mixture is cooked and can be poured.

Heat the oil for deep-frying in a kadhai or deep, heavy-based pan to 180°C/350°F, or until a cube of bread browns in 30 seconds. Put the remaining moong dal flour in a bowl and mix in enough water to make a medium-thick batter. Beat well, preferably with your hands, then working in batches, carefully drop small ladlefuls of the batter into the hot oil and deep-fry for about 2–3 minutes, or until golden brown. Remove with a slotted spoon and add to the yoghurt mix. Simmer briefly, and adjust the seasoning

Heat the ghee or oil for the tempering in a frying pan (skillet) over medium heat, add the cumin seeds and stir-fry for 1 minute, or until the seeds start to splutter, then add the dried red chillies and fry for 2 minutes. Pour over the yoghurt mixture and serve.

Majjida Karhi
Dal & Buttermilk Curry

Origin Coastal
Preparation time 20–25 minutes, plus soaking time
Cooking time 20 minutes
Serves 4

1 teaspoon basmati rice, rinsed and drained
1 teaspoon roasted moong dal
1 teaspoon fresh ginger
500ml / 18fl oz (2¼ cups) sour buttermilk
½ fresh coconut, peeled and ground
pinch of ground turmeric
3 onions, thinly sliced
8 green chillies, de-seeded and cut lengthways into 4 strips each
salt

For the tempering

1 tablespoon vegetable oil
½ teaspoon mustard seeds
3 dried red chillies
½ teaspoon urad dal, rinsed and drained
1 bunch coriander (cilantro) leaves

To garnish

1 bunch coriander (cilantro) leaves, chopped
juice of 1 lime

Soak the rice and roasted moong dal in a bowl of water for 1 hour.

Drain, transfer to a small blender, add the ginger and process to make a paste. Put the buttermilk in a bowl and add the ground coconut, turmeric, ground rice and dal paste, and season with salt. Mix together.

Heat the oil for the tempering in a frying pan (skillet) over medium heat, add all the ingredients for the tempering and stir-fry for 1–2 minutes, or until brown. Add the onions and chillies to the tempering mixture and fry for about 5 minutes, or until the onions are translucent.

Pour the buttermilk into a deep, heavy-based pan, add the onion and tempering mixture and cook, stirring frequently, for about 10 minutes, or until it thickens and is a smooth consistency. Add the chopped coriander and lime juice and mix well before serving.

Borar Jhaal
Black Dal Balls in Mustard Sauce

Origin West Bengal
Preparation time 20 minutes, plus soaking time
Cooking time 15 minutes
Serves 4

100g / 3½oz (½ cup) urad dal, rinsed and drained
4 green chillies
½ teaspoon sugar
½ teaspoon Ginger Paste (see page 57)
pinch of asafoetida
250ml / 8fl oz (1 cup) mustard oil
1 teaspoon kalonji (nigella) seeds
Plain Boiled Rice, to serve (see page 631)
salt

For the mustard sauce
1 teaspoon black mustard seeds
1 teaspoon yellow mustard seeds
2 green chillies
1 teaspoon sugar

Soak the dal in a bowl of water for 30 minutes.

Drain the dal, transfer to a blender or food processor, add 2 chillies, the sugar, ginger paste and asafoetida and season with salt. Process to a paste. Roll the paste into 12 equal-sized balls, about the size of a chocolate truffle. Squeeze the mixture firmly so that it holds together.

Heat the oil in a kadhai or deep frying pan (skillet) to 180°C/350°F, or until a cube of bread browns in 30 seconds, then reduce the heat. Carefully drop the balls into the hot oil and fry for 5 minutes, or until golden brown. Remove with a slotted spoon and drain on kitchen paper (paper towels) while you make the sauce.

Mix all the ingredients for the sauce together in a bowl. Add 750ml / 1¼ pints (3¼ cups) water and stir to combine.

Transfer 3 tablespoons of the oil to a small frying pan. Heat the oil over medium-high heat, then add the kalonji seeds and stir-fry for about 30 seconds, or until they are fragrant. Add the mustard sauce and bring to the boil. Reduce the heat and simmer for about 10 minutes. Add the fried balls, mix well with the sauce and remove from the heat. The borars will absorb some of the sauce, but there should be enough left to eat with rice.

Dal Makhani
Creamy Black Dal

Origin Punjab
Preparation time 30 minutes, plus soaking time
Cooking time 6¼ hours
Serves 4

400g / 14oz (2¼ cups) whole urad dal, rinsed and drained
2 tablespoons vegetable oil
5 teaspoons Garlic Paste (see page 57)
3½ teaspoons Ginger Paste (see page 57)
1 tablespoon chilli powder
400g / 14oz (about 3 medium) tomatoes, puréed
150g / 5oz (1¼ sticks) unsalted butter, plus more to garnish
125ml / 4½fl oz (½ cup) single (light) cream
salt

Soak the dal in a large bowl of water overnight.

The next day, drain the dal and put into a large, heavy-based pan. Add 3 litres / 5¼ pints (12¾ cups) water and the oil and bring to the boil. Reduce the heat to very low, cover and simmer for about 4 hours, or until cooked.

Add the garlic and ginger pastes and chilli powder to the dal and season with salt. Continue to cook, mashing the dal frequently against the sides of the pan with a wooden spatula and scraping any dal clinging to the sides of the pan, for about 1 hour.

Add the puréed tomatoes and 150g / 5oz (1¼ sticks) butter and continue to simmer, mashing and scraping the mixture frequently, for about another 1 hour. Stir in the cream and remove from the heat. Adjust the seasoning, if necessary, and garnish with the remaining butter.

Khare Maash ki Dal
Savoury Split Black Lentil Dal

Origin Awadh
Preparation time 30 minutes, plus soaking time
Cooking time 25 minutes
Serves 4

400g / 14oz (2¼ cups) urad dal, rinsed and drained
2 tablespoons vegetable oil
3 onions, sliced
1 teaspoon garlic, ground
5 green cardamom pods
1 cinnamon stick, about 2.5cm / 1 inch long
4 cloves
¼ teaspoon pepper
1 teaspoon ground cumin
½ teaspoon chilli powder
3 green chillies, slit in half lengthways and de-seeded
1 teaspoon fresh ginger, peeled and ground
1 tablespoon single (light) cream
salt

Soak the dal in a bowl of water for 30 minutes.

Drain the dal, transfer to a large, heavy-based pan, pour in enough water to cover and bring to the boil. Season with salt and cook for about 20 minutes, or until most of the water has evaporated.

Heat the oil in a frying pan (skillet) over medium heat, add the onions and fry for about 5–7 minutes, or until golden brown. Set half the onions aside for the garnish. Add the garlic to the remaining onions in the pan and fry briefly until the garlic is light brown.

Remove the seeds from the cardamom pods and put into a mortar. Add the cinnamon and cloves and pound with a pestle.

Transfer the cooked dal to the pan containing the fried onions and fry lightly. Pour in 250ml / 8fl oz (1 cup) water and all the ground spices and the chillies and ginger and cook over low heat until the dal is soft and there is a thick sauce. Stir in the cream and garnish with the reserved fried onions.

Sukhi Urad ki Dal
Dry Black Lentils

Origin Awadh
Preparation time 15 minutes, plus soaking time
Cooking time 30 minutes
Serves 4

125g / 4¼oz (⅔ cup) urad dal, rinsed and drained
2 teaspoons ghee
1 teaspoon chopped ginger
1 green chilli, de-seeded and chopped
½ teaspoon ground turmeric
pinch of asafoetida
½ teaspoon cumin seeds
2 dried red chillies
salt

Soak the dal in a bowl of water for 1 hour. Drain.

Heat 1 teaspoon ghee in a large, heavy-based pan over medium heat, add the ginger and chilli and fry for about 1 minute. Add the drained dal and turmeric and season with salt. Pour in 500ml / 18fl oz (2¼ cups) water to cover, then bring to the boil, reduce the heat and cook, without stirring, for about 25 minutes or until the water is absorbed and the dal is soft.

Just before serving, heat 1 teaspoon ghee in a small frying pan (skillet) over medium heat, add the asafoetida, cumin seeds and dried red chillies and stir-fry for 1–2 minutes, or until the chillies turn a shade darker. Pour over the dal and gently stir to heat through.

Dal Nizami
'Royal Salute' Dal

Origin Hyderabad
Preparation time 40 minutes
Cooking time 1 hour
Serves 4

---

4 tablespoons chana dal, rinsed and drained

4 tablespoons whole masoor dal, rinsed and drained

4 tablespoons arhar dal or toor (toover) dal, rinsed
  and drained

4 tablespoons moong dal, rinsed and drained

100g / 3½oz (½ cup) urad dal, rinsed and drained

1½ teaspoons chilli powder

1½ teaspoons ground turmeric

5 green cardamom pods

3 black cardamom pods

5 cloves

2 cinnamon sticks, about 2.5cm / 1 inch long

5 bay leaves

3½ teaspoons Ginger Paste (see page 57)

2½ teaspoons Garlic Paste (see page 57)

¼ teaspoon Tamarind Extract (see page 58)

50g / 1¾oz (⅓ cup) wholemeal (whole wheat) flour

2 tablespoons lemon juice

salt

For the tempering

5 tablespoons ghee or vegetable oil

1 teaspoon cumin seeds

8 cloves garlic, peeled and crushed

100g / 3½oz (⅔ cup) sliced onions

crisp golden fried sliced onions

4 green chillies, de-seeded (optional)

10 mint leaves

Put 1 litre / 1¾ pints (4¼ cups) water in a large, heavy-based pan, add the dals, chilli powder, turmeric, cardamom pods, cloves, cinnamon, bay leaves and the ginger and garlic pastes and bring to the boil. Reduce the heat to low and simmer, stirring occasionally and removing the scum that rises to the surface with a slotted spoon, for about 30 minutes, or until all the liquid is absorbed. Set aside.

Heat 2 tablespoons ghee or oil in a frying pan (skillet) over medium heat, add the cumin seeds and garlic and stir-fry for 30 seconds, or until the seeds start to splutter. Pour over the dal and stir.

Heat another 2 tablespoons ghee in the pan, add the onions and fry for about 2–3 minutes, then add the chillies and fry for a further minute. Pour over the dal and stir. Heat the last tablespoon ghee in the pan, add the mint and fry for about 1 minute, or until browned, then pour over the dal and stir.

Remove the whole spices from the dal and puree in a blender or food processor with 250ml / 8fl oz (1 cup) water. Pass through a sieve (strainer) into a separate pan. Return to the heat, add the tamarind extract, wholemeal flour and about 500ml / ¾ pint (2¼ cups) water, then bring to the boil, reduce the heat to low and simmer, stirring occasionally, for a further 2 minutes, or until it is a thin custard consistency. Remove from the heat, add the lemon juice, stir and adjust the seasoning, if necessary.

Tamatar Rasam
Tomato Pepper Water

Origin Tamil Nadu
Preparation time 15 minutes
Cooking time 25 minutes
Serves 4

2 tablespoons vegetable oil
1 onion, sliced
500g / 1lb 2oz (3 medium) tomatoes
pinch of ground turmeric
1 teaspoon sugar
1 teaspoon chilli powder
3 dried red chillies
¼ teaspoon mustard seeds
½ teaspoon cumin seeds
¼ teaspoon urad dal, rinsed and drained
pinch of asafoetida
½ teaspoon ground garlic
8 curry leaves
salt
1 bunch coriander (cilantro) leaves, chopped, to garnish

Heat 1 tablespoon of the oil in a frying pan (skillet) over medium heat, add the onion and fry for about 5–7 minutes, or until light golden brown.

Put the tomatoes, fried onions and turmeric in a large pan. Pour in 750ml / 1¼ pints (3¼ cups) water and bring to the boil. Boil for about 10 minutes, then remove from the heat. Add the sugar and chilli powder and season with salt.

Heat the remaining oil in a small frying pan over medium heat, add the dried red chillies, mustard and cumin seeds, urad dal, asafoetida, garlic and curry leaves and stir-fry for about 2 minutes, or until dark brown. Pour the tempering immediately over the tomatoes and simmer for 5 minutes, or until hot. Garnish with chopped coriander.

Shyama
Mixed Dal

Origin Uttarakhand
Preparation time 1 hour, plus soaking time
Cooking time 2 hours
Serves 6

100g / 3½oz (½ cup) soy beans, rinsed and drained
55g / 2oz (½ cup) French (green) beans
100g / 3½oz (½ cup) kidney beans, rinsed and drained
100g / 3½oz (½ cup) urad dal, rinsed and drained
100g / 3½oz (½ cup) chana dal, rinsed and drained
4 tablespoons kulthi dal, rinsed and drained
4 tablespoons lobiya dal, rinsed and drained
2 tablespoons ground coriander
2 tablespoons ground cumin
salt
1 large sprig coriander (cilantro), to garnish

For the tempering

1 tablespoon ghee or vegetable oil
generous pinch of jambu
or 2 dried red chillies and 4–5 cloves garlic

Soak all the dals in a large bowl of water overnight.

The next day, drain the dal and cook in a pressure cooker with enough water to cover for about 5 minutes. Allow to cool before opening to release the pressure. Alternatively, cook in a large, heavy-based pan for about 20–30 minutes, or until soft. Drain, reserving the cooking water and mash the mixture gently with a spatula.

Transfer the mixture to a kadhai or deep, heavy-based pan, add the cooking water together with the ground spices and season with salt. Cook over low-medium heat for about 2 hours. Remove the dal grains from the soup. Ideally, the mixture should have a thick consistency and a creamy texture.

Heat the ghee or oil for the tempering in a frying pan (skillet) over medium heat, add the jambu or dried red chillies and garlic cloves and stir-fry for 1–2 minutes, or until the jambu releases its aroma or the chillies turn a shade darker. Pour over the mixture and garnish with coriander.

Rasse Misse Rajma
Home-style Kidney Beans

Origin Punjab
Preparation time 2 hours, plus soaking time
Cooking time 45 minutes
Serves 4

250g / 9oz (1⅓ cups) dried red kidney beans, rinsed
   and drained

4 black cardamom pods

2 bay leaves

1 teaspoon ground coriander

1 teaspoon chilli powder

7 tablespoons ghee

4 dried red chillies, wiped with a damp cloth

1½ teaspoons cumin seeds

200g / 7oz (1¼ cups) chopped onions

5 teaspoons Ginger Paste (see page 57)

5 teaspoons Garlic Paste (see page 57)

200g / 7oz (2 small) tomatoes, puréed

1 teaspoon ground black cardamom

½ teaspoon ground black pepper

1× 5-mm / ¼-inch piece fresh ginger, cut into juliennes

2 tablespoons chopped coriander (cilantro) leaves

salt

Soak the kidney beans in a large bowl of
water overnight.

The next day, drain the beans and put into a large,
heavy-based pan. Pour in 1.5 litres / 2½ pints
(6¼ cups) water and bring to the boil. Boil briskly,
removing the scum that rises to the surface with
a slotted spoon, for 10 minutes, then reduce the
heat, add the cardamom pods and bay leaves and
simmer for about 1–1½ hours, or until soft. Remove
and discard the cardamom pods and bay leaves.

Put the ground coriander, chilli powder and a little
salt in a small bowl. Add 4 tablespoons water and
stir until blended.

Heat the ghee in a frying pan (skillet) over medium
heat, add the dried red chillies and cumin seeds
and stir-fry for 1 minute, or until the seeds start to
splutter. Add the onions and fry for 5 minutes,
or until they are light golden brown. Add the ginger
and garlic pastes and fry for 2–3 minutes, or until
the onions are golden brown. Add the ground spice
mixture and stir-fry for about 30 seconds.

Add the puréed tomatoes and stir-fry for about
5 minutes, or until the oil separates out. Now add
the kidney beans and bring to the boil. Reduce the
heat to low and cook for about 7 minutes. Sprinkle
over the ground black cardamom and black pepper
and stir to combine. Remove from the heat and
adjust the seasoning, if necessary.

Serve garnished with ginger juliennes and
chopped coriander.

✳ / 📷 p.193

Rajma
Kashmiri Red Kidney Beans

Origin Jammu and Kashmir
Preparation time 1¼ hours, plus soaking time
Cooking time 30–45 minutes
Serves 8

500g / 1lb 2oz (2¾ cups) dried red kidney beans,
   rinsed and drained

1½ teaspoons Kashmiri red chilli powder

8 green cardamom pods

6 black cardamom pods

4 cinnamon sticks, about 5cm / 2 inches long

3 teaspoons ground turmeric

1½ teaspoons ground ginger

3 tablespoons butter

salt

steamed rice, to serve

Soak the red kidney beans in a large bowl of
water overnight.

The next day, drain the kidney beans and put
into a large, heavy-based pan. Pour in enough water
to cover, bring to the boil and boil briskly for
10 minutes, then drain the beans, rinse and return to
the pan covered with fresh water. Bring to the boil,
then reduce the heat and simmer for a further
45 minutes, or until cooked. Drain and return the
beans to the pan.

Pour in 600ml / 1 pint (2½ cups) water, then add the
chilli powder, cardamom pods, cinnamon sticks,
turmeric and ginger and season with salt. Bring the
mixture to the boil, then reduce the heat, cover and
cook over low heat for 25–30 minutes, or until the
beans are tender and the sauce is quite thick. Add
the butter and serve hot with steamed rice.

Pappu Charu
Spicy Tamarind Pepper Water

Origin Andhra Pradesh
Preparation time 10 minutes
Cooking time 15–20 minutes
Serves 4

pinch of ground turmeric
250ml / 8fl oz (1 cup) Tamarind Extract (see page 58)
1 onion, sliced
½ teaspoon chilli powder
1 green chilli, de-seeded and chopped
½ bunch coriander (cilantro) leaves, chopped
2 tomatoes, chopped
salt

For the seasoning

1 teaspoon vegetable oil
1 dried red chilli
7 curry leaves
¼ teaspoon cumin seeds
¼ teaspoon coriander seeds
¼ teaspoon mustard seeds

Put the turmeric, tamarind extract, onion, chilli powder, chilli, half the chopped coriander and the tomatoes in a pan. Season with salt, add 750ml / 1¼ pints (3¼ cups) water and bring to the boil, then boil for about 5 minutes.

Heat the oil in a frying pan (skillet) over medium heat, add the dried red chilli, curry leaves and cumin seeds and stir-fry for 1–2 minutes, or until the cumin seeds start to splutter. Add the coriander and mustard seeds and stir-fry briefly until they turn dark brown. Add the spices to the pepper water and cover immediately to retain the aroma. Simmer for about 2 minutes, then add the rest of the chopped coriander.

Kairi ki Karhi
Raw Mango Curry

Origin Hyderabad
Preparation time 20 minutes
Cooking time 30 minutes
Serves 4–6

4 raw green mangoes, peeled and cut into bite-sized pieces, stones (pits) reserved
50ml / 1¾fl oz (¼ cup) vegetable oil
¼ teaspoon mustard seeds
¼ teaspoon fenugreek seeds
½ teaspoon cumin seeds
1 onion, sliced
6 curry leaves
¼ teaspoon ground turmeric
1 teaspoon chilli powder
1 teaspoon ground fresh ginger
1 teaspoon ground garlic
500ml / 18fl oz (2¼ cups) natural (plain) yoghurt
2 tablespoons gram (chickpea) flour
1 teaspoon sugar
6 green chillies, de-seeded and chopped
1 bunch coriander (cilantro), leaves only, chopped
salt

Put the mango and all the stones (pits) in a large, heavy-based pan. Pour in 500ml / 18fl oz (2¼ cups) water, add a pinch of salt and bring to the boil. Simmer for 10 minutes, or until the mango is soft. Remove the stones and set aside.

Heat the oil in another large, heavy-based pan over medium heat, add the mustard seeds and stir-fry for about 1 minute, or until they start to splutter. Add the fenugreek seeds, cumin seeds, onion and curry leaves and fry for about 5–6 minutes, or until the onions are soft. Add the turmeric, chilli powder, ginger and garlic, season with salt and fry for a further 1–2 minutes. Pour in 250ml / 8fl oz (1 cup) water.

Put the yoghurt and gram flour in a bowl and whisk together to make a smooth paste. Add the paste to the seeds mixture and cook for 5 minutes. Add the mangoes with the water they were boiled in, the sugar and chopped chillies and simmer over low heat for about 10 minutes. Add the chopped coriander and mix well before serving.

BREADS

Most Indian breads – from the soft paratha, roti and chapati flatbreads to fluffy naan drizzled in butter and fried puri – are unleavened and made with wheat flour, although cornmeal and millet are also popular. Many Indians make fresh bread every day using traditional methods, and cities across the country are renowned for their local varieties and specialities.

6
—

Breads

Lehsuni Naan
Garlic Naan

Origin Punjab
Preparation time 20 minutes, plus standing and
rising time
Cooking time 10–20 minutes
Makes 6

1 egg
½ teaspoon baking powder
1 teaspoon sugar
pinch of bicarbonate of soda (baking soda)
4 tablespoons milk
500g / 1lb 2oz (4 cups) plain (all-purpose) flour, plus extra for dusting
pinch of salt
4 teaspoons vegetable oil, plus extra for oiling
200g / 7oz (1½ cups) chopped garlic

Put the egg, baking powder, sugar, bicarbonate
of soda and milk into a bowl and whisk together.

Sift the flour and salt into a paraat or large bowl.
Make a depression in the centre of the flour, add
the egg mixture and start mixing gradually, adding
in enough water to make a soft dough. When fully
mixed, knead the dough on a lightly floured work
surface for 5 minutes, then transfer to a baking
tray (sheet), cover with a damp cloth or tea (dish)
towel and set aside for 10 minutes.

Add the oil to the dough, then knead and
punch down the dough, cover with a damp cloth
or tea (dish) towel and set aside in a warm place
for 2 hours to allow the dough to rise.

Preheat the oven to 200°C/400°F/Gas Mark 6,
if using.

Divide the dough into 8 equal portions, roll into
balls and place on a floured work surface. Flatten
the balls slightly, then spread the chopped garlic
over the dough. Set aside for 5 minutes.

Lightly oil the palms of your hands. Flatten each ball
between the palms of your hands to make a round,
then stretch it into an elongated oval shape.

To cook the naan, either use a tandoor or oven.
In a tandoor, place the naan on a cushioned pad
and place inside a moderately hot tandoor. Let
the naan bake for 2–3 minutes, then remove it with
tongs. If using the oven, place on an oiled baking
tray and bake for about 10 minutes. Serve hot.

Khurmi Naan
Tomato & Cheese Naan

Origin New
Preparation time 50 minutes, plus cooling time
Cooking time 12–22 minutes
Makes 6

1 quantity Naan Dough (see page left)
plain (all-purpose) flour, for dusting
300g / 11oz (2 medium) tomatoes, puréed
pinch of salt
2 tablespoons sugar
½ teaspoon chilli powder, or to taste
100g / 3½oz (scant 1 cup) grated cheese
butter or ghee, for greasing (optional)

Divide the dough into 8 equal portions and roll
into balls. Place the balls on a floured surface
and cover with a damp cloth or tea (dish) towel.

Heat a heavy-based pan over medium heat, add
the puréed tomatoes and cook for 5–8 minutes,
or until reduced. Add the salt, sugar and chilli
powder and reduce for a few more minutes, until
thick. Remove from the heat, add the grated
cheese, mix and allow to cool.

Preheat the oven to 200°C/400°F/Gas Mark 6,
if using.

Flatten the dough balls between the palms of your
hands, then spread a portion of the tomato mixture
over the center of each. Fold the edges over to
enclose the filling, then roll into balls. Again, flatten
each ball between the palms of your hands to make
a flattened round, then stretch into an elongated
oval shape.

To cook the naan, either use a tandoor or oven.
In a tandoor, place the naan on a cushioned
pad and place inside a moderately hot tandoor.
Let the naan bake for 2–3 minutes and then
remove it with tongs. If using the oven, place the
naan on a greased baking tray (sheet) and bake
for about 10 minutes.

p.593

Poori
Poori

Origin Delhi/Awadh
Preparation time 15 minutes, plus standing time
Cooking time 10 minutes
Serves 6

500g / 1lb 2oz (4 cups) plain (all-purpose) flour
  or wholemeal (whole wheat) flour, plus extra
  for dusting
pinch of salt
1 tablespoon ghee
500g / 1lb 2oz (2¼ cups) ghee or vegetable oil

Put the flour, salt and ghee in a large bowl, mix in enough water to make a pliable dough. Knead well on a lightly floured work surface for about 5 minutes, then transfer to a lightly oiled bowl, cover with a damp cloth or tea (dish) towel and set aside in a warm place for 2 hours.

Knead the dough again, then divide into small lime-sized balls. Roll each ball out on a lightly floured work surface to a round, about 13–16cm / 5–6 inches in diameter.

Heat the oil or ghee in a kadhai, wok or deep, heavy-based pan to 180°C/350°F, or until a cube of bread browns in 30 seconds. Working in batches, carefully add the pooris to the hot oil or ghee and deep-fry for about 1–2 minutes, or until puffed up and pale golden brown. Remove with a slotted spoon and drain on kitchen paper (paper towels). Repeat with the remaining pooris. Serve hot.

p.594

Bervin Poori
Poori Stuffed with Urad Dal

Origin Delhi/Awadh
Preparation time 20 minutes, plus soaking time
Cooking time 15 minutes
Makes 10–12

250g / 9oz (2 cups) wholemeal (whole wheat) flour
pinch of salt
½ tablespoon ghee
625g / 1lb 6oz (2¾ cups) ghee for frying

For the filling

125g / 4¼oz (1⅓ cups) skinned urad dal
2 teaspoons finely chopped fresh ginger
3 teaspoons coriander seeds, crushed
1 teaspoon aniseeds
½ teaspoon chilli powder
2 teaspoons chopped coriander (cilantro)

To make the filling, soak the dal in a large bowl of water for 8–10 hours. Drain, then put into a blender and process to make a smooth, fairly stiff paste. Transfer the paste to a bowl and mix in the remaining ingredients.

To make the dough, follow the instructions for pooris (see page left).

Take 2 tablespoons dough and shape into a small round with your hand. Put 1 level teaspoon dal mixture in the centre and fold over the dough to enclose the filling completely, then roll into a ball. Repeat to make 10–12 balls.

Heat the ghee in a kadhai, wok or deep, heavy-based pan to 180°C/350°F, or until a cube of bread browns in 30 seconds. Working in batches, carefully add the pooris to the hot ghee and deep-fry for about 1–2 minutes, or until puffed up and golden brown. Remove with a slotted spoon and drain on kitchen paper (paper towels).

Poori p.592

Poori Stuffed with
Urad Dal   p.592

Stuffed Round
Gourd   p.302

Layered Paratha
p.609

595

Paratha
p.609

Shallow-Fried Spicy
Potato Stuffed Bread p.611

Curry Leaf
Chutney p.70

Mixed-flour
Bread   p.621

Mixed–flour
Bread   p.621

Dry Khichari
p.638

Fish Biryani
p.646

Coconut and Prawn
(Shrimp) Pulao p.650

Ginger curry
p.322

Lamb Biryani (I)
p.651

Raw Mango
Curry   p.587

Fried Lamb with
Coconut   p.442

Drumstick Sambhar from
Chettinad   p.544

Rice with Moong Dal
              p.665

📷 p.596

Paratha
Paratha

Origin Punjab/Delhi/Awadh
Preparation time 20 minutes, plus standing time
Cooking time 16–20 minutes
Makes 8–10

1kg / 2¼lb (8 cups) plain (all-purpose) flour	
4 green cardamom pods, ground	
100g / 3½ oz (scant ½ cup) ghee	
pinch of salt	

Sift the flour, salt and ground cardamom into a bowl, then mix in enough water to make a soft dough. Knead the dough well for about 5 minutes. Divide the dough into 8–10 balls and cover with a damp cloth or tea (dish) towel for about 15 minutes.

Put the ghee in a shallow pan over low heat and whisk it well by hand to a smooth butter-like consistency. Roll a dough ball out on a lightly floured work surface into a large 20-cm / 8-inch round. Dab a little ghee over the surface, then fold in half and dab a little ghee on the top of the folded side. Roll into a long cigar-like shape and coil into a round.

Heat a griddle, tawa or heavy-based frying pan (skillet) over medium heat. Roll each paratha out to a 18cm / 7 inch flat round. Put a little ghee on the griddle, tawa or in the frying pan and place the paratha on or in the pan and reduce the heat to low. Keep turning the paratha around, pressing down the sides and spooning a little hot ghee around the edges, so they open and separate into layers. Continue to cook over low heat, so that the paratha is well cooked inside. When well browned on one side, turn over to brown the other side. Remember that the more ghee you have in the pan the better the paratha will be. When the paratha is cooked, after 1–2 minutes, remove from the pan and repeat with the remaining parathas.

📷 pp.546, 595

Warqi Paratha
Layered Paratha

Origin Delhi/Agra/Awadh
Preparation time 20–30 minutes, plus standing time
Cooking time 15 minutes
Makes 8–10

250g / 9oz (2 cups) plain (all-purpose) flour, plus extra for dusting	
¼ teaspoon salt	
100g / 3½oz (scant ½ cup) ghee, plus extra for cooking	
2 tablespoons plain (all-purpose) flour	

Sift the 250g / 9oz (2 cups) flour and the salt into a large bowl, then gradually mix in enough water to make a soft dough. Knead on a lightly floured work surface for 5 minutes. Transfer to a lightly oiled bowl, cover with a damp cloth or tea (dish) towel and set aside in a warm place for 30 minutes.

Melt the ghee in a pan and knead 2 tablespoons of it into the dough until the dough is soft and elastic. Put the remaining ghee in a bowl, add 2 tablespoons flour and mix to make a paste.

Divide the dough into 8–10 equal portions, then flatten each portion between the palms of your hands to make a small round. Roll the round out thinly on a lightly floured work surface and fold in half. Spread over a little flour paste and fold lengthways in half again. Roll this strip like a pinwheel, keeping the folded edges outward and forming a cone shape, then press with your hands to flatten and shape into a roti.

Heat a little ghee on a griddle, tawa or in a heavy-based frying pan (skillet), add a paratha and fry, trickling ghee a little at a time down the sides of the griddle or pan. Turn once and cook for 2 minutes, or until golden on both sides. Remove and repeat with the remaining parathas.

Lachha Paratha
Coiled Paratha

Origin Punjab
Preparation time 1 hour, plus standing time
Cooking time 30 minutes
Makes 6–8

360g / 12½oz (3 cups) wholemeal (whole wheat)
    flour, plus extra for dusting

3–4 tablespoons ghee

pinch of salt

melted ghee, for brushing

Sift the flour and salt into a large bowl. Add the ghee, then mix in enough water to make a non-sticky dough. Knead the dough on a lightly floured work surface for 5 minutes, then transfer to a lightly oiled bowl, cover with a damp tea (dish) cloth and set aside in a warm place for about 1 hour.

Knead the dough again and then divide into 6 equal-sized portions and roll into balls, each the size of a large onion. Roll out each ball on a lightly floured work surface to a round of about 20cm / 8 inches in diameter, then spread 1 teaspoon ghee all over the round and dust some flour over it. Now pleat the round lengthways into one collected strip. Coil this strip into a round.

Flatten the coiled round between the palms of your hands or gently roll on the work surface with the rolling pin without applying too much pressure, to make a small, thick paratha about 18cm / 7 inches in diameter.

Brush a little water on the back of the paratha and cook in a moderately hot tandoor. Alternatively, cook on a hot tawa or griddle or in a heavy-based frying pan (skillet). If using a pan, first brown both sides of the paratha lightly on the hot pan, then reduce the heat to low and fry, brushing with ghee, until rich brown on both sides, pressing all over the paratha including the sides with a spoon to make sure that the thick paratha is evenly cooked. Remove from the pan and repeat with all the remaining dough balls

Ulte Tawe ka Paratha
Paratha Cooked on the Griddle

Origin Awadh
Preparation time 55 minutes, plus resting time
Cooking time 10 minutes
Serves 6–8

1kg / 2¼lb (8 cups) plain (all-purpose) flour,
    plus extra for dusting

pinch of salt

1½ teaspoons baking powder

75g / 2½oz Cashew Nut Paste (see page 58)

2 teaspoons khus essence

500ml / 18fl oz (2¼ cups) milk

4 tablespoons sugar

melted ghee, for brushing

Sift the flour and salt on to a wide open tray. Mix the baking powder, cashew nut paste, khus essence, milk and sugar together in a large bowl. Add the mixture to the flour and pour in enough water to make a soft dough. Knead the dough on a lightly floured work surface for about 5 minutes. Divide the dough into 15–16 equal-sized balls, then flatten them with a rolling pin to the size of a poori (see page 592). Pour 1 teaspoon ghee over the dough and spread it evenly with the rolling pin, then dust with flour. Cut the dough into a round shape and then roll it into a conical shape. Now compress it back into the shape of a ball. Repeat with the remaining dough balls. Set aside for about 45 minutes.

Press the dough ball with a rolling pin into a round, about 25cm / 10 inches in diameter. You will need to use some extra flour to roll the dough balls. Heat an ulta tawa, ordinary tawa, griddle or non-stick frying pan (skillet). Transfer the dough to the pan, turn once and spread a little ghee over. Cook for about 20 seconds, pressing with a clean dry cloth, until golden brown. Remove from the pan and keep warm while you cook the others.

Aloo ka Paratha
Shallow-fried Spicy Potato Stuffed Bread

Origin Punjab/Delhi/Awadh
Preparation time 1 hour
Cooking time 30 minutes
Makes 4–5

500g / 1lb 2oz (4 cups plus 3 tablespoons) wholemeal
(whole wheat) flour, plus extra for dusting

pinch of salt

200g / 7oz (¾ cup) ghee

For the filling

250g / 9oz (2 medium) potatoes, unpeeled

1½ tablespoons chopped ginger

6 green chillies, de-seeded and choppped

1 large sprig coriander (cilantro), chopped

1 tablespoon dried pomegranate seeds

1 teaspoon chilli powder

salt

To serve

Mango Pickle with Jaggery (see page 77)

natural (plain) yoghurt

For the filling, cook the potatoes in a large pan of boiling water for about 20 minutes, or until soft. Drain, then allow to cool. Once cool, peel off the skins, return the flesh to the pan and mash. Put the potatoes in a bowl, add the ginger, chillies, coriander, pomegranate seeds and chilli powder, then season with salt and mix well. Set aside.

To make the dough, sift the flour and salt into a large bowl and mix in enough water to make a soft dough. Knead the dough on a lightly floured work surface for about 5 minutes. Divide the dough into 8–10 equal portions and roll into balls. Place the balls on a lightly floured surface and flatten each with a rolling pin into a round shape about 15cm / 6 inches in diameter. Take 2 rounds at a time and spread a portion of the filling in the middle of one round, then place the second round on top and seal around the sides. Flatten again with a rolling pin to a round about 18cm / 7 inches in diameter.

Heat a tawa or heavy-based frying pan (skillet) over medium heat, place a paratha in the pan and half bake for 20 seconds, turning over once. Repeat with the remaining parathas, then add the ghee to the empty pan and heat. Shallow-fry each paratha until golden brown on both sides, then remove and serve immediately with pickle and yoghurt.

Baida Paratha
Shallow-fried Bread with Egg

Origin Hyderabad
Preparation time 40 minutes
Cooking time 1 hour 20 minutes
Serves 4

4 eggs

2–3 green chillies, de-seeded and chopped

2 onions, chopped

1 sprig coriander (cilantro), chopped

300g / 11oz (2½ cups) wholemeal (whole wheat)
flour, plus extra for dusting

4 tablespoons ghee, melted

vegetable oil, for shallow-frying

salt

Put the eggs in a large bowl and beat with a fork. Season with salt and add the chillies, onion and coriander. Set aside.

Sift the flour into a large bowl, add 1 tablespoon ghee and a little salt to the flour and mix, adding a little water to make a medium-soft dough, then knead on a lightly floured work surface for about 5 minutes until smooth. Using 2–3 tablespoons of the dough per ball, roll into 16 equal-sized balls. Dust these balls with a little flour and roll out into rounds of about 18cm / 7 inches in diameter. Brush lightly with ghee and sprinkle over a little flour. Fold over a third of the round from one side, then fold the other side over this and sprinkle over some more flour.

Once again fold a portion from one of the curved sides, overlapping it with the other side to make a layered square. Dust again lightly with flour and roll out into a 15-cm / 6-inch square.

Heat a little oil for shallow-frying on a griddle or tawa or in a heavy-based frying pan (skillet), add the paratha and shallow-fry for about 1 minute on both sides. When the paratha is evenly fried and acquires a rich golden colour, transfer it to a plate and make a slit on one side with a sharp knife to create an envelope. Spread some of the egg mixture inside and seal the opening by pressing the edges together. Place the paratha once again on the griddle, tawa or in the pan and shallow-fry in very little oil for about 1 minute on both sides, or until the egg is cooked. Repeat with the remaining dough balls.

Matar-Paneer ka Paratha
Shallow-fried Spicy Peas
& Paneer Stuffed Bread

Origin Punjab
Preparation time 30 minutes
Cooking time 8–10 minutes
Makes 8–10

160g / 5½oz (1 cup) peas, shelled if fresh

100g / 3½oz (1 cup) Paneer (see page 59), crumbled

1 tablespoon ginger-chilli paste

1 tablespoon chopped coriander (cilantro) leaves

125ml / 4½fl oz (½ cup) soured natural (plain)
    yoghurt, whisked

large pinch of asafoetida

1 teaspoon sugar

½ teaspoon chilli powder

1 teaspoon Garam Masala (see page 31)

500g / 1lb 2oz (2¾ cups) cream of wheat, roasted

plain (all-purpose) flour, for dusting and rolling

200ml / 7fl oz (¾ cup) vegetable oil or ghee

salt

Cook the peas in a pan of boiling water for
5–7 minutes, or until soft, then drain, return to
the pan and mash with a potato masher.

Put the crumbled paneer, ginger-chilli paste,
coriander, yoghurt, asafoetida, sugar, chilli powder
and garam masala in a large bowl, add the peas, then
season with salt and mix together. Set aside.

Put the cream of wheat and a pinch of salt in a
large bowl and mix in enough water to make
a semi-stiff dough. Knead on a lightly floured work
surface for about 5 minutes. Divide the dough into
8–10 walnut-sized balls and lightly roll these
into rounds of about 15cm / 6 inches in diameter.

Place an equal portion of the paneer and pea mixture
in the center of each round, then fold the edges of
the round over the mixture and roll again into a small
ball. Finally, roll out carefully into a round.

Heat a little oil or ghee on a griddle or tawa or in
a heavy-based frying pan (skillet) over medium heat.
Place a paratha on the pan and shallow-fry for
2–3 minutes on both sides, or until golden brown.
Repeat with the remaining dough balls. Serve hot.

Jalebi Paratha
Spiral Paratha

Origin Delhi
Preparation time 1 hour, plus standing
and chilling time
Cooking time 1 hour
Makes 12

---

3 teaspoons fennel seeds

500g / 1lb 2oz (4 cups) plain (all-purpose) flour,
    plus extra for dusting

250ml / 8fl oz (1 cup) milk

180g / 6½oz (¾ cup) ghee

salt

Put the fennel seeds in a mortar and pound with a
pestle, or coarsely grind in a spice grinder. Set aside.

Sift the flour and salt into a paraat or large bowl,
then make a depression in the centre of the flour
and pour the milk and 125ml / 4½fl oz (½ cup) water
into it, then start mixing gradually to make a dough.
When fully mixed, knead the dough for about
5 minutes, then cover with a damp cloth or tea
(dish) towel and set aside for 10 minutes.

Add two-thirds of the ghee to the dough and
incorporate gradually. When fully mixed, knead to
make a soft dough, then add the pounded fennel,
knead again, cover and set aside for 10 minutes.

Divide the dough into 12 equal portions, then roll
into balls, dust with flour, and cover and set aside
for 10 minutes. Place the balls on a lightly floured
work surface and flatten each with a rolling pin into
flattened rounds. Spread 1 teaspoon ghee evenly
over the rounds and dust with flour. Make a radial
cut with a knife and starting with one cut edge,
roll the rounds firmly into conical shapes. Hold
each cone between your thumb and forefinger, 1cm
/ ½ inch above the base and make spiral movements
to compress the rest of the cone to make a small
thick patty. Place on greaseproof (wax) paper in the
refrigerator for 4 hours.

Remove the patties from the refrigerator. Place on
a lightly floured surface and flatten with a rolling pin
into rounds. Place the rounds on individual sheets
of greaseproof (wax) paper and refrigerate again for
30 minutes.

To cook, heat a tawa or heavy-based frying pan
(skillet) over low heat. When hot, add some ghee, then
add a paratha and cook for 2–3 minutes on both sides,
until light golden brown.

Palak Paratha
Spinach Paratha

Origin Punjab
Preparation time 15–20 minutes, plus standing time
Cooking time 20 minutes
Makes 10

600g / 1lb 5oz spinach leaves
500g / 1lb 2oz (4 cups plus 3 tablespoons) wholemeal (whole wheat) flour, plus extra for dusting
pinch of salt
2 tablespoons chopped green chillies
2 teaspoons dried pomegranate seeds
400g / 14oz (1¾ cups / 3½ sticks) butter

To serve
pickle, such as Mild Raw Mango Pickle (see page 77)
natural (plain) yoghurt

Blanch the spinach leaves in a pan of very little water for about 1 minute. Drain and immediately refresh in cold water. Drain and squeeze the spinach to remove any excess water. Transfer the spinach to a food processor or blender and process to make a smooth purée, then transfer to a bowl.

Sift the flour and salt into a paraat or large bowl. Add the spinach purée, chillies and dried pomegranate seeds and mix, adding water if required, to make a soft dough. Cover with a damp cloth or tea (dish) towel and set aside in a warm place for 30 minutes.

Divide the dough into 10 equal portions and roll into balls. Place on a floured surface and flatten each ball with a rolling pin into a flattened round, about 15–18cm / 6–7 inches in diameter.

Heat a tawa or heavy-based frying pan (skillet) over medium heat, place a round in the pan and half-cook for 1 minute, then turn over, add 3 tablespoons butter all around and shallow-fry for a further minute, or until golden brown on both sides. Remove and serve immediately with pickle and yoghurt. Repeat with the remaining parathas.

Dal Paratha
Moong Dal Paratha

Origin Punjab
Preparation time 40 minutes, plus standing time
Cooking time 15 minutes
Makes 8

200g / 7oz (1 cup) moong dal, rinsed and drained
400g / 14oz (3⅓ cups) wholemeal (whole wheat) flour
1 teaspoon chilli powder
1 teaspoon ground turmeric
15g / ½oz (⅓ cup) coriander (cilantro) leaves, chopped
30g / 1¼oz (½ small) onion, chopped
1 tablespoon chopped green chillies
pinch of salt
200g / 7oz (1¾ sticks) butter, melted

Cook the moong dal in a large pan of boiling water for about 30 minutes, or until soft. Drain. Sift the flour into a large bowl, make a depression in the centre of the flour and add the boiled dal and the remaining ingredients, except the butter. Start mixing gradually, adding water if required, to make a soft dough. When fully mixed, knead the dough on a lightly floured work surface for 5 minutes, then transfer to a lightly oiled bowl, cover with a damp cloth or tea (dish) towel and set aside in a warm place for 30 minutes.

Divide the dough into 8 equal portions, then roll into balls. Place on a floured surface and flatten each ball with a rolling pin into a flattened round, about 20–23cm / 8–9 inches in diameter.

Heat a tawa or heavy-based frying pan (skillet) over low heat, then place a paratha in the pan and half-cook for 1 minute, turning once. Pour melted butter all around and fry for a further minute, or until golden brown on both sides. Remove and repeat with the remaining parathas. Serve hot.

Suji Paratha
Semolina Paratha

Origin Awadh
Preparation time 30 minutes, plus standing time
Cooking time 15 minutes
Makes 8

300g / 10oz (2 cups) fine semolina (semolina flour)

6 tablespoons olive oil

salt

Place the semolina in a large bowl and stir in
1 teaspoon salt and 2 tablespoons of oil. Gradually
add enough water to make a soft dough. When fully
mixed, knead the dough on a lightly floured work
surface for about 5 minutes, then transfer to a
lightly oiled bowl, cover with a damp cloth or tea
(dish) towel and set aside in a warm place for about
30 minutes. Divide the dough into 8 equal portions,
then roll into balls and roll out into a roti (a 20-cm
/ 8-inch disc).

Heat a tawa or heavy-based frying pan (skillet)
over medium heat. Add ½ tablespoon oil, heat until
smoking, then add a paratha to the pan and cook on
both sides for about 30 seconds, until golden brown.
Remove and repeat with the remaining parathas.

Malabari Paratha
Paratha from Malabar

Origin Kerala
Preparation time 30 minutes, plus standing time
Cooking time 30 minutes
Makes 8

500g / 1lb 2oz (4 cups) plain (all-purpose) flour,
    plus extra for dusting

pinch of baking powder

pinch of salt

1 egg

125ml / 4½fl oz (½ cup) milk

1½ teaspoon sugar

150g / 5oz (10 tablespoons / 1¼ sticks) butter,
    melted, plus extra for brushing

Sift the flour, baking powder and salt into a large
bowl. Beat the egg in a separate bowl, then add the
milk, sugar and butter. Make a hollow in the centre
of the flour, add the egg mixture and start mixing,
gradually adding water if required, to make a soft
dough, then knead on a lightly floured work surface
for about 5 minutes. Transfer to a lightly oiled
bowl, cover with a damp cloth and set aside in a
warm place for about 1 hour.

Divide the dough into 8 equal portions, then roll
into balls and brush with a little butter. Set aside
for about 30 minutes.

Now roll each dough ball as thinly as possible on
a lightly floured surface into a flattened round.
Pleat the thin roti like a closed flan and then roll it
from one of the short ends into a coil. Set aside for
10 minutes.

Roll out each dough ball again into a flattened round,
about 1mm thick.

Heat a non-stick pan over medium heat, add the
paratha one at a time and cook for about 2–3 minutes
on both sides, brushing with butter until light
golden brown and crisp. Remove and repeat with
the remaining parathas.

Kerala Paratha
Kerala Paratha

Origin Kerala
Preparation time 50 minutes, plus standing time
Cooking time 4–5 minutes
Makes 6

---

2 eggs

150ml / ¼pint (⅔ cup) milk

2½ teaspoons sugar

pinch of salt

4 tablespoons groundnut (peanut) oil, plus extra
   for oiling

450g / 1lb (3⅔ cups) plain (all-purpose) flour,
   plus extra for dusting

pinch of bicarbonate of soda (baking soda)

melted butter, for brushing

100g / 3½oz (½ cup) melted ghee

Put the eggs into a bowl, add the milk, sugar, salt
and oil and whisk together.

Sift the flour and bicarbonate of soda (baking soda)
into a paraat or large bowl. Make a depression in the
centre of the flour, pour the egg and milk mixture
in and start mixing gradually to make a soft dough.
When fully mixed, knead the dough on a lightly
floured work surface for about 5 minutes, then
transfer to a lightly oiled bowl, cover with a damp
cloth or tea (dish) towel and set aside in a warm
place for 30 minutes.

Divide the dough into 6 equal portions and roll
into balls. Flatten each ball with a rolling pin into
a flattened round. Oil a board for rolling out the
dough with oil, then place the flattened dough on it
and stretch evenly on all sides until very thin. Brush
melted butter over the entire surface, dust with flour,
then gather the dough ensuring there are many folds.
Place the dough on the table and roll to make a short
thick round patty, then flatten slightly. Set aside for
5 minutes. Flatten each patty with a rolling pin into
a flattened round, dusting with flour while rolling.

Heat a tawa or heavy-based frying pan (skillet)
over low heat, then place a paratha in the pan and
bake halfway, turning over once. Pour melted ghee
all around and fry until golden brown on both sides.
Remove and repeat with the remaining parathas.

Gurh ka Paratha
Sweet Paratha

Origin Punjab
Preparation time 30 minutes, plus standing time
Cooking time 15 minutes
Makes 8

240g / 18½oz (2 cups) wholemeal
   (whole wheat) flour, plus extra for dusting

ghee, for cooking

For the filling

100g / 3½oz (½ cup) jaggery, crumbled, or soft
   brown sugar

2 tablespoons chopped cashew nuts

1 tablespoon chopped raisins

seeds of 2 black cardamom pods

Mix the flour with enough water in a large bowl
to make a soft dough, then knead well on a lightly
floured work surface for about 5 minutes, or until
smooth. Transfer to a lightly oiled bowl, cover
with a damp cloth or tea (dish) towel and set aside
in a warm place for at least 30 minutes.

Divide the dough into 8 marble-sized balls. Roll out
1 ball on a lightly floured work surface into a very
thin round. Sprinkle 2 tablespoons jaggery or sugar
on it, then sprinkle over 1 teaspoon chopped cashew
nuts, ½ teaspoon chopped raisins and some crushed
cardamom seeds.

Heat a tawa or heavy-based frying pan (skillet)
over medium heat. Roll out another ball into a very
thin round and place it on top of the first round
to cover the filling. Press the edges well to join and
gently flatten a little with the rolling pin. Carefully
transfer the paratha to the hot tawa and cook
for 1 minute until the underside is cooked, then turn
over to cook the other side. Smear a little ghee
over the paratha and trickle some ghee around the
edges, too. Turn and brown both sides. Remove and
make the other parathas in the same way.

Besani Poori
Deep-fried Gram (Chickpea) Flour Bread

Origin Awadh
Preparation time 40 minutes, plus standing time
Cooking time 10–15 minutes
Makes 10–12

200g / 7oz (1⅓ cups) gram (chickpea) flour
120g / 4¼oz (1 cup) wholemeal (whole wheat) flour, plus extra for dusting
¼ teaspoon chilli powder
pinch of asafoetida
pinch of salt
2 teaspoons chopped fenugreek leaves
625g / 1lb 6oz (2¾ cups) ghee

Sift together all the dry ingredients into a large bowl and add the fenugreek leaves. Add cold water, a little at a time, and mix to make a fairly stiff dough. Cover with a damp cloth or tea (dish) towel and set aside in a warm place for 30 minutes.

Pinch off walnut-sized pieces of dough and roll out thinly on a lightly floured board or work surface.

Heat the ghee in a kadhai, wok or deep, heavy-based pan to 180°C/350°F, or until a cube of bread browns in 30 seconds. Working in batches, carefully add the pooris to the hot ghee and deep-fry for about 1–2 minutes, or until puffed up and golden brown. Remove with a slotted spoon and drain on kitchen paper (paper towels).

To make besani roti, add 2 tablespoons chopped onions to the dough, then roll out and cook the roti on a hot griddle, tawa or in a heavy-based frying pan (skillet). With the tip of a sharp knife, prick the roti all over to prevent it from rising. Cook for 1 minute, then turn over and cook the other side. Remove and repeat with the remaining roti.

p.478

Roomali Roti
Handkerchief Bread

Origin Delhi/Awadh/Hyderabad
Preparation time 45 minutes, plus standing time
Cooking time 5 minutes
Makes 5

300g / 11oz (2½ cups) wholemeal (whole wheat) flour
100g / 3½oz (¾ cup) plain (all-purpose) flour, plus extra for dusting
salt

Sift the flours and a pinch of salt together into a flat tray (pan) or large bowl. Make a depression in the centre, then pour in about 125ml /4½fl oz (½ cup) water and start mixing gradually. Add another 125ml /4½fl oz (½ cup) water, and continue mixing to make a soft dough. Knead on a lightly floured work surface for about 5 minutes, or until soft and smooth. Transfer to a lightly oiled bowl, cover with a damp cloth or tea (dish) towel and set aside in a warm place for about 1 hour.

Divide the dough into 8 equal portions and roll into balls. Do not overwork the dough. Place the balls on a lightly floured work surface, then cover and set aside.

Dust the balls with flour, then press and flatten each with a rolling pin into a flattened round, about 10cm / 4 inches in diameter, ensuring that the edges are thinner than the centre. Stretch each round by rotating and flipping from one hand to the other until it is about 35cm / 12 inches in diameter.

To cook the roti, lightly oil a convex tawa, kadhai or wok, and place over high heat. When smoking, add a roti to the pan and cook for 30 seconds. Brush the upper side of the roti with a little oil, then flip and cook for a further 30 seconds. The roti should be cooked through and brown in patches. Serve immediately otherwise the roti will become dry. Repeat with the remaining dough balls.

Khasta Roti
Crisp Bread

Origin Punjab/Delhi
Preparation time 45 minutes, plus standing time
Cooking time 25–30 minutes
Makes 12

125ml / 4½fl oz (½ cup) milk

2 teaspoons sugar

pinch of salt

100g / 3½oz (¾ cup) plain (all-purpose) flour

400g / 14oz (2¼ cups) fine semolina (semolina flour)

½ teaspoon aniseeds

½ teaspoon ajwain seeds

4 teaspoons ghee, melted, plus extra for greasing

melted butter, for brushing

Put the milk in a jug (pitcher), add the sugar and salt and mix together.

Sift the plain flour and semolina into a paraat or large bowl, then add the aniseed and ajwain seeds. Make a depression in the centre of the flour, then pour in the milk mixture and mix it gradually to make a dough. When fully mixed, knead the dough on a lightly floured work surface for 5 minutes, then cover with a damp cloth and set aside for 10–15 minutes.

Preheat the oven to 200°C/400°F/Gas Mark 6, if using.

Add the melted ghee to the dough and knead it in gradually. Divide the dough into 12 equal portions, roll into balls, cover with a damp cloth or tea (dish) towel and set aside for about 5 minutes.

Flatten each ball with a rolling pin to make a flattened round, then prick the entire surface with a fork.

To cook the roti, either use a tandoor or oven. In a tandoor, place the roti on a cushioned pad and place inside a moderately hot tandoor. Let the roti bake for 2–3 minutes and then remove it with tongs. If using the oven, place the roti on a greased baking tray (sheet) and bake for about 10 minutes. Remove and brush with melted butter. Serve hot.

Tandoori Roti
Bread Baked in a Clay Oven

Origin Punjab/Delhi
Preparation time 40 minutes, plus standing time
Cooking time 5 minutes
Makes 8

480g / 17oz (4 cups) wholemeal flour,
    plus extra for dusting

½ teaspoon salt

2 tablespoons ghee or vegetable oil, plus extra
    for greasing

1 tablespoon plain (all-purpose) flour

Sift the wholemeal flour and salt together in a large bowl, then mix in enough water to make a soft dough. Knead the dough on a lightly floured work surface for about 5 minutes, or until smooth. Transfer to a lightly oiled bowl, cover with a cloth and set aside in a warm place for about 30 minutes.

Preheat the oven to 200°C/400°F/Gas Mark 6.

Mix the ghee or oil and plain (all-purpose) flour together in a separate bowl to make a paste. Divide the dough into 8 equal portions and roll into balls. Flatten each ball between the palms of your hands, then roll out on a lightly floured surface with a rolling pin to a round, about 15cm / 6 inches in diameter. Spread the round with a little ghee paste, then using a knife, make a radial cut with a knife.

Now start rolling from one cut edge to form an even cone. Press the cone to get a flattened and coiled round and roll out the round to a diameter of 15cm / 6 inches, carefully applying pressure at the centre only and not on the sides.

To cook the roti, either use a tandoor or oven. In a tandoor, place the roti on a cushioned pad and place inside a hot tandoor. Let it bake for about 2 minutes, or until brown, then remove with tongs. If using the oven, place the roti on a greased baking tray (sheet) and bake for about 5 minutes, or until brown.

Bervin Roti
Plain Stuffed Bread

Origin Awadh
Preparation time 40 minutes, plus standing time
Cooking time 10–15 minutes
Makes 16

1kg / 2¼lb (8 cups) plain (all-purpose) flour or 1kg/ 2¼lb
   (8⅓ cups) wholemeal (whole wheat) flour

pinch of salt

125g / 4¼oz (½ cup) ghee

For the filling
375g / 13oz (2 cups) chana dal, rinsed and drained

½ teaspoon salt

pinch of ground black pepper

Sift the flour and salt together into a large bowl.
Add the ghee and rub it in with your fingertips
until the mixture resembles breadcrumbs, then mix
in enough water to make a soft, not sticky dough.
Knead well on a lightly floured work surface for
about 5 minutes, then transfer to a lightly oiled
bowl, cover with a damp cloth or tea (dish) towel
and set aside in a warm place for 1 hour.

For the filling, cook the dal in a large pan of boiling
water for about 30 minutes, or until soft and dry.
Mash thoroughly with a wooden spatula or potato
masher and season with the salt and pepper.

Divide the dough into 16 equal portions, then roll
into balls and flatten between your palms to make
small rounds. Put a little dal in the centre of each,
then fold over to enclose the filling and roll into
a ball. Carefully roll the balls into rounds, further
flattening with your hands if necessary.

Heat a griddle, tawa or heavy-based frying pan
(skillet) over medium heat. Place a roti on the
griddle or tawa, or in the pan and cook for
1–2 minutes, turning twice until cooked through.
Remove and repeat with the remaining roti.

Akki Roti
Rice Roti from Karnataka

Origin Coastal
Preparation time 20–30 minutes
Cooking time 30 minutes
Makes 6–8

150g / 5½oz (1 cup) rice flour,
   plus extra for dusting

4 tablespoons grated fresh coconut

1 onion, chopped

1–2 tablespoons chopped coriander (cilantro) leaves

3–4 green chillies, de-seeded and chopped

1 × 1-cm / ½-inch piece fresh ginger, peeled
   and grated

1 tablespoon ghee

1 tablespoon soured natural (plain) yoghurt

vegetable oil, for oiling and shallow-frying

banana leaves, cut into pieces

salt

Mix all the ingredients, except the oil and banana
leaves, together in a large bowl. Season with salt,
then gradually sprinkle in 5 tablespoons warm water
and mix to make a soft dough. Knead well on a
lightly floured work surface for 5 minutes.

Heat a tawa, griddle or heavy-based frying pan
(skillet) over medium heat. Place a piece of oiled
banana leaf on the work surface. Pinch off a lime-
sized ball of dough and pat with oiled fingers to
form a 15-cm / 6-inch round roti on the leaf. Gently
lift the leaf and flip it over on to the hot tawa or
pan. The leaf will stick to the roti. When the roti
starts to cook the leaf will come off easily. Drizzle
oil around and over the roti and cook on both
sides until golden brown. Remove and repeat with
the remaining roti.

Makki ki Roti
Corn Bread

Origin Punjab
Preparation time 20–30 minutes, plus standing time
Cooking time 5–10 minutes
Makes 8

500g / 1lb 2oz (4¼ cups) cornmeal

60g / 2oz (½ cup) wholemeal (whole wheat) flour

25g / 1oz (3½ tablespoons) plain (all-purpose) flour,
   plus extra for dusting

pinch of salt

100g / 3½oz (scant ½ cup) ghee or butter, melted,
   plus extra for greasing

Classic Mustard Greens (see page 262), to serve

Sift the cornmeal, flours and salt into a large bowl and mix in enough water to make a soft dough. Knead the dough on a lightly floured work surface for about 5 minutes, then transfer to a lightly oiled bowl, cover with a damp cloth or tea (dish) towel and set aside in a warm place for about 30 minutes.

Divide the dough into 8 equal portions, roll into balls, dust with flour, then cover and set aside for about 5 minutes.

Preheat the oven to 200°C/400°F/Gas Mark 6, if using.

Flatten each ball between the palms of your hands or roll with a rolling pin on a lightly floured surface to make a flattened round, about 20cm / 8 inches in diameter. Sprinkle over a little flour to prevent it sticking.

To cook the roti, either use a tandoor or oven. In a tandoor, place the roti on a cushioned pad, then place inside a moderately hot tandoor. Let the roti bake for about 2 minutes, then remove with tongs. If using the oven, place the roti on a greased baking tray (sheet) and bake for about 6 minutes. When the roti are cooked, brush with ghee or butter and serve with Mustard Greens.

Methi ki Roti
Fenugreek Bread

Origin Punjab
Preparation time 20 minutes, plus standing time
Cooking time 15 minutes
Makes 10

150g / 5oz (2½ cups) fenugreek leaves, chopped

2 tablespoons chopped green chillies

500g / 1lb 2oz (4 cups plus 2 tablespoons) wholemeal
   (whole wheat) flour, plus extra for dusting

pinch of salt

3½ tablespoons melted butter, plus extra for greasing

Mix the chopped fenugreek leaves and chillies together in a bowl.

Sift the flour and salt into a paraat or large bowl. Make a depression in the centre of the flour, then slowly mix in enough water to form a soft dough. Mix in the fenugreek mixture and, when fully mixed, knead the dough on a lightly floured work surface for about 5 minutes, then transfer to a lightly oiled bowl, cover with a damp cloth or tea (dish) towel and set aside in a warm place for 30 minutes.

Divide the dough into 10 equal portions and roll into balls. Place them on a floured surface and flatten each ball with a rolling pin into a flattened round, about 15cm / 6 inches in diameter.

Heat a tawa or heavy-based frying pan (skillet) over medium heat, place the roti in the pan and cook for 1 minute, then turn over and cook the other side until golden brown. Remove and brush with melted butter on one side and serve. Repeat with the remaining roti.

Bajare ki Roti
Millet Bread

Origin Rajasthan
Preparation time 10–15 minutes, plus standing time
Cooking time 15 minutes
Makes 8

500g / 1lb 2oz (4 cups plus 2 tablespoons) millet flour, plus extra for dusting

pinch of salt

5½ tablespoons melted butter, for oiling and serving

Sift the flour and salt into a paraat or large bowl. Make a depression in the centre of the flour, then slowly mix in enough water to make a semi-hard dough. When fully mixed, knead the dough on a lightly floured work surface for about 5 minutes, then transfer to a lightly oiled bowl, cover with a damp cloth or tea (dish) towel and set aside in a warm place for 30 minutes.

Divide the dough into 8 equal portions, roll into balls, cover again and set aside for 5 minutes.

Flatten each ball between the palms of your hands to make a flattened round.

Heat a griddle, tawa or a heavy-based frying pan (skillet) over medium heat.

Place the roti on the hot griddle, tawa or pan and cook for about 1 minute. Turn over and continue to cook, gently pressing with a clean dry cloth. Remove when the bread begins to puff up, changes colour and is marked with dark patches. The edges will begin to crisp. Keep warm while you repeat with the remaining dough balls. Butter each roti lightly before serving.

Missi Roti
Lentil Bread

Origin Punjab
Preparation time 50 minutes, plus soaking and standing time
Cooking time 4–6 minutes
Makes 10

100g / 3½oz (½ cup) chana dal, rinsed and drained

100g / 3½oz (½ cup) moong dal, rinsed and drained

3 tablespoons wholemeal (whole wheat) flour, plus extra for dusting

2 tablespoons plain (all-purpose) flour

5 tablespoons chopped onion

3 green chillies, de-seeded and chopped

1 tablespoon chopped ginger

3 teaspoons chopped coriander (cilantro) leaves

½ teaspoon ground turmeric

1 teaspoon chilli powder

pinch of salt

3 tablespoons ghee or butter, melted, plus extra for greasing

---

Soak the chana dal and moong dal in a large bowl of water for 30 minutes, then drain. Transfer to a pan, pour in enough water to cover and boil for 15 minutes until thick. Allow to cool slightly, then transfer to a food processor or blender and grind to a paste.

Mix the flours together in a bowl and add the dal paste and all the remaining ingredients, except the ghee. Mix thoroughly, adding enough water to make a soft pliable dough. Knead the dough on a lightly floured work surface for 5 minutes, then transfer to a lightly oiled bowl, cover with a damp cloth or tea (dish) towel and set aside in a warm place for about 30 minutes. Preheat the oven to 200°C/400°F/ Gas Mark 6, if using.

Divide the dough into 10 equal portions, roll into ablls, dust with wholemeal flour, then cover with a damp cloth or tea (dish) towel and set aside for about 5 minutes. Flatten each ball between the palms of your hands into a flattened round.

To cook the roti, either use a tandoor or oven. In a tandoor, place the roti on a cushioned pad and place inside a moderately hot tandoor. Let it bake for about 4 minutes, then remove with tongs. If using the oven, place the roti on a greased baking tray (sheet) and bake for about 6 minutes. Serve brushed with ghee or melted butter

Thali Peeth
Mixed-flour Bread

Origin Maharashtra
Preparation time 50 minutes
Cooking time 20–25 minutes
Makes 12

150g / 5oz (1 cup) thali peeth flour, plus extra for
    dusting (see below)

1 tablespoon finely chopped green chillies

1 tablespoon finely chopped ginger

1 onion, finely chopped

1 teaspoon chilli powder

125ml / 4½fl oz (½ cup) soured natural (plain) yoghurt

1 tomato, de-seeded and chopped

1 tablespoon sesame seeds

¼ teaspoon ground cloves

¼ teaspoon ground cardamom

¼ teaspoon ground coriander

¼ teaspoon ground cumin

¼ teaspoon ground black pepper

pinch of salt

5 tablespoons vegetable oil

For the thali peeth flour

200g / 7oz (1 cup) short-grain rice

30g / 1oz (¼ cup) wholemeal (whole wheat) flour

45g / 1½oz (¼ cup) dark millet

45g / 1½oz (¼ cup) white millet

50g / 1¾oz (¼ cup) chana dal, rinsed and drained

½ teaspoon coriander seeds

½ teaspoon cumin seeds

½ teaspoon black peppercorns

½ teaspoon fenugreek seeds

½ teaspoon ground cloves

½ teaspoon ground cardamom

To make the flour, roast all the ingredients and then
process in a spice grinder or blender until ground.
Use as required.

To make the bread, sift the flour on to a large tray
(pan) or into a large bowl and add all the ingredients
except the oil. Make a depression in the centre, pour
in a little water and mix to form soft dough. Divide
the dough equally into small balls. Roll each ball out
on a board and press lightly with your palm to make
small rounds of about 8cm / 3 inches in diameter.

Heat 1 tablespoon of oil on a griddle, tawa or heavy-
based frying pan (skillet) over high heat. Place the
round flat on the hot griddle, tawa or pan, spread
a little oil on the top surface, cover and cook for
2 minutes. Turn over and cook the other side for
about 1 minute until it is light brown, then remove
from the heat. Repeat with the other dough balls.

Bhakri
Maharashtrian Bread

Origin Maharashtra
Preparation time 30 minutes
Cooking time 15 minutes
Makes 10–12

500g / 1lb 2oz (3 cups plus 3 tablespoons) rice flour
    or 500g / 1lb 2oz (4 cups plus 2½ tablespoons)
    millet flour, plus extra for dusting

pinch of salt

Sift the flour and salt into a large bowl, then mix
in 500ml / 18fl oz (2¼ cups) warm water to make a
smooth dough. Knead the dough on a lightly floured
work surface for about 2 minutes, then divide
into 10–12 equal portions and roll into small balls.
Sprinkle some rice flour on a tray (pan) or work
surface and flatten the balls on it, pressing gently
with the palms of your hands. Take care that they
are still round. Sprinkle over some more flour
and shape the flattened balls into roti by pressing
them between the palms of your hands and rotating
them. When you are satisfied with the size and
shape of the breads, set aside.

Heat a flat tawa or a heavy-based frying pan (skillet)
over high heat, then reduce the heat to medium.
Sprinkle some water on the surface of the bhakri and
stretch it a little, then gently place in the pan. Cook
for about 15 seconds, then turn over and cook the
other side for about 15 seconds. If you are using a gas
stove, remove from the pan and hold over a direct
flame on the cooker (stove top). If you are using
an electric stove, cook the bread a little longer in the
pan. Either way, roast until small black burn marks
appear on both sides. Repeat until all the bhakri
are cooked.

Phulka
Puffed Bread

Origin Punjab/Delhi/Awadh
Preparation time 45 minutes, plus standing time
Cooking time 40–50 minutes
Makes 20–25

360g / 12½oz (3 cups) wholemeal
(whole wheat) flour, plus extra for dusting
vegetable oil for greasing

Sift the flour into a flat pan, thali or bowl, then gradually mix in enough water to make a soft dough. Knead and fold the dough for 10 minutes on a lightly floured work surface, sprinkling over a little water during the process. Transfer to a lightly oiled bowl, cover with a damp cloth or tea (dish) towel and set aside in a warm place for 30 minutes.

Knead again thoroughly, then pinch off small pieces of dough, roll into balls and flatten them between the palms of your hands using a little flour. Roll each out thinly on a lightly floured work surface into 15-cm / 5-inch circles, using more flour to prevent sticking.

Heat a griddle, tawa or heavy-based frying pan (skillet) over medium heat. Add a phulka to the griddle, tawa or pan and cook for 1 minute on each side until dry and beginning to brown. Remove the griddle, tawa or pan from the heat, and using tongs, place the phulka over a direct flame for a few seconds until it puffs up. If using an electric stove, cook the phulka for a little longer in the pan, pressing lightly with a clean dry cloth to help it puff up. Turn and cook the other side. Serve immediately. Repeat with the remaining phulkas.

To make a karara, or crisp phulka, hold over the direct flame for a little longer, until burnt patches appear. These semi-burnt phulkas are delicious with dal or a little butter.

Bajari-Methi na Tepla
Shallow-fried Fenugreek & Millet Bread

Origin Gujarat
Preparation time 30 minutes
Cooking time 20 minutes
Makes 12–14

125g / 4½oz (1 cup) wholemeal (whole wheat) flour,
plus extra for dusting
150g / 5oz (1 cup) millet flour
1 teaspoon ground coriander
1 teaspoon ground cumin
¼ teaspoon ground turmeric
1 teaspoon chilli powder
1 teaspoon Ginger Paste (see page 57)
1 teaspoon red chilli paste
2 tablespoons jaggery or soft brown sugar
pinch of salt
4 tablespoons fenugreek leaves
2 tablespoons vegetable oil, plus extra
for shallow-frying
250ml / 8fl oz (1 cup) soured natural (plain) yoghurt

Sift both the flours together with all the ground spices, ginger and chilli pastes, jaggery or sugar and salt in a large bowl. Add the fenugreek leaves and oil and mix, adding enough yoghurt to make a semi-soft dough. Knead the dough briefly on a lightly floured work surface.

Divide the dough into 12–14 equal portions and roll into balls, then flatten these between the palms of your hands and roll with the rolling pin into rounds, about 10cm / 4 inches in diameter.

Heat a little oil for shallow-frying in a heavy-based frying pan (skillet) over medium heat. Add a tepla and shallow-fry for about 2 minutes until it changes colour and is marked with dark patches. Using a spoon, pour a little oil around the edge of the tepla to ensure it does not stick to the pan and burn. Turn over and cook for about 1 minute. Repeat with the remaining dough balls.

Amritsari Kulcha
Baked Bread from Amritsar

Origin Punjab
Preparation time 45 minutes, plus standing time
Cooking time 10–30 minutes
Makes 8

500g / 1lb 2oz (4 cups) plain (all-purpose) flour,
    plus extra for dusting

pinch of salt

125g / 4oz (½ cup) ghee

melted ghee or butter, for greasing and brushing

For the filling

200g / 7oz (1 large) potato, grated

175g / 6oz (⅔ small head) cauliflower, grated

2 tablespoons Paneer (see page 59), grated

2 teaspoons chopped ginger

1 tablespoon chopped coriander (cilantro) leaves

1 teaspoon coriander seeds, roasted
    and crushed

1 tablespoon chopped green chillies

40g / 1½oz (½ small) onion, chopped

1 teaspoon ground black pepper

1 teaspoon dried pomegranate seed powder

1 teaspoon cumin seeds

1 teaspoon ajwain seeds

1 teaspoon dried fenugreek leaves

1 teaspoon Garam Masala (see page 31)

To make the filling, mix all the filling ingredients
together in a large bowl and divide it into
8 equal portions.

Sift the plain flour and salt into an open, stainless
steel platter or large bowl. Add a little water to the
flour and start mixing until a soft dough is formed.
Knead on a lightly floured work surface for about
5 minutes, then transfer to a lightly oiled bowl,
cover with a damp cloth or tea (dish) towel and set
aside in a warm place for about 30 minutes.

Add half the ghee to the dough, knead again,
cover and set aside for a further 10 minutes.

Preheat the oven to 200°C/400°F/Gas Mark 6,
if using.

Now divide the dough into 8 equal portions and roll
into balls, then set aside for about 5 minutes. Next,
put each ball on a floured surface and flatten with
a rolling pin into a flattened round, about 10–12cm
/ 4–5 inches in diameter. Put a little of the filling in
the middle of each round, then fold over to enclose
the filling and press down with your fingertips
to seal the edges. Flatten the round again with
a rolling pin, taking care not to let the filling ooze
out. Do the same with all the dough balls and filling.

To cook the kulcha, either use a tandoor or oven.
In a tandoor, place the flattened round on a
cushioned pad and place inside a moderately warm
tandoor. Let the kulcha bake for 2–3 minutes and
then remove it with tongs. If using the oven, place
the kulcha on a greased baking tray (pan) and bake
for about 10 minutes. After removing the baked
kulcha, brush ghee or butter all over and serve hot.

Chapaati
Chapati

400g / 14oz (3⅓ cups) wholemeal (whole wheat) flour
    plus extra for dusting

pinch of salt

melted ghee or butter, for brushing (optional)

Sift the flour and salt into an open, stainless steel
tray or large bowl. Add about 250m / 8fl oz (1 cup)
water to the flour and start mixing until a soft
dough is formed.

Divide the dough into equal pieces and roll into
balls. Flatten each ball between the palms of your
hands and dust with flour.

Roll each out to about 15cm / 5 inches in diameter.

Heat a flat tawa or a heavy-based frying pan (skillet)
over high heat, then reduce the heat to medium-
low. Add a chapati to the pan and cook for about
10 seconds, pressing with a cloth until the bread
begins to puff up, then turn and cook the other side
in the same way. The chapati is cooked when brown
patches appear on the surface. Serve the chapati as
they are, or brushd with ghee or butter.

Sheermal
Mildly Sweet Milk Bread

Origin Awadh/Hyderabad
Preparation time 15 minutes, plus standing time
Cooking time 12–15 minutes
Serves 24

500ml / 18fl oz (2¼ cups) milk

2 teaspoons dried yeast

4 tablespoons kewra water

1 teaspoon ground green cardamom

3 tablespoons sugar

1kg / 2¼lb (8½ cups) wholemeal (whole wheat) flour

1 teaspoon salt

750g / 1lb 10oz (3¼ cups / 6½ sticks) ghee or butter

Put the milk in a large jug (pitcher), add the yeast, kewra water, ground cardamom and sugar and mix well. Set aside. Mix the flour, salt and ghee or butter together on a large tray or in a bowl, then pour the milk mixture over the flour and mix to make soft dough. Cover and set aside in a warm place for 2 hours.

Divide the dough into 24 equal-sized balls. Roll the ball on a lightly floured work surface with a rolling pin into a round of 15cm / 6 inches in diameter and prick the round with a fork.

Heat a griddle, tawa or heavy-based frying pan (skillet) until hot, then place the round on the hot griddle, tawa or pan and cook for about 10 seconds on both sides until golden brown. Repeat with the remaining dough balls.

Rogani Kulcha
Rich Kulcha

Origin Awadh
Preparation time 40 minutes, plus standing time
Cooking time 25 minutes
Makes 8

1 egg

½ teaspoon baking powder

1 teaspoon sugar

5 tablespoons milk

500g / 1lb 2oz (4 cups) plain (all-purpose) flour, plus extra for dusting

pinch of salt

4 teaspoons vegetable oil

For the rogan

2 tablespoons vegetable oil

1 tablespoon chilli powder

1 egg

Put the egg into a bowl, add the baking powder, sugar and milk and whisk together. Sift the flour and salt into a paraat or large bowl. Make a depression in the centre of the flour, add the egg mixture and start mixing gradually, adding in enough water to make a soft dough. When fully mixed, knead the dough on a lightly floured work surface for 5 minutes, then set aside for 10 minutes.

Add the vegetable oil to the dough, then knead and punch down the dough. Cover with a damp cloth or tea (dish) towel and set aside in a warm place for 2 hours to allow the dough to rise. Divide the dough into 8 equal portions and roll into balls, then set aside.

To make the rogan, heat the oil in a heavy-based pan over medium heat, add the chilli powder and cook for 30 seconds. Strain and allow to cool, then add the egg and mix together.

Preheat the oven to 200°C/400°F/Gas Mark 6, if using. Flatten each dough ball between the palms of your hands to make a flattened round.

To cook the kulcha, either use a tandoor or oven. In a tandoor, place the flattened round on a cushioned pad and place inside a moderately hot tandoor. Let the kulcha bake for 2–3 minutes and then remove it with tongs. If using the oven, place the kulcha on a greased baking tray (sheet) and bake for about 10 minutes. Spread the rogan over the kulcha and serve.

Girda
Kashmiri Fermented Bread

Origin Jammu and Kashmir
Preparation time 1 hour, plus fermenting time
Cooking time 10–15 minutes
Serves 8

250g / 9oz (2 cups) plain (all-purpose) flour
250g / 9oz (2 cups plus 2 tablespoons) wholemeal
    (whole wheat) flour
1 tablespoon ghee
½ teaspoon salt
1 tablespoon sugar
1 teaspoon baking powder
1 tablespoon natural (plain) yoghurt
1 teaspoon poppy seeds

Sift the plain (all-purpose) flour into a large bowl,
then, using your hands, slowly mix in 250ml / 8fl oz
(1 cup) water. Transfer to a pot or bowl, cover and
set aside to ferment overnight.

The next day, preheat the oven to 180°C/350°F/Gas
Mark 4.

Sift the wholemeal flour into a large bowl, add
the ghee, salt and sugar and mix, then mix in the
fermented plain flour. Add some water, if required,
to make the dough into an elastic consistency, which
does not stick to your fingers. At this stage add the
baking powder.

Divide the dough into small balls and shape them
into flat oval-shaped breads. Using a knife, make a
slit along one side of each bread and spread a little
yoghurt inside. Sprinkle some poppy seeds over
the top of the breads. Make small depressions on
the bread and bake in the oven for 10–15 minutes.
Keep checking, and once it starts rising and turns
light brown, it is ready.

Taftan
Flaky Bread

Origin Awadh
Preparation time 30 minutes, plus standing time
Cooking time 6–9 minutes
Makes 8

125ml / 4½fl oz (½ cup) milk
20g / ¾oz (about 7 teaspoons) fast-action dried
    (active dry) yeast
3½ tablespoons sugar
475g / 1lb (3¾ cups) plain (all-purpose) flour
pinch of salt
3 tablespoons natural (plain) yoghurt
2 eggs, lightly beaten
4 teaspoons vegetable oil, plus extra for brushing
    and oiling
1½ tablespoons ghee, melted, plus extra for basting
1 tablespoon kalonji (nigella) seeds
milk, for basting

Mix the warm milk, yeast and sugar together
in a bowl. Set aside until it starts to froth.

Sift the flour and salt into a paraat or large bowl.
Make a depression in the centre of the flour and
pour in the yeast mixture, yoghurt, eggs and oil. Mix
to make a dough, then knead the dough on a lightly
floured work surface for about 5 minutes, until it is
smooth and elastic. Transfer to a lightly oiled bowl,
cover with a damp cloth or tea (dish) towel and set
aside in a warm place for 6 hours.

Punch down the dough and divide the dough
into 8 equal portions. Brush with oil, then set
aside for 20 minutes.

Preheat the oven to 200°C/400°F/Gas Mark 6.
Flatten each ball with the palms of your hands making
it narrow at one end and broad at the other.

Brush with a little ghee and sprinkle over the
kalonji seeds. Put the breads on 2–3 oiled baking
trays (sheets) and bake in the oven for 2–3 minutes.
Remove from the oven and baste with a little milk
and ghee.

📷 p.677

Baqarkhani Roti
Rich Sweet Bread

Origin Awadh/Hyderabad
Preparation time 40 minutes, plus standing time
Cooking time 10 minutes
Serves 12

500g / 1lb 2oz (4 cups) plain (all-purpose) flour,
 plus extra for dusting

1 teaspoon baking powder

pinch of salt

3 teaspoons icing (confectioners') sugar

250ml / 8fl oz (1 cup) warm full cream (whole) milk

1 teaspoon fresh yeast

4 green cardamom pods, ground

2 tablespoons raisins

16–18 almonds, cut into slivers

250g / 9oz (1 cup) ghee, melted, plus extra
 for greasing

1 tablespoon poppy seeds

Sift the flour, baking powder and salt into a large bowl and add the sugar and warm milk. Set aside. Put the yeast in a small bowl, add 5 tablespoons lukewarm water and set aside to rise for about 30 minutes.

Add the yeast mixture to the flour and mix together to make a dough. Knead the dough on a lightly floured work surface for about 5 minutes. Add the ground cardamom, raisins and almonds and knead into the dough. Transfer to a lightly oiled bowl, cover and set aside in a warm place for at least 1 hour, or until risen.

Add half the ghee to the dough and knead again, then divide the dough into 12 equal portions and shape into balls. Transfer to a baking tray (pan), cover and set aside for 30 minutes.

Preheat the oven to 190°C/375°F/Gas Mark 5. Flatten the balls into patties of about 18cm / 7 inches in diameter and about 5mm / 1/4 inch thick. Brush with ghee and fold each into 4. Roll into balls again and leave for 10 minutes. Repeat the entire process three times, then sprinkle the poppy seeds over. Bake in the oven for about 7–8 minutes, or until golden brown.

Bhatura
Deep-fried Bread

Origin Punjab
Preparation time 50 minutes, plus standing time
Cooking time 15 minutes
Makes 15

125ml / 4½fl oz (½ cup) natural (plain) yoghurt

2 teaspoons sugar

500g / 1lb 2oz (4 cups) plain (all-purpose) flour,
 plus extra for dusting

100g / 3½oz (½ cup plus 1 tablespoon) semolina
 (farina)

½ teaspoon baking powder

pinch of bicarbonate of soda (baking soda)

pinch of salt

2 tablespoons vegetable oil, plus extra for oiling
 and deep-frying

Mix the yoghurt, sugar and about 250ml / 8fl oz (1 cup) water together in a bowl.

Sift the flour, semolina, baking powder, bicarbonate of soda and salt into a large bowl. Make a depression in the centre of the flour, then pour in the yoghurt mixture and start mixing gradually to make a soft dough. When fully mixed, knead the dough on a lightly floured work surface for about 5 minutes. Knead 2 tablespoons oil into the dough, then transfer to a lightly oiled bowl, cover with a damp cloth or tea (dish) towel and set aside in a warm place for 10 minutes.

Lightly oil the palms of your hands and flatten each ball into a flattened round, about 13–15cm / 5–6 inches in diameter.

Heat enough oil for deep-frying in a kadhai or deep, heavy-based pan to 180°C/350°F, or until a cube of bread browns in 30 seconds. Carefully add 1 or 2 bhatura to the hot oil and deep-fry until golden brown on both sides and puffed up. Remove with a slotted spoon and drain on kitchen paper (paper towels). Repeat with the remaining bhatura.

Appam
Rice Pancakes with Coconut Milk

Origin Kerala
Preparation time 30 minutes, plus soaking
and standing time
Cooking time 15–20 minutes
Makes 8–10

200g / 7oz (1 cup) rice, rinsed and drained
1 cup cooked rice
¼ teaspoon dried yeast
1 teaspoon sugar
1 teaspoon ground cumin
250ml / 8fl oz (1 cup) coconut milk, fresh (see page 781) or canned
5 tablespoons vegetable oil
pinch of salt

Soak the rice in a large bowl of water for 3 hours,
then drain.

Mix the yeast, ½ teaspoon sugar and 2 tablespoons
lukewarm water together in a bowl or jug (pitcher),
then set aside to ferment for 1 hour.

Put the soaked rice in a blender or food processor,
add the cooked rice, ground cumin, the yeast
mixture and 180ml / 6fl oz (¾ cup) water and
process to make a very smooth paste. Add another
2 tablespoons water if required. Transfer to a large
bowl and pour in the coconut milk. Mix gently and
set aside for about 8 hours.

Just before cooking the appams, add the salt
and remaining sugar.

Brush an appachatti or large non-stick griddle, tawa or
heavy-based frying pan (skillet) lightly with oil
and heat it. Pour in a large spoonful of batter and tilt
and rotate the appachatti to ensure that the batter
is evenly spread. Cover and cook over very low heat
for about 2 minutes. The pancakes should be crisp and
thin at the edges but remain thick and spongy at
the centre. Remove from the pan and keep warm while
you make the remaining appams in the same way.

Traphe Dandan
Buckwheat Flour Pancakes

Origin Tribal
Preparation time 20 minutes
Cooking time 30 minutes
Makes 12–14

vegetable oil, for frying
1 large onion, chopped
2 teaspoons chilli powder
225g / 8oz (1¾ cups plus 2 tablespoons) buckwheat flour
pinch of salt

Heat a little oil in a frying pan (skillet) over medium
heat, add the onion and fry for about 5 minutes,
or until soft. Add the chilli powder and sprinkle in
a little water to prevent it burning, then stir-fry for
about 1 minute. Remove from the heat and drain
off the oil.

Meanwhile, place the flour in a large bowl, add
the salt and gradually beat in enough water to make
a fairly runny batter, beating well to avoid any lumps.
Add the drained onions to the mixture.

Heat a very little oil in a large frying pan over
medium heat, pour in about 2 tablespoons of the
mixture and cook for about 1 minute, then turn
over and cook the other side. Remove from the pan
and repeat until all the mixture is used up.

Rice is known around the world as a staple of Indian cuisine. Although often served as a plain or lightly seasoned accompaniment to a main dish, rice can also be the focus of a wonderful assortment of recipes – the best known is undoubtedly the biryani, a delicious mixture of rice and marinated meat or vegetables cooked to perfection in a sealed pot.

7
—

Rice

Khuska
Plain Boiled Rice

Origin Awadh/Hyderabad
Preparation time 15 minutes
Cooking time 45 minutes
Serves 8

1kg / 2¼lb (5⅓ cups) basmati rice, rinsed and drained
1 teaspoon salt

Bring 3 litres / 5¼ pints (12½ cups) water to the boil in a large, heavy-based pan. When the water begins to boil, add the rice and salt. Stir well with a ladle or wooden spoon, cover and cook for about 12–15 minutes. When the rice is almost cooked but not quite ready, drain through a sieve (strainer) or very fine colander, then return the rice to the pan and sprinkle over 125ml / 4½fl oz (½ cup) water. Stir to loosen the grains and drain again. Put a cloth around and under the lid to absorb the moisture, then leave on a griddle over low heat so that the rice cooks in its own steam for about 30 minutes. Alternatively, cook over very low heat until the rice is cooked.

Saadam
Plain Rice

Origin Tamil Nadu
Preparation time 5 minutes
Cooking time 15–20 minutes
Serves 4

200g / 7oz (1 cup) long-grained rice, rinsed and drained

Put the rice in a pressure cooker, add 375ml / 13fl oz (1½ cups) water and cook under pressure for 5 minutes. Open the cooker lid when the pressure subsides. Alternatively, bring 375ml / 13fl oz (1½ cups) water to the boil in a large pan, add the rice and cook for about 20 minutes, or until soft. Drain.

Serve hot with desired accompaniments.

Makhani Chawal
Buttered Rice

Origin Punjab
Preparation time 10 minutes
Cooking time 10–20 minutes
Serves 8

400g / 14oz (2¼ cups) basmati rice, rinsed
3 tablespoons butter
1 teaspoon black cumin seeds
12 cashew nuts, fried, to garnish
salt

Heat 2 tablespoons butter in a large pan over medium heat. Add the cumin seeds and stir-fry for 30 seconds. Add the rice and fry for 2 minutes. Stir in 700ml / 1 pint ¾fl oz (2½ cups) water and 1 teaspoon salt. Bring to the boil, then reduce to a simmer, cover and cook for 10 minutes.

In the meantime heat the remaining butter in a small frying pan (skillet) and fry the cashews, stirring until golden, for about 2 minutes. Remove from the heat and let stand for 10 minutes before fluffing with a fork onto a serving plate. Top with the cashews.

Puttu
Steamed Rice with Coconut

Origin Kerala
Preparation time 30 minutes
Cooking time 10 minutes
Serves 6

300g / 8oz (2 cups) rice flour
1 coconut, grated
salt

Put the rice flour in a large bowl and season with salt, then mix in enough water and a handful of grated coconut to a smooth batter. Place a 2.5-cm / 1-inch thick layer of grated coconut at the base of a puttukutti and cover with a 5-cm / 2-inch thick layer of the rice flour mixture. Repeat the process until the puttukutti is full. Put the puttukutti on to the metal utensil holding warm water. Increase the heat and steam for 10 minutes. If you don't have a puttukutti, use an ordinary steamer. Form the mixture into rounds and place them on a plate inside the steamer. Steam for 10 minutes.

Thengaai Saadam
Coconut Rice

Origin Tamil Nadu
Preparation time 20 minutes
Cooking time 10 minutes
Serves 8

2 teaspoons vegetable oil

1 teaspoon mustard seeds

1 teaspoon urad dal, rinsed and drained

3 dried red chillies

40g / 1½oz (½ cup) grated fresh coconut

1 cup cooked basmati rice

2 teaspoons broken cashew nuts

1 tablespoon peanuts

10–15 curry leaves

salt

Heat 1 teaspoon oil in a large, heavy-based pan over medium heat, add the mustard seeds, urad dal and red chillies and stir-fry for about 1–2 minutes, or until the seeds start to splutter. Add the coconut and stir-fry for about 1–2 minutes, or until well roasted. Season with salt and remove from the heat. Add the rice and mix well.

Heat 1 teaspoon oil in a frying pan (skillet) over medium heat, add the broken cashew nuts and peanuts and fry lightly for 2 minutes, or until they turn red. Add the curry leaves and remove from the heat. Stir into the coconut rice.

Kobbaraiannam
Savoury Coconut Rice

Origin Tamil Nadu
Preparation time 30 minutes, plus cooling and standing time
Cooking time 30 minutes
Serves 8

500g / 1lb 2oz (2¾ cups) rice, rinsed and drained

3 tablespoons vegetable oil

1 teaspoon black mustard seeds

3–5 dried red chillies, broken into
    2½-cm / 1-inch lengths

2 green chillies, de-seeded

2 cloves garlic, chopped

1 × 1-cm / ½-inch piece fresh ginger, peeled
    and chopped

1 teaspoon urad dal, rinsed and drained

2 tablespoons chana dal, rinsed and drained

1 sprig curry leaves

pinch of ground turmeric

pinch of asafoetida

150g / 5oz (2 cups) grated coconut, roasted

salt

To garnish

chopped coriander (cilantro) leaves

1 tablespoon grated coconut

juice of ½ lime

Cook the rice in a large pan of boiling water for about 5 minutes, then drain well and spread out on a tray to cool.

Heat the oil in a large, heavy-based pan over medium heat, add the mustard seeds, chillies, garlic and ginger and cook for 1 minute, or until the seeds start to splutter. Add both dals, the curry leaves and turmeric and stir-fry for about 1 minute, or until the dals turn golden. Add the asafoetida, grated coconut and rice and mix thoroughly. Remove from the heat and set aside for about 1 hour to allow the flavours to penetrate. Reheat and serve sprinkled with lime juice and garnished with coriander and grated coconut.

Bhagara Bhaath
Fried Savoury Rice

Origin Hyderabad
Preparation time 10 minutes, plus soaking time
Cooking time 45 minutes
Serves 6

500g / 1lb 2oz (2¾ cups) basmati rice, rinsed and drained
100g / 3½oz (scant ½ cup) ghee
1 onion, chopped
½ teaspoon Ginger Paste (see page 57)
½ teaspoon Garlic Paste (see page 57)
6 green cardamom pods
1 cinnamon stick, about 5cm / 2 inches long
6 cloves
salt

Soak the rice in a large bowl of salted water for 20 minutes, then drain.

Heat the ghee in a large, heavy-based pan over medium heat, add the onion and fry for about 5 minutes, or until brown. Add the ginger and garlic pastes, cardamom pods, cinnamon and cloves and season with salt, then fry for about 2 minutes. Add the rice and fry for a further 2 minutes, then pour in enough water to cover the rice by 4cm / 1½ inches.

Stir well, cover and bring to the boil, then half uncover and cook for about 7–10 minutes, or until the rice is half cooked. Reduce the heat to very low, put a cloth around the lid and cover the pan with it so that the moisture seeps into the cloth. Simmer for 20 minutes, or until the water has evaporated and there are holes on the surface of the rice. Loosen the rice in the pan with a long-tined fork.

Zafrani Pulao
Saffron Rice

Origin Awadh
Preparation time 30 minutes, plus soaking time
Cooking time 1 hour
Serves 8

500g / 1lb 2oz (2¾ cups) rice, rinsed and drained
½ teaspoon saffron threads
1 teaspoon warm milk
1 tablespoon ghee
4 cloves
4 green cardamom pods
2 cinnamon sticks, about 2.5cm / 1 inch long
1 onion, sliced
½ teaspoon Garlic Paste (see page 57)
¼ teaspoon ground turmeric
1 litre / 1¾ pints (4¼ cups) chicken stock
salt

Soak the rice in a large bowl of water with 1 teaspoon salt for 15 minutes.

Dry the saffron on a hot griddle or small frying pan, then transfer to a small bowl, add the milk and soak for about 10 minutes. Transfer to a mortar and pound with a pestle or grind in a spice grinder.

Preheat the oven to 140°C/275°F/Gas Mark 1, if using. Heat the ghee in a large, heavy-based pan over medium heat, add the cloves, cardamom pods and cinnamon and stir-fry for about 1 minute, or until the cardamom pods start to splutter. Add the onions and stir-fry for about 5–7 minutes, or until golden brown. Add the garlic paste and stir-fry for 30 seconds. Add the rice and turmeric, mix well and fry for 1 minute. Add the saffron, mix well and cook for 2–3 minutes. Pour in enough water and the chicken stock to cover the rice by 2cm / ¾ inch, then season with salt. Stir, then bring to the boil, reduce the heat, cover and cook for about 18–20 minutes, or until the rice is done and the water has almost evaporated.

Heat a griddle over low heat and place the covered pan on it. Cook for 25–30 minutes. Alternatively, cook in the oven. Serve hot.

Methi ke Chawal
Fenugreek Rice

Origin Punjab
Preparation time 15 minutes
Cooking time 40 minutes
Serves 8

3 tablespoons vegetable oil or ghee

1 teaspoon cumin seeds

1 onion, sliced

1 green chilli, de-seeded and sliced

400g / 14oz (2¼ cups) basmati rice, rinsed

1 tablespoon dried fenugreek leaves

1 teaspoon chilli powder

1 teaspoon ground turmeric

salt

Heat the oil or ghee in a large, heavy-based pan over medium heat, add the cumin seeds and stir-fry for 1 minute, or until they start to splutter. Add the onions and chilli and stir-fry for 5 minutes. Add the rice, 1 litre / 1¾ pints (4½ cups) water, the fenugreek leaves, chilli powder and turmeric, then season. Stir and cook for 25 minutes, stirring occasionally. Reduce the heat lightly, cover and simmer for 5 minutes. When ready, turn off the heat and keep covered until ready to serve.

Molagu Saadam
Pepper Rice

Origin Tamil Nadu
Preparation time 10 minutes
Cooking time 2 minutes
Serves 4

200g / 7oz (1 cup) Plain Boiled Rice (see page 631)

4 teaspoons ghee

3 teaspoons black peppercorns

1 teaspoon cumin seeds

salt

Put the rice in a serving dish. Heat 1 teaspoon ghee in a frying pan (skillet) over medium heat, add the spices and stir-fry lightly for about 1 minute, then transfer them to a small blender and process to make a coarse powder. Add the coarse powder and the rest of the ghee to the rice, then season with salt and mix well.

Ande ki Biryani
Egg & Rice Biryani

Origin Hyderabad
Preparation time 30 minutes, plus soaking time
Cooking time 10–15 minutes
Serves 8

400g / 14oz (2¼ cups) basmati rice, rinsed
  and drained

1 teaspoon saffron threads

125ml / 4½fl oz (½ cup) hot milk

225g / 8oz French (green) beans

250ml / 8fl oz (1 cup) natural (plain) yoghurt

1 tablespoon Garam Masala (see page 31)

6 hard-boiled eggs, shelled and cut in half

125ml / 4½fl oz (½ cup) lemon juice

200g / 7oz (½ cup) sliced fried onions

2 tablespoons raisins

2 tablespoons blanched almonds

20g / ¾oz (½ cup) chopped coriander (cilantro) leaves

125g / 4oz (½ cup) melted ghee, plus extra
  for greasing

Soak the rice in a large bowl of water for about 1 hour, then drain.

Put the saffron in a bowl, add the hot milk and soak until required.

Preheat the oven to 150°C/300°F/Gas Mark 2. Cook the French beans in a pan of salted boiling water for 7–8 minutes, then drain and set aside. Mix the yoghurt, 1 teaspoon salt and the garam masala together in a bowl and set aside.

Put a layer of the rice, a layer of 3 egg halves and a layer of half the beans in a large greased baking dish. Pour over half the yoghurt mixture, then half the lemon juice and sprinkle over half the fried onions, half the raisins, half the saffron milk, half the almonds and half the coriander leaves. Repeat the process, starting with the rice, then when everything is used up, pour over the melted ghee.

Cover the dish and cook in the oven for about 10–15 minutes. Serve hot. Do not mix and carve out a serving from top to bottom, so that you get all the layers of the biryani on your plate.

✳ ✳

—

Kurmu Pulao
Jackfruit Pulao

Origin Hyderabad
Preparation time 25 minutes, plus soaking time
Cooking time 45–50 minutes
Serves 8

1 jackfruit

3 tablespoons vegetable oil, plus extra for oiling

1 tablespoon desiccated (dried flaked) coconut

4 onions, sliced

1 teaspoon sliced ginger

2 teaspoons ground cumin

6 green chillies, de-seeded and chopped

1 teaspoon mustard seeds

400g / 14oz (2¼ cups) basmati rice, rinsed

10–15 curry leaves

6 cloves

2 green cardamom pods

1 cinnamon stick, about 2.5cm / 1 inch long

½ teaspoon ground turmeric

6 green chillies, slit in half lengthways and de-seeded
(optional)

500ml / 18fl oz (2¼ cups) coconut milk, fresh
(see page 781) or canned

2 teaspoons ghee

1 carrot, cut into cubes

50g / 1¾oz (⅓ cup) peas, shelled if fresh

juice of 1 lime

2 green cardamom pods, ground

1 bunch coriander (cilantro) leaves, chopped

salt

Wearing gloves (see page 793), use a sharp knife to remove the white pith from the jackfruit, then remove the seeds. Cut the jackfruit into 6 2.5-cm / 1-inch pieces.

Bring 750ml–1 litre / 1¼–1¾ pints (3¼–4¼ cups) salted water to the boil in a large pan, add the jackfruit, cover and cook for about 10–15 minutes, or until soft, then drain and set aside.

Mix the desiccated coconut, sliced onion, ginger and cumin and 6 chopped chillies with the hot jackfruit.

Heat 2 tablespoons oil in a pan over medium-low heat, add the mustard seeds and 1 sliced onion and cook for about 5 minutes, or until the onion is brown, then remove from the heat. Mix with the jackfruit and cook for 2–3 minutes.

Put the rice in a large bowl, add 750ml / 1¼ pints (3¼ cups) water and soak for 20 minutes, then drain.

Preheat the oven to 140°C/275°F/Gas Mark 1. Heat the remaining oil in a deep, heavy-based pan over medium heat, add the rest of the onions and fry for about 5 minutes, or until brown, then remove from the pan and set aside. Add the whole spices and turmeric to the oil and fry for about 1 minute. Add the slit chillies and fry lightly for about 1–2 minutes, then add the rice and fry for 3–5 minutes. Mix 500ml / 18fl oz (2¼ cups) boiling water with the coconut milk and pour over the rice until 5cm / 2 inches above the rice, otherwise add more water. Add 1 teaspoon ghee, the carrots and peas and mix, then cover and cook for 10 minutes, or until half cooked. Remove from the heat.

Remove half the rice from the pan and spread the cooked jackfruit in its place, then cover with the rest of the rice. Add the lime juice, 1 teaspoon ghee and sprinkle over the ground cardamom and chopped coriander. Cover and cook in the oven for 20–25 minutes until done.

—

Thair Saadam
Plain Yoghurt Rice

Origin Tamil Nadu
Preparation time 20 minutes
Cooking time 2 minutes
Serves 4

400g / 14 oz (2 cups) Plain Boiled Rice (see page 631)

10–12 curry leaves

250ml / 8fl oz (1 cup) natural (plain) yoghurt

250ml / 8fl oz (1 cup) milk

2 teaspoons vegetable oil

1 teaspoon mustard seeds

2–3 green chillies, de-seeded and chopped

1 × 1-cm / ½-inch piece fresh ginger, peeled
and finely chopped

salt

Put the rice in a large serving dish, then crumble a few curry leaves with salt and add to the rice. Add the yoghurt and milk and mix well.

Heat the oil in a frying pan (skillet) over medium heat, add the mustard seeds and stir-fry for about 1 minute, or until they start to splutter. Add the chillies and ginger and fry again briefly, then add to the rice and mix.

Bangla Pulao
Bengali Pulao

Origin West Bengal
Preparation time 30 minutes, plus soaking time
Cooking time 15–20 minutes
Serves 12

2kg / 1¼lb (10¾ cups) basmati rice, rinsed
  and drained

pinch of saffron powder

150g / 5oz (⅔ cup) ghee

100g / 3½oz (⅔ cup) cashew nuts

50g / 1¾oz (⅓ cup) raisins

5g / ⅛oz whole garam masala of cinnamon, cloves
  and green cardamom pods

75g / 2½oz (⅓ cup) sugar

½ grated nutmeg

1 teaspoon ground mace

1 tablespoon ground Garam Masala (see page 31)

1 tablespoon kewra water

1 tablespoon rosewater

rose petals, jasmine flowers or mogra flowers,
  to garnish

salt

Soak the rice in a bowl of water for 1 hour,
then drain.

Bring 3 litres / 5¼ pints (12½ cups) water to the
boil in a large, heavy-based pan, add the rice and
the saffron and return to the boil, skimming off the
scum as it rises to the surface. Cover and simmer
over medium heat for about 10 minutes, or until half
cooked. Drain the rice, reserving the water.

Heat the ghee in a large, heavy-based pan over
medium heat, add the cashew nuts, raisins and whole
garam masala and stir-fry for about 1 minute, or until
fragrant. Add the rice, sugar, nutmeg, ground mace,
ground garam masala, kewra water and rosewater,
then season with salt and mix well. Cover, reduce the
heat to low and cook for a further 5–7 minutes by
which time the rice should be cooked and the grains
separate. If the rice is not quite ready, add a little of
the liquid in which it was cooked, cover and leave
it over low heat for 3–4 minutes. Keep covered until
ready to serve, then heat for 5–7 minutes before
serving. Garnish with a sprinkling of rose petals,
jasmine flowers or mogra flowers.

Kashmiri Pulao
Kashmiri Pulao

Origin Jammu and Kashmir
Preparation time 40 minutes, plus cooling time
Cooking time 25–30 minutes
Serves 4

400g / 14oz (2¼ cups) basmati rice, rinsed
  and drained

1 teaspoon black cumin seeds

4 green cardamom pods

125g / 4oz (½ cup) ghee

For the stock

2 tablespoons vegetable oil

250g / 9oz (2 medium) onions, sliced

3 litres / 5¼ pints (12½ cups) water

6 large bones from a leg of lamb

5 bay leaves

15 black cardamom pods

2½ tablespoons fennel seeds

4 cinnamon sticks, about 5cm / 2 inches long

1 teaspoon black cumin seeds

4 green cardamom pods

salt

For the stock, heat the oil in a frying pan (skillet)
over medium heat, add the onions and fry for about
5 minutes, or until brown, then remove from the pan
with a slotted spoon and set aside.

To make the stock, bring all the ingredients, except
the onion, to the boil in a deep, heavy-based pan.
Cover and continue to boil for 15–18 minutes. Add
the browned onions and boil for a further 5 minutes.
Remove from the heat and allow to cool. Strain
the stock through a muslin cloth (cheesecloth) or fine
sieve (strainer) to get 1.75 litres / 3 pints (7½ cups)
stock, adding more water, if required. Discard the
bones and whole spices.

Pour the strained stock into a deep, heavy-based
pan and bring to the boil. Add the rice, black cumin
seeds and green cardamom pods and season with
salt. Bring the mixture to the boil, then reduce the
heat and cook for about 18–20 minutes, or until the
rice is almost cooked.

Heat the ghee in another deep pan and when hot,
pour in the rice mixture. Cover the pan with a tight-
fitting lid and cook over very low heat until the rice
is cooked.

Kabuli Chaneda Pulao
Chickpea (Garbanzo Bean) Pulao

Origin Punjab
Preparation time 45 minutes–1 hour, plus soaking and standing time
Cooking time 2 hours
Serves 6

250g / 9oz (1⅓ cups) chickpeas (garbanzo beans)
500g / 1lb 2oz (2¾ cups) basmati rice, rinsed and drained
1 teaspoon chilli powder
2 tablespoons ghee
3 teaspoons chopped onions
3 teaspoons Garlic Paste (see page 57)
2 teaspoons Ginger Paste (see page 57)
100g / 3½oz (1 small) tomato, chopped
1 tablespoon lemon juice
½ teaspoon ground green cardamom
1 drop of kewra water or rosewater
4–6 green cardamom pods
1 × 2.5-cm / 1-inch piece fresh ginger, peeled and cut into 1-cm / ½-inch juliennes
4–6 green chillies, de-seeded and cut into strips
2 tablespoons chopped coriander (cilantro) leaves
12 tablespoons chopped mint leaves
salt
about 150g / 5oz dough (optional), for sealing the lid (see page 783)

For the aromatic potli

4–5 black cardamom pods
3–4 cloves
2 cinnamon sticks, about 2.5cm / 1 inch long
2 bay leaves

For the crispy fried onions

2 tablespoons ghee
2 onions, sliced

Soak the chickpeas in a bowl of water overnight. The next day, soak the rice in a bowl of water for 30 minutes, then drain. Drain the chickpeas.

To make the aromatic potli, put all the ingredients in a mortar and pound with a pestle to break the spices, then transfer to a piece of muslin (cheesecloth) and tie in a pouch with enough kitchen string (twine) to hang over the pan edge. Bring 500ml / 18fl oz (2¼ cups) water to the boil in a large, heavy-based pan, add the drained chickpeas and bring to the boil. Continue to boil for about 2 minutes, then remove from the heat and leave to sit in the water for about 1 hour. Drain just prior to cooking, put in a pan, add the aromatic potli and 750ml / 1¼ pints (3¼ cups) water and boil for 30 minutes until cooked.

Preheat the oven to 180°C/350°F/Gas Mark 4, if using. Put the chilli powder in a small bowl, add 1 tablespoon water and mix together.

For the fried onions, heat the ghee in a frying pan (skillet) over medium heat, add the onions and fry for about 5–7 minutes, or until golden brown and crispy, then remove from the heat and set aside.

Heat the ghee in a large, heavy-based pan over medium heat, add the chopped onions and stir-fry for 2 minutes, or until translucent, then add the garlic and ginger pastes and stir-fry for about 1–2 minutes, or until the moisture has evaporated. Add the chilli powder mixture and stir-fry for about 1–2 minutes, or until the moisture has evaporated. Add the tomatoes and season with salt, then stir-fry for about 5 minutes, or until the oil separates out and the tomatoes are mashed. Now add the boiled chickpeas together with their cooking liquid and bring to the boil. Remove from the heat, add half of the lemon juice, the ground cardamom and kewra water, then stir and adjust the seasoning, if necessary.

Bring 1.5 litres / 2½ pints (6¼ cups) water to the boil in a large, heavy-based pan. Add the green cardamom pods and season with salt, then stir, add the rice and bring to the boil. Reduce the heat to medium, add the remaining lemon juice and continue to boil, stirring occasionally, for about 18 minutes, or until almost cooked. Drain and set aside.

Put half the chickpeas and liquor in another large pan, spread half of the boiled rice on top and sprinkle half the ginger juliennes, green chillies, coriander and mint over the rice. Spread the remaining chickpeas and liquor over the rice, then spread the remaining rice on top, and sprinkle the remaining ginger juliennes, green chillies, coriander and mint over the top. Finish with a layer of the fried onions spread evenly over, then cover with a tight-fitting lid and seal with dough. Now cook until steam starts seeping out of the dough. Remove and set aside.

To finish, put a couple of hot charcoals on the lid and leave to stand, or cook in the oven for 15–20 minutes. Break the seal and serve from the pan.

Matar Pulao
Pea Pulao

Origin Punjab/Delhi/Awadh
Preparation time 25 minutes, plus soaking
and standing time
Cooking time 30 minutes
Serves 4

400g / 14oz (2¼ cups) basmati rice, rinsed

1 teaspoon lemon juice

1 tablespoon kewra water or rosewater

1 teaspoon ground green cardamom

generous pinch of ground mace

For the aromatic potli

15–20 black peppercorns

6 green cardamom pods

5 cloves

3 black cardamom pods

2 cinnamon sticks, about 2.5cm / 1 inch long

2 bay leaves

For the peas

large pinch of saffron threads

250g / 9oz (1¾ cups) peas, shelled if fresh

5 tablespoons ghee

50g / 1¾oz (½ small) onion, sliced

3 tablespoon Ginger Paste (see page 57)

1 teaspoon Garlic Paste (see page 57)

6 green cardamom pods

5 cloves

salt

Soak the rice in a large bowl of water for about 15 minutes, then drain.

For the peas, put the saffron threads in a small bowl, add 1 tablespoon water and soak until required. Cook the peas in a pan of boiling water for about 4–5 minutes, or until al dente.

For the aromatic potli, coarsely pound the spices in a mortar or grind in a spice grinder to a coarse powder, then transfer to a piece of muslin (cheesecloth), and tie in a pouch with a piece of kitchen string (twine) long enough to hang over the rim of the pan.

Put the rice in a separate large pan, cover with water, add the aromatic potli and set aside for about 30 minutes. Drain at the time of cooking and reserve the aromatic potli. Bring 375ml / 13fl oz (1½ cups)

water to the boil in a large, heavy-based pan. Add the reserved potli, then season and stir. Sprinkle over the lemon juice, stir and bring to the boil. Add the rice and boil over medium heat for about 18 minutes, or until almost cooked. Drain, discarding the potli and transfer to a separate pan. Sprinkle over the kewra water, cardamom and mace, then cover and set aside for 10 minutes.

Meanwhile, heat the ghee in a frying pan (skillet) over medium heat, add the onions and stir-fry for 2 minutes, or until translucent and glossy. Add the ginger and garlic pastes and stir-fry for about 2 minutes, or until the onions are light golden, then add the peas and season with salt. Stir-fry for about 2–3 minutes, or until the moisture has evaporated. Add the cardamom pods and cloves and stir-fry for a minute. Remove from the heat, transfer to the pan with the rice, sprinkle over the soaked saffron, mix gently and adjust the seasoning, if necessary.

📷 pp.285, 602

Khilwan Khichari
Dry Khichari

Origin Awadh
Preparation time 15 minutes, plus soaking
and standing time
Cooking time 35 minutes
Serves 8

250g / 9oz (1⅓ cups) basmati rice, rinsed

200g / 7oz (1 cup) moong dal, rinsed and drained

100g / 3½oz (scant ½ cup) ghee

1 teaspoon cumin seeds

2 bay leaves

10 cloves

½ teaspoon black peppercorns

250g / 9oz baby (pearl) onions

salt

Combine the rice and dal, then pour over enough water to cover and soak for 20 minutes. Drain and leave to stand for 10 minutes.

Heat the ghee in a large, heavy-based pan over medium heat, add the cumin seeds, bay leaves, cloves and peppercorns and stir-fry for 1–2 minutes. Add the baby onions and stir-fry for 1 minute. Stir in the rice and dal and cook for 1–2 minutes, then season and pour in enough water to come about 4cm / 1½ inches above the surface of the khichari. Red uce the heat to low, cover and cook for 20–25 minutes, or until the rice and dal are soft. Discard the bay leaves before serving.

Gatte ka Pulao
Gram (Chickpea) Flour Dumpling Rice

Origin Rajasthan
Preparation time 1 hour, plus soaking time
Cooking time 45 minutes
Serves 4

For the gattas

150g / 5oz (1 cup) gram (chickpea) flour

1 teaspoon cumin seeds

1 teaspoon chilli powder

1 teaspoon ground turmeric

1 tablespoon ghee or vegetable oil

125ml / 4½fl oz (½ cup) buttermilk (optional)

salt

For the rice

10 cloves garlic

400g / 14oz (2¼ cups) basmati rice, rinsed
    and drained

3 tablespoons vegetable oil

1 teaspoon Garam Masala (see page 31)

3 bay leaves

1 onion, sliced

2 teaspoons chilli powder

pinch of asafoetida

1 teaspoon ground turmeric

2 tablespoons lemon juice

salt

To garnish

1 tablespoon vegetable oil

1 onion, sliced

20g / ¾oz (½ cup) coriander (cilantro) leaves, chopped

For the rice, put the garlic in a small blender or
food processor and process, adding a little water if
necessary, to make a paste. Set aside. Soak the rice
in a bowl of water for about 30 minutes, then drain
and set aside.

To make the garnish, heat the oil in a frying pan
(skillet) over medium heat, add the onion and fry for
about 5–7 minutes, or until golden brown and crisp.
Remove and set aside.

To make the gattas, sift the gram flour into a
large bowl, add the cumin seeds, chilli powder,
turmeric and ghee or oil, then season with salt
and mix together.

Mix in either the buttermilk or enough water to
make a soft dough. Divide the dough into 6 equal
pieces and roll each piece out on a greased board to
form a sausage about 10cm / 4 inches long. Bring a
large pan of water to the boil and when just boiling
slowly lower the sausages into the pan. Boil for
about 10–15 minutes, or until the gattas are cooked.

Remove from the pan with a fork and cut each
one into 2.5-cm / 1-inch long pieces. Set aside. The
cooking water can be used in any vegetable sauce
to make it tastier.

For the rice, heat the oil in a large, heavy-based
pan over medium heat, add the garam masala and
bay leaves, then add the onions and stir-fry
for about 5 minutes. Add the garlic paste and all
the spices and the lemon juice and season with salt,
then stir. Lastly, add the rice and 1.2 litres / 2 pints
(5 cups) water and mix.

Cook either in a rice cooker or in the original pan
for about 20 minutes. Add the boiled gattas and
gently mix into the rice with a fork. Cover and
simmer for a further 10–15 minutes, or until all
the water has been absorbed and the rice is soft.
Remove from the heat and keep covered until ready
to serve. To garnish, sprinkle the reserved fried
onions and chopped coriander over the top.

Zarda Pulao
Sweet Rice

Origin Awadh/Delhi
Preparation time 25 minutes, plus soaking time
Cooking time 20 minutes
Serves 8

pinch of saffron threads

250g / 9oz (1⅓ cups) basmati rice, rinsed
    and drained

100g / 3½oz (scant ½ cup) ghee

1 cinnamon stick, about 5cm / 2 inches long

½ teaspoon ginger

8 green cardamom pods

200g / 7oz (1 cup) sugar

few drops yellow food colouring (optional)

2–3 drops kewra water

salt

Put the saffron in a small bowl, add 4 teaspoons
hot water and soak until required.

Soak the rice in a bowl of water for 20 minutes, then
drain, reserving the water.

Heat the ghee in a large, heavy-based pan over very
low heat, add the cinnamon, ginger and cardamom
pods and cook for 15 minutes.

Remove the pan from the heat, add the sugar,
saffron and food colouring, if using, and stir gently
to distribute the sugar. Add the rice and reserved
soaking water, and season with salt.

Return the pan to low heat and cook for about
20 minutes, or until the rice is soft. Sprinkle
over the kewra water mixed with a little water.

Chitrannam
Rice with Cashew Nuts & Spices

Origin Tamil Nadu
Preparation time 30 minutes
Cooking time 20 minutes
Serves 8

300g / 11oz (1⅔ cups) long-grained rice, rinsed
    and drained

1 tablespoon vegetable oil

1 teaspoon black mustard seeds

pinch of asafoetida

6 curry leaves

½ teaspoon Ginger Paste (see page 57)

½ green chilli, de-seeded and roughly chopped

3–4 dried red chillies

1 tablespoon cashew nuts, halved and lightly fried

1 teaspoon urad dal, rinsed and drained

1 teaspoon chana dal, rinsed and drained
    and lightly fried

½ teaspoon ground turmeric

1½ tablespoons lime juice

salt

1 bunch coriander (cilantro) leaves, to garnish

chutney of your choice, such as Ginger Chutney
    (see page 64), to serve

Cook the rice in a large, heavy-based pan of boiling
water for about 12–15 minutes, or until almost
cooked. Drain thoroughly and set aside.

Heat the oil in a large, heavy-based pan over
medium heat, add the mustard seeds and stir-fry for
about 1 minute, or until they start to splutter. Add
the asafoetida, curry leaves, ginger paste, chillies,
cashew nuts, urad dal, chana dal and turmeric,
then reduce the heat slightly and simmer for 10
minutes, adding a little water if necessary to prevent
the spices burning. Toss in the rice, sprinkle with
the lime juice and heat through for about 5 minutes,
or until the rice is cooked. Garnish with coriander
leaves and serve with a chutney.

Qabooli
Rice & Dried Fruit Kedgeree

Origin Punjab/Delhi/Awadh/Hyderabad
Preparation time 40 minutes, plus soaking time
Cooking time 35 minutes
Serves 8

1kg / 2¼lb (5⅓ cups) basmati rice, rinsed and drained
½ teaspoon saffron threads, warmed to dry
125ml / 4½fl oz (½ cup) milk, plus a little extra
1 teaspoon bicarbonate of soda (baking soda)
500g / 1lb 2oz (3½ cups) blanched almonds, thickly sliced
250g / 9oz (1 cup) ghee
1 onion, sliced
8 green cardamom pods
8 cloves
2 cinnamon sticks, about 2.5cm / 1 inch long
125ml / 4½fl oz (½ cup) natural (plain) yoghurt
salt

Soak the rice in a large bowl of salted water for 20 minutes, then drain.

Put the saffron in a mortar, add 1 tablespoon milk and grind with the pestle. Leave to soak for 15 minutes.

Put the bicarbonate of soda and a little water in a small pan and bring to the boil, then add the almonds and cook until al dente and the water has evaporated.

Heat the ghee in a frying pan (skillet) over medium heat, add the almonds and fry until golden brown, then transfer to kitchen paper (paper towels).

Heat 1 tablespoon ghee in a pan over medium heat, add the onion, cardamom pods, cloves and cinnamon and fry for about 5 minutes, or until brown. Pour in 2 litres / 3½ pints (8½ cups) boiling water, then add the rice, stir and cook for about 18 minutes, or until the rice is three-quarters cooked. Drain and remove half of the rice. Add the sliced nuts, then sprinkle over half the yoghurt and half the milk. Cover with the rest of the rice, then sprinkle over the saffron milk and spread the remaining yoghurt on top. Cover the pan and cook over low heat for about 30 minutes, or until cooked. Serve hot.

Mamri Kaya Pulihora
Spicy Mango-flavoured Rice

Origin Tamil Nadu
Preparation time 40 minutes
Cooking time 15 minutes
Serves 8

2 tablespoons chana dal, rinsed and drained
1kg / 2¼lb (5⅓ cups) rice, rinsed and drained
2 tablespoons vegetable oil
¼ teaspoon ground turmeric
1 teaspoon cumin seeds, roasted and ground
2 teaspoons coriander seeds, roasted and ground
½ teaspoon fenugreek seeds, roasted and ground
1 green mango, flesh cut into small pieces and chargrilled
2 tablespoons peanuts, ground
½ dried coconut, cut into small pieces
4 green chillies, de-seeded and chopped
2 dried red chillies
1 teaspoon mustard seeds
1 teaspoon urad dal, rinsed and drained
8 curry leaves
½ teaspoon asafoetida
salt
Rasam (see page 563), to serve

Put the chana dal in a pan, add 250ml / 8fl oz (1 cup) water, bring to the boil and cook for 10 minutes, or until soft. Drain and set aside.

Cook the rice in a large pan of water for 18–20 minutes, or until soft, then drain and spread out on a clean tea (dish) towel to dry. Transfer to a large serving dish.

Heat 1 tablespoon oil in a large, heavy-based pan over medium heat, season with salt, then add the turmeric and ground spices and fry briefly. Add the mixture to the rice along with the mango, cooked chana dal, ground peanuts, coconut and chopped chillies.

Heat the remaining oil in a frying pan (skillet) over medium heat, add the dried red chillies, mustard seeds, urad dal, curry leaves and asafoetida and stir-fry for about 1–2 minutes, or until they turn dark brown. Add to the rice and mix together. This is eaten at room temperature plain or with Rasam.

Chintakaya Pulihora
Tamarind Rice

Origin Tamil Nadu
Preparation time 30 minutes
Cooking time 50 minutes
Serves 8

1kg / 2¼lb (5⅓ cups) rice, rinsed and drained

6 tablespoons vegetable oil

2 tablespoons peanuts

1 teaspoon cumin seeds

1 tablespoon coriander seeds

5 dried red chillies

2 tablespoons chana dal, rinsed and drained

2 tablespoons fenugreek seeds

½ dried coconut, grated

1 teaspoon jaggery or soft brown sugar

125ml / 4½fl oz (½ cup) Tamarind Extract
    (see page 58)

salt

For the tempering

4 dried red chillies

1 teaspoon mustard seeds

4 curry leaves

pinch of asafoetida

¼ teaspoon ground turmeric

Cook the rice in a large pan of boiling water for about 12–15 minutes, or until the grains are almost cooked. Drain thoroughly and set aside.

Heat about 4 tablespoons oil in a frying pan (skillet) over medium heat, add the peanuts and fry for a few minutes until browned, then remove from the pan and set aside. Add the cumin seeds, coriander seeds and dried red chillies to the pan and fry for about 1 minute, or until the chillies are a shade darker. Transfer to a mortar or spice grinder and pound with a pestle or process until ground.

Heat another 2 tablespoons oil in the frying pan, add the chana dal and fry briefly, then transfer to a pan, add 250ml / 8fl oz (1 cup) water and bring to the boil. Cook for 30 minutes, or until soft, then drain. Mix the ground spices, chana dal, fenugreek seeds, coconut, jaggery or sugar and tamarind extract together in a pan, then cook over low-medium heat for about 2–3 minutes. Heat the oil for the tempering in a frying pan over medium heat, add the dried red chillies, mustard seeds, curry leaves and asafoetida and stir-fry for about 1 minute, or until the seeds start to splutter.

Add the turmeric, then mix with the tamarind and spice mixture. Add the mixture to the rice, stir to mix, and heat through. Sprinkle the fried peanuts on top just before serving.

Tamatar Pulihora
Tomato Rice

Origin Tamil Nadu
Preparation time 30 minutes, plus soaking time
Cooking time 40 minutes
Serves 8

500g / 1lb 2oz (2¾ cups) basmati rice, rinsed
    and drained

1 teaspoon poppy seeds

½ fresh coconut, chopped into pieces

125g / 4oz (½ cup) ghee

1 cinnamon stick

3 cloves

4 cashew nuts

4 onions, chopped

10 green chillies, de-seeded and chopped

1 teaspoon Ginger Paste (see page 57)

2 teaspoons Garlic Paste (see page 57)

7 tomatoes, chopped

1 bunch coriander (cilantro) leaves, chopped

salt

Soak the rice in a large bowl of water for 30 minutes, then drain.

Put the poppy seeds and coconut in a blender or food processor and process, adding a little water if necessary, to make a paste.

Heat the ghee in a frying pan (skillet) over medium heat, add the cinnamon and cloves and fry for about 30 seconds. Add the cashew nuts, onions and chillies and fry for about 4 minutes, or until the onions are lightly browned. Add the ginger and garlic pastes and fry for a further 2 minutes. Add the coconut and poppy seed paste and stir well, then add the tomatoes and cook for 3 minutes. Add the chopped coriander and season with salt.

Measure out twice the quantity of water to the rice, add to the tomato mixture and bring to the boil. Add the rice and cook for about 10 minutes, or until the rice is half cooked, then reduce the heat to very low and cover. Cook for almost 15 minutes.

Aloo ki Tehari
Layered Rice and Potatoes

Origin Awadh
Preparation time 1 hour, plus soaking time
Cooking time 25–30 minutes
Serves 4

For the potatoes

½ teaspoon ground turmeric

½ teaspoon yellow chilli powder

6 potatoes, cut into pieces

6–8 tablespoons vegetable oil, for deep-frying

salt

For the aromatic potli

2 teaspoons fennel seeds

5 green cardamom pods

4 black cardamom pods

4 cloves

2 bay leaves

2 cinnamon sticks

For the liquor

4 tablespoons natural (plain) yoghurt, whisked

3 tablespoons ghee

1 tablespoon cumin seeds

125ml / 4½fl oz (½ cup) vegetable stock

2 green chillies, slit in half lengthways and de-seeded

½ teaspoon yellow chilli powder

½ tablespoon lemon juice

For the rice

500g / 1lb 2 oz (2¾ cups) basmati rice, rinsed
   and drained

salt

½ tablespoon lemon juice

about 150g / 5oz dough (optional), for sealing the lid
   (see page 783)

Soak the rice in a bowl of water for about
45 minutes.

For the potatoes, bring a large pan of water to the
boil, add the turmeric and yellow chilli powder, then
season with salt and stir. Now add the potatoes and
boil for about 10 minutes, or until half cooked. Drain
and pat dry with kitchen paper (paper towels).

Heat the oil for deep-frying in a deep, heavy-based
pan to 180°C/350°F, or until a cube of bread browns
in 30 seconds. Carefully add the potatoes to the hot
oil and deep-fry for about 2–3 minutes, or until
they turn light golden. Remove with a slotted spoon
and drain on kitchen paper.

To make the aromatic potli, put the fennel seeds,
cardamom pods, cloves, bay leaves and cinnamon
in a mortar and pound with a pestle or grind
coarsely in a spice grinder. Transfer the mixture to
a piece of muslin (cheesecloth) and tie in a pouch
with a piece of kitchen string (twine) long enough to
hang over the rim of a pan.

Next, to make the liquor, whisk 2 tablespoons
yoghurt in a bowl. Heat the ghee in a large, heavy-
based pan over medium heat, add the cumin seeds
and stir-fry for about 1 minute, or until they start
to splutter. Pour in the stock and bring to the boil.
Reduce the heat to very low and add the remaining
yoghurt, chillies, chilli powder and lemon juice
and simmer for 5 minutes. Remove and set aside.

To cook the rice, bring about 1.5 litres / 2½ pints
(6¼ cups) water to the boil in a large pan, add
the aromatic potli and season with salt. Stir, add
the rice, bring to the boil, then reduce the heat to
medium. Add the lemon juice and continue to cook,
stirring frequently, for about 18 minutes, or until
almost cooked. Drain and discard the aromatic potli
and set the rice aside.

Finally, put half the liquor in a large pan, then
spread over one-third of the boiled rice and arrange
half the fried potatoes evenly on top. Spread another
third of the rice and arrange the remaining fried
potatoes evenly on top. Spread over the remaining
rice, pour on the remaining liquor and cover with a
tight-fitting lid. Seal with dough, if using, or foil,
and cook over low heat for 25–30 minutes. Remove
from the heat, break the dough seal and serve.

✳ ✳

Vangi Bhaath
Rice with Aubergine (Eggplant)

Origin Karnataka/Coastal
Preparation time 45 minutes, plus soaking time
Cooking time 20 minutes
Serves 8

500g / 1lb 2oz (2¾ cups) rice, rinsed and drained

1 teaspoon ground coriander

3 tablespoons chana dal, rinsed and drained

4 tablespoons vegetable oil

1 tablespoon mustard seeds

1 tablespoon urad dal, rinsed and drained

1 tablespoon chana dal, rinsed and drained

6 curry leaves

4 dried red chillies

500g / 1lb 2oz (1 medium) aubergine (eggplant),
    trimmed and cut into slices lengthways

1 cinnamon stick, about 2.5cm / 1 inch long

4 cloves

¼ dried coconut, ground

1 teaspoon chilli powder

juice of 1 lime

salt

1 tablespoon coriander (cilantro) leaves, chopped,
    to garnish

Soak the rice in a bowl of water for 20 minutes,
then drain. Transfer to a pan, add fresh water, then
season with salt and cook for about 18–20 minutes,
or until cooked.

Stir-fry the ground coriander and the 3 tablespoons
chana dal lightly on a tawa or in a dry frying pan
(skillet) for about 1 minute, or until roasted, then
transfer to a mortar and pound with a pestle or a
spice grinder and process until ground. Set aside.

Heat the oil in a large, heavy-based pan over
medium heat, add the mustard seeds and stir-fry for
about 30–40 seconds, or until lightly browned,
then add the dals and stir-fry for about 1–2 minutes.
Add the curry leaves, dried red chillies and
aubergine and fry for 5 minutes. Add the cinnamon,
cloves, coconut, roasted ground coriander and chana
dal mixture and chilli powder and fry for about
2 minutes. Remove the pan from the heat and add
the lime juice. Stir the mixture lightly into the cooked
rice and garnish with chopped coriander. This
dish can either be served with dal or eaten plain.

Paneer ke Chawal
Indian Cheese Rice

Origin Punjab
Preparation time 30 minutes
Cooking time 35–40 minutes
Serves 8

4 tablespoons vegetable oil, plus extra for deep-frying

1 cup Paneer (see page 59), cut into
    1-cm / ½-inch cubes

2 bay leaves

4 cloves

1 teaspoon cumin seeds

1 onion, sliced

1 tablespoon ground turmeric

2 green chillies, de-seeded and sliced

400g / 14oz (2¼ cups) basmati rice, rinsed
    and drained

80g / 2¾oz (½ cup) peas

2 tablespoons lemon juice

salt

To garnish

2 tablespoons ghee

1 onion, sliced

12 cashew nuts

To make the garnish, heat the ghee in a frying pan
(skillet) over medium heat, add the onion and fry
for about 5–7 minutes, or until golden brown.
Remove and set aside, then add the cashew nuts to
the pan and stir-fry for about 2 minutes, or until
browned. Remove from the pan and set aside.

Heat enough oil for deep-frying in a deep, heavy-
based pan to 180°C/350°F, or until a cube of bread
browns in 30 seconds. Carefully add the paneer
cubes to the hot oil and deep-fry for about 1 minute,
or until golden brown. Transfer with a slotted spoon
to kitchen paper (paper towels).

Heat the oil in a large, heavy-based pan over
medium heat, add the bay leaves, cloves and cumin,
then add the onion and stir-fry for about 5 minutes.
Add the turmeric, chillies, rice, 700ml / 1 pint ¾fl
oz (2¾ cups) water, the peas and lemon juice, then
season with salt and mix well. Bring to the boil, then
reduce the heat to a simmer, cover and cook for
10 minutes. Add the fried paneer cubes and mix with
a fork, then remove from the heat and let stand for
a further 10 minutes, or until the rice is cooked. To
serve, uncover, transfer to a rice platter and garnish
with the fried onions and cashew nuts.

Saboodane ki Khichari
Sago Flavoured with Coconut
& Coriander (Cilantro)

Origin Maharashtra
Preparation time 15 minutes
Cooking time 30 minutes
Serves 6

300g / 11oz (2 cups) sago, rinsed and drained

300g / 11oz (2 cups) peanuts, roasted and crushed

2 tablespoons grated fresh coconut

1 teaspoon cumin seeds

½ teaspoon sugar

2 teaspoons lemon juice

1½ tablespoons ghee or vegetable oil

2 potatoes, chopped

4–5 green chillies, de-seeded and finely chopped

3 tablespoons chopped coriander (cilantro) leaves

rock salt

Put the sago in a large bowl and sprinkle over 250ml / 8fl oz (1 cup) water to loosen the sago and break up any lumps.

Put the peanuts, coconut, cumin seeds, sugar and lemon juice in a large bowl, then season with salt. Mix well and set aside.

Heat the ghee or oil in a heavy-based pan over medium heat, add the potatoes and stir-fry for about 15–20 minutes, or until they become soft. Add the chillies and continue to stir-fry for a few more minutes. Add the sago mixture and mix properly, then reduce the heat to very low, cover and cook for 5 minutes, stirring occasionally. Remove from the heat the moment the sago turns soft and transparent. Add the chopped coriander and mix well.

Baadami Chawal Bariyan
Creamy Spiced Rice with Almonds

Origin Punjab
Preparation time 10 minutes, plus soaking time
Cooking time 35 minutes
Serves 4

250g / 9oz (1⅓ cups) basmati rice, rinsed and drained

½ teaspoon chilli powder

4 green chillies, de-seeded and finely chopped

1 teaspoon ground ginger

1 teaspoon ground coriander

1 teaspoon Garam Masala (see page 31)

1 teaspoon ground succh bari or Kashmiri Garam Masala (see page 56)

3½ tablespoons ghee

1 teaspoon cumin seeds

pinch of asafoetida

3 cloves

15 blanched almonds, cut in half

salt

Soak the rice in a large bowl of water for 1 hour, then drain.

Bring 1 litre / 1¾ pints (4¼ cups) water to the boil in a degchi or casserole, add the rice and cook for about 10 minutes, or until the grains soften, then mix, turning the ladle or wooden spoon in a rotary motion, so that the grains are well crushed and the mixture turns into a pulp. Keep stirring constantly so that it does not stick and burn. If the consistency is too thick, add a little more water so that the mixture acquires a thick, syrupy texture. Add all the spices, except for the cumin, asafoetida, cloves and almonds.

Pour in 500ml / 18fl oz (2¼ cups) water and simmer for 10 minutes, or until the mixture becomes a thick paste.

Heat the ghee in a frying pan (skillet) over medium heat, add the remaining spices and stir-fry for about 1 minute, or until they start to splutter. Pour the mixture over the cooked rice.

✳ ✳ / 📷 p.603

Meen Biryani
Fish Biryani

Origin Kerala
Preparation time 35 minutes, plus standing time
Cooking time 35 minutes
Serves 5–6

500g / 1lb 2oz skinless, firm white fish fillets, cut into chunks
4 teaspoons ground turmeric
250ml / 8fl oz (1 cup) lime juice
125g / 4oz (½ cup) ghee
1kg / 2¼lb (5⅓ cups) basmati rice, rinsed and drained
2 tablespoons raisins
2 tablespoons cashew nuts
3 onions, sliced
2 teaspoons chilli powder
1 teaspoon ground coriander
2 cinnamon sticks, about 2.5cm / 1 inch long
4–6 cloves
2 tomatoes, chopped
250ml / 8fl oz (1 cup) natural (plain) yoghurt, whisked
salt

Put the fish in a large shallow dish and rub with 2 teaspoons turmeric and the lime juice, then cover and set aside in the refrigerator for 45 minutes.

Heat 1 tablespoon ghee in a large, heavy-based pan over medium heat, add the rice and fry for about 10 minutes, then season with salt and add 1 teaspoon turmeric and 1 litre / 1¾ pints (4¼ cups) hot water. Stir gently, then bring to the boil. Reduce the heat, cover and cook for about 15 minutes, or until the water is absorbed.

Heat 4 tablespoons ghee in a frying pan (skillet) over medium-low heat, add the raisins and stir-fry for about 1 minute, then remove from the pan with a slotted spoon. Add the cashew nuts to the pan and stir-fry for about 1 minute, or until brown, then remove from the pan with a slotted spoon and reserve. Add the onions to the pan and fry for about 5–7 minutes, or until golden brown. Reduce the heat, add the chilli powder, coriander, remaining turmeric, 4 teaspoons water, and the whole spices and fry for about 2 minutes, stirring constantly. Add the fish and season with salt, then lightly fry for about 5 minutes. Pour in 250ml / 8fl oz (1 cup) water, bring to the boil and add the tomatoes.

Reduce the heat to low, add the yoghurt and simmer for about 5 minutes to thicken the sauce.

Brush a heavy-based pan with a little ghee and spread a layer of fish over the base, then add a layer of rice and then a layer of raisins and cashew nuts. Repeat the process, until all the fish and rice are used up, ending with raisins and cashew nuts on top. Cover the pan and place on a griddle and cook over very low heat for about 5 minutes. Alternatively, cook over very low heat.

Lemon Rice
Lemon Rice

Origin Tamil Nadu
Preparation time 30 minutes, plus soaking time
Cooking time 5 minutes
Serves 4

500g / 1lb 2oz (2¾ cups) rice, rinsed and drained
3 tablespoons groundnut (peanut) oil
1 teaspoon mustard seeds
10–12 curry leaves
2 teaspoons chana dal, rinsed and drained
4–6 green chillies, de-seeded and chopped
100ml / 3½fl oz (½ cup) lemon juice
1 teaspoon ground turmeric
pinch of asafoetida
50g / 1¾oz (⅔ cup) grated coconut
1 large sprig coriander (cilantro), chopped
salt

Soak the rice in a large bowl of water for about 30 minutes, then drain.

Cook the rice in a large pan of salted boiling water for 18–20 minutes, or until cooked.

Heat the oil in a frying pan (skillet) over medium heat, add the mustard seeds, curry leaves, chana dal and chillies and stir-fry for about 1–2 minutes, or until the dal becomes light brown. Add the lemon juice, turmeric and asafoetida and stir for 15 seconds. Pour the mixture over the rice, add the grated coconut and coriander and mix well

Ilish Maachher Pulao
Hilsa Pulao

Origin West Bengal
Preparation time 35 minutes, plus drying and marinating time
Cooking time 40 minutes
Serves 6

750g / 1lb 10oz (4 cups) basmati rice, rinsed and drained
1 × 2.5-cm / 1-inch piece fresh ginger, peeled
2 onions
6 cloves garlic
350ml / 12fl oz (1½ cups) natural (plain) yoghurt
800g / 1¾lb hilsa or other large firm fish fillets, such as haddock, cut into 1-cm / ½-inch thick steaks
250g / 9oz (1 cup) ghee
2 green cardamom pods
4 cloves
1 cinnamon stick, about 5cm / 2 inch long
4 bay leaves
750ml / 1¼ pints (3¼ cups) warm milk
3 teaspoons sugar
butter, for greasing
salt

Spread the rice out on a clean tea (dish) towel and leave until semi-dried.

Put the ginger, onions and garlic in a blender or food processor and process, adding a little water if necessary, to make a paste. Transfer to a large bowl, add half the yoghurt and a little salt and mix well. Put the fish in a large shallow dish, add the marinade and turn to coat, then cover and set aside in the refrigerator for 1 hour.

Preheat the oven to 150°C/300°F/Gas Mark 2, if using.

Heat the ghee in a large, heavy-based pan until very hot. Reduce the heat, add the cardamom pods, cloves, cinnamon and bay leaves and stir-fry for about 1 minute. Add the fish and marinade and fry for a further 3 minutes. Reduce the heat, pour in 125ml / 4½fl oz (½ cup) hot water and cook for 7 minutes over medium-high heat until the water has evaporated and the fish is cooked. Remove the fish and set aside.

Leave the sauce in the pan and add the rice. Cook over high heat for a few minutes until it changes colour, then pour in 750ml / 1¼ pints (3¼ cups) hot water and add the warm milk and sugar and season with salt. Stir well and bring to the boil, then reduce the heat, cover and cook for 10–12 minutes, or until the rice is almost done. Transfer the rice to a bowl and grease the pan well with butter. Layer the pan alternately with the rice and fish, beginning and ending with rice.

Whisk the remaining yoghurt in a bowl, pour it over the rice and cover with a tight-fitting lid.

Heat a griddle over high heat, then reduce the heat. Transfer the pan to the griddle and cook the pulao for 15 minutes. Alternatively, bake in the oven for 15 minutes.

Fish Qorma Pulao
Fish Korma Pulao

Origin Awadh
Preparation time 30 minutes, plus marinating time
Cooking time 20 minutes
Serves 4

2 tablespoons desiccated (dried flaked) coconut, roasted

2 tablespoons poppy seeds, roasted

1 teaspoon mustard seeds, roasted

100g / 3½oz (1 small) onion, chopped, skin reserved, roasted

30g / 1¼oz (¾ cup) chopped coriander (cilantro) leaves

30g / 1¼oz (⅔ cup) chopped mint leaves

4 green chillies, de-seeded and chopped

5 teaspoons Ginger Paste (see page 57)

3 teaspoons Garlic Paste (see page 57)

100ml / 3½fl oz (½ cup) natural (plain) yoghurt

1 teaspoon chilli powder

1 teaspoon ground cumin

2 tablespoons lemon juice

800g / 1¾lb fish fillets, such as surmai, bhetki or mackerel, cut into chunks

125g / 4oz (½ cup) ghee or vegetable oil

⅛ teaspoon ground green cardamom

⅛ teaspoon ground cloves

⅛ teaspoon ground cinnamon

⅛ teaspoon ground nutmeg

⅛ teaspoon ground black cumin

500g / 1lb 2oz (2¾ cups) cooked basmati rice (see page 631)

salt

Put the roasted coconut, poppy seeds, mustard seeds, onions and onion skins in a blender or food processor and process, adding enough water to make a coarse paste. Transfer to a bowl and set aside.

Put the chopped coriander, mint and chillies in the blender or food processor and process, adding enough water to make a paste. Transfer to the bowl with the coconut paste, add the ginger paste, garlic paste, yoghurt, chilli powder, ground cumin and lemon juice, then season with salt and mix well.

Put the fish in a large shallow dish and rub the paste evenly over the fish, then cover and set aside in the refrigerator for 10 minutes.

Spread the ghee or oil in a flat pan or pot, then layer the marinated fish, including the marinade, over it. Add the ground spices, then cover with a tight-fitting lid and put a couple of pieces of hot charcoal on top of the lid, if you like, and leave to stand over very low heat for 10–12 minutes, or until cooked. Uncover, drain the excess fat and adjust the seasoning, if necessary. Gently heap the cooked rice over the fish. To finish, pour the sauce all over, cover and place on a hot griddle or over very low heat for about 5 minutes.

※ ※
___

Sarangyacha Pulao
Pomfret Pulao

Origin Coastal
Preparation time 45 minutes, plus soaking
and marinating time
Cooking time 45 minutes
Serves 4

400g / 14oz (2¼ cups) long-grained rice, rinsed
    and drained

1 teaspoon ground turmeric

2 teaspoons lime juice

1kg / 2¼lb skinless, boneless surmai or pomfret
    (butterfish) fillets, cut into chunks

½ teaspoon ground cumin, roasted

½ teaspoon ground coriander, roasted

1 teaspoon ground aniseed, roasted

3 tablespoons grated fresh or desiccated
    (dried flaked) coconut, roasted

6 large dried red chillies

1 teaspoon Ginger Paste (see page 57)

8 cloves garlic

1 cinnamon stick, about 2.5cm / 1 inch long

2 cloves

½ teaspoon ground cardamom

4 tablespoons vegetable oil

1 large onion, very thinly sliced

1 bay leaf

pinch of ground mace or nutmeg, to garnish

salt

Soak the rice in a bowl of water for 30 minutes,
then drain.

To make a marinade, mix the turmeric, lime juice
and a little salt together in a bowl. Put the fish
in a large shallow dish and rub the marinade all
over, then cover and set aside in the refrigerator
for 20 minutes.

Put the cumin, coriander, aniseed, coconut, dried
red chillies, ginger paste, garlic, cinnamon, cloves
and cardamom in a blender or food processor and
process, adding a little water if necessary, to make a
smooth paste.

Heat 2 tablespoons oil in a large, heavy-based pan
over medium heat, add the onion and fry for
2 minutes, or until translucent. Add the spice paste
and stir-fry for 2–3 minutes.

Add the marinated fish together with the marinade
and 125ml / 4½fl oz (½ cup) water. Reduce the
heat slightly, then cover and simmer for 5 minutes.
Set aside.

For the rice, heat the remaining oil in a large,
heavy-based pan over medium heat, add the bay leaf
and stir-fry for about 1 minute, or until it starts to
splutter. Reduce the heat, add the rice and stir-fry
very gently for 2 minutes. Add ½ teaspoon salt and
cover the rice with 1 litre / 1¾ pints (4¼ cups) water.
Bring to the boil, then reduce the heat, cover and
simmer for 15 minutes, checking frequently whether
more water is required. Remove from
the heat and set aside.

Transfer half the rice to a large bowl, then spoon
half the fish over the rice left in the pan. Return
the rest of the rice to the pan and spread to cover
the fish. Spoon the remaining fish on top in an
even layer. Cover with a tight-fitting lid and cook
over low heat for 5 minutes. Keep covered until
ready to serve. Sprinkle with ground mace or nutmeg
before serving.

Mahi Pulao
Fish Pulao

Origin Awadh
Preparation time 35 minutes
Cooking time 30–40 minutes
Serves 8

10–12 cloves garlic

1 × 5-cm / 2-inch piece fresh ginger, peeled

125g / 4oz (½ cup) ghee

250g / 9oz (2 small) onions, sliced

2 tablespoons ground coriander

250ml / 8fl oz (1 cup) natural (plain) yoghurt

6 cloves, ground

seeds of 6 green cardamom pods, ground

1kg / 2¼lb fish fillets, cut into bite-sized pieces

3 cloves

3 green cardamom pods

500g / 1lb 2oz (2¾ cups) basmati rice, rinsed
    and drained

salt

about 150g / 5oz dough (optional), for sealing the lid
    (see page 783)

Preheat the oven to 150°C/300°F/Gas Mark 2, if using.

Put the garlic in a small blender or food processor and process, adding a little water if necessary, to make a paste, then remove and set aside. Do the same with the ginger.

Heat the ghee in a large, heavy-based pan over medium heat, add the sliced onions and fry for about 5–7 minutes, or until golden brown. Remove from the pan and set aside. Add the garlic and ginger pastes and the coriander to the pan and cook for 1–2 minutes. Remove the pan from the heat, then season with salt and add the yoghurt, ground cloves and ground cardamom seeds. Crumble in the fried onions, then return to the heat and cook for 5–7 minutes. Add the fish, cover and cook for 5–7 minutes, or until the fish is firm. Remove from the heat and set aside.

Cook the rice in a large pan of boiling water with the whole cloves and cardamom pods for 12–15 minutes, or until almost done. Drain and spread the rice over the top of the cooked fish. Melt the remaining ghee in a small pan and pour over the top. Now cover with a tight-fitting lid and seal with dough, if using, or foil. Put a couple of pieces of hot charcoal on the top of the lid, if you like, and leave to stand. Alternatively, cook in the oven for 30–40 minutes.

📷 p.604

Jhinga Nariyal ka Pulao
Coconut & Prawn (Shrimp) Pulao

Origin Hyderabad
Preparation time 35 minutes, plus soaking time
Cooking time 40 minutes
Serves 8

500g / 1¼lb (2¾ cups) long-grained rice, rinsed
    and drained

1 teaspoon Ginger Paste (see page 57)

2 teaspoons Garlic Paste (see page 57)

10 green chillies, de-seeded (optional)

1 bunch coriander (cilantro) leaves, chopped

juice of 1 lime

500g / 1lb 2oz prawns (shrimp), peeled
    and deveined

1 coconut, ground

125g / 4oz (½ cup) ghee or vegetable oil

2 cinnamon sticks, about 2.5cm / 1 inch long

5 cloves

2 onions, chopped

1 teaspoon chilli powder

salt

Preheat the oven to 140°C/275°F/Gas Mark 1.

Soak the rice in water for 20 minutes, then drain.

Put the ginger and garlic pastes, chillies and coriander leaves in a blender or food processor and process to make a paste. Add the lime juice. Put the prawns in a large shallow dish, add the spice mixture and turn to coat the prawns. Cover and set in the refrigerator for 15 minutes.

Mix the coconut and 250ml / 8fl oz (1 cup) hot water together in a bowl and pass through a sieve (strainer) to extract the thick milk into a clean bowl, then add 1 litre / 1¾ pints (4¼ cups) water and mix together. Set aside.

Heat the ghee or oil in a large, heavy-based pan over medium heat, add the cinnamon and cloves and stir-fry for a few seconds, then add the onions and chilli powder and stir-fry for about 2–3 minutes. Add the prawns and fry for about 3 minutes.

Put the coconut milk into a large ovenproof pan and bring to the boil. Add the rice and cook for about 15 minutes, or until two-thirds cooked, then add the prawns, season with salt and mix. Cover with a tight-fitting lid and cook in the oven for 15 minutes.

pp.604, 607

Biryani (I)
Lamb Biryani (I)

Origin Delhi
Preparation time 40 minutes–1 hour, plus marinating time
Cooking time 35–40 minutes
Serves 8

For stage one

15 cloves garlic

1 × 8-cm / 3-inch piece fresh ginger, peeled

25g / 1oz dried red chillies

50g / 1¾oz (⅓ cup) cumin seeds

6 green cardamom pods

4 black cardamom pods

½ nutmeg

500ml / 18fl oz (2¼ cups) natural (plain) yoghurt

2kg / 2¼lb lamb, cut into large pieces

For stage two

100g / 3½oz (scant ½ cup) ghee

50g / 1¾oz (½ small) onion, finely sliced

For stage three

200g / 7oz (¾ cup) ghee

4 bay leaves

salt

For stage four

1kg / 2¼ lb (5⅓ cup) basmati rice, rinsed and drained

4 tablespoons ghee

150ml / ¼ pint (⅔ cup) natural (plain) yoghurt

about 150g / 5oz dough (optional), for sealing the lid
    (see page 783)

salt

For stage one, put the garlic, ginger, dried red chillies, cumin, cardamom pods and nutmeg in a mortar or spice grinder and pound with a pestle or process until ground. Transfer to a deep glass or ceramic dish, add the yoghurt and lamb and mix together. Cover and set aside in the refrigerator for 2 hours.

For stage two, heat the ghee in a frying pan (skillet) over medium heat, add the onions and fry for about 5–7 minutes, or until crisp and brown. Remove from the pan with a slotted spoon and set aside.

For stage three, heat the ghee in a deep, heavy-based pan over high heat, then reduce the heat, add the bay leaves and stir-fry for about 1 minute, or until they start to change colour. Add the meat and the marinade, and season with salt. Reduce the heat to low and stir-fry until all the natural juices have been reabsorbed and the meat is dry, and the oil rises to the surface. Pour in 1 litre / 1¾ pints (4¼ cups) hot water, stir, cover and simmer for 20 minutes, or until the meat is three-quarters cooked. At this stage, there should be a thick sauce in the pan.

For stage four, preheat the oven to 180°C/350°F/Gas Mark 4, if using. Bring a large pan of water to the boil, add the rice, then season with salt and cook for about 7–10 minutes, or until half cooked. Drain.

Arrange the cooked meat with the sauce in a large heavy-based pan, spreading it out evenly so that there are no gaps between the pieces. Spread half the fried onions over the meat, then spread the rice over the meat and onion layers. Put 250ml / 8fl oz (1 cup) water, the ghee and yoghurt in a bowl and mix together, then spread this mixture evenly over the rice and cover with the remaining fried onions.

Cover with a tight-fitting lid and seal with dough, if using, or foil. Heat a large griddle over high heat, then reduce the heat to low and place the pan of meat and rice on the griddle. Cook for about 35–40 minutes, shaking the pan occasionally to prevent sticking. Alternatively, cook in the oven.

Biryani (II)
Lamb Biryani (II)

Origin Awadh
Preparation time 1½ hours, plus marinating time
Cooking time 2 hours
Serves 8

For stage one

15 cloves garlic

1 × 8-cm / 3-inch piece fresh ginger, peeled

5 green chillies, de-seeded (optional)

50g / 1¾oz (1 cup) coriander (cilantro) leaves

1 × 5-cm / 2-inch square unripe papaya

2 teaspoons cumin seeds

8 cloves

1 teaspoon saffron threads

1kg / 2¼lb lamb, cut into large pieces

½ teaspoon ground turmeric

500ml / 18fl oz (2¼ cups) natural (plain) yoghurt

750g / 1lb 10oz (6 medium) potatoes

salt

For stage two

1kg / 2¼lb (5⅓ cups) basmati rice, rinsed and drained

6 cloves

4 green cardamom pods

¼ teaspoon black caraway seeds

1 cinnamon stick, about 2.5cm / 1 inch long

For stage three

500g / 18oz (2 cups) ghee

750g / 1lb 10oz (6 medium) onions, sliced

2 teaspoons chilli powder

6 dried plums

For the spice powder

3 green cardamom pods

3 black cardamom pods

1 cinnamon stick, about 2.5cm / 1 inch long

2 blades mace

1½ teaspoons black caraway seeds

For stage four

1 tablespoon rosewater

125g / 4oz (½ cup) ghee

180ml / 6fl oz (¾ cup) milk

about 150g / 5oz dough (optional), for sealing the lid
   (see page 783)

For stage one, put the garlic, ginger, chillies, coriander leaves, papaya, cumin seeds and cloves in a blender or food processor and process until ground. Set aside. Put 1 teaspoon saffron threads in a small bowl, add 2 tablespoons hot water and soak until required.

Put the lamb into a large shallow dish and rub with salt, then cover and set aside for 15–30 minutes. Squeeze and rub dry with a clean cloth and coat with a pinch of turmeric. Mix the ground spices and yoghurt together in a bowl and rub all over the meat. Make a cut in the centre of each potato and coat them with a pinch of turmeric. Set aside.

For stage two, bring three-quarters of a large pan of water to the boil, add the rice, cloves, cardamom pods, black caraway seeds and cinnamon and cook for about 5 minutes, or until one-quarter cooked. Drain, reserving the water.

For stage three, while the rice is boiling, heat the ghee in a large, heavy-based pan over medium heat, add the sliced onions and fry for about 5 minutes, or until brown. Remove with a slotted spoon and set aside.

Put all the ingredients for the spice powder in a spice grinder and process until ground. Set aside.

Drain half of the ghee from the pan and reserve, then return to the heat, add 2 teaspoons fried crushed onions and 1 teaspoon chilli powder and cook for 1 minute, then add the potatoes and fry lightly for about 5–10 minutes. Remove with a slotted spoon and set aside.

Arrange the pieces of meat in a tightly packed single layer in a large, heavy-based pan with a flat base. Make sure there are no spaces between the pieces. Pour over 125ml / 4½fl oz (½ cup) drained ghee, then sprinkle over the ground spices and remaining chilli powder. Arrange the potatoes in a single layer over the meat and tuck the dried plums between the potatoes.

For stage four, preheat the oven to 230°C/450°F/Gas Mark 8. Sprinkle the rosewater and 1 teaspoon of saffron water over the potatoes and top with the remaining onions. Spread the rice evenly over this layer, then sprinkle over the ghee, milk, and 300ml / ½ pint (1¼ cups) of the reserved rice water. Pour the remaining saffron water in the centre of the rice. Cover with a tight-fitting lid and seal with dough, if using, or foil.

Place the pan over high heat for 15–20 minutes, then cook in the oven for 20 minutes. Reduce the oven to 180°C/350°F/Gas Mark 4 and cook for a further 1½ hours. When cooked, place the pan again over medium heat for 10–15 minutes.

Kacchi Biryani
Saffron-flavoured Meat
Cooked with Rice

Origin Hyderabad
Preparation time 1 hour 20 minutes, plus marinating and soaking time
Cooking time 50 minutes
Serves 8

100g / 3½oz (scant ½ cup) ghee

3 onions, sliced

1kg / 2¼lb lamb, cut into 5-cm / 2-inch pieces

1 level tablespoon ground unripe papaya

125ml / 4½fl oz (½ cup) natural (plain) yoghurt

1 teaspoon chilli powder

4 green cardamom pods

4 cloves

2 cinnamon sticks, about 2.5cm / 1 inch long

1 teaspoon caraway seeds, ground

2 teaspoons Garlic Paste (see page 57)

1 teaspoon Ginger Paste (see page 57)

1kg / 2¼lb (5⅓ cups) very fine basmati rice, rinsed
    and drained

1 teaspoon saffron threads

250ml / 8fl oz (1 cup) milk, plus a little extra

1 bunch coriander (cilantro) leaves, chopped

1 sprig mint leaves

6 green chillies

1 teaspoon ground green cardamom

juice of 4 limes

about 150g / 5oz dough (optional), for sealing the lid
    (see page 783)

salt

Heat the ghee in a large, heavy-based pan over medium heat, add the onions and fry for about 5–7 minutes, or until golden brown. Remove from the pan and crush half the onions and set aside. Reserve the remaining onions and ghee.

Put the meat in a large shallow dish and rub the papaya over. Add the yoghurt, chilli powder, whole spices, ground caraway seeds, garlic and ginger pastes and the crushed onions, then season with salt. Cover and set aside in the refrigerator for 1 hour, mixing well after about 25 minutes.

Preheat the oven 150°C/300°F/Gas Mark 2, if using.

Soak the rice in a bowl of salted water for about 20 minutes, then drain and cook in a large, heavy-based pan of boiling water for about 12–15 minutes, or until half cooked. Drain, reserving 375ml / 13fl oz (1½ cups) cooking water.

Put the saffron in a small bowl, crush lightly, then add a little milk and mix together.

Spread the meat over the base (bottom) of a large ovenproof pan or casserole. Pour half the milk, the reserved rice cooking water and the saffron milk over the lamb, then sprinkle the fried onions with ghee, coriander, mint leaves, green chillies and ground cardamom over the top. Spread the remaining rice over the mixture, then sprinkle over the ground cardamom and lime juice and season with salt. Cover with a tight-fitting lid and seal with dough, if using, or foil.

Place the pan over medium heat and cook for about 10 minutes, or until the liquid makes slight sounds inside. Remove the pan from the heat. Heat a griddle over low heat, transfer the pan to the griddle and continue to cook for about 35–40 minutes. Alternatively, cook in the oven. To see if the meat is cooked, break the dough and open the lid, then check by putting a long-handled spoon into the pan; if there is liquid at the bottom, cook the biryani a little longer until all the liquid is absorbed. Keep covered until you are ready to serve.

Hyderabadi Dum ki Biryani
Aromatic Slow-cooked Biryani

Origin Hyderabad
Preparation time 1½ hours
Cooking time 1 hour
Serves 4

2 teaspoons saffron threads

2 tablespoons lukewarm milk

250g / 9oz (1⅓ cups) basmati rice, rinsed

3 tablespoons rosewater

1 tablespoon lemon juice

500g / 1lb 2oz leg of kid or lamb, cut into chunks

1 × 5-cm / 2-inch piece fresh ginger, peeled
    and chopped

3–4 green chillies, de-seeded and chopped

6 tablespoons chopped mint

4 tablespoons chopped coriander (cilantro)

4 teaspoons fried onions

1½ tablespoons ghee, melted

salt

about 150g / 5oz dough (optional), for sealing the lid
    (see page 783)

For the aromatic potli

5–6 green cardamom pods, ground

5–6 cloves, ground

For the meat spices

125ml / 4½fl oz (½ cup) natural (plain) yoghurt

1 teaspoon yellow chilli powder

5 tablespoons ghee

5 green cardamom pods

3 cloves

2 cinnamon sticks, about 2.5cm / 1 inch long

2 bay leaves

80g / 2¾oz (1 small) onion, sliced

5 teaspoons Garlic Paste (see page 57)

2 teaspoons Ginger Paste (see page 57)

2 tablespoons lemon juice

4 tablespoons single (light) cream

⅓ teaspoon ground mace

⅔ teaspoon ground green cardamom

1 drop ittar

Crush the saffron threads in a mortar with a pestle, then put them in a small bowl, add the lukewarm milk and stir to make paste. Preheat the oven to 180°C/350°F/Gas Mark 4.

Put all the ingredients for the aromatic potli in a mortar and pound with a pestle to break the spices or grind coarsely in a spice grinder. Transfer to a piece of muslin (cheesecloth) and tie with kitchen string (twine) to make a pouch.

For the meat spices, whisk the yoghurt and yellow chilli powder together in a bowl, then set aside.

Bring 1.5 litres / 2½ pints (6¼ cups) water to the boil in a pan, add the potli and season with salt. Stir, then add the rice and return to the boil. Add the rosewater and lemon juice and continue to boil, stirring occasionally, for about 15–18 minutes, or until the rice is almost cooked. Drain, discarding the potli and set aside.

For the meat spices, heat the ghee in a large, heavy-based pan over medium heat, add the whole spices and bay leaves and stir-fry for about 1 minute, or until the cardamom pods change colour. Add the onion and stir-fry for about 5–7 minutes, or until golden brown. Add the garlic and ginger pastes and stir-fry for about 30 seconds. Add the meat and stir-fry for about 2 minutes, then season with salt. Stir, reduce the heat to low, cover and cook, stirring occasionally, for about 20 minutes, adding water if necessary. Uncover and stir-fry for 10 minutes, or until the liquid has evaporated. Remove the pan from the heat, stir in the yoghurt mixture, then return to the heat and stir for about 1 minute. Cover and simmer, stirring occasionally, for 5–7 minutes, or until three-quarters of the liquid has evaporated. Uncover and simmer, until the liquid has evaporated and the oil separates out.

Add 500ml / 18fl oz (2¼ cups) water and bring to the boil, then reduce the heat, cover and simmer for 20 minutes, or until the meat is almost cooked. Remove the meat and squeeze the sauce through fine muslin (cheesecloth) or sieve (strain) into a separate pan. Sprinkle over the lemon juice, stir, then add the cream and stir again. Adjust the seasoning if necessary and reserve a quarter of the sauce.

Return the meat to the remaining sauce, arranging it in the middle of the pan. Add the ground mace and cardamom, then stir. Return the pan with the meat to the heat, sprinkle over half the chopped ginger, chillies, mint, coriander, fried onions and saffron, arrange half of the partially cooked rice around the meat, pour over the remaining ginger, chillies, mint, coriander, fried onions and saffron, then cover with the remaining rice and sprinkle over the reserved sauce. Pour on the ghee, bring to the boil and remove from the heat. Add the ittar, then cover with a tight-fitting lid and seal with dough, if using, or foil. Put a couple of pieces of hot charcoal on top of the lid, if you like, and leave to stand or bake in the oven for 15–20 minutes.

Awadhi Gosht Biryani
Lamb Biryani from Lucknow

Origin Awadh
Preparation time 1½ hours
Cooking time 50 minutes
Serves 6

For the lamb

125g / 4oz (½ cup) ghee

1½ teaspoons ground cumin

1 teaspoon ground green cardamom

¾ teaspoon ground cinnamon

¾ teaspoon ground cloves

very small pinch of ground nutmeg

½ cup Boiled Onion Paste (see page 57)

2 tablespoons blanched almond paste

3 teaspoons Ginger Paste (see page 57)

3 teaspoons Garlic Paste (see page 57)

1 tablespoon Poppy Seed Paste (see page 58)

2 teaspoons chilli powder

1kg / 2¼lb lamb, cut into pieces

125ml / 4½fl oz (½ cup) natural (plain) yoghurt,
   whisked

salt

For the rice

½ teaspoon saffron threads

1 tablespoon milk

500g / 1lb 2 oz (2¾ cups) basmati rice, rinsed
   and drained

2 cinnamon sticks, about 2.5cm / 1 inch long

4 green cardamom pods

2 tablespoons ghee

1 onion, sliced

½ teaspoon kewra water or rosewater

1 teaspoon black cumin seeds

125ml / 4½fl oz (½ cup) single (light) cream

about 150g / 5oz dough (optional), for sealing the lid
   (see page 783)

To garnish

2 tablespoons raisins

2 tablespoons blanched almonds, slivered

For the rice, put the saffron in a small bowl, add the milk and soak until required.

For the lamb, heat the ghee in a large, heavy-based pan over high heat, add all the spices for the meat together with the pastes and the chilli powder.

Stir constantly for about 2 minutes, or until the oil separates out. Add the lamb, then season with salt and continue stirring so that the spices coat the lamb pieces. This may take about 10 minutes. Add the whisked yoghurt and 1.25 litres / 2 pints (5 cups) water and cook for 1 hour until the lamb is tender and the sauce has a thick consistency.

Bring a deep pan of water to the boil, add the rice, cinnamon and cardamom pods and cook for about 12–15 minutes, or until the rice is almost done and all the water is absorbed.

Heat the ghee in a flat, heavy-based pan or pot over medium heat, add the sliced onion and fry for about 5–7 minutes, or until golden brown, then remove from the pan and set aside. Spread the rice over the base (bottom) of the pan, then pour over half of the saffron milk, half of the kewra water, half the black cumin seeds and half the cream. Spread half of the cooked lamb over the top and repeat the process for the second layer. Now cover with a tight-fitting lid and seal with dough, if using, or foil. Put a couple of pieces of hot charcoal on top of the lid, if you like, and leave to stand until cooked. Alternatively, omit the charcoal and cook over very low heat for 30–35 minutes, or until cooked.

Uncover, adjust the seasoning, if necessary, then scatter over the reserved fried onions, raisins and almonds to garnish.

Shahi Biryani
Imperial Biryani

Origin New
Preparation time 2 hours
Cooking time 45 minutes
Serves 8

pinch of saffron threads

250g / 9oz (1 cup) ghee

2 tablespoons Garlic Paste (see page 57)

2 tablespoons Ginger Paste (see page 57)

½ teaspoon cloves

½ teaspoon black peppercorns, crushed

seeds of 6 black cardamoms, crushed

2 cinnamon sticks, about 2.5cm / 1 inch long

4 bay leaves

1kg / 2¼lb lamb, cut into pieces

100ml / 3½fl oz (½ cup) natural (plain) yoghurt,
   whisked

1kg / 2¼lb (5⅓ cups) basmati rice, rinsed and drained

large pinch of ground turmeric

salt

about 150g / 5oz dough (optional), for sealing the lid
   (see page 783)

Preheat the oven to 150°C/300°F/Gas Mark 2, if using.
Put the saffron in a small bowl, add 4 teaspoons hot
water and soak until required.

Heat the ghee in a large, heavy-based pan over
medium heat, add the garlic paste and stir-fry for
about 1 minute, or until golden. Stir in the ginger
paste and spices and cook for 1–2 minutes. Add the
lamb and cook for 10–15 minutes, or until lightly
browned. Add the yoghurt, then season with salt and
pour in 1.5 litres / 2½ pints (6¼ cups) water. Cook
over medium heat for 1 hour, or until the meat is
tender, adding more water if necessary. When the
meat is done there should be approximately 250ml
/ 8fl oz (1 cup) liquid left in the pan.

Cook the rice in a large pan of boiling water for
about 10 minutes, or until half done. Stir through the
turmeric, then drain.

Spoon the rice on top of the cooked lamb and
sprinkle over the saffron and a few drops of food
colouring, if you like. Now cover with a tight-fitting
lid and seal with dough, if using, or foil. Put a couple
of pieces of hot charcoal on top of the lid and leave
to stand over very low heat or omit the charcoal
and cook in the oven for 45 minutes. Stir the biryani
to mix the rice and meat together before serving.

Qorma Pulao
Curried Lamb Pulao

Origin Punjab
Preparation time 40 minutes, plus soaking time
Cooking time 45 minutes
Serves 8

500g / 1lb 2oz (2¾ cups) basmati rice, rinsed
   and drained

¼ teaspoon saffron threads

1 tablespoon milk

2 green cardamom pods

1 cinnamon stick, about 2.5cm / 1 inch long

3 cloves

500g / 1 lb 2oz lamb from Lamb Korma (II)
   with about 250ml / 8fl oz (1 cup) sauce
   (see page 450)

juice of 1 lime

1 tablespoon natural (plain) yoghurt

3 green cardamom pods, ground

150g / 5oz dough (optional), for sealing the lid
   (see page 783)

salt

To garnish

1 tablespoon ghee

2 onions, sliced

Soak the rice in a bowl of water for 20 minutes, then
drain. Put the saffron in a mortar, add the milk and
grind with a pestle. Set aside.

Bring 1.5 litres / 2½ pints (6¼ cups) water to the boil
in a large, heavy-based pan. Add the cardamom
pods, cinnamon and cloves and season with salt. Add
the rice and cook for about 15 minutes, or until two-
thirds cooked, then drain.

Spread the lamb korma over the base (bottom) of
a large, heavy-based pan, then cover with rice.
Sprinkle over the saffron, lime juice, yoghurt and
ground cardamom, then cover with a tight-fitting lid
and seal the lid with dough, if using, or foil. Cook
over very low heat for 40 minutes.

Meanwhile heat the ghee for the garnish in a frying
pan (skillet) over medium heat, add the onions and
fry for about 5–7 minutes, or until golden brown and
crisp, then remove and set aside. Garnish the cooked
rice with the fried sliced onions.

Keema Khichari
Savoury Minced (Ground) Meat Pulao

Origin Hyderabad
Preparation time 45 minutes, plus soaking time
Cooking time 45 minutes–1 hour
Serves 8

For the mince

125ml / 4½fl oz (½ cup) vegetable oil

2 green cardamom pods

3 cloves

1 cinnamon stick, about 5cm / 2 inches long

4 onions, sliced

1 tablespoon Ginger Paste (see page 57)

1 tablespoons Garlic Paste (see page 57)

1 teaspoon ground coriander

2 tablespoons poppy seeds, ground

500g / 1lb 2oz minced (ground) lamb

1 tomato, chopped

250ml / 8fl oz (1 cup) natural (plain) yoghurt

½ bunch coriander (cilantro) leaves, chopped

½ teaspoon saffron threads

For the rice

500g / 1lb 2oz (2¾ cups) rice, rinsed and drained

pinch of saffron threads

1 teaspoon milk

1 tablespoon vegetable oil

2 onions, sliced

1 clove

3 green cardamom pods

1 cinnamon stick, about 2.5cm / 1 inch long

4 teaspoons natural (plain) yoghurt

1 bunch coriander (cilantro) leaves, chopped

2 cardamom pods, ground

juice of 1 lime

small knob (pat) of butter (optional)

Soak the rice in a bowl of water for 20 minutes, then drain. Put the saffron threads in a small bowl, add the milk and soak for about 10 minutes, then transfer to a mortar and grind with a pestle.

For the mince, heat the oil in a large, heavy-based pan over medium heat, add the cardamom pods, cloves and cinnamon and fry for about 1 minute. Add the onions and fry for about 5–7 minutes, or until golden brown. Add the ginger and garlic pastes, ground coriander and poppy seeds and cook for a few minutes until well fried.

Sprinkle over a little water and stir if the mixture is sticking to the base (bottom) of the pan. Add the mince and fry for about 5–10 minutes, or until well-browned. Add the tomato and mix, then stir in the yoghurt. Reduce the heat to low and cook for 15 minutes. Add the chopped coriander and saffron and cook for a further 1–2 minutes, then remove from the heat.

For the rice, heat the oil in a frying pan (skillet) over medium heat, add the onions and fry for about 5–7 minutes, or until golden brown, then remove from the pan and set aside. Reserve the oil.

Bring a large pan of water to the boil. Add the cloves, cardamom pods, cinnamon and rice, and cook for 10 minutes or until half cooked. Drain and return half the rice to the pan. Spread the mince over the rice in the pan, add 2 teaspoons yoghurt, half the chopped coriander, a little ground cardamom, a dash of lime juice and a dash of saffron milk. Spoon the rest of the rice evenly over the mince, then sprinkle over the remaining chopped coriander, yoghurt, ground cardamom, saffron milk, the fried onions and a little of the oil that the onions were fried in or the butter. Cover with a tight-fitting lid, and stand the pan on a hot griddle or place over low heat and cook for about 10 minutes.

Kaleji Pulao
Liver Pulao

Origin New
Preparation time 15 minutes
Cooking time 20 minutes
Serves 8

500g / 1lb 2oz pig's liver, cut into 5-cm / 2-inch pieces

600g / 1lb 5oz (3¼ cups) basmati rice, rinsed
and drained

2 onions, sliced

2 teaspoons garlic, chopped

1 teaspoon ground black pepper

salt

Place the liver in a large, heavy-based pan with 500ml / 18fl oz (2¼ cups) water and bring to the boil. Add the rice and the remaining ingredients. Return to the boil, then reduce the heat and simmer for about 20 minutes, or until the rice is done.

Moti Pulao
Pearl Pulao

Origin Awadh
Preparation time 3½ hours, plus soaking and standing time
Cooking time 1 hour
Serves 6

For the stock

2 cups lamb bones
2 bay leaves
1 cinnamon stick, about 2.5cm / 1 inch long
10 cloves
5 black cardamom pods
½ teaspoon cumin seeds
½ teaspoon black peppercorns
pinch of mace flakes
salt

For the meatballs

500g / 1lb 2oz very finely minced (ground) lamb
2 green chillies, de-seeded and finely chopped
1 tablespoon chopped coriander (cilantro) leaves
pinch of salt
1 egg, beaten
100g / 3½oz (scant ½ cup) ghee
1 sheet silver leaf (optional)

For the rice

500g / 1lb 2oz (2¾ cups) basmati rice, rinsed and drained
pinch of saffron threads
2 tablespoons ghee, plus extra for greasing
1 × 5-cm / 2-inch piece fresh ginger, peeled and finely chopped
6–8 cloves garlic, ground
few drops kewra water
about 150g / 5oz dough (optional), for sealing the lid (see page 783)

To make the stock, put the lamb bones, bay leaves, whole spices and a little salt in a large, heavy-based pan. Cover with 1.75 litres / 3 pints (7½ cups) water, bring to the boil, then reduce the heat and simmer for 1 hour. Return to the boil, then reduce the heat and simmer for a further 1 hour. Strain and discard the bones and spices. You should have about 750ml / 1¼ pints (3¼ cups) stock. Set aside.

Preheat the oven to 150°C/300°F/Gas mark 2, if using. Soak the rice in a bowl of water for 20 minutes, then drain and leave for 10 minutes. Put the saffron in a small bowl, add 3–4 teaspoons water and soak until required.

For the moti, mix the mince, chillies, coriander, salt and egg together in a large bowl. With damp hands, shape the mixture into small pea-sized balls.

Heat the ghee in a frying pan (skillet) over medium heat, then, working in batches, fry the meatballs for 3–4 minutes until golden. Set aside and allow to cool slightly. Carefully open out a sheet of silver leaf, if using, and roll the balls of mince on it until covered. Set aside.

For the rice, heat the ghee in a large, heavy-based pan over medium heat, add the ginger and garlic and stir-fry for 1–2 minutes. Stir in the rice and fry for a further 1–2 minutes. Pour in the lamb stock to come 2.5cm / 1 inch above the surface of the rice, then reduce the heat, cover and cook for 15 minutes, or until the rice is almost done.

Layer the rice and meatballs in a greased pan, sprinkling over a little saffron and kewra water on each layer and ending with a layer of rice. Cover with a tight-fitting lid and seal with dough, if using, or foil. Put a couple of pieces of hot charcoal on top of the lid, if you like, and leave to stand or omit the charcoal and cook in the oven for 20–30 minutes.

Mutanjan Pulao
Sweet Lamb Pulao

Origin Awadh
Preparation time 2¼ hours, plus soaking time
Cooking time 40 minutes
Serves 8

½ teaspoon saffron threads
1kg / 2¼lb lamb, cut into bite-sized pieces
10 cloves
10 green cardamom pods
1 teaspoon cumin seeds
½ teaspoon black peppercorns
1 cinnamon stick, about 2.5cm / 1 inch long
250g / 9oz (1 cup) ghee
250g / 9oz (2 small) onions, sliced
1 × 10-cm / 4-inch piece fresh ginger, peeled and thinly sliced
3 teaspoons ground coriander
2 litres / 3½ pints (8½ cups) milk
1kg / 2¼lb (5⅓ cups) basmati rice, rinsed and drained
250g / 9oz (1¾ cups) blanched almonds
250g / 9oz (1¾ cups) sultanas (golden raisins)
500g / 1lb 2oz (2½ cups) sugar
salt
about 150g / 5oz dough (optional), for sealing the lid (see page 783)

Soak the saffron in a small bowl of hot water until required.

Put the lamb into a large, heavy-based pan with 5 cloves, 5 cardamom pods, the cumin, peppercorns and cinnamon and season with salt. Pour in 3½ litres / 6 pints (15 cups) water, bring to the boil, then reduce the heat and simmer for 1½ hours, or until the meat is tender. Drain the meat, reserving the stock, and discard the spices. You should have about 2–2½ litres / 3½–4½ pints (8½ –10½ cups) stock.

Heat 2 tablespoons ghee in a small frying pan (skillet) over medium heat, add the remaining cloves and stir-fry for about 1 minute, or until black, then pour into the stock. Set aside.

Heat the remaining ghee in a large, heavy-based pan over medium heat, add the onions and fry for about 5–7 minutes, or until golden brown. Stir in the ginger and coriander and the remaining cardamom pods and cook for 1–2 minutes. Add the lamb, stir and cook for 10 minutes, or until brown. Set aside.

Meanwhile, bring the milk to the boil in a pan, then reduce the heat and simmer until reduced to a quarter of its original volume. This will take about an hour. The milk will be very thick, having a consistency of porridge.

Put the almonds and 125ml / 4½fl oz (½ cup) stock in a food processor or blender and process until the almonds are ground, then mix into the thickened milk.

Soak the rice in a large bowl of water for 15 minutes, then drain and leave to stand for 10 minutes.

Remove the cloves from the stock, bring to the boil and add the rice. Reduce the heat, cover and cook for 12–15 minutes, or until the rice is almost done and the liquid is absorbed.

Put one-third of the rice on top of the cooked meat, then spread over half the milk mixture and scatter over half the sultanas and sugar. Sprinkle over a little of the saffron. Add another third of the rice, the remaining milk, sultanas and sugar and a little more saffron. Finally, top with remaining rice and saffron. Now cover with a tight-fitting lid and seal with dough, if using, or foil.

Put a couple of pieces of hot charcoal on top of the lid, if you like, and leave to stand or omit the charcoal and cook over very low heat for about 15 minutes, or until the rice is cooked. Stir gently to mix before serving.

Yakhni Pulao
Lamb Stock Pulao

Origin Awadh
Preparation time 1 hour, plus soaking time
Cooking time 30 minutes
Serves 8

500g / 1lb 2oz (2¾ cups) basmati rice, rinsed and drained
1 large onion, sliced
3 tablespoons ghee
5 green cardamom pods
8 cloves
2 cinnamon sticks, about 2.5cm / 1 inch long
1 teaspoon Ginger Paste (see page 57)
1 teaspoon Garlic Paste (see page 57)
500ml / 18fl oz (2¼ cups) lamb stock (see page 636)
3 tablespoons natural (plain) yoghurt
juice of 2 limes
4 bay leaves
250ml / 8fl oz (1 cup) milk
4 tablespoons cream
salt

To garnish

4 hard-boiled eggs
225g / 8oz (1½ cups) boiled peas

Soak the rice in a large bowl of salted water for 30 minutes, then drain.

Preheat the oven to 140°C/275°F/Gas Mark 1.

Put the onion in a blender or food processor and process to make a paste. Set aside.

Heat the ghee in a frying pan (skillet) over medium-low heat, split open the cardamom pods and add half of them with half the other spices, onion, and ginger and garlic pastes to the pan and cook for about 5 minutes. Do not allow the onions to brown. Add the stock to the mixture and season with salt to make a thick sauce. Add the yoghurt and lime juice and cook for a further 5–10 minutes, then remove from the heat and pass through a sieve (strainer) into a clean pan.

For the rice, put the bay leaves, remaining cloves, cardamom pods and cinnamon in a square of muslin (cheesecloth) and tie with kitchen string (twine) to form a pouch. Add the pouch and 2 teaspoons salt to a large, heavy-based pan with 1.75–2 litres / 3–3½ pints (7½–8½ cups) water and bring to the boil.

Add the rice, stir immediately and cook, stirring occasionally later, for about 5 minutes. Remove and discard the spice pouch, then drain through a sieve into a clean pan. Add the prepared stock and the milk and cream. Adjust the seasoning, if necessary, then cover and cook in the oven for about 30 minutes. Serve garnished with hard-boiled eggs and boiled peas.

Bengali Mutton Biryani
Bengali Lamb Biryani

Origin West Bengal
Preparation time 1 hour
Cooking time 50 minutes
Serves 5

250ml / 8fl oz (1 cup) vegetable oil
100g / 3½oz (1 small) onion, sliced
2 teaspoons Ginger Paste (see page 57)
½ teaspoon ground nutmeg
½ teaspoon ground mace
2 teaspoons chilli powder
2 cinnamon sticks, about 2.5cm / 1 inch long
10 white cardamom pods
500ml / 18fl oz (2¼ cups) natural (plain) yoghurt
1kg / 2¼lb lamb, cut into cubes
3 potatoes, cut into large cubes
800g / 1¾lb basmati rice, rinsed and drained
1 teaspoon kewra water or rosewater
12 cloves
8–10 dried plums
few saffron threads
salt

Heat about half the oil in a wide pan over medium-low heat, add the onion and fry for about 5 minutes, or until light brown. Add the ginger paste, nutmeg, mace, chilli powder, cinnamon and cardamom pods, then slowly add the yoghurt, stirring constantly. Season with salt. Stir thoroughly for 5 minutes, then add the lamb and cook for 1½ hours, or until tender. Remove the pan from the heat and set aside.

Heat the remaining 125ml / 4½fl oz (½ cup) oil in a kadhai, wok or deep, heavy-based pan over medium heat, add the potatoes and stir-fry for about 10 minutes, or until golden brown. Remove from the pan with a slotted spoon.

Add the rice to the pan and stir-fry for 2–3 minutes. Add 1.2 litres / 2 pints (6 cups) water, the kewra water and cloves and cook for about 15 minutes, or until three-quarters of the water has evaporated. Reduce the heat to low, add the fried potatoes and dried plums, then spread the cooked lamb on top. Sprinkle over the saffron threads sparingly, then cover and cook for 30 minutes.

Murga ka Safed Pulao
White Chicken Pulao

Origin Awadh
Preparation time 1 hour
Cooking time 30 minutes
Serves 8

3 cloves
3 green cardamom pods
1 cinnamon stick, about 2.5cm / 1 inch long
1 × 800-g / 1¾-lb chicken, cut into 12 pieces
1.25 litres / 2 pints (5 cups) milk
½ tablespoon Ginger Paste (see page 57)
½ tablespoon Garlic Paste (see page 57)
1 bunch coriander (cilantro) leaves, chopped
2–3 green chillies, de-seeded and sliced
200g / 7oz (¾ cup plus 2 tablespoons / 1¾ sticks) butter
500g / 1lb 2oz (2¾ cups) basmati rice, rinsed and drained
juice of 2 limes
salt

To garnish

200g / 7oz (1⅓ cups) freshly cooked peas
3 hard-boiled eggs, shelled and cut in half lengthways

Preheat the oven to 140°C/275°F/Gas Mark 1.

Put the whole spices in a spice grinder and process until ground, then set aside.

Cook the chicken, milk, ginger and garlic pastes, coriander, chillies, ground spices and a little salt in a large, heavy-based pan over medium heat until the milk is reduced to half and the chicken is almost cooked.

Melt the butter in a frying pan (skillet) and pour over the chicken.

Bring 1.5 litres / 2½ pints (6¼ cups) water to the boil in a large, heavy-based pan, add the rice and cook for about 15 minutes, or until two-thirds cooked. Drain and spread a layer of rice over the base (bottom) of a large, heavy-based casserole or ovenproof pan. Spread a layer of the chicken and milk mixture over the rice, then cover with the remaining rice. Pour over the lime juice, then cover and cook in the oven for about 30 minutes, or until cooked. Serve garnished with lightly boiled peas and halves of hard-boiled eggs.

Murg Biryani
Chicken Biryani from Lucknow

Origin Awadh
Preparation time 3 hours
Cooking time 35 minutes
Serves 6

For the chicken

180g / 6oz (¾ cup) ghee
1 tablespoon ground cumin
1½ teaspoons ground green cardamom
1 teaspoon ground cinnamon
¾ teaspoon ground cloves
very small pinch of ground nutmeg
1 cup Boiled Onion Paste (see page 57)
2½ tablespoons almond paste
1½ tablespoons Ginger Paste (see page 57)
1 tablespoon Garlic Paste (see page 57)
1½ tablespoons Poppy Seed Paste (see page 58)
2 teaspoons red chilli powder
1kg / 2¼lb chicken breast and leg pieces
175ml / 6fl oz (¾ cup) natural (plain) yoghurt, whisked
salt

For the rice

¾ teaspoon saffron
1 tablespoon milk
600g / 1lb 5oz (3¼ cups) basmati rice, rinsed and drained
3 cinnamon sticks, about 2.5cm / 1 inch long
7 green cardamom pods
2½ tablespoons ghee
2 onions, sliced
1 teaspoon kewra water or rosewater
175ml / 6fl oz (¾ cup) single (light) cream
3 tablespoons raisins
about 150g / 5oz dough (optional), for sealing the lid (see page 783)

For the rice, put the saffron in a small bowl, add the milk and soak until required.

For the chicken, heat the ghee in a large, heavy-based pan over high heat, add all the spices, the pastes and the chilli powder. Pour in 250ml / 8fl oz (1 cup) water if the mixture sticks to the base (bottom) and fry for about 2 minutes, or until the oil separates out and rises to the top. Now add the chicken, season with salt and continue stirring over high heat until the spices coat the chicken pieces. This will take about 6–7 minutes. Reduce the heat, add the whisked yoghurt and cook until the chicken is tender and the sauce has a thick consistency.

Bring a deep pan of water to the boil, add the rice, cinnamon and cardamom pods and cook for about 12–15 minutes, or until the rice is almost done and all the water is absorbed.

Heat the ghee in a flat, heavy-based pan or pot over medium heat, add the sliced onions and fry for about 5–7 minutes, or until golden brown. Remove from the pan and set aside.

Spread the rice over the base of the pan, then pour over half of the saffron milk, half of the kewra water and half the cream. Spread half of the cooked chicken over the top and repeat the process for the second layer. Now cover with a tight-fitting lid and seal with dough, if using, or foil. Put a couple of pieces of hot charcoal on top of the lid, if you like, and leave to stand until cooked. Alternatively, omit the charcoal and cook over very low heat for 30–35 minutes, or until cooked. Uncover, adjust the seasoning, if necessary, then sprinkle over the reserved fried onions and raisins to garnish.

Odi Pulao
Andhra Chicken Pulao

Origin Andhra Pradesh
Preparation time 1¾ hours
Cooking time 40 minutes
Serves 8

For the chicken

2 × 750-g / 1lb 8-oz chickens

3 large onions, sliced

250g / 9oz (1 cup) ghee

2 large tomatoes, chopped

1 tablespoon fresh ginger, ground

½ tablespoon ground garlic

8 green chillies, slit in half lengthways and de-seeded

2 cinnamon sticks

10 cloves

6 cardamom pods

3 bay leaves

375ml / 13fl oz (1½ cups) natural (plain) yoghurt

125ml / 4½fl oz (½ cup) coconut milk, fresh
    (see page 781) or canned

12 cashew nuts

1 tablespoon poppy seeds

1 tablespoon chironji kernels

juice of 4 limes

salt

For the rice

1kg / 2¼lb (5⅓ cups) basmati rice, rinsed and drained

7 cloves

5 green cardamom pods

2 cinnamon sticks

½ teaspoon caraway seeds

4 bay leaves

125g / 4oz (½ cup) ghee

125ml / 4½fl oz (½ cup) single (light) cream

500ml / 18fl oz (2¼ cups) milk

salt

Cook the chickens in 1–2 large pans of boiling water for about 2 minutes, then drain and rinse in cold water and remove the skin. Cut the chicken into pieces.

Heat the ghee in a large, heavy-based pan over low heat. Add the onions and cook until tender and light brown, stirring constantly. Add the chicken, tomatoes, ginger, garlic, chillies, cinnamon, cloves, cardamom pods and bay leaves, then season with salt. Cook for about 5 minutes, then increase the heat to brown the chicken. Cover and cook over low heat for about 45 minutes, stirring occasionally. When the oil starts to separate, add the yoghurt, stir and simmer again for 8–10 minutes, then add the coconut milk, cashew nuts, poppy seeds, chironji kernels and bring almost to the boil. Add the lime juice, remove from the heat, mix and cover.

Meanwhile, for the rice, soak the rice in a large bowl of salted water for about 20 minutes, then drain. Put 2 litres / 3½ pints (8½ cups) water in a large, heavy-based pan over high heat and add the cloves, cardamom pods, cinnamon, caraway seeds and bay leaves. When the water boils, add the rice and stir so that the rice cooks evenly. Season with salt, reduce the heat slightly, and cook, stirring occasionally, for 15 minutes, or until the rice is two-thirds cooked, then drain and discard the whole spices.

Spread 4 tablespoons ghee over the base (bottom) of a deep, heavy-based pan. Spread half the rice over this, then spread the chicken and sauce over the rice. Cover with the remaining rice, then pour 4 tablespoons ghee on top along with the cream. Pour the milk evenly over the rice, then cover, weigh down the lid and place over low heat for about 40 minutes, or until the rice is cooked.

Sofiyani Pulao
Bohri Muslim Pulao

Origin Gujarat
Preparation time 1 hour, plus marinating time
Cooking time 30 minutes
Serves 4

5 green cardamom pods
5 cloves
2 cinnamon sticks, about 2.5cm / 1 inch long
500g / 1¼lb (2¾ cups) basmati rice, rinsed
4 tablespoons ghee
125ml / 4½fl oz (½ cup) milk
about 150g / 5oz dough (optional), for sealing the lid (see page 783)
salt

For the chicken

2 green chillies, slit in half lengthways and de-seeded
2½ teaspoons Ginger Paste (see page 57)
2 teaspoons Garlic Paste (see page 57)
8 green cardamom pods
5 cloves
2 cinnamon sticks, about 2.5cm / 1 inch long
2 teaspoons lemon juice
4 tablespoons ghee
16 chicken drumsticks
3 tablespoons almond paste
3 tablespoons Khoya (see page 58) or milk powder (dry milk)
375ml / 13fl oz (1½ cups) natural (plain) yoghurt, whisked
salt

Preheat the oven to 180°C/350°F/Gas Mark 4.

For the chicken, mix the chillies and the remaining ingredients, except the chicken, almond paste and khoya, with the yoghurt in a large bowl. Add the drumsticks and mix well ensuring they are evenly coated. Set aside to marinate.

Transfer the drumsticks together with the yoghurt mixture to a large, heavy-based pan and bring to the boil. Reduce the heat to medium-low and simmer, stirring occasionally and very carefully, for 25 minutes until the yoghurt is absorbed, ensuring the chicken does not break up or change colour. Add the almond paste and khoya, then stir quickly to incorporate and remove from the heat. Adjust the seasoning, if necessary, and set aside.

Bring 1.5 litres / 2½ pints (6¼ cups) water to the boil in a large, heavy-based pan. Add the cardamom pods, cloves and cinnamon and season with salt. Stir, add the rice, bring to the boil and continue to boil, stirring occasionally, for 15 minutes, or until almost cooked. Drain and set aside.

Arrange the chicken in a large, heavy-based pan, spread the partially cooked rice on top, pour on the ghee and milk, then cover and seal with dough, if using, or foil. Put a couple of hot charcoals on top of the lid and leave to stand or omit the charcoal and cook in the oven for 30 minutes or until the rice is cooked. Break the dough seal just before serving.

Ar Sawchiar
Chicken Pulao with Mustard Leaves

Origin Tribal North East India
Preparation time 40 minutes, plus soaking time
Cooking time 55 minutes
Serves 8

200g / 7oz (1 cup) basmati rice, rinsed and drained
1 whole chicken
1 green cardamom pod
1 black cardamom pod
2 bay leaves
2 fresh red chillies
3 sticks (ribs) celery leaves, chopped
1 handful mustard leaves
½ teaspoon ground black pepper
2 tablespoons rice beer or rice wine
salt

Soak the rice in a bowl of water for 30 minutes, then drain. Roast the chicken over a charcoal fire for about 20–30 minutes, turning frequently until the skin turns brown. Alternatively, roast the chicken in an oven preheated to 120°C/250°F/Gas Mark 1 for 20 minutes.

Remove the chicken and cut into 8 pieces.
Bring 600ml / 1 pint (2½ cups) water to the boil in a large pan, add the cardamom pods, bay leaves, red chillies, celery, leeks and mustard leaves, then reduce the heat and simmer for 15 minutes. Add the rice and bring to the boil, then simmer for 10 minutes, or until half done. Add the chicken and simmer for 20–30 minutes or until the rice is soft and the chicken is cooked through. Stir in the rice beer or wine.

Murg Pulao
Chicken Pulao

Origin Punjab
Preparation time 1½ hours, plus soaking time
Cooking time 45 minutes
Serves 8

1 × 1-kg / 2¼-lb chicken, cut into 10–14 pieces,
    neck, bones and giblets reserved
2–3 bay leaves
1 cinnamon stick, about 5cm / 2 inches long
6 black cardamom pods
6 cloves
1½ teaspoons black peppercorns
½ teaspoon cumin seeds
500g / 1lb 2oz (2¾ cups) basmati rice, rinsed
    and drained
10 cloves garlic
250g / 9oz (1 cup) ghee
2 onions, sliced
1 × 2.5-cm / 1-inch piece fresh ginger, peeled and
    finely chopped
2 teaspoons ground coriander
6 cloves, ground
6 green cardamom pods
100ml / 3½fl oz (½ cup) natural (plain) yoghurt,
    whisked
salt

Put the chicken neck, bones and giblets in a large, heavy-based pan with the bay leaves, cinnamon, black cardamom pods, cloves, peppercorns and cumin. Pour in 2 litres / 3½ pints (8½ cups) water and bring to the boil. Reduce the heat and simmer for 1 hour. Strain and discard the bones and spices. Measure the stock and set aside.

Soak the rice in a bowl of water for 20 minutes, then drain and set aside.

Put the garlic in a small blender or food processor and process, adding a little water if necessary, to make a paste. Set aside.

Heat the ghee in a large, heavy-based pan over medium heat, add the onions and fry for about 5–7 minutes, or until golden brown. Stir in the garlic, ginger, coriander and cloves and cook for 1–2 minutes. Add the green cardamom pods and yoghurt and season with salt, then cook for 5–7 minutes. Add the chicken pieces and rice and cook for 10 minutes. Pour in enough chicken stock to come 2.5cm / 1 inch above the surface of the rice, then reduce the heat to low, cover and cook for 20–30 minutes, or until the rice is soft and the chicken is cooked. Garnish with the onions.

📷 p.608

Venu Pongal
Rice with Moong Dal

Origin Tamil Nadu
Preparation time 15–35 minutes
Cooking time 20 minutes
Serves 8

150g / 5oz (¾ cup) moong dal, rinsed and drained,
    then roasted
200g / 7oz (1 cup) rice, rinsed and drained
3 teaspoons ghee
1 teaspoon black peppercorns
1 teaspoon cumin seeds
½ teaspoon asafoetida
pinch of ground turmeric
20 cashew nuts
10–15 curry leaves
salt

Mix the roasted moong dal and rice together, add water, then cook in a pressure cooker until soft. Alternatively, bring a large pan of water to the boil, add the dal and rice and cook for about 20 minutes, or until the dal and rice are soft.

Heat ½ teaspoon ghee in a large, heavy-based pan over medium heat, add the peppercorns, cumin seeds, asafoetida and turmeric, then season with salt and stir-fry for about 1 minute, or until the seeds start to splutter. Remove from the heat and add the cooked dal and rice and mix well.

Heat ½ teaspoon ghee in a frying pan (skillet) over medium heat, add the cashew nuts and fry for about 1–2 minutes, then add to the pongal. Heat ¼ teaspoon ghee in the frying pan, add the curry leaves and stir-fry for about 30 seconds, then add to the pongal. Add the rest of the ghee and mix well.

※ ※ / 📷 p.548

Bisi Bele Huli Anna
Rice with Lentils

Origin Karnataka
Preparation time 50 minutes–1 hour
Cooking time 15–20 minutes
Serves 6

10 dried red chillies
½ teaspoon coriander seeds
½ teaspoon fenugreek seeds
¼ dried coconut, ground
1 tablespoon chana dal, rinsed and drained
2 tablespoons vegetable oil
250g / 9oz (2 small) tomatoes, chopped into 4-cm / 1½-inch pieces
2 (vegetable) drumsticks, peeled and cut into 5-cm / 2-inch pieces
2 carrots, chopped into 4-cm / 1½-inch pieces
4 baby aubergines (eggplant), trimmed and chopped into 4-cm / 1½-inch pieces
10 French (green) beans, topped and tailed (trimmed) and chopped into 4-cm / 1½-inch pieces
4 potatoes, chopped into 4-cm / 1½-inch pieces
250g / 9oz (3 small) onions
125ml / 4½fl oz (½ cup) Tamarind Extract (see page 58)
2 green chillies, de-seeded and chopped into 4-cm / 1½-inch pieces
¼ teapoon ground turmeric
400g / 14oz (2¼ cups) basmati rice, rinsed and drained
200g / 7oz (1 cup) whole (sabut) masoor dal
salt

For the tempering

1 tablespoon vegetable oil
10 curry leaves
1 teaspoon mustard seeds
pinch of asafoetida
6 dried red chillies

Roast the dried red chillies, coriander seeds, fenugreek seeds, coconut and chana dal lightly on a tawa or in a dry frying pan (skillet) for about 1 minute or until roasted, then transfer to a blender or food processor and process until ground. Set aside.

Heat the oil in a deep, heavy-based pan over medium heat, add the vegetables including the onions and fry for 3–4 minutes. Add the tamarind extract together with the roasted ground spices and the turmeric, then season with salt.

Heat the oil for the tempering in a frying pan, add the curry leaves, mustard seeds, asafoetida and red chillies and stir-fry for about 1 minute, or until dark brown, then add to the vegetables. Add the rice and dal and pour in about 2 litres / 3½ pints (8 cups) water. The water and tamarind extract should be about three times the quantity of the rice and dal. Cook for about 15–20 minutes, or until the rice and dal are soft.

Moong Dal Khichari
Khichari with Moong Dal

Origin West Bengal
Preparation time 10 minutes
Cooking time 20 minutes
Serves 4

100g / 3½oz (½ cup) rice, rinsed and drained
100g / 3½oz (½ cup) moong dal, rinsed and drained
1 tablespoon Ginger Paste (see page 57)
2 teaspoons aniseed paste
2 teaspoons ghee
1 teaspoon aniseeds
2 bay leaves
salt

Bring a deep pan of water to the boil, then add the rice, dal, ginger paste and aniseed paste and season with salt. Cook until the mixture reaches a soft thick consistency.

Heat the ghee in a frying pan (skillet) over high heat, then reduce the heat. Add the aniseeds and bay leaves and stir-fry for about 1 minute, or until the bay leaves change colour. Pour over the rice mixture and cover.

Sarvari
Rice with Urad Dal, Chickpeas
(Garbanzo Beans) or Peas

Origin Hyderabad
Preparation time 1 hour, plus soaking time
Cooking time 30–45 minutes
Serves 4

100g / 3½oz (½ cup) chickpeas, urad dal or peas, rinsed and drained
¼ teaspoon bicarbonate of soda (baking soda) (optional)
150g / 5oz (¾ cup) basmati rice, rinsed and drained
3½ tablespoons ghee
1 teaspoon ground cumin
2–4 cloves
salt

If you are using chickpeas or urad dal, soak them overnight in a bowl of water with the bicarbonate of soda.

The next day, rinse the chickpeas or urad dal in fresh water, then cook in a heavy-based pan of boiling water for about 20–40 minutes, or until soft, then drain. Set aside. If you are using peas, cook them in a pan of boiling water for about 5–7 minutes, or until soft, then drain and set aside.

Soak the rice in a bowl of water for 1 hour, then drain.

Cook the rice in a large pan of boiling water for about 18–20 minutes, or until done. When cooked, drain and turn the rice out on a thali or plate and sprinkle over some salt. Heat the ghee in a frying pan (skillet) over medium heat, add the cumin and cloves and stir-fry for about 1 minute, or until the cumin seeds start to splutter, then pour over the rice. Now add either the chickpeas, urad dal or peas and mix well with a ladle or wooden spoon, being careful not to break the rice. Return the rice mixture to the pan and cover. Place a few hot charcoals on the lid and leave until heated through. Alternatively, cook over very low heat for about 5 minutes, or until hot.

Chane ki Dal ki Tehari
Rice Cooked with Chana Dal

Origin Awadh
Preparation time 30 minutes, plus soaking and standing time
Cooking time 20–25 minutes
Serves 8

200g / 7oz (1 cup) chana dal, rinsed and drained
500g / 1lb 2oz (2¾ cups) basmati rice, rinsed and drained
200g / 7oz (¾ cup) ghee
2 bay leaves
10 cloves
6–8 green cardamom pods
2 cinnamon sticks, about 2.5cm / 1 inch long
½ teaspoon black peppercorns
salt

Soak the dal in a large bowl of water for 8–10 hours, then drain and leave to stand for 10 minutes. Soak the rice in a large bowl of water for 15–20 minutes, then drain and leave to stand for 10 minutes.

Heat the ghee in a large, heavy-based pan over medium heat, add the bay leaves and spices and stir-fry for 1–2 minutes. Stir in the dal, then reduce the heat, cover and cook for 5 minutes.

Add the rice to the pan and season with salt. Stir for 1 minute, then pour in enough water to come about 2.5cm / 1 inch above the surface of the rice. Reduce the heat to low, cover and cook for 20–25 minutes, or until the rice and dal are soft.

Discard the bay leaves and cinnamon before serving.

DESSERTS

Perhaps the best-known Indian desserts are milk based – such as sweetened yoghurts, rice puddings and creamy kulfi – but there is a world of other tastes to explore, from sticky, deep-fried morsels dripping in syrup, to sesame cakes and sweet dishes made from vegetables and fruit.

8
—

Desserts

📷 p.673

Khopra Paak
Coconut Toffee

Origin Coastal
Preparation time 20 minutes, plus standing and cooling time
Cooking time 30 minutes
Makes about 34

400g / 14oz (5 cups) grated fresh coconut
125ml / 4½fl oz (½ cup) heavy (double) cream
1 tablespoon vegetable oil or ghee
300g / 11oz (1½ cups) sugar
150g / 5oz Khoya (see page 58), grated
1 teaspoon ground green cardamom
2 tablespoons unsalted pistachio nuts, blanched and slivered, to decorate

Mix the coconut and cream together in a large bowl and set aside for about 30 minutes. Brush a large baking tray (pan) lightly with the oil or ghee.

Put a pan over low heat, pour in the coconut-cream mixture and cook for about 10 minutes.

Add the sugar and khoya and continue cooking over low heat for about 20 minutes.

Sprinkle over the ground cardamom, then mix well and pour into the prepared baking tray. Decorate with the pistachios. Allow to cool and set, then cut into desired shapes.

Khoobani ka Meetha
Stewed Apricots with Clotted Cream

Origin Hyderabad
Preparation time 1½ hours, plus soaking and cooling time
Cooking time 15 minutes
Serves 10

500g / 1lb 2oz (2¾ cups) dried apricots, preferably Hunza
150g / 5oz (¾ cup) sugar
250g / 9oz (1 cup) clotted cream or heavy (double) cream

Put the dried apricots in a bowl, add 75g / 2½oz (⅓ cup) sugar, then pour in enough water to cover and soak overnight.

The next day, put the apricots in a pan together with the soaking water and bring to the boil. Reduce the heat and simmer for about 1 hour, or until the apricots are soft and pulpy.

Remove from the heat and allow to cool. When cool, remove and discard the stones (pits) and mash the apricots well.

Cook the mashed apricots with the remaining sugar in a large pan of 500ml / 18fl oz (2¼ cups) boiling water for about 10 minutes over medium heat, stirring constantly. Serve with clotted cream.

Palpayasam
Rice Flour Dumplings in Sweet Milk

Origin Kerala
Preparation time 1 hour, plus cooling time
Cooking time 30 minutes
Makes 15

200g / 7oz (1⅓ cups) rice flour
3 tablespoons groundnut (peanut) oil, plus more for deep-frying
1 litre / 1¾ pints (4¼ cups) milk
125g / 4oz (½ cup) sugar
1 teaspoon ground green cardamom
½ teaspoon ground nutmeg

Put the flour into a large bowl, add the oil and mix in with your fingers until well incorporated, then mix in enough water to make a soft dough. Knead the dough on a lightly floured work surface for about 5 minutes, then divide into 15 pieces and roll each into a small ball.

Heat enough oil for deep-frying in a kadhai or deep, heavy-based pan to 180°C/350°F, or until a cube of bread browns in 30 seconds. Carefully lower a dumpling into the hot oil and deep-fry for 2–3 minutes until golden brown. Remove and drain on kitchen paper (paper towels). Repeat with the remaining dumplings, one at a time.

Bring the milk to the boil in a large, heavy-based pan and boil for about 30 minutes until it is reduced to half its original volume. Add the sugar and boil until reduced to one-third. Add the ground cardamom and nutmeg and remove from the heat. Allow to cool until lukewarm.

When the milk mixture is lukewarm, add the dumplings and allow to soak for a few minutes. Serve warm or cold.

Rava Laddu
Sweetened Semolina & Coconut Balls

Origin Karnataka/Tamil Nadu
Preparation time 20 minutes, plus cooling time
Cooking time 15 minutes
Makes 15–20

125g / 4oz (½ cup) ghee
280g / 10oz (1⅔ cups) semolina (semolina flour)
120g / 4½oz (1 cup) wholemeal (whole wheat) flour
1 dried coconut, grated
600g / 1lb 5oz (3 cups) sugar
½ teaspoon lime juice
pinch of saffron threads, warmed and ground
50g / 2oz (⅓ cup) raisins or sultanas (golden raisins), fried
50g / 2oz (⅓ cup) cashew nuts, fried

Heat the ghee in a frying pan (skillet) over medium heat, add the semolina and fry lightly for about 2 minutes. Remove from the pan. Add the flour to the pan and fry lightly for about 2 minutes.

Put the coconut, semolina and flour in a mortar or spice grinder and pound with a pestle or process briefly until ground.

Pour 500ml / 18fl oz (2¼ cups) water into a large, heavy-based pan, add the sugar and heat gently, stirring, until the sugar has dissolved. Increase the heat and bring to the boil. Continue to boil, removing the scum that rises to the surface with a slotted spoon, until it reaches two-thread consistency (see page 59). Stir in the lime juice. Add the semolina mixture, saffron, raisins or sultanas and cashew nuts and cook over medium heat for 4–5 minutes until thick. Remove from the heat and allow to cool slightly, then while the mixture is still warm, pinch off pieces of the mixture and roll into walnut-sized balls.

Stewed Apricots with
Clotted Cream   p.671

Hanging
Yoghurt p.782

Creamy, Chilled
Yoghurt   p.693

Syrup–soaked
Pancakes   p.689

Coconut Rice
Pudding p.696

Dough of and finished
Saffron, Coconut &
Cashew Biscuits P.714

Carrot Dessert p.715

Thandai, p.721

Milk-based Sherbet p.721

Sweet Mango Drink p.724

Masala Tea
p.726

Tangy Tamarind &
Pepper Aperitif   p.727

p.676

Yel Adai
Coconut & Rice Pancakes

Origin Tamil Nadu/Kerala
Preparation time 1 hour, plus soaking time
Cooking time 20 minutes
Serves 4

500g / 1lb 2oz (2¾ cups) rice, rinsed and drained

4 banana leaves (optional)

250g / 9oz (1¼ cups) jaggery or soft brown sugar

½ teaspoon lime juice

4 tablespoons grated fresh coconut

150g / 5oz (⅔ cup) ghee

1 teaspoon ground green cardamom

salt

Soak the rice in a bowl of water for 20 minutes. Drain and set aside. Cut the banana leaves into 10-cm / 4-inch squares and set aside. If you can't find banana leaves, you could use pieces of foil or clean, moist muslin (cheesecloth).

To make a syrup, pour 750ml / 1¼ pints (3¼ cups) water into a large, heavy-based pan, add the jaggery or sugar and heat gently, stirring until the jaggery has dissolved. Increase the heat and boil. Continue to boil, removing the scum as it rises to the top with a slotted spoon, until the syrup is reduced to one-quarter of its original volume and reaches one-thread consistency (see page 59). Stir in the lime juice.

Add the grated coconut to the syrup and cook over medium heat for about 7 minutes, then stir in the ghee, reserving about 2 tablespoons.

Put the rice in a blender or food processor and process, adding enough water to make a batter of dropping consistency. Season with salt and add the ground cardamom.

Smear the reserved ghee over the banana leaves. Heat a tawa, griddle or heavy-based frying pan (skillet), then briefly place the leaves on the hot pan to soften. Pour some rice batter into the centre of each banana leaf, then spread the coconut syrup over the top and fold into parcels.

Steam the parcels in a steamer for 20 minutes. If you don't have a steamer, use a large pan with a lid and place an upside-down plate in the base (bottom). Pour in enough water so it stays below the top of the plate. Place the parcels on a plate and carefully put the plate on top of the upside-down plate, cover and steam for 20 minutes. Serve hot or cold.

Malpoa
Syrup-soaked Pancakes

Origin West Bengal
Preparation time 15–20 minutes, plus cooling time
Cooking time 20–30 minutes
Makes 8

250ml / 8fl oz (1 cup) natural (plain) yoghurt

2 tablespoons plain (all-purpose) flour

1 teaspoon aniseeds

200g / 7oz (1 cup) sugar

125g / 4oz (½ cup) ghee

Mix the yoghurt and flour together in a bowl, add the aniseeds and mix well.

To make the syrup, pour 500ml / 18fl oz (2¼ cups) cold water into a large pan, add the sugar and heat over low heat, stirring, until the sugar has dissolved. Increase the heat and boil until the syrup reaches one-thread consistency (see page 59). Remove from the heat and allow to cool.

Heat the ghee in a kadhai, wok or deep, heavy-based pan over medium heat. Add a tablespoon of yoghurt batter at a time and fry for 2–3 minutes until brown and crisp at the edges. Remove the mini pancakes from the pan using a slotted spoon and drain on kitchen paper (paper towels).

Dip the pancakes in the syrup, one at a time, as they are fried.

Ale Bele
Coconut-filled Pancakes

Origin Coastal
Preparation time 15–20 minutes, plus standing time
Cooking time 15–30 minutes
Serves 4

180ml / 6½fl oz (¾ cup) milk
125g / 4oz (1 cup) plain (all-purpose) flour
pinch of salt
1 egg, beaten
1 teaspoon vegetable oil
2 tablespoons butter

For the filling

2 tablespoons sugar
1 tablespoon coconut water
1 half-ripe tender coconut, grated
few sultanas (golden raisins) and cashew nuts, chopped
seeds of 3 green cardamom pods, ground

Mix the milk and 5 tablespoons water together in a bowl. To make the batter, sift the flour and salt into a large bowl, add the egg, milk and water mixture and oil and whisk together. Let the batter stand for about 2 hours, then just before cooking dilute the batter with 2–3 tablespoons water.

Melt the butter in a large frying pan (skillet) over very low heat. Pour a spoonful of batter into the pan and tilt the pan to spread evenly. Cook for 1–2 minutes, or until the batter has just set, then turn with a spatula and cook for 1–2 minutes on the other side. Remove from the pan and keep warm while you repeat the process until the batter is used up.

To make the filling, put the sugar and coconut water in a heavy-based pan and stir until the sugar has dissolved, then bring to the boil and boil until the syrup thickens. Stir in the remaining ingredients.

To complete the pancakes, place a little filling along one side of each pancake and roll up.

Patisapta
Sweet Pancakes Filled with Dried Fruit

Origin West Bengal
Preparation time 30 minutes
Cooking time 15–20 minutes
Serves 4

few saffron threads
3½ tablespoons hung natural (plain) yoghurt (see page 793) or Chhena, crumbled (see page 59)
150g / 5oz (1 cup) rice flour
3–4 green cardamom pods

For the filling

4 dried figs
3 tablespoons raisins
2 dates, stoned (pitted)

Soak the saffron in a few tablespoons of water. Set aside. Soak the figs for the filling in a bowl of water for 30 minutes.

To make the filling, chop all the ingredients finely, then put into a bowl, add the yoghurt or chhena and mix to combine.

Put the flour in a large bowl and stir in 150ml / ¼ pint (⅔ cup) water, the saffron water and cardamom pods, and whisk to make a batter. Heat a non-stick frying pan (skillet) over low-medium heat. Gently pour in a ladleful of the batter and tilt the pan so the batter evenly coats the base (bottom) of the pan to make crepe-like pancakes. Cook for 1–2 minutes, or until light brown, then turn with a spatula and cook for 1–2 minutes on the other side. Remove from the pan as soon as they start blistering.

Place a portion of the filling in the centre of each pancake, then pat to spread evenly and fold into parcels.

📷 p.677

Kulfi
Ice Cream

Origin Delhi/Punjab/Awadh
Preparation time 50 minutes, plus cooling
and freezing time
Serves 4

2 litres / 3½ pints (8½ cups) full cream (whole) milk

150g / 5oz (¾ cup) sugar

50g / 1¾oz (⅓ cup) ground almonds

few drops kewra water

Bring the milk to the boil in a large, heavy-based
pan, then reduce the heat and continue to cook,
stirring frequently, for 45 minutes, until the milk
is reduced to less than half its volume. Remove from
the heat, add the sugar and stir until the sugar
has dissolved. Add the ground almonds and kewra
water and allow to cool.

When the milk mixture is cool, pour it into kulfi
moulds leaving about a 2.5-cm / 1-inch space at the
top for the frozen kulfi to expand. Seal firmly with
lids and freeze for 8–10 hours, or until frozen.

To serve, hold the cones under tepid water briefly,
then remove the lid from the mould, run a sharp
knife around the inside edge and slip out the kulfi
onto a plate. Kulfi must be served semi-frozen and
not soft like ice cream.

Kulfi is a very popular Indian dessert and comes
in many different flavours, such as mango,
cardamom and pistachio. Use this recipe as a base
and experiment by adding your favourite flavours.
Special lidded containers, called kulfi moulds,
are used for this dessert, but you can use either
individual freezerproof moulds or one large
freezerproof container with a lid.

Pista Kulfi
Pistachio-flavoured Ice Cream

Origin Delhi
Preparation time 45 minutes, plus cooling
and freezing time
Serves 8

1 litre / 1¾ pints (4¼ cups) milk

100g / 3½oz (½ cup) sugar

3 tablespoons unsalted pistachios, crushed

125ml / 4½fl oz (½ cup) double (heavy) cream

¼ teaspoon kewra water or 1 tablespoon rosewater

¼ teaspoon ground green cardamom

Bring the milk to the boil in a large, heavy-based
pan and cook for 25 minutes to reduce to 750ml /
1¼ pints (3¼ cups). Put the sugar in a heatproof bowl,
add 125–180ml / 4½ –6½fl oz (½–¾ cup) hot milk
and stir until smooth. Mix with the rest of the milk,
then stir and cook over low heat until thick and
creamy. Add the crushed pistachios and cook for
1 minute, then remove from the heat and allow to
cool completely.

Whip the cream in a large bowl until smooth and
thick but not stiff, then mix the cream, kewra water
or rosewater, and cardamom into the milk and
pour into cone-shaped containers or kulfi moulds,
leaving about a 2.5-cm / 1-inch space at the top for
the frozen kulfi to expand. Seal firmly with lids and
freeze for 8–10 hours, or until frozen.

To serve, hold the cones under tepid water briefly,
then remove the lid from the mould, run a sharp
knife around the inside edge and slip out the kulfi
on desserts plates or in shallow bowls. Kulfi must
be served semi-frozen and not soft like ice cream.
Cut into quarters, if you like.

Kalakand
Creamy Milk Sweets

Origin Rajasthan
Preparation time 10 minutes, plus setting time
Cooking time 5 minutes
Makes 1kg / 2¼lb

ghee or butter, for greasing

1kg / 2¼lb Khoya (see page 58), grated

200g / 7oz (1 cup) sugar

1 tablespoon unsalted pistachio nuts, blanched
    and slivered

Grease a large baking tray (sheet) with ghee or butter.

Heat the khoya in a kildhai or large, heavy-based
pan, then bring to the boil over medium heat,
stirring constantly with a flat spoon for 5 minutes.
Remove from the heat, add the sugar and stir
until dissolved.

Transfer the mixture immediately to the greased tray
and level with a spatula. Sprinkle the pistachios
over the top and thump the tray on a table or on
the floor to remove any air pockets. Leave in a cool
place to set for 15 minutes, then cut into pieces.

Gil e Behisht
Milky Clay of Paradise

Origin Hyderabad
Preparation time 15 minutes
Cooking time 30 minutes
Serves 7–8

1 teaspoon saffron threads

2 tablespoons milk

2 tablespoons raisins

150g / 5oz (1 cup) rice flour

125g / 4oz (½ cup) ghee

500g / 1lb 2oz (4 cups) icing (confectioners') sugar

100g / 3½oz Khoya (see page 58), grated

250ml / 8fl oz (1 cup) hung natural (plain) yoghurt
    (see page 793)

1 teaspoon ground green cardamom

Put the saffron in a small bowl, add the milk and
soak until required.

Put the raisins in another bowl, add 2 tablespoons
water and soak for 15 minutes. Drain.

Bring a medium-sized pan of water to the boil, add
the rice flour, ghee and sugar and cook for about
10 minutes, stirring constantly to make sure it does
not stick to the base (bottom) of the pan and burn,
until the mixture is a uniform consistency. Sprinkle
over the saffron mixture.

Mix the khoya and yoghurt together in a bowl, then
beat well, adding a little lukewarm water to thin
the mixture slightly. Add this to the contents of the
pan and cook over very low heat until the dish
has the consistency of porridge. Remove from the
heat and allow to cool.

Sprinkle the soaked raisins and ground cardamom
on top before serving.

Nimish
Frothy Delight

Origin Awadh
Preparation time 2 hours, plus chilling time
Serves 4–6

500ml / 18fl oz (2¼ cups) full cream (whole) milk
100ml / 3½fl oz (½ cup) heavy (double) cream
½ teaspoon cream of tartar
50g / 1¾oz (⅓ cup) icing (confectioners') sugar
¼ teaspoon rosewater
1 tablespoon unsalted pistachio nuts, blanched
    and slivered

Blend the full cream milk, cream and cream of tartar together in a large bowl, then chill in the refrigerator overnight.

Early the next day, remove the bowl from the refrigerator and add 4 teaspoons icing sugar and the rosewater, then whisk at high speed. Transfer the foam on top of the bowl to a tray (pan) and sprinkle with a little icing sugar. Repeat the process until all the milk is used up. This dessert can be served in small bowls. Sprinkle slivered pistachios on top.

📷 p.675

Shrikhand
Creamy, Chilled Yoghurt

Origin Maharashtra
Preparation time 20 minutes, plus chilling time
Serves 6

1 teaspoon saffron threads
1 tablespoon milk
1 litre / 1¾ pints (4¼ cups) hung natural (plain)
    yoghurt (see page 793)
100g / 3½oz (½ cup) caster (superfine) sugar
1 teaspoon green cardamom seeds, crushed
8–10 unsalted pistachio nuts, blanched and slivered

Put the saffron in a small bowl, add the milk and soak until required. Put the hung yoghurt in a bowl, gradually add the sugar and whisk. Stir in the saffron mixture and then sprinkle over the cardamom seeds and pistachio nuts and whisk. Chill in the refrigerator before serving.

Mishti Doi
Sweet Yoghurt

Origin West Bengal
Preparation time 10 minutes, plus setting and chilling time
Cooking time 15 minutes
Serves 10

500ml / 18fl oz (2¼ cups) milk
100g / 3½oz (½ cup) sugar
1 tablespoon natural (plain) yoghurt

Bring the milk to the boil in a large, heavy-based pan and boil until reduced to half its volume. Stir in the sugar and reduce the heat to low, stirring, until the sugar has dissolved completely. Remove from the heat and set aside until the milk is lukewarm.

Heat the reduced milk in a heavy-based pan. Add the yoghurt and stir thoroughly, then remove from the heat, cover and set aside in a warm place to set.

When the yoghurt is set, transfer to the refrigerator for about 2 hours before serving.

Payesh
Sweet Rice & Milk

Origin West Bengal
Preparation time 10 minutes
Cooking time 30 minutes
Serves 4

1 tablespoon rice
green cardamom pods to taste
1 litre / 1¾ pints (4¼ cups) milk
75g / 2½oz (⅓ cup) sugar

Put the rice in a blender and process until ground, then remove and set aside. Put the cardamom pods in a spice grinder and process until ground. Set aside.

Bring the milk to the boil in a deep, heavy-based pan and add the ground rice. Cook, stirring frequently, for 20 minutes, or until reduced by half and almost blended. Remove from the heat, add the sugar, stir well, then return to low heat for 5 minutes, taking care that the payesh does not boil. Sprinkle the ground green cardamom over the top.

📷 p.678

Kheer
Rice Pudding

Origin Punjab/Delhi/Awadh
Preparation time 10 minutes, plus soaking time
Cooking time 1 hour 10 minutes
Serves 4

4 tablespoons rice
1 litre / 1¾ pints (4¼ cups) milk
200g / 7oz (1 cup) sugar
10 unsalted pistachios
10 almonds
4 green cardamom pods, crushed
1 teaspoon kewra water
pinch of saffron threads
4 edible silver leaves, to decorate

Soak the rice in a bowl of water for 20 minutes. Drain and set aside.

Bring the milk to the boil in a heavy-based pan over low heat and cook for 30 minutes until reduced by half. Add the rice, then bring to the boil and boil for 1 minute. Reduce the heat and continue to simmer, stirring gently, for about 30 minutes.

Sprinkle over the sugar, nuts, crushed cardamom, kewra water and saffron. Mix, remove from the heat and decorate with edible silver leaf.

Rabri
Thickened Milk

Origin Awadh
Preparation time 15 minutes, plus chilling time
Cooking time 1½ hours
Serves 8–10

4 litres / 7 pints (17 cups) full cream (whole) milk
300g / 11oz (1½ cups) sugar
10 green cardamoms seeds, ground
2 drops of rosewater
15–20 blanched almonds, slivered
15–20 unsalted pistachio nuts, blanched and slivered

Bring the milk to the boil in a large, heavy-based pan, then reduce the heat and simmer for 1 hour, stirring frequently, until the milk is very thick and reduced to about a quarter of its original volume. Keep scraping the film of milk that clings to the sides of the pan, and stir it back into the simmering milk. Add the sugar, then remove from the heat and stir to dissolve.

Sprinkle over the ground cardamom, rosewater and nuts and chill in the refrigerator for 1–2 hours before serving.

Badaam ki Kheer
Almond Milk Pudding

Origin Punjab
Preparation time 15 minutes
Cooking time 25–30 minutes
Serves 6

1 litre / 1¾ pints (4¼ cups) milk
200g / 7oz (1½ cups) blanched almonds, slivered
100g / 3½oz (½ cup) sugar
¼ teaspoon ground green cardamom

Bring the milk to the boil in a large, heavy-based pan, then reduce the heat and simmer for 15–20 minutes, or until thickened. Add the sliced almonds and cook for a further 10 minutes.

Remove the pan from the heat, add the sugar and stir to dissolve, then stir in the ground cardamom.

Bajre ki Kheer
Pearl Millet & Milk Pudding

Origin Rajasthan
Preparation time 10 minutes
Cooking time 40–50 minutes
Serves 6–8

pinch of saffron threads
1 tablespoon ghee
4 tablespoons millet grains
1 litre / 1¾ pints (4¼ cups) milk
100g / 3½oz (½ cup) sugar

Put the saffron in a small bowl, add 2–3 teaspons water and stir to mix, then set aside.

Heat the ghee in a heavy-based pan over medium heat, add the millet and fry for 1–2 minutes.

Bring the milk to the boil in a separate large, heavy-based pan, add the millet and reduce the heat to low. Cook, stirring occasionally, for 40–50 minutes, or until thickened. Remove from the heat, add the sugar and stir to dissolve, then stir the saffron into the pudding. Serve warm.

Rawa Payasam
Semolina & Milk Pudding

Origin Tamil Nadu
Preparation time 10 minutes
Cooking time 10–15 minutes
Serves 4

4 teaspoons ghee
140g / 4¾oz (¾ cup) semolina (semolina flour)
250ml / 8fl oz (1 cup) milk
200g / 7oz (1 cup) sugar
5–6 green cardamom pods, crushed
12–15 cashew nuts, to decorate

Heat the ghee in a heavy-based pan over medium heat, add the semolina and fry for about 2–3 minutes until it is a reddish brown colour. Pour in the milk in a slow stream to avoid lumps and stir well. When the semolina is about to 'set' sprinkle over the sugar and cardamom. Decorate with cashew nuts and serve warm or at room temperature.

Double ka Meetha
Hyderabadi Bread Pudding

Origin Hyderabad
Preparation time 50 minutes
Cooking time 1¼ hours
Serves 10–15

pinch of saffron threads
2 tablespoons rosewater
250g / 9oz (1¼ cups) sugar
½ teaspoon lime juice
500ml / 18fl oz (2¼ cups) milk
125ml / 4½fl oz (½ cup) cream
10 slices white bread
150g / 5oz (⅔ cup) ghee, plus extra, melted for brushing
20 blanched almonds
1 teaspoon unsalted pistachio nuts, blanched and slivered
4–5 edible silver leaves, to decorate

Preheat the oven to 150°C/300°F/Gas Mark 2. Put the saffron in a small bowl add the rosewater and soak until required.

Fill a heavy-based pan with water, add the sugar, and heat over low heat, stirring, until the sugar has completely dissolved. Increase the heat and bring to the boil. Continue to boil, removing the scum that rises to the surface with a slotted spoon, until it reaches a one-thread consistency (see page 59). Stir in the lime juice. Remove from the heat and set aside.

Bring the milk to the boil in another pan with the cream and cook for about 45 minutes, or until reduced by half.

Heat the ghee in a frying pan (skillet) over medium heat, add the bread slices and shallow-fry for 2–3 minutes on both sides until golden. Brush 2 baking trays (pans) with a little ghee. Place the bread slices in the tray and pour the milk, saffron and sugar syrup over them, then sprinkle over the almonds and pistachios. Let stand for 3–5 minutes for the bread to absorb the liquids, then bake in the oven for about 1 hour, or until the liquid dries up. Decorate with edible silver leaf.

p.679

Nariyal ki Kheer
Coconut Rice Pudding

Origin Hyderabad
Preparation time 40 minutes, plus soaking time
Cooking time 35 minutes
Serves 8

100g / 3½oz (½ cup) rice, rinsed and drained
2 fresh coconuts, peeled and grated
250g / 9oz (1¼ cups) sugar
8–10 green cardamom pods, ground
1 tablespoon ghee
2 tablespoons blanched almonds
2 tablespoons unsalted pistachio nuts, blanched
2 tablespoons raisins

Soak the rice in a large bowl of water for 1 hour, then drain.

Put the rice and coconut in a blender or food processor and process, adding a little water to make a thick paste. Transfer the paste to a large, heavy-based pan, and cook over low heat for 10 minutes. Pour in 250ml / 8fl oz (1 cup) water, add the sugar and simmer for 20 minutes, or until the mixture has a porridge-like consistency. Sprinkle over the ground cardamom and mix well. Spoon into a glass bowl.

Heat the ghee in a frying pan (skillet) over low heat, add the nuts and stir-fry for about 3 minutes, or until light brown. Remove and add the raisins to the pan and stir-fry lightly for about 1–2 minutes. Sprinkle over the pudding, then allow to cool completely and serve cold.

Sheer Birinj
Regal Milk & Rice Dessert

Origin Awadh
Preparation time 30 minutes
Cooking time 1 hour
Serves 5–6

3.5 litres / 6 pints (14¾ cups) milk
60g / 2oz (⅓ cup) basmati rice, rinsed and drained
200g / 7oz (1 cup) sugar
200g / 7oz Khoya (see page 58)
1 tablespoon kewra water or rosewater
100g / 3½oz (½ cup) ghee, melted
200g / 7oz (1 cup) clotted cream
50g / 1¾oz Cashew Nut Paste (see page 58)
½ teaspoon ground green cardamom

To decorate

50g / 1¾oz (⅓ cup) blanched almonds, slivered
50g / 1¾oz (⅓ cup) unsalted pistachio nuts, blanched and slivered

Bring the milk to the boil in a large, heavy-based pan, add the rice and cook for about 20 minutes, or until done. Add half the sugar, stir, and cook for few minutes.

Crumble the khoya slowly into the pan, ensuring that there are no lumps. Sprinkle over the kewra water or rosewater and the remaining sugar, stirring constantly, and cook until the mixture thickens and clings to the spoon. Pour in the ghee and stir. Add the clotted cream together with the cashew nut paste. Spoon onto a serving plate, sprinkle over the ground cardamom and decorate with slivered almonds and pistachios.

Zarda
Sweet Yellow Rice

Origin Awadh/Delhi
Preparation time 1 hour
Cooking time 45 minutes
Serves 6–8

½ teaspoon saffron threads

1 tablespoon milk

1kg / 2¼lb (5 cups) sugar

¾ teaspoon lime juice

7 cloves

2 cinnamon sticks

10 small green cardamom pods

4 black cardamom pods

500g / 1lb 2oz (2¾ cups) basmati rice, rinsed
    and drained

100g / 3½oz (½ cup) ghee, melted

2 tablespoons kewra water

150g / 5oz Khoya (see page 58), grated and fried

about 150g / 5oz dough (see page 783) (optional),
    for sealing the lid

To decorate

4 tablespoons almonds

4 tablespoons unsalted pistachio nuts

3 tablespoons raisins

4 edible silver leaves

Put the saffron in a small bowl, add the milk and soak until required.

Put the sugar and 2 litres / 3½ pints (8½ cups) water in a deep, heavy-based pan over low heat and heat gently, stirring until the sugar has completely dissolved. Increase the heat and bring to the boil. Continue to boil, removing the scum as it rises to the top with a slotted spoon, until the syrup reaches one thread consistency (see page 59). Stir in the lime juice. Remove from the heat and set aside.

To make an aromatic stock for the rice, bring about 2 litres / 3½ pints (8½ cups) water to the boil in a large, heavy-based pan and add the cloves, cinnamon, cardamom pods and saffron. Boil over medium heat for about 15 minutes, then strain through a sieve (strainer) into a bowl and set the water aside; discard the whole spices.

Put the rice and aromatic stock in a large pan and bring to the boil. Parboil the rice for about 10 minutes, then drain and put the rice into another pan. Add the sugar syrup and boil for about 1 minute. Now cover with a tight-fitting lid and seal the pan with dough, if using, or foil. Put a couple of pieces of hot charcoals on the lid, if you like, or omit the charcoal and cook in a low oven for about 30 minutes, or until the rice is cooked.

Break the seal, uncover and pour over the ghee. Stir very gently with a fork, then sprinkle over the kewra water and khoya. Turn onto a serving plate and decorate with almonds, pistachios, raisins and edible silver leaf.

Jauzi Halwa
Rich Wheatgerm Dessert

Origin Awadh
Preparation time 30 minutes
Cooking time 1½ hours
Makes 20–25

5 litres / 1.1 gallons (21 cups) milk

250g / 9oz (2 cups plus 2 tablespoons) wheatgerm
    extract

500g / 1lb 2oz Khoya (see page 58)

1.5kg / 3¼lb (7½ cups) sugar

½ teaspoon kewra water

1kg / 2¼lb (4½ cups) ghee

1 teaspoon saffron threads

¼ teaspoon ground cinnamon

¼ teaspoon ground nutmeg

1 teaspoon ground green cardamom

Blend the milk and wheatgerm extract in a large, heavy-based pan and cook over low heat, stirring constantly, for 45 minutes until the milk is reduced by half. Add the khoya. Keep stirring constantly over low heat for about 30 minutes to blend the mixture.

Add the sugar together with the kewra water and stir constantly for 5 minutes until the sugar is dissolved. Add the ghee and saffron and mix well, ensuring that the mixture does not stick to the pan. Remove the pan from the heat and spread its contents on a large baking tray (pan). Sprinkle the ground cinnamon, nutmeg and cardamom over the top and cut into 20–25 squares or diamonds.

Makki ka Halwa
Corn Dessert

Origin Rajasthan
Preparation time 30 minutes
Cooking time 1 hour
Serves 6–8

2 teaspoons saffron threads
500ml / 18fl oz (2¼ cups) milk, plus extra for soaking
250g / 9oz (1 cup) ghee
500g / 1lb 2oz (3¼ cups) sweetcorn (corn) kernels
100g / 3½oz Khoya, grated (see page 58)
50g / 1¾oz (⅔ cup) grated fresh coconut
500g / 1lb 2oz (2½ cups) sugar
1 teaspoon ground green cardamom
100g / 3½oz (⅔ cup) raisins
35g / 1¼oz (⅓ cup) unsalted pistachio nuts, blanched and slivered

Put the saffron in a small bowl, add 2 tablespoons milk and soak until required.

Heat the ghee in a large, heavy-based pan over low heat, add the sweetcorn kernels and stir-fry for 2–3 minutes. Add the milk and khoya and continue to stir-fry for 2–3 minutes until the milk is completely absorbed. Mash well with the back of a ladle or spatula to combine. Add the coconut and stir-fry for about 1 minute, then add the sugar and stir-fry for 1–2 minutes, or until the mixture becomes thick and leaves the sides of the pan. Sprinkle over the ground cardamom, raisins, pistachios and saffron and mix well. Serve immediately.

Shahi Tukra
Sweet Morsel for the Prince

Origin Awadh
Preparation time 40 minutes, plus soaking time
Cooking time 20 minutes
Serves 4

35g / 1¼oz (¼ cup) raisins
pinch of saffron threads
2 tablespoons rosewater
2 teaspoons ghee or vegetable oil
4 slices white bread
2 tablespoons condensed milk
4 tablespoons sugar
1 teaspoon kewra water or rosewater
½ teaspoon lime juice
250ml / 8fl oz (1 cup) milk
¼ teaspoon ground green cardamom
1 teaspoon blanched almonds, slivered
1 teaspoon unsalted pistachio nuts, blanched and slivered
4 edible silver leaves, to decorate

Soak the raisins in a bowl of hot water for 15 minutes, then drain and set aside. Put the saffron in a small bowl, add the rosewater and soak until required.

Heat the ghee or oil in a frying pan (skillet) over medium heat, add the bread slices in batches and fry for 2–3 minutes until golden. Remove from the pan and drain on kitchen paper (paper towels). Set aside.

Put the condensed milk in a bowl, add 2 tablespoons sugar together with the kewra water and stir.

Fill a heavy-based pan with water, add the remaining sugar, and heat over low heat, stirring, until the sugar has completely dissolved then bring to the boil. Continue to boil, removing the scum that rises to the surface, until the syrup reaches a one-thread consistency (see page 59). Stir in the lime juice.

Place the fried bread slices in a shallow pan, pour over the milk and sugar syrup and cook over low heat for about 10 minutes, or until the milk thickens considerably and changes colour. Stir gently to prevent the milk from burning, taking care that the bread slices don't break. Turn the slices over carefully and delicately during cooking to ensure the thickened milk coats the slices evenly. Sprinkle over the saffron and spread the condensed milk on top of the slices. Sprinkle over the almonds, pistachios and raisins and decorate with edible silver leaf.

Churma Laadoo
Fried Bread Sweets

Origin Rajasthan
Preparation time 45 minutes, plus standing time
Cooking time 1½ hours
Makes 20

180g / 6½oz (1½ cups) wholemeal (whole wheat) flour

½ teaspoon baking powder

2 tablespoons ghee, plus extra for deep-frying

6 blanched almonds, slivered

15g / ½oz candied sugar (rock candy), crushed,
    or 1 tablespoon sugar

1 tablespoon grated fresh coconut

1 teaspoon ground green cardamom

salt

Sift the flour, baking powder and a pinch of salt into a tray or large bowl. Make a depression in the centre, add 1 tablespoon ghee and start mixing gradually, adding enough water to make a soft dough. Knead the dough on a lightly floured work surface for about 5 minutes until smooth. Divide the dough into 20 equal portions, roll into balls, then cover with a damp cloth or tea (dish) towel and set aside for 10 minutes.

Now flatten the balls between the palms of your hands to make patties. Dust a baking tray (sheet) with flour and arrange the patties on it, then cover with a damp cloth or tea (dish) towel and set aside until ready to cook.

Heat enough ghee for deep-frying in a kadhai, wok or deep, heavy-based pan to 180°C/350°F, or until a cube of bread browns in 30 seconds, then reduce the heat slightly if necessary. The patties should be deep-fried at low-medium heat. Working in batches, carefully lower the patties into the hot oil and deep-fry for 2–3 minutes until golden. Remove from the pan with a slotted spoon, transfer to kitchen paper (paper towels) and allow to cool.

When the patties are cool, coarsely grind them in a food processor. Transfer the mixture to a bowl, add 1 tablespoon of the deep-frying ghee and the remaining ingredients and mix well. Sprinkle over a little water, and with damp hands, roll the mixture into balls, then cover and set aside for 15 minutes before serving. They can also be stored in an airtight container in the refrigerator for up to 3 days.

Tilgul
Sweet Sesame Balls

Origin Punjab
Preparation time 10 minutes
Cooking time 15 minutes, plus cooling time
Makes 30–35

1kg / 2¼lb (6⅔ cups) white sesame seeds

30g / 1¼oz (⅓ cup) desiccated (dried flaked) coconut

70g / 2½oz (½ cup) peanuts, with skins on

500g / 1lb 2oz (2½ cups) jaggery or soft brown sugar

1 teaspoon ghee

1 teaspoon ground green cardamom

vegetable oil, for oiling

Place a frying pan (skillet) over low heat, add the sesame seeds and stir-fry for about 1–2 minutes, or until golden. Remove from the pan. Add the coconut to the pan and stir-fry for about 2 minutes, or until light brown. Remove from the pan. Add the peanuts to the pan and stir-fry for about 2 minutes, or until golden, then remove from the pan, remove the skins and crush.

Heat the jaggery or sugar in a heavy-based pan over low heat for 2 minutes. Add the ghee and cook for 1–2 minutes until the jaggery changes colour. Add the sesame seeds, coconut, peanuts and ground cardamom, then mix well.

Oil the palms or your hands with a little oil and roll the mixture into small equal-sized balls, then set on a tray. This has to be done when the mixture is hot because it hardens very fast. Set the balls aside to cool.

Mawe ki Kachori
Sweet Stuffed Kachori

Origin Rajasthan
Preparation time 1½ hours, plus standing and cooling time
Cooking time 15 minutes
Makes 12

For the dough

250g / 9oz (2 cups) plain (all-purpose) flour

¼ teaspoon bicarbonate of soda (baking soda)

pinch of salt

5 tablespoons vegetable oil

ghee, for deep-frying

For the filling

350g / 12oz Khoya (see page 58)

100g / 3½oz (½ cup) sugar

½ teaspoon ground green cardamom

50g / 1¾oz (⅓ cup) raisins

1 tablespoon chironji kernels

1 tablespoon unsalted pistachio nuts

salt

For the syrup

1kg / 2¼lb (5 cups) sugar

¾ teaspoon lime juice

¼ teaspoon rosewater

To make the syrup, put 1 litre / 1¾ pints (4¼ cups) water and the sugar in a large, heavy-based pan and heat gently, stirring, until the sugar has dissolved. Increase the heat and bring to the boil. Continue to boil, removing the scum that rises to the surface with a slotted spoon, until it reaches a one-thread consistency (see page 59). Add the lime juice and rosewater and set aside.

To make the dough, sift the flour, bicarbonate of soda and salt together in a large bowl. Make a depression in the centre, pour in the oil and start mixing gradually. When fully mixed, add enough water to make soft dough. Knead the dough on a lightly floured work surface for about 5 minutes, then cover with a damp cloth or tea (dish) towel and set aside for 15 minutes.

Meanwhile, to make the filling, heat a heavy-based pan, add the khoya and stir-fry over medium heat for 5–6 minutes, stirring constantly, until it begins to change colour and release fat. Stir constantly to prevent overcooking. Stir in the sugar slowly, mixing well, then sprinkle in the cardamom, raisins, chironji kernels and pistachio nuts and stir to blend. Remove from the heat and allow to cool.

Divide the reserved dough into 12 equal portions, roll into balls, then cover with a damp cloth or tea (dish) towel. Flatten each ball between the palms of your hands into rounds about 8cm / 3 inches in diameter, making them thinner around the edges.

Place a portion of the filling in the middle of each round, fold over to enclose and pinch off the excess dough to seal the edges, then flatten between the palms of your hands into rounds.

Heat enough ghee for deep-frying in a kadhai, wok or deep, heavy-based pan to 180°C/350°F, or until a cube of bread browns in 30 seconds. Working in batches, carefully lower the kachori into the hot oil and deep-fry for 3–4 minutes, or until golden brown and crisp. Remove from the pan with a slotted spoon and drain on kitchen paper (paper towels).

Put the kachori in the reserved sugar syrup to soak, then remove and allow to cool before serving.

Mung Dal ka Halwa
Moong Bean Dessert

Origin Punjab/Delhi/Awadh
Preparation time 30 minutes, plus soaking time
Cooking time 1 hour
Serves 6–8

200g / 7oz (1 cup) moong dal, rinsed and drained
500ml / 18fl oz (2¼ cups) milk
200g / 7oz (1 cup) sugar
1 teaspoon saffron threads
125g / 4oz (½ cup) ghee

To decorate

10 almonds, slivered
10 cashew nuts, slivered
seeds of 10 green cardamom pods, crushed

Soak the dal in a bowl of water overnight.

The next day, drain the dal, then transfer to a blender or food processor and process, adding a little water if necessary, to make a smooth paste.

Bring the milk to the boil with sugar and saffron in a large pan for 10 minutes.

Heat the ghee in a kadhai, wok or deep, heavy-based pan over very low heat, add the dal paste and stir-fry for 5 minutes until it turns brown. When the dal starts to brown, add the hot milk and stir continuously. It should not stick to the wok. Keep stirring for about 30 minutes, until the milk dries up and the ghee separates out.

Transfer the halwa to a silver platter or other serving plate and decorate with the almonds, cashew nuts and crushed cardamoms. Serve hot.

Rosogolla
Rosogolla

Origin West Bengal
Preparation time 10 minutes
Cooking time 45 minutes
Makes 12–15

250g / 9oz (1 cup) Chhena (see page 59)
500g / 1lb 2oz (2½ cups) sugar

Knead the chhena into a soft dough, then roll into balls slightly smaller than the desired size of the rosogollas.

Fill a heavy-based pan with water, add the sugar and place over low heat. Heat gently, stirring until the sugar has dissolved, then increase the heat and boil until the syrup reaches one-thread consistency (see page 59). Strain through a sieve (strainer) into a heatproof bowl. Return the syrup to the pan and return to the boil.

Slide the balls carefully into the boiling syrup. Cover the pan and cook for a further 30 minutes. Uncover and gently remove the rosogollas from the pan with a slotted spoon. Serve at room temperature.

Puran Poli
Shallow-fried Bread with Sweet Filling

Origin Maharashtra
Preparation time 45 minutes, plus soaking
and cooling time
Cooking time 50 minutes
Makes 10

250g / 9oz (1⅓ cups) chana dal, rinsed and drained

200g / 7oz (1⅔ cups) icing (confectioners') sugar

1 teaspoon ground green cardamom

¼ teaspoon ground nutmeg

200g / 7oz (1⅔ cups) wholemeal (whole wheat) flour

4 tablespoons vegetable oil

2 tablespoons plain (all-purpose) flour, for dusting

4 tablespoons melted ghee

Soak the chana dal in a large bowl of water overnight.

The next day, drain the dal. Bring 500ml / 18fl oz
(2 cups) water to the boil in a large, heavy-based
pan, add the chana dal, reduce the heat to medium
and cook for 20 minutes until the water is absorbed.
Remove from the heat and allow to cool. When
cool, transfer to a blender or food processor and
process to make a smooth paste.

Place a heavy-based pan over medium heat, add
the chana dal paste, sugar, ground cardamom and
nutmeg and mix well. Cook over medium heat
for 5–10 minutes, stirring, until the water released
by the sugar is absorbed. Remove from the heat
and transfer the mixture to a shallow dish and allow
to cool.

Put the wholemeal flour in a large bowl and mix in
enough water and 2–3 tablespoons of the oil to
make a soft and springy dough. Knead the dough on
a lightly floured work surface for 5 minutes.

Divide the dough and the chana dal mixture each into
10 equal portions. Take one portion of the dough
and roll into a ball. Brushing lightly with oil, then roll
it out to a diameter of about 10cm / 4 inches on
a lightly floured surface. Place one portion of the
chana dal mixture in the centre, then lift the dough
from all sides and seal over the filling. Roll it
once again, brushing a little oil on the surface, to
a diameter of about 15cm / 6½ inches.

Heat a tawa, griddle or heavy-based frying pan
(skillet) over medium heat. Place one bread in the
pan and cook for 2 minutes on both sides, then
brush with 1 teaspoon ghee and cook for a further
1 minute on both sides, until golden brown. Remove
from the pan and repeat with the remaining dough
and chana dal.

Pinni
Bonbons

Origin Punjab
Preparation time 30 minutes
Cooking time 15 minutes
Makes 20

250g / 9oz (1 cup) ghee

280g / 8½oz (2 cups) wholemeal (whole wheat) flour

2 cups crumbled Khoya (see page 58)

300g / 11 oz (1½ cups) sugar

15–20 raisins

10 pistachio nuts, blanched and slivered

10 blanched almonds

Heat the ghee in a kadhai, wok or deep, heavy-based
pan, add the flour and stir for 3–4 minutes until
it turns light brown, then remove the pan from the
heat. Dry-roast the crumbled khoya in another
kadhai, wok or deep, heavy-based pan, stirring
it constantly, for 5–7 minutes until it also turns light
brown. Remove the pan from the heat and add
the fried flour. Stir in the sugar, raisins and nuts,
then shape into round balls while the mixture is
still warm.

Moticoor Laddu
Sweet Globes

Origin Punjab/Delhi/Awadh
Preparation time 20 minutes, plus soaking time
Cooking time 20 minutes
Makes 30–35

few saffron threads
1 tablespoon rosewater
500g / 1lb 2oz (3⅓ cups) gram (chickpea) flour
250g / 9oz (2¼ cups) sugar
½ teaspoon lime juice
ghee, for deep-frying and greasing
1 tablespoon dried melon seeds
1 teaspoon ground green cardamom
edible sliver leaf, to decorate

Put the saffron in a small bowl, add the rosewater and soak for 20 minutes.

Put the gram flour in a bowl and mix in enough water to make a smooth batter with a uniform pouring consistency.

To make a syrup, fill a heavy-based pan with water, add the sugar and heat gently, stirring, until the sugar has dissolved. Increase the heat and bring to the boil. Continue to boil, removing the scum that rises to the surface with a slotted spoon, until the syrup reaches a one-thread consistency (see page 59). Stir in the lime juice and saffron soaked in rosewater and set aside over a low heat.

Heat enough ghee for deep-frying in a kadhai, wok or deep, heavy-based pan to 180°C/350°F, or until a cube of bread browns in 30 seconds, then reduce the heat to low-medium. Working in batches, if necessary, pour the batter carefully into the hot oil through a steel strainer with medium-sized holes, forming droplets, called boondis, and deep-fry for 3–4 minutes until golden. Remove from the pan with a slotted spoon and drain the excess oil. Grease your hands with a little ghee, then roll the boondis into small balls.

Transfer the boondis to the warm syrup and mix well, then remove from the heat and allow to cool.

When cool, remove the boondis from the syrup, spinkle over the melon seeds and ground cardamom and decorate with edible silver leaf.

Jalebi
Sweet Pretzels

Origin Punjab/Delhi/Awadh
Preparation time 20 minutes, plus fermenting time
Cooking time 30 minutes
Makes 20–25

6 tablespoons plain (all-purpose) flour
2 tablespoons gram (chickpea) flour
2 tablespoons natural (plain) yoghurt
1 tablespoon vegetable oil, plus extra for deep-frying
200g / 7oz (1 cup) sugar
½ teaspoon lime juice

Mix the plain flour, gram flour, yoghurt, 1 tablespoon oil and enough water to make a thick batter in a large bowl. Cover and set aside to ferment overnight.

To make a syrup, fill a heavy-based pan with water, add the sugar and heat gently, stirring, until the sugar has dissolved. Increase the heat and bring to the boil. Continue to boil, removing the scum that rises to the surface with a slotted spoon, until the syrup reaches a one-thread consistency (see page 59). Stir in the lime juice. Set aside over low heat while you cook the jalebi.

Heat enough oil for deep-frying in a kadhai or deep, heavy-based pan to 180°C/350°F, or until a cube of bread browns in 30 seconds. Beat the fermented flour batter and transfer to a piping bag or clean plastic bag with a small hole in one corner. Working in batches if necessary, slowly squeeze the bag over the hot oil. Starting at one side of the pan and working across, try to make small coils, about 8cm / 3 inches in diameter, starting from the outer ring and ending at the centre, on top of the oil – the coils should be linked together in a line. Deep-fry for 2–3 minutes until both sides are golden and the jalebi is crisp. To turn over, use a metal skewer. Remove the jalebi gently with tongs and drain on kitchen paper (paper towels).

Transfer the jalebi to the warm syrup and soak for about 5 minutes, then remove and serve hot, broken into individual coils.

Gulab Jamun
Khoya Bonbons in Syrup

Origin Delhi/Awadh
Preparation time 45 minutes
Cooking time 30 minutes
Makes 10–12

pinch of saffron threads
1 teaspoon rosewater
300g / 11oz Khoya (see page 58)
50g / 1¾oz (4 tablespoons) Chhena (see page 59)
4 tablespoons plain (all-purpose) flour
1 teaspoon baking powder
1 tablespoon ghee
6 teaspoons cardamom seeds
12 unsalted pistachio nuts
1kg / 2¼lb (5 cups) sugar
¾ teaspoon lime juice
500ml / 18fl oz (2¼ cups) vegetable oil, for deep-frying

Put the saffron in a small bowl, add the rosewater and soak until required.

Crumble the khoya and chhena to remove any lumps, then put into a large bowl, add the flour, baking powder and 1 tablespoon ghee and mix together to make a soft dough. Knead the dough on a lightly floured work surface for about 5 minutes. Pinch off pieces of dough and roll into balls, about 2.5cm / 1 inch in diameter. Place a few cardamom seeds and a pistachio nut in the centre of each.

To make a syrup, fill a heavy-based pan with water, add the sugar and heat gently, stirring, until the sugar has dissolved. Increase the heat and bring to the boil. Continue to boil, removing the scum that rises to the surface with a slotted spoon, until the syrup reaches a one-thread consistency (see page 59). Stir in the lime juice and saffron soaked in rosewater. Set aside.

Heat the oil for deep-frying in a kadhai or deep, heavy-based pan to 180°C/350°F, or until a cube of bread browns in 30 seconds. Working in batches, carefully add the balls to the hot oil and deep-fry for 3–4 minutes until rich brown, then remove from the pan with a slotted spoon and drain on kitchen paper (paper towels).

Transfer the balls to the syrup to soak. Serve hot or at room temperature.

Phirni
Milk & Rice Dessert

Origin Delhi/Awadh
Preparation time 30 minutes, plus soaking time
Cooking time 30–35 minutes
Serves 4

3 tablespoons rice
750ml / 1¼ pints (3¼ cups) milk
6 tablespoons sugar

To decorate

8–10 blanched almonds
2 tablespoons unsalted pistachio nuts, blanched and slivered
few drops of kewra water or 1 teaspoon rosewater (optional)

Soak the rice in a small bowl of water for about 30 minutes. Drain the rice, transfer to a blender or food processor and process to make a paste. Set aside.

Bring the milk to the boil in a large, heavy-based pan, then reduce the heat and simmer for 2–3 minutes. Stir in the rice paste and sprinkle over the sugar. Continue cooking over low heat for about 20 minutes until the milk is reduced by one-third.

Remove the pan from the heat, pour the dessert into serving bowls and decorate with almonds and pistachio nuts. You can also sprinkle a few drops of kewra water or rosewater over the top, if you like.

Mysore Pak
Rich Gram (Chickpea) Flour Confection

Origin Karnataka/Tamil Nadu
Preparation time 15 minutes
Cooking time 30 minutes
Makes 25–35

400g / 14oz (2 cups) sugar
½ teaspoon lime juice
8–10 green cardamom pods, ground
500g / 1lb 2oz (2¼ cups) ghee
65g / 2½oz (½ cup) plain (all-purpose) flour
175g / 6½oz (1¼ cups) gram (chickpea) flour

To make a thick syrup, pour 250ml / 8fl oz (1 cup) water into a large, heavy-based pan, add the sugar and heat gently, stirring, until the sugar has dissolved. Increase the heat and bring to the boil. Continue to boil, removing the scum that rises to the surface with a slotted spoon, until the syrup reaches a two-three-thread consistency (see page 59). Stir in the lime juice and ground cardamom and set aside.

Heat the ghee to boiling point in a heavy-based pan, then remove from the heat and set aside.

Carefully transfer 100g / 3½oz (½ cup) of the ghee to a second large, heavy-based pan over low heat. Add the gram and plain flours and fry for about 5 minutes, or until the ghee separates out. Add the sugar syrup and keep stirring for 1 minute, then add the remaining ghee, 1 tablespoon at a time. When the mixture stops sticking to the spoon, pour it into a 5cm / 2 inch deep tray (pan) brushed with a little ghee or oil, and let it settle for about 5 minutes. Tilt the tray and drain off the excess ghee. Cut the sweets (candies) into 5-cm / 2-inch squares and serve at room temperature.

Kesari Bhaath
Saffron-tinged Semolina (Farina)

Origin Tamil Nadu
Preparation time 10 minutes
Cooking time 10–15 minutes
Serves 4

large pinch of saffron threads
5 tablespoons hot milk
250g / 9oz (1 cup) ghee
280g / 10oz (1⅔ cups) coarse semolina (farina)
10 cashew nuts
400g / 14oz (2 cups) sugar
7–8 green cardamom pods, ground

Put the saffron in a small bowl, add the hot milk and soak until required.

Heat the ghee in a large, heavy-based pan, add the semolina and fry until golden brown. Remove from the pan and set aside. Add the cashew nuts to the pan and fry for about 2–3 minutes, or until golden. Return the fried semolina to the pan and pour in 500–750ml / 18–24fl oz (2–3¼ cups) water, or as much as necessary depending on the quality of the semolina used. Stir well and cook for 3–4 minutes until most of the water is absorbed. Add the sugar and cook, stirring, for 5 minutes until the mixture starts to stick to the spoon and leave the sides of the pan. Remove from the heat and sprinkle over the ground cardamom and saffron and mix well. Serve at room temperature.

Kadalaparippu Payasam
Chana Dal Dessert

Origin Kerala
Preparation time 45 minutes
Cooking time 1 hour
Serves 5–6

500g / 1lb 2oz (2½ cups) jaggery or soft brown sugar

½ teaspoon lime juice

125g / 4oz (½ cup) ghee

500g / 1lb 2oz (2⅔ cups) chana dal, rinsed
    and drained

1.4 litres / 2½ pints (5½ cups) coconut milk, fresh
    (see page 781) or canned

500ml / 18fl oz (2½ cups) coconut cream, fresh
    (see page 781) or canned

6–8 green cardamom pods, ground

1 coconut, grated

3 tablespoons raisins

2 tablespoons cashew nuts

Pour 500ml / 18fl oz (2¼ cups) water into a large,
heavy-based pan, add the jaggery or sugar and heat
gently, stirring, until the jaggery has dissolved.
Increase the heat and boil. Continue to boil,
removing the scum as it rises to the top with a
slotted spoon, until the syrup reaches one-thread
consistency (see page 59). Stir in the lime juice.

Heat 1 tablespoon ghee in a large, heavy-based
pan over medium heat, add the dal and fry for 3–4
minutes until brown. Pour in the syrup with 500ml
/ 18fl oz (2¼ cups) water, then mix well and bring to
the boil. Reduce the heat to medium and boil for
about 30 minutes.

Add most of the remaining ghee, stir and continue
cooking over medium heat until the mixture is
the consistency of a thick porridge. Remove the
pan from the heat and gradually add 625ml / 1 pint
(2½ cups) coconut milk. Bring to the boil and
continue boiling until the mixture thickens a little,
then pour in the remaining coconut milk and return
to the boil, stirring constantly. Finally, pour in
the coconut cream, then sprinkle over the ground
cardamom and remove from the heat.

Heat the rest of the ghee in a frying pan (skillet) over
medium heat, add the grated coconut and stir-fry
for about 1–2 minutes, or until brown. Remove from
the pan and set aside.

Add the raisins to the pan and stir-fry for about 1–2
minutes, then remove and set aside. Add the cashew
nuts to the pan and fry for about 2 minutes, or until
golden. Add all the fried ingredients to the payasam
before serving.

Parippu Payasam
Green Moong Dal Flavoured
with Coconut Milk

Origin Andhra Pradesh
Preparation time 20 minutes
Cooking time 50 minutes
Serves 10

250g / 9oz (1⅓ cups) split green moong dal, rinsed,
    drained and dried

750ml / 1¼ pints (3¼ cups) coconut milk, fresh
    (see page 781) or canned

750g / 1lb 10oz (3¾ cups) crumbled jaggery
    or soft brown sugar

5 tablespoons ghee

¾ teaspoon ground green cardamom

To decorate

50g / 1¾oz (⅓ cup) raisins

50g / 1¾oz (⅓ cup) cashew nuts

Stir-fry the green moong dal in a dry pan over
medium-low heat for about 2–3 minutes, or until
light brown. Add the coconut milk, bring to the boil
and boil for about 30 minutes.

Add the jaggery or sugar and continue to boil,
stirring frequently, for 10 minutes, or until thick.
Now add the coconut milk and simmer for about
10 minutes, then add the ghee. Sprinkle over the
cardamom and stir, then remove from the heat.
Decorate with raisins and cashew nuts and serve hot.

Neyappam
Deep-fried Rice Flour Balls

Origin Kerala
Preparation time 15 minutes
Cooking time 15–30 minutes
Serves 4–6

150g / 5oz (1 cup) rice flour

---

4 green cardamom pods

150g / 5oz (¾ cup) ground jaggery
    or soft brown sugar

---

3 teaspoons ghee

---

1 tablespoon plain (all-purpose) flour

30g / 1¼oz (⅓ cup) desiccated (dried flaked)
    coconut

---

vegetable oil, for deep-frying

Put the rice flour, cardamom pods and jaggery in a blender or food processor and process with enough water to make a thick paste. Transfer to a bowl and add the ghee and plain flour together with the desiccated coconut.

Heat enough oil for deep-frying in a kadhai or deep, heavy-based pan to 180°C/350°F, or until a cube of bread browns in 30 seconds. Pour small quantities of the paste carefully into the hot oil and deep-fry until dark brown. Remove from the pan with a slotted spoon and drain on kitchen paper (paper towels).

Sakin Gata
Rice Cakes Steamed in Banana Leaves

Origin Coastal
Preparation time 40 minutes, plus soaking time
Cooking time 20 minutes
Serves 5–6

1kg / 2¼lb (5 cups) sticky (glutinous) rice, rinsed
    and drained

---

5 teaspoons sugar

---

3 banana leaves (optional)

---

1 tablespoon black sesame seeds

Soak the rice in a bowl of water overnight.

The next day, drain and spread out to dry on a clean tea (dish) towel. When dry, transfer to a blender or food processor and process to make a powder.

Place the rice powder and sugar in a bowl, add 500–750ml / 18–24fl oz (2¼–3¼ cups) water and mix to make a soft dough, then knead the dough for about 5 minutes.

To soften the banana leaves, hold them over the low flame of a gas cooker (stove-top gas burner) for a few seconds, or until soft. Alternatively, use a cook's blowtorch or dip each leaf in a pan of boiling water, then rinse under cold water and dry well. Cut the banana leaves into 15-cm / 6½-inch squares. If you can't find banana leaves, you could use pieces of foil.

Spread about 2 tablespoons of the dough on each banana leaf square and sprinkle over the sesame seeds. Fold the leaves to form neat parcels and tie with kitchen string (twine). Place the parcels in an earthen pot or steamer and steam for about 20 minutes. If you don't have a steamer, use a large pan with a lid and place a trivet or upside-down plate in the base. Pour in enough water so it stays below the top of the trivet and cover with the lid. Place the parcels on a plate and carefully put the plate on top of the trivet or upside-down plate, cover and steam for 20 minutes.

Jangir
Syrup-soaked Pretzels

Origin Tamil Nadu
Preparation time 20 minutes, plus soaking and chilling time
Cooking time 20 minutes
Makes 20–30

400g / 14oz (2 cups) urad dal, rinsed and drained
200g / 7oz (1 cup) basmati rice
large pinch of saffron threads
1 tablespoon rosewater
1kg / 2¼lb (5 cups) sugar
1 teaspoon milk
vegetable oil, for frying

Soak the lentils and the rice in a large bowl of water overnight.

The next day, drain, then transfer to a blender or food processor and process to make a paste. Set aside. Put the saffron in a small bowl, add the rosewater and soak until required.

To make a syrup, put 500ml / 18fl oz (2¼ cups) water in a large, heavy-based pan, add the sugar and heat gently, stirring, until the sugar has dissolved. Increase the heat and bring to the boil. Add the milk and boil, removing the scum as it rises to the top with a slotted spoon, until the syrup reaches a two-thread consistency (see page 59). Stir in the saffron and rosewater and reduce the heat to low while you cook the jangir.

Take a wide pan and fill it three-quarters with oil, then heat to 180°C/350°F, or until a cube of bread browns in 30 seconds, but do not let it get any hotter.

Transfer the lentil-rice paste to a piping (pastry) bag or clean plastic bag with a small hole in the corner, then gently squeeze out concentric circles into the hot oil. Fry for 2–3 minutes until rich-red and crisp, turning to cook evenly on both sides. Using tongs, remove the hot jangir from the pan, add to the warm syrup and soak for about 5 minutes. Remove from the syrup, chill in the refrigerator and serve cold.

Parval ki Mithai
Wax Gourd Sweets

Origin Awadh
Preparation time 1½ hours, plus cooling, soaking and chilling time
Cooking time 30 minutes
Serves 12–15

1kg / 2¼lb wax gourd
400g / 14oz (2 cups) sugar
1 litre / 1¾ pints (4¼ cups) milk
juice of 2 limes
200g / 7oz (1 cup) caster (superfine) sugar
1 teaspoon rosewater
70g / 2½oz (½ cup) blanched almonds, finely chopped
4 tablespoons unsalted pistachio nuts, blanched and finely chopped
Paneer
2 tablespoons crushed sugar candy (rock candy)
seeds of 8 green cardamom pods, crushed
pinch of saffron threads, crushed

Put the wax gourd into a large pan of water and bring to the boil, then reduce the heat and simmer for about 10 minutes. Drain and allow to cool. Make a slit along one side of each wax gourd and de-seed, then remove the pulp.

Pour 500ml / 18fl oz (2¼ cups) water into a large, heavy-based pan, add half the sugar and heat gently, stirring, until the sugar has completely dissolved. Bring to the boil, then reduce the heat to medium and cook for 2 minutes. Remove from the heat and stir in the rosewater, then add the wax gourd and soak for 3–4 hours.

Transfer the paneer to a blender or food processor, add the remaining sugar and process to make a paste. Put the paste into a bowl and mix in the sugar candy, chopped nuts and crushed cardamom.

Remove the wax gourd from the sugar syrup and stuff with the paneer filling, then sprinkle a little crushed saffron on top. Chill in the refrigerator until ready to serve, and serve cold.

Nariyal ke Laddu
Sweet Coconut Balls

Origin New
Preparation time 10 minutes, plus cooling time
Cooking time 10 minutes
Makes 15–25

250g / 9oz (2⅔ cups) desiccated (dried flaked) coconut
½ teaspoon butter
150g / 5oz Khoya (see page 58)

Set aside 50g / 1¾oz (½ cup) of the coconut. Heat the butter in a large pan, add the remaining coconut and the khoya and cook over low heat for about 10 minutes, or until the mixture leaves the sides of the pan. Remove from the heat and allow to cool.

When cool, spread the reserved coconut on a large plate, then with greased hands, roll the mixture into small balls, and coat in the coconut.

Ragi Halwa
Sweet Coarse Grain Dessert

Origin Tamil Nadu
Preparation time 10–15 minutes
Cooking time 10 minutes
Serves 4

200g / 7oz (1 cup) ghee
500g / 1lb 2oz (4 cups plus 3 tablespoons) millet flour
300g / 11oz (1½ cups) jaggery or soft brown sugar
1 teaspoon ground green cardamom

To decorate

2 tablespoons cashew nuts, fried
2 tablespoons raisins, fried

Heat the ghee in a large, heavy-based pan over medium heat, add the flour and stir-fry for about 5 minutes, stirring constantly.

Mix the jaggery or sugar with 1 litre / 1¾ pints (4¼ cups) water in another pan and bring to the boil. Gradually stir the jaggery mixture into the flour making sure that there are no lumps, then cook for about 5 minutes, or until it reaches the desired thickness. Sprinkle over the ground cardamom and decorate with fried cashew nuts and raisins.

Aloo ki Kheer
Milk & Potato Dessert

Origin Awadh
Preparation time 10–20 minutes, plus cooling time
Cooking time 20 minutes
Serves 4–6

2 large potatoes
1 litre / 1¾ pints (4¼ cups) milk
5 tablespoons sugar
large pinch of ground green cardamon
1 tablespoon butter or ghee
1 tablespoon raisins or sultanas (golden raisins)
2 teaspoons rosewater
6 unsalted pistachio nuts, finely slivered, to decorate

Finely grate the potatoes and put into a large bowl of water to prevent them from turning black.

Bring the milk to the boil in a large, heavy-based pan, add the sugar and cook until the mixture is thick and reduced by half, then add the ground cardamom.

Heat the butter or ghee in a frying pan (skillet) over medium heat, add the grated potato and stir-fry lightly for about 2–3 minutes to remove the raw smell, then add to the milk and continue to boil over medium heat for 7–8 minutes. Add the raisins or sultanas and simmer for a further 5 minutes. Remove the pan from the heat and allow to cool.

When cool, sprinkle over the rosewater and decorate with slivered pistachios.

Suji Halwa
Semolina Halwa

Origin Punjab/Delhi/Awadh
Preparation time 15 minutes, plus standing time
Cooking time 30 minutes
Serves 6–8

140g / 4¾oz (¾ cup) semolina (semolina flour)
250ml / 8fl oz (1 cup) clotted cream or heavy (double) cream
2 teaspoons raisins
200g / 7oz (1 cup) sugar
10 tablespoons ghee
seeds of 3–4 green cardamom pods, ground
60g / 2oz (½ cup) chopped mixed nuts

Mix the semolina, cream and raisins together in a large bowl. Cover and set aside for at least 1 hour.

Mix the sugar and 875ml / 1½ pints (3¾ cups) water together in a large, heavy-based pan, then place over low heat and stir until the sugar dissolves. Remove from the heat and set aside.

Heat the ghee in a kadhai, wok or deep, heavy-based pan, add the semolina mixture and fry for 5 minutes until the mixture is light brown and fragrant. Add the sugar and water mixture and mix well to remove any lumps. Cook for 6–7 minutes, stirring constantly, until the ghee separates out. Remove from the heat and sprinkle over the ground cardamom and chopped nuts. Mix well and serve hot.

Gajar Burfi
Carrot Halwa

Origin New
Preparation time 20 minutes, plus cooling and setting time
Cooking time 30 minutes
Serves 6

125g / 4oz (½ cup) ghee
8 green cardamom pods, crushed
1kg / 2¼lb carrots, grated
200g / 7oz (1 cup) sugar
few drops kewra water
¾ cup dried Khoya (see page 58)
40g / 1½oz (⅓ cup) icing (confectioners') sugar

Heat half the ghee in a large pan over medium-low heat, add the crushed cardamom and stir-fry for about 2 minutes. Add the carrot and fry for 5 minutes. Pour in 250ml / 8fl oz (1 cup) boiling water, cover and simmer for 7–8 minutes. Uncover and cook for about 5 minutes until the moisture has evaporated.

Add the remaining ghee and stir-fry for 5 minutes. Sprinkle over the sugar and continue stirring to mix well and cook for 2–3 minutes until the carrots are dry. Remove the pan from the heat, add the kewra water and mix, then allow to cool.

When cool, blend with the khoya, then spread the mixture out on a large greased baking tray (pan) and level the surface. Leave to set, then cut into desired shapes.

Nishashte ka Halwa
Wheatgerm Halwa

Origin Sindh
Preparation time 10 minutes, plus cooling time
Cooking time 15–20 minutes
Serves 6

125g / 4oz (½ cup) ghee, plus extra for greasing
250g / 9oz (1¼ cups) sugar
120g / 4oz (1 cup) wheatgerm
2 teaspoons lime juice
2 tablespoons blanched almonds, chopped
2 tablespoons unsalted pistachios, blanched and chopped
pinch of ground green cardamom

Grease a large baking tray (pan) with a little ghee, then set aside.

Pour 500ml / 18fl oz (2¼ cups) water into a large heavy-based pan, add the sugar and heat gently, stirring, until the sugar has dissolved. Increase the heat and boil for 5–8 minutes until the syrup reaches one-thread consistency (see page 59). Strain through a piece of muslin (cheesecloth) or fine sieve (strainer) into a clean heavy-based pan.

Mix the wheatgerm with 250ml / 8fl oz (1 cup) water in a large bowl to make a smooth dough-like paste, then add it to the syrup and keep stirring and cooking for 4–5 minutes until the mixture forms a pliable lump. Add the lime juice and continue stirring for 5–7 minutes until the mixture begins to stick to the base of the pan. Add the ghee and keep stirring for 7–8 minutes until it does not stick to the sides of the pan. Mix in the chopped almonds, pistachios and ground cardamom, then spread the mixture out on the prepared baking tray and level the surface.

Allow to cool, then cut into desired shapes with a damp knife.

Ande ki Piyosi
Baked Egg Halwa

Origin Hyderabad
Preparation time 15–25 minutes
Cooking time 30 minutes
Serves 8–12

125g / 4oz (½ cup) ghee or butter, plus extra for greasing
20 eggs
1kg / 2¼lb (8 cups) icing (confectioners') sugar
140g / 4¾oz (1½ cups) almonds, coarsely ground
1kg / 2¼lb Khoya (see page 58), crumbled
¾ teaspoon saffron threads, finely ground

Preheat the oven to 150°C/300°F/Gas Mark 2 and grease a flat baking dish (pan), at least 4cm / 1½ inches deep with a little ghee. Separate the egg yolks and whites, then whisk the egg whites in a clean grease-free bowl until soft peaks form.

Mix the yolks and sugar together in a separate bowl and beat until creamy. Fold in the whites and mix, then add the ground almonds, khoya, ghee and saffron and mix well to combine.

Pour the mixture into the prepared baking dish and place it on a baking tray (sheet), so that the base does not get too brown. Bake in the oven for about 30 minutes, or until the top starts to brown. Remove from the oven, allow to cool slightly, then cut into diamonds or squares and serve while still warm.

Kahoor ka Halwa
Dessert of Dates

Origin Hyderabad
Preparation time 5 minutes, plus cooling time
Cooking time 10 minutes
Serves 8–10

125g / 4oz (½ cup) ghee or butter
1kg / 2¼lb (7 cups) dates, stoned (pitted) and chopped into small pieces
500ml / 18fl oz (2¼ cups) milk
4 green cardamom pods, ground
12 blanched almonds, coarsely chopped
12 cashew nuts, coarsely chopped
12 unsalted pistachio nuts, blanched and coarsely chopped
heavy (double) cream, to serve

Heat the ghee in a large, heavy-based pan over low heat, add the dates and fry for a few minutes. Pour in 500ml / 18fl oz (2¼ cups) water and the milk and simmer, adding more water if required, for 5 minutes, until the dates are soft. Mash the dates to a pulp, then add the ground cardamom and simmer for 1 minute. Add the nuts and mix well, then cook for 1–2 minutes until the mixture has a porridge-like consistency. Allow to cool and serve with cream.

Baadam ki Jaali
Almond Marzipan

Origin Hyderabad
Preparation time 30 minutes, plus cooling time
Cooking time 45 minutes
Serves 6

500g / 1lb 2oz (3½ cups) blanched almonds
375ml / 13fl oz (1½ cups) milk
6 green cardamom pods, ground
250g / 9oz (1¼ cups) sugar
½ teaspoon lime juice
150g / 5oz (1¼ cups) icing (confectioners') sugar
3–4 edible silver leaves, to decorate

Put the almonds in a food processor, add the milk and process to make a very smooth paste. Set aside.

To make a sugar syrup, put 250ml / 8fl oz (1 cup) water and the ground cardamom together in heavy-based pan, then add the sugar and heat gently, stirring until the sugar has dissolved. Increase the heat and bring to the boil. Continue to boil, removing the scum that rises to the surface with a slotted spoon, until the syrup reaches a one-thread consistency (see page 59). Add the lime juice and almonds, reduce the heat to low and cook until the syrup and almonds are well blended and become like dough. Remove from the heat and allow to cool.

Preheat the oven to 150°C/300°F/Gas Mark 2. Sprinkle a little icing sugar on a work surface. Roll the sugar mixture into small balls and then, using a rolling pin, roll out each one to about 5cm / 2 inches in diameter and less than 5mm / ¼ inch thick. Cut with a serrated-edged cutter. Separate half of them and cut out geometric shapes or flower patterns with a knife or special biscuit (cookie) cutter in the centre. Sprinkle icing sugar over them again.

Place the almond sweets (candies) on a large baking tray (sheet) and bake in the oven for about 15 minutes. Allow to cool, then decorate with edible silver leaf.

Meve ki Gujiya
Sweet Nutty Pastry

Origin Delhi/Agra
Preparation time 45 minutes, plus standing time
Cooking time 35–45 minutes
Makes 20

250g / 9oz (2 cups) plain (all-purpose) flour, plus extra for dusting
5 tablespoons ghee, plus extra for deep-frying
2 tablespoons chironji kernels
2 teaspoons marsh melon seeds
50g / 1¾oz (⅓ cup) blanched almonds, slivered
4 tablespoons unsalted pistachio nuts, blanched and slivered
2 tablespoons raisins
2 teaspoons sugar

Put the flour in a large bowl, add the 5 tablespoons ghee and rub together until the mixture resembles breadcrumbs, then mix in enough cold water to make a soft dough. Knead on a lightly floured work surface for 5 minutes, then cover with a damp cloth or tea (dish) towel and set aside for 20 minutes.

Lightly roast the chironji kernels and melon seeds on a tawa, griddle or in a dry frying pan (skillet) for about 2–3 minutes, then transfer to a bowl. Add the nuts, raisins and sugar and mix together.

Roll the pastry out on a lightly floured surface into 20 x 8-cm / 3-inch rounds and place a teaspoon of the nut mixture in the centre of each. Fold the rounds into crescent shapes, then dampen, seal and crimp the edges.

Heat enough ghee for deep-frying in a kadhai or deep, heavy-based pan to 180°C/350°F, or until a cube of bread browns in 30 seconds, then reduce the heat to very low. Working in batches, carefully lower the pastries into the hot oil and deep-fry for 3–4 minutes until golden. Remove with a slotted spoon and drain on kitchen paper (paper towels).

Rajbhog
Giant Rosogollas

Origin West Bengal
Preparation time 30 minutes, plus standing time
Cooking time 25 minutes
Makes 12

200g / 7oz (1 cup) Chhena (see page 59)
1 teaspoon plain (all-purpose) flour
1 teaspoon semolina (farina)
60g / 2oz Khoya (see page 58)
seeds from 1 black cardamom pod
1kg / 2¼lb (5 cups) sugar
1 teaspoon rosewater

Knead the chhena gently until smooth, then mix in the flour and semolina and knead again. Divide the mixture into 12 equal portions, then roll into smooth tightly packed balls and flatten a little by pressing between the palms of your hands.

Mix the khoya and black cardamom seeds together in a separate bowl, then divide into 12 equal portions.

Put the sugar and 750ml / 1¼ pints (3¼ cups) water into a large, heavy-based pan over low heat, and heat gently, stirring, until the sugar has dissolved completely. Increase the heat and bring to the boil, then continue to cook until the syrup reaches one-thread consistency (see page 59).

Place one portion of the khoya mixture in each flattened chhena ball and roll into tight smooth balls to seal in the filling.

Put the chhena balls into the syrup and simmer until they swell up to a much larger size. Sprinkle the syrup with 1 teaspoon hot water and continue cooking over high heat for 7–8 minutes, or until the surfaces of the rosogollas start to crack. Remove from the heat.

Sprinkle over the rosewater and allow the rosogollas to soak for at least 4 hours before serving.

📷 pp.680, 681

Boorelu Appalu
Jaggery Biscuits (Cookies)

Origin Andhra Pradesh
Preparation time 2¼ hours
Cooking time 25 minutes
Makes 24–30

1 tablespoon ghee, plus extra for greasing
1 banana leaf (optional)
900g / 1½lb (3 cups) crushed jaggery or soft brown sugar
120g / 4½oz (1 cup) wholemeal (whole wheat) flour
450g / 16oz (3 cups) rice flour
vegetable oil, for deep-frying

Grease a banana leaf, if using, with a little ghee and set aside. You can also use greaseproof (wax) paper.

Bring 1 litre / 1¾ pints (4¼ cups) water to the boil in a large, heavy-based pan. Add the ghee and jaggery and return to the boil, then remove from the heat and stir in both the flours, whisking to make sure that there are no lumps. Return to low heat, cover and simmer for 1½ hours, stirring occasionally.

Taking care not to touch the mixture directly, scrape it onto a piece of greaseproof paper. Cover with a second piece of paper and press lightly to flatten. Set aside to cool.

Roll the mixture into 24–30 walnut-sized balls. Press each ball on the banana leaf or greaseproof paper to form a patty.

Heat the oil for deep-frying in a kadhai or deep, heavy-based pan to 180°C/350°F, or until a cube of bread browns in 30 seconds. Working in batches, carefully lower the patties into the hot oil and deep-fry for 2 minutes until golden brown, turning once. Remove with a slotted spoon and drain on kitchen paper (paper towels).

Chandrakanthalu
Saffron, Coconut & Cashew Biscuits (Cookies)

Origin Andhra Pradesh/Tamil Nadu
Preparation time 1 hour, plus soaking time
Cooking time 30 minutes
Makes 20–25

225g / 8oz (1 cup plus 3 tablespoons) moong dal, rinsed and drained
½ fresh coconut, grated
225g / 8oz (1 cup plus 2 tablespoons) sugar
pinch of ground green cardamom
few saffron threads
pinch of edible camphor
12 cashew nuts
vegetable oil or ghee, for deep-frying

Soak the dal in a bowl of water for 1 hour. Drain, transfer to a blender or food processor, add a little water and process to make a smooth paste. Put the paste into a large pan, add the grated coconut and sugar and mix together. Cook over low heat for about 15 minutes, stirring constantly, until the mixture no longer clings to the sides of the pan. Add the ground cardamom, saffron, camphor and cashew nuts and mix well.

Take a thick cloth or tea (dish) towel, dip it in water and squeeze it dry. Spread it on a flat surface, then spread the mixture evenly out over it and ress down to form a thin flat layer. Cut out desired shapes.

Heat enough oil or ghee for deep-frying in a kadhai or deep, heavy-based pan to 180°C/350°F, or until a cube of bread browns in 30 seconds. Working in batches, carefully lower the biscuits (cookies) into the hot ghee and deep-fry for 2–3 minutes until golden brown. Remove with a slotted spoon and drain on kitchen paper (paper towels).

p.682

Gajar ka Halwa
Carrot Dessert

Origin Punjab/Delhi
Preparation time 15 minutes
Cooking time 1 hour
Serves 8

1 litre / 1¾ pints (4¼ cups) milk
1kg / 2¼lb carrots, grated
200g / 7oz (1 cup) sugar
60g / 2oz (¼ cup) ghee
1 teaspoon ground green cardamom

To decorate

60g / 2oz Khoya (see page 58)
10–15 blanched almonds, slivered
10 pistachio nuts, blanched and crushed
20–25 raisins

Bring the milk to the boil in a large, heavy-based pan, add the grated carrots and cook over medium heat, stirring constantly, for about 25 minutes, or until the carrots are soft and most of the liquid has evaporated. Add the sugar and cook for another 20–25 minutes until it dissolves and the milk is completely absorbed.

Add the ghee and stir-fry for 5 minutes, then add the ground cardamom and stir. Turn out onto a serving plate and decorate with khoya, almonds, pistachio nuts and raisins. Serve hot or at room temperature.

Ganne ke Ras ki Kheer
Rice Cooked in Sugarcane Juice

Origin Awadh
Preparation time 15 minutes
Cooking time 20 minutes
Serves 10–12

1 litre / 1¾ pints (4¼ cups) sugarcane juice
250g / 9oz (1⅓ cups) basmati rice, rinsed and drained
100g / 3½oz (½ cup) sugar
3 tablespoons cashew nut halves
3 tablespoons raisins
25g / 1oz chironji kernels

Strain the sugarcane juice into a large, heavy-based pan, add the rice and bring to the boil. Reduce the heat to medium and simmer for 10 minutes. Stir in the sugar and mix, then simmer for a further 2–3 minutes. Add the cashew nuts, raisins and chironji kernels and stir to combine.

Given the heat of India's climate and the piquancy of the dishes it's no surprise that many Indian beverages are refreshing and thirst quenching. *Chai* (tea) remains the most popular drink in India and water is often the preferred accompaniment to a meal, but a wide range of milk-based drinks, such as *lassi* and sherbets (cooling and refreshing blends of fruit juice, nuts or spices with milk, cream or egg whites), are also served with or without food.

9
___

Drinks

Meethi Lassi
Sweet Yoghurt Shake

Origin Punjab
Preparation time 20 minutes
Serves 4

500ml / 18fl oz (2¼ cups) natural (plain) yoghurt

2 tablespoons sugar

½ teaspoon ground green cardamom

800ml / 28fl oz (3½ cups) cold water

½ teaspoon rosewater

pinch of saffron threads

Put all the ingredients in a blender and process until well mixed. Serve this thick foamy drink in any glass you like.

Masala Milkshake
Spicy Milkshake

Origin New
Preparation time 15 minutes
Serves 6

12 blanched almonds

1.2 litres / 2 pints (5 cups) milk

1 teaspoon rosewater

pinch of saffron threads

8 teaspoons sugar

1 teaspoon ground green cardamom

few pistachio nuts, to garnish

Put the almonds in a blender and process, adding a little water to make a paste. Pour in the milk and add all the remaining ingredients and process until mixed together. Pour the mixture into 6 clay pots or thick ceramic mugs or glasses and garnish with the pistachios just before serving.

Namkin Lassi
Salty Yoghurt Shake

Origin Punjab
Preparation time 20 minutes
Serves 6

500ml / 18fl oz (2¼ cups) natural (plain) yogurt

1 teaspoon ground cumin, roasted

dash of ground black pepper

salt

Put all the ingredients in a blender, add 800ml / 28fl oz (3½ cups) water, season with salt and process until well mixed. Pour into a jug (pitcher) and serve.

Lassi Masalewali
Spicy Yoghurt Shake

Origin Punjab
Preparation time 20 minutes
Serves 4

1 tablespoon blanched almonds

1 tablespoon pistachio nuts

500ml / 18fl oz (2¼ cups) natural (plain) yoghurt

½ teaspoon ground ginger

½ teaspoon ground cumin

¼ teaspoon ground black pepper

small pinch of rock salt

2 green chillies, de-seeded and chopped

salt

To garnish

4 small sprigs coriander (cilantro)

large pinch of dried mint leaves

edible rose petals

Stir-fry the almonds and pistachios lightly on a tawa or non-stick frying pan (skillet) over medium heat for 2–3 minutes, or until roasted. Whisk the yoghurt and 250ml / 8fl oz (1 cup) water together in a large jug (pitcher) until well blended. Add the ground spices together with the rock salt and chillies and whisk to combine.

Pour the drink into individual tall glasses and garnish with the roasted nuts, a coriander sprig, dried crumbled mint leaves and rose petals.

Baadam ka Doodh
Almond Milkshake

Origin Awadh
Preparation time 15 minutes
Serves 6

1.2 litres / 2 pints (5 cups) milk

seeds from 6 green cardamom pods, crushed

12 teaspoons sugar

30 almonds

pinch of saffron threads

Pour the milk into a blender, add all the remaining ingredients and process until mixed together. When thoroughly mixed, pour into individual mugs and microwave at medium power until desired temperature, or heat in a small pan over medium heat before serving. If you want to serve it cold, transfer the milk to a covered jug (pitcher) and chill in the refrigerator until cold, then stir before serving.

Kele ka Doodh
Banana Milkshake

Origin Awadh
Preparation time 15 minutes
Serves 6

6 ripe bananas

3 eggs

dash of ground nutmeg

pinch of salt

1.5 litres / 2½ pints (6¼ cups) cold milk

Put the bananas together with all the other ingredients in a blender and process until frothy. Serve immediately in crystal glasses.

Adrak ka Sherbet
Ginger-lemonade Sherbet

Origin Awadh
Preparation time 10 minutes
Cooking time 10 minutes
Serves 8–10

300g / 11oz fresh ginger, peeled and coarsely cut

250g / 9oz (1¼ cups) sugar

juice of 12 limes

Put the ginger in a food processor or blender and process, adding a little water to make a thick paste.

Bring 500ml / 18fl oz (2¼ cups) water to the boil in a large, heavy-based pan, add the sugar and while stirring, pour in the lime juice. Keep stirring, then add the ginger paste and mix well. Dilute with water to serve.

Baadam ka Sherbet
Almond Sherbet

Origin Punjab/Rajasthan
Preparation time 15 minutes
Cooking time 15 minutes
Serves 10–12

500g / 1lb 2oz (3½ cups) blanched almonds

500g / 1lb 2oz (2½ cups) sugar

Put the almonds in a blender or food processor and process, adding a little water to make a smooth paste.

Put the almond paste in a heavy-based pan, then pour in enough water to cover and bring to the boil. Reduce the heat to medium and continue to boil for about 5 minutes. Remove from the heat and strain through a piece of muslin (cheesecloth) or fine sieve (strainer) into a pan. Return to the heat, add the sugar and bring to the boil over medium heat. Continue boiling and stirring until thick.

Remove from the heat. Strain again through the muslin or fine sieve, then pour into sterilized bottles (see page 791), seal and refrigerate. Dilute with water to serve.

Doodh ka Sherbet
Milk-based Sherbet

Origin Awadh
Preparation time 30 minutes, plus soaking time
Cooking time 5–8 minutes
Serves 8

1 tablespoon saffron threads
2 litres / 3½ pints (8½ cups) milk
1 tablespoon dried rose petals
1 teaspoon ground green cardamom
sugar to taste
20 pistachio nuts, blanched and finely sliced
20 blanched almonds, finely sliced

Put the saffron in a bowl, add one-quarter of the milk and soak overnight in the refrigerator.

The next day, drain the saffron, reserving the milk, add the rose petals, then blend together to make a paste using a little of the soaking milk if necessary. Set aside.

Bring the remaining 1.5 litres milk to the boil in a large, heavy-based pan, then reduce the heat to medium. Continue boiling, stir in the saffron and rose petal paste and cook for 2 minutes. Sprinkle over the ground cardamom and remove from the heat. Add sugar to taste, then add the nuts and stir once to mix.

Chill in the refrigerator for at least 30 minutes before serving.

Thandai
Thandai

Origin Awadh
Preparation time 30 minutes
Serves 6

8 blanched almonds, soaked
8 pistachio nuts, blanched
1 teaspoon poppy seeds
4 black peppercorns
½ teaspoon ground cinnamon
1 teaspoon aniseeds
pinch of ground nutmeg
12 dried melon seeds
750ml / 1¼ pints (3¼ cups) cold milk
6 teaspoons sugar
few edible pink rose petals, to garnish

Put the nuts and all the spices, including the melon seeds in a blender or food processor and process, adding 125ml / 4½fl oz (½ cup) water to make a thick paste. Transfer the paste to a bowl, pour in 500ml / 18fl oz (2¼ cups) cold water and mix well. Strain through a piece of damp muslin (cheesecloth) into a large jug (pitcher), then add the milk and sugar and chill in the refrigerator for at least 30 minutes.

Serve garnished with rose petals floating on the top.

Kairi ka Sherbet
Green Mango Sherbet

Origin Hyderabad
Preparation time 25 minutes, plus cooling time
Serves 10–12

4 unripe green mangoes, peeled
400g / 7oz (2 cups) sugar, plus extra if necessary
pinch of salt
4–6 green cardamom pods, ground

Bring 750ml / 1¼ pints (3¼ cups) water to the boil in a large pan, add the mangoes and cook for about 5 minutes, then remove from the heat and let cool.

When the mangoes are cool, squeeze them over a clean pan or chop the flesh to a pulp and transfer to a pan. Add the sugar and salt and heat over low heat to dissolve the sugar. Remove from the heat and allow to cool.

When cool, strain through a piece of muslin (cheesecloth) or fine sieve (strainer) into a bowl and add the ground cardamon. Add more sugar, if necessary, then transfer to a blender and process briefly until smooth. Dilute with water to serve.

Tulasi Sherbet
Sweet Basil Seed Sherbet

Origin Awadh
Preparation time 20 minutes, plus soaking and cooling time
Serves 8–10

4 tablespoons sweet basil seeds
120g / 4oz (½ cup) sugar
1 teaspoon kewra water or rosewater
500ml / 18fl oz (2¼ cups) cold milk

Put the seeds in a large bowl, pour in 750ml / 1¼ pints (3¼ cups) water and soak for about 1 hour, or until they swell up. Drain off any excess liquid.

Heat 1 litre / 1¾ pints (4¼ cups) water in a large heavy-based pan over low heat, add the sugar and stir until dissolved. Remove from the heat and cool.

Add the basil seeds and stir until well blended, then stir in the kewra water and milk before serving.

Sherbet-e-Gulab
Rose Cordial Sherbet

Origin Delhi
Preparation time 20 minutes, plus cooling time
Cooking time 30 minutes
Serves 4

750g / 1lb 10oz edible red roses
3kg / 6lb 8 oz (15 cups) sugar
250ml / 8fl oz (1 cup) rosewater
1.5 litres / 2½ pints (6¼ cups) milk, boiled and cooled

Break off the rose petals and wash thoroughly, then put into a large pan with 2 litres / 3½ pints (8½ cups) water and cook over low heat for about 20 minutes, or until the liquid has reduced by half.

Strain the mixture into a clean pan and add the sugar. Return to low heat and stir to dissolve the sugar, then bring to the boil. Remove from the heat and allow to cool.

When cool, add the rosewater. Stir in the milk, pour into a jug (pitcher) and chill in the refrigerator until ready to serve. Serve chilled.

Annanas ka Sherbet
Pineapple Sherbet

Origin Delhi/Awadh/Hyderabad
Preparation time 30 minutes, plus chilling time
Serves 8

180ml / 6½fl oz (¾ cup) lemon juice
375ml / 13fl oz (1½ cups) orange juice
100g / 3½oz (½ cup) sugar
6 canned pineapple slices, chopped
1 litre / 1¾ pints (4¼ cups) soda water (club soda)
1 litre / 1¾ pints (4¼ cups) ginger ale

Mix the lemon juice, orange juice and sugar together in a bowl, then cover and place in the refrigerator for about 2 hours.

Strain the mixture through a fine sieve (strainer) into a clean bowl, then add the pineapple, soda water and ginger ale and mix with a large spoon. Serve in a punch bowl with lots of crushed ice.

☀ / 📷 p.688

Leechi ka Sherbet
Lychee Squash Sherbet

Origin Awadh
Preparation time 20 minutes, plus cooling time
Serves 10–12

1.25 litres / 2 pints (5 cups) lychee juice
1kg / 2¼lb (5 cups) sugar
1½ teaspoons citric acid

Set the lychee juice aside in a jug (pitcher).

Bring 750ml / 1¼ pints (3¼ cups) water to the boil in a large, heavy-based pan, add the sugar and citric acid and boil for 5 minutes. Remove from the heat and strain through a piece of muslin cloth (cheesecloth) or fine sieve (strainer) into a large bowl to remove the scum. Allow to cool, then stir in the juice. Pour the drink into a sterilized bottle (see page 791). Store for up to 2 weeks in the refrigerator. Dilute with water, to serve.

Seb ka Ras
Apple Juice

Origin Punjab/Delhi/Awadh
Preparation time 15 minutes
Cooking time 10 minutes
Serves 10–12

1kg / 2¼lb (7 medium) apples, peeled, cored and cut into pieces
1kg / 2¼lb (5 cups) sugar
2 teaspoons citric acid

Put the apples and 750ml / 1¼ pints (3¼ cups) water in a large, heavy-based pan. Add the sugar and citric acid and cook for 10 minutes, or until the apples become soft. Allow to cool slightly. Transfer to a blender and process until mixed together, then pour into a sterilized bottle (see page 791). Store for up to 1 week in the refrigerator. Dilute with water, to serve.

Pappu Charu
Tangy Tamarind & Pepper Aperitif

Origin Andhra Pradesh
Preparation time 30 minutes
Cooking time 15 minutes
Serves 4

2 tomatoes, chopped
1 tablespoon Tamarind Extract (see page 58)
pinch of ground turmeric
1 teaspoon ground black pepper
½ bunch coriander (cilantro) leaves, chopped, plus extra to garnish
2 green chillies, de-seeded and chopped
salt

For the tempering

1 teaspoon vegetable oil
8–10 curry leaves
¼ teaspoon cumin seeds
¼ teaspoon coriander seeds
¼ teaspoon mustard seeds
1 dried red chilli

Bring 1 litre / 1¾ pints (4¼ cups) water to the boil in a large, heavy-based pan. Add the tomatoes, tamarind extract, turmeric and black pepper and season with salt. Continue to boil for about 5 minutes over medium heat, then add the coriander and green chillies.

To make the tempering, heat the oil in a frying pan (skillet) over high heat, add the curry leaves and cumin seeds and stir-fry for about 30 seconds, or until they start to splutter. Add the coriander seeds and mustard seeds and stir-fry for about 30 seconds, or until they are dark brown and start to splutter. Add the dried red chilli and stir-fry for about 1 minute, or until it turns a shade darker. Pour the tempering over the pepper water and cover immediately to retain the aroma. Simmer for about 2 minutes, then garnish with chopped coriander.

p.686

Nimboo ka Sherbet
Lemon Sherbet

Origin Pan-India
Preparation time 20 minutes, plus standing time
Serves 10–12

1kg / 2¼lb (10 medium) lemons
500g / 1lb 2oz (2½ cups) sugar

Squeeze the juice from the lemons into a jug (pitcher). Fill a clean sterilized bottle (see page 791) with the sugar, then add the lemon juice. Keep the sherbet in the sun for about 10 days or, if there is no sun, on the kitchen windowsill for a little longer, shaking the bottle daily. The sherbert is ready when the sugar has almost dissolved and the lemon juice is not as tart. Dilute with water to serve.

Kesar Elaychi Sherbet
Saffron & Cardamom Sherbet

Origin Awadh
Preparation time 20 minutes, plus soaking and cooling time
Serves 20–25

2 teaspoons saffron threads
2kg / 4½lb (10 cups) sugar
pinch of turmeric
seeds of 20–30 green cardamom pods, ground

Put the saffron in a small bowl add 125ml / 4½fl oz (½ cup) water and soak for about 2 hours.

Bring 1.8 litres / 3¼ pints (8 cups) water to the boil in a large, heavy-based pan, add the sugar and boil, removing the scum with a slotted spoon as it rises to the top, to make a syrup. Remove from the heat and allow to cool.

When the syrup is cool, add the turmeric, saffron and ground cardamom. Pour into a sterilized bottle (see page 791). Store for up to 1 week in the refrigerator. Dilute with water to serve.

Aamras
Sweet Mango Drink

Origin Maharashtra/Andhra Pradesh
Preparation time 15 minutes, plus chilling time
Serves 4

4 ripe mangoes, peeled
500ml / 18fl oz (2¼ cups) milk
sugar to taste
100g / 3½oz (½ cup) clotted cream or double (heavy) cream
125ml / 4½fl oz (½ cup) milk, for topping up (optional)

Peel the mangoes and chop the flesh, taking care around the stone (pit), then chop to a pulp with a knife or in a blender. Add the milk and sugar to taste and blend together. Chill in the refrigerator.

When cold, top up with cream or add the extra milk.

Shikanji
Lemonade

Origin Punjab/Delhi/Awadh
Preparation time 20 minutes
Serves 6

3 lemons
6 tablespoons sugar
pinch of salt
large pinch of ground black pepper

Squeeze the juice from the lemons into a large jug (pitcher). Pour 1.2 litres / 2 pints (5 cups) water into a large pan, add the sugar and stir to dissolve, then cook over low heat for about 10 minutes. Add the salt and pepper and the sugar water to the lemon juice and stir. Chill in the refrigerator until ready to serve.

Kharbuje ka Panna
Musk Melon Drink

Origin Punjab
Preparation time 25 minutes
Serves 6

1 musk melon or cantaloupe
4 tablespoons sugar
1 teaspoon rosewater
1.2 litres / 2 pints (5 cups) water

Peel the melon, de-seed and cut into dice. Transfer to a bowl, add the sugar, rosewater and 125ml / 4½fl oz (½ cup) cold water and stir. Serve in tall glasses with ice cubes and a spoon for the melon cubes.

Imli ka Soda-Paani
Tamarind Soda Water (Club Soda)

Origin New
Preparation time 30 minutes, plus standing time
Serves 6

1 tablespoon fresh ginger, peeled and roughly chopped
125ml / 4½fl oz (½ cup) Tamarind Extract (see page 58)
1 tablespoon sugar
1 teaspoon ground cinnamon
few drops of red food colouring
500ml / 18fl oz (2¼ cups) soda water (club soda)
salt

Put the ginger in a small blender and process, adding a little water if necessary, to make a paste.

Put the tamarind extract, ginger paste, sugar and cinnamon in a large heatproof bowl and season with salt. Pour in 1 litre / 1¾ pints (4¼ cups) boiling water, then cover and set aside until cold.

Strain the mixture through a piece of damp muslin (cheesecloth) into a jug (pitcher), add the red food colouring and stir. Chill in the refrigerator until ready to serve. To serve, add the soda water and some crushed ice.

Aam ka Panna
Mango Water

Origin Punjab/Awadh/Rajasthan
Preparation time 30 minutes
Serves 6

3 raw mangoes, peeled
3 tablespoons sugar
1 teaspoon ground cumin, roasted
½ teaspoon chilli powder
salt

Boil the mangoes in a pan of water for 5–10 minutes, then using your hands separate the pulp from the stones (pits). Put the pulp into a large bowl and mix with 1.2 litres / 2 pints (5 cups) water and the sugar. Strain the liquid through a piece of wet muslin (cheesecloth) into a clean bowl and add the remaining ingredients. Season with salt, stir well, then chill in the refrigerator until ready to serve.

Kaapi
Cold coffee

Origin Anglo-Indian
Preparation time 20 minutes, plus cooling time
Serves 6

6 tablespoons instant coffee
150g / 5oz (¾ cup) sugar
2 tablespoons cold milk

To serve

ice cream
dash of cream (optional)

Put the coffee in a large heatproof jug (pitcher). Pour in 1.25 litres / 2 pints (5 cups) hot water, add the sugar and mix well. Allow to cool completely, then add the milk. Transfer the mixture to a blender and process until well mixed.

Serve immediately in tall glasses with a dollop of ice cream on top. Cream or ice cream can also be blended with the coffee mixture, if you wish.

Filter Kaapi
Coffee

Origin Tamil Nadu/Karnataka
Preparation time 20 minutes
Serves 4

1 tablespoon ground coffee powder
500ml / 18fl oz (2¼ cups) milk
sugar, to taste

Put the coffee powder in the filter of a coffee press, place the inverted umbrella over it and gently press the powder. Pour boiling water over until the cup is filled and cover with the lid. Wait until a thick decoction collects in the cup below. Empty the decoction cup and pour some more boiling water into the upper cup, to extract a thinner version of the decoction.

Fill a cup or tumbler one-third full with the coffee, then add freshly boiled milk as desired to get a perfect filter coffee. Add sugar to taste.

Thandi Chai
Iced Tea

Origin Anglo-Indian
Preparation time 15 minutes
Serves 6

3 tablespoons tea leaves
few mint leaves
3 tablespoons lemon juice
3 tablespoons sugar
6 lemon slices, to garnish

Bring 1.5 litres / 2½ pints (6¼ cups) water, the tea and mint leaves to the boil in a large, heavy-based pan. Boil for 5 minutes, or until the tea acquires a rich hue, then strain through a fine sieve (strainer) into a heatproof jug (pitcher). Add the lemon juice and sugar and allow to cool a little, then chill in the refrigerator until ready to serve. To serve, float a lemon slice on top of each cup or glass and add some ice cubes.

Elaichi ki Chai
Cardamom Tea

Origin Gujarat
Preparation time 25 minutes
Serves 6

3 tablespoons tea leaves
150g / 5oz (¾ cup) sugar
6 green cardamom pods, crushed
250ml / 8fl oz (1 cup) milk

Put all the ingredients in a large, heavy-based pan, pour in 1.25 litres / 2 pints (5 cups) water and bring to the boil for about 5 minutes. Strain through a fine sieve (strainer) into a heatproof jug (pitcher) and serve hot in earthenware pots or in ceramic mugs.

📷 p.687

Masala Chai
Masala Tea

Origin Gujarat
Preparation time 20 minutes
Serves 8–10

6–8 cloves, coarsely ground
8 green cardamom pods, ground
1 cinnamon stick, about 2.5cm / 1 inch long, broken into pieces
1 teaspoon ground ginger
1 teaspoon ground fennel
6 teaspoons tea leaves
1.25 litres / 2 pints (5 cups) milk
150g / 5oz (¾ cup) sugar, or to taste

Bring 1.5 litres / 2½ pints (6¼ cups) water to the boil in a large, heavy-based pan. Add all the spices and boil for about 2 minutes over medium heat. Add the tea leaves and boil for a further 1 minute, then reduce the heat and simmer for about 5 minutes. Pour in the milk and return to the boil, then reduce the heat and simmer for a further 2 minutes. Remove from the heat and stir in the sugar. Strain through a fine sieve (strainer) into cups or mugs and serve hot.

Nimbuwali Chai
Lemon Tea

Origin Anglo-Indian
Preparation time 15 minutes
Serves 4

6 teaspoons sugar
4 teaspoons tea leaves
juice of 1 lime

Bring 1.25 litres / 2 pints (5 cups) water to the boil
in a large, heavy-based pan, add the sugar and stir
to dissolve, then add the tea leaves. Cover, remove
from the heat and let the tea steep for 2 minutes.
Pour in the lemon juice and stir.

Sheer Chai
Salty Cream Tea

Origin Jammu and Kashmir
Preparation time 20 minutes
Serves 4

1 teaspoon green tea leaves
pinch of bicarbonate of soda (baking soda)
375ml / 13fl oz (1½ cups) milk
salt
1 tablespoon double (heavy) cream, to serve

Put 250ml / 8fl oz (1 cup) water in a large, heavy-
based pan, add the tea leaves and the bicarbonate
of soda and bring to the boil. Boil for 8–10 minutes,
or until only 5 or 6 teaspoons of liquid remain. Now
add another 250ml / 8fl oz (1 cup) water and boil
until only a little is left. Next, add 1 litre / 1¾ pints
(4¼ cups) water and season with salt. Boil for a few
minutes, until the tea becomes pink. Pour in the milk
and continue to boil for 90 seconds. Do not cover
the tea while it is cooking. To serve, add the cream.

Jal Jeera
Cumin Water

Origin Punjab/Delhi/Awadh
Preparation time 20 minutes, plus soaking time
Serves 6

500ml / 18fl oz (2¼ cups) Tamarind Extract (see page 58)
few sprigs of fresh mint, ground
½ teaspoon chilli powder
½ teaspoon ground black salt
2 tablespoons lemon juice
1 tablespoon icing (confectioners') sugar
2 tablespoons ground cumin seeds, roasted
salt
6 lemon slices, to garnish

Put all the ingredients along with 1 litre / 1¾ pints
(4 cups) water in a large bowl and whisk to mix.
Chill in the refrigerator until ready to serve. To
serve, spread some salt out on a plate, then wet the
rims of 6 glasses and dip them upside down into the
plate of salt, so that the rims are coated with salt.
Carefully pour the cumin water into the glasses and
put a lemon wedge on the edge of each glass. Serve
with ice cubes.

Gajar Kaanji
Carrot Water

Origin Punjab
Preparation time 30 minutes, plus soaking time
Serves 4

450g / 1lb (8 medium) carrots, preferably black, cut lengthways into 6 long slices
2 tablespoons black mustard seeds
1 teaspoon chilli powder
salt
carrot slices, to garnish

Put the carrots in a large glass jar, add the spices
and pour in 3 litres / 5 pints (12¾ cups) cold water.
Tie a muslin cloth (cheesecloth) on top of the jar and
place in the sun for 2–3 days, or on the windowsil
for a week, shaking daily. When tangy, dilute if
prefered and serve with a slice of carrot in each
glass. Store in the refrigerator.

This section includes signature dishes from some of the most highly regarded Indian chefs working around the world. Each has contributed to today's high standard of excellence within Indian cuisine.

—

Guest Chefs

Anirudh Arora, Moti Mahal, London

Anil Ashokan, Qmin, Sydney

Ajoy Joshi, Nilgiri's, Sydney

Ashish Joshi, Paatra, New Delhi

Vikrant Kapoor, Zaafran, Sydney

Joy Kapur, Maharani, San Francisco

Alfred Prasad, Taramind, London

Suvir Saran, Dévi, New York

Vivek Singh, Cinnamon Club, London

Miraj-ul-Haque, Radisson's, New Delhi

Vikram Vij & Meeru Dhalwala, Vij's, Vancouver

Anirudh Arora
Moti Mahal

45 Great Queen Street
London WC2B 5AA
United Kingdom

Anirudh Arora's obsession with detail, along with
a passion for the cuisine of India, has made him
one of London's best Indian chefs. The son of an
Indian army officer, he spent his formative years
between Kashmir, Ladakh, Lucknow and Kolkata and
has translated this experience into a broad culinary
repertoire. At the age of 25, he was personal chef
to the prime minister of India. Each dish on Moti
Mahal's menu is inspired by the culinary roots of
rural India, particularly along the Grand Truck
Road, and is created with quality ingredients based
on seasonality and freshness.

Menu

1 **Kararre Bhyein**
Stir-fried Lotus Stem

2 **Qabali Seviyan**
Vermicelli & Masala Chicken

3 **Paturee**
Pan-fried Crab & Prawn (Shrimp) Cakes

4 **Suvey aur Palak ka Gosht**
Stewed Lamb with Spinach & Dill

5 **Titari**
Guinea Fowl with Cumin,
Garlic & Red Chillies

Kararre Bhyein
Stir-fried Lotus Stem

Preparation time 15 minutes
Serves 4

600g / 1lb 5oz lotus stems, peeled
1 litre / 1¾ pints (4¼ cups) oil, for deep-frying
few sprigs coriander (cilantro)
70g / 2½oz (½ cup) peanuts
1 heaped teaspoon chilli powder
2 teaspoons amchoor powder
1 heaped teaspoon ground cumin, roasted
1 × 2.5-cm / 1-inch piece fresh ginger, cut into julienne
1 lemon
salt

Slice the lotus stems, place in a sieve (strainer) and
rinse under cold running water, then drain.

Heat the oil for deep-frying in a deep pan to
180°C/350°F, or until a cube of bread browns in
30 seconds. Working in batches, if necessary,
carefully lower the lotus stems into the hot oil and
deep-fry until crisp. Remove with a slotted spoon
and drain on kitchen paper (paper towels). Set aside.

Carefully add the coriander to the hot oil and
deep-fry for a few seconds until crisp. Remove with
a slotted spoon and drain on kitchen paper.

Put the peanuts in a dry frying pan (skillet) and roast
over low heat for a few minutes until golden brown.
Watch them carefully as they may burn. Remove
the pan from the heat and allow to cool. When the
peanuts are cool, transfer them to a blender and
crush. Set aside.

Put the chilli powder, amchoor powder, roasted
ground cumin, roasted peanuts, deep-fried lotus
stem and ginger julienne in a bowl and season with
salt to taste. Squeeze over the lemon and mix well
to combine.

Check the seasoning, garnish with the deep-fried
coriander and serve warm.

Qabali Seviyan
Vermicelli & Masala Chicken

Preparation time 40 minutes
Cooking time 6–8 minutes
Serves 4

For the vermicelli

2½ tablespoons ghee
½ teaspoon caraway seeds
1 red onion, sliced
1 green chilli
1 × 3-cm / 1¼-inch piece fresh ginger, cut into julienne
1½ teaspoons chilli powder
1 heaped teaspoon ground turmeric
100g / 3½oz vermicelli
few sprigs coriander (cilantro), chopped
1 lemon
salt

For the chicken stuffing

3 tablespoons vegetable oil
1 × 2-cm / 1-inch piece fresh ginger, chopped
2 tablespoons chopped green chilli
80g / 2¾oz (½ cup) chopped onion
2 scant teaspoons chilli powder
2 scant teaspoons ground coriander
¾ teaspoon ground turmeric
80g / 2¾oz (½ cup) chopped tomatoes
2 boneless, skinless chicken supremes or breasts, cut into thin strips
1 heaped teaspoon Garam Masala (See page 31)
few sprigs coriander (cilantro), chopped
2 teaspoons pine nuts
1 lemon
salt

For the egg custard

2 eggs
1½ tablespoons chopped onion
1 tablespoon de-seeded and chopped tomato
½ tablespoon chopped green chilli
few sprigs coriander (cilantro), chopped
2 teaspoons grated cheese
½ teaspoon chilli powder
½ teaspoon crushed black pepper
salt

Preheat the oven to 180°C/350°F/Gas Mark 4.

For the vermicelli, heat the ghee in a large, heavy-based pan over medium heat, add the caraway seeds and let them infuse (steep) in the hot ghee. Add the onion, green chilli and ginger and cook for about 5 minutes, or until the onions are translucent.

Add the chilli powder and turmeric and season with salt. Cook for 1 minute, then add the vermicelli and hot water to cover. Cover and cook for about 3–4 minutes, or until the vermicelli becomes soft.

Add the chopped coriander, then squeeze over the lemon and check the seasoning. Set aside.

For the chicken, heat the oil in a large, heavy-based pan over medium heat, add the ginger and green chilli and sauté briefly. Add the onion and cook for about 5–7 minutes, or until the onions are golden brown. Add the chilli powder, ground coriander and turmeric, then season with salt to taste. Cook for 1 minute then add the chopped tomatoes and cook for a few minutes until they become soft.

Add the chicken strips and cook until done. Sprinkle over the garam masala, chopped coriander and pine nuts, then squeeze over the lemon and check the seasoning. Set aside.

For the egg custard, beat the eggs in a bowl, then add the onion, tomato, green chilli, coriander, cheese, chilli powder and crushed black pepper and season with salt. Beat well and check the seasoning.

Spread a layer of the vermicelli over the base (bottom) of an ovenproof dish, then add a layer of the chicken mixture. Repeat the layers until the vermicelli and chicken are used up. Pour the egg custard over the top and bake in the oven for 6–8 minutes.

Paturee
Pan-fried Crab & Prawn Cakes

Preparation time 30 minutes
Cooking time 8–10 minutes
Serves 4

1 banana leaf
200g / 7oz raw prawns (shrimp), peeled and deveined
200g / 7oz white crabmeat
60g / 2oz (⅓ cup) boiled grated potato
few sprigs curry leaves, chopped
few sprigs coriander (cilantro), chopped
2 tablespoons mustard oil
30g / 1¼oz (¼ cup) grated cheese
½ teaspoon ground turmeric
¾ teaspoon chilli powder
2 teaspoons Garam Masala (see page 31)
½ teaspoon dried red chilli flakes
1 lemon
salt

Trim, cut and wipe the banana leaf with a damp cloth.

Put the chopped prawns, crabmeat, potato, curry leaves, coriander, mustard oil, cheese, turmeric, chilli powder, garam masala and dried red chilli flakes in a bowl and season with salt to taste. Mix well, then squeeze over the lemon and check the seasoning.

Divide the mixture into equal-sized cakes and wrap them in the banana leaf, making sure that the mixture does not come out.

Heat a large, non-stick frying pan (skillet) over medium heat. Working in batches, add the wrapped cakes and cook for about 8–10 minutes, turning once during cooking. Serve hot.

Suvey aur Palak ka Gosht
Stewed Lamb with Spinach & Dill

Preparation time 1 hour
Cooking time 1½ hours
Serves 4

3 tablespoons vegetable oil
whole spices
2 onions, chopped
1kg / 2¼lb diced boneless leg of lamb
2 teaspoons Ginger Paste (see page 57)
2 teaspoons Garlic Paste (see page 57)
1½ teaspoons chilli powder
2 teaspoons ground coriander
1 teaspoon ground turmeric
4 tomatoes
80g / 2¾oz (⅓ cup) natural (plain) yoghurt
100g / 3½oz baby spinach
few sprigs dill, chopped
1 × 1-cm / ½-inch piece fresh ginger, cut into julienne
½ teaspoon ground black cardamom
1½ teaspoons Garam Masala (see page 31)
juice of 1 lemon
salt

Heat the oil in a flat-based pan over medium heat and add the whole spices. Add the onions and cook for about 5–7 minutes, or until golden brown. Add the lamb and cook until well seared. Add the ginger and garlic pastes and sauté briefly, then add the chilli powder, ground coriander and turmeric cook for about 2–3 minutes.

Put the tomatoes into a blender and process to make a smooth purée. Add them to the pan along with the yoghurt and cook until the oil separates. Pour in enough water to cover the lamb and gently simmer until the lamb becomes tender.

Add the baby spinach, dill and ginger to the pan and cook for a further 2 minutes. Finish with the ground black cardamom, garam masala and lemon juice. Check the seasoning.

Titari
Guinea Fowl with Cumin, Garlic & Red Chillies

Preparation time 1 hour, plus soaking and marinating time
Cooking time 30 minutes
Serves 4

25g / 1oz dried Kashmiri red chillies

1 skinless guinea fowl, cut into 8 pieces

4 tablespoons malt vinegar

1 teaspoon chilli powder

1 × 1-cm / ½-inch piece fresh ginger

10 cloves garlic

3 tablespoons mustard oil

90g / 3¼oz (⅔ cup) hung natural (plain) yoghurt
   (see page 793)

½ teaspoon caraway seeds

¾ teaspoon Garam Masala (see page 31)

salt

Soak the chillies in a bowl of water.

Using a sharp knife, make incisions on the breast and legs of the guinea fowl.

Put the vinegar and chilli powder in a large, non-metallic shallow dish or bowl, season with salt and add the guinea fowl. Mix well, cover and allow to marinate for about 15–20 minutes.

Preheat the tandoor, charcoal barbecue or grill (broiler) to moderately hot.

Meanwhile, put the ginger, garlic, mustard oil and soaked chillies in a food processor or blender and process to make a smooth paste. Transfer to a bowl, add the hung yoghurt and caraway seeds and mix well. Check the seasoning. Spread this paste over the guinea fowl, then thread the guinea fowl pieces through metal skewers and cook in the preheated tandoor, on the barbecue or under grill for 15–25 minutes or until done. Serve hot.

Anil Ashokan
Qmin

207 Pacific Highway
St Leonards
NSW 2065
Australia

Raised in Mumbai Anil Ashokan graduated from the Taj Mahal Hotel in Mumbai and then spent several years honing his skills in Hong Kong, Paris, Japan and Switzerland. When he moved to Australia, he spent six years as Executive Sous Chef at the ANA Hotel (now called the Shangri La Hotel) before opening the highly regarded and innovative Sydney restaurant, Qmin. As head chef and author of a successful cookbook, Ashokan is best known for his spicy and aromatic innovative interpretations of regional cuisine.

Menu

1 **Elumikkai Sadam**
Lemon Rice

2 **Methi Suva Macchi**
Tuna with Fenugreek & Dill Leaves

3 **Tulsi ke Tikke**
Marinated Chicken with Basil

4 **Nalli Rogan Josh**
Braised Lamb Shanks

5 **Bathak Peri-Peri**
Roast Duck with 'Peri-Peri'

6 **Anjeer aur Akhrot ki Kulfi**
Frozen Parfait with Figs & Walnuts

Elumikkai Sadam
Lemon Rice

Preparation time 20 minutes
Cooking time 10 minutes
Serves 4

500g / 1lb 2oz (2⅔ cups) basmati rice, cooked
2 tablespoons oil
1 teaspoon black mustard seeds
3g / ⅛oz whole dried red chillies, broken in half
1 teaspoon split yellow dal
1 sprig curry leaves
½ teaspoon ground turmeric
1 teaspoon very finely chopped ginger
2 tablespoons peanuts
juice from 1½ lemons
salt

Spoon the hot rice into a serving bowl. Heat the oil in a heavy-based pan over medium heat, add the mustard seeds and sauté for about 1 minute, or until they start to splutter. Add the chillies, dal, curry leaves, turmeric, chopped ginger and peanuts and cook until the dal and peanuts are golden brown. Remove the pan from the heat and stir in the lemon juice. Pour over the rice then season with salt and toss well until the rice is coated and turns an even yellow colour.

Methi Suva Macchi
Tuna with Fenugreek & Dill Leaves

Preparation time 20 minutes
Cooking time 8–10 minutes
Serves 4

---

1 teaspoon fennel seeds

5 tablespoons chopped fresh fenugreek leaves or
    1 teaspoon dried fenugreek leaves

5 tablespoons chopped fresh dill leaves

3½ tablespoons chopped fresh mint leaves,
    preferably spearmint

4 tablespoons chopped coriander (cilantro) leaves

2 tablespoons de-seeded and finely chopped
    green chillies

600g / 1lb 5oz yellowfin tuna fillets, cut into
    thick steaks

1 tablespoon lemon juice

vegetable oil, for pan-frying and oiling

salt

Preheat the oven to 180°C/350°F.

Fry the fennel seeds in a dry frying pan (skillet) over gentle heat for about 1 minute, or until very lightly roasted. Transfer to a mortar and crush with a pestle. Put them in a bowl, add the chopped herbs and chillies and mix together, then season with salt.

Heat a large, heavy-based pan over high heat. Season the tuna with salt, then add to the very hot pan and quickly fry for a few minutes to seal well on all sides. Remove the pan from the heat and sprinkle the lemon juice over. Transfer the tuna one by one to the chopped herbs mix and roll to coat. Press down with the palms of your hands to get all the herbs to stick to the tuna. Place the tuna on an oiled baking tray (sheet) and cook in the oven until done to your liking.

Tulsi ke Tikke
Marinated Chicken with Basil

Preparation time 30 minutes, plus soaking and marinating time
Cooking time 12 minutes
Serves 4

500g / 1lb 2oz chicken thighs, cut into cubes

For the marinade

2 tablespoons cashew nuts

1 × 1-cm / ½-inch piece fresh ginger, puréed

6–7 cloves garlic, puréed

1 bunch basil, leaves only

1 green chilli, chopped

2 tablespoons oil

heaped 1½ teaspoons Garam Masala (see page 31)

heaped 1½ teaspoons Chaat Masala (see page 31)

salt

For the marinade, put the cashew nuts in a bowl, pour in enough warm water to cover and allow to soak for 30 minutes, then drain.

Put the ginger, garlic, basil, cashews and chillies in a blender or food processor. Add 1 tablespoon of the oil and process well to make a smooth paste. Remove from the blender or food processor and add the garam masala and chaat masala.

Put the chicken in a large shallow dish, add the marinade and mix well until the chicken is thoroughly coated. Season with salt and add the rest of the oil. Cover and allow to marinate in the refrigerator for at least 4 hours.

Preheat a tandoor, charcoal barbecue or grill (broiler) to moderate. Alternatively, preheat the oven to 190°C/375°F/Gas Mark 5.

Thread the chicken on to several metal skewers and cook in the preheated tandoor, on the barbecue, or under grill for 12 minutes. Alternatively, cook in the oven for 15 minutes.

Serve with Roomali roti (traditional thin bread that is cooked on a griddle) and some salad.

Nalli Rogan Josh
Braised Lamb Shanks

Preparation time 30 minutes
Cooking time 30 minutes
Serves 4

¼ teaspoon saffron threads

2½ teaspoons Ginger Paste (see page 57)

heaped 1 tablespoon Garlic Paste (see page 57)

½ teaspoon ground coriander

3 tablespoons paprika

1 teaspoon chilli powder

6 tablespoons oil

1 cinnamon stick

4 cloves

2 bay leaves

3 black cardamom pods

240g / 8½oz (1⅔ cups) finely sliced red onions

4 lamb shanks

250g / 9oz (2 small) tomatoes, puréed

½ teaspoon ground mace

2 sprigs coriander (cilantro)

salt

Put the saffron in a small bowl, add a little water and allow to soak until required.

Put the ginger and garlic pastes, ground coriander, paprika and chilli powder in a bowl, add 2 tablespoons water and mix to form a paste.

Heat the oil in a large, heavy-based pan over medium heat, add the cinnamon, cloves, bay leaves, cardamom and sliced onions and sauté, stirring well for about 5–7 minutes, or until the onions are golden brown. Remove a third of the mixture with a slotted spoon and set aside for the garnish.

Put the shanks in the pan and cook for a few minutes until sealed on all sides. If required, cover and cook for a minute until the oil starts to separate out. Season with salt and pour in about 1 litre / 1¾ pints (4¼ cups) water, or enough to cover the meat, and bring to the boil over high heat. Add the puréed tomatoes, return to the boil, then reduce the heat and simmer for at least 30 minutes, or until the lamb is cooked. Stir in the ground mace and soaked saffron and garnish with the reserved onion mixture.

Bathak Peri-Peri
Roast Duck with 'Peri-Peri'

Preparation time 30 minutes, plus soaking and marinating time
Cooking time 30 minutes
Serves 4

8 whole dried red chillies, slit in half
    lengthways and de-seeded

150ml / ¼ pint (⅔ cup) malt vinegar

1 × 1.8-kg / 4-lb duck

50g / 1¾oz (½ small) onion, chopped
    into large chunks

50g / 1¾oz (1 medium) carrot, chopped
    into large chunks

1 cinnamon stick

1 tablespoon chopped cloves

2 teaspoons black peppercorns

4 tablespoons cumin seeds

1 × 2.5-cm / 1-inch piece fresh ginger, chopped

50g / 1¾oz tamarind

2 teaspoons cardamom

salt

Put the chillies into a bowl, pour over the vinegar and allow to soak for at least two hours.

Separate the legs and breasts of the duck. Chop the neck and all the bones and trimmings into chunks and place in a roasting tray (sheet). Add the onions and carrots to the roasting tray and mix together.

Stir-fry the whole spices in a dry frying pan (skillet) over low heat for a few minutes until roasted. Set aside. Transfer the chillies, including the vinegar, the tamarind, ginger and all the spices into a blender or food processor and process to make a smooth paste. Don't add any water.

Rub the spice mix over the duck, season, then cover and allow to marinate in the refrigerator for 1 hour.

Preheat the oven to 200°C/400°F/Gas Mark 6. Place the duck on top of the bones, carrots and onions and bake in the oven, basting occasionally, until the duck starts to brown. Reduce the heat to 180°C/350°F/Gas Mark 4 and continue to roast, basting occasionally, until the duck is soft and fully cooked. Remove the roasting tray from the oven and gently lift out the duck with a slotted spoon and set aside in a serving dish. Strain the juices into a pan, skim off the fat, then simmer, skimming occasionally, to reduce the juices. Pour over the duck and serve.

Anjeer aur Akhrot ki Kulfi
Frozen Parfait with Figs & Walnuts

Preparation time 20 minutes plus chilling
and freezing time
Cooking time 45 minutes
Serves 4

100ml / 3½fl oz (scant ½ cup) milk
100ml / 3½fl oz (scant ½ cup) pouring (light) cream
seeds from 4 green cardamom pods, crushed
300ml / ½ pint (1¼ cups) condensed milk
60g / 2oz (⅓ cup) dried figs, chopped into small pieces
60g / 2oz (½ cup) walnuts, chopped into small pieces
2 tablespoons pistachio nuts, sliced
3 tablespoons slivered almonds
2 tablespoons rose syrup, to serve

Put the milk and cream in a heavy-based pan, add
the crushed cardamom and bring to the boil, then
reduce the heat and simmer, stirring constantly,
until the mixture is reduced by nearly half. Add the
condensed milk and stir. Add the figs and walnuts
(saving some for the decoration), then remove the
pan from the heat and allow to cool.

When the mixture is cool, chill in the refrigerator
for 3 hours.

Once the mixture is very cold, transfer to an ice
cream machine and churn according to the
manufacturer's instructions. When the mix starts to
set in the machine, scoop out and put into kulfi
moulds, ramekins or dariole moulds. Transfer the
moulds to the freezer and freeze for 4 hours, or until
well set. Decorate with the reserved figs and walnuts
and serve with the rose syrup. You can remove
the kulfi from the moulds or serve in the moulds.

If you don't have an ice-cream machine, reduce the
quantity of milk to 4 tablespoons and increase the
quantity of cream to 150ml / ¼ pint (⅔ cup). Follow
the same cooking method, then after chilling, pour
directly into moulds and freeze until well set.

Ajoy Joshi
Nilgiri's

81–83 Christie Street
St Leonards
NSW 2065
Australia

Nilgiri's reputation has come about through Ajoy Joshi's culinary vision, which includes books, branded spice mixes and ready-made meals. Teaming his international culinary expertise with a contemporary flair, Ajoy produces regional food that is steeped in Indian tradition.

———

Menu

1 **Pudine ka Raita**
Mint Raita

2 **Kakdi ka Raita**
Cucumber Raita

3 **Pathar ka Gosht**
Grilled Marinated Lamb

4 **Yerra Varuval**
Prawn (Shrimp) Fry

5 **Meen Kozhambu**
Fish Kozhambu

6 **Dum ka Murgh**
Rich Chicken Curry

7 **Murgh Biryani**
Chicken Biryani

Pudine ka Raita
Mint Raita

Preparation time 10 minutes
Serves 8–10

¼ bunch mint leaves, chopped

¼ bunch coriander (cilantro) leaves, chopped

½ tablespoon crushed fresh ginger

½ tablespoon roughly chopped green chillies

565g / 1lb 4oz (2½ cups) full-fat natural
    (whole plain) yoghurt

salt

Put the mint and coriander leaves, ginger and green chillies in a blender and process until ground.

Add the yoghurt, season with salt and process until all the ingredients are mixed together.

Season to taste and serve as an accompaniment.

———

Kakdi ka Raita
Cucumber Raita

Preparation time 10 minutes
Serves 8–10

565g / 1lb 4oz (2½ cups) full-fat (whole) yoghurt

2–3 cucumbers, peeled, de-seeded and grated or
    4–6 Lebanese cucumbers, finely chopped

1 teaspoon cumin seeds, lightly roasted and ground

¼ bunch coriander (cilantro) leaves, chopped

salt

Put the yoghurt in a bowl and whisk. Add the cucumber and ground cumin and mix well. Season with salt, then add the chopped coriander leaves and mix to combine. Serve as an accompaniment.

Pathar ka Gosht
Grilled Marinated Lamb

Preparation time 15 minutes, plus marinating time
Cooking time 10–15 minutes
Serves 4

1kg / 2¼lb lamb cutlets

2–3 onions, sliced into rings

2–3 lemon wedges

1 bunch mint leaves

For the marinade

1 teaspoon fresh ginger, crushed

1 teaspoon garlic clove, crushed

6–8 green chillies, crushed to a paste

1 teaspoon cassia buds, ground

1 teaspoon black peppercorns, ground

salt

Put all the ingredients for the marinade in a bowl and mix together. Season with salt.

Put the lamb in a shallow non-metallic dish and spread the marinade over. Cover and allow to marinate in the refrigerator for 30 minutes.

Heat a granite stone, preferably on a charcoal barbecue. Place the marinated cutlets on top of the hot stone and cook on both sides for 5–7 minutes. Serve hot with the onion rings, lemon wedges and mint leaves.

Yerra Varuval
Prawn (Shrimp) Fry

Preparation time 10 minutes
Cooking time 5–7 minutes
Serves 4–6

1kg / 2¼lb prawns (shrimp), peeled and deveined

vegetable oil, for frying

juice of 1 lemon

For the marinade

½ tablespoon crushed fresh ginger

½ tablespoon crushed garlic clove

1 tablespoon tamarind paste

½ teaspoon ground turmeric

½ teaspoon chilli powder

2 tablespoons coriander seeds, ground

½ tablespoon black peppercorns, crushed

1 sprig curry leaves

2–3 tablespoons vegetable oil

salt

For the mint and coriander (cilantro) chatni

1 bunch mint leaves

1 bunch coriander (cilantro) leaves

1 green chilli, stem removed

1 tablespoon lemon juice

4 tablespoons natural (plain) yoghurt

salt

Put all the ingredients for the marinade in a shallow bowl and mix together. Season with salt to taste. Add the prawns and turn to coat, then cover and set aside for 5 minutes.

Meanwhile, to make the mint and coriander chatni, put all the ingredients in a food processor, season with salt and process to make a smooth paste. Set aside.

Heat the oil in heavy-based pan over medium heat. Add the prawns and stir-fry until cooked. Remove the pan from the heat and add the lemon juice.

Serve hot with the mint and coriander chatni.

Meen Kozhambu
Fish Kozhambu

Preparation time 20–30 minutes
Coking time 15–20 minutes
Serves 4–6

4 tablespoons vegetable oil

1 teaspoon black mustard seeds

½ teaspoon fenugreek seeds

2–3 whole dried red chillies

500g / 1lb 2oz (3 medium) onions, sliced

2 tablespoons crushed fresh ginger

2 tablespoons crushed garlic

2 sprigs curry leaves

1 tablespoon ground turmeric

2 teaspoons chilli powder

4 tomatoes, roughly chopped

1 tablespoon tamarind paste

1kg / 2¼lb fish fillets, preferably barramundi,
   snapper or flathead, skinned and cut into fingers

225ml / 7½fl oz (scant 1 cup) coconut cream

juice of ½ lemon

salt

Heat the oil in a heavy-based pan over medium heat. Add the black mustard seeds and fry for about 1 minute, or until they start to crackle. Add the fenugreek seeds and stir until they turn light golden brown, then add the whole dried red chillies. When the chillies turn deep brown, add the sliced onions and sauté for about a minute. Add the crushed ginger and garlic and cook for a further 2 minutes, or until they release their flavours. Add the curry leaves, turmeric and chilli powder, then season with salt and cook over gentle heat for about 30 seconds.

Add the chopped tomatoes and cook for about 5 minutes, or until they turn soft, then add the tamarind paste and mix well.

Add the fish fillets, cover and simmer in the sauce for about 10–15 minutes, or until the fish is cooked. Add the coconut cream and warm through. Sprinkle over the lemon juice and serve hot with steamed rice.

Dum ka Murgh
Rich Chicken Curry

Preparation time 45 minutes, plus marinating time
Cooking time 45–60 minutes
Serves 4–6

1kg / 2¼lb boneless chicken thighs

100ml / 3½fl oz (scant ½ cup) vegetable oil

3 onions, sliced

juice of 1–2 lemons

For the marinade

500g / 1lb 2oz (generous 2 cups) full-fat natural
   (whole plain) yoghurt

1 teaspoon crushed fresh ginger

1 teaspoon crushed garlic

1 tablespoon crushed green chillies

½ teaspoon ground turmeric

1 tablespoon white sesame seeds, ground

50g / 1¾oz cashew nuts, roasted and ground

salt

For the spice mix

1 teaspoon cassia buds

2 green cardamom pods

4 cloves

½ teaspoon black cumin seeds

Put all the ingredients for the marinade in a large shallow dish and mix together. Season with salt. Add the chicken and turn to coat, then cover and allow to marinate in the refrigerator for 1–2 hours.

To make the spice mix, put all the spices in a spice grinder, small food processor or mortar and pestle and grind together. Set aside.

Heat the oil in a heavy-based pan over medium heat, add the sliced onions and saute for about 5–7 minutes, or until the onions turn golden brown. Add the marinated chicken and stir well. Moisten with a little water and cook for 25–30 minutes, or until the chicken is tender. When the chicken is cooked, add the freshly crushed spices and sprinkle over the lemon juice.

Murgh Biryani
Chicken Biryani

Preparation time 45 minutes
Cooking time 1¼ hours
Serves 4–6

1 teaspoon saffron threads
1½ teaspoons hot milk
250ml / 9fl oz (1 cup) oil
500g / 1lb 2oz onions, sliced
50g / 1¾oz ginger, crushed
50g / 1¾oz garlic cloves, crushed
100g / 3½oz green chillies, slit
600ml / 1 pint (2½ cups) natural (plain) yoghurt
1 × 1-kg / 2¼-lb chicken, cut into large pieces
50g / 1¾oz roasted cashew nuts
25g / 1oz raisins
juice of 1 lemon
1 bunch coriander (cilantro) leaves, chopped
1 small bunch mint leaves, chopped
2 teaspoons Garam Masala (see page 31)
1kg / 2¼lb premium grade basmati rice
salt

Preheat the oven to 220–240°C/ 425–475°F/Gas mark 7–9.

Put the saffron threads in a small bowl, add the hot milk and allow to soak until required.

Heat the oil in a large heavy-based casserole or ovenproof pot over medium heat, add the sliced onions, season with salt and cook until the onions have caramelized. Add the crushed ginger and garlic and slit chillies, then add the yoghurt and stir. Now add the chicken and cook for a few minutes to seal. Add the roasted cashew nuts, raisins and lemon juice and cook for about 5 minutes.

Add the chopped coriander and mint leaves to the chicken together with the garam masala, then cover with a lid and set aside.

Cook the basmati rice in a large heavy-based pan of boiling salted water until al dente, then drain and spoon over the chicken. Sprinkle with the saffron-infused milk and cover the rice with a damp clean tea (dish) towel.

Cover with a lid and transfer the casserole dish or pot to the oven and cook for about 10 minutes, or until the chicken is cooked.

Remove from the oven and serve hot with cucumber raita.

Ashish Joshi
Paatra

Jaypee Vasant Continental
Basant Lok, Pratik Market
New Delhi
India

The menu at Paatra showcases a diverse collection of dishes from Punjab and traces the ancient culinary route from Amritsar to Lahore. At the helm of the operation is chef Ashish Joshi who — with nearly 20 years of experience — creates a vibrant collection of recipes made with freshly-ground spices and cooked in authentic vessels to preserve the real flavours. Joshi has worked all over Asia, organized culinary festivals in India and appeared on various cookery shows.

___

Menu

1 **Bhunee Chaat**
Paatra Indian Salad

2 **Matterwali Tikki**
Pan-grilled Pea Patties

3 **Shadras Subziyan**
Stir-fried Vegetables

4 **Amritsari Tawa Murg**
Pan-fried Amritsari Chicken

Bhunee Chaat
Paatra Indian Salad

Preparation time 1¼ hours, plus marinating time
Cooking time 6–8 minutes
Serves 4

---

2 large potatoes

1 teaspoon ground turmeric

salt

2 sweet potatoes

1 pineapple, peeled and cut into 5 × 5 × 2.5-cm /
    2 × 2 × 1-inch thick chunks

oil, for deep-frying

2 guavas, cut into chunks

2 pears, cut into chunks

3 apples, cut into chunks

6 mushrooms, blanched

2 each of red, yellow and green peppers, cored
    and cut into 5 × 5 × 2.5-cm / 2 × 2 × 1-inch
    thick chunks

butter, for basting

1 teaspoon Chaat Masala (see page 31)

For the marinade

2 teaspoons sugar

2 teaspoons ground pomegranate

2 teaspoons balsamic vinegar

2 teaspoons white (malt) vinegar

salt and black salt

2 tablespoons hung natural (plain) yoghurt
    (see page 793)

1 teaspoon red chilli, roasted and crushed

1 teaspoon paprika

2 teaspoons red chilli paste

½ teaspoon ground amchoor

1 teaspoon Chaat Masala (see page 31)

½ teaspoon Garam Masala (see page 31)

½ teaspoon black peppercorns, crushed

4 tablespoons oil

1 teaspoon roasted ground ajwain

½ teaspoon black cardamom

Cut the potatoes into barrel shapes, then into slices 1cm / ½ inch thick. Blanch the potato slices in a large pan of water with the turmeric and salt to taste. Drain and pat dry with kitchen paper (paper towels).

Meanwhile, boil the sweet potatoes in a pan of water for about 20 minutes, or until soft. Drain and leave until cool enough to handle. Peel off the skins and cut into 1-cm / ½-inch thick slices.

Heat enough oil for deep-frying in a kadhai or large, deep pan to 180°C/350°F, or until a cube of bread browns in 30 seconds. Carefully add the potatoes and deep-fry over medium heat until nearly cooked. Remove with a slotted spoon and drain on kitchen paper.

Carefully add the sweet potatoes to the hot oil and deep-fry over medium heat until light brown, then remove with a slotted spoon and drain on kitchen paper.

To make the marinade, put the sugar and ground pomegranate on a flat tray and add the vinegars. Mix with the palms of your hands until the mixture is smooth. Now add all the remaining ingredients and mix well. Add the prepared fruits and vegetables to the marinade and mix well until each piece is coated. Set aside for 15 minutes.

Preheat the oven to 190°C/395°F/Gas Mark 5. Thread the fruits and vegetables alternately onto several metal skewers.

Roast in the oven for about 5 minutes or until the kebabs change colour. Remove from the oven and baste with butter then roast again for 1 minute. Remove the fruit and vegetables from the skewers, sprinkle with chaat masala and serve hot.

—

Matterwali Tikki
Pan-grilled Pea Patties

Preparation time 1½ hours
Cooking time 8–10 minutes
Serves 6

1kg / 2¼lb green peas
1 large potato
100g / 3½oz (scant ½ cup) ghee, plus extra for shallow-frying
4 teaspoons cumin seeds
½ teaspoon ground turmeric
½ teaspoon asafoetida
1 × 10g / ¼oz piece fresh ginger, peeled and finely chopped
3 green chillies, de-seeded and finely chopped
½ teaspoon yellow chilli powder
1 teaspoon ground cumin, roasted
½ teaspoon Garam Masala (see page 31)
20g / ¾oz cornflour (cornstarch)
30g / 1¼oz breadcrumbs
Chaat Masala (see page 31), for sprinkling
salt

For the filling

25g / 1oz processed cheese, grated
1 teaspoon fresh mint, chopped
25g / 1oz paneer, grated
½ teaspoon chopped ginger
½ teaspoon chopped green chilli
¼ teaspoon yellow chilli powder
1 teaspoon raisins, roughly chopped

Cook the peas in a pan of boiling water for about 5 minutes, or until tender. Drain and allow to cool, then roughly chop.

Cook the potato in a pan of boiling water for about 10 minutes or until tender. Drain and leave to cool, then peel and grate. Set aside.

Heat the ghee in a wok over medium heat, add the cumin seeds and sauté for about 1–2 minutes, or until they start to crackle. Add the turmeric and asafoetida then season with salt and stir. Add the roughly chopped green peas and sauté until the moisture has evaporated. Add the grated potatoes and stir-fry for 3 minutes. Remove from the heat and leave to cool.

Add the chopped ginger, green chillies, yellow chilli powder, roasted ground cumin, garam masala, cornflour and breadcrumbs, mix well and season with salt. Divide the mixture into 16 equal portions and set aside.

To make the filling, mix all the ingredients together in a bowl and season.

Flatten each portion of pea mixture against the palms of your hands and place a little filling in the centre. Seal and flatten again into patties. These cakes can be made smaller in size if required.

Heat enough ghee for shallow-frying in a non-stick pan, add the patties, in batches, and shallow-fry over low heat for about 8–10 minutes, turning occasionally until both the sides have a golden-coloured crust. Remove from the heat, sprinkle with chaat masala and serve hot.

Shadras Subziyan
Stir-fried Vegetables

Preparation time 1½ hours
Cooking time 6 minutes
Serves 4

1 small broccoli, cut into florets
1 small courgette, trimmed and cut into diamond shapes
50g / 1¾oz baby corn, cut into diamond shapes
10 asparagus spears, cut into diamond shapes
50g / 1¾oz mushrooms
1 red and yellow (bell) pepper, cut in half, cored and cut into diamond shapes
3 tablespoons oil
1 teaspoon cumin seeds
3 teaspoons coriander seeds, crushed
1 large onion, finely chopped
100g / 3½oz tomatoes, finely chopped
4 tablespoons tomato purée
20g / ¾oz garlic cloves, finely chopped
1 teaspoon black peppercorns, crushed
2 teaspoons mustard paste
2 teaspoons chilli powder
1 teaspoon ground turmeric
1 teaspoon cumin seeds, roasted and crushed
1 teaspoon ground fenugreek
1 × 15-g / ½-oz piece fresh ginger, peeled and finely chopped
5 green chillies, de-seeded and finely chopped
15g / ½oz coriander (cilantro), finely chopped, plus extra to garnish
1 teaspoon Garam Masala (see page 31)
salt

Blanch the broccoli in a pan of boiling water for a few minutes, then drain and refresh under cold running water. Set aside.

Blanch the courgette, baby corn and asparagus in a pan of boiling water for a few minutes, then drain and refresh under cold running water. Set aside.

Blanch the mushrooms in a pan of boiling water for a few minutes, then drain and refresh under cold running water. Set aside.

To make the red gravy, heat 2 tablespoons oil in a pan, add the cumin seeds and half of the crushed coriander and sauté over medium heat for about 1–2 minutes, or until the seeds start to crackle. Add the chopped onion and sauté over medium heat for about 5–7 minutes, or until light brown. Add the chopped tomatoes and season with salt. Cook for about 3–5 minutes, or until the tomatoes are soft. Add the tomato purée and cook until the oil separates out. Remove from the heat and set aside.

Heat the remaining oil in a frying pan (skillet), add the garlic and sauté until light brown, then add the remaining crushed coriander seeds and the peppercorns and cook until golden brown. Add the blanched vegetables and stir-fry over medium heat.

Now sprinkle over the mustard paste, chilli powder, turmeric, roasted ground cumin, ground fenugreek, ginger and green chillies and stir-fry for a few minutes until the moisture has evaporated. Add the red gravy, increase the heat to high and stir-fry. Add the chopped coriander and garam masala then check and adjust the seasoning.

Transfer to a bowl, garnish with the extra coriander and serve hot.

Amritsari Tawa Murg
Pan-fried Amritsari Chicken

Preparation time 1 hour, plus marinating time
Cooking time 20 minutes
Serves 6

5 teaspoons Ginger Paste (see page 57)
5 teaspoons Garlic Paste (see page 57)
1 teaspoon chilli powder
1 teaspoon ground dried fenugreek
1kg / 2¼lb boneless chicken legs, cut into 7–8 pieces
4 tablespoons ghee
1 teaspoon black cumin seeds
1 teaspoon coriander seeds, crushed
1 tablespoon black peppercorns, crushed
20g / ¾oz garlic cloves, finely chopped
2 large onions, finely chopped
1 × 20-g / ¾-oz piece fresh ginger, peeled and finely chopped
2 green chillies, de-seeded and finely chopped
4 fresh red chillies
1 large tomato, finely chopped
200g / 7oz (1½ cups) tomato purée
½ teaspoon chilli powder
1 teaspoon ground cumin, roasted
3 tablespoons chicken stock
1 teaspoon Garam Masala (see page 31)
30g / 1¼oz coriander (cilantro), finely chopped, plus extra to garnish
juice of 1 lemon
salt

To make the marinade, mix the ginger paste, garlic paste, chilli powder and half of the ground fenugreek in a shallow dish and season with salt. Add the chicken pieces and turn to coat well. Cover and set aside in the refrigerator for at least 30 minutes.

Heat the ghee in a tawa or large frying pan (skillet), add the black cumin seeds, crushed coriander and black peppercorns and sauté over medium heat for about 1–2 minutes, or until they start to crackle. Add the marinated chicken, together with the marinade and stir-fry over medium heat for 8–10 minutes. Remove from the pan and set aside.

Add the chopped garlic to the ghee in the pan and sauté for 2 minutes, then add the onions, ginger, green and red chillies, and stir-fry for 5 minutes.

Now add the chopped tomato and sauté until soft, then add the tomato purée, remaining ground fenugreek, chilli powder and roasted ground cumin and cook until the oil separates out.

Return the chicken to the pan and cook for 2 minutes, then sprinkle with the chicken stock, garam masala and chopped coriander and stir. Check and adjust the seasoning, then sprinkle with the lemon juice. Mix and transfer to a flat serving dish. Serve hot garnished with extra chopped coriander.

Vikrant Kapoor
Zaafran

Level 2, 345 Harbourside
Shopping Centre
Darling Harbour 2000
Sydney
Australia

Lobster curry, baked salmon and baby snapper roasted in the tandoor oven may not be the hallmarks of conventional Indian cuisine, but Zaffran's unconventional menu has earned praise from patrons and critics alike. Drawing inspiration from the most basic dishes to the most complex, Vikrant Kapoor modernizes each dish without compromising the traditional methods of Indian cooking.

—

Menu

1 **Lasooni Tali Machli**
Pan-roasted Barramundi

2 **Badanjoon Nirali**
Aubergine (Eggplant) Discs with Spiced Lentil & Bean Topping

3 **Mirch ka Chaap**
Lamb Cutlets with Chilli & Tamarind

4 **Bhuni Salmon Machchi**
Baked Salmon

5 **Zaaffran Kay Jheengey**
Tandoori King Prawn (Jumbo Shrimp)

6 **Soya-Sarasonwala Daliya Bharta**
Dill & Wholegrain Mustard Mash

Lasooni Tali Machli
Pan-roasted Barramundi

Preparation time 20 minutes, plus marinating time
Cooking time 3–5 minutes
Serves 4

2 skinless boneless baby barramundi fillets
juice of ½ lime
vegetable oil, for pan-frying
salt

For the marinade

juice of ½ lime
1½–2 teaspoons Garlic Paste (see page 57)
½–1 teaspoon green chilli paste
½–1 teaspoon ground cloves
1 teaspoon cornflour (cornstarch)
pinch of ground white pepper

Cut each baby barramundi fillet in half and remove all the bones. Put the fillets in a shallow non-metallic dish. Season with salt and sprinkle with lime juice.

Mix all the marinade ingredients together in a bowl then rub the marinade all over the fillets. Cover and leave to marinate in the refrigerator for 2 hours.

Brush a little oil on a non-stick pan and heat the pan over medium heat. Add the fish and pan-fry for 3–5 minutes on both sides, or until cooked.

Badanjoon Nirali
Aubergine (Eggplant) Discs with Spiced
Lentil & Bean Topping

Preparation time 20–25 minutes
Cooking time 20 minutes
Serves 4

2 aubergines (eggplants)

½ teaspoon chilli powder

vegetable oil, for deep-frying

cornflour (cornstarch) and flour, for dusting

chilli powder, for sprinkling

Chaat Masala (see page 31), for sprinkling

salt

For the mixture

60g / 2oz (⅔ cup) sprouted mung beans

60g / 2oz (⅔ cup) sprouted whole brown lentils

4 tablespoons vegetable oil

5 garlic cloves, chopped

40g / 1½oz (¼ cup) chopped onions

1 teaspoon chilli powder

small pinch of ground turmeric

100g / 3½oz (1 medium) tomato, blanched
    and chopped

home-made date and tamarind chutney

For the mint and coriander (cilantro) chutney

1 bunch mint

1 bunch coriander (cilantro)

1 green chilli

1 small piece fresh ginger

1–2 garlic cloves

juice of ½ lemon

1 teaspoon sugar

salt

For the yoghurt topping

100g / 3½oz (½ cup) natural (plain) yoghurt

1–1½ teaspoons sugar

ready-made sev

salt

First, make the mint and coriander chutney. Pick
off the leaves from the mint and coriander and
cut some of the tender stems into small pieces. Put
all the ingredients in a blender or food processor
and process, adding just enough water to make a
smooth paste. Adjust the seasoning, then set aside.

To make the yoghurt topping, put all the ingredients
in a bowl and whisk together, then set aside.

For the mixture, blanch the mung beans and brown
lentils in a pan of hot salted water, then refresh in
iced water. Set aside.

Heat the oil in another pan over medium heat, add
the garlic and onions and sauté for about 5 minutes,
or until translucent. Add the chilli powder and
turmeric and stir for 30 seconds. Add the tomatoes,
then increase the heat to high and stir-fry for
about 2 minutes. Reduce the heat and simmer for
a further 2–3 minutes. Finally, add the blanched
mung beans and brown lentils, stir and adjust the
seasoning. Cover and set aside.

Peel the aubergines and cut widthways into approximately 1-cm / ½-inch thick discs. Using a sharp
knife, make gashes on the discs, then sprinkle over
the chilli powder and season with a little salt.

Spread the cornflour and flour out on a large plate,
add the aubergine discs, one at a time, and toss to
coat. Set aside.

Heat the oil for deep-frying in a deep, heavy-based
pan to 190°C/375°F or until a cube of bread browns
in 30 seconds. Working in batches, carefully
lower the aubergine slices into the hot oil, and
deep-fry for about 5 minutes, or until golden.
Remove with a slotted spoon and drain on kitchen
paper (paper towels).

To assemble the dish, place 2 aubergine discs on a
plate. Sprinkle lightly with chilli powder and chaat
masala, then place a large spoonful of the warm
lentil and onion mixture on to the discs and spread
evenly. Spoon over a little of both the chutneys
and then the seasoned yoghurt topping. Sprinkle
with sev and serve.

Mirch ka Chaap
Lamb Cutlets with Chilli & Tamarind

Preparation time 35–40 minutes
Cooking time 3–4 minutes
Serves 4–8

8 lamb cutlets, trimmed and lightly beaten
1 tablespoon chilli powder
½ tablespoon ground turmeric
50g / 1¾oz (½ cup) ground coriander
8–10 curry leaves
1½ tablespoons vinegar
1 teaspoon tamarind paste
½ tablespoon Ginger Paste (see page 57)
½ tablespoon Garlic Paste (see page 57)
1–2 tablespoons white sesame seeds
juice of ½ lime
salt

For the coorgi-style masala powder

2 green cardamom pods
1 clove
1 bay leaf
½ star anise

To make the coorgi-style masala powder, blend all the ingredients in a spice grinder to make a powder.

Put the lamb cutlets in a large shallow non-metallic dish. Put all the spices in a bowl, add the vinegar, tamarind, ginger and garlic pastes and mix together. Pour over the lamb and massage, then cover and set aside in the refrigerator for 30 minutes or overnight as preferred.

Preheat a charcoal barbecue or grill (broiler) to moderately hot. Spread the sesame seeds out on a plate and use to coat the lamb cutlets. Cook on the preheated barbecue or under the grill for 3–4 minutes on each side until medium or well-done, depending on how you like your lamb.

Alternatively, preheat the oven to 200°C/400°F/Gas Mark 6. Put the lamb cutlets in a large non-stick pan and sear over high heat until browned, then transfer to a roasting tin (pan) and roast in the oven for about 5–7 minutes until medium or well-done, depending on how you like your lamb.

Squeeze the lime juice over the lamb cutlets and serve hot with a cucumber raita and a salad.

Bhuni Salmon Machchi
Baked Salmon

Preparation time 10–15 minutes
Cooking time 5–7 minutes
Serves 4

4 skinless boneless salmon steaks, about 140–160g / 4¾–5½oz each

For the marinade

100g / 3½oz (½ cup) natural (plain) yoghurt
1 tablespoon gram (chickpea) flour, roasted
1 teaspoon ajwain seeds
1 tablespoon Ginger Paste (see page 57)
1 tablespoon Garlic Paste (see page 57)
1 teaspoon green chilli paste
1 teaspoon Garam Masala (see page 31)
1 tablespoon mustard oil
1 tablespoon chilli powder
1 teaspoon ground fenugreek
juice of ½ lemon
salt

For the tartar of prawns (shrimp)

4 small prawns (shrimp), chopped
4 tablespoons chopped onions
4 tablespoons chopped tomatoes
1 teaspoon chopped fresh ginger
1 tablespoon fenugreek leaves
4 tablespoons chopped coriander (cilantro) leaves
1 tablespoon chopped green chilli
½ teaspoon ajwain seeds

Preheat the oven to 200°C/400°F/Gas mark 6. Put the salmon in a large shallow non-metallic dish. Mix all the ingredients for the marinade together in a bowl. Rub the marinade liberally over the salmon, then cover and leave to marinate in the refrigerator for 30–45 minutes.

Mix all the ingredients for the prawn tartar together in a bowl and season with salt. Uncover the salmon and spread the prawn tartar over the top of the steaks.

Bake the salmon in the hot oven for 5–6 minutes, or until cooked but still slightly pink in the centre.

Remove from the oven and set aside for 2–3 minutes. Serve with mint chutney.

Zaaffran Kay Jheengey
Tandoori King Prawn (Jumbo Shrimp)

Preparation time 10 minutes, plus marinating time
Cooking time 10 minutes
Serves 4

4 king prawns (jumbo shrimp), peeled with tail intact
juice of ½ lime
1/6 teaspoon Tabasco sauce
salt

For the marinade
2 tablespoons cream cheese or Cheddar cheese
     mixed with cream
juice of ½ lime
½ –1 tablespoon natural (plain) yoghurt
½ –1 teaspoon Ginger Paste (see page 57)
½ –1 teaspoon Garlic Paste (see page 57)
½ –1 teaspoon ground green cardamom
½ –1 teaspoon ground mace
soaked saffron
salt

Put the prawns in a shallow non-metallic dish,
season with salt and sprinkle with the lime juice
and Tabasco sauce. Cover and set aside for
10–15 minutes.

Mix all the ingredients for the marinade together
in a bowl, season with salt and rub over
the prawns. Cover and leave to marinate in the
refrigerator overnight.

The next day, preheat a tandoor or grill (broiler)
to moderately hot. Thread the prawns through metal
skewers and roast in the preheated tandoor or
under the grill for 2–3 minutes, or until cooked.

Soya-Sarasonwala Daliya Bharta
Dill & Wholegrain Mustard Mash

Preparation time 30 minutes
Cooking time 10 minutes
Serves 10–12 portions

500g / 1lb 2oz (4–5 medium) potatoes, peeled
     and diced
150g / 5oz (10 tablespoons) butter
100g / 3½oz (⅔ cup) chopped onions
4 tablespoons wholegrain mustard
150–200ml / 5–7fl oz (⅔–scant 1 cup) cream
150–200ml / 5–7fl oz (⅔–scant 1 cup) milk
1 bunch dill, chopped
salt

Put the potatoes in a large heavy-based pan, pour
in enough water to cover and bring to the boil. Cook
for about 15 minutes, or until soft and mashy. Drain,
return to the pan and mash, then set aside.

Heat the butter in another heavy-based pan over
medium heat, add the chopped onions, then reduce
the heat and cook, stirring occasionally, for about
7 minutes, or until onions are translucent.

Add the mustard and potato mash and cook for
3–5 minutes, stirring constantly. Pour in the cream
and milk and cook for a further 3–5 minutes stirring
constantly. Finally, add the chopped dill.

Joy Kapur
Maharani

1122 Post Street
San Francisco, CA 94109
United States

Born in India, Joy Kapur moved to San Francisco in 1967 and, after finishing a business degree from Golden Gate University, plunged into the restaurant business. Since 1971 he has opened nine restaurants in the Bay Area. In its fifteenth year of business, Maharani continues to bring traditional cuisine to San Francisco with a varied menu of authentic Indian dishes served in a unique and creative environment.

___

Menu

1 **Channa Masala**
Chickpea (Garbanzo Bean) Curry

2 **Murg Tikka Masala**
Chicken Tikka Masala

3 **Goawali Machchali**
Goan Fish Curry

4 **Bakare ke Gosht ka Vindaloo**
Lamb Vindaloo

5 **Gajar Halwa**
Carrot Halwa

Channa Masala
Chickpea (Garbanzo Bean) Curry

Preparation time 20 minutes, plus cooling time
Cooking time 8–10 minutes
Serves 4

1 large potato, unpeeled
1 tablespoon ghee or oil
1 large onion, chopped
1 large tomato, puréed
1 teaspoon Ginger Paste (see page 57)
1 teaspoon Garlic Paste (see page 57)
½ teaspoon ground cumin
½ teaspoon ground coriander
½ teaspoon ground turmeric
½ teaspoon chilli powder
450g / 1lb canned chickpeas (garbanzo beans)
1 teaspoon salt or to taste
coriander (cilantro) leaves, to garnish

Cook the potato in a pan of boiling water for about 10 minutes or until tender. Drain and allow to cool, then peel and cut into cubes. Set aside.

Heat the ghee or oil in a frying pan (skillets), add the onion, tomato, ginger and garlic pastes, cumin, coriander, turmeric and chilli powder and cook for 2 minutes. Add the potatoes and chickpeas and 125ml / 4½fl oz (½ cup) lukewarm water and cook for 5 minutes or until hot. Garnish with coriander.

Murg Tikka Masala
Chicken Tikka Masala

Preparation time 30 minutes, plus marinating time
Cooking time 40 minutes
Serves 4

1.2kg / 2½lb skinless boneless chicken breast

freshly ground black pepper

4 tablespoons vegetable oil or ghee

onion

2 cloves garlic, chopped

1 × 2.5-cm / 1-inch piece fresh ginger, peeled
  and chopped

2 teaspoons Garam Masala (see page 31)

1 teaspoon chilli powder

1 teaspoon cayenne pepper

tomatoes

1 teaspoon sugar

250ml / 9fl oz (1 cup) cream

1 tablespoon ground almonds

salt

For the masala marinade

225ml / 7½fl oz (1 cup) natural (plain) yoghurt

2 garlic cloves, minced

1 tablespoon finely grated fresh ginger

1½ teaspoons ground cumin

1½ teaspoons ground coriander

¼ teaspoon ground cardamom

¼ teaspoon cayenne pepper

¼ teaspoon ground ground turmeric

½ teaspoon freshly ground pepper

2 tablespoons tomato purée

salt

To garnish

coriander (cilantro) leaves

lime

First make the masala marinade. Combine the yoghurt, garlic, ginger, cumin, coriander, cardamom, cayenne and turmeric in a large stainless steel bowl. Season with salt and pepper.

Using a sharp knife, make a few shallow slashes in each piece of chicken. Add the chicken to the marinade, turn to coat and marinate in the refrigerator overnight.

Preheat the grill or the tandoor and position a rack about 23cm / 9 inches from the heat. Remove the chicken from the marinade and scrape off as much of the excess marinade as possible. Sprinkle the chicken with salt and pepper and spread the pieces on a baking tray (sheet). Grill the chicken, turning once or twice, for about 10 minutes until just cooked through and browned in spots. Transfer to a chopping board and cut into 5-cm / 2-inch pieces.

Heat 2 tablespoons of oil or ghee in a large enamelled cast-iron casserole until shimmering. Add the onion, garlic and ginger and cook over medium heat, stirring occasionally, for about 8 minutes until tender and golden. Add the garam masala, chilli powder and cayenne and cook, stirring, for 1 minute. Add the tomatoes with their juices and the sugar and season with salt and pepper. Partially cover and cook over medium heat for about 20 minutes, stirring occasionally, until the sauce is slightly thickened. Add the cream and ground almonds and cook over a low heat for a further 10 minutes, stirring occasionally, until thickened. Stir in the chicken and simmer gently for 10 minutes, stirring frequently, until the chicken is cooked through. Garnish with coriander and lime.

Goawali Machchali
Goan Fish Curry

Preparation time 15 minutes
Cooking time 40 minutes
Serves 4

2 tablespoons mustard powder
2 tablespoons oil or ghee
1 large onion, chopped
1 teaspoon ground turmeric
4 garlic cloves, chopped
1 × 7.5-cm / 3-inch piece fresh ginger, peeled and chopped
1 teaspoon salt
4 green chillies
900g / 2lb catfish fillets, cut into pieces
4 teaspoons lime juice

Put the mustard powder in a small bowl, add an equal amount of water and mix together. Heat the oil or ghee in a non-stick frying pan (skillet), add the onions and mustard paste and fry, stirring, for 10 minutes. Add 750ml / 1¼ pints (3¼ cups) lukewarm water and all the spices and chillies. Bring to the boil and add the fish fillets. Reduce the heat to medium-low and cook for 30 minutes, or until the fish is cooked. Squeeze over the lime juice.

Bakare ke Gosht ka Vindaloo
Lamb Vindaloo

Preparation time 10 minutes
Cooking time 35 minutes
Serves 4

1–2 teaspoons chilli powder
1 teaspoon ground turmeric
2 teaspoons cumin seeds
2 teaspoons coriander seeds
125ml / 4½fl oz (½ cup) vinegar
6 tablespoons oil or ghee
2 teaspoons ground mustard seeds
2 teaspoons cayenne pepper
2 teaspoons Garam Masala (see page 31)
1 large onion, finely chopped
2 garlic cloves, minced
4 tablespoons oil
900g / 2lb lean boneless leg of lamb, cut into pieces
coriander (cilantro) leaves, to garnish
salt

Put all the spices and vinegar in a bowl and mix together.

Heat the oil or ghee in a large pan, add the spice and vinegar mixture and fry for 10 minutes. Add the lamb and continue to cook, stirring, for 20 minutes. Add some water and cook for a further 5 minutes on low heat. Garnish with coriander.

Gajar Halwa
Carrot Halwa

Preparation time 20 minutes
Cooking time 55 minutes, plus cooling
Serves 4

125g / 4¼oz (½ cup) ghee
220g / 7½oz (2 medium) carrots, grated
60g / 2oz (¼oz) double (heavy) cream
125g / 4¼oz (½ cup) sugar
2 tablespoons slivered blanched almonds
½ teaspoon ground cardamom
1 teaspoon rosewater, optional
¼ cup chopped pistachios and slivered almonds, to decorate

Heat the ghee in a large, heavy-based pan, add the grated carrots and bring to the boil, stirring frequently. Reduce the heat and cook, uncovered, at a slow boil for 20 minutes, stirring frequently.

Add the cream and continue to cook, uncovered, for 15 minutes, stirring frequently. Add the sugar and almonds and cook for a further 10 minutes, stirring frequently, until the mixture begins to stick to the base of the pan. Remove from the heat and allow to cool to room temperature. Stir in the cardamom and rosewater, if using. Serve decorated with chopped pistachios and slivered almonds.

Alfred Prasad
Tamarind

20 Queen Street
London W1J 5PR
United Kingdom

Alfred Prasad's original take on traditional Indian cuisine has earned him the title of youngest Indian chef to receive a Michelin star. Aiming to use the freshest of locally available produce, organic foods and sustainable ingredients, Prasad prides himself on his creative combinations and believes each meal should be presented as a complete sensory experience.

Menu

1 **Sada Chaawal**
Steamed Rice

2 **Bhindi Channa**
Spiced Okra & Chickpeas
(Garbanzo Beans)

3 **Hariyali Macchi**
Monkfish Kebabs

4 **Murgh Makhni**
Chicken Tikka in Creamed Fresh
Tomatoes

5 **Ajwaini Jhinga**
Marinated Tiger Prawns (Shrimp)

Sada Chaawal
Steamed Rice

Preparation time 10 minutes, plus soaking time
Cooking time 15 minutes
Serves 4

490g / 1lb (generous 2 cups) basmati rice

salt (optional)

1 tablespoon vegetable oil (optional)

Measure the rice in a measuring jug, then transfer to a bowl and pour twice the quantity of water as rice into a large heavy-based pan. Set aside.

Rinse the rice under cold running water, then pour over enough cold water to cover and allow to soak for about 20 minutes.

Drain the rice and add it to the boiling water, stir gently, cover with a lid, reduce the heat and allow to simmer for 15 minutes.

Remove the pan from the heat, uncover and set aside for a further 5 minutes. Using a flat wooden spoon, turn the rice from the edges before serving.

Bhindi Channa
Spiced Okra & Chickpeas (Garbanzo Beans)

Preparation time 40 minutes
Cooking time 10 minutes
Serves 4

1 tablespoon vegetable oil
1 teaspoon cumin
200g / 7oz canned chickpeas (garbanzo beans)
650g / 1½lb okra, cut into 2-cm / 1-inch pieces
½ teaspoon channa masala
½ teaspoon Garam Masala (see page 31)
¼ bunch coriander (cilantro) leaves, chopped

For the masala sauce

3 tablespoons vegetable oil
2 sticks cinnamon
2 cardamom pods
2 cloves
2 onions, chopped
1½ teaspoons Ginger Paste (see page 57)
1½ teaspoons Garlic Paste (see page 57)
½ teaspoon chilli powder
1 teaspoon ground coriander
½ teaspoon ground turmeric
4 tomatoes, chopped
½ tablespoon tomato purée
salt

Make the masala sauce first. Heat the oil in a large, heavy-based pan over medium heat, add the whole spices and sauté for a couple of minutes. Add the chopped onions and cook for about 5–7 minutes, stirring occasionally, until the onions are golden brown. Add the ginger and garlic pastes and sauté briefly, then add the ground spices followed by the fresh tomatoes and tomato purée. Sauté over high heat for about 15 minutes, stirring occasionally. Season with salt, then remove the pan from the heat and set aside.

Heat the remaining oil in another pan over medium heat, add the cumin, chickpeas, okra and channa masala and sauté for a few minutes. Add the masala sauce and sauté for a further few minutes.

Add a sprinkling of garam masala and the chopped coriander, then check the seasoning and serve hot.

Hariyali Macchi
Monkfish Kebabs

Preparation time 30 minutes, plus marinating time
Cooking time 10 minutes
Serves 4

2 tablespoons vegetable oil
1 tablespoon gram (chickpea) flour
12 chunks monkfish
juice of 1 lemon
1 tablespoon Ginger Paste (see page 57)
1 tablespoon Garlic Paste (see page 57)
½ bunch mint leaves, chopped
1 bunch coriander (cilantro) leaves, chopped
1 handful of spinach, chopped
2 lime leaves, chopped
½ teaspoon ground turmeric
3 tablespoons lemon juice, plus extra for sprinkling
1 tablespoon ground cumin
1 tablespoon ground coriander
3 green chillies, chopped
½ teaspoon Chaat Masala (see page 31), to serve
salt

Heat 1 tablespoon of the oil in a heavy-based pan over low heat, add the gram (chickpea) flour and stir constantly until it turns light brown. Remove the pan from the heat and allow to cool. Put the monkfish in a large, non-metallic dish and sprinkle over the juice of 1 lemon, then add the ginger and garlic pastes and season with salt. Mix well, cover and set aside.

Put the mint, coriander, spinach and lime leaves in a food processor or blender, add the remaining oil, the turmeric and 3 tablespoons lemon juice and process until smooth.

Put the browned gram flour, ground cumin and coriander, chillies and the green paste in a large bowl and mix together, add the monkfish, mix well and put in the refrigerator for 30 minutes. Preheat the tandoor, charcoal barbecue or grill (broiler) to moderately hot.

Cook the fish in the preheated tandoor, on the barbecue or under the grill for 3 minutes, then turn over and cook for a further 2 minutes. Increase the heat and cook for a further 2 minutes on each side or until browned.

Serve hot sprinkled with some extra lemon juice and the chaat masala.

Murgh Makhni
Chicken Tikka in Creamed
Fresh Tomatoes

Preparation time 40 minutes, plus marinating time
Cooking time 10 minutes
Serves 4

For the chicken tikka

16 boneless chicken thighs

1 tablespoon Ginger Paste (see page 57)

1 tablespoon Garlic Paste (see page 57)

225g / 8oz (1 cup) natural (plain) yoghurt

1 tablespoon Kashmiri chilli powder

1 teaspoon Garam Masala (see page 31)

salt

For the makhni sauce

3 tablespoons vegetable oil

4 sticks cinnamon

5 cardamom pods

5 cloves

4 green chillies

1 × 2.5-cm / 1-inch piece fresh ginger

2 bay leaves

12–15 ripe tomatoes

1 tablespoon Kashmiri chilli powder

1 tablespoon honey

25g / 1oz (2 tablespoons) butter, plus extra for frying

½ tablespoon tomato purée

2 teaspoons dried fenugreek leaves

250ml / 8fl oz (1 cup) single (light) cream,
    plus extra to garnish

For the chicken tikka, put the chicken thighs in a large shallow dish, add the ginger and garlic pastes and season with salt, then mix well.

Put the yoghurt in another bowl, add the chilli powder and garam masala and whisk to combine. Pour this mixture over the chicken, turn to coat, then cover and allow to marinate in the refrigerator for at least 4 hours. Preheat a tandoor, charcoal barbecue or grill (broiler) to moderately hot.

Cook the chicken in the preheated tandoor, on the barbecue or under the grill for 4 minutes, then turn over and cook for a further 3 minutes or until cooked through. Set aside.

To make the makhni sauce, heat the oil in a heavy-based pan over medium heat, add the whole spices, then the green chillies, ginger and bay leaves and sauté for 2 minutes.

Add the whole fresh tomatoes and simmer over a medium heat until the tomatoes have cooked to a pulp. Remove the pan from the heat and transfer the mixture to a blender. Process until smooth, then pass the purée through a sieve (strainer) into a clean pan.

Return the pan to the heat and bring to the boil. Add the chilli powder, honey, butter and tomato purée, then season with salt to taste and simmer for a further 20 minutes. Sprinkle over the fenugreek leaves.

To finish, heat a little butter in a large, heavy-based pan over medium heat, add the chicken thighs and sauté until piping hot. Add the makhni sauce and the cream, reduce the heat and simmer for a few minutes before serving garnished with a swirl of cream.

Ajwaini Jhinga
Marinated Tiger Prawns (Shrimp)

Preparation time 15 minutes, plus marinating time
Cooking time 10 minutes
Serves 4

12 raw tiger prawns (jumbo shrimp), peeled and deveined
juice of 1 lime
4 tablespoons vegetable oil
2 tablespoons gram (chickpea) flour
225g / 8oz (1 cup) natural (plain) yoghurt
3 teaspoons paprika
½ teaspoon ajwain seeds
1½ teaspoons Ginger Paste (see page 57)
1½ teaspoons Garlic Paste (see page 57)
½ bunch chives, chopped
salt

Put the prawns in a non-metallic dish. Sprinkle the lime juice and ½ teaspoon of salt over the prawns and mix well. Set aside.

Heat 2 tablespoons of the oil in a heavy-based pan over low heat, add the gram (chickpea) flour and stir constantly until it turns light brown. Remove the pan from the heat and allow to cool.

Put the yoghurt, paprika, ajwain seeds, ginger and garlic pastes, the remaining oil and the gram flour paste in a bowl and season with salt. Mix well then add the prawns.

Add a sprinkling of chopped chives, then cover and leave to chill in the refrigerator for about 20 minutes.

Preheat a tandoor, charcoal barbecue or grill (broiler) to moderately hot.

Cook the prawns in the preheated tandoor, on the barbecue or under the grill for about 10 minutes, or until cooked through. Serve hot accompanied with salad.

Suvir Saran
Dévi

8 East 18th Street
New York, NY 10003
United States

Suvir Saran is a respected restaurant owner and authority on Indian food in America. His upscale New York restaurant, Dévi, offers the authentic flavours of Indian home cooking and received a Michelin rating in 2007 and 2008, as well as a three-star rating from *New York* magazine and two stars from *The New York Times*.

―――

Menu

1 **Kararee Bhindi**
Crispy Okra Salad

2 **Teekhe Achari Jhinge Wale Luqme**
Prawn (Shrimp) Balchao Bruschetta

3 **Gobi-Matar-Mithee Lal Mirch**
Stir-fried Cabbage with Red (Bell) Peppers & Peas

4 **Dhansaak**
Lentil & Vegetable Stew

5 **Devi ki Mashhoor Chaampen**
Devi's Famous Lamb Chops

6 **Jhingha Poha Pulao**
Prawn (Shrimp) Poha Paella

Kararee Bhindi
Crispy Okra Salad

Preparation time 15 minutes
Cooking time 5–7 minutes per batch
Serves 4

corn oil, for deep-frying
700g / 1lb 8½oz okra, stems removed and thinly sliced lengthways
½ small red onion, thinly sliced
3 small or 1 large tomato, cored, de-seeded and thinly sliced
5g / ⅛oz chopped coriander (cilantro)
juice of ½ lemon, or more to taste
1½ teaspoons Chaat Masala (see page 31)
1 teaspoon salt, or to taste

Heat 5cm / 2 inches of oil in a large heavy-based pan to 180°C/350°F or until a cube of bread browns in 30 seconds. Add one-third of the okra and fry for about 5–7 minutes until browned and crisp. Remove with a slotted spoon and drain on kitchen paper and repeat with remaining okra, making sure the oil temperature comes back to 180°C/350°F before frying additional batches.

Toss the okra in a large bowl with the onion, tomato, coriander, lemon juice, chaat masala and salt. Taste for seasoning and serve immediately.

Teekhe Achari Jhinge Wale Luqme
Prawn (Shrimp) Balchao Bruschetta

Preparation time 15 minutes
Cooking time 15–20 minutes
Serves 8

For the prawns

450g / 1lb medium prawns (shrimp), peeled and deveined
juice of 1 lemon or lime
2 teaspoons salt
½ teaspoon cracked peppercorns
½ teaspoon cayenne pepper

For the sauce

3 tablespoons corn oil
16 curry leaves, roughly torn
4–8 dried red chillies (optional)
1½ teaspoons cumin seeds
¼ teaspoon cracked peppercorns
2 red onions, chopped
2 teaspoons salt
1 tablespoon sugar
1 tablespoon white-wine vinegar
350g / 12oz boxed or canned chopped tomatoes
1 tablespoon unsalted butter
4 slices of bread, preferably brioche, brushed with melted butter, toasted and sliced diagonally into 8 pieces

Place the prawns in a large resealable plastic bag. Add the lemon or lime juice, salt, pepper and cayenne and shake to incorporate. Put into the refrigerator while you prepare the sauce.

Put 60ml / 2½fl oz water next to your hob. Heat the corn oil, curry leaves, chillies (if using), cumin seeds and cracked pepper in a large pan over medium-high heat until the cumin browns, about 2 minutes. Add the onions and salt and cook for 7–10 minutes, or until they are browned and sticky. When the onions start sticking to the base of the pan, splash with water and stir and scrape up. Stir in the sugar and vinegar and cook for 1 minute. Add the tomatoes and cook for about 4 minutes until the texture of the sauce is thick and jammy. Add the butter and once melted, add the prawns, cooking until curled and opaque, about 2–4 minutes. Place 3 or 4 prawns on each toasted brioche, spoon some sauce over the top and serve.

Gobi-Matar-Mithee Lal Mirch
Stir-fried Cabbage with Red (Bell) Peppers & Peas

Preparation time 15 minutes
Cooking time 15–30 minutes
Serves 6

3 tablespoons corn oil
1½ teaspoons cumin seeds
1 teaspoon ground turmeric
3 dried red chillies
1.6kg / 3½lb head of cabbage, cored and finely chopped
2 red (bell) peppers, de-seeded and finely chopped
120g / 4oz frozen peas
1½ teaspoons salt

Heat the corn oil with the cumin seeds, turmeric and chillies in a large pan or wok over medium-high heat, stirring occasionally, until the chillies become smoky, about 3 minutes. Add half of the cabbage and all of the red peppers and peas and stir to combine with the spices. After a couple of minutes the cabbage will start to wilt. Now stir in the remaining cabbage. Cook, stirring frequently, until the volume has reduced by one-third and the cabbage looks very browned, about 15–30 minutes (depending on your pan or wok). Mix in the salt and serve warm or at room temperature.

Dhansaak
Lentil & Vegetable Stew

Preparation time about 1¼ hours
Coking time 45 minutes
Serves 8–10

For the spice blend

1 cinnamon stick, 2.5cm (1-inch) long

8 cardamom pods

1 tablespoon coriander seeds

1½ teaspoons cumin seeds

1 teaspoon fennel seeds

1 teaspoon mustard seeds

1 teaspoon turmeric

½ teaspoon whole black peppercorns

¼ teaspoon fenugreek seeds

¼ teaspoon whole cloves

For the herb paste

45g / 1½oz coriander (cilantro)

25g / 1oz mint

1 × 7.5-cm / 3-inch piece fresh root ginger, peeled
and roughly chopped

1 jalapeño chilli, de-seeded and roughly chopped

3 dried red chillies

6 garlic cloves, roughly chopped

For the stew

60ml / 2½fl oz (¼ cup) extra-virgin olive oil,
plus 3 tablespoons

1 teaspoon cumin seeds

2 red onions, finely diced, plus 1 red onion, chopped

1 tablespoon salt, plus 2 teaspoons

450g / 1lb lentils (a combination of brown, green, red
and yellow)

3 large tomatoes, chopped

600g / 1lb 5 oz aubergine (eggplant)
cut into 2.5-cm / 1-inch chunks

350g / 12oz frozen or fresh sweetcorn kernels

Grind the spice blend ingredients in a coffee grinder or small food processor until a fine powder forms and set aside.

Blend the herb paste in a food processor with 60ml / 2½fl oz (¼ cup) water until smooth and set aside.

Place 225ml / 7½fl oz (1 cup) water next to your hob. Heat the 60ml / 2½fl oz (¼ cup) olive oil and the cumin seeds in a large pan over medium-high heat until the cumin is toasted and browned, about 2 minutes. Add the finely diced onions and the salt and cook for about 12–15 minutes until the onions are deep brown. Stir frequently and splash with water, scraping up any browned bits from the base of the pan when the onions begin to stick. Add whatever water remains in the jug and cook until it evaporates, about 3 minutes.

Reduce the heat to medium, add the lentils and 3 tablespoons of the spice blend and cook for 2 minutes, stirring frequently. Add 2 litres / 3½ pints water and bring to the boil. Reduce the heat to medium-low, cover and simmer for 30 minutes, stirring frequently.

Meanwhile, heat the remaining 3 tablespoons of olive oil in a medium frying pan (skillet) over medium-high heat for 30 seconds. Add the coriander paste and cook for 2 minutes, stirring. Once the lentils have cooked for 30 minutes, add the cooked coriander paste and the tomatoes, aubergine, sweetcorn and chopped onion to the pan. Bring everything to the boil and add the remaining spice blend. Reduce the heat to medium-low, cover and cook until the aubergine is completely soft, about 45 minutes, stirring every 10 minutes. Taste for seasoning and serve.

Devi ki Mashhoor Chaampen
Devi's Famous Lamb Chops

Preparation time 15 minutes plus draining and
marinating time
Cooking time 20 minutes
Serves 4

225ml / 7½fl oz (1 cup) natural yoghurt, drained,
    sour cream or crème fraîche

900g / 2lb lamb rib chops (8–10), cut into 2.5–4cm /
    1–1½ inches thick

60ml / 2½fl oz (¼ cup) malt vinegar

juice of 1 lemon

8 garlic cloves, finely chopped

1 × 7.5-cm / 3-inch piece fresh root ginger,
    peeled and grated

1 tablespoon Garam Masala (see page 31)

1 tablespoon toasted cumin

1 teaspoon ground cardamom

½ teaspoon cayenne pepper

¼ teaspoon ground mace

¼ teaspoon ground nutmeg

2 tablespoons corn oil

3 tablespoons unsalted butter, melted

Drain the yoghurt (if using) in a muslin (cheesecloth)-
lined sieve (strainer) or coffee filter for 2–4 hours.

Cut 3 or 4 deep slashes in each of the lamb chops
(take care not to cut all the way through the chop).
Mix all of the remaining ingredients except for the
oil and butter in a large resealable plastic bag. Add
the chops and turn to coat in the marinade. Seal
and allow to marinate in the refrigerator overnight.

Heat the grill to medium-high (you should be able to
hold your hand 13cm / 5 inches above the grate for
no more than 3–4 seconds). Add the oil to the bag,
reseal and, using your hands, massage the chops on
the outside of the bag to incorporate. Remove the
lamb from the marinade, place on the grill and cook
for 4–5 minutes on each side. Transfer to a baking
sheet and let the lamb rest for 5 minutes. Brush
with melted butter and grill until each side is evenly
browned, about a further 5 minutes per side.

Jhingha Poha Pulao
Prawn (Shrimp) Poha Paella

Preparation time 10 minutes
Cooking time 10–15 minutes
Serves 8

900g / 2lb peeled and deveined large prawns (shrimp)

juice of ½ lemon

salt

1½ teaspoons ground turmeric

¼ teaspoon cracked peppercorns

4 tablespoons unsalted butter

36 curry leaves, roughly torn

1 tablespoon mustard seeds

1½ teaspoons cumin seeds

2 medium red onions, quartered and
    thinly sliced crossways

200g / 7oz (1½ cups) frozen peas

4 cups thick poha, rinsed in cold water and drained

¼ teaspoon cayenne pepper

30g / 1¼oz chopped coriander (cilantro)

½ lemon, cut into wedges, to serve

Place the prawns in a large bowl and mix them with
the lemon juice, 1 teaspoon of salt, ¼ teaspoon of
turmeric and the pepper and set aside.

Melt the butter with the curry leaves, mustard seeds
and cumin seeds in a large pan or wok over medium-
high heat, stirring frequently, until the cumin begins
to darken, about 2–3 minutes. Add the onions, ¼
teaspoon turmeric and 1 tablespoon of salt and cook,
stirring occasionally, for 5 minutes. Add the peas and
cook for 2 minutes, then add the prawns and cook
for a further 2 minutes. Stir in the cayenne pepper
and poha and cook for 1½ minutes. Drizzle 125ml /
4½fl oz (¼ cup) water around the edges of the pan,
then reduce the heat to medium-low, cover and
cook for 7 minutes. Remove the lid and fluff. Taste
for seasoning and sprinkle with chopped coriander.
Serve with lemon wedges.

Vivek Singh
Cinnamon Club

The Old Westminster Library
30 Great Smith Street
London SW1P 3BU
United Kingdom

Since it first opened its doors in 2001, the Cinnamon Club in Westminster has established itself as the one of the world's best Indian restaurants. Chef Vivek Singh has challenged the perceived boundaries of Indian food and his menus successfully marry Indian flavours and spicing with Western culinary styles.

——

Menu

1 **Kali Daal**
Black Lentils

2 **Khumb aur Kumhdey ka Phool**
Courgette (Zucchini) Flower Stuffed with Corn & Mushroom

3 **Quinoa Upma**
Curry Leaf & Tomato Quinoa

4 **Banjara Chakoor**
Peanut & Dried Mango Crusted Partridge

5 **Imli Mein Lipatee Strawberri Wala Shrikhand**
Shrikhand Cheesecake with Tamarind-Glazed Strawberries

——

Kali Daal
Black Lentils

Preparation time 10 minutes, plus soaking time
Cooking time 1 hour 25 minutes
Serves 4–6 people

250g / 9oz (1⅓ cups) black urad dal
1 teaspoon Ginger Paste (see page 57)
1 teaspoon Garlic Paste (see page 57)
1 teaspoon salt
1 teaspoon chilli powder
2 tablespoons concentrated tomato purée (paste)
150g / 5oz (10 tablespoons) slightly salted butter
1 teaspoon Garam Masala (see page 31)
½ teaspoon ground dried fenugreek leaves
½ teaspoon sugar
2 tablespoons single (light) cream

Soak the dal in a bowl of water overnight.

The next day, drain the dal and transfer to a pan. Pour over 1 litre / 1¾ pints (4¼ cups) water and cook for about 1 hour until the lentils are thoroughly cooked but not completely mashed.

Add the ginger and garlic pastes, salt and chilli powder and boil for a further 10 minutes. Add the tomato purée and butter and cook for further 15 minutes, or until the dal is thick. Take care that the mixture does not split – the butter should not separate from the dal. Add the garam masala, dried fenugreek leaves and sugar and check the seasoning. Add the cream.

Khumb aur Kumhdey ka Phool
Courgette (Zucchini) Flowers Stuffed
with Corn & Mushrooms

Preparation time 25 minutes
Cooking time 10 minutes
Serves 4

4 courgette (zucchini) flowers

oil, for deep-frying

For the filling

1 tablespoon corn or vegetable oil

1 tablespoon finely chopped red onion

1 tablespoon canned corn kernels

½ green chilli, finely chopped

2 tablespoons assorted finely chopped mushrooms

½ teaspoon ground turmeric

1 teaspoon salt

1 tablespoon chopped coriander (cilantro) leaves

juice of ½ lemon

½ teaspoon Garam Masala (see page 31)

2 tablespoons boiled grated potato (optional)

For the batter

2 tablespoons cornflour (cornstarch)

½ teaspoon salt

½ teaspoon cumin seeds or black cumin seeds

juice of ½ lemon

Open the courgette flowers, taking care not to tear
the petals, and remove the stigmas and any insects
from inside. Pat the flowers dry with kitchen paper
(paper towels) and set aside.

For the filling, heat the oil in a heavy-based pan
over medium heat, add the onion and sauté for
about 5 minutes, or until it is soft and starts to
change colour. Add the corn kernels and the green
chilli and sauté for a further 2–3 minutes. Add the
mushrooms and cook for a further 1–2 minutes, then
add the turmeric and sauté for 1 minute. Add the
salt, coriander, lemon juice and garam masala. If
the mix is too coarse remove the pan from the heat
and allow to cool. When cool add the grated boiled
potato for more binding and mix well to combine.

Fill the flowers evenly with the mixture.

Put the flour, salt, cumin, lemon juice and
1 tablespoon water in a bowl and mix together
to make a batter.

Heat the oil for deep-frying in a deep pan to
190°C/375°F, or until a cube of bread browns in
30 seconds. Dip the flowers lightly into the batter
then carefully lower them into the hot oil and
deep-fry for a few minutes until the batter is crisp
and the filling is cooked through. Remove with a
slotted spoon and drain on kitchen paper.

Serve with tamarind chutney and mango purée.

Quinoa Upma
Curry Leaf & Tomato Quinoa

Preparation time 40 minutes, plus soaking time
Cooking time 10 minutes
Serves 4 as an accompaniment, 2 as a main course

100g / 3½oz (⅔ cup) quinoa

salt

For the tempering

2 tablespoons vegetable or corn oil

1 whole dried red chilli, broken into 3 pieces

1 teaspoon mustard seeds

20 curry leaves

1 large onion, finely chopped

1 fresh green chilli, finely chopped

1 × 1-cm / ½-inch piece fresh ginger, peeled
   and finely chopped

1 tomato, coarsely chopped

¼ teaspoon chilli powder

½ teaspoon sugar

1 tablespoon finely chopped coriander (cilantro)
   or basil

juice of ½ lemon

Soak the quinoa in a bowl of water for 15 minutes, then drain and refresh in cold water. Pour about 300ml / ½ pint (1¼ cups) water into a large, heavy-based pan, season with salt, add the quinoa and bring to the boil. Cook for about 15–18 minutes, or until the grains are cooked but still retain some bite. Quinoa develops a white ring on the outer circumference of each grain when ready. If there is any excess water left in the pan, drain the quinoa through a colander.

For the tempering, heat the oil in a large, heavy-based pan over medium heat, add the dried red chilli and mustard seeds and allow them to crackle and splutter for about 30 seconds. Add the curry leaves and fry for about 30 seconds, or until they turn crisp. Add the onion and cook for 6–8 minutes, or until it starts to turn golden. Now add the finely chopped green chilli and ginger and stir for a minute. Add the chopped tomato, 1½ teaspoons salt and the chilli powder and cook for a further 8–10 minutes until most of the moisture from the tomatoes has evaporated and the onion and tomato mixture begins to come together. Add the cooked quinoa and mix for a minute or two until heated through. Finish with the sugar, a sprinkling of coriander or basil and the lemon juice. Serve hot.

Banjara Chakoor
Peanut & Dried Mango Crusted Partridge

Preparation time 20 minutes, plus marinating time
Cooking time 6–7 minutes
Serves 4

---

4 whole partridges, cut in half lengthways

1 teaspoon salt

3 tablespoons malt vinegar

1 tablespoon Ginger Paste (see page 57)

1 tablespoon Garlic Paste (see page 57)

200g / 7oz (scant 1 cup) Greek yoghurt

2 teaspoons amchoor powder

1 teaspoon cumin seeds, roasted and crushed

3 tablespoons roasted peanuts, coarsely crushed

2 green chillies, finely chopped

1 tablespoon vegetable oil

2 tablespoons chopped coriander (cilantro) stems

juice of ½ lemon

Put the partridges in a large shallow, non-metallic dish. Add the salt, vinegar and the ginger and garlic pastes. Put the yoghurt, amchoor powder, cumin seeds, crushed roasted peanuts, chopped green chillies and oil in a bowl. Add the coriander stems, then pour over the partridges and mix well. Cover and marinate in the refrigerator for 30 minutes. Put several wooden skewers in a bowl of water and allow to soak for 30 minutes.

Preheat the oven to 200°C/400°F/Gas Mark 4 and preheat the grill (broiler). Thread the partridges on to the soaked wooden skewers and cook in the oven for 3–4 minutes, then finish under a hot grill for 3 minutes.

Remove the partridge from the skewers and serve with curry leaf and tomato quinoa.

Imli Mein Lipatee Strawberri Wala Shrikhand

Shrikhand Cheesecake with Tamarind-Glazed Strawberries

Preparation time 50 minutes, plus chilling time
Serves 8

For the tamarind glaze

160g / 5½oz (¾ cup) sugar

450ml / 15fl oz (scant 2 cups) tamarind purée

1 × 2.5-cm / 1-inch piece fresh ginger, finely chopped

4 tablespoons lime juice

finely grated zest of 2 limes

20 mint leaves, cut into fine julienne

For the cheesecake

250g / 9oz (generous 1 cup) hung natural (plain) yoghurt (see page 793)

100g / 3½oz mascarpone cheese

100ml / 3½fl oz (½ cup) double (heavy) cream, whipped

80g / 2¾oz (heaped ⅓ cup) caster (superfine) sugar

1 teaspoon ground green cardamom

For the crumble

500g / 1lb 2oz (3⅔ cups) plain (cake) flour

500g / 1lb 2oz (2½ cups) caster (superfine) sugar

315g / 11¼oz (3⅓ cups) ground almonds

500g / 1lb 2oz (4½ sticks) butter

For the spice mix

30g / 1¼oz (⅓ cup) coriander seeds

30g / 1¼oz (¼ cup) fennel seeds

To serve

6–8 strawberries per person

mint sprigs

Preheat the oven to 180°C/350°F/Gas Mark 4.

To make the tamarind glaze, put the sugar in a flat pan over low heat and cook until caramelized, then add the tamarind purée. Cook over low heat until thick, then add the ginger and remove the pan from the heat. Whisk in the lime juice and zest and allow to cool. Once cooled, fold in the mint. Set aside.

For the crumble, put the flour, sugar and ground almonds in a bowl and mix together to combine. Add the butter and rub it in with your fingertips. Place the crumble on a baking tray (sheet) and bake in the oven for 5 minutes, or until crisp. Allow to cool, then break into small pieces. Transfer to the base (bottom) of 8 individual ring moulds.

For the cheesecake, put all the ingredients in a bowl and fold together gently. Half-fill the ring moulds with the mixture, making sure the top is smooth. Chill in the refrigerator until set.

To make the spice mix, roast the spices then crush in a mortar with a pestle. Set aside.

To serve, unmould the cheesecakes and place them in the centre of a serving plate. Hull the strawberries and slice them in half, then put them in a mixing bowl, add a spoonful of the tamarind glaze and mix gently, ensuring all the strawberries are evenly glazed. Spoon in an even fashion around the cheesecake and lightly sprinkle the roasted and crushed spices over the top. Decorate with a sprig of fresh mint or strawberry.

Miraj-ul-Haque
Radisson's

Swarna Jayanti Marg
New Delhi
India

Within an impressive 25-year career and advanced culinary skills, Meraj-ul-Haque specializes in the cuisine of Lucknow. Several generations of his family have worked in the restaurant business and it was no surprise that cooking was a natural calling. As the head chef of Radisson in New Delhi, he has created a vibrant menu of richly spiced and intensely flavoured dishes.

Menu

1 **Murg Kandahari**
Chicken with Pomegranate

2 **Dum ki Makai**
Spiced Tomatoes & Corn

3 **Achari Machhi Tikka**
Boneless Fish Cubes in Pickling Spices

4 **Kaju Subz ke Shami**
Vegetarian Shami with Cashew Nuts

Murg Kandahari
Chicken with Pomegranate

Preparation time 20 minutes, plus marinating time
Cooking time 10 minutes
Serves 4

40g / 1½oz (⅓ cup) gram (chickpea) flour, roasted
150g / 5oz pomegranate seeds
50ml / 2fl oz pomegranate juice
50ml / 2fl oz beetroot purée
50ml / 2fl oz hung natural (plain) yoghurt (see page 793)
3g red chilli powder
salt
1kg / 2¼lb chicken, skinned and cut into 8–10 pieces
5g / ⅛oz Chaat Masala (see page 31)

Put the roasted gram flour and hung curd in a large shallow dish and mix together, gradually incorporating all the other ingredients except the chicken and chaat masala. Season with salt to taste. Add the chicken pieces and spread the marinade over until coated. Cover and allow to marinate in the refrigerator for about 2 hours.

Preheat a charcoal grill or oven, if using. Remove the chicken from the marinade and thread onto metal skewers. Grill until done to your taste. Sprinkle with chaat masala and serve hot.

Dum ki Makai
Spiced Tomatoes & Corn

Preparation time 15 minutes
Cooking time 15 minutes
Serves 4

1 tablespoon oil
1 bay leaf
1 black cardamom pod
1 × 1-cm / ½-inch cinnamon stick
½ teaspoon black peppercorns
2 cloves
1 medium-sized onion, chopped
2–3 garlic cloves, crushed
½ teaspoon ground coriander
½ teaspoon ground cumin
¼ teaspoon Kashmiri red chilli powder
a small pinch of ground turmeric (optional)
1 teaspoon sugar
salt
100g / 3½oz tomatoes, diced
200g / 7oz baby corn, medium-sized cobs
2 green chillies, de-seeded, to garnish
phulka or boiled rice, to serve

Heat the oil in a pan, add the bay leaf together with the other whole spices and stir-fry until they start to change colour. Add the onions and garlic and stir-fry over medium-high heat for about 5 minutes until the onions are translucent. Add the ground spices together with salt to taste, the sugar and tomatoes. Continue cooking until the sauce is slightly thickened. Add the baby corn and mix well, then cover, reduce the heat to low and simmer for about 5 minutes. Garnish with the green chillies and enjoy with phulka or boiled rice.

Achari Machhi Tikka
Boneless Fish Cubes in Pickling Spices

Preparation time 30 minutes, plus marinating time
Cooking time 5 minutes
Serves 4

30g / 1¼oz gram (chickpea) flour, roasted
2 tablespoons hung natural (plain) yoghurt (see page 793)
4 teaspoons single (light) cream
1kg / 2¼lb boneless fish, cut into chunks
2 teaspoons mustard oil
8g / ⅓oz fennel seeds
2g kalonji seeds
2g fenugreek seeds
3g cumin seeds
3g caraway seeds
10g / ½oz Garam Masala (see page 31)
20g / ¾oz pickle paste with oil
salt
5g / ⅛oz Chaat Masala (see page 31)

Put the roasted gram flour, curd and cream into a large shallow dish and mix together. Add the fish and stir until the fish chunks are coated. Cover and leave to refrigerate for 1 hour.

Heat the mustard oil over high heat in a heavy-based pan to smoking point. Add the spice seeds and stir-fry for about 1 minute or until they start to crackle, then remove them from the pan and put them in another large shallow dish with the pickle paste and mix together. Season with salt to taste.

Remove the fish from the first marinade and remove the excess marinade. Add the fish to the second marinade and stir until the fish is coated.

Preheat a charcoal grill or grill, if using. Remove the fish from the marinade and thread through several metal skewers then grill until done to your taste. Sprinkle with the chaat masala and serve hot.

Kaju Subz ke Shami
Vegetarian Shami with Cashew Nuts

Preparation time 40 minutes
Cooking time 10 minutes
Serves 4–6

200g / 7oz potatoes, unpeeled
oil, for shallow-frying
200g / 7oz beans
200g / 7oz cauliflower florets
100g / 3½oz carrots, sliced
150g / 5oz paneer (see page 59, grated)
150g / 5oz peas
50g / 1¾oz gram (chickpea) flour, roasted
100g / 3½oz cashew nuts, broken and roasted
5g / ⅛oz cumin seeds, roasted and ground
5g / ⅛oz Garam Masala (see page 31)
salt
2–3 green chillies, de-seeded and chopped
5g / ⅛oz fresh root ginger, peeled and chopped
5g / ⅛oz coriander (cilantro), chopped

Cook the potatoes in a large pan of boiling water for about 10–15 minutes, or until tender. Drain and leave until cool enough to handle, then peel off the skins. Set aside.

Heat the oil in a karhai or heavy-based frying pan (skillet), adds the beans and fry until cooked. Remove the beans with a slotted spoon and drain on kitchen paper. Add the cauliflower to the same oil and fry until cooked, then remove with a slotted spoon and drain on kitchen paper (paper towels).

Now add the carrots to the oil and fry until cooked. Remove with a slotted spoon and drain on kitchen paper. Add the peeled potatoes and fry until golden brown, then remove with a slotted spoon and allow to drain on kitchen paper. Add the paneer to the oil and stir-fry for about 2 minutes.

Put the vegetables and paneer in a bowl and add the peas. Mix to combine, then pass the mixture through a mincer into a clean bowl. Add the roasted gram flour and cashew nuts together with the ground spices and season with salt to taste.

With damp hands, shape the mixture into balls and press between the palms of your hands to form patties.

Heat enough oil for shallow-frying. Add the patties, in batches if necessary and shallow-fry until a crisp crust is formed on the outside. Turn the patties over carefully and shallow-fry the other side until a crisp crust is formed. Remove with a slotted spoon and drain on kitchen paper.

Vikram Vij and Meeru Dhalwala
Vij's

1480 W 11th Ave
Vancouver, BC V6H 1L1
Canada

Vikram Vij and Meeru Dhalwala, the husband-and-wife team behind Vancouver's top-rated restaurant Vij's, are devoted to seasonal recipes, sourcing much of their produce within the province and making an effort to serve only local, sustainable seafood and organic poultry and meats. Vij's has earned numerous accolades since opening in 1994.

———

Menu

1 **Chownki Mausami Sabziyan**
Seasonal Vegetables Sauteed in Ghee & Cumin, Kalonji & Yellow Mustard Seeds

2 **Sarasondane wali Phali aur Alu**
Green Beans & New Potatoes in Mustard Seed Curry

3 **Khatta Mitha Barhe ka Salan**
Beef Tenderloin Marinated in Demerara Sugar & Tamarind, with Black Cumin Curry

4 **Saunfiya Kalaunji wala Gosht**
Oven-braised Goat Meat in Fennel & Kalonji Curry

Chownki Mausami Sabziyan
Seasonal Vegetables Sauteed in Ghee &
Cumin, Kalonji & Yellow Mustard Seeds

Preparation time 10 minutes
Cooking time 8–10 minutes
Serves 4

1 tablespoon cumin seeds
1 teaspoon kalonji seeds
2 tablespoons yellow mustard seeds
125g / 4½oz (½ cup) ghee
1 small tomato, finely chopped
1 tablespoon ground coriander
1 tablespoon salt
½ teaspoon crushed cayenne pepper
1 large turnip, about 225g / 8oz, cut into thin rounds then cut into quarters
1 small head of green cabbage, cut into 1-cm / ½-inch wide and 5-cm / 2-inch long strips
1 small head of purple cabbage, chopped
6 tablespoons lemon juice

Put the cumin, kalonji and yellow mustard seeds
in a small bowl and mix to combine. Heat the ghee
in a medium-sized pan over high heat for 1 minute.
Reduce the heat to medium and immediately add
the mixed seeds.

Stir well and allow to sizzle for 1–2 minutes, or until
you can hear the first popping sound of the mustard
seeds. You basically want to cook the seeds, but not
burn them.

Immediately add the tomato and stir. Add the
coriander, salt and cayenne and cook for 3–4
minutes. At this point add your choice of vegetables,
depending on their cooking times. For this particular
recipe, add the turnips and cook, stirring frequently,
for 2 minutes.

Just before serving, add the cabbages and cook over
medium-high heat for 2–3 minutes. Stir in the lemon
juice and serve with plain basmati rice.

Sarasondane wali Phali aur Alu
Green Beans & New Potatoes in
Mustard Seed Curry

Preparation time 15 minutes, plus soaking time
Cooking time 20–25 minutes
Serves 4

250g / 9oz (5–6) new potatoes
125ml / 4½fl oz (½ cup) vegetable oil or ghee
6 large tomatoes, puréed
1 tablespoon ground cumin
1 tablespoon black mustard seeds, ground
2 teaspoons salt
1 tablespoon crushed dried red chilli flakes
1 teaspoon ground turmeric
250g / 9oz (1⅔ cups) green beans, strings removed, cut in half lengthways

Soak the potatoes in a large bowl of water for
10 minutes to loosen any dirt. Drain and thoroughly
wash, then cut each one into 4–6 slices. Set aside.

Put a medium-sized pan over medium-high heat, add
the oil or ghee and tomatoes and stir. Add the cumin,
ground mustard seeds, salt, chilli flakes and turmeric
and stir well. Sauté for 5–8 minutes, or until you see
the oil glistening on top.

Pour in 1 litre / 1¾ pints (4¼ cups) water and bring
to the boil. Reduce the heat to medium and boil for
12–14 minutes, stirring occasionally. The spices and
water should be very well mixed together at the end
of cooking.

Gently add the potatoes, cover with a lid and cook
at a medium boil for 5–8 minutes. Uncover, add
the green beans, stir well and cook for a further
5 minutes. Serve piping hot.

Khatta Mitha Barhe ka Salan

Beef Tenderloin Marinated in
Demerara Sugar & Tamarind,
with Black Cumin Curry

Preparation time 40 minutes, plus marinating time
Cooking time 4–8 minutes
Serves 4

150g / 5oz (¾ cup) demerara (raw brown) sugar
80g / 3oz (⅔ cup) tamarind paste
3½ tablespoons ground coriander
1 tablespoon cayenne pepper
½ tablespoon salt
6 tablespoons vegetable oil
6 beef tenderloin steaks, about 150–175g / 5–6oz each

For the black cumin curry

125g / 4½oz (½ cup) ghee
1 tablespoon cumin seeds
400g / 14oz (2½ cups) finely chopped onions
75g / 2½oz (⅔ cup) plain (all-purpose) flour
1 tablespoon salt
½ teaspoon cayenne pepper
1 tablespoon ground cumin
1 tablespoon ground coriander
1 large tomato, finely chopped
1.25–1.5 litres / 2–2½ pints (5–6¼ cups) organic chicken stock

The key to this recipe is the balance between the sugar and the tamarind. Mix the two ingredients together, then taste. Adjust the sweetness or tartness according to personal preference. Add the coriander, cayenne salt and oil in a large bowl and mix to combine. Pierce each tenderloin steak 5 or 6 times with a knife, then put the steaks into the sugar-tamarind mixture and turn to coat. Make sure the steaks are well covered. Cover and allow to marinate in the refrigerator for at least 3 hours, and ideally 6–8 hours.

For the curry, heat the ghee in a medium-sized pan over medium-high heat, add the cumin seeds and allow them to sizzle for 30–45 seconds, or until they are darker brown, but not quite black. Don't let them turn black. Alternatively, dry roast the cumin seeds in a dry, small, heavy-based frying pan (skillet) over high heat for 1–2 minutes, or until they are dark brown.

Add the onions to the melted ghee with the cumin seeds and sauté for 8–10 minutes, or until the onions are browned. Add the flour, stir well and reduce the heat to low. Cook, stirring frequently, for 6–7 minutes, or until the flour darkens to a tannish-brown colour. Add the salt, cayenne, ground cumin, coriander and tomato. Stir well and sauté for 5 minutes. This masala will be quite doughy. Add the chicken stock and stir well, then increase the heat to medium. Bring to the boil, uncovered, then turn off the heat.

To finish the beef, preheat the grill (broiler), or barbecue or a stovetop cast-iron grill (griddle) pan to high. Grill the marinated steaks on one side for about 2 minutes, then turn and grill the other side for a further 2 minutes for medium-rare. If you prefer your steaks well-done, continue cooking each side for another minute or two.

Spoon the curry over each steak and serve with rice. You could serve the Green Beans & Potatoes in Mustard Seed Curry (see page 770) as a side dish.

Saunfiya Kalaunji wala Gosht
Oven-braised Goat Meat in Fennel
& Kalonji Curry

Preparation time 2 hours 50 minutes,
plus cooling time
Cooking time 15–20 minutes
Serves 8

about 4.5kg / 10lb leg of goat, fat trimmed
900g / 2lb (about 4 large) tomatoes, chopped
2 onions, chopped
1 tablespoon salt
½ tablespoon cayenne pepper
½ teaspoon ground black pepper
1 tablespoon Garam Masala (see page 31)

For the fennel and kalonji curry

2 tablespoons fennel seeds
1 tablespoon cumin seeds
1 teaspoon kalonji seeds
1 teaspoon ajwain seeds
125ml / 4½fl oz (½ cup) vegetable oil
6 large tomatoes, puréed
2 teaspoons salt
1 teaspoon ground turmeric
½ teaspoon cayenne pepper

Preheat the oven to 220°C/425°F/Gas 7.

Place the leg in a large roasting tin (pan) and add the tomatoes, onions, salt, cayenne, black pepper, garam masala and 1 litre / 1¾ pints (4¼ cups) water. Mix well, then cover with a lid or seal tightly with foil and cook in the oven for 2 hours. Remove from oven and allow the meat to cool.

To make the fennel and kalonji curry, put the fennel, cumin, kalonji and ajwain seeds in a heavy-based pan and cook over medium heat, stirring constantly, until the fennel develops a yellowish tinge, about 2–3 minutes. Transfer the spices into a bowl and allow to cool.

When the spices are cool, put them in a spice grinder and grind to a powder.

Combine the oil and puréed tomatoes in a medium to large pan over medium-high heat, add the ground spice mixture, salt, turmeric and cayenne, stir and cook for 5–8 minutes, or until you see the oil glistening on the tomatoes and they have become more 'paste like'.

Pour in about 1.2 litres / 2 pints (5 cups) water and stir well. Bring to the boil, then reduce the heat to low and simmer for 10 minutes. Remove the pan from the heat and set aside.

To finish, wearing plastic gloves, peel the meat off the bone (be sure to get all the meat stuck on the bone), then discard the bone and stir the meat back into the roasting tin. Place on the hob (stove top), cover again and bring to the boil over medium-high heat. Uncover and boil for about 10 minutes, until there is enough liquid to keep the meat, onions and tomatoes moist, but the mixture is not soupy.

Return the curry to medium heat and add the goat meat, tomatoes and onion. Mix well and heat until beginning to boil.

Serve with rice, naan or fresh baguette.

Talk to your butcher when purchasing goat. An older goat will take longer to cook and, in terms of cooking, is defined as more than a year old.

GLOSSARY

Glossary

Ajwain

A seed similar to thyme in flavour, and similar to caraway or cumin seed in appearance. Used dry roasted to give a pungent flavour to dishes.

Alkaline water

Water that is neither acidic nor neutral. Used in north Indian cooking, and thought to have health benefits by helping balance the acidity in the human body. Alkaline, or ionized, water can be purchased, or produced from a tap (faucet) with an alkalizer attached. Ordinary water can be substituted.

Allspice

A spice made from the dried berries of a small tree. The name is derived from the berry's fragrance, thought to resemble a blend of cinnamon, cloves and nutmeg. A key flavouring for kebabs.

Almonds

The seed of the fruit of the almond tree, which has a nutty flavour and texture. Used raw, blanched or roasted, in whole, flaked, slivered or ground form, in both savoury and sweet dishes.

Alum

A chemical compound with many applications, alum powder is dissolved in water and used in cooking to reduce the bitterness or astringency of some ingredients, and in pickling foods. It can often be found in the spice section of grocery stores.

Amaranthus

An exotic plant, also known as *bathua* or pigweed, the leaves and grains of which are edible and highly nutritious. The leaves are eaten as a vegetable in many areas of the world. Use spinach instead.

Amchoor

A flavouring made from raw unripe mango, which has been dried and powdered. It is used as a garnish for sprinkling on savoury dishes, or for making chutneys.

Amla

Also known as Indian gooseberry, a greenish-yellow fruit that has a sour, astringent taste. It is often pickled. It is also eaten raw or cooked in various dishes.

Aniseed

The fruit or seed of an annual flowering plant, used to add a liquorice flavour to dishes. Also thought to aid digestion. Known as *saunf* in India.

Apricots

A small yellow-orange coloured stone fruit, used fresh or dried in Indian cooking in drinks and sweets and also in some meat dishes. Hunza apricots are small, round, hard and beige in colour. They come from wild apricot trees in Kashmir, Afghanistan and Turkey, where the fruit is dried on the tree before harvesting, and need to be soaked before using.

Arhar

Whole or split yellow lentils, also called *toor* or *toover* lentils. Can be bought whole, but is usually sold skinned and split. Has a mild, nutty flavour.

Asafoetida

Made from sap from a plant, which can be obtained as an amber-coloured resin, or crushed into powder. Uncooked, it has a strong unpleasant odour, but it takes on a pleasant, onion-like smell after heating.

Ash gourd

Thought of as one of the many varieties of gourd, but actually a fruit, eaten in India, where it is known as *petha*. The white flesh is most often used as a vegetable in curries, but the immature fruit can be quite sweet, and is sometimes used as an ingredient in sweets.

Badhi

A dried spice tablet made from ground lentils and spices, eaten fried or used as an ingredient. If you cannot buy them, use a spice mixture instead.

Bael fruit

Also known as Indian quince, and grown throughout India and most of the southeast countries. Greatly valued for its therapeutic qualities.

Bamboo shoots

The edible shoots of some types of bamboo plants. Used most often in Asian cooking. Fresh shoots require careful preparation, but canned and frozen shoots are bought ready to use. Bamboo shoots are used as a vegetable in many different types of dishes.

Banana leaves

Used as plates in India, and also to wrap food in for cooking. Can be bought frozen, and thawed under warm running water. If you cannot buy them, use foil instead, although the subtle flavour of the banana leaf will be absent from the finished dish.

Banana stems

The tender core of the banana plant, used as a vegetable in curries.

Basmati

A variety of long-grain, polished rice grown extensively in India. With a unique fragrance, it is used extensively in pulaos and biryani. The basmati rice of Dehradoon is particularly noted.

Bay leaf

The leaf of the bay tree, used fresh or dried to give curries a flavour similar to strong cinnamon. The leaf is used for flavour only, and is not eaten.

Belan

A type of rolling pin, used most often with a circular rolling board to roll out breads.

Bengal gram

Black chickpeas (garbanzo beans), also called *kala channa* in India. More a deep red colour than black, used in the same way as regular chickpeas but with a slightly nutty flavour.

Bhojwar masala

A Hyderabadi spice mixture, which is a ground blend of spices including coriander, sesame seeds, cumin and bay leaf, commonly used in Hyderabadi dishes.

Biryani

Literally 'fried rice', biryani is arguably the best-known rice dish in Indian cuisine. It has many regional variations, but the *dum ki* (slow-cooked in a sealed pot) recipe from Hyderabad is the most prized.

Bitter gourd

A bitter vegetable with a knobbly green skin, known as *karela* in India. Comes in many varieties ranging from short to long, dark green and pale green. Cooked as a vegetable throughout India. It can be found in Asian grocery stores.

Black cumin

A spice made of the dried seeds of a plant from the same family as cumin, known as *shahi jeera*, *siyah jeera* or *kala jeera* in India. Darker in colour than regular cumin, and with a more complex, sweeter flavour. Traditionally used extensively in small quantities in dishes from the royal kitchens of Awadh and Hyderabad.

Black rock salt

A purplish-brown coloured rock salt with a smoky flavour, known as *kala namak*.

Black-eyed beans

See Lobiya beans.

Blanching nuts

To blanch nuts yourself, put them in a bowl and cover with boiling water. Leave for 2 minutes, then drain and allow to cool slightly. Use a clean cloth to rub off the skins.

Boora

An unrefined Indian sugar, produced by boiling the juice of the sugar cane, skimming away impurities, and drying and then powdering the resulting syrup. Caster (superfine) sugar can be used instead.

Boti

A sharp cutting tool from Bengal, used to cut meat before cooking.

Bottle gourd

A bottle-shaped pale green fruit, with a nutty flavour. Used in curries throughout India, where it is known as *lauki*. Squash can be used as an alternative.

Broken rice

Rice whose husk has been cracked during harvesting or milling. Broken rice absorbs more moisture during cooking.

Broken wheat

Wheat that has been coarsely milled. Broken wheat, also called cracked wheat or *dalia*, is prepared with un-boiled wheat grain, and is sold both roasted and un-roasted. Most commonly prepared as sweet or savoury porridge for breakfast, and considered the best diet for the infirm, ailing or convalescent, as it is easily digested.

Buttermilk

A fermented milk drink. In India, buttermilk is the liquid left over when yoghurt is churned to make butter. It is known as *chaas* and is used primarily in milk-based drinks. Outside India, artificial, or 'cultured', buttermilk is readily available and is a fine substitute, although possibly thicker than the traditional version.

Cambodge petals

Petals from the fruit of *Garcinia combogia*, or Malabar tamarind, also known in India as brindleberry. The petals and dried berries are used as a spice and a souring agent in cooking. *Kokum* can be used as an alternative.

Camphor

White resin with a strong aroma and pleasant cool taste. Used in miniscule quantities in cold drinks, sweets and some aromatic spices. Some forms of camphor are hazardous to health, and only the variety clearly labelled 'edible camphor' should be ingested.

Candied sugar

Unrefined sugar available in two forms: crystalline and in lumps. Known as *misri* in India.

Caraway seeds

A spice used to flavour rice dishes, breads, biscuits and cakes, and also in many fish recipes. Also valued for its carminative, digestive properties.

Cardamom

A spice made from the dried pods of the cardamom plant, used in both sweet and savoury dishes, and known as *elaichi* in India. The most common variety has green pods, while the other has black-brown pods with a more astringent flavour. Ground green cardamom is also available from Asian grocery stores.

Cassava

Obtained from palm roots, like sago, cassava is the edible root of a tropical plant enclosing white starchy flesh within brown rind. Originally from Brazil, Cassava was imported to India to combat famine by a prince in Kerala in the 19th century. It is eaten boiled or cooked (like potatoes) as a curried vegetable.

Chaar magaz

A mixture of four seeds – pumpkin, melon, squash and watermelon. It is a used as a paste to give flavour and thickness to curries.

Chaat

Savoury street-side finger food, including *tikki, papri, gujiya, gol gape, pani puri, alu,* and many more. Chaat are served with an assortment of sweet and tangy chutney and spice powders, and are commonly prepared at and served from *khumcha* and *redhiwallahas* (vendors with a portable kiosk or pushcart).

Chabaina

A snack or a very light meal, literally something to nibble on.

Chakki or chakla

A round flat disc or rolling board made of wood or stone, and often mounted on small low legs, on which breads are rolled out with the help of a rolling pin, known as a *belan.*

Chana dal

Split black chickpeas (garbanzo beans), produced by skinning and splitting the yellow kernel of black chickpeas, chana dal is sweet and nutty and the most commonly used pulse in India. Regular chickpeas or yellow lentils can be used as an alternative.

Chayote

A gourd, also known as custard marrow, that grows on climbing vines and is shaped like a large green-white pear. It has a sweet, mild-flavoured flesh.

Chhena

Fresh curd cheese, produced by boiling milk, then curdling it and hanging it in muslin (cheesecloth) to produce a semi-solid product that is kneaded until smooth. Used in desserts. See page 59 for recipe.

Chicken, dressed

A chicken with the internal organs and head removed, and plucked.

Chickpeas (garbanzo beans)

A round, pale yellow pulse (legume), often used whole in dal and in a dry tangy, strongly spiced dish with or without potatoes. Chickpeas are also ground in India to make gram flour, which is used frequently in Indian cooking. Canned cooked chickpeas are readily available, and can save much time in the kitchen.

Chigur

The tender shoots of the tamarind plant, used in Hyderabad and elsewhere in Andhra Pradesh as a souring agent in dishes.

Chillies

The fruits of certain varieties of capsicum plant, with a unique hot flavour essential to many curry dishes. They may be green, yellow or red in colour, according to their ripeness. The hottest parts of the chilli are the seeds, which are often discarded before use. Chillies may be used whole, slit open or chopped, and may be either fresh or dried.

Many varieties of chilli are used in India. Fresh green chillies, both small round ones called birdseed and longer ones are common. Dried whole red chillies from Rajasthan (Nagori) and Andhra Pradesh (Rasampatti) are particularly prized for their pungent flavour.

Kashmiri red chillies are very mild and valued for giving dishes a scarlet hue without increasing the heat of a dish. Red chilli powder is almost as commonly used across India in everyday cooking as turmeric and ground coriander. Chilli powders, flakes and pastes are also widely available.

Chippe

An earthenware pot used in Hyderabad to cook a meat speciality.

Chironji

Also known as priyala seeds, these seeds have a mild flavour similar to almonds. They are used whole in desserts and ground as a thickener in other dishes.

Cinnamon

A spice made from the thin dried inner bark of the cinnamon tree, with a warm flavour suitable for sweet and savoury dishes. Known as *dalchini* in India. It is used ground, or in sticks that are cooked with dishes to release their flavour, but not eaten.

Citric acid

A naturally occurring acid found in citrus fruits. Used in Indian cooking in powdered form as a souring agent instead of fresh lime juice. It can also be used to add flavour and to tenderize meat.

Clarify

To remove impurities from a liquid, as with butter, which can be melted to remove the milk solids and obtain the purified fat (ghee).

Cloves

A strong spice made from the dried buds of a tree, known as *laung* in India. Used to give flavour to vegetables, pulses, meat dishes or rice. Used whole or ground, often in combination with black cardamoms, or as an ingredient in garam masala.

Cluster beans

A plant native to India, the fresh tender pods of which are used as green beans. The beans can also be ground and used as a thickening agent, as can the gum from the plant.

Coconut

An oily nut grown on a coconut palm, with a coarse brown exterior and white flesh. The flesh can be used fresh or dried in large or small pieces, or grated and dried (dessicated), and is added to dishes to give flavour and texture. The liquid inside the fruit is called coconut water. Alternatively, liquid can be extracted from the coconut meat to make coconut milk, or a slightly thicker version, coconut cream.

To make fresh coconut milk, grate the flesh of a fresh coconut into a bowl. Cover with water and leave to soak for 30 minutes. Pour the mixture through a clean piece of muslin (cheesecloth) or into a clean bowl. This first extract is thick, and is used like coconut cream. It requires careful handling when cooking, and should be added to dishes slowly only after reducing the heat. Otherwise it will curdle.

To make a thinner coconut milk, return the soaked coconut to the bowl, cover with water and repeat the soaking and straining process. This coconut milk can be boiled for longer periods

Coconut feni

A liquor made from the sap of the coconut palm.

Coconut vinegar

Made by fermenting the coconut water found inside
the nut with yeast and a culture. It has low acidity
and a musty taste.

Colocasia

A tropical plant, grown mostly for its root, or tuber,
and also called taro root. In India, the stem, roots
and leaves are eaten. The entire plant contains a
chemical that can irritate the skin and should be
carefully prepared before it can be eaten.

Coriander (cilantro)

An annual herb, the entirety of which is used in
Indian cooking: the fresh leaves as a garnish or
in green chutney; the whole seeds in temperings,
pickling spices and some non-vegetarian dishes; the
powdered seeds, or ground coriander, is among the
most commonly used spices in everyday cooking.

Cornmeal (corn flour)

Made from whole dried corn kernels that have been
hulled, dried and ground. Used to make breads, and
in combination with other flours in baking. Not to be
confused with cornflour (cornstarch), which is made
from the endosperm part of the kernel only, and is
used for binding or thickening.

Cowpeas

See Lobiya beans.

Cream of tartar

A by-product of wine making and used in powdered
form in cooking to help stabilize, to give beaten
whites volume, in some baking powders and in sugar
syrup to prevent crystallization.

Cumin

An essential ingredient in Indian cooking, available
ground or as whole seeds, with a nutty, warm
flavour. Known as *jeera* in India. Used in all
mixed spices and curry powders, and to flavour
a range of pulses and vegetable dishes, as well as
yoghurt dishes.

Curd

See Yoghurt.

Curry leaves

An aromatic leaf known in India as *kadipatta*,
similar in appearance to the bay leaf, but much
smaller in size, with a warm, lemony smell. In south
India, curry leaves are used to flavour vegetables,
lentils and breads. They are available fresh or dried.

Dal

A collective term in India for dishes prepared with
lentils, pulses (legumes) and dried beans. Also refers
to dried split pulses before they are cooked. See
individual entries.

Dekchi

A broad circular pot used to cook rice dishes, such
as pulao and biryani. The larger, profession version
of this pot is called a *deg*.

Dhungar

A smoking technique that adds flavour to cooked
meats by placing them around a small dish of
burning charcoal, to which spices and a few drops of
oil are added, producing smoke. The entire dish is
then covered for a few minutes.

Dough seals

To seal a pot with dough, put 120g / 4oz (1 cup) flour in a bowl and slowly add about 60ml / 2fl oz (¼ cup) water, or enough to make a soft dough. Knead the dough on a lightly floured work surface for a few minutes, then shape into a long sausage. Press the dough onto the rim of the pot, cover with the lid, and pinch to seal.

Drumsticks

An extremely popular vegetable in south Indian cuisine as an ingredient in sambhar, drumsticks are the immature long green pods of the Moringa tree, known as *sahjan ki phalli*. The flowers and leaves of the tree may also be eaten.

Dry roasting

See Roasting.

Dum

A traditional method of slow cooking in which the food is steamed in a sealed container, retaining all its cooking juices. During cooking, charcoals are placed on top of the lid to distribute the heat evenly. On some occasions the pan is also placed on a bed of hot coals. Used extensively in Mughal cuisine.

Fennel seed

A herb with a liquorice-like flavour. The leaves of the plant are edible, but in Indian cuisine it is the seeds which are used most often, and sometimes form part of garam masala. Fennel seed is used extensively with dried ginger powder in Kashmiri cuisine.

Fenugreek

An aromatic bittersweet spice known as *methi* in India. The seeds have a strong flavour, and the chopped and dried leaves (*kasoori methi*), are milder. Both the seeds and leaves are used to add a wholesome touch to curries, pickles and chutneys.

Fermented fish

Fish that is left for several months to ferment and which sometimes reduces to a paste or liquid. Used as the main flavouring in many dishes in northeast Indian cuisine.

Flour, plain (all-purpose)

Made from highly refined ground wheat, high in nutrition and fibre. Used to make snacks, pastries, breads and other baked goods.

Flour, wholemeal (whole wheat)

Made from whole ground wheat. Used as an alternative to plain (all-purpose) flour.

Garam masala

A blend of spices used mostly in north Indian cooking, and particularly in meat dishes. Common ingredients include cinnamon sticks, bay leaves, cloves, cardamom pods, mace blades and black peppercorns. The spice mixture may be fried in hot oil or ghee (before other ingredients, such as meat, are added), or tied together in a small piece of clean muslin (cheesecloth) and added to a pot during cooking. See page 31 for recipes.

Garlic

The bulb part of the garlic plant, which can be divided into cloves which have a pungent white flesh. Used in a wide range of savoury dishes.

To make garlic water, soak 2 tablespoons crushed garlic in 125ml / 4½fl oz (½ cup) water for 5 minutes, then strain through a piece of fine muslin (cheesecloth) or fine sieve (strainer).

Gentlemen's toes

See Round gourd.

Gongura leaves

A bitter acidic leaf vegetable that comes in two varieties, green stemmed and red stemmed. The latter is more sour. Gongura is often used in pickles, and also in curries.

Ghee

Butter which has been clarified to remove the milk solids and obtain the purified fat. Used to prepare cooked desserts and to cook many Mughal dishes.

Ginger

A vital ingredient in Indian cooking, ginger has a strong pungent flavour. The fresh root of the ginger plant, which is used grated or pounded gives a warm, citrus flavour to dishes. Dried ginger (*saunth*) is a spice made from ground ginger roots, with a more woody, less pungent flavour than fresh ginger.

Gold leaf

An extremely thin, edible sheet of gold used to decorate sweet dishes and some exotic savoury vegetarian and non-vegetarian delicacies.

Gourd

Many varieties of gourds, also called marrows or squash, are cooked in India. See individual entries for more detail.

Gram flour

Known as besan in India, gram flour is made from ground dried chickpeas (garbanzo beans), sometimes roasted, then ground into a powder. It is often used in batters for deep-frying. It is also known as chickpea flour.

Grinding spices

The best way to grind spices is in a mortar with a pestle, or in a clean spice grinder kept especially for spices. Ground spices are best used fresh, although they can be stored in an airtight container for a short time.

Handi

A traditional cooking vessel with a narrow neck, originally made from clay. Often covered and sealed and used in *dum* (slow) cooking.

Hatha

A ladle made of wood, which is used to stir dishes.

Hemp seeds

The seeds of Cannabis plants, hemp seeds are not toxic. Ground to a paste, they are used to thicken gravies and to impart a nutty flavour to dishes. Combined with pomegranate seed they make a tangy chutney.

Idli

Steamed dumplings made with a lightly fermented batter of rice flour and ground lentils, and usually served with powdered spices and coconut chutney or sambhar. This ancient dish is very popular as a light breakfast all over Tamil Nadu, Karnataka, Kerala and Andhra Pradesh.

Idli thattu

A traditional metallic steamer used to cook idlis. *Idli* moulds are now made to fit inside pressure cookers.

Ittar

Fragrant edible essences, such as rosewater or kewra water, used in small quantities in desserts, and in some savoury dishes.

Jackfruit

A large fruit which grows on a tree. It can be cooked into curries or used raw to make a variety of vegetable dishes. It can be found in Asian grocery stores. Jackfruit contain a white substance that numbs the hands. Some Indian stores sell cleaned and cut jackfruit, but if you buy a whole fruit you might like to wear gloves when handling it.

Jaggery

An unrefined sugar made from sugar cane, in which the sugar crystals are not separated from the molasses. Mainly used in sweet preparations in south India and Bengal.

Jambu

A strongly aromatic grass valued in Uttarakhand for its unique aroma. Traditionally used as a tempering for dal. It can also be substituted for garlic.

Jharji

A large, long-handled slotted spoon used to remove items from hot oil.

Kachri

A member of the melon family, grown in the desert areas of India, mainly in Rajasthan. It is has a bittersweet flavour and is used both as a vegetable and as a meat tenderizer. It can be dried and also ground and sold as a powder.

Kalonji seeds

Small black seeds, also known as nigella seeds or black onion seeds, which have a peppery flavour, and are used extensively in vegetable dishes, breads and pickles.

Karhai

A wok-like cast-iron vessel, used for deep-frying breads, snacks and sweets.

Kashmiri chilli water

Water in which whole dried red Kashmiri chillies have been soaked and then squeezed to extract the colour of the chillies.

Kashmiri red chilli powder

A special type of red chilli powder used as a spice in many Kashmiri dishes. Milder than other chilli powders, and it is also used as a colouring.

Katori

Small and large serving bowls used mainly for dishes with sauce. A number of *katori* arranged on a *thali* allow diners to eat as much as they want in the order they want, according to their mood.

Kewra water

An essence extracted from the leaves and flowers of a plant of the screw pine family. Gives a delicate, floral taste to desserts and some savoury dishes. Rosewater can be used instead, although it has a different flavour.

Khand

A type of unrefined sugar, similar to jaggery or palm sugar, which is sold in crystalline lumps rather than small crystals.

Khoya

A powdered product made from milk, by gradually heating whole milk and then drying it. Used extensively as an ingredient in many sweet dishes throughout India, and also known as *mawa*. See page 58 for recipe.

Khoya can also be grated before being added to dishes, and milk powder may be used as an alternative if necessary.

Khus

Vetiver, a grass plant grown throughout India, from which an essence is extracted that is widely used to flavour savoury Mughal dishes and many sweet dishes.

Kidney beans

Dark red coloured beans with a strong nutty taste. Kidney beans from Kashmir are well known for their unique taste and colour. Known as *rajma* in India.

Kofta

Small meatballs, sometimes sausage-shaped, served in gravy. There are many regional variations of kofta, including numerous vegetarian recipes prepared with bottle gourd, unripe plantains, potatoes or paneer.

Kohlrabi

A member of the cabbage family, with a similar taste to turnip. Can be eaten raw or cooked in the manner of other types of turnip.

Kokum

The plum-like fruit of a tree grown on the western coast of India. It gives a purple colour and sour flavour to fish dishes and some vegetarian curries.

Korma

A dish in which the meat has been marinated, then slowly braised in a thick sauce. Korma are considered subtler and more aromatic than other non-vegetarian dishes.

Kulcha

A type of bread from Punjab that is mostly deep-fried, but sometimes cooked in a tandoor. Usually served with chickpeas (garbanzo beans), or stuffed with paneer or potatoes. In Amritsar, the making of kulcha is considered an art form.

Kulthi

A small oval-shaped bean, often with a wrinkled appearance, ranging in colour from black to brown to red. Most often used whole, it has an earthy flavour. Channa dal can be used as an alternative.

Kurcha

A flat spatula with a long or short handle, used to scrape the food that sticks to the sides or bottom of a cooking vessel when a dish is fried or boiled for a long period of time.

Lobiya

Black-eyed beans or cowpeas. Medium-sized, oblong beans that are creamy white with a black 'eye' on one side. Their skin is quite thick and they need to be soaked overnight before cooking. They have a nutty aroma and a creamy taste that is slightly earthy.

Lotus puffs

Puffed-up lotus seeds known as *taal makhana*, used to prepare a *kheer* (rice pudding) or paired with dried fruits and nuts, and even green peas, to make a vegetarian delicacy.

Lotus roots

The roots, or stems, of the lotus flower, which grow under the water. Known as *kamal kakadi, nadru* or *bhain* in India. They can be boiled or fried, in the same way as other vegetables, and cooked into curries; those from Kashmir are particularly renowned.

Mace

The aromatic fruit surrounding the nutmeg kernel, which can be used whole and dried, or ground, in sweet and savoury dishes. Known as *javitri* in India.

Malai

A type of clotted cream obtained from boiled milk, used in many sweets. It is also used into enrich pulses (legumes) and other vegetable dishes.

Masala

This term can be used to describe any spiced dish, or to refer to a combination of spices (spice mixture).

Masoor

When whole, these lentils are green-brown in colour and take a long time to cook. The split version are red and take much less time to cook, although they actually turn golden brown during cooking. The split version is called masoor dal.

Millet

A variety of cereal crop and its grains, used as an alternative to rice. The seeds can be used whole or ground and have a slightly nutty taste. Hulled millet is also often called birdseed in the US.

Millet flour

Made from ground millet grains, with a slightly nutty flavour. Used to make breads including chapatis and roti, and in other dishes.

Mint

A leafy, aromatic herb used fresh or dried in chutneys, salads, fruit drinks or as a garnish.

Mixed pickle

Literally a five-coloured variety of mixed pickle, popular all over north India. The most common combination is mango, lemon, green chilli, carrots in oil. In Punjab, turnips, cauliflowers and carrots are pickled in vinegar and oil and a little sugar. Mixed pickles are served with paratha instead of vegetables or as an accompaniment.

Mizo anthurium

A local herb in Mizoram, northeast India. Mustard leaves can be used instead.

Mogodi

Mildly spiced dried lentil dumplings made with moong beans, and cooked as dal or paired with vegetables. Popular in Rajasthan, *mogodi* were traditionally made at home but are now available ready-made from stores throughout India.

Mogra flowers

A variety of jasmine valued for its delicate fragrance. The petals are used as a garnish and the essence, or *ittar*, is used to aromatize Awadhi and Hyderabadi delicacies.

Mooli

A pleasantly pungent type of white radish used fresh in salad and raitas, as well as cooked and paired with potatoes and tomatoes, or served on its own.

Moong dal

A type of green lentil (which is yellow once the skin has been removed). Slightly larger and coarser than whole yellow lentils. It has a stronger flavour — nutty and sweet — than most other lentils.

Morel mushrooms

A highly sought-after edible fungus with a spongy appearance. In India, it is found almost exclusively in Kashmir and Himachal Pradesh.

Mowal extract

Obtained by soaking mowal flowers, also called cockscomb flowers, in water to extract the colour. The extract is used to add colour to Kashmiri delicacies, such as Roghanjosh.

Mustard

Mustard seeds, both yellow and black, are widely used in Indian cooking. Oil pressed from these is the preferred cooking medium in large parts of rural north India and in Bengal. The seeds and oil are commonly used in tempering and are an essential ingredient in pickling spices. The fresh green leaves of the plant are a popular vegetable.

Nutmeg

An aromatic spice derived from the kernel of the mace fruit, which can be used freshly grated or ground. It is a key ingredient in garam masala.

Okra

Also known as *bhindi* or ladyfingers, a long, green, pod-like fruit with a ridged and slightly furry skin. Used as a vegetable in curries and also stir-fried with spices, or pickled.

Paatra

A dish that is cooked wrapped in a leaf, usually a banana leaf. In this way meats or vegetables can be steamed, pan-grilled or roasted without losing any of their cooking juices.

Paanch phoren

This is a mixture of five spices, consisting of fennel, cumin, kalonji, mustard and fenugreek seeds. It is the preferred tempering in Bengal. See page 55 for recipe.

Paneer

A cheese made by coagulating milk using heat and acid, and then draining off the whey. It has a crumbly texture and mild flavour. It is used to make starters such as tikkas and kebabs, stuffings for breads, or is often mixed with vegetables or salads. See page 59 for recipe.

Papad

Dried mango, also known as mango leather, a mixture of mango pulp and sugar that has been left in the sun to dry. Traditionally eaten as a snack, it is sweet and chewy, with a consistency similar to leather.

Papita

A sweet fruit with orange flesh and black seeds, *papita*, or papaya, is an indispensable part of the fruit chaat, a spicy fruit salad. The raw flesh is also often used in marinades as a meat tenderizer. It is easy to make: just process washed unripe papaya skin with a little water in the food processor or blender to a paste. Alternatively, use a mortar and pestle.

Paraat

A large, round metal tray used in bread making to hold the dry ingredients and to knead the dough on. Also used by professional sweet sellers to display their produce.

Parkia seeds

Cluster bean seeds commonly used in North Eastern Indian cuisine. Usually dry roasted with ginger and garlic, or mixed with shrimp.

Pasandas

Boneless fillets from a leg of lamb, either cut thinly or pounded until thin. Used to prepare delicate kebab and korma dishes, and especially popular in Awadh, Delhi and Hyderabad.

Pateeli

A cooking vessel with a small mouth, used to slow-cook food in its own steam (*dum*). Also known as a *deg*. It is often used to prepare pulao or biryani dishes. The *pateeli* is often made with aluminium or stainless steel, and clad with copper or lined with tin.

Pav

Mini loaves of bread that are served with spicy *bhaj* as a street-side snack. Derived from the Portuguese '*pau*', which means bread.

Pipli

The original pepper that provided the pungency in Indian dishes before the Portuguese introduced chilli peppers to the subcontinent.

Pistachio

A green nut with a distinctive flavour, used in many savoury and sweet dishes and as a garnish.

Plantain

A term which refers to both the smaller, yellow fruit that is eaten raw (banana), and its larger relative (plantain), which is cooked in curries. Plaintains can be found in Asian grocery stores.

Pomegranate seeds

The sweet, ruby-coloured seeds of the pomegranate fruit. Used either partly dried, or fully dried and ground, the seeds add a tart and tangy flavour to dishes and chutneys.

Poppy seeds

The small black seed of the poppy flower. Lightly toasted and ground, they are used to give texture to sauces, and to flavour breads, as well as meat and vegetable dishes.

Pressed rice

Also called flattened, beaten or flaked rice, this is rice that has been hulled, cleaned, soaked, pressed and dried. Bland on its own, pressed rice absorbs large quantities of liquid (and therefore flavour) when added to dishes.

Plums (dried)

Known in India as *alubukhara*, dried plums are used as a souring agent.

Puffed rice

Produced by heating rice grains under pressure until they heat up. Often used as a garnish for snacks.

Pulao

A dish in which rice is cooked together with meat or vegetables.

Pulses (legumes)

A generic term for all varieties of lentils, dried beans and split peas, pulses (known as dal) are the principal source of protein for most Indians. See individual entries for more detail.

Raita

A dish of yoghurt mixed with vegetables and fresh or dried fruits, served as an accompaniment.

Rasam powder

A blend of piquant spices used to prepare soupy pepper water in south India.

Rice flour

Made from finely ground rice. Used, along with ground lentils, to produce a batter that is fermented to prepare dosai and *idli* in south India. Also used as a thickening agent in sauces or in a batter used to prepare crisp fritters.

Ridged gourd

Long, dark green ridged fruit, with a think skin and a soft interior. The skin can be made into chutney, but it is often removed and discarded, and only the interior is used as a vegetable in curries.

Roasting spices

To roast spices heat a small, clean, dry frying pan (skillet) over medium-low heat. Add a little ghee and the spices, seeds or nuts and cook, stirring frequently, until aromatic and lightly browned. Remove immediately from the pan. To dry-roast ingredients, omit the ghee and cook in a clean dry pan.

Rose petals

Sun-dried rose petals that are ground for use in savoury dishes, sprinkling on rice dishes or to make cooling sherbets.

Rose water

Distilled from fresh rose petals, this fragrant essence is used for flavouring sweets and cold drinks. It is also used in some Mughal dishes.

Round gourd

Also called gentlemen's toes, Indian round gourd or baby pumpkin. It is native to India, where it features in many dishes. The seeds are also edible and are often roasted.

Sago

Small white pearls of starch made from the pith of a palm-like tree, with a bland but creamy taste. They are soaked in water and cooked, then incorporated into savouries or sweets.

Saffron

A spice made from the dried stigmas of the saffron crocus. With a unique, delicate flavour, saffron is also used as a colouring. It is one of the most expensive spices, but a tiny pinch is enough to flavour a dish.

Semolina flour

Made from semolina and often used in place of wheat flour.

Sesame seeds

The seed of the sesame plant, found in black and white varieties. They have an oily, nutty flavour and are used in small quantities as a thickening agent and for making sweet dishes and snacks.

Sharashi

Caliper-shaped iron tongs used to handle hot pots and pans safely. Also known as *sandesi*.

Sherbet

Flavoured sugar syrup blended with the juice or pulp of fruit or flowers.

Silver foil

A very fine, edible silver sheet used to decorate sweet and savoury dishes, or betel leaf (*paan*).

Sirka

A vinegar, which may be made from coconut, sugar cane and rosehip (*jamun*). A popular souring agent, it also acts as a preservative.

Soya beans

Small round legumes (pulses) that can be eaten fresh (green) or dried (yellow and black), and also made into a variety of products, including tofu and soya milk. In India, black soya beans predominate, and are cooked like lentils in Uttarakhand, and also eaten dry roasted as a nutritious snack.

Sorrel leaves

See Gongura.

Snake gourd

A very long, green, soft-skinned fruit with a white interior. Slightly bitter in flavour, used in large quantities as a vegetable in Indian cooking.

Star anise

A spice made from the dried fruit of a shrub native to East Asia. It is shaped like a five-pointed star, with shiny seeds that have a flavour similar to anise. Sometimes used in Kashmiri, Chettinad, and Goan dishes, the star anise should be cooked with the dish to release its flavour, but not eaten.

Sterilizing jars

To sterilize jars, wash the jars and lid thoroughly in hot, soapy water. Rinse well, then place jars and lids open-side up, without touching, on a baking tray. Transfer to an oven preheated to 120°C / 250°F, and leave for at least 30 minutes. Alternatively, boil the jars and lids in a large pan of water for 15 minutes. Take care to ensure that the jars are already warmed before placing them in a hot oven.

Succh bari

A combination of aromatic and flavourful spices, shaped into a cake, that impart a distinctive flavour to various Kashmiri delicacies. A small piece of *succh bari* is broken off and crumbled into the dish being cooked. Traditionally made at home, *succh bari* are now available ready-made at Indian stores.

Sugar cane juice

The liquid produced when sugar cane is pressed. Popular in India as a drink (often sold by street sellers), or as a sweetening ingredient in recipes, particularly desserts and drinks.

Sugar syrup

A mixture of sugar and water, produced when sugar is dissolved into hot water. The mixture is then boiled to achieve the desired consistency. See page 59 for recipe.

Tamarind

A fruit used extensively in India as a souring agent, where it is known as *imli*. It can be bought as a concentrate, or de-seeded and dried. The dried fruit is ground, pulped or soaked in water to extract its flavour.

Tandoor

The clay tandoor oven used in the Indus valley dates as long ago as 3,000 BC. Traditionally they were heated with burning charcoal, but modern tandoor ovens are often heated with electricity. A skilled tandoor cook can manipulate the heat of the oven to bake, roast or grill a variety of foods.

Tandoori masala

A blend of aromatic and piquant spice powders to be sprinkled over dishes prepared in a tandoor (clay oven).

Tawa

A flat iron griddle used to cook many Indian breads, such as chapatis, parathas and dosas. It is also used for very shallow-frying and pan-grilling. Tikki or tikka (spiced patties) are also finished on a *tawa*.

Tempering

A mixture of spices that has been fried in oil or ghee to release the flavour, and which is added to a dish before serving.

Thali

A large circular eating plate, traditionally made of metal, brass and bell metal, now often made of stainless steel.

Tinda

See Gourds.

Toddy

A drink comprising water, spirits, sugar, spices or lemon, or fermented coconut water. Considered restorative for the ill or infirm.

Toor

Split yellow lentils. See Arhar.

Turmeric

A spice made from the rhizome of the turmeric plant, which is ground to make a bright yellow powder. It has a warm, dry flavour and is found in almost all curries and pickles. It also has antiseptic properties.

Ulta tawa

Literally 'upside-down griddle', a curved griddle used in Awadh to cook a particular type of paratha.

Urad dal

Whole or split black lentils, also called black gram. They are small and oblong in shape with a black skin and a creamy white flesh, often used in curries. Skinned urad dal is white and has a milder flavour, and is often ground into flour or paste.

Vada

Deep-fried lentil dumplings, which are a popular snack in south India. They are also eaten in north India, often with curd or chutney.

Water chestnuts (green)

Eaten raw and also cooked in spicy aromatic sauce. Also consumed in the form of flour, after drying and grinding.

Waxy gourd

Known as *parval* in India, waxy gourd has a whitish waxy skin, which means it can be stored for several months if needed. The white flesh is eaten as a vegetable in pickles, curries and other dishes.

Wearing gloves

Some ingredients, such as colocasia in its raw form, contain toxins. These are destroyed by cooking (or, in the case of colocasia, by soaking the roots overnight), but you might want to wear gloves when dealing with the raw leaves, which are acidic and can cause irritation.

Similarly, jackfruit contains a white substance that numbs the hands. Most grocery stores sell cleaned and cut jackfruit, but if you buy a whole fruit, you might like to wear gloves when handling it.

Wheat germ

The embryo of wheat kernels, which are separated out before wheat is ground into flour. It is used in baking along with other flours, in particular for rich, chewy desserts from Awadh.

Yam

Elephant's foot yam, cooked dry or with a sauce, is popular all over India, where it is known as *zimikand* or *suran*.

Yoghurt

A milk product made by coagulating milk with the help of a fermenting agent. Usually called curd in India. It can be eaten plain, sweetened with sugar or fruits, or mixed with water to make lassi.

To cook yoghurt, heat a little ghee in a pan over low heat. Pour in the yoghurt and saute until it is light brown, then remove from the heat and set aside.

To hang yoghurt, line a sieve (strainer) with a piece of clean muslin (cheesecloth). Holding the sieve over the sink, pour in the yoghurt. Bring the sides of the muslin together to form a pouch and tie with kitchen string (twine). Hang over a container to catch the draining liquid, for 30 minutes for slightly thickened yoghurt, and up to 1 day in the refrigerator to produce a solid.

To make sour yoghurt, add a few drops of lemon juice or vinegar and stir to combine.

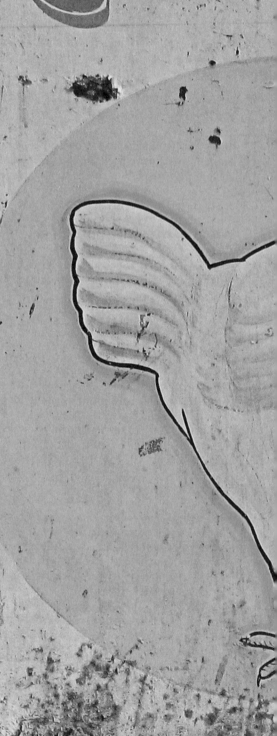

Many of the ingredients and equipment listed in the glossary that you will need for the recipes are widely available in markets, grocery stores and supermarkets in major cities, as well as in Indian stores. If they are not available near you, here is a list of selected online suppliers specializing in Indian ingredients, utensils and cookware.

—

Directory

UK

www.hampshirefoods.co.uk/home
Stocks Asian and Indian foods and spices as well
as kitchen utensils.

www.indianmart.co.uk
Email: info@indianmart.co.uk
Stocks Indian food (including fresh fruit and
vegetables) and spices.

www.itadka.com
Email: info@itadka.com
Indian food (including fresh vegetables), spices
and a limited range of kitchen utensils are available.
Regional Indian products are also stocked.

www.siras.co.uk
Email: info@siras.co.uk
Stocks Indian food (including fresh fruit and
vegetables), Halal butchers and kitchenware.

www.spicesofindia.co.uk
Email: sales@spicesofindia.co.uk
Stocks Indian food (including spices, fresh fruit and
vegetables as well as freshly made sweets), cookware,
and utensils.

www.theasiancookshop.co.uk
Email: customerservices@theasiancookshop.co.uk
Stocks Indian and Asian food, spices, cookware
and utensils.

USA

www.indianblend.com
Email (general): info@indianblend.com
Email (sales): sales@indianblend.com
Good for spices and lentils, and has a small selection
of cookware and kitchen utensils.

www.indianfoodsco.com
Has a good supply of Indian food with organic
alternatives.

www.indiaplaza.com
Email: service@Indiaplaza.com
Stocks a wide range of cookware and kitchen utensils
for Indian cooking.

www.ishopindian.com
Stocks Indian food (including fresh breads) and
organic spice blends.

www.kalustyans.com
Email: sales@kalustyans.com
An international speciality food store specializing
in south Asian and Middle Eastern products.
Indian food, spices, cookware and kitchen utensils
are available.

www.patelbrothersusa.com
E-mail: info@patelbrothersusa.com
E-mail (orders): orders@patelbrothersusa.com
Good for canned, dry and powdered Indian
food products as well as sweets, snacks, spices
and cookware.

Canada

www.indiaauthentic.com
Email: contactus@indiaauthentic.com
Stocks Indian food and spices.

www.eastwestbazaar.com
Email: custserv@eastwestbazaar.com
Good for Indan sweets, canned products and spices.

Australia

www.indiangroceriesonline.com.au
Stocks a small range of Indian food and spices.

www.hindustan.com.au
Email: spices@hindustan.com.au
Email: vs@hindustan.com.au
Stocks Indian food, including rice, flour, oil, dried
fruit, nuts, herbs, spices and pulses (legumes).

www.indiabazaar.com.au
Email: sales@indiabazaar.com.au
Primarily stocks Indian herbs and spices as well as
some Indian food (rice, lentils, flour, sweets, pickles,
chutneys, oils, teas).

A

Pushpesh Pant was born in 1946 in Nainital, northern India, and is a professor at the Jawaharlal Nehru University in New Delhi. A regular recipe columnist and author of many cookbooks in India, he has spent two decades collecting authentic family recipes from all over the country, which have been carefully edited, tested and collated to produce a remarkable collection documenting the rich diversity of Indian cuisine.

———

Author's acknowledgements

I would like to dedicate the book to the fond memory of my mother, Jayanti Pande, whose brilliance as a scholar was matched by amazing creativity in the kitchen.

I am indebted to many people who have assisted me in various ways while I was working on this book. I would like to thank first of all my son Indrajit who shares my passion for Indian food and has been a research associate and invaluable aid in the trial kitchen.

Gifted chefs Muhammad Farouk and Miraj ul Haq of Lucknow, Javed Akbar the gourmet from Hyderabad, Qamar Agha and the late Pt Arun Kaul and Rashmi Dar have been generous with recipes and insights about Awadhi, Hyderabadi and Kashmiri cuisines.

HK Dua's invitation to write a food column for his newspaper *Tribune* provided much needed encouragement, and readers' feedback, often critical, helped me fine-tune the recipes.

Rai An and Krishna of Varanasi opened my eyes to the lost riches of vegetarian food. Mahavir and Govind have rendered invaluable assistance in tidying up an unwieldy mass of information and shaping the manuscript.

I would also like to thank Promod Kapoor of Roli Books for inspiration and support, and for introducing me to the wonderful editorial team at Phaidon Press who have transformed my ugly duckling into a beautiful swan!

Recipe Notes

Unless otherwise stated, eggs and individual vegetables and fruits, such as onions and apples, are assumed to be medium.

Cooking times are for guidance only, as individual ovens vary. If using a fan oven, follow the manufacturer's instructions concerning oven temperatures.

Some recipes include raw or very lightly cooked eggs or meat. These should be avoided particularly by the elderly, infants, pregnant women, convalescents and anyone with an impaired immune system.

Both metric and imperial measures are used in this book. Follow one set of measurements throughout, not a mixture, as they are not interchangeable.

All spoon and cup measurements are level, unless otherwise stated. 1 teaspoon = 5ml; 1 tablespoon = 15 ml.

Australian standard tablespoons are 20ml, so Australian readers are advised to use 3 teaspoons in place of 1 tablespoon when measuring small quantities.

Phaidon Press Limited
Regent's Wharf
All Saints Street
London N1 9PA

Phaidon Press Inc.
180 Varick Street
New York, NY 10014

www.phaidon.com

First published 2010
© 2010 Phaidon Press Limited
ISBN 978 0 7148 5902 6

A CIP catalogue record for this book is available from the British Library.

Designed by Frost Design
Recipe photographs by Andy Sewell
Food preparation and styling by Nikita Gulhane with
    Sarojini Gulhane
Other photographs by Shubhangi Athalye 538–539; Ian Cowe 668–669; Jan Enkelmann 60–61; Indrajit 6–7; Meena Kadri front endpaper, 4–5, 28–29, 88–89, 224–225, 588–589, 716–717, 728–729, 774–775, 798–799; Max Lieberman 794–795; Pau Sarradell back endpaper; Karen Stockert 628–629.
Printed in Italy